THE COMPLETE BOOK OF GARDENING

THE COMPLETE BOOK OF GARDENING

Edited by
Michael Wright

Consultant editors
Frances Perry,
John E. Elsley and Lizzie Boyd

Ebury Press and Michael Joseph

This book was conceived, edited and designed by New Leaf, 38 Camden Lock, Commercial Place, Chalk Farm Road, London NW1

Director:	Michael Wright	Art director:	Michael McGuinness
Assistant editor:	Helen Varley	Designer:	Malcolm Smythe
Sub-editors:	Vivianne Croot Yvonne McFarlane Sally Walters	Assistant designers:	Sue Rawkins Eric T. Budge
Assistance and admin:	Chrissie Revell Betty Leslie Jo Foster	Editorial and picture research:	Viv McCausland Jan Jones Malcolm Hart Neil Ardley

First published in Great Britain in 1978 by Ebury Press, Chestergate House, Vauxhall Bridge Road, London SW1, and Michael Joseph Ltd, 52 Bedford Square, London WC1

ISBN 0 7181 1555 4

Copyright © 1978 by New Leaf Books Ltd

Set in Mergenthaler Times and Helvetica by Filmtype Services Ltd, Scarborough, Yorkshire, and printed in England by Cripplegate Printing Company Ltd, Edenbridge, Kent; binding by Hunter & Foulis Ltd, Edinburgh, Scotland

In memory of E.D.W.

Consultant editors
This book was planned and created with the advice and guidance of Frances Perry, MBE, FLS, VMH, gardening correspondent of *The Observer* (London) and former principal of Norwood Hall College of Agricultural Education. She is also a widely travelled lecturer and broadcaster, having visited some 70 countries 'looking for plants and gardens', and the author of 15 books. She is the first woman council member of the Royal Horticultural Society and holder of its Veitch Gold Medal. She was also the first Briton to be awarded the Sarah Frances Chapman Medal of the Garden Club of America, and is a Member at Large of that club. She is married to Roy Hay.
Consultant editor for North America, and responsible for revising the text for the American edition, was John E. Elsley, curator of hardy plants at the Missouri Botanical Garden (Shaw's Garden), St Louis, Missouri. A graduate of the University of Leicester and the Royal Botanic Gardens, Kew, both in England, he has undertaken botanical work and horticultural collecting in Greenland, Iceland, Japan and Scandinavia.
Acting as coordinating editor and responsible for cross-relating the work of the many contributors was Lizzie Boyd, Danish-born editor and author of many books on gardening and cooking.

Contributors
The text was contributed by the following:–
Lizzie Boyd (see above);
Philip Damp, general secretary of the National Dahlia Society (UK) and dahlia correspondent for a number of magazines and journals;
Frederic Doerflinger, American-born representative in Britain of the International Flower-bulb Centre, of Hillegrom, Holland, and author of *The Bulb Book*;
John Dyter, a director of Notcutts Nurseries, Woodbridge, Suffolk, and first recipient of the Bowles Memorial Scholarship;
Roy Elliott, editor of the *Bulletin* of the Alpine Garden Society (UK) and author of several books on alpine plants;
Alfred Evans, assistant curator, Royal Botanic Garden, Edinburgh, and author of *The Peat Garden and its Plants*;
Ray Evison, OBE, VMH, former Director of Parks and Gardens for Brighton and author of *Gardening by the Sea* and other books;
Michael Gibson, editor and horticultural writer specializing in roses, and author of *Shrub Roses for Every Garden*;
A. J. Halstead, entomologist to the Royal Horticultural Society;
Roy Hay, MBE, VMH, gardening correspondent of *The Times* and *The News of the World* (London), writer and broadcaster, former editor of *Gardener's Chronicle*, and author or editor of many books;
Arthur Hellyer, MBE, FLS, VMH, gardening correspondent of *The Financial Times* (London) and former editor of *Amateur Gardening*, author of many books, including *The Amateur Gardener* and *The Collingridge Encyclopedia of Gardening*; his contributions were written jointly with his wife, Gay, who sadly died during the creation of this book;
Phil Kumba, specialist in plant diseases and pests;

F. P. Knight, FLS, VMH, VMM, former director of the Royal Horticultural Society's Garden, Wisley, Surrey, and co-author of *The Propagation of Trees and Shrubs*;
Roy Lancaster, FLS, VMM, curator of the Hillier Gardens and Arboretum, Hampshire, one of the largest collections of woody plants in the world, and author of several books on trees and shrubs;
Alan Mitchell, VMH, forest research officer and author of *Field Guide to Trees of Great Britain and Northern Europe* and of a similar guide (in preparation) to trees of North America;
John Negus, horticultural writer and journalist, and enthusiastic believer in organic gardening;
Anthony du Gard Pasley, landscape architect and author of *Summer Flowers*;
Frances Perry (see above);
Noël J. Prockter, former assistant editor of *Amateur Gardening* and author of *Climbing and Screening Plants* and *Simple Propagation*;
Rosemary Roberts, head of the Department of Amenity Horticulture at Capel Manor Institute of Horticulture, Hertfordshire;
Peter Russell, garden designer and gardening correspondent of *House and Garden* magazine (London);
Moira Savonius, horticultural and natural history writer and co-author of *Create a Butterfly Garden*;
Donald Smith, head of glasshouse and field services at the John Innes Institute and horticultural writer and broadcaster;
James F. Smith, chrysanthemum specialist and writer of several books and many articles on the subject;
Lionel P. Smith, former president of the Commission for Agricultural Meteorology of the UN World Meteorological Organization and author of several books and bulletins on agriculture, horticulture and climate;
John Street, writer and broadcaster on gardening and third-generation member of a horticultural family;
Mrs Desmond Underwood, VMM, proprietor of a nursery specializing in silver-leaved plants and hardy pinks, and author of *Grey and Silver Plants*;
Andrew S. White, research gardener at the Nuffield Orthopaedic Centre, Oxford, whose work involves studying and teaching handicapped gardeners how to continue their hobby;
and Robin Williams, landscape designer and writer, illustrator and lecturer on garden design.

Other assistance
Detailed acknowledgements of the sources of photographs and the artists responsible for drawn illustrations are given at the end of the book. Special thanks for assistance of various kinds are due to Allwood Bros (Hassocks) Ltd, Anglo-Aquarium Plant Co Ltd, Bees Ltd, Tom Blake, Alan Bloom of Bressingham Gardens, The Bulb Information Desk, G. Culpan of Murphy Chemical Ltd, Elm House Nurseries Ltd, Jim Fisk of Fisk's Clematis Nursery, Fisons Ltd, Fox Pool International, Stadt Frankfurt am Main, Eric Gray and W. L. Maxim of Suttons Seeds Ltd, David Grigg at Capel Manor Institute of Horticulture, Gary Hincks, Christine Oram of Thompson and Morgan (Ipswich) Ltd, the director of the Royal Horticultural Society's garden at Wisley, and F. J. Unwin Ltd.

Contents

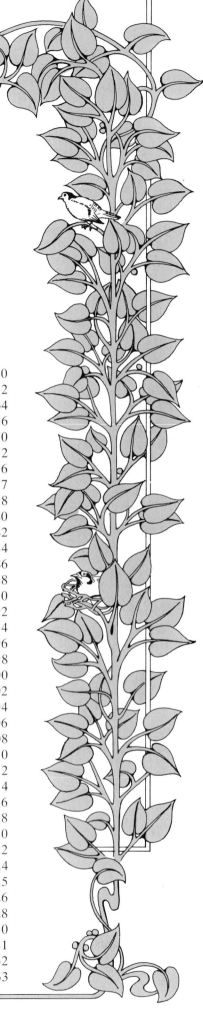

Chapter 1
Designing your garden

Chapter 2
Major garden features

Chapter 3
Decorative garden plants

Chapter 4
The vegetable and fruit garden

Chapter 5
Gardening techniques and technicalities

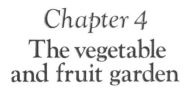

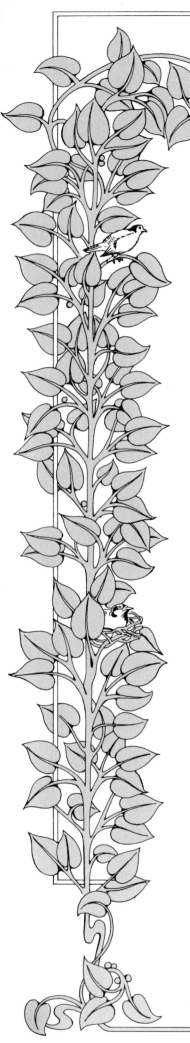

Introduction

Gardening is probably the most popular pastime in the world, and there is no shortage of books to guide the amateur. Why, therefore, create another? There are various reasons, but the main one concerns the presentation of information in a way that is both attractive and geared to the user's needs. It is an approach we first used in *The Complete Indoor Gardener**, aiming to create a book that would be both a valuable reference work, in which all the facts relating to particular topics were collected into a series of self-contained two-page articles, and one that would be fascinating to browse in of a winter's evening. As buyers of that previous book (and there are now some three-quarters of a million worldwide) will see, this new guide to outdoor gardening is organized and designed in a similar way, though there are differences of detail.

The most important differences are the result of the greater scope of the present volume. This book begins more or less where *The Complete Indoor Gardener* (which, in spite of its title, encompasses window boxes, balconies, patios and roof gardens as well as indoor plants) left off. It is geared primarily to the needs of the gardener with a plot of moderate size, rather than the lucky owner of an acre or more of grounds, and to the relative beginner rather than the green-fingered expert. Nevertheless, the scope is still very wide – all aspects of decorative outdoor gardening and also the growing of vegetables, herbs and fruit – and both experts and owners of large gardens should find plenty of interest. (As some indication of the scope, the index of plant names contains some 6,000 entries.)

The greater scope of this new book has necessitated a marked increase in size: it has 60 per cent more pages than its predecessor, with a similar increase in the number of illustrations and virtually twice as many words. Although we have kept to the principle of giving all the information on a particular topic in one or more self-contained articles, it has been necessary to extend the length of such articles beyond two pages in a number of cases. On the other hand, a number of articles occupy just a single page. The whole book comprises some 200 articles, which are grouped into five chapters dealing with garden design, garden construction and maintenance, decorative plants, food-growing, and gardening techniques, respectively.

The advantage of this arrangement can be seen in the section of the book dealing with decorative plants, where the many types are grouped according to their uses and characteristics rather than alphabetically or by botanical grouping. (There are a few exceptions in the cases of important and well-known botanical groups, such as roses, clematis, and rhododendrons and azaleas, which also have closely related charac-

Published in Great Britain by Pan Books and in the United States by Random House

teristics and needs.) Thus the point of view is that of the gardener who wants to create a particular effect or to plant a particular section of the garden. Details of a wide range of suitable plants will be found grouped together in one or more articles. If, on the other hand, you want to find out about a particular named plant, you should refer to the comprehensive index of common and botanical names at the end of the book. (There is a separate index of general topics, including broad groupings of plants.)

Plant names
You will find that the index of plant names is organized according to the botanical (Latin or Latinized Greek) names as far as decorative plants are concerned, cross-references being given from common names. Similarly, in the main body of the text, plants are largely referred to by their botanical names. The reason for this is not perversity. Nor are we trying to blind you with science. It is simply a question of avoiding ambiguity – a particular problem in a book like this that is designed for use in many countries. 'Common' English names often refer to a number of different plants, some related and some not. Black-eyed Susan, for example, is the common name of a climber known botanically as *Thunbergia alata* and also of several kinds of rudbeckia which are herbaceous plants closely related to each other but not to the thunbergia; the only thing they have in common is orange flowers with black centres.

When one crosses national frontiers even more confusion can arise. *Impatiens sultani* is a plant commonly grown in both Britain and North America, but whereas British gardeners know it as the busy Lizzie, to Americans it is patience or patient Lucy. Even more confusing, the rose of Sharon is well known on both sides of the Atlantic, but this name is used for two quite different plants: the low-growing *Hypericum calycinum* in Britain and the bushy hardy hibiscus, *Hibiscus syriacus*, in the United States. By using the botanical names, usually in addition to common ones, such ambiguities can be ruled out (though botanists are not altogether blameless, for botanical names are sometimes changed).

By international convention, the principal botanical names are printed in italic type. To define a distinct kind of plant needs two names (rather like a person's family name, or surname, and Christian, or given, name). The first name, always shown with an initial capital letter, is the genus name. A genus can contain as few as one or as many as several thousand distinct plants, all with basic botanical similarities. Examples of genera are *Hedera* (the ivies), *Rosa* (roses) and *Campanula* (bellflowers). Distinct types of plants within a genus are termed species, and the species name is always printed second, in small letters – for

example, *Hedera helix* (the common English ivy) and *Hedera canariensis* (Canary Islands ivy). It is common practice, where there is no risk of ambiguity, to abbreviate the genus name after the first time it appears in a particular paragraph or section – for example, *Hedera helix, H. canariensis*.

Even species can be subdivided, though here the differences are only minor – a different leaf form or pattern, a different flower colour or size, and so on. Naturally occurring (or wild) variations of this type are termed subspecies or varieties, and their name is added to the genus and species names in small italic letters. For example, the Irish ivy is classified as a subspecies of the English and is called *Hedera helix hibernica*, though it is sometimes listed in catalogues as *Hedera hibernica* – an example of confusion caused by botanists' own change of mind. (Where a plant does have two or even more botanical names, the alternatives may be given in brackets.)

Such natural varieties are comparatively rare among outdoor garden plants. Far more common are varieties that have resulted from selection or cross-breeding by gardeners and nurserymen. Such forms are correctly termed cultivars (*culti*vated *var*ieties), and by international agreement their names are printed in single quotation marks, in Roman (non-italic) type, and with an initial capital letter. An example is the form of English ivy known as *Hedera helix* 'Glacier'. Hybrids – plants resulting from cross-breeding two distinct types – are named in a similar style, but where the parents belong to two different species or where (as is often the case with garden plants) the exact parentage is obscure, no species name may be given before the cultivar name – as, for example, in *Rhododendron* 'Kirin'. In some cases, a group of hybrids may have established characteristics as distinct as those of a true species; then they may be given a botanical-style name, but with an × sign between the genus and 'species' name to indicate that this is a hybrid. An example is the garden pansies, which are classified as *Viola × wittrockiana*. The same sign is used where a hybrid between two genera occurs, as in × *Fatshedera lizei*, which is a hybrid between an ivy and a species called *Fatsia japonica*.

Common names are always printed in Roman type without quotation marks and without capital letters (except where a proper name is involved). This is the case, too, when a botanical name is used in the style of a common name, whether it is in truly common usage (as with rhododendrons and violas) or not (as with thunbergias and fatsias). There is one more case where names are printed in Roman type, but this time with an initial capital letter. These are the names of well-defined groups (or races) of cultivars or hybrids within a genus. Examples include Floribunda and Hybrid Tea roses and Parrot tulips.

International scope

All this may seem a little confusing at first (not least because nurserymen's catalogues do not always follow the international convention), but you will find as you read that the style of naming – and many of the names themselves – will become familiar. The species and variety names often have a certain amount of logic behind them that quite quickly becomes apparent. 'Variegata' means variegated, for example, *scandens* means climbing, *chinensis* Chinese, *japonica* Japanese, *vulgaris* common, *rubra* red, and so on. The great advantage of such names is that they are completely international – not only throughout the English-speaking world, but in other languages also.

This is of particular importance in this book because it is designed for an international readership. Although created in Britain, it should be of use to gardeners in all places with temperate climates. Continental areas, such as North America, suffer much greater extremes of climate – both hot and cold – than such relatively benign areas as the British Isles, and this brings both advantages and disadvantages. With the help of our North American consultant editor, the book has been made broad enough in scope to encompass the needs of gardeners in most parts of the United States and Canada, with the exception of those in the arctic north and the subtropical south, and the text of the North American edition has been specially revised and adapted for them.

In a similar way, gardeners in New Zealand, much of Australia and South Africa should find most of their needs catered for, though most of them will not have to preoccupy themselves so much with protecting their plants from winter cold as their fellow enthusiasts in northern climes. The climatic differences of the various regions encompassed by the book are discussed in the article on page 338, and the climatic maps printed on the endpapers give more specific data. Because the seasons come at different times in different parts of the world – and because plants respond to seasonal weather changes, not the calendar – you will find that throughout the book we refer to the seasons rather than to specific dates.

Apart from these differences, the only barriers between gardeners of most of the English-speaking world are likely to be ones of language – spelling and in a few cases terminology. (A British gardener's seed-tray is an American's flat, while what Americans call peat moss is known in Britain simply as peat, and so on.) We hope we have managed to anticipate the more important of these and have given the equivalents in the glossary on page 392. In any case, we trust that they are no barrier to your sharing with us the enjoyment of gardening. From all who helped to create this book – writers, artists, photographers, editors, designers and others – good growing!

1
Designing
your garden

The most fascinating, demanding but also rewarding
aspect of gardening is the design of your garden.
It is the area where artist and plantsman meet,
for a successful garden design forms a unified whole
that is much more than the sum of its individual parts.
It combines the static, fixed architectural features
and the dynamic, living structure of the garden:
the trees, shrubs, hedges, herbaceous plants, grass and others.
It takes account of harmony of form, texture and colour,
together with the changing aspect through the seasons.
However large or small your garden,
there is no reason for it not to have impact and originality.
The solutions you choose will depend on the
characteristics of the site, your needs and personal taste,
but in this chapter you will find plenty to stimulate your ideas,
including examples of many historical and geographical styles
and a large number of practical, well-designed gardens.

The purpose of garden design

Your garden is part of your living space. Like any room in your house, it should be both functional and attractive, at once a comfortable outdoor extension of your home and a visually satisfying composition. It can be a small-scale private landscape with a dimension that no indoor room has: it changes continually with the light, the weather, the time of day and the seasons, eternally reflecting the varying moods and atmospheres of nature.

Design should be the simple means by which you make the very most of your garden-making opportunities. Some gardens just seem to evolve over the years in a haphazard way. They begin with a lawn, perhaps, and a few flower beds. Then other features are added as needs arise and tastes dictate – rock garden, vegetables, a display of

Cohesive design will give a garden an essential flow, a fundamental life and interest that provides scope for thoughtful and effective planting. Trees, shrubs and other plants will make a positive contribution only if they are chosen in relation to the garden as a whole. They can be used to alter perspective, to create atmosphere and to emphasize style; they can mask ugly features and soften hard lines. Many beautiful gardens seem full almost to bursting point with plants, but thoughtless planting will inevitably result in erratic display and wasted opportunities. By planning the selection of plants, you can bring colour, contrast and variety to the overall scheme, maximize the decorative possibilities of your garden and, above all, ensure that interest is maintained, season by season.

self with its characteristics and details. Apart from shapes and dimensions, you will need to record such key factors as the lie of the land and the existence of any permanent features and structures – all of which are likely to affect the end result. The article on page 14 explains the importance of these and other influences, such as climate, enclosures, type of soil, and even the surroundings.

But you cannot begin to design your garden until you have thought a little about what you want from it. A garden can have many uses, both decorative and practical, and these are considered on page 16. Decide what you would like to have and draw up a list of priorities. Larger features may have to be excluded if the site is small, but you may find that a single area can be made to serve several

roses. This approach can be successful in a large garden where there is plenty of space to accommodate each new feature. But a garden should not just be a random collection of lawns and borders; it needs a certain unity that only forethought will ensure. And smaller gardens – the vast majority – have no space to waste and are best spared the haphazard approach that leads at best to an unsatisfactory compromise and at worst to overcrowding and fussiness.

The importance of planning can be seen in many suburban gardens, which are commonly awkward in shape, limited in size and lacking in privacy. Here the object is to escape from the box, to mask the frame and to allow the land to express itself – within its scale – to best effect. By abandoning stereotyped, fence-following lines and introducing rhythm and freedom into their layout, such gardens can be rescued from the ranks of the ordinary.

Designing your garden should save you time and money. You can calculate costs in advance and spread them over any period, for the various stages of your design can be begun or postponed – and expenses expanded or contracted – according to circumstances. It should help you to avoid costly mistakes, and a garden planned to fall well within your capabilities and inclination to care for will never become a millstone.

Keep simplicity and scale in mind when designing your garden, and it will succeed from the very beginning.

Planning the garden

Producing a simple plan of your existing site is a good way to begin designing a new garden; the article on page 66 explains how to go about it. This will form a basis for your subsequent design, and will give you an opportunity to explore your garden and familiarize your-

different purposes. With ingenuity you can probably make space for most of the things you want.

Having made your list, try allocating space for the various items on copies of your plan. You can make sketches; or cut out pieces of paper to represent features, and arrange them in different ways as your ideas progress.

Principles of garden design

A sense of space is an important element in garden design. This involves emphasizing the dimensions of a large, broad garden, blending it subtly into the landscape around, and bringing a feeling of openness to a small one. The best way of doing this is to lead the garden easily away from the house, so make a start by allocating an area just beyond as a lawn or paved area. This will open up even the smallest plot, and will also visually unite the various garden areas. From a practical point of view, it may become the most used part of the garden – a place to sit and a conveniently visible play area for children.

An area such as this will be most effective if it opens away from the line of vision, especially if the land slopes upwards away from the house. So avoid visual trip-wires, such as transverse beds or screening patio walls, that obstruct the immediate sight-lines and close in the aspect.

The use of perspective will help to create a sense of space in a small or enclosed garden. Beds and borders of fluent outline and scaled size disposed in and around the central area will give it form and can be used to carry the eye outwards, towards a distant tree or another feature outside the garden boundaries. Perspective can be used in other ways,

from the beginning, but remember that the length and breadth of a lawn or patio must be in proportion to the overall size and shape of the garden; that borders and beds must be in proportion with the areas they surround; and that vertical structures such as enclosures, pergolas, shrubs and trees must be in scale with the dimensions of both house and garden, or they will dominate too much.

The practicalities of working in the garden must always be kept in mind. There must be access to all parts (but avoid drawing too many paths into your design) and you must be able to manoeuvre barrows and mowers. Do not forget to allow some space for the service features – a compost heap, shed and so on. These can be assigned to a separate service area (see p 78) sited near to the house for

family garden if rigidity is to be avoided and the very most is to be made of the space that is available.

Informal gardens have a role to play in softening rigid lines and masking ugly features – of both landscape and architecture. You can mix styles in a garden by setting aside a part of a garden away from the house as, say, a rough grass and woodland area. But take care – harmony and unity are essential to the success of garden design.

Choosing plants
The walls, fences and paths are the backbone of your garden; they define the space of your outdoor room. The plants are another kind of structure; like the wallpaper and furnishings in your living room they emphasize its style

Different approaches to garden planning: **far left** Careful choice and positioning of trees and shrubs lies behind the apparently careless design of this luxurious, informal garden. **left** Geometrical formality imposed upon a rectangular site: the gardens at Sissinghurst Castle in England. **right** Bold curves and easy, flowing lines form the basis of suburban informality while **far right** bold sculptural shapes, subdued colours and interesting textures are the essence of the modern style.

too: to divert the eye in different directions in the case of an awkwardly shaped garden, or to shorten the apparent length of a long, narrow one by obstructing the gaze with an interesting focal point – an island bed, perhaps, a pool with a fountain, or a planted screen (see p 14). Changes in level can also be emphasized to bring interest to a garden.

Strength of line is all-important if you are going to be successful in your use of perspective. Keep the lines of your garden simple, but promote the sense of flow by using curves rather than hard, straight edges. One or two boldly shaped borders are more imposing than a series of small beds, and focal points must be kept to a minimum if they are to achieve their desired effect. Aim at elegance of line, and avoid a cluttered and trivial effect.

If there is room, large-scale features that represent a radical change of mood – such as a vegetable or fruit garden, a woodland area or perhaps a swimming pool – can be sited beyond the central area. They can be separated by shrubs, hedges, planted walls or fences, or climbers grown on trellis, to create a series of small gardens in one, and so add an element of surprise.

But remember always that, in order to be a pleasing environment, a garden must be easy on the eye. Try to maintain a harmonious relationship between the various features and areas within your garden. Working within the accurate outline and scale provided by your survey will help you to keep proportions right

easy access. Or if there is no room for one, you will have to allocate unobtrusive places around the garden for each of these features.

Back gardens tend to be given most consideration in a design, at least in countries like Britain where houses are commonly sited close to the roadway. But a similar approach can be brought to the front or sides of the house. Front gardens (see p 46) pose the special problems of drives and entryways, and if your whole garden fronts onto the street, you will have to give this special consideration in evolving a design.

Garden style
If your garden is to form a visually satisfying composition, it must have style. Style gives cohesion and harmony to a garden design. It is expressed to some extent in the garden layout, but also in the specific types of surfaces and enclosures used (see pp 70 to 75), in the types of furniture, ornaments and other embellishments you introduce (see p 80), and even in the plants chosen.

The architecture of your house might suggest a style for your garden, especially if it is of definable character, such as a country cottage (see p 43), a period house or a very modern building. But do not make the common error of trying to impose a particular garden style where it is unsuitable. Symmetry is a feature of many garden styles. Many grandiose schemes of the past were based on it. But such formality is best abandoned in the suburban

and line, and give it atmosphere. The significance of this living structure is examined in the series of articles beginning on page 22.

Plants provide mass in the garden; they define its spaces and emphasize or obliterate its lines. Together with the materials that make up the hard structures and surfaces, they also provide texture, and they are the main source of colour. For best effect, they must be used positively, according to significance and size.

The art of plantsmanship in the garden involves putting the right plants in the right place for maximum effect, appreciation and good performance. Yet every plant you introduce will have a greater or lesser influence on the overall design, and will thus affect to some degree the appearance of all the others. A sound basic framework (in the form of a well thought-out plan) will, however, point to many logical solutions.

Unless you are already an expert gardener, you will need to find out something about plants before you can begin to select. Chapter three of this book is planned to aid your choice, grouping the descriptions of plants primarily according to their major features and applications. You will, of course, have to take into account the soil, natural conditions and aspect of your garden when choosing, for no plant will grow well in a situation that is not to its liking. But there is virtually no garden need that cannot be satisfied by the right choice of plants.

The site and its surroundings

Quite clearly, your garden site, with all its quirks and peculiarities, is going to have an important influence on the design of your garden. But turning problems into advantages is half the fun of design, so if you are faced with a site of such odd proportions that you cannot attempt the ideal garden you always had in mind, do not despair: a difficult proposition may well stimulate the creation of a garden of very special interest.

The location and land form of the site may well have a bearing on its design, too – whether it is in an exposed position or by the sea, demanding shelter belts of trees and shrubs; in a city, overlooked by close buildings and plagued by pollution; or on a steep slope, demanding terracing. The soil and climatic conditions will exert an influence mainly on the type of plants grown, and these of course have a strong bearing on the garden's appearance. Overlying all these intrinsic influences on garden design are the extrinsic ones – cost and time availability and, above, all, the use to which the garden-maker wants to put the garden (see p16).

Size of the site

Large and small gardens present two different sets of design problems, and they have to be approached with different aims in mind. A large garden has many advantages. Where space is no object you can let your imagination run riot with rolling lawns, pools and exotic flower beds. But if you have little time for gardening and cannot find or afford staff to do the work, your garden will be a headache to maintain. The overall shape of the site will rarely pose a problem if it is large – informal features flow naturally into irregular boundaries and successfully obscure them – but achieving unity of design is a major challenge.

A small garden has the advantages of low initial cost and cheap and simple maintenance. Here the aim will be to enlarge the site visually, while using the available space fully. Keeping the centre open will create an illusion of space. Use a pleasant view, if there is one, as if it were an extension of the garden; this will enlarge perspective and so make the garden appear larger. If the site is enclosed, you may be able to emphasize a fine tree in an adjoining plot by planting something eye-catching nearby to draw attention to it. You will have to think vertically in a small enclosed

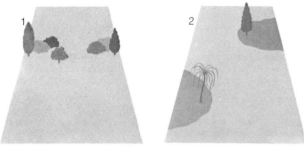

Perspective and garden shape
Parallel lines formed by the side boundaries of a long, narrow garden tend to draw the eye into the distance and emphasize its length. You can foreshorten the perspective simply by sectioning off an area at the end with a low planted wall or a sweeping line of shrubs or small trees 1. Beyond you could place a vegetable garden or orchard.
Straight borders and long lawns also emphasize length, but if side borders are allowed to swing out in sweeping curves at strategic points on either side 2, 3, the garden can be made to meander along its length. If opposite border peaks are staggered and are accented with striking plantings, the eye will pause and, again, the garden will appear shorter.
A path or expanse of paving crossing a long site will appear to widen it. Changes of level can have ths same effect 4.
Using terracing, timber decking, raised beds or even rock gardens, they may be created artificially on a flat site. Similar solutions can be applied to gardens that narrow along their length.
If the site widens away from the house, use perspective in the opposite way, narrowing it by screening off one or both sides. If it is short but wide, emphasize the diagonal – the longest sight-line – by planting beds in diagonally opposite corners 5. A specimen plant in one of the farthest corners will draw the gaze in that direction.
A circular lawn or paved area surrounded by tall plantings is a bold device to alter the shape of a triangular garden, obliterating the sharp corners.

garden. You can plant small trees, cover walls in climbers, plant hanging baskets. Changes in level create interest in a tiny site, and, effectively chosen enclosures and paving will unify.

Garden shapes

Gardens are most commonly rectangular or, if they surround a corner house, L-shaped. But they can be triangular, wedge-shaped or tapering, a succession of shapes thrown together, or simply undefinable. Regular-shaped sites are the most simple to plan. Rectangles provide the proportions for an easy, balanced design and effective plant display, for unless they are very small they may only require some softening along the hard lines of walls or fences.

It is when the overall proportions of the garden are unrelated in scale – when the site is too long or too wide in relation to its depth – or awkwardly irregular, that shape becomes a problem. Proportion and balance will then have to be achieved artificially by the use of line and perspective, as shown in the diagrams on this page.

Regular proportions and pleasing variety can be achieved in a garden of any shape by breaking it up into small units or modules of a determined size and shape – squares, diamonds or circles. Patios, lawns, borders and beds will then reflect the dimensions of the basic module, providing a series of strong visual lines that will impose their own pattern

upon an awkward shape. Alternatively, irregularities of shape and proportion can be lost in a series of flowing curves, making for a generally more informal appearance but effectively masking hard boundary lines. These techniques are described in more detail on page 18.

House and garden

As an integral part of the design, the house should always be considered in relation to the garden as a whole. An open garden provides the most pleasing setting for a fine house, though this does not mean that plants cannot be used tastefully to enhance it. An ugly or nondescript building may be effectively camouflaged, but no house of this kind is going to be improved by burying it under plants. Indeed, an open and relaxed garden may provide the necessary grace to redeem a hideous pile. Wall shrubs to soften sharp corners and restrained plantings to ornament the entranceway may be all that is required.

Very small gardens in partnership with a large house – a combination often found in cities – are best treated as one, and their relationship emphasized by extending the living room into the garden by means of a conservatory or garden room leading out onto paving. Whatever the size of the garden, this association of features can be the making of a house and garden relationship, though patios and terraces need to be adequate in size to do their job effectively. Loggias and pergolas can also link house and garden, but if they carry climbing plants make sure that they do not rob the house of light.

Soil and natural conditions

Soil type will influence garden design to a degree, but it is only extremes that will exert an overriding influence, and common sense will usually tell you what is possible and what is not. It would be foolish, for example, to try to create a woodland garden – whose characteristic plants thrive in a rich soil containing a lot of humus – on a site that is almost pure

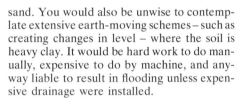

left An informal design is the best solution to the problems of maintaining a large garden; here a stream makes a central feature in a woodland setting. right A semi-wild hillside garden that makes the most of an exceptionally lovely view. below left A pergola entwined with climbing roses and an ornamental open gate are the devices used to integrate this garden and adjoining house. below right The unusual shapes and textures of cacti and palms impress gardens in hot, dry and desert regions with their own distinctive character.

sand. You would also be unwise to contemplate extensive earth-moving schemes – such as creating changes in level – where the soil is heavy clay. It would be hard work to do manually, expensive to do by machine, and anyway liable to result in flooding unless expensive drainage were installed.

It is when you come to decide upon individual plantings that soil influences become more important, and although soil conditions can be modified (see p 332), it is better to work with nature than against it. Plan your plantings in accordance with prevailing conditions – of both soil and climate – and your chosen plants will grow well and display themselves to best advantage. If you have limy soil, for example, it is pointless to try growing rhododendrons and azaleas, but there are other flowering shrubs such as *Abelia* × *grandiflora*, *Choisya ternata* and *Osmanthus delavayi* that will grow on lime and give much the same visual effect. Other recommendations of plants for particular conditions are given in the tables starting on page 386.

The combination of climate and local soil conditions will tend to impress a garden with a certain character. The distinctive cactus and succulent gardens of hot, dry Mediterranean lands make a good example. So do the lush, verdant gardens of mild, wet maritime areas such as western Ireland. But there are few areas where the gardener cannot exert a helpful influence. Soil improvement – lightening heavy soils and enriching light ones – is one aspect of this. Another is to create a microclimate within the garden – or in just part of it – that is conducive to the healthy growth of particular plants.

The influence of climate on plants is discussed on page 340, but you should remember when planning your garden that parts of it – whether the result of natural features or your own efforts – will be colder or warmer, drier or wetter, than average. Their position depends on the site and its geographical location – north-facing walls are generally cold and damp in Britain and North America but hot in Australia – but careful observation through the seasons will help you to understand the microclimatic variations within the site and to avoid, for example, putting a rock garden in a cold, damp, shaded place.

The greatest range of plants thrive in equable conditions where variations are not too extreme. You can do a great deal to create such a microclimate by building enclosures, planting shelter belts of trees, shrubs and hedging plants, and making good use of climbers. The light cover of high, thin trees such as birch is particularly valuable, providing dappled shade in summer and protection from radiation frosts in winter.

The surroundings

The view from your garden may be delightful, even spectacular. Low, unobtrusive walls and fences and adroit planting will frame the view and allow vistas beyond the garden at selected points, creating an extrovert effect (see p 36).

But if the view from the garden is unpleasant it will need to be screened, and the two-way gaze between neighbours may also have to be obscured for privacy. This is best effected by a tall fence or screen wall, and completed with trees and tall shrubs planted in the borders at strategic points. Unless they are impossibly oppressive, however, try to consider the surroundings as a visual extension of your own garden: take advantage of your neighbours' garden-making skills!

Garden purpose and usage

A garden design should evolve from the various needs of its users. Some will be purely decorative places serving to display the skills of those for whom gardening is a hobby or as places of seclusion and escape from the outside world; others will be put to many varied uses by large and active families. The layout of your garden must include areas for the various activities, so if your design is going to be successful, you must have a clear idea from the outset of what you want in it.

Gardens for decoration and display

If you want a purely ornamental garden for sitting outdoors and for quiet reflection, you will be free to develop the full decorative potential of your site. Uninhibited by economies of space, lawns can be allowed to surge between borders, or around beds or

landscaping will give maximum scope for the kinds of plants you particularly want to grow. The inexperienced gardener need not be resigned to a bare or uninteresting garden, for the range of easy, straightforward flowers, trees and shrubs is vast, and a well-designed site will provide a framework for planting schemes that can increase in sophistication as knowledge develops. Gardens and borders devoted to unusual colour-schemes (see p 28) require no special skills. A bed of white and green plants, or purples and reds, or even in different tones and shades of a single colour, is effective, however simple the plants.

Specialist gardens devoted to a particular family, such as heathers, or even a single genus, as in a rose garden, can also exhibit an astonishing variety of form and colour, and this can be emphasized to great effect. Per-

Utility and display are blended successfully if walls and fences are used to display certain attractive cane fruits and trees trained as espaliers or fans. Cordons and espaliers make interesting garden dividers, and there is a role for bush fruits as screens and even enclosures in sheltered situations. Standard fruit trees – particularly apples, pears, plums and peaches – can be used as specimens in a vegetable or flower garden. They will contribute a glorious profusion of delicate blossom in early spring, dappled shade in summer and mellow-coloured summer or autumn fruit.

An orchard, however small, is a pleasant place, and will soften a nearby vegetable patch. The ground beneath can be roughly grassed so long as an area about 2 m (7 ft) across is left clear around young trees for the first few years, to allow them to establish their

Today's ornamental gardens are luxuries for those with the time to devote to them: **left** a family garden will become a retreat for quiet reflection when the children grow older. **below** A display garden for plants in which the owner has a special interest and **right** a multi-purpose fruit and flower

garden tended by someone for whom gardening is a hobby. **centre right** A well-planned city garden used as an outdoor room for rest, recreation and perhaps also entertainment. **far right** Sports and games can only be accommodated in large gardens. Here a games lawn has been set aside for croquet.

specimen trees and shrubs. An ornamental pool, or perhaps a rock garden or scree bed, can be positioned for best visual effect and growing conditions. Any plants in which you have a special interest can be introduced into the landscape in places where they will be most effectively displayed.

You may feel inspired to give free rein to your own ideas of seasonal planting to make your garden attractive throughout the year, to experiment with unusual colour schemes, or try out original combinations of plants of different shapes and sizes, and imaginative associations of textures. Some ways in which these elements of design can be used to bring life, character and originality to your garden can be found in a series of articles beginning on page 22.

If gardening is your your hobby, creative

golas, pools and other features will bring atmosphere to such a garden, and tasteful choice of associated plants will ensure that interest is maximized and prolonged.

A decorative garden is there to be enjoyed, so extra patio or lawn space for sitting outdoors is likely to be well used. Seats and benches placed at selected viewpoints around the garden will encourage quiet moments of therapeutic contemplation.

Gardens for food crops

There is rarely any difficulty in adapting part of an ornamental garden for the production of vegetables, fruit and herbs. Conversely, if a garden is to be devoted almost entirely to crops, it should be possible to avoid a totally utilitarian appearance by finding room for a decorative area near to the house.

feeding roots. The grass can then be planted with bulbs for spring, summer, autumn and even winter colour. A hive of bees adds an extra dimension and aids pollination of fruit trees as well as yielding honey.

Grass walks through a predominantly vegetable garden help to give it charm, though paving of some kind may be more practicable where conditions are liable to turn muddy. An area of flowers (such as gladioli, dahlias and cosmos) grown for cutting will provide colour. And while the most attractive crop plants, such as artichokes and runner beans, can be planted for ornamental effect, a range of herbs give a vegetable garden a special decorative – and fragrant – quality. Ideas for herb gardens can be found on page 270, and all aspects of fruit and vegetable gardening are dealt with in detail in chapter four.

Family gardens

Plenty of open space for recreation is a major prerequisite for a family garden, especially if there are children. Some beds and borders may need to give way to extra space for lawns and patios to be used for children's games, for sitting and eating out, for entertaining friends and as extra space for overspill from parties. Correctly positioned, patio or terrace walls can also be used to create a sun trap for sunbathing. Shady places can be contrived too, if required, especially in hot climates. Open areas should be large enough to do their job properly, particularly if they are to be used for sports and games; when in doubt and where space permits, make patios larger rather than smaller.

Efficient use of space is the secret of a garden that is both decorative and functional. There should be no difficulty in adapting part of the garden for vegetables and soft fruit if they should be required, perhaps by shortening the lawn to make extra planting space, or by screening off some border space. Walls and greenhouses can be utilized for fruit-growing, and if space is limited patches of flowers for cutting can be scattered among ornamental beds and herbs grown as edgings. Summerhouses doubling as garden sheds (see p 79) are also useful for storing garden furniture

Gardens for families with very young children may need to be planned with the children's needs more emphatically in mind. Such gardens spring largely from common sense: ornamental pools can be dangerous and should really be omitted, or covered with wire netting or an ornamental metal grille. Swimming pools must be enclosed within a strong barrier, too tall to be climbed over by growing youngsters and fitted with a gate that is readily lockable. Thorny shrubs such as berberis and pyracantha and poisonous plants like foxgloves, primulas, laburnum, and monkshoods (*Aconitum* spp) are, perhaps, best avoided. (Check carefully before you plant; see the table on page 52.) Garden gates that close firmly, preferably with the aid of a spring and a self-locking latch, are essential.

Under these circumstances the children can play safely, surrounded by beauty and increasingly aware of the need to respect it. As long as the garden is basically well-structured it can always be altered – borders widened, a pool built in or its guard removed, areas replanted – when the children are older.

Sports and games in the garden

Although many games can be played on a lawn in a garden of average size, gardens to be used specifically for sporting activities really

for such games, be sure to use a hard-wearing seed mixture (see p 84).

Tennis and other hard-surfaced permanent ball courts are only for the very largest of gardens, where their obtrusiveness can easily be camouflaged. Groups of fairly tall trees and shrubs are most appropriate and will blend well with the rest of the garden. Practice areas for such sports as cricket and baseball and driving ranges for golf addicts can be worked into a large garden if required, but are better if screened off in the same way.

Gardens intended for recreation more commonly include a swimming pool, particularly in warm climates. Carefully sited and appropriately landscaped, a pool (see p 82) can give an air of luxury to a garden large enough to take it. A smooth lawn running up to the surrounding area is both decorative and comfortable, and colourful flower beds and planted tubs placed at a discreet distance are also appropriate. Ornamental hedges make effective baffles against prevailing winds, and may help form a suntrap. Tall conifers planted along an appropriate boundary make an elegant windbreak and provide privacy. Windbreaks of all kinds will screen the pool from the rest of the garden; emptied or covered over in winter, it will not be so pleasant to look at.

when a small lawn is needed for children's games. Energetic children can roller-skate or ride bicycles along an access path surrounding the house or garden.

Many family gardens are planned along general decorative lines and any children in the household fit in very successfully. Individual play areas for children can be arranged within a basically ornamental garden – a sandpit can be worked quite discreetly into a patio or lawn near enough to the house for easy observation. Border space may need to be reduced and plants used that are tough and relatively undemanding, but given a lawn of reasonable size, children will play happily and safely enough with or without the swings, slides, climbing frames and other items of equipment made especially for children's gardens and described on page 52.

need to be large. Not only do most sports occupy a lot of space, but since the playing areas are not usually attractive, they are best sited beyond the ornamental garden area, and also screened off. It helps if there is room for adornment in between what might be termed functional areas: a mid-garden patio with a statue or ornament of essential merit, planted around and blended in, for example, or perhaps a formal rose garden.

Lawn games such as croquet can be scaled for play on almost any good lawn of reasonable size, although a full-size croquet lawn measures 32 by 25.6 m (35 by 28 yds). Though equally space-consuming, the paraphernalia for lawn tennis is portable and can easily be set up when people want to play, and then dismantled and stored in a shed or summer-house. If a lawn is to be used much

Practical factors

Whatever purposes you want your garden to fulfil, do not forget to think about the realities of aftercare when you are making your plan. Arrange the garden to fit your time and budget, as well as your life-style. If you begin with a strong but simple layout, detail can always be added; if the design is fluid, it will not be too difficult to add a new feature later on by readjusting the sizes of other features such as lawns or flower beds, to make space.

Ease of access and maintenance is particularly important for those who, through age or disability, are not so agile or energetic as the average person. The particular needs of elderly and handicapped gardeners are examined on page 56, and these will point up some useful practical considerations for fit gardeners, too.

The garden's structural elements

The structural elements of your garden are like the floor, walls and ceiling of an indoor room: they give it form and define the space within it. Horizontal features, such as patios, paths, terraces, steps, and also lawns and soft surfaces, form the garden floor and make up the ground pattern; vertical elements, such as walls, fences, gates and screens, enclose and divide the site; and overhead structures – and the visible expanse of sky – can be thought of as its ceiling.

Enclosures, pavings and roofs have utilitarian functions to fulfil, but they also have an important aesthetic role in the garden. They are the foundation of the garden design, providing a framework for the other, softer elements – soil and water, and the garden's living structure, the plants. Arranging the elements of garden architecture into a visually pleasing composition is the first stage of the design process, for your design will work best if its component parts are laid out in a simple, well-ordered way.

Establishing the garden pattern

One simple way of building up your garden pattern, as the illustrations show, is by using a modular system to divide your site into a number of interconnecting shapes. Divide your plan into small squares, rectangles, circles, triangles or diamonds of consistent size, and use the grid these form to define the

triangular or wedge-shaped site, especially if you obscure the sharpness of the apex with flower beds, or screen it off and use it as a vegetable plot. By making use of diagonals – the longest sight-lines – you can give greater depth to a short wide garden. Here, diamond-shaped or triangular modules will probably be most successful.

The curve is another great ally in overcoming problematical garden shapes, and tends to produce a less formal feeling than the use of modules. It creates flow and allows almost infinite directional variation. In eccentric form, the edges of beds and borders can be

central area is not 'pinched' too narrowly.

You will have to design around any immovable structures and any established trees and shrubs that are to be retained, and blend them into the pattern. If you have inherited a straight row of trees that you want to keep, a lawn curve or diamond-shaped area of paving made to run between some of them can ease the problem quite surprisingly. Half in the lawn or paving and half in the border, the row will not look so straight.

Remember that vertical and horizontal elements work together to create the visual effects you are trying to achieve with your

Using curves in the garden
left Curving flower beds and stepping stone path balance each other in an informal arrangement; the curve of this garden's natural slope adds a subtle three-dimensional element. **right** The bold sweep of a circular lawn brings perspective interest to this flat, straight-sided garden. **centre right** Scallops can be decorative, but curves must be bold to effectively alter perspective. **far right** A path curving out of sight invites the visitor to explore.

Forming shapes with curves
right The curve is the garden designer's most flexible tool, but it probably calls for greater artistic sense than the modular system if it is to be really successful. The outline plans drawn here illustrate some of the almost infinite number of ways that curves can fit into boundaries of various shapes and sizes.
In a long, narrow suburban plot **1**, border peaks help the garden to meander gracefully, and make it look wider than it really is, but in a very small garden **2** there may be room for just a

The modular system

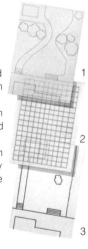

To divide up your garden into modules – units of consistent size – impose a graph-paper grid **2** on a scale plan of the garden **3**. The scale of the grid should fit the scale of the plan so that each grid square represents, say, a 25 cm or 12 in square on the ground. The grid lines can run parallel to the garden edges, or you can turn them to an angle of 45° (or any other angle) if you want to base your layout on diagonal sight-lines. Make a grid of sharply pointed diamonds by drawing parallel diagonal

lines, and use a compass to inscribe circular modules on the grid.
If you want to try out various garden schemes, draw your site plan in ink on a white card, and your grid on a sheet of tracing paper pinned on top. Then you can draw trial plans in pencil on successive sheets of tracing paper laid over the grid sheet **1**. The advantage of the modular system is that it gives you a basis for a flexible garden plan

that will be easy to set out later on the ground. Begin your plan by marking off along appropriate grid lines the edges of lawns, paved areas, beds and borders. Even with a square grid all edges do not need to be straight; you can introduce curves most easily by using a pair of compasses to draw arcs of a circle. If you are dissatisfied with the first plan, simply start again on a fresh sheet of tracing paper.

spaces occupied by the various features you have decided to include in your garden; each of these should occupy one or more of the basic units or modules. Working to a grid will help you to achieve regular proportions between the different elements of the design, and so ensure a pleasing visual balance.

The modular shape you choose need not echo the shape of your garden site. The object of the pattern is to create a series of secondary forms within the outline of your site; you can use it to maximize visual interest within a site of regular proportions, or as a useful device for overcoming the problems of an awkwardly-shaped garden (see p 14). In a square site, however large or small, a modular system based on circular units will soften the straight lines, producing curved borders to fill in the corners. Circles will also work well in a

swung and looped around a garden and swirled in and out of awkward corners. Curves can relieve hard straight boundaries and soften the effect of fences and shed or garage walls that jut out into the garden. They provide marvellous scope for imaginative planting in borders that alternately widen and narrow into peaks and hollows, sculpting the lawn or the expanse of paving within it.

Try out a curved scheme on a copy of your site plan. Starting from a point on one of the side boundaries that seems a convenient distance from the house, swing an easy arc out. Bend the curve back to form the first border peak of suitable depth, and the beginning of the first loop. Continue making further peaks and loops to fit the available space and your own requirements. Peaks on opposite sides of the garden are best staggered, so that the

garden pattern. As a two-dimensional representation of the garden picture, your plan cannot possibly give you an accurate idea of how the garden will look when you are walking or sitting in it. You will have to try to imagine the visual effect of tall structures and changes in level. Make sure that enclosures and dividers do not counteract the perspective effect you are aiming to achieve with lawns, borders and areas of paving, and use the garden pattern to direct the eye away from garage walls, service areas, neighbours' high fences and other obtrusive objects that might otherwise interfere with it.

An enormous variety of materials can be used for paving and walling, and many of these are described on pages 70 and 72 respectively, but do not introduce too many disparate materials into the garden or it will lose its essential unity. Cost and function are bound to influence your choice, but if in doubt let aesthetic considerations prevail.

The horizontal elements

Simple and uncluttered paving has the effect of opening up a garden area and making it appear larger than it really is – a very useful point to remember when planning a small garden. A broad sweep of paving leading the eye towards a focal point at the far end of the garden – or a view beyond it – will emphasize perspective and visually extend the length of a small or shallow garden. You could even

and view your private landscape. Always make as large as space will allow; a mean ribbon of paving skirting the house wall looks entirely unsatisfactory and leaves little or no room for seats, tables or recreational activities. Garden architects of the neoclassical style thought that a terrace should be as wide as half the height of the house. When determining the ratio of length to width, bear in mind that a proportion of eight units to five is known to be visually pleasing, but you need not adhere too rigidly to these rules; much will depend upon the shape and dimensions of your site, and your individual needs.

patio or terrace – and also your garden paths – remember that their size should be in proportion to the size of the area to be paved. Very large paving units can look incongruous in small areas and very small ones tend to look extremely fussy if used to cover a large area. But for some unaccountable reason, bricks look well in any situation.

Garden paths and steps

The golden rule for planning garden paths is to keep them to a minimum. Too many bold lines will look confusing and destroy any sense of space, particularly in a small garden. Some

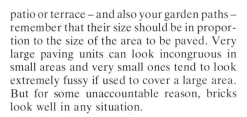

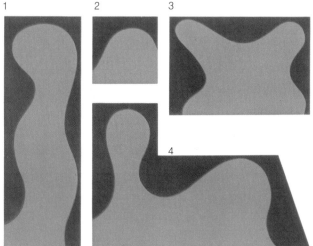

create a false perspective by skilfully narrowing a path or an area of paving towards its farthest point, but remember that this ploy is only effective from one viewpoint.

Paving is the ideal labour-saving alternative to a lawn in a small garden. A diminutive courtyard garden could well be entirely paved. But in a large garden, extensive paved areas tend to lose their visual impact and look monotonous, an effect that is easily overcome by confining the hard surfacing to paths, patios, terraces and subsidiary areas such as rose or herb gardens, and turning the main body of the site over to a lawn. Lawns can be shaped in innumerable ways to link the various garden areas.

A spacious terrace or patio provides an easy transition from house to garden, and – provided they have a sunny aspect – a place to sit

single curve or loop to scythe across the garden and die into the fence on the opposite side to where it began. A lawn or paved area can be strongly looped in and out of the top corners of a short, wide garden **3**. Specimen plants positioned at the extremes of the diagonal sight-lines will help direct attention to them. The curve system provides contoured lines and a flowing effect in a large, L-shaped street-corner garden **4**, and wedges and other awkward and irregular garden outlines can all be lost in easy curves.

Your terrace or patio need not be rectangular – some very pleasing effects can be achieved here with curved or other shapes, and changes in level can add a great deal of interest, even in a small area. Like an indoor room, it can be quite formal in design, even though the garden beyond may be planned along informal lines. This formality may be expressed in its furnishings – many terraces have balustrades and are decorated with statuary, or plants in containers of formal design – and also in the type of material used to pave it. A tiled garden room extending out onto a patio floored in the same material and decorated with leafy plants in geometrically-shaped containers represents a modern kind of formality and a charming exchange of indoor/outdoor space.

When ordering paving units to lay your

gardens need two kinds of paths – those for general access, service and maintenance, and those for casual wandering and exploration – but with ingenuity you should be able to combine the two into a single scheme.

Some landscape designers plan large schemes initially without paths because they know that trodden routes will soon appear as people take the most convenient course from point to point. These natural routes are sometimes referred to as desire lines, and it is over these that the designer will ultimately lay his surfaced paths, knowing them to be correctly positioned for maximum convenience. You could well carry out this exercise on a small scale. You will probably find that the majority of desire lines cross the central body of the garden and can be lost in a large paved area or lawn. Never allow paths to obtrude unless they have a well-defined role in the garden pattern. Many a narrow garden is ruined by a hard, straight path of disproportionate width laid right down the middle.

Avoid straight paths unless you want a formal garden. In most situations curved paths – even if they curve only slightly – will blend in more easily and add charm to the garden. But try to make a bold smooth curve; a series of wiggles will only look contrived. Casual paths should take you quite literally around the garden, winding past special features and turning unexpectedly, perhaps, into a shady grove or hidden rock garden. Where they run into straight maintenance paths, the hard lines can be softened by allowing plants to flop over the edging here and there. Make all paths wide enough for two people to walk side by side.

Make the most of steps. You/*continued*

The garden's structural elements (continued)

can use the slightest slope as an excuse for making even a shallow flight, for they add elegance and character to both house and garden. A broad flight of steps descending elegantly from terrace to garden was a device employed by many landscape designers of the past. Extending the terrace wall or balustrade down the steps to a stone or brick pier decorated with a planted vase or a finial will give a graceful finish, especially at the front of the house. Semicircular steps make a formal introduction to a lawn below the terrace.

In less imposing situations, steps turning at an angle or gently curving out of sight will add an air of mystery, and steps offset to right or left, or from side to side, are more interesting than a straight flight. Wherever possible, construct garden steps of the same materials as you use for the paths and terraces they extend, and make sure that they reflect the overall garden style and atmosphere.

fence or high walls you can lessen their overpowering effect by covering them with plants and masking their sharp corners with the delicate branches of ornamental trees. And if you really need a tall enclosure for reasons of privacy, or to screen an unattractive view, you can use trellis or horizontal beams, firmly attached to a wooden frame, to raise the height of a fence, which can then be clothed with a curtain of climbers.

Never attempt to screen a single exterior feature, such as a factory chimney, by raising the height of the wall or fence that faces it. A specimen tree will do the job far more efficiently and attractively. But as long as you keep proportion in mind you can quite effectively lower part of a wall or fence to frame a beautiful feature or pleasant view beyond the garden. Reduce the height of the enclosure by stages on either side of the feature to be framed to draw the eye towards it.

stone wall makes an unusual garden feature.

You can use the stylistic associations of certain materials to advantage when choosing the type of wall or fence you want. Concrete walls undoubtedly have a contemporary look, and so do straight-lined wooden rail fences painted white, but rough-cut wood has a rustic air. Dressed stone walls have a classical appearance, while dry stone is more informal.

A gate should be in keeping with the wall or fence in which it is placed, otherwise a visual contradiction may occur, perhaps making the gate look ostentatious in comparison with a simple fence, or vice-versa. A wrought-iron gate between brick piers can be beautiful against a background of foliage or flowers, or a well-laid path – inviting the visitor to enter and explore further. At the other extreme, ultra-modern styles in such materials as glass, aluminium and stained hardwood can look good in the context of modern architecture.

Vertical elements

Proportion is an important factor in the success of a three-dimensional design, for this determines its scale – or apparent size – and its line – or apparent shape. So garden boundaries should relate in height to the size of the area they enclose. Tall, solid boundaries will emphasize the size of a small garden, giving it a walled-in appearance, but seen from a distance they are less imposing and give an air of intimacy to a large site. Fairly low boundaries of open-work pattern which permit you to see the plants in neighbouring borders are more suitable for the smaller garden.

Because garden boundaries are usually necessary for demarcation purposes – and to keep stray animals out and children in – it is difficult to prevent them from emphasizing the outline of an awkwardly-shaped garden. Parallel lines formed by the side boundaries of a long narrow site will inevitably emphasize its length. In such cases, try to make them as inconspicuous as possible by choosing styles and materials that blend into borders on either side; wooden palings, for example, will be almost invisible behind a cluster of tree trunks, even in winter.

But if you have inherited a neighbour's tall

above left Pergolas provide shade and a chance to display climbing plants, but should lead to some ornamental feature. **centre** Raised beds emphasize a slight change in level in this flat garden. **right** An archway and ornamental wall lead charmingly into a separate area with its own point of central interest.

Walls, fences and gates

Whether to choose a wall or a fence for your garden will depend largely on considerations of cost, function and maintenance, but inevitably appearance will often be an overriding factor. As a rule, walls tend to look more formal than fences, and psychologically a solid wall provides the greatest sense of security; the higher the wall, the more forceful is its visual impact. The next best thing to a solid wall is a solid fence, but it has a rather more homely appearance.

Fences have the effect of separating and yet blending at the same time, and make the most suitable boundaries in gardens with an open, extrovert appearance; where a beautiful view is to be appreciated anything but the lowest of walls would be inappropriate. In Japanese gardens the two are often combined. A creeper-entwined fence constructed on a low

The design of the gateway is also important; for example, a rounded arch can look very attractive, and frames the vista beyond.

Garden divisions

Arches and pergolas make charming frames for vistas planned within the garden, leading the visitor to the edge of a formal pond or into a rose garden. It is often a good idea to emphasize the garden's natural divisions in this way – special features screened off with open-work walls or decorative fences make gardens within gardens.

Partial division is a way of disposing of space in a large garden, making areas of special interest, and is the best way to avoid a crowded effect in a smaller one. Small gardens can be made to appear larger by dividing them with a low hedge or dwarf wall because this prevents the eye from taking in the whole area at once.

Vistas planned throughout the garden will make it attractive from all viewpoints. These are easily created if each garden area has a focal point in the form of a specimen plant, fountain or other ornament. But keep focal points to a minimum – one to each garden area is a useful rule of thumb.

Garden slopes

Unless you want the kind of formal garden that is traditionally made on flat ground, you can adapt any garden style to a slope, though naturally the degree and direction of slope will affect its treatment. A very steep garden is a difficult proposition and requires some radical solutions, such as those described on page 48, but a gentle slope offers both a challenge to your skill and an opportunity for imaginative exploitation.

Downward-sloping gardens
A terrace at house level from which you can enjoy a commanding view of both garden and countryside is almost essential to a garden that slopes down from the house. Shape it in harmony with the projection of the house to emphasize the link between house and garden, but lead the steps down from one side of the terrace; they might lose their graceful effect if they appear to chase a falling slope. The terrace height should depend upon the gradient of the slope – if this is shallow a patio will look less dominating.

Falling slopes tend to lengthen perspective, and a large expanse of lawn is likely to emphasize this effect. Levelling a very wide terrace across the centre of the slope is a way of foreshortening it. As the main body of the garden, you can treat it in quite a formal way with a lawn and ornamental beds, and link it with steps to the upper terrace. A pool makes an effective focal point when seen from above. Should cross-winds be a nuisance, install screens or plant groups of shrubs on either side to moderate their effect and to hide a service area or vegetable plot and ramps for manoeuvring machinery.

You can landscape the lower part of the garden with shrubs and rough grass with naturalized bulbs, but because you can see almost the entire site from its highest point you may prefer to design an informal layout that seems to move, disappear and change continually, to create and foster interest. Terraced walks are a delight to explore if you make full use of slopes and retaining walls for planting. Hidden dells have their own special fascination, especially if they have the kind of dappled shade in which many woodland plants thrive, and a compelling mystery is presented by the sparkle of water glimpsed through a thin screen of green foliage.

Rising ground
Land rising from the house shortens perspective quite decidedly, so make room for a patio adjoining the house to give a sense of space. You could turn it into a special feature with an unusual shape and unusual trees, shrubs and foliage plants in containers. If the garden slope is gradual there may be room for a lawn and borders beyond the patio, but if the slope runs right to the edge try not to bring it to an abrupt halt before a frontal wall. This will only succeed in shutting the house in and the garden out. If possible, leave a margin of lawn and make a gentle incline or two to more shallow terraces, and level off the slope if you wish, to make a plateau.

Be careful not to mar the informal effect of

the scheme with a straight flight of steps leading centrally up the slope. A flight on one or both sides will look better. Decorative grasses growing on the slope will make patterns in the wind, and many other plants, such as miniature bulbs, may, to their great advantage, be seen here at eye level.

Make any plateau as broad as possible and treat it as an ornamental feature, remembering that you will be able to look down on it from the upper windows of the house. An informal curved scheme will overcome an awkward shape. Unless it is very large, paving may prove more suitable than a lawn. Put a bench in the sunniest spot and position a specimen tree or raised bed to one side as a focal point. A background of planted trellis, tall shrubs or trees will shelter the site and obscure the unyielding lines of surrounding walls or fences.

A well-sited terrace will always have a stabilizing effect on a sloping garden; the example **above**, decorated with plants and a fountain, makes a strong focal point to distract the eye from the unevenly-sloping lawn. **below** An unusual sunken garden with traditional formal layout and planted walls has great charm.

Transverse slopes
You can solve the problem of balance in a site with a gradual transverse slope by treating it in a similar way. If you level off the central part of the slope to make a lawn, you can use the surplus earth to raise the lower part to a slightly higher level. You can plant borders here and landscape the rising part of the slope into a bank and plateau or series of shallow terraces as described above, using excavated material to extend it in a sweep across the bottom of the garden. A low terrace skirting the house will emphasize its horizontal lines and you can use tall border plants, rock features, island beds and specimen trees to balance the composition where necessary.

A pronounced transverse slope will need terracing on a larger scale if the part of the garden seen from the house is to look horizontal. Use a bank to retain the lawn on the lower side and perhaps build a rock garden or plant a shrubbery along the top and down the sides of it. Plant a few specimen trees to form a flowing curve across the lower corner of the garden for balance.

Undulating and sunken gardens
Some levelling of the area in front of the house, and terracing elsewhere, may be called for in a site that slopes in all directions, but a rolling lawn looks positively majestic in an undulating garden. You can plant ornamental grasses and bog plants, or make little pools in the dips, and excavate earth to form a sunken garden in the largest hollow or at the bottom of the site (see p 76).

A sunken garden is always a pleasant surprise. It creates a welcome sheltered spot in a sloping garden, and a shallow sunken lawn or terrace of suitable shape makes a small-scale change in level to enliven a flat garden without looking out of place. Use the walls for planting as you would in a courtyard garden (rock gardens make magnificent retaining walls), and make the most of steps as a decorative feature. Imaginative bedding schemes, a covered walk, and perhaps a central pool and fountain or a fine statue will give the sunken garden an air of elegance.

The living structure of the garden

The structure of a garden consists, in essence, of a balance between masses and voids. A mass is formed by an object or group of objects above ground level, a void by any surface or space on which one can look down. Masses are essentially vertical, voids horizontal, and it is the interplay of these two complementary forms – vertical mass, horizontal void – which gives the garden its underlying shape. A mass does not have to be solid; the typical clumps of the 18th-century landscaped park or the scattered trees on a suburban lawn create a feeling of partial enclosure. Space flows around them like water, forming rivers of light between the tree trunks or open pools where it is dammed up by some solid mass, and it is this flow which brings a sense of vitality and movement to the garden design.

The artificial shapes formed by the demarcation lines between lawns, paved areas and flower beds, and by such structures as walls, fences and screens, represent one kind of structure, as shown on pages 18 to 20. But the major part of garden structure is formed by plant material. This defines space, creates a background for more detailed decorative planting, provides shelter, shade and privacy, and forms the major horizontal and vertical masses which complement the other structural forms of building and ground shaping.

Structures with trees

The largest element available for this purpose is the tree, which gives a sense of vertical scale to even the smallest enclosure. As you plan your garden you should always be thinking about the finished effect in three dimensions, so that the placing of trees and the way in which they balance or contrast with architectural forms must be considered from the outset of the design process.

Perhaps the most obvious use for trees in many gardens is that of screening undesirable features that are outside the site and therefore beyond your control. In that case you must remember not to use trees with very striking shapes – like Lombardy poplars (*Populus nigra* 'Italica'), for instance, which are frequently used for the purpose but which attract the eye from a long distance and so draw

attention to what they seek to hide. A solid bank of trees along the boundary is often unnecessary, and a careful examination may reveal that one or two, strategically placed, will so soften the outlines of what is to be hidden that it is no longer in evidence even though not completely concealed. The nearer you can place your tree to the observer and the farther from the object to be hidden, the smaller the tree – or even large bush – required to do the job: an important fact to remember where there is only a limited range of vision or number of viewpoints.

Wind shelter and privacy

Shelter from wind is another vital element in many gardens, and again trees are most generally used for this purpose. Where the site is exposed and there is space available, a fairly wide belt of two- to three-year-old saplings used in forestry work, closely planted, is more effective than a smaller number of bigger trees, which may be unable to re-establish themselves under adverse conditions. In really exposed positions it is necessary to protect your shelter planting with wattle hurdles or some other device that will filter the force of the wind, and to plant your trees small. Plant them closely, too, so that they help to protect one another and the branches will eventually interlace, giving mutual support. Suitable species are suggested on page 91.

Where space is limited and exposure not too great, both shelter and privacy can be

top The heather garden in the foreground, the house and the curving tree and shrub borders in the background are the masses in this garden, serving to sculpt and balance its spacious central void, the shapely lawn, and create vistas from the windows of the house, while enabling the garden to retain an open, spacious air. left A screen of evergreen *Thuja plicata* whose conical shapes break the outline and distract the gaze from the building behind. right A group of shrubs and a rocky pool oblige a garden path to take a more inviting, serpentine course around them.

The plants you choose for your garden should make a positive contribution to the visual balance of the overall scheme. **right** Tall, irregularly shaped plants make a secluded and informal garden 'room'. **far right** Informal balance achieved with mounds of straggling silver flowers and foliage planted either side of these cottage garden steps, softening the grey severity of the stone and providing a tonal link between house and garden. **bottom** Stately but delicate verbascum spikes contrast with the dark solidity of their background.

obtained by pleaching trees to form a solid mass of green above the level of the boundary wall or fence (see p 90). Such a feature does not have to follow the line of the boundary, of course, but can divide areas of garden above eye level while allowing space to flow beneath them. Fastigiate, or columnar, varieties of trees, if fairly closely planted, can form tall and unusual screens which need little trimming, as can feathered trees. In that case you buy them with twiggy branches right down to the ground – before the nurseryman has formed them into standards – and plant them in a line at about 1 m (3 ft) apart. Simply allow them to grow together, stopping off the tops when they reach the desired height and giving the sides a light trim now and again to keep them tidy. For further information on the use of trees, see page 88.

Structure with hedges
Probably the most obvious structural element in the garden is the hedge, and before choosing any particular plant material it is essential to decide the purpose which the hedge is to fulfil. If it is to be kept clipped into trim architectural shape, then the chosen shrubs must be capable of achieving and retaining such a shape, preferably with only one trim per year. If it is to form a background to other planting, then it must have a matt texture and a recessive quality when cut. For instance, yew is an admirable background hedge plant, with small dark leaves and close-growing neat habit, while the common laurel (*Prunus laurocerasus*), with large pale shiny leaves and a looser habit of growth, is not.

If the hedge is to form an element in its own right, then there is more freedom of choice, and hedges with coloured leaves, flowers and fruit are a possibility. In every case, however, whether the hedge is to be clipped or not – and if it is to be both clipped and flowering you must remember to adjust the cutting programme to the period of formation of flower buds – the chosen shrub must have a basically neat and regular habit of growth. Straggling and floppy shrubs, even when planted in line, will never make satisfactory hedges or space-dividers. For more information on hedges, see page 90.

Structure by balance
There are two kinds of balance in the garden, symmetrical and asymmetrical. The first is generally a matter of strict formality. The second is apparently informal, but should be just as carefully controlled in a less obvious way. Both require the use of structural planting. The formal treatment can range from a simple pair of conifers or clipped bay trees (*Laurus nobilis*) on either side of a garden door to a whole avenue or a series of garden 'rooms' with walls formed from hedges. Such applications of planting to structural purposes are simple and, providing that the right plant material is used, fairly easy to achieve. The asymmetric style is more difficult because it requires a greater appreciation of the visual quality of plants, factors considered in more detail on page 24.

In essence, it is a matter of relating the forms of plants to one another, making use of complementary shapes or contrasts and relating these to the shape of the ground and adjoining buildings. For instance, you might place a tree that would grow round-topped and wide-spreading with age on a little knoll of ground, around which curves a path set in a slight valley formation. In that case the tree on its raised ground gives a reason for the curve of the path; subsequently, as the branches

spread and cast a patch of shade, it will draw attention to the path emerging into the sunlight on the other side. Such a tree might be balanced on the far side of the path – either nearer or farther from the observer, but not directly opposite the tree itself – by a rounded group of shrubs like rhododendrons, which will grow naturally into a dome-shaped formation. If a group of spiring cypresses were planted on the knoll and balanced by a strongly horizontal group of *Viburnum plicatum* the result would be equally effective but totally different.

A group of delicate trees of strong character – such as silver birch (*Betula pendula*) or the golden-leaved false acacia, *Robinia pseudoacacia* 'Frisia' – might be placed in front of a solid mass of evergreens or a plain, dark-coloured wall. In that case the eye would be attracted to the foreground plant, but because of its lightness and the impression of space between and beyond, the adjoining mass would appear to be farther away. Conversely, a heavy, striking plant – for instance, a large dark-coloured conifer – placed near the observer with a background of light-foliaged, delicate plant masses, would also create an effect of greater distance beyond, but in quite a different way.

Structural use of shadows
It is not only trees and shrubs – or even herbaceous plants of strong outline – that can be used structurally, but also the shadows that they cast. Looking from dark to light, or from light through dark to light beyond, is very effective and adds drama to the most ordinary scene. Even in cool temperate climes there is sufficient sunlight to make it worthwhile planning effects of this kind.

Shadow can also be used to conceal the many unattractive things that have to be accommodated in the average small garden. Dust and coal bins, sheds and garages can all be lost if they are painted black or dark brown and then have their hard outlines broken by planting which, casting its shadows on their dark surfaces, makes them almost disappear. However, you must be careful not to make the mistake of half-hiding them with a plant that is so striking as to attract attention.

Plant form and texture

In the days before colour photography became a simple matter, even the most inexperienced photographer realized that in order to make a satisfactory picture the arrangement of forms, textures, lights and shadows were all-important. If any of these elements were missing or not considered properly, a picture in black and white could not be a success. Although gardeners tend to be obsessed by colour, this is generally fleeting and changes from season to season, while forms and textures remain to give stability to the garden picture at all times of year.

Plants as abstract shapes
Looked at through half-closed eyes, almost every plant from the largest tree to the smallest alpine has a very specific outline which, once you have appreciated it, is quite unmistakable. A very large number of plants have shapes which are almost geometric, and one can see triangles, both upright and inverted, globes, half-circles, pyramids, cubes, columns, rectangles, and other shapes, as well as forms more generally related to plants. When you are looking at a plant for the first time, its outline shape should be appreciated and should be the immediate thing you think about when the name of that plant is mentioned in the future. Also remember that a group of the same plants, if fairly closely planted, will take on the outline of a single specimen, only on a larger scale.

Having trained your eye to appreciate and categorize plant form in this way, your first consideration when designing plantings should be the satisfactory arrangement and grouping of abstract shapes. There is no need to worry, at this point, what the forms represent – it is enough to arrange them firstly to create the structure and then to infill with complementary decorative groupings in the same way. Many people find the arrangement of plants difficult because they become too confused by the plants themselves, but thinking about them in the abstract allows one to regard them simply as objects in space.

These objects can be grouped not only with one another, but also with land-form and buildings. The 18th-century landscape designer Humphry Repton noted that certain types of architecture composed best with trees that had opposite characteristics. He propounded a rule that round-headed and horizontally-branched trees should be used in association with Gothic architecture – always basically spiky and vertical – while upright, pointed trees were best with the mainly horizontal lines of classical designs.

Although the shapes of modern architecture are not as diverse as those of past styles, the rules for the relationship between buildings and their immediate plantings remain the same. Few buildings look well rising straight from naked grassland or hard surfaces, but almost all can be reconciled to their surroundings by the careful use of trees, shrubs and ground-shaping, all of which help to give them an appearance of stability and belonging.

Plant textures
The next thing to notice about plants is that they all have a well-defined texture, partly as a result of the size, shape and angle of the leaves and partly depending on their ability to reflect the light. So much emphasis is placed on the appearance of flower and fruit that the importance of foliage – unless highly coloured –

above Trees, shrubs and leafy plants of almost every possible shape and size, ranging from tall, leafy deciduous trees to one species of weeping habit, fine-textured conical evergreens, dense, compact bushes and rounded and spreading shrubs, have both structural and decorative roles in this unusual scheme.
left The contrasting textures of ferns and foliage plants and a young Japanese maple (*Acer palmatum* 'Atropurpureum') are strikingly emphasized by their contrasting colours.
right The dappled texture of the variegated Japanese honeysuckle, *Lonicera japonica* 'Aureoreticulata', is made doubly interesting by the lustrous yellow leaf veins.

tends to be forgotten. In fact it is one of the most vital elements in a garden composition and repays careful study: not only the close-up appearance of an individual leaf – although many of these, with their strange shapes, markings and textures, can be absolutely fascinating – but their general effect when seen from a distance.

The larger and shinier the leaf, the coarser is the apparent texture of the plant, because large leaves hold strong shadow beneath them, increasing the contrast between the shiny upper surface and the dark under-side. Even when large, a matt-textured leaf does not produce such a coarse effect because the contrast between upper and lower surfaces is much less; smaller shiny leaves, like those of

Among plants that combine an interesting growth habit with attractive texture is *Picea abies* 'Reflexa', a creeping bush which naturally forms a low, wide-spreading mound **right**. Its unusual form and dense evergreen colour suggest its use as a specimen plant against a background of pale concrete or stone in a modern paved garden – and, an excellent carpeting shrub, the fine-textured branchlets may be pleasingly contrasted with plants of more dramatic form.

holly, for instance, may give a coarser reading than large dull ones. Naturally, the finest textures are those of plants such as conifers which have small, light-absorbent dark needles.

Qualities in combination
The abstract shapes which you have already arranged can therefore be given a texture – fine, medium or coarse, light-reflecting or light-absorbent – so that a satisfying combination of shapes and textures results. The next thing to take into consideration is colour, and this is examined more fully on pages 26 to 29. One word of warning at this stage, however: Any two of the three main attributes of plant material – form, texture and colour – can be contrasted to advantage, but to contrast all three at once produces such a striking effect that it should not be attempted too frequently or the result will be restless and spotty.

Generally speaking, you will find that a 'coarse' plant or group is best used as the major feature in a setting of 'fine', because fine foliage is recessive and most suitable for creating a background, while the coarse plant will appear highlighted as though it were a sculptured object.

Plants as sculpture
Few people can afford good sculpture in their gardens, so focal points have to be created in a simpler way. There are many plants, both evergreen and deciduous, that have exactly the quality of carving and, if well placed against a neutral background or deep shadow, can create suitably dramatic incidents without

the use of any hard materials. Some plants of this kind earn, by reason of their angular form or other attributes, the epithet 'architectural' (see p 252), but plants do not have to be so idiosyncratic in shape to be worthy of display as specimens.

Among evergreen shrubs of this type are such mahonias as *Mahonia bealii, M. japonica* and the hybrid 'Charity', the false castor-oil plant (*Fatsia japonica*), *Viburnum rhytidophyllum* and *Yucca gloriosa*, together with the evergreen perennial New Zealand flax (*Phormium tenax*). On a smaller scale, there is *Viburnum davidii,* while *Aralia chinensis,* the stag's-horn sumach (*Rhus typhina*) and *Sorbaria aitchisonii* are deciduous shrubs of equally strong character. *Vitis coignetiae* and the various fruiting figs (*Ficus carica*) can be used to create a sculptured panel against a suitable plain wall, while hostas, bergenias, *Macleaya cordata* (the plume poppy) and acanthus – from which the ancient Greeks derived the Corinthian capital – will do the same in the flower bed.

Growth patterns
Plants have not only form and texture, but also have very specific habits of growth which in many cases give them an added dimension.

This most often occurs with an open-branched structure – as, for instance, in *Rhus typhina* – where the pattern formed by the branches, particularly in winter, has an attraction beyond the striking foliage and fruit. Such plants are best used against a plain, pale-coloured background or rising from a simple carpet of close texture which does not create competition for the eye.

Into this category, though with rather different results, come the strongly regular horizontal branch patterns of *Cornus kousa, Viburnum plicatum tomentosum* and, on a very large scale, the cedar of Lebanon (*Cedrus libani*). Some weeping trees which have a rather open 'willow-pattern' effect, like the weeping ash (*Fraxinus excelsior* 'Pendula'), share the same quality of interest, but many weeping forms have such a thick and confused pattern that they read only as shapes.

While the general outline stays the same, the texture of the plant and the amount of its structure which is revealed naturally change from season to season. There is the bare tracery of winter, with its emphasis on skeletal patterns and the often unexpectedly rich textures of tree trunks, branches and twigs. In spring the interest of the pattern remains but is lightly veiled by the rising tide of deciduous foliage which, being juvenile, tends to give a preponderance of fine texture to the general scene. Summer and autumn vary rather in colour range than in their strong textures and solid outlines.

Each of these periods and its special effects have to be borne in mind when considering a planting plan; and this is examined in the article on page 30. But if you have studied the visual as well as the cultural aspects of plants as you encounter them, you need not flounder about helplessly in a confusing mass of catalogues and conflicting ideas. Having decided on abstract shapes and complementary textures, you will probably find that there is only one plant which you can use under the particular set of growing conditions – and the problem is solved!

Plants with sculptural form include the spiky yuccas; **below left** *Yucca filamentosa* 'Variegata' as a specimen plant set off by the fine-foliaged masses of surrounding shrubs and ground-cover plants. The stiff-leaved form and striking colouring of these evergreen plants make them suitable substitutes for modern garden sculpture. **below right** The art of converting plants into sculpture by topiary is a very old one; evergreen, bushy and slow-growing, yew is ideal for clipping into complex shapes like the popular corkscrew.

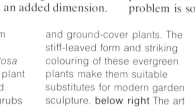

Colour in the garden

The cry 'I do like a nice splash of colour' is commonly heard, but a splash is only a splash and it is not the colour that is important but the exact function of that colour in relation to its surroundings. Colour can do nothing by itself and it is the way in which colour is used that is all-important: a fact too often forgotten by eager planters, to judge by some of the extraordinary effects to be seen in very many parks and gardens.

Colour and light

The first thing to remember is that, like everything else in the garden, colour is not static but constantly changing. The intensity of light varies not only from season to season but from hour to hour, and it is light that gives life to all colour. Without light, colour is invisible, and depending on the quality of light so colours change and take on new dimensions. In much of northern Europe and northern North America the atmosphere is always slightly blue – sometimes visibly so – however bright the sun, and this blue light has a powerful effect on the appearance of many flowers. Not only blue flowers and foliage but all the mauves, purples and bluish-pinks gain an intense vitality from the blue in the atmosphere, whereas, in the brilliant white or yellow light of other parts of the world, they look faded and washed out. Conversely, the gentle, misty quality of such light can make the dashing colour contrasts which look so stimulating in warmer climes appear tawdry and vulgar.

Pale colours look best in shade or semishade because they gain in intensity from contrast with the surrounding darkness, whereas in full sunlight they appear merely drained. Most strong colours, especially those like crimson and purple that have a touch of darkness in their make-up, need brilliant sunlight to give them life, while in shade they seem dowdy and muddy-looking. The placing of colour in relation to the strength and intensity of light is all-important if you are to achieve the best possible effects in your garden with the means available.

above left The yellow colour range: yellowish-green aralias and veratrums and yellow lilies giving way to salmon-pink varieties. **above right** The blue range, including bluish-pinks in association with silver-grey foliage, mauves, magentas and brilliant white. **below** A border planted in varying shades of green, including a yellowish-green robinia and a clump of yellow-margined hostas, a *Juniperus chinensis* 'Kaizuka' in a more 'conventional' shade of green, a blue-green *Juniperus horizontalis* and pampas grass.

Then there are seasonal variations in the colours themselves. You only have to think of the sharp, shrill greens of grass and trees in springtime and compare them with the sober, heavy green of midsummer to realize the possible extent of variation. Even evergreens, which one thinks of as being largely static in their effect, can change considerably when they are covered in young shoots and tufts of juvenile foliage. On the whole, spring colours are cool and a little thin, summer colours opulently rich and autumn colours brilliant, with a tendency for summer foliage to be rather muted. Winter colour too should not be neglected, for although the palette is restricted it is much more subtle, and without other distractions the eye can appreciate the greys, browns, reds and purples of twigs and bare branches, the rich greens of moss and lichen, the warm tones of earth and stone.

Colour quality

So often, colour is considered to be almost anything other than green, but green itself is a colour of infinite variety which extends through a wide range of bluish and yellowish tones to the more 'conventional' greens and near-black. A very satisfying garden – especially in a city, which tends to confuse the eye with too much garish colour in shops and on advertisement hoardings – could be made from greens alone, with perhaps a few pale lilies or paeonies as occasional highlights. Then there are the warm colours of brick walls and buildings, of cultivated soil and gravel paths, or the cool ones of painted stucco, natural concrete and stone flags. All these form a background but they are colours in their own right and have to be thought about as a major part of any composition.

Many people fail in their use of colour because they do not understand the need to decide on the relative importance of the various elements. Just as in cooking no good cook would think of throwing a number of ingredients into a pot and allowing the flavours to fight it out between them, so one cannot amass a number of colours – however pleasant they may be individually – and expect them to achieve a good effect. The situation is aggravated by packets of seed sold in 'mixed colours' – or, even worse, 'mixed varieties'. These mixtures create an impossible problem for the creative gardener. They simply result in a mess rather than a mass of colour, and make any form of colour-scheming very difficult. In any successful scheme there is always a dominant note, supported by subdominants of differing degrees against a more neutral background. Firstly one must decide on the overall theme, then consider how this is to be carried out to the best effect.

Simplicity in the use of colour

In its simplest form you can use colour as a pure mass, just as in nature the bluebell wood, the embankment solid with primroses or the clearing a sea of spiring foxgloves makes the greatest impact. In a small garden such simplicity may seem out of place, but with careful interplanting several such effects can be created in the course of a season.

One of the easiest and most striking ways to use colour is to design a small garden – or a section of a large one – in a single colour. This need never be dull, for you can use every shade and tone of that colour, playing off light against dark, brilliant against pale, and setting the whole thing against a neutral background or one subtly contrasted to bring out the quality of the theme colour.

A good example of this approach is to be seen at Hidcote Manor, in Gloucestershire, where borders with flowers in every shade of red from light scarlet to deep crimson are set against dark tapestry hedges formed from yew, holly and purple-leaved beech. Yellow is an excellent colour to use in this way, with a setting of grey or silver foliage – all the easier as many grey-leaved shrubs have yellow flowers. A similar scheme would be possible with orange, but in that case purple, crimson and dark green would provide the most effective background.

If you have great self-control, a garden of white flowers, white-variegated leaves and silver foliage can be very beautiful; but white is a very strong colour and too much contrast between white flowers and dark green foliage should be avoided or the result can be very spotty and disturbing. The white garden at Sissinghurst Castle, Kent (see p 240) and the white borders at Crathes Castle, Banchory, in Kincardineshire, are fine examples of this rather unusual colour range. Blue is good, too, but needs a very carefully contrived setting if it is not to appear too cold, while purple looks dull unless livened up with touches of red and magenta as in the big purple border at Sissinghurst. With pink one enters another realm, for there are two distinct ranges of pink flowers, one biased towards mauve and blue, the other towards salmon and yellow.

All flower and leaf colours appear to tend either to blue or to yellow. In the yellow range are all the warm whites and creams, yellow, orange, salmon and apricot-pinks, all the various sunset colours and pure scarlet. With these are associated all the yellow and yellowish-green leaves – a quality which is particularly noticeable in spring. On the blue side are the hard, brilliant whites which always contain a touch of blue to bring out their whiteness, all the blues, the bluish-pinks from 'apple-blossom' to 'old rose', the magenta and fuchsia colours, and all the purples, mauves and crimsons. With these go most grey and silver leaves, all the leaden blues and the (generally rather dark) blue-greens like those of holly and rhododendrons.

The indiscriminate mixing of these two ranges of colour can produce clashes that are ugly rather than stimulating, but when imaginatively used they can create many exciting effects (see p 28).

Colour and space

Colour is not something which you add, like icing on an already completed cake, but is basic to your designing. It can be used to alter the proportions or feeling of the space on which you are working. If your garden is too long, strong colour at the far end will make it appear much shorter, while pale, misty colours at the end of a short enclosure will make it look farther away. If the space is too confined – a fault with many modern gardens, particularly in urban areas – the boundaries can be darkened, then lost in the shadows of free-growing plant material placed in front of them, while the eye is held within the space so enclosed by a group of bright flowers or strong foliage cunningly placed where it will catch the light.

A gloomy area lacking much direct sunlight can be lightened by introducing flowers and foliage in shades of yellow, while one which seems cold – as do many north-facing gardens in the northern hemisphere – can be warmed with pale oranges and flame-pinks. The too-hot garden – for instance a walled courtyard catching all the brilliance of the midday sun – will look much cooler if planted with frosty blues, whites and silver foliage.

Artificial colour

Although one thinks of garden colour largely in terms of flowers and foliage, there are other elements in the scene that deserve equal consideration. Dust and coal bins, sheds, garages and greenhouses all tend to compete for attention, when under ideal conditions one would not wish to see them at all. Except for the greenhouse, which is a special case, the best solution is to paint them a dark colour and cast shadows over them (see p 23). The greenhouse, of course, cannot be placed in shadow because that would nullify its function, but if it must be positioned conspicuously, some semi-transparent structure such as a pergola can usually be placed between it and the viewer, to hold the attention and discourage the eye from penetrating further.

Even a well-designed garden with careful planting can be spoiled by lack of attention to the final details. Badly-chosen garden furniture with garish coverings may fight the eye. Even in an entirely green garden, fabrics patterned with bright flowers, wine bottles, advertisements and other irrelevant things would be disturbing; in a garden already gay with flowers and coloured foliage they can be a disaster. You would do better to choose from the excellent range of plain canvas and sailcloth – the natural, undyed variety is particularly attractive.

Plastic plant containers in improbable shades of green are also very unpleasant. On the whole, green is best left to nature, and paintwork and other colouring carried out in simple earth and stone colours, or white, or made to tone with adjoining buildings if these are also coloured. Texture plays its part here, too, and it is best to avoid objects which have an offensive artificial sheen, for they never weather to a mellow tone, but merely grow dirty and look sordid.

Colour, texture, light and shadow are essential ingredients of the garden picture and it is only through careful observation and constant experiment that you will find how best to use them to advantage.

Bold but simple use of colour is the secret of a striking garden: **above** A mass of white flowers with silver-grey and green foliage makes a very effective monochromatic border. **below left** Pale yellow verbascums take on a luminous quality in shade. **below right** Frosty blues, such as this jacaranda, and cool greens look restful and shady in a hot, sunny climate.

Plant associations for colour effects

Good cooks know that it is not only the choice of ingredients that makes a delectable dish, but the way these are combined and the whole presented. So it is with the colour composition of a garden. The article on page 26 discusses the basic qualities and functions of colour in the garden, and colours are (along with plant form and texture; see p 24) the creative gardener's principle ingredients. This article moves on to the 'cooking' and presentation stages: the choice and positioning of actual plants to create pleasing visual effects, in particular colour effects.

It is this, the art of skilful plant association, that distinguishes the creative gardener from the plantsman. The latter may be an expert at growing and nurturing his specimens, but it takes a different kind of skill to produce an effect that can be truly termed artistic.

One of the most common but inane statements about gardening – and one doubtless responsible for many horticultural visual dis-

There can be problems with spring-flowering azaleas, however, which many gardeners group without thought, producing a discordant effect of magenta, red, orange and purple. These then become rivals for attention rather than partners working towards a harmonious whole.

Some of the loveliest spring effects are obtained by teaming blues and yellows; or soft pinks and reds with blue or cream. In the Keukenhof Gardens in Holland one finds in most years a winding path of blue grape hyacinths (*Muscari armeniacum* 'Heavenly Blue') wending through a plantation of sprouting hazelnut trees. These are undercarpeted with white *Anemone nemorosa*.

Rhododendron × *praecox* bushes, 1 to 1.5 m (3 to 5 ft) high, planted on a grassy bank present a delightful picture when underplanted with *Narcissus cyclamineus* or blue *Scilla sibirica* or grape hyacinths. When these are all in bloom the effect is charming. Other

asters – is that 'flower colours never clash'. Of course they do, particularly if you team, say, orange, scarlet and magenta-purple in close proximity. Those with a good understanding of colour and well-trained eye can, however, mix colour ranges successfully and create clashes which stimulate rather than stun. But to work well such climaxes must be built up through a series of carefully related tones, and be separated by stretches of rather neutral and recessive colouring. Flowers in pastel shades or green and silver foliage are ideal for such muting purposes. Another basic principle, as explained in the article on planning herbaceous borders on page 104, is to use bold areas of colour and avoid spotty effects.

Nevertheless, whatever the principles, it remains a fact that some of the most successful colour effects in gardens come about by chance, the happy juxtaposition of complementary flowers and foliage. Experienced gardeners remember these groupings and

top A small spring grouping of bright blue scillas, primroses, red polyanthus and grape hyacinths. above left Delphiniums and other blue, white and pink summer flowers teamed with grey-green foliage. above right The blue and yellow border in the gardens of Clare College, Cambridge.

repeat them in future seasons, and they also keep a watchful eye for similar combinations in other people's gardens – both grand and small. These can either be photographed for future reference, or detailed in a notebook. When you do this, be sure to note the particular season to which each relates and any circumstances – like weather conditions or aspect – that may have influenced the result.

Ideas for spring

Apart from the strident shades affected by certain tulip cultivars, few bulbs create colour problems. They team well with most plants – shrubs, grass, perennials and other bulbs.

suggestions worth trying are formal beds of pink 'Clara Butt' tulips and a late-flowering poet's narcissus, such as the white 'Actaea', interplanted with a froth of blue forget-me-nots; or yellow primroses and blue scillas in front of red polyanthus and blue hyacinths.

Yellow doronicums and blue pansies mix well, as do snowdrops and the wine-red *Crocus tomasinianus* massed in a shrubbery setting. A blend of tall golden *Fritillaria imperialis* 'Lutea', yellow daffodils and deep orange wallflowers provide a sunshine symphony. Similar plays on simple colour themes are achieved by using all blue flowers – hyacinths, pansies, scillas and grape hyacinths – or by mixing these with blocks of white narcissi or white violas.

Summer blends

There is such a wealth of bloom in summer that a succession of combinations can be made on a framework of permanent plants. Many people favour one-colour borders, like the red border at Hidcote Manor, Gloucestershire, or ones of restricted colour range in which white and cream flowers predominate (see p 27). There are blue and yellow borders at Clare College, Cambridge. Pyrford Court, Surrey, has a silver border in which a weeping silver pear (*Pyrus salicifolia* 'Pendula') dominates the scene, with bold groupings of *Senecio laxifolius* and *Stachys olympica* (*S. lanata*) with silvery cotton thistles (*Onopordum acanthium*) balanced by *Verbascum bombyciferum* – tall spire plants both – at the back; the spaces between are filled with curry plants (*Helichrysum serotinum*, or *H. angustifolium*), lavenders and Jerusalem sages (*Phlomis* spp).

A gold border can have year-long interest if the main features of the design consist of shrubs – for example, gold-variegated hollies, golden yews, *Elaeagnus pungens* 'Maculata' and even common golden privet. In season

Small groupings
It is always more difficult to create effective plant associations in restricted areas such as window-boxes and other containers, or small patio beds. However, here are a few suggestions for such plantings:–
 Pink, mauve and blue petunias
 Lemon-yellow lupins with rich blue perennial flax (such as *Linum narbonense* 'June Perfield')
 Blue or white hyacinths and blue forget-me-nots
 Pink and red astilbes with blue *Iris sibirica*
 Salvia farinacea 'Blue Bedder', white foxgloves and silver *Senecio cineraria*
 Pale pink pelargoniums (geraniums) such as 'Cleopatra' teamed with mauve-purple heliotropes

Autumn effects
Although more ephemeral, the autumn tints of certain deciduous trees and shrubs (see p 242) can be as brilliant as many flowers. Liquidambars (sweet gums), maples, *Parrotia persica* and the spindle tree (*Euonymus europaeus*), with their vivid scarlet, orange, crimson and gold foliage, gleam like flames in late autumn. They become most effective when backed by a few green or gold-variegated, columnar conifers, especially where there is water in front to mirror their beauties. The Sheffield Park Gardens in Sussex are noted for this combination of lakes with water-lilies, shrubs and trees that show brilliant autumn tints.

For late effects in the herbaceous border, mauve, pink, purple and lilac michaelmas daisies (*Aster novae-angliae* and *A. novi-belgii* forms) look well in a bed by themselves or can be interplanted with pink *Chrysanthemum rubellum*.

these may be interplanted with daffodils, wallflowers and golden pansies, followed by yellow antirrhinums and calceolarias, and later still by yellow and gold dahlias and chrysanthemums.

For a pleasing waterside picture try pink and rose candelabra *Primula pulverulenta* hybrids interspersed with the rich blue of *Meconopsis betonicifolia*, plus a few *Ranunculus lingua* 'Grandiflora'. Grow pink climbing roses with purple *Clematis* × *jackmanii* so that the two intermingle, or team deep blue delphiniums, rosy-pink *Papaver orientale* 'Mrs Perry' and cream *Lilium regale* behind blue irises or multicoloured aquilegias. A touch of red brings life to silver foliage – for example a few scarlet pelargoniums (geraniums) among groupings of *Helichrysum petiolatum*, *Senecio greyi* or *S. laxifolius*, and *Artemisia maritima*. Or let a red clematis wend its way through the gold-netted foliage of *Lonicera japonica* 'Aureoreticulata'.

above left A gentle waterside grouping of yellow-green *Alchemilla mollis* and *Carex stricta* 'Bowles' Golden' with a contrasting clump of blue-green *Hosta sieboldiana*. above right Green, bronze and brilliant red autumn foliage colours at the Sheffield Park Gardens in Sussex.

Irises grown in colour blocks, gradating from pastel shades to the deeper colours of the spectrum, are exquisite in early summer. Or for a quiet corner try *Alchemilla mollis*, which has yellow-green, feathery flowers, with the blue-green foliage of *Hosta sieboldiana* (not to be confused with *H. sieboldii*) and the golden-yellow grass-like sedge *Carex stricta* 'Bowles' Golden'. Around the same time, mauve, white and blue delphiniums associate pleasantly with pink foxgloves, blue, mauve and pink cup-and-saucer Canterbury bells, plus a few clumps of the cerise cranesbill *Geranium psilostemon* or deep blue *G. meeboldii* (*G. grandiflorum*).

Colour in winter
Although the bright colours of summer cannot be matched in winter yet there are compensations in the green, gold and silver of evergreen shrubs and trees, particularly amongst conifers. When these are spangled with hoarfrost or snow they can be magnificent. Many lend themselves to topiary and are colourful against grass in winter. Colourful bark also assumes importance.

Winter-flowering heathers form ground carpets of colour; their flatness is easily broken by the papery trunk and lacy twigs of a silver birch. As the days begin to lengthen, dwarf irises like the blue *Iris histrioides* or yellow *I. danfordiae* blend beautifully with the purplish-red of the heathers, and later come snowdrops and snowflakes to fill any gaps. Bamboos fronted by red or pink camellias with red and cream *Helleborus orientalis* at their feet also make an effective combination for late winter.

Time: the fourth dimension

In any design involving the use of plants, time is always the fourth dimension that has to be taken into account, for in spite of the (often doubtful) charms of 'instant' gardening, there are many effects that only years of care can achieve. There are no instant cedars of Lebanon, for example, and these can be enjoyed only by the third or fourth generation after the planter. Even in your own lifetime you must plant a garden when you are fairly young, and remain with it, if you are going to enjoy to the full the great pink flowers of *Magnolia campbellii* or a high wall covered by the rich foliage of *M. grandiflora*.

Gardens are not ephemeral things to be thrown away and forgotten when you are no longer in charge of them; they continue from one generation to another. Buildings may be pulled down or change their use, large gardens may be broken up into smaller units, but generally the major elements of planting – large trees, mature hedges and massive shrub groups – remain. Fortunately there is a strong feeling for conservation that helps to ensure that this is so. Even the trees planted in small gardens are often saved and remain to be incorporated into more spacious landscape schemes when streets of houses are cleared for redevelopment.

Time layers

The garden designer therefore has a duty towards the future as well as to his own immediate pleasure, and it is essential that he thinks in terms of time as well as space. The answer is to plant in 'time layers' ensuring that as far as possible you plant for continuity, although the effects of your foresight will differ in different decades. The longest-lived things generally grow most slowly, and if you put them at the correct distance apart for their final spacing, there will be vast areas of bare ground between them. However, if you position them at the correct spacing and then infill with things which mature more quickly and possibly infill again with yet quicker subjects interspersed with herbaceous plants and bulbs, you can achieve considerable continuity without sacrificing immediate gain or final effect.

For instance, if your land is large enough you might decide that a certain knoll would look well crowned by a group of evergreen oak (*Quercus ilex*). Of course, these are very slow and will scarcely be more than big bushes in your own lifetime; they will also look ridiculous sitting in little round beds on the grass mound. You might therefore take the bold decision to plant the whole of the knoll, placing the oaks where they will be required for the final effect, interspersed with groups of magnolias and rhododendrons. But these, too, are comparatively slow so that in some places drifts of broom or tree lupins (*Lupinus arboreus*) could fill the growth gaps, to be removed when they outgrow their strength in about five years, while in other gaps groups of ground-cover plants and bulbs could be started so that they could creep across and make a complete cover when the temporary shrubs are pulled out. For the first year or two,

pockets of annuals or even bedding plants might hide the remaining bare soil. Planting of this kind has only one disadvantage: You must keep watch to ensure that the temporary plants do not grow so vigorously that they suppress the slower permanent ones.

This system of infill can also be used to advantage when planting trees for shelter, particularly those that can only be moved when they are small. If you plan a windbreak using mainly pines (*Pinus* spp), you will find that it is best to put them in as young plants, which will give no cover to begin with and will themselves need protection in the early stages. For this reason it is best to interplant with shrubs such as the sea buckthorn (*Hippophae rhamnoides*), which will make a thick screen 2 or 3 cm (7 to 10 ft) in height, or with quick-growing trees like silver birch. With careful maintenance, the pines will be protected and encouraged to grow upwards faster than they could have done if left alone and

Winter Surprisingly strong colours can appear in the winter garden; here frost rims the evergreen leaves and red berries of a pyracantha.

left Until the permanent occupants of this long border – the relatively fast-growing cypresses and other trees and shrubs – have reached their mature height and spread, the dwarf shrubs, foliage plants, herbaceous perennials and roses that have been planted as infill in the gaps between them will continue to clothe the soil, give necessary height, depth and density to the area and provide the seasonal colour and interest that would otherwise be lacking.
right During most of the day the pink spires of these shade-tolerant astilbes bring eye-catching colour to a green and shady woodland clearing, but planted where they are, at certain times shafts of sunlight act as spotlights to bring out new fiery qualities in their waving plumes.

exposed, while the fillers will create screening and shelter in the early stages. As the pines grow, the other material can be gradually cut out until the pines are dominant. It must be remembered in such a case that the visual balance of the plantation will change over the years from being almost purely deciduous to almost purely evergreen, and this may affect the pattern of long-term planting that you arrange in front of it.

The seasons

As well as evolving slowly over the long time-scale of the years, gardens change cyclically over the shorter one of the seasons. The garden year is generally divided, rather roughly, into four, and one must plan for a complete – and different – effect in each. Today, with the great range of plant material from all over the world available to gardeners, and with hybridizers constantly producing plants that flower out of their normal season, it would be

Spring Yellow and cream polyanthus carpet the ground beneath the misty mauve blossom and delicate branches of a *Rhododendron augustinii*.

technically possible to make a garden that was changeless or that went against the indications of seasonal variation, but it would hardly be worthwhile. Each season has its particular character, and you will get the most satisfaction if you acknowledge this and try to underline the essential qualities of each in your garden planting.

Winter is not a dead season. Indeed, for those with a perceptive eye it can be the most beautiful of all. Firstly one sees the underlying 'bone-structure' of both landscape and garden, the shape of the land and the elegant patterns of trees and shrubs, all of which are lost in the more verdant seasons. Then there are the subtle colours of winter; although you may think of tree trunks and branches as being basically brown, they have a wide colour range from silver grey to rich chestnut. Many of the maples such as *Acer davidii* and *A. griseum*, cherries like *Prunus serrula* and almost all the birches – from silver to red and bronze – are particularly effective.

Young twigs are even more diverse, and many are brilliant scarlet, plum, yellow, green or purple, giving a rich haze of colour which gains in intensity from the misty light. On a large scale, a wood of silver birch, particularly when seen against a blue-green background of Scots pine (*Pinus sylvestris*) has both the colour and bloom of a ripe plum – an effect repeated with greater intensity in the shrub layer by groups of the dogwood *Cornus alba* 'Sibirica'. As a contrast to these low tones, a bank of the scarlet willow (*Salix alba* 'Chermesina'), particularly if pruned severely to increase the production of young shoots, will make a sheet of flame to warm the coldest day. Texture, too, is important, and with less to divert the eye the intricate details of bark and the varied tones of conifers and broad-leaved evergreens can be enjoyed to the full.

Winter flowers tend to be small, but many are sweetly scented and at that time of year one can appreciate their exquisite detail. It is well worth gathering your winter flowers together in some place near the house, where they can be enjoyed without too much effort, but keep them sheltered both from cold winds

and from the early morning sun so that the flowers are not damaged by thawing too quickly in frosty weather. Between them and in the front of the borders you can make drifts of all the small early-flowering bulbs which, when scattered in groups about the garden, are totally lost, but together can make a tapestry of colour over the bare soil. Because they are mostly low-toned, strict colour-scheming is not necessary, but a good arrangement of textures and a satisfactory balance between evergreen and deciduous subjects is essential.

This is true of the rest of the garden, too – at least those sections of it that can be seen from the house – and if you are going to enjoy the winter season to the full the apparent emptiness of beds and borders needs to be concealed or furnished by the careful placing of groups of evergreens or well-arranged dwarf hedges.

Spring is a frail time, the outlines of winter being only lightly veiled and the flowers themselves, though very numerous, have a thin-textured look, delicate and airy as though constantly poised for flight on the rough winds. That is why the large solid daffodils in shades of brass-yellow and the lumpy double tulips of strident colouring may look out of place. The essence of early spring is perhaps more difficult to capture than that of any other time of year, partly because plant-breeders have been almost too busy, and the richness of material is difficult to handle.

High summer shines gloriously. Ample and glowing, it merges almost imperceptibly into the bonfire brilliance of autumn. These seasons are easier because, used with taste, almost any association of plants and colours can succeed. But care is still needed, and the false note struck by too-early-flowering chrysanthemums, for instance, should be avoided. See also page 28.

Light and shade

Even during the course of a single day, the passage of time is important. Within the confines of your garden you should have a clear idea of the pattern of sunlight and shade at different periods, because the sun can be used as a spotlight to emphasize some special effect against a background of dark shadow.

As the sun moves round, so the emphasis will shift and the scene appear different from hour to hour. If you have any choice in the matter – and most of us do not have the space to create different areas for various times of day – your bedroom should overlook an arrangement containing groups of flowers which open each day and close again at night. This factor emphasizes the freshness of early morning, when the summer garden is at its most beautiful and least visited. At night the garden becomes another world, all colour lost and only the pale glimmer of white flowers and silver leaves weaving a pattern of light against varying degrees of blackness.

Summer Bold colours of every hue characterize the crescendo of the gardening year; here there are roses, California poppies, lavender and more.

Autumn Many flowers still linger, but the peak is the brilliant foliage of many trees; here a maple sheds its leaves like petals on the grass.

Water in the garden

In any garden, water exercises a magnetic spell. Its surface is constantly changing, at one moment calm and still, reflecting sun, sky and waterside trees and plants like a mirror, the next ruffled by the wind. Reeds growing near the margins bend and sway, while small brightly-coloured fish dart among the underwater vegetation, providing a living interest. No other garden feature can compare with the changing moods of a water garden.

Not only is there movement, there is sound, too – of moving water lapping and splashing over rocks or tumbling over a waterfall, of poolside reeds and grasses rustling in the breeze, but above all of the birds and other

creatures lured by the presence of water. In addition, there is the fascination of the plants themselves, distinctive and beautiful, many of which cannot be grown except in close proximity to water.

Styles of garden pools

A garden pool can be formal, with or without raised sides, but always of regular shape and in a conventional setting. Alternatively, it can be informal and of irregular outline – a form best suited to natural surrounds. Such pools are excellent in wild gardens or linked to streams, and are particularly appropriate when teamed with rockwork.

Rock and water are common companions in nature, and with a little skill can be made to represent a natural formation – complete with waterfall, rills, and a stream running down to a pond at the lowest level. Such ventures need not be extravagant of water or rock. Electrically-driven pumps ensure that the same water is used over and over again, and, in the absence (or prohibiting expense) of real rock, lightweight synthetic simulations are available. While these cannot be compared with the real thing, they do tone down pleasantly with age and help to bring this type of gardening within everyone's reach.

The essence of an informal pool is that it should appear to be a natural feature. Its shape can range from a simple oval or kidney shape to quite indefinable forms. Its margins should be masked with rockwork, overhanging grass verges or waterside plantings of moisture-loving species. (Some of these, as mentioned on page 256, will scramble in and out of shallow water and wet soil.) Above all, it should be positioned and landscaped so as

not to appear in any way artificial – in a hollow or at the foot of a slope rather than on a rise, and never with raised, artificial-looking edges or with the method of construction showing. Ornamental fountains look out of place here.

A formal pool is generally rectangular, circular, or rectangular with semicircular ends. Such a pool makes an effective focal point in the garden. It looks best in an open position with pavement surround, for example on a terrace that has crazy paving interplanted with small rock plants, or set in grass with an edging of stone paving, so that the feet remain dry in inclement weather. In expansive surroundings, a pool with an area of paving around it can look very effective sunk a little below the general level of a terrace, with two or three steps leading down all round.

Formal pools should always be accessible and planting kept low. Frequently, water-

above A luxuriant pool in the grounds of Brodick Castle in Scotland reflects its setting of open woodland.
above left A small pool and cascade teamed with rockwork bring colour, sparkle and sound to a sloping suburban garden.
above right Although blatantly artificial, this tear-shaped pool is effectively landscaped into a garden terrace, making a feature of a change in level.
left A shallow pool of stark outline nevertheless imparts an air of tranquility to this modern city-centre garden. It needs draining in hard winters.

lilies alone are sufficient ornamentation, but if a figure or fountain is installed, a few narrow-leaved plants such as reeds or water irises can be introduced near to such a feature.

A formal pool can also be built close to the house, with a wall fountain providing interest and movement. Or it can be constructed half in and half out of a room in the building (linked by a channel), a device that calls for skill in lighting the indoor section, but which can be most effective when properly installed. But water is always liable to attract mosquitoes – a good reason, apart from their attractiveness, for keeping fish in all ornamental pools. The other general rule for all garden pools – formal or informal – is to site them where there is plenty of sunshine; otherwise the water may become brackish and will certainly lack sparkle, and aquatic plants will flower poorly.

There are various methods of constructing garden pools, and these are described on page 128. The principal methods use concrete, plastic sheeting and glass-fibre. It is even possible for very small town gardens to have a pool, for any receptacle capable of holding water may be looked upon as a potential water garden. Baths, tanks, cisterns or sawn-down casks are all possibilities and, when sunk into the ground and their edges masked with low-growing land plants, can look most attractive. Even apartment-dwellers with balconies, roof gardens or basement wells can keep free-standing tubs containing aquatic plants. Aquatics need special techniques of

planting, and these are described on page 130. The articles on pages 254 to 256 describe various kinds of plants for the water garden.

Streams and bogs

A stream lazily wending its way between green lawns on a summer's day sounds delightful, and those who are blessed with such a natural feature possess a great asset. The garden can be built around such features, but unfortunately, since many aquatics dislike running water, only the most sluggish streams will grow water-lilies satisfactorily. Whilst in artificial streams the rate of movement can be controlled, problems may occur when a natural stream has to take a sudden spate of flood water, or dries up in summer – a common occurrence in some areas. Methods of overcoming some of these are described on page 132, along with information on constructing water-courses in conjunction with more conventional water gardens.

The margins of natural streams, however, remain suitable for such bog perennials as candelabra primulas, calthas and astilbes which, in the absence of static or running water, can still be grown wherever there is constantly moist, humus-rich soil. Such plants prefer to feel the influence of water rather than sit in it, so to ensure the right conditions make provision as outlined on page 133.

A final possibility, particularly in areas where frosts are rare, is to construct a shallow water feature – about 15 to 20 cm (6 to 8 in) deep – for growing marginal aquatics such as water irises, reedmaces and bulrushes. Such a pool can look well on a patio or in a courtyard, perhaps with stepping stones or areas of large pebbles between groups of plants.

Water gardens in history

Since primitive man tended to settle near lakes and streams, it is not surprising that aquatic plants received early attention and many have strange histories. For example, some authorities have suggested that the swastika and cornucopia symbols were derived thousands of years ago from the twisted sepals and bursting seed-pods of water-lilies. And the biblical phrase 'Cast thy bread upon the waters for thou shalt find it after many days' refers to the early Egyptian practice of wrapping the seeds of the lotus (*Nelumbo nucifera*) in balls of clay and then throwing them into the Nile. In time the harvested flower seeds were crushed to make flour.

The story of water plants is linked with many creeds and civilizations. The ancients venerated water-lilies, seeing in their chaste flowers and annual revival from the mud and slime of dried summer ponds a miracle of purity, hope and regeneration. It is small wonder that all the world's great gardens included water. The Hanging Gardens of Babylon were largely water features. The fabulous pools and canals of the Taj Mahal are legendary. Vaux le Vicomte and Versailles in France have their playing fountains. In Spain and Persia, Colombia and Mexico men build their courtyard gardens around a pool or fountain, and there are walls of water in New Orleans and vast lily pools at the Longwood Gardens, Pennsylvania. In Britain such famous gardens as Sheffield Park, Bodnant and Stowe owe much of their magnificence to a cunning use of water. Sometimes this blends in naturally with the landscape, but on occasions is blatantly artificial – as at Blenheim and Chatsworth.

The earliest artificial pools were probably dewponds made of puddled clay. After excavation, they were made waterproof by kneading heather roots or similar plants with wet clay – generally by having cart-horses trample over the area until the basin became watertight. Later came shallow stone containers designed to catch the drips from fountains, but in the late 19th century pools were being installed as an aesthetic feature. This development came about for two reasons – the invention of concrete and the researches of a French engineer called Marliac.

The availability of Portland cement and the simple technique of concrete-mixing meant that anyone so minded could have a pool in his garden. The material is malleable before setting, tough and strong on hardening; and with its aid a miscellany of shapes, sizes and depths became possible. Around this period Bory St Vincent Latour-Marliac became interested in the genus *Nymphaea*, the water-lilies. Reading an article in the *Revue Horticole* about a consignment of blue water-lilies which had recently arrived at the *Jardin Botanique* in Paris, Marliac dreamt of decorating the Seine with similar floral treasures.

He systematically set to work, combing the world for water-lilies – tropical varieties as well as hardies – and then hybridizing, selecting and trying out the resultant cultivars. He had unique success; new colours appeared, fresh shapes and flower sizes varying between that of a wedding ring up to a teaplate. His achievements remain unparalleled. Altogether Marliac gave the world some 70 hardy water-lily cultivars, and helped create the current interest in water gardening.

Japanese water gardens
Water has for centuries been an integral part of Japanese gardens, and in such a mountainous country there is little difficulty in making it seem appropriate to the landscape. This traditional-style house and water garden are so adeptly landscaped that the two form a harmonious whole and the large pool, though artificial, looks completely natural in its site. This is helped considerably by the sensitive marginal planting and the use of elegantly shaped overhanging trees, together with the use of natural materials in the construction of the house, so that even building over the water does not strike a false note. Even in more formal and stylized Japanese gardens, water is often present, possibly trickling from a bamboo pipe into a *tsukubai*, or water basin. Or its presence may be represented by pebbles.

Attracting wildlife to your garden

Every garden, however small, attracts wildlife of some kind. Animals and plants are so interdependent that even a window box on a town balcony will attract wild creatures, most probably insects such as aphids at first, soon followed by their predators the ladybirds. Eventually a surprise visitor such as a hummingbird hawkmoth may probe into the petunias with its long tongue. A suburban or country garden has much more potential as a haven for wildlife, and it is not difficult to encourage welcome insects, birds and even small animals.

Wild creatures are not interested simply in a colourful display. Their needs are basic, and what they are looking for is firstly food and water, then shelter, and finally undisturbed breeding places. If your garden can provide some or all of these you are certain to have a number of passing visitors and probably also some permanent residents.

Such creatures are not only decorative and interesting, they are also useful to have around the garden, since many of them feed upon insects and pests that cause so much damage to plants. But pesticides and weed-killers – in fact all substances that have a warning on the container to keep them away from pets – can be a danger to wildlife. Such chemicals should be used with great care in the garden, and whenever possible avoided altogether. They can cause enormous damage to the natural balance between the animal and plant life of the garden, making little distinction between friend and foe. (Most insecticides, for example, kill butterflies and bees as readily as aphids and other pests.)

Plants to attract insects

Honey-bees and wild bees are attracted to flowers rich in nectar and pollen. In temperate regions they will visit winter-flowering heathers, then crocuses in early spring. Later on in the year they will search for aubrieta, wallflowers, *Hesperis matronalis* (sweet rocket) and any plants of the cabbage family – both edible and ornamental varieties – that have been allowed to run to flower. They are fond of herbs, especially thyme, lavender, marjoram and rosemary, and love nearly all flowers belonging to the daisy family, from

dandelions and thistles to Michaelmas daisies and sunflowers. Shrubs such as buddleias, cotoneasters, hebes and berberis, and citrus and eucalyptus trees all have plenty to offer insect visitors, as do the flowers of soft fruits like raspberries and currants, and apple, plum and cherry blossom. Generally speaking, bees prefer single to double flowers and a border of mixed annuals to a rose garden.

Butterflies have similar tastes, and like bees they also visit many wild flowers. If you have enough space in your garden to allow even a small area, such as a sloping bank, to become a natural garden of red and white clover, bird's foot trefoil, garlic mustard (*Alliaria petiolata*) and ox-eye daisies (*Chrysanthemum leucanthemum*) among rough grass, you may well be rewarded by butterflies such as orange-tips, meadow browns, small heaths and even common blues laying their eggs in your garden. And if you are courageous and unconventional enough to allow a clump of stinging nettles to flourish somewhere in a sunny corner, you will provide a nursery for four colourful butterflies: the peacock, the red admiral, the small tortoiseshell and the comma. A few thistles and a burdock plant nearby might even tempt a passing painted lady butterfly to deposit a few eggs on the leaves.

Encouraging birds into your garden

There must be some degree of order in a garden if it is not to revert to a complete wilderness, but many wildlife visitors, especially the shyer birds, feel more at home in a garden where there is adequate cover and shrubs are allowed to grow naturally. Resist the temptation to trim and train them too much. Nesting is a very private business for most small birds. Although many of them are prepared to tolerate the coming and going of people, they like their nests to be hidden as much as possible from view.

If you have an ivy-covered wall, think twice before you tear the foliage off and leave a bare surface where no creature can find shelter. Thick clumps of ivy on trees and walls provide wonderful nesting-places for birds and offer

winter shelter to hibernators. The blossom of English ivy (*Hedera helix*) also provides the last big nectar feast of the season for innumerable insects.

The hole-nesters – such as Old World redstarts, nuthatches and all the tits, and the chickadees of North America – appreciate nesting boxes in a garden. The entrance hole must be small enough to prevent squirrels and predatory birds such as jays from entering, and the box should preferably be in the shade, especially in a climate where the summer temperature is high.

A bird table in a garden will prove a great attraction, particularly during the winter when food is scarce. Generous feeding in severe weather – together with a constant supply of unfrozen water – often saves the lives of birds which might otherwise perish. Bird seed, nuts of all kinds, apples and apple cores are appreciated by many birds; bread crusts, grated cheese and porridge oats are also excellent foods, and bacon rind and suet are ideal in cold weather. But during the nesting season it is better not to feed too liberally, especially with nuts, bread and fatty foods which are often fatal to nestlings. If food is not offered in the summer when there are plenty

Features to attract wildlife
Food, water, shelter and breeding places – these are wild visitors' prime needs. **left** A 'flowering meadow' sounds like a feature for a large garden, but even a small area of wild flowers amid long grass will attract butterflies and bees. **above** Any gardener can provide food and shallow water (for drinking and bathing), nesting boxes for tits and plenty of shrubs and climbers for nest-builders. Keep the bird table stocked in winter with fatty foods and thawed water. In summer, let some plants go to seed; grow plenty of nectar-rich annual flowers.

of insects about, the birds will revert to their natural diet and rear their broods successfully – and will rid your garden of many pests.

Don't be too fussy about dead-heading your flowers. Leaving some of the seeds to ripen on the plants is the most satisfactory way of assuring that the garden can provide plenty of natural food during the growing season. Both herbaceous plants and shrubs produce an abundance of seed, and finches of all kinds will very quickly come and harvest it, even before it is fully ripe. When you notice that the seed pods have been torn open and emptied you can remove the unsightly old stems with a good conscience.

Many fruits and berries will also tempt birds into the garden. Apart from fruits which you want for yourself (and would be wise to protect with nets), birds delight in elderberries (the black and red fruits of the *Sambucus* species), berries of the *Sorbus* species – the mountain ash, whitebeam and rowan – berries of the hawthorn, various viburnums and hollies, rose hips, crab apples and many more. Every country has its own shrubs and trees whose seeds and fruits birds find palatable. A little bird-watching in your own area will quickly give you a clue to the kinds of things you should plant to please flying visitors.

Water to attract wildlife

Clean water is essential all the year round, but especially so in hot summer weather or in dry climates where drinking places may be hard to find, and in winter when ponds and puddles may be frozen over. A shallow bird bath where birds can both drink and bathe should

have a place in every garden where there is no suitable pond. A formal pool can provide drinking water if it is filled right up to the brim, but it is useless as a bathing place for small birds, who much prefer a shallow puddle where there is no danger of drowning. A tiny fountain sending up a fine and not too forceful spray will also be used by birds wanting a shower.

Bees and butterflies prefer to drink from drops of water sprayed over herbage, or from a shallow trickle between stones in a little stream. If you cannot provide this, a tray filled with shingle and kept constantly wet will make an ideal 'refreshment bar' for thirsty insects. Even quite a small garden pond will act as a magnet for water insects, and various

beetles, pond skaters, dragonflies and damselflies will often appear of their own accord. Larvae and eggs are frequently introduced with water plants, or they can be bought, together with water snails, from dealers.

Frogs are becoming scarce in Britain, but are still common in many countries and should certainly be welcomed. The attractive tree frogs also breed in water; they like a pool which is partly overhung by trees or shrubs. Far from being unpleasant, toads are most engaging creatures, and once settled in a garden they may remain there for years, asking nothing more than to be left undisturbed in their cool hiding places during the day. In the evening they set out on their rounds, hungry for large quantities of various garden pests.

Wild animals in your garden

Small lizards, skinks and geckos are delightful to watch in a garden. They will often move in if you have a suitable sunny stone wall or rocky bank where they can hide and chase insects. In Britain, tortoises are classified as pets, but in countries where they are native they may well find their way in and sample some of the garden plants. The damage they do is seldom serious.

The hedgehog is one of the most useful visitors to a European garden. It hunts assiduously for slugs, beetles and worms, and is quite uninterested in flowers or vegetables. You can encourage it by providing a saucer of milk when dusk falls. Squirrels can be very attractive too, but fruit cannot be protected against their ravages. In some gardens both badgers and foxes are welcomed and fed with various scraps. This can be fun, but they are fairly large animals and if they begin to feel too much at home they may start excavations which – though tolerable in a large garden – can cause considerable damage in a small one.

Every garden has room for at least some wildlife; the way to live happily with wild visitors is to encourage only those that can fit into your garden picture without spoiling it – and make it clear to the rest that they are not welcome.

Garden style and atmosphere

A garden of character and distinction generally has a definable style. It may reflect the personality and lifestyle of its creator, or it may bear a direct relationship to the style of the house to which it is attached. It may slot precisely into an established historical garden style or one of the stereotypes – almost clichés – such as the cottage garden, or it may be describable loosely as modern and informal. It may be brim-full and overflowing with plants, or stark and relatively empty. It may have an intimate, cosy atmosphere in which the visitor feels comfortably at home, as in the well-furnished rooms of a country cottage, or it may be open and expansive, a relaxed private landscape that acknowledges and uses the larger landscape beyond to enhance its own beauties.

Garden atmosphere is the most difficult of attributes to create deliberately. It is not something that can be imposed, but springs directly from layout and plantings, hard structures and contouring, furnishings and ornament – in fact from all the elements that contribute to a successful design – so it demands the combined skills of designer and plantsman. At its simplest, meandering, fluent lawns set about with bushy shrubs and overhanging trees, will have that softness and relaxed feeling that cannot be matched, for example, by straight-sided lawns and trees of more rigid habit. The latter may, on the other hand, produce a kind of static calm. A still pool also engenders a placid, peaceful atmosphere very well, and while a geometrically designed formal herb or rose garden can have a charm of its own, neither can match the ease emanating from a garden laid out in relaxed bed and border shapes.

Style is not, however, something that can be considered in isolation. It should, if it is to be convincing and successful, stem at least in part from the shape and land-form of the site, and it should make a contribution to the solution of the garden's design problems. Clearly, a formal design involving long, straight borders that have the effect of lengthening perspective would be quite wrong for a long, narrow garden. On the other hand formal bedding can be very effective in an enclosed courtyard garden. As long as it is subtly done, without changes that are too abrupt, it is possible to effectively incorporate areas of both formal and informal style in a large garden, but as a general rule smaller gardens are best given a more coherent treatment.

Formal and informal gardens

Formal styles – the traditional garden styles of Europe and also of Islam – consist of beds, fountains and other features laid out in symmetrical patterns and geometrical shapes within a site of regular proportions. Changes of level may be incorporated by means of terraces and connecting steps, while trees and other large plants are commonly of rather severe outline – if necessary imposed by careful trimming – and may be planted in balanced pairs or straight avenues. Large formal gardens, of which those of André le Nôtre at Versailles in France are the supreme example

left The informal garden style is characterized by curved or free-form design, asymmetrical layout and plants encouraged to grow into their natural shapes. below Formal styles are based on geometrical shapes and have a symmetrical layout.
right An extrovert garden usually has an external feature or view of particular interest or beauty ¬ here a river runs along the bottom – that forms a natural focal point for the composition. Introvert gardens far right, as the name implies, have no exterior focus, so interest has to be created within. If there is no natural focal point, an artificial one such as this wrought iron well-head may be introduced.

in history, have an atmosphere of stately grandeur. At the other end of the scale, small knot gardens and the Dutch town gardens of the 17th and 18th centuries, with parterres (flat areas of intricate formal beds) often of bulbs, decorative topiary, lead statues and trees in tubs, both have a characteristic air of elegant charm.

Informal styles, traditional in China and Japan (see p 50) and popular in the Western world from the 18th century, are infinitely more flexible where small gardens and sites of irregular and awkward shape are concerned. Nature is the model here. Man-made features are kept to the minimum, or are contrived to blend in subtly with the plants, which are in any case the major decorative features and are arranged in as naturalistic a way as possible. The spacious, romantic English parklands designed in the 18th century by 'Capability' Brown and Humphry Repton were as grand in their way as the great formal gardens of the same period on the European continent, but small informal gardens have an easy, relaxed atmosphere and a subtle beauty that have come to be thought of as modern.

You can extend the interest of an informally laid out garden by creating something along the lines of John Claudius Loudon's 'gardenesque' style, in which flowers, shrubs and trees were selected for their special interest, and each specimen was planted where it would be most effectively displayed. In the 19th-century gardens inspired by William Robinson and Gertrude Jekyll, harmonious yet unusual plant associations and colour schemes (see p 28) were of great importance, the herbaceous border became pre-eminent and hardy exotic plants were introduced among the traditional varieties to add an eclectic air.

Extrovert and introvert gardens

If your garden has a beautiful view, it calls for an outward-looking, or extrovert, style. Even a small garden will have an open, spacious atmosphere if it appears to extend outwards into the surrounding landscape. The formal gardens of the Italian Renaissance and the picturesque landscapes of 18th-century England were both extrovert in style.

To design such a garden, however, calls for

consideration of what lies outside and to landscape the garden in a sympathetic manner. In an area of rolling, wooded countryside, a large garden that contained a grove of trees or possibly a stream could very well be developed in one of the natural garden styles described on page 40; it would then link naturally with the countryside beyond. A garden in a wild mountainous area or on the edge of a desert would clearly need quite different treatment. Scandinavian garden architects have mastered the art of making semi-wild gardens for second homes built on the fringes of their vast spruce and birch forests; wooden terracing and a rough grass clearing in front of the house provide recreation space, and by planting cultivated plants among the wild varieties growing out towards the edge of the garden the natural atmosphere is retained. Following the same principle, gardens in arid zones may be planted with palms and other shade trees, and cacti and various other succulents introduced among the natural drought-resistant desert scrub and spiky grasses.

Clearly, the boundary around an extrovert garden needs to be low or virtually non-existent, at least in the direction of the view that is to be opened up. With the opposite situation, where ugly views have to be screened or where (as with many city gardens) buildings hem them in, the style will naturally become introverted, or inward-looking. There are many historical precedents here, for in every age small enclosed gardens have served as private oases for seclusion and retreat from the distractions of the outside world. Even the grand formal gardens of Renaissance Italy had their small, enclosed *giardini segreti* (secret gardens) of flowers and herbs, their green theatres (enclosures of clipped evergreen hedges) and their grottoes and shaded walks, all with an intimate atmosphere quite distinct from that of the surrounding formal grandeur.

An enclosed city courtyard can be easily converted into a cheerful, colourful oasis informally planted with permanent and potted specimens, but there are other interesting possibilities. In a warm climate, the airy stillness of the Islamic courtyard garden (see p 50) might be an appropriate style to emulate; in cooler regions the model might be the fragrant calm serenity of the medieval monastery garden, with its shaded walks bordered by raised beds of flowers and herbs, and a still, deep well, a fish pond or a quietly splashing fountain as a focal point.

With less severely enclosed gardens, the simple device of opening up the centre while losing the boundaries behind plantings of shrubs, climbers and herbaceous plants in borders of informal outline will concentrate interest within the garden. The result will be to create an introverted style almost without the user and visitor being aware of it. This is a solution applicable to a large proportion of small modern gardens, combining informality with privacy.

Garden and architectural style

A building of distinctive historical style – whether venerable or extremely modern –

This luxuriant spot in the Compton Acres gardens, in south-west England, is opulent with exotic plants and represents the ultimate in the eclectic, informal style of garden design.

may call for a garden to complement it. This does not necessarily mean mimicking exactly the garden style of the house's period; a modern re-interpretation that is sympathetic to the architecture may have more vitality. (The situation is the same as in interior design, where well-designed modern furniture can look extremely effective in a period setting and *vice-versa*.) Furthermore, the large formal gardens that accompanied many houses of the 16th to 19th centuries needed a great deal of upkeep, and a simpler, more labour-saving style would be more appropriate today. Such a garden will, in any case, make the more elaborate architectural styles seem less fussy, while more elaborate and colourful layouts may be used to set off a plain façade.

Utterly modern architecture can be complemented by gardens of quite new design – not the relaxed informal style of curving beds and swirling lawns mentioned earlier as the most appropriate solution to many of today's gardens, but the new asymmetric style that blends formality and informality. These could be termed architectural gardens, for they use shapes, materials, ornaments and furnishings that are uncompromisingly modern and have more in common with building than landscaping. These may be set off by plants also of 'architectural' form, with striking silhouettes, often large, luxuriant foliage and exotic appearance (see p 252).

In such gardens, the geometrical forms of modern architecture are echoed in the shapes of plant beds, lawns, patios, pools and clusters of rocks (see p 13). Such features sited near to the house give the whole garden a formal appearance, yet its layout is usually asymmetrical, and away from the house this informality predominates. The link with the building is emphasized more than at any time in history, for water gardens may extend from the patio through to a glassed-in garden room, and indoor plants grouped to complement the exterior landscape. Yet modernity is eclectic, containing elements of traditional Chinese and Japanese styles; little in garden design is totally new.

The landscaped garden

Space brings the garden designer new possibilities and challenges, but new problems, too. With plenty of room to spare, it is possible to try out some of the more ambitious landscaping ideas that often have to remain dormant when treating a smaller site. But your garden does not need to be a stately park to benefit from some of the techniques used in large-scale landscaping; an area of, say, 2000 m² (½ acre), though not particularly large – and quite commonly to be found attached to a country house or a large suburban one – allows ample scope for free, even flamboyant, design.

Such a garden brings with it the problems of care and maintenance; unless you can obtain help, it would be wise to keep these factors firmly in mind when making your plans. With spacious gardens, of course, labour-saving machinery, such as ride-on lawn-mowers, cultivators and the like (see p 376), really comes into its own. Nevertheless, keep to a minimum the area occupied by labour-intensive features such as formal beds, velvet lawns and herbaceous borders; if you want to include these, site them near the house where they will be most appreciated, and landscape the rest of the garden in a more informal, easily maintained style.

Structure and form
Another pitfall to avoid is to allow a large garden to lapse into aesthetic anarchy; its space needs to be organized but at the same time unity maintained. The structural elements of flat surfaces and vertical screens and divisions will have to work doubly hard to unify a large and rambling garden into a satisfying whole. Style plays a vital role, too. If your house has a distinctive style – whether it be a fine period property or an uncompromisingly modern one – it will give a clear lead to developing a suitable garden style; otherwise, you will have to strive to create a garden that enhances the house's best features.

Boundaries are less obtrusive in a large site than a small one, and can be built as high as you wish for privacy. A high wall will even serve as a visual reminder of the property's unity, especially if its material echoes that of the house. If you have inherited an inappropriate wall or fence, of course, it can be obscured with shrubs or trees. A ha-ha – a sunken wall backed by a deep, wide ditch – may create an adequately secure boundary while allowing a view out onto attractive countryside.

Grand gates that would appear pretentious in any other setting will not look out of place in a large property. If the house is set some distance back from the public road, they could lead to the first piece of landscaping to greet the visitor – the broad sweep of a drive, perhaps flanked by shrubberies or a grove of trees and surfaced with gravel, brick or granite setts. It may be wise to provide separate pedestrian access, for safety, and if there are separate entrance and exit drives, make it clear which is which. A drive-in walled entry court may be an attractive alternative to a front garden in a large suburban property. With adequate space, complex patterns in

such materials as brick and stone paving have room to develop. On the other hand, a more open front garden, perhaps with a lawn and formal pool with a fountain, will set off to perfection the façade of a beautiful house.

Within the large garden, divisions and screens may create various distinct areas, possibly linked by grassy walks. Plants – both formal hedges and plantings of tall shrubs – can form such divisions, or you can use ornamental screen walling, mellow brick, trellis and so on. Try not to introduce too many diverse materials, or anarchy may threaten, but there is less need for strict uniformity of style and material than in a smaller garden. A pergola flanked by shrubs might lead to a walled garden, parts of whose walls are covered with trellis. The key when using diverse materials – as when creating garden areas of diverse style – is to make the transition easy and natural by using intermediate linking materials or areas of more subdued, neutral character.

House and garden
A patio or terrace can stretch out more spaciously from the house in a large garden, providing ample area for sitting out. A low house may look better for the addition of a roomy verandah, or you might wish to build a conservatory or sun-lounge – which may be no more than a glassed-in verandah – to increase the season of use of the patio area. Any of these may be paved in the same material as the patio or terrace – a material sympathetic to the style of the house. In many cases, you can extend the terrace all the way around the building; at the front it will provide a transition from drive to front door. Furnish the terrace, verandah or garden room with plants that echo or complement those in the garden.

An open garden is the best setting for a fine house. It would be quite possible to landscape this private side of the garden with symmetrical formality, or you can make full use of wide, sweeping curves. Where space is plentiful a lawn can become more than just a green platform for recreation, but a major feature set off with a majestic tree, such as a cedar or a variety of the common European beech (*Fagus sylvatica*), that can be seen here to full advantage. Should open recreational space not be required, areas of lawn can swirl between island beds of varied shapes. Planted with herbaceous perennials in pleasing colour patterns, they will look particularly attractive seen in perspective from the terrace or windows. (Island beds are inherently easier to maintain than the traditional one-sided herbaceous border; see p 108). At a greater distance, these can give way to plantings of larger specimen plants, rough grass with naturalized bulbs, shrubs and trees.

Special features opening off to the sides of the terrace and lawn will be seen from above by anyone looking out of upstairs windows, and can make exciting little 'secret gardens' for the visitor to explore. You may want to make a traditional enclosed kitchen garden or a formal herb garden – both are most useful if sited near the house. In other places you may be tempted to create a formal, ornamental rose garden with seats for visitors to enjoy the seclusion and perfume and perhaps with a

Water in the garden

Water is to many people an almost essential element in any landscaping scheme. A pool of geometrical shape makes a perfect centrepiece for a formal layout, whether it is stocked with fish and water-lilies or simply ornamented in the centre with a statue or fountain. It could be illuminated at night (see p 83). In less formally landscaped areas, a pool can harmonize in shape with nearby flower beds, and the link can be accentuated with marginal plantings and an adjacent bog garden. A distinctive specimen plant at the waterside – even something as well known as pampas grass – will look magnificent reflected in a still pool.

If the garden is large enough, a wider expanse of water – even a small lake or series of lakes – will make a real impact, around which the rest of the garden design will revolve. Try to use a natural hollow, or you will need to excavate the site mechanically. Large ponds and lakes can be waterproofed with puddled clay, or you can use synthetic rubber sheeting for even quite extensive areas (see p 128). You can landscape the banks with grassy walks or paths of gravel or perhaps

so screening shrubs or a belt of trees may be needed to deflect it.

You will probably want to sit and entertain visitors beside the water, so a small paved area with garden furniture in the lee of such a screen would be much used. In many cases a boathouse and landing stage may be fitted in, while a smaller stream or river may be bridged attractively. Where the water is shallow, stepping stones or rocks may be placed strategically, creating a gurgle of sound as well as visual interest. Always bear safety in mind where there is water, however; make sure that young children cannot reach it unsupervised, and if the water is deep provide a prominently positioned lifebelt.

The outer garden

Beyond the area of trim lawns, flower beds and shrub plantings, the larger garden may merge smoothly into rough grass cut only once or twice a year and planted with trees, shrubs and naturalized wild flowers and bulbs. Paths and mown walks through rough grass will provide links and will help to emphasize the feeling of unity. In a rural district, this area can run on towards the boundaries, and if

Schemes for the larger garden may be as imaginative as you wish: **above left** A serpentine lawn meanders between borders, island beds and a lily pond. **far left** A grand paved terrace is set off with flowering climbers, shrubs and plants in containers. **left** A stretch of water makes a focal feature around which the rest of the garden design can be planned. **right** Many of the techniques of landscaping can be applied to gardens of moderate size, especially where there are changes of level. **far right** In the country, the garden can be opened up to its surroundings.

centre piece of a sundial or circular pool. Elsewhere there may be a small medieval-style enclosed orchard, a heather garden, a moss and fern garden in a shady spot, a sunken garden or even a topiary garden with arches and statues. Particularly where changes of level already exist, a dramatic rock garden may be worked into the scheme.

Sports and games can be absorbed into a large garden with little difficulty (see p 17). Informal ball games and croquet may perhaps be allowed to take temporary charge of a main lawn, and this may run through in one direction to form a grass tennis court shielded by soft netting and partly concealed by border plants or shrubs; hard courts will need firmer screening. You could construct a pergola to lead towards a swimming pool constructed neatly within a paved area or lawn in a suitably sheltered spot (see p 82). A small combined sauna and changing cabin would not be inappropriate here, as long as its style suited that of the garden.

pine-needles or wood chips, and position a seat or bench here and there. You can merge waterside and marginal plantings as with a smaller pool, but there is room here for the more rampant marginals such as the larger bulrushes and reedmaces (*Scirpus* and *Typha* spp). Make a feature of handsome waterside trees such as weeping willows or the swamp cypress, *Taxodium distichum* (see p 140), or the imposing herbaceous *Gunnera manicata* and other bog plants described on page 257.

You may be lucky enough to have a garden in which water is a natural feature. Many suburban gardens back on to rivers, canals or creeks, while rural gardens may be similarly situated or may even have streams running through. Although the latter may need management to avoid problems of flooding and drought (see p 132), you should take advantage of any natural water by opening the garden pattern out towards it and landscaping the margin as described above for a lake. Wind can be a problem over any expanse of water,

plenty of sightings are allowed through the boundaries to the landscape beyond, the garden will seem to drift on into the countryside. Groups of trees, planted strategically to conceal surrounding houses but to admit views through to beautiful features of neighbouring gardens, will do a similar job for the large suburban garden.

A very large garden can be landscaped as a wild garden (see p 40), with woodland groves and dells, areas of trees and ground cover, grassy knolls with rock outcrops, drifts of heather or banks of rhododendrons, and paths winding through the site. Plant bulbs for extra colour in clearings, on sunny slopes and beneath deciduous trees, and woodland perennials wherever they will grow. The more precious features of the grand garden of past centuries – pagodas, Palladian temples, mock ruins, obelisks and so on – would look very out of place, but a simple summer-house in a picturesque spot can look appealing and make an idyllic place to pass a few quiet hours.

The 'natural' garden

Wild landscapes as diverse as Scotland's heather slopes, Swiss alpine meadows, rolling English woodlands and the vast spruce and birch forests of Scandinavia have inspired many gardeners of the past to try and imitate them. Today, the wild or natural garden has its own place in the range of garden styles as the most informal of informal gardens, an obvious choice for any lover of the open countryside who is faced with an overgrown and unkempt – or a new and uncultivated site. If your garden is already structured and landscaped, trying to create a natural garden from scratch would be an arduous task and hardly worthwhile; for example, trees planted to make the woodland garden described opposite – one type of natural garden – will take decades to mature. But you may enjoy making a wild place somewhere within a more conventional garden.

Because the aim in creating a natural garden is to simulate nature as closely as possible, there are no formal lawns or flower beds, few

associations observed in the surrounding countryside, if the site is bare; otherwise, accentuate or enlarge some aspect of the existing scheme: take advantage of natural changes in level, planting grasses or marsh plants in low spots, rock plants in stony places, or meadow flowers in drifts down a slope.

In many countries it is illegal to collect certain protected plants or even seeds from the wild, but if you live in country regions native plants often seed themselves naturally, and those that survive can be encouraged to spread. Garden centres and nurseries may offer collections of native wild plants suitable for your natural garden, and you can successfully combine garden varieties and suitable modern hybrids with them to add colour and seasonal interest. But choose only those that are indigenous to the area; too much cultivation will make a wild garden lose its natural appearance.

Paths in a natural garden can be mere tracks, perhaps with stepping stones, which

cultivation today are almost exact counterparts of those still growing in the wild, a large rock outcrop, whether natural or artificial, if planted convincingly, can look as if it is part of a wild mountain.

The person who first thought of planting a shrubbery was perhaps looking for a way to reproduce a thicket in a garden setting; if you observe the natural association of plants on a nearby heath or natural open place you can make an unusual area – or garden – based on a similar scheme, adding evergreens perhaps, or early-flowering shrubs to prolong the season, and with ground-covering plants or rough grass and seasonal bulbs to provide colour and interest until the garden is established.

An area of rough grass is a versatile feature that can serve as a link with more formal and cultivated areas of the garden. Allowed to run wild it becomes a grass garden, one of the easiest natural gardens to make since it requires only clearings and paths cut out with

left A semi-wild garden of flowers, shrubs and long grass beneath sparse trees. **below** A heather garden has a rather more 'cultivated' appearance but is almost maintenance-free.

walls and fences to construct or paths to lay, and straggling hedges and a few weeds are accepted as part of the wild setting. So these gardens are easier both to develop and to maintain than any laid out along formal lines.

Planning a natural garden

Take your cue from nature when planning a natural garden and let the soil and natural conditions determine the kind of garden you make: you may need to clear the site of undergrowth, rubble and rampant weeds, but do not attempt any changes in level; soil conditions may have to be improved, but again do not make any wholesale changes. The natural effect is brought about largely by careful choice, association and positioning of plants and features such as rock outcrops, a fallen tree trunk or a stream or waterfall, all of which can be artificially introduced but must look as if they belong in their surroundings.

You can build up planting schemes from basic ideas, perhaps derived from plant

also make very satisfactory steps. Simple stone or brick walls, or a stout post and rail fence softened with evergreen shrubs or climbers, will make strong boundaries if necessary, and a tree screen or an informal hedge of native flowering shrubs makes an effective and natural-looking windbreak.

Features of natural gardens

A mossy patch as a foil for a cluster of ferns will make a cool, restful spot at the bottom of a small garden; you can include clumps of *Cystopteris fragilis* and other lacy miniatures, evergreen ferns such as *Blechnum spicant* and the taller moisture-loving *Polystichum acrostichoides* for the winter garden, and if the soil and weather are moist the majestic *Osmunda regalis* will even provide autumn colour.

Soil conditions permitting, a heather garden with a winding rocky path can be colourful throughout the year, and a bog garden is as peaceful as a woodland pool and less difficult to maintain. And because many rock plants in

a rotary mower. It will have three lives if you time the cuttings – scything, if you can manage it, will lay a meadow low without disturbing wildlife – to early and late summer and mid-autumn. Spring bulbs, violets, primroses, cowslips and bluebells will make carpets of colour from very early spring until early summer, when ox-eye daisies and similar flowers burst into full bloom. Sprinkle seed of suitable annuals such as cornflowers, harebells, flax and poppies in patches to augment the wild flowers that dot the garden in midsummer, and plant autumn-flowering bulbs such as colchicums in the grass to end the season.

If your garden is by the sea you can plant the kinds of coarse grasses that grow on dunes and bind the soil, and intersperse them with the lovely salt-tolerant herbaceous plants such as sea-thrift and sea-hollies. Trees always associate well with shrubs and grassy areas, and fast-growing types such as the silver birch or suitable conifers in small groves will add another dimension to your garden.

The woodland garden

The gardener whose land includes or is set in an area of woodland – whether it is extensive or merely a small copse – is extremely fortunate, for the woodland garden forms an environment where a very special type of plant can be successfully grown. It can, if handled wrongly, be dull and weed-infested, but with a proper understanding of its characteristics a wide range of introduced species will thrive.

Shade brings a coolness appreciated by many plants, but you must remember that in dull, rainy weather woodland usually remains cold, wet and still – conditions not at all to the liking of many plants that are not indigenous to this type of terrain. Furthermore, the shady conditions favour the development of robust plants, and if you introduce vigorous kinds you must restrict their progress if they are not to overwhelm the smaller, choicer species.

Basic features

It is obvious that the light intensity is very much reduced in a garden where trees grow thickly. So you should select only plants that will tolerate – even favour – shade; apart from those mentioned in this article, the charts beginning on page 386 indicate such plants. On the fringe of the woodland or small

copse, you can grow plants requiring a little more light. And where the trees are deciduous, some early-flowering bulbs – most notably scillas, snowdrops, eranthis and wood anemones – will almost certainly thrive.

Coniferous evergreens and deciduous broad-leaved trees create rather different environments, with different problems. The light, of course, differs considerably, that under conifers varying much less through the seasons than that under deciduous trees. Soil conditions vary, too; in deciduous woodland the soil may be extremely rich in leaf-mould and more fertile than under conifers. The shedding of foliage from deciduous trees in autumn can cause problems unless you spend a period constantly tidying up; this will prevent the damp, decaying leaves affecting small evergreen ground-covering plants.

Although a woodland scene or glade is not formal and therefore calls for a more casual line than in most gardens, a definite means of access to the area is important. The path or

Plantings of drumstick primulas such as *Primula pulverulenta* left, foxgloves **above** and shade-loving rhododendrons **right** can bring bright colour to an area of deciduous woodland.

paths, however, generally look best wandering informally. While one that is grass-covered may present a cool, pleasing picture, a track strewn with pine needles or bark chippings can be equally effective. In addition, plants growing by the sides of such non-grassy areas may be allowed to spill over onto the path without fear of damaging the path's surface or of being mutilated by mowing.

Cultivation and maintenance

Plants growing naturally in an arboreal setting are treated to a rich woodland soil – one full of decaying leaves, twigs, and even larger branches. Clearing up removes all this natural humus, so, to preserve ideal conditions, this must be re-introduced. Let the leaves you collect in autumn rot down for six months and then dig in the resultant leaf-mould. If this is not sufficient, well-made garden compost and peat are excellent substitutes. Apart from humus, a supply of water will be necessary, especially in a garden where, due to a low rainfall, conditions in summer are too dry. You will not need to use artificial fertilizers to any extent where ample humus is present.

As in all other garden features, the standard of tidiness is set by the gardener, but to be classed as a garden at all the woodland garden needs some degree of cultivation and control. It is important to restrict the colonizing species, so that they do not swamp the less vigorous kinds. Some of the other tasks to be performed include dividing and transplanting when necessary, and spraying and irrigating to keep the plants healthy and growing sturdily.

Plants to grow

Natural woodland comprises various layers of vegetation, and below the tree canopy tall shrubs provide both shelter and background. In a garden setting, large rhododendrons,

hydrangeas, shrubby loniceras (honeysuckles) and species of *Rubus* and *Ribes* (ornamental brambles and currants) can provide this. These may be flanked by coarser-leaved herbaceous plants, of which filipendulas, rodgersias, cranesbill geraniums, polygonums (knotweeds) and hostas are good examples. But these simply set the scene; from now on the choice of species becomes personal. You may opt for an effective ground-covering type of planting, needing the minimum of maintenance. Or you may prefer a plantsman's garden, where interest in plants is the yardstick, and the rarer and more difficult they are to grow the better; here the plants should be more accessible and visible as individuals.

There is a compromise between these two which can be completely satisfying. Bergenias, arums, euonymus, hypericums, species of *Lamium* (dead nettles), lunarias and pachysandras are typical inhabitants of the ground-cover type, but the enthusiastic gardener requires more for his labours than mere effect. For him the sylvan setting could hold bold groupings of the perennial blue Himalayan poppy, *Meconopsis betonicifolia*, and the golden and silver rosettes of the once-flowering *M. regia* and *M. superba*.

These may be punctuated by stands of Asian, European and North American lilies, uplifting the whole quality of the surroundings. Add to these some day lilies (*Hemerocallis* spp) and a few drifts of the Asiatic primulas, and a true garden is created.

Having reached this stage, the collector need not stop, for there are many other choice plants that are natural inhabitants of this type of arrangement. Notable are anemones, trilliums, many ferns, and species of *Clintonia, Corydalis, Hacquetia, Disporum, Mertensia* and *Polygonatum*. They give ample scope for development of the enthusiast's interests.

Woodland not only allows the gardener to be less formal and plant-tidy than elsewhere; it even encourages this. As a result, plants may be allowed to grow through each other to some extent – and this may, in fact, be difficult to prevent. Consequently the setting is such that, when properly staged, it will provide a completely closed plant association, a truly self-supporting community.

The secluded and shady garden

Shade may occur in varying degrees in any garden, in isolated patches or extensive areas, and is often – quite wrongly – considered to be restrictive. Think of it as an asset rather than a matter for concern, for shade is precisely what a great many plants enjoy. In addition to those specially suited to sunless conditions (see the charts starting on page 386), so many others will tolerate shade that its presence in your garden will actually increase the range of plants you can grow. You may even need to create it artificially (see p 77) if your garden is very hot, to make a kind of cool, green retreat from the sun. Shade has certain peaceful, still qualities that can be accentuated in a garden that receives little or no direct sunlight, to give it a very distinctive air.

Types of shade
Plants are not just shade-loving or shade-tolerant. Shade varies considerably in degree, and this is important to the gardener, for plants that will thrive under one set of conditions may be a failure under others. The shade cast by walls and other vertical structures is known as open shade. Enclosed gardens in fact admit quite a lot of light because they are open to the sky, but they may receive little direct sunlight. Few plants fail to grow in open shade, though merely shade-tolerant species and varieties may fail to flower or fruit as well as in sunnier places, or they may grow unduly tall, with rather weak stems. But there are many plants, particularly some climbers, wall shrubs and certain rock plants, that positively thrive in this type of shade and shelter.

Dappled shade, the sort that occurs under trees whose branches and leaves form a lacy, open pattern, suits woodland shrubs and flowers (see p 41) so well that you could develop the area beneath a few silver birches, dogwoods, redbuds or hazels, for example, into something of a woodland garden. Closely-planted trees and those with large or overlapping leaves provide the kind of dense shade in which only a limited number of plants will grow. Beeches, the Norway maple and the fragrant, flowering yellowwood (*Cladastris lutea*) are all ideal shade trees for exposed gardens, and you can underplant them with evergreen shrubs such as laurel and yew, the colourful butcher's broom (*Ruscus aculeatus*), or ground-covering English ivy (*Hedera helix*) and vincas.

Damp shade occurs if the ground is very moist, or where the atmosphere is humid and there is no sunshine to dry it out, and could mean making a feature of a bog garden (see p 133), or moisture-loving ferns or grasses.

Ideas for shady gardens
Certain lawn grasses grow well in semi-shade (see p 85), but none do so where the light is dim, so it is better to surface the over-shadowed garden with a light-toned material – something that harmonizes with the garden walls. If these are dark you can brighten them with paint or stucco tinted with off-white shades that are more restful than bright white. Textured paving is least slippery in damp conditions and is attractive in a garden lacking

above Shade-loving plants grouped in unusual combinations of colour and texture enliven **left** an enclosed rock garden and **right** an overshadowed border. **below** *Osmunda regalis*, the royal fern, in a patch of autumn sun.

sunlight. For additional interest, combine different types of paving materials, such as stone or concrete paving slabs and gravel. A patch of white sand, stone chippings, or cobbles will bring a dim corner to life, especially if you train winter jasmine (*Jasminum nudiflorum*) up the wall above it.

Textural contrasts are eye-catching, and you can introduce some quite spectacular effects by planting large patches of leafy ground ivy (*Nepeta* [*Glechoma*] *hederacea*) or the flowering *Claytonia virginica* in borders or shallow raised beds. There is a place here for wall sculptures or elegant marble statues in wall cavities to break the monotony of high enclosures. Think of texture too when

you choose outdoor furniture; rough stone or concrete benches, or wrought-iron chairs and tables could make a beautiful addition.

Colour in the shady garden
There is no lack of colour among shade-loving plants, but use it carefully in a sunless garden. Very brilliant colours may tend to look gaudy – or may simply lose their effect – in dim light, while pale, delicate colours will take on a magical luminous quality. You can brighten the garden with woodland flowers and shade-loving bulbs such as scillas in early spring, and herbaceous perennials such as hostas and astilbes in later seasons. Make the most of walls with jasmine, honeysuckle and hydrangeas, wall shrubs such as camellias, and euonymus or hypericums for autumn foliage. Where you do want something stronger-coloured, fuchsias thrive in open shade.

Green is a particularly tranquil colour, and certain evergreen plants suited to shady conditions would make the basis of an unusual evergreen-and-white garden. Use English ivy or *Pileostegia viburnoides* to clothe walls and fences, shrubs such as hollies for winter colour and the daisy bush (*Olearia × haastii*), camellias and *Rhododendron* (*Azalea*) 'Daviesii' for white spring and summer flowers. *Arenaria balearica* is a splendid white-flowering ground cover, and you can plant lilies of the valley in drifts to perfume spring air.

Using some of the shade-loving ornamental grasses (see p 244), you can turn a dark, secluded plot into a rippling grass garden, with the feathery *Stipa pennata* and the charming silver *Holcus mollis* 'Variegatus' in borders and beds. For special effect plant the majestic pampas grass (*Cortaderia selloana*), or varieties of *Miscanthus* or *Eulalia*. Alternatively, you can make an unusual fern garden (see p 238) with evergreen scolopendriums, *Dryopteris borreri* varieties and many others. Water ferns or moisture-loving grasses around a small fountain make a delightful central feature in a shady garden, and take on an entirely different atmosphere if illuminated at night. Mosses, too, will thrive in this environment; in many gardens they are considered weeds, but in shady spots you can make a feature of them.

The country cottage garden

A cheerfully disordered little plot, over-flowing with colourful flowers, is the traditional idea of a cottage garden, and although this popular image is a very romantic one, old cottage gardens were indeed very full. Rural cottagers of the English Victorian era, the unwitting originators of the style, grew a little of anything that could be useful. Forced by an austere existence to be self-sufficient, they cultivated bright and scented flowers to provide nectar for bees, and collected their petals for pot-pourris and muslin bags to perfume the house and keep flies and moths away. Nasturtium and dandelion leaves made salads, sunflower seeds made winter fodder and pinks were used to flavour ale. But vegetables, fruits and culinary herbs took up as much if not more space than flowers and, isolated from city sophistication, the influence of folk medicine could be seen in the range of medicinal herbs.

The rambling beauty and peaceful atmosphere of these gardens first gave rise to their imitation, and any modern adaptation that captures these qualities will echo something at least of the original character of the most spoilt rural area. The style is easily adapted to very small gardens and, surprisingly, to modern house styles, so long as plants growing close to new materials are selected with care. And cottage-style gardens, once established, are quite easy to maintain.

Planning the garden

An old cottage will give you a rare opportunity to disobey some of the most sacrosanct rules of garden design. Overshadowing the walls with Virginia creeper – or hollyhocks so tall they reach the eaves – will probably make it look all the more picturesque. And if your design consists of little more than a straight path from door to garden gate between two beds of gaily unsegregated crop plants and flowers, all jostling for room to spread, you will merely be following an old tradition.

But if you plan a more sophisticated scheme, it should be in keeping with the atmosphere of rustic simplicity you are aiming to create. If the garden is large, rolling lawns will seem too grand. You would do better to keep lawns small and include an area of pav-

above Cottages and gardens in Somerset, England. below A colourful mixture of old-fashioned flowers left, herbs, and wayside plants such as the tall heracleum right, characterize the cottage-garden style.

ing, a herb garden, a display of old-fashioned roses, even a small orchard, in your design, using the natural divisions as a fitting excuse for screens and arches of trellis or rustic woodwork displaying heavily perfumed climbing roses such as 'Zéphirine Drouhin', which is thornless, or the semi-evergreen 'Félicité et Perpétue'.

Crazy paving looks right in a cottage garden, but if your house has a more modern design, stone slabs, rustic bricks or shingle might be more appropriate. Paths can be straight, intersecting at right-angles, or gently winding like country lanes. It would be difficult to find fault with a dry stone wall, whether planted or not, or a picket fence used as a support for runner beans or sweet peas. You can also plant space-saving hedges such as beech, perfumed hedges of sweetbriar, lavender or rosemary, or a mixed farm-style hedge of holly and thorn or elder and hazel. Cottagers delighted in topiary, clipping box or privet into plump cockerels or other shapes.

Well-designed wrought iron or wooden gates make a fine introduction to the garden,

but take care not to overplay the country style with wagon-wheel gates, for example. And make sure that textures and colours of pavings and enclosures complement those of nearby flowers and leaves, rather than compete for attention as artificial colours so often do.

Cottage-garden plants

An air of natural, gay profusion is a most difficult thing to achieve because there is no clear design. The secret lies in introducing into practically every inch of space genuinely old-fashioned varieties of flowers and ornamental herbs (many of which are becoming popular and easier to obtain again), improved varieties and modern hybrids – particularly dwarf forms that need no staking – and a sprinkling of plants naturalized from hedgerow, field and woodland.

So you can surround the doorway or windows of your house with the rustic perfumed honeysuckle, or a combination of the common white summer-flowering jasmine and winter-flowering jasmine, *Clematis montana* or one of the other small-flowered clematis mentioned on page 144, or a wisteria. Fruit espaliers look well against its walls, as do traditional shrubs such as japonica (*Chaenomeles* spp), or firethorn (*Pyracantha* spp). Plant cushion plants among paving stones and around the edges of paths and patios; old-fashioned pinks (see p183) are particularly appropriate and sweetly scented.

A large fruit tree such as an apple, pear or crab apple will make a fine basis for the design, and a vigorous climbing rose or glory vine (*Vitis coignetiae*) entwined around the trunk epitomizes the spirit of the cottage garden. You can plant winter aconites, snowdrops, bluebells and other scillas, primroses and unusual summer-flowering bulbs in rough grass underneath.

Crowded beds bring their own rewards in that weeds have little opportunity to become a problem; a well-maintained soil bed given regular applications of both well-rotted organic material and fertilizers is an essential foundation. The traditional cottage-garden perennials such as bergamot (*Monarda* spp), Michaelmas daisies, marguerites, heleniums, lupins, delphiniums, border phlox, gaillardias and a host of others set the atmosphere of a flowery paradise. The Madonna lily (*Lilium candidum*) and crown imperial (*Fritillaria imperialis*) have for centuries had a special place in cottage gardens. Patches of hardy annuals and bedding plants can be planted here and there – plants such as pot marigolds, mignonettes (*Reseda odorata*), night-scented stocks (*Matthiola bicornis*), snapdragons, pansies, and sweet Williams – to ensure full seasonal interest, colour and fragrance.

Cottagers were not given to ornamenting or furnishing their gardens, so you will have to use some discretion here. An old well-head or ivy-entwined pump would be most suitable, or even a beehive or dovecot. Planted tubs, crocks, sinks and specimen trees make good cottagey ornaments. Furniture has no need to be rustic, but let simplicity be your guide in choosing it.

The suburban garden

Gardens in suburban areas vary enormously in situation, size and shape; some are large enough to suit many of the landscaping ideas described on page 38, while those on city outskirts may have a pleasant rural view to make a focal point for the design. Sloping gardens in hilly suburbs can be landscaped in a variety of different ways (see p 21).

It is not difficult to make interesting gardens in sites such as these, but the average suburban plot is a more challenging task. Generally modest in size and oblong in shape, it is usually uninspiringly flat, a dull box hemmed in by rows of similar houses and gardens. Every gardener wants his garden to look original, but the suburban situation is one in which one garden with patio, lawn, space for vegetables and so on can all too easily end up looking much like another, and imaginative design is particularly necessary. The designer will be called upon to fit all the features necessary to what is usually a family garden into a scheme that looks spacious, restful and uncrowded, and that is also relatively simple to maintain.

Individuality and style

Before you begin to think of allocating the available space for different purposes, give some thought to a style for your garden, for a well-chosen style will endow the flattest garden in the dullest surroundings with atmosphere and distinction. The article on page 36 gives a brief survey of different garden styles, past and present, and books, magazines and visits to gardens of special interest will help you to assess the merits and defects of those that appeal to you. Choose something that is adaptable to your garden, suitable for your lifestyle and practical to maintain.

As a general rule, informal styles are more applicable to the suburban garden than formal, symmetrical designs, just because they are more flexible. The simpler kinds of natural gardens (see p 40), Japanese gardens, even your own version of the gardenesque style (see p 36) can all be adapted to a small site and are comparatively easy to look after. If you want to be more conventional, borders of shrubs and herbaceous plants can be made to curve obligingly around an open central recreation area while screening out neighbouring gardens and unsightly objects.

But if your garden is wanted purely for decoration and relaxation, you may enjoy making and tending a formal garden. There are many historical examples, but these should not be copied down to the finest detail – simply adapt the basic layout to your garden, and furnish it with representative plants and decorative features that will recreate its essential atmosphere. A simple paved garden surrounded by a rustic brick wall or a clipped hedge, with geometrically shaped beds and perhaps a round pool as a focal point would not look pretentious in a small site. In a larger site, it would also make an attractive formal feature in an otherwise informally landscaped garden, as long as the transition from one style to the other were eased by appropriate dividing structures.

But the modern garden styles, with their

interesting blend of formality and informality, are infinitely varied and adaptable. Designed with the suburban garden in mind, they are undoubtedly most congruous with modern styles of living.

Adapting the style

If, like many suburban houses, yours has no determinate style, you will have to look for subtle ways to establish a visual unity between your house and garden. Paving plays a major part in setting the garden style, and a small terrace or patio – useful in any garden – or an entirely paved site, can do much to lay the foundations of a harmonious design.

Pave the garden with the same materials used to build the house if these will suit your garden style; if not, choose something unobtrusive in a similar colour. Keep the size of the paved area strictly in scale with the house, but shape it in keeping with the garden pattern and echo its shape in the lawn, if you have one. Use the same materials for paving and paths, but only make paths where they are essential or make a real artistic contribution to the garden – straight paths alongside a washing line cannot really be included in this category. A slightly raised terrace will add extra interest to a flat garden.

Enclosures too have an important stylistic and unifying role, and you may be able to install walls or fences in keeping with the type and colour of the paving. But faced with the problem of breaking down the rigidity of confining enclosures and also providing dis-

creet privacy from neighbours, a simple paling fence may be less likely to emphasize the boundary lines. It will permit an agreeable view through to plants in adjoining borders, and will not quarrel with your garden style if masked in places by tall shrubs or small groups of trees worked here and there into the garden pattern.

But enclosures are all too often an unwelcome inheritance in a suburban garden. It is sometimes worthwhile to raise the height of a solid wall or fence by adding a top section of some material more suited to your garden, and screening the lower part behind border plants. Masking with climbing plants or hedging shrubs may be the only solution to enclosures that are too high or dominating.

Colour-washing the façade of house and garden walls is a more radical way of achieving unity of house and garden style, and may succeed in bringing character to a dull or undistinguished dwelling, but only attempt it if you are sure it will be an improvement. The addition of a small porch or even a balcony may make a house look more in keeping with a formal garden, and building a sun lounge linked with a patio, rather than buying a summer-house, may provide the perfect connection between a modern garden and a house of indefinite style.

Creating interest with plants will make an ugly façade go almost unnoticed. Plant a low-growing, spreading shrub beneath a window, or install a window box planted with trailing plants. Position a group of dwarf coni-

left An informal layout with flowing beds containing plants of varied size, form and colour effectively masks the rigid, box-like shape of many suburban gardens. **above** Massed plantings mask oppressive boundaries and give the overlooked garden a self-contained character. **above right** Where there is no need to accommodate children, a stylish formal garden can be effective in a small site. **right** A verandah can both open up a house to its garden and also unify the two.

plants should fulfil some clear decorative role. The main body of the planting structure should be used to create interest in a flat garden, so use colour in blocks and masses; a unified planting scheme consisting of flowers in tones of a single colour (see p 26), or of two or three colours only, can make a small garden look very distinctive. Plants chosen for accent, contrast and display as specimens should be outstanding examples of the particular form, texture, or other quality that is required of them.

Even in a new housing development where each property is almost identical in size and shape, no two gardens are exactly alike; each plot will have subtle dissimilarities of climate, aspect, light and shade, the result of their slight differences in situation. You can emphasize your garden's essential individuality if you can identify such influences and accentuate them in your garden design. Make a feature, if you can, of a shady area, or plant a sunset-coloured shrub where it will catch the light at the close of the day. And give careful thought to seasonal colour and interest, or the garden will lose all its effect in winter.

Do not create too many focal points in a small garden, and these, whether ornaments or specimen plants, should belong to the garden style; carefully chosen, they can be its making. And take care not to destroy the effect of a carefully planned scheme with a feature such as a rock garden or a rose arbour that simply does not belong in it. If you particularly enjoy growing rock plants or marsh plants, choose a scheme that suits them, or make a feature of them in the front garden instead, although this should not differ in style too much from the garden on the other side of the house.

And do not forget the side of the house; many suburban houses have two side passages, and if one is not necessary you can make a useful storage area there, and turn the other into a path bordered by shade-loving shrubs or ferns, or a decorative, plant-entwined archway.

fers around a sharp corner, or train an evergreen climber to arch over a door and trail across a wall. Plant white or silver-grey plants and soft blue flowers against light red brick, and add pinks and yellows if the brick is dark red. Bright, bold colours and green foliage stand out against white concrete and paint, and pinks, reds, blues and purples will brighten a dull grey house wall. Use the same shades and colours as a basis for your colour-scheme to emphasize unity with the body of the garden.

Layout and planting schemes
The layout of the rigidly suburban garden needs to be shapely and simple to be effective. The smaller the garden, the more vital it is to keep the design simple. You can make an easily identifiable garden pattern using simple geometrical shapes for lawn and plant beds, or create equally bold sweeps of more informal outline; avoid indecisive wiggles. Areas for vegetables and service features are often both required, but screen these out effectively; odd glimpses of unsightly features and objects will spoil the effect. You can use planted trellis, groups of large shrubs, a tall evergreen hedge, an ornamental wall or some other device suggested by the garden style, even a screen of red or white runner beans, sweet peas or ornamental gourds. A wall or divider made of planted trellis or bamboo can form an entrance arch between a patio and the garden proper on one side, and a screen for a small service area on the other, and will conceal the

seating area of the garden from the houses on either side. Patio and lawn should together provide adequate play space for children; sand-pits and items of play equipment are not unsightly; you can find room for them on the lawn until the children are too old for them.

Every garden style has certain plants closely associated with it; from among these select a limited number – do not clutter the garden with too many different plants – and use them boldly; every plant or group of

Coastal gardens
Gardens on the coast will have the whole range of different soils but two things in common: the winds are likely to be strong and salt-laden during at least half the year, but the climate will be generally sunnier and milder than for inland areas in the same region. You will have to plant a windbreak before you can establish the garden; consider Scots, stone or Monterey pines, which will also provide shade, or hedges of tree purslane (*Atriplex halimus*) or the various species of daisy bush (*Olearia* spp).

Stone is most appropriate for paving gardens on rocky coastlines, and you can make an unusual rock garden using smooth sea-worn rocks planted with spiky sea hollies and pretty salt-tolerant perennials. Many suitable plants are identified in the tables beginning on page 386. Deep evergreens, soft silvery greys and the clear

blues and pinks of seaside flowers are colours that can predominate in a garden on the coast, where the light tends to be stronger and harsher than inland.

Eryngium variifolium, an evergreen sea holly

The street-front garden

The front garden is the public part of your garden, serving mainly to provide access and a decorative introduction to your home, and yet, oddly, it is often neglected. Perhaps this is because busy householders prefer to devote their spare time to parts of the garden used for recreation or food-growing, and also because the architecture of many houses isolates the front garden. The main living rooms often overlook the back, and patios and French doors serve to link the back garden more directly to the interior. Yet the need for a balanced, well-scaled design is just as important in front of the house.

You may enjoy making your house look as individual as possible, especially if it is very

perhaps plant a narrow but sweeping screen of open-textured shrubs – bamboos would be ideal – around the perimeter. Feathery foliage and a natural break for a gate will inhibit cross-street views without blocking out daylight. You can lead the visitor on a diagonal – but still direct – route from a combined garage/garden gate on one side to the door.

Cushion and specimen plants set in pockets left in the paving and planted containers placed where they will catch the eye may be used to bring colour to a paved garden, and trellis planted with self-clinging climbers will mask expanses of garage wall. But do not disturb the unity of your composition by introducing too confusing a variety of plants.

shrub bed to an exit on the opposite side is ideal, but do not sacrifice too much space for car access. Remember that drives should be about 3 m (10 ft) wide if possible.

Slopes and awkward shapes
Rock gardens are commonly used to landscape a sloping front garden. If well constructed and adequately drained and supported, these can be very striking, and so long as the plants are carefully chosen, they will not need a lot of care. A single specimen tree, such as a weeping birch (*Betula pendula* 'Youngii'), planted off-centre on an elegantly paved or rocky slope will provide screening in a garden that slopes down to the street. A

similar to the other houses in the street. A house that fronts directly on to the street can be made gay with planted pots and window boxes (bracketed onto the house wall if you have no window-ledges), and a narrow strip of garden between house and pavement planted with spring bulbs, summer-flowering bedding plants and a berrying wall shrub such as *Cotoneaster horizontalis* will give cheerful year-round colour. The front of the house itself can support a climber.

Avoiding stereotypes
A bold and unified yet essentially simple design is the key to a distinctive front garden, whatever its size. Make effective, practical and decorative use of all available space, and avoid the typical, wasteful sectioned arrangement of border, straight path and ineffectual lawn – and maybe shrub border and garage approach, too. An open-plan scheme consisting of a well-tended, unfenced lawn, perhaps extending to the next-door garden, crossed by a brick or stone path, and a single ornamental specimen tree for decoration and screening, can make a very effective front garden, but an enclosed plot can look spacious if entirely paved.

Vertical structures, including tall plants, should look in scale, but avoid dwarf walls and hedges, even in a small site, if you need to keep pets and children in or stray animals and wind-blown rubbish out. A 1.25 m (4 ft) wall or fence and gate will not look forbidding if screening plants obscure its line in places. Keep the centre of a paved garden open, but

above left An open-plan front garden with sweeping lawn and a few imposing shrubs, such as these rhododendrons, makes a simple, relaxed approach that suits many house styles. **above right** Even an almost non-existent front garden can be made to look bright and cheerful.
above Raised beds and an ornamental gateway give this entrance court a distinguished air.

The same principle applies equally to large front gardens. You can plan a gracious, informal scheme by constructing a wide, sweeping gravel driveway, with plenty of turning space in front of the house, and giving the remaining area over to ground-cover plants or an expanse of lawn, though this would need more maintenance. Tall grasses, shrubs or one or two trees will create contrast. Where there is room, a drive curving from an entrance facing the garage around a semi-circular

contoured slope planted with low-growing ground covers will not block the light from a garden that rises from the house. Awkward transverse slopes can be contoured or terraced into an L-shape (see p 21), planted with low cover and balanced with tall trees and shrubs opposite the rise. A driveway with steps down the centre or at the side makes an ingenious entrance path for a sloping garden if you need access to a garage.

Shrub borders can visually erase any eccentricities in boundary lines, but L-shaped sites on street corners are harder to deal with. Tall hedges are best here for shelter and privacy, and a street-front door set in a wall, instead of a gate, looks enticing. You can make a curved scheme (see p 18) to encompass front and side gardens, but a more interesting idea would be to turn the front part of the garden into a separate entrance court, screened from the side garden by an ornamental screen or planted trellis. This is also a graceful device for landscaping a garden that lies entirely at the front of the house.

You can let your imagination run riot in designing such a garden, making a relaxed, informal shady or Japanese-style garden (see pp 42 and 50). Or create a more formal arrangement with a pool, statuary and exotic plants and tender wall shrubs, for the walls may provide an environment in which the latter will flourish. Changes in level are appropriate here too. A sunken patio will provide an unusual seating area and will separate the recreational part of the courtyard garden from the means of access to the house.

Allotments and leisure gardens

Leisure garden is an apt new name for the modern allotment; in recent years these useful but traditionally uninspiring vegetable plots have undergone a complete transformation. In many north European countries they have been converted into neat and attractive gardens, often complete with chalets, for use as second homes by families living in apartments and gardenless housing developments.

As leisure gardens, modern allotments approach more closely the ideal of their German originator, Dr Moritz Schreber, who first advocated the use of gardens for family recreation and exercise, and whose followers began the European allotment movement as long ago as the 1860s. Today, *Schrebergärten* – now more popularly called *Kleingärten* – are to be seen around every West German industrial city, and they are equally popular in Holland (where they are called *volkstuinen*) and Denmark (called *kolonihaver*). But in the British Isles, and to some extent in Belgium and the other Scandinavian countries, the allotment movement was in a sad state of decline until inflation of the 1970s gave a boost to vegetable-growing. Even so, many people feel that it is still hampered by the old industrial working-class image, and could benefit from a new lease of life.

Using the leisure garden
The majority of leisure gardens on the continent of Europe are rented by families who want space for children to play and parents to sit and relax, beds of flowers for ornament and for cutting, and perhaps also some room for vegetables and fruit crops. Some room must be found too for the utility features necessary to any garden, but since the size of these plots ranges from a mere 200 m² to around 450 m² (approximately 250 to 550 sq yd), the division of space is a major problem.

Luckily, an open central area for recreation, essential to a family with young children, is also a sound design idea for a small garden and should reduce the need for paths to a few paving slabs leading into the site and perhaps also onto a vegetable patch. A small lawn is easily maintained by the weekend gardener and is softer for play than paving.

Boundaries are not common (and are sometimes prohibited) on municipal sites, so the leisure garden has no problems of shade and dry soil so often found along the perimeters of enclosed gardens. You can make side borders as narrow as 1 m (3 ft) to give as much space as possible to a lawn. Tall plants or fruit bushes are a good substitute for boundaries to provide privacy; if enclosures are permitted, a chain link fence would make a useful espalier on which to train fruit trees (see p 375), and open wooden fences make attractive foils for plants. Dwarf hedges look neat and attractive, but tall hedges will exhaust the soil in your own – and neighbouring – borders.

Even in a small garden you can make a lawn

above A Dutch leisure garden used for growing fruit and vegetables and also as an ornamental garden for weekend relaxation and enjoyment. above right A picturesque chalet garden on the outskirts of Amsterdam, Holland, is laid out and planted in a way reminiscent of the versatile English cottage garden style. below Open-plan *Kleingärten* adjacent to a housing development in Frankfurt, West Germany, are more utilitarian but still provide space for relaxation.

of unusual shape, perhaps curved to distract the eye from the rigid lines of a rectangular site. Danish leisure gardens are often oval in shape, and these present some interesting design possibilities. Shorten the lawn by as much as you require to make a vegetable patch at one end, and screen it off with a narrow planted border. Alternatively, you can plant some of the more ornamental vegetables among the border plants (see p 261). With ingenuity you should be able to include a paved utility corner near the entrance path, and screen it with climbers or a small shrub.

Planting the garden
Plants have a particularly important role in a garden with a minimum of hard structural elements. Establish a definable garden pattern (see p 18) by planting your favourite flowers in visually effective masses, and back

them up with bulbs, edging plants and well-placed evergreens for seasonal colour and interest. Regular feeding and cultivation of the soil will be essential in an area of such intensive planting.

You will have to use colour to achieve a basic unity of design. The article on page 26 may inspire ideas for building up a scheme on the basis of a single colour, with the green of grass, shrubs and foliage plants as a foil. Do not omit to consider the effect of colourful plants in neighbouring gardens; if they clash with your scheme you may need to mask their effect with one or two tall screening plants placed at strategic points.

Shade may be a problem in an open site during a hot summer. The planting of trees is permitted on most sites and an ornamental fruit tree or a shade tree such as a weeping silver birch will add a vertical element to a flat garden – but remember that all trees have hungry roots that may affect other plants over quite a wide area. Plants in containers, or handsome specimen plants, will become the ornaments in gardens where pools may be prohibited and statues may look out of place. Unless you have a chalet, such a plant will form the only focal point.

Chalet gardens
In Britain an allotment must, by law, be used primarily for food production, but that does not mean that needs to be unattractive; if you erect a shed, try to ensure that it looks pleasing or at least inconspicuous. In other European countries, building on the sites is actively encouraged, and the erection of small chalets, often with heating, cooking and sleeping facilities, is popular. Many families build their own chalets, but Scandinavian prefabricated wooden cabins are also popular, with small wooden sun decks around the outside. On a small site a summer-house (see p 79) with a small stove would make an adequate substitute, and would provide the necessary storage space too for garden furniture, a few tools and other equipment.

Steeply sloping gardens

Designing a garden for an acutely sloping site will give full scope to your ingenuity and imagination, for a hill site presents a stark challenge to the garden designer. But sloping land always offers interesting landscaping possibilities, and like all gardens on awkward sites a hillside or hilltop garden can be quite spectacular if treated boldly.

House and site

Maintaining elegance of line is all-important in a steep garden, so give some initial thought to the relationship between house, garden and surrounding landscape. A terrace can transfigure the appearance of a house built on an incline; without one it may look as if it is about to slide downhill. If conditions permit, extend the terrace all around the building to maximize the stabilizing effect – and to make extra space for utility features. Make the terrace as broad as proportion allows, to give an impression of spaciousness.

A formal or fussy terrace will look odd in a wild landscape, so keep its decoration simple, while making the most of its planting possibilities. Conifers and fast-growing shrubs along the edging wall will soon give protection from high winds. An ornamental gate or archway, and steps leading onto the hillside, could make the link with the garden.

Landscaping a slope

The ease or difficulty of future maintenance is a vital factor in deciding how best to landscape a steep garden. A lawn may be ruled out, but rough grass makes a perfect foil for naturalized bulbs and flowering shrubs, giving a steep transverse or upward-sloping site the appearance of an alpine meadow. The binding roots of coarse grasses such as creeping red fescue and rough-stalked meadow grass (see p 85) help to retain the soil and prevent erosion. When the grass does need attention, a rotary grass-cutter that rides on a cushion of air (see p 86) will be the easiest to use.

Terracing (see p 76) is an excellent alternative, especially for sites that slope steeply downwards from the house. Let the terraces curve and undulate naturally, following the contours of the site. Retaining walls laid dry blend in well, but mortared walls may be required where slopes are very steep. Soften the faces with plants that spill over the top or from holes left for them during construction. Alternatively, some or all of the slope can be made into a dramatic rock garden, with vertical rock faces for trailing plants and planting pockets for smaller alpines (see p 118).

Terraces and slopes give unlimited scope for informal areas of ground-covering plants and spreading shrubs, such as perennial candytuft (*Iberis sempervirens*), *Bergenia cordifolia*, Spanish gorse (*Genista hispanica*), and rose of Sharon (*Hypericum calycinum*), that will more or less look after themselves. You can punctuate these with larger berberis, olearias, potentillas and brooms. Rambler roses and other trailing plants (see pp 148 and 236) can be pegged down onto slopes or allowed to cascade over walls. In acid or neutral soils the whole range of heathers (see

p 152) could turn a slope into a complete heather garden, dotted with small junipers and other conifers. Fruit trees and vegetables can be grown successfully on terraces and gentle slopes, but hilly places are usually windy, so arrange screening features where necessary to protect them.

A little stream with waterfalls can be made in areas of high rainfall to cascade down the slope and culminate in a pool or a bog garden. Line the downhill course of the stream with river stones and ferns and other woodland plants so that it looks attractive even when dried out, and build little bridges or make stepping-stones where paths cross it. If a natural water supply is not reliable, you can use an electric pump to recirculate the water from the pool at the bottom (see p 132).

Enclosures and boundaries

Walls and fences are likely to be conspicuous, so choose unobtrusive materials that blend in well. Wood is most suitable for regions devoid of natural stone, though palings or rustic fences adapt to a slope more easily than solid fencing. Hedges, perhaps combined with chain-link fencing, make effective contour-hugging, windbreaking enclosures. Dry stone walls are traditional in many mountainous areas, and they too make excellent enclosures, but they are difficult to build.

Windbreaks formed with tall trees (see

p 90) may be essential to protect hilltop or very exposed gardens, but all boundaries can be broken at intervals with specimen trees or groups of tall shrubs. Where possible, however, leave gaps to allow sightings through to a pleasant view.

Ornamental access

Because many paths and cross-walks will be needed for access and general garden maintenance, their decorative qualities should be exploited to the full. They need to be solidly constructed with non-slip surfacing, but this does not preclude the use of gravel, pine-needles, wood chips and other attractive materials in flat places, or the occasional interconnecting stretch of stepping-stones.

If the size of the site permits, use an entrance path to take a visitor on a gently meandering route through the garden, along terraces lined with banks of flowers or planted raised beds, through rocky outcrops, rock gardens and scree beds, through shady avenues of trees or tall shrubs, plant-entwined archways or covered walks or pergolas leading out to viewpoints furnished with a seat or bench to view the landscape.

You may have to build ramps for moving wheelbarrows and other equipment, but make a special feature of steps. They can be constructed from the same materials as the paths or terrace walls and edged with plants.

A steep garden is an excuse to make the most of steps **left**, in short flights connected by stretches of path. They need non-slip surfacing to be safe, but a handrail can be as much an ornament as a necessity. A slope can be converted into a series of informal terraces by using rocks and small boulders **bottom left**, but where changes of level are more abrupt, it will probably be necessary to construct proper retaining walls **bottom right**. These can still be of fluent, informal shape, however, and contain beds of fine plants.

The city garden

Ingenuity in garden design is nowhere more evident – nor more necessary – than in a city, where gardens are tucked in between buildings, behind walls, on roof-tops, in basement courtyards and a host of other odd and awkward places. At their best, they bring character and colour to areas where they may least be expected to be found. It sometimes appears as if defying the odds is as much responsible as anything else for the creation of a city garden, but even if it consists of little other than a planted patio, everything that grows is certain of maximum appreciation.

Roof gardens, though beyond the scope of this book, offer a unique opportunity – and sometimes the only opportunity – for city dwellers to create a unique garden style. Special problems arise with exposure to wind, the need to grow everything in containers and restrictions on weight, but roof gardens do not lack light in the way most other small, enclosed city gardens do.

City garden style
Just because urban land is so costly, city gardens tend to be small and overshadowed by the walls of adjoining buildings. Informal

be built in the same materials as the house to emphasize the garden's role as an outdoor room; if privacy is a problem, a screen of ornamental trees is likely to be as much a pleasure for your neighbours as for yourself. These will be invaluable for shade too during a hot summer. Tolerant of polluted atmospheres, the purple-leaved cherry plum *Prunus cerasifera* 'Pissardii' will enliven the greyest spring with its early blossom, and the stag's-horn sumach (*Rhus typhina*) has striking form and fiery autumn foliage. *Ailanthus altissima*, the tree of heaven, is an easy city tree.

You can increase the light in an enclosed garden with pale-coloured walls and paving. White-painted trellis will bring a dark corner into focus. Bright white walls and a floor of white stone chippings will give a Mediterranean atmosphere to a dingy basement courtyard, English ivy (*Hedera helix*) or a variety of *Euonymus fortunei* making a striking contrast. There are ample colourful shade-loving plants, but you may prefer to create a cool oasis of green among the city concrete.

Surprisingly perhaps, a small garden is one place where changes in level – a sunken central area, large raised beds, a balcony or raised

and bracketed on walls, neat window boxes on ledges and hanging baskets blossoming just above eye level offer their own distinctive and often indispensible kinds of decoration. An enormous number of plants will tolerate even polluted city atmospheres; the charts beginning on page 386 indicate many of these.

Healthy soil is the key to the success of such intensive cultivation. City soils have generally been cultivated for many years, and may be thin and exhausted. You may well find that the soil needs a good deal of improvement (see p 332) before you can begin to plant. Try to find room for a compost bin that will provide a steady supply of humus-forming organic material to prevent the soil from becoming dusty and impoverished. It is even more important to mulch around trees and shrubs and to apply adequate quantities of fertilizers (see p 352) than with less intensively used ground.

Remember to choose plants – and especially shrubs and trees – that will remain in scale with the garden when they have grown to their mature height. It is all too easy to overshadow a small garden.

Ornament and decoration
As long as you do not overcrowd the garden or interfere with ease of movement through it, an 'architectural' specimen plant set in a space left for it in the paving, or planted in a decorative container, can be used to provide a focal point in the garden. Alternatively, an ornamental pool or fish pond can be the making of a city garden that is not too shaded; the movement and sound will be very appealing. Many forms of statuary look appropriate in city surroundings, and you can combine two attractive features by ornamenting a pool with a small statue. Where space is lacking, a wall fountain or statue may be fitted into a niche.

Storage space is often a problem in diminutive gardens, so any garden furniture should not take up too much space. White-painted cast iron or aluminium chairs and tables are useful, as they form decorative elements in their own right. If you have somewhere to store them when not in use, folding canvas chairs are also good, and you may be able to build a wooden-seated bench into raised beds of brick or stone.

below left In crowded city situations, high dividing walls and ornamental screening trees are commonly essential. **below**

right A balcony enlivens the façade of a town house and, furnished with plants, creates three-dimensional interest in its

garden. **above right** A still, quiet spot is created by a water feature in a diminutive city-centre roof-top garden.

styles suit these gardens best; a modern design brings contrasting colours, shapes and textures to flat expanses of concrete and the currently popular Japanese garden (see p 50) is easily adaptable to diminutive sites.

Some of the landscaping ideas for suburban gardens (see p 44) are equally applicable to larger city gardens where a well-kept lawn can be the making of the layout, but paved gardens are most practical where space is limited, because they can better withstand concentrated use. Remember that small paving units look most appropriate in a small area, and glazed bricks or paver tiles will look sophisticated. Patches of contrasting materials such as cobbles or gravel can be used to emphasize special features or specimen plants, and to relieve the starkness of a concrete surface.

Whenever possible the garden walls should

terrace with a well-proportioned climber-covered balustrade, and gracefully descending steps – can be created artificially yet will not look superimposed. Even a small grassy mound planted Japanese-style with a white azalea, or a cluster of lichen- or moss-covered boulders, can be effective.

Plants and pollution
The secret of creating your city oasis is to plant every inch of space without seeming to clutter the garden. Establish cushion plants in pockets in paved areas, fill surrounding borders with evergreen berrying and early-flowering shrubs for winter and early spring colour, and plant masses of colourful flowers for summer. Use containers to fill any seasonal gaps and train climbers along walls and over windows, doors and gates. Pots, hung

Other cultures, other styles

Gardens are as old as civilization, and there is no need to restrict your design ideas to the mainstream of Western styles that originated in Europe. The gardens of Asia and the Islamic world, in particular, offer garden-makers fresh inspiration. To capture their essence and translate it into a practical design will entail greater effort, but the result can be a garden of refreshing originality.

Persian gardens

Paradise gardens of beautiful plants and roaming animals like the imagined garden of Eden, and the terraced hanging gardens of the fabulous city of Babylon were the traditions behind the renowned pleasure gardens of ancient Persia. These gardens were based on a square plan and, like the formal enclosures of the Egyptian gardens, surrounded by high walls and formally laid out. They were divided into quarters by raised irrigation channels representing the four rivers of life; each channel was lined with straight rows of cypresses, representing eternity, and fruit trees which typified the springtime revival of life decorated the four quarters; a roofed pavilion in the centre provided a cool place for quiet thought, and roses and other perfumed flowers added to the beauty of the trees.

The gardens of Islam

The Arab invaders of medieval Persia, who like the ancients also thought that paradise was a garden, were so influenced by these shady Persian oases that they adopted their style and spread it through the entire Islamic empire. Rectangular, formal and architectural though their gardens were, Muslim garden designers were concerned to achieve a perfect balance between man and nature rather than to demonstrate man's mastery as the designers of the European Renaissance were to do. Regularity of form seems to promote a universal feeling of tranquility, and a shady courtyard is the perfect place for a garden where the climate is hot and dry.

In the shadow of high walls Muslim gardeners planted dense screens of evergreens, and elsewhere verdant trees – planes and sycamores were greatly loved – made cool areas where other plants could grow. Palms, citrus and other fruit trees, roses and scented flowers in pots and vases softened the straight lines of tile and marble architecture and added an air of romanticism to temper its austerity.

Except in dry Khorasan, where blue and grey pebbles were used to represent it, every garden had a central reflecting pool of geometrical shape, made shallow but kept brimming, and lined with blue tiles to make it look deeper. Spray from fountains cooled the air and their sound gratified the ear. Roofed colonnades, balconies, tents, awnings and tiled pavilions or kiosks – or the Spanish *glorieta*, an arbour covered with vines or a circle of cypresses trained onto arches – all provided shade. Statuary was rare, but beautiful coloured tiles adorned the walls and were used for paving, their intricate geometrical patterns a foil and echo of plant forms.

above The medieval Ryoan-ji temple garden in Kyoto, Japan, consists of 15 rocks arranged in 5 groups to represent islands in a sea of raked white gravel. below The qualities of relaxation and versatility inherent in Japanese gardens have long appealed to Westerners, who try to capture the essence of the style in their modern garden designs.

Gardening in the Far East

Nature was accorded the dominant role in the traditional gardens of the Far East. For millennia, gardens were made in imitation of the asymmetrical natural landscape: rivers were dug out, lakes excavated, hills constructed and among them dwellings and pavilions were fitted as unobtrusively as possible.

The gardens of old China were essentially open, extrovert gardens, merging as imperceptibly as possible into the surrounding landscape. They were picturesque compositions, like delicate landscape paintings, forming a series of pictures that merged gradually into each other. Rustic twisting paths, bridges and seats, wooden buildings at points of particular beauty and strange old weathered stones were the ornaments of a Chinese garden.

The Japanese evolved their own distinctive forms of the Chinese style, discovering in the process a set of aesthetic rules governing the design of gardens. In the hill garden, mounds of earth or boulders, and suitably scaled plants were positioned to give the impression of a hilly landscape seen from a distance. In the level garden, stones, small trees and perhaps a stream would be used to represent a wild valley or moor. Dry landscape gardens were built as contemplative exercises by the Zen Buddhist monks of medieval Japan. They used raked sand and groups of rocks in asymmetrical arrangements, within sober earthen walls, to represent islands in the sea, and often devoid of plants. Water featured prominently in many other gardens, however (see p 33).

The beauty of these gardens lies in their essential intimacy – no large garden is without it, and no space is too small for a garden – their natural asymmetry of layout and their subtle, hidden symmetry seen in the interplay between light and shade, contrasting textures, bright and muted colours; and in the essential harmony of scale, shape and form.

The rules governing the features and layout of the Japanese gardens were strict. Each style had its requisite number and relative positioning of different features, and could be laid out according to a *shin* (elaborate), *gyo* (semi-formal) or *so* (abbreviated and informal) treatment. The literary man's garden evolved as a style through which persons of sensitivity could enjoy the tranquillity of nature in a limited space, and might consist of little more than a group of rocks and a flowering tree or a clump of bamboos in a yard.

The 17th-century *chaniwa* or tea garden, on the other hand, was a more elaborate style – often containing elements of all the others. Its role was to lead the visitor to the *chaseki* or tea house, and the front garden or entrance was always accorded great importance in the design. It was planted to induce feelings of harmony and contemplation in the visitor. Paved with rough stones and moss and planted with evergreen and flowering trees, but very few flowers, the atmosphere of the tea garden was rustic and natural, its ornament consisting of little more than a water basin and perhaps a stone lantern.

Gardens for warm climates

The garden-maker in an area of Mediterranean climate, where frosts are rare or non-existent and summers are hot, is fortunate in being able to grow a great range of beautiful and colourful plants, many of them described in the articles beginning on pages 173 and 222. These make it possible to have a garden that is full of interest and colour throughout the year.

But he faces challenges, too. The garden under a hot sun should ideally be a haven of cool shade and luxuriant greenery – sometimes a problem if drought is common and irrigation expensive or forbidden. It may be necessary for all rainwater to be collected and stored in a cistern during wet seasons, or even to collect waste water from baths, basins and sinks; so long as this is allowed to cool and does not contain chemicals, it is quite safe to give to plants. Increasing the water-retaining properties of the soil by digging in plenty of organic material and using thick mulches of peat, shredded bark or similar material will help, but drought-resistant plants should be chosen as far as possible. Cacti and succulents are obvious candidates, but many other plants

that would die in open ground in drought may survive if planted in a container or raised bed and kept watered. Planting drought-resistant shade trees helps to create conditions in which other plants can thrive (see below).

Garden style

Such problems apart, the design opportunities in warm climates are exciting. Garden designers from the Mediterranean to the Far East have long been masters at creating styles to suit such climates, so some of those described opposite may be a source of inspiration. An old house of traditional design may well have a shady inner court that can be turned into a green oasis by planting permanent and potted plants. Walls can be clothed with climbers in great diversity, and a pool and cool fountain can form a central focal feature, leaving plenty of room for furniture.

Present-day architects often bow to tradition and design houses in warm regions with adjoining courtyards. You can take advantage of cheap and readily available local materials to build your own outer courtyard – or even a

series of interconnected courts at different levels on a sloping site. You can create some picturesque sculptural effects with rounded whitewashed or stuccoed walls of clay and rubble, or with adobe blocks.

A hillside garden overlooking the sea can be landscaped as a series of open terraces planted with almond, walnut, cypress or fig trees – or roofed with pergolas – for shade; you will be able to enjoy the view and your garden will look very much part of the countryside in areas where agriculture is traditionally carried out on terraces. If you have a modern house you can use concrete (which somehow seems to look right in an arid region, but can also be painted white) to make a contemporary open-plan arrangement of low, angled walls, shallow sweeping terraces and steps, all of which throw shapely shadows that can be used to spectacular effect as part of the garden pattern.

above left Succulent mesembryanthemums and aloes together with bright gazanias decorate a rock feature in a Mediterranean garden.
centre Palm trees such as *Trachycarpus fortunei* provide elegant shade in a hot climate, while **right** plumbago adds to the coolness of this courtyard.

Creating shade

Shade is an essential in any area where sunlight is strong. You can build roofed walks around a courtyard garden, and bamboo strips or wooden slats entwined with a vine can be used to shade part of an open patio or terrace. Arbours and pergolas – perhaps extending into walks covered with climbers and leading to an ornament or stone seat – will make additional shady features. Fast-growing acacias, palms, eucalypts, umbrella pines (*Pinus pinea*) and many others make good shade trees.

A number of architectural features create pleasant shaded areas at the point where house and garden meet. Balconies, planted with bougainvilleas or vines, provide a first-floor vantage point from which to view the

garden, and are traditional to many houses in warm regions; they catch any air movement. Open-sided ground-floor verandahs and porticos, and loggias (built into many grander houses in sunny climes) can all be furnished with chairs and tables and ornamented with plants at the outer edges where there is most light. The *lanai*, native to Honolulu, is a kind of glassed-in verandah that can be opened to the air or shaded with blinds when necessary, and makes an ideal extension for a modern house in hot, windy districts.

Features for outdoor living

Room for recreation is essential for any garden in a warm climate. A lawn will be much used, but be sure to choose suitable warm-climate and/or drought-resistant grasses (see p 85). In very dry regions a paved area – or even synthetic grass of the kind used for sports arenas – might be a more practicable, if expensive, alternative. A barbecue (see p 83) will be a useful feature, but provided water is in adequate supply a swimming pool (see p 82) and possibly a paddling pool for children will be the most popular of all. It will be in use

for much of the year, so you can make a central feature of it, with a poolside terrace with seats and umbrellas for shade and tubbed or potted plants for decoration. These could include, for exotic effect, a banana plant or *Monstera deliciosa* (the so-called Swiss cheese plant or split-leaf philodendron commonly grown as a houseplant) trained up a moss-covered pole; both should be taken under cover in winter unless it is very mild.

With or without a swimming pool, a garden under the sun can be a very appealing outdoor room, with furniture of such materials as cane, wicker and rattan that will not rot if the air is dry. Colourful awnings and canvas chairs will not look gaudy in bright sunlight. For outdoor meals a permanent table can be constructed of brick and concrete, possibly surfaced with colourful tiles. With a background of citrus trees in pots, deliciously night-scented climbers, the dramatic silhouettes of a cactus and succulent garden, statues and a tinkling fountain, all subtly lit at night, a garden can be created that is the envy of anyone who has to live under grey skies.

Children's gardens

While most children think of the garden as a place for play and adventure, many parents want it to be a haven of tranquillity and beauty. This conflict of interests is fundamental, for the parents are likely to have a fixed idea of how they want their garden to look, and will work steadily towards that end, while the children's needs evolve as they develop mentally and physically. Compromises need to be worked out carefully in the planning stages.

If you have a large garden, you can easily set aside a plot of suitable size entirely for the children's use, and even screen it off altogether if they are old enough to be left to play alone. You will still have a substantial area of garden to landscape as you wish. But in a small garden, even if a portion is designated for the children's use, some overspill is inevitable and the 'play area' may turn out to be more of a theory than a practical reality. In families where there are toddlers and teenagers together, the problems are compounded, for the toddlers will be pushing and riding wheeled toys at the same time as the older children are playing ball games, roller skating and riding bicycles.

You will also find that allowing the children the run of the entire garden with perhaps the exception of a flower bed or two is not a satisfactory compromise. A garden consisting largely of flat play areas is by no means beautiful. But it is possible to produce a flexible design for a family garden that will adapt to the changing needs of the whole family (see p 17). You can reduce the widths of borders and so enlarge a lawn to make space for children to play. You can lay access paths to double as cycling or roller-skating tracks. And you can at the same time create secluded corners where you can sit and enjoy a pleasant view when you have time to rest. In later years, certain elements can be reconstructed to perform a more ornamental role.

The play area

Very small children will play happily with their toys on a patio or lawn near the house doors or windows, needing no more than a blanket or waterproof sheet to sit on. But eventually, when the noise of their play becomes a nuisance, they may be given their own larger play area sited at a more discreet

(though still visible) distance from the house.

Siting a children's play area within a garden calls for some thought. It will need to be somewhere fairly sheltered from strong winds, and should be at least partly shaded in hot and sunny climates. In cooler regions, it should receive as much sunshine as possible. If you have a small garden you can make a play area on a lawn or central paved area, using canvas beach screens if necessary as windbreaks. You can equip the area with movable apparatus – an ideal solution on a lawn since you can then ensure that different parts of the lawn are used equally, and so avoid bare patches.

For shade or shelter, the children's play area may need to be partly roofed. Canvas makes a good protection against both rain and glaring sunshine. Wooden latticework or plants growing on a pergola will also provide some shade. A soft grass surface is ideal for playing upon, but because rain and intensive use can easily turn it into mud – an attractive

but rather too tenacious a material for children's play – an alternative form of flooring may be needed.

Open-surface materials such as shredded fir bark, pine needles or wood chips are soft, clean and inexpensive, but you should perhaps avoid gravel; even rounded beach shingle tends to be rather uncomfortable to play on. Concrete or stone pavings, though hard and cold, are cleaner. Warm, quick-drying and pleasant to walk on – even with bare feet – wood that has been treated to give it a non-slip finish is an excellent choice. Whatever flooring material you select, the play area must be very well drained.

Suitable materials for building an enclosed play shelter are described on page 74. The cheaper materials only need be used – old planks, wooden trellis, wattle fencing, larch poles or even timber oddments. With the help of a little juvenile imagination it will soon become a fort or a Wendy house, or the headquarters of a secret society.

Plants to beware

The garden plants listed below are to a greater or lesser extent poisonous; unless otherwise stated, all parts may be harmful. Apart from these, many weeds and wild plants are also dangerous. It is wise to teach children not to pick and eat *any* leaves or berries unless known for certain to be harmless – as with cultivated crops.

Aconitum spp (monkshood); *Actaea* spp (baneberry); *Aesculus* spp (horse chestnut; leaves, fruits); *Anemone* spp; *Aquilegia* spp (columbine); *Arum* spp; *Baptisia* spp (false indigo); *Buxus* spp (box); *Caltha palustris* (kingcup, marsh marigold); *Caesalpinia* (*Poinciana*) spp (pods); *Colchicum* spp (autumn crocus, meadow saffron); *Convallaria majalis* (lily of the valley); *Daphne laureola* (spurge laurel); *D. mezereum* (mezereon); *Datura stramonium* (thorn-apple); *Delphinium* spp (larkspur);

Dicentra spp (bleeding heart; root); *Digitalis purpurea* (foxglove); *Eranthis hyemalis* (winter aconite); *Euonymus europaeus* (spindle tree); *Euphorbia* spp (spurge; sap also irritates skin); *Fritillaria meleagris* (snake's-head fritillary; bulb); *Galanthus* spp (snowdrop; bulb); *Hedera* spp (ivy; berries, leaves); *Helleborus* spp (hellebore, Christmas rose; leaves); *Hyacinthus orientalis* (hyacinth; bulb); *Hydrangea* spp (root); *Hypericum* spp; *Ilex* spp (holly; berries); *Iris* spp; *Kalmia latifolia* (calico bush; leaves); *Laburnum* spp (golden rain); *Lathyrus* spp (sweet pea; pods); *Leycesteria formosa* (Himalayan honeysuckle; seeds); *Ligustrum vulgare* (common privet; sap, leaves, berries); *Lobelia* spp; *Lonicera* spp (honeysuckle); *Lupinus* spp (lupin; seeds); *Mirabilis jalapa* (four-o'clock plant, marvel of Peru; root, seeds); *Narcissus* spp (daffodil, narcissus, jonquil; bulb); *Nerium*

oleander (oleander); *Ornithogalum umbellatum* (star of Bethlehem; bulb); *Phoradendron serotinum* (berries); *Phytolacca* spp (pokeweed; berries, root); *Podophyllum* spp (May apple, American mandrake); potato (*Solanum tuberosum*; green parts and especially berries); *Primula* spp; *Prunus laurocerasus* (common or cherry laurel); *Ranunculus* spp (buttercup, crowfoot); *Rhamnus* spp (buckthorn; berries); *Rhododendron* spp (including azaleas); rhubarb (*Rheum raponticum*; green leaf blades); *Rhus* spp (poison ivy, sumach); *Robinia pseudoacacia* (false acacia, black locust); *Sanguinaria* spp (bloodroot; root); *Scilla* (*Endymion*) *non-scripta* (bluebell; bulb); *Skimmia* spp; *Symphoricarpos albus* (snowberry; berries); *Taxus baccata* (yew); tomato (*Lycopersicon lycopersicum*; green parts) *Trollius europaeus* (globe flower); *Viscum album* (mistletoe)

Simple play equipment

Often the simplest everyday equipment provides the greatest fun and best encourages a child to use his or her imagination, so the play area need not be full of expensive apparatus. Quite ordinary things can be used for sitting on – logs placed on end or laid flat, or large smooth stones (but not in cold climates). Planks supported by a couple of bricks and wooden stools are useful as tables.

A bowl of water, plus a few cups, funnels, plastic bottles and floating toys, will provide endless fun for young children in warm weather – though toddlers need supervision for safety. A sand-box is popular with children of many ages. You can simply fill a fairly large box with clean sharp sand and provide buckets and spades. Alternately you can build a sand-box from boards, logs or bricks – it can be used as a raised bed later on.

Larger items

A sand-pit can be accommodated in a large play area, or will make a self-contained one in a small garden. It is easy to build; the most important thing to remember is that, whether at ground level or below, it must be well drained. This can be achieved with a base of compacted gravel or open-jointed paving slabs. Clean, sharp horticultural sand is the best to use; soft builders' sand is often dirty. Spread it about 30 cm (12 in) deep. If the surface is at ground level the pit should have a rounded edging to prevent the sand spilling out. Wood is simplest and perhaps best, but you may prefer to use brick or stone. A cover is essential; apart from keeping out debris when the pit is not in use, it will prevent cats and dogs fouling the sand.

A paddling-pool is another popular item of play equipment, but you should never install one in the garden until your children are old enough to use it safely. Even shallow water is a danger to a toddler. A paddling area can be built on to a swimming pool (see p 82), but a safety barrier between the two is essential, and the whole pool should be enclosed with a tall, unscaleable fence and a gate that is kept firmly locked when the pool is not in use.

Collapsible or inflatable paddling-pools can be moved around to take advantage of the available sunshine, and they are easily cleaned and stored. When damaged, the better quality sort can be repaired with a special repair kit. Some swimming-pool manufacturers also make paddling-pools, or you can build your own using a metal, glass-fibre or plastic liner, or poured concrete. It should have a good non-slip surround made of paving slabs or concrete, and the pool floor should also have a non-slip surface. A permanent pool must be easily drained and cleaned.

Old favourites such as swings and slides are still popular items of play equipment. Swings can be bought or made – the simplest kind is an old tyre slung from a strong tree branch – but slides should really be bought from a reputable manufacturer. Both are best stood on a surface of grass, sand, fir bark or some other soft material because children are bound to have falls. Do not place them anywhere near a

path or paved area where other children could be walking, and be sure to anchor them firmly. Make sure that tree branches and other overhead supports are very strong, and that ropes and seats are very well secured. They must be checked regularly for wear and replaced when necessary. If equipment such as this is purchased in kit form, make sure that the manufacturer's instructions for assembly and anchoring are followed.

Children love to climb, and climbing frames are always popular. If you buy one, make sure that it is sturdy and, again, well anchored. An excellent climbing structure (doubling as a fort, den or whatever) can be improvised from logs, but secure them very firmly. The ultimate structure of this type is a tree house – which needs both a strong tree of suitable shape and a high degree of woodworking skill.

Water gardens are fascinating to most children, but with young ones fit a strong protective grille through which the aquatic plants can grow.

Plants for children's gardens

Fast-growing flowers	*Calendula officinalis* (pot marigold); *Centaurea cyanus* (cornflower); *Clarkia elegans; Convolvulus minor* (*C. tricolor*); *Crocus* cvv; *Eschscholzia californica* (Californian poppy); *Helianthus annuus* (sunflower); *Hyacinthus orientalis* (hyacinth; bulbs poisonous); *Iberis amara* (candytuft); *Linaria maroccana* (toadflax, bunny rabbits); *Malcolmia maritima* (Virginia stock); *Narcissus* cvv (daffodils; bulbs poisonous); *Nigella damascena* (love-in-a-mist); *Papaver rhoeas* (poppies, especially Shirley strain); *Tagetes* spp (African and French marigolds); *Tropaeolum majus* (nasturtium); *Tulipa* cvv (tulips)
Unusual plants	*Dipsacus* spp (teasels); *Ecballium elaterium* (squirting cucumber); *Kochia scoparia* (burning bush); *Lagenaria* spp and *Cucurbita* spp (gourds); *Luffa aegyptiaca* (loofah); *Oxalis acetosella* (wood sorrel); *Physalis alkekengi* (Chinese lantern); *Physostegia virginiana* (obedient plant); *Trifolium repens* 'Purpurascens Quadriphyllum' or 'Purpureum' (four-leaved ornamental clover); tree seedlings from stones (eg, apple, cherry, chestnut)
Plants to eat	Alpine strawberries; beans (especially runner); carrots; corn salad (lamb's lettuce); lettuces (especially dwarf varieties); mustard and cress; nasturtiums (*Tropaeolum majus*; for edible leaves, flowers and seeds); peas (dwarf); potatoes (tops poisonous); radishes; spring onions; dwarf tomatoes (eg, 'Tiny Tim'); wheat

The child's own garden

Children learn as they play, and the family garden will provide a valuable source of opportunity and information, so they should not be too confined within their own play area, or cut off from the rest of the garden. Older children will probably appreciate a wild area at the bottom of the garden – perhaps equipped with a cabin or summer-house.

A shallow pool stocked with plants and other pond life (see p 32) will be a never-ending source of interest. If it is small and positioned where it cannot easily be fallen into – preferably with raised sides – it will not be a danger to older children, but it should have a grille or wire safety netting for younger ones. A garden planned and planted to attract wildlife (see p 34) will also be a fascinating place for both children and parents.

Most children like to watch seeds they have sown grow and develop into flowers and vegetables, and if gently encouraged will take an interest in caring for their own plot. If you decide to give your child his own patch of ground to care for, make sure that it is large enough to yield an attractive result – and avoid allocating space under a hedge or in some other obscure place where nothing will grow. A plot of 2m² (20 sq ft) is as much as most ten-year-olds can manage easily, and younger ones need less. If sited near the house it will be easily accessible while not interfering with the layout of the garden.

Children usually want to see quick results from their horticultural efforts, or their enthusiasm quickly wanes; the table on this page lists some plants that are particularly quick and easy to grow. Show the children how to prepare the ground, plant the seeds, and keep them watered. Then leave them to their own devices; they will be delighted with the results, and will learn, too.

Labour-saving gardens

Many people think of labour-saving in the garden solely in terms of mowing machines or rotary cultivators. These have their part to play, but there is far more to it than mechanization: Careful planning is the secret of the garden that almost looks after itself.

Every gardener would be wise to plan his garden with future ease of maintenance in mind. But broadly speaking, gardeners who would benefit most from a time and motion study on their garden fall into four categories: the young and frantically busy who can devote only limited time to their garden, people who have a second garden at their country or sea-side home, people with large gardens, and older people who usually have plenty of time, but who no longer have the physical strength

for the work they used to do, and so need to economize on labour. Gardeners in this last category may also find some useful hints in the article on gardens for the elderly and handicapped (see p 56).

Planning a labour-saving garden
Begin by deciding what you want from your garden – and also how much time and effort you can afford to put into it. When you have listed your priorities, look around your garden and decide which features to eliminate and what to put in their place.

The garden's most labour-intensive features are formal beds and borders, rose gardens, lawns, hedges, grassy paths and banks, rock gardens full of rare plants, and fruit and vegetable plots. They need a lot of regular feeding and weeding, staking and tying, disbudding, dead-heading, trimming, pruning, mowing, clipping, spraying, protecting for winter and so on. These features can be eliminated altogether from your garden or your plan – or at least diminished in scope – and garden chores consequently lessened. In their place you can substitute informal plantings of shrubs, with ground-cover plants or trouble-free bulbs and perennials, planted patios and

paved areas, rough grass or woodland patches, walls and fences brightened with climbers, coniferous and other hedges that need only an annual trim, if any, and other work-reducing schemes.

If you find that you really do want a lawn, however, or if you want to devote all your time to a large flower bed, you can still plan or reorganize the rest of the garden along labour-saving lines, while ensuring that your lawn or flower bed is planned, built and maintained as efficiently as possible.

Beds, borders and backgrounds
The traditional herbaceous border is nearly always planted in front of a wall, fence or hedge. The result is charming, but the back-

ground causes the plants to draw towards the light and produce longer stems than they would if grown in a more open, light and airy situation. Thus many plants that do not usually need staking must be given support in such a one-sided border. Moreover, clipping the hedge is awkward and time-consuming.

Transferring the plants to a free-standing island bed (see p 108) is a good labour-saving idea, for the plants grow stockier and sturdier, and far fewer kinds need staking. Alternatively, if there is room in front of it, the border edge could be extended outwards by, say, 0.9 to 1.25 m (3 to 4 ft), the plants moved forward, and a path of similar width laid between the border and the wall or hedge. This leaves the size of the border unchanged, but positions it well away from the background, so that the plants are not drawn upward so much.

Another way to reduce work is to eliminate all hardy herbaceous plants that need anything but minimal staking. Similarly, hardy annuals and biennials require very little maintenance if the shorter varieties are chosen, and most hardy bulbs need little attention for a number of years.

Formal hedges entail a great deal of work in clipping at least once or twice a year. Where

expense is no object, a hedge can be replaced by a handsome wall. At less cost, there is much to be said for planting a less formal screen of shrubs, attractive for their flowers or foliage or both, that need little or no pruning. The old hedge can be pulled up when the new shrubs are big enough to take over. Such a screen will probably occupy a wider strip around the garden than a formal hedge, but shrubs can be chosen that are not too wide-spreading. Philadelphus (mock orange), lilac, weigela, diervilla, evergreen berberis and pyracantha would be ideal. Laurel, too, is good, only needing light trimming once a year, and 'Queen Elizabeth' is a popular rose for hedging (see p 99). On acid soils, rhododendrons such as *Rhododendron pon-*

Ways of reducing work
far left Use of ground-cover plants is one of the best ways of reducing garden chores; here heathers and primulas are interplanted with dwarf conifers for variety. **left** Low-growing perennials need no staking, and flanking the bed with a hard edging and gravel path minimizes the problem of plants flopping over the edge. **above right** Ground-hugging evergreens can be used to great effect at the front of a house, maintaining an attractive appearance with the minimum of attention.
far right A well-planted wild garden needs little care; here only a narrow strip of grass is mown. **below right** In a small garden, paving can eliminate the chore of lawn maintenance.

ticum would flourish, as well as azaleas and other lovely shrubs (see p 91). In front of and among them you can plant heathers, vincas and many other ground-covering, weed-smothering plants (see p 232).

All roses have to be pruned and sprayed, tied and trained, and the beds must be kept clear of weeds and underplanted with other subjects to give interest in the rose bed when the flowering season is over. If you really love roses, the shrub varieties (see p 158) tend to be large but are the least demanding.

A combination of trees, shrubs and permanent ground-covering plants offers the best approach to a truly labour-saving garden. A mixture of ornamental fruit trees such as almond, cherry or peach, which flower in the spring, summer-flowering shrubs, trees and shrubs that turn colour in the autumn, and evergreens, will provide year-long interest; and ground-covering plants can take the place of annuals and perennials, fill in the awkward gaps and discourage weeds.

Labour-saving lawns
The lawn is a hard taskmaster; it needs weekly cutting and edging for at least half the year. With large lawns, you can compromise and

save yourself labour: leave most of the grass rough, and cut it with a rotary mower three or four times a year, setting aside just a small area near the house to cut short. The contrast between the rough and the mown parts is very pleasing. Bulbs and other plants can be naturalized in the long grass, and one or two beds of shrubs planted in it, with a winding path or two cut through to them.

In a small garden there is much to be said for replacing the lawn with paving, leaving gaps in which to grow dwarf plants (see p 235). Indeed, you can grow a wider assortment between the paving stones and in containers stood on the paved area – you cannot plant them in a lawn! Weeds between paving stones can be avoided by setting the stones in concrete, leaving pockets of soil for planting.

But if you find that a lawn is essential to your garden life, make sure that you choose the most suitable grass (see p 84). Also, careful construction and initial maintenance can save you much effort later, and there are many mechanical devices to make the recurrent tasks of lawn maintenance easier.

Building jobs to reduce work

A simple job that is often worth doing is to lay paving 40 to 45 cm (15 to 18 in) wide, or a double row of bricks, along the length of a flower border that is flanked by a lawn. Plants in the front of a border generally need to be cut back or supported in some way, if they are not to encroach on the grass and cause bare patches. With a stone edging they can flop to

their heart's content, and this also eliminates the need to trim lawn edges by hand, as the wheels of the mower can run on the paving.

Grass banks are a nuisance – they are difficult to cut and not usually very attractive. They can be covered with shrubs or ground-cover plants, but if you are prepared to go to the trouble of building, perhaps over a year or two, retaining walls of brick, peat blocks or stone, the bank could be terraced. Depending on the height of the bank, one or two raised borders may be created in which to grow plants, and in the spaces between the bricks or stones other plants can be set (see p 124). People getting on in years will appreciate being able to grow a good range of rock plants without having to stoop or kneel too much.

Rock gardens require a surprising amount of attention, but that is partly because some of the rarer alpine plants are difficult to grow. Many rock plants, once properly established, need little enough care, especially if some weed-smothering kinds that spread over the ground, forming a mat, are chosen. The rarer alpines could be grown in a small raised sink or trough that is easier to get at, or in pots in a cold frame (see p 122).

Steps, though often charming, make it difficult to move heavy loads or equipment around the garden. You can make a portable ramp from wooden boards, but it is also easy to make a gently sloping permanent ramp at one side of the steps.

Diminishing garden chores

Most routine garden chores that cannot be eliminated altogether can at least be made easier with the aid of specialized tools and machinery. Many of these are described on pages 376 to 379. Garden equipment stores and catalogues can be scoured for useful labour-saving gadgets – you will find devices to pick up leaves, to spread fertilizers and to help with a host of other tasks that are a nuisance to the fit and may be beyond the

capabilities of the elderly and handicapped.

Weeds, pests and plant diseases are the most difficult garden problems to eliminate. Modern chemical weedkillers (see p 356) are the most effective solution to the first. They have revolutionized weed control in the garden, although few amateurs realize what splendid labour-savers they are when handled correctly. Ground-covering plants and mulches will help to prevent weeds. Fruit cages (see p 267) will help with the larger pests, such as birds, and the use of spraying devices (see p 360) is the quickest way of dealing with the rest. By choosing certified disease-free plants, especially in the fruit garden, you can reduce the problem of dealing with diseases.

The garden at the second home

People with a second home out of town will particularly need a minimum-care garden. Certain gardens are naturally labour-saving, after an initial investment of time and effort in creating them. The 'natural' garden (see p 40) in particular falls into this category, as does the heather garden (see p 152) when the soil is the right type. In coastal areas, an attractive garden can be built with stones and pebbles interplanted with grasses and suitable salt-tolerant shrubs. Inveterate 'second-homers', the Scandinavians solve the problem with semi-natural gardens of silver birch and forest conifers, rough grass areas planted with bulbs, gorse and shrub roses, and shrubs that are drought- and frost-resistant.

For lawns at second homes, a rotary lawn-mower is almost obligatory because a cylinder mower would probably not be able to cope with two or three weeks' growth if for any reason the owner were unable to visit the property regularly. Similarly, watering presents a problem, particularly in coastal gardens with light, sandy soils. Here, the use of thick moisture-retaining mulches and a choice of plants that do not require much watering seem the best solutions.

Gardens for the elderly and handicapped

Any well-planned garden should be constructed and planted in a way that takes account of the gardener's abilities and the amount of time he is able or prepared to spend on its maintenance. When planning for the disabled or the elderly, these considerations may be paramount – though there is no reason why such a garden should not be extremely attractive at the same time.

A number of tools and other items of equipment are available, as described on page 378, that help such people carry out various garden tasks. As that article explains, handicaps vary widely and thus, correspondingly, do elderly or handicapped gardeners' needs for special aids. Much the same applies to the garden itself: The gardener's particular abilities and disabilities must be taken into account. This article describes the most important ways in which planning and construction can make such peoples' gardening easier and more enjoyable. (Gardening can be an excellent form of occupational therapy.) The numbers in bold type refer to features shown in the illustration of a hypothetical garden, which is rectangular in plan for clarity; there is no reason why some features should not be built in sweeping curves for a softer effect.

Terrace and paths

A terrace or paved patio **1** should be readily accessible from the house and sheltered from cold winds. It may be the only part of the garden a disabled person can reach in bad weather, and should be attractive as it may be the only part visible from inside. The terrace can be surrounded by raised beds **2** about 40 cm (15 in) high and 60 cm (2 ft) wide, which can be planted with bulbs and seasonal bedding plants (see p 112) for bright colour through nine months of the year. A narrow border 30 cm (12 in) wide between the house and the terrace will allow for climbing plants to be trained on the house walls. Alternatively, these can be grown in large tubs **3**. Also on this terrace is a water garden **4** with raised sides for safety and seating in a sunny spot **5**.

If the ground slopes up or down from terrace to garden, one or more gentle ramps **6** are preferable to steps. Provide handrails on each side, and make the gradient no steeper than 1:15 (1 in 15). Any ramp longer than about 10 m (33 ft) should have a midway level area of 1 m (3 ft) so that a wheelchair gardener can take a rest. A main path in the centre of the garden **7** will provide access to all areas. All paths and ramps should be at least 90 cm (3 ft) wide for wheelchair users or those using walking frames or crutches.

The hard surfaces can be built from either precast concrete slabs or concrete laid *in situ*. Either must have a non-slip surface; you can give *in situ* concrete a rough texture by brushing the surface 30 minutes after the concrete is laid. Take care to allow a sufficient 'fall' for rainwater to drain off the terrace and paths; this is particularly important in winter, when an icy surface can be extremely dangerous. The raised beds can be built of brick or from paving slabs stood on edge and braced against

the edge of the terrace paving by ballast (see p 124). The pool is constructed from poured concrete (see p 128).

The ornamental garden

Beyond the terrace, a formal rose garden **8** can be laid out with crossing paths so that the roses can be tended from a wheelchair. Half-standards are easy for wheelchair gardeners to reach; standards are easier if you cannot bend. Ground-cover plants reduce the need for weeding. A lawn **9** is pleasing but needs regular maintenance. More raised beds **10** are best used for plants that need or benefit from close attention – such as annuals, bedding plants, smaller herbaceous perennials and alpines. They should be 60 cm (2 ft) high and up to 1.25 m (4 ft) wide. Shrubs and other easy-care plants can occupy ground-level beds **11**.

Fruit and vegetables

Fruit trees **12** add colour to the garden in spring as well as fruit later in the year. Apples and pears can be grown as cordons or dwarf pyramids, or trained as espaliers. Plums, cherries and peaches make attractive fans. All can provide cover for fences or protection in the vegetable garden.

To keep the width of the growing area to a maximum of 2 m (7 ft), the kitchen garden **13** can be divided into sections. This allows all cultivations to be carried out from the paths without the gardener having to walk on the dug soil. It is easiest to use a hoe or tined cultivator by a push-pull action, so rows of vegetables should be short so that the gardener can stand or sit at the ends and cultivate all the way along. A seat **14** provides a welcome resting place.

A raised bed **15** can be used to grow herbs or as a seed-bed for vegetable plants. Soft fruit such as gooseberries and currants **16** can be trained as half-standard bushes on 30 to 60 cm (1 to 2 ft) stems. These will be easy to handle and will produce top quality fruit.

The greenhouse

If gardening is to be enjoyed throughout the year, a greenhouse **17** is an essential feature, and for the elderly and disabled siting is extremely important. Provided that it is not in deep shade, the nearer the house it is the easier it will be for the gardener to reach in winter. (A few hours spent tending plants in a heated greenhouse can provide a welcome change of scene for a housebound person.) In these circumstances, a lean-to greenhouse

built on to the house – forming a kind of conservatory – may be best. Otherwise, it may be better for appearances' sake to position the greenhouse between the ornamental and kitchen gardens, to form a screen, as shown in the illustration.

For a wheelchair gardener, the doorway should be at least 75 cm (2½ ft) wide and have no step or door rail to obstruct passage. The inside path should be equally wide, so a fairly large size of greenhouse is needed. Staging can be lower than normal.

It is worthwhile providing a number of automatic features, such as capillary watering devices and thermostatic heating and ventilation, so that greenhouse maintenance does not become a chore. But ensure that services such as electricity and water are installed safely by experts. All electrical apparatus should be operated from one insulated control panel within easy reach but above the level of the staging. A spare socket can be used for an electric lawn-mower, hedge-clippers or other equipment.

As well as a water supply in the greenhouse, fit an outside standpipe connected to a hose reel **18** of the type that allows water to flow through the hose while it is uncoiling. Placed near the middle of the garden, the hose can easily reach every part. When watering is finished, it is easy to re-coil the hose by turning the reel handle.

Shed and frame

To help screen the vegetable patch, a shed **19** can be positioned opposite the greenhouse, their doors facing each other across a 3 m (10 ft) paved area **20** providing ample turning space for a wheelchair. Again, the shed door must be wide and uncluttered. Ideally, a window at the opposite end will give light for potting and other jobs, which can be carried out on a full-width bench beneath it. Part of the bench top can form the lid of a bin for storing potting mixture. Provide a safe, lockable cupboard for garden chemicals and a wall rack for tools. Electric lighting is useful.

On the outside, climbing plants can be trained over the side nearest the house. On the other side, you can build a raised bed 60 cm (2 ft) high (with a solid back so that the shed does not rot). Filled with soil to a depth of 45 cm (18 in) and provided with lights hinged to a wooden plate screwed onto the shed, this becomes a convenient cold frame **21**. Corrugated clear plastic is lighter and easier to handle than glass, and the height minimizes bending to tend the plants.

The area behind the shed **22** can be used for rubbish disposal and unsightly objects. It can house a dustbin for broken glass, stones and other non-burnable rubbish; a compost bin for weeds, grass cuttings and the like; and a wire cage incinerator for woody rubbish. Plastic sacks are useful for collecting extra rubbish in autumn, and a two-wheeled wheelbarrow can be used even from a wheelchair.

The front garden

Most people want the area of garden fronting onto the street to present an attractive and tidy appearance at all times. For the elderly and disabled the best solution is to plant evergreen ground-cover plants that need minimal maintenance and will smother weeds. A variety of heathers (see p 152) will provide colour in every season provided the soil is not limy. If it is, you can choose lime-tolerant spreading conifers such as the prostrate *Juniperus communis* 'Hornibrookii' and *J. horizontalis* in such forms as 'Glauca' and 'Douglasii', and the slightly taller *J. sabina* 'Tamariscifolia' and *J. chinensis* 'Pfitzeriana'. The forms of *J. horizontalis* have blue-green foliage, while the others have blue-black or brownish berries, so considerable colour variations are possible. Taller conifers will add interest.

2
Major
garden features

From the last chapter's examination of garden design,
this chapter moves on to the practicalities of garden-making:
how to plan and construct a new or renovated garden
and the creation, planting and maintenance of major features.
It covers the permanent architectural structure,
from paths, walls, fences and gates to pergolas, swimming pools
and other features for garden decoration and enjoyment.
You will find details of how to use and look after
trees, hedging plants, climbers, shrubs, herbaceous plants,
bulbs, temporary bedding plants, alpines and aquatics.
You will discover how to design and make
such features as lawns, shrub and herbaceous borders,
rose gardens, rock gardens, peat gardens and water gardens.
It covers planting, and garden maintenance, too:
how to keep these features looking their best from year to year.
Unusual features are covered, as well as the more conventional,
including bog gardens, scree beds and planted walls.

The evolution of a new garden

Faced with the opportunity of making a new garden on a more or less empty site, your first feelings may well be a combination of bewilderment and impatience: bewilderment as to how to set about creating on this patch of earth the idyllic spot you can imagine in your mind's eye, and impatience to get on with the job. The temptation is very strong to start laying lawns, building paths and fences, and planting beds and borders in a piecemeal fashion. The result is likely at best to be unsatisfactory, at worst chaotic and possibly very expensive and time-consuming, as you alter or remove features that you realize too late were mistakes.

The answer – even if it does delay a little the putting of spade into ground – lies in planning: not just planning the garden layout, though that is part of the job, but planning the whole process of building the new garden. For the best way of ensuring that it evolves without unnecessary trouble is to work out a logical sequence of operations. The evolution of the garden can take place as a continuous operation, or in instalments over a much longer period as time and money allow. In the latter case it is even more important that a plan and scheme of operations are to hand to ensure that all the work is directed towards the desired result.

Certain aspects of the development may be beyond your capabilities, so that you will need to consult a contractor. Be sure to use a reputable landscape contractor, preferably a member of a landscape or trade organization, and if possible obtain a detailed quotation for the work in advance. Two or three quotations from various member firms are even better, but remember when comparing prices to ensure that they are for carrying out exactly the same job.

Planning on paper

Measuring the garden is the first job to undertake, followed by the preparation of a detailed site plan; these operations are described in detail in the article on page 66. This will enable you to clarify your ideas about the design of the garden (the subject of the previous chapter), and to draw the design plan. This is the time to change your mind, to try out various ideas and see how they translate onto the ground by inserting temporary pegs or canes corresponding to your proposed layout. After an appropriate amount of thought – and probably a good deal of time – you should arrive at a final decision. When you do, stick to it! Changing your mind half-way through the development of your new garden – unless, of course, you realize that you have made a serious mistake that has to be rectified – can lead to as unsatisfactory a result as working with no plan at all.

Apart from deciding on ground layout, you should prepare a planting plan for the whole garden and possibly also, at a larger scale, for individual beds and borders. This will enable you to order plants well in advance if you plan to buy by mail-order – though in this case you will have to be sure that all the groundwork will be finished before the plants are de-livered. Alternatively, you can prepare shopping lists for visits to garden centres (a job for winter weekends, perhaps). In preparing planting plans, you will have to make decisions on spacing, particularly of trees and shrubs. As explained on page 65, shrubs are often planted closer than really necessary to achieve an effect of 'instant' maturity – though even this can take several years. It is better in the long term, however, to space the

major subjects at their correct final distances and to fill in with short-lived or temporary bedding and ground-cover plants

Onto the ground

The first stage of garden construction proper, after the paper-work, is the preparation and marking out of the site. This is, literally, the foundation-laying of the new garden, and is necessary both for the health of your plants and the success of your design. For example, the site may have to be cleared of brushwood or certain trees, and weedkillers may need to be applied to eradicate the more pernicious weeds (see p 356). All rubbish ought to be cleared at this stage, too; otherwise you may find yourself constantly moving it from place to place to make way for other operations. (In practice, you may have found it necessary to do a certain amount of ground clearance in order to carry out your initial survey.)

Major ground contouring will be next if this forms part of your plan (and, as explained on page 76, you would be well advised to avoid it if possible). To ensure that good topsoil does not become mixed with infertile subsoil (see p 330), it is essential to remove the topsoil first and stack it to one side. Consider carefully where you position this 'spoil' heap; it will be time-consuming and heavy work if you have to move it again to make way for further work. Even if you do not plan major earthworks, make sure that building work has not resulted in subsoil being dumped on top of topsoil or being mixed with it, and that an unscrupulous

A gently sloping site that needs no major earth-moving **left**, and on which a rock garden is the only construction job to be tackled, will only need to be cleared of weeds and debris and the soil improved and cultivated before lawns, trees and plant beds can be planted **below**. But considerable construction work has gone into contouring the sloping lawn and its supporting terrace with a rock garden, pool and steps **right**. The appearance of both gardens will change considerably over the next few growing seasons as trees, shrubs and other plants mature.

builder has not removed a large part of the topsoil and sold it. You may need to correct compaction of the soil caused by heavy equipment, and a general soil-improvement programme, as described on page 332, may be necessary.

Excavation of such features as a lily pond or swimming pool will form part of the soil contouring, and the subsequent concreting or lining should be carried out almost to the point of completion at this stage, too. Another feature that may be begun at this point is the construction of a rock garden – particularly if it is a large one whose stones may need moving mechanically. However, a smaller rock garden with easily handled stones can be constructed without much trouble at the final levelling or raking stage, just before lawn-seeding and planting (see below). At this latter point, too, the final soil in-filling of a large rock garden may be completed.

Laying foundations for paved areas and walls will be the next job, and to some extent may be combined with general contouring. Soil levels will in many cases dictate the level of these structures, but in others – especially near the house, where you must consider the position of the damp-proof course, which should be at least 15 cm (6 in) above the final level of any terrace – soil contouring will need to finish at a predetermined level. Material excavated from foundations can, of course, be used in contouring, but it is best to remove any surplus as soon as possible to leave the way clear for further measuring and setting out. Remember to shore up any excavations more than about 1 m (3 ft) deep – less in light soils – for safety and to prevent soil collapse. Then the foundations themselves – hardcore, concrete or both – can be laid and firmed down.

It is sensible to leave the installation of services or drainage if needed (see p 333) until major contouring is complete, particularly if you have to use heavy mechanized plant. It is very easy for machinery to damage or cut underground water pipes or electricity cables, though if either of these have to cross areas where paving or walls are to be installed,

It is best to complete walls, pergolas and fences before paths; then the latter's foundations can be used for access and will be well compacted before the final surfacing is applied. The latter will come next, except in the case of tarmacadam or bitumen paths; these are easily stained by mud or mortar and, unlike such surfaces as concrete and paving slabs, cannot be washed clean. In some cases, mud left to dry on tarmacadam and then removed will lift the tarmacadam beneath it, leaving a hole. For this reason, leave such paths until the very end. At the same time as you lay paving, you can finish pool surrounds.

Final stages
When the paths and paving are completed, final spreading of topsoil to finished levels can take place. This may simply mean shifting and raking existing soil, or it may involve importing topsoil if there is insufficient on site. If possible, you should aim for a depth of at the very least 30 cm (12 in) and preferably 45 cm

trunk) either before or after sowing or planting, depending on the season and the availability of the young trees. For the sake of convenience and tidiness it is a good plan to plant trees at the time of final raking but before seeding or turfing. Hedges may be planted even earlier, especially if no major contouring is to take place; then they can begin to become established and provide shelter for subsequent plantings.

You can cultivate the areas of beds with hand tools, preferably double digging their whole area (see p 334) unless you have already cultivated the subsoil, or with a mechanical cultivator. If possible, aim to do this in autumn so that the soil can lie rough over the winter to be weathered. (This does not apply to the same extent if earth-moving has taken place, resulting in the topsoil being thoroughly turned over.) Once dug or cultivated, or in the following spring, you can roughly rake over the beds to their final levels. It is not necessary to take too much trouble over raking at this point once levels are established, as the ground will inevitably be well trampled during planting.

Planting and finishing touches
Articles later in this chapter deal with methods of planting various types of plants, but as a general rule you can plant container-grown plants at any time when the ground is not frozen or waterlogged (and preferably not when the weather is too hot, either). Provided they are well watered, you can keep them as long as necessary in their containers. Other plants should be planted only when dormant and the ground is workable; usually the best time is late autumn or early spring – particularly the latter in areas with harsh winters or on heavy soils. They can be stored for a while with their roots in moist peat in a cool, frost-free place, but if there is going to be a delay of more than a few days heel them in (plant them temporarily) in an out-of-the-way place.

Following the planting plan, space out the plants over the bed. With bare-rooted specimens do not space out more than can be planted without fear of the roots drying out. Then commence planting, making final adjustments to spacing as necessary. After any necessary watering in, rake over the bed as you go; if planting in late spring or summer, apply a mulch of moist peat or other organic material to retain soil moisture.

On completion of planting, the finishing touches may be put to the garden: tubs and other containers positioned, and garden furniture and ornaments installed. Assuming that the foundations have been installed earlier in the programme, a shed, summer-house, greenhouse and any other garden buildings can be erected. And of course as soon as any stage of planting is completed, maintenance work begins almost immediately, with watering, feeding, trimming, grass-cutting and so on. In this respect, no garden is ever 'finished'; however, a systematic and logical programme of work in the construction stages will make sure that subsequent work will be as minimal and straightforward as possible.

you will need to lay the relevant part of the system as the foundation work is done. In the case of land drainage, not only can the pipes be broken by machinery but you may find that contouring has altered the water table, making premature installation unnecessary or ineffective.

Re-spreading of topsoil – at least on areas where further building work is not to be done – comes next in the sequence of operations, though you may find it convenient to deal with part of the garden at a time, and indeed to finish those areas away from any further building work before digging foundations; in this way, the size of the spoil heap may be reduced. However, before doing so be sure to correct any compaction of the subsoil caused by earth-moving machinery. It is worthwhile, if the topsoil is exposed, to dig in humus-forming material such as garden compost, manure or peat (easiest with a rotary cultivator; see p 377), as this will increase the ultimate depth of the fertile soil. Delay final soil levelling adjacent to paths, walls, fences and the like until these are completed.

(18 in) of good fertile topsoil over all cultivated areas of the garden. Usually, if the soil is to form a shrub or flower bed against a path, the soil is left just below the path's surface level. In the case of grass, the soil level should be at or just above the level of the paving; this will ensure easy mowing later on without the need to trim the edges every time the grass is cut. (If you plan to use turves, remember to make allowance for their thickness.)

Once the soil has been graded finally you can prepare the lawn areas for sowing or turfing. In either case, a good fine bed must be prepared as described on page 84, including the application of a fertilizer as necessary. Normally, the cultivation of flower and shrub beds can follow laying of the lawn. However, in some cases the only means of access to a bed may be across the lawn area, and if this is seeded it should be walked upon as little as possible for its first season. In this case, it is as well to reverse the order if planting time is pressing. Provided the final levels have been achieved, trees may be planted in grassed areas (leaving an area of bare soil around the

Renovating an old garden

It is likely that at some time or another you will inherit a garden that was laid out by someone else. Since people's tastes vary widely it is also likely that your inheritance will not be entirely to your liking. If you are fortunate, the previous owner will have been a gardener who conscientiously and lovingly tended the garden. It may then need a minimum amount of work and perhaps only simple modifications to bring it to your idea of perfection. On the other hand, you may feel that major reconstruction work is necessary, in which case the process of renovation may be very similar to that of creating an entirely new garden, as described on page 60.

Even worse, perhaps, there may have been a considerable delay between the previous occupier leaving and the new one taking over. This delay can have serious effects on a garden, particularly if it is left for more than a

carefully so that shrubs, trees and other plants that are individually sound are not damaged. This is often difficult, as weeds and desirable plants grow together, making it hard to distinguish between the two. If in doubt, it may be best to consult a nurseryman or specialist landscape contractor.

Having cleared the jungle sufficiently, measurements can be made and a plan of campaign worked out. It is particularly important when working on an existing garden to write down on the site plan the relative positions of the existing features, such as paths, buildings, trees, shrubs and other plants. Do so in pencil so that it is easy to change as you decide to remove particular plants. It may take a considerable time to plot all the worthwhile plants – perhaps up to a year, as each plant grows, develops, flowers and possibly fruits, enabling you to identify it and take a

from neglect, and can be replaced or repaired and treated with preservative.

This is the time for new constructional work, too – path-laying and wall-building. But first remove any large trees that are obviously unwanted or are diseased. To be on the safe side, check first whether there is any tree-preservation order in force in the case of large specimens.

The felling and removal of large trees is usually beyond the skill of the gardener, and in almost every case it would be wise to call in a specialist contractor. Make sure that he is a member of a recognized arboricultural association and that he is fully insured. Obtain a quotation first, and make sure that it includes removal of the main root, for the sake of both convenience and garden health, for dead roots can encourage diseases such as honey fungus in many areas. Unless you want

Some features of a run-down garden may be obviously worth renovating. Here, a programme of cutting, feeding and the application of weedkiller brought visible results to the lawn in a matter of months.

Weeds were cleared from the rose beds and the soil improved by fertilizing and mulching. Most important, the overgrown rose bushes were pruned hard and all weak or diseased specimens removed.

year. During this time, considerable uncontrolled growth can take place and features deteriorate. Worst of all, the previous occupier may have neglected the garden for a considerable period, leaving it in a state of dereliction. To cover all eventualities, it is best to assume that the garden has reached this state; what can be done to bring it to some semblance of order?

Basic planning and clearance

As with any major work in the garden, a basic plan will be helpful – that is, a plan showing the layout of the garden and how you want it to be and a plan of operations to enable the work to be carried out in a logical and efficient sequence (see p 60). To prepare a ground plan, however, it will be necessary first to survey and measure the garden (see p 66). If it has been long neglected this may be impossible, as high overgrowth and undergrowth may prevent it. If this is so, then initial clearance work must be undertaken, but undertaken

note of its characteristics. This is particularly true of bulbs and herbaceous plants if you take over the garden out of season, when they have died back.

Take note of other features, too: areas of light and shade, dry and moist areas, and the general orientation. If the previous occupier is contactable and cooperative, however, you will be able to glean a great deal of information that will save hours of work and possibly months of waiting.

Foundation tasks

If you do have to wait to observe the garden through the seasons, there is plenty that can usefully be done during this plant identification period. You could start with the messy jobs or those that are likely to cause a lot of disturbance. Unwanted paths and areas of paving and concrete can be removed; where necessary, land drainage can be installed; walls can be repaired and re-pointed. Fences, too, will very likely have suffered

to use any of the timber for construction work ensure that removal of the tree from the site is also included. Smaller trees and branches can be dealt with separately and may be used for firewood; the roots may be burned.

Some trees may well need surgery rather than felling, and provided that the season is right this may usefully be done at the same time, as great piles of cuttings will undoubtedly arise (see p 89). It is even more important to check credentials in the case of tree surgery, as it is very skilled work that can ruin a tree if done badly. Again, check insurance and ensure that the quotation includes removal of lopped branches unless you want to burn them. A point worth bearing in mind if a healthy hardwood tree needs felling is that it may well have a commercial value; some timber merchants will fell and remove free of charge.

Another job for the 'waiting' period is to start reclamation of grassed areas. After even a comparatively short period of neglect, the

grown and poorly shaped, although its position is acceptable, that severe pruning may give it a new lease of life. This is particularly true of many evergreens (see p 373).

The period spent clearing beds and borders is a good time to make soil tests as described on page 332, to establish how acid or alkaline the soil is and whether it has a deficiency of nutrients. A plot that has been gardened for many years may well be depleted of plant foods and need a systematic programme of soil improvement with fertilizers and bulky manures or compost. Take great care in cultivating the soil around established shrubs, as it is easy to damage shallow roots. To avoid this risk, it is best to apply garden compost or peat as a mulch rather than digging it in. For the same reason, remove weeds carefully by hand; alternatively, you can use certain weedkillers, as described on page 356.

The kitchen garden
Unlike the ornamental sections of the garden, work can start on the fruit and vegetable garden almost immediately. Certain fruit bushes or trees may be preserved if they are worth keeping – possibly being given restorative pruning in the appropriate season (see p 371). With the rest, however, it will probably be desirable to make an absolutely clean sweep of it and continue through to final cultivation. The main areas may need treating with weedkillers, or the top growth burning down, or you may be able to double dig the whole plot immediately, incorporating skimmed-off grass and annual weeds into the lower spit as green manure (see p 334).

Planning of the vegetable garden is covered in the article on page 262, but bear in mind that it is a good idea to plant a large crop of potatoes in the first year as a 'groundbreaker'; the frequent cultivations involved in earthing up the potato plants expose soil pests to predators and allow the germination and removal of annual weeds.

Short-term face-lifts
During the restoration work on an old garden, which at times can make it look more like a battlefield, short-term plantings can take place in selected areas. It is perhaps in the part fronting the street and in the area immediately outside the house – where visitors may see something colourful and beautiful that will draw their attention from elsewhere – that most people will want to make such displays. Bulbs and annual bedding plants are most suitable for this purpose (see pp 110 and 112).

Although not always the most logical place to commence operations, restoration work on an existing garden usually starts near the house. It is understandable that the new occupier should want to make this attractive as soon as possible. The advantage of such a garden, of course, is that the larger shrubs or trees will lend it an air of maturity. With skill you will be able to progress from temporary in-filling in the first season or two to permanent replanting and restructuring while maintaining continuity.

n the side garden of the same ouse **top**, a combination of estoration and new building ork was undertaken. The lematis clinging to the eaves as saved by hard pruning, but nost of the other shrubs were removed and a new patio and garden pool installed. Behind the latter, an area was thoroughly double dug before being planted with perennials. In the area destined to become the kitchen garden **above**, the new owner made an almost completely clean sweep; very few existing plants were kept, and the soil was thoroughly cultivated and all perennial weeds removed before planting the first crop of vegetables.

rasses will be long and may be infested with eeds. However, provided no damage has ccurred to the soil surface all is not lost. As xplained in the article on page 84, an area of eglected grass can be turned into a beautiful reen sward; in some instances, the unintenonal period of rest from cutting and tramling does some good.

Broadly, the improvement programme onsists of cutting, feeding, the use of weedkilrs, top dressing to fill small depressions, and arifying and aerating as necessary. Cutting particular should be relatively gentle, educing the length of the overgrown grass ver a sequence of three or four cuts with a and scythe, power shears or a rotary mower. the grass cuttings do not contain too many eed seeds they can be dug into other areas of e garden as green manure; otherwise they n be composted (see p 334). In some cases, owever, the grass area may be too far gone to lvage and you will have to cultivate the ound and start again.

Beds and borders
By now, a sufficient time may have passed to return your attention to the beds and borders. Armed with your plan and list of what is what and where, judicious pruning and thinning out can take place. In the case of many perennials, lifting and dividing clumps, discarding the old central portions and replanting the rest, may completely revitalize them. In other cases, plants may need to be moved to a different part of the garden – not generally feasible with large, well-established shrubs because of root disturbance – or discarded altogether.

In clearing out unwanted shrubs, as with trees, it is better to remove the entire root system as far as possible rather than hacking off at ground level. Leaving the roots can make replanting of new shrubs difficult, while encouraging disease. Alternatively, the roots may make a vigorous attempt to grow again, possibly producing a thicket. It is worth bearing in mind, however, if you are tempted to remove a shrub simply because it is over-

The 'instant' garden

Making a new garden or remaking an old one can be a lengthy process. If major restructuring jobs have to be undertaken, or if the plantings chosen are slow or difficult to establish, a garden can take years to reach maturity. Yet many people move house frequently these days, and want an attractive, well clothed garden at once. They may not be willing to put up with the tastes or the wilderness left behind by former occupants, nor to tolerate an untidy, unfinished patch for months or even years.

If money is no object you could have a new garden almost before you move in, by employing a garden architect to draw up a plan and a landscape contractor to carry it out. This would be very expensive, but the entire job could be done in a few weeks.

A more economical alternative is to plan your own instant garden. Theoretically you can plant a bed or border – or even a complete garden – at any time, providing the ground is not frozen, waterlogged or covered with snow, by buying bedding plants and container-grown herbaceous perennials, shrubs and trees from a nursery or garden centre. Even these plants are not cheap, however, and careful, informed selection, planting and siting are necessary to avoid unwelcome losses. They need a lot of care and attention, especially during the first year after planting, and you will have to arrange to have them watered when you go away or they may quickly die.

Planning an instant garden

Whether you are creating a new garden or converting an existing one, building the permanent features – or tearing them down – will be the first problem, and probably the most expensive one. Boundaries and screens are a priority because new plantings will need their protection. A strong boundary (see p 72) will be necessary in exposed gardens, and wattle hurdle fencing makes a reasonably cheap and effective screen. If necessary, polythene attached to stakes will make temporary shelter. Among the quickest-growing hedging plants are privet (*Ligustrum ovalifolium*), Leyland cypress (× *Cupressocyparis leylandii*) and western red cedar (*Thuja plicata*).

If you are renovating an old site, you have the advantage that there will be existing trees, shrubs, lawns and border plants, some at least of which can be salvaged to add an air of maturity. A shrub border or hedge, for example, can usually be transformed very quickly – in many cases merely by pruning, combined with cultivation and enrichment of the ground. Shrubs up to about five years old will generally transplant successfully, as will larger specimens of slow-growing or shallow-rooting kinds such as rhododendrons. But do this only during the dormant season. With judicious underplanting with bulbs or bedding plants restoration can be effected very quick-

ly. For further discussion of the problems of renovating an old garden, see page 62. For information on how to renovate a lawn, see page 85.

Whatever you decide to do, it pays not to be too purist or ambitious when planning your 'instant' garden. A herbaceous border can take years to establish, but a few quick-growing herbaceous plants in a mixed border can give the garden that elusive air of maturity. Similarly, a rose bush underplanted with low-growing annuals or ground-covering plants will not be an eyesore even when not in flower, but a beautiful rose garden cannot be created overnight.

Planting the 'instant' garden

The 'instant' lawn (see p 84) is a boon for anyone with a new garden to lay out. Traditional turves, 90 cm (3 ft) long, 30 cm (1 ft) wide and 4 cm (1½ in) thick, can be in use within a month of laying, but they represent the most expensive method of lawn-making. Remember, too, that very thorough preparation of the underlying ground is vital.

Bedding plants (see p 112) are especially valuable for providing colour in the 'instant' garden. They are ideal for the odd bed or two in a key situation, for infilling among newly planted shrubs, for container planting and for generally occupying gaps that are to be dealt with permanently at a later date. They principally consist of biennials (see p 210) for autumn planting and half-hardy annuals (see p 214) for spring, though certain hardy annuals and some perennials are sold in the same way. They include foliage plants for contrast and background as well as flowering subjects.

Hardy annuals (see p 206), sown where

they are to flower, are equally colourful an much cheaper, but generally not so long flowering as the half-hardies. Certain hard annuals, such as candytuft, larkspurs and fla (*Linum grandiflorum*) take only six to eig weeks from sowing to flowering. If you pla some dwarf French or African marigol (forms of *Tagetes*), dwarf chrysanthemum such as 'Denise', and other late-flowerir plants in an odd corner of the garden, they ca be transplanted to replace the summer ann als at the end of the season.

Bulbs are a boon to anyone with a ne garden, providing almost instant colour. The are covered in detail on pages 188 to 205. you move into your new home in late summe or autumn, you can plant many bulbs to flowe from midwinter onwards. Some bulbs, such a tulips and daffodils, that do not object t being transplanted, can be planted in pots an moved to their flowering positions when th garden is ready and they are about to flowe Summer bulbs, such as anemones, gladi and *Acidanthera bicolor*, can be planted spring to flower only a few months later.

There is always a strong temptation f anyone faced with a virtually empty garden buy too many plants and crowd the availab

Doctrine of expendability

For quick impact while allowing for long-term effect, you might plant Brewer's spruce (*Picea breweriana*) and Leyland cypress (× *Cupressocyparis leylandii*) with ground cover of heathers and bulbs **left**. After 8 to 10 years **right**, the cypresses would have reached a substantial size while the spruces would not yet be large enough to show their weeping habit. After five more years **far right**, the cypresses could be discarded, their job done.

left For the most 'instant' colour, plant half-hardy annual and perennial bedding plants such as salvias, rudbeckias, nicotianas, begonias, geraniums, tagetes and ageratums. **above** One of the quickest climbers for a pergola is the 'mile-a-minute' plant, *Polygonum baldschuanicum*.

space with plantings. Very often a single specimen, or scattered groups of two or three, can be more effective. When planting for ground cover, for example, a better effect is achieved in the long run if small plants are spaced an even distance apart over a large area. A few bulbs dotted about – or clusters of bedding plants – will help to fill the ugly gaps during the years while the ground cover is taking hold, and they will help to prolong the flowering season in that part of the garden.

With shrubs and trees, there is always a danger of buying the largest specimens to be found. This policy is often unsuccessful because with most plants younger specimens establish themselves better and grow more quickly than older plants. Certainly, if you do buy substantial specimens, you must take much greater care in ground-preparation, planting and subsequent attention (see p 96). A much better plan is to buy a vigorous young seedling or well-rooted cutting growing in a container. If this is intended to enhance the garden in future years as an exceptional specimen tree, you could position it in an island bed and surround it – though not so closely as to compete for moisture and nutrients – with colourful bedding plants or

annuals. As a rough guide, most shrubs will give a worthwhile show of flowers three seasons after planting, and young trees will take between five and seven years.

The doctrine of expendability

A common way of obtaining a quick effect in a new garden is to plant shrubs and ground covers more thickly than usual, and then remove some of the plants later, before they interfere with those to be retained and spoil their shape. This can be termed the doctrine of expendability.

You can, for example, buy some fast-growing shrubs or herbaceous plants and interplant them with slower-growing varieties. A fast-growing conifer such as the Leyland cypress (× *Cupressocyparis leylandii*) or one of its varieties, which will reach 7.5 m (25 ft) in ten to twelve years, can be neighboured by a much slower-growing conifer such as *Picea pungens glauca,* which will take the same time to reach a height of 3 to 3.5 m (10 to 12 ft). The two should be planted at least 4 m (13 ft) apart and the cypress would have to be moved after about 12 years.

There are many more such combinations of fast- and slow-growing conifers and other trees and shrubs grown for their flowers or foliage or both (for dual-purpose plants, see page 166). The charming witch hazels (species and varieties of *Hamamelis*) are very slow-growing, but some of the viburnums such as *Viburnum farreri* (*V. fragrans*) grow fast. So does the Portugal laurel, *Prunus lusitanica*. Escallonias and weigelas grow fairly fast in good soil if fed and watered well.

The same idea can be applied to rock gardens and to mixed borders. A good compromise is to plant fairly large temporary shrubs in rock gardens and interplant them with low-growing heathers, shrubby hypericums and the like. In a herbaceous border, dwarf Michaelmas daisies, day lilies, heleniums or rudbeckias can be discarded or moved to another site when the more permanent occupants have grown.

Overcrowding is one of the dangers of the doctrine of expendability. It will be hard to part with the temporary plants when the time comes, but perhaps you could find a spare place for them in a neighbour's garden. Or maybe new beds could be created in previously grassed areas of your own garden.

The movable garden

You can make much use in the 'instant' garden of window boxes, tubs and other containers. Instructions on planting them and suggestions for plants to grow in them will be found on page 116. Provided the containers are light enough to be moved about when full of potting mixture and plants (light plastic inner containers can be inserted into a larger 'show' container), you can ring the changes with great effect.

If there is room somewhere out of sight, you can plant a succession of containers to provide a continuous show from early spring bulbs through summer flowers to dwarf chrysanthemums at the end of the season. If you have a greenhouse or garden frame you can raise all the half-hardy or bedding plants you need to fill pots, tubs and window boxes, hanging baskets to brighten up doorways terraces and patios, and pots to hang in holders from monotonous walls and fences.

'Instant' coverings

Movable trellis will provide a temporary support for climbers to cover an unsightly wall. This consists of square-meshed plastic-covered wire panels that can be wired to long vine eyes or nails driven into the wall, so that there is a space of about 10 cm (4 in) between the panel and the wall.

Perhaps the quickest-growing permanent wall cover is supplied by the Russian vine, *Polygonum baldschuanicum*, often aptly called the mile-a-minute plant. In a couple of seasons it will cover an unsightly coal bunker, shed or a screen over a dustbin. You can cut it back as hard as you like and it smothers itself with a white foamy mass of flowers in summer. To cover walls and fences you can plant a vigorous climbing rose, a honeysuckle, clematis or any of the more vigorous climbing or wall shrubs described on pages 142 to 149.

Alternatively, you could apply the doctrine of expendability again, planting some quick-growing annual climbers such as *Cobaea scandens* (the cup-and-saucer plant), *Tropaeolum peregrinum* (the Canary creeper), a climbing variety of its relative, the nasturtium (*T. majus*), or even runner beans. White-flowered beans such as the self-pollinated variety 'Fry' look well against red-brick walls, and red-flowered varieties against white walls. See also page 212.

The site plan

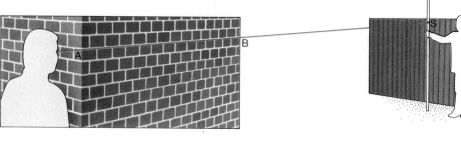

Before making any attempt to prepare a design for a new garden, or to renovate or remodel an existing one, an accurate plan of the site, drawn to a convenient scale, will be very useful. It will clarify and bring together the site's geometrical information, such as the length of the boundaries, the outline measurements of the house, the juxtaposition of the house and boundaries, and any changes in ground level. It will enable you to record the existing features – trees, shrubs, paths and outbuildings – and to position the less tangible elements, such as areas of shade and full sun, the damp and dry areas, the direction of prevailing winds, and good or bad views. Finally, it makes it easier to consider these groups of information together in order to formulate design ideas and judge their feasibility.

Prior to setting out with a tape-measure, however, make sure that an outline plan of the garden does not already exist; even a basic plan showing just the boundaries can save hours of measuring time. There are various possible sources of a plan. If the house is new or has been altered, the architect or builder will be your most likely source; it is probable that a site plan had to be submitted for building permission. The next most likely source is the solicitor, lawyer or other person who handled the purchase or renting of the house; the lease or other legal documents probably include a site plan, though this may be to too small a scale to be of much use. The surveyor's department of the town or county authority is another possibility. If the garden is very large and beyond your surveying capabilities, firms specializing in aerial photography can often be very helpful. While it would be expensive to commission a special photograph, you may well be able to obtain one of your neighbourhood from stock, enlarged to a specified scale; a tracing can easily be made of this.

Should a site plan not already exist, then it will be up to you to draw one. Tackled the right way, it can be informative and fun. It is at the point of measuring that the design process begins, albeit unconsciously. Every point of the garden will be visited and seen from every angle, and new ideas will result.

Basic needs and decisions

To start measuring, you will need a tape-measure, if possible one 30 m (100 ft) long; this will be much more convenient and accurate for measuring a garden even of moderate size than, say, a 3 m (10 ft) tape. With the latter, you will have to keep stopping, marking and moving on again. Long tapes are expensive, but it may be possible to hire one. If not, one alternative is to use a short tape in conjunction with a tough cord that will not stretch (the type used for clothes-lines is suitable) with knots every 3 m (10 ft); this will not be so accurate, but it will be a lot cheaper! The next piece of basic equipment is a large, fairly heavy piece of paper pinned to a smooth board. With most gardens, a sheet about 45 by 60 cm (1½ ft by 2 ft) will be big enough to include a useful amount of information while not being too unwieldy. Provided you choose a suitable scale (see below), graph paper is the

Plotting regular outlines
If the edges of both house and garden are straight and fairly regular, you can use the walls as surveying 'instruments'. First measure and plot the outline of the house on paper, then use the walls as sight-lines to plot points on the boundaries.
above Look along one wall (such as AB) and ask a helper to insert a cane on the far boundary in line with your sighting – point S. Do the same along wall DC to plot point T. Measure the distances BS and CT, and you can plot points S and T accurately on your scale plan **below left**. Do the same for points U, V, W, X, Y and Z. Then

draw a straight line though points S and T and extend it in both directions; do the same for the other pairs of points to complete the site outline.
Cross-check by measuring the distances between the corners.

Plotting by triangulation
With irregular shapes, where obstructions prevent using the walls for sighting, or for plotting points within the garden, use triangulation **below right**.
Again, the house walls make a good starting point, so measure and plot these first if possible; otherwise, start from a straight boundary wall or fence whose length you can measure. From

one end of the wall, B, measure the distance to the point you want to plot, P. Scale this and, using a pair of compasses, draw an arc (part) of a circle with its centre at B. Then measure the distance to P from the other end of the wall, C. Scale this distance and draw another arc of a circle, centred at C. The point where the arcs cut represents point P. You can plot point Q – and the whole of the garden – in the same way, using any convenient and already plotted pairs of points as the base-line for your imaginary triangles. Cross-check by taking measurements between points as you plot them.

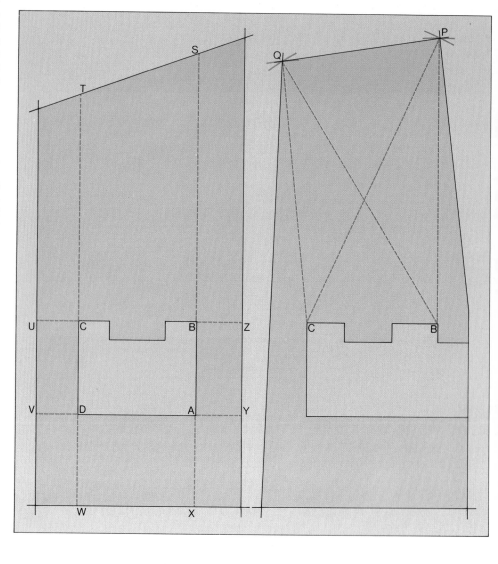

best to use; it will act as a guide and reminder to you of the scale. You will also need a pencil that is neither so soft as to constantly need resharpening nor so hard that the lines are difficult to see, and an eraser. A pair of compasses, preferably with an extension arm, is also very useful, and a scale rule. This last item is obtainable from drawing office suppliers, and enables you to translate measurements on the ground directly onto paper at a chosen scale without having to make calculations.

The choice of scale is important, on the one hand because you will want to fit the whole garden plan onto the one sheet of paper without having to stick on more half-way through measuring, and on the other because the drawing should be big enough to show clearly all the information you require. Therefore, if you do not already know the overall dimensions of the site, make one or two quick, rough measurements to enable you to choose a suitable scale so that the plan will comfortably fit.

The scale will depend on whether you are using the metric or Imperial (yard-foot-inch) system of measurement. The former is the easiest, and the most useful scales are 1:50 (2 cm to 1 m) for small gardens and detailed plans of flower beds, patios and so on; 1:100 (1 cm to 1 m) for medium-sized gardens; and 1:200 (5 mm to 1 m) for large gardens. Scale rules are easily obtainable with these scales – often with all three on the same rule. The corresponding scales in the Imperial system are ¼ in to 1 ft (equal to 1:48), ⅛ in to 1 ft (1:96) and ¹⁄₁₆ in to 1 ft (1:192). One fairly obvious but important point is to make all your measurements in the same system and to use the corresponding – metric or Imperial – graph paper! To prevent confusion and mistakes, particularly if you carry out your survey over a period of days or weeks, write down the chosen scale at the top of your sheet of paper.

Measuring and plotting

When you actually start surveying, there are two possible ways of working. You can make a rough site plan, write in on this the measurements as you take them, and then later draw the accurate scale plan from these. Or you can draw the site plan accurately to scale while measuring. The latter method has the advantage of eliminating the confusion that may occur as the rough plan becomes covered with figures; also, drawing as you go provides a useful built-in check that you have measured accurately, because you can quickly see (or take check-measurements to confirm) that lines join up in the right places.

Start measuring and plotting from a convenient fixed, straight line; the house walls are usually the best choice. Include all doors and steps, and all important windows; you may wish to take advantage of certain views, and this is valuable information to be used later in your final design. Having drawn in the house walls, next draw in the boundaries. If the overall shape of the house is rectangular and the site has three or four straight boundaries, the job is relatively simple. By using the house walls as sight-lines to mark points on the boundaries as illustrated, and then measuring the distance from the corresponding house corner to each marked point, it is easy to plot the positions of these points on your plan. By marking two such points on each boundary, joining these with straight lines and extending the lines until they meet, you can plot the garden's boundaries.

Should the house or site not be regular in shape, and in order to plot the positions of features such as trees and paths, you will need to use the method of surveying known as triangulation. This is much easier than it sounds. As illustrated, it consists of taking measurements to the point you want to plot (such as a corner of the site) from each end of a straight base-line (such as the ends of the house's wall). If you then convert these measurements to the scale of your plan and use a pair of compasses to draw arcs of circles centred at the ends of your base-line, the point you wish to plot lies where the two arcs cut. Even very irregular or curving boundaries or features can be plotted in this way, by taking measurements to points at convenient intervals, plotting all the points on your plan and then joining them.

The only essentials for triangulation are a straight base-line of known length and a clear, unobstructed line for measurement. The method is called triangulation because the base-line forms the base of an imaginary triangle, the opposite corner of which is the point being plotted. Once plotted accurately, a point can of course be used as the end of a new base-line for further triangulation. If the house is very irregular in shape, and also when plotting features within the garden, it may be more convenient to use the site boundaries themselves, once plotted, as base-lines.

Finalizing the plan

Unless the site is flat, the next information you will need for the site plan is details of levels. If the garden is to be laid out mainly with grass and plants, only very rough information will be needed, but walls, steps and other constructions need more accurate measurement. In the absence of expensive surveying equipment, a little improvisation will be necessary. Since the information you require is the fall – the difference in level – over a given distance, you can measure the vertical distance to the ground from two points that are exactly level, and subtract one from the other. As illustrated, you can use pegs, a straight-edged board and a spirit level over short/continued

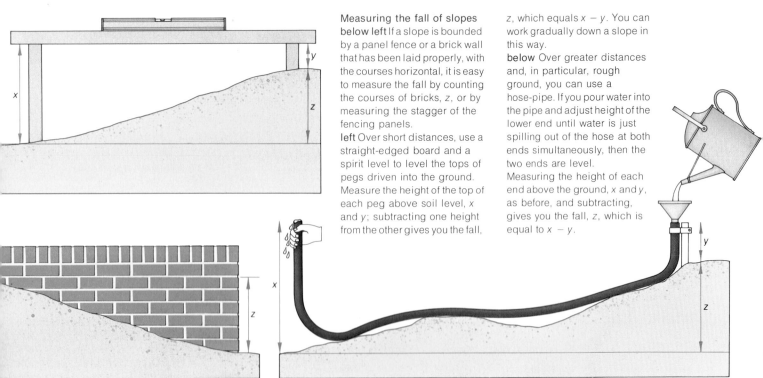

Measuring the fall of slopes
below left If a slope is bounded by a panel fence or a brick wall that has been laid properly, with the courses horizontal, it is easy to measure the fall by counting the courses of bricks, z, or by measuring the stagger of the fencing panels.
left Over short distances, use a straight-edged board and a spirit level to level the tops of pegs driven into the ground. Measure the height of the top of each peg above soil level, x and y; subtracting one height from the other gives you the fall,

z, which equals $x - y$. You can work gradually down a slope in this way.
below Over greater distances and, in particular, rough ground, you can use a hose-pipe. If you pour water into the pipe and adjust height of the lower end until water is just spilling out of the hose at both ends simultaneously, then the two ends are level. Measuring the height of each end above the ground, x and y, as before, and subtracting, gives you the fall, z, which is equal to $x - y$.

The site plan (continued)

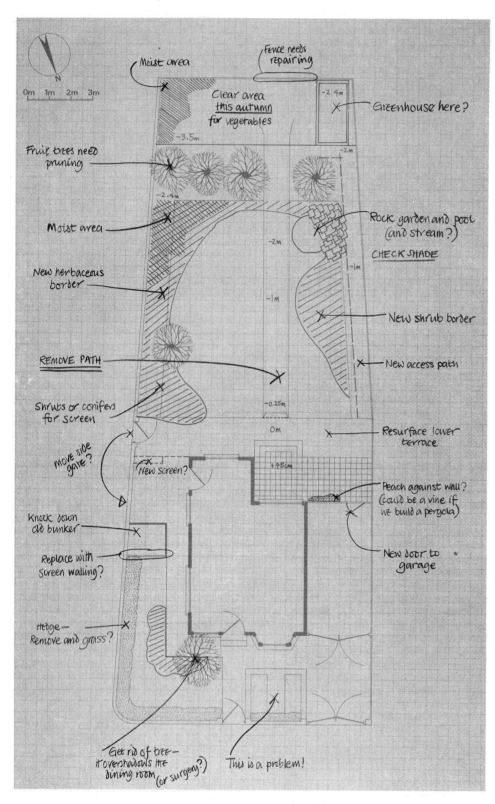

Moist area

Fence needs repairing

Clear area this autumn for vegetables

-2.4m

Greenhouse here?

-3.5m

Fruit trees need pruning

-2.4m

-2m

Moist area

Rock garden and pool (and stream?)

CHECK SHADE

-2m

-1m

New herbaceous border

-1m

New shrub border

-1m

REMOVE PATH

New access path

Shrubs or conifers for screen

-0.25m

0m

move side gate?

New screen?

Resurface lower terrace

+45cm

Knock down old bunker

Peach against wall? (could be a vine if we build a pergola)

Replace with screen walling?

New door to garage

Hedge— Remove and grass?

Get rid of tree— it overshadows the dining room (or surgery?)

This is a problem!

The completed site plan

Ink in boundaries and features that you intend to retain, but leave anything you are undecided about in pencil. You may find it useful to mark levels above or below a fixed point of reference (such as a terrace) in one colour (here they are in red) and general observations about the site in another (here black).

Indicate the spread of trees as well as the positions of their trunks. Include notes of such features as views (good and bad), the height of existing walls and fences, the positions of drains, water pipes, cables and other services, and conditions of soil, areas of sunshine and shade, and so on. You can then cover the basic

drawing with tracing paper on which you can try out your design ideas. These should be drawn accurately but need not be elaborate at this stage; it may, however, help you to visualize the final effect if you colour in your design plan, using green for grass, light brown for paths and terraces and dark brown for flower beds.

distances. Or you can use a hose-pipe filled with water; when water is just trickling out of both ends the ends are level. Noting and adding together the falls in level panels of fencing or brick walls – and do check that they are level – is yet another way of accurately establishing the degree of slope in a garden.

After the falls have been calculated, you can add the remainder of the information as desired to the site plan, and ink in the permanent features, together with the boundaries. Anything that is likely to be removed can be left in pencil as a point of reference. Add the points of the compass and mark in – possibly in coloured pencil – site information such as damp, dry, sunny or shady spots and so on. You can then pin tracing paper over the basic site plan and either make copies to use for trying out design ideas or simply superimpose these ideas over the outline plan (see p 18).

Using photographs

In association with the site plan, a series of photographs from important viewpoints are invaluable. You can take photographs at various seasons and times of the day from various windows of the house and points within the garden. These can be used in association with the site plan as a visual reminder of width, distance and perspective, and will later help you to formulate ideas for the design. A photograph is exact and analytical, whereas the eye tends to adapt, causing the viewer to see only what he wants to see. In particular, the eye tends to shorten perspective in the horizontal plane while exaggerating the height of verticals.

Probably the most useful for aiding design are black and white pictures enlarged to a size of about 20 by 25 cm (8 by 10 in). If you want to visualize the effect of tree or shrub plantings, you can draw over the photographs with a wax pencil; this can be wiped off with a cloth moistened with lighter fuel. Alternatively, draw on tracing paper pinned over the photograph. If a person stands in the proposed position of a tree, you will be able to draw the tree's outline in scale by relating it to the person's height. In the same way, you can gauge the effect of walls and screens and numerous other features.

From paper onto the ground

To take the possibly very big jump from planning to execution, laying out your final design on the ground needs to be carried out just as accurately as the initial survey; otherwise the time you have spent surveying and planning will have been wasted. The same method of triangulation can be used, inserting canes or pegs or simply positioning bricks at points you wish to mark. The simplest way to plot these is obviously to use two tape-measures to take simultaneous measurements to each end of your base-line. In the absence of these there are two alternatives. You can use a series of markers to plot points at the correct distance from each end of the base-line; these will form arcs corresponding to those drawn with a pair of compasses on paper, and where they cross is the point you require. Alternatively, you can work by trial and error, repeating the measurements as often as necessary to get them both right.

With many features, of course – such as a patio of regular outline – such elaborate methods are unnecessary. But with others, such as flower beds of irregular, flowing shape you will have to insert a whole series of pegs or canes. In practice, it may only be certain points of these, such as the ends, that will need to be positioned accurately according to your design plan; you can simply move the other markers around until you are satisfied that the outline is pleasing. With certain more geometrical shapes, such as right-angles, circles and ovals, there are a number of 'tricks' that make setting-out easy; these are illustrated.

The end result will be a series of pegs or other markers on the ground; you can stretch string between them. In the same way, pegs (levelled by using a spirit level, as in surveying) and string can be used to mark contouring of slopes and the positions of steps and other features to be constructed. The strings will not only provide lines to work to but an outline picture of the delights to come.

Using site photographs
Black and white photographs taken from various viewpoints within the garden and from the windows of the house can be a very useful aid to visualizing a design. The anticipated mature outline of trees, shrubs, beds and borders can be drawn directly on the photograph with a wax pencil or can be drawn on tracing paper laid on top. If a person or object of known size is stood at the position of a proposed feature, it will help you to draw the feature to scale. (But it will be no help for scaling features nearer or farther away unless you take the differing distance accurately into account.)

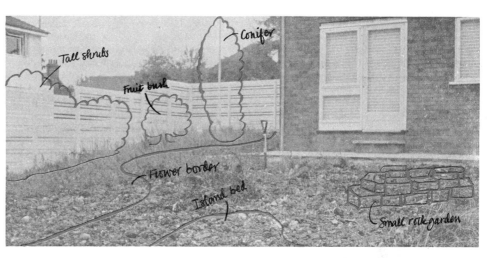

Marking geometrical shapes
1 To form a right-angle, knot a rope into sections exactly 3 m, 4 m and 5 m long (or 3, 4 and 5 feet, yards or any other consistent unit of measurement). If you peg it out in a triangular shape as shown, with each section taught. The angle between the two shorter sides will be an exact right-angle.
2 It is easy to mark out a circular flower bed by driving a peg into the ground and using a cord like a giant pair of compasses. If marking the circle in cultivated ground, use a second peg to scrape a furrow, but to avoid obliterating it sprinkle lime, sand or flour in it. When marking out on grass, you will need to drive a series of pegs into the ground.

To mark out a regular oval-shaped bed, **3** first insert two pegs (A and C) to indicate the ends of the oval (its longest axis), together with a central peg O. Then mark the width of the oval at its narrowest point by inserting two more pegs (B and D) at the ends of a line through the centre and at right-angles to AC. Stretch a length of cord from A to C and tie a knot at each end.
4 Double this cord to find the mid-point between the two knots and loop this point around peg B. Now stretch out the cord so that the knotted ends just come to the line AC. Drive in a peg where each knot reaches

the line and slip the knots over the pegs (X and Y). You can now remove all the other pegs, and will be left with a loop of cord between X and Y.
5 Use a loose peg Z to keep the cord stretched taut; as this peg moves around the two fixed pegs it will trace out an ellipse, or oval shape.

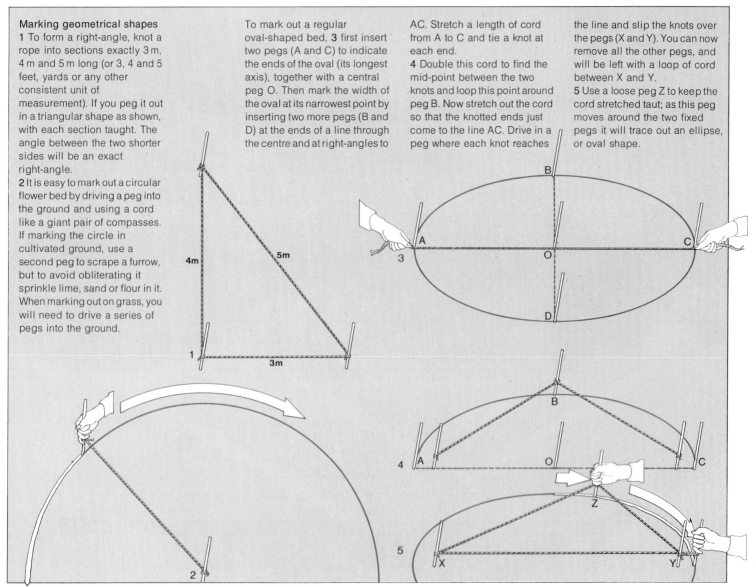

Paths and hard surfaces

Where a part of the garden is used extensively by foot and wheeled traffic, some kind of hard-wearing surface is essential for safe, easy and dry passage. Grass, the most widely used garden surface, is not suitable for the most heavily-trodden areas, but stepping-stones set just below grass level will save wear on those parts of a lawn that are crossed frequently. Openwork concrete blocks of the type used for screen-walling (see p 73) can be laid face-up in grassed areas that need to be crossed only occasionally by vehicles; the blocks give support but grass can grow through and be mown in the normal way. Elsewhere, more durable finishes are needed.

Choosing materials

Laying paving is among the most expensive jobs in the garden, so think carefully before choosing your materials. Apart from cost, the main factors to consider are appearance and function. Natural stone is probably the ideal choice – being attractive and very hard-wearing – but it is expensive and often difficult to obtain, though you may be able to buy second-hand paving stones. Broken pieces, or 'crazy paving', are cheaper and more readily available than regular-shaped slabs, and some modern imitation stone paving looks good.

Textured concrete makes a good non-slip surface and is cheaper. Concrete paving slabs are available in many shapes, sizes and colours, or you can cast your own at even less cost. Poured concrete is hard work to mix and lay, but can be bought ready-mixed and quickly makes a permanently paved area. Colouring can be incorporated when mixing, and the wet surface can be brushed to give a more attractive finish.

Well-laid brick paving is always beautiful. As long as you choose kinds suitable for outdoor use they will make an ideal surface for a path or patio, but, like tiles, they tend to be costly and time-consuming to lay because of the quantities needed. Granite setts are even more expensive.

Choosing garden pavings

Brick pavings rely for strength on their foundations, so bricks may be laid flat or on edge, in bonds chosen for decorative effect. Shown here are **1** a straight bond, **2** a basket-weave pattern and **3** a herring-bone design. Stable tiles **4** are thin pavers with drainage grooves that provide a non-slip surface. Italian glazed tiles **5** have gay patterns, and heavy-duty, frost-resistant quarry tiles **6** come in many sizes and dark, earthy colours.

Stone slabs of regular size can be laid in a stretcher pattern **7** and slabs of two sizes **8** can be coursed. Random-sized slabs must be laid correctly to look well, the large stones being set around smaller 'key' stones **9**. Cobbles **10**, like setts, are hard to walk on unless deeply embedded in soil and sand. A dull expanse of poured concrete can be scored **11** or stippled for an attractive finish, or sectioned with bricks or strips of wood. Gravels **12**, **13** and **14** include rounded river or beach shingle, sharp-edged stone chips and fine-grade types that bind firmly. They come in a wide range of colours.

Old railway sleepers or wooden planks make an unusual path if laid diagonally **15** and can be raised to make a deck; they have a warm and homely feeling but need anti-rot and anti-slip treatment. Granite setts are grey-coloured and look like bricks but do not come in standard sizes; half-setts can be laid in a so-called fish-scale pattern **16**.

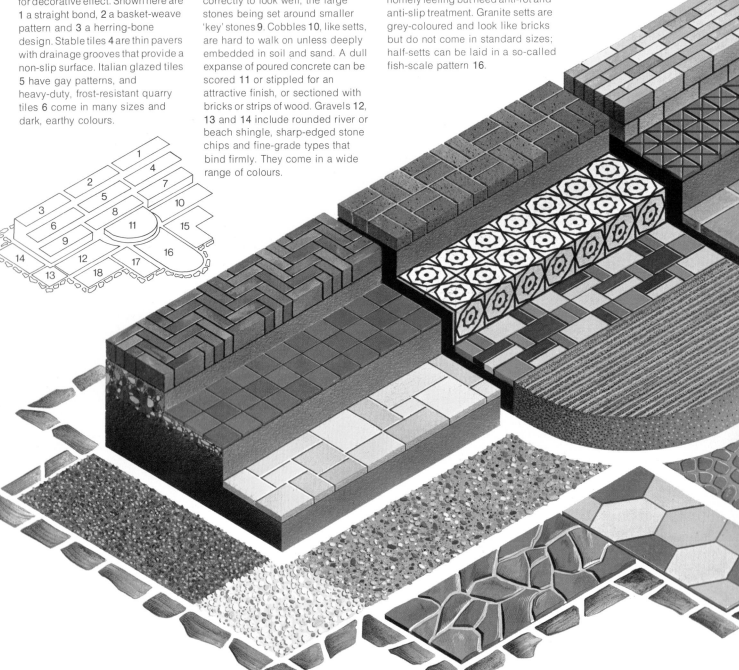

One of the cheapest surfacing materials for paths and drives, gravel is free-draining and very quick and easy to lay – you simply pour it between edging boards or bricks, and spread it evenly to a depth of 5 cm (2 in). If you roll a layer of fine gravel firmly into a layer of coarse, the surface will bind better. It requires regular raking over and topping up, and an occasional application of weedkiller.

If you like the colour, asphalt and tar-macadam make good permanent surfaces for drives, and look better if loose stone chippings of contrasting colour are rolled into the surface. They are best laid professionally, but for small jobs you can buy bags of cold-laid mat-

Concrete paving slabs can be cast at home, or bought in many sizes and shapes including hexagons 17, circles and rectangles. Irregular stone pieces 18, and broken concrete slabs make cheap 'crazy' paving or stepping stones in grass.

erial that need flattening only with a heavy hand roller.

Wood is an unusual paving material, and is liable to decay and be slippery unless treated with preservative and an anti-slip finish. However, old railway sleepers, logs sawn across the grain to make round stepping-'stones' and split logs can make attractive paths. A raised deck of wooden planks forms an interesting patio for a modern garden.

In areas likely to be affected by frosts it is particularly important to choose paving with a non-slip finish, such as rough-surfaced stone or textured concrete. The same applies on slopes and in shady places or areas of high rainfall where it may become slippery with algae. The slime can easily be removed with proprietary solutions, but beware of home-made remedies that may discolour and damage the surface, as may salt in winter.

Laying the foundations
The strength and durability of a paved area depends upon its foundations, so the thicker and firmer you make them, the stronger the load-bearing surface will be. Soil expands and subsides surprisingly in wet, dry or frosty weather – especially heavy clay – and the paving may move and crack if the foundations are not firm. Where earth-moving has taken place (as around a newly-built house), allow plenty of time for settling before starting work, or firmly consolidate in layers up to 25 cm (10 in) thick to save waiting. Drives will obviously require the deepest foundations, about 15 cm (6 in) thick; paths and patios need 5 to 10 cm (2 to 4 in) foundations, depending on the expected wear and type of subsoil.

Unless the path is to be raised above the surrounding area, dig out the ground to the depth of the foundations plus the thickness of the paving and its embedding material, if any. Ram down the soil, and lay a layer of hardcore – pieces of broken brick or stone – followed by a layer of smaller rubble. Firmly tamp down each layer. For some paving materials, a final embedding layer of sand, ashes or cement is needed; with others you can lay direct.

Drainage
All impervious paving materials, such as mortar-bedded paving stones, bricks with mortared points, concrete and asphalt, must be adequately drained. Where paving extends up to or close to a house wall, the finished surface should be a minimum of 15 cm (6 in) below the house's damp-proof course to prevent the dampness rising through the walls.

Lay patios or paths so that they slope away from the house – in several directions if necessary. A gentle gradient of 1:100 (1 cm in 1 m, or 1 in in 8 ft) is usually sufficient and quite unobtrusive. Drives can be gently cambered, and if gaps are left in the edgings, surface water will drain off into the garden.

Laying paving
Wood, paving stones and bricks can be embedded in a 5 cm (2 in) layer of sand, ashes or soil, but paving slabs are best laid on mortar spots. (This is quicker than laying on sand and

there is less risk of movement later.) Like bricks, they can also be bedded solid in mortar over a concrete base 2.5 cm (1 in) thick, for a firmer base. Follow a line stretched between pegs to provide an even fall, levelling each paving unit with a spirit level. Keep the joints narrow and even in width, and where possible form a pattern like the bonds in brickwork (see p 72). If you leave planting pockets, many plants can be grown, varying the monotony of a large paved area (see p 235).

Edgings are sometimes needed for paths, especially in formal situations or to contain loose surface materials. Concrete, stone slabs, bricks and tiles can all be used. They should be buried to half their depth in a bed of concrete. Wooden planks can be secured with galvanized nails to pegs at intervals of about 1.25 m (4 ft), and there are simple, if rather unattractive, edgings of corrugated aluminium strips and similar materials.

Garden steps
Most paving materials can also be used to construct garden steps. Even gravel can be packed tightly between risers (the vertical parts of the steps) of wood or concrete. But it is essential that steps should be safe to use, so the treads (the parts of the steps you walk on) must always have a non-slip surface. Rough-textured concrete is probably the safest, and precast concrete and stone slabs are the easiest to use.

Whatever material you choose, make your steps consistent in height and spacing for safety's sake. Let them rise as gently as topography permits, with treads of 30 cm (12 in) or more if possible. Risers should if possible be about 10 cm (4 in) high, and no more than 15 cm (6 in), but very shallow risers are awkward to use. So are widely spaced steps whose treads are not a multiple of a normal stride, about 75 cm (2½ ft). A good general rule is that twice the height of the riser plus the depth of the tread should equal at least 60 cm (2 ft). Steps, like paths, should be wide enough for two people to use side by side. Handrails are a must for the elderly or disabled, and where possible substitute a slope (see p 56).

The treads must be accurately levelled for safety, but they must drain well. Before beginning construction, mark out the positions of the steps with accurately levelled and spaced pegs and string. Then cut each step out of the soil by digging back and down to the marked lines.

Most materials for steps can be embedded directly into the soil if they are firmly hammered down, but for greater stability, pack small rubble into the soil and bed the paving into a layer of mortar. Start building the steps at the bottom of the slope, making sure that the first risers are firmly in place before laying the treads. If two different materials are used for risers and treads, the treads should overhang the risers by up to 5 cm (2 in) for better drainage and a tidy effect. Railway sleepers, logs and the like need to be anchored with stakes driven deeply into the foundations, while temporary shuttering must be erected for concrete cast *in situ*.

Walls, fences and gates

A wisely chosen wall or fence can form a harmonious and functional asset to your garden. A strong fence should last for a quarter-century and a wall will endure many generations, so bear this in mind when making your choice. A mistake could prove too expensive to rectify, and you will have to live with it for a very long time.

Do not forget to check your national and local regulations governing the height of private boundaries, and the kinds of materials you can use for them, before starting work, and have a word with the neighbours about joint boundaries. They may share costs – but they may also have their own ideas!

Materials, styles and costs

From a practical point of view, solid walls make the strongest enclosures. If your garden looks out over a busy highway, a wall will cut out noise and pullution more effectively than a fence. But solid barriers are not suitable for exposed gardens. When winds are high, gusts rush over the top and cause severe turbulence inside. A pierced wall or openwork fence – or a hedge (see p 90) – will filter the wind and reduce its force.

In sheltered areas, ornamental walls and fences can be used to define a boundary. Bricks and wooden palings are equally suitable for straight or curved boundaries, and

above A high brick wall can present a rather forbidding appearance, especially when situated close to the roadway or path. One way of softening the hard line is to make small pockets near the top, fill them with soil and install plants that will cascade down the face of the wall. Here the golden-yellow *Alyssum saxatile* is used.

split-bamboo and cleft chestnut pale fencing (sold in rolls) are inexpensive. Within the garden, the more decorative enclosures have a useful role as screens and dividers. Free-standing solid structures, such as double walls filled with soil and planted, are best kept low. Taller dividers are useful as backgrounds for bold foliage plants, and as hosts for climbers.

Choose materials that harmonize with the architecture of your house and the atmosphere of your garden. Examples abound of walls and fences that bear no relation to the rest of the property and look as though they have been stuck on as an afterthought. Certain materials have a natural affinity: dark-coloured wood and red brick, for example, or weather-boarding and stucco. Brick, wood and stone are versatile materials, and can be used in many different ways to suit almost any garden style. The best way to ensure harmony with the surroundings is to use local materials in a traditional way.

As a rule, a brick or stone construction will be more expensive than a timber one chosen to perform the same function. But it will also be more durable and need virtually no maintenance if properly built. Fences will require replacement more frequently – the cheaper types in perhaps as little as five to ten years. All painted structures will need attention at intervals of three to five years.

Patterns in brickwork

The various patterns in which bricks are arranged in walls are called bonds. Each layer of bricks is a course, and several courses may have to be laid before a bond becomes apparent. Proper bonding is essential for the strength and stability of a wall. It ensures that vertical and horizontal loads are distributed over a large number of bricks, and reduces movement. The stretcher bond **1** is the simplest. Only the long, narrow sides of the bricks – the stretchers – can be seen. This is the width of a single brick, and must have supporting piers if it is more than 75 cm (2½ ft) high. The other bonds shown here are all double this thickness. English bond **2** is the strongest. A stretcher course alternates with a

course of headers (in which only the ends of the bricks are visible). These must be laid so that the vertical mortar joint never runs directly through two courses, but is staggered. In the English garden bond **3**, the header course alternates with three or five courses of stretchers.
Flemish bond **4** is very attractive. A stretcher alternates with a header in each course. These are staggered over the same arrangement in the course below. In the Flemish garden bond **5**, each course consists of one header followed by three or five stretchers and another header. The headers are positioned between the centres of the middle stretchers in the courses above and below.

Mortar joints are commonly 1 cm (⅜ in) thick. You can buy ready-mixed mortar, but a mixture of Portland cement, lime and builder's sand in the proportions 1:1:6 will give good colour and strength. On a damp or exposed site, use one part cement to three parts sand.

Mortar joints

bottom The way the mortar joints between bricks are finished off affects both the appearance and durability of a wall. Useful in exposed walls are the flush joint **1**, formed by rubbing with sacking, the rubbed or keyed joint **2**, made with a piece of rounded metal and the bucket-handle joint **3**, shaped with a bent piece of bucket handle.

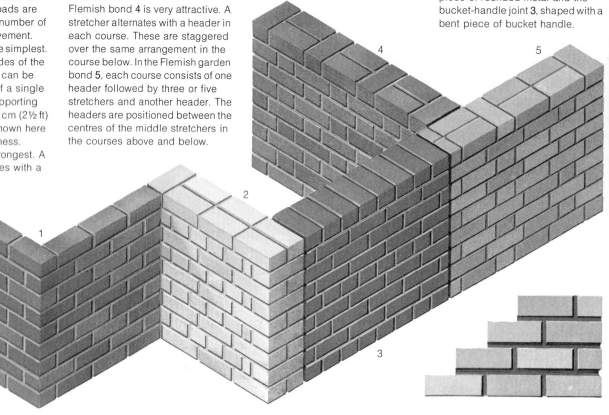

Building it yourself

You can reduce costs considerably by building your own garden walls or fences, but it makes good sense to seek professional advice before starting. Building information services run by manufacturers, trade bodies and independent organization are a good source of free help. Skilled advice becomes more important the larger and more complex the structure.

A wall is only as strong as its foundations, and the depth needed depends on soil type as well as the wall's dimensions. High, long walls may need buttresses or piers building in at intervals. Retaining walls not only need extended foundations and proper drainage to prevent water building up at the rear, but the stones or bricks are best set at an angle so that the wall slopes back towards the top (see p 76). Curved walls are more difficult to build than straight, and may need special curved bricks known as radial stretchers.

Expert guidance can help you find solutions to problems like these, and to the equivalent problems when building a fence or gate. Fence posts need embedding to an adequate depth, in concrete or directly in the soil, and those under tension at the end or a corner may need bracing with angled struts. Gate posts must be even stronger, for a swinging gate imposes more strain than a static fence, and if the post does sag the gate will not shut prop-

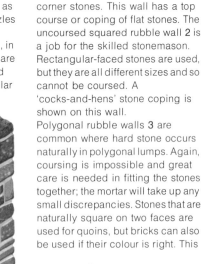

above A retaining wall can make an eye-catching feature at a change of garden level. Here the surface is given texture with flints, while planting on top provides emphasis. The conifer is *Chamaecyparis pisifera* 'Plumosa Aurea'; the trailers include *Juniperus procumbens* (foreground), a dwarf phlox and yellow alyssum.

erly. There is a vast range of materials and methods for building gates and fences, many of the modern prefabricated types being ideal for the do-it-yourself enthusiast.

Using bricks and blocks

There are so many types of bricks in so many shades, shapes and textures that you are sure to find one to suit any situation. But not all bricks are suitable for use in the garden, so it is wise to discuss your choice with a builder's merchant. Used bricks have a mellow appearance, and can sometimes be bought cheaply in demolition yards (though you will probably have to transport them yourself and possibly clean off the old mortar).

For adequate strength, all brick walls must be bonded – built to an established pattern – so that the vertical mortar joints are staggered and never appear one above the other. Some useful and decorative bonding patterns are shown on page 72. Never build a mortar-bound wall in freezing weather. Special bricks are available for copings to finish the top of a wall, but these are not essential in the garden, although they do give a more professional – and possibly formal – appearance. Stone or concrete copings can also be used.

Concrete building blocks can make attractive, inexpensive and quickly built garden walls. They are least expensive/*continued*

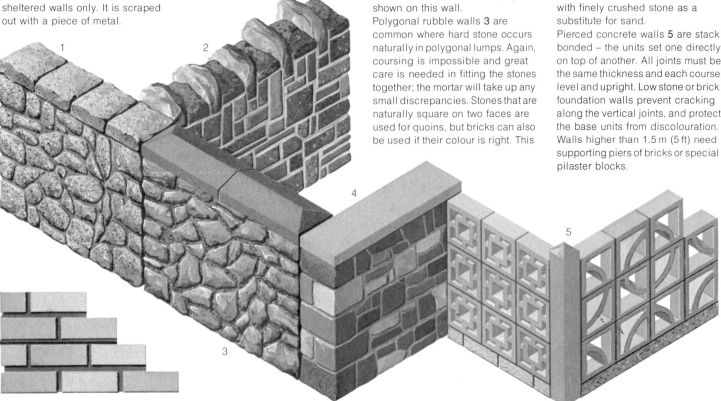

The weathered joint **4** directs rain down the wall face; the horizontal mortar layers overhang the lower bricks and the vertical ones slope from one side to the other. The 'bird-beak' or twice-weathered joint **5** deflects rain away from the wall. It is formed with a special implement. The recessed joint **6** is useful for sheltered walls only. It is scraped out with a piece of metal.

Stone and concrete walls

Natural stone (otherwise known as rubble) walls are like jigsaw puzzles in stone. The simplest is the uncoursed random rubble wall **1**, in which irregularly-shaped stones are laid in an attractively haphazard way. The largest and most regular pieces are used for the quoins, the corner stones. This wall has a top course or coping of flat stones. The uncoursed squared rubble wall **2** is a job for the skilled stonemason. Rectangular-faced stones are used, but they are all different sizes and so cannot be coursed. A 'cocks-and-hens' stone coping is shown on this wall.

Polygonal rubble walls **3** are common where hard stone occurs naturally in polygonal lumps. Again, coursing is impossible and great care is needed in fitting the stones together; the mortar will take up any small discrepancies. Stones that are naturally square on two faces are used for quoins, but bricks can also be used if their colour is right. This

wall has a concrete coping. Coursed squared rubble walls **4** are expensive. All stones used are dressed, or rectangular, and there must be enough of a certain size to complete each course. Dressed quoins are also needed. A sawn natural stone coping is shown. Mortar for stone walls is often made with finely crushed stone as a substitute for sand.

Pierced concrete walls **5** are stack bonded – the units set one directly on top of another. All joints must be the same thickness and each course level and upright. Low stone or brick foundation walls prevent cracking along the vertical joints, and protect the base units from discolouration. Walls higher than 1.5 m (5 ft) need supporting piers of bricks or special pilaster blocks.

Walls, fences and gates (continued)

if you cast them yourself, but you can buy precast blocks or broken slabs. The cheaper types are best cement-rendered to give a rough-textured surface that will weather to a mellow appearance within a few months. Pierced concrete screen blocks are usually square, each unit having an identical pattern, but several different units may be needed to build up a design. Unlike brick walls, the blocks are stacked in vertical rows, not staggered, and if more than 1.5 m (5 ft) high need reinforcing with a lateral metal strip.

If you are faced with a drab wall, you can brighten it up with stucco or cement-based masonry paint. Ceramic tiles and mosaics are cheerful in patios and small gardens. Frost-proof tiles should be used in cold areas, and must be properly fixed.

Using stone
Stone can be prohibitively expensive in areas where it does not occur naturally, but if read-ily available it can be as cheap as brick. It can be hard like granite or soft like limestone, and ranges in colour from off-white to yellow, brown, red, grey and black, and can even be multi-coloured. If you buy it from the quarry, it can be fully-dressed, or shaped, but it is cheaper if roughly or semi-dressed. You can also dress it yourself with club hammer and bolster. As with bricks, second-hand stone is sometimes available from demolition work.

Natural stone should be laid on bed – that is, with the grain running in the same direction as when it was part of a rock formation. This maximizes the natural durability of the mat-erial, and the grain can be very attractive. Unless the stone used is uniform in shape and size, mortar-bound stone walls are difficult to build (see p 73). Dry stone walls are even more complicated, but are very pleasing in the garden if they have a soil core and more soil is packed into the crevices and rock and trailing plants grown (see pp 124 and 236).

The most ordinary fencing materials can be enlivened by suitable climbing plants. Here, a woven panel fence and its abutting wall support a profusion of climbing roses.

Reconstructed (reconstituted) stone is made of crushed stone bound by cement. The regularly-shaped blocks are easier to handle – and cheaper – than real stone, and have a more natural appearance than concrete blocks. The same material is used to make balustrading and decorative features such as ball finials.

Making fences
Many kinds of fences are sold in kit form or as prefabricated panels, but you can also design your own. Timber for outdoor use in less for-mal situations need not be of first quality in terms of straightness of grain, freedom from knots and smoothness of finish. But for dura-bility choose the more long-lived softwoods such as cedar or larch, or such hardwoods as oak or chestnut. The cheaper grades of soft-wood generally sold as deal can also be used for garden fencing, but they will need rela-tively frequent attention with paint or preser-

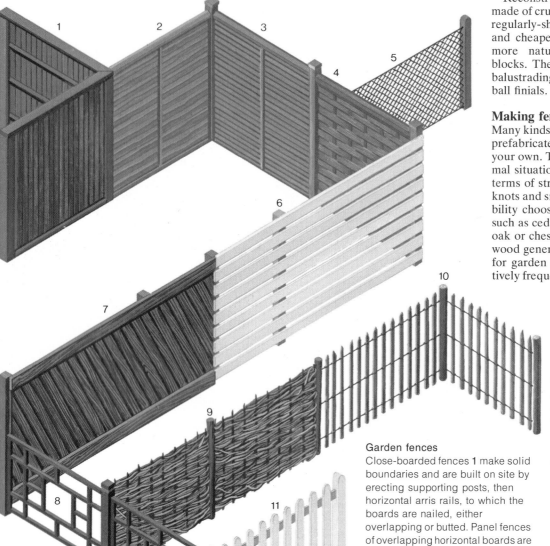

Garden fences
Close-boarded fences **1** make solid boundaries and are built on site by erecting supporting posts, then horizontal arris rails, to which the boards are nailed, either overlapping or butted. Panel fences of overlapping horizontal boards are prefabricated and may have wavy lower edges **2** or a more regular slatted appearance **3**. They are often built of a cheaper softwood such as larch. The popular woven wood fences **4** are also sold in panel form.

Chain-link fencing **5** makes a good host for climbing plants, but if possible obtain the black plastic-coated type, which is the least obtrusive. The post-and-rail ranch-style fence **6** may have from two to nine or more rails; it combines strength with a formal appearance, especially if painted white. A board fence with diagonal slats **7** is unusual and attractive, and is also strong. An ornamental fence of oriental appearance **8** is useful as a decorative screen within a garden; it is made of narrow hardwood sections. Wattle hurdle fencing **9** has a soft rustic appearance and is inexpensive. One of the cheapest and simplest of all fences to erect is cleft chestnut fencing **10** sold in rolls. Palisade or picket fences **11** may have pales with rounded or pointed tops; they are ideal for cottage gardens, painted white or left their natural colour.

A rounded archway makes a distinctive garden entrance, furnished with an iron gate of simple, elegant design. Red brick and wrought iron make a pleasing combination of materials.

relatively cheap, but should never be used on fences that support plants. Water-borne and organic-solvent preservatives are available that do not harm plants. The latter smell initially but do not corrode metal fittings; the former cannot be over-applied, are non-combustible and when dry do not bleed. Choose a colour sympathetic to the timber and surroundings. White paint looks good on certain kinds of fences.

Gates and gateways
The size, position and style of gateways in the garden should be governed by aesthetic as well as practical considerations. Obviously, main entrance gates must be positioned where access is needed, and must be wide enough for their purpose – a minimum of 75 cm (2½ ft) for pedestrians and 2 m (7 ft) or more if possible for vehicles. But gates can form decorative focal features in their own right – from the rustic simplicity of the five-bar gate to classic

styles in wrought iron. Whatever style you favour, make sure that it is sympathetic to the style of the wall or fence (see p 20).

Apart from dimensions, such practical details as the strength of the gate posts are vital. Wooden supporting posts commonly need to be 10 by 10 cm (4 by 4 in) thick, and must be sunk deeply into the earth and braced across the top if possible. For wrought iron and very heavy wooden gates – particularly if they are tall – you will probably need to erect brick or stone piers set on substantial foundations for stability. Most wooden gates need to be braced diagonally to prevent sagging. Strong hinges are also necessary – with forged iron straps for heavy gates. Ensure that your gate opens into the garden and not out into the street. Finally, choose latches, bolts or locks – and other gate furniture, such as knobs and knockers – that are in sympathy with the style of the gate as well as able to do the job demanded of them.

vative. Timber is available that has been pre-treated with preservative.

Apart from a wide variety of timber panelling styles, some of which are illustrated, you can use concrete or plastic panels; wooden rails; glass; woven reeds, twigs or bamboo; trellis; even canvas. One of the most utilitarian materials is chain-link fencing, which can be galvanized or plastic-coated; this can be masked by growing lightweight climbing plants though the mesh. Iron railing is decorative but expensive.

Whatever the infilling, the most important part of a fence is the posts. Even if you are using cheap panelling timber, try to afford hardwood posts. If you do not mind the appearance, of course, concrete posts are the most durable of all. Bore post-holes with an earth auger, or dig holes and embed the posts in concrete. In either case, treat the buried part of timber posts with creosote. Depth of post-holes depends on various factors, but as a general rule set posts 75 cm (2½ ft) deep for a 1.8 to 2.5 m (6 to 8 ft) fence, and 60 cm (2 ft) deep for one up to 1.25 cm (4 ft) high. Spacing depends on the size of the prefabricated panels if you are using these – they are usually 1.8 to 2 m (6 to 7 ft) wide – but for other fences it can vary from 1.8 to 3 m (6 to 10 ft).

For most kinds of fence made from sawn timber, two or more horizontal rails will be needed between the posts. They can be nailed in position or preferably tenoned into mortises formed in the posts. Close-boarding can be butted (nailed edge-to-edge) or feathered (thinned at one edge) and overlapped. A timber capping nailed over the top edge of the fence will help prevent water penetration and retard rotting. A gravel board running horizontally along the bottom, above a bed of gravel, ensures good drainage and also prevents premature rotting. Use galvanized nails for attaching boards.

Red cedar and larch are naturally resinous and need treating with preservative only after some years. Hardwoods can be left to weather naturally, but other timbers need treatment every two to three years. Creosote is good and

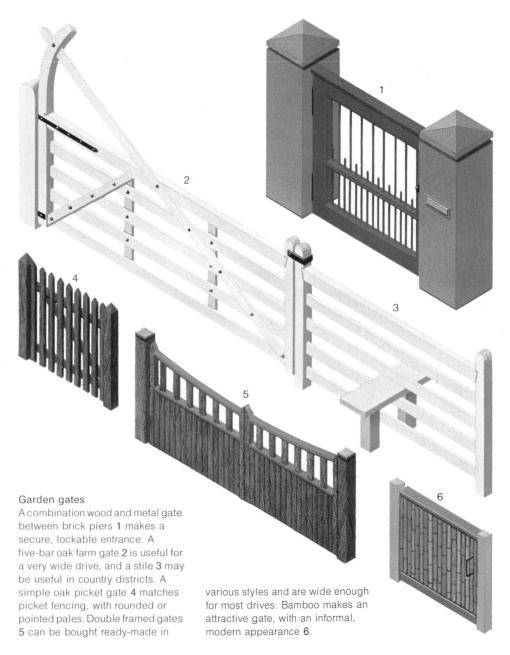

Garden gates
A combination wood and metal gate between brick piers 1 makes a secure, lockable entrance. A five-bar oak farm gate 2 is useful for a very wide drive, and a stile 3 may be useful in country districts. A simple oak picket gate 4 matches picket fencing, with rounded or pointed pales. Double framed gates 5 can be bought ready-made in various styles and are wide enough for most drives. Bamboo makes an attractive gate, with an informal, modern appearance 6.

Changes in garden level

Any reshaping of the contours of your garden site will be the first major construction job to be tackled if you are making a new garden or restructuring an existing one, and because earth-moving is such a weighty task you would be wise to attempt it only if absolutely essential. Major contouring should only be necessary in extreme situations – on a site with a pronounced transverse slope, for example, or in a garden that rises steeply from the house – and the creation of artificial slopes or hills is best attempted only if the lie of the land suggests it.

If you terrace an existing slope, or excavate a natural hollow to make a sunken garden, these features when completed will look as if they belong (though a good deal of a downward-sloping garden can be lost visually over terracing), but large-scale changes in level tend to look out of place if introduced into a level site. A good way of landscaping a slope without major building work is to construct a rock garden (see p 118).

Reshaping the ground

Work out a detailed plan for your new scheme (see p 66) and mark out the proposed new levels on site with stakes and string before you begin the spade-work. Any reshaping you do carry out will involve removing the fertile topsoil (see p 330); stack it in a convenient place for later replacement or use elsewhere. (This applies equally when terracing or excavating a sunken garden.)

(12 in), with extra topsoil brought in if necessary, and the area left to settle. Correct any resulting depressions before replanting.

Terracing a slope

Terracing a sloping site is more complex, and may involve a considerable amount of earth-moving, so work out convenient routes for transporting excavated earth, and ways of disposing of any surplus, before you begin. As a general rule, work from the bottom of the slope upwards.

Take the natural lie of the land as your guide when planning the terracing. You can aim for a gently undulating effect, with wide flat terraces and curving gentle banks, on ground that slopes gently. To avoid soil erosion – especially where the soil is light – the banks should not be steeper than about 1:2 (1 in 2, or an angle of 30° from the horizontal), and must be planted for stabilization. Steep banks can be paved and planted as described on page 125.

Terracing on steeply sloping sites will involve building one or more retaining walls, with flat planting areas between. Such walls must be very strong, with extensive foundations, and unless you have considerable experience of bricklaying are best constructed by an expert. They should have a slight batter (backwards tilt), and drainage pipes must be inserted between the bricks or blocks of stone, so that any water behind can seep away – eventually to a ditch or drain. If planting holes

least 15 cm (6 in) deep for turfing and 30 cm (12 in) deep for planting. Begin the planting immediately the ground has settled, to prevent soil erosion. On exposed sites erect windshields of hurdles across the slopes until the plants are established.

Where the ground around a house slopes away downwards, a paved terrace may be built in much the same way, with a strong retaining wall going down well into the soil and steps leading down to the garden. Fill in with a layer of hardcore at least 15 cm (6 in) thick, ram it down firmly and allow it to settle for as long as possible before finishing the surface. This can be of almost any of the paving materials mentioned on page 70, but ensure that the final level is at least 15 cm (6 in) below the house's damp-proof course and that it slopes slightly away from the house for good drainage. Leave planting pockets if you wish (see p 235), and finish off with some kind of parapet, such as a balustrade.

Sunken gardens

Even where there is a natural hollow that suggests the construction of a sunken garden, this is only practicable if drainage is good. Test for this first by digging a trench at the lowest point as described on page 332. If water seeps into the trench from the surrounding land after rain, some kind of artificial drainage will be required. Either install one or more deep soakaways or lay a system of land drains leading to a yet lower spot (see p 333).

left A grass 'staircase' is a striking and unusual way of treating a slope but one that needs a great deal of upkeep. right Conventional retaining walls must be strong and based on wide concrete foundations with a 'toe' that projects well back into the bank so that the weight of soil pressing down stabilizes the structure. Give the brickwork a batter, and generally make its thickness one-third the wall's height; only the lowest retaining walls can be one course thick. Inset drainage pipes to prevent the build-up of water, and treat the back with bitumen paint to avoid staining of the bricks.

Divide the area to be restructured into easily workable sections, then cut away or build up the subsoil, section by section, to a depth of about 30 cm (12 in) below the proposed new level. When building up the ground, spread the new soil (obtainable from a garden centre, building contractor, or perhaps from excavations in other parts of the garden) in thin layers, each about 15 cm (6 in) deep, and allow to settle before laying the next. (Firming down too heavily can cause drainage problems.) If the area is to be planted, take the opportunity to improve the soil by digging in humus-forming material (see p 334). The topsoil can then be replaced to a depth of 30 cm

are left in the walls, suitable trailing plants can be inserted (see pp 124 and 236).

As before, work from the bottom and follow as closely as possible the natural contours of the land. Build the first retaining wall and then level off the terrace behind. You will have to construct steps as you progress, but you can leave the laying of the paths and the building of edging walls or raised beds along the top of the terrace until the excavations are complete. Begin the second terrace after the first one is completed, and continue in the same way until you reach the top of the slope.

When the basic work is complete, with or without retaining walls, replace the topsoil at

If this seems too daunting, you may do better to construct a pool or bog garden instead (see pp 128 and 133).

Even if drainage is adequate, you could take the opportunity, when moving earth to form the sunken garden, to excavate farther and lay 15 to 30 cm (6 to 12 in) of coarse rubble all over the site. Follow this with finer rubble and then paving or, for planting or grassing, a layer of gravel, a layer of inverted turves and finally a 30 cm (12 in) layer of topsoil. Support the sides of the garden with retaining walls, or slope the sides to form grass banks; the latter are more difficult to maintain but less expensive to construct.

Vertical garden structures

There are various types of free-standing structures that will form attractive garden features and, in many cases, also have practical purposes. For example, pergolas and other forms of garden 'roofing' can provide very welcome shade, particularly in hot climates; whether or not they are planted with climbing plants, as described on page 92, they will also contribute to the garden's visual impact. Archways and similar structures can make attractive garden dividers and can be used to frame a pleasant view or obscure an ugly one.

Most structures of this kind are fairly straightforward to build yourself. Most of the

of shade. Also, if the planks are orientated north-south, they will provide minimal shade at midday; east-west orientation gives the maximum shade. In sunny climes, you can fix planks on the flat in staggered rows.

In hot climates, where adequate shade is the paramount consideration, a roof of woven bamboo fencing supported on strong wires or timber cross-pieces provides shade while letting air circulate; it can be rolled up and stored away in winter. But here, even more than in cooler climates, a living 'roof' of lightweight climbing plants is ideal for both appearance and practicality.

1.25 m (4 ft) as a minimum – but can be twice this width if the site allows and you use strong enough cross-pieces. The height should be a minimum of 2 m (6½ ft). Apart from timber uprights, you can construct brick or stone supporting piers. The wooden cross-pieces may be cemented directly into the brickwork (after being treated with preservative), supported on metal joist-hangers or fixed to metal bolts cemented vertically in place. You can leave the sides of the pergola open, or fix trellis or larch poles in a rustic pattern. Loops of thick rope slung between the uprights are excellent for training climbing roses, and ivy on the shady side.

Other features
Many other architectural features of grand landscaped gardens can be adapted to more domestic surroundings if kept in scale and style. For example, trellis can be attached to a wooden framework to make treillage, which can take various forms. An arbour – a kind of small open-fronted summer-house, usually with a seat – can be built in this way, and clothed with plants. Or one can be made of rustic poles. On a larger scale, a pergola does not have to form a straight walk; a circular version, with poles radiating out from one central support to a ring of outer ones, can be extremely attractive. A wrought iron wellhead – whether or not it tops a real well – can form the focal point of a formal paved area or an interesting feature in an informal setting.

materials and styles suitable for walls and fences (see pp 72 to 74) are adaptable to these features, so it is not difficult to harmonize with other house and garden architecture. One over-riding principle is to ensure strength and stability. Brick or stone piers must have good foundations and be vertical; wooden uprights must be treated with preservative and sunk firmly at least 60 cm (2 ft) into the ground – at least 1 m (3 ft) if the soil is light – and preferably embedded in concrete. All cross-members must be securely fixed with rustproof screws or nails and must be strong enough to support both themselves and any climbing plants. Sawn softwood should be treated with a nontoxic preservative or painted, but only the sawn ends of bark-covered rustic poles need to be treated.

Shading for patios
A roof that will give some protection against sun and wind without inhibiting vertical air circulation can make a welcome difference to a terrace or patio. Attractive canvas canopies with metal rod or pipe supports need no complex supporting structures and can be dismantled when not needed. Alternatively, you can construct a sturdy frame of timber to support a 'roof' of planks arranged on edge in the manner of floor joists. Planks 15 by 2.5 cm (6 by 1 in) are suitable. The closer together they are, the more 'solid' and shady the roof will be, but bear in mind that the closer to the tropics you live, the higher is the angle of the midday summer sun, so the closer together must the planks be for an equivalent amount

Arches and pergolas
Simple archways built of larch poles or other timber and clothed with roses, clematis or other climbers make charming garden features, but they must be sited logically if they are not to look pretentious. Straddling a path leading from one section of your garden to another – perhaps flanked by hedges or shrubs – an arch will serve a proper aesthetic and practical purpose. A pergola – which is, in essence, generally a series of linked arches – is a big enough structure to stand as a feature in its own right, perhaps flanking a lawn, but it should still if possible lead somewhere – at least to a terminal focal point. As well as permanently planted climbers and ground plantings, it can (if strong enough) support hanging baskets of summer flowers.

A pergola or arch should be wide enough for two people to walk side by side – say

Pergolas can take varied forms from the semi-circular arch **above left**, which forms an alley between two parts of the garden, to the more purely decorative wooden structure **above**, which serves simply to support climbing plants that are part of the overall scheme. In hot regions **above right**, a bamboo roof can provide shade. An octagonal pergola **right** is less common than the rectangular type, but is easy to build with brick and wood.

The 'business' end of the garden

Cold frames and compost heaps, tool sheds and piles of unburnt refuse are obtrusive things. They are essential to the garden's smooth running but difficult to fit into its design. Manhole covers, taps and cables fall into this category, too, and you can add dustbins, wood piles and any other unsightly items that have to be stored in the garden. With ingenuity and planning, some of these objects can be concealed and others camouflaged, and the rest can, if space permits, be kept to one utility area: a place where equipment can be stored and garden jobs done.

Siting the utility area

Better out of sight, the utility area is almost invariably relegated to the bottom of the gar-den, where it becomes inaccessible and is usually still visible. Put near to the house – behind a shed or garage, or adjoining a vegetable patch along a side wall of the garden – it is handier and less conspicuous. It can be screened off from the rest of the garden with evergreen shrubs, or screen walls or fences planted with evergreen climbers.

The utility area should not be so close to the house or any garden seating area that smoke from a bonfire or incinerator, and smells from a compost heap or dustbins, become a nuisance. Just underneath a tree or too near to unscreened plants is also unsuitable, because rising heat can easily scorch foliage. It should be supplied with paths wide enough for garden machinery, and needs a hard surface to facilitate compost shovelling and other tasks. This will also encourage hygiene. If pots or seed boxes are stored there, cross-infection can occur in dirty conditions; a paved or concreted area can easily be swept or washed down periodically.

Garden camouflage

A hinged timber screen 1 or an easily erected trellis 2 that can be covered with evergreen climbers will conceal any unsightly garden object. Or you can store a whole cache behind a narrow raised bed 3 with a side gate 4. Camouflage an incinerator or dustbin with a three-sided concrete bay 5; a brick version 6 can be built higher, but dustbins are least unhygienic if kept in a cupboard 7 with a lifting or sliding top for filling and a door at the front for emptying.

You can hide broken paving under movable brick planting boxes 8 and inspection or manhole covers under a water-lily tub set among pebbles 9, or light rocks 10 that can be easily moved aside. Multi-purpose planting units 11 of bricks stacked on a paving slab foundation and filled with movable container plants will also serve; they are easily dismantled. Planted containers made of lightweight asbestos cement and other materials 12 will also hide ugly ground features, especially if grouped.

A small shed adjacent to the utility area will provide storage for tools, pots and other small items. Alternatively, large cupboards or even a set of shelves will provide storage and working space. If you have to store garden machinery in the utility area, a roof will give protection against rain, and screening around the area will also keep out the wind.

Concealment and camouflage

It is difficult to hide a garage, but the bleak walls of these structures can be softened with container shrubs, smothered in creepers or edged with borders of wall shrubs. A flat roof can be extended outwards with beams, supported with pillars, and so converted into a pergola. Again, if evergreens are used, the screening and camouflaging will be effective the year round.

Drain and manhole inspection covers are eyesores that appear in the most inconvenient places, and sometimes in groups. There may be several in a garden. These covers must always be immediately accessible and easy to identify, so they cannot be hidden completely. In a border they can be camouflaged with prostrate shrubs, and for paved areas a special cover is available. This has a recessed top to allow a piece of paving material to be set into it. Apart from a narrow metal rim it will then blend almost unseen into the patio, terrace or path.

Deception is not so easy in the lawn; you cannot bury these objects under the grass. Deeply recessed and turfed they might be dangerous, and the turf will turn brown in dry weather. Painting the cover green does little to help, as green paint looks unnatural and the green of grass varies almost weekly with cutting and weather conditions. The best solution is to make virtue out of necessity, and put something eye-catching on top – perhaps loose pebbles or gravel, rocks, or a tub or sink garden. These can be moved aside when the need arises, particularly if on a wheeled base in the case of a tub.

Drainage systems and cables near the lawn surface will cause brown marks in dry weather, so bury these deeply. A layer of protective tiles placed over an underground cable in other parts of the garden will prevent damage and will mark their position. It is better to use armoured cables for such services. Always take the advice of a qualified electrical engineer before bringing electrical fittings into the garden; special waterproofing precautions are necessary, and overhead cables have to be supported.

The washing line is easily overlooked in a garden plan. This is one of the most difficult items to integrate. It has a strong visual impact, particularly if it is associated with a service path. Unfortunately, its function dictates that it should be near to the house, where it is easily accessible. Unless the garden is large and the clothes line can be put in an unobtrusive place, a rotary clothes drier should be considered. It is the least obtrusive type because it can be set in a socket and is easily folded, removed and stored away when it is not in use.

Garden sheds

Tool and potting sheds are rarely objects of beauty, and like the service area they can be sited least conspicuously to one side of the garden, near the house, or beside a vegetable garden. Plants can provide camouflage. Before erecting a shed, however, check whether building regulations govern its siting, size and materials.

Sheds can be bought ready-made in a variety of sizes and styles, but they are less expensive if they are bought in kit form and erected on site. They can be made in a variety of materials: hard and softwoods, also hardboard proofed with a rubber bitumen compound, waterproof plywood, bricks and many others. Floors are usually of wood resting on simple brick piers at intervals – ensure that these are square and level – but concrete floors and foundations with a damp-proof membrane can also be laid and are more permanent.

Roofs can be of wood, roofing felt, corrugated iron or asbestos-cement, or tiled. Wooden shingles make a very attractive and durable roofing material. Pitched roofs are easier to waterproof than flat ones. If possible, fit guttering to catch rain-water and feed it into a butt.

Sizes of sheds vary considerably. An average size, giving adequate room for storage of machinery as well as tools and other garden equipment would be 2.5 m by 1.5 m by 2 m high (8 ft by 5 ft by 7 ft), but they can be smaller if necessary – and consequently cheaper. Sliding doors can be fitted so that the shed need occupy the minimum possible space in a very small garden.

Styles of sheds

A recent trend has been the production of multi-purpose sheds – garden buildings that combine the functions of storage shed, greenhouse, summer-house and even conservatory. Some examples are illustrated. Glass roofs and doors, large windows that open, even French and picture windows and sun porches can be attached to a home-made shed to extend its use.

Internal furnishings of a garden shed will vary according to personal need. A bench for potting and other odd jobs is almost essential. A peg board with hooks to hang tools is a useful feature, as are bins for seed, potting mixture and so on. If you are going to store weedkillers and other chemicals, make sure that the door has a lock, so that children can be kept away. Then, as an added precaution, keep these poisons on an inaccessible shelf or in a locked cupboard.

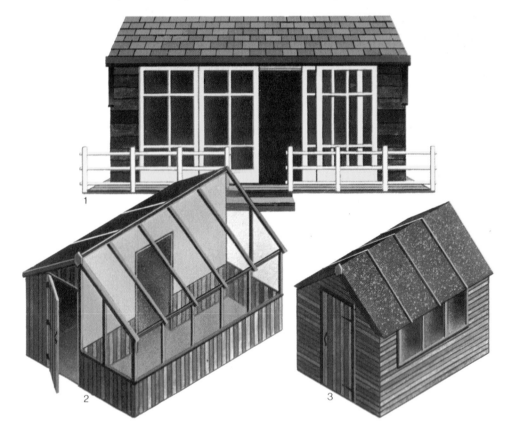

Multi-purpose sheds
A summer-house 1 with a tiled or shingled roof, sliding glazed doors and a surrounding wooden deck or balcony can also double as a tool and garden furniture store and potting shed. It is more expensive than ordinary sheds, but is more attractive – an advantage in a small garden where it may be impossible to site a shed inconspicuously. A lean-to shed built against a wall is both cheap and space-saving; free-standing versions 2 are available in which the shed backs onto a greenhouse, again saving cost and space. Given a firm, level base, the easiest type to erect is a simple cedarwood shed with a pitched roof 3 covered in roofing felt.

Garden ornaments and furniture

Ornaments have long been a very important tool in the garden designer's art – they figured prominently in the informal gardens of the 18th-century English landscape movement, when the ideal garden was as 'natural' in appearance as an undisturbed landscape. Mock buildings, ruins and even dead trees were used to decorate these gardens but they were, nevertheless, ornaments.

An ornament can be defined as any feature used for decorative purposes, but as far as this article is concerned living plants are excluded. Its job is usually to adorn and embellish, but in the context of garden design ornaments are usually called upon to do rather more than this. A small bronze figure – or a tub filled with brightly coloured flowers – are both ornamental features. They could well be positioned – on a patio or terrace, for example – in a spot where they will be most effectively displayed, and admired for their own intrinsic beauty. But they should also form an integral part of the overall garden design, and they may also have a functional role within it.

A device often employed by garden architects is to make use of an ornament as a focal point. Used in this way it does more than merely decorate; it serves to draw one's attention – or oneself – to a particular spot in the garden. A number of ornaments strategically positioned about a garden will subtly draw the visitor from one place to another until he has wandered all the way through it. Many old gardens have arrangements of statues, temples and grottoes which do just this.

Conversely, many functional objects can also be used as ornaments. An attractive seat, for example, can be used to make a focal point and it will also be used for sitting on. Bridges, summer-houses, wells and stone lanterns are frequently used as functional ornaments.

Choosing garden ornaments

Choose an ornament for the garden as you would choose one for a room in your house. Proportion, harmony, style and function are the key points to consider. You would reject anything that was inappropriate to the decor, or out of scale with your living room, so think of the garden as an outdoor room and apply the same rules. A chubby stone cherub or a rustic log seat would obviously look incongruous in a clean-lined, formal setting. A large statue would be out of scale and would most likely seem pretentious in a small garden – and a tiny stone urn would be virtually invisible at the far end of a long walk and thus fail to do its job in providing a focal point. Although rules of taste can be surprisingly flexible, try to imagine your proposed purchase *in situ* before you make an irrevocable decision.

The range of objects that can be used for ornamenting a garden is vast and includes many natural as well as man-made features. Logs or tree stumps (treated with preservative) make excellent decorative features. The use of pebbles, stones and rocks to create visually interesting garden compositions is an idea borrowed from the Orient. Embedded in moss or covered in lichens and positioned

Furniture and ornaments should subtly accent garden style and atmosphere. **above** Bronze urns and a wooden bench arranged symmetrically suggest calm formality. **above right** A traditional statue makes a more effective focal point framed by a wrought-iron arbour. **below left** An ornate or lead figures are available, and while not truly sculptures are excellent lightweight, low-cost substitutes, if carefully made. sundial in the form of an armillary sphere enhances a herb garden's old-fashioned dignity. **below right** A dovecot ornaments an old cottage wall.

carefully, they can provide a more natural and less expensive alternative to a stone sculpture.

A still, reflective expanse of water is both pleasing and restful, and streams and fountains add sound and sparkle to the garden composition. A jet of water issuing from and returning to a circular dish of pebbles – both elements completely natural – together make a most attractive ornament.

Sculpture in the garden

Sculptures, both modern and traditional, readily spring to mind when thinking of ornaments. They may be made of many materials: a whole range of metals, many kinds of stone or, latterly, glass-fibre. Bronze, lead and stainless steel are the best metals for exterior use as they do not deteriorate in contact with the elements. Glass-fibre imitations of bronze

or lead figures are available, and while not truly sculptures are excellent lightweight, low-cost substitutes, if carefully made.

The durability of stone sculptures will depend much upon the type of stone used and climatic and atmospheric conditions. Some stones, such as soft limestone, do not respond well to damp or extremes of temperature, while others – notably marble – may quickly deteriorate in industrial or maritime positions in cold or temperate climates. Concrete and simulated stone replicas (of which there are very good and very bad examples) are considerably cheaper than real stone.

Both modern and traditional wooden sculptures are very attractive in the garden, perhaps because, like stone, wood is a natural material and has an affinity with trees, grass and flowers. But this material too is easily

affected by climatic extremes, and in damp climates particularly it should be regularly treated with preservative or paint.

Some sculptures need a plinth to increase their height, while others look best standing on their own. Each piece should be considered individually, but since a plinth can affect the appearance of a sculpture in the same way as a frame can spoil or enhance the effect of a picture, it is essential that besides giving (and appearing to give) adequate support to the sculpture, it should be in proportion to its shape and size, and should be of a suitable material, colour and style.

Decorating walls
Wall sculptures, usually in stone, concrete or metal, are sometimes used to decorate the walls of modern buildings. Tiles and mosaics also make attractive wall decorations. In an appropriate setting, you can give an elegant

below A stone slab set on blocks makes a simple ornamental seat. **right** Patio furniture in warm, earthy shades looks colourful yet unobtrusive.

appearance to a wall with the addition of balustrades, carved finials, urns and vases, and even small statues – all of which can be purchased, in real or simulated stone, along with obelisks, scrolled benches, wall plaques and other classical devices, from specialist suppliers. They will be expensive, so be sure that they will suit the style of your garden before you consider buying. Copings, gates and steps (see pp 70 to 75) can also have great ornamental value, as can pots, tubs and other plant containers (see p116)

Siting garden ornaments
The position of an ornament in the garden very much depends upon the job it has to do. A sundial, for example, will appear blatantly useless if it is sited where the sun hardly shines. If some decoration seems necessary in a shady place, a Japanese stone lantern would be most appropriate, suggesting a source of light in an area of darkness. An ornamental bird-table or bird-bath would be sensibly put near a favourite seat, or within sight of the house windows so that the garden's users can see the birds rather than merely provide a facility for them.

Not all ornaments can be so obviously placed, of course; you will have to rely upon your own taste and judgement, and perhaps try placing a particular piece in two or three different places before you find the right position for it. There are, however, a few helpful guidelines to follow. An ornament positioned so that it is encountered on rounding a bend or corner will generate drama in the garden, and an element of surprise can do much to enhance its appeal. A marble statue set back so that it is seen through a light tracery of twigs or leaves can be more attractive than a cold, uncompromising confrontation. Background is an important consideration. A stone figure standing out from a soft leafy background will look quite different from the same figure placed in front of a tightly clipped yew hedge or a brick wall. The latter will make the figure appear to stand out in contrast, suggesting formality, while the leafy background will suggest integration and informality.

Garden furniture
Garden furniture, too, can be highly ornamental. Clearly, if it is to remain permanently outside it must also be weatherproof. Stone furniture is ideal in this respect. Manufacturers usually give hints on the aftercare of their products and these should be closely followed, but as a rule, overtreatment is better than undertreatment. Wooden tables, chairs and benches should be treated even if they are made of durable hardwood, and log furniture should, if possible, be stripped of bark. This will usually fall off in time, but until it does it may harbour pests or dampness.

Cast iron has been in vogue for over 100 years as a material for garden furniture, but it is unfortunately extremely heavy and requires frequent painting to prevent rust. Its manufacture has largely been replaced by that of very light aluminium alloy pieces, requiring paint only for cosmetic, rather than protec-

tive, purposes. Such furniture includes both modern designs and replicas of Victorian styles. Garden furniture can also be made of logs or concrete, and pieces can easily be constructed *in situ* by the handyman. You can finish concrete furniture in various ways: giving it plain smooth surfaces, textured finishes or imitation stone facings, for example. Bricks and paving slabs, too, make good, robust items of furniture and many interesting effects are possible. They will require very little, if any, maintenance.

Plastic and glass-fibre furniture is available in many designs and styles, and even plastic-covered cushions can safely be left outside. Plastic used as a covering for metal combines the strength of the metal with the weatherproof, maintenance-free plastic surface. Furniture in softer materials, such as cane, rattan, bamboo or wicker, and seats, swings and sunshades covered in cloth or canvas, come in interesting shapes and a wide range of colours, but they should not be left out for any length of time in temperate climates. Except for the larger pieces, this furniture is normally lightweight and can easily be carried under cover after use. Some types – canvas chairs and tables in particular – can usually be folded for storage.

Consider the decorative as well as the practical aspects of any garden furniture you are thinking of buying. Try to achieve a harmony of style between the various items of furniture in your garden, and with the garden itself, even if you choose different materials for, say, the patio and for a single bench used as a focal point.

Many items of furniture are brightly coloured – either painted or covered in patterned cloth. If used with taste, this can add an element of gaiety and interest to a garden, especially to a large paved terrace or a swimming-pool surround, but beware of creating clashes; most gardens are furnished primarily with plants, and the colours of these are all too easily overpowered by the strident tones of plastic and paint. If you would have subtle effects, go for the neutral tones of brick, stone, wood and cane, and natural undyed cloth. But do not be too much afraid to exercise your own judgement and taste – it is primarily yourself that you have to please.

Features for outdoor living

Among the most ambitious features to install in your garden, a swimming pool is probably the most rewarding. Few garden recreations can be as satisfying as bathing in the waters of your own pool. A barbecue alongside the pool, or installed on its own on a patio, is well worthwhile for outdoor meals on warm summer evenings. And to make the most of both features – and of the decorative parts of the garden – you can install outdoor lighting.

Planning a pool
Even the least expensive type of swimming pool involves considerable outlay, and it is as well to be aware of the problems that may arise before deciding to invest in one. Not every garden has room for a swimming pool, in any case. The pool needs to be at least 3 by 5.5 m (10 by 18 ft), with an area of trim and decking up to 1.8 m (6 ft) wide all round, and if possible should be 5 by 9 m (15 by 30 ft) or more. If you have a small plot, therefore, check whether a pool will fit; few people will want to give up the whole of the garden area. Then check subsoil conditions and whether any electricity cables, gas pipes and so on cross the proposed site; they will be costly to move. And check whether there are any local laws or regulations governing the siting and construction of a pool.

It is well worth consulting a swimming pool contractor at an early stage. He may offer an advisory service for a small fee that is waived if you accept his quotation. He will advise where to site the pool in order to keep costs to a minimum. He will check whether the ground is liable to subsidence – as where recent earth-moving has taken place – whether it will be easy to excavate and whether it is corrosive (as with soils containing a lot of sulphur).

A pool will necessarily dominate a small garden, but with a careful choice of shape and imaginative landscaping, it can make an effective central feature. In a large garden there may be many suitable positions. If possible, choose a place that receives maximum sun-

shine – at least at the time of day when the pool will be most used, such as late afternoon.

Pools should always be sheltered from prevailing winds for comfort and to prevent debris from being blown into the water. You may need to put up a screening wall or fence, or plant a hedge at least around the sunbathing area, though this will increase the overall cost. In areas of persistent high winds a pierced screen wall and hedge would together be better than a solid wall.

A pool sited near the house will benefit from its shelter and from the accessibility of water and electricity supplies and drainage systems. Children playing will be easily visible, especially if the shallow or paddling area faces the windows. But if you live in a place where winters are cold, do not forget how forlorn a pool looks under grey skies, even with its cover installed. If children's safety is not a factor, you may prefer to position your pool somewhere out of sight, or screen it off with trees or shrubs.

Selecting a pool
Swimming pools can be either free-standing or sunk into the ground. Free-standing pools need very little excavation other than levelling. Usually made of a metal or timber framework supporting a plastic liner, they are often supplied in kit form and may be installed by an amateur with a little assistance in just a few days. The advantages are obvious: They provide an almost instant pool at relatively low cost.

But they are difficult to integrate into a garden design, for the side structures are always visible. These can be banked up with soil or screened with plants, but this is rarely very successful. They are most attractive when used on a sloping site where changes in level can be used to effect; a pool half in and half out of the ground can be very appealing if carefully landscaped.

The traditional sunken pool is easily landscaped and can be quite beautiful, but because

of the enormous amount of excavation necessary is costly to install. It is not advisable for an amateur to attempt to build such a pool unaided. Even the simplest (and cheapest) types, using plastic liners, require careful excavation and the sides have to be well supported with a compacted soil backfilling. This will require at least the advice, if not the assistance, of a professional.

A concrete floor may be required to provide the base for a supporting framework of concrete blocks, and this must be professionally laid or the entire structure may later crack. In one technique, concrete is shot from a special gun into and over shaped steel reinforcing mesh, and the hard-packed technique, of using dry concrete to build up the walls, can only be carried out by skilled operators. A concrete pool should be finished attractively, and for this polished composite stone or marble pastes, glazed tiles (the most expensive) or paint (the cheapest) can be used.

On the whole a concrete pool, if properly constructed, will be the most expensive type. Cheaper materials include glass-fibre, which, like concrete, can be applied on site to the sides of the excavation, or can be installed as a preformed shell, and aluminium and steel which are assembled on site by an engineer. All preformed shell systems need extremely accurate excavation, but are ideal for use on problem sites such as the side or top of a hill.

Pools vary a great deal in cross-sectional shape. Some are an equal depth all over, while others have a shallow end for beginners and increase in depth to a section for diving. Some have a paddling section for children, but to prevent accidents this should be blocked off from the main swimming area. Before installing a diving board, make sure that the pool is deep and wide enough, or accidents are bound to occur. A springboard at 1 m (3¼ ft) above water-level needs at least 3 m (10 ft) depth of water, and there should be 5.3 m (17½ ft) of water surface forward from the board. A fixed board is safe with slightly shallower water.

Auxiliary equipment
Besides the pool itself, there are many available 'extras' – some necessary and others less so. Choose with care, for they can easily double the overall cost. A filter is essential, and some kind of system, such as an overflow channel to clear floating debris, is usually included in the pool design. Pumped filters using sand or other material will remove fine particles suspended in the water and debris lying on the pool floor. Some filtration systems have skimmers that clean the water surface or a 'vacuum cleaner' attachment to use on the bottom.

A comfortable water temperature for swimming is at least 18°C (64°F) and preferably 21 to 24°C (70 to 75°F), so heating is useful in cool climates. Systems include gas, electricity, oil and solar heating, and the installation cost is second only to that of the filtration unit. (It may be worth checking with a heating engineer whether one system can heat both the house and the pool.) Unfortunately, heating will add considerably to the

Types of lighting
Decorative garden lanterns 1, to illuminate dark corners or accent plants, come in various designs, but use a wide-beam fitting 2, as high or low as necessary, to light gateways, drives, paths or steps. Spotlights 3 can highlight a statue or plant, but several light sources are used to give depth to a tree or shrub group in contour lighting 4. Floodlighting 5 is effective for large areas such as patios, but the light is softer if reflected. It can be installed under water to light a pool. For silhouette effects 6, light a wall behind the object to be shown up. In etched lighting 7, a broad beam is aimed to skim along the surface of an object to emphasize its texture.

cost of running the pool, but special pool covers will help to conserve heat. In the interests of economy, site the heating and filtration units as near to the deep end of the pool as possible. Normally they are housed in a separate building, and if large enough this can also include a changing room.

Other accessories include such essentials as steps or stairs, safety equipment such as rings, hooks and floating pool alarms, underwater lighting (which must be installed with the pool), and water games equipment, diving boards and slides. Other essentials that will need to be bought regularly are water-purifying chemicals – chlorine and algicides.

Landscaping the pool

It can be very upsetting to see new and expensive deckwork slowly sink or crack at the pool edge as the soil originally used as backfill begins to settle. Apart from the unsightliness, uneven decking can mean a very real danger of someone tripping and falling – perhaps into the pool! To overcome this problem special reinforced paving units can be fitted which are supposed to resist subsidence, but it is more important to ensure that the pool surround is properly laid over a well-consolidated base.

Much depends on the thoroughness of the backfill consolidation.

Most paving materials are suitable for decking – tiles, exposed aggregate concrete, stone or concrete slabs, and wood. The paving should provide a good walking surface, particularly when wet, so avoid smooth, shiny surfaces. The paving should slope away from the pool so that dust and leaves are not washed into it by rainfall. When choosing materials make sure that the colours complement the large, uninterrupted expanse of (usually blue) water. The decking can be extended to form a sunbathing area equipped with suitable furniture.

Small trees, shrubs, ornamental grasses and flowers – all growing in containers – add a luxurious and slightly exotic air to a swimming pool, but position (or move) them far enough away that leaves do not scatter on the water in autumn. These plants can serve as a bridge to integrate the pool and its windbreak plantings into the rest of the garden.

Installing a barbecue

Portable barbecues are so readily available that an adequate area of hardstanding – perhaps of engineering bricks – is all that is

really necessary. But a barbecue can be designed as an integral part of the shelter wall around a patio or pool – an ideal place for it. Elsewhere in the garden, a sheltered place should be found; an excavated barbecue pit makes an interesting feature.

A barbecue can be built as small or large as required. A cooking surface 30 by 50 cm (12 by 20 in) is adequate, but it is worth making it bigger if you plan to hold barbecue parties. Fireproof bricks make a good base, and the walls (on three sides only) should be built of similar bricks or of walling stone. Set the grill (which must be rigid) about 15 cm (6 in) clear of the fire. If it rests on projecting bricks it can be removed for cleaning. The wall should extend a few courses above the grill to protect the cooking area from draughts.

Lighting the garden

Unless you use a low-voltage system with an indoor transformer giving a supply at 12 volts, the installation of outdoor lighting is strictly a job for a professional electrician. Special armoured cable and waterproof fittings must be used, and this is particularly important with underwater lighting in a swimming pool. This and patio lighting need to be bright to be useful, so have to run at mains voltage.

Low-voltage systems are sold in kits. The transformer may be plugged into the main house supply and light fittings on spikes simply stuck into soft ground. The cable needs only to be hidden among shrubs and flowers or buried shallowly – but make sure you know where it is when digging. Such lighting can be used to balance floodlighting or to subtly illuminate other parts of the garden.

When working out a lighting scheme, divide your garden plan into sections – entryway, paths and steps, patio and lawn, water features, ornaments, specimen plants and so on – and work out a way of illuminating each area and feature. Try out alternative arrangements and intensity levels until you get the effect you want before finalizing the installation.

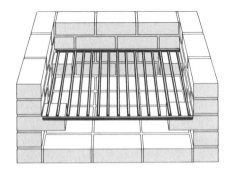

left A free-standing barbecue can make an ornamental as well as a functional feature for the patio. above A simple version can easily be built with fireproof bricks and a metal grille.

Making a lawn

A well-kept lawn is at once beautiful – swirling in a rich carpet of green between beds and borders, setting off the colours of flowers to perfection – and utilitarian, providing an all-encompassing playing, lounging and walking surface. It is no wonder that most gardens include a lawn of some kind, and in many it is the major feature.

Grasses grow almost everywhere, but there is all the difference in the world between a 'patch of grass' and a beautiful sward. The latter needs as much care and attention as any other garden feature. Though it is perfectly feasible to cultivate wild grass growing on the site, in many cases the best solution is to start from scratch and create a new lawn. There are three ways of doing this: by laying ready-grown turf, by planting tufts of creeping grass, and by sowing grass seed. In each case, however, site preparation is the most important part of the job.

Preparing a lawn site
The aim of the initial work is to make a level (or evenly sloping), well-cultivated area of fertile, weed-free soil with a light, crumbly surface. This is just as important when using turves – to encourage the grass roots to grow through and bind them to the underlying soil – as when sowing seed or planting grass plants. If your garden is attached to a newly-built house, therefore, the first priority is to remove any builder's rubble and excavated subsoil. If much soil movement is then necessary for levelling, remove the topsoil first, level the subsoil, let it settle thoroughly, and then replace the topsoil evenly all over.

If the site contains many difficult weeds, such as convolvulus, couch grass, docks and nettles, eliminate these with herbicides before starting to cultivate the soil. Do not use any weedkiller (such as simazine) that will leave harmful residues in the soil. The best type to use is a non-selective one such as paraquat that is inactivated by the soil and works only through leaves (see p 356).

If turf is to be laid, no additional weedkilling should be necessary, though you should remove all weed roots, dead or alive, when cultivating. If seed is to be sown or grass tufts are to be planted, you can save trouble later on by waiting a few weeks for weed seeds to germinate, and then killing the seedlings with a non-persistent herbicide before sowing or planting the grass.

Except where site grass is being used, lawn sites should always be well cultivated by digging, forking or rotovating. Aim to break up the soil to a depth of at least 20 cm (8 in). Remove stones from the surface only, and rake this to leave a well-graded, crumbly surface. A week or so before sowing, planting or turfing, rake in a proprietary lawn fertilizer at the rate advised by the maker.

Making a lawn with turves
This is usually the most expensive method, and unless the turf has been specially grown for lawn-making, it may contain coarse grasses and many weeds, so inspect before buying if possible. Turves cut in the traditional way – in strips 1 m by 30 cm by 4 cm (3 ft by 1 ft by 1½ in) – are heavy and slow to lay. But turf can also be obtained in long, thin carpet-like rolls 75 cm (2½ ft) wide, which are much lighter and quicker to use. A turf lawn can generally be used in a month or so.

Provided rainfall is adequate, or the lawn can be well watered until established, you can lay turf at any time of the year when the soil is not frozen or waterlogged, but spring and autumn are usually the most favourable seasons. Lay turves cut in narrow strips lengthwise in straight staggered rows. Give the new lawn its first cutting when the grass is growing and is 4 to 5 cm (1½ to 2 in) high.

Making a lawn with grass plants
This method is used mainly where it is difficult to get grass to establish readily from seed, such as in hot climates or on steep banks. Very creeping species, such as creeping bent or (in hot regions) Bermuda grass, must be used, and these are not always ideal lawn grasses. They are unsuitable for close mowing, but can make excellent lawns cut at 2 to 2.5 cm (¾ to 1 in) or even more above soil level. They take several months to create a usable lawn.

Since creeping grasses vary greatly in character (even among forms of one species), it is important to obtain one of known lawn-making quality. Spring is usually the best season for planting. Plant tufts about 20 cm (8 in) apart all over the site. Keep well watered in dry weather. It may be a few weeks before the plants begin to spread and two or three months before there is complete cover. Do not mow until this is achieved, and then never so closely as to expose the surface roots.

Making a lawn with seed
Sowing grass seed gives the gardener the opportunity to select grasses to suit the soil and situation and the purpose for which the lawn is required. For example, fine grasses can be chosen for a very smooth surface, hard-wearing grasses for rough use, shade- or moisture-loving grasses where appropriate.

Types of grasses
No one grass species is ideal for all uses. Upright, tufted types, such as most fescues 1, make springy turf but do not spread quickly. Bents 2 grow outwards and then up, but if encouraged to grow closely by frequent watering, feeding and cutting they make fine, close turf. Creeping grasses, such as Kentucky bluegrass 3, have horizontal rhizomes or stolons and spread to form strong turf. Rye grass 4 is short-lived and coarse, but quick-growing and cheap. Timothy sprawls, and is best used for sports fields. Grasses also vary in shade tolerance, but none will thrive in deep shade. Lawn seed generally contains a mixture to combine good features, and also to ensure that at least one component will thrive in the varied conditions found in parts of one lawn. Finally, a disease that strikes one species of a mixture will not destroy the whole lawn.

In most cases, a mixture of species with complementary characteristics is best, and ready-formulated blends are available to suit most situations; the table with this article will enable you to predict results. Lawns made from seeds are unlikely to be usable in under three months, though they may have a good appearance in as little as one month.

The best seasons for sowing are spring and early autumn, but you can sow grass seed at any time when the soil temperature is high enough for germination – about 10°C (50°F) – provided there is also enough natural moisture or the seed-bed and lawn can be kept adequately watered. Seeding rates vary from about 15 to 70 g/m² (½ to 2 oz/sq yd) according to the species used and how quickly complete cover is required.

Spread seed evenly over the prepared site, scattering it by hand or putting it through a fertilizer distributor adjusted for the right rate of flow. When hand-sowing, it is best to mark out the site in metre- or yard-wide strips or squares, each to be sown individually with a measured quantity of seed. Cover the seed by raking lightly or by scattering sifted soil over the site. Most commercial grass seed is treated with bird-repellent, but you can protect it with black cotton criss-crossed between pegs about 5 cm (2 in) above the surface.

Sown grass should be cut when about 4 cm (1½ in) high, preferably the first time with a sickle, rotary grass-cutter or shears. A cylinder mower, unless very sharp and well-adjusted, may drag out some of the seedlings. It helps to roll lightly a day before mowing. Mowing will eliminate annual weeds that germinate with the grass. Others can be killed with special selective weedkillers developed for seedling grass, but do not use ordinary

Laying turves
Kneeling on a plank laid on turves that are already in position, unroll each turf and push it firmly against its neighbour. Beat it down lightly onto the prepared site with the back of a spade. Stagger each row so that the joints between turves do not fall opposite each other. Trim the edges with a half-moon tool after laying. Complete the operation by scattering a mixture of equal parts of fine sifted soil and finely milled damp peat along the joints between the turves. Brush this in lightly with a broom. Roll lightly a few days after laying, and keep well watered until established.

selective lawn weedkillers until the grass is well established.

Improving site grass
Cultivating the grass growing naturally on the site is the cheapest method initially, though not necessarily in the long term. It has the merit that if the grass has survived for a considerable time on the site it is likely to be composed of species suited to the soil and situation. A lawn made in this way can be used from the outset.

Little or no turf or soil disturbance will be necessary unless the site is very uneven. Then the quickest way to get a good effect will be to lift all the turf with a spade or, preferably, a turfing iron; stack it carefully to one side and then dig and level the exposed soil. The turf can then be relaid. In many cases, you will be able to restrict lifting and relaying to a few small areas.

Whether lifted and relaid or left undisturbed, the treatment to improve the quality of the turf is the same, and will take many months. Regular, frequent mowing at about 2 cm (¾ in) above soil level (higher in hot climates or hot weather) will gradually eliminate some weeds and coarse grasses. Weed-clearance can be hastened by application of selective lawn weedkillers. Feeding with a lawn fertilizer (fairly high nitrogen in spring and summer; low nitrogen, high phosphate, medium potash in autumn; see p 352) will improve the growth and quality of the turf.

Top dressing with finely milled peat – and, on heavy, poorly-drained soil, sharp sand – will improve soil texture, especially if combined with slitting or spiking, for which special tools are available. If patches of coarse grass prove persistent they should be lifted and replaced with good turf. For further information, see page 86.

Recommended lawn grasses

	Name	Soil	Situation	Characteristics
For wet, mild climates	*Agrostis canina* (velvet bent)	Moist moist	Open	Narrow leaves; spreading; thick; fine-textured
	A. canina montana (brown bent)	Moist moist	Open	Narrow leaves; spreading; thick; fine-textured
	A. stolonifera (creeping bent)	Most moist	Open; semi-shady	Leaves vary, usually narrow; very spreading; thick; fine-textured
	A. tenuis (browntop bent; colonial bent)	Most moist	Open	Narrow leaves; fairly spreading; forms clumps; fine-textured
For cool climates	*Cynosorus cristatus* (crested dog's-tail)	Poor, chalky	Open	Fairly broad leaves; slightly tufted; wiry flower stems; hard-wearing
	Deschampsia flexuosa (wavy hairgrass)	Acid	Open; shady	Narrow leaves; tufted
	Festuca ovina vulgaris (sheep's fescue)	Porous, acid	Open	Tough, needle-like leaves; tufted; fairly drought-resistant
	F. rubra (red fescue)	Porous, acid	Open	Tough, needle-like leaves; fairly spreading; fairly drought-resistant
	F. rubra fallax (Chewing's fescue)	Porous, acid	Open	Tough, needle-like leaves; tufted; fairly drought-resistant
	F. rubra genuina (creeping red fescue)	Porous, acid	Open	Tough, needle-like leaves; slightly spreading; fairly drought-resistant
	Lolium perenne (perennial rye grass)	Most	Open	Broad leaves; erect; wiry flower stems; fast-growing; short-lived
	Phleum pratense (Timothy; cat's-tail)	Most, even heavy clay	Open	Broad, soft leaves; semi-decumbent; recovers well after wear
	Poa compressa (Canadian bluegrass)	Most	Open; shady	Fine leaves; spreading; tough; withstands extreme cold
	P. pratensis (smooth-stalked meadow grass; Kentucky bluegrass)	Most	Open	Broad leaves; spreading; fine-textured; drought-resistant
	P. trivialis (rough-stalked meadow grass)	Most moist	Shady	Broad leaves; spreading; not wear-resistant; withstands cold well
For hot climates	*Axonopus affinis* (carpet grass)	Most	Open; semi-shady	Coarse leaves; spreading; herbaceous (brown in winter)
	Cynodon dactylon (Bermuda grass)	Most	Open	Fine leaves; very spreading; dense; herbaceous; salt-tolerant
	Eremochloa ophiuroides (centipede grass)	Acid	Open	Rather coarse leaves; spreading; slow-growing; herbaceous
	Lolium multiflorum (annual rye grass)	Most	Open	Coarse; very fast-growing; used to overseed herbaceous lawns for winter
	Stenotaphrum secundatum (St Augustin grass)	Moist, neutral	Open; shady	Coarse; very spreading; herbaceous in cold; salt-tolerant
	Zoysia japonica (Japanese lawn grass)	Most	Open; shady	Rather coarse leaves; spreading; herbaceous; salt-tolerant
For arid climates	*Bouteloua gracilis* (blue grama)	Most	Full sun	Small leaves; tufted; spreading; dormant (brown) in hot, dry weather
	Buchloë dactyloides (buffalo grass)	Most dry	Full sun	Narrow leaves; creeping; dormant (brown) in hot summers; slow-growing

Lawn care and maintenance

A lawn needs care and attention to thrive, but it will then reward its keeper with a beautiful and smooth, strong, dense and springy surface. The most time-consuming operation is mowing, which is really a kind of continual pruning that promotes strong, dense growth and discourages tall-growing grasses and many weeds. But equally important are feeding, watering, aeration and the treatment of pests, diseases and persistent weeds. Most lawns are composed of a mixture of grass species or varieties that are constantly altering their proportions one to another, and this natural fluctuation in population will be affected by management.

Mowing and trimming

Frequent – though not necessarily close – mowing is the first key to producing and maintaining a beautiful lawn. It is necessary throughout the period of growth, usually from early spring to mid-autumn, with possibly one or two further light cuts – or even more in particularly mild conditions – in late autumn and winter. You should also regularly trim the lawn's edges.

Precisely how often and how closely you should cut your grass will depend on climate and season – in warm, moist conditions in late spring it may be necessary two or more times a week – and on the kind of lawn you want and the grasses it contains. A putting green requires far closer, more frequent mowing than grass that is used solely as a foil for other plants. Fine grasses such as the fescues and some bents should be mown more closely than coarser grasses such as perennial rye, meadow grass (Kentucky blue) and crested dog's-tail.

Very close mowing weakens the turf, and under no circumstances should you mow closer than 6 mm (¼ in) to the soil. Cut the coarser grasses no closer than 12 mm (½ in) and for general ornamental purposes 2 to 2.5 cm (¾ to 1 in) is sufficient. Leave the grass longer in dry or hot conditions, and generally cut warm-climate grasses such as Bermuda grass to 3 to 4 cm (1¼ to 1½ in) or even more.

Most lawn-mowers are of either the cylinder (reel) or rotary type. Both must have sharp blades, or the grass will be bruised and torn, and the former must be kept properly adjusted. Do not mow when the grass is wet, particularly with a cylinder machine. When mowing in parallel strips, carry out alternate mowings at right-angles if possible, to avoid forming ridges. Even with a long, narrow lawn, perform at least occasional mowings cross-wise or on the diagonal. In general, it is best to remove lawn clippings as these look unsightly and may spread weeds and diseases. However, a light covering of weed-free cuttings will act as a mulch in hot weather, protecting the grass roots from the sun and conserving soil moisture.

Feeding and top dressing

Like all other plants, grass removes nutrient chemicals from the soil, and unless these are returned – either by letting the lawn clippings lie and rot, or by feeding with chemicals or other top-dressings – the grass will eventually starve. Fertilizer must be spread evenly; mix concentrated chemicals with sand, and water in if it does not rain within a day or two. Branded lawn fertilizers are available, but are not essential.

For spring and summer feeding, use readily soluble, quick-acting chemicals and apply every six to eight weeks, except in drought conditions. As a rule, use a compound fertilizer containing roughly equal percentages of nitrogen, phosphate and potash (see p 352). For an analysis of 7:7:7, the rate of application should be about 70 g/m² (2 oz/sq yd), but with branded fertilizers follow the maker's instructions. In late summer or early autumn, use slower-acting chemicals, with a low proportion of nitrogen, fairly high phosphate and medium potash. This will promote strong root growth during the autumn. One application, according to label instructions, is generally sufficient; with an analysis of about 3:12:6, apply 70 g/m² (2 oz/sq yd).

The humus content of the soil may also become impoverished, causing loss of soil texture, poor bacterial and fungal activity, and slow breakdown of complex chemicals into the simple salts that feed grass. Humus is most readily replaced as finely-milled peat. Spread this thinly over the surface, preferably in spring and autumn after spiking (see below), and work it down into the turf with a broom or the back of a rake. Never apply so much that some of the grass is completely covered. Heavy soils benefit from a dressing of coarse sand mixed with the peat and similarly applied after aerating.

Watering

In spring and summer, grass needs a lot of water which in many places will not be supplied by natural rainfall. Some watering will be needed both to meet this requirement and to dissolve chemical fertilizers, which are only useful in solution. However, in persistently dry regions, special drought-resistant grasses are generally grown (see p 85), and these may suffer from fungus diseases if they receive too much water.

The ideal watering system is one that simulates rainfall, delivering a fine spray at the rate of 1 cm (½ in) or less per hour, so that it has time to soak into the soil and not run uselessly off the surface. At least 1 cm (½ in) of water is likely to be necessary at each watering, but frequency of watering will vary greatly according to soil and weather. If possible, do not allow grass to become so dry in spring and summer that growth stops and it turns yellow.

Aeration and scarifying

Grass roots need air, and may suffer if the soil becomes very hard or if a thick mat (or thatch) of dead grass and grass roots forms under the sward. Such a mat can also prevent water

Types of lawn-mower

1 Cylinder (reel) mowers may be powered by hand, petrol engine or electricity (mains or battery). Amateur models range in cutting width from 30 to 60 cm (12 to 24 in) or more. In general, the bigger your lawn the more worthwhile it is to buy a big mower. With a battery-powered model, make sure that you can cut your whole lawn on one charge.

Usually, the wheels and blades are geared together, thus fixing the number of cuts per metre or yard. Low-geared mowers (about 25 cuts per metre) are generally cheap, light to push and useful for rough cutting because they do not clog easily. The highest gearing (about 140 cuts per metre) gives the smoothest surface but needs much more power, clogs easily, and is necessary only for sports greens. A good compromise for garden use is about 45 cuts per metre (40 per yard) if hand-propelled and 80 per metre (72 per yard) if powered.

2 Rotary machines that have whirling horizontal blades do not produce such a smooth cut as the cylinder type, but are more versatile and easier to use. They can be adjusted to cut grass of any length, wet or dry, and can be powered by petrol or electricity, with or without the wheels also being driven. 3 Other rotary mowers support themselves on a cushion of air rather than running on wheels. This type is particularly useful for cutting grass on banks, since it can be swung along from the top, if necessary on a rope. The main

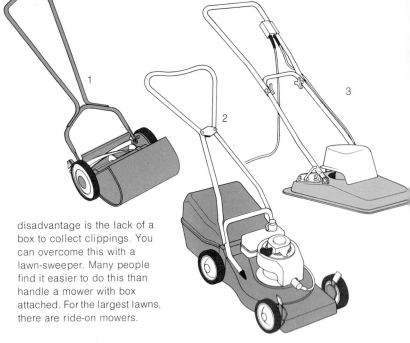

disadvantage is the lack of a box to collect clippings. You can overcome this with a lawn-sweeper. Many people find it easier to do this than handle a mower with box attached. For the largest lawns, there are ride-on mowers.

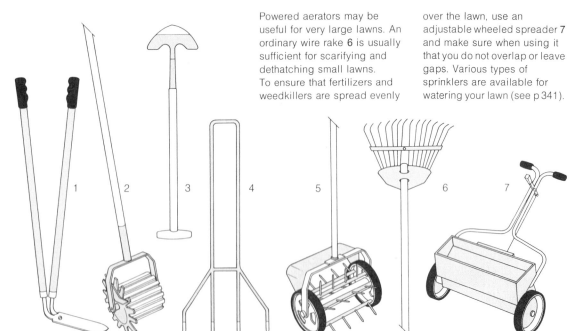

reaching the roots. You should rectify these faults by perforating or slitting the turf and by scarifying (vigorously raking the surface); severe cases of matting may need treatment with a power rake. Carry out these treatments whenever necessary, but it is generally most convenient to do them in late summer or early autumn, just before the late feeding and top dressing.

At its simplest, perforation consists of pushing an ordinary garden fork 5 to 8 cm (2 to 3 in) into the turf and levering it slightly backwards. Do this every 10 to 15 cm (4 to 6 in). For quicker, more effective results, use one of the many lawn spiking tools available. The best types have hollow tines that remove thin cores of soil; brush up the cores and add them to the compost heap. Tools are also available to slit the turf, cutting through the mat of dead material so that you can rake it out. Power rakes and dethatchers will do this job in one operation, and may be hired.

Dealing with weeds

Numerous herbicides are available that are relatively harmless to grass but will kill a wide range of weeds commonly found in lawns. They include 2,4-D, MCPA, mecoprop and dicamba. No one chemical will control all weeds, however, so manufacturers often prepare mixtures of two or more herbicides. It is wise to ring the changes, since what one misses another may kill. Even so, tap-rooted weeds such as dandelions may need to be dug up by hand.

You can use selective lawn weedkillers at any time from spring to early autumn, but they are most effective when weeds are growing fast in spring and early summer. Do not use in very dry or very wet conditions. For best results, apply a lawn fertilizer about a week beforehand; this is better than using a combined fertilizer-weedkiller. Always follow the maker's instructions, and apply on a windless day, taking care not to let the weed-

Levelling dips and bumps
Smooth out minor hollows over a period of several years by top dressing with a sifted mixture of loam, very well-rotted farmyard manure or other organic material and sharp sand. Spread the mixture thinly so as not to smother the grass, and work it in with a broom or heavy sack dragged across the area. The best time for this treatment is early autumn, after raking and aerating.
To eliminate mounds and deeper hollows, **1** cut the turf with an edging tool into 30 cm (12 in) strips. **2** Using a turfing iron or spade, roll back the strips. Then add or remove soil to the correct level, firm down and replace the turves. **3** Brush a mixture of sifted soil and fine peat into the cracks.

killer drift or splash onto border plants or shrubs. A sprinkler bar attached to an ordinary watering can will give quick, even coverage. One all-over application in spring should be enough, followed by spot treatment of individual weeds and weed colonies. Do not cut the grass for at least three days after applying weedkiller, and allow the clippings to rot for at least six months before using them as compost.

Moss may be a problem in very wet or shaded lawns, or where aeration is needed or mowing is too short. Mercurized lawn sand (which also contains fertilizer) is the best chemical cure, followed by raking out of the dead moss and reseeding with grass seed. You should also correct the causes mentioned above. Where moss results from poor soil fertility, treatment with lawn sand (see p 393) – if necessary followed by reseeding – may be enough. Never rake out live moss, or you will spread the spores to other parts of the lawn.

Pests and diseases

As a rule, these do not present a serious problem on home lawns. Most diseases caused by fungi can be controlled with mercurized lawn sand, which also kills moss. Lawn fungicides are also available. Soil pests such as leatherjackets (tipula larve), cutworms (caterpillars),

wireworms (agriotes larvae) and chafer grubs can be killed by watering the turf with an insecticide such as BHC, diazinon, trichlorphon or carbaryl.

Earthworms are normally friends, not foes, but in excess can foul lawns with their casts, which may also kill small patches of grass. You can remove casts by brushing or raking, and excess worms can either be driven to the surface by top dressing with mowrah meal (if obtainable), followed by heavy watering, or destroyed underground with a worm-killer such as chlordane applied according to the maker's instructions.

Overseeding

A regular maintenance task that faces gardeners who want a year-round green lawn in warm climates (such as the southern United States) is overseeding. In these parts, the usual lawn grasses die down and turn brown when cool winter weather comes. To maintain a green lawn through the winter, seed of a quick-growing annual grass (usually annual rye grass; see p 85) may be sown over the lawn in autumn. The normal rate is about 25 g/m^2 (¾ oz/sq yd). The grass germinates and grows in a few weeks, to be overtaken by the permanent grasses when the warm weather of spring comes.

Other lawn equipment
Unless it has a paved or similar surround, the edges of your lawn will need regular trimming to keep them tidy. The most widely used edge-trimmers are like shears with long handles **1**. When buying, make sure that you can use them without uncomfortable stooping; the best type have the blades cranked at an angle. Rotary edge-trimmers **2** simply need to be pushed along the verge; electric versions are also available. You will occasionally need to use a half-moon edge-cutter **3** to cut the edge back to a firm line.
Aerators include simple fork-like devices **4** and rotary spikers **5**. For best results, particularly on heavy soils, choose one with hollow tines rather than solid spikes.

Powered aerators may be useful for very large lawns. An ordinary wire rake **6** is usually sufficient for scarifying and dethatching small lawns.
To ensure that fertilizers and weedkillers are spread evenly over the lawn, use an adjustable wheeled spreader **7** and make sure when using it that you do not overlap or leave gaps. Various types of sprinklers are available for watering your lawn (see p 341).

Trees for many purposes

Trees are the vital element in the design of gardens. They make, frame and often end vistas and glades. They form large-scale features like clumps and avenues, as well as smaller features and focal points. And they act as general background and, when evergreen, backbone and winter features of the whole garden design.

Trees add the dimension of height, as well as variety of form, texture, foliage, flower, fruit, bark and autumn colours. Few gardens are too small for one or two diminutive trees. Although a handy definition of a tree is a plant capable of a height of 6 m (20 ft) or more on a single, woody stem, there is, in practice, a complete gradation in heights at maturity from dwarf conifers and willows less than 1 m (3 ft) tall to conifers 55 m (180 ft) and broad-leaved trees 40 m (130 ft) tall. There are thus tree species and cultivars available to suit any scale of planting.

Trees for shelter
New gardens are often bleak and exposed. Expensive large trees, guyed and staked to prevent them toppling over, are all too often seen struggling to survive in conditions like these, where only a few robust species can succeed. It is much better to plant groups and belts of small, cheap, dispensable trees; in two or three years, these will give shelter in which the desired trees can thrive. Birch, willow and larch, costing very little if obtained two years old and 1 m (3 ft) tall, will soon give a clothed appearance. They will grow 1 m (3 ft) a year, creating the woodland conditions in air and soil that more choice trees require. Later they can be gradually removed, or just a few of the more shapely specimens retained.

Most shrubs require the same help in becoming established, and some woodland plants of all kinds need the high shade provided by lightly crowned trees – such as larch and birch – for protection against both sharp late frosts and strong sunshine. The shelter of trees is particularly important in windy coastal sites. Against strong sea winds, the bishop pine (*Pinus muricata*) is even better than the commonly used Monterey pine (*P. radiata*) and holm oak (*Quercus ilex*). Other suitable deciduous trees include the sycamore (*Acer pseudo-platanus*) and the white poplar (*Populus alba*). In smoky air the European sycamore and its semi-dwarf colourful form 'Brilliantissimum' thrive, as will the locust tree (*Robinia pseudoacacia*; also called the common acacia or false acacia), the bean tree (*Catalpa* spp), the foxglove or princess tree (*Paulownia tomentosa*), the unusual late-flowering *Euodia hupehensis,* the attractive keaki of Japan (*Zelkova serrata*) and the unique, primitive ginkgo.

Trees as focal points
A focal point – or an eye-catcher to divert attention from an ugly feature – can be made with a single tree of striking aspect or with a group of columnar trees. The latter can be uniform in kind, or of highly contrasted colours – such as bright yellow and silvery-blue Lawson cypress (*Chamaecyparis lawsoniana*)

cultivars. Depending on the size of the garden and its planting, focal-point trees can be on any scale from dwarfs to giant sequoias or cedars of Lebanon (*Cedrus libani*) well over 30 m (100 ft) tall.

The tree for the site
Before a tree can be chosen for a site, you should decide, first, exactly what the tree is required to do, and then what limitations of choice are enforced by the site itself. Ultimate size is a vital factor that is often neglected, leading to endless trouble. Shading of windows or neighbours' gardens is to be avoided, and on clay soils a house within 30 m (100 ft)

will preclude the planting of poplars, willows or ash because of possible damage to foundations from roots shrinking the soil during droughts. Where other trees already grow, inspect the site in summer, as the degree of shade cannot be appreciated in winter, and few trees of interest can grow in any but the lightest overhead shade.

Dry sandy soils are unsuited to many trees, and soils dried by the roots of big trees are unsuited to any. Poorly-drained soils liable to hold water in winter restrict planting to com-

mon alder (*Alnus glutinosa*), the swamp cypress (*Taxodium distichum*), the American arbor-vitae (*Thuja occidentalis*) and some willows. But if less severely impeded, such soils may grow good spruce, oaks, hornbeams, poplars, wing-nuts (*Pterocarya* spp) and many other trees. Shallow soils over chalk and limestone have their well-known restrictions (see p 331), but grow a good range of trees.

Regional and local climates affect the choice of less usual trees rather than those like birch, oak, ash and beech, which thrive in a wide range of conditions. Cool, damp, maritime areas – on west coasts in the northern hemisphere – favour most conifers. In extremely mild areas, such as Ireland and western Scotland, evergreens from the southern hemisphere and China thrive, when they cannot grow at all in more continental climates – even in other parts of the British Isles. Many fine trees from the eastern United States, however, do not need mild maritime winters but do require hot summers. Catalpas, hickories (*Carya* spp), scarlet and pin oaks (*Quercus coccinea* and *Q. palustris* respectively), the black walnut (*Juglans nigra*) and sassafras, for example – all from North America – and many trees from northern China, such as the tree of heaven (*Ailanthus altissima*) and the golden rain tree (*Koelreuteria paniculata*), will reach large size and flower well only in regions with less maritime climates. Local frost-pockets can reduce possible sites for some species to the upper slopes (see p 339), but broad rules on hardiness are worthless, for many warm corners harbour trees that should not be there at all.

Where few can be planted, each tree should combine several good points. Examples of good all-rounders include the paperbark maple, *Acer griseum*, with attractive bark, foliage, flowers and autumn colour; the madrona, *Arbutus menziesii* (bark, flowers, fruit and year-round foliage); and the Chinese privet, *Ligustrum lucidum* (glossy year-round foliage and a long season of highly fragrant flowers). For descriptions of some of the best garden trees, see pages 136 to 141.

Buying and planting

The prime needs in buying a tree are health, vigour and shape, all shown critically by the leading shoot. This central shoot must be dominant and straight, long and strong, as future growth and shape depend on it. Trees without a good leader are worthless in conifers and little better in others.

For best survival after planting, and the most rapid, shapely growth into a sturdy large tree, the smallest vigorous (and therefore very

left Conifers are among the best trees for background and screening, with their subtle variations of colour and texture and interesting shapes. below left Flowering trees such as this Indian horse chestnut (*Aesculus indica*) make splendid focal features, but you should also consider the flowerless appearance. below right For more enduring effect, a less flamboyant tree of highly distinctive form – even a form that is maintained artificially – may be more appropriate. right Just as important as the visual impact of trees is their effect on the garden's microclimate. Silver birches are attractive and fast growing, and create the ideal conditions of dappled shade in which many smaller plants can thrive.

young) plant is essential. Such a tree will generally be two years from seed, and should never need to be staked. Eucalypts are planted out only three months after sowing, when some 20 cm (8 in) tall, and since they should grow at least 2 m (7 ft) in their first year they do often need a stake. Many Japanese cherries and, regrettably, some rowans, whitebeams and others, are top-worked – that is, grafted at 1.5 to 2 m (5 to 7 ft) as standards – and these cannot be obtained until too large for good planting. In areas subject to vandalism only 'heavy' standards or grown-on stock is likely to survive. All such trees need very careful planting, staking and after-care.

The method of planting trees is very similar to that for shrubs (see p 96). The hole must always be wider and deeper than the root system. In heavy soils, break up the bottom and sides of the hole to a depth of at least 15 cm (6 in) and dig in light soil, sand and leaf-mould. In poor, sandy soils, replace the bottom 15 cm (6 in) with pieces of turf (grass side down), garden compost or leaf-mould. Before planting, prepare a planting mixture to fill in around the root-ball of the new tree. It should consist of good loam mixed with organic matter, such as well-rotted manure, garden compost or leaf-mould. Add a handful of bonemeal per tree.

The root ball of very large trees should be left intact, but with smaller trees some of the roots should be brought out and placed in the enriched new soil used to fill the planting hole. This induces stability and prevents the root ball remaining isolated, dry and liable to rock about. The use of peat should be sparing, and it should be well mixed with the other soil or this too may remain dry and prevent new roots from growing out into the new soil.

Trees grown in – and not just sold in – containers can be planted, with plenty of water, at any time. Transplants if deciduous need no moisture (and thus no active roots) between mid-autumn and early spring, so they can be planted at any time during that period when there is no frost. Evergreens of all kinds do use some moisture and need active roots at all times. Roots can still grow in late autumn, so evergreens can be planted then in light soils. Growth of roots ceases from then until spring, so planting must then wait until roots are growing again, in mid-spring. This is, in any case, a better planting time in heavy soils.

Where trees have to be planted in grass, an area around the tree at least 2 m (7 ft) in

diameter should be kept clear. This is where the tree's new feeding roots will be – just a few centimetres down, where grass roots are dense and take the nutrients, especially nitrogen that the tree needs for growth. Where possible, keep this area free of other plants (though a few colourful bulbs or annuals will do no harm), and make it retain moisture by applying a heavy mulch. This can be done with leaf-mould, or with nettles, bracken or other weeds cut from around and heaped up in a circle, making sure that none lie against the bole of the tree, or they will encourage rotting fungi to attack.

Care and pruning

In their first year, trees should be watered copiously in the growing season, from spring to the end of summer, or heavily mulched. Except on already rich, fertile soils, a small dose – up to 100 g (3½ oz) – of a general compound fertilizer (analysis about 7:7:7; see p 352) should be spread carefully around the tree as growth starts in late spring, before rain. Repeat about a month later, in early summer. Where browsing by deer, rabbits or hares is a risk, each tree should be given a sleeve of chicken-wire, securely fixed at the base and protecting the trunk up to 1.5 m (5 ft).

Ornamental trees should not normally need pruning, but twinned leading shoots must be reduced to a single leader. Rarely, an over-strong branch threatens to dominate the leader or to spoil the shape of the crown, and must be cut back to its origin. Trees destined to grow in the open with canopy to the ground will, if planted when very young and small, need to have the bole cleaned of branches for the first metre (3 ft) or so, or these will become a nettle-infested tangle of dead wood as the branches above grow out and shade them. These higher branches will later sweep down to near the ground. Trees planted among shrubs or in a group need their boles cleaned to 2 m (7 ft) as soon as possible, once the tree is 4 to 5 m (13 to 16 ft) tall, before the branches become so stout as to leave a big scar. Such pruning can be done at any time, but the scars smooth over quickest if the cutting is done in early spring. Scars less than 5 cm (2 in) across heal too quickly to need any dressing, but larger ones benefit from a sealant. See also page 369.

Mature trees must usually look after themselves unless dangerous. Otherwise, dead wood is quite natural and is essential for many forms of wildlife. Only large dead branches that are unsightly or dangerous need to be removed. Trees that fork, or have cup-shaped crowns, have an inherent weakness at the point of division. Before senility is apparent these should be braced professionally; a tree-surgeon will do this almost invisibly with eye-bolts and high-tensile wire.

Apart from such special attention, one of the great attractions of well-chosen trees is that, after a few seasons of attention to ensure that they become established, they can be left virtually untouched to grow into their role of providing the major structural and focal features in the garden.

Hedges, screens and windbreaks

Although walls and fences can be quickly constructed, to form permanent boundaries and divisions around and within the garden, hedges and other screens formed by living plants often look more attractive. As a backdrop and foil to more flamboyant displays – whether of roses and other flowering shrubs, or of herbaceous perennials – nothing looks so good as a dense, dark green clipped hedge or the subtly varying tones and textures of screening conifers. Hedges of flowering shrubs allowed to sprawl informally, their branches crowded with blossom or berries, make superb decorative features in their own right, and can be chosen to blend subtly with the garden's other plants.

Hedges perform more utilitarian functions, too. As barriers to noise and pollution they can, if thick and dense, be more effective than walls or fences. An excellent way to reduce road noise is to plant a double hedge, with a space of about 1.5 m (5 ft) between each hedge and the outer lower than the inner. Sound is deadened between the two. An outer hedge plus a screen of trees can also greatly reduce noise and can lessen the force of prevailing winds.

A hedge or a shelter-belt of trees is much more effective as a wind barrier than a solid screen, as it reduces and filters the wind's force rather than causing turbulence, making the garden a much more pleasant place to sit and work in. This is particularly important in windy coastal and elevated districts, and perhaps least so in hot climates, where cooling breezes are welcomed. Many hot regions suffer blustery or stormy winds, however, and here a living barrier that lets some air pass through is just as welcome as in colder climes. And for plants as well as for human occupants, a hedge or windbreak creates an equable microclimate in its lee in which many plants thrive – though you should beware of soil dryness caused by the hedge's roots combined with its rain-shielding effect.

Kinds of hedges and screens

The table with this article gives details of a wide range of deciduous and evergreen plants commonly and not so commonly used for

hedges and taller screens and windbreaks. To make a successful formal hedge, a plant must stand clipping to size and shape without dying back – and preferably not need trimming too frequently. Evergreens or those that keep their dead leaves over winter (such as beech and hornbeam) are best. They should remain clothed with leaves down to ground level, so that they can be trimmed over the years to shape – narrower at the top than the bottom.

There are fewer restrictions with informal hedges, though these should retain their shape – and grow down to the ground – with minimal pruning. Such hedges are more commonly used within a garden than as boundaries. Dwarf hedges of box edging (*Buxus sempervirens* 'Suffruticosa'), lavender or cotton lavender make pleasant frames for beds – particularly in old world cottage gardens and where formal beds are desired. Their use dates back to Elizabethan knot gardens.

When planting a tall screen or windbreak, decide first whether you need evergreens or

Hedges in most gardens are functional, serving as screens (both visual and protective), but they can form attractive features in their own right. An informal flowering hedge is generally more sprawling than one that is clipped into severe formality, but if space is available it can be just as dense and functional. For the best combination of beauty and practicality, choose a species such as *Berberis darwinii* **left**. This has small, glossy, holly-like evergreen leaves, yellow or orange spring flowers and later attractive blue-black berries.

Where space is more limited, charming features can be made with dwarf hedges of box edging **bottom**. These can edge paths and beds, or can form an elaborate knot garden in Elizabethan style. The effect is generally rather formal.

deciduous plantings and whether a slow-growing screen is sufficient or fast-growing species are necessary to obscure tall objects and filter the wind. If the site is exceptionally windblown or is in a coastal area where salt spray may burn foliage, the choice of species will be restricted. If you have room, a double staggered row will make a more effective windbreak than a single row of plants.

There is no harm in planting as closely as your pocket will permit, but the trees should be thinned out before they start growing into one another. As a general rule, plant single rows of broad-leaved species 60 to 90 cm (2 to 3 ft) and conifers 1.5 to 3 m (5 to 10 ft) apart. Where planting double rows, the distances between plants and between rows should be about 0.9 to 1.25 m (3 to 4 ft) and 1.5 to 3 m (5 to 10 ft) respectively. Generally, little pruning is needed, except for some trimming in the early years in the case of broad-leaved evergreens (such as common laurel) and such conifers as Lawson cypress.

A screen of pleached trees

An efficient and attractive way to make a summer screen above a fence or wall – or an avenue in a larger garden – is to plant lime trees that are pleached, or interlaced. Plant the trees 2.5 to 3.5 m (8 to 12 ft) apart. Once they have grown enough, remove all branches up to the top of the wall and train the higher branches horizontally along canes or wires. Tie in the side branches and prune every autumn or winter.

The common European lime (*Tilia* × *vulgaris* or *T. europaea*) can be used, but is prone to aphid infestation, resulting in sticky honeydew falling to the ground. Alternatives are the Caucasian lime (*T.* × *euchlora*) and the hornbeam. Wisteria and ornamental vines can also be pleached.

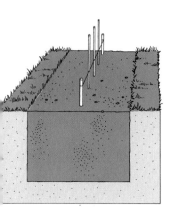

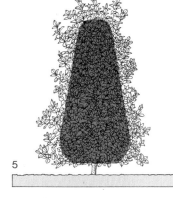

according to species, but 30 to 60 cm (1 to 2 ft) is normal. Space the plants more widely if you want to form a tall screen.

2 Plants less than 60 cm (2 ft) tall transplant best, become established most quickly and generally form a mature hedge more

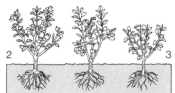

readily than larger specimens. Where possible, plant in autumn or early spring. As a planting mixture, add two handfuls of bonemeal and one of hoof and horn to a bucketful of moist peat. Work the mixture around the root ball when planting. Spread out the roots of bare-rooted deciduous plants, but keep the root

Establishing a hedge

Deep, thorough cultivation is essential, as the hedge will be in position for many years. Double dig a strip of ground 1.25 m (4 ft) wide if possible, incorporating about 50 kg (1 cwt) of well-rotted farmyard manure or garden compost into each 5 to 10 m² (6 to 12 sq yd). Peg out a straight line and insert canes at regular intervals to indicate planting positions. A single row is adequate in most modern gardens unless an exceptionally thick hedge is needed. Planting distance varies

ball of evergreens and all container-grown plants intact. Tread in firmly. Staking is rarely necessary, except on windswept sites or with over-large plants.

3 Prune all except conifers and slow-growing evergreens after planting. With fast growers such as privet, cut back hard to promote bushy growth. With intermediate types such as beech, prune the tips by one-third but trim the sides harder. 4 The following winter, trim the new growth of fast and intermediate growers to a similar extent and shape the sides even of

conifers and slow growers, leaving the top to grow until the desired height is reached.

5 Once established, trim formal hedges two or three times a year, informal ones once (generally after flowering unless berries are wanted). Trim formal hedges to a string between two stakes, tapering towards the top to encourage a dense base. With large-leaved species, use secateurs rather than shears to avoid slicing leaves in half. Feed, water, weed and mulch a hedge well, as with other shrubs.

Plants for hedges and screens

Evergreen formal hedges and screens

Buxus sempervirens (box; FF*; T; WD; C); *Chamaecyparis lawsoniana* (Lawson cypress; some forms CF; ND; C); *Cotoneaster lacteus* (FF; W; C); × *Cupressocyparis leylandii* (Leyland cypress; some forms CF; FG; NA; NS; W; C); *Cupressus macrocarpa* (Monterey cypress; some forms CF; NA; W; C; NH); *Erica* spp (heaths; FF; some forms CF; most NL; C; some NH); *Euonymus japonicus* (FF; CF; W; C; NH); *Griselinia littoralis* (CF; W; C; NH); *Hebe* spp (shrubby veronicas; FF; W; C); *Ilex* spp (hollies; some forms FF; some forms CF); *Laurus nobilis* (sweet bay or bay laurel; AF; C; NH when young); *Ligustrum japonicum* (Japanese privet; W; C; NH); *L. ovalifolium* (oval-leaved privet; some forms CF; deciduous in cold winters; W; C); *Picea abies* (Norway spruce; ND); *Pittosporum tenuifolium* (FF*; C; NH); *Prunus laurocerasus* (common laurel or cherry laurel; FF;); *P. lusitanica* (Portugal laurel; FF; some forms CF); *Quercus ilex* (holm oak; W; C); *Taxus bacata* (yew; T; poisonous; C); *Thuja* spp (arbor-vitae; some forms CF); *Tsuga heterophylla* (western hemlock; NL; NS)

Deciduous formal hedges and screens

Acer campestre (field maple; AC; NA); *Alnus glutinosa* (alder; FF; NA; ND); *Atriplex halimus* (tree purslane; CF; WD; W; C; NH); *Carpinus betulus* (hornbeam; AC; retains old leaves well into winter; FF; WD; W; C); *Corylus avellana* (hazel; FF); *C. maxima* 'Purpurea' (purple hazel; CF); *Cotoneaster* spp (AC; FF; W; C); *Crataegus oxyacantha* (hawthorn; AC; FF; W; C); *Fagus sylvatica* (beech; AC; some forms CF; retains old leaves well into winter; W; C); *Larix decidua* (larch; AC; FF; C); *Ligustrum vulgare* (common privet; some forms CF; FF; often retains old leaves well into

winter; W; C); *Metasequoia glyptostroboides* (dawn redwood; AC; FG; needs frequent trimming); *Prunus cerasifera* (myrobalan plum; some forms CF; FF); *Sambucus nigra* (elder; CF in 'Aurea'; FF)

Evergreen informal hedges and screens

Bamboos (various species; see p 243; some CF; rustling sound; ND); *Berberis* spp (barberries; FF; C); *Escallonia* spp (FF; W; C; some NH); *Mahonia aquifolium* (Oregon grape; AC; FF); *Olearia* spp (daisy bush; FF; W; C; some NH); × *Osmarea burkwoodii* (FF; C); *Pyracantha* spp (FF; C); *Rhododendron ponticum* (common rhododendron; FF; NL; W; C); *Rosmarinus officinalis* (rosemary; AF; FF; C; NH); *Senecio greyi* (CF; FF; WD; W; C); *Viburnum tinus* (laurustinus; FF; W; C)

Deciduous informal hedges and screens

Cornus spp (cornels and dogwoods; AC; CB; FF); *Forsythia* × *intermedia* (FF; C); *Fuchsia magellanica* (FF; W; C; NH); *Hydrangea macrophylla* (AC; FF; W; C); *Hypericum* spp (St John's wort; AC; FF; W; C); *Leycesteria formosa* (Himalayan honeysuckle; FF; W; C); *Philadelphus* spp (mock orange; FF*); *Potentilla fruticosa* (FF); *Rhododendron luteum* (*Azalea pontica* or yellow azalea; AC; FF*; NL); *Ribes sanguineum* (flowering currant; FF; W; C); *Rosa* spp & vars (roses, especially Floribundas and certain shrubs; see p 99) (FF*; C); *Salix caprea* and *S. cinerea* (willows; some CB; CF; FF); *Spiraea* spp (AC; FF); *Syringa* spp (lilac; FF*); *Tamarix* spp (tamarisk; CB; FF; NL; C; W); *Viburnum farreri* (*V. fragrans*; CF; FF*) *V. lantana* (wayfaring tree; FF); *Weigela florida* & hybrids (FF; C)

Windbreaks and/or tall screens

Acer platanoides (Norway maple; D; AC; NA); *A. pseudo-platanus* (sycamore; D; AC; FF; W; C); *Alnus glutinosa* (see above); *Betula pendula* (silver birch; CB; C); *Carpinus betulus* (see above); *Chamaecyparis lawsoniana* (see above); × *Cupressocyparis leylandii* (see above); *Cupressus macrocarpa* (see above); *Eucalyptus* spp (gum trees; E; CF; FG; NL; W; C; some NH); *Fagus sylvatica* (see above); *Fraxinus excelsior* (ash; some forms AC; ND; W; C; do not plant near buildings); *Larix decidua* (see above); *Picea* spp (spruces; E; ND; W); *Pinus* spp (pines; E; some lose lower branches; W; most C); *Populus nigra* 'Italica' (Lombardy poplar; D; W; C; do not plant near buildings); *Prunus laurocerasus* (see above); *Quercus ilex* (see above); *Sorbus* spp (whitebeams and rowans; D; AC; FF; C); *Tilia* × *euchlora* (Caucasian lime; D; FF); *Tsuga heterophylla* (see above); *Viburnum rhytidophyllum* (E; FF)

Dwarf hedges

Berberis spp (some; see above); *Buxus sempervirens* 'Suffruticosa' (box edging; E; WD); *Erica* spp (some; see above); *Lavandula* spp (lavender; E; AF; FF*; C); *Prunus* × 'Cistena' (*P.* 'Crimson Dwarf'; D; AD; CF; FF); *Rosmarinus officinalis* (see above); *Santolina chamaecyparissus* (cotton lavender; E; CF; FF; WD; C)

*Characteristics: AC = autumn colour; AF = aromatic foliage; CB = coloured bark (including silver); CF = colourful foliage (including variegated, silver, gold, etc); D = deciduous; E = evergreen; FF = flowers and/or fruit (including berries, catkins, cones, etc); * = scented; FG = fast-growing; T = suitable for topiary*

Soil needs: Unless otherwise stated, grows on any soil; NA = not acid; ND = not dry or sandy; NL = not limy; NS = not shallow (may be unstable in winds); WD = should be very well-drained
Suitability: C = good for coastal gardens; NH = not hardy in cold areas; W = wind-hardy, for particularly exposed sites

The vertical dimension

There can be few gardens unable to accommodate – and benefit from – one or more climbing plants. Even the apartment dweller with a tiny patio can grow, say, a clematis in a tub, and where space is limited in any way it makes good sense to clothe walls and other vertical structures with colourful climbers. But in larger gardens, too, climbers have abundant uses. These include uses that may be termed positive, where the climbers form decorative features in their own right, as well as negative, where they are used to hide eyesores and convert these into harmonious parts of the garden composition.

The term climber covers a surprisingly wide variety of plants. There are true self-clinging climbers (see p 142) – plants like Virginia creeper with aerial roots that attach their stems to walls, trees or other supports. Others (see p 144) have twining tendrils or stems (like clematis and honeysuckle) or, as in the case of climbing roses (see p 148), hooked thorns so that they can scramble up and through trees, trellis, netting and so on; these last often need tying in to their supports. Climbers include both shrubby types with woody stems that persist over winter (though some tender species may be cut down by frost) and herbaceous perennials that die to the ground in winter but send up new climbing stems each spring. Then there are annual climbers (see p 212) – quick-growing, cheap and ideal for temporary cover or show.

Apart from these true climbing plants, there are others useful for decorating walls and other vertical surfaces. Wall shrubs (see p 170) include both species that are somewhat tender and benefit by being grown against a warm wall, and others that can easily be trained – as fans, espaliers and so on – to cover a wall. Finally, there are trailing plants (see p 236) which, if planted in soil pockets at the top or part-way down a wall, will trail gracefully over its surface. These find particular uses in hanging baskets (see p 116) and dry walls (see p 124).

Climbers on walls and fences

Boundary walls and fences and the walls of buildings are perhaps the most commonly used supports for climbing plants. Unless you choose self-clinging plants, some kind of support, to which the stems can attach or be tied, will be necessary. This can range from simple loops of strong fabric nailed to the wall, through wires strung between vine eyes, to trellis of wood, metal or plastic. If you will later need access to the wall or fence for painting, avoid using self-clinging climbers and choose a form of support – such as the type of plastic trellis sold in panels – that can be easily detached and swung away from the wall while the work is done.

The height of a dividing fence can be increased by fixing trellis at the top. The resulting structure will not make such a dense enclosure as a high fence would. If light climbers, such as jasmine or climbing roses, are grown on the trellis, plenty of light will penetrate into the garden in the gloomy days of winter. Trellis can also be used on its own,

so long as it has stout supports. A chain-link fence – a utilitarian but unattractive form of barrier – makes an excellent support for light-stemmed, low-growing climbers such as ivy and *Euonymus fortunei*. In a few seasons, these will all but obscure the fence, turning it into a 'fedge'.

Other uses of climbers

A wide range of other pre-existing or specially-constructed supports can accom-

Climbers can mask unattractive walls **above** (here supporting *Clematis montana* and *Eccremocarpus scaber*), soften the line of a gateway **below** (a climbing rose) or disguise the bare trunk of a tree **right** (*Euonymus fortunei*).

modate climbing plants. Among the former, trees living or dead make excellent hosts for vigorous climbers to grow and clamber through their branches. A Virginia creeper, for example, growing through a tall specimen of Lawson cypress (*Chamaecyparis lawsoniana*) can be a magnificent sight in autumn when the foliage is a blaze of red. Old apple trees make good hosts for such climbers as clematis, wisteria, honeysuckle or vigorous climbing roses. But be sure that the tree is sound enough to support the climber's weight; with an old tree that is partly rotten, the extra weight and wind resistance can be disastrous.

So long as they are sound, tall tree stumps may similarly be used. Where you want a tall, relatively narrow focal feature, you can install a vertical spruce or larch pole that has some of the branches left on, though cut back to a length of about 15 cm (6 in). These will allow a climber to scramble up the post and hang down in a natural manner. An alternative is to erect three poles in a tripod formation, firmly tying the tops together.

Then there are the more elaborate decorative features commonly erected in gardens specifically to form supports for climbing plants. These include arches and pergolas, and in hot climates serve the additional purpose of providing welcome shade. They may be of wood – rustic or otherwise – or of wood combined with brick or stone. Thick rope may also be looped between vertical pillars. In all cases, adequate strength in relation to the weight of the climbers is again essential. For further information, see page 77.

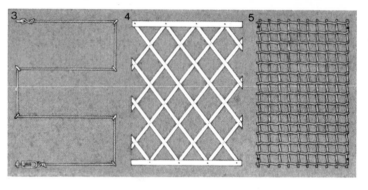

urpose-built supports for climbers
iclude pergolas **above** (here with
asminum officinale) and tripods of
rch poles **above right** (with
lematis 'Jackmanii'). **right** There
re various methods of supporting
on-self-clinging plants on walls.
raditional techniques include
anvas strips **1** looped around the
ems and nailed to the wall and
pecial nails with strips of soft lead
tached **2** that can be bent over the
ems. Strong galvanized or
plastic-coated wires **3** can be strung
horizontally and/or vertically
between vine eyes spaced about
1.8 m (6 ft) apart. Space the wires
about 45 cm (18 in) apart, and tie in
the stems with soft fillis string, raffia
or twist ties. Wooden trellis **4** is an
excellent support for many types
of climbers, while modern
plastic versions **5** come in various
colours and styles. Space these
about 10 cm (4 in) away from the
wall, to allow air to circulate.

lanting and routine care

epending on the type of plant – shrubby,
erennial or annual – the technique of plant-
g a climber is no different from that of plant-
g the equivalent non-climbing type, as
escribed on other pages. However, ground
reparation is even more important than
sual because it encourages the plant to
ecome quickly established – and only then
ill it start climbing properly. Greatest care of
l is needed when planting against a wall, for
e foundations will extend out some dis-
nce. Moreover, walls and fences shield the
ound from rain, so always plant at least
5 cm (10 in) away from the base; provide a
ne leaning towards the wall for the young
lant to bridge the gap. The same rules apply
hen planting climbers that are to scramble
rough the branches of a tree.

Providing adequate root moisture is a con-
uing problem. If you install a length of clay
pe (the type used for land drainage) verti-
lly in the soil beside the climber, and fill it
ith stones or gravel, you can easily direct
ater to the roots. Help retain moisture by
ulching thickly around the stem with well-
tted manure or garden compost, lawn clip-
ngs or peat – but ensure that the soil is moist
st. If you use farmyard manure, further
eding will probably be unnecessary, but in
her cases give a light dressing of fertilizer –
ther a balanced synthetic kind or a mixture
bonemeal and dried blood – in spring and
rly summer. Bear in mind that climbers are
ot, in general, gross feeders.

With newly-planted climbers, frost can
cause damage to roots where the soil becomes
loosened after frost leaves the ground. When
this happens, tread the soil down again. Marginally hardy plants will in any case need protection from cold winter winds and frost.
Where the weather is not too harsh, sacking or
a wigwam of straw or fern fronds around the
base of the plant will generally be sufficient. In
areas with severe winters, however, you may
need to give protection as described for roses
on page 101.

Equally important for some climbers – notably clematis – is a cool root run, while having
their heads in the sun. You can achieve this by
positioning a slab of stone on the ground in
front of the main stem. Alternatively, position
a small shrub in front; suitable types include
lavender, rosemary and *Ruta graveolens*
'Jackman's Blue'.

Training and pruning

After planting a climber, train out young
shoots so as to produce good general coverage
of the wall or fence. Tie in the developing
shoots regularly, and inspect the ties from
time to time to make sure that they are not
damaging the stems. (The same applies to
crossing stems, which may rub.) Depending
on whether the climber is self-clinging or adequately twining, this tying-in and training may
have to be continued even when it is mature.
At least once a year, inspect ties and renew as
necessary.

With vigorous shrubby climbers, annual
pruning may also be necessary, both to keep
them within bounds and to encourage flowering. The former depends on the space available and whether the climber needs to be
specially trained over a pergola or other structure. The latter depends on whether the
climber flowers on new or old wood, and you
should follow the same principles as when
pruning non-climbing shrubs (see p 369). For
the special techniques of pruning climbing
roses, see page 149; for clematis, page 145.
Methods of training applicable to wall shrubs
are described on page 374.

Shrubs in the garden

Shrubs – particularly flowering shrubs – have enjoyed an enormous increase in popularity in recent decades. It all began in 1883, when William Robinson wrote in the first edition of *The English Flower Garden*: 'If one-tenth of the trouble wasted on "carpet bedding" and other fleeting and costly rubbish had been spent on flowering shrubs, our gardens would be the better for it.' Yet if Robinson and his disciple Gertrude Jekyll killed the artificiality of carpet bedding – annual plants, often in garish colours, set out in geometric patterns – it was not immediately to be replaced by plantings of flowering shrubs. The fashion changed to the herbaceous border, largely through the influence of Miss Jekyll. This did not entail as much work as bedding out, but there was still plenty to occupy the paid gardeners of houses both large and relatively small: staking, tying, cleaning up, weeding, replanting every few years, and so on.

Then came the slump of the 1930s, and fewer and fewer garden owners could afford paid help – a trend that has gone on, except on the very largest estates, in almost every country. Shrubs came into their own because they saved work. Not that they were newcomers to gardens. The shrubbery was a popular feature of Victorian gardens, but it tended to consist largely of rather dreary evergreens in spite of the fact that plant collectors had for years been bringing a wide range of shrubs from Asia back to Western nurserymen. Such collecting continued up to World War II, and plant breeders were also busy producing more decorative cultivars, so that by the middle

years of this century the range of shrubs available to gardeners was enormously improved.

They went from strength to strength, and many a gardener was converted to the view that they are easy to grow, need little maintenance, last a long time and give year-round colour. All this is true, but it is not the whole truth, and the planting of all or part of your garden with flowering shrubs needs just as much forethought and preparation as creating any other garden feature. You cannot hope to

All shrubs have an individual character that must be taken into account when choosing and placing them in the garden. Azaleas and other relatively low-growing shrubs **left** are ideal for smaller borders. They can also be used to bring variations of height in a larger shrubbery **below left**, by occupying bays between the taller subjects. Evergreens such as the golden-leaved hebe **below right** are useful in mixed beds and borders to fill gaps and extend the season of interest. Small conifers and other evergreens also make good screens for unsightly objects such as a shed **below far right**. When planting a somewhat tender species such as *Buddleia globosa* **right**, choose a spot by a sunny wall.

transform the garden by buying a nurseryman's 'special collection' without thought to the soil, surroundings and setting. Such collections often do contain some of the easiest-to-grow shrubs, so that most of them will very likely survive if planted and maintained properly (see p 96). But they are rarely the most rewarding, and, as a very general rule, the better the shrub the more care it needs. So it will pay you to plan carefully and choose the plants on the basis of your needs and theirs.

Basic characteristics and needs

Shrubs, like trees, have woody stems and branches that remain alive all through the year (even if in many cases they are dormant in winter). The fundamental difference between shrubs and trees is that the latter have solitary trunks from which the branches grow – commonly but not necessarily starting some distance from the ground. Shrubs have no trunk, but branch below, at or a little above ground level. Height is, strictly speaking, immaterial – a 1 m (3 ft) Japanese maple is a tree, while a 6 m (20 ft) rhododendron is a shrub – but to the gardener a dwarf tree will perform much the same function as a small shrub, while a giant shrub can be treated much like a tree except for its more spreading habit.

Things are, moreover, confused by the fact that some slightly tender shrubs are cut to the ground by frosts but spring up again in the manner of herbaceous plants. Then there are the in-between plants – the sub-shrubs that have semi-woody stems, and plants like geraniums (pelargoniums) that develop woody stems in hot climates but are soft-stemmed elsewhere.

Climatic and environmental needs in general are the fundamental characters governing your choice of shrubs. There is the over-riding consideration of whether the soil is acid or alkaline – vital because some of the best flowering shrubs, such as rhododendrons, camellias and most heathers – will only grow on non-alkaline (lime-free) soil. Similarly

avoid choosing a sun-loving shrub for a shady place, or a less hardy type in a windy, cold place. The microclimate varies even from one part to another of a single garden, but a study of what grows well in local gardens and parks will provide basic guidance.

Against this, it is worth being a little adventurous. Except in areas with severe winters, many beautiful shrubs that have the reputation of being tender can be grown in a sheltered spot – against a sunny wall, for example. The heat of nearby buildings in suburban gardens can alone make a difference of 2 or 3°C (4 or 5°F) in the two most damaging frosts of the year – the first and last – as compared with an open site.

Selecting to suit your needs

Beyond the basic question of whether or not it will survive – or, hopefully, thrive – in your garden, you have to choose your shrubs on the basis of what they will contribute to your overall garden picture. Their permanence and the fact that they are, very broadly, among the larger plants in the garden means that they form major structural elements and provide variations of height and interest, while unifying the garden's planting scheme through all four seasons. This makes it all the more important to consider fully the characteristics of each candidate – whether it is deciduous or evergreen; the character and colour of its foliage and bark; whether it produces conspicuous flowers and/or fruits, and if so in which colours and which seasons; and its overall form and pattern of growth. This last characteristic is much more variable than the straightforward distinction between the erect, sprawling, round or weeping, and in many cases elegance of form and beauty of leaf is enough to earn a place in the garden – these features are, after all, far less ephemeral than flowers.

Even if they are not as distinctive as this, all shrubs have a character of their own. They can be broadly divided into 'star' plants and 'crowd players'. The star plant, at its best, is the shrub that will stand out on its own in an isolated, carefully chosen position – on a lawn, perhaps – where it will add to the general plan and give flower at the same time. It must be a distinctive plant and one that will grow well. A good example is *Magnolia grandiflora*, with large evergreen leaves and a long display of large, white, scented flowers – sporadic, perhaps, but none the less beautiful for this position. The crowd player is gregarious, and needs to grow and be seen in a group. The blue-berried *Callicarpa bodinieri giraldii* is typical. Not only does it look better in a group of three, five or seven (Gertrude Jekyll's magical numbers) but the plants will also carry more berries.

Then there are shrubs for the mixed border (see p 106), which need other qualifications. First of all, they should save work, by growing close to the ground so that they keep down weeds. They should not be obtrusive, but fit in happily with the perennials, bulbs and annuals, adding something to them all. Yet they must make a contribution of their own, both in form and foliage. Curiously enough, that often-despised plant, golden privet (*Ligustrum ovalifolium* 'Aureum') is one of the best for this purpose. It can be cut to fit, and the yellow leaves are an excellent foil to the other plants. Shrubs for the rock garden or heather garden need choosing particularly carefully if they are to fit in, for sophisticated modern hybrids – often with large or brilliantly coloured flowers – may overpower the subtler beauty of alpines and heathers.

plants to fill in the gaps, both on the ground and between the flowering periods of the shrubs. To have a really worthwhile display of flowers all the year round needs quite a lot of shrubs which, in turn, need a lot of space.

If you do have the space, you can form groups of shrubs (there can be as few as three in each) for each of the seasons of the year. Or you can plan your planting so that there is always some shrub in flower, in some part of the garden. A well-planned shrub border comes somewhere between these approaches. To avoid a 'spotty' effect, it is best to group together shrubs of interest at particular seasons. Intersperse them with evergreens – particularly ones with variegated foliage – to extend the interest. This is especially important in sections visible from the house, to provide a pleasing winter aspect. Aim for contrasts in shape and texture, too, and make the most of the available space by using shrubs that will contribute more than one characteristic, such as flowers, berries and attractive foliage. Underplanting with bulbs and carpets of ground cover sweeping through the border are other ways of increasing variety and interest.

There is no substitute for a carefully prepared scale plan – along much the same lines as that suggested for herbaceous borders on page 104 – when working out your planting scheme. An informal outline to the border is usually best, but in a small garden a straight edge may be unavoidable; this can be broken by the odd branch here and there, kept well above ground level. Broadly speaking, the tal-

Planning a shrub border

One of the attractions of using shrubs in the garden is that they enable you to extend the period of interest beyond the summer flowering season of most perennials. Shrubs are available that will flower in any month of the year, and evergreens of course have year-round foliage interest. But it is quite unwarranted to assume from this that you only have to buy a half-dozen shrubs to be assured of a gorgeous display from January to December. You might just be able to achieve this with double the number, but you would have to be very selective and employ ground-cover

lest shrubs should go at the back, but do not aim for an even gradation. Remember to leave adequate room between the shrubs for future growth, interplanting temporarily as described on page 30 if necessary. As a very rough guide, allow three shrubs per 5 m² (50 sq ft), but give each shrub the space its growth rate and spread demand. Then it will not need otherwise unnecessary pruning and the border will not become the amorphous mass common in the last century. Each specimen will be able to display its own individual character while contributing to the overall visual effect.

Growing and caring for shrubs

The great majority of shrubs grown in gardens are adaptable and easy to grow, but if you want the best from them you should plant the right subjects in the right positions (see p 94) and should be sure to give them all proper after-care. Good cultivation extends from the initial choice of healthy, well-grown plants to the regular watering, feeding and pruning needed to keep your shrubs in good shape. The advice given in this article on planting and immediate after-care applies equally to trees.

Choosing and buying

You can buy shrubs in two main ways: from a garden centre or shop, or by mail-order. The former enables you to examine and choose the actual plant you buy, but the range of species and cultivars will usually be much more restricted than if you buy from the mail-order catalogue of a specialist nurseryman. If you buy from a garden centre, the plant will probably be sold in a container, such as a plastic or whalehide (tarred paper) pot. Container shrubs are also sold by mail-order, or they may be 'balled and burlapped' – dug up with a good quantity of soil around the roots, which is wrapped in burlap (sacking) – or similarly dug up but left bare-rooted.

Try to ensure that any container shrub has actually been growing in the container long enough to be well rooted into the potting mixture, so that the container will not fall away if you lift the plant by the stem. Such a shrub can be planted – with care not to disturb the roots – at any time of year when the soil is not frozen, but it is best to avoid very dry or very wet spells. The potting mixture in the container provides nutrients while the new feeding roots are growing out into the surrounding soil, and this is a distinct advantage in poor or heavy soils.

Some shrubs sold in containers are dug up from open ground and merely potted immediately before sale; such treatment is no better than balling and burlapping (and, if the supplier is so unscrupulous as to pass off such plants as container-grown, they may well have been treated worse). Shrubs not grown in containers should be delivered and planted only in the dormant season. For deciduous types, this is any time between mid-autumn and early spring; the plants come to no harm with-

out soil around their roots. Evergreens, which are never completely dormant, resent much root disturbance, so the ball of soil around the roots should be kept intact. Also, it is best to plant at a time when the plant is losing little water by transpiration (see p 336) but the soil is warm enough for some root growth to take place after planting; the best times are middle to late autumn, or mid-spring.

The size of shrub you buy should be in proportion to the ultimate size. A small plant of a tall-grower is acceptable if well rooted, but a large plant of a small species may take

longer to become established and may need harder initial pruning. As a general rule, evergreen shrubs suitable for planting range from about 30 cm (12 in) as a minimum for slow growers up to about 60 cm (2 ft) as a maximum for the faster types. Deciduous shrubs may range up to a maximum of 90 cm (3 ft) for the most vigorous kinds. Strong, healthy shrubs have well-defined branches, usually with ample side shoots; evergreens should have leaves free from blemishes as well as a good branching habit. Avoid sparsely shooted, misshapen or diseased plants.

Planting shrubs

1 Thoroughly cultivate the planting site by double digging a wide area, incorporating ample rotted organic matter. Allow the ground to settle, then take out a planting hole about twice the size of the shrub's root ball. Fork over the bottom of the hole, then test for depth by standing the shrub in position. The soil level should be the same as in the container, or as shown by the soil mark on the stem. If the shrub is growing in a pot or other rigid container, water it well and then carefully remove the pot. Stand the shrub

in position in the hole. Loosen the roots of dormant deciduous shrubs, but keep the root ball of others intact.

2 With shrubs growing in a thin plastic or whalehide container, water and then slit down the side of the container with a knife. Place it in position, then remove the rest of the container.

3 Balled and burlapped shrubs should have the sacking carefully removed from around the root ball only when in position in the hole. If necessary, soak the whole root ball, in its sacking, in a bucket of water beforehand.

Soil preparation and planting

A shrub is destined to occupy the same ground for a number of years, so thorough soil preparation is vital. Clear weeds and double dig the planting site (see p 334), working in plenty of humus-forming material – well-rotted farmyard manure or garden compost, leaf-mould, peat or chopped turves. For a shrub border, work the whole area, but for individual specimen shrubs prepare an area at least 1.25 cm (4 ft) across. Do this several weeks before planting, to allow the soil time to settle.

Do not unpack plants that arrive in frosty weather, but put them in a shed or sheltered place, covered with sacks. If frost is prolonged, retain the packing material at the roots, but loosen that covering the branches to admit air. If the ground is not frozen, heel in bare-rooted shrubs that cannot be planted immediately; dig a trench, spread the roots and cover them with moist soil. With container-grown shrubs, merely prevent the container from freezing solid or drying out.

When planting, prepare a planting mixture of two parts soil and one part leaf-mould, garden compost or peat, with a handful or bonemeal per plant mixed in. Use canes to mark planting positions spaced so that the shrubs will not overgrow each other's positions when they reach their mature size. When planting near a fence or wall, allow a gap of at least 30 cm (12 in) or the shrub's roots are liable to remain chronically dry.

Dig adequate planting holes and put each shrub in position. Do not plant too deeply – just up to the level of the potting mixture in a container or the soil mark on the stem. Use the prepared planting mixture to fill in around the roots or root-ball, ensuring that you leave no air spaces. Spread out the roots of bare-rooted deciduous shrubs, and loosen slightly the root-ball of container-grown deciduous shrubs that are dormant, but keep the soil intact around the roots of evergreens. It is best to cut away the container or burlap only when the plant is in position in its hole. Tread the soil down firmly all round, and add more planting mixture if necessary. In dry regions, leave a slight depression around the plant to catch moisture.

If exposed to strong winds, insert a sturdy

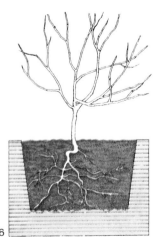

When planting a shrub border **left**, be sure to space the plants wide enough apart so that they do not encroach upon each other when mature. A specimen shrub planted in a lawn, such as the *Buddleia alternifolia* **above**, should have an area 1 m (3 ft) across kept clear of grass and weeds.

stake before positioning the shrub (to avoid root damage), and tie the stem to this with a patent tie. Then, if necessary, erect a protective screen of sacking or wattle hurdles (see p 354) until the roots have taken a firm hold. Water well after planting, and keep moist for some months, until you are sure that the shrub is well established. Do not allow grass or weeds to grow in an area at least 1 m (3 ft) in diameter around each shrub for at least two years. Mulching with organic material helps to retain soil moisture and keeps down weeds.

Newly transplanted shrubs, especially conifers and other evergreens planted in spring, benefit from a daily overhead spraying of luke-warm water for a few weeks. This is particularly true of such plants as hibiscus, which may not break into leaf until midsummer after spring planting. (You can check whether such a shrub is alive by scraping the bark with your thumbnail or knife blade; in living plants, the layer just beneath the surface is moist and green. Make the test low down.)

Once your shrubs are well established, it is a good idea – for both practical and aesthetic reasons – to plant ground-cover plants (see p 232) in the spaces around and between them. These will keep down all but the most persistent perennial weeds, will shade the

ground and prevent it drying out too much, and will mask unattractive bare earth. However, they will take some nutrients from the soil, so compensate by giving a little extra fertilizer (see below).

Routine care

In spring, after the soil has begun to warm up but when it is still moist, apply a mulch of well-rotted organic material or peat around your shrubs. Before this, rake in a little balanced proprietary fertilizer around any that have been neglected or grow on poor soil, and especially those that flower on new wood. Beware of stimulating too much stem and leaf growth on shrubs that flower on spurs or buds formed the previous year – especially by giving a fertilizer too high in nitrogen (see p 352).

Some shrubs may need winter protection in certain areas. With only marginally tender types in regions that do not experience winters that are too severe, it may be enough to erect a tripod of canes around the shrub and weave bracken fronds in between the shrub's branches. Or an open-topped screen of sacking, held by four vertical canes, can be erected around the shrub; this gives protection mainly from cold winds. For shrubs grown against a wall, you can erect a semi-circular screen of chicken-wire stuffed with bracken or straw. In regions with more severe climates, you may have to resort to the methods described for roses on page 101.

The main regular maintenance job with shrubs, however, is pruning. Apart from maintaining shape and good health, this may help to ensure prolific flowering. But shrubs vary widely in their pruning needs. On all types, you should cut out dead or badly diseased branches, unwanted suckers and straggling branches that unbalance the shape; these jobs can be done at any time of year. Some may need to have dead flowers removed regularly, but most evergreen shrubs need no further pruning until and unless they grow too big or congested. With deciduous shrubs, pruning time and technique varies according to the flowering season and whether flowers appear on new or old wood. Full details are given in the article on page 369.

Propagation

With most garden shrubs, you can increase your stock quite easily by propagating from cuttings or seed. For most kinds, hardwood cuttings taken in late autumn or semi-hard cuttings in summer are the easiest methods. The former are rooted in the open, the latter under glass. With some species, leaf-bud cuttings yield large numbers of plants from a small amount of material, while layering enables you to grow new shrubs from stems still attached to the parent. Suckers represent an easy way of growing new plants of many shrubs, provided that they are not grafted but grow on their own roots. Growing from seeds and berries is generally more difficult and time-consuming, but perfectly feasible if you have a cold frame or greenhouse. For full details of all these methods, see the articles on pages 344 to 350.

4 Bare-rooted deciduous shrubs should have any diseased or injured roots cut back cleanly to healthy wood.
5 Stand the roots in a bucket of water for a few hours before

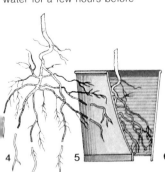

planting. Hold the shrub in position in the planting hole and spread the roots well out. **6** Fill in around the roots or root ball with a prepared planting mixture (see text). Work the mixture in carefully so that there are no air pockets and tread down firmly. Fill in the depression with more planting mixture and tread again. After planting, cut back damaged or diseased branches to a healthy outward-facing bud. Cut any stumps of wood flush with the stem. Keep well watered, and regularly spray the foliage of evergreens with water.

The rose garden

Roses are the most popular garden plants in the world, their beauty, range and adaptability appealing to the ordinary gardener and the specialist alike. Depending on your degree of enthusiasm, there are three equally attractive choices open if you share this love of roses. You can have roses, together with other plants, in your garden; you can set aside a part of your garden for growing roses only; or you can make your whole garden a rose garden.

The last of these alternatives may seem extreme, but there are worse ways of planning a garden. Although all roses are species and hybrids of a single genus, *Rosa*, the number of varieties in cultivation runs into thousands. If you make good use of the range available, you will have flowers from spring until autumn or even later, with colours ranging from white and the softest pastel pinks, mauves and apricots to blazing scarlet, bright daffodil-yellow, and deep, dusky red. Only blue is missing (though there are lavender roses). The flower of the rose ranges from the single five-petalled beauty of the wild species to the huge, high-centred, very double bloom of the modern Hybrid Tea. No plant has more rewarded the efforts of breeders.

Hybrid Tea and Floribunda roses can be used as permanent bedding plants that are almost always in flower, the more vigorous varieties for hedges of varying heights, and the low-growing ones for edging paths and flower beds. Climbers and ramblers can cover the walls of your house, or wander in glorious profusion over arches and pergolas or up trees. Shrub roses can make handsome specimens on a lawn, be used for wide, informal and very colourful hedges or for group plantings, and many of them will mix well with – and even scramble up through – other shrubs, giving midsummer colour to an evergreen like a holly.

There are even creeping roses that hug the ground and root as they go. These are useful for groud-cover, as are others that grow up to 1 m (3 ft) tall, but spread far and wide, smothering weeds and themselves smothered in blossom. The smallest miniature roses are no more than 12 cm (5 in) high, and are ideal for rock gardens and stone troughs, and for edging. For detailed information on types of roses, and recommended varieties, see page 148 and pages 158 to 163.

Roses for bedding

Bedding schemes, formal or informal, are probably the commonest way of displaying bush roses. Most people mix a number of varieties in a small bed, though the massed planting of a single variety adds impact in formal surroundings. Apart from colour, take into account size when choosing varieties. For a small bed – unless against a wall or fence, where tall roses can grow at the back and short at the front – avoid the more leggy growers. A bushy variety that does not top 75 cm (2½ ft) is best. To achieve variety and movement for the eye, you can plant standard or half-standard roses, perhaps in a contrasting colour, as the centrepiece for a round or square bed, or in a line down the centre of a long one,

spaced at intervals of about 1.25 to 1.5 m (4 to 5 ft). Do not, however, use weeping standards, as their pliable canes will whip around in a wind, tangling with – and probably damaging – the blooms of the bush roses.

Nothing looks better for edging rose beds than the green of well-tended grass. But a small rose garden – perhaps below a terrace, with steps leading down into it – can look most attractive with paths running through it of paving or fine gravel, particularly if the stones are grey. However, roses with a tendency to sprawl – such as 'Europeana' and 'Percy Thrower' – should be kept away from the edges of beds with only a narrow path between. Rough stonework for surrounding walls can also add charm to rose beds.

Roses as specimens

Weeping standard roses are best used as solitary specimen plants, perhaps in the middle of a lawn, or as a colourful corner feature. But remember that the commonest varieties –

such as 'Sander's White', 'Excelsa' and 'Crimson Shower' – being ramblers, flower only once a year, albeit spectacularly. Some so-called weepers derived from climbers – such as 'New Dawn', 'Leverkusen' and the climbing sport of 'Allgold' – have prolonged flowering but are too stiff to droop without training.

Where space is limited, choose for specimen planting one of the tall long- or repeat flowering shrub roses, such as 'Golden Wings' or 'Chinatown', or one of the Hybrid Musk roses like 'Penelope' or 'Vanity'. For a large garden, creamy-white 'Nevada' or its pink sport 'Marguerite Hilling', or 'Frühlingsmorgen', with its marvellous pink, single flowers, which shade to soft yellow in the centre, are unbeatable. If you plant any of these in a lawn, cut a fairly wide circle of earth for them to grow in, and keep it clear of grass and weeds, which will rob the rose of its nourishment and keep rain from the roots.

Roses with other plants

A rose bed is not always a thing of beauty – particularly after pruning – and many people like to improve its appearance by underplanting with other plants. The wisdom of this depends on how close together you grow your roses. With close planting – 45 cm (18 in) or closer – underplanting makes it difficult to cultivate the roses properly. Wider spaces, however, give room for other low-growing flowers to flourish comparatively unharmed. Best are annuals such as violas, which bloom early and are a favourite for underplanting rose bushes. Aubrieta, thrift (*Armeria* spp), old-fashioned pinks and dwarf varieties of lavender make excellent edgings for rose beds, their cool colours setting off the roses to perfection. The upright stance and rather

Kinds of roses
The term shrub rose is given to the taller types **1** that will not fit into bedding schemes. They include species, old and new hybrids and even some extra-vigorous Floribundas. Bush roses **2** are generally up to 1 m (3 ft) tall, and include Hybrid Teas (with one or a few large blooms per stem) and Floribundas (with clusters of smaller flowers).
Sometimes called tree roses, standards **3** are bush roses grafted onto a 1 to 1.25 m (3 to 4 ft) 'trunk'; the stem of a half-standard is only 60 cm (2 ft) tall. A weeping standard **4** is similar, but is derived from a rambler rose, whose flowering canes droop.
Miniature roses **5** range from 12 to 40 cm (5 to 15 in) tall; there are miniature climbers.
Ramblers **6** produce only one flush of flowers a year, on new wood. Climbers **7** flower over a long period on old and new wood, including side shoots.

Styles of rose-growing
left Climbing and shrub roses, with their informal habit of growth, help to create the idyllic picture of a country cottage garden in summer.
right In stark contrast, the geometrically shaped and arranged beds of a formal rose garden, filled with rows of bush roses, make an equally arresting scene, whether large in scale, as here, or intimate. The idea that roses can only be grown with other roses perhaps arose when 19th century enthusiasts segregated their exhibition roses to give them individual attention. In fact, roses associate well with many other kinds of plants.
below left 'Canary Bird' trained as a weeping standard makes an imposing specimen planting in a corner bed.
below right Certain species and varieties of roses, such as 'Raubritter', make excellent ground cover, forming undulating carpets of blossom.

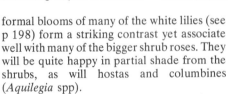

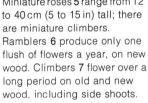

formal blooms of many of the white lilies (see p 198) form a striking contrast yet associate well with many of the bigger shrub roses. They will be quite happy in partial shade from the shrubs, as will hostas and columbines (*Aquilegia* spp).

And, as already mentioned, roses themselves can be used for ground cover. 'Max Graf' grows completely prostrate, the canes rooting where they touch the ground, and gradually spreads out until it is trimmed back to keep it in bounds. *R. × paulii* is an example of a rose that comes from a single root, keeps below 1.25 m (4 ft) and yet spreads out to 3.5 to 4.5 m (12 to 15 ft) if grown in a situation that suits it.

Roses for hedging
For hedges of almost any kind, roses are hard to beat. No other hedging plant gives so much colour over such a long period. Low hedges for the sides of paths or drives, or for dividing one part of your garden from another, can be formed by Floribundas in all their variety, by some of the taller miniature roses, or by many of the Gallica group of shrub roses. The vigorous Floribunda 'Queen Elizabeth' makes a fine tall, narrow hedge, and can be bushed out reasonably well and kept below 1.8 m (6 ft) if it is hard pruned to just over 1 m (about 3½ ft) each year. The Gallicas have the advantage that you can clip them over gently in winter with shears, rather than pruning them, but they flower only once a year.

You can also use shears on many of the Japanese Rugosa roses, if they are used for hedges, but they, like the Gallicas, cannot be trimmed with the severity of conventional hedging plants, such as box or privet. Such treatment would, in any case, ruin their

informal charm. They are very spiny, and the beautiful leaves, which colour in the autumn, cover the plants right to the ground. There are many other shrub roses that can also be used for hedges, such as the Hybrid Musks, but they are too vigorous for a small garden.

Other uses of roses
Climbing and rambling roses have a multitude of uses apart from the most common one of covering walls. Many of the less vigorous varieties, such as 'Aloha', make good free-standing shrubs, or they can be trained on pillars or tripods of rustic poles to achieve variety in a bedding scheme in the same way as standard roses. They will effectively disguise an old and unsightly fence or shed, but you should not forget that almost all roses lose most of their leaves in winter. New leaves – and flowers – come early on most climbing roses, however.

There are many roses that will mix quite happily with border plants and other shrubs, as opposed to being underplanted with them. A bed of carefully chosen heathers (so that there are some in flower right through the year; see p 152) is made even more perfect with pink, white and purple shrub roses dotted here and there through it. It is, however, as well not to pick roses that grow too densely or are very lax in habit so that they cast a heavy shadow low down, for heathers like the sun just as much as roses.

The old roses, with their soft, muted colours, and some of the modern ones, such as the blush-pink 'Fritz Nobis' and the sumptuous deeper pink 'Constance Spry', mix in well with any general shrub planting, provided once again that they have their share of sun for a good many hours a day. The grey-green leaves of the Alba race, the elegant pointed leaves, often bronze-tinted, of many of the China roses, and many of the rose species all blend well with philadelphus (mock orange), holly, forsythia, berberis, spiraea and others. And some of the less vigorous kinds of clematis (see p 144) will weave happily through the branches of a climbing or rambling rose, extending the season of colour.

Not only are roses among the most beautiful of garden flowers, but they are also among the most adaptable.

Growing beautiful roses

When planning to plant almost any kind of rose – whether a solitary specimen shrub, or a whole garden of modern hybrid bush roses, or one or more climbers to clothe a wall, pergola or other structure – the first essential is to choose a sunny spot. With the exception of a few tree-climbing sorts, which thrive in partial shade, and some other climbers that do well on sunless, but otherwise well-lit walls, roses cannot have too much sun and will produce a poor display without it.

They also like plenty of air, but not exposure to strong winds that will rock the plants and loosen their roots. They need adequate moisture, but good drainage; they will not thrive in waterlogged soil. Given these limitations, roses will grow well in most types of soil, though they are not fond of chalk.

Soil preparation and planting

Before planting, a heavy clay soil should have plenty of peat or other humus-forming material dug into the lower spit to improve drainage and to lighten it. Light, sandy soils will benefit from the same treatment to increase their retention of water. Both should have farmyard manure or garden compost added, for your roses will be in position for a long time and these, when broken down, provide many of the nutrients the roses need.

Never plant new roses straight into a bed that has grown other roses for some years past. The soil will have become what is known as 'rose-sick', and the new plants will never do well. The soil can, of course, be replaced, but this could be a big undertaking with a large bed. If replacing a single rose bush, remove soil from an area about 45 cm (18 in) in diameter and 30 cm (12 in) deep, and replace it with new. Otherwise, it is best to allow a bed that has supported roses to 'rest' for several seasons – growing annuals, perhaps, or herbaceous plants – before replanting with a new collection of roses.

Carry out the preliminary preparation of your new rose beds in early autumn, to allow the earth to settle again before the roses arrive. Roses can be planted at any time between late autumn and early spring when the ground is neither frozen nor waterlogged. In practice, the best time in areas that experience only moderate winters (such as the British Isles) is late autumn, with early spring as second best. In regions where winters are harsh (such as northern North America), plant in early spring, while in warm climates you must take advantage of the plants' brief dormant period in the middle of winter.

If you cannot plant your roses immediately they arrive, do not unpack them. Keep them in a cool, frost-proof shed for up to a week or ten days, but for a longer wait than this they should be heeled in. This means putting them in a shallow trench in a spare corner of the garden with at least 15 cm (6 in) of earth over the roots. Like this, they will be quite happy for several weeks if need be, but do plant them properly as soon as possible, choosing a mild, frost-free period.

On unpacking, the roses should be inspected, and any broken or unhealthy-

looking canes cut back to healthy, undamaged wood. Long, tough roots should be shortened by about one-third, to encourage fine, feeding roots to sprout from them once the rose is planted. Any leaves still on the plants should be cut off, and if the bushes look dry, they should be stood in a bucket of water for at least an hour before planting.

While they are soaking, you can be making up a planting mixture, which will help to give them a good start. This should consist of about one large shovelful per rose of an equal mixture of fine, moist soil and moist granulated peat, into which a handful per rose of bonemeal has been stirred.

The planting holes should be wide enough for the plants' roots to be spread out as evenly as possible all round, and deep enough for the budding union (a thickening of the stem just above the roots, from which the canes sprout) to be just below soil level. Do not plant your roses in deep, narrow holes.

Once the rose is in position in the hole, hold it upright and put your planting mixture over the roots. Tread it lightly, and rake in the soil which you dug from the hole. Then tread once more, firmly but not too hard, especially on heavy soils that might compact. Water well if the ground is dry. If you have to carry out a late planting in spring, prune straight away. With autumn planting, leave pruning till the spring. For details of how to prune roses see the articles on the various kinds, on page 148 and pages 156 to 163.

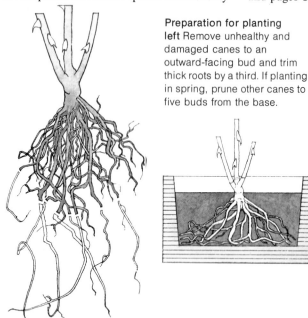

Preparation for planting
left Remove unhealthy and damaged canes to an outward-facing bud and trim thick roots by a third. If planting in spring, prune other canes to five buds from the base.

The perfect rose
To obtain a succession of beautiful blooms from bush roses such as 'Blessings' **left**, remove old flowers promptly. **above** Cut just above a bud, which will develop into a new flowering shoot.

Tending established roses

To get the best from your roses, you must give them proper attention – particularly as regards feeding, pruning and protecting them from pests and diseases.

A small handful of a proprietary rose fertilizer, lightly hoed in round each rose in early spring, late spring and midsummer, will do nothing but good. Such fertilizer is rich in phosphate (having an analysis of about 5:10:5; see p 352) to encourage flower and root growth. Roses can also be given a foliar feed; this is particularly useful if underplanting makes access to the soil difficult.

Mulching with a layer no more than 8 cm (3 in) thick of manure, garden compost or peat, after rain and when the soil has begun to

Planting
far left Dig a fairly shallow but wide hole and spread out the rose's roots. Cover with prepared planting mixture and tread in. Rake soil into the hole and tread again. Just cover the budding union except in frost-free areas, where exposure gives bushier growth.

Removing suckers
left Suckers look different from top-growth, often with seven (not three or five) leaflets per leaf. Trace to the origin on the rootstock, if necessary removing earth, and pull completely off.

Winter protection for roses
The budding union is the most vulnerable part, so cover the crown with well-drained soil. **below left** Down to −18°C (0°F), twine straw or bracken through the bush, cover with burlap (sacking) and tie with string. **centre** Down to −35°C (−31°F) you can tie the branches and mound well-drained soil at least 30 cm (12 in) deep all over the rose. **right** In particularly harsh regions, enclose the rose in a tar-paper bin filled with dry peat or shredded bark; cover with burlap and pile earth around. **bottom** Loosen the roots of standard roses in harsh areas, lay them over and protect with piled earth or other methods. Treat climbers similarly after removing them from their supports and tying the canes in a bundle. Remove all protection when the weather begins to warm up again.

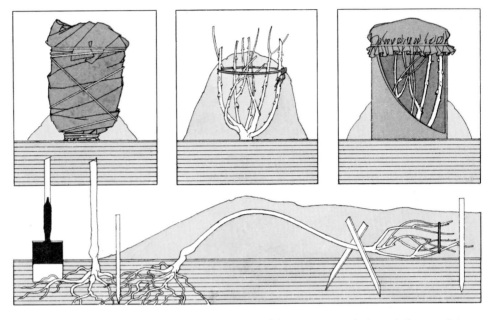

warm up in spring, will help to retain soil moisture, smother weed seedlings, and add goodness to the soil when what remains is hoed in during the autumn clean-up of the garden. It also helps to keep the roots cool.

The removal of spent flowers and hips (or heps) will ensure that you get more flowers in the second flush. This should be done by cutting just above the first healthy bud below the old flower, and not by simply pulling off the old flower head. If cutting roses for indoor display, cut in a similar way to a bud lower down. Suckers too, should be removed promptly. These are growths coming from the wild rose stock (root and stem) onto which your cultivated variety has been budded to give it extra vigour. They come from below the budding union, and should be pulled off completely. Cutting suckers merely encourages them to grow more vigorously.

Pruning is important to maintain vigorous growth, and may be carried out in autumn or spring in a mild climate. In cold regions, spring pruning is advisable, when the tops of any frost-damaged canes can be cut away; earlier pruning might result in frost damage to the pruned canes, destroying some of them altogether as they will be much shorter. However, to avoid wind-rock in winter gales loosening and damaging the roots, cut back all tall-growing Hybrid Teas and Floribundas by about one-third late in the autumn. (As already mentioned, detailed pruning instructions are given in the next chapter.)

In a cold climate, where there is prolonged frost and snow, it is necessary to give roses winter protection. Even in some moderately cold areas, strong drying winds may damage roses; straw and burlap gives sufficient protection here. In colder areas Hybrid Teas and Floribundas should be earthed up, well over the crown of the plant, and standard roses should have straw or bracken woven through the canes of the head. Burlap, or dry peat encased in burlap, may be used in combination with earthing-up in severe cold. In extreme cases the roots of standard roses may need to be eased from the soil on one side so that the whole stem can be laid flat and earth piled over it. The same methods can be used with climbers and ramblers, but these may first need the canes untying from trellis or a fence and retying with raffia into a bundle. Remove winter protection once severe frosts are over.

Rose varieties vary widely in their susceptibility to disease, but every rose-grower should watch out for such fungal diseases as canker, powdery mildew, black spot and rust (see p 367). Many insect pests may also plague the plants, particularly aphids (greenfly and blackfly), thrips, capsid bugs, leafhoppers, scale insects, caterpillars, sawflies, chafers, leaf miners and certain beetles (see p 364).

The months from spring to autumn are the worst period for rose troubles, and many gardeners spray their roses regularly, at weekly or two-weekly intervals, in this period, using a combination of an insecticide and a fungicide – for example, malathion plus Benlate. However, sprays are expensive, so with insect pests you need only spray at the first sign of damage; however, preventative spraying is advisable for many diseases.

The herbaceous border

Herbaceous borders are garden features at which, thanks to a moist and reasonably mild climate, the British excel. They even coined the term, when George Nicolson of Kew Gardens suggested in the late 19th century that 'best results from planting are obtained when the border is mainly made up of herbaceous perennials'.

Of course, flower beds had been known for many centuries and in many countries. Ancient Persians reputedly 'bordered their walks with tufts of flowers', and in medieval times they were common – mostly as a hotch-potch of flowers, shrubs and bulbs in season. But no one before Nicolson had suggested segregating herbaceous perennials from other plants. As writers and practical gardeners like Gertrude Jekyll and William Robinson extolled the virtues of the herbaceous border, plant collectors and nurserymen introduced new varieties, and the herbaceous border came to stay – and indeed spread all over the world.

Basic characteristics

Herbaceous perennials are plants that last for an indefinite number of years, but certainly more than two, and die to the ground annually. Some, such as *Dictamnus* and paeonies, are extremely long-lived and can remain many years in the same bed without the need for division or replacement. Others, such as Michaelmas daisies (*Aster novi-belgii* and its varieties), must be regularly and frequently split up and replanted, or they will lose their flowering qualities. Others again, such as delphiniums and *Meconopsis* (blue poppies), are short-lived and need to be replaced every few years, or need to be given greater cultural care in other ways.

A few plants that are not strictly herbaceous are included in such borders for the sake of convenience, like the sub-shrubby (semi-woody) border pinks (*Dianthus*), the rhizomatous and generally evergreen bearded irises, and red-hot pokers (*Kniphofia*). The last of these also retain their foliage in winter, which thus protects the vulnerable crowns, but it withers away as the new leaves come through the ground in spring. In regions where winters are frosty, tender perennials are included in permanent borders only for seasonal effect or to prolong display.

Using herbaceous perennials

Although plants with similar cultural demands are thus conveniently grown together, herbaceous borders need not be extensive. They should be of a size to suit the garden, but include bold groupings. One Michaelmas daisy plant makes little visual impact, whereas four or five do, so concentrate on more plants in fewer varieties if the garden is small.

Given room, however, a 3.5 m (12 ft) deep, flower-filled border, backing on to a wall or close-clipped evergreen hedge, presents an unforgettable picture. Twin borders with a grass path between are still more striking, particularly when they weave through a lawn and so can be seen from both sides. Years ago, double borders were frequently used as divid-

ers in kitchen gardens, partly to mask and relieve the monotony of rows of vegetables and fruit bushes, and partly to provide a source of cut flowers for the house. Island beds are another way of using herbaceous perennials (see p 108). Or they can be grouped between shrubs, used as container plants outdoors, or brought into a greenhouse for forcing to provide indoor decoration.

The only situation where failure might be anticipated with hardy herbaceous perennials is beneath or near to tall trees, particularly evergreens. The far-reaching roots of these leach the soil of water and nourishment; drips from their leaves damage plants underneath and their heavy shade robs the perennials of light and air. However, where gaps occur between trees, frequent applications of leaf-mould or peat may be provided to enrich the topsoil; then woodland perennials like trilliums, hostas and polygonatums (Solomon's seal) do well and spread with happy abandon.

Preparing the ground

Because of the long years that herbaceous perennials occupy the same piece of ground, it is essential for them to have a good start. Whatever the nature of the soil, it must first be

top The herbaceous border in high summer can be a glorious sight, with bold colour masses forming pleasing associations, and variations of height, form and texture that add greatly to the impact. Traditionally it backs onto a hedge, fence or wall which, if high enough, can support climbers (such as the clematis here) that form part of the colour-scheme. Another good situation for a herbaceous border is along one or both sides of a path left. Here, compact, low-growing plants are allowed to spill informally over the paving. Where the background is dark, as with the hedge opposite, tall pale-coloured plants such as verbascums (mulleins) make both a perfect contrast to the background and a foil to the colourful low-growing plants.

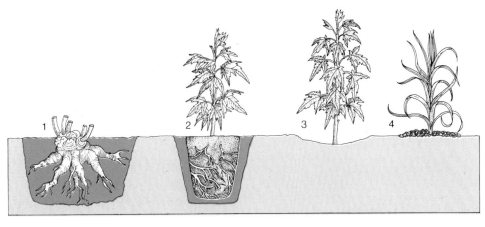

cleaned and then made rich and fertile by digging and working in plenty of organic material. In later years, mulches can make up for lost nourishment, but deep preliminary cultivation facilitates rooting and also makes it easier to rid the area of perennial weeds. Suitable sources of humus include well-rotted farmyard manure, ripe garden compost, leaf-mould, peat and spent hops. Work these through the top 20 to 30 cm (8 to 12 in) of soil. A dressing of bonemeal at 135 g/m² (4 oz/sq yd) scattered over the ground when digging is completed provides a slowly released source of phosphate, which is particularly valuable for this class of plants.

Lime should not be applied as a routine dressing. Some border plants, such as meconopsis, are calcifuges and allergic to lime. Most perennials prefer slightly acid conditions, and those that do benefit from its presence – such as pinks and bearded irises – can be dealt with separately.

If possible, prepare the ground in the autumn and leave it alone to settle until spring. If this is not possible, cultivate as before; then firm the ground with a very light roller, or else 'tread' it – by shuffling sideways all over the border, bringing one foot against another so that every piece of ground is trodden down. In either case, rake the ground prior to planning, and then outline the allotted space of each group of plants with sand or pieces of string. These should be set out according to a pre-drawn plan (see p 104). Such planning will make it easier to position the plants exactly as you want them, especially if each section is labelled with the name of its prospective inmates. In dry gardens, water the ground well the night before planting.

Planting the border

According to climatic conditions, herbaceous perennials can be planted in autumn in mild to warm zones, or left until spring in very cold situations. Even in the milder areas there are certain kinds that transplant better in spring than autumn – particularly hollow-stemmed or hairy-leaved plants like catananches, oriental poppies, gaillardias, delphiniums and *Aster amellus* varieties. For some reason, these seem less prone to bacterial diseases and slug and millipede attack in spring.

Today, nurseries supply many herbaceous plants grown in containers. Provided these are not root-bound, nor have broken soil balls, they can be established at any season except under severe winter conditions. Stand them in water for an hour beforehand, then turn them carefully from the pots and plant them, using a trowel. Open-ground plants sold more or less bare-rooted must be planted only during dormant seasons. They should have their roots well spread before planting – again with a trowel. Firm them well.

Satisfy individual requirements at this time – for example, by leaving moisture-loving perennials in saucer-like depressions so that rain and irrigation water runs down to their roots. Plants needing sharp drainage should have a little sand or grit worked around the roots and possibly a similiar mulch around

Planting perennials
1 Plant bare-rooted plants lifted from open ground when dormant in late autumn or early spring. Spread out the roots in a large hole and work a mixture of soil, peat and a little bonemeal between them. 2 Container-grown plants can be planted at any time the soil is not frozen if the root ball is kept intact; use the same planting mixture. 3 Leave a depression around the stem of moisture-lovers. 4 Give those prone to winter stem rot a collar of grit, and lime-lovers a top-dressing of chalk.

their stems. This will prevent the lower leaves resting on wet ground, a common cause of infection and winter losses. Lime-lovers can have a top-dressing of chalk or limestone chippings. Sensitive plants can be given temporary shade whilst rooting by pushing a few leafy twigs into the ground nearby.

Immediately after planting, give the soil a good watering, unless it is already reasonably moist, and next day hoe the ground between the plants to remove footprints and break up soil compacted by watering.

Caring for the border

During their first season, most borders are apt to be weedy, simply because the plants are too small to link up with their neighbours and so smother weed seedlings. Hoeing is the best way to keep these down, preferably whilst they are still tiny (see p 357). Even such tough weeds as thistles and docks can be 'bled' to death by constant hoeing. In later seasons, hoe wherever possible and remove large weeds by hand.

Give tall plants ample support, especially in one-sided borders. (In island beds, as shown on page 108, plants tend to grow more evenly upright, and get all-round support from their neighbours.) Species plants rarely need staking anyway, but cultivars have often achieved more or larger flowers at the expense of vigour. Unless they are supported, their weak stems snap or break down in high winds or heavy rains.

Providing support is a task best undertaken when the growths are only a few centimetres high, the ideal support being twiggy sticks pushed in between the shoots. These should be slightly shorter than the ultimate height of the plants, so that they are not seen when the plants come into flower. Delphiniums, foxtail lilies (*Eremurus*), hollyhocks and similar 'spired' flowers are best secured to canes, coloured green to make them inconspicuous. There are also patent wire supports with movable grilled tops. These are pushed into the ground, the shoots grow up through the grilles, and the top is pulled upwards on its stake as the stems extend.

Feeding and watering are vital for the health of herbaceous perennials. In hot dry summers even the healthiest plants feel a need for extra water. A stressed plant can soon succumb to pests and disease. Keep up the moisture content of the soil by applying organic mulches – such as peat or garden compost – in late spring or early summer, and water when necessary in the cool of the evening or early in the morning. A dressing of general fertilizer (analysis about 7:7:7 or 7:10:7; see p 352), hoed into the top soil layer at 70 to 135 g/m² (2 to 4 oz/sq yd), can be useful when plants are slow to start growing in a cold spring, or to help them along prior to flowering. Foliar feeds give rapid results and benefit most plants; spray these over the leaves on a still, sunless day.

Apart from staking, one area where herbaceous borders generally demand more attention than other garden features, such as shrubberies, is in winter care. When frost blackens stems and foliage, you should tidy the borders for winter. In warm to mild climates, cut all herbage (except that of irises, pinks, kniphofias and the like, which are more or less evergreen) to ground level, fork between the plants and leave till spring. In cold climates leave the dead tops as winter protection and heap dry leaves, bracken (or salt hay in North America) over the doubtfully hardy kinds. Remove this material, plus the old stems, in early spring, and fork or hoe between the plants. Any which need dividing can be lifted and separated at this time, to ensure an even better display in the coming season.

Planning a herbaceous border

Making a successful herbaceous border can be compared to planning a tapestry picture or painting, and there is also some resemblance to a jigsaw puzzle. Most of the points to be considered are common to any form of art, and include colour, texture, balance and design.

For good effects, the border should be as deep as possible; between 2.5 and 4.5 m (8 and 15 ft) is ideal. Length is less important. A second basic rule is that haphazard planting is never successful; there has to be a master plan, prepared long before the plants arrive. A good method is to draw a scaled map of the border on a sheet of graph paper. Then cut out irregular shapes in coloured paper and slot these into the plan – like pieces in a jigsaw puzzle. Start at the back and work towards the front, dovetailing the sections into one another informally. Avoid straight lines or any suggestion of rigidity. Move the pieces about freely at this stage, and when the pattern is to your liking stick them down in place.

Each section represents one kind of plant, and the next essential is to fill in their names – a task calling for specialized knowledge regarding each plant. The next chapter of this book contains details of scores of plants suitable for herbaceous borders, including some for special effects, such as tones of silver and grey (see p 240). However, the major articles containing descriptions of hardy herbaceous perennials, grouped broadly by size and colour, will be found on pages 176 to 185.

Size and growth span

One of the most important considerations when positioning a plant is its ultimate height. A border that backs on to a wall, hedge or fence presents only one face to the viewer; consequently the tallest specimens should go towards the back. Medium-sized plants, between about 0.3 and 1.25 m (1 and 4 ft) tall, will have central positions, with the shorter kinds going in front. Although such gradation is desirable, since it presents an unbroken front of colour at peak-time viewing, it need not be adhered to too rigidly. The odd slender spire piercing the foliage of shorter plants can be very attractive and break the flatness. Thalictrums, eremurus, and crown imperials

(*Fritillaria imperialis*) particularly can be used in this way, since their leaves are unobtrusive and disappear after flowering.

In the case of two-sided borders, the position is somewhat different, for then the tallest plants must have a central position and gradate outwards on both sides. The ends also may merit attention and be graded in a similar way; it all depends on their relationship to the rest of the garden.

Considerations of height and growth rate determine the number of plants to be grouped in each section. Only rarely is a single plant impressive enough to stand alone; details of such are given on page 177. Normally five or seven – sometimes more – plants of the same kind are needed to make a bold display; the object is to present a brilliant mass of colour, not a speckled effect. Odd numbers are easier to place and seem to give more pleasing results than even numbers.

Every plant must be given enough room to develop its full stature in two or three years. A specimen listed in a catalogue as requiring,

say, 30 cm (12 in) square (or having such a planting distance) must not be planted nearer than 30 cm (12 in) from its neighbours in any direction. Even within these limits avoid straight-line planting; stagger the plants to give more natural effects.

Colour harmony and contrast

Colour is highly important in all herbaceous borders, and although it is said that flowers never clash, hot strident shades in close proximity can be offensive. Scarlet oriental poppies, the cerise *Geranium psilostemon* and orange alstroemerias make poor neighbours, although all are excellent plants in the right setting. Installing late-flowering perennials between such plants with strong clashing colours provides a green barrier of foliage and softens the impact. Similarly, a group of silver-foliaged plants can be used, or perennials with white or pale flowers.

Colour harmony is not always easy to achieve, and should be linked with shapes and textures. Avoid having too many round,

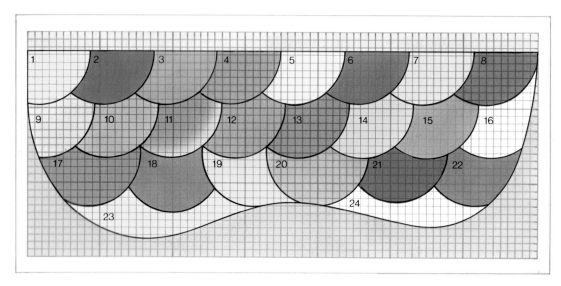

Designing the border
To visualize the colour-scheme you can use cut-out coloured paper shapes, as described in the text, or work directly on a scale plan of the border **left**; here, each large square represents 1 m (3¼ ft). Divide the area into irregular shapes, each big enough to hold at least three (and preferably five or seven) plants of one species or variety. Colour in the areas to represent your choice of flower colours, and finally select suitable plants. The plants in the completed scheme **right** are listed. In most cases, a wide range of colours is available, and one particular variety has been chosen; nor do they in fact flower together.
1 *Hemerocallis* hybrid;

'daisy' flowers together; interplant them with irregular-shaped flowers like penstemons, monardas and salvias, and also a few spiky plants like lupins, delphiniums and kniphofias. Again, the many shades of green assumed by leaves are as varied as flowers' colours – some have a reddish hue, and there is a whole range of perennials with variegated foliage. Their shapes range from simple ovals to deeply cut kinds with finger-like leaflets; they can be broad, or long and narrow; very large or very small; plain, hairy or patterned; and come directly from the ground or grow on the flower stems in a variety of patterns.

The many points to be considered presuppose background experience or warrant preliminary study of the plants. However, as knowledge grows so will the flair for making interesting plant associations. Some groupings can be sheer delight – for example, deep blue delphiniums with double pink paeonies in front and soft blue *Iris sibirica* coming up here and there, the whole edged with a border of blue violas. Another suggestion is yellow lupins, blue flax (*Linum narbonense*) and deep blue *Campanula glomerata*. Other ideas are outlined on page 28. It is groupings like these that give herbaceous borders character and lift them out of the realm of the 'ordinary' to something distinctive and lovely.

Season and individual needs

Flowering time is important background information when making plans. A few people opt for peak periods of bloom, such as early or later summer, and are not concerned with between-times. This may be either because they have large gardens and plenty of alternative features, or because they only use the house and garden at odd times. Most, however, demand rather more from borders, so need to spread the interest by working in a certain number of early and late bloomers with the bulk of the plants flowering between late spring and late summer. This can be done by careful choice of herbaceous plants, but the longest season of interest comes by compromising the principle of the 'pure' herbaceous border, and creating a mixed border that contains flowering shrubs or other plants

as well as herbaceous perennials (see p 106).

When finalizing your plan, you should also take account of individual needs and peculiarities. For example, some plants die badly, the foliage becoming an unsightly brown before disappearing. Oriental poppies and anchusas are typical examples, and should never be given a front-row position. Plant a late developer nearby so that its new growth masks the dying-down process of the poppy. Other plants need lime, or sharp drainage or very moist soil; some require staking, mulching or winter protection. Record these facts on the plan and get to know them. It will save untold trouble later on.

For special effects

When planning a border for some special effect, such as fragrance, colour tone or seasonal interest first study the descriptions on pages 176 to 185, and then draw a scale plan of the area. Drawing on your knowledge of the plants' height and growth span, fill in the gaps as suggested for ordinary borders. Here are some of the most important types of special-effect borders:

Colour borders   A pleasant conceit prior to World War I was the one-colour border, an idea that has recently been revived. Very pleasing effects are obtained for example by using only plants with blue, mauve or purple flowers (sometimes associated with silver foliage as well); or shades of pink – from flesh to scarlet; or creams, yellows and oranges. The gardener who plans such colour borders ultimately becomes a collector of plants spanning the chosen specialities, which adds to his or her interests.

Fragrance   There are not so many fragrant perennials as occur in bulbs and flowering shrubs, but sufficient exist to make the idea of a fragrant herbaceous border feasible. Paeonies, bergamot (*Monarda*), pinks and irises will provide the main plantings, and other suggestions can be found on page 248.

Cutting borders   After working hard to produce a masterpiece of colour grouping, few people will wish to cut the plants about for home decoration. The solution may be to make small cutting beds in some out-of-the-

way spot, possibly in the kitchen garden. These need not be wide; 75 to 90 cm (2½ to 3 ft) allows for picking, staking and weeding without treading all over the soil. Such beds should contain only reliable perennials like Michaelmas daisies, alstroemerias, paeonies and the like. See also page 246.

Permanent borders   These will be made up of 'no-trouble' plants, kinds that require little attention for years on end. Whereas Michaelmas daisies (asters) and golden rods (*Solidago*) exhaust the ground and have to be frequently lifted and divided, the permanents increase slowly and do best when left alone. They also form the hard core of normal herbaceous borders, and include such plants as paeonies, dictamnus and oriental poppies. The idea can be extended to a non-staking border – a boon to the busy gardener, since all the perennials included will have sufficiently stout stems to make supports unnecessary.

Paths and backgrounds

Grass paths are undoubtedly the most attractive for providing access to perennial borders, their green carpet providing a perfect foil for the brilliance of the flowers. But their upkeep is continuous, for grass must be cut, fed, watered and weeded, and have the edges kept in order throughout the summer (see p 86).

Gravel paths are durable, but these again need periodic weeding, and also need rolling and repairing from time to time. Frost has a tendency to lift gravel, which creates other problems. Crazy paving or hard paths of concrete, brick, cobbles, and the like provide fewer problems, although bricks can chip and cement turn slippery in wet weather.

Nothing beats a wall as background for a herbaceous border, although it can be dry close to the foundations, so leave a space between it and the first row of plants. It may be worth providing a narrow path or stepping stones in between, to ease access for attending to your plants. If a hedge is to be planted, go for an evergreen kind, such as yew, cypress or holly. These look attractive but leach food and moisture from the border, so again do not plant the border nearer than 60 to 90 cm (2 to 3 ft) from the hedge.

2 *Campanula lactiflora*;
3 *Miscanthus sinensis* 'Variegatus' (a grass); 4 *Helenium autumanale*;
5 *Anemone hupehensis japonica*;
6 *Salvia nemorosa* 'Superba';
7 *Heliopsis helianthoides scabra*;
8 *Lythrum virgatum*; 9 *Phlox paniculata*; 10 *Crocosmia masonorum*; 11 *Kniphofia* hybrid;
12 *Papaver orientale*; 13 *Phlox paniculata*; 14 *Rudbeckia fulgida*;
15 *Scabiosa caucasica*;
16 *Filipendula vulgaris*;
17 *Potentilla fruticosa*; 18 *Geranium pratense*; 19 *Coreopsis grandiflora*;
20 *Armeria maritima*; 21 *Sedum spectabile*; 22 *Tradescantia* × *andersoniana*; 23 *Oenothera missouriensis*; 24 *Anaphalis triplinervis*

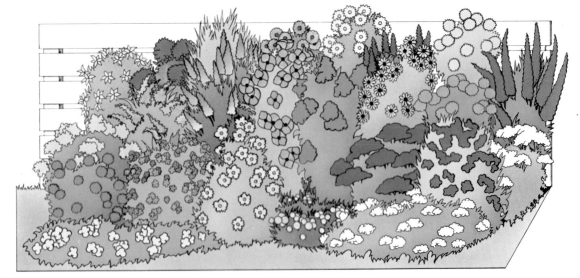

Mixed beds for prolonged interest

Those with only a small garden – and that includes most of us – have a particular need to plan for displays that span a long season. Whilst there is no scarcity of flowering perennials between the end of spring and midsummer, or in late summer, the choice is considerably narrowed at other seasons, particularly between autumn and spring. Obviously, early and late perennials have to be included when borders are designed for extended interest, but many people prefer to augment sparse displays of these with temporary or permanent plants from other groups – such as annuals, shrubs and bulbs. They then become mixed borders rather than herbaceous borders in the narrow sense of the term.

Shrubs and climbers

Shrubs are particularly useful for borders that back onto a fence or building, especially late-blooming shrubs and climbers. They provide a pleasing background and also out-of-season interest. Useful examples include *Viburnum farreri* (*V. fragrans*), which blooms on and off all winter, and being of upright, rather restricted habit, never becomes a top-heavy nuisance; the yellow-flowered, winter-blooming *Jasminum nudiflorum*, which can be trained up trellis; *Garrya elliptica*, a small-leaved evergreen with green and gold catkin-like inflorescences in late winter; the sweetly fragrant wintersweet (*Chimonanthus praecox*): and the evergreen, late winter-flowering *Clematis armandii*.

In summer, climbing roses, when trained up 2.5 to 3 m (8 to 10 ft) posts, will carry their blooms on a higher level than the perennials and make vivid splashes of colour – red, pink, white, yellow and orange. Their fragrance is an added attribute. If teamed with *Clematis* × *jackmanii* or one of its cultivars, the latter will use the roses for support, and climb up into the bushes, covering these, after the roses have had their day, with a profusion of velvety purple blooms. (The Jackmanii varieties are the most suitable for this purpose as, unlike certain other clematis, the old stems can be

cut down each spring and so are out of the way before the roses need pruning.)

It is also possible to introduce long-blooming shrubs at the ends of borders, and possibly in central positions as well. Hydrangeas are very suitable as they remain attractive for weeks. The blue spiraea (*Caryopteris* spp) is commonly planted in perennial borders, partly for its feathery blooms in late summer but mainly because the stems become herbaceous in cool climates. Even moderately severe winters cut them to

ground level, an occurrence that is duplicated by other shrubs in the eastern United States, particularly silvery-leaved, Mediterranean kinds like rosemary, lavender and santolina.

In a front-row position, clumps of winter-flowering heathers (see p 152) are invaluable for extending the flowering season and, being evergreen, remain attractive at all times.

Bulbs for mixed borders

In mild climates, one way to cheat winter is to plant pre-cooled daffodil bulbs. These flower several weeks earlier than normal, and even if bowed nightly by frosts, soon recover and remain attractive until the untreated daffodils take over. They will not, however, flower early where the ground lies under snow for weeks, so they are less useful in cold climates.

Later come tulips: first the water-lily kinds derived from *Tulipa kaufmanniana* in late winter, followed by the bright scarlet *T. fosteriana* hybrids, which provide vivid patches of colour at the same time as narcissi and doronicums come to bloom. Darwins are later still and, as with every section, should be grouped for maximum effect. Never line tulips out in straight rows in mixed borders, nor use them for edging purposes.

At the front of the border, small groups of single-colour hyacinths delight the eye and perfume the air, whilst snowdrops may be used informally throughout the area. A few bulbs of the latter may be disturbed by seasonal cultivation, but many remain and eventually spread to small colonies through self-set seedlings.

herbaceous perennials. On the other hand, bedding and Cactus dahlias, Shirley poppies, gaillardias and foxgloves fit in with many planting schemes.

Perhaps bedding plants are most useful in 'one-colour' borders (see p 105), where it commonly proves difficult to maintain continuity of display. In a cream, yellow and gold border, for instance, yellow antirrhinums, gloriosa daisies (rudbeckias) and dwarf single gold or yellow bedding dahlias help to tide over bleak periods. Pink stocks, rose-pink nasturtiums and pink 'cup-and-saucer' Canterbury bells (*Campanula medium*) do the same for a pink border.

Most bedding plants will be discarded after flowering, although some – such as dahlias – may be lifted and overwintered in a frost-free place. The spaces they leave can then be filled again with bulbs, or such spring-flowering plants as polyanthus, wallflowers and double daisies (*Bellis perennis* varieties).

Reserve beds
Even the best of herbaceous borders look rather drab at times, and the introduction of temporary bedding plants represents one useful method of brightening them up. Another, but more laborious, method of filling blanks – one much used in the past, when labour was cheaper and more plentiful – is to grow spare perennials in pots. For herbaceous plants in the 60 to 90 cm (2 to 3 ft) range, you will need at least 18 cm (7 in) pots. Grow them in a good potting mixture – preferably a loam-based type with ample nutrients. Keep the pots ready in a reserve bed, plunged to their rims in ashes or peat. Just before the plants come into flower, lift the pots and drop them into blank spaces in the border, again buried to the rim. When flowering is over, take them out again and return them to the reserve bed.

With feeding and top-dressing, such plants can sometimes be encouraged to continue for a second or third season without repotting. Remove up to 5 cm (2 in) of the topsoil – it washes out easily and harmlessly with a hose – and replace it with fresh potting mixture. Such pot-grown perennials can be easily increased by such techniques as root division and cuttings (see pp 346 to 350).

Purists may disapprove of mixed borders of herbaceous plants, bulbs and shrubs, but they offer the ordinary gardener greater variety and continuity of display and are often less laborious to maintain than the 'pure' herbaceous border. The shrubs may predominate, as with the azaleas in the small

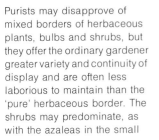

border **below left**, or they may be used to provide background and variety of height and form, as in the large border **left**, which even includes rose bushes. Perennials can also be planted in bold groups in 'bays' between groups of shrubs, as with the blue herbaceous veronica **above**.

Another way of keeping up appearances is to grow plants in large pots **above** that can be plunged to the rim in the border for their season, and then replaced with others brought on to flowering point in other pots in an out-of-the-way place, preferably plunged in moist peat or ashes.

Several tall bulbous plants are commonly planted in herbaceous borders and left there indefinitely, being treated in fact like normal herbaceous perennials. Good examples are the stately crown imperial (*Fritillaria imperialis*) and its purple counterpart *F. persica* 'Adiyaman'. These are spring-flowering, but in midsummer the summer hyacinths (*Galtonia*, or *Hyacinthus*, *candicans*) are equally useful, particularly when their tall spires of white, bell-shaped flowers are grouped near scarlet red-hot pokers.

Others worth remembering are bluebells for shady borders, nerines in warm spots and of course lilies. Many of these bulbs can remain *in situ* after flowering, but narcissi, tulips and hyacinths should be carefully lifted, laid in soil in an out-of-the-way spot, and after watering be left to ripen their bulbs. The spaces they vacate will then be ready to take other short-season later-blooming subjects.

Bedding plants
Annuals and tender bedding plants (see pp 206 to 223) are usually at their best in summer, so a select few may well take the place of ousted bulbs in mixed borders. Their use should be restrained, however; you can easily plant too many, and only those that blend or fit in with the perennials should be included. Pelargoniums (geraniums), for example, are too exotic; they look wrong with

Small herbaceous borders
It is neither essential nor always possible for herbaceous borders to be long and wide. Certainly, just as one can create more colourful designs and patterns on a big carpet than on a small rug, so a large area offers more scope than a small one. Yet, even so, there is no reason why the border of restricted size should not be as perfect within its own limitations.

The greatest danger lies in making a narrow border two-deep – that is, using only two rows of plants and setting these in straight lines. Regardless of its length, make the border as wide as possible, taking in the neighbouring path if necessary, and leave the front edge informal – in a series of

curves, not a straight line. This allows for a third row of plants to spread naturally here and there over the front.

Pay particular attention to plant textures when planning small borders. Foliage assumes even greater importance than usual, since it should not be so dense as to shade the more delicate plants, and coloured and variegated leaves pay dividends for the whole of the season. Plants like *Sedum maximum* 'Atropurpureum', with its purplish leaves and stems, and the variously coloured ajugas are real prizes in this respect. Select plants of varied height and form, and try to obtain as much variety and contrast as is feasible. Climbers can provide a backing.

Further uses of herbaceous perennials

Island beds

Flower borders need not be long and narrow, nor do they have to back onto a hedge or building. It is true that many follow this pattern, but they are not necessarily the most successful. Most herbaceous perennials are sun-lovers; they need plenty of light and air, but also cool roots. Instead, they often suffer competition from hedge roots. Or the walls and buildings they front dry out at the foundations and reflect the heat. Also, all backgrounds tend to 'draw' plants upwards and outwards, so that some may need staking. Plants grown in the open invariably do better and need less support, because they develop shorter, sturdier stems.

A very pleasant method of achieving airy conditions is by making island beds, cutting these out of an existing or previously prepared lawn. There can be one or several beds – it all depends on the size of the garden. They can be large or small, or in a variety of sizes, but always make them informal in shape. A set of circles, for example, would look absurd for

mixed border perennials; the ideal are rough lozenge or kidney shapes, which are easily turned one way or another to make a variety of patterns.

Be careful to relate the shapes of the beds, and the pattern they form, to the overall shape of the garden and its major features. Repeat a curved lawn line in the shape of the bed, and avoid too narrow a strip of grass between the bed and the lawn's edge. Also take into account the boundary walls, fences or hedges, and any plantings of trees or substantial shrubs. In medium to large gardens especially, you may be able to use a belt of trees some distance from the new beds to form a backcloth to the colourful plantings of perennials when these are viewed from the house or another important vantage-point. In others, a single specimen tree – or perhaps a clump of bamboos or tall, majestic grasses – spaced 3 m (10 ft) or more (depending on the size) from a carefully shaped and planted island bed, can form a balancing or accent point to the whole composition.

Island beds can be used for a miscellany of plants and purposes. If you have several in one garden, contrasting colour schemes are a practical proposition; for example, one could

Island beds are adaptable to many purposes. They can accommodate a single imposing specimen plant such as pampas grass (*Cortaderia selloana*) **left** or a massed planting of smaller species such as *Liatris spicata* **above right**. But for the greatest scope create a bed of fluent shape **above** and plant a harmonious collection of hardy perennials. The design principles are the same as for a conventional herbaceous border (see p 104).

be blue and silver, another have only white and green flowers and so on. Or they can be geared to seasons, with perhaps early summer the peak period for one bed, early autumn for another. Bulbs, annuals and even rock plants may be included, and occasionally pieces of stone, but only if the beds link into a rock garden or fit in with surrounding features in other ways. A further idea is to devote each bed to a single class of plant, for example grasses, or different species and varieties of irises, or plants with variegated and coloured foliage. The whole point about island beds is their adaptability. At the more conventional extreme, they can be treated as a kind of two-sided herbaceous border (see p 104).

Accent plants

An accent plant is one that is distinctive enough to draw attention to another feature in the garden and so double its impact. The right grouping can add importance to a wrought-iron gateway, a patio or a well-head, or set off a picture window. Accent plants can either be planted directly in the ground near the object concerned, or grown in containers of good soil. The last are particularly useful to stand about on paths or hard surfaces, and plants to consider for such treatment include delphiniums, red-hot pokers and astilbes.

There are also special plants particularly suitable for special places – for example, at the edge of a pool, where ligularias, rodgersias, rheums and hostas are ideal; or near the house, where a stately New Zealand flax (*Phormium tenax*) commands instant attention. Another specimen plant is worthy of a bed to itself. This is *Ferula communis,* the so-called giant fennel. A graceful giant whose branching flower stems are topped by masses of yellow flowers, this plant grows to 3 to 3.5 m (10 to 12 ft) in three months. The huge

Creating an island bed

Mark the outline with white tape or white-painted pegs. Then, using a half-moon edging tool, cut the outline into the turf. The tape or pegs can then be removed if you wish. Next, using the half-moon tool and a turfing iron or spade, cut the grass into turves 5 cm (2 in) thick. Set them aside for turfing or patching, or chop them into small pieces. Then double dig the bed (see p 334), incorporating the pieces of turf or ample manure. It is best to prepare the bed in the autumn, then plant in spring.

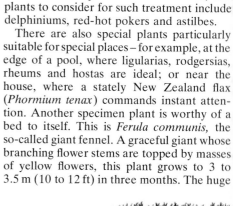

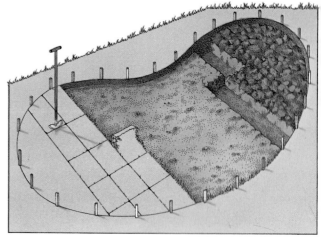

leaves, cut into myriads of thread-like segments, belie their size, for they have an airy, lacy appearance unique amongst tall plants.

In Sweden, small island beds are commonly devoted to a single specimen plant, much as other gardeners use shrubs and trees. The kinds selected are usually fairly bold, for fine foliage remains attractive even after the flowers are gone. Acanthus, phormiums, macleayas or even (for a shady spot) a clump of *Kirengeshoma palmata* are typical and very desirable for summer interest. Such plants invariably do well since they receive plenty of light and air. However, you should select plants that do not require staking. Normally, specimen plants are set in grass, but they look equally well planted in a hole in crazy paving or flagstones. When planting in a lawn, prepare the ground as thoroughly as for a large island bed.

Hardy plants with trees and shrubs
Herbaceous perennials are often used as fill-ins for shrub borders, as well as the other way round (as in the more conventional mixed border). The best kinds for such situations are those that tolerate a reasonable amount of shade, for they are bound to be at least partly overshadowed by their neighbours. Because shrubs and trees have far-reaching roots, the soil must be kept damp and fertile, which necessitates an annual mulch of leaf-mould, moist peat or garden compost. This is highly important. Many plants will grow in moist shade, but very few in dry shade.

At the beginning of the season, before the foliage develops on deciduous trees, a number of early perennials flower, even when set far back close to the trees' trunks. White-flowered dentarias, for example, gleam like small stars in the dim undergrowth, and the coarse *Trachystemon orientalis* is not to be despised, since it will grow in poor light. It is true that the large leaves, which follow the purplish-blue borage-like flowers, are not very inspiring and the plant is invasive, but it is not difficult to keep in bounds if all unwanted shoots are regularly hoed off.

Towards the front of the border, where the light is dappled or sunny for part of the day, the choice is greater. Here, Lenten roses (*Helleborus orientalis*) will make a weed-defying carpet of evergreen leaves topped from mid-winter to spring by masses of cream, green,

pink or purplish flowers. Some ground-carpeting plants (see p 232) also thrive, as well as some campanulas and primulas, *Helleborus lividus corsicus* and *H. foetidus*, Solomon's seal, hostas and dicentras.

As summer advances, clumps of day lilies (*Hemerocallis*) are useful, although these flower better where the light is good; also oriental blue poppies (*Meconopsis*) and jeffersonias. In late summer or early autumn the fine foliage and yellow, snapdragon-like flowers of *Corydalis lutea* and the ubiquitous *Anemone hupehensis japonica* make attractive groupings.

Border edgings
Edgings for herbaceous or mixed borders can be living or inert; the choice depends to a great extent on the setting and surroundings. Herbaceous perennials in patio beds, for example, will probably need a course of bricks or concrete blocks to hold soil back from the paved sitting area. Pieces of rock or large flints, although sometimes used, are less satisfactory since they are uneven in shape and attract slugs and snails. Cost can also be a prohibitive factor.

The simplest natural edging is a narrow strip of good turf, kept an even width. But achieving this takes time and patience, necessitating weeding, feeding, grass-cutting and edging. Where borders run on to a lawn the question of edging need not arise; the plants themselves billow out between grass and border very naturally and satisfactorily. (Though for ease of maintenance a narrow edging of bricks or paving may be placed in between.) With paving, it is often preferable to let plants have their will, clipping them back occasionally to keep them tidy.

If a uniform finish is required, an edging of pinks (*Dianthus* cultivars) is ideal as these remain green (or grey) all winter. Nepeta (catmint) can be used on well-drained soil, but tends to rot off in winter on wet land. Armeria (thrift), another evergreen, is always neat, with short grassy foliage. Polyanthus can be used for spring effects and *Stachys olympica* (*S. lanata*), the lamb's tongue, which thrives on the poorest soil, is valuable because of its silver leaves. More dwarf perennials will be found on page 184.

Herbaceous perennials have a multitude of uses in various parts of the garden. For underplanting trees and shrubs and edging shrub borders it is wise to choose shade-tolerant species such as *Trillium grandiflorum* **left**. Make sure that they receive adequate moisture. Perennials of striking form can be used as accent plants in key situations, emphasizing the impact of a decorative feature such as the Chinoiserie false bridge **right**, here flanked by *Gunnera manicata* and the sword-like *Phormium tenax* 'Variegatum'.

Growing and using bulbs

If you want plenty of flowers all round the year, diversified form and lavish colour, quick and virtually guaranteed success with minimum effort – as well as a challenge to the creative instinct – the simple and short solution is to plant bulbs. There are bulbs for every gardener, whether beginner, experienced enthusiast or skilled horticulturist. They are easy to obtain in great variety, and although they may appear to be relatively expensive to buy they provide good value for money, particularly in that the vast majority readily multiply. A few types require particular cultivation procedures or specific conditions, but most are easy to grow and will flourish in any well-drained soil. Provided that a little care is taken in selecting and planting them, they can be sited in sun or partial shade in any garden location in all but the most extreme climates.

No other group of plants yield so many floral styles with such subtle combinations of colour and texture and such heterogeneous foliage, over such a lengthy flowering season, as bulbs. The variations of stem height range from a few centimetres (an inch or two) to over 3 m (10 ft). And there is a bonus too in that many bulb blooms make long-lasting subjects for home flower arrangements.

Bulbs are popular because they give so much for so little effort. Begin bulb growing by choosing from those that local suppliers offer in quantity, for these will reflect successful local planting patterns. As familiarity with their few simple needs is acquired, any gardener can then graduate to the rarer bulbs.

Basic characteristics

A bulb is quite different from a seed, although both represent dormant phases in a plant's life-cycle. Inside every bulb there is a whole tiny plant – roots, stem, leaves and flower-bud – and all the nutrient necessary for it to grow. All it needs is a proper home in the ground and sufficient water.

The word bulb has become a generic term encompassing all bulbous plants. These include true bulbs, such as hyacinths, tulips and lilies; corms, such as crocus and gladioli; tubers, such as dahlias and many begonias; and rhizomes, such as eranthis, some anemones and many irises. They vary in size and shape, even among each type, but they all possess common components and an identical life-cycle. The difference between them simply lies in the precise structure of the food storage organ that enables them to survive through a dormant or resting period. In true bulbs, for example, food is stored in swollen leaf bases, while rhizomes are swollen underground stems.

Bulbs are so valuable to the gardener because they perpetuate themselves in a number of ways – depending upon the kind of bulb and the exterior conditions. All bulb flowers produce seeds, but raising bulbous plants from seed is the most time-consuming and difficult method of propagation.

Most bulbs have other ways, of greater benefit to the everyday gardener. Narcissus and daffodil bulbs, for example, divide and produce offsets in the form of small bulbs. Crocus and gladioli corms disappear after flowering, but produce a new corm to provide bloom the following year, together with a number of small cormlets that will flower in later years. Some lilies and tulips produce stolons at the end of which a small bulb forms, and other lilies produce aerial bulbils in leaf axils. These just fall to the ground and develop into new plants.

Many bulbs can be left alone to form expanding colonies which only require lifting, segregating and replanting every three to five years. Clumps of tender bulbs that require annual lifting and frost-free winter storage can be separated according to size at lifting time and planting again at the appropriate time the following year. Both rhizomes and tubers can be divided with a sharp knife. Each piece of rhizome should contain a bud or eye, and tubers should be divided so that each section contains part of the original stem.

These divisions can be replanted to form a whole new plant the following season. Little skill is needed to increase stocks of bulbs in these ways.

Bulbs can be successfully grown anywhere in the world except in the coldest climates, and, with minor exceptions, their sequence of flowering is the same everywhere. The precise date of bloom and the length of the flowering season will, of course, be

affected by variation in climate. Although some types of bulbs or some varieties are not particularly prolific in certain climates, every gardener will, nevertheless, find a wide choice available. Local suppliers and regional bulb catalogues will indicate which bulbs are best suited to relevant climatic zones.

Buying, planting and cultivation

Bulbs are dormant but nevertheless living plants, and should always be handled with care. A quality bulb is weighty for its size, plump, firm and unscarred, although peeling of the tunic (the dry outer skin) is natural and not an indication of a defect. There should be no sign of mould.

The largest bulbs of each variety invariably produce the showiest blooms, but there are wide variations between species, and even between some cultivars of the same genus. For outdoor cultivation, however, you can save money by purchasing so-called

bedding-size hyacinths, which yield entirely adequate results, and it is a sensible economy to buy the smaller grades of, say, daffodils if these are intended for naturalizing in grass. With the exception of daffodils and narcissi, which are available as single-nose or double-nose bulbs (the latter producing two flowering stems), bulbs are sold according to their circumference in centimetres. Many retailers, however, simplify matters by listing their bulbs as top, first or good flowering size.

There are two major sales seasons for bulbs, coinciding with planting seasons. Buy and plant spring-flowering bulbs – those that bloom from winter through to late spring – during the autumn. For best results, however, plant daffodils and narcissi by mid-autumn, and delay planting tulips until late autumn. Buy and plant the more tender summer-flowering bulbs from middle into late spring. Planting of some types must be delayed until there is no longer any danger of frost, but some lilies may be planted in the autumn in areas not subject to severe winters. There is also a limited range of autumn-flowering bulbs available in the shops from midsummer, and these should be planted immediately.

Ideally, all bulbs should be planted as quickly as possible after purchase. If planting must be delayed, keep bulbs with tunics in open bags in a cool, dark, well-ventilated place. Bulbs with scales or fleshy roots should be temporarily stored in flat boxes of damp peat or sand until it is convenient to plant them out.

All hardy spring-flowering bulbs require a six-week period of weather below 5°C (41°F) to maintain their growing cycle. Gardeners living in consistently warm areas can still enjoy the whole range of spring bulb bloom, however, by pre-cooling the bulbs before planting. This simply involves placing the bulbs in ventilated bags in that section of a domestic refrigerator where a temperature of 5°C (41°F) can be maintained for six to nine weeks before planting. Alternatively, you may be able to buy prepared bulbs that have been pre-cooled by the grower or seller.

Because bulbs develop extensive root systems, it is a wise precaution to plant them in well-dug ground. But the most important requirement is soil that drains well. As a rule,

conditions, the size of the bulb and the stature of the plant. The diagram gives general guidance, but bulbs should be planted on the deeper side in light soils and on the shallow side in heavy soils or very warm climates. Spacing is a matter of artistic licence provided that the bulbs do not touch each other, but a spacing identical to the depth of planting is generally effective. In outdoor containers, where concentrated display is usually desired, bulbs can be planted much closer together than in the open ground.

Thorough watering is essential immediately after planting and throughout the active growth of the plants. Taller-growing plants should be staked to prevent wind and storm damage. A peat mulch, 8 to 15 cm (3 to 6 in) thick, helps to retain moisture and discourage weeds, and is also effective for winter protection. When flowers pass their peak, remove the flower-heads to prevent seeds from forming. Whether bulbs are left in place or lifted,

For bulbs left *in situ*, such fertilizers can be applied as a top-dressing at any time after flowering and before top growth appears again the following season. Or they can be mixed with the soil before replanting bulbs that have been lifted for winter storage. Watering with liquid manure every week or two until buds show colour will contribute to perfection of bloom.

Where to plant bulbs

Bulbs may be effectively planted alone or with other plants in formal and informal beds, in all types of borders, in woodland areas and wild gardens, in lawns and rough grass, in rock gardens, in cutting beds, beneath deciduous trees, beside paths, pools and steps, between shrubs and paving stones, on slopes, atop hollowed-out walls, in outdoor containers – indeed in virtually every garden location enjoying full sun or partial shade.

Every variety is suited to a number of appli-

left and far left Tulips are ideal for a short-lived but flamboyant spring display in containers and patio beds. below left Delicate nodding heads of *Fritillaria meleagris* look charming beside the still water of a pool. right The popular spring-flowering bulbs – hyacinths, daffodils and narcissi, tulips and muscari – provide the first great colour show of the gardening year. far right Many bulbs, such as this *Narcissus cyclamineus* 'Jack Snipe', can be naturalized in grass or woodland.

bulbs will flower in any soil from sand to clay, but a good friable soil with plenty of humus will help bulbs to do their best. If your soil is too sandy or too heavy, dig in some peat or sand as conditions dictate. Most bulbs will tolerate both neutral and slightly acid soils, although hyacinths prefer chalky soil and some lilies will not tolerate lime.

The specific depth at which each bulb should be planted varies according to the soil

make sure not to cut the foliage until it has died down naturally. When lifted bulbs are stored, remove all dead foliage and earth, and keep them in a dry, well-ventilated and cool but frost-free place.

For first-year bloom no fertilizer is needed, except for notably greedy bulbs such as lilies, gladioli and dahlias. Slow-acting fertilizers other than animal manure are particularly recommended for feeding bulbs (see p 352).

cations, essentially determined by its flowering time, size, habit and colour. You will find descriptions of all the important types, together with suggestions for uses and more detailed cultural instructions, on pages 188 to 205. The scope for individual taste is infinite – a simple matter of determining when and where flowers are wanted, and then selecting from those bulbs which best lend themselves to particular garden locations.

Planting bulbs

Plant single bulbs with a dibber, trowel or special tool, ensuring that the base rests on soil 1 and does not hang in 'mid-air'. For large groups, excavate soil, break up the bottom, position bulbs and re-cover. Plant to the correct depth; depths shown are for average conditions: 1 tulip; 2 cyclamen; 3 base-rooting lily; 4 rhizomatous iris; 5 anemone; 6 crocus; 7 ranunculus; 8 tuberous begonia; 9 *Iris reticulata*; 10 dahlia; 11 daffodil; 12 gladiolus; 13 *Fritillaria meleagris*; 14 hyacinth; 15 stem-rooting lily

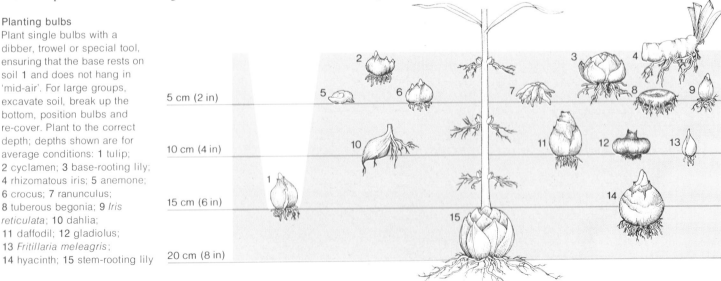

5 cm (2 in)

10 cm (4 in)

15 cm (6 in)

20 cm (8 in)

Seasonal bedding for quick colour

In Victorian times, when labour was plentiful and cheap, both public and private gardens used to plant lavish displays that were renewed once or twice a year. These usually consisted of half-hardy plants grown in a nursery, reserve garden, greenhouse or frame, and planted out in a specially prepared bed just before they were ready to begin blooming. Exotic plants were often used for these displays. In carpet bedding, the most elaborate form, potted plants were buried rim-deep in ornately shaped beds.

Rising costs have cut back these bedding displays, except in showpiece public gardens. More and more beds and borders, in private gardens particularly, are being planted with roses, flowering shrubs and other permanent occupants. But a striking and continuous show of colour from spring until the autumn frosts (and even in winter in the warmer regions of the world) can still be managed if you are prepared to go to the trouble.

Bedding plants are indispensable in the modern garden whenever additional colour is required. They can be interplanted in mixed borders and among shrubs or roses. They are excellent for edging paths, lawns and borders of all kinds, and for every type of container – from ornamental urns to hanging baskets. They are also particularly useful to the owner of a new garden who wants an established and colourful display almost overnight.

Growing bedding plants

Bulbs, tubers, hardy and half-hardy annuals, biennials and some perennials are used in bedding schemes. For spring display, bulbs, seeds of hardy annuals and young plants are usually planted where they are to flower in early to mid-autumn, except in the most severe climates. In order to maintain a continuous display, half-hardy annuals and other tender plants for summer bedding must be started under glass in late winter and early spring, and grown on in pots or boxes so that they are ready for planting out when the spring display is over.

A greenhouse or frame, preferably heated, is essential for raising half-hardy flowers from seed. If the seeds are sown indoors, perhaps in a small propagator, and the seedlings pricked out in due course, they will still need the protection of a greenhouse or frame until they can be hardened off (gradually accustomed to cooler temperatures) ready for planting out from late spring to early summer, depending upon local climate. Seedlings raised in a cold greenhouse or frame will flower later than plants sown and grown on in heat.

You can, of course, buy young plants for summer bedding direct from garden centres, but in cooler regions it is important not to purchase the less hardy kinds too early, in case of late frosts. Also, try to ensure that the plants have been properly hardened off.

Preparing the bed

Display beds should generally be sited in sunny and relatively sheltered areas of the garden, although calceolarias, tobacco plants (*Nicotiana*) and tuberous begonias are shade-tolerant, and Siberian wallflowers will survive in exposed positions.

Soil for bedding plants should not be too rich. It should be well dug, and then, unless conditions are dry, lightly mounded towards the centre to show off the planting scheme to best advantage. It is best to give beds and borders their annual dressing of manure, hop manure, mushroom compost, garden compost or other organic material in the early summer, after the spring flowers have been lifted. Autumn manuring may promote rapid, soft growth that will not stand up well to severe winter weather. Generous manuring in spring should sustain the summer flowers, and there should be enough nourishment left in the soil for the autumn-planted flowers and bulbs. Give one or two feeds with a proprietary general fertilizer during the summer, and two or three foliar feeds just after planting, at intervals of 10 to 14 days, to help the roots become established (see p 352). A light dressing of bonemeal at, say, 135 g/m² (4 oz/sq yd) is all that is needed in autumn.

Planting and care

If spring bedding plants are to be planted in the autumn in their flowering positions, it is essential to clear the beds of summer flowers and complete the replanting by mid-autumn, while the soil is still fairly warm. This gives the plants an opportunity to make some new roots before the cold weather sets in. If the autumn is fine and free from frosts, and the summer flowers are still making a good show, there is the temptation to leave them there. But you should be hard-hearted and lift them in early autumn, fork over the bed or border, and plant the bulbs and spring flowers. (The planting of tulips can be left until late autumn, however, to lessen the risk of slug damage.)

In exposed gardens, it is best to leave planting the spring flowers until after the end of winter, when all risk of severe frosts is past. However, remember that in exposed windy gardens the Siberian wallflowers (*Erysimum*, or *Cheiranthus, × allionii*) usually overwinter better than ordinary wallflowers. They make small plants in the autumn, but grow very fast in the spring. They take over as the bulbs fade, and will carry the display on into late spring or even early summer.

Planting out the summer bedders can be a delicate operation. Whenever possible, choose fairly cool weather to make the transfer. Take out the holes to receive the plants in the evening, and if the soil is dry fill them with water. Also water thoroughly the plants to be moved next day. When transplanting the young plants, disturb the roots as little as possible, and leave as much soil as you can adhering to them, to protect them during their ordeal. Then water the plants in and – unless the weather is very hot and dry, when they will require a daily watering – the plants will hardly know they have been moved.

Many bedding plants are now bought or grown in peat pots, and are planted out pot and all. (The roots grow through the peat.) This ensures less shock to the plants, and there is less danger of damaging the roots, but it is most important when planting these out to see that the soil in both the bed and the peat pot is really moist. Also, cover the top of the peat pot with 2.5 cm (1 in) of soil; otherwise it will act as a wick and evaporate away water needed by the plant.

A series of cold nights may occur in late spring or early summer, just after tender plants like geraniums and dahlias have been planted out. The foliage goes pale, or even yellow, but a few foliar feeds will usually start the plants growing again. In the autumn it is necessary to lift geraniums, bedding fuchsias, cannas, begonias and other tender perennials before there is danger of frost. These plants

Spring bedding: pansies and tulips planted with hardy perennial doronicums (yellow daisies)

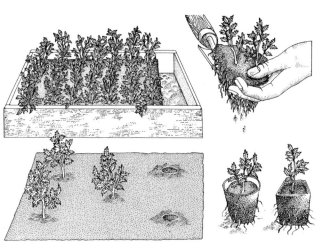

Setting out bedding plants
The day before planting out, thoroughly water plants raised or bought in boxes, peat pots or flower-pots. At the same time, take out planting holes spaced according to the plants' size, and fill with water. Carefully remove and separate boxed plants, minimizing root disturbance. Plant firmly and water in. Plants in peat pots should be planted complete with the pot, covering this entirely with soil.

are expensive and worth saving. The top growth of the herbaceous and shrubby subjects should generally be cut back, and the plants should then be potted. In most cases, the cut shoots can be rooted in a peat and sand mixture to provide extra stock. The tubers of begonias and cannas should be stored in a frost-free place over winter, ready to bring into growth again in spring.

Spring bedding
Traditional spring bedding consists of such flowers as wallflowers, primulas and primroses, forget-me-nots, large-flowered English daisies (*Bellis perennis* Monstrosa varieties) and ornamental pansies, interplanted with bulbs – crocuses, daffodils, narcissi, tulips, hyacinths and scillas.

Bulbs are now expensive, but you can plant clumps of daffodils that will, hopefully, increase over the years (see p 190). Leave them in the ground after flowering, and if they are watered well in dry spells from the time the flowers fade until the foliage dies down, they should increase. Spraying with a foliar feed several times at ten-day intervals in spring is also beneficial. The Darwin Hybrid

tulips flower in mid-spring (see p 192). They have large flowers, so can be planted 12 to 15 cm (5 to 6 in) apart, and if they are lifted after flowering and heeled in to ripen off they may be replanted in the autumn.

Summer bedding
Half-hardy plants such as petunias, marigolds, salvias, zinnias, annual rudbeckias, fibrous-rooted begonias (*Begonia semperflorens*), ageratums, cosmeas, cleomes and asters, bought as young plants or raised from seed, will replace the spring bedding. Antirrhinums can be raised and planted out (after hardening-off) earlier than these half-hardy annuals; they are hardy in milder areas, but are usually treated as half-hardy annuals.

A small stock of tender perennials – such as zonal and ivy-leaved geraniums, tuberous begonias and lantanas – together with such shrubby subjects such as hydrangeas, tender fuchsias and the lovely blue *Plumbago capensis,* may be grown in a cool greenhouse kept to a minimum temperature of 7°C (45°F), and used for bedding out during the summer (see p 222). All of them are easily propagated by cuttings, and from a modest outlay on a small

selection of plants you can soon work up a substantial stock.

It is unfortunate that dahlias do not succeed very well if planted among other plants; they prefer a bed on their own. But some of the dwarf dahlias that are easily raised from seed grow reasonably well in the front row of a border (see p 189). An easy (and cheap) alternative to traditional summer bedding is to sow a few clumps of hardy annuals in the spaces left by the spring flowers (see p 114).

Dot plants, grown on a tall stem so that they rise above the main plantings, give height to a summer bed, and serve to make it more interesting (see p 221). Fuchsias, lantanas and heliotrope can be trained as standards up to 1.25 m (4 ft) high. The plumbago may be trained up a tripod of canes, and all these examples can be planted out for the summer and brought back to the greenhouse before the coming of the autumn frosts. Geraniums too can be grown as short standards on a stem, say, 60 cm (2 ft) high. The dwarf forms of the grey and silver *Senecio cineraria* (*Cineraria maritima*) provide a good contrast with vividly coloured plants such as geraniums, salvias and begonias in summer bedding schemes.

Late-season bedding
Like the hardy annuals, some bedding plants raised from seed, including alyssum (*Lobularia*), pot marigolds (*Calendula*), linaria, and lobelia, may be clipped over hard with shears when their first flowering is over, to induce a second crop. In some seasons they may even be trimmed over a second time, and will give a third crop of flowers. The regular removal of faded flowers to prevent all plants from setting seed not only keeps the beds looking tidy, but will prolong the flowering period of most plants.

Late-flowering plants such as marigolds or dwarf chrysanthemums, raised in a reserve bed if there is space in the garden, will be useful to replace the early summer flowers. Again, transplanting must be done with care.

In warm climates, where frosts are rare or non-existent, however, bedding can be continued right through the year. In such places, all the plants that are considered in cooler regions to be half-hardy or tender may be grown outdoors at any time. South African plants such as gazanias, arctotis and venidiums are colourful and free-flowering. *Chrysanthemum frutescens* is a popular year-round bedder in Mediterranean countries. The cannas, geraniums, heliotropes, plumbago, bougainvilleas, daturas, oleanders, fuchsias and similar plants that in cool climates are used only for temporary bedding-out in summer, and are then returned to a greenhouse for the winter, may be left out all the time. Indeed, in the subtropical climates, these plants, being perennials, are often left to form the framework, as it were, of a bed or border and to maintain a succession of flowers, and spaces in between are filled with the more ephemeral annuals.

For descriptions and cultural details of many plants suitable for bedding schemes, see pages 214 to 223.

Summer bedding: red salvias, silver cinerarias, mauve ageratums, marigolds, petunias, geraniums

Using hardy annuals and biennials

Most people took their first faltering steps in gardening by sowing some seeds of easy hardy annuals – perhaps Virginia stock or nasturtiums – in their first child's plot. Certainly, hardy annuals and biennials are highly adaptable plants, thriving in most soils and situations where they receive a good deal of sun. They can be sown directly where they are to flower (though this is not usual in the case of biennials). They require the minimum of care; weeding, dead-heading, watering in dry spells and staking of the tallest specimens is all the attention they ask for. They are also wonderful value for money; a few packets of seed will cheer up any garden from spring until the autumn frosts, and can provide an inexpensive supply of cut flowers.

Basic characteristics

An annual plant completes its entire life cycle (from germination, through growth and flowering, to seed-ripening) within one growing season, and then it dies. Biennials take two years. They are sown during the first year, and produce foliage; during the second they flower, produce seed and then die. To ensure an annual display, it is necessary to sow fresh seed – of both annuals and biennials – every year. The seed used should preferably be commercially produced, since seed gathered from plants pollinated at random in your own garden rarely gives good results.

Hardy annuals and biennials can, by definition, withstand frost. They do not need high temperatures for seeds to germinate, so these can be sown in open ground. The annuals are normally sown in their flowering positions, either in spring and early summer or, in

centres and nurserymen. In either case, they are treated from then on like bedding plants (see p 112). The same is true of half-hardy annuals, which cannot withstand frost, and must not be sown outdoors in cool regions until summer; to obtain worthwhile flowers they must generally be raised under glass and planted out after hardening-off.

Except where otherwise indicated, the rest of this article relates to the use of hardy annuals. Individual kinds of these are described on pages 206 to 210. Kinds of hardy biennials are covered on page 210. For details of how to grow them from seed, see page 344.

see p 112; pages 206 to 210; page 210; page 344

few flowers; some, such as nasturtiums, fairly thrive on poor soil.

Such annuals as the now rarely-grown clary (*Salvia horminum*), the dwarf strains of cornflowers, eschscholzias (Californian poppies), love-in-a-mist (*Nigella*) and the dwarf lupin *Lupinus* 'Lulu' do best when sown in early to mid-autumn, while the soil is still warm and friable. You can thin them to, say, 2.5 cm (1 in) apart after the seedlings come through, but leave final thinning until the spring, as slugs and other pests may take their toll of the seedlings during the winter. If not sown in the autumn, the seed of early-

Cheap and cheerful colour
left For an inexpensive and quick show of colour in a new garden or an unusual, semi-wild (though short-lived) effect in an established one, simply scatter a packet of mixed hardy annual seed over a prepared seed-bed and wait for it to come into flower. Broadcast the seed thinly in early spring for a midsummer display, rake over the surface and keep the bed moist and weed-free while the plants are establishing themselves.
right For a more planned effect, group a number of plants of the same kind in irregular patches or drifts through the border, creating pleasing colour contrasts or gradations between adjacent groups.

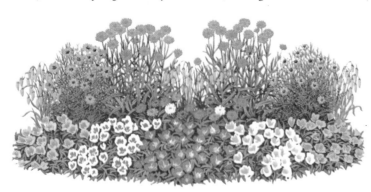

Planting schemes for annual beds For a predominantly blue and pink effect **left**, cornflowers (*Centaurea cyanus*) and love-in-a-mist (*Nigella damascena*) can be planted with pearl grass (*Briza maxima*) and an edging of a dwarf pink variety of *Godetia grandiflora*.

You can make an old-fashioned cottage-garden-style perfumed bed **right** by planting Virginia and night-scented stocks (*Malcolmia maritima* and *Matthiola longipetala* [*M. bicornis*]) with mignonettes (*Reseda odorata*) and an edging of pansies (*Viola* × *wittrockiana*).

areas where winters are not too harsh and with plants that are hardy enough, in the autumn for flowering the subsequent year. Where possible, autumn sowing generally produces sturdier, earlier-flowering plants. Even in cold climates, many annuals can be sown in autumn if given some protection with cloches over winter.

Since hardy biennials produce no flowers in their first year, they are generally sown and grown on in rows in a reserve bed in an odd corner of the garden. If you have no room, plants can bought in the autumn from garden

Planting and care

Generally speaking, hardy annuals prefer a sunny position, although a few will tolerate partial shade. They like well-drained soil that has been cultivated thoroughly and reduced to a fine tilth before sowing. If you plan to sow in the spring, do your rough digging before winter begins, so that the winter frosts and rain can break the lumps of soil down. Then, before sowing, use a tined cultivator (see p 376) and rake to make the soil fine and crumbly. Hardy annuals do not like over-rich soils, which tend to produce leafy plants with

flowering annuals should be sown in early spring, as soon as the ground is workable. It should be moist but not wet. Later-flowering types are sown throughout the spring and early summer.

To obtain sturdy, free-flowering plants, hardy annuals must not grow too close together. Dwarf plants, such as candytuft, can be grown as close as 15 cm (6 in), but larger types, such as lavateras, should be at least 45 cm (18 in) apart. Sow the seed thinly in the first place (see the illustration), and be sure to thin out the seedlings as soon as they are big

Sowing an annual bed
below Using sand or a sharp stick mark patches from 50 cm (20 in) across for small plants up to 1 m (3 ft) for large. Cast seed thinly over each patch, cover lightly with soil and thin out when the plants are big enough. Or make parallel drills in each patch with a draw hoe, spacing them the distance apart recommended for final thinning and running them in different directions in adjacent patches. Sow thinly; this is easiest if pelleted seeds or a seed tape **above left** are used. Rake soil over the drills, and keep well watered until germination takes place.

enough to handle. The same applies to biennials grown in a reserve bed.

Both annuals and biennials need ample moisture throughout their period of growth. Water them with a fine rose whenever the ground shows signs of drying out. Mulching the soil around the plants will help to prevent water loss from the soil, and will also keep the roots cool and discourage weeds (see p 356). The annual bed should, in any case, be weeded from time to time – by hand, as the roots could be damaged by a cultivating tool.

The flowering season of some of the hardy annuals is rather short, but with many kinds the season can be extended by sowing seed successively, at intervals of two to three weeks. And with a little care in cutting them back immediately after flowering, some may be persuaded to give a second or even a third crop of flowers. You can snip off the dead flowers of toadflax (*Linaria*), alyssum, lobelia and pot marigolds (*Calendula*) with shears, and they will soon be in flower again. Sedulous removal by hand of dead flowers is generally feasible only with small numbers of plants in a small garden. Once the plants have stopped flowering, pull them out ruthlessly – perhaps replacing them, if the season is not too late, with late-flowering bedding plants.

Hardy annual beds

Beds or borders solely of annual flowers can be charming, but are not generally showy for very long periods. Even with a combination of hardy annuals sown *in situ* and half-hardy annuals raised under glass and planted out when danger of frost is past, you cannot expect to see much colour until early summer. But if you raise them yourself, such plants can give a brave show reasonably cheaply.

It is tempting to grow annuals in a border with a background of a hedge, wall or fence. It looks attractive, but the plants will tend to lean towards the light and may need the support of twiggy sticks that would not be needed in a bed out in the open. Obviously, if the bed is to be viewed only from the front, the taller annuals are best placed at the rear, those of medium height in the middle and the dwarfs in the front. There is no need to be slavish about this; a drift of low-growing annuals like linarias, dwarf asters, dwarf marigolds or dahlias can be allowed to extend from the front half-way back here and there. A bold patch of, say, larkspurs, annual rudbeckias or sunflowers will give height to parts of the bed. If the bed is free-standing, one can naturally make greater play of contrasting heights.

The use of foliage plants here and there adds variety. There are several good kinds easily raised from seed, among them the castor-oil plant (*Ricinus communis*), burning bush (*Kochia scoparia*), *Euphorbia marginata* (*E. variegata*), *Senecio cineraria* (*Cineraria maritima*), *Centaurea candidissima* (*C. ragusina*) and various silver or golden pyrethrums. See also page 221.

Whether to have beds of single kinds of annuals – antirrhinums, asters, marigolds or whatever – is obviously a matter for personal preference. Much depends on the space available. Where this is limited, it is probably best to go for combinations of plants that last longest in flower – for example, calendulas with rudbeckias. Two planting schemes designed for pleasing colour effects are illustrated on the opposite page.

Other uses for annuals and biennials

Hardy annuals are so easy and adaptable that they have many uses – particularly as 'fillers'. Time was when it would have been unheard of to 'cheat' with herbaceous borders, for example, by planting patches of annuals or biennials among the perennial plants. But now that most gardens are so small, flower borders are more commonly in full view of the house, and it is desirable to have some colour in them for as long as possible.

Patches of forget-me-nots and wallflowers provide early spring colour. Siberian wallflowers – the yellow and golden varieties of *Erysimum* (*Cheiranthus*) × *allionii* – will carry on the show into early summer. Sweet Wil-

liams and Canterbury bells will also flower in early summer before the full flush of herbaceous plants comes along.

The forget-me-nots and wallflowers can be removed in late spring and replaced with half-hardy annuals raised under glass (see p 344). The gaps left by the sweet Williams are more difficult to fill, and it may be worthwhile growing on in pots some *Begonia semperflorens* or dwarf dahlias, to drop in when the sweet Williams are removed.

Ground-covering plants such as vincas and heathers are often planted between the taller shrubs in a shrub border. These may take two or three years to cover the ground and make an effective weed-smothering carpet. Hardy annuals and biennials can help enormously in these years to produce colour and interest in the meantime. Eschscholzias (Californian poppies), larkspurs, clarkias, godetias, cornflowers and Shirley poppies (varieties of *Papaver rhoeas*) and other annuals can be used to fill the empty spaces.

It is anathema to suggest to alpine plant enthusiasts that annual or biennial flowers could be interplanted with their rock plants. But rock gardens are usually at their best in the spring, and tend to be rather dull from midsummer on, unless planting is carefully planned (see p 120). The rock hybrid or 'Magic Carpet' antirrhinums, only about 10 cm (4 in) high, look well in a rock garden, as do Livingstone daisies (*Mesembryanthemum criniflorum* or *Dorotheanthus bellidiformis*), alyssum, lobelia and similar low-growing plants. Similarly, forget-me-nots, pansies, dwarf eschscholzias (such as 'Mission Bells'), alyssum and *Mesembryanthemum criniflorum* are all excellent for underplanting rose beds.

Annuals with special properties

Climbing annuals (see p 212) have many uses, especially in a new garden. You can plant clumps of sweet peas, *Cobaea scandens* (a perennial usually grown as an annual) or even white- or red-flowered runner beans (commonly used as decorative plants in Finland and the United States) to ramble over pea sticks and give height to a border. Half-hardy annual climbers such as the beautiful morning glories (varieties of *Ipomoea*) can be used to clothe a wall or fence, as can climbing varieties of nasturtiums and the closely related Canary creeper (*Tropaeolum peregrinum*) – both fully hardy.

Annual flowers seem to rely more on bright colours than on scent to attract the insect visitors they need to ensure pollination. Some, however, are powerfully scented but, as in the case of mignonettes (*Reseda odorata*) and night-scented stocks (*Matthiola longipetala* or *M. bicornis*), not very showy. Sweet alyssum combines attractive, if tiny, white flowers with a delicious honey scent, but the less colourful types are best interplanted with more showy flowers – for example, Virginia stocks (*Malcolmia maritima*) with the night-scented ones. A few of these plants grown near the house will scent the air delightfully on a warm summer evening.

Pots, tubs and other containers

Plants grown in containers – ranging from ordinary flower-pots to decorative tubs and vases – present an effective method of cultivating flowers, herbs, vegetables or fruits in difficult or impossible situations, such as on terraces, balconies, concrete aprons and forecourts, or suspended from buildings and lamp-posts. They are also useful to maintain small gardens in peak condition, since directly one set of plants passes from flower they can be immediately replaced by others that have been planted and grown to flowering point in an inconspicuous corner.

The most important preliminaries to success are a good growing mixture, or compost, which in most instances needs changing annually; provision for drainage; adequate watering; and the regular removal of dead leaves and spent flowers to prevent seeding. (Seed-production depresses further flowering so this is highly important.) Also, all containers should be deep enough to keep plant roots cool and moist, especially where they stand in full sun. Pots of low-growing evergreens will help to shade larger containers stood behind.

The growing mixtures most commonly used for container culture are either soil-based or loamless (peat-based); soil taken straight from the garden is unsatisfactory. The former type may be mixed at home – normally with equal quantities of good loam, coarse sand and moist peat or leaf-mould, together with some dried blood and bonemeal. Or they can be obtained from garden centres or nurseries prepared to a formula. Loamless mixture are basically peat with added fertilizers and sometimes sand. They are clean and light to handle, and give excellent results provided the material is neither overwatered nor allowed to get bone-dry. See also page 345.

Hanging baskets

Hanging baskets provide bright spots of colour in unorthodox situations, such as the corners of buildings, hanging from lamp-posts or over doorways. One kind, which is semi-circular, with one side flattened, can be hung against a wall. They are not suitable for plants during the winter months since the roots are too exposed and can be killed in cold weather. So plant hanging baskets in late spring and grow them along under cover until it is safe to hang them up outside on strong supports.

Hanging baskets made of wire look best lined with sphagnum moss, but they dry out very quickly, so need frequent watering – twice a day in hot weather. A lining of plastic (either in addition to or instead of the moss) will retain moisture, but holes are necessary to prevent waterlogging. The best method of watering is to lower the basket and suspend it in a bath of water for about 20 minutes. Suitable plants for hanging baskets include trailing lobelias and nasturtiums, ivy-leaved geraniums (pelargoniums), small-leaved ivies, pendent fuchsias and tuberous begonias, and various trailing house-plants.

Window boxes

Window boxes when pleasingly planted do a great deal for a house with a plain façade and,

unlike hanging baskets, can provide year-round interest. They may be constructed of various materials – such as timber, terracotta, reinforced plastic, glass-fibre or concrete – the main essential being that they are very firmly attached to their supports. Apart from window sills, plant boxes can be fastened to brackets on a boundary wall; there they look particularly effective when staggered at various heights.

Although drainage holes are not essential – and perhaps are undesirable in some situations – they nevertheless provide an insurance against overwatering. Whether they are there or not, always provide a 2.5 cm (1 in) drainage layer of broken flower-pots, stone or brick rubble, covering this with dry leaves, bracken or coarse peat debris to stop fine soil filtering down and so defeating its purpose. Then fill with growing mixture and plant.

Some boxes have detachable liners, which is very convenient when a quick change is desired. Suitable plants for window boxes include the winter cherry (*Solanum capsicastrum*), *Erica carnea* cultivars and small kinds of aucubas and *Euonymus radicans* for winter display. In spring come various bulbs, polyanthus, forget-me-nots and wallflowers, followed if required by cinerarias and primulas. For summer there are geraniums (pelargoniums), stocks, fuchsias, trailing lobelia, shrubby calceolarias, petunias and a wide range of other annuals and bedding plants (see pp 214 to 223). It is also possible to grow alpine strawberries, various herbs and small salad plants like 'Tom Thumb' lettuce, 'Pixie' tomatoes, and mustard and cress.

Tubs and plant boxes

For many years, sawn-down wine and beer casks have been used for the cultivation of plants, for they are comparatively cheap to buy and deep enough to take plants with

extensive root systems like rhododendrons, azaleas, hydrangeas and the half-hardy agapanthus and daturas. Their term of life however depends on how they are treated; extreme dryness, for example, causes the staves to shrink and fall out, so many people today purchase the virtually indestructible glass-fibre models. Many of these are extremely attractive (and expensive), especially those fashioned as replicas of old lead vases and cisterns, or based on the wooden containers used for growing orange trees in the gardens at Versailles in France.

There are jardinières for balconies or for standing at the corners of a formal pool, pedestal vases for raised positions and boxes of various shapes, sizes and designs to stand about on patios, steps, entrances to rose gardens, by front doors and in other key positions. Apart from glass-fibre and wood, plant boxes can be made of concrete, aluminium or terracotta. Most expensive of all are those made from real or reconstructed (reconstituted) stone.

Tubbed and potted plants
Whether forming a whole pot garden **left** or specimens such as the impatiens **below** and *Mimulus glutinosus* **below right**, plants in containers combine impact and versatility.

right 1 Strawberry pots are easiest to water if you fit a wire netting core. **2** Always provide adequate drainage topped with a layer of fibrous peat; if possible, raise off the ground. Re-pot permanent plants each spring, carefully replacing a third of the growing mixture. Or scrape or hose away the top 5 cm (2 in) and replace with fresh, adding bonemeal. **3** Sempervivums live for years planted in bricks.

Strawberry and parsley pots
There are various sizes of strawberry pots, all with lipped openings about 5 cm (2 in) across around their sides. Small plants are inserted in these and firmed, and more arranged around the top. The containers are ideal for strawberries (especially the alpine kinds), petunias and other annuals, herbs – plant a different kind in each opening – and also hyacinths and double tulips for spring display. White-painted strawberry barrels, with 5 cm (2 in) round holes cut at various points in the sides, also make good containers. Parsley pots have very small holes, so only plant seedlings in these, and in a few weeks the pot will be completely hidden by a bower of delicate greenery.

Most strawberry and parsley pots are made of terracotta, which is porous, so that they often dry out unless adequately watered. Some gardeners overcome this by making a narrow roll of wire netting, as long as the height of the pot. This is then stood in the centre of the pot and filled with stones. The rest of the space is taken up by planting mix-ture, and when water is poured into the top of the core it spreads in all directions and so moistens the soil. Another idea is to stand the pot in a large terracotta saucer, keeping this filled with water. This is a simple but most effective method since the water is drawn into the container and up through the soil by capillary action. Strawberry pots made of glass-fibre are not porous, so the core method is best for these.

Sink gardens and other ideas
Old stone sinks make excellent receptacles for small alpine plants and dwarf conifers, and since they can be raised on brick piers or a low wall they are easy to tend. They can be used for a miscellany of rock plants, or devoted to one genus – like saxifrages or gentians. It is then easy to provide special plants with the right soil. For more details, see page 122.

Another idea is to make a miniature rose garden, complete with pygmy rose bushes and tiny standards, small flagged paths and pergolas. Or one can make a whole miniature garden, complete with summer-house, lawn and miniature pool, using tiny plants and cutting the lawn when required with scissors.

Other plant containers to use outdoors include old chimney pots, stood on a flat surface and filled with trailing as well as upright plants. Some chimneys have side vents that can be planted up in the same way as strawberry pots.

Tower pots consist of plastic sections with extended pocket-like appendages. The base of each section can be fitted into the top of another so that it is possible to build the towers to various heights. A range of plants can be used in the pockets, including petunias, geraniums and alpine strawberries.

The kind of builder's bricks that have holes through them can also be used for growing plants. Fill the holes with soil and put a small houseleek (*Sempervivum* spp) in each. Stand them about in unsightly corners such as on manhole covers. They persist for years and years, the brick completely hidden by the houseleeks after a period of time.

Hanging baskets
left Planted with colourful specimens and combined with window boxes, these brighten a dull facade. If using wire baskets **right**, first line with damp sphagnum moss, installing a saucer to retain moisture. Or use green or black plastic instead of or inside the moss, making ample drainage holes. Half-fill with planting mixture, and gently thread the shoots of trailing plants through the lining and wire, leaving the roots inside. Fill to within 2.5 cm (1 in) of the top and plant the other plants. Water.

Growing bags
These comparatively new innovations consist of bolster-shaped plastic bags filled with loamless growing mixture. They can be laid on any hard surface, an opening made in the top (the bought bags have special areas for cutting) and after watering planted up. They are excellent for tomatoes – about four plants to each bag under glass, or five outdoors – aubergines, marrows and other vegetables, also herbs and flowers. They need regular watering but produce stupendous crops in areas where normal vegetable cultivation is impracticable. After harvesting, the growing mixture can be used to mulch choice garden plants.

The rock garden

Many people return from holidays spent in mountainous regions entranced with the beauty and profusion of the spring flowers and filled with a desire to recreate such pleasures in their own garden. When they discover that a wide variety of mountain plants from many parts of the world can transform the beauty of spring into a beauty lasting through all four seasons, their love of rock gardening is born.

The rock garden offers perhaps the most intimate pleasures of horticulture and the closest involvement of the gardener with his plants. It is the closest to nature, too, for the successful rock garden captures the essence of the alpine landscape – with its harsh outcrops of rock, gently sloping meadows and flowing screes – as well as supporting the most beautiful of its plants, many of them delicate and frail-looking but in reality extremely tough. To achieve the first aim requires considerable skill, and it will help you to clarify your ideas before beginning to design a rock garden if you study those at some of the great gardens open to the public, to see how the rock formations can be positioned. To grow alpine plants successfully requires special conditions – most notably sharp drainage and a fairly open aspect – but is otherwise straightforward.

Site preparation

Given a sloping site and the ready availability of local stone, the battle to create an effective rock garden is half won, but do not be deterred if you have less than ideal conditions. A city rock garden cannot be truly natural, so you must contrive to make it look as natural as you can. It must have height – at least one-fifth of the maximum width – so, if a natural slope does not exist, pathways must be excavated downwards and the rock bed built up. Contrive varied aspects if possible, for not all rock plants like full exposure to sun; this is best provided by a site running north and south. Avoid overhanging trees, with their menace of drips in winter, though a rock garden partially protected by the shade of distant deciduous trees is often ideal. To be aesthetically satisfying, the rock garden needs to be an entity by itself, and must have its own background, preferably dark.

The more care that is taken with the initial preparation of the site and soil, the longer the rock garden will remain in good condition and the better the plants will grow. The first essential is to free the site completely of perennial weeds, but, as already mentioned, good drainage is the vital factor. On heavy soils, particularly on a flat site, provide artificial

drainage consisting of rubble, broken bricks and large stones in a layer 30 cm (12 in) thick. This can be laid in trenches where the rock garden is to follow a natural slope, but where it is to be built up from flat ground the drainage can be partly dug down and partly built up to form a core to the rock garden.

The soil itself must drain well too, and this is usually achieved by mixing in stone chippings: small gravel or granite chips for most plants, limestone chippings for lime-lovers. Many 'everyday' rock plants and dwarf shrubs will thrive in any good garden soil, and special preparation for these is a waste of time. But the real jewels of the high mountain crags call for special soil conditions, such as a scree mix-

ture comprising up to two parts stone chippings with one part each of loam and peat. Many of the shade-lovers, on the other hand, need a 'woodland' mixture of loam, leaf-mould and sand. Make up ample quantities of suitable soil mixtures (using topsoil excavated when installing drainage) before beginning construction work.

The stone

Stone is obviously needed for a rock garden, though it is not essential for growing rock plants, as is shown on pages 122 to 125. Its value lies in the cool root-run it provides for the plants, its artistic merit if properly used, and the fact that, by staggering the pieces horizontally and vertically and leaving soil pockets, it facilitates three-dimensional planting and a satisfying overall effect.

Always choose a local stone, for economy's sake. (A moderate-sized rock garden 3 by 5 m [10 by 16 ft] will need some 2 tonnes of stone

in assorted sizes up to 25 kg [½ cwt].) Preferably use a local sandstone, yellow or red; it is porous, attractive and the plants like it. On environmental grounds, avoid any stone quarried in an area of great natural beauty. Limestone is not ideal in city gardens, because the acid atmosphere makes it remain white and stark. Tufa, if you can get it, is ideal. Of limestone origin, it is not truly a rock for it is deposited from water in much the same way as stalactites and stalagmites. It has one drawback – cost – but, bulk for bulk, it weighs only a quarter as much as many rocks. It is porous, moisture-absorbent and easily worked, and plants can be established directly in holes drilled into it (see p 123). Whatever stone you

choose, do not mix different types. And never use broken concrete, although artificial rocks of hypertufa (see p 123) are acceptable if skillfully shaped.

Construction

When placing the rocks, much depends on the site, size and layout of the rock garden, and on the choice of stone, but there are a number of general principles. First and foremost, the rocks must never lie on the soil surface; they should appear to emerge from it, as in a natural rock outcrop. Tilted in this way, they will also direct rainwater back to the plants' roots. On a sloping site, the rock strata can be more or less horizontal, forming a series of terraces. On a built-up flat site, have the rocks sloping gently, as in an outcrop. Just as in a natural formation, they should all slope at the same angle; avoid the 'broken-back' look that occurs if you tilt the rocks at opposite ends of the rock garden in opposite directions in an

Building a rock garden
right The prime essentials are good drainage and rocks angled so that they seem to form outcrops from the ground. This is relatively simple on a slope but needs careful planning on the flat. **centre** A rock garden can be effectively combined with a pool and peat bed. **far right** Construction is easy in the angle of two walls.

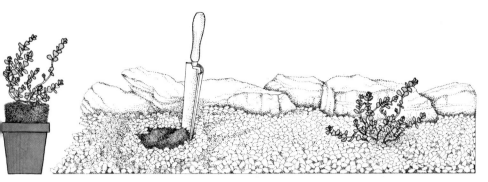

Planting a rock garden
above Alpines are generally sold in small pots. Water the plant well, then remove it from its container without disturbing the root ball; if it is pot-bound, tease out some of the roots at the base. Scrape back the top-dressing of gravel from the planting site, and make an adequate-sized hole. Place the plant in position, fill in around with soil mixture, firm down and water again. With sun-lovers like *Penstemon bridgesii* **left**, re-spread chippings around the neck of the plant.
When creating a rock-garden planting scheme, make use of trailing plants such as *Phlox douglasii* **far left** to form cascades of colour over rocks. A completed rock garden **right** should combine plants and stone into a pleasing three-dimensional composition.

effort to arrange that both appear to emerge from the soil. Differences in slope of this kind should never be visible from one viewpoint. Also in keeping with nature, the natural stratum lines of the rock should always be horizontal, never vertical. Arrange the rocks in relation to each other to form strongly horizontal (but not too regular) strata.

Every stone must be firm and steady to walk on, but avoid using cement; many rock plants bind stones together naturally. Never try to lift heavy rocks; manoeuvre them onto stout planks and then manipulate them into position with a long crowbar. Pack the prepared soil mixture (see above) behind each rock and ram it firm; never leave air pockets behind or under stones that can harbour slugs and wood-lice. Where you place rocks one on top of another, a cushion of soil will help make the joint firm. It is sensible to place suitable crevice plants in these joints at the time the rockwork is being built; establishing plants in

such positions is difficult later. Sempervivums (houseleeks) and silver saxifrages are ideal plants for providing this sort of living cement.

It is not only the rocks that make a good rock garden, of course, but also the soil pockets in which the plants grow. These may range from a broad 'plateau' on the higher reaches to smaller level areas on the terraces; from small pockets, open to the sun but sheltered on all sides from the wind, to vertical crevices where rosette-forming plants do well. Form and fill these with soil mixture as you go, and gently firm it. After a week or two the soil should have settled. Top up as necessary, and then spread a top-dressing of 5 to 6 mm ($^{3}/_{16}$ to $^{1}/_{4}$ in) rock chippings about 1 cm ($^{1}/_{2}$ in) thick that will help retain soil moisture but prevent the necks of the plants rotting. They will also keep the plants' roots cool and suppress weeds. Choose limestone chippings for lime-loving plants; gravel or granite chippings for others; but do not top dress peat beds.

Sun and shade; scree and water
Just as one side of the rock garden (to the south in the northern hemisphere) should be angled for those plants that revel in the maximum possible sun, so should the reverse slopes accommodate the shade-loving plants. The degree of shade may not be very much – even the slight shade cast by a rock is often sufficient – but it commonly helps if the shady side is more steeply sloping.

A scree – in nature, virtually a river of small, loose stones down a mountainside –

should always be in the sun. It should flow down from some height, between breaks in the rock strata, spreading outwards as the slope lessens at the bottom. Position occasional rocks almost buried in the scree mixture (see above) to act as stepping-stones and to give a cool root-run to the plants. The scree mixture should be about 30 cm (12 in) deep.

At the foot of the shady slope, a water-retentive peaty soil mixture should replace the scree. Here you can place a small pool (see p 128), possibly with a cascade (see p 132). This provides not only an attractive feature but also a moist microclimate for the plants that are to grow here. Many enthusiasts choose to blend the rockwork into blocks of peat with just the occasional rock as a stepping-stone in a bed of lime-free peaty soil, forming a peat garden (see p 126).

Planting and maintenance
Once the rock garden is constructed and the soil mixtures have settled, you can begin planting. Nurserymen grow all alpines in pots or other containers, so you can plant them at any time of the year when the soil is not frozen. Make sure they receive ample water in dry or hot weather until they are established, however; do not confuse the need for sharp drainage with a lack of need for moisture.

The choice of rock plants is the subject of the article on page 120, but there are general principles to bear in mind. A rock garden should be labour-saving; it never has to be dug over and the plants seldom need dividing. The newcomer to rock gardening, however, often makes the same mistake – of putting in too many plants without considering their mature size. This is all part of the fun, of course, and in any case there is no better form of weed-control than close planting, but aim always at saving work.

Avoid free-seeding plants with tap roots, the Welsh poppy, *Meconopsis cambrica*, being a supreme example. If the rock garden is small, avoid the rampant 'everyday' rock plants such as helianthemums or aubrieta, which are constantly in need of cutting back; concentrate instead on the real alpines, four or five species of which can grow in the space required by a single helianthemum. These can give you four or five times the enjoyment as well as needing less attention. If you do include rampant growers, place them where they are hemmed in by rocks and least able to overrun their neighbours.

You can save trouble in other ways, too. Rocky outcrops rising from an immaculate lawn are all very well at major horticultural shows, but they make the grass impossible to mow; have a paved path, scree bed (see p 125) or narrow channel of gravel between grass and rockwork. Finally, if the rock garden is not too large and your pocket not too small, top dress all but the peat beds annually with rock chippings and bonemeal – a fine long-term fertilizer, except for lime-haters. For the peat bed and the shade-loving and lime-hating plants, a top-dressing each year of leaf mould or peat plus some hoof and horn meal is equally advisable.

Planting the rock garden

Anybody, it has been said, can have an attractive and colourful rock garden in the spring, but the whole joy and essence of this form of gardening lies in making the garden attractive in every season of the year. The alpine enthusiast is helped in this by not being restricted to using nurserymen's plants. He can go out into the world's mountains and see and choose his plants, for his love is of wild species in their vast variety. He can choose them for their colour or form, or for the period at which they flower. He should not, if he has any feeling for the natural environment, take plants – or even cuttings or seed – from the wild, but, having identified his choice, he can obtain seed or nursery-raised plants from specialist suppliers.

In broad outline, rock-garden plants fall into four main categories. Firstly, there are the mat-forming, creeping and spreading species that cover the ground in sheets of colour and in many cases will cascade down over a rock face. In direct contrast are the smaller beauties, some forming cushions or hummocks studded with flowers, others simply poking their heads up through the ground or holding their flowers above a cluster of leaves. Thirdly there are the rosette-forming plants that are most at home growing in vertical crevices and, finally, the larger, more 'architectural' plants – dwarf shrubs, trees and herbaceous types – that give height and bulk.

Colour in the rock garden

Colour is a difficult concept to handle in any part of the garden. Green is the basic colour of plant life, and you must first create a basic backcloth of green before blending in the colour masses that the green so admirably frames. This applies just as much in the rock garden as elsewhere – not that the rock gardener relies on green alone, for foliage plants of gold and silver also play their part.

Just as colour masses and foliage need blending together in carefully planned asociation, so do different colours need blending. This is particularly important in the rock garden, for rock plants are not always easily moved once they are planted, so that good associations of colour and foliage need planning in advance. Such planning must encompass the time element as well as position. In the rock garden more than in any other feature, you must give constant thought to the amount of colour and interest you can produce from the same piece of ground.

For example, a patch of the evergreen mat-forming *Dryas octopetala* (best, incidentally, in its form 'Minor') might have bulbs of *Chionodoxa luciliae* planted below it. The season would then commence in early spring with the blue of the bulbs, followed by the white flowers of the dryas, and then in mid-summer would come its attractive feathery seed-heads to carry the interest on into autumn. In the same way, plantings of snowdrops can be intermingled with dwarf willows such as *Salix herbacea* or the red-catkinned North American *S. nivalis,* whose new leaves appear on its bare stems just as the untidy leaves of the snowdrops are passing.

Rock plants for winter

Key	Botanical name	Colour(s)	Remarks
1	*Crocus flavus* (*C. aureus*)	Orange-yellow	Well-drained soil and sun
	Crocus laevigatus	White; lilac	Well-drained soil and sun; scented
	Cyclamen coum	Pink; white; carmine	Half-shade; gritty soil
	Daphne mezereum	Purple-rose	Sweet-scented shrub; eventually rather too big for most rock gardens
	Helleborus atrorubens	Maroon-red	Half-shade; flowers very early
	Helleborus niger	White	Half-shade; ordinary soil; the Christmas rose, but only selected forms flower in early winter
	Hepatica transsylvanica	Blue	Half-shade; gritty soil
2	*Iris unguicularis cretensis*	Blue-violet	Narrow-leaved dwarf form of *I. unguicularis*; must be starved and sun-baked to flower freely
	Iris histrioides	Blue	Hot, dry position; likes lime
3	*Narcissus asturiensis* (*N. minimus*)	Yellow	Well-drained soil and sun; the smallest trumpet daffodil, less than 8 cm (3 in) tall
	Ranunculus calandrinioides	White flushed pink	Well-drained but moist soil in sheltered spot; crepe like petals: glaucous foliage
4	*Saxifraga* × *apiculata*	Yellow	Sun and scree; white in the form 'Alba'

Rock plants for spring

Key	Botanical name	Colour(s)	Remarks
1	*Aubrieta deltoidea*	Purple to rose-lilac	Well-drained soil and sun; likes lime; good forms include 'Gurgedyke' and 'Mrs Rodewald'
	Clematis (*Atragene*) *alpina*	Blue	Grow from seed, to push up through dwarf shrubs
2	*Cytisus ardoini*	Yellow	Good garden soil and sun; a dwarf species of broom only 15 cm (6 in) tall
	Gentiana acaulis	Blue	Superlative spring gentian of Alps; leafy soil and sun; if fails to flower, try *G. verna*
	Haberlea spp	Blue; white	Lime-loving crevice plant for cool, shady slope
	Iris pumila; *I. chamaeiris*	Wide range	Superb colour forms available; well-drained soil and sun
	Lithodora diffusa (*Lithospermum diffusum*)	Blue	Lime-free soil and sun; 'Heavenly Blue' and 'Grace Ward' are among finest of all rock plants
	Primula denticulata forms	Wide range	Moist soil; sun or partial shade
	Primula × *pubescens* forms	Wide range	For sunny scree
3	*Pulsatilla vulgaris* (*Anemone pulsatilla*) forms	Wide range	Sun and scree; the pasque flower
4	*Ramonda* spp	Blue; white	Lime-loving crevice plant for cool, shady slope
	Saxifraga oppositifolia	Rose-purple	For damp shade; 'Ruth Draper' is outstanding

Another aspect to consider when planting is the way you want to cover the ground. Although the aim of rock gardening at its best is to capture the essence of a natural landscape, there is room for different interpretations. There are rock gardens where every plant is an entity in itself, surrounded by a top-dressing of chippings and in splendid isolation from its neighbours. In others there is a carefully contrived disarray, where plants merge together in a splendour of colour. Perhaps these alternatives show the difference between a plantsman and a gardener.

Plants for each season

The tables with this article list a dozen or so of the best rock plants for each season, and were you to restrict your planting to these your rock garden could have colour and interest in every month of the year. However, they represent only a small selection of many dozens of excellent rock plants that are available. You will find details of a wide range in the series of articles starting on page 224. For details of how to plant alpines, see page 119.

There are all too few flowers to be enjoyed in the bleak months of winter, but they give a great deal of pleasure. The few flowers of the first snowdrop of winter (or perhaps it is the last of autumn), *Galanthus nivalis reginae-olgae*, are infinitely more satisfying than all the alyssum and iberis of spring. The alpine enthusiast looks forward each year too to the unfailing appearance of *Helleborus atrorubens*, often before the shortest day.

To choose a dozen of the best plants for spring flowering is an invidious task, for there are simply too many of them. Make your choice with care and restraint, remembering that the beauty of your rock garden does not depend on spring colour alone, but on foliage, architectural plants, plants of interest and above all on the provision of colour in the other three seasons of the year.

Again, the choice of plants for summer display is so vast that you might well consider specializing. Many gardeners – and probably most keen rock gardeners – tend to specialize in particular genera. *Dianthus* species and hybrids – the rock pinks – can alone provide colour galore in summer, and the vast realm of campanulas (bellflowers) would carry the colour well into the autumn.

Autumn is the difficult period in the rock garden, when tumbling leaves make a sodden mat on plants that are used to the clear air and drying winds of the mountains. Yet the last of the little cyclamen and the first of the crocuses add a sparkle to the fading tones of the gardening year's end. Those gardeners with a deep, peaty loam can provide a home for the fantastic carpets of blue formed by Asiatic gentians such as *Gentiana sino-ornata*. Yet even if those who garden on a sun-baked limy soil cannot raise these plants, there are always the zauschnerias from California to mingle their orange-red flowers with the blue of ceratostigmas from China.

The well-planned rock garden is never bereft of colour, even when other garden features are at their emptiest.

Rock plants for summer

Key	Botanical name	Colour(s)	Remarks
	Acantholimon venustum	Pink	Scree and sun; the finest of the genus, the so-called prickly heaths; starry flowers
1	*Alyssum (Ptilotrichum) spinosum*	White	Delicate spiny shrublet with grey foliage; for hot, dry spot; pale to deep rose-pink in 'Roseum'
	Androsace sarmentosa	Pink	A trailing plant for scree
2	*Campanula × haylodgensis*	Blue	Gritty soil; double flowers
3	*Dianthus neglectus*	Pink	A compact, delicate rock pink for acid soil
4	*Dryas octopetala* 'Minor'	White	Ordinary soil; evergreen
5	*Gentiana septemfida*	Blue	An easy gentian; ordinary soil in sun or shade
	Gypsophila 'Rosy Veil'	Rose	Ordinary soil; immensely long-lived; a microform of *G. paniculata* much less vigorous than the type
	Linum alpinum	Sky-blue	Ordinary soil; a delicate, gently waving flax
	Penstemon roezlii	Rosy-red	Gritty soil and sun
6	*Phlox* 'Chattahoochee'	Lilac	Half-shade; a new North American woodlander
	Potentilla nitida	Rose-pink to white	Mat-forming, with silvery appearance; for well-drained, limy soil in full sun
	Saxifraga longifolia 'Tumbling Waters'	White	Probably the finest of a magnificent genus; lime-loving, for scree and sun

Rock plants for autumn

Key	Botanical name	Colour(s)	Remarks
	Ceratostigma plumbaginoides	Blue	Poor soil and sun; rampant
	Colchicum autumnale	Rose-pink; lilac; white	Hot, dry site, chosen carefully where large leaves in spring will not look ugly; blooms without leaves
1	*Crocus speciosus*	Blue; purple; white	Any soil; full sun
2	*Cyclamen hederifolium* (*C. neapolitanum*)	Pink to red	Leafy, well-drained soil in partial shade; will seed itself; beautifully marbled leaves
	Disporum oreganum	Orange berries	Shady site and peaty soil
3	*Gentiana sino-ornata*	Blue	An all-time great; for peaty, lime-free soil
	Kniphofia nelsonii	Orange	Any soil in full sun; a dwarf red-hot poker
4	*Lapeirousia laxa* (*Anomatheca cruenta*)	Crimson-scarlet	A South African for a sunny, sheltered spot; lift the corms in winter in harsh climates
5	*Polygonum vacciniifolium*	Pink	Any soil, in sun or shade
	Saxifraga fortunei	White	Damp soil; protected position; superb foliage
	Schizostylis coccinea forms	Pink to red	Kaffir lily from South Africa; any good soil in sun; give winter protection in cold areas
	Zauschneria californica	Orange-red	Full sun in protected position; the Californian fuchsia

Alpines without a rock garden

There is no doubt that if you have the space, conditions and inclination, a well-constructed rock garden makes the most appropriate setting for alpine plants in all their diversity. But it is not the only way to grow them. For the shade-loving, lime-hating types that thrive in a 'woodland' type of soil, the peat bed (see p 126) is ideal. One of the most popular ways of growing alpines of all kinds without a rock garden is in a raised bed (see p 124). Some kinds can also be grown between paving stones – on the level or on a slope – or in a scree bed (see p 125).

This article deals primarily with growing alpines in containers of one sort or another, either in the open or under glass. These have the universal advantage of making it easy to give individual plants their ideal soil conditions. However, they represent not just alternatives to the rock garden but a genuine extension of the gardener's opportunities. For example, the keen alpine plantsman who wishes to grow the really choice, often difficult, high alpines in a region with high winter rainfall or other adverse conditions has few options open. These plants are used to a blanket of snow to protect them from winter wet, or from drying winds, for many months of the year, and the nearest he can get to such conditions is to grow them in pots in a frame or alpine house. This calls for much dedication, expense and hard labour, but, fortunately, there are alternative methods suitable for the less dedicated.

Alpines under glass
The alpine house is virtually a greenhouse with additional ventilation – both along the ridge and at bench level – and no heat. It involves the maximum of year-round interest and pleasure, but a great deal of work. Pots must be kept clean, and be plunged to their rims in sand or chippings to prevent drying-out. Annual re-potting is needed, which even-

tually means space problems, and pests and diseases are always worse under glass than in the open. But it is all worth it to the enthusiastic alpine plant-lover.

It is possible to adapt the same type of alpine house by making the plunge beds for pots into open scree beds. Filled with suitable drainage material and soil mixtures, the same plants can be grown without pots, making a degree of 'landscaping' possible (with some rocks if desired). Here again, certain problems arise; freed from the restriction of pots, some plants grow too quickly. Many plants like to have their roots restricted, either by pots or by close root association with other plants, and the sudden freedom of an open bed brings problems. Watering is more difficult to control, and the art of watering is the art of growing where alpines are concerned – never too much, especially in the resting season; never too little especially in the growing season. Many alpine gardeners compromise – or perhaps compound their problems – by having a plunge bed along one side of the alpine house and a scree bed along the other.

Although some form of glass protection is needed to grow the whole range of alpine plants in most climates, you need not go to the expense of constructing or adapting a special greenhouse. A cold frame (see p 380) is quite satisfactory, though not so convenient. Even an ordinary Dutch light – a solid-walled frame with lift-off glass top – straddling a sand plunge bed will grow plants just as well as the most expensive alpine house. In some ways, it even has advantages in that the lights can be lifted off in the summer and the labour of watering avoided.

Alpine troughs
One of the most attractive and popular ways of growing the more compact treasures of the mountains is to build up a collection of stone troughs – feeding troughs, watering troughs, stone sinks, even old stone coffins. These attractive containers, once so widespread, are now hard to find, however, and some alternatives are mentioned below. They are all best

mounted on a pedestal to keep slugs out, and can be planted with mixed genera and perhaps a dwarf conifer to give height and form. Alternatively, the specialist may wish to plant each trough with a collection of related plants, such as Kabschia saxifrages, silver saxifrages or a variety of sedums (stonecrops). Pieces of rock can be included to make a miniature landscape. These look best if few and comparatively large, even in a moderate-sized trough; every crevice between the rocks can be planted with suitable specimens.

Free drainage is vital to success, so one or more drainage holes must be drilled in the bottom if they do not already exist. Since troughs vary widely in depth, a good general rule is to place a minimum of 8 cm (3 in) of drainage material – either broken crocks or chippings – in the bottom, having first covered the drainage hole with a piece of perforated zinc. Between this and the actual growing mixture should be a coarse fibrous layer to

*Sink gardens can be planted to form a complete miniature landscape **top**; slow-growing dwarf conifers are ideal for adding height. Rocks and scree can be introduced **below**; the pink-flowered trailing plant is Saponaria × olivana.*

An alpine house allows the enthusiast to grow even the most difficult of alpine plants in pots in their ideal soil and protected from winter wet. They are exposed to the maximum light, air flows freely, but there is no artificial heat.

Planting an alpine trough

If necessary, drill one or more drainage holes in the base. Cover these with strips of perforated zinc and spread an adequate layer of drainage material – broken flower-pots, brick pieces and stones – over the bottom. Cover this with a layer of inverted thin turves, leaf-mould or fibrous peat to stop the growing mixture clogging the drainage material. Fill with a good loam-based potting mixture that contains plenty of grit. Mix in stone chippings (to improve drainage) if the trough is deep, extra peat (for moisture retention) if it is particularly shallow. For lime-loving plants,

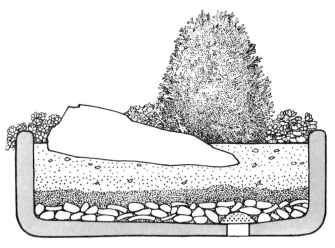

mix in limestone chippings. Embed one or more carefully chosen rocks in the surface, arranging them to form naturalistic outcrops. Plant the trough's inhabitants in the same way as with a full-sized rock garden (see p 119), finally top-dressing with rock chippings. Water regularly; alpines need extremely good drainage but ample moisture.

prevent the soil mixture washing down among the drainage material and defeating its purpose. Suitable materials include coarse leaf-mould, peat blocks or thin shaved turves laid grass-side down.

If you cannot obtain a genuine stone trough – or are not prepared to pay the high price usually asked – you may have to compromise. One adaptation is to take a large rectangular stone paving slab, raise it on supports, and build retaining walls of rock pieces. Hold these to the base and to each other with mortar, and build up until a suitable depth is reached. Leave gaps around the base for drainage. Once the mortar has set the trough can be filled and planted as above, but if you plan to grow lime-haters, let it stand in the open for a few months for the mortar to cure.

Even glazed kitchen sinks can be adapted by disguising the glaze and the harsh outlines with a mortar mixture that weathers to an appearance close to that of stone. First clean

and dry the sink thoroughly, then brush with a suitable adhesive such as Polybond or Unibond. When this has completely dried, make a mixture of equal parts (by bulk, not weight) of cement, silver sand and sifted peat. Mix these together when dry, and then make into a thick paste by adding the minimum amount of water. Apply the mix thickly to the sink by hand, and shape as necessary.

A rather similar mixture is used to make hypertufa, a kind of pseudo-concrete that looks attractive and is not inimicable to plant life. Troughs, tubs and other containers can be moulded from it, reinforced with wire netting (see the illustration).

Alpines in tufa

A fascinating method of growing small alpines, such as Kabschia saxifrages, without a rock garden is to obtain (and this is not easy) a large block of tufa. Tufa is a soft, extremely porous rock, and planting holes can be drilled

or chiselled into it. These should be about 10 cm (4 in) deep, 2.5 to 4 cm (1 to 1½ in) in diameter and 10 to 12 cm (4 to 5 in) apart; they can be positioned on the top and all sides, but should all slope at least slightly downwards. Prepare or buy rooted cuttings of the required plants, and hold them with the roots dangling into the holes. Pour dry silver sand in around the roots until the hole is filled, then water in. The plants will quickly root from the sand into the pores of the tufa, and no further attention is needed apart from watering.

You can, of course, stand such planted tufa blocks in various parts of the garden or on a terrace, but it helps to prevent too-rapid drying out if they are embedded 2.5 cm (1 in) deep in soil or sand. You must never forget that tufa is almost pure limestone, albeit in a different form from the usual; lime-haters may appear to grow in it for a time, but chlorosis is soon apparent and the plants eventually die.

A small trough is ideal for growing a collection of plants of one genus, such as sedums **top**. A block of tufa **below** can be drilled and the holes planted directly with small alpines; in this case they are Kabschia saxifrages.

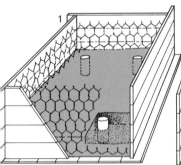
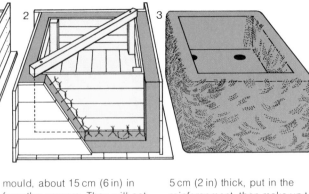

Making a hypertufa trough

First make wooden moulds. The outer one should be like a box whose sides can easily be dismantled. Make the inner one similarly box-like and 10 cm (4 in) smaller all round than the outer; a cross-piece makes removal easier. Cut four 10 cm (4 in) lengths of round- or square-section wood about 4 cm (1½ in) thick. Stand these on the bottom of the outer

mould, about 15 cm (6 in) in from the corners. They will act like legs to support the inner mould and, when removed, form drainage holes. Cut heavy chicken-wire for reinforcement. Make a dry mixture of one part cement, one part silver sand and two parts sifted peat (all by bulk). Add water to make a mortar that just pours.
1 Cover the bottom of the outer mould with a layer of mortar

5 cm (2 in) thick, put in the reinforcement, then make up to 10 cm (4 in). **2** Install the inner mould and pour mortar for the walls, tamping down to avoid air pockets. When almost set, carefully dismantle the outer mould and use a sharp tool to round off the corners and give a 'hand-hewn' look **3**. Then leave it to set for some days before removing the inner mould. Allow it to weather.

Raised beds and planted walls

There are immense advantages to be gained from growing plants, and in particular rock plants, in raised beds, and this is becoming an increasingly popular form of gardening. The difficulties caused by an alpine plant's need for effective drainage are very easily solved; choice plants are brought nearer to eye level, where both they and their attendant pests can more readily be seen; the gardener does not have to work on hands and knees (for disabled gardeners, a most valuable advantage; see p 56); and the fact that special soil mixtures can be made up for each bed means that the needs of acid-loving plants can be catered for even in the limiest of districts.

With certain kinds of raised beds, particularly those built from dry stone walling without mortar and those made with peat blocks (see p 127), the retaining walls themselves can be planted. This vertical planting adds an attractive new dimension. The principle can in fact be extended to the free-standing dry wall; if built with a core of soil and planted as it is built this becomes in effect a very narrow raised bed. Depending on orientation, it can be planted with sun-lovers on the top and one side and shade-lovers on the other side.

Types of raised bed

The gardener who possesses a brick wall in the garden is lucky indeed, for a further wall, about 75 cm (2½ ft) high and a similar distance away from the original wall, will provide the perfect raised bed with the minimum of expense and trouble. You can also, of course, build a free-standing brick raised bed if you have no existing wall. New brickwork can look rather harsh, and occasional planting holes should be left about two to three courses down, so that the vertical face can be utilized; such holes should be the size of the header (end) of a brick. Similar walls can be built with pieces of broken paving laid like bricks.

One of the simplest ways of making a raised bed is with stone or concrete paving slabs stood vertically. These always look stark and harsh, however, and fit best the style of a modern patio garden or paved yard. Here, the vertical slabs can be braced against the straight edges of the paving. Sink them 30 cm (12 in) into the ground and, when you are sure that they are level and vertical, pack hardcore behind the slabs both to hold them vertical and to provide drainage for the bed.

Natural stone walls constructed dry (without mortar) make the most attractive raised beds, but they can be tricky to build. It is easiest to use squared stone laid to a bonding pattern as you would a brick wall (see p 73). Use a suitable soil mixture in place of mortar, leaving the occasional gap (bridged by a stone in the course above) and carry out vertical planting as you go. Tilt the stones back slightly to direct rainwater inwards into the bed, and give the whole wall a slight batter, so that it tilts inwards to the top by about 8 cm (3 in) in 75 cm (2½ ft).

Possibly the ultimate in raised beds is formed by a tufa cliff – an almost vertical rock garden built with tufa (see p 123) – with a glass roof cantilevered from a rear retaining

Raised scree beds **above** make a good home for alpines where the soil is heavy, as drainage is automatically improved and planting mixtures can be adapted to plants' needs. These are at Kew Gardens, near London, but small versions are possible for home gardens. If you can obtain tufa, you can make a tufa cliff **bottom**. Here, the rock face as well as the bed can be planted. Dry stone walls look extremely attractive with planted crevices **right**.

wall. Here many of the most difficult alpines can be grown to perfection. A suitable soil mixture packed behind binds the rock and provides additional growing medium. The glass protects the plants from rain, but you will of course have to water the bed regularly.

Filling and planting

Whatever the height of the raised bed, and whatever the soil mixture to be used in it, a good rule of thumb is that one-third of the depth should be of coarse drainage (such as rubble and broken bricks) covered with reversed turves or peat blocks to prevent the soil mixture getting into the drainage and clogging it. (Further drainage should be installed below ground level on heavy soils, and any solid base broken up.)

What soil mixture you use above the drainage depends on the plants to be grown. The same mixtures recommended for rock gardens (see p 118) are suitable, though you may prefer to use a ready-made potting mixture such as the John Innes type. Add considerable extra grit (sandstone, granite or limestone to choice) for the small choice alpine plants that so delight in a bed of this kind. For ordinary bedding plants, small shrubs and perennials, any well-draining garden soil, enriched with peat or leaf-mould, is adequate.

Planting the top of a raised bed is no different from planting a rock garden or flower bed, though you should allow the soil to settle first. As already mentioned, the best time to plant the vertical walls is during construction, when the roots can be snugly embedded in soil mix-

Building a raised bed
A simple if stark raised bed is made with paving slabs braced against the edge of a paved area. Pack hardcore behind the bottom edge of the vertical slabs **right**; when firm and vertical, top with smaller stones and soil **below**.

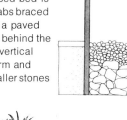

Rock plants on the flat

ture. Later planting is not difficult if the planting holes are big enough, though you may need to introduce some extra soil mixture and wedge it into place with a block of peat cut to size and gently rammed home.

A similar method can be used to plant narrow crevices. First make sure that the back of the crevice has enough soil for the plant's roots. Then cut two pieces of peat block to fit loosely around a rooted cutting and wedge the whole lot into the crevice, making sure that the roots are in contact with the soil behind. Water and spray regularly.

Plants for the wall

Apart from such crevice plants as sempervivums, species of *Ramonda* and *Haberlea* and others commonly used in rock gardens, a number of trailing and creeping plants are excellent for clothing the sides of a raised bed. *Cotoneaster dammeri*, with small white flowers followed by red berries, is one of the few shrubs that will grow away from the sun to cover a shady wall. *Daphne cneorum* 'Eximia', one of the choicest of creeping shrubs, should be planted at the top edge of a raised bed and again in a vertical slot below; then it will quickly form a mat with, in spring, a profusion of fragrant pink flowers.

Among other shrubs, *Hypericum empet-*

rifolium will, if planted in a crevice of a dry wall on the sunny side, gradually make a superb evergeen carpet, covered with yellow stars in summer. *Rubus calycinoides* (*R. fockeanus*) forms a dense carpet of attractive glossy evergreen leaves and can be trained downwards in sun or light shade.

Campanula isophylla is a perennial that is hardy only in mild regions, and even there may prefer a piece of glass over its crown in winter. But it is a superb trailer that is smothered in white or blue star-shaped flowers in late summer. *C. garganica* is hardier and equally good. Plant the tuber of *Tropaeolum polyphyllum* 30 cm (12 in) deep, and it will eventually thrust its panicles of yellow through every cranny in the bed or wall in early summer. It is quick to come and quick to disappear. Among commoner plants, aubrieta and *Alyssum saxatile* make a good show in spring. For others, see page 236.

Given their need for excellent drainage, it is not surprising that alpines are normally grown in garden features raised above the general ground level, such as rock gardens and raised beds. But this need not be the case. Provided drainage is good and water never lies there, they can be grown on flat surfaces too. In particular, you can use scree beds and the spaces between paving stones, either level or on a bank. Plants that form cushions or hummocks are good in such situations – especially ones that can take some crushing, if grown in paving – but you should try to introduce the occasional taller specimen to break the flatness and monotony. For some recommendations of plants to grow, see page 235.

Planting between paving

Provided that surface water runs away quickly and that the soil underneath is free-draining, plants growing between paving stones have the near-ideal conditions of a cool root-run, air and light for their heads, and protection for their necks from winter wet. The best method is generally to leave planting pockets about 15 cm (6 in) across and provided with a good soil mixture to a depth of 30 cm (12 in). When working on an already existing paved area, you may need to break and lift portions of stone and excavate with a trowel. It is generally best to point (fill with mortar) the cracks between the paving, apart from where you intend to plant, in order to stop weeds growing. If you do not want to do this, however, you can mix the seed of suitable plants with silver sand and sprinkle it into the cracks.

Steep slopes can also be paved and planted (here pointing is essential). As the bank will not be walked upon, more substantial plants can be used – for example, a prostrate juniper for evergreen cover, dwarf brooms such as *Cytisus procumbens* and *C.* × *kewensis*, *Potentilla fruticosa* in its many colour forms and the berrying *Cotoneaster horizontalis*. Such treatment offers useful alternatives to grassing (with the resultant problem of cut-

ting), terracing with walls or rockwork or the direct planting of ground-covering shrubs.

Scree beds

A scree bed is simply an independent, level or slightly sloping version of the scree often built as part of a rock garden (see p 119). It is a convenient way of growing alpines in a small garden where there is no room for a rock garden and you do not wish to build a raised bed. Construction consists essentially of excavating a bed 60 to 90 cm (2 to 3 ft) deep; installing drainage material 15 cm (6 in) thick, covered with reversed turves or peat blocks; and filling with a scree mixture of two parts rock chippings to one part loam and one part leaf-mould or peat. If possible choose a sunny, gently sloping site; it is vital to choose one where water will not collect and fill the bed.

top A level scree bed is a good way of growing alpines, but water must never collect in it.
below Gaps in crazy paving can be planted with trailers like *Nierembergia repens* (*N. rivularis*).

The peat garden

Peat beds can form extensive terraced features **left** or small raised beds **above** and **below**. The plants below include *Rhododendron* 'Carmen' (red), the pink *Primula farinosa* (to its right), *Andromeda polifolia* 'Nana' (right foreground) and *Erythronium* 'Pink Beauty' (background).

Peat is commonly used in the garden for mulching and soil-improvement, but it is only relatively recently that whole garden features have been made using peat blocks or logs and a soil mixture containing a high proportion of granulated peat. These can range from simple raised beds built with retaining walls of peat blocks or other materials to much more extensive features, generally built on a slope and incorporating 'outcrops' of peat somewhat like the stone outcrops of a rock garden. The natural model for the peat outcrops is, however, those worn by water in the peat beds of moorland rather than the rock outcrops of the mountains. Another big difference is that, whereas the stones of a rock garden can at most be partly obscured by trailing and mat-forming plants, the roots of suitable plants will rapidly grow through moist peat blocks, knitting them together and covering them with flourishing and colourful vegetation.

Where peat blocks are difficult to obtain, as in North America, suitable substitutes include logs, small tree-trunks and untreated railway sleepers. These cannot, of course, be directly planted, so the result is more like a conventional rock garden (see p 118) or raised bed (see p 124), but they have the advantage of being more durable in extreme climates than peat blocks. Apart from construction and direct planting of the blocks, other details in this article remain the same.

Like the rock garden, the peat garden appeals to the lover of small things, the gardener who enjoys paying close and individual attention to his plants. It can be used to grow all manner of plants that like an acid, peaty soil, but the enthusiast's peat garden is rather more sophisticated. It is populated with naturally occurring plants from alpine and sub-arctic heathlands all over the world, rather than with nurserymen's hybrids. It is not surprising that many peat gardens are built by rock garden enthusiasts – often as a shaded continuation of the rock garden.

One word of warning, however: the peat garden is often quoted as a means of growing lime-hating plants on chalky soil. In fact, this will only succeed for more than a short period if you construct the raised-bed type of peat garden and use soft (lime-free) water – such as rainwater – for watering.

Siting and construction

The site chosen for a peat garden depends on local conditions – particularly on rainfall. Peat blocks shrink when dry, so it is essential that if you use these they should remain moist. Where summer watering is no problem, either from rainfall or a piped source of soft water, you can choose an open, sunny site. Otherwise it is best to choose a partly shaded position. In the northern hemisphere, a gentle north-facing slope is ideal, for this will allow banks or terracing walls of peat blocks to be built. Alternatively, choose an area shaded by a wall, shrubs or trees (but not overhung).

The bigger the peat blocks you can obtain and handle, the more stable the construction will be. Cubes 30 cm (12 in) in each direction are ideal for fairly large peat gardens, but brick-shaped blocks about 40 cm (15 in) long by 20 to 25 cm (8 to 10 in) wide and deep are easier to buy, and you may not be able to obtain ones much larger than a house-brick in all such cases, lay the blocks flat, not on edge. They are best positioned when wet, so avoid dried blocks meant for fuel. Fill any gaps between the blocks with wet peat to seal air channels that would otherwise hasten drying out. The walls look more natural if they are not laid absolutely straight, as in steps, but are built to resemble fairly large, level outcrops, the front face sloping back slightly. Lay the blocks in a bonding pattern, as for brickwork (see p 72). If using logs, arrange these similarly to form shallow terraces.

In order to aid stability, sink the lowest course of blocks half into the soil, and pack soil mixture behind the walls as you progress.

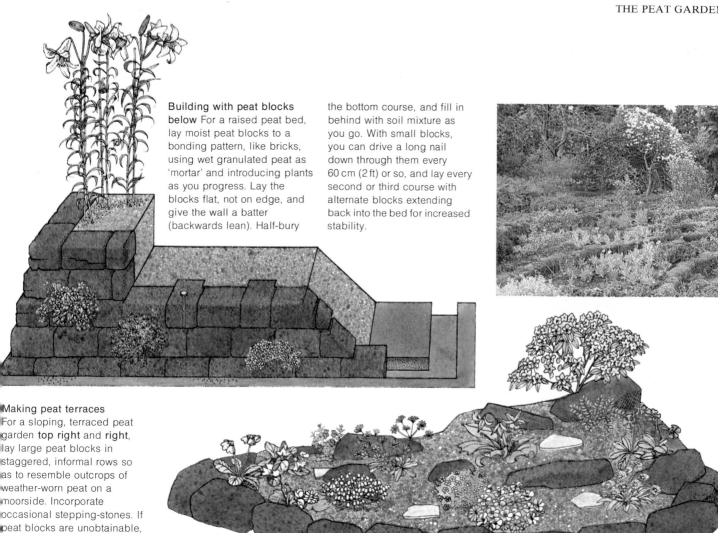

Building with peat blocks below For a raised peat bed, lay moist peat blocks to a bonding pattern, like bricks, using wet granulated peat as 'mortar' and introducing plants as you progress. Lay the blocks flat, not on edge, and give the wall a batter (backwards lean). Half-bury the bottom course, and fill in behind with soil mixture as you go. With small blocks, you can drive a long nail down through them every 60 cm (2 ft) or so, and lay every second or third course with alternate blocks extending back into the bed for increased stability.

Making peat terraces For a sloping, terraced peat garden **top right** and **right**, lay large peat blocks in staggered, informal rows so as to resemble outcrops of weather-worn peat on a moorside. Incorporate occasional stepping-stones. If peat blocks are unobtainable, use logs or baulks of rough timber to form shallow terraces.

The soil on the terraces between the walls and on the gentle slopes can consist of half granulated peat (the medium-coarse type commonly used for mulching) and half topsoil (which must be lime-free). This mixture retains a certain amount of moisture but at the same time, if the garden is sloping, will drain well and not become stagnant. In other situations it may be better to use equal parts of peat, topsoil and coarse sand. Before actual planting, it is worthwhile to place stepping-stones at convenient intervals so that you never need to step on the soil or peat walls.

Planting and maintenance

This environment will accommodate a wealth of fascinating plants. For furnishing the peat blocks, such genera as *Andromeda*, *Arcterica*, *Gaultheria*, *Pernettya*, *Schizocodon*, *Shortia* and *Vaccinium* include dwarf shrubby creepers, while among the herbaceous types certain species of *Cornus*, *Cyananthus*, *Ourisia*, *Polygonatum* and *Pyrola* will provide summer vegetation and cover. If you then distribute a few small shrubby species of *Chamaedaphne*, *Kalmiopsis*, *Phyllodoce*, *Pieris* and *Rhododendron* informally over the area they will create useful microclimates in which some real treasures will thrive. These include members of such genera as *Gentiana*, *Nomocharis*, *Notholirion*, *Orchis*, *Paris*, *Primula*, *Sanguinaria*, *Streptopus* and a host of others. Many of these are rare in cultivation, and are only obtainable from specialist nurserymen.

Obviously, as the plants grow and expand, some replanting will be necessary if peat blocks are used, for these offer no physical restrictions to plant expansion, unlike rocks. Do this while the plants are still healthy and strong. It is also important to retain a balance between the shrubby, dominating species and the more vulnerable herbaceous plants, even at the expense of removing some of the former. Weeding will be a regular chore, while top dressing in spring with a mixture of equal parts of peat and good lime-free topsoil will be beneficial and will compensate for any soil removed in weeding. Fertilizer should rarely be needed, and then at half the rate normal in other parts of the garden; hoof and horn is a good lime-free type.

Plants for a small peat garden

Shrubby evergreens	*Andromeda polifolia* (pink; creeping); *Cassiope lycopodioides* (white); *C. selaginoides* (white); *C. wardii* (white); *Gaultheria cuneata* (white; whitish fruits); *G. nummularioides* (pink; purple fruits); *Kalmiopsis leachiana* (pink); *Leiophyllum buxifolium* (pink); *Pernettya tasmanica* (yellow, white or crimson fruits); *Phyllodoce aleutica* (yellow); *P. breweri* (rosy-red); *P. caerulea* (purple); *P. nipponica* (white); *Rhododendron calostrotum* (crimson-purple); *R. campylogynum* (pink); *R. chameunum* (rosy-purple); *R. chryseum* (yellow); *R. fastigiatum* (dark blue); *R. hanceanum* (cream); *R. keleticum* (purple); *R. microleucum* (white); *R. nitens* (reddish-purple); *R. pemakoense* (pink); *R. sargentianum* (yellow); *Vaccinium delavayi* (neat foliage); *V. nummularia* (pink)
Herbaceous plants	*Adonis vernalis* (yellow); *Cyananthus lobatus* (purple); *C. microphyllus* (blue); *Dodecatheon meadia* (rose-pink); *Gentiana sino-ornata* (blue); *G. veitchiorum* (deep purple); *Glaucidium palmatum* (pinkish-mauve); *Incarvillea mairei* (reddish-purple); *Meconopsis betonicifolia* (blue); *M. integrifolia* (yellow); *M. quintuplinervia* (lilac); *M. villosa* (yellow); *Primula aurantiaca* (orange); *P. aureata* (yellow and cream); *P. capitata* (purple); *P. frondosa* (pink); *P. involucrata* (white); *P. nutans* (lilac); *P. sinopurpurea* (purple); *P. vialii* (lavender); *Shortia uniflora* (pink); *Trientalis borealis* (white)
Bulbs and rhizomes	*Clintonia andrewsiana* (pink; purple fruits); *Disporum smithii* (white); *Erythronium revolutum* (pink); *E. tuolumnense* (yellow); *Fritillaria pallidiflora* (greenish-cream); *F. pyrenaica* (purple to yellow); *Lilium columbianum* (orange); *L. japonicum* (pink); *L. mackliniae* (pink); *L. oxypetalum* (yellow); *Nomocharis farreri* (pink); *N. saluenensis* (rosy-purple); *Trillium chloropetalum* (white to purple); *T. grandiflorum* (white); *T. ovatum* (white)

Building a garden pool

There is nothing particularly difficult about constructing a garden pool and thus bringing to your garden the unique combination of beauty and sound, serenity and movement, that only water can give. Pools can be built in four main ways, although one of them – the oldest, clay puddling – is rarely practised today since the necessary materials are cumbersome and messy. Moreover, it is difficult to make such pools really watertight, and this is definitely a technique for the professional.

The other three methods – using concrete, a preformed glass-fibre shell or heavy-duty waterproof fabric – are all within the capabilities of most home handymen. Each has its advantages and disadvantages.

Concrete pools

Although there are more modern methods of pool-making, concrete still has many uses, especially for large pools or for formal pools with raised edges. The most important factors for success are a good thick lining and a correct mixture of cement and other ingredients. To ensure watertightness, use only the best materials: best Portland cement, coarse but clean builder's sand, and aggregate (which gives the concrete strength) that is free from loamy or organic substances, and of a size graduating between 2 cm (¾ in) and 5 mm (³⁄₁₆ in). Various mixtures are recommended by builders – a good one consists of one part cement to two each of sand and aggregate – but seek your local supplier's advice before setting about the operation. You can save a great deal of time and labour if you obtain the concrete ready-mixed. But you must work quickly; remember that concrete starts to set in 20 minutes.

Steel reinforcement is rarely necessary, except with very large pools, but where used it should cover the whole of the base plus a turn-up of at least 15 cm (6 in) at the sides. It should be inserted half-way through the thickness of the floor. This means laying half the floor concrete, then the reinforcement, and finally the rest of the concrete – all at the same time, with one making of wet concrete.

If the pool is to be a formal one with raised sides, the concrete will of course be built up with shuttering well above the general ground level. The outside of the raised portion can be finished with facing bricks and a coping laid on top. An informal pool can be finished with irregular slabs of paving or with turf. Or a few pieces of rock can be introduced and some trailing rock plants.

In all cases, leave the pool for at least a week before filling it with water and leaving it again to test for leaks. Then empty it by syphoning off the water with a hose, and paint the whole interior with a proprietary waterproofing compound designed for garden pools – one that is capable of neutralizing the alkalinity of the new concrete. Once this has dried, the pool is ready for filling and planting.

Prefabricated pool shells

These represent the simplest and quickest method of making a pool; indeed a small one can be installed and planted in the space of

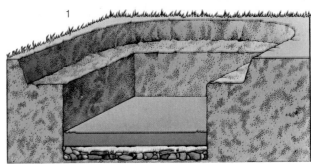

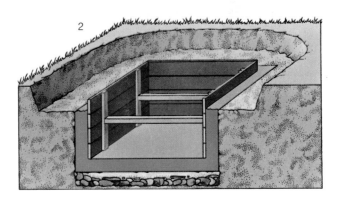

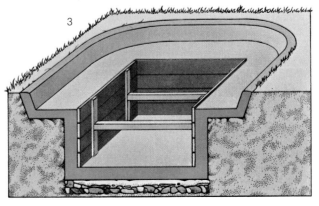

Building a concrete pool

After excavating the site of the pool, work on the deep-water section first. **1** Ram down a layer of hardcore, followed by sand or ashes firmed with the back of a spade. Spread 15 cm (6 in) of concrete over the base working quickly and evenly and incorporating reinforcement if necessary (see text). Smooth the surface, but leave the outer 15 cm (6 in) rough to form a key to take the sides.

2 Next install shuttering to form the sides of the deep section. The easiest to use is a prefabricated box without a bottom or roof and 30 cm (12 in) smaller across than the hole; this leaves a 15 cm (6 in) gap all round. Work fresh concrete round and round in the space ramming it down particularly well at the corners, where leaks commonly occur.

3 For an informal pool, continue with the shallow area, where a 10 cm (4 in) layer of concrete sufficient and no reinforcement is necessary. When all the concrete has set, after a few days, withdraw the shuttering; this will be easier if it was oiled beforehand.

It is easier to allow each stage to set before going on to the next than to pour all the concrete at one session, but there is a greater risk of leakage unless the joints between sections are well keyed (roughened).

one afternoon. Although aluminium and other materials have been tried for the purpose, it was not until man-made fibres became generally available that the idea of prefabricated pools really took on. Nowadays they are almost invariably made of resin-bonded glass-fibre, cast in moulds of various shapes, depths and sizes. Circular, square, rectangular, kidney-shaped and various other patterns are now available.

Most of them are fairly shallow, and this is their greatest drawback, since in a bad winter the water can freeze solid, killing both plant and animal occupants. Rarely do prefabricated pools have deep areas where fish can be safe from freezing in winter, or can hide in a hot summer.

Nevertheless, they have a place in a small plot, such as a city or suburban garden, or on a roof garden or terrace. The problem of freezing can be overcome with a special insulating mat laid over the pool, or a small thermostatically controlled electric heater can be installed. A definite advantage is their lightness; they can be taken up without damage and easily moved to another site if required, or stored in a shed.

When installing such a pool, be absolutely sure that it is stable and level; if the pool tips to one side it will drive you mad! Edging finishes can be formal or informal, just as for a concrete pool, and once installation is complete the pool can be immediately planted and filled. Most prefabricated pools have punched out sections to take the roots of water-lilies and other aquatics, but rarely do these have rims capable of holding the soil in place. As a consequence, the roots emerge after one season, soil washes out, and the plants require frequent lifting and replanting if they are to survive. You would do well to build up the sides of the planting pockets with a false rim of bricks or a metal hoop.

Plastic sheeting

The easiest and cheapest method of pool-making that is fully satisfactory is to line an excavation with strong plastic or synthetic rubber sheeting. This is the newest of the recommended methods, and is ideal for small gardens, particularly for an informal pool adjacent to a rock or bog garden. But it is also being increasingly used for storage tanks, lakes and other large-scale water features.

Briefly, the method consists of taking out the soil to the required depth – or series of depths – and then lining the excavation with the reinforced sheeting. After the soil is removed, check carefully for unevenness. Since a single litre of water weighs a kilogram (a gallon weighs 10 lb), there will be great pressure on the fabric when the pool is full, and if it rests on stones or in a depression it may wear through in time and cause a leakage. To prevent this happening, cover the soil with a layer of coarse sand or sifted ashes. In the finished pool, the fabric lining can be tucked away out of sight, under soil, turves, rocks or paving, so the artificial nature of the pool is not apparent.

Two important points to remember with plastic sheeting are, firstly, its vulnerability to any sharp tool such as a garden fork and, secondly, that sunlight can degrade the fabric, so it is important to keep such pools filled with water. Some of the better-made fabrics can be patched if damaged, however, in much the same way as you would mend a bicycle tyre. It is easy to do away with such pools without a great deal of effort and, provided the fabric has not become too brittle, it can be rolled up and used again somewhere else.

Planning and preparation

Before finally choosing a method, decide the approximate size and location of your pool, and whether it is to be formal or informal in style (see p 32). You can then estimate the materials you will need and compare costs. Specialist suppliers of water-garden materials, equipment and plants will usually offer free advice if you remain undecided.

When starting to excavate, mark out the pool area with pegs or short stakes, moving these about until you are satisfied with the shape. Unless your pool is to be a very shallow feature – on a sheltered patio, perhaps, and designed for growing only marginal aquatics – it should have an inner deep-water section for water-lilies and fish. How deep this should be depends on climate. It must not freeze solid in winter, and yet should be shallow enough to warm up quickly in spring and promote growth of the water-lilies. In areas without frost or with fairly mild winters (such as most of Britain) the water should be 60 cm (2 ft) deep, but in more extreme climates at least 75 cm (2½ ft) is necessary. Informal pools also need shallow areas for marginals plants about 15 to 20 cm (6 to 8 in) deep.

The deep-water section should be straight-sided and preferably of rectangular shape if the pool is to be made of concrete. This is easier to construct and make watertight than one of irregular outline – and the rest of the pool can anyway be less regular in the case of an informal pool. When excavating, allow for a layer of hardcore and 15 cm (6 in) of concrete in the deep water section, 10 cm (4 in) elsewhere. The hole for a prefabricated pool should be slightly larger than the shell, to allow for sand to be packed in between. When using plastic sheeting, make slopes and curves more gentle, so that the fabric is not strained too much.

Installing a prefabricated pool
1 Excavate a hole slightly larger than the shell, and deep enough for its rim to lie just below the surrounding soil level. Make the base firm,

ideally spreading a thin layer of sand and tamping this down.
2 Install the pool, test for levels with a spirit level, work soil or sand into the space around the edges to hold it firm, and again

test for levels. When you are quite sure that it is level and firm, and that the space between the shell and the cavity is filled, lay paving stones or other edging material.

Using a plastic pool-liner
1 Excavate your pool to the required size and shape, rounding all corners smoothly. Line it with sand or ashes.

2 Lay sheeting over the whole excavation, pulling it taught and weighting it at intervals with slabs of paving stone or heavy weights. The fabric stretches, and at this stage should have a surplus on all sides equal to at least the pool's maximum depth. Now run in water, preferably from

a hose placed near the centre of the fabric. As the weight of water builds up, the sheeting will sink and stretch, taking on the contours of the cavity.
3 When the pool is quite full, trim the edges with scissors, leaving about 15 cm (6 in) of sheeting all round. Tuck this out of sight under the edging.

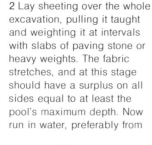

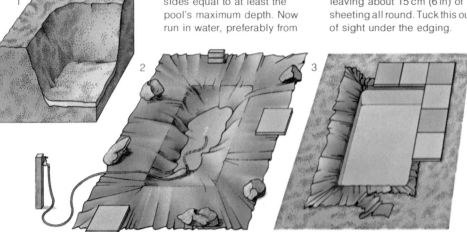

Stocking a water garden

Although a formal pool need not necessarily contain any plants or fish, most garden pools have both. The key to healthy, clear water is to achieve a balance between the various inhabitants. The plants absorb mineral salts and carbon dioxide from the water and, in the presence of sunlight, create food materials and oxygen. The fish absorb oxygen and release carbon dioxide through their gills; apart from their aesthetic attraction they feed on such pests as water-lily beetles, mosquito larvae, aphids and caddis flies. They also fertilize plants with their excreta.

So long as the plants – particularly the submerged oxygenators (see p 255) – get plenty of light and have to compete for minerals, the microscopic algae that make water murky will have little chance to thrive. On the other hand, there must not be too much light in relation to the number of oxygenators. It is vital, therefore, to carefully work out the number and size of the pool's inhabitants. There cannot be too many underwater oxygenators, especially in the first year or two; after that, any surplus can be removed. But floating and deep-water aquatics (such as water-lilies) must never cover more than about a half of the pool's surface, so as not to create too much shade. As a general rule for working out quotas, for each 5 m² (50 sq ft) of pool surface (that is, a pool about 2.5 m [8 ft] in diameter or 2 by 2.5 m [7 by 8 ft]) you can allow one or two water-lilies (depending on their vigour; see p 254), about twenty submerged oxygenators and ten marginal aquatics (see p 256).

Do not overstock with fish. A rough guide is to allow 20 litres of water for every 10 cm of fish (an inch of fish per gallon of water, or six inches per cubic foot). Bear in mind their further growth, and if in doubt consult an aquatic supplier.

Methods of planting

With small pools the best method of planting water-lilies is in plastic aquatic baskets. These hold about two bucketsful of soil and have openwork perforations around the sides – an important refinement since water-lily roots like to feel the influence of water. In confined containers they never seem to do as well, for after a time the roots grow out of the top and into the water instead of going downwards. When it becomes necessary to divide the plants it is also much easier to lift plants in baskets than to grub them out of the silt at the bottom of the pool.

With large natural ponds or lakes, however, the position is more flexible. Here there will be a natural accumulation of soft, loose mud, dead leaves and other debris into which the plants can root. In such cases the tubers can sometimes be pushed down into the soil, or they can be tied between turves (with the grass shaved and turned inwards) and then dropped into the water at the appropriate depth. This method is not advocated for small pools, since there is no natural subsoil and the rotting turf encourages algae. Baskets are equally suitable for large pools, however.

Marginal aquatics can be planted in special

pockets installed during the making of the pool, or else in pots or baskets. A few of the most prolific types, like typhas and glycerias, should always have their roots confined, otherwise they tend to take over small pools. Underwater oxygenators, which are nearly rootless, are 'planted' by the simple expedient of gently clipping narrow strips of lead (obtainable from aquatic dealers) around two or three stems at a time and dropping these into the water. The lead brings them down to the floor of the pool, after which they adapt and keep their own level. Floaters present no problems. All you do is place them on top of the pool; they get all their nourishment from dissolved salts in the water.

Potting and planting

If your pool is built of concrete, make sure that it is neutralized, so that lime is not released into the water, before stocking. This can be done chemically, as described on page 128, or by allowing the pool to stand, filled with water, for six months, then emptying, scrubbing, rinsing and refilling. Glass-fibre and plastic-lined pools can be filled and stocked immediately. Planting should be done in late spring.

Water-lilies require a fairly stiff growing medium, rich but free from fibrous organic matter such as peat, leaf-mould or fibrous loam. All of these release mineral salts into the water in rotting down, and cause discoloration. The best mixture is heavy loam (preferably stacked for six months, so that any grass roots and so on have disappeared) plus one-sixth of its bulk of rotted cow manure. Alternatively, add a handful of coarse bonemeal to each bucketful of loam. Marginal aquatics do best in plain soil without added ingredients.

When planting water-lilies, cover the soil with shingle to hold down the roots and to prevent fish from digging into the mud and making the water cloudy. Also, lower them only gradually into deep water – over a period of weeks – or they may not flower in their first season, nor even make much growth. Marginals can be installed directly in their permanent positions, the crowns covered by a few centimetres (an inch or two) of water.

Introducing fish

Fish should not be put into a new pool until six to eight weeks after it is planted. Do not handle or net the fish when introducing them. They are commonly transported from the supplier in large sealed plastic bags of water, a concentrated 'dose' of oxygen – enough for about 48 hours – being pumped in immediately before despatch. Immediately on arrival, place the whole bag, unopened, on the pool, shading it from the sun if necessary. Leave it for a few hours to reach the same temperature as the pool water. Then undo the seal or cut a corner of the bag and allow the fish to swim out. With fish in open containers, similarly stand these in the pool for a few hours before turning them on one side. Do not be alarmed if the fish hide for a few days after the trauma of their journey.

Planting aquatics

Plant water-lilies in baskets lined with rot-proof nylon netting, to stop soil seeping out into the water through the perforations. 1 Half-fill a basket with growing mixture (see text) and insert a water-lily tuber; set it 2 vertically or 3 horizontally according to type (see p 254). Add more soil up to its crown. Plant very firmly and top dress with a 2.5 cm (1 in) layer of clean pea-sized shingle.
At first, the lily should not be too deeply submerged. Prop the basket on bricks 4 so that it is covered by only 2.5 cm (1 in) of water. When the plant recovers from the shock of being transplanted and begins to grow, remove the bricks one at a time. After six to eight weeks it can stand on the floor of the pool 5.
Plant submerged oxygenators

by bunching their stems together with thin lead strips 6 and dropping them gently in the water. Marginal aquatics must not be planted too deeply; stand their containers on a shelf 7 so that the water will just cover their roots.

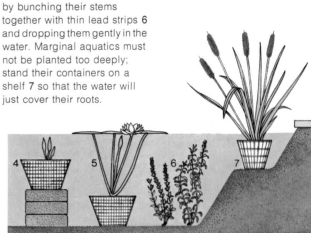

Water-garden maintenance

The essence of a balanced pool is that it should be more or less self-supporting and self-regulating. Nevertheless, a certain amount of care and attention is almost always needed. Plant pests cause few problems; any that attack the emergent leaves of aquatics – such as aphids on water-lilies – should be hosed into the water for the fish to eat. Any plant disease should be dealt with promptly, before it can spread, by destroying the affected part – or the whole plant if necessary.

A common problem is the growth of algae (see opposite). You can easily remove the filamentous type – blanket weed – by hand or with a stick, and flooding over the pool gets rid of brown or green floating scum. But murky green water indicates that there are too few underwater oxygenating plants to compete for the available light and minerals, or that too little shade is cast by water-lilies. Correct these causes of imbalance, and then if necessary use permanganate of potash to clear the water. Make a saturated solution by shaking the crystals in a jar of water until they all dissolve. Stir in a maximum of one teaspoonful (5 ml) of the solution for every 50 litres (2 cu ft) of water in the pool. The water should not turn more than the very palest pink and should clear in a few days; if necessary, repeat later in the season.

Trimming the plants

Aquatics are prolific growers, and from time to time need cutting back in order to keep them in check. Inveterate seeders like typhas (reedmaces), alismas and cyperus species should have the old flower-heads removed before they scatter their fruits, and plants like *Iris pseudacorus*, sagittarias, and *Pontederia cordata* will need dividing occasionally to keep the clumps compact. Slips of plants frequently break away from the parent stock and set up a separate existence elsewhere in the pool; *Crassula (Tillaea) recurva* and *Nymphoides peltata* are particularly prone to this, and unless checked can become weeds.

If the leaves of water-lilies cover too much space they may need thinning, and any yellow or dead leaves should be removed on sight. Take these off as near the roots as possible, and do the same with old flower heads. All such material fouls the water whilst rotting down. When water-lily leaves huddle and push their way up from the water, and so hide the flowers, it is an indication that they need replanting. Do this in late spring.

In early autumn, most of the marginal aquatics will die down, when the old stems should be cut to water level. Not only does this give the pond a tidy appearance, but it prevents pests from hibernating in the dead stems.

Autumn and winter protection

Do not let leaves from nearby trees fall into the water; constantly dredge them out in autumn with a rake. With small pools it is worth constructing a light framework of wooden battens slightly larger than the pool, and tacking galvanized or strong nylon netting from side to side. In early autumn lay this over the pool and it will catch the leaves as they fall.

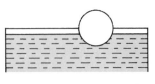

Protection from freezing below A rubber ball frozen into the surface can easily be removed with boiling water, to leave a hole. Bale out some water and cover the hole with sacking; then the ice will act like a greenhouse, preventing further freezing, and air can pass to and from the water. Apart from seasonal measures, a balanced pool **left** is self-supporting and should need little attention.

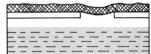

In moderate climates, you can keep the pool filled with water throughout the winter. In the event of freezing, make a hole in the ice, and keep it open to admit air to the fish and plants. Never use a hammer to break the ice; sharp shocks from this can injure fish and even damage the structure of the pool. Instead, float a rubber ball or block of wood in the water; when freezing takes place pour boiling water over it, and lift it out, leaving a hole. With fairly thick ice – 2.5 cm (1 in) and over – remove a few centimetres of the water underneath (with a syphon or by baling), and cover the hole with a sack. The ice then acts like a greenhouse, protecting the fish and plants underneath, but directly a thaw sets in the pool must be filled again. An alternative is to use an electric pool heater to keep one area always above freezing point.

Most hardy water-lilies will withstand the amount of frost normally experienced in the British Isles and countries with similar or milder climates, if they are planted 45 to 60 cm (1½ to 2 ft) deep. This is far enough down to avoid a complete freeze-up, yet not too deep for easy flowering. The miniature sorts in tubs or rock-garden pools may need extra protection, and here the framework recommended above for leaf-catching will again prove useful. Lay this over the water surface, cover it with plastic sheeting and heap pine-branches, mats or even straw or bracken on top. Directly the weather turns mild remove the covering, or the plants beneath may start into premature growth.

In extremely cold districts this may not be enough even for full-sized pools. In such cases they must be drained of water, the fish and oxygenators transferred to aquariums or indoor pools, and the lilies and other aquatics protected with boards, or layers of leaves and bracken. They respond quite well to waterless conditions for a time. In spring the covering should be removed, the pool cleaned over,

and just enough water run in to start the plants into growth. Add more water as they develop, until the pond is again brim-full.

Sometimes semi-hardy aquatics like *Thalia dealbata* and certain isnardias are used in outdoor pools for the summer. These should be grown in pots so that they can be lifted in and out according to the weather. They store for winter quite well in a greenhouse if the tops are cut back and the soil is kept just moist. The floating water hyacinth (*Eichhornia crassipes*) is not winter-hardy and is difficult to keep even under glass unless the roots are potted in damp soil in late summer and kept barely moist at a minimum temperature of 13°C (55°F) until spring. It may then be lifted, the roots washed and dead leaves removed, and floated in fresh water in a warm but light situation until the weather is warm enough for it to go outdoors.

Caring for fish

Goldfish and their relatives are surface-feeders and can often be trained to feed from the hand. Always feed in one place, several times a week, and never give more food than can be consumed in five minutes, otherwise this falls to the bottom and rots. Fish appreciate a varied diet; flies, pulverized hard-boiled egg yolk, rubbed raw meat and proprietary foods are all useful. Cease feeding in the depth of winter. The fish are then naturally sluggish and cannot assimilate a lot of food; they can find enough nourishment in the pond for their immediate needs.

Various diseases and parasitic organisms can afflict pond fish, and the main signs to look out for are general sluggishness, inflamed or damaged gills or fins, and white spots or film on the fish's body. If you suspect such troubles, consult a specialist book or supplier. But remember that fish can also be killed by cats, by rough handling and by weedkiller or pesticide sprays seeping or drifting into the water.

Streams and natural ponds

A natural stream or pond can be an enviable possession or a worrying one. If it floods in winter and/or dries up in summer there can be great problems, certainly in utilizing it to create a water garden feature and quite possibly in managing the adjacent land. With such cases it is impossible to generalize. It may be necessary to divert land drains to take the overflow, or to line the pond with plastic sheeting (as described on page 129) to retain summer losses due to drainage. Every case must be taken on merit and the help of a landscape architect or drainage expert sought where such difficulties get out of hand.

Two possibilities are worth bearing in mind, however. Land prone to slight periodical flooding (as long as water does not lie there for long) may be adaptable to make a bog garden (see opposite). And a stream can sometimes be partially diverted into a plastic-lined pool with a dam at the inlet end to control the flow. Such a static, controlled water feature is much easier to manage.

Plants for streams

A major problem with flowing water is that it severely limits your choice of decorative plants. Water lilies dislike swiftly running water, so it is useless to plant them in such situations. However, the less spectacular nuphars can take their place. These generally have yellow flowers that smell alcoholic, and include the British native yellow pond lily, *Nuphar lutea*. Other good species are *N. advena* from North America and *N. japonica* from Japan. Among other plants that are likely to succeed in running water are bulrushes (*Scirpus* spp), sparganiums, the water crowfoot (*Ranunculus aquatilis*) and the willow moss (*Fontinalis antipyretica*). If you have exceptionally clear, unpolluted flowing water, you can grow watercress (see p 307).

To extend the possibilities, stream banks may be levelled in places to make planting pockets. After being supplied with a good planting mixture (see opposite), these may become home for a wide range of colourful plants – drifts of candelabra bog primulas, astilbes, irises, hemerocallis, *Lobelia fulgens*, rodgersias and lysichitons, to name but a few. Specimen plants of *Gunnera manicata* and *Rheum palmatum* may also be grown, as may clumps of bamboos to create shelter for birds and plants, and to provide rustling effects. In expansive surroundings, the swamp cypress (*Taxodium distichum*; see p 140) makes a majestic waterside tree. Such plants thrive in the vicinity of water but not in it, although the occasional short period of flooding may not do much harm.

Artificial streams

Various methods of constructing artificial pools are described on page 128, but in the case of artificial streams concrete provides the strongest and most flexible material. There are prefabricated stream sections on the market, made from glass-fibre-reinforced plastic, but these do not look very convincing. And plastic sheeting is difficult to arrange in folds for a winding stream.

Let your stream flow down into a pool, with or without small intermediate pools on the way. Unless your garden has a natural slope down which the stream can be routed, the best arrangement is to build up earth and rocks at one side of the pool to form a rock garden (see p 118). If constructed at the same time as the pool, of course, you can use earth excavated from the pool, but pay attention to the need for good drainage for the rock plants. Make sure that the foundations are really strong, to support the heavy weight of rocks, mounds of earth and concrete.

Arrange the top stones in such a way that they mask a pump house, connected to a supply of electricity and to a buried pipe to carry

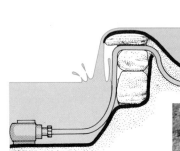

water from the pool. Alternatively, use a submersible pump in the pool. When the pump is switched on, water is drawn from the lowest pool and pumped up to the highest point of the watercourse. It then floods over and starts its way downwards, tumbling over the falls and through the stream as it goes. Thus the same water is used over and over again. Pumps of various capacities are obtainable from aquatic dealers, who will advise on suitable sizes. Similar pumps can be used to power fountains.

Building a rock cascade
Mark a slope with the outline of a stream and excavate it to the required length and depth, widening it at intervals to form pools and making sure that the edges are level. Lay hardcore and concrete, setting rocks at the pools' lower edges to form waterfalls **right**. Or, if you simply want a series of small pools, use plastic sheeting **above**. Prefabricated cascades are also available. A submersible pump in the lowest pool recirculates water.

Nuphar advena

Making an artificial stream
Mark out and excavate the course of the stream, making sure that the ground will not subside. Lay foundations of broken bricks and clinker, building up the sides to about 20 cm (8 in). Line it with concrete 5 cm (2 in) thick, and mask the edges with rocks, earth and plants **right**.

Bog gardens and waterside plantings

Some of the garden's most arresting and unusual plants are denizens of the waterside. In order to give of their best they demand special provisions – rich moist soil which never dries out even in the hottest summer, full sun or light shade to suit individual needs, and, in the case of small minorities like *Iris kaempferi,* the contrary requirement of comparative dryness in winter.

These are the bog plants. Unlike aquatics, they do not thrive in standing water, which rots their roots and prevents them functioning. Their chief desiderata is well-drained soil containing plenty of organic matter, but damp and soft so that their roots easily penetrate its spongy texture. Such plants are extremely varied, from the more adaptable hostas, hemerocallis, trollius and astilbes, which also do well in the drier ground of herbaceous borders, to the rather more demanding bog primulas, rodgersias, ligularias and cardamines. These make beautiful companions to the true aquatics of the garden pool.

The same guidelines apply to the design and planting of a bog garden as for a herbaceous border or island bed (see pp 104 and 108), depending on site and surroundings. Constraints may be imposed where the garden is adjacent to a stream or pond. When positioning the plants, keep them in uneven drifts of one sort, with the tallest kinds at the back, and the smaller, more precious kinds near the path, where they can be supervised. Slugs and snails may prove a nuisance in perennially damp areas, but can be deterred by surrounding choice plants with a ring of granite chippings or ashes, or by using slug bait.

An artificial bog garden

A bog garden looks particularly well near a garden pool, making a natural transition between the water-loving aquatics and the drier-ground land plants. If sited at a lower level than the pool, the latter can be flooded over in summer from time to time to moisten the occupants. (This is an unnecessary proce-

(3 in). The water gradually drains away, leaving the soil moist enough to support the plants. In the garden, you can line an excavated bed with a very weak concrete mixture (made with one part Portland cement to five or six parts aggregate).

Plants for bog gardens

There is a wide variety of herbaceous perennials suitable for bog culture (see p 257), many of them, such as gunneras and arum lilies (*Zantedeschia* spp), of exotic appearance. Also suitable are certain trees and shrubs – such as willows (*Salix* spp), alders (*Alnus* spp) and bog myrtle (*Myrica gale*) – various bamboos and grasses, and even a few bulbs, such as *Lilium canadense, L. pardalinum* and *Allium tuberosum* (*A. angulosum*).

Some marginal aquatics (see p 256) can also be grown. These are plants that normally need to have their roots lapped by water all through the year – not necessary to any great depth, but sufficient to eliminate any risk of

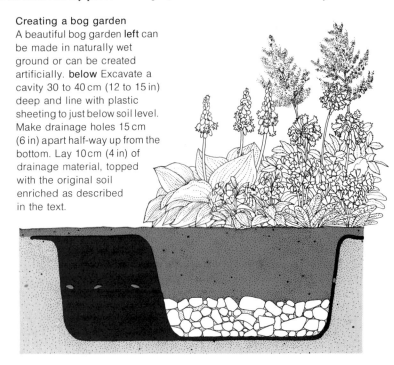

Creating a bog garden
A beautiful bog garden **left** can be made in naturally wet ground or can be created artificially. **below** Excavate a cavity 30 to 40 cm (12 to 15 in) deep and line with plastic sheeting to just below soil level. Make drainage holes 15 cm (6 in) apart half-way up from the bottom. Lay 10 cm (4 in) of drainage material, topped with the original soil enriched as described in the text.

A natural bog garden

Boggy areas may occur naturally in damp, low-lying ground, especially in the vicinity of rivers, lakes and marshes. Land drainage seeping down maintains the level of moisture and organic salts, although surrounding trees may make the area too dark for many flowering plants to flourish.

The first essential with such a site is to clear the ground of scrub bushes, light-blocking trees and shrubs. Then fork over the site or make flower beds. Lay paving stones on sand (for easy removal) between these for access paths to keep your feet dry in bad weather. Improve the soil in the beds with a good planting mixture composed of some coarse sand, some moist peat or leaf-mould, some well-rotted animal manure or mushroom compost and some loam – more or less in equal parts. Work this into the existing soil.

dure in winter in most climates.) One can also install an underground water system using a so-called 'leaky hose' (see p 341) which, at the turn of a tap, will release small jets of water at various points.

But a bog garden does not have to be in the vicinity of standing or flowing water. If you want to grow bog plants in free-draining soil, make a 'leaky pool' lined with plastic sheeting, as shown in the diagram above. Such a bed will always retain a certain amount of water but will never become waterlogged, since any surplus will seep away through the holes in the plastic lining.

The same result can be achieved by lining the excavation with porous concrete. In Uppsala, Sweden, there is a tank in the Botanic Gardens full of rare bog orchids. It is made of porous concrete, and every week or so in summer is flooded to a depth of 8 cm

drought. Certain species are adaptable to both worlds, however. The golden club, *Orontium aquaticum,* for example, given deep water has floating, elongated, very glaucous leaves and floating flowers, but in a bog produces huge green leaves and few flowers.

Normally, marginal aquatics should be given between 8 and 20 cm (3 and 8 in) of soil, according to their size and vigour, the large tuberous-rooted kinds needing the greatest depth. Extremely vigorous kinds should not be encouraged to encroach on the territory of others, so confine their roots in some sort of container, such as a pot or box, or thrust pieces of slate sideways into the soil so as to form a barrier.

Manuring is unnecessary with bog plants. The plants should, however, be lifted and divided occasionally in order to maintain their quality and vigour.

3
Decorative garden plants

Plants are the most important features in every garden.
In any garden created for enjoyment and beauty,
decorative plants form major structural elements in the design
and are the primary source of decoration and colour.
There are the more or less permanent types,
from trees and shrubs that will last many decades to
perennials that will need renewing or replanting every few years.
At the other extreme are the most ephemeral of plants,
the annuals that give a brief splash of colour and are then gone.
There are plants with special qualities of form, fragrance,
seasonal interest or usefulness in flower arrangements.
This chapter contains details of thousands of types.
Apart from the most important kinds, such as roses and heathers,
which have one or more individual articles of their own,
they are grouped according to their characteristics and uses.
The aim is to make it as easy as possible for you
to choose the best plants to fulfil your particular needs.

Evergreen garden trees

Evergreen trees provide the main features – background, framework, screening and foliage – during the winter months, and form perhaps the most important structural element in the design of a garden. A great variety of colours, forms and textures is available, and there is no excuse for relying on excessive plantings of Lawson cypress, thuja and the now over-used Leyland cypress. Evergreens include both broad-leaves and conifers.

Broad-leaved evergreens

Tall-growing broad-leaved evergreens are scarce in cool climates. By mild seaboards (west coasts in the northern hemisphere) the holm oak, *Quercus ilex,* is valuable in exposed areas. In some shelter, it can reach 27 m (90 ft) in 100 years, but it is a dull tree in numbers. The Lucombe oak, *Q. × hispanica* 'Lucombeana', is less oppressive and makes a broader tree. It is a hybrid between the cork oak and Turkey oak. The Chilean beech, *Nothofagus dombeyi,* has decorative, small, nearly black leaves. It grows extremely rapidly near mild oceanic coasts to 20 m (65 ft) in 30 years, and is hardy but slower in less maritime areas. It needs lime-free soil.

Smaller trees of great all-round merit are the strawberry trees. The madrona, *Arbutus menziesii,* reaches 15 m (50 ft) in 40 years, and has bold foliage, massed cream flowers in spring, orange-red fruit in summer, and smooth red bark stripping away to pale yellow. The hybrid strawberry tree *A. × andrachnoides* has smaller leaves and deep red bark. Unlike *A. menziesii,* it will tolerate lime, but neither is fully hardy when young.

The hollies provide medium to small trees of great variety and exceeding hardiness. The Highclere hybrids are good even in bad pollution and against strong sea winds. Hodgins's form, *Ilex × altaclarensis* 'Hodginsii', is a male, and so lacks berries, but it makes a broad column, up to 15 m (50 ft) tall, of glossy broad leaves. 'Camelliifolia' bears berries and makes a conical tree of light green, with big, glossy, narrow leaves. For gold variegation

Quercus × hispanica 'Lucombeana'

Eucalyptus globulus

Cedrus atlantica 'Glauca'

Picea beweriana

there is 'Golden King' (also a female), among others, whilst among the white-variegated hollies the best are forms of *I. aquifolium,* 'Handsworth New Silver' and 'Perry's Weeping' being particularly decorative.

A very choice tree excellent in cities and towns is the Chinese privet, *Ligustrum lucidum,* which reaches 12 m (40 ft) in about 40 years. It bears fragrant plumes of cream flowers almost hiding the broad, glossy leaves from later summer until the winter.

One of the best-known eucalypts is the Tasmanian blue gum, *Eucalyptus globulus,* which runs wild around San Francisco, California, growing to 60 m (200 ft) in 80 years. This and scores of other species thrive in the western half of the British Isles and in southern Europe. *E. globulus* can survive only slight frosts, but many others are hardy down to about −15°C (5°F). *E. niphophila* and *E. gunnii,* for example, are fully hardy everywhere in Britain, and *E. dalrympleana* is only slightly less so. Eucalypts generally grow 2 m (7 ft) a year on well-drained open sites, but are difficult to place in a landscape, with their hard blue-grey foliage and bright, pale blue-white or yellow bark.

The cypress family

The most useful conifer in gardens in regions where temperature variations between summer and winter are not too extreme is the Lawson cypress, *Chamaecyparis lawsoniana.* Uniformly conical in shape and sea-green in colour in its small native stands in the Siskiyou Mountains in California and Oregon, it soon became the most variable of all the conifers when seedlings were raised in nurseries.

There are now Lawson cypresses of every stature from minute buns to 40 m (130 ft) trees, from brightest gold to powdery blue, from open or fernlike to congested and bunched or drooping, thread-like foliage, and from narrow spires to round bushes. Furthermore, these are all peculiarly indifferent as to soil, and thrive in acid sands and peats as well as in chalky loams and clays – provided only that water does not lie there during floods. All are good against moderate sea winds and exposure, and only really harsh, cold winter winds burn them. Birds find them ideal for early nesting.

Recommended cultivars among the golden forms include 'Lutea', which is somewhat pendulous and may scorch in intense sun, since it is not seen in the hotter parts of the United States, but is common in the northwest and in the British Isles; 'Winston Churchill', which is upswept at the base; 'Stewartii', with long ferny sprays and much grown in San Francisco; and 'Lanei' ('Lane'), with thin feathery sprays.

Among the blue-grey kinds, try 'Triumph of Boskoop', vigorous to 25 m (80 ft); 'Col-

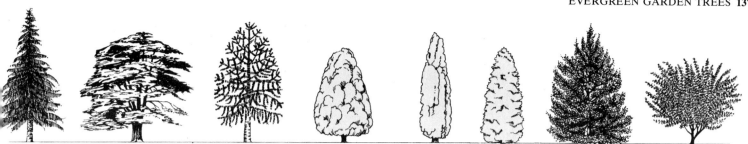

umnaris', neat and narrow to at least 12 m (40 ft) in 40 years; 'Pembury Blue', often bushy and a lovely powder-blue; 'Allumii', a less blue cultivar, conical from a bushy base; or 'Wisselii', which forms a tall, columnar, turretted crown of dark blue congested foliage and grows rapidly to 25 m (80 ft) in 60 years. Among the narrow green forms are 'Youngii', a conical tree growing to 20 m (65 ft), with highly decorative ferny sprays; and 'Green Pillar' ('Jackman's Erecta'), a very tight column, bright green in colour, from a shiny-barked stout trunk.

The weeping Nootka cypress, *C. nootkatensis* 'Pendula', has long, dark green shoots hanging in curtains from upcurved branches, and is much planted in Switzerland and north-western North America. Cripps's golden Hinoki cypress, *C. obtusa* 'Crippsii', is a bright yellow, broadly conical tree of medium-small growth. There are also useful cultivars of the Sawara cypress, *C. pisifera*, generally up to 10 m (33 ft) tall.

Members of the genus *Chamaecyparis* are distinguished from the related cypresses of the genus *Cupressus* in having flattened sprays of foliage rather than branchlets in plumes from all round the shoots. Among the latter, the smooth Arizona cypress, *Cupressus glabra*, is a splendid neat tree, blue-grey in colour and remarkably hardy and tolerant of heat and drought.

The Leyland cypress, × *Cupressocyparis leylandii*, is a bigeneric hybrid between the Nootka cypress, *Chamaecyparis nootkatensis* (from cool, moist summers), and the Monterey cypress, *Cupressus macrocarpa* (from hot, very dry summers, but really preferring damper summers than it has at Monterey, California). The hybrid grows with the utmost vigour in most soils and situations, and can reach 30 m (100 ft) in 50 years. It is easily raised from cuttings, and there are twelve cultivars. The two most recent are superb golden trees: 'Castlewellan', with feathery foliage that is yellow all the year on the exterior, and 'Robinson's Gold', with flattened foliage sprays intensely gold in early summer.

Also in the cypress family, the junipers are a dull, slow group, best for their excellent dwarf forms (see p 231). But they are resistant to heat, drought and lime, and can thus be valuable in some gardens. The golden Chinese juniper, *Juniperus chinensis* 'Aurea', forms a column – sometimes two columns – of gold. The Syrian juniper, *J. drupacea*, makes a very narrow column of big, fresh green leaves, silvered on the inside. The cultivar 'Glauca' of the red cedar, *J. virginiana*, makes a rather open tree with upswept branches of pale grey.

The golden barred thuja, *Thuja plicata* 'Zebrina' ('Aureovariegata'), a form of western red cedar, is a fine golden tree of neat conical form and moderate growth, but it is not suited to hot dry areas. The Chinese thuja, or Chinese arbor-vitae, *T. orientalis*, is more

Evergreens of varied form
Left to right: *Tsuga heterophylla*; *Cedrus libani*; *Araucaria araucana*; *Thuja orientalis*; *Juniperus chinensis*; × *Cupressocyparis leylandii*; *Ilex* × *altaclarensis*; *Ligustrum lucidum* (not to scale)

tolerant but is dull and of bushy shape. The form 'Elegantissima' is however a fine, upright, narrowly ovoid tree changing from bright yellow to mossy yellow-green in winter.

Other conifers
The silver firs, *Abies* species, are mostly majestic trees of humid mountain regions. The cork fir, *Abies lasiocarpa arizonica*, can, however, make a neat narrow tree of metallic blue, and *A. concolor* 'Violacea' a rather larger tree of pale grey. They are good in almost any garden. The Korean fir, *A. koreana*, may be put in a shrub border, for it usually grows to only about 2.5 m (8 ft) in 20 years, and it flowers freely well before that. The female flowers are cylindrical, up to 5 cm (2 in) tall, and may be yellow-green, pink or purplish. They are crowded along the upper shoots and ripen into 5 to 8 cm (2 to 3 in) cones, dark blue but largely obscured by brown bracts. The undersides of the leaves are silvery-white. Occasional plants grow strongly to 10 m (33 ft) or more in 20 years.

The monkey-puzzle, or Chile pine, *Araucaria araucana*, has its detractors, but a group on a rocky knoll or a strongly growing tree well placed on a lawn can look splendid. Even at its best, in very mild maritime conditions, it is relatively slow-growing and will rarely achieve 15 m (50 ft) in less than 50 years. Female trees may bear 15 cm (6 in) globular, green, gold-spined cones after some 40 years. The Chile pine is highly tolerant of strong winds and of varied soils.

The blue Atlas cedar, *Cedrus atlantica*

Chamaecyparis lawsoniana 'Winston Churchill'

'Glauca' is extremely accommodating, and makes a big tree almost anywhere. The deodar, *C. deodara*, needs mild winters, being abundant in gardens in southern and western North America and the British Isles. It has dark green, pendulous foliage.

The Japanese red cedar, *Cryptomeria japonica*, has unusually bright green scale-like foliage and an orange-brown bark. Where thriving, in areas of high summer rainfall, it grows too fast and too big for most gardens, but the form 'Elegans' rarely attains 15 m (50 ft). Its bark is bright orange-red and stringy, and it has fluffy blue-green foliage that turns red-purple for the winter. It may sprawl with age, but the foliage is useful for winter flower arrangements.

Among the many spruces, few are suited to small gardens or to any but damp sites. The beautiful weeping Brewer spruce, *Picea breweriana*, slowly makes a tree that grows best in rather maritime countries and is up to 15 m (50 ft) tall in parts of Britain. The golden new shoots of the neat-foliaged *P. orientalis* 'Aurea' ('Aureospicata') make this rather slow tree worthwhile. The blue Colorado spruce, *P. pungens* 'Koster', prefers moist soils but thrives in gardens across the entire northern half of the United States and in the British Isles and western Europe.

The pines are mostly tolerant of dry heat or cool moist summers, and the Swiss arolla pine, *Pinus cembra*, and the similar Korean pine, *P. koraiensis*, make attractive young trees. Few others are worth a place in a small garden, but the golden Scots pine, *P. sylvestris* 'Aurea', forms a tower of gold through winter and early spring, but is blue-green at other seasons, and the neat, dark, blue-coned Bosnian pine, *P. leucodermis*, thrives on any soil from acid peat to limestone.

The hemlocks (*Tsuga* spp) are Asiatic and American conifers of few species but great variety. The western hemlock, *Tsuga heterophylla*, is the giant of the group, an elegant tree growing to over 70 m (230 ft) in North America and 45 m (150 ft) in Scotland, where it has been grown for only 120 years. The Carolina hemlock, *T. caroliniana*, is a much smaller tree, reaching 14 m (45 ft) in cultivation, but has dense luxuriant foliage that is deep shiny green with narrow bright white bands beneath the leaf. The female flowers are little ovoids of rich rosy-purple. The mountain hemlock, *T. mertensiana*, is an exceedingly hardy, tough tree making a tall narrow cone of hanging blue-grey foliage.

An oddity from Japan, the umbrella pine, *Sciadopitys verticillata*, is a redwood relative with 12 cm (5 in) leaves fused together in pairs, each a rich, glossy green and radiating in whorls. In reasonably equable climates with damp summers, this makes an attractive tree or large bush. It usually bears numerous cones, fleshy and green, 8 cm (3 in) long, but soon turning brown and disintegrating.

Trees for flowers and fruits

Deciduous trees, by their very nature, cannot provide the year-round structural framework for a well-planted garden that is a major attribute of evergreens (see p 136). Some make up for this, however, by their decorative features – often beautiful leaves, flowers, colourful berries or decorative bark. This article deals with some good garden trees with attractive flowers or fruits – or both – while the next article deals with those grown primarily for their foliage and form.

Flowering cherries and plums

The cherries (*Prunus* spp) provide the richest array of opulently flowering trees in spring, but they are poorly shaped and dull in summer. Two, however, have beautiful bark but lack spectacular flowers. These are the Tibetan cherry, *Prunus serrula,* which has shining mahogany-coloured bark if it is regularly stroked and not allowed to turn to black scales, and the Manchurian cherry, *P. maackii*, with honey-brown bark becoming orange. Sargent's cherry, *P. sargentii*, has an early mass of good pink single flowers, and makes up for hanging its dull, abruptly tipped leaves all summer by an early autumn blaze of scarlet and ruby-red foliage. One of its hybrids, 'Accolade', has clouds of soft pink, hanging double flowers that open even earlier than in the species. It makes a low, spreading tree with sparse, narrow dark leaves.

Prunus maackii

Prunus 'Amanogawa'

Prunus 'Pink Perfection'

The big-flowered cherries of middle and late spring are Japanese cultivars of partly obscure parentage, so they are generally known by their cultivar names alone. 'Kanzan' (or 'Kwanzan') is the universal one; sumptuous though it be, it is so common that one of the lesser known forms is to be preferred. 'Shimidsu Sakura' is a superb late-season cherry, its long-stalked pink buds opening into double, pure white flowers. These hang among leaves that start violet-flushed, then turn green, on a spreading low crown. Crossed

with 'Kanzan', it gave the glorious 'Pink Perfection', with big, globular, late double flowers in red and pink, and green leaves. 'Shirofugen' is a more pendulous 'Shimidsu Sakura', with red leaves above the opening pink buds. The flowers become white, then fade pink again at the very end of the season. 'Ichiyo' is the most superb but rarely seen mid-season tree, with huge globular clusters of big, pale pink, frilled, double flowers.

'Tai-haku' was lost to cultivation in Japan for 150 years and turned up in a Sussex garden. From among deep red leaves, there emerge in mid-season the largest white, single flowers of any cherry; they are wreathed along new shoots, and in globular clusters on old. 'Ukon' is similar, but the flowers are semi-double and open the palest yellow beneath pale brown leaves. 'Hokusai' has been swamped in recent years by 'Kanzan', but it remains a fine tree, in flower two weeks before 'Kanzan' and much paler pink; whilst 'Horinji' flowers after 'Kanzan', has whitish-pink flowers glistening amongst dark pink buds, and spreads on wide ascending branches. 'Amanogawa' flowers in mid- to late-season, with pale pink, fragrant and double flowers; it takes up practically no room, as the branches grow almost vertically.

The plums also belong in the genus *Prunus*. The myrobalan plum, or cherry plum, *P. cerasifera*, is the earliest in flower; its starry white little flowers appear among the emerging green leaves in late winter. They are often mistaken for those of the blackthorn, *P. spinosa*, a dense shrub that flowers up to two months later and without leaves. Pissard's plum, *P. cerasifera* 'Pissardii' ('Atropurpurea') makes dreary purple-brown patches all the summer in suburban roads all over Britain and the northern United States. It bears a mass of flowers (if bullfinches let it) that pale to white from pink buds as the leaves unfold. The form 'Nigra' blooms a week later

with bright pink flowers, but is just as dull in leaf. So, alas, is the pretty-flowered hybrid double cherry-plum *P. × blireana*, which has double flowers eventually showing a red boss.

Apples, pears and rowans

The ornamental apples are very tough little trees flowering in late spring. They are tolerant of extremes of heat and cold, and numerous flowering crab apples have been planted in the North American prairie regions. The prairie crab itself, *Malus ioensis,* has fine, soft pink, fragrant flowers from globular buds, but the forms 'Plena' and 'Klehmii' are more showy doubles. The related *M. coronaria* has the form 'Charlottae', which bears big clusters of large, rich pink, semi-double flowers, and from a distance resembles a well-flowered pink semi-double cherry.

The Chinese species *M. hupehensis* is a sturdy, rather spreading tree with pink buds and beautiful large white flowers. 'David', 'Snowdrift' and 'White Angel' are among the very freely flowering crabs grown in North America. They are small and upright, with white single flowers. 'John Downie', from England, is similar but has pink buds and brilliant scarlet and yellow glossy fruit that makes a jelly of superb colour and flavour (see p 323). For the smallest space, there is the pillar apple, *M. tschonoskii,* from Japan. This is nearly erect, and its broad leathery leaves turn glorious scarlet and crimson in autumn.

The weeping willow-leaved pear, *Pyrus salicifolia* 'Pendula', is a favourite small tree with silvery-grey foliage and creamy-white flowers. It is very resilient. Even more robust in town conditions are the two commonest forms of the Chinese pear, *P. calleryana*: 'Bradford' is much planted in city streets in North America, and is a neat ovoid-crowned tree with pale green leaves. 'Chanticleer' is similar, but more upright and less regular. Both have orange and red foliage in autumn.

Also related to the apples and pears are the *Sorbus* species, the whitebeams and rowans or mountain ashes). Among these, the choice trees are two rowans from China. *Sorbus* 'Joseph Rock' is a slender tree up to 9 m (30 ft) tall that bears bunches of lemon-yellow berries in autumn, amongst leaves that are turning crimson and purple. The berries remain after leaf-fall. Sargent's rowan, *S. sargentiana,* is a spreading tree with big, glossy red buds that weep resin, and large pinnate leaves that turn bright scarlet in autumn. It bears some 200 small, bright red berries on each head.

Another fine rowan is a form of the common European species, *S. aucuparia,* called 'Beissneri'. It has well-cut leaflets which colour amber-yellow in autumn, but its main feature is the pink or orange-red bark. The Hupeh rowan, *S. hupehensis,* is a sturdy tree, reaching 15 m (50 ft) in 50 years or less. It is distinctive in summer with its large grey-green leaflets – bluish beneath – on red central stalks. Its fruits are white or pink-tinged and hang in large bunches. Birds leave them alone, apparently regarding them as unripe.

Other flowering and berrying trees

The Indian bean tree, *Catalpa bignonioides,* from Louisiana, is valuable in cities for its late summer flowers, which are white and fragrant, its long bean-like fruits and its big

upper sides of the level sprays of foliage, erect cream-white bracts fading to dark pink over a long season. The centre boss remains atop its upright stalk and becomes a fleshy, dark red, strawberry-like fruit. The Japanese form, *C. kousa* itself, is shorter, with whiter and less densely packed flowers.

The American dogwood, *C. florida,* is a common woodland, roadside, garden, park and town tree across all the northern and eastern United States and in southern Canada. It is usually a low rounded tree of 6 m (20 ft) or so, but can be 12 m (40 ft) tall. It differs from *C. kousa* in that the smooth bark on the ribbed bole becomes dark brown and deeply cracked. Also, its flowers are less dense and the fruits are short-stalked bunches of scarlet berries. In Europe, the form 'Rubra' is generally grown. It is a little unreliable in its flowering, but in a good year makes a spectacular cloud of pale pink. The biggest dogwood is the Pacific dogwood, *C. nuttallii.* In mild maritime areas this can be 15 m (50 ft) tall, but it is sometimes short-lived. It bears four to six big white bracts around each flower head, and bears more flowers as the leaves turn red in autumn.

Of the innumerable thorns (or hawthorns), the best are the Washington thorn, *Crataegus phaenopyrum,* which is much planted in streets in North America, and the hybrid *C. × prunifolia,* which is common in Europe. The

round, pale leaves, and its flowers are in spikes. *Halesia monticola* (*H. carolina monticola*), the snowdrop tree, can reach 27 m (90 ft) in the Tennessee woods, but a rather snaky 15 m (50 ft) in cultivation. It bears rows of hanging white flowers in spring, followed by winged fruit.

Ash trees are mostly too big for gardens, but the flowering ash or manna ash, *Fraxinus ornus,* is a good street and garden tree with smooth grey bark and highly fragrant plumes of creamy-white flowers in early summer. Many magnolias are either pure shrubs or trees that become too big. *Magnolia salicifolia,* however, is a tree of modest size bearing copious white flowers on bare shoots in early spring, and has peculiarly bronzed-green, aniseed-scented leaves.

Oxydendrum arboreum, the sorrel tree, can be grown only on acid soils, where it soon bears long narrow sprays of little white flowers above long glossy leaves. In the autumn, the ivory-white fruits are set off by bright and deep red leaves. For brilliant abundance of autumn flowers in every shade of pink, the crape myrtle, *Lagerstroemia indica,* has few rivals. It is a common street tree in the South of the United States, and in France, but it does not receive enough sun to do well in the British Isles.

The Japanese pagoda tree, *Sophora japonica,* which is used freely in north-eastern

Sorbus aucuparia

yellowish-green leaves. The western catalpa, *C. speciosa,* from Illinois, is planted less but makes a taller tree with longer leaves. The Judas tree, *Cercis siliquastrum,* needs hot summers to give its best displays of densely bunched, rosy-pink pea-flowers, which erupt from shoots, branches and boles in late spring. The nearly round leaves are attractive, and the large pods turn purple in the summer. The redbuds of North America are very similar, the eastern redbud, *C. canadensis,* having very slightly smaller and darker flowers.

The dogwoods, or cornels, (*Cornus* spp) are largely shrubs, but a few make small trees. These have showy inflorescences which are really a boss of minute flowers surrounded by four to six large ovate bracts. The most free-flowering is the so-called Chinese strawberry tree, *Cornus kousa chinensis,* a small tree sometimes 10 m (33 ft) tall, with very flaky brown bark. The flowers are packed along the

Cercis canadensis

Washington thorn has deeply lobed little leaves, long slender thorns and small bunches of bright red berries. *C. × prunifolia* has broad, glossy leaves, purple thorns 5 cm (2 in) long and in autumn is an unusual coppery-orange colour, turning crimson, with red berries. It makes a broad bushy tree.

The storax family has some good small trees. *Styrax japonica* is a neat rounded tree with small, light green leaves, and is liberally hung in summer with a myriad of little white bell flowers. *S. obassia* has very big, nearly

Euodia hupehensis

American cities, flowers in late summer. Big open panicles of white pea-flowers are followed by pale green pods that are thickened at each seed like beads on a string. The leaves are up to 25 cm (10 in) long, each with 9 to 15 leaflets. The laburnums are poor trees when not in flower, but the hybrid Voss's laburnum, *Laburnum × watereri,* is too good to miss, combining as it does the long 30 cm (12 in) flower heads of *L. alpinum,* one of its parents, with the large, densely held flowers of *L. anagyroides,* the other parent.

Finally, a superb all-rounder: a tree of the highest quality in foliage, growth, health, in usefully late flowering, and even in fruit. *Euodia hupehensis,* a tree able to thrive in city parks, has a smooth grey bark and opposite pinnate leaves with leathery, glossy leaflets on pink stalks. In late summer it bears numerous heads of nearly white flowers, followed by upright heads of orange-red berries.

Trees for foliage effect

Deciduous trees grown primarily for the beauty of their foliage should be chosen with even greater care than most other plants. A tree that has, say, brilliantly coloured leaves for a week or two in the autumn needs other attractive features to earn its place in the garden through the rest of the year. The leafless winter appearance and the form and colour of its foliage throughout the whole season are important factors.

Deciduous conifers
Few conifers are deciduous, but those that are make excellent garden trees. The swamp cypress, *Taxodium distichum*, is usually planted beside water, but it does not need to be. Very late into leaf, it is a fresh light green colour until it turns fox-red in late autumn. Eventually a tree over 30 m (100 ft) tall, this is relatively slow-growing and can be a feature of a small garden for a long period.

The Chinese *Metasequoia glyptostroboides* (dawn redwood) is somewhat similar, but has bigger leaves and shoots that are borne in opposite pairs. In cultivation only since 1948, this has shown that it does best in some shelter and on damp sites with long, rather hot summers. The buds open pale green in early spring, and in autumn the foliage turns pink and then deep red. The bark is orange, brick-red flakes peeling off and littering the ground beneath the tree. Both the above look best as specimens standing apart from other trees.

The larches are invaluable in gardens, but are seldom used. The rapid early growth of the best ones, even in exposed areas, makes them very suitable for quick, expendable shelter in new gardens. The fresh green leaves appear early, just after the little pink, cream or red flowers, and remain late to give fine colours at the very end of autumn. Under larches, bluebells and other bulbs, or good grassland, can be grown, and many birds feed or nest in these trees.

The European larch, *Larix decidua*, is the freshest colour and is the best on fertile sheltered sites, whilst the Japanese *L. kaempferi* has darker foliage, dark red or orange shoots and a denser crown, and is more robust in hard conditions. The hybrid between these, *L. × eurolepis*, is intermediate except that it grows faster than either. The golden larch from China, *Pseudolarix amabilis*, may be slow to start and hard to acquire, but it is an ideal tree for a fairly small garden, and is bright orange-brown in autumn.

The maple family
The maples (*Acer* spp) include more small trees of high quality than any other single genus, with year-round features and few foibles. They are best known for their colourful or autumn-tinted leaves, but many also have attractive bark and some have attractive flowers. The paperbark maple, *Acer griseum*, is always in demand for its orange or red peeling bark, its yellow-flushing leaves and flowers, and its scarlet and crimson autumn colours. In the same group, with leaves of three leaflets, the Nikko maple, *A. nikoense*, colours similarly and thrives on limestone.

Taxodium distichum

The ash-leaved maple, or box elder, *A. negundo*, grows wild right across the United States, and everywhere has a rich green, fine foliage with three to seven leaflets per leaf. In Europe the species is a little dull, but the variety 'Variegatum' makes a splash of white variegation and 'Auratum' is a splendid gold.

The snakebarks are a remarkable group of maples. All come from China and Japan except for the moose-bark, *A. pensylvanicum*, which comes from the north-eastern United States. This has grey or green bark, bold striped blue-white, and big broad leaves which turn lemon-yellow in early autumn. The best of the Asiatic species are *A. capillipes*, with scarlet stalks to the glossy parallel-veined leaves, and orange and crimson autumn colours; and *A. hersii*, an olive green tree with broad dark leaves turning orange and red. All snakebarks grow fast for a few years, then fan out attractively. They seldom exceed 12 m (40 ft) in height, but do need some space.

Two species of Japanese maple are grown in numerous forms, most of which are shrubs (see p 164). The type species of the commonest, *A. palmatum*, can however attain 15 m (50 ft), and has well-cut small leaves colouring well in autumn. *A. japonicum* 'Vitifolium' makes an upright twisting tree of similar height, with big, many-lobed leaves colouring scarlet, gold and purple. A curious and attractive maple from Japan is the hornbeam maple, *A. carpinifolium*. It has slender unlobed but sharply toothed leaves, each with 22 or more parallel veins. It is rather bushy and turns yellow in the autumn. The Chinese trident maple, *A. buergeranum*, is a superb tree for a small garden, with a mass of pretty leaves that are bluish beneath and turn crimson in the autumn. The tree forms a domed crown up to 10 m (33 ft) tall.

Lobel's maple, *A. lobelii*, is useful because it grows very fast, but its rather few branches are almost vertical, so it takes up little room. The leaves are broad, with five whisker-tipped lobes. The Norway maple, *A. platanoides*, is too big for a small garden but the form 'Columnare' is strictly upright and used in some city streets. The form 'Globosum' grows a dense, low, globular crown. Both have bright green leaves that turn yellow in autumn.

The sugar maple, *A. saccharum*, (the source of maple syrup and maple sugar) forms a large tree in its native habitat of eastern North America. But it has two varieties that are slender spires, 'Newton Sentry' being almost

Acer rubrum

Acer psuedo-platanus 'Brilliantissimum'

ingle unbranched pole and 'Temple's Upright' a little more furnished. Both achieve brilliant autumn colours. The red maple, *A. rubrum,* has the variety 'Columnare' of columnar form and fast attaining 20 m (65 ft) and more, but the type tree grows slowly enough to find a place in medium to small gardens. With red flowers before the leaves, and pretty leaves turning yellow and scarlet or deep purple, it has a long season.

The European sycamore, *A. pseudoplatanus,* has yielded many forms, many as dull as the type, but 'Brilliantissumum' is a superb tree for the smallest garden. Forming a dense small head at first, if grafted onto a trunk about 1.8 m (6 ft) tall, it bushes out and becomes globular. The leaves emerge bright pink, then with a reddish tinge turn orange, then yellow, and after three weeks turn white before relapsing to a dull greyish-green. 'Prinz Handjery' is similar, a little less dense, and flowers well, yellow catkins hanging among pink leaves that are purple beneath.

The birch family

The birches make graceful trees, mostly of moderate size. The common silver birch, *Betula pendula,* is ideal for early temporary shelter when establishing a garden on open land. It grows rapidly to 20 m (65 ft) in about 25 years. On light sandy soils its roots are invasive, but on stronger soils they allow shrubs and bulbs to grow beneath the trees. The foliage provides high light shade which keeps radiation frosts from tender plants. It will make a good specimen tree with the bole cleared early of side shoots to encourage the white bark, but the Swedish or cut-leaf birch – the form 'Dalecarlica' – is superior. It has whiter bark, a smoother trunk and long, pendulous shoots of small, deeply cut leaves. It is very tolerant of heat. The weeping form, 'Youngii', is popular, although it makes rather an untidy mound of small foliage hanging from a spindly trunk.

B. medwediewii is a choice plant, almost a shrub but usually springing low from a single bole. The many stems form a cup shape and bear substantial, rather alder-like leaves and big catkins. In autumn it is a blaze of gold. *B. utilis,* from the Himalayas, makes a fine tree with glossy leaves on red stalks, and the bark is a blend of smooth rich browns or clear white. *B. jacquemontii,* from farther west, has pure white shiny bark.

Also in the birch family are the alders, most of which like damp situations. The best for a small garden is *Alnus incana* 'Ramulis Coccineis', which has sealing-wax-red buds in winter and golden leaves in summer. It is a low domed tree, and tolerates any soil.

Other foliage trees

One horse chestnut remains small enough in stature for the average garden and has merit in the colour in which the leaves emerge. This is the sunrise horse chestnut. *Aesculus × negecta* 'Erythroblastos', which comes into leaf bright pink. It stays a good pink for barely a week, then pales and turns bright green.

The honey locust, *Gleditsia triacanthos,* is grown, usually as the form 'Inermis' without spines on the bole, in every city in the United States and many in Canada. It is one of the few able to thrive in canyons among skyscrapers and with hot paving over its entire root-run. There are also a few in London. The species is a useful but uninteresting tree, but the form 'Sunburst' ('Inermis Aurea') is striking in spring. In the American Midwest it comes into leaf a rich orange-yellow and fades to pale yellow. In Britain it leafs out fairly bright yellow, then becomes green, and is still an attractive small tree for a sunny position.

A tree from the Allegheny Mountains in the east of the United States, the tupelo, *Nyssa sylvatica,* can tolerate a little lime and

Nyssa sylvatica

rather slowly makes a pendulous tree. Its glossy leaves turn in autumn to shining gold and scarlet, then deep red. It seems to need a good damp soil to grow well.

Trees grown primarily for foliage in a small garden can include few oaks, but the blackjack oak, *Quercus marilandica,* has strikingly big shiny leaves with two huge side-lobes, and remains a small tree. Room can usually be found also for the cypress oak, *Q. robur* 'Fastigiata', a form of the common English oak that has the shape of a Lombardy poplar. Variably narrow, some are very slender and will take some 60 years to exceed 20 m (65 ft) in height.

The best willow for foliage is the bay willow, *Salix pentandra,* a native of northern Europe. It has glossy brown shoots and bright glossy green leaves, whilst yellow catkins emerge when it is in leaf. *S. magnifica,* from China, has huge, broad leaves and very big catkins. It is in the sallow group, with upright flowers. The best weeping willow of cooler

parts is *S. alba* 'Tristis'. This has yellow shoots and whitish-blue, velvety undersides to the leaves. In warmer areas, the commonest is *S. babylonica,* a Chinese tree with brown shoots and smooth, nearly green undersides to the leaves. Both are very vigorous growers with roots able to spread far enough to find adequate moisture on any but the driest soil.

The sweet gum, *Liquidambar styraciflua* is as good in summer, with its bright, shiny, prettily lobed and toothed big leaves, as it is in autumn with its scarlet, ruby, dark red or plum and gold colours. It needs, to grow best, a deep, rich, rather moist soil; it may then reach 20 m (65 ft) in 40 years. The most attractive ash is the Caucasian ash, *Fraxinus oxycarpa,*

Ginkgo biloba

with bright, glossy green leaves and shiny, pale grey bark. In the form 'Raywood' the leaves turn rich purple in autumn, but this is too vigorous a tree for a small garden.

Lastly, there is the ginkgo, *Ginkgo biloba* – neither conifer nor broad-leaved tree, but just a ginkgo. Like nothing else alive today, it represents a primitive family of trees common 160 million years ago. This maidenhair tree (its leaves resemble those of the maidenhair fern) will rarely outgrow a garden within 50 years of being planted, although it can reach 30 m (100 ft). It is usually narrow, except in some parts of the eastern United States, and is often very narrow – especially in the 'Sentry Ginkgo' or 'Fastigiata'.

In virtually every city in North America, ginkgos abound and thrive. In Britain, it thrives only in the south, but it can be grown, if slowly, in southern Scotland. Leafing out bright fresh green and signing off with bright butter-yellow, this unique plant should be grown wherever it has a chance of surviving.

Self-clinging climbers

There is such a varied collection of climbing plants to choose from that the gardener needs to have a clear idea of his requirements before selecting. You must first decide where the plant is to grow – in particular, the aspect and exposure of the supporting wall or other structure – and how much space the plant will occupy when established. Is an evergreen plant required, or can it be bare in winter? Are you attracted by autumn tints, or by flowers, fragrant or otherwise. (Fragrance is a great asset where a plant is to clothe the wall of a house and grow near its windows.)

Hedera helix 'Sagittaefolia'

Finally, to what extent can you help the climber on its way? Some twist or twine their way up trellis or through the branches of a tree or hedge. Some have self-clinging aerial roots, while others need to be regularly tied in to supports.

Twining and twisting perennial climbers, together with those that need tying-in, are covered on pages 144 to 147. Annual climbers and others easily grown from seed are covered on pages 212 to 213. This article deals with those with aerial roots, which absorb atmospheric moisture as well as attaching their shoots and stems to walls, trees and so on. For general information on the use and cultivation of climbers, see page 92.

The ivies
Many people think of ivies (*Hedera* spp) as plants that will climb over anything in a matter of moments. This is far from the truth, as ivies can take at least a year to become thoroughly established – though once they have got going all will be well. All are hardy evergreens with glossy leaves, though the Canary Island (or Algerian) ivy, *Hedera canariensis,* is more tender than the others and will be cut back in a harsh winter; it will usually shoot again from ground level. Some varieties of ivy need the leading shoot pinched out in spring to encourage branching.

The common or English ivy, *H. helix*, has produced a multitude of green and variegated forms, with leaves of various sizes. A delightful small-leaved variety is 'Goldheart' (also called 'Jubilee'). Its rich green-edged leaves

Parthenocissus tricuspidata 'Veitchii'

Hedera canariensis 'Gloire de Marengo'

are enhanced by a splash of gold in the centre. 'Glacier' has grey variegations, while the pretty 'Marginata' ('Argentea Elegans') has triangular leaves with creamy-white edges that take on a pink tinge in winter. All-green varieties can also look attractive, particularly those with sharply lobed leaves, such as 'Sagittaefolia' and 'Digitata'.

Another beautiful but somewhat tender variegated ivy is *H. canariensis* 'Variegata' ('Gloire de Marengo'). Its dark green leaves are bordered with silvery-grey and creamy-

white. Where you want a really large-leaved ivy, plant the dark green *H. colchica* (*H. amurensis*), the Persian ivy. The lustrous leaves are 20 cm (8 in) long and 10 cm (4 in) wide, and it is a vigorous grower. So too is *H. colchica* 'Dentatovariegata', whose soft green leaves are handsomely variegated with pale yellow. Another large-leaved dark green ivy is the Irish ivy, *H. helix hibernica* (sometimes listed as *H. hibernica*). An attractive bronze-purple ivy is *H. helix* 'Purpurea', while *H. helix* 'Tricolor' ('Elegantissima' or 'Marginata Rubra') is rather similar to 'Marginata'.

Virginia creepers
Among the most colourful – though deciduous – self-clinging wall climbers are the Virginia creepers (*Parthenocissus* spp). Probably the best known and most widely planted, however, is not a true Virginia creeper at all but is more properly known by its American common name, Boston ivy. It is *Parthenocissus tricuspidata* 'Veitchii' (*Ampelopsis,* or *Vitis, veitchii* or *V. inconstans*), which was introduced from the Far East in 1862. It adheres to its host by sticky discs at the end of the leaf tendrils. In mature plants the foliage is large and coarse, being dark green during the summer, but it is unsurpassed for its mantle of red and crimson in autumn. Where space is

limited, the small-leaved variety 'Beverley Brook' is the best.

The true Virginia creeper from eastern North America is *P. quinquefolia*. Its leaves are composed of five leaflets, are bright green in summer, turning in autumn to brilliant orange and scarlet. It is ideal for growing on high walls or in lofty trees. *P. inserta* is similar, but less vigorous and having twining rather than adhesive tendrils. It is also North American.

Another Far Eastern wonder is *P. henryana*. The three to five leaflets making up each leaf are a dark velvety green, enhanced by silvery-white and pinkish-purple on the main veins. In autumn it turns a brilliant warm red. It is happiest on a shady wall. Always plant a container-grown specimen, for it dislikes having its roots disturbed.

For the closely related *Ampelopsis* and *Vitis* species, see p 147.

Hydrangea family

The climbing hydrangeas are useful plants for growing up trees or against the walls of buildings. They withstand polluted air, and are happy in sun or shade. The deciduous *Hydrangea anomala* has toothed leaves and creamy-white flower heads. An evergreen, *H. integerrima* has leathery green leaves and small creamy-white flowers borne in panicles 8 to 15 cm (3 to 6 in) long in summer. It is best grown against a wall. Perhaps the best known of the climbing hydrangeas is the deciduous *H. petiolaris*, which is also known as *H. scandens* but is now officially classified as a sub-species of *H. anomala*, *H. anomala petiolaris*. With its large flat white flower heads up to 25 cm (10 in) wide from early summer onwards, it can climb to 18 m (60 ft).

Tree trunks make superb hosts for climbing plants, and two suitable climbers with fragrance, though not frequently seen, are the decumarias. *Decumaria barbara*, which attaches itself by aerial roots, has small white fragrant flowers, borne above glossy green foliage, in early to mid-summer. It grows to 9 m (30 ft). It is deciduous, though sometimes semi-evergreen. A lower-growing species is the evergreen *D. sinensis*; its small honey-scented white flowers are borne in late spring. It grows satisfactorily on an east or west wall, reaches 3 to 4.5 m (10 to 15 ft), but is a rare plant in cultivation.

A late-flowering evergreen self-climbing shrub with aerial roots like ivy is *Pileostegia viburnoides*. This accommodating climber will clamber over a tree stump or up a medium-sized tree, though it is happier when growing against a sheltered wall. The panicles of creamy-white flowers, up to 12 cm (5 in) wide, are backed by 10 to 15 cm (4 to 6 in), dark green leathery leaves. Container-grown plants put out in spring do best. It needs a well-drained loamy soil.

Two further hydrangea-like self-clinging climbers are the schizophragmas. *Schizophragma hydrangeoides* has large, coarsely-toothed leaves and flower-heads up to 25 cm (10 in) across consisting of pale yellow bracts encircling the small yellow flowers. In the variety 'Roseum' the bracts are pink-flushed.

Even larger flower-heads appear on *S. integrifolium*, whose bracts are creamy-white. Both of these species flower from mid-summer to early autumn.

Other kinds

For a really spectacular self-clinging climber, you can grow the trumpet vine, *Campsis* (*Tecoma*) *radicans*. It produces clusters of orange or red trumpet-shaped blooms, up to 8 cm (3 in) long, from late summer, providing any garden with exotic splendour. It likes a sunny spot, but will climb well over a wall or tree trunk. For other species of *Campsis*, which are not self-clinging, see p 146.

The evergreen dwarf spindles are especially useful in small gardens, forming either prostrate free-standing shrubs good for ground-cover, or self-clinging low climbers. The most widely grown is *Euonymus fortunei radicans* (often listed simply as *E. fortunei* or *E. radicans*). The variety 'Silver Queen' has bright silver-variegated foliage. 'Variegatus' is similar but not quite so bright, though in autumn the foliage takes on a pinkish tinge. The leaves of 'Coloratus' are tinged purple in winter.

Schizophragma integrifolium

Euonymus fortunei radicans 'Variegatus'

Hydrangea petiolaris

Clematis, the 'virgin's bower'

No garden should be without one or more species or varieties of clematis. These moderately vigorous climbers can provide flowers through every season if you choose the right varieties. They are excellent for growing on walls, pergolas or old tree stumps. They support themselves with twining petioles (leaf stalks), which wind round any available slender support, so it is best to provide trellis – either wooden or plastic panels – where no natural support exists.

Clematis flowers range from little more than 2.5 cm (1 in) across to 15 cm (6 in) or more. Colours are generally muted, associating well with many other plants, and range from white and pink, through violet, mauve and purple, to blue and red. There are also some yellow and orange kinds. Many are bar-

Clematis tangutica 'Gravetye'

red or edged in contrasting shades. A happy combination is to plant a clematis along with a climbing or rambling rose – especially a rose that has only one flush of flowers, such as 'Mme Grégoire Staechelin' or 'Albertine'. In this way, the clematis has natural support, and – provided a suitable clematis is chosen – the period of colourful display is lengthened.

There is a vast range of species and hybrids of the genus *Clematis,* and the table lists a selection that should assure any gardener of a good display from late winter right through to autumn.

Clematis montana 'Elizabeth'

Three large-flowered hybrid clematis

Cultivation

First and foremost, clematis like their roots to be shaded and if possible cool, but their stems and flowers to be in the sun. Therefore, when planting beside a sunny wall or fence, shade the roots with a large stone or slab. Or plant a bushy evergreen such as rosemary, lavender or the attractive rue, *Ruta graveolens* 'Jackman's Blue'. Some clematis will, however, thrive even on a cool, shady wall (north-facing in the northern hemisphere).

The large-flowered named hybrids are generally more difficult to establish than the species and their varieties, but all appreciate good living. So prepare the ground well, digging in plenty of well-rotted farmyard manure or garden compost, plus two good handfuls of bonemeal per plant.

Recommended clematis species and varieties

Season	Name	Flower colour; remarks	Aspect	Vigour*	Pruning*
Late winter to spring	*Clematis cirrhosa*	Off-white; evergreen	Any	Great	A
	C. cirrhosa balearica	Greenish-yellow; evergreen	Any	Great	A
Mid- to late spring	*C. alpina* 'Columbine'	Soft lavender-blue	Any	Low	A
	C. alpina 'Pamela Jackman'	Oxford-blue	Any	Low	A
	C. alpina 'Ruby'	Rosy-red	Any	Low	A
	C. alpina 'White Moth'	White; double	Any	Low	A
	C. armandii 'Snowdrift'	White; scented; evergreen	Sheltered	Great	A
	C. macropetala 'Markham's Pink'	Soft pink	Any	Moderate	A
Late spring to early summer	*C. chrysocoma*	Soft pinkish-mauve	Any	Great	A
	C. macropetala 'Lagoon'	Deep lavender; semi-double	Any	Moderate	A
	C. montana	White	Any	Great	A
	C. montana 'Elizabeth'	Pink; richly fragrant	Any	Great	A
	C. × vedrariensis 'Highdown'	Deep pink	Any	Great	A
Summer to autumn	*C. flammula*	White; small; fragrant	Not sunless	Great	C
	C. orientalis (orange-peel clematis)	Thick, orange-yellow hanging sepals	Not sunless	Strong	C
	C. rehderiana	Straw-coloured; bell-shaped	Not sunless	Strong	C
	C. tangutica 'Gravetye'	Bright yellow	Not sunless	Strong	C
	C. texensis 'Gravetye Beauty'	Rich, deep red	Not sunless	Moderate	C

Recommended large-flowered hybrid clematis

Season	Name	Flower colour; remarks	Aspect	Vigour*	Pruning*
Late spring, repeating in early autumn	'Barbara Jackman'	Violet-purple, crimson bar	Any	Moderate	B
	'Elsa Spath'	Blue; free-flowering	Not sunless	Moderate	B
	'Lasurstern'	Purplish-blue	Not sunless	Moderate	B
	'Nelly Moser'	Mauve-pink, carmine bar	Some shade	Moderate	B
	'The President'	Deep violet; paler bar	Any	Moderate	B
Early summer to midsummer	'Sealand Gem'	Mauve; purple bar	Any	Moderate	B
	'William Kennett'	Lavender-blue; crimped edges	Not sunless	Strong	B
Early to late summer	'Etoile Violette'	Deep violet; medium-sized	Any	Strong	C
	'Marie Boisselot'	White; large; free-flowering	Any	Moderate	B
Middle to late summer	'Jackmanii'	Violet-blue; free-flowering	Any	Strong	C
	'Madame Edouard André'	Deep red; pointed sepals	Any	Low	C
	'W. E. Gladstone'	Lavender; free-flowering	Sheltered	Strong	C
Early summer to autumn	'Comtesse de Bouchaud'	Soft pink, flushed mauve	Any	Moderate	C
Midsummer to early autumn	'Ernest Markham'	Glowing red; difficult to establish	Not sunless	Moderate/strong	C
	'Lady Betty Balfour'	Rich violet-blue	Full sun	Strong	C
	'Ville de Lyon'	Bright carmine-red; deeper-coloured edges	Not sunless	Moderate	C

*Vigour: In average growing conditions, those marked low can be expected to reach a maximum of about 2.5 m (8 ft); those marked moderate to 3.5 to 4.5 m (12 to 15 ft); strong to about 6 m (20 ft); great to 9 m (30 ft) or more. Pruning: For details and key to treatment, see text.

Climbing and rambling plants

Clematis 'Ernest Markham'

Clematis 'Lasurstern'

Pruning needs vary, and recommended treatment is indicated in the table by the letters *A, B* and *C*. All newly-planted clematis should be cut back during late winter or early spring to within 15 to 30 cm (6 to 12 in) of ground level, pruning immediately above a pair of buds. Species and hybrids in group *A* will flower from late winter to late spring, and should be pruned immediately after flowering. Where there is ample room for the plant to spread as it wishes, little pruning will be required apart from cutting away any surplus or unwanted growth. Where space is limited, cut out old flowering growth and tie in new young shoots, which will give the following season's flowers.

Those species, varieties and large flowered hybrids that flower from late spring, throughout the summer and up to early autumn form group *B*. They are pruned in late winter or early spring. When buds start to show, all weak growth should be cut out to a strong pair of buds. But do not cut back any shoot more than one-third of its total length. Also cut out all dead wood. In many cases only a minimum of pruning will be required. The species, varieties and hybrids in group *C*, which flower from early summer to autumn, are also pruned in late winter or early spring. But they can be cut back fairly hard to within 90 cm (3 ft) of ground level, or even harder if required.

A great many climbing plants used in the garden are not self-clinging in the sense of those described on page 142 – that is, they do not have aerial roots that can attach themselves directly to walls or other supports. Many do, however, have twining tendrils or stems, and will scramble up or through trees, shrubs, trellis, wire netting and so on. But in many cases the gardener needs to tie them in for extra support (see p 92).

Pale-coloured flowers
The actinidias include three interesting deciduous climbers. *Actinidia arguta* has large, shining green leaves and slightly fragrant white flowers, enriched by purple anthers, in summer. It later bears greenish-yellow berries 2.5 cm (1 in) long. This very vigorous climber is ideal to scramble through trees. The Chinese gooseberry, *A. chinensis,* is not quite so vigorous, bearing fragrant creamy-white flowers, later changing to buff, 4 cm (1½ in) across, during the late summer. These are followed by edible egg-shaped fruits covered with brownish hairs. Even more exciting are the tricoloured variegated leaves of *A. kolomikta,* the Kolomikta vine. In spring, the leaves are a striking metallic green, but they become even more beautiful during the summer when the foliage is suffused with pink and white. To obtain the best colour, plant *A. kolomikta* against a sheltered wall in full sun. The flowers are small and white.

There are few climbers that can enrich the garden from early summer to early autumn, and fill the air with their fresh fragrance, so much as the common white jasmine, *Jasminum officinale.* This semi-evergreen twining shrub with pure white flowers is hardy and a rapid grower. It needs to be pruned after the flowers have faded, when the growths should be thinned. Or this can be done in winter. Other good jasmines for the garden include the well-known yellow winter jasmine, *J. nudiflorum,* whose cheerful yellow flowers appear on the bare, dark green stems throughout the winter; it needs some support. Another is *J. × stephanense,* a hybrid related to *J. officinale.* This hybrid is semi-evergreen in mild winters, and young leaves are often

Actinidia kolomikta

Jasminum nudiflorum

Lonicera periclymenum 'Belgica'

variegated. The pale pink fragrant flowers come in early summer.

Honeysuckles (*Lonicera* spp) are always favourites, and many of them have richly scented flowers. Among the most attractive evergreen kinds is *Lonicera japonica* 'Aureoreticulata', which has prettily netted golden-yellow variegated foliage (see p 24), turning in autumn to gold and bronze. It has fragrant white to creamy flowers. Also sweetly scented and evergreen is *L. japonica halliana,* with white flowers that pale off to a creamy-yellow; it blooms from early summer to autumn. This and the golden variegated form may be pruned each spring, when all shoots can be cut back to the last year's growth. If some pruning is not done the plants will soon grow out of hand.

Two more fragrant beauties are varieties of the deciduous woodbine or common honeysuckle of Europe, *L. periclymenum.* 'Belgica', the early Dutch honeysuckle, has tubular flowers flushed reddish-purple on the outside, fading to yellowish within. 'Serotina', the late Dutch honeysuckle, though similar, has a darker purplish-red flower colouring that becomes paler with age. The inside of the flowers is creamy-white, later changing to yellow. The former blooms in early summer, the latter from summer until the autumn.

Other worthwhile honeysuckles include the fragrant goat-leaf honeysuckle, /continued

Climbing and rambling plants (continued)

L. caprifolium, the slightly tender evergreen *L. sempervirens,* which has scentless orange-scarlet flowers, and the deciduous *L. tragophylla,* which is also without scent but a bright golden-yellow. Among many excellent hybrids are the fragrant *L.* × *americana,* with white flowers fading to yellow, and *L.* × *brownii,* the scarlet trumpet honeysuckle, which is unscented.

Polygonum baldschuanicum, the Russian vine, is sometimes called the mile-a-minute plant, an apt name for a quick-growing deciduous climber that will grow as much as 4.5 m (15 ft) in a season. It is a superb plant for covering a wall, old tree or stump, though it sometimes takes a year or two for a new specimen to become established. Prune only when the plant has filled its allotted space. It has masses of white flowers tinged with pink. *P. aubertii* is very similar, but the flowers are all-white.

Red and orange flowers

A beautiful evergreen, *Berberidopsis corallina,* the coral plant, was introduced in 1862 from Chile, but is little planted. Its crimson-red globose flowers in late summer show up against the background of its dark green leathery leaves, which are glaucous beneath. Although it is semi-twining, it does require support. It also needs shade and protection from cold winds, and does not like lime or starved soils. Before planting be sure that the soil has adequate humus in the form of moistened peat or leaf-mould. No regular pruning is needed, but if it has to be pruned do so either in spring or autumn. It is not hardy in extreme climates.

There is no need for garden walls, fences or pergolas to be drab or unattractive, and where a twiner or scandent climber is wanted, and there is room for growth, plant the deciduous *Campsis grandiflora* (*C. chinensis*). It produces clusters of drooping orange-scarlet trumpets, 8 cm (3 in) wide at the mouth, in late summer and early autumn. It needs to be planted against a sunny wall. It is tolerably hardy, though not as hardy as *C. radicans* (see p 143). It will reach a height of some 6 m (20 ft). A beautiful hybrid of *C. grandiflora*

Tropaeolum speciosum

and *C. radicans* is *C.* × *tagliabuana* 'Madame Galen'. The large, vivid salmon-red trumpets are borne on short crowded panicles from late summer onwards. Where plants have to be restricted, cut back all side shoots to the old wood; otherwise remove old, worn-out wood in spring.

Closely related to the campsis is the vigorous semi-evergreen *Bignonia capreolata.* It has tubular orange-red flowers in early summer, and climbs vigorously against a sunny, sheltered wall. However, it is only hardy down to about −12°C (10°F).

Another colourful climber for a sheltered, warm spot is the deciduous *Mutisia decurrens.* It is difficult to establish, but where suited produces brilliant orange or vermilion daisy

Passiflora edulis

flowers throughout the summer. Equally beautiful, but lower-growing and salmon-pink in colour, is *M. oligodon.*

The flame flower or flame creeper, *Tropaeolum speciosum,* is an attractive hardy deciduous climber or twiner. The small, scarlet, nasturtium-like flowers have abruptly clawed spurs, and appear throughout the summer. It has fleshy, rather brittle roots, which need a cool root run. But the flowers and foliage should be in the sun. An ideal support is an evergreen such as yew or box. Sometimes it is difficult to establish. It is a herbaceous perennial, and dies down in winter. *T. tuberosum* has flowers of similar colour, but more tubular in shape. It is cut down by frost, so be sure to plant the early-flowering variety (it has no other varietal name), which begins to bloom in early summer, to ensure a good period of display.

Other climbers with red or orange flowers include certain species of honeysuckle (*Lonicera*; see above) and the Chilean glory vine, *Eccremocarpus scaber.* Although often treated as a half-hardy annual (see p 214), it is perennial where winters are not too harsh. It is best grown against a warm, sheltered wall or through a bush. In favourable years, it will begin producing its pretty tubular flowers – in racemes of 10 to 20 blooms, each 2.5 cm (1 in) long – in late spring, continuing to late autumn or the first frosts.

Blue, purple and brown flowers

A pretty semi-evergreen is *Akebia quinata,* which has fragrant chocolate-purple flowers in spring. It makes a useful trellis or pergola plant, and does best in an acid or loamy soil. It will reach a height of 9 to 12 cm (30 to 40 ft). After a long, hot summer it will produce purple sausage-shaped fruits. The almost evergreen *A. trifoliata* (*A. lobata*) is an elegant climber with three leaflets to each stalk. The flowers are dark purple, the fruits pale violet. It will reach about 9 m (30 ft).

Aristolochia macrophylla (*A. durior*) is aptly known as the Dutchman's pipe, for the flowers are tubular and flaring, but bent so that they look rather like an old Dutch pipe. They are yellowish-green, the flared mouth

Wisteria sinensis 'Plena'

being brownish-purple, and appear in early summer. It is vigorous, deciduous and hardy and was introduced to European gardens from the eastern United States in 1783.

The passion flower, *Passiflora caerulea,* is a vigorous evergreen climber, but it must have support to which it can cling by its tendrils. The palmate leaves have five to seven lobes and are dark green. It has a remarkable flower, which consists of five sepals and five petals, both blue-white in colour, with a central corona of purplish stamens and pistils of extraordinary shape. It blooms from early summer to early autumn. The common name comes from the fact that Spanish priests in its native Brazil claimed religious significance in its flowers; the various parts, they said, represented various aspects of the Easter story. The flowers may be followed by edible orange fruits the size of plums.

Although normally evergreen, the passion flower is not fully hardy, and may be cut down or even killed by a sharp frost. It therefore does best against a sunny, sheltered wall. The variety 'Constance Elliott', with white flowers, is slightly hardier. In frost-free regions other species may be grown, including *P. edulis* (the granadilla) and *P. quadrangularis* (the commercial passion fruit). All dislike lime. Prune in late winter, when secondary growths should be cut back to within a few buds of the base and new shoots tied in.

The potato vine or jasmine nightshade, *Solanum jasminoides,* is a rambling evergreen climber that requires the protection of a wall and needs to be planted in full sun. Its slate-blue flowers are produced from midsummer through to autumn. Fairly hard pruning should be carried out each spring, but it will still reach a height of 6 m (20 ft). *S. crispum* is hardier but less vigorous, having rich purple flowers that are freely produced throughout the summer. It will climb to 4.5 m (15 ft). The variety 'Glasnevin' ('Autumnale') has deeper-coloured purple flowers and blooms from early summer to early autumn, more freely than *S. crispum* itself.

Among the most beautiful of all deciduous climbers are the wisterias, with their exquisite drooping racemes of pea-flowers in purple, blue, pink or white appearing from spring to early summer. Although named after a Dr Wistar, they were originally named *Wisteria,* so this rather than *Wistaria* is the correct spelling. Although vigorous once established, a specimen of *Wisteria sinensis* (*W. chinensis*) grown from seed may take 20 years to flower, and then very sparsely. So always buy a good form propagated by cuttings or layering. Also, correct pruning is vital for proper flowering. During the summer, regularly pinch out the growing tips of all laterals or young shoots when about 30 cm (12 in) long. Then in winter cut back all side shoots to within two or three buds of the main stems, leaving only those shoots needed to extend the climber farther.

Given such treatment, *W. sinensis,* the most popular species, should give an abundance of deep mauve or heliotrope-blue scented flowers. The variety 'Alba' is white, while 'Black Dragon' is dark purple. The Japanese wisteria, *W. floribunda,* is less vigorous, reaching up to 9 m (30 ft) rather than the 30 m (100 ft) of the Chinese species. For pristine beauty, plant the pure white *W. floribunda* 'Alba', whose racemes are 45 to 60 cm (1½ to 2 ft) long. Even more magnificent is the variety 'Macrobotrys' (also called *W. multijuga*), whose fragrant lilac flowers, tinged with bluish-purple, come in racemes as much as 90 cm (3 ft) long. An attractive hybrid with violet-pink flowers is *W.* × *formosa.*

Among other climbers with purple or red flowers are the everlasting sweet peas, *Lathyrus latifolius* and *L. grandiflorus.* These are commonly grown at the back of herbaceous borders, and are described among the taller herbaceous perennials on page 177.

Autumn colour

Where you want a colourful autumn display of fruit and foliage, a superb choice would be *Celastrus orbiculatus.* Its orange and yellow fruit capsules split open when fully ripe and display their bright scarlet seeds. It also has pure yellow foliage in autumn. This vigorous, deciduous twining climber is at its best when scrambling up a tree or through a large shrub. It will reach 9 to 12 m (30 to 40 ft). *C. scandens* displays similar seeds. It is less vigorous, only reaching about 6 m (20 ft), and is useful for a wall or trellis.

No climber can surpass the autumn brilliance of the glory vine, *Vitis coignetiae,* introduced to France from Japan by a Madame Coignet in 1875. In summer, its dark green leaves, 25 cm (10 in) wide, have a rusty-brown felt beneath, but they change to a rich warm crimson in autumn. The small grape-like berries are black with a purple bloom. It will climb to 18 m (60 ft) or more and, like other members of the genus, is deciduous.

The northern fox grape or skunk grape, *V. labrusca,* has three-lobed dark green leaves 8 to 18 cm (3 to 7 in) wide. Its autumn tints are less spectacular than those of *V. coignetiae,* but the sweetly-scented flowers are followed by edible purple or amber fruits having a foxy or musky aroma. A variety of the common grape, *V. vinifera,* called 'Brandt' has large

Vitis coignetiae

green leaves changing in autumn to brilliant tints that range from yellow and orange to rosy-crimson and scarlet. It has the bonus of good-flavoured blue-black fruits. The purple-leaved grape, or the claret vine, *V. vinifera* 'Purpurea', is even more beautiful. Its foliage is at first claret-red, deepening later to a vinous-red, and before falling turns a deep purple. When planted against a warm wall the black fruits will ripen.

Related to these, and at one time classified in the same genus, are the species of *Ampelopsis.* They are grown for their attractive foliage, which is often a glossy green. After a long, hot summer they develop orange, red, purple or dark blue fruits. *A. brevipedunculata* is one of the best types.

Climbing and rambling roses

No roses are true climbers in the sense that they do not twine round their supports, nor cling to them as ivy does. In their natural state, they hook their thorns over twigs and branches of trees and shrubs, as they scramble up through them. In the garden, they have to be tied in to wires, pillars or trellis.

Although used for much the same purposes, climbing and rambling roses have more or less distinctive characteristics which mean that they need somewhat different treatment. Rambler roses are closely related to wild species such as *Rosa wichuraiana,* and have clusters of small flowers, produced only at midsummer, mainly on the long new canes that come up from the base of the plant each year. Climbers have larger flowers that do not always come in clusters, and many varieties are recurrent (flowering more than once a year). New wood takes the form of strong side shoots from the main canes, though some may come from the base, too. Unlike ramblers, they flower well on the old wood.

Apart from true ramblers and climbers, a

erican Pillar' (pink), 'Albertine' (coppery-pink), 'Albéric Barbier' (creamy-white), 'Sanders' White', and 'Excelsa' ('Red Dorothy Perkins'), are hybrids of *R. wichuraiana*, but they are much less popular nowadays than they used to be. This is largely because they flower only once, though they do give a spectacular display over quite a long period. Also against them is their tendency to mildew, and for this reason they should never be planted against a wall, where air circulation will be poor. They stand a much better chance of keeping healthy on pillars, arches and pergolas, but it is as well not to let them ramble too high, when they would be difficult to spray.

Although descended from the same rose, there are two distinct types of rambler related to *R. wichuraiana*. 'Excelsa' is an example of one that sends up strong new growth from the base each year, which bear the best flowers the following summer. It can be a daunting task, but the old canes should be cut right out to the ground after flowering, and the new ones tied in, in their place. However, should

strong-growing and will reach 9 m (30 ft) or more, so make sure that you choose a really strong tree to support them. The weight and wind resistance of a fully grown rambler of this type is enormous, and could easily bring down an aging and perhaps partially rotten apple tree, which on the face of it might be an obvious choice as a support. Plant the rose on the windward side of the tree you do choose, so that the prevailing wind will tend to blow the long canes into the tree, rather than away from it. The rose may need a little training at first, but will soon begin to weave its way into the branches and be self-supporting.

Ramblers like this are not, of course, suitable only for growing up trees. They can also be used for pergolas and arches, but the strength of the support, whatever it is, must still be borne in mind. The less vigorous Wichuraiana ramblers can be used in smaller trees, though it will be virtually impossible to prune them to achieve maximum flowering. The white 'Seagull' is a good tree-climbing rambler up to about 3.5 m (12 ft).

Rosa 'American Pillar'

Rosa 'Aloha'

number of shrub roses, as mentioned on page 158, can be trained against a wall, and some, such as the beautiful yellow *R. ecae*, are best treated in this way.

Well-known ramblers
Some rambling roses are true species, and the close relationship of the others to species gives them not only their vigour and ability to take readily from cuttings, but also their once-flowering habit. *R. wichuraiana* is an example of a species rambler that, although it will scramble up through other shrubs, or can be trained to climb, grows naturally prostrate on the ground, its long canes – which may grow 1.8 to 2.5 m (6 to 8 ft) in one season – rooting where they touch the ground. It makes a fine ground-cover plant, and is ideal for covering a bank which may otherwise be difficult to keep tidy. The flowers are single and white, and do not appear until mid- or even late summer. A pink hybrid from it is called 'Max Graf'.

Most of the ramblers commonly grown in gardens, such as 'Dorothy Perkins' and 'Am-

there be only a few of these in some seasons, a number of the old ones can be left. They probably will flower, but not as profusely.

'Albertine' is an example of the second type, and here new growth is more likely to take the form of very strong side shoots from the old wood. In this case the old wood should, again after flowering, be cut back to the point where the new cane has sprouted. When buying a rambler, check with your supplier which group it belongs to.

Ramblers for growing up trees
There are a whole group of ramblers with different and varying ancestry from the above, and which are less commonly seen. Most of them are white, and many have truly enormous sprays of tiny flowers each no more than 2.5 cm (1 in) across. Grown up trees, these sprays of flowers will hang down from the branches in creamy waterfalls and scent the air for yards around. Examples of this kind of rose are *R. longicuspis, R. filipes* 'Kiftsgate' and 'Rambling Rector'.

Many of these ramblers are tremendously

Climbing roses
The group of roses generally known as climbers can be subdivided into two kinds: those descended from *R. gigantea* and other Far Eastern species and which have the long canes of the typical climbing rose, and the climbing sports of what are normally bush roses.

A rose that sports either produces a cane with flowers quite different from those on the rest of the bush, or else suddenly sends out the long canes of a climber, carrying the same flowers as before. Both kinds of sport can be propagated to produce others of its kind, but many climbing sports are much more shy in flowering than their bush counterparts, and may not produce a second crop of bloom at all. Care is needed in choosing your varieties, but a selection of generally reliable ones are listed in the table.

Many, though not all, of the older true climbers are repeat-flowering, though no climbing rose is really continuous – despite what some catalogues claim. Some of the old roses are tremendously vigorous – far more so than is needed for the walls of small modern

Rosa ecae

Rosa 'Climbing Iceberg'

at least 45 cm (18 in) away from the wall, fanning the roots outwards rather than spreading them evenly all round. Supports on both walls and fences should be strong galvanized iron wires. Space them about 30 cm (12 in) apart horizontally, and string them tightly between galvanized nails on a fence, or vine eyes (metal rings) on a wall, so that the wires are about 15 cm (6 in) clear of the surface. Vine eyes can be driven into the mortar between the bricks, though it is rather easier if a small guide hole is drilled first. Being tapered, the vine eyes will wedge firmly in the holes.

To prevent the flowers of your rose coming only at the top, fan out the canes as horizontally as possible, tying them loosely to the outside of the support wires with plastic-

houses – so breeders have recently been aiming to produce varieties with good second flush of bloom, combined with moderate vigour. As a result, a number of the new climbers like the deep pink 'Aloha' and 'Golden Showers', if given the support of a stake or two, make excellent shrubs as well. And of course they are fine roses for pillars or tripods of rustic poles.

When choosing a climber, it is worth asking your supplier (if he is a specialist who really knows his roses) whether it sheds its petals cleanly when the flowers have died off. Nothing looks worse than a mass of sodden brown petals on the side of a house, and they may be difficult to get at for removal. For cutting flowers for the house, long stalks are desirable, but there are plenty of Hybrid Teas and Floribundas to supply these needs (see pp 160 to 163). Climbers should ideally be grown for the beauty of their massed blooms. The weight of the flowers of a climber like the pale yellow 'Elegance', with 30 cm (12 in) stalks, makes them hang far out from a wall, and the whole plant can look rather untidy. On a pillar, of course, they can be tied in.

Planting and training climbers

When planting a climber against a wall, particularly the wall of a house that has an overhanging roof, do not forget that this will probably be the driest place in the garden. The wall itself will absorb water, and the roof will keep off at least some of the rain. So plant your rose

Recommended climbing roses

White	'Climbing Iceberg'† ('Climbing Schneewitchen'); 'Swan Lake' ('Schwanensee'); 'White Dawn'*
Light pink	'Climbing Mme Caroline Testout'†; 'Climbing Queen Elizabeth'†; 'Coral Dawn'*; 'Galway Bay'; 'New Dawn'*; 'Pink Perpétue'; 'Rosy Mantle'*
Deep pink	'Aloha'*; 'America'*; 'Climbing Caprice'*† (cream reverse); 'Climbing First Prize'*†; 'Dublin Bay'
Red	'Altissimo'; 'Blaze'; 'Climbing Crimson Glory'*†; 'Climbing Ena Harkness'*†; 'Climbing Super Star'*†; ('Climbing Tropicana'); 'Copenhagen'*; 'Danse du Feu' ('Spectacular'); 'Don Juan'*; 'Dortmund' (single; white eye); 'Parkdirektor Riggers'; 'Sympathie'*
Orange	'Compassion'; 'Schoolgirl'*
Yellow	'Casino'*; 'Climbing Golden Dawn'*† (buff); 'Climbing Goldilocks'*†; 'Climbing Peace'† (tinged pink); 'Climbing Spek's Yellow'*† ('Climbing Golden Scepter'; golden); 'Golden Showers'*; 'High Noon'; 'Mermaid'*; 'Royal Gold'*
Bicolours and tricolours	'Climbing Masquerade'† (red, pink, yellow); 'Climbing Shot Silk'*† (salmon, carmine, yellow); 'Climbing Talisman' (orange, scarlet, yellow); 'Handel' (cream, pink); 'Joseph's Coat' (yellow, orange, red)

Scented variety; †climbing sport of bush rose

covered garden wire. When the canes are bent over like this the sap flow to the ends is restricted and the side buds will break into growth, making plenty of flowering side shoots. If these in turn are trained to the horizontal, the same thing will happen again, and gradually the rose will spread upwards, but well branched all the way. Some climbers, like ramblers, make new basal growth, but some never do. These can become rather bare lower down, and will probably look better with a low shrub (this could be a rose bush) planted in front of them. When growing a climber (or a rambler) on a pillar or tripod, twine the canes around the support in a spiral. This will encourage side shoots to grow.

Pruning climbers

All climbers flower well on old wood, and make, in time, a strong framework from it, so they should not be cut to the ground when pruning, except for the occasional removal of an old, worn-out cane that is not producing any worthwhile laterals. This should encourage a strong new replacement to grow. Carry out the pruning after flowering has finished. Simply shorten lateral growths by about two-thirds, cutting just above a bud. Many climbers live quite happily and flower well with little or no pruning at all, so it may be worth waiting to see what happens with yours before doing anything.

For winter protection, and other aspects of growing and using roses, see pages 98 to 101.

Evergreen shrubs for year-round beauty

Leaves are more important than flowers – especially evergreen leaves. They offer beauty all the year round, even after the flowers have faded, and evergreen shrubs are invaluable for giving the garden a clothed appearance between autumn and spring. The flowers of some evergreens are so insignificant as to pass unnoticed, yet the shrubs are worth growing for their leaves alone. In others, leaf beauty is allied to an attractive overall form; such shrubs are described on page 164. Some other evergreen shrubs are described on pages 166 to 169.

Evergreen shrubs need to be treated differently in planting from deciduous flowering shrubs. For details of planting, see page 96. They generally need no pruning beyond that needed to keep them the size and shape you want. Unless otherwise stated, all those described here will grow in any good garden soil, acid or alkaline.

For foliage interest

Supreme among the evergreen shrubs whose leaves rather than flowers are the main attraction are the laurels. But what is the true laurel? It is doubtful if it is the one we know best, the hedge plant correctly known as *Prunus laurocerasus*. This, the common laurel or cherry laurel, is a much maligned plant. It is used largely in a utilitarian role, but if it is allowed to grow into a big specimen, up to 4.5 m (15 ft) tall, it is a magnificent evergreen shrub. There are various forms with differing habits and shapes of leaf; one of the best for specimen planting is 'Mischeana', with lustrous dark green leaves. Equally good as a specimen, and sometimes forming a small tree, is the Portugal laurel, *P. lusitanica*. It is hardier than the cherry laurel, and has reddish leaf-stalks. Both have variegated forms and bear white flowers followed by berries.

Then there is the laurel of the ancients, the green bay tree, *Laurus nobilis*. Its leaves are smaller and are very aromatic; they are

Laurus nobilis

invaluable in the kitchen. But it is important not to confuse it with the common laurel. The latter can also be used for flavouring – but only with extreme care, because the leaves contain a small amount of prussic acid, a deadly poison. Bay responds well to clipping, and can be trained into cones, round-headed standards and so on that are good in formal settings. But it is not very hardy and should be grown in a tub in regions with cold winters, so that it can be moved under cover. 'Aurea' is a beautiful yellow-leaved form.

A third so-called laurel is *Aucuba japonica*, whose variegated forms are known as spotted laurel (see p 164). Lastly there is the Alexandrian laurel, *Danae racemosa*, carrying its long pointed glossy leaves in arching sprays.

Mahonia japonica

This was the laurel used in ancient times for crowning poets and victorious soldiers. All four genera are quite unrelated to each other.

Early spring flowers

Progressing through the seasons, evergreen flowering shrubs begin to give a display that overlaps the winter (see p 250) with the 2.5 m (8 ft) tall *Viburunum tinus*, the laurustinus. This may well have been showing its flat heads of white flowers since the end of autumn, and will carry on until mid-spring. The mahonias flower over the same long period, with yellow sprays like those of the lily of the valley and a delightful scent. The two best known are *Mahonia bealii* and *M. japonica*, which grow to 1.5 to 1.8 m (5 to 6 ft) and as much through. They later bear attractive berries.

The next group of evergreens to make a display in the early spring, the pieris, also have flowers similar to the lily of the valley, but they need a lime-free soil. There are three main species, *Pieris floribunda*, *P. formosa* and *P. japonica* (all sometimes classified as *Andromeda*). There are various forms of all these, generally with white flowers, but one of the most useful introductions is *P. japonica* 'Blush', with flowers that are rose-pink in bud, opening to a pale blush-pink. They grow to about 1.5 m (5 ft). See also page 167.

Early in the spring, one of the most beautiful of all flowering evergreens opens its mass of tiny white flowers, which have a delicious scent and look particularly well against the

dark green box-like foliage. This is *Osmanthus delavayi*, growing 1.8 to 2.5 m (6 to 8 ft) high and as much through. This has been crossed with another evergreen called *Phillyrea decora* (*P. vilmoriniana*), which is about the same height but more spreading. The resulting white-flowered hybrid is called × *Osmarea burkwoodii*, named after the man who raised it in about 1930. The second parent, *P. decora*, is a graceful evergreen with long branches of slender dark green leaves that are a delight to the flower arranger. It has white flowers, also scented, as are those of the offspring.

The raiser of × *Osmarea burkwoodii*, Mr Albert Burkwood, has also produced many other fine shrubs. Probably the best of all is

Cistus sp

Viburnum × *burkwoodii*, a strong-growing evergreen up to 2.5 or 3 m (8 or 10 ft) tall, with whorls of small flowers that are pink in bud, white when fully open and, again, beautifully scented.

The British Isles have very few native evergreen flowering shrubs, but there is one that gives a lavish display of yellow flowers in spring – the double-flowered form of the common gorse, *Ulex europaeus* 'Plenus'. Like the gorse, yellow and orange are the colours of the evergreen berberis (barberries) that flower a little later. *Berberis darwinii*, growing to about 1.8 to 2.4 m (6 to 8 ft), was discovered in South America by Charles Darwin on the voyage of the *Beagle*. The leaves are small and dark green, the flowers deep yellow – almost orange – with a faint suggestion of red at the tips. There is also a beautiful hybrid called *B.* × *stenophylla*, with longer arching branches, smaller leaves and yellow flowers (see p 169).

Rosemary (*Rosmarinus officinalis*) is grown mainly for its use as a herb, but its beauty in the garden should not be overlooked. The leaves are probably well known – small, narrow and greyish-green, covering the stem completely and with a delightful aromatic smell. It carries blue flowers in spring and grows to about 1 to 1.5 m (3 ft to 5 ft). It is not hardy in cold climates. There are now many varieties like 'Benenden Blue', with deeper blue flowers but even less hardy than the type, and 'Fastigiatus', which has an upright habit.

Escallonia 'Donard Radiance'

Hebe speciosa 'La Seduisante'

Spring and summer colour

Spring is dominated by those popular evergreen flowering shrubs, the camellias and rhododendrons (see pp 153 and 154). The most spectacular of all other evergreens at this time is *Kalmia latifolia,* the calico bush, which needs the same lime-free soil as a rhododendron. It will grow to a height of about 1.5 m to 1.8 m (5 to 6 ft) in time, and it carries bunches of pink flowers like umbrellas, deeper in bud than when they are fully open.

The cistus, commonly known as rock roses or sun roses (a name also used for helianthemums, which are dwarf shrubs suitable for rock gardens; see p 225), are evergreen flowering shrubs with aromatic foliage that are not planted as much as they might be. Perhaps the reason is that they are short-lived and resent severe frost. Even so, they are well worth replacing every ten years or so. They have the considerable advantage of enjoying a limy or chalk soil, and are long-flowering, giving crop after crop. There are many excellent species and varieties. *Cistus laurifolius* is the hardiest, carrying white flowers with a yellow centre, and *C. ladanifer* (gum cistus) has white flowers with a purple spot. These will grow

into fairly big shrubs from 1.5 to 2 m (5 to 7 ft) tall. But *C. × corbariensis,* another relatively hardy variety, which has deep pink buds that open pure white, grows only to around 50 cm (20 in), although spreading fairly wide, and *C. × pulverulentus* (sometimes called 'Warley Rose') is a little taller, with cerise flowers. Among named cultivars, 'Silver Pink' is a beautiful hardy shrub about 90 cm (3 ft) tall (see p 168).

Perhaps the most easy-going of all evergreen flowering shrubs are the escallonias. They demand so little but give so much. A particular favourite is *Escallonia* 'Apple Blossom', with the flowers aptly described by the name appearing on a compact shrub up to about 1.5 m (5 ft) tall. Many new varieties have been raised by the Slieve Donard nursery in Northern Ireland: 'Donard Gem' has large pink scented flowers on compact growth, and 'Donard Radiance' is deeper in colour with deep green leaves.

A group of easily grown shrubs that look as appealing as their common name are the daisy bushes (*Olearia* spp). They come from Australasia, but many are hardy except where winters are severe. They stand up well to

windy coastal conditions and like chalky soil, but some kinds may need trimming in early spring to retain their shape. The lustrous leaves have white felt beneath. Probably the best known kind is *Olearia × haastii,* which stands up to polluted air and is covered with white, fragrant daisy flowers in midsummer. It reaches about 2 m (7 ft). More vigorous, reaching 3 m (10 ft), is the New Zealand holly, *O. macrodonta,* which has a musky smell and clusters of tiny white flowers against holly-like leaves. Although rather tender, *O. stellulata* is notable for the variety 'Splendens', which has flowers like those of Michaelmas daisies in shades from blue to rose-pink.

Once known as the shrubby veronicas, the hebes give an excellent show over a long period, but dislike severe winters. Probably the best for garden decoration are the cultivars *Hebe* 'Autumn Glory', with dark purple flowers from midsummer to the first frost, and a plant sold under the names of 'Bowles' Hybrid' or 'Eversley Seedling', which gives a continuous performance of sprays of mauve-pink flowers for the same period. Both grow up to about 60 cm (2 ft). Many shorter types are suitable for ground cover.

Autumn and winter colour

There are many more flowering evergreens in autumn than might be imagined. Two of the finest in their own right, as evergreen shrubs, flower at this time of year: *Elaeagnus macrophylla* and its hybrid *E. × ebbingei.* Both have silver-grey leaves and silver flowers with a delightful perfume. The former reaches 2 to 3 m (7 to 10 ft), the latter 3 to 4.5 m (10 to 15 ft). For *E. pungens* 'Maculata', a beautiful foliage evergreen, see page 165.

Winter is the time for holly (*Ilex* spp), of which there are numerous forms. Two interesting cultivars are *Ilex aquifolium* 'Golden King', with bright gold-edged leaves, some pure gold, and 'Golden Queen', gold variegated with green. The strange paradox is that 'Golden King' is a female variety, bearing berries, but 'Golden Queen' is male. If you want to plant a green holly in your garden from which you can be sure of picking a sprig of berries for the Christmas pudding, then choose 'J. C. van Tol', a hermaphrodite form which berries almost without fail. Excellent forms of the American holly, *I. opaca*, include 'Miss Helen' and the yellow-berried 'Xanthocarpa'. All these can form trees up to about 6 m (20 ft) tall, but are easily kept within bounds as large bushes if the leading shoot is stopped when the plants have reached the required height and they are given an annual trim in summer. Always plant small plants, and position variegated kinds in a sunny spot.

Lastly there is one of the oldest evergreens of all, surrounded by the Norse myth of Baldur or Balder, son of the great God Odin, who was killed by an arrow made from a branch of mistletoe, *Viscum album.* If you want to cultivate your own mistletoe, it is easy enough. You merely insert some seeds in cuts in the bark of a suitable tree. But you must sow them in the same type of tree from which they were taken – poplar to poplar, apple to apple.

Ilex aquifolium 'Golden Queen'

Heaths and heathers

For those who garden on neutral or acid soil, heathers represent some of the easiest and most labour-saving of all garden plants. With a careful selection of varieties, there can be colour and interest – of flower and foliage – throughout every month of the year. If you add to these qualities their value in smothering the ground, virtually eliminating all need for weeding so long as spacing is correct, their importance is obvious.

Altogether, there are over 600 species of heaths and heathers, but the great majority grow only in southern Africa and are unsuitable for outdoor culture in cool climates. There are less than 20 hardy garden species but numerous cultivars. The use of the terms heath and heather is confused, but, botanically, heaths belong to the genus *Erica* and heathers to *Calluna*. However, *Erica cinerea* is commonly called the bell heather, and *Daboecia cantabrica* is the Connemara, or St Dabeoc's, heath. In any case, to most people they are all simply 'heathers'.

Uses in the garden

The best way of growing heathers is to form a heather garden in scale with its setting. In small gardens, the individual groups may need to consist of no more than, say, seven plants of a kind, and this basic plan can be adjusted by increasing the number in each group where larger areas are to be planted. The best-known heathers range in height from a mere 10 cm (4 in) to about 90 cm (3 ft), but for greater variations of height there are species of so-called tree heaths that grow to 3 m (10 ft) – or even double this height in warm, Mediterranean climates.

If it is not practicable to devote an area to forming a whole heather garden, the next best alternative is to plant groups of heathers in association with suitable shrubs – particularly evergreens. One way is to form planting bays in shrub borders and beds. Many kinds of shrubs are suitable, including the smaller rhododendrons and many slow-growing conifers. Do not overshadow the heathers, however, for they need the maximum possible sunlight. A third use is for covering banks that are troublesome to mow if grassed. Many of the less vigorous kinds are also useful in rock gardens (see p 228).

Planting and cultivation

All heathers grow best in a peaty, acid soil, and although a certain success is claimed for growing the winter-flowering kinds – such as *E. carnea* and its derivatives – and the Corsican tree heath, *E. terminalis,* on limy soil, only rarely do the plants really thrive. There is little harm in the venturesome gardener with only slightly alkaline soil experimenting, but a safer course is to create a raised peat bed with peat blocks and filled with a lime-free growing mixture (see p 126).

When preparing a bed for heathers, dig in plenty of moist peat and spread a further layer of peat on the newly dug surface so that this can be worked in around the roots of the plants. Container-grown plants can be planted at any time when the soil is not frozen,

The heather garden at the Royal Horticultural Society's gardens at Wisley in southern England

but it is as well to avoid the height of summer and depth of winter. Spacing depends on the size to which the particular varieties will grow, but as a general rule plant the majority at about 40 cm (15 in), with the tree heaths at 75 cm (2½ ft). If, after a few seasons, bare ground is still showing, low branches can be pegged down and covered with soil to induce rooting and the formation of new plants. (This is known as layering; see p 349).

Subsequent maintenance is very simple. Water in dry weather, but do not give fertilizer. An annual top-dressing of dry granulated peat gives good results. (Wet peat sticks to the plants.) Scatter the peat among the plants in early spring and shake them gently so that it reaches the soil surface. Once a year,

cut off dead flower-heads with sharp shears. Deal with the summer-flowering kinds in early spring, the winter-flowering varieties about a month later. Trim just below the lowest flowers, and do not cut into old wood.

Apart from rabbits and the effects of too much soil alkalinity (which causes yellowing of foliage and stunted growth), the most important problem with heathers is erica wilt (browning or die-back). The foliage turns silvery-grey, wilts and then turns brown and dies. It is caused by a fungus and is difficult to control; affected plants should be burned. However, poor soil conditions can cause similar symptoms, so it is best to send a sample of affected plants to a plant pathology laboratory for positive diagnosis.

Recommended summer-flowering heathers

Calluna vulgaris cultivars	'Alba Plena' (white; double); 'Alportii' (crimson-purple); 'Barnett Anley' (petunia-purple); 'County Wicklow' (pink; double); 'Hammondii' (white; single; good for cutting); 'J. H. Hamilton' (fuchsia-pink; double); 'Peter Sparkes' (cyclamen-purple, fading; double)
Daboecia cantabrica cultivars	'Alba' (white); 'Atropurpurea' (rich reddish-purple); 'Bicolor' (purple, white and purple-and-white flowers on same plant); 'William Buchanan' (reddish-purple)
Erica cinerea cultivars	'C. D. Eason' (bright rosy-red); 'Eden Valley' (white flushed purple); 'Knap Hill Pink' (pinkish-purple); 'P. S. Patrick' (reddish-purple; foliage tipped dark red); 'Pink Ice' (pink; foliage tinted bronze in winter); 'Rosea' (bright rose); 'Vivienne Patricia' (purple; foliage tipped dark red in summer)
Erica vagans cultivars	'Lyonesse' (white, brown anthers); 'Mrs D. F. Maxwell' (deep cerise, dark brown stamens); 'St Keverne' (rose-cerise, tinged white, with brown anthers)

Recommended winter-flowering heathers

Erica carnea cultivars	'Ann Sparkes' (reddish-purple; foliage tipped yellow); 'December Red' (cyclamen-purple); 'King George' (deep rose-pink; compact); 'Pink Spangles' (reddish-purple); 'Springwood White' (white); 'Vivellii' (carmine-red; bronze foliage)
Erica × darleyensis cultivars	'Arthur Johnson' (deep pink; long flower spikes); 'Darley Dale' (pale mauve; vigorous); 'Silberschmelze' ('Silver Beads', 'Silver Bells', 'Silver Mist'; white, tipped pale pink

---

Recommended heathers for foliage effect

Calluna vulgaris cultivars	'Golden Feather' (golden-yellow tipped red; mauve flowers); 'Gold Haze' (golden-yellow; white flowers); 'Hirsuta Typica' (glaucous greyish-green, sometimes silvery; purple flowers); 'Robert Chapman' (orange-red to scarlet in winter; rose-purple flowers)
Other kinds	*Erica carnea* 'Aurea' (green and lemon-yellow; pink flowers); *E. ciliaris* 'Aurea' (golden; pink flowers); *E. cinerea* 'Golden Drop' (golden); *E. vagans* 'Valerie Proudley' (golden; white flowers)

The beautiful camellias

Kinds to grow

Broadly, heaths and heathers fall into three groups: those that flower in summer and autumn, those that flower in winter and early spring and those grown for foliage effect. Most of the first group are intolerant of any lime, and include the wild heather or ling of northern Europe, *Calluna vulgaris*. This grows up to 90 cm (3 ft) tall and thrives in moist soil, but most of the cultivars derived from it are less vigorous. A number of modern cultivators have strikingly coloured winter foliage. *Daboecia cantabrica* and its cultivars are also summer-flowering, as are its hybrids (such as 'William Buchanan') with *D. azorica*.

The main summer-flowering ericas are forms of the 30 cm (12 in) *Erica cinerea* (bell heather) and the more vigorous *E. vagans* (Cornish heath), but others include *E. ciliaris* (Dorset heath), which is low-growing and long-flowering, and *E. tetralix,* known as the cross-leaved heath because its leaves are arranged in fours around the stem, forming a cross. Among the tree heaths, *E. arborea*

Erica cinerea 'C. D. Eason'

flowers in spring and will reach more than 3 m (10 ft), while *E. terminalis* is summer-flowering and varies from 1.25 to 1.5 m (4 to 8 ft).

The principal heathers for winter flowers are forms of *E. carnea* (*E. herbacea*), which rarely exceed 30 cm (12 in) in height, and the hybrids of *E. carnea* with *E. mediterranea* (*E. erigena*) called *E.* × *darleyensis*. The original plant – now named 'Darley Dale' – grew at a nursery at Darley Dale in Derbyshire. These are rather taller than *E. carnea*.

Erica cinerea 'Golden Drop'

With their glossy evergreen leaves and exquisite early blooms, camellias are among the most desirable of shrubs. Many forms are hardy down to at least −12°C (10°F), yet little more than half a century ago the exotic appearance of their flowers made gardeners in cool climates think that they were too tender for anything but greenhouse culture.

Species and cultivars

The hardiest and best-known camellias are *Camellia japonica* and its numerous cultivars. But for cold gardens a better choice would be one of the hybrids listed under the name *C.* × *williamsii*. These flower more freely in cold conditions, and also have the advantages of being earlier-blooming than most cultivars of *C. japonica* and of casting off dead flowers (which persist unattractively on *C. japonica* forms). The name comes from the pioneer breeder J. C. Williams, who first produced these hybrids by crossing forms of *C. japonica* with the Chinese species *C. saluenensis*.

In sheltered gardens, with the protection of a wall, you can also grow some forms of *C. reticulata* – including 'Captain Rawes' (Turkey-red) and 'Robert Fortune' (rose-red) – the hybrid *C.* × 'Cornish Snow' (pink in bud, opening white) and the varieties of *C. sasanqua,* which has small single flowers throughout the winter. Somewhat hardier is the semi-double rose-pink *C.* × 'Leonard Messel', a hybrid between *C.* × *williamsii* 'Mary Christian' and *C. reticulata*.

Cultivation

Camellias are easy to grow given a humus-rich, lime-free soil. They thrive in tubs provided you use a lime-free potting mixture and water them with rainwater, so this is the answer if you garden on chalk. Like rhododendrons, they appreciate a thin canopy of open

Camellia × *williamsii* 'Donation'

Recommended camellia cultivars

Camellia japonica cultivars	'Adolphe Audusson' (blood-red, yellow stamens; semi-double); 'Alba Plena' (white; double); 'Alba Simplex' (white; single); 'Apollo' (rose-red, sometimes blotched white; semi-double); 'Contessa Lavinia Maggi' (white to pink with cerise stripes; double); 'Donckelarii' (red mottled white; semi-double); 'Elegans' (deep peach-pink; anemone-flowered); 'Gloire de Nantes' (rose-pink; semi-double); 'Lady Clare' (rose-pink; semi-double; spreading habit); 'Nagasaki' ('Lady Buller') (carmine spotted white; semi-double); 'Preston Rose' ('Duchesse de Rohan'; a salmon-pink; paeony-flowered); 'Rubescens Major' (crimson; double)
Camellia × williamsii cultivars	'Donation' (silvery-pink; semi-double); 'Golden Spangles' (pink; single; yellow-centred leaves); 'J. C. Williams' (phlox-pink; single); 'Mary Christian' (bright pink; single); 'November Pink' (pink; single); 'St Ewe' (purplish-pink; single)

deciduous trees. In areas with frosty winters, position the plants where they will not receive the early morning sun; too rapid thawing damages the flowers. In the northern hemisphere, a wall or border of northerly or westerly aspect is ideal.

Mulch in spring with humus-forming material. If growth is poor and the leaves are yellowish, the soil may be too alkaline. Provided the problem is only slight, watering in sequestered iron (see p 353) may correct this. Otherwise, the main problems are mealy bugs, scale insects and aphids (see p 363); birds that peck through the base of the flowers, mainly of *C.* × *williamsii* varieties, for nectar; and the poorly understood problem of bud drop. Little or no pruning is needed.

Camellia japonica 'Donckelarii'

Rhododendrons and azaleas

Rhododendrons and azaleas are among the most spectacular and important flowering shrubs of the late spring and early summer everywhere except on limy soil. There are kinds, too, that flower as early as midwinter, and others into midsummer. Some deciduous types give spectacular autumn tints, and a mass planting of low-growing kinds can rival any heather garden for a carpet of colour.

Although regarded separately by most gardeners, azaleas are botanically part of the genus *Rhododendron*. This includes more than 500 species – mostly natives of the Himalayas and western China – a wide range of which are in cultivation. They vary from small, almost mat-like plants a few centimetres high, with tiny leaves, to trees 12 m (40 ft) or more high, some with leaves measuring nearly 60 cm (2 ft) in length by 40 cm (15 in) wide. In addition there are many hundreds – probably thousands – of hybrids, and it is these that are most widely cultivated.

Provided that the soil is not alkaline or waterlogged, there are rhododendrons suitable for nearly all gardens, varying from those in maritime climates with a high rainfall, such as on the western side of the British Isles and much of the North American West Coast, to the harder, drier conditions in other parts. Mostly having evergreen leaves – generally leathery and in many cases extremely decorative – the flower colours of rhododendrons range from pink, mauve and red to yellow, white and even blue.

Rhododendrons are not difficult to cultivate, although those with larger leaves require

Rhododendron 'Gomer Waterer'

shade and shelter from hot sun and cold winds, and are at their best in woodland gardens. Most of the mass of hardy hybrids will thrive in open sunny positions, but require particular care in the preparation of the soil to conserve moisture. The dwarfs with small leaves will be happy in the rock garden and along the frontal margins of beds and borders.

Azaleas are usually divided into two main groups: firstly the deciduous kinds – those which lose their leaves, which change to brilliant colouring before leaf-fall – and secondly the evergreen or semi-evergreen kinds still often referred to as Japanese azaleas. The flower colours of the deciduous group are among the brightest of all flowering shrubs, and provide a blaze of rich yellow, orange and red in the spring as well as softer pinks and

whites. The evergreens produce colours not found in the other group: mauve, purple, magenta and dark crimson, as well as bright pink, white and salmon.

Choice and cultivation

It is wise to seek a specialist grower's advice on types of rhododendrons and azaleas to grow in your region and on good forms of the various species. When planning a planting scheme, remember that these are by nature social plants, so group them if you can. They are shallow-rooted, so do not position other plants where they will compete for nutrients and moisture. If you want mixed plantings, position groups of such shrubs as pieris, vaccinium, kalmia and gaultheria, or such herbaceous plants as lilies, hostas, trilliums and willow gentian (*Gentiana asclepiadea*) between – but not under – the rhododendrons or azaleas.

With the modern commercial practice of growing and supplying rhododendrons and azaleas in containers, planting can be carried out during most months of the year when the ground is not frozen – even when the shrubs are in flower. It is wise to avoid the depth of winter and the height of summer, however, and the ideal time to plant is autumn. Next best is early spring, taking precautions to protect from drying winds.

In woodland gardens, rhododendrons and azaleas should be planted in suitable holes excavated from the soil. The size depends on the ultimate size of the plant, but an average would be 1.25 m (4 ft) in diameter and about

Recommended rhododendrons and azaleas

	Name	Final height	Final spread	Flower colour	Season*	Remarks
Evergreen species for shelter and shade	*Rhododendron calophytum*	7.5 m (25 ft)	4.5 m (15 ft)	Lilac-pink	Early	Flowers vary from whitish to pink; leaves 40 cm (15 in) long by 12 cm (5 in) wide
	R. falconeri	9 m (30 ft)	6 m (20 ft)	Creamy-yellow	Early/middle	Leaves rust-coloured beneath, 30 cm (12 in) long
	R. macabeanum	9 m (30 ft)	6 m (20 ft)	Yellow	Early	Leaves glossy above, white below, 30 cm (12 in) long; flowers bell-shaped
Evergreen species for open or shady positions	*R. aberconwayi*	2.5 m (8 ft)	1.5 m (5 ft)	White	Middle/late	Flowers saucer-shaped and sometimes pink-tinged
	R. ciliatum	1.25 m (4 ft)	1.25 m (4 ft)	Blush-pink	Early	Flowers vary from white to pale pink; attractive bark
	R. cinnabarinum	3 m (10 ft)	2.5 m (8 ft)	Cinnabar-red	Middle to late	Several good named forms, such as 'Mount Everest' (pale apricot)
	R. lutescens	3.5 m (12 ft)	1.8 m (6 ft)	Yellow	Very early/early	Select good forms such as 'Bagshot Sands'; leaves yellowish-bronze
	R. racemosum	1.5 m (5 ft)	1.25 m (4 ft)	Pink	Early	Select a good form such as 'Rock Rose'
	R. rubiginosum	4.5 m (15 ft)	2.5 m (8 ft)	Rosy-lilac	Middle	Very free-flowering; makes a good informal hedge
	R. wardii	3 m (10 ft)	2.5 m (8 ft)	Yellow	Middle	Variable; select a good form such as 'Ellesstee' or 'Meadow Pond'
	R. yakusimanum	1.25 m (4 ft)	1.25 m (4 ft)	Pale pink	Middle	Compact and slow-growing; white flowers when mature; striking foliage; parent of many good hybrids
Evergreen hybrids	'Azor'	3.5 m (12 ft)	2.5 m (8 ft)	Salmon-pink	Late	Valuable for late flowering
	'Blue Peter'	3 m (10 ft)	2.5 m (8 ft)	Lavender-blue	Middle	Flowers spotted with maroon
	'Britannia'	3 m (10 ft)	2.5 m (8 ft)	Crimson	Middle	Spreading habit; light green foliage
	'Carmen'	1 m (3 ft)	1.25 m (4 ft)	Dark red	Middle	Compact, rounded bush; best seen against sunlight
	'Cynthia'	4.5 m (15 ft)	3.5 m (12 ft)	Rosy-crimson	Middle	Very reliable in open positions
	'Elizabeth'	1.5 m (5 ft)	1.5 m (5 ft)	Light blood-red	Early/middle	Grows slowly; can be used in rock gardens
	'Fastuosum Flore Pleno'	4.5 m (15 ft)	3.5 m (12 ft)	Mauve	Middle/late	Unusual in having double flowers
	'Gomer Waterer'	3.5 m (12 ft)	3.5 m (12 ft)	White/mauve	Late	Flowers flushed mauve at edges; valuable for late flowering
	'Lavender Girl'	3.5 m (12 ft)	4.25 m (14 ft)	Pale lavender	Middle	Flowers sweetly scented
	Loderi 'King George'	6 m (20 ft)	6 m (20 ft)	Pink to white	Middle	Very large, scented flowers; best in woodland
	Naomi 'Exbury'	5.5 m (18 ft)	4.5 m (15 ft)	Lilac/yellow	Middle	Flowers tinged yellow; one of the best Naomi cultivars
	'Pink Pearl'	4.5 m (15 ft)	3.5 m (12 ft)	Rose-pink	Middle	The best-known hardy hybrid rhododendron
	'Purple Splendour'	3 m (10 ft)	2.5 m (8 ft)	Deep purple	Late	Slow, compact grower; effective among lighter colours
	'Sappho'	4.5 m (15 ft)	4.5 m (15 ft)	White	Middle/late	Flowers have dark blotch; spreading habit; striking evening effect
	'Susan'	3.5 m (12 ft)	5 m (16 ft)	Lavender	Middle	Attractive foliage with light brown under-sides

A mixed planting of evergreen azaleas

operation, neglect of which will soon be apparent in the production of short, stubby growths with inferior flowers and foliage.

In the open garden, the preparation of single holes for planting is the same as that for woodland specimens, but there is less fear of root invasion from trees. If plants are to be grouped together in beds or borders these should be dug at least 45 cm (18 in) deep. If the soil tends to remain wet, raise the surface of the beds slightly above the level of the surrounding land to improve drainage. Mix peat or leaf-mould in with the soil and work a liberal quantity in among the roots at planting time. Loosen the ball of soil in which each plant was growing so that the ends of the roots are exposed and will more easily grow into the new soil. Never plant more deeply than the old soil level shown on the plant's stem.

In dry conditions, water in well at planting time. Water, too, in prolonged dry spells, especially during the main growing season from early spring to the middle of summer. Your plants will enjoy a spray of water over the foliage in the evening in spring and summer – but never in strong sunshine in hot weather. Mulching will help retain soil moisture and replenish soil nutrients; the best mulches for rhododendrons and azaleas are beech or oak leaf-mould, peat, pine-needles or shredded bracken fronds.

If you wish to fertilize your plants, choose a low-nitrogen kind with an analysis of about 5:10:10 (see p 352). Foliar feeding is excellent for restoring to health plants that have deteriorated in flower colour and growth rate.

Rhododendron calostrotum

An annual dose of sequestered iron and other minerals (see p 353) will be beneficial on soils that are not as acid as the plants prefer. Otherwise, the only necessary routine is to pick off old flower heads. Pruning is only needed if a plant becomes too big or straggly.

Propagation

It is not easy to propagate rhododendrons and azaleas from seed or cuttings, except in the case of evergreen azaleas, which can be grown from summer cuttings rooted in a warm frame. The best method for the gardener who wants just a few extra plants is layering (see p 349). Peg down a suitable branch to the ground in autumn. After about 18 months, the branch should have rooted enough to be severed from the parent plant.

75 cm (2½ ft) deep. Sever any tree roots that encroach into the planting hole. Roughen the sides of the hole so that the rhododendron roots can penetrate into the surrounding soil and avoid becoming 'pot-bound'. To make a planting mixture, mix peat or leaf-mould with the excavated soil rather than making up a completely new mixture which will be spongy and may become waterlogged. When filling in the hole, take care not to create a sump into which water will drain and stand.

Competition from the invading roots of nearby trees – especially those of birch – must be expected, and at intervals these should be drastically severed with a spade at the point where they begin to penetrate into the new soil in which the rhododendron has been planted. This is an important maintenance

	Name	Final height	Final spread	Flower colour	Season	Remarks
Evergreens for rock gardens	R. calostrotum	0.6 m (2 ft)	0.6 m (2 ft)	Rosy-purple	Middle/late	Colour varies; 'Gigha' (bright rose-crimson) is a good form
	R. ferrugineum	1 m (3 ft)	0.6 m (2 ft)	Rosy-crimson	Late	Commonly called the alpenrose; there is a white form, R. ferrugineum album
	R. hanceanum 'Nanum'	15 cm (6 in)	25 cm (10 in)	Yellow	Early/middle	Slow-growing
	R. racemosum 'Forrest 19404'	0.6 m (2 ft)	0.6 m (2 ft)	Pink	Early	Fine, free-flowering dwarf form of species listed above; known by its original collector's number
	'Chikor'	0.3 m (1 ft)	0.6 m (2 ft)	Deep yellow	Middle	Dwarf and compact habit
	'Sapphire'	1 m (3 ft)	1.25 m (4 ft)	Blue	Early/middle	Free-flowering
Evergreen azaleas	'Hinodegiri'	1.25 m (4 ft)	1.25 m (4 ft)	Bright crimson	Middle	An old favourite
	'Hinomayo'	1.25 m (4 ft)	1.25 m (4 ft)	Soft pink	Early/middle	Very free-flowering
	'John Cairns'	1 m (3 ft)	1 m (3 ft)	Dark orange-red	Middle	Does best in shade; good for regions with cool summers
	'Kirin'	0.6 m (2 ft)	0.6 m (2 ft)	Deep rose-pink	Middle	'Hose-in-hose' flowers; colour lightens with age
	'Mother's Day'	0.6 m (2 ft)	1 m (3 ft)	Red	Middle	Semi-double flowers
	'Palestrina'	1.25 m (4 ft)	1.25 m (4 ft)	White, green eye	Middle	Striking large flowers
	'Rosebud'	0.6 m (2 ft)	0.6 m (2 ft)	Rose-pink	Middle	Double 'hose-in-hose' flowers; a lovely formal buttonhole flower
Deciduous azaleas	R. luteum	3 m (10 ft)	3 m (10 ft)	Yellow	Middle	Fragrant; the common yellow azalea widely known as Azalea pontica
	'Cecile'	2.5 m (8 ft)	2.5 m (8 ft)	Salmon-pink	Middle	Each flower has an attractive yellow blotch
	'Coccinea Speciosa'	3 m (10 ft)	2.5 m (8 ft)	Orange-red	Middle	Brilliant colouring; scented; the most popular Ghent azalea
	'Daviesii'	3.5 m (12 ft)	3.5 m (12 ft)	White, yellow eye	Middle/late	Sweetly scented
	'Exquisitum'	2.5 m (8 ft)	2.5 m (8 ft)	Cream/pink	Middle/late	Sweetly scented; an Occidentale hybrid; flowers cream, flushed pink
	'Golden Oriole'	1.8 m (6 ft)	1.8 m (6 ft)	Deep yellow	Middle	Sweetly scented; young leaves bronze-tinted
	'Golden Sunlight'	2.5 m (8 ft)	2.5 m (8 ft)	Golden-yellow	Middle	Also called 'Directeur Moerlands'; buds white, opening bright golden-yellow
	'Homebush'	2.5 m (8 ft)	2.5 m (8 ft)	Deep carmine	Middle	Well-shaped tight round trusses of double flowers
	'Koster's Brilliant Red'	2.5 m (8 ft)	2.5 m (8 ft)	Orange-red	Middle	Colour variable; best selected when in flower
	'Norma'	3.5 m (12 ft)	2.5 m (8 ft)	Bright rose-pink	Middle/late	Double flowers
	'Satan'	2.5 m (8 ft)	1.8 m (6 ft)	Scarlet	Middle	Dark buds; very free-flowering
	'Spek's Orange'	1.5 m (5 ft)	1.5 m (5 ft)	Orange	Middle	Very brilliant colour
	'Whitethroat'	1.8 m (6 ft)	2.5 m (8 ft)	Pure white	Middle	Compact growth; double flowers

Very early: from late winter; early: early to mid-spring; middle: middle to late spring; late: early summer

Deciduous flowering shrubs

The beauty of flowering shrubs is that they need little attention once they are planted and established. Furthermore, a collection of ten or a dozen, well chosen, will provide colour and interest throughout the seasons. Yet because they are so easy to grow they may suffer through neglect. They must be treated well from the start, or they will deteriorate into so much scrub. They may well occupy the same position for as much as 20 years, so the soil needs to be prepared thoroughly, and they must be planted with all care and attention (see p 94). Correct pruning is also vital to best performance (see p 369).

Early spring
The season for flowering shrubs begins in the depths of winter with a number of beautiful shrubs described in the article on colour in the winter garden (p 250). Among the first shrubs to flower in the spring are the forsythias, which reach about 2.5 m (8 ft). It is, perhaps, a little unfortunate that their flowers should be yellow, when there are so many other yellow flowers at this time of year – from daffodils to the fragrant shrubs of the genus *Corylopsis*. Even so, there are now many forsythias that are great improvements on the older species and cultivars. One that is still good is *Forsythia × intermedia* 'Spectabilis', although this has probably been superseded by 'Lynwood', with larger flowers in a richer yellow. It was discovered in a cottage garden in Northern Ireland in 1935.

It is at this point that the flowering shrub range breaks down. For what is needed to contrast with all the yellow of the spring is a good mauve or purple flower. This can only be found among the rhododendrons (see p 154), except for *Daphne mezereum,* the mezereon, with its deliciously scented purple-pink flowers, which are followed in autumn by red berries. (There is also a good white form.) It grows to about 1.5 m (5 ft). There is another opportunity for a good colour combination by using a rambling forsythia, such as *F. suspensa* (see p 172), to clamber through the branches of *Prunus × blireana* grown as a bush. This latter is flowering plum with purple leaves and double pink flowers (see p 138).

After the forsythias come the ribes, or flowering currants. These are 2 to 3 m (7 to

Daphne mezereum

10 ft) shrubs with lovely flowers but a pungent smell – so hesitate before using them in the house. If you want the best for a small garden, choose the cultivar *Ribes sanguineum* 'King Edward VII' or, if you have a bit more space, 'Pulborough Scarlet'.

Then comes the vivid red of the old japonica, cydonia or Japanese quince, correctly known as *Chaenomeles japonica.* The basic species is a small shrub, up to 1.8 m (6 ft) tall, which produces bright orange-scarlet flowers, followed by big quince-like fruits that are useful for jellies and jams (where they aid setting). It makes an excellent substitute for azaleas on a neutral or chalky soil. Among the excellent varieties of the Chinese *C. speciosa* (which is often confused with the above) are

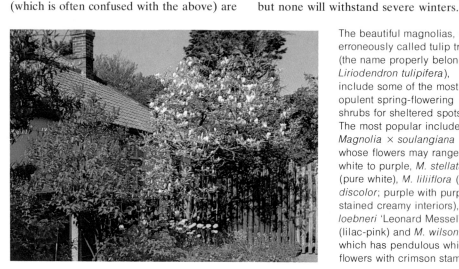

the pink and white 'Moerloosii' and the pure white 'Nivalis'. Many other free-flowering forms are classified under *C. × superba,* ranging in colour from pale pink to deep crimson.

Later spring
Spring reaches its full beauty with *Spiraea × arguta,* the so-called foam of May or bridal wreath, a 2 m (7 ft) shrub with delicate green foliage and a mass of white flowers. At this time of year, too, one of Britain's native plants, *Viburnum opulus,* or the guelder rose (known to Americans as the European cranberry bush), is giving a fine show of heavily fragrant white flowers, to be followed in the autumn by red berries and rich red foliage. There is now an even better form for smaller gardens called 'Compactum', which gives the same performance but does not grow nearly as big (reaching about 1.8 m [6 ft] rather than 4.5 m [15 ft]). Another variation is 'Sterile' (the snowball bush), with larger flowers but no berries.

Many berberis (or barberries) are evergreen (see p 150) or have beautiful leaf colourings instead of or in addition to flowers and berries (see pp 165, 167 and 169). Among the deciduous kinds grown primarily for their spring flowers, however, is *Berberis montana* (*B. chillanensis*), whose drooping yellow and orange blooms, resembling those of a Tazetta narcissus, are 2.5 cm (1 in) across. It makes a good 2 m (6 ft) shrub.

The ornamental brooms (*Cytisus* spp),

developed from another European native, have been improved remarkably in recent years. They now come in all colours from white through yellow, pink and buff to red – and even mauve in the cultivar 'Mrs Norman Henry'. Most of the novel colour forms have been the result of hybridizing *Cytisus scoparius* 'Andreanus', which has flowers that are half yellow and half crimson. It was found growing wild in Brittany at the end of the 19th century. 'Burkwoodii' and 'Windlesham Ruby' are two good reds. 'Lady Moore' has flowers of creamy-yellow touched with pink and scarlet, and 'Donard Seedling' is a combination of yellow and mauve-pink. Most of these reach a maximum of about 2 m (7 ft), but none will withstand severe winters.

The beautiful magnolias, often erroneously called tulip trees (the name properly belongs to *Liriodendron tulipifera*), include some of the most opulent spring-flowering shrubs for sheltered spots. The most popular include *Magnolia × soulangiana* left, whose flowers may range from white to purple, *M. stellata* (pure white), *M. liliiflora* (*M. discolor*; purple with purple-stained creamy interiors), *M. × loebneri* 'Leonard Messel' (lilac-pink) and *M. wilsonii*, which has pendulous white flowers with crimson stamens.

The lilacs (*Syringa* spp) close this season of the year. The many cultivars now available make the choice confusing. But you could go for *Syringa vulgaris* 'Congo', single and the deepest purple of them all, 'Souvenir de Louis Späth', again single and wine-red, and the beautiful double white 'Madame Lemoine', all of them deliciously scented and 2.5 to 3.5 m (8 to 12 ft) tall.

Spring into summer
As late spring moves into early summer, there start the flowering shrubs that give a continuous performance, often flowering for many weeks. The potentillas begin to flower at this

Cystisus hybrids

time, among them the new and beautiful *Potentilla fruticosa* 'Red Ace', with red flowers that go on right through the summer. It had the distinction of making newspaper headlines in 1975, when someone attempted to steal a cutting from the first plant shown in front of the Royal Horticultural Society, in London. There are many others, and two that are good are *P. fruticosa* 'Friedrichsenii', pale yellow with grey-green foliage, and *P. fruticosa* 'Tangerine', the colour described by the name. They vary from 0.6 to 1.25 m (2 to 4 ft).

Another long-flowering plant is the rich yellow *Spartium junceum*, or Spanish broom. The flowering time of this shrub can be controlled by pruning. It needs to be cut back hard in the spring, but the earlier you cut it

Potentilla fruticosa 'Goldfinger'

back, the earlier it flowers, and vice versa. Allowed its head, it reaches 3 m (10 ft), but it will not tolerate severe winters.

Closely allied to the cytisus, and also known as broom, are the genistas. Some are mere dwarfs for the rock garden, but others, such as *Genista cinerea* and *G. tenera* (*G. virgata*; Madeira broom) make substantial shrubs. Both of these are covered in fragrant yellow flowers in early summer. For *G. aetnensis*, see page 169.

Among the most popular and easily grown fragrant shrubs of early summer are the hybrid philadelphus, or mock orange, generally listed as *Philadelphus × virginalis*. There are

Philadelphus 'Innocence'

Weigela hybrid

numerous named forms ranging from 1 to 3 m (3 to 10 ft) in height. The white flowers often have purple or maroon basal blotches.

Equally or even more popular are the weigela hybrids, which grow up to about 1.8 m (6 ft) and whose branches are covered in clusters of white, pink or red flowers from early summer. Among the best are *Weigela* 'Abel Carriere' (rose-pink), 'Bristol Ruby' (ruby-red), 'Eva Rathke' (bright red) and 'Newport Red' (dark red).

High summer

Buddleias are superb shrubs, mostly 3 m (10 ft) tall, for the summer. *Buddleia davidii* is often called the butterfly bush because its fragrant flowers, in arching plumes, attract butterflies. Two varieties in sharp contrast are 'Royal Red' and 'White Profusion'. *B. alternifolia* grows like a small weeping willow with grey leaves and pale mauve flowers, and *B. globosa* carries deep yellow flowers in globular clusters like tiny oranges.

There are many hardy fuchsias for summer flower where winters are not too cold, and the best known is *Fuchsia magellanica* 'Riccartonii', with red and purple flowers, the plant that makes hedges in mild districts. 'Chillerton Beauty', with white and rose-pink flowers, is a cottage-garden plant from the Isle of Wight, in southern England, and the dwarf 'Mrs Popple' is a striking mixture of scarlet and violet. Less hardy fuchsias can be used for temporary bedding (see p 222).

Hydrangea paniculata 'Grandiflora' is very hardy, and produces big panicles of flowers in the late summer. They start green, turn to white and end with a delicate flush of pink. The better known hydrangeas are the Hortensia cultivars, which are often listed under *H. macrophylla*. There are many excellent forms for milder gardens, reaching a height of 3 m (10 ft) in particularly favourable conditions. Two that are equally good in performance, giving pink flowers on alkaline or neutral soil, blue on acid, are 'Marechal Foch' and 'Altona'. (If you want blue hydrangeas but have neutral soil, water in a proprietary 'blueing' compound or simply a weak solution of alum.) 'Ami Pasquier' is dwarf and deep red.

A third group, known as the Lacecaps, are more hardy, and have a centre of tiny flowers, surrounded by a ring of the conventional hyd-

rangea florets. 'Bluewave' and 'Whitewave' are two that are both described by their names, and are among the most attractive of all flowering shrubs for the late summer.

In the full heat of midsummer, there comes one of the most delightful colour combinations in the whole spectrum of flowering shrubs: ceanothus and hypericum (rose of Sharon). There are two types of ceanothus: the evergreen varieties, which prefer to climb up a wall (see p 172), and the deciduous varieties, which make better plants for a border. The best of the latter is *Ceanothus × 'Gloire de Versailles'*, because it throws delightful powder-blue flowers from midsummer right through to the late autumn. Another shrub that gives the same continuous performance,

Fuchsia magellanica

with waxy-yellow flowers to make a delightful contrast, is *Hypericum patulum* 'Hidcote'. It reaches about 1.8 m (6 ft), the ceanothus slightly more. Ceanothus are not hardy where harsh winters occur.

To finish the season of flower there come the 2 m (7 ft) hardy hibiscus, *Hibiscus syriacus*. Among the best of these are 'Woodbridge', a rich pink with a dark eye in the centre, and 'Ardens', a double flower in near blue, with a maroon blotch. These end the parade of deciduous flowering shrubs, to the point where those that provide colour from their foliage and berries take over, as described on page 166.

Hibiscus syriacus 'Mauve Queen'

Shrub roses old and new

All roses are shrubs, so the term shrub rose is rather a confusing one. For want of a better, however, it is used to cover all roses (apart from climbers and ramblers) that are not normally used for bedding – all, that is, except the bush roses, standards and miniatures. The term generally includes all the larger species and old roses bred before, roughly, the beginning of the 20th century, Modern hybrid shrub roses, and even, confusingly, such Floribundas as 'Chinatown' and 'Fred Loads', which are too tall for the average garden bedding scheme.

There are two common beliefs about shrub roses that are only partially true. The first is that they flower but once a year. This is true of practically all species roses, and also, among the cultivars, of the Gallicas, Damasks, Albas, Centifolias and Moss roses. It is not true, with a few exceptions, of the Bourbons, Hybrid Perpetuals, China roses, Rugosas, Hybrid Musks, and most of the Modern shrub roses. And many that do flower only once put on a display for a month more spectacular than that of any other kind of flowering shrub.

The second fallacy is that all shrub roses are far too large for a small garden. This is true only of most species, some of the Damasks, Albas, Centifolias, Moss roses, Bourbons, Rugosas, Hybrid Musks and Modern varieties, and a very few of the Gallicas and China roses. A few species are even of rock-garden size, but an important point to bear in mind, if you do choose a rose which you know will make a big plant, is that a great deal of the charm of shrub roses is in their informal habit of growth. Many species, for instance, have long arching canes, spangled with blossom along their entire length. They require no pruning except for the removal of dead wood as and when it occurs, and to cut them about to reduce their size, simply because you have not allowed enough room for them, will not only reduce the amount of bloom, but ruin their appearance as well.

Few of the roses grown in gardens today are true species, though many of them have been given botanical names as if they were. The majority are the result of crosses between species in the wild, or which took place quite by chance in gardens or nurseries, for it was only in the last century that it was realized that new varieties of plants can be produced by cross-pollination.

Species roses

These are the original wild roses, true species and their natural hybrids and varieties, generally having single flowers of five petals. Interesting garden species and hybrids include the yellow *Rosa foetida* and its sport, the scarlet and yellow *R. foetida bicolor*. These have just about the brightest colour of any rose, and all modern bright yellow and orange roses are descended from them. Open-growing, they will reach 1.5 m (5 ft), but really need the shelter of a warm wall in colder climates. And watch out for black spot.

R. × harisonii ('Harison's Yellow') and 'Canary Bird' (a cultivar of *R. xanthina*) are both yellow roses of late spring, the flowers of

Rosa moyesii 'Geranium' (hips)

the former being semi-double and cupped, and of the latter single and coming all along the canes. Both will reach 1.8 m (6 ft) in height and spread, and the small, ferny foliage of 'Canary Bird' especially is attractive all the summer.

R. moyesii 'Geranium' makes a 2.5 m (8 ft) upright and rather open shrub, with bright red single flowers, followed by enormous scarlet, bottle-shaped hips. *R. × paulii* and the *R. ×* 'Macrantha' hybrid 'Raubritter' are both good roses for ground-cover and sprawling down banks. The latter becomes absolutely covered with semi-double, cupped pink flowers, will reach about 90 cm (3 ft) high, but will cover about 25 m (8 ft) of ground. *R. rubrifolia*, at 1.8 m (6 ft), has rather insignificant pink flowers, followed by bunches of more showy red hips, but it has ruby-red canes and leaves in a mixture of mauve and grey.

Gallica roses

The oldest cultivated race of roses, the Gallicas date back to before the 16th century, and derive from the wild *R. gallica*. In the main they are small, upright shrubs, not exceeding

Rosa 'Frühlingsgold'

1.25 to 1.5 m (4 to 5 ft), and are ideal for the front of the shrub border or for low hedges. The flowers are carried erect above the foliage, which is rough and rather coarse. They have few thorns, but numerous hair-like bristles. If grown on their own roots, they will sucker, and with most of them you must watch for mildew.

Good varieties that come true to type include 'Charles de Mills', with large, flat quartered flowers in crimson-purple; *R. gallica* 'Officinalis' (known variously as the Provins rose, the apothecary's rose and the red rose of Lancaster), with bright pink semi-double flowers and golden stamens; and its sport *R. gallica* 'Versicolor' ('Rosa Mundi'), with pink striping on a blush-pink ground. 'Belle de Crécy' and 'Tuscany Superb' are like those mentioned above, only 1.25 m (4 ft) tall, but this is because they are much more lax growers. The flowers of the former, very fragrant, are creamy-mauve, of the latter crimson-purple. 'Complicata' is possibly a hybrid of *R. ×* 'Macrantha', and has huge single, pink flowers with a white eye. It will reach 1.8 m (6 ft), or scramble much higher into a neighbouring shrub or tree.

Damask and Bourbon roses

A very old and comparatively small group, the Damasks have no obvious common feature to anyone other than a botanist. They are related to *R. × damascena*, and the name is said to refer to Damascus, from where they were supposedly brought to Europe by the crusaders. Good examples include the 1.5 to 1.8 m (5 to 6 ft) 'Celsiana', with semi-double, fragrant, pale pink flowers in clusters, and the 2.5 m (8 ft) 'Ispahan', one of the roses used for hundreds of years for the production of attar of roses, which has bright pink, very double flowers. 'Mme Hardy', reaching 1.5 m (5 ft), has strongly scented, quartered, pure white flowers with a green eye, or pointel.

Strong-growing, lusty shrubs, Bourbons are

the product of a cross between the unique twice-flowering Autumn Damask and the China roses, which introduced perpetual-flowering garden roses to the West. Most types flower from early summer until autumn frosts. They generally need the support of a stake or pillar, and many can be grown as short climbers. They were first raised in the early 19th century on the island of Réunion (then called the Île de Bourbon).

'Boule de Neige' has creamy-white, full, rounded, very fragrant blooms. 'Commandant Beaurepaire' ('Panachée d'Angers') is bright rose-pink, streaked and marbled with violet and white, but is not certain to flower again in the autumn. The soft pink 'La Reine Victoria' certainly will. It has cupped blooms with delicate, shell-like petals and is rather lax in growth, reaching 1.8 m (6 ft) with the support of a pillar. 'Zéphirine Drouhin' is a popular shrub or climber up to 3 m (10 ft) tall with scented cerise-carmine flowers that recur all summer if dead-headed. It is almost thornless.

Hybrid Perpetual roses
Generally rather similar in habit to the Bourbons, these were one of the parents of the Hybrid Teas (see p 160). 'Ferdinand Pichard', at 1.5 m (5 ft), has cupped blooms of white, striped with scarlet-pink. 'Mrs John Laing' is soft pink, full and fragrant, and 'Paul Neyron' a deeper pink. 'Reine des Violettes' will make a bigger shrub up to 1.8 m (6 ft) and spreading wide; the flowers are violet-crimson, opening flat, and quartered. It repeats well, but needs quite hard pruning and good soil to give its best.

Alba roses
Having reached the parents of the Hybrid Tea, Albas represent a jump back to another line descended from the Damask rose, crossed with *R. canina* (the dog rose). Albas are mostly large, with distinctive grey-green leaves, and all are scented. 'Königin von

Rosa 'Golden Wings'

Rosa 'Ferdinand Pichard'; 'Roger Lambelin'

Dänemark' ('Queen of Denmark') has soft pink, very full, reflexing blooms, salmon-pink in the centre. It will reach 1.8 m (6 ft), but *R. × alba semiplena* (the white rose of York), semi-double and white, and its double white sport *R. × alba maxima* (the so-called Jacobite rose), will go up to 2.5 m (8 ft) and scramble into trees if given the chance.

Centifolia and Moss roses
Mostly large shrubs with lax, drooping canes, full, sweetly scented flowers, and very large leaves, Centifolias, also known as Provence or cabbage roses, will certainly need support. 'Fantin Latour', in palest pink and reaching 1.5 m (5 ft), is one of the loveliest, almost equalled by *R. centifolia* 'Cristata' ('Crested Moss'), which has an unique crested, mossy calyx. 'Petite de Hollande', again pink, is only 1.25 m (4 ft) tall and one of the smallest.

The first Moss rose sported from a Centifolia, and they are generally very similar, except for the glandular, mossy growth on the flower stalks and calyx of the former. The common Moss rose ('Old Pink Moss', or *R. centifolia* 'Muscosa'), in soft pink, 'Henri

Martin' (crimson) and the giant, heavily mossed and very fragrant 'William Lobb', in purple-magenta, fading to lilac-grey and reaching 2 m (7 ft), are some of the best.

China roses
Small, light and generally airy shrubs, the China roses are descendants of *R. chinensis*. Almost constantly in flower from early summer until late autumn, they have attractive, very healthy, narrow, pointed leaves. 'Old Blush' (sometimes called the common monthly rose, and supposedly the inspiration for Thomas Moore's song 'The Last Rose of Summer') has clusters of globular, silvery-pink, fragrant blooms and will reach 1 to 1.25 m (3 to 4 ft). *R. chinensis* 'Mutabilis' ('Tipo Ideale') is completely different, except in height. The single, buff-yellow flowers change to orange-red, salmon and then crimson. Against a warm wall, it will climb to about 2.5 m (8 ft).

Rugosa roses
Big, tough roses that will grow in the poorest soil and have handsome, wrinkled, completely disease-proof foliage, the Rugosas – relatives of the wild *R. rugosa* – make first-rate hedges. The single and semi-double varieties bear enormous hips, like small tomatoes. 'Blanc Double de Coubert', with papery, double white flowers, and 'Roseraie de l'Hay' ('Plena'), in wine-red, are two of the best. 'Frau Dagmar Hastrup', with pale pink single flowers with cream stamens, is smaller at 1.5 m (5 ft).

Hybrid Musk roses
Like giant Floribundas in many ways, with enormous heads of flowers – scented and either single, semi-double or double – these also make good hedges. 'Penelope', in shades of cream and apricot, and 'Pink Prosperity' are both well worth having.

Modern shrub roses
There is no common factor with these, and they range from the 2.5 m (8 ft), once-flowering, scented 'Frühlingsgold', with its arching canes of semi-double, pale yellow blooms; its 1.8 m (6 ft), often repeat-flowering cousin, 'Frühlingsmorgen', in deep pink, shading to a yellow centre with maroon stamens; the creamy-white 'Nevada' – 2 m (7 ft) in height and spread – and its pink sport 'Marguerite Hilling' ('Pink Nevada'); through the rather smaller 'Golden Wings' at 1.5 to 1.8 m (5 to 6 ft), which is covered all summer with large, scented, pale yellow blooms; down to the 90 cm (3 ft) 'Ballerina', with its masses of small pink flowers. 'Constance Spry', once-flowering, is vigorous but needs support, and has very large, full, fragrant, rose-pink blooms in the style of the old roses. 'Cerise Bouquet' has cerise-pink, semi-double fragrant blooms which open flat. The bush is fairly open, arching, and 1.8 m (6 ft) tall. Other varieties are mentioned with the Floribunda roses (see p 162).

For more information on displaying and growing roses, see pages 98 to 101.

Bush roses: the exquisite Hybrid Teas

The best-known roses are the compact types used mainly in bedding schemes and generally known as bush roses. They fall into two main groups today, the Hybrid Teas and the Floribundas – both generally upright growers not more than 1 to 1.25 m (3 to 4 ft) tall, but in some cases quite a bit shorter and in a few somewhat taller. Hybrid Teas have large, double flowers, in some varieties one to a stem, in others forming small clusters. They have a long flowering period, but are particularly showy in early and late summer. Floribundas (see p 162) have large trusses of comparatively small blooms, though the modern breeding tendency is towards larger flowers and fewer in a truss, so it is difficult to tell whether some roses belong to the Hybrid Tea or the Floribunda group.

Many varieties of both types are grafted on to tall-growing rootstocks to make standard and half-standard roses. The only difference between these two is the length of base stem below the bushy top. In a standard (sometimes called a tree rose), it is generally about 1 to 1.25 m (3 to 4 ft); a half-standard has only a 60 cm (2 ft) stem.

Development of the Hybrid Tea

The Hybrid Tea rose has been with us since 1867. That was the year in which the first variety, 'La France' – a soft, silvery-pink and very sweetly scented rose – was introduced. There are other claimants for the title, and the picture is rather confused because a number of the early Hybrid Teas looked very like the Hybrid Perpetuals (see p159) from which they were descended. But 'La France' gets the popular vote even though it has the globular blooms and something of the same habit of growth as the earlier roses.

The story of the Hybrid Tea goes back another half-century, however. In the early part of the 19th century, Tea roses were arriving in the West from the Far East. These had the perpetual-flowering properties of all China roses, and large flowers of much greater elegance than the rather cabbage-like blooms of the Hybrid Perpetuals. The centre petals were longer, so that for the first time were seen the high, pointed centres to rose blooms that are considered essential today. Some of them were of a creamy-yellow or buff colour, which was also a new thing in garden roses, but they were not very hardy in the colder northern climates. They would flourish only against a warm wall or in a greenhouse.

Crossing Tea roses with Hybrid Perpetuals brought the robustness of the latter to the resulting roses and, in time, the more refined flowers of the Tea. The new race was the Hybrid Tea group. (Tea roses, incidentally, got their rather strange name from the fact that they were supposed to smell like the newly-opened tea containers arriving from China and Burma, though it takes some imagination nowadays to believe this.)

Although some of the Tea roses were creamy-yellow, all other cultivated roses at that time were either white, pale or deep pink, lilac, maroon or purple, though some crimson varieties were beginning to appear as a result

Rosa 'Grandpa Dickson'

of crosses with earlier China roses. It was not until 1900 that the first really strong yellow garden rose came on the market, a Hybrid Perpetual called 'Soleil d'Or'. At such a comparatively recent date one might expect it to have been a Hybrid Tea, but it was not until some years of this century had passed that the Hybrid Tea succeeded in ousting the earlier race. 'Soleil d'Or' was the result of crossing the double form of the bright yellow Persian species, *Rosa foetida persiana*, with a Hybrid Perpetual, though it took the French nurseryman who achieved the breakthrough many years before he managed to produce anything worthwhile. Modern yellow Hybrid Teas (and yellow Floribundas and climbers) are all descended from this one wild rose, and a red and yellow bicolour form of it gave rise to all the modern orange, flame and bicolour roses.

R. foetida thus has quite a place in rose history, but it has passed on one attribute that rose-growers could do without. It was, and is, a great rose for black spot, which was a com-

Rosa 'Rose Gaujard'

paratively rare disease before it came on the scene. However, the exciting new roses derived from *R. foetida* were soon crossed with every imaginable other colour in the search for further novelties, and black spot began to spread like the plague it is, and has never stopped.

For a reason that no one has so far fathomed, some Hybrid Teas are to a greater or lesser degree healthy, under most conditions keeping free from both black spot and mildew. Top of the list come 'Pink Favourite' and its yellow-pink sport 'Honey Favourite' and others include 'Peace', 'Grandpa Dickson', 'Wendy Cussons', 'Rose Gaujard', 'Ernest H. Morse', 'Red Devil', 'Fragrant Cloud' and 'Chicago Peace' (see the table). Breeders today are much more careful to use healthy varieties for breeding, though there is clearly a long way to go before rose-growers can put away their sprays.

Choosing Hybrid Teas

Before choosing roses for any purpose, it is wise to see them growing in garden conditions; only in this way can you really judge whether they are what you want. Some Hybrid Teas, for instance, have much less continuity of bloom than others, and the different varieties vary greatly in height. If you are planting a mixed bed, with perhaps five varieties in groups of six of each, it is important to decide whether you want them all at their flowering peak together and to choose accordingly. And you would not want one variety to grow twice as tall as the others.

A thorough pre-knowledge of the roses will help, too, in blending the colours together to make an attractive whole. The colours of a few roses do actually clash with others if they are placed side by side, but more often it is a case of one with a strong, vivid colour simply

ushing one with more delicate tones into the
background, so that it is scarcely noticed. This
can often happen to the lilac and mauve roses,
which can look very washed-out if planted
incorrectly. It is only with other pastel colours, and in contrast with white and yellow
roses, that they are able to give of their best.
The stronger carmine-pinks, such as 'Wendy
Cussons', also need careful placing, for they
do not blend well with many other roses. If
you want to separate bright colours, use
cream or white roses between them, as these
will tone in, or contrast attractively with, practically anything else.

It is often said that modern roses have no
scent, but this is much less true of Hybrid Teas
than it is of Floribundas, the ancestry of which
is different. It is probably the very rapid rise in
the popularity of the Floribundas since World
War II (in a number of countries they are now
more widely grown than Hybrid Teas) that
has led to the idea that all modern roses are
the same in their lack of fragrance, but
remember that scent in all flowers depends to
some extent on the time of day, the heat of the
sun and the humidity of the air. Most Hybrid
Teas, if the conditions are right, have some
scent, but some of those that can be relied

Rosa 'Whisky Mac'

seems that yellow and orange roses in general
– however many petals they have – stand up
better to both rain and the damp autumn
mists. There are some Hybrid Teas in other
colours that are also reasonably good, and
they are marked in the table.

Really hard pruning should only be carried
out by the average gardener when dealing
with an old, neglected bed of roses, but this is
to try to encourage them to send up strong
canes from the base of the plant, after which
they can be dealt with much more gently. For
most purposes, and with most Hybrid Teas,
cutting the main canes to a suitable eye about
20 to 25 cm (8 to 10 in) from the ground will
give the best results and provide a first-rate
show of flowers later on.

Hybrid Teas make the most beautiful of cut
flowers, but they seldom last more than a few
days. Various proprietary products are sold to
increase this period, most of them based on
glucose, a spoonful of which mixed in the
water in the vase produces just as satisfactory
results. It is better still to stand the roses,
immediately after cutting, up to their necks in
a bucket of nothing but pure water in a cool
place for about eight hours. Then, fully
charged with water, they will really give of
their best and remain fresh and beautiful for
the maximum length of time.

For further information on using and growing roses, including methods of winter protection and general principles of pruning, see
pages 98 to 101.

**Pruning Hybrid Teas
above left** First remove any
dead, diseased, damaged or
weak canes, cutting back to
strong, healthy wood. **centre** If

any canes cross closely, cut
back one of them. **right** Then
cut back other canes, normally
to about 20 to 25 cm (8 to 10 in)
from the ground; prune strong

shoots more gently than weak
ones, and with 'Peace' and its
offspring prune less severely.
inset Cut to an outward-facing
bud to keep the bush open.

upon at all times to have more than the average are marked in the table.

Not all of these, however, are the best of
garden roses, except in a long, hot summer.
'Red Devil', 'Bonsoir' and 'Royal Highness'
are really exhibitors' roses, and have petals
that are easily damaged by rain, so they may
not open properly when wet. They are,
nevertheless, very lovely roses and worth taking a chance with even if you do not show,
which is why they are included in the list.
Generally speaking, the more petals a rose
has and the slower it is to open, the more
likely it is to rain damage, though there are
notable exceptions like 'Stella', 'Gail Bor-
den', 'Rose Gaujard' and 'Grandpa Dickson',
which seem to revel in showery weather. The
last of these is a yellow Hybrid Tea, and it

Pruning and cutting

How severely you should prune your Hybrid
Tea roses depends to some extent on what you
want from them. The old idea of very drastic
pruning down to about 8 to 10 cm (3 to 4 in),
or two or three eyes from the base, has been
recognized as being far more drastic than is
needed for ordinary garden display. It is only
carried out nowadays by some exhibitors, as it
results in bigger blooms – which is what they
want – but fewer of them. However, such hard
pruning will actually result in a very poor performance from some varieties; 'Peace', and a
number of roses which have been bred from it,
are examples of this. 'Peace' does much better
if never cut back below about 90 cm (3 ft) –
except, of course, for the removal of old, diseased or spindly wood.

Recommended Hybrid Tea varieties

White	'Blanche Mallerin'*; 'Message' ('White Knight'); 'Pascali'
Light pink	'Blessings'*† (coral); 'Bonsoir'* (peach); 'Honey Favourite' (yellowish); 'Mischief'*† (coral); 'Royal Highness'* ('Königliche Hoheit'); 'Silver Lining'* (silvery); 'Stella'† (cream centres)
Deep pink	'Lady Seton'†; 'Mala Rubinstein'*; 'Mullard Jubilee'*† ('Elektron'); 'Pink Favourite'; 'Prima Ballerina'*† ('Première Ballerine'); 'Red Lion'*; 'Tiffany'*; 'Wendy Cussons'*†
Lilac	'Blue Moon'* ('Mainzer Fastnacht'; 'Sissi')
Red	'Alec's Red'*; 'Ernest H. Morse'*†; 'Fragrant Cloud'* ('Duftwolke'; 'Nuage Parfumé'); 'John Waterer'*; 'National Trust'†; 'Red Devil'* ('Coeur d'Amour')
Dusky red	'Mister Lincoln'*
Vermilion	'Summer Holiday'†; 'Super Star'† ('Tropicana')
Orange	'Beauté'; 'Just Joey'*†; 'Troika'†; 'Typhoon'†
Apricot blends	'Apricot Silk'†; 'Chicago Peace' (pink flush)
Yellow	'Adolf Horstmann'; 'Grandpa Dickson'† ('Irish Gold'); 'King's Ransom'*†; 'Peace'† ('Gioia'; 'Gloria Dei'; 'Mme A. Meilland'); 'Whisky Mac'*
Red/white	'Rose Gaujard'
Red/yellow	'My Choice'*† (pastel colours); 'Piccadilly'†

* Strongly scented; †weather-resistant

Bush roses: the free-flowering Floribundas

If you want a massed display of bedding roses, rather than a smaller number of exceptionally beautiful blooms, your best choice is to plant Floribundas. These are of much more recent origin than Hybrid Teas (see p 160), and have really become popular only since World War II, largely through such varieties as 'Masquerade', 'Fashion' and 'Goldilocks', which were produced by the American hybridist Gene Boerner. He brought double blooms and startling new colours to a group of roses already distinguished by their large clusters or trusses of comparatively small flowers and by exceptional continuity of bloom. Also from America came the name Floribunda.

Before that time, Floribundas had been known as Hybrid Polyanthas because they are directly descended from the wild rose *Rosa polyantha*. Today this is known as *R. multiflora*, and its cluster-flowering habit has been passed on to its children. *R. polyantha*, probably crossed with a perpetual-flowering China rose, produced the first Polyantha rose in 1875. This and others that followed were dwarf-growing bushes about 30 cm (12 in) tall. The rosette form their flowers often took led to the extension of the name to Polyantha-Pompon, or simply Poly-Pom.

Not many are grown today, as a number were rather prone to mildew, but among those still worth a place in the garden are 'The Fairy' (pink), 'Baby Faurax' (mauve, scented), 'Coral Cluster' (coral-pink), 'Ideal' (velvety crimson) and 'Paul Crampel' (orange-scarlet). They make excellent low hedges or edging plants for paths or drives, or they can be used for bedding, being especially suitable for small gardens.

Early in this century, work was being done in Denmark to try to increase the size of the flowers on the Polyantha roses by crossing them with Hybrid Teas. In 1924 came 'Else Poulsen' and 'Kirsten Poulsen', the first of the Hybrid Polyanthas and the first roses resembling the Floribunda as we know it today. In addition to having bigger flowers, these new roses were also taller than the Polyanthas.

The change in name from Hybrid Polyantha to the rather simpler Floribunda came about purely for commercial reasons, and under protest from botanists, as it was

Rosa 'Elizabeth of Glamis'

Rosa 'Dearest'

not botanically valid. Also for commercial reasons, a decision was later made in the United States to separate out the very tall-growing Floribundas like 'Queen Elizabeth', which have larger flowers than the average and fewer in the truss, and to call them Grandifloras. This term has not been accepted in all countries, but in Britain those Floribundas with large flowers, closely resembling in form those of the Hybrid Tea, are known officially (and rather clumsily) as Floribunda Hybrid-Tea-type. Moves are afoot, if international agreement can be reached, that all roses of this type, other than the large-flowering Hybrid Teas, be called cluster-flowered roses.

Floribundas in the garden

Floribundas make excellent bedding plants. Generally speaking, they are more continuously in flower than Hybrid Teas, because the

flowers in their trusses open in succession and a new truss is ready to bloom by the time the first ones are over. As their flowers usually have fewer petals, they are as a rule much better at opening in wet weather, and they also last longer when cut for vases. This latter attribute may have something to do with the petal thickness, which tends to be greater on Floribundas than Hybrid Teas.

Some varieties of Floribundas have smaller trusses on the first flush of bloom than they do later on, even the odd flower or two coming one to a stem. This is quite normal, but over the whole summer period they will certainly have far more flowers than a Hybrid Tea, which concentrates on quality rather than quantity. The one serious drawback of Floribundas is their lack of scent. However, there are some fragrant varieties, including those indicated in the table.

Among the roses in the table, 'Chinatown' and 'Fred Loads' are really Floribunda shrubs and are so tall (1.5 m and 1.8 to 2 m [5 ft and 6 to 7 ft] respectively) that they are – together with 'Queen Elizabeth', 'Dorothy Wheatcroft' and 'Iceberg' – more suitable for the back of the border, for specimen planting, or for hedging. For this last purpose they can be planted closer together than normal – at perhaps 60 cm (2 ft) intervals, or, for a thicker, more substantial hedge, staggered in two rows about 45 cm (18 in) apart, but still with 60 cm (2 ft) between each plant.

At the other end of the scale, rose-breeders are now concentrating on low-growing, bushy Floribundas for the smaller garden. Most of these, though vigorous and spreading, reach no more than 60 cm (2 ft) in height, and examples of those on the market are 'Topsi', 'Marlena', 'Paddy McGredy' and 'Stargazer'.

Recommended Floribunda varieties

White	'Iceberg' (Schneewittchen); 'Fée des Neiges'; tall); 'Ice White' ('Vison Blanc')	**Scarlet**	'Evelyn Fison'† ('Irish Wonder'); 'Korp'† ('Prominent'); 'Topsi'
Light pink	'Dearest'* (salmon); 'Elizabeth of Glamis'*; ('Irish Beauty'; salmon); 'Michelle'*; 'Pink Parfait'†; 'Queen Elizabeth'† (tall)	**Vermilion**	'Dorothy Wheatcroft' (tall); 'Fred Loads'* (tall); 'Orange Sensation'*; 'Stargazer'
		Orange	'Dame of Sark'; 'Southampton'†
Deep pink	'City of Leeds' (salmon); 'Paddy McGredy' (carmine)	**Yellow**	'Allgold'†; 'Arthur Bell'†; 'Chinatown'*† ('Ville de Chine'; tall); 'Sunsilk'
Lilac	'Escapade'*† (white eye); 'Yesterday'†	**Red/white**	'Eye Paint'; 'Matangi'; 'Old Master'; 'Picasso'
Red	'City of Belfast'†; 'Marlena'†; 'Stephen Langdon'†	**Yellow/red**	'Masquerade'; 'Redgold' ('Rouge et Or')
Dusky red	'Europeana'; 'Frensham'; , 'Rob Roy'†		

Scented variety; †disease-resistant

Roses in miniature

Floribundas from cuttings
Unlike most Hybrid Tea roses, Floribundas grow well on their own roots, and can be raised outdoors from cuttings. In late summer, choose strong, ripe shoots of the current year's growth. Trim them with a sharp knife just above a leaf, and again just below a bud about 25 cm (10 in) farther down. Leaving two or three leaves at the top, plant the cuttings in a narrow trench about 15 cm (6 in) deep, adding coarse sand to the bottom if the soil is heavy. Fill in the trench, leaving only 10 cm (4 in) of the cuttings above the surface. Using hormone rooting powder increases the chance of the cutting taking, and by late autumn of the next year they should be ready for transplanting to their permanent quarters.

There is a considerable need for this type of rose, because for a long time new varieties of both Floribundas and Hybrid Teas have tended to get taller, or even leggy.

The wide-open flowers of many Floribundas have the added attraction of gold or cream-coloured stamens, but they have also given the hybridists the chance of introducing exciting colour variations into the petals. McGredy's nurseries, first in Northern Ireland and then in New Zealand, have been the pioneers here, starting with 'Picasso', which has a distinct patterning of carmine and silvery-white on each petal, changing as the flower ages. 'Picasso' has been followed by 'Old Master', 'Matangi' (an exceptionally healthy rose), and 'Eye Paint'. And 'Escapade' is a lilac-mauve Floribunda from Harkness that has an attractive white eye to each flower. 'Matangi' is perhaps top of the list of disease-resistant Floribundas, but others are indicated in the table.

Pruning Floribundas
The pruning of Floribundas follows in its general pattern that for Hybrid Teas (see p 161), except that the cutting back can be lighter. When dead-heading, the whole flower truss should be removed, cutting back to the first healthy bud below the truss. Removing only the spent flowers or hips will leave an unsightly framework of useless, twiggy growth, and so prolific are the majority of these roses that a new truss will be just about ready to take the place of the old. For hedging with Floribundas, prune the main canes very lightly indeed, until a substantial framework has built up, for it is height that is needed.

For more information on using and growing roses, see pages 98 to 101.

Few plants are as dainty as the miniature rose. With the best of them, everything is tiny and perfectly in scale – the flowers no more than 1 cm (½ in) in diameter and the leaves and stems in proportion. Apart from their special uses in rock and sink gardens, they make charming edgings for paths and beds of larger roses. And in spite of the common belief that they are delicate little plants that need nursing along, they are in fact just as tough and hardy as their bigger relations. Though commonly sold in pots, they are not houseplants. You can, if you keep them in their pots, take them indoors when they flower, but they should be put back outdoors immediately afterwards; keep them well watered.

Sizes of miniature roses
The smallest miniature roses, such as 'Tom Thumb', are only about 12 cm (5 in) tall, but all of them tend to grow much larger if they are budded on to a more vigorous rootstock. As they take very readily from cuttings, it seems a pity that this should so often be done, but, for a commercial nursery, propagation by cuttings is really too slow. The result is that a number of the miniatures that you can buy grow to 25 or even 40 cm (10 to 15 in), and extra-vigorous varieties like 'Baby Masquerade' will top 60 cm (2 ft), with 2.5 cm (1 in) flowers – so that it is really getting into Polyantha or Floribunda territory.

Crossing miniatures with Floribundas has had the effect in a number of cases of increasing the flower size, though not necessarily that of the plant, so that one looks too big for the other. It has, however, brought a wider range of colour and flower form to the little roses. The blooms of miniatures range from single, through semi-double and the cupped shapes of the old roses, to the high-centred flowers of classic Hybrid Tea shape. American breeders have even produced miniature varieties with red and white striped flowers – only single at the moment – and miniature Moss roses (see p 159). Generally, the blooms of miniatures are in small trusses.

Recommended miniature roses

White	'Easter Morning'
Pink	'Cinderella'; 'Eleanor' (coral); 'New Penny' (coppery-salmon); 'Rouletii'; 'Sweet Fairy'*
Lilac	'Lavender Lace'*; 'Mr Bluebird'
Red	'Coralin' ('Carolin'); 'Darling Flame'; 'Perla de Alcanada' ('Baby Crimson'; 'Pearl of Canada'); 'Scarlet Gem' ('Scarlet Pimpernel'); 'Starina'; 'Wee Man'
Orange	'Baby Darling'; 'Colibri'
Yellow	'Bit o' Sunshine'*; 'Gold Coin'; 'Rosina' ('Josephine Wheatcroft'; 'Yellow Sweetheart'); 'Yellow Doll'
Red/white	'Little Buckaroo'; 'Toy Clown'
Red/yellow	'Little Flirt'

*Scented variety

Miniatures in the garden
In the garden, miniature roses can be used to line paths, or as rock garden plants – though for the latter use they must have a good pocket of soil, for they like a deep, cool root run. For stone sinks in patio gardens and for window boxes, miniatures are ideal, though once again depth of soil is important. It should not be less than 25 cm (10 in) and must not be allowed to dry out.

One of the most attractive ways of using miniature roses is to plant a complete miniature rose garden. The paths between the beds are probably best made from small paving stones or fine gravel; grass would be difficult to cut and keep neat if the paths were narrow enough to be in keeping. Bush miniatures, with either Hybrid Tea or Floribunda-type flowers, should be planted about 20 cm (8 in) apart, and miniature standards can be bought to give height and variety to the bed.

If backing onto a low wall or fence, this can be clothed with miniature climbers, such as 'Nozomi' (palest pink, almost white), 'Pompon de Paris' (rose-pink; sometimes called 'Climbing Rouletii'), 'Pink Cameo' ('Climbing Cameo'; rich rose-pink) or 'Magic Wand' (red). All these climb to 1 to 1.25 m (3 to 4 ft), with delicate foliage and small flowers that are in proportion.

Rosa 'Perla de Alcanada'

Rosa 'Pompon de Paris'

Shrubs for form and foliage

There is more to a flowering shrub than its flowers. Obviously, the leaves are important – their colour, shape, size, arrangement along the branches and so on. But so, too, is the habit of the plant. This alone can be enough to justify a place in the garden. Another aspect, often overlooked, is the winter outline, particularly of deciduous trees and shrubs. It is a quality dramatically portrayed by D. H. Lawrence when he wrote in the poem 'Bare Almond Trees' of 'almond trunks curving blackly, iron dark, climbing the slopes'.

Some of the shrubs that have this almost strange beauty are described in this article. Others – many of which might more accurately be termed striking rather than beautiful – will be found among the 'architectural'

Cornus alba 'Gouchaltii'

plants described on page 252. For general information on planting and after-care of shrubs, see page 96. Unless otherwise stated, all the plants in this article are deciduous.

Manipulating plants

The most spectacular foliage effects can be produced by playing tricks with plants, largely by the simple process of pollarding. This means that you cut the shrub or tree hard to the ground every year. It then throws up strong young growth to give leaves that are bigger and better than if it is left alone.

Sometimes a little more manipulation is necessary. For example, if *Ailanthus altissima* (tree of heaven) is cut right back every year, then only allowed to send out one shoot, it will produce leaves 1.5 m (4 ft) long which have something of a tropical splendour about them. The same may be done with *Paulownia tomentosa*. This tree will give enormous heart-shaped leaves, as much as 60 cm (2 ft) across, and the stem will reach 3 m (10 ft).

There are many more that can be improved by the simple method of pollarding alone, including forms of *Salix alba* (white willow) and *Cornus alba,* and some poplars: *Populus alba* and its variety 'Richardii' and *P. candicans* 'Aurora'. The result may sometimes be a wonderful foliage plant that is virtually unrecognizable – as, for example, when the common European hornbeam, *Carpinus betulus,* is treated in this way.

The more hardy eucalyptus, or gum trees,

Eucalyptus coccifera and *E. gunnii,* give beauty in a reverse way. When pollarded they will always throw their juvenile foliage, the small rounded leaves that are so attractive in flower arrangements, rather than the long narrow leaves of the fully grown tree. But it is not generally known that the popular grey-leaved foliage shrub *Senecio greyi* is best if it is given a somewhat similar treatment, but in a small way, and more often. This shrub is grown more for its silver-grey leaves than for its flowers – which are not much better than those of the weed groundsel. Consequently, the best effect is obtained by constantly pinching out the young growth to make it bush out. This improves the colour of the foliage, and makes the plant tougher and hardier.

Acer palmatum var

Ligustrum lucidum 'Excelsum Superbum'

Leaf pattern, colour and texture

The Japanese maples are entirely dependent upon their leaves for their beauty. They are among the most distinguished shrubs for both leaf pattern and habit. Even the common form, *Acer palmatum,* has a certain charm in its shape – and good autumn colour. But the most delicate are the low-growing Dissectum group with leaves so finely cut that they are like filigree metalwork. The two best known are the green form, *A. palmatum* 'Dissectum', and the dark purple form, *A. palmatum* 'Dissectum Atropurpureum'. Another section is known as Heptalobum, and one of the best of these is *A. palmatum* 'Heptalobum Osakazuki'. This has green leaves, rather in the shape of the original *A. palmatum,* but they

turn fiery-scarlet in the autumn – perhaps the brightest colour of any autumn foliage.

The stag's-horn sumach, *Rhus typhina,* is a well-known plant, particularly in urban areas where it seems to thrive. Not so well known is the cut-leaved form called *R. typhina* 'Laciniata', with long leaves that are like delicate fern fronds, turning brilliant yellow and orange in the autumn. Both reach a height of about 3.5 m (12 ft).

There are not many evergreen flowering shrubs distinguished for leaf and form, but one that does have leaves that are more finely cut than the rest is *Berberis gagnepainii,* with yellow flowers followed by black berries. It grows to about 1.8 m (6 ft).

Glossy leaves are a considerable advantage in towns because the rain washes grime from the shiny surface. *Aucuba japonica* 'Variegata' ('Maculata'), the common spotted laurel, has leaves with this texture, brightly coloured in gold and green. There are a number of other named forms, making rounded bushes 2 to 3.5 m (7 to 12 ft) tall.

The privets offer similar advantages. The common hedging plant *Ligustrum ovalifolium* and its golden form, 'Aureum' (golden privet), are well known, but these are not the only privets. *L. lucidum,* the Chinese privet, is a taller-growing and stronger plant up to 3 m (10 ft) tall. Its most decorative cultivar is called 'Tricolor', whose green leaves are bordered with white and touched with pink when they are young.

Many beautiful effects can be obtained in the garden by using leaves with different textures. *Phlomis fruticosa,* the Jerusalem sage, is a low-growing shrub with very furry sage-like grey-green leaves and yellow flowers in the summer. Being a Mediterranean plant, however, it is not hardy in cold climates.

Lavender, too, can play a part in this contrast of texture, and there are many varieties

Elaeagnus pungens 'Variegata'

of old English lavender from which to choose. These are usually listed under *Lavandula spica,* though they are more correctly hybrids of *L. angustifolia* (*L. officinalis*) and *L. latifolia.* Probably two of the best are 'Munstead' and 'Twickel Purple', both about 75 cm (2½ ft) tall. For neat growth and good foliage, but with some loss of scent, *L. spica* 'Vera' (Dutch lavender, sometimes listed as *L. vera*) is a compact form with larger leaves than the rest.

The angelica trees (species of *Aralia*) have huge leaves – 1.25 m (4 ft) or more long and half as much wide – but these are doubly pinnate, divided into small leaflets, so they are more delicate than they sound. In *Aralia elata,* the Japanese species, the leaves grow like ruffs at the end of the stems. In the form 'Aureovariegata' they are irregularly blotched and margined in yellow. There is also a Chinese species, *A. chinensis,* with spiny stems. Generally forming tall, suckering shrubs, they also have large panicles of small white flowers in late summer or early autumn.

There are many plants with golden and variegated leaves, but some are inclined to become tatty with age and are often less hardy. The best evergreen is undoubtedly *Elaeagnus pungens* 'Maculata', growing to 2 to 3 m (7 to 10 ft). Here the gold dominates the leaves, being surrounded by only a thin border of green. An excellent golden-leaved plant is the golden form of the common elder, *Sambucus nigra* 'Aurea'. The reason why it is so good is that instead of the leaves becoming tarnished

with age, they improve in colour throughout the summer, especially if it is pruned hard in the spring.

Shrubs that give brilliant colour in the autumn from their foliage need to provide some other form of beauty at another time of the year (see the article on two-way shrubs on page 166), unless the colour is so startling that it is worth giving space to that alone. One plant that does this is *Berberis thunbergii* 'Erecta'. It also has the advantage of being a narrow-growing plant, reaching about 1.5 m (5 ft), but similar in shape to a Lombardy poplar. It has small yellow flowers in spring, followed by red berries. In the form 'Atropurpurea', the leaves are a rich reddish-purple throughout the season, intensifying as winter approaches. It is much more spreading, however.

Useful shapes

Another upright plant and a valuable evergreen for a small garden because it is not quick-growing, reaching only 1.5 m (5 ft) in 10 to 15 years, is the golden upright yew *Taxus baccata* 'Standishii'. The colour of the leaves is bright gold, and it is a female form carrying the red berries of the yew. Like all yews, it is poisonous in all its parts.

The opposite in habit is *Cotoneaster salicifolius floccosus,* an evergreen shrub with wide-spreading branches, white flowers in the spring and bunches of red berries in the autumn. It reaches 3 m (10 ft) or more, but its graceful form makes it a valuable plant in many positions. Similarly with the Warminster broom, *Cytisus × praecox,* which forms a cascade of grey stems that are covered in pale yellow flowers in the early spring. The form of cherry laurel called *Prunus laurocerasus* 'Zabeliana' is another spreading plant, with dark green leaves and white flowers that are relatively large for a laurel.

Then there are shrubs which grow naturally

Juniperus × media (*J. chinensis*) 'Blaauw'

into rounded shapes without clipping. *Genista hispanica,* the Spanish gorse, forms a neat round hummock about 50 cm (20 in) high by as much through, and is covered with a mass of yellow flowers in the spring. A bigger plant with this same shape is a holly called *Ilex aquifolium* 'Watereriana', with yellow-variegated leaves usually without spines.

There is a curious attraction, especially in modern gardens, in shrubs that have a stark and gaunt outline. *Berberis sargentiana* grows with long, groping branches carrying vicious spines, narrow evergreen leaves and yellow flowers in the spring. It will reach as much as 2.5 m (8 ft) in height and as much through. *Cotoneaster microphyllus* is a shorter evergreen with branches of small, dark green

Corylus avellana 'Contorta'

leaves that form angular growths, carrying big red berries in the autumn.

Corylus avellana 'Contorta', the corkscrew hazel, or Harry Lauder's walking stick, is an oddity with twisted branches – as may be gathered from the common name. It is slow-growing to about 3 m (10 ft) and carries attractive catkins in the winter. Somewhat similar in growth is a form of the Peking willow, *Salix matsudana* 'Tortuosa'. Both are useful for flower arrangements.

Coniferous shrubs

There are a number of conifers of medium growth which also have interesting outlines. The most useful of them all in this role is *Juniperus × media* (*J. chinensis*) 'Pfitzeriana'. This juniper grows to a height of about 1.5 m (5 ft), spreading to 2 m (7 ft) and more. The branches grow out in layers, slightly weeping at the end. There is also a golden form. *J. × media* 'Blaauw' is similar but more stiff in growth, the branches ascending at an angle of about 45°. Its beauty lies in the metallic-grey lustre of the leaves.

An excellent small Sawara cypress, *Chamaecyparis pisifera* 'Boulevard' is similar in colour during the summer, but turns purple in the winter. It is conical in habit. Its leaves are softer and smaller than those of *J. × media* 'Blaauw', but both grow to about 1 to 1.5 m (3 to 5 ft). Other low-growing conifers will be found among the rock plants described on page 231.

Two-way shrubs

The days of big gardens, with special borders for one flower or one colour, are gone. Small gardens cannot afford to give space to big specimen shrubs that give just one glorious burst of colour. Consequently, shrubs that give two displays, or serve two purposes, give the best value. An outstanding example is the common yellow azalea, *Rhododendron luteum* (see p 155), which provides a wonderful show of deliciously scented yellow flowers in spring and brilliant foliage colour six months later. This article describes a number of shrubs that similarly give double value, although many comparable plants will be found elsewhere in this book. For general information on planting and caring for shrubs, see page 96. Unless otherwise stated, all the shrubs mentioned here are deciduous.

Flower and leaf colour

Liking the same lime-free soil as rhododendrons and azaleas, *Amelanchier lamarckii*, the snowy mespilus or June berry, gives three forms of beauty – a mass of white flowers (pink-tinged in 'Rubescens') in spring, sweet black berries in early summer and beautiful autumn tints through to leaf fall. It grows about 3 m (10 ft) tall. It is often mistakenly sold as *A. canadensis*, a different species, as is the beautiful *A. laevis,* which may form a small tree and whose white flowers emerge at the same time as the delicate pink young foliage; it also has good autumn tints.

Both the hamamelis (witch hazels) described in the article on the winter garden (p 250) and the fothergillas offer star-shaped yellow flowers in the winter and early spring, and colourful autumn foliage which, particularly with *Fothergilla major, F. monticola* or *F. gardenii,* can be startling in its brilliant yellow and orange tones. In several witch hazels, such as *Hamamelis × intermedia* 'Hiltingbury' and 'Jelena' ('Copper Beauty'), the flowers are coppery or orange in colour. Except for *F. gardenii,* which is a dwarf, all the above reach about 2.5 m (8 ft).

The smoke tree or Venetian sumach, *Cotinus coggygria* (*Rhus cotinus*), makes a 2.5 m (8 ft) rounded shrub that is smothered in fluffy purplish inflorescences in early summer. They fade to smoke-grey. The foliage is

Fothergilla major

light green in the species, but dark purple in 'Foliis Purpureis' and 'Royal Purple'. The leaves of all of them turn a brilliant orange-red in autumn.

There is a new shrub which does duty as a foliage plant and as a flowering shrub all through the summer: *Abelia × grandiflora* 'Frances Mason'. Raised in New Zealand, this new abelia has golden-variegated foliage with a continuous show of small mauve flowers. It is also useful because it only grows to 1 m (3 ft). In a way, it is similar to the old *Weigela florida* 'Variegata', with silver-variegated leaves, although this shrub grows somewhat taller and does not carry its pink flowers for such a long period.

The golden form of the mock orange,

Leycesteria formosa

Philadelphus coronarius 'Aureus', is another that is as beautiful for its leaves as it is for its flowers – but it must be cut back hard every year after it has finished flowering. It will then keep to a height of about 1.8 m (6 ft). The colouring is retained best if it is grown in full or semi-shade.

It is not generally known that the popular summer-flowering shrub, *Spiraea × bumalda* 'Anthony Waterer' will produce attractive leaves of pink and cream provided it is lightly clipped (not cut back hard) when the red flowers have finished. This helps to keep it to a useful height of around 50 cm (20 in).

Flower and berry

There are one or two shrubs that will give as many as four different displays. *Leycesteria formosa* is a shrub that needs to be cut back hard every year in the spring. It will then throw strong green stems, attractive for winter bark effect, which produce white flowers followed by red bracts and purple berries. The overall height is about 1.8 m (6 ft). *Stranvaesia davidiana* is an evergreen shrub growing to as much as 3 m (10 ft) but, curiously for an evergreen, some of the leaves colour red in the autumn. At the same time, it is carrying red berries that follow the white flowers.

A good range of shrubs combine spring

flowers with attractive autumn berries. Among the best are the cotoneasters, of which there are a number of species that form shrubs 2 m (7 ft) or more tall, as well as prostrate and wall-hugging kinds such as *Cotoneaster horizontalis* (see p 171). All have small white or pink spring flowers and conspicuous red berries in autumn and winter. Among the best bushy kinds are the evergreen *C. conspicuus* and the semi-evergreen *C. simonsii* and *C. × watereri.* Some deciduous types, such as the low-growing *C. adpressus* and the large *C. bullatus,* also have autumn leaf tints.

The ornamental thorns (*Crataegus* spp) similarly have spring flowers and colourful autumn fruits, or haws. Many of them form good-sized trees (see p 139), but the haw-

Crataegus laevigata (C. oxyacantha)

thorns or May trees of Europe, *Crataegus monogyna* and *C. laevigata* (often listed as *C. oxyacantha* or *C. oxyacanthoides*), together with their various named cultivars, make excellent large shrubs. They are very showy when covered in white, pink or red blossom – often fragrant. This appears in late spring – in May in its native Europe, hence one of the common names.

Skimmias are evergreen shrubs of neat habit, generally about 1.25 m (4 ft) tall, that give flowers – sometimes scented – in the spring and berries in the autumn, on female plants. Since the sexes are separate, be sure to plant at least one male among the females. Among the excellent males is *Skimmia japonica* 'Rubella' (sometimes listed as a form of *S. reevesiana* [*S. fortunei*] and possibly derived from both species), which has pink buds all winter that open to white flowers. Vigorous female forms include *S. japonica* 'Foremanii' and the free-fruiting 'Nymans'.

Skimmias prefer an acid soil, as does *Pernettya mucronata*, a smaller-growing shrub up to 50 cm (20 in) tall with small bell-shaped white flowers in the spring and large berries – red, white, pink and purple – in the autumn. This shrub will occasionally pollinate itself, but it is best again to include a proven male form among a group to make sure that you obtain a good crop of berries.

Flower, foliage and form

Attractive young foliage is an attribute of some of the cultivars of pieris – even more beautiful than the flowers, which are like those of lilies of the valley. *Pieris* 'Forest Flame', growing to about 2 m (7 ft), starts with bright red young leaves, which turn to pink and then creamy-white before they become green. And there are many more. *P. formosa* 'Jermyns' has vinous-red young growth, *P. formosa* 'Wakehurst' red leaves at the same time as the large white flowers, while *P. japonica* 'Bert Chandler', raised in Australia, has salmon-pink young leaves. All the pieris need an acid soil, the same as for rhododendrons and azaleas, but like some shelter. They are also evergreen shrubs, and it is surprising

Pieris formosa 'Wakehurst'

how many evergreens do provide more than one form of beauty.

Berberis verruculosa grows to a neat round bush about 1.25 m (4 ft) tall with a good display of yellow flowers in the spring. Although it, too, is an evergreen, many of the leaves colour red in the autumn. The tree heathers, forms of *Erica arborea*, which grow up to 3 m (10 ft), or even more in mild, maritime regions, are similarly dual-purpose. They are often thought to be more attractive for their

Yucca gloriosa

long sprays of evergreen foliage, which give the effect of a small conifer rather than a heather, than for their white and pale pink flowers in early spring. Perhaps the best form is *E. arborea* 'Alpina'.

A big evergreen shrub growing to 3 m (10 ft) and as much through, *Viburnum rhytidophyllum* would be worth growing for its large dark green leathery leaves alone – especially as it enjoys a chalk soil and will substitute for a big-leaved rhododendron. It also carries white flowers which are followed by red berries that later turn black. It is another of those shrubs that have a sex problem, and to enjoy the berries at their best it is necessary to plant two together. *V. davidii* is somewhat similar but much lower-growing, reaching only 60 to 90 cm (2 to 3 ft).

The yuccas (Adam's needle) are shrubs which can also be grown solely for the beauty of their form – large sword-like evergreen leaves that give a subtropical effect. They also flower freely, particularly in a hot summer, giving a magnificent spike of creamy-white flowers, somewhat similar to the madonna lily. It is a complete myth that these shrubs only flower once in seven years. The best-known species are *Yucca gloriosa, Y. recurvifolia* and the smaller and hardier *Y. filamentosa*, which has grey-green leaves. They thrive on dry, sandy soils.

Among the deciduous shrubs which offer more than one form of beauty, *Viburnum plicatum tomentosum* grows in a distinctive manner, with tier upon tier of branches which carry flowers in the spring somewhat similar to those of the Lacecap hydrangeas. They have a central group of buds surrounded by open florets. It has all this and autumn colour, too, with red berries turning black, which are produced in a hot summer.

Moving on to shrubs which also give some other display in the winter, *Euonymus alatus* is one of the most brightly coloured of all autumn foliage shrubs. But when the leaves have fallen they display the cork-like branches which have a curious attraction of their own, reaching up to 1.5 m (5 ft).

Cornus alba 'Elegantissima' is the odd man out of this group, for its beauty lies in the silver-variegated leaves and in the colour of its stems in the winter; the flowers are insignificant. It is probably the most striking of all deciduous variegated shrubs, and the colour of the bark, particularly on the branches in the middle of the shrub, is a bright cerise-pink – darker on the outside. This makes a big shrub 1.5 m (5 ft) high by 3 m (10 ft) in diameter. 'Westonbirt' ('Sibirica') is similar except for the leaf variegations. For best bark colour, prune to the base in spring.

Multi-purpose shrubs

Some shrubs are so versatile that they can be used almost anywhere in the garden, and few have more uses than *Mahonia aquifolium*, the Oregon grape. This is a compact plant growing to little more than 75 cm (2½ ft), with purple-green holly-like leaves, turning an even deeper colour in the winter. The flowers in early spring are bunches of yellow, and are

Mahonia aquifolium

followed by blue-black edible berries (see p 315) that give the shrub its common name. It can be planted as a decorative shrub in its own right, it can be used for ground cover among taller shrubs and trees, and it will make an excellent hedge.

The pyracanthas, or firethorns, are evergreen shrubs with more uses than the usual one of climbing up a wall. If planted at intervals of about 1.8 m (6 ft), and the branches trained along wires, to be kept clipped, they make a good hedge that will not take too much nourishment from the soil because the plants are so far apart. They can even be grown as standard trees. Some varieties, particularly *Pyracantha* 'Watereri', give three displays – from the flowers, like those of the May tree in the spring, from the young growth throughout the summer, which is bronze, and from the red berries, for which it is best known, in the autumn. Prune in winter as for a fruit tree.

Sage is generally thought of as a herb, but if it is allowed to grow into a shrub and flower, the common sage, *Salvia officinalis*, is a beautiful sight with its small pale mauve flowers in early summer. Even better for evergreen foliage is a cultivar called 'Purpurascens' – the purple-leaved sage – which, when it is growing happily in a sunny situation, will have leaves as good as those of any houseplant. Like the ordinary variety, these leaves can be used for flavouring.

Salvia officinalis

Shrubs rare and beautiful

Do not be put off by the title of this article. These plants are not difficult to grow, and at one time they were reasonably plentiful. But, with the advent of garden centres, they have become more difficult to obtain than those that can be bought on a cash-and-carry basis, grown and 'packaged' in containers. That is to say, if you want to buy one of the plants described here, it will probably be necessary to write to a specialist nursery and have it sent by post or rail. This adds to the cost, and is the prime reason why most plants are now sold through garden centres.

But there are other reasons for rarity. Some plants are not easy to propagate, although they can be grown without fuss or bother in any good garden soil, in almost any situation. The best illustration of this problem is *Daphne cneorum,* the garland flower, which has been cultivated as a garden plant for more than 200 years. At one time, this was easily obtainable in England, because there was one man, working for one firm, who had the knack of rooting the cuttings as easily as privet. That firm sent thousands of small plants of *Daphne cneorum* to Covent Garden market, to be bought by nurseries and garden centres to sell to their customers.

Then the man who held the secret of the garland flower died, and the nursery was sold for building land. So this delightful little evergreen shrub, only growing to about 30 cm (12 in), but covered in pink flowers with a wonderful scent in the spring, suddenly became elevated to the rarity bracket.

Low-growing kinds
All of these grow to less than 75 cm (2½ ft). Working up from *Daphne cneorum,* there is *Polygala chamaebuxus* 'Grandiflora'. This is even more attractive than *Daphne cneorum,* except that it lacks the scent. It is a minute evergreen plant, sometimes called the ground box, which gives pea-shaped flowers of yellow and mauve in the early spring. Even earlier, sometimes in the winter, another evergreen flowering shrub with a difficult name, *Sarcococca hookeriana digyna,* produces its white scented flowers. This has narrow leaves

Nandina domestica

and later carries black berries. Neither thrives where winters are harsh, however.

Leucothoë fontanesiana, also evergreen, is a delight for the flower arranger. This plant colours well in the winter and there are now a few cultivars, like 'Rainbow' ('Multicolor'), with leaves variegated in cream, yellow and pink. It will grow only on acid soils. Still down on the ground, there is one of the shrubby veronicas – the hebes mentioned on page 151 – called *Hebe anomala* that is an excellent ground-cover plant, largely because it has light green leaves that look fresh throughout the whole year. Another good type, though not a rarity, is *H.* 'Pagei' (often listed under *H. pinguifolia*), which has glaucous leaves and small white flowers.

Again going back to a plant mentioned on page 151, *Cistus* 'Silver Pink' is only rare because it is wanted by so many people and the supply is limited. It is a rock rose, or sun rose, with flowers aptly described by the name. It is no more difficult to grow than the rest when it is planted in the garden, but it is not as easy to produce.

Medium height
In the range from 0.75 to 1.5 m (2½ to 5 ft), *Corylopsis spicata* and *C. pauciflora* are shrubs that give catkin-like yellow flowers in early spring. They are much like those of the hazel nuts (*Corylus* spp), but more glamorous and attractive. *Stachyurus praecox,* with pendent racemes of pale yellow flowers, is somewhat similar. It might well be considered the best of all the early flowering shrubs with catkin-like flowers.

Surprisingly, two close relations of the blackberry are among the finest of all flowering shrubs, but much more difficult to obtain. These are known by the correct botanical names of *Rubus deliciosus* and *R.* × *tridel.* They carry big single white flowers in the summer, similar to those of the dog rose but more glistening. Both are thornless. *R.* × *tridel* may reach as much as 3 m (10 ft).

Then there is the shrub with autumn colour to outshine all plants that offer beauty in their dying leaves – *Disanthus cercidifolius.* It is difficult to describe the colour of the leaves of this plant in the autumn, but perhaps crimson splashed with dark purple might be near the mark. They are so beautiful that the mauve flowers produced at the same time are pale in comparison. It needs moist but well-drained soil and a semi-shaded position.

Desfontainia spinosa

Corylopsis pauciflora

Kolkwitzia amabilis

It would be a tragedy for ornamental gardening if *Corokia cotoneaster* – sometimes called the wire netting bush – should be lost from nurserymen's catalogues, because it might drop out of general circulation. The common name does it a disservice. It is a plant that is interesting at all times of the year because it has twisted, wiry black stems carrying grey leaves and, in the spring, yellow flowers. It is not hardy in very cold areas.

Nandina domestica, known as the Chinese sacred bamboo – though it is not a true bamboo – is another unusual plant that is easy to grow. An evergreen somewhat resembling a bamboo, it has good autumn foliage, and berries in warm areas. It is used in China as a decoration in houses for the Chinese New Year. Like the corokia, it will not stand very cold winters.

Another little-known but extremely beautiful shrub – a member of the heather family – is *Zenobia pulverulenta.* An evergreen with glaucous-grey leaves, it carries large white lily-of-the-valley flowers in early summer. They are aniseed-scented. Like most ericaceous plants, it will not tolerate lime.

The last of the evergreens is among the rarest of rarities. *Desfontainia spinosa,* with holly-like leaves and orange-scarlet flowers in summer, is a slightly tender South American shrub. It is well worth growing if you can obtain it.

Moving over to deciduous flowering shrubs, *Deutzia × kalmiiflora* has flowers similar to the umbrella-shaped blossoms of the kalmia (see p 151), but it is easier to grow on any soil. The flowers appear in early summer, and are white, flushed with carmine. There are a number of other worthwhile deutzias to be

found in nurserymen's catalogues, all flowering at about the same time, mainly in pink and white. In many, the young shoots may be damaged by late spring frosts, but they are otherwise fairly hardy.

At this same time of the year, too, *Kolkwitzia amabilis,* the beauty bush, is in flower. One of the most attractive shrubs for this period, it has pale pink snapdragon flowers and the leaves are covered in a furry down. The whole effect merits the common name.

Spiraea prunifolia is another beauty that is not to be seen in every garden centre. Like *Daphne cneorum,* it is not easy to propagate, but it is a beautiful plant with double white flowers in summer, and the orange or red autumn colour is magnificent.

Eucryphia × nymansensis 'Nymansay'

Tall shrubs
Among the shrubs growing to a height of more than 1.5 m (5 ft), *Caragana arborescens* 'Lorbergii' is in a situation rather like that of *Daphne cneorum.* That is to say, it was grown in Britain for years by one nursery which has now gone out of business; even so, it is still grown here and there. Its beauty is in its spring foliage, as delicate as that of a maidenhair fern. Yet it is very tough.

Sycopsis sinensis is one of the few evergreens related to the witch hazels (*Hamamelis* spp). It has similar flowers, very early in the year, which are partly hidden by the leaves. However, a little judicious stripping makes it a useful plant for flower arrangement, and it is a good shrub simply as an evergreen.

There are several interesting forms of *Berberis × stenophylla.* 'Autumnalis' produces a second crop of flowers in the autumn, while 'Semperflorens' will go on flowering throughout the summer. But perhaps one of the best of all is 'Pink Pearl', with leaves mottled and striped with pink and cream, and flowers either creamy-yellow, verging on orange, pink, or bicoloured – all on the same bush.

Carpenteria californica is a handsome evergreen shrub with glossy leaves carrying white flowers with yellow anthers in early to midsummer – a time of year when there are not all that many interesting flowering shrubs. It is slightly tender, but does well against a sheltered wall.

Genista aetnensis, the Mount Etna broom, is either a large shrub or a small tree, up to 3 m (10 ft) tall, flowering in high summer with typical yellow broom-like flowers. But its main value in the garden is that it has a habit similar to that of the weeping willow but does not grow nearly as big and is not as greedy.

Perhaps the only evergreens that are rare because they are new are the recently introduced hybrids of *Photinia × fraseri*: 'Birmingham' from America, 'Red Robin' from New Zealand and 'Robusta' from Australia. These all have bright red young foliage, similar to that of some of the pieris, but with the considerable advantage that they will grow on a lime soil. They do best in a sheltered, warm position, 'Robusta' being the hardiest.

Eucryphia × nymansensis is a semi-evergreen flowering shrub growing to 3 m (10 ft), while *E. glutinosa,* one of its parents, is deciduous. Both carry large white flowers throughout the late summer, and *E. glutinosa* colours well in the late autumn. They prefer moist, lime-free soil and some shelter.

As with the photinia, there are new forms and varieties of *Cornus florida,* the flowering dogwood, which give flowers and bracts in spring, followed by brilliant foliage in the autumn. Among them are 'Apple Blossom' (pale pink), 'Cherokee Chief' (rose-red) and 'White Cloud' (pure white). *C. kousa* is another flowering dogwood which is attractive in the same way, but these are large shrubs, only seen at their best when the flowers can be viewed from underneath. *C. kousa* is, however, one of the finest multipurpose shrubs, combining attractive habit, flowers, fruits, autumn colour and bark.

Shrubs for sheltered walls

There are many extremely beautiful shrubs that are not hardy enough to be grown in exposed positions in regions with cold winters. Unprotected, they will suffer frost or wind damage, but in many areas they will thrive against a sunny, sheltered wall or fence. The ideal aspect varies with geographical location, but in the British Isles, for example, the warmest walls are those that face south or south-west. Again, there are shrubs that do well when trained over a wall, secured to trellis or wires and helped to take on the right form by judicious pruning. Such shrubs may also require the wall's protection, but some are perfectly hardy and may be grown against cold as well as sheltered walls.

For general information on planting, growing and pruning shrubs, see page 96. Remember when planting against a wall or fence – especially beside a house – that the roots are liable to become very dry. So dig in plenty of moisture-retaining, humus-forming

plant, but is well worth growing. The fragrant white flowers, 7.5 cm (3 in) wide, are produced from early summer to midsummer. Plant it in spring in a sunny spot sheltered from cold winds. It will reach a height of about 2.5 m (8 ft).

Winter sweet, *Chimonanthus praecox* (*C. fragrans*), is one of the most fragrant of winter-flowering deciduous shrubs. It blooms on the bare branches, the yellow outer petals being tinged green, the inner petals purple. The foliage is rough to the touch. It will grow in most soils to about 2.5 to 3 m (8 to 10 ft), but is not happy in acid conditions.

Choisya ternata, the Mexican orange-blossom, is a superb evergreen having lustrous, dark green foliage adorned by sweet hawthorn-like scented white flowers. These appear first in spring and often again in autumn. The foliage is excellent for floral arrangements and lasts well in water, as do its flowers. When grown against a wall or fence it

wires or trellis, and will reach a height of 2.5 to 3 m (8 to 10 ft).

The evergreen Bull Bay, or laurel, magnolia, *Magnolia grandiflora*, has outstandingly handsome glossy, dark green, leathery leaves and is ideal where space is no object. It will grow to as much as 12 m (40 ft). From midsummer to autumn, its large creamy-white, waxy, globular flowers fill the air with an exotic fragrance. Unlike most magnolias, *M. grandiflora* tolerates a lime or chalk soil, but choose a wall sheltered from cold winds.

An evergreen to enhance any garden where a sheltered wall is available, *Trachelospermum asiaticum* will reward with small, fragrant, creamy-white flowers produced against a background of dark glossy-green oval foliage. They appear in summer.

White, pink or red flowers
The abelias are beautiful shrubs that need a warm, sheltered wall, to which they must be

Choisya ternata

Itea ilicifolia

material, such as well-rotted farmyard manure, garden compost or leaf-mould. And always plant 20 to 30 cm (8 to 10 in) away from the foot of the wall or fence.

Fragrant flowers
The forsythia-like shrub *Abeliophyllum distichum* is a comparative newcomer to Western gardens, having been introduced from Korea in 1924. In late winter it bears fragrant white flowers, tipped with pink, on the leafless branches. It needs a warm, sunny wall or fence, and reaches a height of 1.25 to 1.8 m (4 to 6 ft).

A rarely seen evergreen, also needing warmth and shelter, is *Azara serrata*. The fragrant yellow flowers in midsummer look well among the shining green oval leaves. It thrives best in chalk or sandy soil, and reaches 2.5 to 3.5 m (8 to 12 ft).

A rather tender evergreen from California is *Carpenteria californica*. It is not a long-lived

needs to be tied to wires or trellis. In winter the foliage is sometimes scorched by frost, but it soon grows out of this in spring. Its height is 1.8 to 3 m (6 to 10 ft).

A charming evergreen shrub seldom grown as a wall plant, though it makes a most successful one, is *Daphne odora* 'Aureomarginata'. When neatly tied to wires or trellis on a sheltered, sunny wall, it reaches a height of 0.9 to 1.25 m (3 to 4 ft) and may spread as much as 2.5 m (8 ft). Its sweetly fragrant reddish-purple flowers, which are paler or nearly white within, are something to look forward to every year, appearing from midwinter well into spring. The foliage is faintly margined with pale yellow.

A tender, handsome evergreen, *Itea ilicifolia* is suitable only for warm, favoured localities. The glossy, holly-like foliage makes a pleasing background to the sweetly scented greenish-white flowers that droop like long catkins in late summer. It needs tying in to

secured by wires or trellis. They are not fastidious over soil and will grow satisfactorily on chalk. A semi-evergreen, *Abelia floribunda*, has brilliantly coloured rosy-red tubular flowers in midsummer. It likes sun, and reaches a height of 1.8 to 3 m (6 to 10 ft). *A. × grandiflora* is also semi-evergreen, and has white flowers, tinged with pink, that are freely produced above dark, glossy foliage. It reaches only 0.9 to 1.8 m (3 to 6 ft), however. It flowers from midsummer to early autumn. *A. schumannii* is deciduous and grows about 1.5 m (5 ft) tall. Its soft rose-lilac flowers are borne from early summer to mid-autumn.

The deciduous Japanese quince has been given many different botanical classifications in the past 200 years: first *Pyrus*, then *Cydonia* and *Malus*, and at the end of the 19th century *Chaenomeles* – the name it is called by today. *Chaenomeles japonica* is a small hardy shrub bearing bright orange-flame flowers in spring. These are followed in autumn by

Chaenomeles speciosa

greenish-yellow fruits which make an excellent jelly. A dwarf form, *C. japonica alpina*, has bright orange flowers and grows 60 to 75 cm (2 to 2½ ft) high.

There are also many varieties of *C. speciosa* that vary in height from 60 cm to 3 cm (2 to 10 ft). They all grow well standing free or against a sunny wall in any good garden soil – chalky or otherwise – though a well-drained loam is best. Included among these is the white 'Nivalis', which grows 1.8 to 2.5 m (6 to 8 ft) tall, and the crimson 'Simonii', only about 75 cm (2½ ft). Among the hybrids listed as *C. × superba*, 'Crimson and Gold' is rich crimson with a boss of golden stamens and 1.8 to 3 m (6 to 10 ft) tall; 'Knap Hill Scarlet' is mandarin-red and 1.5 m (5 ft); 'Pink Lady' is a clear rose-pink, 1 to 1.8 m (3 to 6 ft) tall and late winter-flowering against a sheltered wall (but otherwise spring-flowering); and 'Rowallane' is deep red and 0.9 to 1.25 m (3 to 4 ft) tall. All make excellent wall shrubs, and when grown this way should be pruned immediately after flowering by cutting back secondary shoots.

Abelia schumannii

Cotoneaster horizontalis

The lobster claw or parrot's bill, *Clianthus puniceus*, is an unusual New Zealander. The brilliant red flowers appear from early to mid-summer. Their extraordinary shape, from which the common names derive, produces a quite exotic effect. Unfortunately this semi-evergreen is extremely tender, and needs a warm, sheltered wall or fence and protection in winter. It grows to a height of 1.8 to 2.5 m (6 to 8 ft).

Cotoneasters are many and varied, some forming substantial shrubs (see p 166). But by far the most useful for a small or medium-sized garden is *Cotoneaster horizontalis*. Its herring-bone arrangement of shoots and branches are covered with white star-like flowers, suffused with pink, followed in autumn by bright red berries and colourful foliage. The joy of this deciduous shrub is that it grows flat against its backing wall without any training or support, and will reach a height of up to 1.8 m (6 ft). It is easily raised

from seed which should be stratified (see p 345) and sown in spring.

Where the climate is kind and the garden is free of at least severe frost, *Feijoa (Acca) sellowiana* is an interesting and unusual ever-green. It is a native of Brazil. Among the dark grey-green foliage, the solitary myrtle-like flowers are borne on the current season's shoots in midsummer. They are red and white, with a central boss of crimson stamens. Height is up to 4.5 m (15 ft).

Those living in frost-free localities who have a warm, sheltered wall can plant a pomegranate, *Punica granatum*. This decidu-ous shrub has scarlet-red funnel-shaped flowers which are borne singly or in pairs at the ends of short shoots. They appear from early summer to early autumn. In good condi-tions it will reach 4.5 m (15 ft), but avoid chalk soils. There is also a double form, 'Flore Pleno'. See also page 325.

An aptly named group of excellent wall

Pyracantha rogersiana 'Flava'

shrubs are the firethorns (*Pyracantha* spp). These hardy evergreens have thorny branches, small dark green glossy leaves and white hawthorn-like flowers from late spring to early summer, followed in autumn by bril-liant orange, red or yellow berries. They are not fussy over soil or locality, but always plant pot-grown plants. They will easily reach 2.5 to 4.5 m (8 to 15 ft). Prune in spring by shorten-ing the longest side shoots; where space is at a premium more severe pruning will be needed, but this will reduce the crop of berries. *Pyracantha* 'Watereri' is more compact than most, but free-flowering and free-fruiting. *P. rogersiana* is similar but larger, while its form 'Flava' has bright yellow berries.

Yellow flowers
Abutilon megapotamicum is a charming ever-green shrub when its yellow flowers with red calyces hang down like Chinese lanterns from spring to late autumn. In early/*continued*

Shrubs for sheltered walls (continued)

spring, cut out any shoots that have been frosted and tie in new growths. The variety *A. megapotamicum* 'Variegatum' has prettily mottled golden-variegated foliage. When well grown, plants will reach 1.8 cm to 2.5 m (6 to 8 ft). A number of hybrids with white, yellow or red flowers are classified as *A.* × *hybridum*.

Although *Forsythia suspensa* is rather lax in habit it makes a useful deciduous wall or fence shrub, its golden-yellow flowers being freely produced in spring. To combat its tendency to sprawl, secondary shoots need to be cut back, after the flowers have faded, to within one or two buds of the old wood, tying in any new shoots where necessary. It may reach a height of up to 6 m (20 ft).

Even if everyone cannot enjoy Californian sunshine it is possible in many gardens to grow the semi-evergreen Californian shrub *Fremontodendron californicum* (*Fremontia californica*). Though not fully hardy, it grows satisfactorily against a warm, sheltered wall. It has curiously curled, waxy, golden-yellow sepals from late spring to midsummer, and grows up to 3 m (10 ft) high.

One of the best-loved wall shrubs with yellow flowers is the winter jasmine, *Jasminum nudiflorum*. It will thrive whatever the aspect – sunny or not – producing its bright yellow flowers on bare branches from early winter right through to early spring. In exposed positions, however, the flowers may be damaged by cold winds. It will grow up to 3 m (10 ft), but needs some support. When grown as a wall shrub, you can prune back long growths after flowering.

Kerria japonica, the Jew's mallow, is a bushy deciduous shrub that needs the protection of a wall in cold regions. It has bright green toothed leaves and yellow-orange spring flowers rather like those of wild roses. It reaches 1.8 m (6 ft) or more, and its green stems look effective in winter. There is a vigorous double form, 'Pleniflora', and a low-growing, more tender form called 'Variegata' that has white-edged leaves.

The New Zealand laburnum or kowhai, *Sophora tetraptera*, although evergreen in its

Abutilon × *hybridum* 'Canary Bird'

native home, is deciduous when grown in colder climates. It must have the protection of a warm, sunny wall. The golden-yellow tubular flowers are produced from late spring to early summer, and are followed by pea-shaped winged pods 5 to 20 cm (2 to 8 in) long. The leaves each consist of up to 40 leaflets. It will grow to 4.5 to 12 m (15 to 40 ft), depending on conditions.

Other wall shrubs

Caryopteris × *clandonensis* is a 0.6 to 1.25 m (2 to 4 ft) deciduous shrub that needs wall protection in cold areas. It combines aromatic grey-green foliage with bright blue tubular flowers that appear in late summer. Good forms include 'Arthur Simmonds', 'Heavenly Blue' and 'Kew Blue'.

The evergreen ceanothus make a glorious show with their varying shades of blue, generally from late spring to midsummer, but sometimes later. Where space is limited, plant *Ceanothus* × 'Burkwoodii', whose rich blue flowers are freely borne from summer through to autumn; it reaches 1.8 to 2.5 m (6 to 8 ft). *C. dentatus* is grey-blue and 1.8 m (6 ft) tall. The small bright blue flowers of *C. impressus* appear against small dark green leaves. Its height is 4.5 m (15 ft). Another more compact species is *C. rigidus*. Not fully hardy and needing a warm, sheltered wall, it has tightly packed clusters of purplish-blue flowers. It reaches 1.8 to 2.5 m (6 to 8 ft). *C. thyrsiflorus* has pale blue flowers and grows 3.5 to 4.5 m (12 to 15 ft) tall; it is hardier than the others. Where an even taller plant is wanted grow *C.* × 'Cascade'. Its bright clus-

Ceanothus impressus

ters of sea-blue flowers are borne on long stems in late spring, and it will reach as much as 6 m (20 ft).

An evergreen that will adorn your walls from early spring to late winter or early spring is the tassel bush, *Garrya elliptica*. Be sure to plant a male specimen as the 15 to 25 cm (6 to 10 in) greyish-green catkins are finer than the female ones. The foliage is a dull matt grey-green. Garryas will flourish in any soil and any position, reaching up to 3.5 m (12 ft). Always plant pot-grown specimens.

Laburnum is well known by many gardeners, but not the so-called evergreen laburnum, *Piptanthus laburnifolius*. In spite of its name it becomes deciduous in severe winters. Its leaves, which are composed of three leaflets, are enhanced in late spring and early summer by bright yellow, pea-shaped flowers in erect clusters 5 to 8 cm (2 to 3 in) long. It grows in all soils except chalk, but always plant pot-grown plants. It grows up to 2.5 to 3.5 m (8 to 12 ft) high.

Among other shrubs that do well treated as wall shrubs are forms of *Euonymus fortunei* (see p 143), certain ornamental rubus, such as *Rubus phoenicolasius* (the Japanese wineberry), and many camellias (see p 153). When growing camellias against a wall or fence select a site with westerly aspect, so that the early morning winter sun does not reach the plant until frost has gone off the foliage and flower buds. Train them on wires well away from the wall. This method is ideal for the many varieties of *Camellia japonica* and also of *C. sasanqua*, which can be espalier-trained (see p 375).

Woody plants for warm regions

The potential for gardeners in regions enjoying a Mediterranean climate – ranging from the Mediterranean basin itself to California and much of Australia and South Africa – is enormous. A huge variety of ornamental plants thrive in warm (as opposed to cold or tropical) climates, and this article can only be very selective. Some others, which can be grown in cooler regions if given special treatment, are described elsewhere in this book. Tender perennials will be found on page 222.

Tender climbers

The first thing one notices where frosts are unknown is the wealth of vines and other cover on walls, fences and pergolas. Perhaps the most popular and easily recognized are the bougainvilleas, whose brilliant-bracted flowers are produced in great cascades over many months. Most are varieties of the deciduous South American *Bougainvillea glabra* in colours ranging from purple to orange, red and rose. They will even scramble high into a tall tree if initially trained.

Streptosolen jamesonii is an evergreen from Colombia and climbs by means of twining stems. The clusters of tubular flowers are a brilliant orange. The South African *Plumbago capensis* is equally vigorous, but its gentle powder-blue flowers bring a piece of sky into the garden. It is a scandent evergreen shrub needing the support of a wall or pergola, and is very effective trained into the branches of a small tree. Both are sometimes trained as small standards with informal, if artificial, heads. The plumbago can also make an attractive low hedge. *Tecomaria capensis,* also evergreen, similarly serves several purposes, and its clusters of orange-scarlet tubular flowers positively glow with the warmth of its native South African sun.

Some of the most reliable and attractive of all vines for warm regions are the evergreen kennedias, especially *Kennedia comptoniana* and *K. ovata.* Both have clusters of pea-shaped flowers; they are violet-blue and white in the former and red in the latter. They may be trained over walls or on the

Bougainvillea glabra

ground where they soon make a dense cover.

Fragrance may be provided by several evergreen jasmines which twine their slender stems through latticework and over walls. *Jasminum polyanthum, J. azoricum* and *J. sambac* all have showers of white or pink-flushed flowers which fill the air with a delicious perfume.

Overpowering in its strength rather than its scent is the Argentinian bird-of-paradise plant, *Caesalpinia (Poinciana) gilliesii,* a strong-growing deciduous scrambling shrub with thorn-clad stems. If its vigour can be accommodated on a large wall or outhouse it

will amply reward its captor with large, handsome, fern-like leaves and numerous dense racemes of rich yellow flowers with long scarlet stamens. There is a slightly hardier relative, *C. japonica*, from Japan. Both are imposing if difficult to control.

Strong-growing, deciduous and also scandent are the Chilean *Solanum crispum* and *S. jasminoides* (see p 147), which grow much taller in warm climates than in cool regions. Another climbing species is *S. wendlandii*, whose prickle-clad stems enable it to climb into trees, from where its lilac-blue flowers hang in large conspicuous clusters./*continued*

Plumbago capensis

Solanum wendlandii

Woody plants for warm regions (continued)

S. rantonnetii is a shrub of elegant habit and the typical violet-blue, yellow-beaked flowers. It makes a handsome lawn specimen.

Finally, two evergreen vines with deeply divided leaves and loose clusters of yellow flowers are *Cassia obtusa* and *C. corymbosa*, the former with golden-yellow, the latter with lemon-yellow flowers. Both are excellent when trained against a wall or pergola.

Tender trees
The palm is the tree most associated with warm regions, and there can be no denying its bold and characteristic presence in the landscape. The variety available to gardeners in such regions is considerable, but small gardens are more restricted in choice, and apart from the Mediterranean native fan palm, *Chamaerops humilis*, the only other generally available is *Cycas revoluta*. Strictly, this is not a palm at all, but is a cycad more nearly related to the conifers; however, it is sufficiently palm-like in appearance to give the desired effect.

For larger gardens there are *Phoenix canariensis* and *Jubaea chilensis*, both stout-stemmed and bearing impressive heads of enormous feather-like leaves. Of the fan-leaved palms, *Livistona australis* and *Sabal palmetto* are popular and effective, whilst the Chusan palm, *Trachycarpus fortunei* (*Chamaerops excelsa*) is both impressive and hardy as far north as the British Isles. *Erythea armata* resembles a short-stemmed trachycarpus, but the leaves are a striking silvery-blue and are carried on viciously-spined stalks.

Rattling its pods in the slightest breeze, *Brachychiton acerifolium*, the flame tree of Australia, is the perfect deciduous tree to bring the often rare element of sound into the garden. Added to this are the small, brilliant scarlet bell-flowers which cluster the naked

Chamaerops humilis

Nerium oleander

branches before the maple-like leaves appear. The evergreen gum trees (*Eucalyptus* spp) also produce sound from the shaking of their large, often scimitar-shaped leaves. There are so many of these Australian trees suitable for gardens that there is only room to mention two examples. The first is *Eucalyptus globulus*, the blue gum, which eventually attains a very large size (see p 136). Its trunk has piebald flaking bark, and its flowers are white. Very different is the red gum, *E. ficifolia*, which makes a smaller tree with green leaves and large clusters of spectacular scarlet or crimson flowers. If you cannot accommodate a large tree, try hard pruning to near ground level every two to three years, to produce an abundance of sucker shoots.

One of the most brilliant small flowering trees for gardens in warm regions is *Spathodea campanulata*, the African tulip tree. Its large evergreen leaves are handsome enough, but the large terminal clusters of goblet-shaped flowers assail one with their flamboyance, being a rich coral-red edged with gold. The jacaranda, *Jacaranda mimosifolia*, is another tree guaranteed to cause instant admiration when its violet-blue funnel-shaped flowers appear in large clusters, afterwards falling to form a colourful pool over the ground. The deciduous leaves, too, are beautifully divided like a filigree fern, and turn gold in autumn.

Few who have visited the Mediterranean region in winter are likely to forget the wonderful displays created by the mimosas – *Acacia dealbata* and *A. decurrens*. Here these evergreens flood valleys and gild hillsides, as in the wild in their native Australia, with their rich yellow flower clusters, filling the air around with a delicious perfume. There are many others suitable for gardens, including the silver-leaved *A. baileyana* and *A. podalyriifolia*. All are best planted when

small, preferably from pots or containers.

Perhaps one of the best answers to a weeping willow in warm regions is *Schinus molle* – the pepper tree of South America. It is excellent for light shade beneath which to sit, and its elegant drooping branches form an ever-moving curtain of evergreen, daintily divided leaves. Female trees, when pollinated, bear cheerful coral-red fruits.

Tender shrubs
When it comes to choosing shrubs suitable for warm regions, the choice is immense and only a small selection can be described here. The

Cycas revoluta

oleander, *Nerium oleander*, is an easily grown and rewarding evergreen subject equally at home in containers as in the ground, and tops each leafy stem with a voluptuous cluster of single or double rose, pink, white or buff flowers. *Lagerstroemia indica* – the crape myrtle – is another shrub with richly coloured pink or mauve flowers whose crimpled petals add to its attraction, as does the white bark of mature specimens. It is deciduous.

For speed of growth, *Abutilon vitifolium*

some of the most useful and exotic shrubs for warm regions. Most members of the protea family have handsome foliage and their flowers may be cut for use indoors.

Although the evergreen lantanas have the reputation of being a nuisance in situations where they thrive, there is no doubting their value when carefully used, and few shrubs are more dependable or free-flowering. *Lantana camara*, with orange, yellow, white or lilac flowers, makes an attractive and effective low

evergreen sword-shaped leaves which bring a bold, almost aggressive element to the garden. Some of the hardier species are used in colder climates to create a subtropical effect, but it is in the warmer regions that the yuccas are seen at their best. Three of the best species are *Yucca glauca* for its stemless clumps of narrow blue-grey rapiers, *Y. gloriosa* for its bold piles of grey, spine-tipped swords, and the tree-like *Y. guatemalensis* (*Y. elephantipes*) for its exotic heads of loose green straps.

Acacia sp

Leucospermum conocarpodendron

Lantana camara

has few rivals among deciduous shrubs. Its grey-green woolly stems and vine-shaped leaves are admirable foil for the large, open, lavender or white flowers, which are produced over a long period. Then there are the several forms of *A. × hybridum* with large, nodding bell-shaped flowers of yellow, red or white.

Although buddleias are popular flowering shrubs in colder areas, there are several choice species that are seen at their best only in warm regions. These include the sweetly scented *Buddleia asiatica* and the popular *B. madagascariensis*. Both are large evergreens with long panicles of flowers of white and yellow respectively. They are best trained against a wall or fence, as are the evergreen bottlebrushes (*Callistemon* spp) of Australia. Their long slender stems are clothed with narrow leaves and bear dense cylindrical clusters of red or yellow flowers whose long colourful stamens are the chief attraction.

South Africa is a well-known fund of unusual and exotic shrubs, and none more so than the evergreen proteas and their relatives. All have densely packed heads of tubular flowers surrounded by colourful bracts. They are easy to grow in warm regions and demand no more than full sun and a well-drained soil of an acid nature. Some of the most satisfactory species include *Protea aristata, P. barbigera, P. compacta, P. cynaroides, P. longiflora, P. nerifolia* and *P. repens*. The leucadendrons are closely related and rather similar in effect, and include the evergreen silver tree, *Leucadendron argenteum*, whose silvery foliage and sweetly scented, star-like, male flower heads are startling to behold. Varying in habit from prostrate to large shrubs of 3 m (10 ft), the leucospermums mainly differ from the proteas in the absence of bracts around the flower-heads. This in no way detracts from their effect and the many species provide

hedge, whilst the prostrate *L. sellowiana*, with its rosy-lilac, yellow-eyed flowers, is useful for planting on steep banks or wall-tops.

A favourite evergreen shrub for warm regions is *Datura suaveolens*, the angel's trumpet from Mexico. The large, pendent, trumpet-shaped flowers are white and deliciously fragrant, especially at night. It attains a large size but responds favourably to pruning if necessary. Other equally exotic species include *D. cornigera* and its double form 'Knightii' (both white), *D. chlorantha* (yellow), *D. sanguinea* (orange-red), and *D. versicolor* (peach-pink).

Fragrance in the garden is especially desirable in the early evening when dinners on the patio are made more memorable by the presence of such flowers. A favourite at such times is *Cestrum nocturnum*, a comparatively small evergreen shrub of loose habit with showers of small, tubular, cream-coloured, sweetly-scented flowers. *C. parqui* is another of similar growth with fragrant yellow flowers.

The yuccas are woody-based plants with

Hibiscus rosa-sinensis

All have handsome erect panicles of ivory-white flowers.

Purple is an uncommon flower colour in most gardens, and when this is accompanied by bold foliage it is a combination not to be ignored. *Eupatorium atrorubens* is such a shrub from Mexico, developing into a large mound of rounded, flannel-like evergreen leaves topped by the large flattened flower-heads. *E. ianthinum* (*E. sordidum*) is similar in effect but lower-growing and with lilac flowers. Coming from a woodland habitat, both prefer a little shade and shelter from the hot sun.

Large leaves are also the trademark of *Sparmannia africana*, a popular houseplant in northern countries. It is certainly tolerant of adverse conditions and makes a striking large shrub in warm regions, with its downy, maple-shaped evergreen leaves and large clusters of white, yellow-stamened flowers.

Erythrina crista-galli, the deciduous coral tree from Brazil, produces large terminal racemes of large, waxy, deep scarlet pea-flowers on stiffly arching stems. It loves the sun and is best planted where its sparsely leafy shoots may surge through lower vegetation. There are also several exotic African species, of which the dwarf kaffirbloom, *E. humeana*, is the most satisfactory.

To a northern gardener, few shrubs conjure up visions of warm regions more than the hibiscus. Evergreens, the most commonly grown species in such areas is *Hibiscus rosa-sinensis*, with its large scarlet, trumpet-shaped flowers, from the centre of which thrusts a long tongue of yellow-anthered stamens. There are several other colour forms including yellow and pink. Left alone it develops into a large shrub of over 4 m (13 ft), but it may be controlled by pruning, and makes a delightful, if vigorous, informal hedge.

The taller hardy perennials

Wherever its ultimate placement, the height of a plant is of paramount importance. When planning mixed borders it is best to select the tallest plants first, then those for the front row and finally the plants needed for central situations; there are many more of the last than of the others. All the plants described in this article grow to 1.25 m (4 ft) or more, and are among the most important in the garden, whether placed at the back of a one-sided border, in a midway position in an island bed, as a solitary container specimen or as an accent plant in a key position.

It is also imperative to know the colour of the flowers when selecting. In mixed borders these can be varied and balanced, although strong shades of cerise, scarlet and orange, for example, are best separated by plants with pastel flowers or silver foliage. Similarly with one-colour beds, spread the various tints along the border, or else gradate them evenly.

Unless otherwise stated, all perennials mentioned here can be propagated from seed (especially the species), by division or by soft cuttings rooted under glass (see p 346).

White and green flowers

These have a cool look in summer, and show up well in twilight, so they are especially popular in tropical and warm temperate climates. Few bloom in spring, an exception being *Eremurus himalaicus*, the foxtail lily, which has fleshy, octopus-like roots. These need planting about 15 cm (6 in) deep, packed around with sand, in a position with good drainage and full sun. It has lax, ground-hugging, strap-shaped leaves and tall spikes of starry white flowers.

In an open situation a single plant of the giant seakale, *Crambe cordifolia*, makes an impressive display in midsummer, with large grey-green leaves and huge branching sprays – up to 1.8 m (6 ft) across – of four-petalled flowers. *Veratrum viride* has green, and *V. album* white, flower trusses containing myriads of small blooms, and pleated leaves. In late summer the bugbanes (*Cimicifuga* spp) bear white or cream bottlebrush flowers on branching stems. All have deeply divided pungent leaves, and the common name refers to their property of repelling insects. *Cimicifuga dahurica*, *C. simplex* and the 2 m (7 ft) *C. racemosa* are the showiest; all should be planted in moist soil.

Artemisia lactiflora, the white mugwort, is a useful late-summer perennial for a damp situation, and there are also white varieties of hollyhocks, delphiniums, foxgloves and tall Michaelmas daisies in this range.

Lilac, blue and mauve flowers

Important summer bloomers of tall stature include the noble delphiniums, which delight in deep, rich, moist soils with some lime, and full sun. The large-flowered hybrids, derived in part from *Delphinium elatum* and known as the Elatum group, come in all shades of blue, from pale to navy, on 1.25 to 2.5 m (4 to 8 ft) stems. Many have white or black 'bee' centres or eyes, and there are also white, pink and near-red flowers, either single or double, with

Veratrum viride

a contrasting eye. The Pacific Hybrids are another reliable race that are mainly seed-grown, in shades of blue, lilac, pink and white. All delphiniums require early staking and protection from slugs.

Monkshoods (*Aconitum* spp) grow in sun or light shade, but the ground must be moist. They have helmet-shaped flowers and glossy leaves shaped like those of the buttercup. Recommended kinds are mostly of hybrid origin like *Aconitum carmichaelii wilsonii*, 'Barker's Variety' and 'Kelmscott' – all 1.8 m (6 ft) tall and deep blue. *A. napellus* grows to 1.5 m (5 ft) and has a white form, 'Album', and another with violet and white flowers called 'Bicolor'.

Campanula latifolia, the great bellflower,

Delphinium 'Vespers'; 'Blue Nile'; 'Lord Butler'

with rough lanceolate leaves and large pendent bluish-purple flowers, grows to 1.5 m (5 ft) and likes semi-shade, but its more garden-worthy cultivars with violet, purple or pale blue flowers are usually shorter. The chimney bellflower, *C. pyramidalis*, makes a splendid container specimen, with rosettes of rather small leaves from which rise spikes of sky-blue flowers; there is also a white form. Given deep, rich soil, it grows up to 1.8 m (6 ft) tall. It is best treated as a biennial, or propagated annually from the non-flowering side shoots that appear close to the ground.

The meadow rue, *Thalictrum delavayi* (the *T. dipterocarpum* of gardens, but not of botanists, since another species claims that name) has fine branching stems spangled with tiny lilac, golden-stamened flowers; its double mauve cultivar 'Hewitt's Double' is particularly fine. There are also many tall Michaelmas daisies of the *Aster novi-belgii* group that are invaluable in late summer, but being top-heavy may need staking. They have single or double flowers in all shades of blue, from light to deep purple. The many-petalled *A. novae-angliae* flowers are usually rosy-purple, although there is a fine rose-pink cultivar called 'Harrington's Pink'. *Boltonia asteroides*, with mauve, purple or occasionally white Michaelmas-daisy-like flowers, grows 1.5 to 1.8 m (5 to 6 ft) tall and does well in rough places – such as wild gardens or between shrubs. Such a situation also suits the giant lettuce, *Lactuca bourgaei*, a plant with rough leaves and 1.5 to 1.8 m (5 to 6 ft) panicles of soft blue florets.

Globe thistles (*Echinops* spp) are good back-of-the-border perennials. They have branching stems terminating in round, prickly flower heads that look like drumsticks. The grey-green divided leaves are commonly white-felted beneath. *Echinops ritro* has steel-blue flowers, but the more richly coloured cultivar 'Veitch's Blue' and the vigorous 'Taplow Blue' are better garden plants.

Pink and red flowers

Hollyhocks, *Alcea* (or *Althaea*) *rosea*, are noble perennials that are best grown as annuals, since this lessens the risk of contracting a disfiguring rust disease (see p 367) on the foliage. There are single and double sorts – both easily raised from seed – with variously coloured rosettes of flowers on lofty 1.8 to 2.8 m (6 to 9 ft) spikes. The red and pink kinds are most popular, but whites and yellows are also available. *Filipendula rubra* (*Spiraea palmata*) is a giant moisture-loving meadowsweet, 1.8 to 2.5 m (6 to 8 ft) tall, with deeply cut leaves and fluffy plumes of pinkish-purple flowers – or strawberry-pink in the variety 'Venusta'.

Eupatorium purpureum, the Joe Pye weed, is a moisture-lover with its leaves arranged in whorls and heads of fluffy, purplish flowers on 1.8 to 2.5 m (6 to 8 ft) stems. It blooms in late summer, as does the giant mallow, *Malva alcea*. This carries cup-shaped, hollyhock-like, rich rose flowers on 1.25 m (4 ft) stems. Another late bloomer is *Phygelius capensis*, the Cape figwort, a shrubby plant which frost

Phormium tenax 'Atropurpureum'

Rheum palmatum 'Atrosanguineum'

Fritillaria imperialis

cuts to ground level in winter but which later sprouts 1 to 1.5 m (3 to 5 ft) wand-like stems carrying small oval leaves and tubular scarlet flowers. Planted 60 cm (2 ft) apart, it makes a splendid wall plant.

Macleaya (*Bocconia*) *microcarpa*, the plume poppy, has a running rootstock, so it has to be kept in bounds – although a quick jab with a hoe soon eliminates unwanted shoots. It grows to 2 m (7 ft), and has beautiful grey-green leaves that are silvery beneath. The branching stems carry many tiny buff-pink flowers; the variety 'Coral Plume' is more pinkish and *M. cordata* creamy. They are suitable for sun or light shade.

Among climbing perennials are three species of sweet peas. *Lathyrus grandiflorus* has fuchsia-pink and red flowers, usually two to a stem, as large as those of annual sweet peas (see p 212); it makes a good 1.5 m (5 ft) 'hedge' when trained over trellis or peasticks. *L. latifolius*, given support, goes even higher – to 3 m (10 ft). It has more but smaller rosy flowers on each stem, and boasts a white vari-

ety called 'White Pearl'. *L. rotundifolius* is rose-pink and 1.8 m (6 ft) tall.

Rheums are related to culinary rhubarb and, like crambes, can be used as specimen plants in beds by themselves as well as at the back of the border. *Rheum palmatum* 'Atrosanguineum' is one of the best, with huge, deeply cut leaves that are vivid red until the plant flowers, and then turn green. The branching heads of deep red flowers are borne on 1.8 m (6 ft) stems.

There are also pink and red Michaelmas daisies, and a few tall red hot pokers like *Kniphofia praecox* (*K.* 'Nobilis' of gardens) and the 1.5 m (5 ft) scarlet and gold *K. uvaria*.

Yellow, gold and bronze flowers

Since spring is too early for tall herbaceous perennials to make sufficient height for flowering, the bulbous crown imperial, *Fritillaria imperialis*, is commonly used in spring borders. It grows 1 to 1.25 m (3 to 4 ft) tall, with leafy stems each carrying a whorl of large pendent orange (or yellow in the variety

'Lutea'), bell-shaped flowers. Above these, the stem terminates in a tuft of leaves reminiscent of a pineapple-top. The bulbs should be planted 15 to 20 cm (6 to 8 in) deep in late summer, in sun or light shade.

The 1.5 m (5 ft) *Eremurus stenophyllus* has soft yellow flowers in late spring, and there are a number of garden hybrids such as 'Shelford Hybrids' and 'Highdown Hybrids' with orange, buff and apricot as well as pink and white flowers. These are of varying heights, but can be planted well forward, as they die down before most border perennials develop to flowering size.

The tall yellow mulleins (*Verbascum* spp) are good background plants for mid- to late summer, as are *Achillea filipendulina* 'Gold Plate' and 'Parker's Variety', similar cultivars with aromatic leaves and flat heads of yellow flowers – which can be dried for winter arrangements. *Helianthus salicifolius*, a perennial sunflower, is yellow; and there are two showy rudbeckias, *Rudbeckia laciniata* and *R. nitida* 'Herbstsonne', the latter a 1.8 m (6 ft) cultivar whose large yellow flowers have backward-hanging 'petals' (after the manner of a cyclamen flower) and green thimble-like protruding central cones.

Other tall yellows include *Centaurea macrocephala*, which has very leafy stems and large thistle-like flowers protected by hairy brown scales; yellow hollyhocks; *Cephalaria gigantea*, a giant scabious with soft yellow blooms; and the moisture-loving ligularias, particularly *Ligularia stenocephala* 'The Rocket', a fine-foliaged plant with black-stemmed spikes of bright gold, ragged-petalled flowers, and *L. dentata* (*Senecio clivorum*) 'Desdemona', which has large, round, purplish leaves and deep orange daisy-like flowers.

Tall perennials for specimen planting

A plant impressive enough to stand alone has many uses, as shown on page 108. In key situations it should be afforded plenty of room and light (unless it is shade-loving), and the soil should be regularly mulched to keep up the quality of flower and foliage. Sometimes leaves are more important than flowers, witness *Phormium tenax* (New Zealand flax) and its variegated and purple-leaf forms; *Ferula communis* (commonly known as the giant fennel, though not related to the true fennel); and *Euphorbia characias wulfenii*, a handsome spring bloomer with narrow, dark green leaves clothing 1.25 m (4 ft) stems and terminating in heavy heads of yellowish-green flowers. The latter then die but are regularly replaced by new basal shoots.

Among the flowering plants, rheums, verbascums, crambe and hollyhocks (already mentioned) can be used as specimens. So can the cardoon, *Cynara cardunculus*, which has large, deeply cut silvery leaves and stout 1.8 to 2.5 m (6 to 8 ft) branching stems. These carry large mauve, thistle-like flowers – much visited by bees – backed by spiny, silvery calyces. The shrubby *Lavatera olbia*, a tree mallow growing 1.5 to 1.8 m (5 to 6 ft) high and as much across, is spangled all summer with rich rose hollyhock flowers.

The 'midway' hardy perennials

Herbaceous perennials that reach a height of about 0.3 to 1.25 m (1 to 4 ft) are the 'backbone' of borders. They are the important middle-of-the-road plants that provide substance and colour, their general effect highlighted by a framework of background and frontal plants. Nevertheless, to provide strong impact they must be grouped, for very few are sufficiently dramatic to stand alone.

White and green flowers

There are few white-flowered sorts for spring, apart from several that do best in deep moist soil and semi-shade. These include the toothwort, *Cardamine heptaphylla* (*Dentaria pinnata*), which grows about 40 cm (15 in) tall, with short-stalked, jagged leaves arranged in whorls of three, and spikes of four-petalled flowers. Another, *Ranunculus aconitifolius* 'Flore Pleno', a double buttercup commonly known as fair maids of France, has 45 cm (18 in) branching sprays of small white rosettes and glossy, deep green leaves. Drought is fatal, so keep the roots always moist.

The false spikenard, *Smilacina racemosa*, and Solomon's seal, *Polygonatum multiflorum* (*P. × hybridum*), are somewhat similar, both growing about 90 cm (3 ft) tall, with white and green flowers (tubular in the latter, fluffy in the former) on leafy stems. Both require light shade, humus-type soil and planting 30 cm (1 ft) apart. *Actaea alba*, the white baneberry (whose berries are poisonous), likes cool moist soil and grows 60 cm (2 ft) tall with buttercup-like leaves. Its fluffy white flower heads are succeeded by white berries on scarlet stalks. The similar *A. rubra* has scarlet berries.

Later come paeonies: first the unpleasant-smelling European *Paeonia officinalis* 'Alba', with large double flower heads like giant snowballs; then the deliciously fragrant Chinese paeonies derived from *P. lactiflora*. These have large, showy single or double flowers of white, pink, red or vermilion atop 90 cm (3 ft) mounds of deeply cut leaves. Good white forms include the doubles 'La Lorraine' and 'Cheddar Cheese', the latter an American variety with ruffled petals speckled with yellow, and *P. obovata* 'Alba', a superb single white. Dependable and trouble-free, paeonies can remain in borders for many years, requiring only an occasional mulch.

The false goat's beard, *Aruncus dioicus* (*A. sylvester*), can grow 1.5 to 1.8 m (5 to 6 ft) tall, with large and heavy plumes of creamy, honey-scented flowers and deeply cut foliage. This is a plant that can be used alone if required. The white burning bush, *Dictamnus albus*, and its purple counterpart, *D. albus* 'Purpureus', have lobed leaves and 60 to 90 cm (2 to 3 ft) flower spikes. All parts of the plants are pungently aromatic when touched; the oil given off is inflammable – hence the common name (shared with the annual *Kochia scoparia*; see p 221).

Asphodelus albus and *A. microcarpus* are the Greek asphodels, only suitable for dry, poor soils. They then produce handsome, stiffly strap-shaped leaves and 90 cm (3 ft) tough branching flower spikes bearing white

funnel-shaped flowers with a purple stripe running down each petal segment. *Anthericum liliago*, the St Bernard's lily, has lax grassy leaves and several white lily-like flowers on 45 cm (18 in) stems. It grows best in light, rich soil and once established should be left undisturbed.

Gypsophila paniculata, or baby's breath, is a useful plant to establish near *Papaver orientale* (the oriental poppy), pulmonarias and other plants untidy after flowering; its froth of tiny flowers provide just what is needed to mask bare soil and dead leaves. The more arresting variety 'Bristol Fairy', a double white, is usually grafted on the rootstock of the species. Full sun and sharp drainage is essential; they like lime.

Two late summer bloomers are the 60 to 90 cm (2 to 3 ft) creamy red-hot poker *Kniphofia* 'Maid of Orleans', and a bulbous plant with long narrow leaves and 60 to 90 cm (2 to 3 ft) spikes of pendent white bells called *Galtonia candicans*, or summer hyacinth.

Tree-poppies like the 90 cm (3 ft) *Romneya trichocalyx* and the 1.25 to 1.5 m (4 to 5 ft) *R. coulteri* are plants for full sun and well-drained soil. They produce silvery, somewhat leathery leaves and huge poppy-like flowers up to 15 cm (6 in) across. These are bowl-shaped, with crinkly white petals, the inner cups filled with long golden stamens. Once established they should be left alone; transplanting almost invariably kills, so propagate from seed sown in small pots and plant the

Phlox paniculata 'White Admiral'

Aruncus dioicus (*A. sylvester*)

seedlings out without root disturbance. Or separate any suckers. The plants remain attractive from midsummer to early autumn.

Good white astilbes for moist situations include *Astilbe* 'Bridal Veil' ('Brautschleier'), 75 cm (2½ ft), and 'Professor van der Wielen', 1.25 m (4 ft). There are also several white cultivars of *Phlox paniculata*, such as 'White Admiral' and 'Mount Fujiyama', both 75 cm (2½ ft); although mauve-flowered, 'Harlequin' has such heavy cream variegations on the foliage as to appear white. Phlox rarely need staking but must have moist soil. Dead stems and leaves are an indication of eelworm damage, so propagate only from root cuttings that do not harbour these pests.

Additionally, there are white irises (including Sibiricas as well as rhizomatous kinds; see p 196), white poppies and foxgloves, a white *Centranthus ruber* (see p 181), white autumn anemones (*Anemone huphensis japonica*), and white Korean and Rubellum chrysanthemums like 'Bridal Veil' and the dependable cultivars of *Chrysanthemum maximum* such as 'Esther Read' and 'Wirral Supreme', which are good for cutting.

Many hostas have white or almost white flowers, notably *Hosta plantaginea, H.* 'Royal Standard' and *H. sieboldiana*. There are also several with white leaf borders or variegations (although lilac-flowered): *H. crispula, H. albomarginata, H. fortunei* 'Marginato-Alba' and a cultivar called 'Thomas Hogg'. There is also a white *Achillea ptarmica* called 'Perry's

pale azure to lilac, mauve, rich blue and violet. *Phlox paniculata* and Michaelmas daisies are particularly useful, as they flower late in the season and associate pleasantly in mixed borders with pink chrysanthemums and red-hot pokers. One can even devote a whole bed to Michaelmas daisies – *Aster amellus* as well as the *A. novi-belgii* and *A. novae-angliae* sorts – since they come in various heights from 20 cm to 1.5 m (8 in to 5 ft), as well as in a range of colours.

Bearded irises (see p 196) are unexcelled in early summer, but have a short flowering season, so some gardeners interplant them with gladioli (p 195) or tigridias (p 205), which have similar foliage. To maintain free flowering properties, iris rhizomes should be lifted

uncertain origin known as 'Johnson's Blue'.

Some *Delphinium* Elatum cultivars also come into this height range, as do the 1 m (3 ft) Belladonna cultivars like 'Blue Bees' (Cambridge-blue), 'Lamartine' (purplish-blue) and 'Wendy' (cobalt-blue). Mauve erigerons (*Erigeron speciosus* varieties) are good for cutting, and produce their daisy flowers spasmodically after the first spring flush through to autumn. *Scabiosa caucasica* is a favourite cut flower with round pincushion-like flower heads of lavender-blue in 'Clive Greaves' but almost indigo in 'Moerheim Blue'. Plant scabious in spring (they often die off following autumn planting) in well-drained soil containing chalk, in full sun.

For partial shade there is no more beautiful

Sisyrinchium striatum

Scabiosa caucasica 'Clive Greaves'

Meconopsis betonicifolia

White' and a white non-seeding form of the willowherb, *Epilobium* (*Chamaenerion*) *angustifolium* 'Album', which blooms for weeks. *Gaura lindheimeri* has rosy-white, very slender spikes 1 to 1.25 m (3 to 4 ft) high. *Libertia grandiflora* needs shelter and sun, and then produces 30 to 60 cm (1 to 2 ft) spikes of small white flowers and evergreen grassy leaves, and *Sisyrinchium striatum* has iris-like foliage and small, yellowish-white, tightly packed flowers on 60 cm (2 ft) spikes.

Blue, mauve and purple flowers

Some of the most important plants in these colours are found among the bearded irises, phlox and Michaelmas daisies – all of which have cultivars in a miscellany of shades from

and divided every third or fourth year. Summer is also campanula time, starting with the clustered heads of the violet-purple *Campanula glomerata*, which grows 30 to 60 cm (1 to 2 ft) high and needs grouping at 60 cm (2 ft) spacing for maximum effect, and then the taller *C. lactiflora*, one of the finest, with great branching heads of lilac-blue flowers on 1.25 m (4 ft) stems.

Anchusas (principally *Anchusa azurea* and its varieties) are unreliable perennials that need frequent renewal from root cuttings. Their rough stems and leaves and 1.25 m (4 ft) inflorescences of rich blue associate well with the violet-blue cranesbills, such as *Geranium meeboldii* (*G. grandiflorum*), with open, saucer-like flowers, or a rich blue hybrid of

plant than the Himalayan blue poppy, *Meconopsis betonicifolia*. The crimped, taffeta-like, sky-blue flowers, each 5 cm (2 in) across, are set off by central bosses of golden stamens. They grow 0.6 to 1.25 m (2 to 4 ft) high and need damp, rich but light soil. They are unreliable perennials (lasting one year or ten), but are easily replaced from fresh seed. Two other worthwhile species are *M. grandis* and *M. quintuplinervia*. *Mertensia virginica*, the Virginian cowslip, also needs partial shade. It is a beautiful plant with soft, blue-green lanceolate leaves and 60 cm (2 ft) stems weighted down by large, vivid blue flowers like those of forget-me-nots.

Camassias are liliaceous plants commonly planted in mixed borders, but also/*continued*

The 'midway' hardy perennials (continued)

naturalized in damp meadows. *Camassia leichtlinii*, a variable species, has blue flowers on 75 cm (2½ ft) stems in early summer. Given full sun, *Baptisia australis*, the false indigo, grows well in most soils. It has a very compact habit, the stiffly erect 1 to 1.25 m (3 to 4 ft) stems carrying many indigo-blue flowers similar to those of lupins.

An old-fashioned perennial widely grown in Tudor times for its fragrant flowers is the sweet rocket, or damask violet, *Hesperis matronalis*. It blooms in early summer with 60 to 90 cm (2 to 3 ft) spikes of violet, mauve or purple flowers, which resemble those of honesty (*Lunaria annua*). Double forms exist but are rare in cultivation. Frequent renewal from seed is necessary, because the plant is a rather poor perennial.

Clematis are generally considered climbers, but there are a few erect border perennial species that do well in well-drained soil, particulary in chalk. The stems of these die down and disappear in winter. They are of bushy

Many salvias are blue, and at least two are suitable for individual planting – namely *Salvia sclarea*, the herb clary, a 90 cm (3 ft) biennial with hairy stems, large heart-shaped leaves and huge panicles of bluish-white flowers, and *S. pratensis haematodes,* a broad-spreading plant 90 cm (3 ft) tall with corrugated leaves and rich lavender-blue flowers on wide branches. *S. farinacea* is a slender sage, 90 cm (3 ft) high, with deep blue, lavender-like flowers; *S. nemorosa* 'Superba' (sometimes listed as *S.* × *superba* or *S. virgata nemorosa*), a popular bushy perennial of 60 to 90 cm (2 to 3 ft), has many spikes of violet-blue; and the rather tender *S. patens* is deep pure blue on 45 cm (18 in) stems. To ensure holding this plant over winter, either lift some roots and keep them in a frame, or else maintain stock by means of late summer cuttings kept until spring in a greenhouse.

Eryngiums, or sea hollies, are suitable for most gardens; their prickly seed-heads are also useful for drying. *Eryngium* × *oliverianum* and *E.* × *zabelii* are two of the best, with large metallic-blue flowers on 60 cm (2 ft) stems. *E. giganteum,* a beautiful silvery-blue, is a biennial but is commonly used in borders, since self-set seedlings make propagation unnecessary. Agapanthus, with large umbels of pale to deep blue flowers, make good tub subjects as well as border plants, especially the hardier *Agapanthus* 'Headbourne Hybrids'. These are hardy down

Pink, red and crimson flowers

Among the 'hottest' colours in this section are the brilliant reds of *Phlox paniculata* – brighter than most other perennials in the height of midsummer. Particularly recommended are 'Starfire' (rich scarlet), 'Vintage Wine' (purple-red) and 'Pastorale' (rich pink with purple eyes) – all about 75 cm (2½ ft) tall and all requiring full sun and moist soil.

Papaver orientale 'Marcus Perry' is the best of the perennial poppies, with huge, brilliant scarlet, bowl-shaped, stamen-filled flowers on sturdy stems that do not require staking. There is a softer pink variety, 'Sultana', and a rich rose-pink called 'Mrs Perry'. All are 75 cm (2½ ft) tall. *Lobelia fulgens* has scarlet flowers and crimson stems and leaves; to safeguard the stock in cold wet winters, a few roots should be overwintered in frames. Cultivars include 'Queen Victoria' (scarlet), 'Will Scarlet' (bright red) and 'Cherry Ripe' (cerise-red); all of them are 75 to 90 cm (2½ to 3 ft) tall.

Salvia nemorosa 'Superba' (S. × superba)

Platycodon grandiflorum

Liatris spicata

habit, although they topple in wind and so are best staked. *Clematis heracleifolia* has purplish-blue tubular flowers; *C. integrifolia* is indigo-blue, but its hybrid *C.* × *durandii* has very large violet flowers and is the best member of this group.

Centaureas, or knapweeds, have thistle-like flowers and deeply cut and lobed leaves. They are suitable for sun or shade but, because of a tendency to spread, should not be given rich soil. *Centaurea dealbata* has rosy-purple flowers on 60 cm (2 ft) stems; they are intensified to cyclamen-purple in the hybrid 'Steenbergii'. *C. montana* is variable, but mostly deep blue with reddish centres, and the 30 cm (12 in) *C. stricta* is clear blue with mauve centres.

to about −10°C (14°F) but will survive −15°C (5°F) if the roots are protected with a deep layer of leaves or straw.

Among other blue-flowered middle-of-the-border perennials are *Galega officinalis*, with lilac, vetch-like flowers on 1 m (3 ft) stems; the herbaceous veronicas (*Veronica* spp), which have 30 to 90 cm (1 to 3 ft) spikes of small blue florets; *Tradescantia* × *andersoniana* hybrids, with three-petalled flowers of mauve and blue (also white) and grassy leaves; blue lupins; the 60 cm (2 ft) *Platycodon grandiflorum* 'Mariesii', with inflated campanula-like flowers; *Nepeta* (*Dracocephalum*) *sibirica*, a tall (1 m; 3 ft) catmint; and *Cynoglossum nervosum,* which is like a large forget-me-not.

Several red-hot pokers, such as *Kniphofia* 'Red Start' and 'Bressingham Torch', gleam like tongues of flame in quiet borders, whilst in late summer the scarlet tubular flowers and narrow silvery leaves of the 30 cm (12 in) Californian fuchsia, *Zauschneria californica*, bring cheerful colour to the border until frost ends its blooming.

For summer borders there are pink and red paeonies (both *Paeonia officinalis* and *P. lactiflora* kinds) and bearded irises; also the scarlet nettle-like *Monarda didyma*, a fragrant-leaved plant of 90 cm (3 ft) that needs sun and constant root moisture. Varieties with pink flowers, such as 'Croftway Pink' and the salmon-red 'Prairie Glow', are also available.

Earlier still, pink and red lupins (*Lupinus*

THE 'MIDWAY' HARDY PERENNIALS **181**

varieties, particularly the Russell strain) bring gay splashes of colour to herbaceous borders, although spent flowers should be removed to prevent seeding, which weakens the plants. In early summer the bleeding heart, *Dicentra spectabilis*, has 0.6 to 1.25 m (2 to 4 ft) arching stems hung with rosy-red and white 'locket' flowers and deeply cut leaves. Give this plant rich, moist soil in sun or light shade, but protect the succulent young shoots from slugs.

Alstroemerias, or Peruvian lilies, are brilliant mid-season perennials, with clustered heads of tubular, lily-like flowers. They are orange in *Alstroemeria aurantiaca* (the hardiest) but pink, salmon or rose in the beautiful hybrids derived from *A. ligtu*. The usual height is 1 to 1.25 m (3 to 4 ft). Sharp drainage

Lobelia fulgens 'Red Flame'

cranesbill with black basal petal spots, looks best planted away from scarlets and oranges. *Liatris spicata* and *L. callilepis*, the Kansas gayfeather, have many fuchsia-cerise flowers – like small shaving brushes – atop 60 cm (2 ft) leafy stems.

Sidalceas resemble small hollyhocks with satiny-pink flowers in midsummer. They grow 45 cm (18 in) tall in most soils and situations. *Sidalcea* 'Loveliness' (shell pink) and 'Rose Queen' (rosy-red) are good cultivars. *Dierama pulcherrimum*, or wand flower, has grassy evergreen leaves and wiry 1 to 1.5 m (3 to 5 ft) stems that bend like fishing rods under the weight of tubular, pale pink to deep rose or red flowers. There are also rose and red valerians, *Centranthus ruber*, on 60 cm (2 ft) stems, good for dry banks; pink and purple foxgloves, *Digitalis purpurea*; pinkish columbines (*Aquilegia* hybrids); and the 60 cm (2 ft) *Sedum telephium maximum* 'Atropurpureum', which has insignificant flowers but fleshy leaves that start green, then develop to rich crimson.

Saponaria officinalis, the common soapwort, or bouncing Bet, is a rampageous subject for odd corners; its pink or rose double flowers on 75 cm (2½ ft) stems are in character for weeks in summer. The shade-tolerant *Phytolacca clavigera* has 1.25 m (4 ft) vivid crimson stems with terminal heads of pink flowers succeeded by juicy black poisonous berries.

The burnet, *Sanguisorba obtusa*, has greyish pinnate leaves and pink bottlebrush-like flowers on 1.25 m (4 ft) stems. *Physostegia virginiana* is the obedient plant, so called because its pink tubular flowers can be moved around and then stay as placed. It blooms in late summer on 90 cm (3 ft) stems – or only 30 cm (12 in) in the case of the deeper pink 'Vivid'. Moist soil is advisable.

Agastache mexicana is like a refined monarda (see above) with slender 60 cm (2 ft) stems and small dark pink sage-like flowers. The 45 cm (18 in) *Erodium manescavii*, or heron's bill, with carrot-like foliage and magenta, geranium-type flowers with black basal spots, blooms all summer in good soil and sun; and the 90 cm (3 ft) *Chelone obliqua*, or turtle's head (the name alludes to the shape of the flowers), is lilac-pink and flowers in the autumn.

Centranthus ruber

and full sun is essential; the Ligtu hybrids grow well on raised beds, but provide winter protection in cold or exposed gardens. Plant the roots 20 cm (8 in) deep.

There are pink to purplish-red chrysanthemums that are good for cutting, and other daisy-type flowers useful in this respect are the pyrethrums, *Chrysanthemum coccineum*, with feathery foliage and many colour forms. These include the light pink 'Eileen May Robinson', the salmon 'Evenglow' and deep pink 'Brenda' – all singles – and the double crimson 'Lord Rosebery' and deep pink 'Vanessa'.

Autumn-flowering anenomes, *Anemone hupehensis japonica* forms such as the single pink 'Queen Charlotte' or the double pink

'Lady Gilmour', do well in shade and can be increased from root cuttings. They grow about 90 cm (3 ft) tall. *Echinacea purpurea* 'Bressingham Hybrids' are a race of cerise, red-purple or magenta 'daisies' with protruding mahogany-coloured centres on 90 cm (3 ft) rough-leaved stems.

Particularly dazzling reds are found in *Potentilla* 'Gibson's Scarlet', a 45 cm (18 in) branching plant with strawberry-like flowers and leaves, which blooms on and off all summer; and also in *Lynchnis chalcedonica*, the sunloving Maltese cross (so called because of the shape of the flowers) with congested heads of brilliant vermilion blooms on 1 to 1.25 m (3 to 4 ft) stems. *Geranium psilostemon* (*G. armenum*), a 1.25 m (4 ft) magenta-crimson

Yellow, orange and bronze flowers
In general, gold and yellow flowers seem most plentiful in spring and autumn, and almost the first are the bright golden daisy flowers of doronicums. They appear with the daffodils and are as good as these for cutting. Suitable for sun or light shade, given the essential of moist soil, *Doronicum plantagineum* 'Harpur Crewe' grows to 75 cm (2½ ft), the hybrid 'Miss Mason' to 45 cm (18 in) and *D. pardalianches* to 90 cm (3 ft). Planted 60 cm (2 ft) apart, the last is suitable for naturalizing in thin woodland.

Trollius are also early bloomers, and of erect habit with round, yellow or gold, buttercup-like flowers. As well as thriving in borders they can be planted near/continued

The 'midway' hardy perennials (continued)

streams or naturalized in moist meadows. Cultivars of *Trollius europaeus* are the most commonly grown, including 'Alabaster' (light primrose), 'Canary Bird' (lemon), 'Gold-quelle' (rich yellow), 'Commander in Chief' (deep orange), and 'Earliest of All' (butter-yellow). All grow about 75 cm (2½ ft) tall.

Isatis tinctoria is woad, a poor perennial best treated as biennial. It is the plant from which indelible juices were extracted by the Ancient Britons to stain their bodies. It makes a spreading plant 60 cm (2 ft) high and as much across, liberally spangled in early summer with small yellow flowers.

Later come a whole series of composite flowers (that is, members of the daisy family), most of them good for cutting. *Helenium*

Crocosmia masonorum

autumnale cultivars will grow in most soils, but prefer a stiff loam and full sun. They have stout leafy stems with flowers in autumnal shades of yellow, bronze and coppery-red. Representative varieties include 'Butterpat' (clear yellow), 'Wyndley' (copper-orange), 'The Bishop' (buttercup-yellow), 'Moerheim Beauty' (bronze-red) and 'Coppelia' (coppery-orange). All reach 75 to 90 cm (2½ to 3 ft).

Perennial sunflowers, *Helianthus* species, are useful but rather coarse plants for late summer and autumn. *Helianthus decapetalus* 'Loddon Gold', 'Miss Mellish' and 'Soleil d'Or' are all golden, double and 1.25 m (4 ft) high, with rough leaves.

Others for late-season colour include golden rods (*Solidago* spp) – particularly the

shorter (90 cm; 3 ft) hybrids between *S. cutleri* (*S. brachystachys*) and × *Solidaster* (the latter a bigeneric hybrid between *Solidago* and *Aster*) such as 'Goldenmosa' and 'Leraft'. *Heliopsis helianthoides scabra* is like a refined golden sunflower; it has several named cultivars including 'Golden Plume', 'Light of Loddon' (both fully double) and 'Gold-greenheart', which has near-double flowers tinged with green. Heliopsis dry well for winter decoration and grow about 1.25 m (4 ft) tall.

Rudbeckia fulgida speciosa is a sturdy little plant with rough stems and leaves, and golden daisy flowers with large dark brown centres on 60 cm (2 ft) stems. *Coreopsis grandiflora* 'Sunburst', 'Badengold' and 'Perry's Variety'

Solidago 'Lena'

Alstroemeria Ligtu hybrids

all make good cut flowers and have smooth leaves, 60 to 75 cm (2 to 2½ ft) stems and semi-double, rich yellow to golden daisy flowers. Given full sun they grow in most gardens, but since they tend to sprawl may need staking. This is a trait not shared by the delightful little *C. verticillata* 'Golden Shower', which has 60 cm (2 ft) stems, needle-like leaves and small golden flowers all through the summer.

Anthemis tinctoria is like a gold marguerite with pungent, parsley-like leaves. It grows 60 to 90 cm (2 to 3 ft) tall and has a number of yellow cultivars such as 'Grallagh Gold' (the best, but a poor perennial and often shy-flowering), 'E. C. Buxton' and 'Perry's Variety'. *Lathyrus aureas* (*Orobus aurantiacus*) is

useful in early summer, when the compact clumps of yellowish-green, pinnate foliage are overtopped by spikes of small coppery-orange pea-flowers on 45 cm (18 in) stems.

Gaillardias, or blanket flowers, come as perennials as well as annuals, but fail if planted in cold wet ground or in shade. A few good cultivars derived in part from *Gaillardia aristata* are 'Mandarin' (flame-orange), 'Ipswich Beauty' (yellow and mahogany-red), 'Croftway Yellow' (a bright yellow self) and 'Wirral Flame' (brownish-red, tipped with yellow). All grow to 75 to 90 cm (2½ to 3 ft).

Some of the most important gold and yellow perennials in this range are the day lilies, *Hemerocallis* species and cultivars. Hardy, dependable and long-lasting, they are suitable for a wide range of soils, climates and situations and, having neat grassy leaves, remain attractive even when out of flower. The blooms last only a day, but appear in constant succession over a period of several weeks. They are lily-like, often fragrant, and come in lemon, gold, orange and bronze – also dusty pink and red shades – mostly between 75 and 90 cm (2½ and 3 ft) tall.

Yellow and gold are also basic colours amongst hardy chrysanthemums (see p 181). *Alstroemeria aurantiaca* (see above) is rich red-gold; the 90 cm (3 ft) *Thermopsis montana* looks something like a yellow lupin, but having running rootstocks needs controlling; and *Phlomis samia* has velvet-textured, silvery leaves and branching 90 cm (3 ft) spikes carrying whorls of fragrant, butter-yellow flowers. *Oenothera tetragona*, an 'evening primrose' that flowers in the day, grows 45 to 60 cm (1½ to 2 ft) tall, with slender stems and yellow flowers from reddish buds. Named garden seedlings include 'Yellow River' and 'Fireworks'.

Kirengeshoma palmata is the yellow waxbell, a plant of great beauty in early autumn, with 90 cm (3 ft) stems, maple-like leaves and loose sprays of pendent, cool yellow flowers like long earrings. It will grow in partial to deep shade in deep, moist soil, but dislikes lime. *Asclepias tuberosa* also blooms in autumn with compact heads of brilliant orange flowers on 45 cm (18 in) stems, but is only hardy in light soils and sunny places. *Chelidonium majus* 'Flore Pleno' – a double form of the giant celandine – has yellow sap in its 60 cm (2 ft) stems, deeply cut leaves and many small yellow florets. Owing to its propensity for seeding, the plant needs careful siting, but it is useful in rough places or wild or natural gardens.

Crocosmia masonorum, a cormous member of the iris family, is a real charmer for late summer, with spikes of brilliant vermilion-orange flowers poised at right angles at the tops of 90 cm (3 ft) stems. The leaves resemble those of gladioli. The species is suitable for sun or light shade in any good moist soil. Recently hybrids from this plant and montbretias and antholyzas have produced some fine colour forms such as 'Spitfire' (fiery-orange), 'Bressingham Blaze' (flame-red), 'Emberglow' (burnt orange-red) and 'Citronella', (lemon-yellow).

Border carnations and pinks

No flowers are more evocative on the one hand of elegance and on the other of the old-world informality of the Victorian cottage garden than the border carnations and garden pinks. They combine beautiful form, a wide range of colours, often a delightful fragrance, and neat silvery evergreen foliage. They are valuable for herbaceous beds and borders, and the smaller types are excellent for edging. All make superb cut flowers.

Carnations and garden pinks both belong to the genus *Dianthus*. Their close relatives include the dwarf rock pinks (see p 225), a number of kinds that are very easily raised from seed as half-hardy annuals (see p 218) and the biennial sweet William (*Dianthus barbatus*; see p 211). Border carnations and pinks are also grown as biennials in regions with hot climates, but elsewhere they are perennials – albeit rather short-lived ones that must be propagated every few years. The great majority are hybrids, but carnations derive mainly from *D. caryophyllus,* garden pinks from *D. plumarius*.

Types and characteristics
Border carnations are the largest, both in flower and in height, growing about 60 cm (2 ft) tall. The flowers are double, heavy and 5 cm (2 in) or more across. They differ from those of the closely related perpetual carnations – the buttonhole carnations grown in greenhouses in cool climates – in having smooth-edged rather than crinkled petals and in flowering only once a year, in summer. Colours include almost every shade except true blue. They are classified principally into selfs, which have an all-over single colour,

Dianthus 'Doris'

There are two main groups of garden pinks. The old-fashioned varieties of Victorian gardens bloom once a year, in early summer. Like border carnations, they produce a single flowering stem the first year, more in subsequent years. Though less vigorous than modern kinds, they are long-lived and have a delicious scent and tidy habit. Modern pinks originated when Montagu Allwood crossed an old-fashioned garden pink with a perpetual carnation. The resultant plants are now called *D. × allwoodii*. They have a longer flowering season – from early summer to late autumn – and are often fragrant. They grow more vigorously and if the growing point is pinched out produce many flowering stems, but are shorter-lived. Related groups include show pinks, intermediate in habit between modern pinks and border carnations, and London pinks, which are vigorous and long-flowering,

Dianthus 'Beauty of Cambridge'

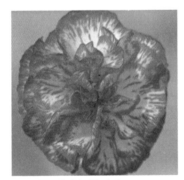
Dianthus 'Robin Thain'

Dianthus 'Inchmery'

Dianthus 'Prudence'

fancies, in which there are stripes or other markings in a contrasting colour, and picotees, in which a pale main colour is edged intricately by a contrasting darker shade. Many varieties are scented, those described as cloves having a delicious spicy fragrance.

Garden pinks are more dainty, growing about 25 to 30 cm (10 to 12 in) tall. Their flowers may be smooth-edged or fringed, single or double. The colour range is more restricted – from white and pink to dark red and purple – but markings are more varied. They include selfs, fancies, bicolours (with a central contrasting 'eye') and laced varieties (where the eye extends to form a ring around each petal; the name pink, incidentally, does not refer to colour, but is an old word for eye).

but generally with the old-fashioned form of flower – often laced.

Cultivation and propagation
Garden pinks are extremely hardy, border carnations slightly less so, particularly in wet conditions. Both like an open, sunny but sheltered situation. Good drainage and a little lime are their main needs. Excessive wet in winter rots the stems, as does a damp peat mulch or dead leaves. Grow them in a raised bed on badly drained soil. The best fertilizer is bonemeal or a synthetic fertilizer high in potash (see p 352). Plant in spring or autumn, making sure not to bury more than 5 mm (¼ in) of stem. Insert stakes for the taller-growing kinds, and pinch out the growing tips

of modern pinks but not of the other types. Border carnations can be disbudded in early summer to leave only the crown bud on each stem. When tidying the garden, do not cut back into the hard, woody stems or the plants may not shoot again.

Modern pinks and border carnations need renewing every two to three years, old-fashioned pinks every four to five years. In summer, take cutting of side shoots about 10 cm (4 in) long and root in peat and coarse sand. Alternatively, increase border carnations and tall pinks by layering. Cut a slit in a side shoot just below the lowest leaves, peg it down and cover with soil. Once rooted, separate it. All types can also be grown from seed, but colours are unpredictable.

'Front-row' hardy perennials

Most of the plants used for the front of the herbaceous or mixed border will naturally be low-growing (even ground-hugging) and under 30 cm (12 in), but sometimes individuals slightly taller than this are planted in frontal positions because of their light habit, which would be masked behind others. Such plants may also be necessary to hide the untidy remains of perennials such as anchusas and oriental poppies as these die down after they finish flowering.

White and green flowers

Hellebores are early bloomers in this section, especially the Christmas rose, *Helleborus niger*, which needs more light than the closely related, shade-loving lenten rose, *H. orientalis*. These come in various colours from greenish-yellow and white to pink, rose and purple, and are easily reproduced from self-set seedlings. Lilies of the valley (*Convallaria majalis*) also do well in light shade, given annual top-dressings of leaf-mould or compost. 'Fortin's Giant' is one of the best, with 20 cm (8 in) stems and larger, tubbier flowers, and there are also pink-flowered, double and variegated-leaved forms.

Front-liners with greenish-yellow flowers include the lady's mantle, *Alchemilla mollis*, whose frothy plumes of tiny florets rise over round, scalloped-edged leaves; *Euphorbia myrsinites*, which has glaucous-grey stems and foliage; and *E. cyparissias*, with needle-like leaves and heart-shaped bracts.

Two late-season perennials used at the

Alchemilla mollis

front of borders are the white everlastings *Anaphalis triplinervis* and *A. yedoensis*, which both grow about 40 cm (15 in) tall, with papery flowers atop leafy, silvery-green stems. The St Bruno's lily, *Paradisea liliastrum*, has white, lily-like flowers – several to a stem – in early summer, and clumps of lax grassy leaves.

There are also white violas and white polyanthus (see below); a small creamy-flowered antirrhinum-like trailer called *Asarina procumbens*, which is suitable for excessively dry places; and of course white pinks (*Dianthus* cultivars) like the fragrant double 'Mrs Sinkins' and 'White Ladies'. These last can either be grouped in clumps or used as a continuous edging.

Blue, lilac and mauve flowers

For sunny situations, blue polyanthus (hybrids of *Primula* spp) are unexcelled for spring display, although they have to be lifted after flowering and grown in moist shade all summer. Almost every hue is available from light blue to gentian-blue and violet, and there are also white, yellow, orange, pink and red varieties. Seeds can be bought in these shades and come reasonably true, although good sorts are best propagated by division.

Vying for popularity with the polyanthus are the violas, violets and pansies – all species and hybrids of *Viola* – which come in a wide range of colours from the blues and violets suggested by the name to shades of pink, red, orange, bronze, yellow and white, as well as bicolours. Best for the front of borders are the spring-flowering scented *V. odorata*; the larger summer-blooming *V. tricolor* (heartsease); and the latter's derivatives, the hybrid garden pansies now classified as *V. × wittrockiana*. These last include summer- and winter-flowering sorts which reach a maximum of 20 cm (8 in). They are often treated as biennials (see p 114). All violas need moist but well-drained soil in a sunny or partially shaded position.

The blue forget-me-not-like *Brunnera macrophylla* (*Anchusa myosotidiflora*), which has rough heart-shaped leaves and needs moist shade, flowers in spring, as does the 15 cm (6 in) vivid blue *Omphalodes verna*, a gem for a damp spot. In sunny places, the cowslip-like lungworts give a good account of themselves; several have rich blue flowers, including *Pulmonaria angustifolia* and its cultivars 'Azurea' and 'Munstead Blue'. These all have rough green leaves, whereas those of the vivid blue *P. longifolia* are conspicuously spotted with white. In the case of *P. mollis* the deep blue florets change with age, first to purple and then to red, although blue is always the dominant colour.

Other early plants include the ground-hugging bugles; *Ajuga reptans*, a European native, has small oval green leaves but more garden-worthy are its foliage forms like the wine-red 'Burgundy Glow', the green and white 'Variegata', and 'Multicolor' ('Rainbow'), where the basic green is marbled with dark red, purple and yellow. All have 15 to 20 cm (6 to 8 in) spikes of deep blue flowers. A long-flowering woodlander for poor soils, in sun or shade, is *Borago laxiflora*, a borage with light blue flowers – occasionally used in fruit cups and salads – and rosettes of rough hairy leaves.

Pasque flowers, *Pulsatilla vulgaris* (but often called *Anemone pulsatilla*), are beautiful plants for spring, normally with mauve flowers but sometimes lilac-pink or purple. These are succeeded by silky seed-heads. The filigree texture of the deeply cut leaves and the softly hairy stems are other attractions.

For summer borders there are various hostas with lilac or purple flowers, although most of these are grown for their foliage (see p 242); also the strong-smelling, lavender-mauve catmint, *Nepeta × faassenii* (*N. mussinii*), and the cupid's love-dart, *Catananche*

caerulea. The flowers of this last resemble deep mauve cornflowers backed by silvery bracts, which rustle when touched. Catananches must have full sun and sharp drainage, and are propagated from root cuttings. *Stokesia laevis* looks something like a dwarf china aster (*Callistephus*), with 10 cm (4 in) mauve-purple, blue or white flowers on 30 to 40 cm (12 to 15 in) stems. It will grow in sun or shade provided the drainage is good, and is also increased by root cuttings.

Liriope muscari, or lily-turf, blooms in autumn, the dense spikes of violet flowers looking something like those of a grape hyacinth (*Muscari*). The narrow, dark green foliage is normally evergreen. It grows 30 cm (12 in) high and is suitable for sun or partial shade. Although the sky-blue flowers of the flax, *Linum narbonense*, only open in sun and the plants may reach 45 cm (18 in), they are so delicate as to need a frontal position. The cultivars 'June Perfield' and 'Six Hills' are deep blue on light branching stems. *Stachys grandiflora* (*Betonica grandiflora*, or *B. macrantha*) makes rosettes of oblong, corrugated leaves from which emerge 45 cm (18 in) stems bearing whorls of sage-like violet flowers.

In addition to these, there are mauve and blue dwarf asters; also *Buglossoides* (*Lithospermum*) *purpureo-caeruleum*, a deep blue shade-lover of 20 to 30 cm (8 to 12 in); *Roscoea purpurea*, a curious plant with purple hooded flowers in late summer atop leafy 30 cm (12 in) stems; and *Codonopsis ovata*, a ground-hugger with small oval leaves and

Viola tricolor 'Bowles' Black'

pale blue, pendent, bell-shaped flowers, speckled like a bird's egg inside with gold and green. This needs a sheltered, well-drained but sunny spot.

Pink and red flowers

Bergenias make good edging plants, with their large, smooth, heart-shaped leaves and spikes of flowers in early spring. *Bergenia cordifolia* 'Purpurea' has magenta flowers and leaves that turn purplish in winter, and there are many fine sorts of German origin such as 'Abendglut' ('Evening Glow'; crimson with maroon foliage), 'Silberlicht' ('Silver Light'; white) and *B. × schmidtii* (pink).

Heucheras have heart-shaped evergreen

Stokesia laevis 'Wyoming'

Saxifraga umbrosa

eaves and slender stalks of small, pendent, bell-like flowers. *Heuchera sanguinea* cultivars include the deep red 'Firebird', the clear pink 'Pretty Polly', the carmine and white 'Sparkler' and the deep pink 'Hyperion'. The fringed bleeding heart, *Dicentra eximia*, has rosy-purple blooms above fern-like foliage, and both it and the fuchsia-red *D. formosa* 'Bountiful' flower on and off all summer – as does *Geranium endressii*, a 20 to 30 cm (8 to 12 in) cranesbill with clear pink flowers.

Pink thrift, *Armeria caespitosa*, makes a low evergreen edging, and flowers in spring. *Oenothera caespitosa* is a pink, scented, long-blooming evening primrose about 30 cm (12 in) high, and there are plenty of red and

Pulsatilla vulgaris (Anemone pulsatilla)

pink polyanthus (see above), as well as double border pinks like the red *Dianthus* 'Emperor', the rosy-pink 'Excelsior' and the light pink 'Mrs Pilkington'.

In summer, *Incarvillea mairei* (*I. grandiflora*) and *I. delavayi* strike an exotic note with their rosy-purple, gloxinia-like flowers and striking pinnate leaves, although the roots may need protecting in a bad winter. *Mimulus cupreus* cultivars, such as the scarlet 'Bee's Dazzler' and the crimson 'Red Emperor', are ideal for damp sunny places, but the Himalayan whorlflower, *Morina longifolia*, needs sun, sharp drainage and winter shelter. It produces low rosettes of spiny-edged leaves and 60 cm (2 ft) spikes of red and white tubu-

lar flowers arranged in whorls around the stems. They fade to crimson-purple.

Although generally reckoned as bedding plants, *Penstemon barbatus* hybrids are useful near the front of mixed borders on account of their long flowering season, which is prolonged through summer and autumn; also, some are hardy enough to leave outside in gardens that do not experience sharp frost. *Schizostylis coccinea*, the Kaffir lily, has crimson flowers like those of small gladioli on 30 to 45 cm (12 to 15 in) stems. These appear in late autumn and are good for cutting; 'Mrs Hegarty' and 'Viscountess Byng' are pink. Kaffir lilies do best in moist to wet ground, but are not reliably hardy in cold areas.

Saxifraga umbrosa, the London pride, has red and white flowers on slender stems; the white and purple flowers of the bastard balm, *Melittis melissophyllum* hold great attraction for bees; and, although a hybrid, *Geum* 'Mrs Bradshaw', with bright scarlet flowers and strawberry-like leaves, comes true from seed. *Lamium maculatum* is an almost ground-hugging dead nettle with white-blotched leaves and rose or purple flowers; there is also a form with golden foliage.

Late in the summer, the large, flat, rich pink flower-heads of *Sedum spectabile* 'Brilliant' prove irresistible to butterflies, and there are several good polygonums – notably *Polygonum affine* 'Darjeeling Red' and the bright pink *P. vacciniifolium*. Although popular as rock plants, they also have a place at the front of herbaceous borders.

Yellow, orange and gold flowers
Among spring bloomers with yellow flowers are violas and polyanthus (see above) and the cushion spurge, *Euphorbia epithymoides* (*E. polychroma*), which makes a brave show when seen *en masse* because of the brilliance of the golden bracts surrounding the clustered flowers. There are also yellow primroses (*Primula vulgaris*) for shady spots, and many gardeners employ a few clumps of the silver-leaved *Alyssum saxatile,* for its rich golden flowers bring a touch of sunshine to bare borders as well as rock gardens.

Stylophorum diphyllum is the celandine poppy, a handsome plant with large, bright yellow poppy-like flowers on black-haired

30 cm (12 in) stems. The glaucous leaves are handsomely cut, and the plant grows best in rich damp soil, where it makes a wonderful team-mate for the Virginian cowslip, *Mertensia virginica* (see p 179).

Adonis vernalis, the spring adonis, has large yellow, buttercup-like flowers on 20 to 30 cm (8 to 12 in) stems in late spring, but earlier still *A. amurensis* and the double form 'Plena' steal the scene. Their blooms are nearly 5 cm (2 in) across, and the finely cut foliage resembles that of fennel. *Corydalis lutea* flowers all summer with fern-like leaves and countless tubular yellow blossoms on 30 cm (12 in) stems. It will grow anywhere, even amongst stones and gravel – a handy plant in poor dry

Mimulus luteus 'Hose-in-Hose'

soils, but a problem at times on good land, where it may be too vigorous.

Mimulus luteus (see p 256) is summer-blooming and suitable for a damp spot as well as for the water garden, and, although not hardy, *Gazania* hybrids are frequently used in herbaceous borders because of their long flowering season. They have a wide colour range, often displaying several hues in the same flower, although yellows, oranges and tangerines dominate. The narrow leaves are silvery and the plants require full sun – or the flowers will not open – and sharp drainage. Cuttings should be taken in late summer and overwintered in a frost-free place to maintain stock. They are easily raised from seed.

Chysanthemums, the 'golden flowers'

Chrysanthemums must be among the earliest flowers cultivated by man, for records have been traced as far back as 500 BC in China. At that time their form was single and their colour yellow; the very name chrysanthemum (which serves as both common and botanical name), when translated from botanists' Greek, means golden flower. With their present-day variations in form, colour and size, chrysanthemums hold a fascination for many, and the old belief that they are only useful as exhibitor's blooms or for funeral wreaths has long gone in many countries.

The genus *Chrysanthemum* includes annual, hardy perennial and alpine species, many of which are described elsewhere in this book. This article deals with those members of the large group of mainly half-hardy perennial hybrids, commonly known as florists' chrysanthemums, that can be grown outdoors even in cool regions. (The tender varieties that need greenhouse cultivation except in warm regions are beyond the scope of this book.)

Because of their versatility for border decoration, as bedding plants or cut flowers, no garden today is complete without hybrid chrysanthemums. They are among the most valuable of late-season flowers, producing a riot of colour from midsummer to autumn. The amount of work needed to produce good results in any garden is minimal; it is only the fanatic who makes the art of growing chrysanthemums appear to be hard work.

Growing chrysanthemums in borders

The best effect in the herbaceous border is achieved by leaving spaces large enough to take small groups of chrysanthemums, and setting out well-rooted plants once frosts have ceased. Prepare the ground carefully in early spring so that the roots of permanent residents are not disturbed. Fork over the top 15 cm (6 in) of soil, and add some humus-forming material, such as garden compost, manure or peat, plus a handful of general fertilizer per square metre. Chrysanthemums like slightly acid soil, so lime should be applied only if a soil test shows it to be extremely sour (see p 332). (In any case, do not lime at the same time as you apply fertilizer or manure.) If space permits, and you want to grow a larger number of plants to provide cut flowers, allocate a separate bed; then it will be easier to prepare the ground adequately during the autumn.

Healthy, well-rooted young plants can be obtained from reputable nurserymen, including many who specialize in chrysanthemums. When ordering, it is best to state clearly when you want delivery; most modern hybrid chrysanthemums are not fully hardy, and if delivered in late winter or early spring, when frosts are still liable to occur, you will need to protect them in a greenhouse or cold frame until you can plant them out. In subsequent years, you can raise your own new plants by taking cuttings from plants stored through the winter in a frost-free place. It is best not to replant overwintered plants.

Plant out in late spring, when all danger of frost is past. Place the plants 30 to 45 cm (12 to 18 in) apart, just cover the root ball with soil and firm it down gently with your knuckles. Water in well. For the taller-growing types, which will need support, provide 0.9 to 1.25 m (3 to 4 ft) stakes or canes. It is advisable to protect young plants from birds immediately on planting or they will peck them to pieces; wind black cotton between the stakes. Water the plants regularly to maintain steady growth, giving liquid manure every two weeks; alternatively, sprinkle general fertilizer around the plants two or three times during the summer, to be washed into the soil by rain or watering if necessary. Tie in as necessary to the supporting stakes, using raffia or soft string. Some types (see below) need disbudding – that is, removal of small buds around the central flower bud on each stem – to encourage large blooms to form.

Pests, particularly aphids (such as greenfly and blackfly) and leaf miners (see p 364), can be troublesome, and it is worthwhile spraying the plants every 10 to 14 days as a precaution; alternate insecticides to ensure maximum control. If eelworms attack, plants should be destroyed and the ground sterilized; use a new site for next year's chrysanthemums. The main disease that troubles these plants is powdery mildew (see p 367).

At the end of the autumn, before severe frosts begin, carefully lift the plants without damaging the roots. Cut back the main stem to about 25 cm (10 in) and trim off all basal growths. Store them in boxes or trays, filling in around the roots with potting mixture. Keep them only slightly moist, in a cold frame, cool greenhouse or other well-lit frost-free place. Watch out for mildew, slugs and other troubles. When warmer weather comes in late winter, start watering to bring the dormant

Chrysanthemum Spray varieties

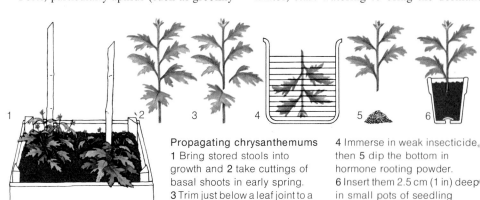

Propagating chrysanthemums
1 Bring stored stools into growth and 2 take cuttings of basal shoots in early spring.
3 Trim just below a leaf joint to a length of 5 to 6 cm (2 to 2½ in), removing the lowest leaves.

4 Immerse in weak insecticide, then 5 dip the bottom in hormone rooting powder.
6 Insert them 2.5 cm (1 in) deep in small pots of seedling mixture. Water in, but give no more water till roots form.

plants, or stools, into growth. They will send up new shoots from the base. Take cuttings from these; their youth and vigour means that they will form a good root system. Cuttings 5 to 6 cm (2 to 2½ in) long can be rooted successfully in a cold frame, especially if treated with hormone rooting powder, using a soil- or peat-based seedling mixture in small pots or a seed tray, but a cool greenhouse is better.

Spray chrysanthemums
Possibly the most suitable group of chrysanthemums for garden decoration are those specially grown as Sprays. (They are sometimes known in North America as Cushion chrysan-

Chrysanthemum 'Cricket'

Recommended border chrysanthemums

Spray varieties	'Anna Marie' (white); 'Ellen' (white); 'Gerrie Hoek' (pink); 'Grandchild' (pink); 'Lillian Hoek' (bronze; red and yellow sports); 'Lucida' (yellow); 'Margaret' (pink); 'Nathalie' (purple); various 'Pennine' varieties (wide colour range)
Pompons	'Bright Eye' (yellow, reddish centre); 'Cameo' (white); 'Denise' (yellow); 'Fairie' (pink; bronze, purple and salmon sports); 'Solly' (lemon-yellow)
Koreans	**Double** 'Blush' (salmon); 'Copper Nob' (bronze-red); 'Falgate' (light bronze); 'Janice Bailey' (pink) **Single** 'Ada Miles' (cream); 'Fairy Rose' (pink); 'Lemon Tench' (lemon-yellow); 'Wendy Tench' (salmon)
Disbudded varieties	**Incurved** 'Iris Riley' (pink); 'Marjorie Boden' (yellow); 'Martin Riley' (yellow); 'Ruby Wren' (pale pink); 'Woolley Wonder' (yellow); 'Yellow Nuggett' **Reflexed** 'Alice Jones' (bronze); 'Bronze Eve Gray'; 'Eve Gray' (pink); 'Karen Rowe' (pink); 'Redhead' (red); 'Timmy Gray' (pink); 'White Karen Rowe'; 'Woolley Dandy' (red); 'Yellow Value' **Intermediate incurving** 'Cricket' (white; yellow and pale yellow sports); 'Gladys Sharpe' (yellow); 'Harry Wren' (yellow); 'Keystone' (purple); 'Mac's Delight' (yellow); 'Red Keystone'; 'Shirley Victoria' (light bronze)

themums.) These are available in many colours and forms, and have a long flowering period from midsummer to autumn, depending upon variety and weather. They do not require disbudding, as their beauty relies upon a mass of small flowers. To ensure a bushy effect, stop the plants – that is, pinch out the growing tip of the main stem – when they are 20 to 30 cm (8 to 12 in) high, to encourage the production of side growths as early as possible. No further restriction is necessary. The ultimate height of the plants will be in the range of 1 to 1.25 m (3 to 4 ft) depending upon variety; Sprays are practically self-supporting when planted fairly close together. The list of varieties is almost unending. Indeed, almost any chrysanthemum can be grown as a spray, but a selection of Spray varieties is listed in the table.

Pompons and semi-pompons
These are treated in the same manner culturally as Sprays, though many of them, being smaller, are ideal for planting at the front of a border. These delightful chrysanthemums are distinguished by having small spherical or half-spherical blooms approximately 2.5 cm (1 in) in diameter. Again, varieties are many.

Koreans
Reasonably dwarf in habit, these are most useful as bedding plants and for growing in the front of a border. They form bushy plants with small single or double flowers in a wide range of colours. They have the advantage of being fairly hardy and will often survive the winter without loss if left outside, though it is as well to give some protection in very cold spells or in places where winter temperatures fall below about −5°C (23°F).

Disbudded varieties
Chrysanthemum varieties that give blooms most like those seen at flower shows call for a little more attention, though their usefulness in border decoration or as cut flowers is indis-

Stopping and disbudding
1 Stop chrysanthemums when 20 to 30 cm (8 to 12 in) tall by pinching out the growing tip. 2 This encourages branching; with disbudded varieties, restrict to six or eight side shoots. 3 Secure their main buds by gradually removing smaller ones. 4 Leave other types after initial stopping.

putable. They require both stopping (as with Sprays) and disbudding, in order to produce one individual bloom on each stem. This is done by pinching out the main growing tip in late spring in the same manner as with Sprays; but instead of allowing the plant to grow in a bushy manner, the number of side shoots which develop is restricted to six or eight. As stems form, side shoots will grow from their leaf axils, and these should be removed when about 2.5 cm (1 in) long.

By late summer or early autumn a flower bud will have formed on each of the individual stems, and is usually surrounded by a cluster of other smaller buds or shoots. Allow these

Chrysanthemum 'Fairie'

to grow until large enough to handle, then gradually remove one at a time over a period of days until only one bud is left. This procedure is known as securing the bud. Individual blooms produced in this way are usually about 10 to 15 cm (4 to 6 in) across.

The form of these more sophisticated blooms is classified under three headings; all have their own devotees according to personal preference. The Incurved blooms are the most elegant, being characterized by close, tightly incurving florets which give a mature bloom the appearance of a perfect globe. One slight handicap for garden decoration is that larger blooms of this type tend to hold rain, making them so heavy that their stems bend over and they seem to hang their heads in shame. The smaller-flowered varieties are less susceptible.

The Reflexed group is possibly the most popular of the disbudded varieties for garden decoration. Their florets fold outwards from a central tuft to give an umbrella-like effect, making it easier for rain to run off the bloom. Blooms in the Intermediate group (also known in North America as Irregular Incurves) can be loosely incurving in formation – more open than a true Incurve – or semi-reflexing. The latter tend to be untidy in appearance, so recommendations in this case are given for the incurving blooms.

The table with this article gives a representative selection of named cultivars. A considerable number of varieties are introduced each year, so that any suggestions can soon become out of date – although those named are expected to last for several years.

The dazzling dahlias

Blooming with unmatched brilliance from the middle of summer to the first frosts, dahlias bring a touch of tropical splendour to the garden. Although originating in Mexico (from where the Spanish conquistadors introduced them to Europe in the 18th century), they grow successfully from Iceland to the Antipodes. The rich foliage makes an excellent background for the flowers in all their variety of colours and forms. Their easy-growing habit makes them suitable for beginners and professionals alike, while the enthusiast can produce exquisite exhibition blooms. They make superb cut flowers.

Garden dahlias are complete hybrids, and are classified by horticulturalists as *Dahlia variabilis*. They will not reproduce themselves exactly from seed, though a number of strains of seed-raised types are grown as half-hardy annuals (see p 215). These so-called bedding dahlias are generally quite short – 30 to 50 cm (12 to 20 in) tall – and may be single- or double-flowered. The seed of other types can, of course, be saved, but the resultant seedlings will bear little or no resemblance to the parent – though there is always the chance of raising a winner. But if replicas of favourite plants or particular named varieties are to be grown in succeeding seasons, you must propagate from cuttings or by division.

Tuberous-rooted, dahlias love rich soil and moisture but will perform satisfactorily under even the harshest conditions. They do not like frost, however; just a few degrees will severely damage the soft leaves and stems, and you must always take this into account when growing dahlias. In frost-free areas, the tubers (or roots, as they are sometimes called) may be left in the ground throughout the winter. Elsewhere, you should lift them as soon as the first autumn frosts blacken the leaves, store them in a dry, cool but frost-free place, and bring them back into growth the following spring.

Raising and planting

In areas where spring frosts preclude outdoor propagation, you should make a start indoors two months before all danger of frost is past. You can bring overwintered dormant tubers into growth and then take cuttings of the new shoots. Or you can simply divide up a large root into pieces. Both methods are illustrated. It is not usually satisfactory simply to replant an old large root without division, for this inhibits new root growth and results in leafy plants with poor blooms.

The seed for bedding and other dahlias should also be sown under glass in early spring. Prick out the seedlings into trays or pots as soon as they are big enough to handle. However you raise your plants, grow them on under glass until they are sturdy and there is no more risk of frost. For the last week or two before planting out, put them in a cold frame to harden off.

Dahlias will grow in almost any sort of soil, but they are greedy feeders and it pays to fork in plenty of decayed manure or garden compost during autumn digging of the dahlia beds. And when forking over prior to planting, add

Dahlia Ball variety

a top-dressing of bonemeal at 135 g/m² (4 oz/sq yd) to ensure a full season's success.

These are fairly rampant plants, and need room to grow. Space the smaller tuberous types at least 60 cm (2 ft) apart, the larger 90 cm (3 ft). Bedding dahlias can be spaced as close as 40 cm (15 in). Avoid positioning the plants where high trees or shrubs, walls or fences will overshadow and 'draw' the plants. When planting, take out planting holes about

10 cm (4 in) deep and wide enough to take the spread-out roots; work some peat enriched with organic fertilizer around the root ball. Water well and insert a strong stake tall enough to support the plant when fully grown. Alternatively, insert several stout canes around each plant. Two or three weeks after planting, pinch out the growing point to encourage bushy growth.

Summer care

It is essential that the plants do not go short of water in the early stages of growth, and ample water is a priority need during the whole growing season. (In fact, it is more important than additional fertilizer.) If the summer is dry, a mulch of straw or garden compost around the roots will help to keep the soil moist. As the plants grow, tie them in to the supporting stake or canes. Watch out for pests; aphids, thrips, earwigs, capsid bugs, slugs and snails all find the dahlia's foliage and buds to their liking. For advice on treatment, see page 364.

By midsummer, the first blooms will appear. To maintain a spectacular display remove dead and dying flower heads promptly. Cut back well into the stronger bushes, to a point where new buds can grow into flowering shoots to replace the stem that has been

Raising dahlias from cuttings above 1 In late winter or early spring, plant stored tubers in boxes of damp peat at 16°C (61°F). New growth will show in about two weeks. **2** As the shoots elongate to about 10cm (4in), sever them from the old tubers and trim just below a joint. Dip the ends in hormone rooting powder and **3** insert in a mixture of moist peat and sand. Keep the cuttings warm and shaded. In two or three weeks roots will have formed. **4** Pot the plants individually in potting mixture and grow on until it is time to plant out.

 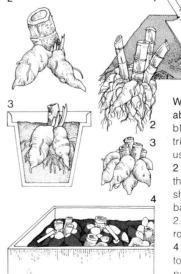

Dividing dahlia roots above and right 1 In early spring, cut stored roots into pieces, making sure that each has a section of stem with an eye from which new growth will emerge. **2** Generally, divide into single large tubers or clumps of two or three smaller ones. Dust cuts with lime and flowers of sulphur to prevent rotting. **3** Pot each section in potting mixture and keep moist at about 16°C (61°F). grow on until planting time.

Winter storage of roots above and left 1 When frost blackens leaves and shoots, trim back the dead stems and use a spade to lift the roots. **2** Remove loose soil and hang them upside-down in an airy shed to dry. **3** When dry, cut back the hard stems to about 2.5 cm (1 in) and remove thin roots, leaving just the tubers. **4** Dust with flowers of sulphur to discourage rotting and pack away in peat, straw or dry soil in a cool place.

Dahlia Decorative variety

Dahlia Semi-cactus variety

removed. To encourage extra-large blooms on long stems – for cutting or exhibition – remove all but one of the buds that appear on each flowering stem. The one flower that does develop will be large and intensely coloured.

When gathering blooms for indoor display, cut long stems – about 60 cm (2 ft) for the largest varieties – and plunge them immediately into cold water almost to the top of the stem. Then cut another 2.5 cm (1 in) off

Dahlia Cactus variety

the bottom of the stems while they are submerged, and leave them in the water for a few hours before transferring to a vase.

As autumn comes, be ready to lift the roots when frost blackens the plant tops. Some exhibitors lift their roots earlier, as soon as the tubers ripen and the flowers and the plant generally show signs of weakness. This avoids any possible losses through disease in damp, cold weather, but such worries need not unduly concern the average gardener.

Types and uses

The dahlia has a multitude of forms and colours that offer a choice to satisfy even the most fastidious gardener. Form is international, and one of the most satisfying aspects of growing dahlias is that varieties raised in Australasia or North America can soon be seen growing just as successfully in Europe, and vice-versa. Among the recommended

---

Recommended dahlia cultivars

Decorative 'Alvas Supreme' (pale yellow; giant); 'Evelyn Foster' (white; medium); 'Hamari Girl' (pink; giant); 'Meiro' (lavender shades; small); 'Rothesay Robin' (dark pink; small); 'Kung Fu' (scarlet; small)

Cactus 'Banker' (glowing red; medium); 'Doris Day' (deep red; small); 'Klankstad Kerkrade' (lemon-yellow; small); 'Match' (creamy-white, tipped magenta; small); 'Polar Sight' (white; giant); 'Rokesley Mini' (white; miniature); 'Worton Harmony' (pink and yellow; medium)

Semi-cactus 'Cheerio' (cherry-red tipped silver; small); 'Cryfield Bryn' (butter-yellow; small); 'Davenport Pride' (apricot; medium); 'Hamari Bride' (white; medium); 'Frank Lovell' (lemon-yellow; giant); 'Surprise' (soft pink; giant); 'Symbol' (bronze; medium)

Ball and pompon 'Alltami Supreme' (yellow; small); 'Downham Royal' (purple; miniature); 'Jo's Choice' (scarlet; miniature); 'Nettie' (pale yellow; miniature); 'Opal' (pink and white; small); 'Small World' (white; pompon); 'Willo's Violet' (violet; pompon)

Bedding 'Coltness Hybrids' (mixtures and separate colours; single); 'Early Bird' (mixed colours; double and semi-double); 'Redskin' (mixed colours; semi-double; bronze foliage)

Size refers to blooms, though overall height is usually in proportion. Giant=25 cm (10 in) or more in diameter; medium=15 to 20 cm (6 to 8 in); small=10 to 15 cm (4 to 6 in); miniature=5 to 10 cm (2 to 4 in); pompon=up to 5 cm (2 in).

---

cultivars listed in the table with this article there are varieties raised in Australia, England, Holland, Japan, New Zealand, Scotland and the United States. These represent only a brief selection, however; there are hundreds of other worthwhile sorts.

As with other garden plants of complex parentage, dahlias are classified into various groups according to flower form. The most popular forms internationally are the Decoratives, which have broad, flat petals; the Cactus forms, where the petals are tightly rolled; the

Semi-cactus, a form midway between the two previous types; and the Ball dahlias, where – as the name suggests – the mature bloom is globular in form. The tiny Pompon dahlias, popular in every part of the world, are miniature forms of the Ball type. All the above have fully double blooms.

Rather less popular are the single and semi-double types, which include the Anemone-flowered group, where flat outer

Dahlia Single-flowered variety

petals surround tight-packed inner ones; Collerettes, which have two rings of petals, one larger than the other; the Paeony-flowered type, where the two rings of flat petals are more or less equal in size; and the Single-flowered group, with a single row of flat petals surrounding the central disc.

Most dahlias – and certainly the larger varieties – are best grown in a bed or border of their own. The medium-sized kinds can be grown successfully in the herbaceous border, while the short, so-called bedding dahlias – generally raised from seed – are even more adaptable. The flower form of bedding dahlias can, in theory, fall into any of the groups listed above; most, however, are of the Single-flowered, Decorative or Cactus type. Although not so exotic-looking as the larger dahlias raised from tubers, they represent an easy and cheap introduction to these flamboyant flowers.

Daffodils, the heralds of spring

Though regarding them with affection as the heralds of spring, the average gardener tends to think of daffodils and narcissi as rather common. Perhaps this is because they are relatively inexpensive, multiply rapidly, are so widely and easily grown, and are so extensively used as cut flowers. Yet the genus *Narcissus* (which includes both the flowers commonly called narcissi and the trumpet-flowered daffodils) contains endless variety and a host of exciting forms and colours. (Except where the distinction is obvious, the name daffodil is used in the rest of this article to include narcissi.)

Daffodils thrive virtually everywhere – in the sun, shade or partial shade – bringing rewards of enchanting bloom year after year. Put them in any well-drained soil near water or on a rocky ledge or wall. Naturalize them in tall grass or under trees. Interplant them among shrubs or in the rock garden. You can even place them in 'problem' spots where conventional flowers perform poorly, or

Narcissus 'Birma'

deploy them in outdoor containers. They can last as long as three weeks, and when cut in bud for floral arrangements they will last in water for a week or more.

Buying and growing
There are no grades or sizes of daffodil bulbs; they are generally sold as round (single-nosed) or double-nosed. The latter have two distinct points on top, indicating that two flowering stems will emerge; they are actually two bulbs fused together. The bulbs vary significantly in size among the various species and varieties, as they do in the colour of the tunic, or outer papery covering.

They are simplicity itself to cultivate, and make few demands on the gardener. They prefer cool, well-drained but moist conditions, and although light feeders appreciate humus-rich soils. The bulbs should be planted in late summer or early autumn, and always before mid-autumn. Set them 10 to 15 cm (4 to 6 in) deep, according to the size of the bulb. They can be sited in sun or in all but the densest shade; shade will make for somewhat later but longer flowering and slightly longer stems. Application will determine spacing, but the shorter-stemmed cultivars can generally be spaced about 10 cm (4 in) apart in the open garden and in containers, while the

Narcissus 'Unsurpassable'

taller-stemmed varieties can be planted about 15 cm (6 in) apart.

All daffodil bulbs should be watered immediately after planting to induce good root growth. Supplement rainfall whenever necessary, particularly if plantings are naturalized or in sandy soil. Pick off old blossoms before the seed pods develop, and keep the bulbs growing after flowering. Let the foliage mature fully before removing it, to provide food to build up next year's bulbs.

Daffodils increase rapidly by offsets, and prefer not to be disturbed. Where used in temporary bedding schemes or where space is precious, lift them soon after flowering finishes, and heel them into an odd corner of the garden until the foliage dies down. No fertilizer is required with initial plantings, but spraying with foliar feed (see p 352) after flowering will help to build up large bulbs for next year, and they will appreciate an annual winter top-dressing of bonemeal when left *in situ*. Clumps may be divided in midsummer after three to four years, and the bulbs replanted immediately, reserving the smaller offsets for growing on in a reserve bed until they reach flowering size.

Daffodils may suffer from fungal disease or from attack by bulb eelworms and narcissus fly. Should plant growth appear stunted, or should foliage and floral stems be covered with grey mould, the bulbs will be suffering from basal or grey rot. Such bulbs must be destroyed and the soil sterilized. There is another mould that hibernates in fragments of infected leaves lying on the soil, but does not attack the bulb. Burn all foliage and sterilize the soil.

Classification of varieties
Narcissi and daffodils are officially classed in 12 divisions (many of them sub-divided) according to their characteristics, mainly of flower form. Ten comprise garden types (including one that is not yet widely available); one division contains all the species, or botanical narcissi, and their wild forms and

Anatomy of a daffodil flower
In spite of their different appearance, all daffodil and narcissus flowers have two rows of petals, the corona 1, which may be cup- or trumpet-shaped, or multiplied in the double varieties, and the outer perianth 2.

hybrids; and one contains all the miscellaneous types that have not been allocated to other groups. Most catalogues and retail outlets now list cultivars under their respective divisions, or at least indicate the type of flower, and so does the table with this article.

As shown in the drawing, there are two major parts to the daffodil flower. The back row of six petals is called the perianth, and varies somewhat in size, shape and colour. Attached to this is another row, often growing together and resembling a tube. This is the cup, corona or trumpet. It varies even more than the perianth, and petal edges can be serrated, split or rolled.

Daffodils and narcissi come both short

Recommended daffodils and narcissi

Trumpet daffodils (Div 1)	'Dutch Master'†‡ (soft yellow; E); 'Explorer'† (yellow; M); 'Golden Harvest'† (golden-yellow; very large; E); 'Joseph MacLeod'† (yellow; large; M); 'Magnet' (white/yellow; M); 'Mrs E. H. Krelage'† (creamy/white; M); 'Mount Hood' (white; M); 'Queen of Bicolors' (white/canary-yellow; M); 'Spellbinder' (greeny-yellow/white; E); 'Unsurpassable'† (golden-yellow; large; M); 'W. P. Milner'‡ (sulphur-white; miniature; 20 cm [8 in]; VE)
Large-cupped narcissi (Div 2)	'Carlton'† (soft yellow; M); 'Flower Record' (white/yellow edged orange; M); 'Fortune' (yellow/orange-red; E); 'Gigantic Star' (mimosa-yellow/lemon-yellow; E); 'Ice Follies' (white; M); 'Mrs R. O. Backhouse'† (ivory/apricot-pink; M); 'Professor Einstein' (white/orange; VE); 'Rushlight' (lime-yellow; M); 'Semper Avanti'† (creamy-white/orange; E); 'Yellow Sun' (golden-yellow; E)
Small-cupped narcissi (Div 3)	'Barrett Browning'‡ (white/red; M); 'Birma' (yellow/orange-scarlet; M); 'Edward Buxton' (yellow/deep orange; M); 'Engadine' (white,

stemmed and tall; with tiny blooms or massive flowers. There are many shapes and forms, some with double flowers and some with three to eight or more blooms per stem. Quite a number of daffodil blooms are scented. Fragrance is greatest in some species and in the Jonquil, Poeticus and Tazetta hybrids. It is barely noticeable in the trumpet daffodils and large- and small-cupped varieties, and rare in the Cyclamineus and Triandrus hybrids.

The miniature types flower earlier than the larger cultivars, and also provide greater scope in garden applications. The table identifies miniatures, in terms of both stature and size of flower, and gives an indication of flowering time. The genus as a whole blooms earlier in warmer climates, but they still appear in sequence. In more continental climates, the whole daffodil season is shortened.

Uses of narcissi and daffodils

Size – both overall height and flower size – is the major factor governing the uses of the various species and cultivars. The miniatures are ideal for rock gardens, for mass foundation plantings, to grow between paving stones, for edging and in outdoor containers, and some species are well suited to naturalization in grass. They will thrive among ground-cover plants and will even do well between light-leaved shrubs. Most miniatures, like their bigger sisters, make long-lasting cut flowers.

Many varieties of the taller trumpets, large-cupped and small-cupped divisions, as indicated in the table, can effectively compete with both smooth and rough grass, and look lovely when scatter-planted as if growing wild. The larger daffodils are ideal border subjects, but do remember that the bright clear blooms will last longer and stay fresher if planted where sunlight is filtered. Narcissi are equally attractive interplanted between evergreen and flowering shrubs, or grouped under deciduous trees.

Wherever you plant them, they provide garden glory, either on their own or with other bulbs like early tulips and hyacinths, chionodoxa, muscari, scillas and others. Colourful combinations can be similarly achieved with many bedding plants and perennials flowering at the same time. Always plant at least five bulbs of the same variety in a group for maximum impact. In larger gardens, drifts of daffodils in their hundreds through parts of the lawn or borders can truly produce 'a host of golden daffodils . . . fluttering and dancing in the breeze'.

Species narcissi

Almost all the wild forms have flowers of miniature type, and most are small in overall stature. The smallest of all is *N. asturiensis* (*N. minimus*), whose tiny yellow trumpets stand less than 8 cm (3 in) tall. It is very early-flowering, as are two varieties of the common English wild daffodil or Lent lily, *N. pseudonarcissus lobularis* (with white perianth and yellow trumpet) and the Tenby daffodil, *N. pseudonarcissus obvallaris* (bright

Narcissus 'Texas'

Narcissus 'Thalia'

Narcissus 'Actaea'

Narcissus cyclamineus

	centre tinged green; M); 'Verger'† (white/deep orange; M)	**Jonquil narcissi** (Div 7)	'Golden Perfection'*‡ (golden-yellow; miniature; M); 'Golden Sceptre'*‡ (deep golden-yellow; miniature; E); 'Suzy'* (yellow; M); 'Sweetness'* (yellow; M); 'Trevithian'* (yellow; M)
Double narcissi (Div 4)	*N. albus plenus odoratus** (snowy-white; gardenia-like; L); 'Cheerfulness'* (creamy, orange edge; multi-flowered; L); 'Flower Drift' (white/yellow; M); 'Mary Copeland' (creamy-white/lemon-yellow and orange; L); 'Texas' (pale yellow/orange-red; M); 'Van Sion'†‡ ('Telemonius Plenus'; golden-yellow; E); 'White Lion' (white, creamy centre; M); 'Yellow Cheerfulness' (primrose-yellow; multi-flowered; L)	**Tazetta and Poetaz narcissi** (Div 8)	'Cragford'* (white/orange; multi-flowered; E); 'Geranium'* (white/deep orange; multi-flowered; L); 'Silver Chimes'*‡ (white/creamy-yellow; multi-flowered; miniature; 25 cm [10 in]; L)
		Poeticus narcissi (Div 9)	'Actaea'*† (white/yellow edged red; M); 'Cantabile'* (white/green edged red M); 'Winifred van Greven'* (white/yellow edged red; M)
Triandrus narcissi (Div 5)	'April Tears'*‡ (yellow; multi-flowered; miniature; M); 'Dawn'*‡ white/lemon-yellow; multi-flowered; miniature; M); 'Hawera'‡ (bright yellow; multi-flowered; miniature; M); 'Thalia'‡ (white; multi-flowered; miniature; M); 'White Marvel' (white; double; multi-flowered; 45 cm [18 in]; M)		
Cyclamineus narcissi	'February Gold'†‡ (yellow; miniature; E); 'Jack Snipe'†‡ (white/orange-yellow; miniature; E); 'March Sunshine'†‡ (golden-yellow; miniature; E); 'Peeping Tom' (yellow; 35 cm [14 in]; E/M)		

Scented variety; †suitable for naturalizing in grass; ‡suitable for outdoor containers
Colours: Where two colours are given, first refers to outer perianth; second to inner cup
Sizes in words refer to flowers themselves
Heights: Except where otherwise stated, heights are as follows: Triandrus and Cyclamineus narcissi, 20 to 30 cm (8 to 12 in); others, 35 to 48 cm (14 to 19 in)
Flowering season: VE = very early (late winter); E = early (early spring); M = mid-season (mid-spring); L = late (late spring to very early summer)

yellow). They are 18 and 25 cm (7 and 10 in) tall respectively.

The bulk of the species and their forms flower a little later, in early spring. They include the hoop-petticoat daffodils, *N. bulbocodium* (bright yellow; 15 cm [6 in]) and its forms *N. bulbocodium citrinus* (lemon-yellow; 15 cm [6 in]) and *N. bulbocodium conspicuus* (golden-yellow; 15 cm [6 in]); the type species of the Cyclamineus narcissi, *N. cyclamineus* (yellow; 15 cm [6 in]); the tiny trumpet-type *N. minor conspicuus* (*N. nanus*) (yellow; 10 cm [4 in]); the scented campernelles, *N. × odorus* 'Campernelli' and its double form 'Campernelli Plenus' (both golden-yellow; multi-flowered; 25 cm [10 in]); and the angel's-tears narcissus, *N. triandrus albus* (creamy-white; multi-flowered; 18 cm [7 in]), with its back-swept outer petals.

Among the late-flowering kinds, all of them strongly scented, are *N. canaliculatus* (white perianth, golden-yellow cup; multi-flowered; 15 cm [6 in]); *N. × gracilis* (pale yellow; multi-flowered; 30 cm [12 in]); the jonquil, the parent of the Jonquil cultivars, *N. jonquilla* (golden-yellow; multi-flowered; 30 cm [12 in]); and the poet's narcissus, *N. poeticus* (perianth white, cup pale yellow with red edge; 38 cm [15 in]), which is the parent of the Poeticus cultivars.

The flamboyant tulips

The tulip is one of the most popular bulb flowers in the world, with a long flowering season and a most spectacular range of colours and forms. A member of the lily family, the genus *Tulipa* consists of some 100 species, but there are about 4,000 recognized cultivars ranging from 10 cm (4 in) to nearly 1 m (3 ft) in height.

Their colours range from white to near-black, from soft pink to lilac and purple, from palest yellow and green-tinged tones to flaming scarlet. They can be self-coloured, or striped, streaked, shaded or tinged with other colours. Tulip flowers have six petals and are basically cup-shaped, but variations are wide. Some are egg-shaped, some are like turbans, and some open wide. In some the petals are frilled or fringed. Most have one flower on each stem, while a few species are multi-flowered. A few are scented, and most make excellent cut flowers. The main challenge is to use their flamboyant colours effectively.

Uses and cultivation

The flowering time, height, form, colour and habit of a tulip will suggest ways in which it can be used effectively in the garden, in groups by itself or with other bulbs or plants that complement or contrast with it. By selecting varieties from different classes, you can enjoy months of tulip flower. They create great impact planted in informal or formal beds, in mixed borders or rock gardens, between paving stones, roses or shrubs, beside walls, fences or steps, to form a foundation

Tulipa 'Texas Gold'

planting or in window-boxes or other outdoor containers. Plant some just for cutting, too.

Tulips prefer light, rich, porous and well-drained soil and sunny positions. Always plant the bulbs late – from mid-autumn into early winter. If possible, plant them in a fresh site where tulips did not grow the previous year. If you must grow them in the same ground annually, use a suitable fungicide such as quintozene (see p 361) to prevent disease. A fungal disorder called fire disease is tulips' main enemy (see p 367).

Plant the taller types (including all garden cultivars) 15.5 to 15 cm (5 to 6 in) deep and at

Tulipa 'Absalon'

least 10 cm (4 in) apart. Shorter species and their hybrids can be slightly shallower and closer. Like all bulbs, they like plenty of water during growth, and a foliar feed (see p 352) after flowering helps to boost the build-up of the bulbs for the next season. After the foliage has withered, you can lift the bulbs, clean them and store them in a cool, well-ventilated place until autumn. But lifting is not essential every year except in extreme climates. They are hardy in most climates and do not need winter protection, but are better lifted annually in damp conditions. Thin out naturalized colonies every few years.

Garden tulips

The official classification of tulips lists 15 divisions – 11 of the so-called garden tulips, three of cultivars derived from the species, and the last comprising true species and their direct hybrids. The first two divisions contain the early-flowering garden cultivars, the first to bloom being the Single Early tulips, from mid-spring. They are cup-shaped, with strong 25 to 38 cm (10 to 15 in) stems, and are good for massing in beds or borders. The Double Earlies flower slightly later, with large, wide-open double flowers on 25 to 30 cm (10 to 12 in) stems. They are generally longer-lasting, and are ideal for massed display in sheltered beds.

Among the mid-season group, Mendel tulips have single flowers, some of them bicolours, on slender 40 to 60 cm (16 to 24 in) stems. They flower from middle to late spring, and are best planted in groups in sheltered positions. Triumph tulips, also singles, are of similar height but are sturdier. The blooms, commonly shaded and margined in contrasting colours, are virtually weather-resistant and ideal for exposed positions.

Earlier than the Darwins themselves and boasting the biggest blooms of all tulips are the Darwin Hybrids. They are equally outstanding for their brilliant colours and superb stature. The flowers are massive single cups, especially noted for glowing shades of red, standing stalwart and spectacular on stems 55 to 70 cm (22 to 28 in) tall.

Tulipa 'Princess Margaret Rose'

Among the late-flowering tulips, most of which start to flower in late spring, the Darwin tulips are the most weather-resistant. They have long been famous for their large-cupped squared-off flowers, their wide colour range and satiny texture, and their tall, sturdy stems – up to 80 cm (32 in). In direct contrast, the Lily-flowered tulips, graceful and elegant, have beautifully reflexed and pointed petals. The blooms stand on wiry 45 to 60 cm (18 to 24 in) stems in rich, full and glowing colours.

The Cottage tulips, which are particularly varied in form, are also late-flowering. The

Recommended tulip cultivars

Single Early (Div 1)	'Bellona'* (golden-yellow; E); 'Brilliant Star' (scarlet; E); 'General de Wet'* (fiery-orange, stippled scarlet; E); 'Prince of Austria'* (orange-red; E); 'Prins Carnival'* (yellow flamed red; E); 'Yokohama' (yellow; M)
Double Early (Div 2)	'Carlton' (deep Turkey-red; M); 'Electra' (cherry-red; E); 'Mr van der Hoef' (golden-yellow; E); 'Orange Nassau' (orange-scarlet; E); 'Peach Blossom' (rosy-pink; E); 'Schoonoord' (white; E)
Mendel (Div 3)	'Apricot Beauty' (salmon-rose tinted red; M); 'Athleet' (white; M); 'Olga (violet-red edged white; M); 'Pink Trophy' (pink flushed rose; E); 'Van der Eerden' (red; M)
Triumph (Div 4)	'Attila' (violet; M); 'Danton' (deep carmine; L); 'Garden Party' (white edged carmine; M); 'Golden Melody (buttercup-yellow; M); 'Hibernia' (white; M) 'Kees Nelis' (red edged yellow; M); 'Orange Wonder'* (orange; M); 'Peerless Pink' (satiny-pink; M)
Darwin Hybrids (Div 5)	'Apeldoorn' (orange-scarlet; E); 'Dover (poppy-red; E); 'Elizabeth Arden' (salmon; M); 'Golden Apeldoorn' (golden-yellow; E); 'Gudoshnik' (sulphur-yellow tinted red; E); 'Holland's Glory' (deep carmine edged poppy-red, interior mandarin-red; M); 'Lefeber's Favourite' (scarlet; E); 'Red Matad (carmine flushed scarlet; E)

Tulipa fosteriana 'Red Emperor'

Tulipa greigii 'Red Riding Hood'

Species and their hybrids

A large number of species tulips are available to gardeners, but the most important in breeding have been *Tulipa fosteriana, T. greigii* and *T. kaufmanniana.* The Kaufmanniana hybrids have inherited their parent's 'water-lily' flowers, which open out flat on short 10 to 25 cm (4 to 10 in) stems. Many have also retained mottled, striped or spotted leaves.

Fosteriana hybrids, noted for their flamboyant, glowing colours and massive blooms, have sturdy stems ranging from 20 to 45 cm (8 to 18 in) tall. The Greigii hybrids are remarkable for their long-lasting, brilliant 'oriental'-coloured blooms and beautifully marked leaves. The cup-shaped flowers can be 12.5 cm (5 in) or more across, the stems varying from 10 to 50 cm (4 to 20 in), but mostly at least 25 cm (10 in).

Among the many species tulips worth growing, some of the best are as follows. *Tulipa pulchella violacea* ('Violet Queen'), with crocus-like blooms in violet-pink on 15 cm (6 in) stems, flowers as early as late winter. For early spring bloom try the flame-scarlet multi-flowered *T. praestans* 'Fusilier', just 15 to 20 cm (6 to 8 in) tall; or the large, bell-shaped, shiny scarlet *T. eichleri* on 30 cm (12 in) stems. For mid-spring there is the dainty, scented, star-shaped, orange-pink *T. aucheriana,* only 8 cm (3 in) tall; the graceful buttercup-yellow and cherry-rose *T. clusiana chrysantha,* 15 cm (6 in) in height; the multi-flowered *T. kolpakowskiana,* about 20 cm (8 in) tall and golden-yellow shaded copper-

large, primarily pastel-coloured flowers are basically egg-shaped, with long, pointed petals. They include some multi-flowered cultivars, as well as a growing range of Viridiflora, or green tulips. Most are 45 to 80 cm (18 to 32 in) tall, but a few are less than 25 cm (10 in) in height. They are ideal for mass plantings, the multi-flowered types being most effective as focal groups in sheltered locations.

Rembrandt tulips, with their 'broken' colours, are limited in variety and supply, but make exotic groups in the garden and are

valued for flower arrangements. All have large single cups on 45 to 70 cm (18 to 30 in) stems. Parrot tulips are actually all sports from tulips of other divisions, having massive flowers with fringed, waved or scalloped petals. They come on sturdy stems 50 to 60 cm (20 to 26 in) tall. They look dramatic in groups sheltered from winds.

The final garden division consists of Double Late tulips, dubbed paeony-flowered because of their big, squat, double flowers on strong 40 to 60 cm (16 to 24 in) stems. They do best in sheltered positions.

Darwin (Div 6)	'Clara Butt' (salmon-pink; L); 'Demeter' (plum-purple; E); 'Dix's Favourite' (glowing red; M); 'Greuze' (violet-purple; L); 'Landseadel's Supreme' (cherry-red; M); 'Pink Attraction' (silvery violet-rose; L); 'Queen of Night' (velvety-maroon; L); 'Sunkist' (deep yellow; L)	Double Late (Div 11)	'Eros* (deep rose; E); 'Gold Medal' (deep yellow; M); 'Lilac Perfection' (pearly-lilac; M); Mount Tacoma' (white; M); 'Orange Triumph' (rich orange, rimmed gold; M); 'Uncle Tom' (maroon-red; M)
Lily-Flowered (Div 7)	'Aladdin' (scarlet edged yellow; M); 'China Pink' (satin-pink; M); 'Queen of Sheba' (red edged orange; M); 'Red Shine' (deep red; L); 'West Point' (primrose-yellow; M); 'White Triumphator' (white; M)	Kaufmanniana hybrids (Div 12)	'Alfred Cortot' (carmine-red and deep scarlet; mottled leaves; VE); 'Goudstuk' (carmine edged yellow, interior golden-yellow; E); 'Heart's Delight' (carmine-red, interior pale rose; mottled leaves; E); 'Shakespeare' (salmon, apricot and orange; E); 'The First' (white flushed red, interior ivory; E)
Cottage (Div 8)	'Artist' (salmon-rose and green; 25 cm [10 in]; L); 'Balalaika' (Turkey-red; M); 'Burgundy Lace' (wine-red; fringed edge; L); 'Golden Harvest' (lemon-yellow; M); 'Groenland' ('Greenland'; green edged rose; L); 'Maureen' (marble-white; L); 'Princess Margaret Rose' (yellow edged orange-red; L)	Fosteriana hybrids (Div 13)	'Galata' (orange-red; E); 'Princeps' (orange-scarlet; E); 'Purissima' (white; E); 'Red Emperor' ('Madame Lefeber'; vermilion-red; E); 'Yellow Empress' (golden-yellow; E)
Rembrandt (Div 9)	'Absalon' (coffee-brown on yellow; L); 'Black Boy' (dark chocolate on garnet brown; M); 'Dainty Maid' (magenta-purple on white; M); 'Victor Hugo' (cherry-rose on white; M)	Greigii hybrids (Div 14)	'Cape Cod' (apricot edged yellow, interior bronze-yellow; 20 cm [8 in]; 'Golden Day' (lemon-yellow tinged red; M); 'Oriental Beauty' (carmine-red; E); 'Perlina' (silvery salmon-rose; M); 'Red Riding Hood' (carmine-red; 12.5 cm [5 in]; M); 'Yellow Dawn' (old rose banded yellow, interior yellow; E)
Parrot (Div 10)	'Black Parrot' (purplish-black; L); 'Blue Parrot' (bright violet; L); 'Comet' (orange-red edged yellow; M); 'Fantasy' (rose, sometimes streaked green; L); 'Orange Favourite'* (orange blotched green; L); 'Red Champion' (blood-red; L); 'Texas Gold' (deep yellow; L)		

*Scented variety
Height: Except where otherwise stated, heights are within the range described in the text
Flowering season: VE = very early (early spring); E = early (mid-spring); M = mid-season (middle to late spring); L = late spring to very early summer)

Tulipa clusiana

red; and the bunch-flowered *T. tarda (T. dasystemon)*, with white and yellow starry blooms on a 15 cm (6 in) stem.

For late spring you can choose from the unusual *T. acuminate,* with long, thin, curled, spidery petals of yellow streaked with red on a stem 45 to 50 cm (18 to 20 in) tall; *T. linifolia,* with a glossy scarlet pointed flower, or the very similar pale yellow species *T. batalinii,* both with 10 to 15 cm (4 to 6 in) stems. The latest to bloom is *T. celsiana (T. persica)*, with several scented, star-like flowers of pale yellow with bronze exteriors on each 8 to 12 cm (3 to 5 in) stem.

The dependable, fragrant hyacinths

The delightful fragrance of its heady perfume, its clear translucent colours, its perfect form, its timely bloom in mid-spring and its ease of cultivation have endeared the hyacinth to flower-lovers and gardeners for many centuries. Today, it is among the most popular of indoor plants and is enjoying a renaissance in modern labour-saving gardens.

It is derived from *Hyacinthus orientalis*, prevalent in ancient times in many areas of the eastern Mediterranean. This is the parent of the present-day garden or Dutch hyacinth, and is the only species of its genus; related plants still often listed under *Hyacinthus* are now classified in other genera (see below).

The wild species has 5 to 15 individual florets, small and widely spaced, on weak stems about 25 cm (10 in) tall. The original colour was blue, but in cultivation the plant soon developed bud variations of white and purple. It was in 1612 that the first double-flowered hyacinths derived from the species

Hyacinthus orientalis 'City of Haarlem'

were mentioned, and a few double cultivars are still obtainable from specialist suppliers. The species itself is no longer widely cultivated, but over 300 years of breeding and selection have produced today's rich, thickly-flowered hyacinths, with sturdy stems and greater fragrance.

Uses and cultivation

Dutch hyacinths are suited to any garden, large or small, in many locations. They can be used in formal beds or borders; in informal groups near the house, along garden paths or at the base or top of walls. They do well in raised beds, in foundation plantings, between shrubs, at the base of light-leaved trees, among ground covers and in outdoor containers. Their pastel colours blend or contrast beautifully with tulips, narcissi, muscari and other bulbous and non-bulbous plants flowering in mid-spring.

Hyacinths like sandy, well-drained soils, and will produce superior blooms in well-dug humus-rich soils in sunny positions in all but the most extreme climates. They may be planted at any time in autumn, about 12 to 15 cm (5 to 6 in) deep and between 10 and 15 cm (4 and 6 in) apart according to application. Water well after planting and maintain adequate moisture throughout growth. No fertilizer is needed with newly planted bulbs.

Hyacinthus orientalis 'Blue Jacket'

Bulbs described as bedding-size are ample for garden use. All Dutch hyacinths bloom outdoors in mid-spring, but for the longest succession of flower choose a selection of varieties from the early, mid-season and late-flowering groups, as indicated in the table.

Because growers give their bulbs hot-air treatment after harvesting, gardeners rarely come across the yellow, black, white or root rot that can affect hyacinths. Should any plant's growth appear stunted, malformed or parched or bear black spots, or should bulb scales become sticky white, the only solution is to destroy the bulbs and sterilize the soil. The appearance of grey fluffy mould demands a weekly spray of copper fungicide (see p 361) and the burning of all rotted blooms and foliage.

Dead blooms should be removed immediately after flowering, but it is not essential to lift bulbs annually except in areas prone to severe winters. When bulbs are left *in situ*, apply a generous top-dressing of bonemeal before the buds emerge the following spring. If lifting your bulbs, delay this until foliage has completely died down. Then clean and store the bulbs in a cool, dry, well-ventilated place until planting time returns.

Hyacinths degenerate more rapidly than any other bulbs, particularly in regions where the spring is very warm. When left *in situ* they produce fewer and smaller flowers, but these are ideal for flowering arrangements. It is less

Recommended Dutch hyacinths

Early	'Bismarck' (porcelain-blue); 'Colosseum' (white); 'Jan Bos' (blood-red); 'Orange Boven' ('Salmonetta'; apricot-salmon); 'Pink Pearl' (clear pink)
Mid-season	'Blue Jacket' (dark blue); 'Lady Derby' (shell-pink); 'L'Innocence' (white); 'Myosotis' (light sky-blue); 'Perle Brillante' (ice-blue); 'Yellow Hammer' (creamy-yellow)
Late	'Amethyst' (lilac-violet); 'Carnegie' (white); 'City of Haarlem' (primrose-yellow); 'Eros' (rosy-red); 'King of the Blues' (indigo-blue); 'Marconi' (deep rose-pink); 'Queen of the Pinks' (bright rose-pink)

Flowering season: All hyacinths flower over a period of about a month in mid-spring, but in the sequence indicated above

expensive to buy new bulbs than to attempt t maintain big, fat bulbs. Propagation is com plicated and best left to professionals.

Related species

The best-known hyacinth-relatives are th Roman and summer hyacinths. The forme now officially *Bellevalia romana* though ofte listed as *Hyacinthus romanus* or *H. oriental albulus*, has scented white bell-flowers i spring. They grow on stems up to 25 cr (10 in) tall; it thrives in a rock garden. Th multi-flowered fairy hyacinths were derive from this species, but with rare exceptions ca only be cultivated successfully indoors. Th closely related *B.* (*H.*) *dalmatica* produces i spring an inflorescence of many small, pa blue flowers on a 15 cm (6 in) stem. It is rock-garden gem.

Galtonia (*Hyacinthus*) *candicans*, th summer hyacinth, bears racemes of 15 to 2 large, scented, drooping, milk-white bells o

Hyacinthus orientalis 'L'Innocence'

sturdy 0.75 to 1.25 m (2½ to 4 ft) stems i middle and late summer from spring plant ings. It is ideal for borders, naturalization an as a cut flower. *Hyacinthella azurea* (*Hyacin thus azureus* or *Muscari azureum*) is similar t a grape hyacinth, with a close-packed 22 cr (9 in) spike of small, bright blue, bell-shape scented flowers in spring. It is superb in sunny rock garden. For true grape hyacinth (*Muscari* spp), see page 201.

Galtonia candicans

Gladioli: sword lilies of summer

Apart from the lilies, gladioli are the most important of the summer-flowering bulbous plants. They are best known for the large-flowered hybrids that are so popular for garden decoration and make superb cut flowers. These have been produced in great variety in an almost unlimited range of colour.

Gladioli are sometimes called sword lilies because of their distinctive narrow, pointed leaves. The flower consists of three large upper segments and three smaller lower ones, but in one group – the Primulinus varieties – the central uppermost petal is hooded. The whole flower is curved and funnel-shaped. The spikes of flowers, ranging in height from 0.6 to 1.8 m (2 to 6 ft), each carry from 1 to 14 or more florets, all facing the same way at regular intervals along the spike. They open in succession from the bottom upwards, maintaining bloom for several weeks. The species gladioli are equally beautiful but produce smaller and less flamboyant blooms. Most,

Primulinus gladioli have flowers less than 8 cm (3 in) in diameter, but the triangular florets, which are commonly blotched, are most graceful, on a thin, flexible 75 to 90 cm (2½ to 3 ft) stem. They make dainty cut flowers and handsome clumps in beds and borders. Butterfly gladioli are a blotched and bicoloured race from Holland with 8 to 9 cm (3 to 3½ in) wide ruffled florets on a 90 cm (3 ft) spike. Like the early and mid-season Primulinus varieties, they bloom in mid- and late summer, and have identical uses.

Cultivation of hybrid gladioli

Plant plump, firm corms in sheltered positions in full sun in any well-drained, humus-rich neutral soil. Ideally it should be double-dug (see p 334), incorporating 135 g/m² (4 oz/sq yd) of a complete garden fertilizer of analysis about 10:10:10 (see p 352). Plant in groups of 10 to 25, about 15 cm (6 in) apart in circles for easy staking or utilization of a

patent ring support. Begin planting in spring after frost is out of the soil, setting the corms 10 to 15 cm (4 to 6 in) deep, on a thin layer of sand. To extend the flowering season to as much as three months, continue planting at regular intervals until early summer. Prevent thrips from streaking the foliage and mottling the blooms by rolling the corms in a dust containing BHC before planting.

Water well after planting and liberally during growth, adding liquid manure as buds form. Frequent shallow cultivation and mulching is advisable. When the foliage is dead, lift the plants, cut off the tops above the corms and dry them off. After a few weeks, separate the corms and place them in a well-ventilated frost-free winter store.

Hardy species gladioli

The early-flowering species gladioli available for outdoor application are limited. Cultivation is similar to that for the hybrids, but

Gladiolus Large-flowered hybrids

Gladiolus 'Aldebaran'

Gladiolus 'Fidelio'

Gladiolus Primulinus and Butterfly hybrids

however, are too tender for anything but greenhouse cultivation in temperate zones.

Hybrid gladioli

The hybrid gladioli are classified according to size of flower, colour and conspicuous markings, the systems varying somewhat between Britain, Australia, Holland and North America. There are three main types, however: the Large-flowered, the Primulinus and the Butterfly hybrids. All are good for cutting.

The Large-flowered types provide the biggest choice and longest flowering season, from midsummer to early autumn if planted in succession. The flowers, often ruffled or semi-ruffled, are over 11.5 cm (4½ in) in diameter, and are carried on strong spikes between 1 and 1.8 m (3 and 6 ft) tall. They are effective at the back of borders, against fences or walls, or interplanted between shrubs.

Recommended gladiolus cultivars

Large-flowered	'Ardent' (cherry-red); 'Bloemfontein' (salmon blotched yellow); 'Blue Conquerer' (violet-blue, lighter throat); 'Eurovision' (light vermilion-red); 'Flos Florium' (salmon-pink); 'Flowersong' (yellow, carmine throat); 'Grock' (purple); 'Memorial Day' (reddish-magenta); 'Morning Kiss' (white); 'My Love' (old rose shaded rose-white); 'New Europe' (geranium-red); 'Pink Sensation' (light pink blotched white); 'President de Gaulle' (orange-red); 'Vink's Glory' (canary-yellow)
Primulinus	'Columbine' (soft carmine-rose shaded pink); 'Harmony' (cyclamen-purple marked white); 'Little Jade Green' (green and yellow); 'Pretoria' (coral-red flecked apricot and gold); 'White City' (white); 'Yellow Special' (sunflower-yellow)
Butterfly	'Ares' (creamy-white blotched red); 'Dancing Doll' (soft pink blotched carmine-pink); 'Gallant Lady' (deep yellow); 'Green Woodpecker' (greenish-yellow blotched red); 'Pink Pearl' (shell-pink); 'Salina' (burgundy-red splashed yellow)

corms of the species should be planted in autumn about 8 cm (3 in) deep and 15 cm (6 in) apart. A protective mulch is mandatory in areas with severe winters.

Gladiolus byzantinus has 5 to 12 trumpet-shaped purple-red flowers on a 60 cm (2 ft) stem in early summer, and is ideal for rock gardens, borders, naturalizing and cutting. There is a pure white form, *G. byzantinus albus. G. imbricatus* is an equally hardy species with dark purple blooms on stems 45 to 60 cm (1½ to 2 ft) tall. It flowers in early summer, and has identical applications.

The group of hybrids sometimes listed under *G. nanus* or *G. × colvillei* have delicate small flowers on 45 to 60 cm (1½ to 2 ft) stems in early summer. The colour range is extensive, and you can buy either mixtures or named cultivars. Use them in border clumps or drifts, or plant *en masse* for cutting.

The varied, versatile irises

Irises are among the most important and diverse of all bulbous plants, ranging from jewels that bring a sparkle to the winter rock garden to the tall, stately 'flags' of summer flower borders. Their gorgeous blooms – quite unlike any others – are noted for their dramatic colour variations. Altogether, there are 300 *Iris* species and many more hybrids.

The iris flower is unique, having six perianth segments linked by a short tube above the ovary. The outer three segments have reflexed (bent-under) petals known as falls, which in some types have a 'beard' of fleshy hairs. The inner three are smaller and, except in the Juno group, stand vertically; they are the standards. Three lipped styles – looking rather like petals and often having a crest – project between falls and standards.

Cultivation and uses

The diversity of irises can be confusing, but there are two main types: those with true bulbs, which include types useful for beds and borders, for rock gardens and as cut flowers; and those with rhizomes that grow on or below the soil surface, which are mostly border plants, but also include types that are at home in the rock garden or wild garden and some aquatic and semi-aquatic kinds. With the exception of one or two winter-flowering

Iris 'Professor Blaauw' (Dutch)

types, the flowering season of the various kinds extends from spring to midsummer.

Although cultivation requirements vary somewhat, all irises like open sunny positions, good drainage, plenty of moisture during their relatively short growing and flowering season, and a long period of baking on the sun after growth has died down. A few like acid soil, some appreciate a little lime but the majority do best on neutral soil.

The rhizomatous types should be planted from midsummer to early autumn, or in spring; in the latter case, no flowers can be expected in the first year. Trim the leaves by about half before planting. After three or four years, the rhizomes are liable to become overcrowded. Lift the whole clump in late summer or autumn, and cut the rhizomes with a sharp knife into sections, each containing at least

Iris 'Marquette' (Dutch)

one 'eye'; discard the old woody centre of the rhizome. Set the pieces about 60 cm (2 ft) apart in well-worked soil, with the roots well spread out. Except for the cushion and related types, which should be covered with 2.5 cm (1 in) of soil, only partly cover the rhizomes, leaving the top exposed.

Plant bulbous irises in autumn, the smaller types 5 to 8 cm (2 to 3 in) deep, the larger Dutch, English and Spanish irises about 10 cm (4 in) deep. Planting distances range from 5 to 30 cm (2 to 12 in) according to size. All the bulbs multiply by offsets or from lateral rootlets, and most can be left in the ground until overcrowded. The Spanish irises should, however, be lifted once the foliage dies down, to assist ripening, and replanted in autumn.

Irises are generally sturdy, although bulbs and rhizomes may be attacked by fungal infections that cause rotting. Badly affected plants must be burnt, though bulbs that are only slightly infected by ink disease – in which black patches appear on the outer scales –

Iris 'Wabash' (Bearded)

Anatomy of an iris flower
The upper petals **1** are called standards, the lower **2** falls; these may have a beard **3**. In some, the style **4** is visible.

may be treated by soaking in weak (1:300 formalin solution.

Rhizomatous irises

There are four main groups of irises that have rhizomes. They are the bearded, the beardless, the cushion (or Oncocylus) and related irises, which are sometimes classed in the bearded group, and the crested.

Bearded irises This group, with hairy beards on the falls, have flowers that resemble those of some orchids. They include a few mainly late-spring-flowering species of garden value and a large number of hybrids, and range from 10 cm (4 in) dwarfs to the flag irises 90 cm (3 ft) or more tall. Among the species, *Iris pumila* is the smallest and earliest, its stemless flowers – purple, white or yellow and 5 to 8 cm (2 to 3 in) across – appearing in mid-spring. A little later, *I. chamaeiris* shows its flowers of bright and pale yellow, white or purple, on 15 cm (6 in) stems.

The taller species include *I. biflora* (*I. aphylla*), with scented purple and white flowers on 40 cm (15 in) stems, and *I. variegata,* with chestnut and yellow flowers on 45 cm (18 in) stems and tufts of fine leaves. The tallest species include *I. germanica,* the purple flag iris, and the fragrant *I. pallida,* which is lavender-blue. They grow to 90 cm (3 ft).

The biggest choice is provided by the hardy hybrids, which range in stem height from around 15 cm (6 in) to 1 m or more (over 3 ft) and in flower size from about 8 to 15 cm (3 to 6 in). The flowering season is from late spring to early summer, and specialist growers list dozens of modern named cultivars, in shades of white, yellow, brown, pink, rose, blue, violet and purple. Avoid old, inferior cultivars.

Beardless irises These also have big, showy flowers. They like sunny, sheltered positions and some kinds need protection in winter. Most like neutral or slightly acid soil. Th group includes such aquatic and semi-aquatic kinds as the blue *I. laevigata* and the yellow *I. pseudacorus* and some, such as *I. kaempferi* (purple and yellow) and *I. sibirica* (blue), which do well in moist border soil as well as at the margins of pools (see pp 256 and 257). The same applies to *I. chrysographes*, a variable species whose flowers range from almost black to reddish-purple and blue, with gold markings. Most of the above have named forms, particularly notable being the Sibirica hybrids, ranging from light blue to deep purple, with some white forms as well, and the varieties of *I. kaempferi* raised in Japan, which have a wide range of self- and multi-coloured forms. The above range in height from 45 to 90 cm (1½ to 3 ft).

One of the smallest of the group is *I. unguicularis* (*I. stylosa*), which has scented lavender-blue flowers in winter on 30 cm (12 in) stems. Even shorter is the hybrid 'Mary Barnard', also winter-blooming, with deep purple flowers on 15 to 20 cm (6 to 8 in) stems. *I. foetidissima*, about 60 cm (2 ft) tall, has small lavender-blue flowers in early summer, but the pods of big orange seeds are the main attraction. It is ideal beside water or in a wild garden, but beware of bruising the evergreen leaves; their unpleasant smell gives the plant its common name of stinking gladwyn.

Iris 'White Excelsior' (Dutch)

I. hexagona has soft lilac flowers in summer on 1.25 m (4 ft) branching stems. It and the 45 cm (18 in) *I. fulva,* with brick-red flowers, come from the lower Mississippi region of the United States. They are related to the Louisiana hybrids, which come in a wide colour range and grow 60 to 90 cm (2 to 3 ft) tall. In warm climates, these like very moist, rich soil, but prefer drier conditions where it is cooler. Protect with a peat mulch in winter.

Also in the beardless group are the rather tender Spuria species and hybrids, in a wide colour range, and the so-called Pacific Coast irises. The latter include such species as *I. douglasiana* and *I. innominata* and the Californian hybrids, most of which are raised from mixed seeds. They are good for cutting.

Cushion and related irises The Oncocyclus group are beautiful but difficult to grow. They

Iris chrysographes (Beardless)

have large, silky flowers with standards that curve inwards and a soft, diffuse beard (hence the term cushion) and a dark patch, on stems from 40 to 60 cm (15 to 24 in) tall. They flower in late spring or early summer. Plant the rhizomes in well-drained raised beds in humus-rich limy soil. Protect from rain with cloches in summer to ensure ripening of the rhizomes. The species include *I. gatesii,* with large greenish-white flowers speckled with reddish-brown and purple, and *I. susiana* (the mourning iris), which is silver-grey, veined with purple that looks almost black, and has a black patch on the falls.

Related to these, but easier to grow, are the Regelia types, which should be cultivated like bulbous irises and are sometimes catalogued with them. They are superb in sunny borders, and include *I. hoogiana* (fragrant, lavender-blue with a yellow beard) and *I. stolonifera* (cobalt-blue, brown and purple), both flowering in late spring and about 60 cm (2 ft) tall. Probably the best types, however, are the hybrids between the Oncocyclus and Regelia irises, which combine the flamboyance of the former with the easier culture of the latter. They are sometimes known as Oncogelias or Regeliocyclus. They come in shades of blue, violet, purple, brown and cream, often veined; they flower in late spring on 30 to 45 cm (12 to 18 in) stems.

Crested irises These have a crest rather like a cockscomb in place of the beard. They have glossy evergreen leaves. *I. japonica* is probably the best-known species, with bright blue flowers tinged with gold in late spring. They grow on thin 45 cm (18 in) stems. Give some winter protection. The 15 cm (6 in) *I. cristata* is hardier, and has flowers of lavender, white and orange; it is good for the rock garden.

Bulbous irises

Again, this group is subdivided, the various sub-sections being covered here in order of flowering, from late winter to midsummer.

Reticulata group These hardy, dwarf species, with rush-like leaves and mostly scented flowers, are excellent for rock gardens, the front of borders and containers. They are easy to grow and naturalize readily.

The smallest species, both 8 cm (3 in) tall, are *I. danfordiae,* with brown-spotted yellow flowers, and *I. histrioides* 'Major', white-spotted gentian-blue but unscented. Only slightly taller are *I. bakeriana,* which has ultramarine-blue standards and violet-blotched yellow falls, *I. histrio* (bright blue) and the well-known *I. reticulata* (violet splashed with gold). There are also over a dozen named hybrids in shades of blue, violet and purple.

Juno group These have small standards growing out horizontally, often below the falls. They do best in rather heavy soils, but increase very slowly from thick lateral roots which must not be broken off. They are multi-flowered, with several blooms on stems 30 to 60 cm (1 to 2 ft) tall. *I. bucharica* has scented cream flowers marked with yellow, while *I. graeberiana* is silvery-mauve and cobalt-blue. *I. magnifica* is pale lavender with orange markings. *I. aucheri* (*I. sindjarensis*) is another fragrant species, pale steel blue with a narrow yellow midrib; it needs glass protection in winter.

Dutch, English and Spanish irises These form the largest cultivated group of bulbous irises, being available in a wide range of colours and growing up to 60 cm (2 ft) tall. They are excellent for cutting, having flowers up to

Iris 'Violet Beauty' (Reticulata)

12 cm (5 in) across. They are all hybrids, the Dutch and Spanish being derived largely from *I. xiphium,* the English from *I. xiphioides.* The Dutch are the first to flower, and have more delicate blooms than the fragrant Spanish irises. Last come the English irises, which have the largest blooms, in midsummer. Bulb merchants list many forms of all three types.

Hermodactylus tuberosus

The so-called widow iris or snake's-head iris is sometimes listed as *I. tuberosa,* but is now properly called *Hermodactylus tuberosus.* The quaint solitary flowers have greenish standards, speckled with purplish-brown, and black falls. It blooms in mid- to late spring on 20 to 25 cm (8 to 10 in) stems. Grow it as for the Reticulata irises. It is ideal for the rock garden and unusual in flower arrangements.

The aristocratic, easy lilies

Exotic and beautiful, lilies are the hardiest of all summer-flowering bulbs and despite their delicate appearance are mostly easy to grow. Their bulbs may be relatively expensive, but they produce prolific bloom annually without lifting, provide an extensive range of forms and colours – many fragrant – and a flowering season from the beginning of summer into early autumn.

The genus *Lilium* consists of some eighty species native to the northern hemisphere in both the New and Old Worlds. They occur naturally from the tropics to the arctic. Derived from these are a vast number of hybrids. The flowers always have six petals, but these can be arranged in a variety of ways, so that the flowers may be open-faced, bowl-shaped, trumpet- or turban-shaped (as in the Turk's-cap varieties), and upright or pendent. According to their parentage and flower form, the various kinds are classified in nine divisions, not all of which are suitable for gardens in temperate regions, however. Those which are are mostly sun-lovers, but some will flourish in partial shade.

The flowers almost invariably appear as clusters of a few up to dozens of blooms on a stem. The delicate yet bright colours exclude only blue, and the petals are commonly beautifully veined, spotted or starred. Stem heights generally range from 60 cm to 2 m (2 to 7 ft), with some as small as 30 cm (12 in) and some as big as 3 m (10 ft). The closely related *Cardiocrinum giganteum* (sometimes called *Lilium giganteum*) is a woodland plant that can reach 4 m (13 ft), with twenty or more cream or greenish blooms to a stem. It flowers only once before dying, but new plants develop from offsets of the bulb.

Lilium 'Mrs R. O. Backhouse'

Lilium 'Fire King'

Cultivation

A lily bulb is quite unlike any other, consisting of overlapping fleshy scales and having no papery tunic. Unlike other bulbs, too, many lilies send out roots from the stem that emerges from the top of the bulb; these so-called stem-rooting lilies need to be planted deeper than those which only send out roots from the base. Another distinction is that lilies are never completely dormant, so it is doubly important to buy plump, firm bulbs and to plant them immediately. Plant in early spring or, in mild climates, late autumn.

Good drainage and rich soil are vital. Dig a hole deep and wide enough to accommodate the bulb and allow for root spread. Break up

the bottom and dig in garden compost, leaf-mould or peat. Surround the bulb with sand to help drainage and discourage slugs, and fill in with soil enriched with humus-forming material. Cover base-rooting lilies with 10 cm (4 in) of soil, except for *L. candidum* and *L. × testaceum*, which need only 5 cm (2 in). (Some growers leave the neck of the former above ground.) Stem-rooting lilies need at least 15 cm (6 in) of covering and a 5 cm (2 in) surface mulch of peat or leaf-mould. Plant cardiocrinums shallowly, grouping bulbs of varying sizes if possible, to establish a succession as the parent bulbs die.

Space the smaller types about 30 cm (12 in) apart, the larger ones about 45 cm (18 in);

Recommended lily hybrids and species

	Name	Colour	Height (metres [feet])	Stem/base rooting	Flowering season	Flower type; comments (for key, see footnotes)
Asiatic hybrids (Div 1)	'Brandywine'	Orange	0.9–1.25 (3–4)	Stem	Early	Outward-facing; C; LT; OC
	Fiesta Hybrids	Yellow, red, orange	0.9–1.5 (3–5)	Stem	Mid	Pendent; C; LT; OC
	'Fire King'	Nasturtium-flame	0.6–0.9 (2–3)	Stem	Mid	Outward-facing; C; LT; OC
	Harlequin Hybrids	Pink, red, purple, cream, yellow	0.9–1.25 (3–4)	Stem	Mid	Pendent; C; LT; OC
	'Maxwill'	Orange-red	1.5–1.8 (5–6)	Stem	Mid/late	Pendent; C; LT; OC
	Mid-Century Hybrids	Yellow to maroon-red	0.6–1.25 (2–4)	Stem	Early/mid	Upright; C; LT; OC
	'Orange Triumph'	Orange-yellow	0.6 (2)	Stem	Early	Outward-facing; C; LT; OC
	'White Gold'	Apricot	0.6–0.9 (2–3)	Stem	Mid	Pendent; C; LT; OC
Martagon hybrids (Div 2)	'Marhan'	Rich orange	1.25–1.5 (4–5)	Stem	Early/mid	Pendent, Turk's-cap; LT; PS
	'Mrs R. O. Backhouse'	Orange-yellow	1.25–1.5 (4–5)	Stem	Early/mid	Pendent, Turk's-cap; LT; PS
	Paisley Hybrids	White to orange, brown and lilac; spotted	0.9–1.5 (3–5)	Stem	Early	Pendent, Turk's-cap; PS
Candidum hybrids (Div 3)	*Lilium × testaceum**	Apricot	1.25–1.5 (4–5)	Base	Mid/late	Trumpet; plant very shallowly
American hybrids (Div 4)	Bellingham Hybrids*	Yellow to orange-red	1.5–2 (5–7)	Base	Mid	Turk's-cap; C; N; PS
	Del Norte Hybrids*	Shades of pink	1.5 (5)	Base	Mid	Turk's-cap; C; PS
Aurelian (Trumpet) hybrids (Div 6)	Black Magic strain*	Purple-brown; white inside	1.25–1.5 (4–5)	Stem	Mid/late	Funnel-shaped; LT; PS
	Golden Clarion strain*	Yellow to gold	0.9–1.5 (3–5)	Stem	Mid	Funnel-shaped; LT; PS
	Golden Splendor strain	Deep gold	1.25–1.8 (4–6)	Stem	Mid	Funnel-shaped; C; PS
	Golden Sunburst strain	Golden-yellow	1.25–1.5 (4–5)	Stem	Mid/late	Star-shaped; C; LT
	'Green Dragon'*	Chartreuse-green	0.9–1.8 (3–6)	Stem	Mid	Funnel-shaped; C
	Heart's Desire strain	White, cream, yellow-orange	1.5–1.8 (5–6)	Stem	Mid	Pendent; C; LT; PS
	'Limelight'*	Chartreuse-yellow	1.25–1.8 (4–6)	Stem	Mid	Funnel-shaped; C; LT; PS
	Olympic Hybrids*	Pink to green	1.25–1.5 (4–5)	Stem	Mid	Trumpet; C; LT; PS
	Pink Perfection strain	Violet to purple	1.5–2 (5–7)	Stem	Mid	Funnel-shaped; C; PS

Lilium speciosum 'Grand Commander'

Lilium 'Bright Star'

Lilium tigrinum

plant in groups of at least three. The larger kinds may need staking; insert the stakes at planting time to avoid damaging the bulbs. Do not allow the bulbs to dry out; water well after planting and then give an occasional soaking rather than frequent sprinklings. All lilies should receive a 5 cm (2 in) summer mulch of peat or leaf-mould to shade the roots. The proximity of shrubs such as rhododendrons or azaleas is helpful, and a ground cover of low-growing plants also helps conserve moisture.

Remove faded flowers as necessary, but do not cut stems completely back until autumn; otherwise they may harbour disease. Bulbs should not be lifted after the foliage has died down but left *in situ*, the dried foliage removed and bulbs given a winter mulch.

Apart from such vermin as squirrels, which may eat the bulbs, lilies' main enemies are slugs, aphids (which may carry a virus disease that distorts leaves), eelworms and two forms of fungal disease. One attacks leaves, the other the base of the bulb; benomyl fungicide will control both. See pages 358 to 367.

Types and applications

Because lilies are so varied in form, habit, height, colour and flowering time they lend themselves to a great many applications in the garden. When planting lilies, however, remember that, while they like their heads in the sun at least part of the time, they do best when their roots are shaded. Also take into account whether or not a particular kind will tolerate lime.

There are lily cultivars suited to beds, borders, rock gardens, wild gardens, outdoor containers and for interplanting between shrubs, ground covers and other plants. Others are ideal for naturalizing, to create vertical accents or to transform the appearance of a pond or stream. Most lilies make long-lasting cut flowers, and the entire flowering section of a plant may be taken provided the stem is cut above the leaves. These various characteristics and needs are indicated in the table with this article.

	Name	Colour	Height (metres [feet])	Stem/base rooting	Flowering season	Flower type; comments (for key, see footnotes)
Oriental hybrids (Div 7)	'Bonfire'	Crimson and white	1.25–1.5 (4–5)	Stem	Late	Bowl-shaped; C; OC
	Imperial Crimson strain*	Crimson and white	1.25–1.5 (4–5)	Stem	Late	Flat-faced; C
	Imperial Gold strain*	White, gold stripe	1.25–1.5 (4–5)	Stem	Late	Flat-faced; C
	Jamboree strain*	Crimson and white	1.25–1.5 (4–5)	Stem	Late	Recurved; C; OC
Species and their forms (Div 9)	L. auratum*	White and gold	1.25–2 (4–7)	Stem	Late	Open; C; PS; OC
	L. candidum* (Madonna lily)	Satin-white	0.9–1.25 (3–4)	Base	Early/mid	Chalice-like; C; LT; plant with nose exposed
	L. cernuum*	Purple-violet	0.3–0.6 (1–2)	Stem	Early/mid	Reflexed; LT; OC; R
	L. davidii	Cinnabar-red	1.25–1.8 (4–6)	Stem	Mid	Turk's-cap; C; LT; PS
	L. hansonii*	Golden-yellow	1.25 (4)	Stem	Early	Turk's-cap; N; PS
	L. henryi*	Orange-yellow	2 (7)	Stem	Late	Recurved; C; LT; N; PS
	L. longiflorum* (Easter lily)	Pure white	0.6–0.9 (2–3)	Stem	Early/mid	Trumpet-shaped; C; LT; OC; various forms
	L. martagon (Turk's-cap lily)	Purple or pinkish	0.9–1.25 (3–4)	Base	Early/mid	Turk's-cap; LT; PS; 'Album' white
	L. monadelphum*	Yellow; sometimes spotted	1.25–1.5 (4–5)	Stem	Early	Pendent, Turk's-cap; LT; PS
	L. pardalinum (leopard or panther lily)	Orange shading to crimson	1.25–1.5 (4–5)	Base	Mid	Turk's-cap; C; N; PS
	L. pumilum	Scarlet	0.3–0.6 (1–2)	Stem	Early	Turk's-cap; C; LT; OC; R
	L. regale*	White; carmine exterior	0.9–1.25 (3–4)	Stem	Mid	Funnel-shaped; C; N; PS; 'Album' earlier and pure white
	L. speciosum*	White to crimson	0.9–1.5 (3–5)	Stem	Late	Turk's-cap; C; N; OC; PS; various forms
	L. tigrinum (tiger lily)	Lemon to orange; some spotted	1.25–1.5 (4–5)	Stem	Late	Turk's-cap; C; LT; N; PS; various forms

*Fragrant variety
Seasons: Early = late spring to early summer; mid = midsummer; late = late summer to early autumn
Comments: C = suitable for cutting; LT = lime-tolerant; N = suitable for naturalizing; OC = suitable for outdoor containers; PS = likes partial shade; R = suitable for rock gardens

The invaluable 'minor' bulbs

Many people tend to think of bulbs in terms of hyacinths, daffodils and tulips, and to a lesser extent irises, gladioli and lilies, and to overlook the great host of minor bulbs, many of them inexpensive and the majority so easy to cultivate that at any time of year some undemanding bulb can be found in bloom. They are generally hardy and can be left *in situ* or naturalized to increase rapidly over the years. With a few exceptions all can be planted about 8 to 10 cm (3 to 4 in) deep and the same distance apart, and general cultivation and after-care is similar to that of other bulbs.

Such bulbs, rich in colour, beauty and often scent, are a boon to creative gardening, for they are as infinite in application as in character. Dwarf kinds, up to 20 cm (8 in) tall, flourish in rock gardens, between paving stones, at the edge of woodland and paths and beneath light-leaved trees and shrubs. They can also be naturalized in drifts in orchards, meadowland and lawns, while the taller intermediate bulbs 20 to 60 cm (8 to 24 in) high are often excellent as cut flowers, provide gay accents in beds and borders, and create vistas of colour on slopes and changing levels of the garden.

In addition to those described here, you will find details of a number of unusual, often slightly tender, bulbs mainly for summer display on page 204.

Winter-flowering kinds

In the midst of winter comes the first promise of spring when tiny bulbs push their heads through the covering of snow. The aptly named glory of the snow (*Chionodoxa* spp) is admittedly one of the last to appear, but it bursts forth with exquisite starry, bright blue and white-centred flowers, especially where it is naturalized in a sunny spot. *Chionodoxa gigantea* is 20 cm (8 in) high while *C. luciliae* is only 10 to 15 cm (4 to 6 in); it is pale blue in the species, white in the cultivar 'Alba' and soft pink in 'Pink Giant'. The porcelain-blue *C. sardensis* is similar in stature to *C. luciliae*.

Crocus chrysanthus 'E. A. Bowles'

Chionodoxa sardensis

The majority of crocuses are true spring-bloomers, but for welcome colour and grace in winter, it is worthwhile to set out some of the dwarf species crocuses, all 5 to 10 cm (2 to 4 in) tall, such as the orange-yellow *Crocus ancyrensis*, often listed as 'Golden Bunch', or the white, purple-flushed *C. biflorus*. *C. laevigatus*, at only 5 cm (2 in), is usually the first of the winter crocuses to flower, with pale lavender, purple-veined blooms. It is followed by *C. imperati*, striped purple outside, satin-pink inside, and *C. susianus*, whose flowers open to stars, golden on the inside, bronze outside. The golden-yellow *C. chrysanthus* is a little gem, equally dainty in the numerous cultivars in shades of yellow, blue and purple, usually with contrasting markings.

The florists' cyclamen is a popular winter pot-plant, but it is not often realized that it has several relatives, hardy and ideal for naturalizing in woodland or shady rock gardens, where the attractive marbled leaves remain for months after the flowers have finished. *Cyclamen coum* (*C. orbiculatum*), with white, pink or carmine blooms on 8 cm (3 in) stems from midwinter, thrives beneath deciduous trees. *C. neapolitanum* (sometimes listed as *C. hederifolium*), slightly taller and with silvery-green leaves, comes into flower in the autumn, and the pink or mauve blooms continue into early winter; there is also a white form. Other species flower in spring (*C. repandum* or *C. vernale*) and summer (*C. europaeum* or *C. purpurascens*).

Winter aconites (*Eranthis* spp) are at their most glorious planted 2.5 cm (1 in) deep in drifts beneath trees and shrubs, and associate well with snowdrops. They are undemanding as to soil, but need plenty of moisture in spring to build up the tubers. All bear yellow buttercup flowers set above a ruff of finely cut, pale green leaves. *Eranthis cilicica* is the smallest, with only 5 cm (2 in) pink stems, and is the latest to flower. *E. hyemalis*, the most common species, is pale yellow. The hybrid *E.* × *tubergenii* combines the features of these two, with large, late, deep yellow buttercups.

Probably no winter flower is greeted with more joy than the graceful little snowdrop (*Galanthus* spp). The white bells are com-

posed of three short and three long petals. They flourish in heavy soil, preferably moist, and in sun or shade. Plant the small bulbs immediately on receipt as they dry out rapidly. On *Galanthus elwesii* the flowers, on 20 cm (8 in) stems, are deep green on the inner petals, while *G. nivalis*, the common snowdrop, 15 cm (6 in) or less tall, is pure white with green markings. 'Flore-pleno' is a double form; 'S. Arnott' is single, but with much larger, sweetly scented flowers.

Types for spring

Alliums, or ornamental onions, bring beauty to the garden for several months, most of them flowering in early summer, but two species appear earlier. *Allium karataviense*, only 20 cm (8 in) tall, bears its dense umbels of lilac-purple flowers and mottled green and purple leaves from late spring on. *A. moly* is golden-yellow and 30 cm (12 in) high.

Anemones, ideal for rock gardens, naturalizing and for cutting, flower in spring from an autumn planting or in autumn if planted in spring. Set them 5 cm (2 in) deep and 15 cm (6 in) apart. *Anemone appennina*, 15 cm (6 in) high, has sky-blue single daisy flowers of pale blue, mauve, pink or white. Derived from *A. coronaria* are two strains known as De Caen and St Brigid, both suitable for cut flowers, having stems 15 to 25 cm (6 to 10 in) tall. De Caen cultivars bear single saucer-shaped blooms, available in single colours or as mixtures; St Brigid cultivars are double, but less free-flowering. *A. nemorosa*, the wood anemone, is more suited for naturalizing in open woodland; the single flowers, on 15 cm (6 in) stems, are white, blue or pink.

One species of brodiaea flowers in spring, before its taller summer-flowering relatives. This is *Brodiaea uniflora* (more correctly *Ipheion uniflorum*), a dwarf plant up to 15 cm (6 in) tall with sweetly fragrant starry flowers, white to violet-blue. Flowering at the same time, *Bulbocodium* (*Colchicum*) *vernum*

Erythronium dens-canis

Crocus vernus 'Remembrance'

opens its cup-shaped rose-violet blooms before the leaves and seldom grows more than 12 cm (5 in) tall; it thrives in the same conditions as the later lily of the valley (*Convallaria*; see p 184).

Close on the heels of the winter crocuses come the Dutch crocuses, raised from *Crocus vernus*. These have larger flowers, often up to 10 cm (4 in) high, and are available in a large selection which includes 'Enchantress' (silvery-blue), 'Joan of Arc' (pure white), 'Little Dorrit' (silvery-lilac), 'Negro Boy' (dark purple), 'Pickwick' (pale lilac with deeper stripes), 'Purpureus Grandiflorus' (rich purple), 'Remembrance' (violet with a silvery sheen), 'Striped Beauty' (white and purple), and 'Yellow Giant' (golden-yellow). Equally outstanding, though slightly smaller, are *C. etruscus* 'Zwanenburg' (blue), *C. sieberi* 'Violet Queen' (violet-blue) and *C. tomasinianus* 'Ruby Giant' (purple and silver) and 'Whitewell Purple'.

Ideal for clumps in the rock garden, the bulbs of erythroniums should be planted in autumn, 10 to 15 cm (4 to 6 in) deep in moist, shady and sheltered spots to establish themselves. The nodding flowers are characterized by pointed reflexed petals like a Turk's-cap lily. *Erythronium californicum*, up to 30 cm (12 in) high, is creamy-white; *E. dens-canis*, the dog's-tooth violet, is best in the named forms, 15 cm (6 in) tall, such as 'Lilac Wonder' (pink-purple, blotched brown), 'Purple King' (purple, dappled brown) and 'Rose Queen' (pink). *E. revolutum* 'White Beauty', 30 cm (12 in) tall, is outstanding, with massed cream anthers drooping from between the white petals, and marbled leaves. The species *E. tuolumnense* has been superseded by the hybrids 'Kondo', primrose-yellow, cinnamon at the base, and 30 cm (12 in) tall, and 'Pagoda', up to 40 cm (16 in), canary-yellow, with bronze leaves.

The crown imperial, *Fritillaria imperialis*, is the most imposing of all spring bulbs, its statuesque habit seen to advantage in the mixed border (see p 177). Among its relations are *F. latifolia*, a dwarf, 10 to 20 cm (4 to 8 in) high, with single purple-maroon or yellow pendent flowers. The charming *F. meleagris* (the snake's-head fritillary) is a little taller,

eye-catching with its chequered purple blooms; named forms are available in white, deep red, violet and purple, all veined.

After the snowdrops have disappeared comes the spring snowflake, *Leucojum vernum*, with white, green-tipped bells on 15 cm (6 in) stems. The summer snowflake, *L. aestivum*, up to 45 cm (18 in) tall, appears in late spring, with the bells borne in umbels and particularly large in 'Gravetye Giant'.

Late spring is symbolized in the bright blue muscaris, or grape hyacinths; they look charming planted in clumps at the front of beds and borders or in the rock garden, and also last well as cut flowers. Plant in autumn. *Muscari armeniacum*, 15 to 25 cm (6 to 10 in) high, bears dense spikes of scented cobalt-blue flowers rimmed with white; 'Blue Spike' is flax-blue and yellow. *M. botryoides* is white

Puschkinia scilloides libanotica

in the form 'Album', sky-blue and honey-scented in 'Heavenly Blue'. In *M. comosum* 'Plumosum' the flower spikes are composed of sterile violet-blue filaments. *M. tubergenianum*, the Oxford and Cambridge muscari, is bright blue at the top, deep blue on the lower half.

Unlike the white-flowered chincherinchee (*Ornithogalum thyrsoides*), which flowers in summer and should be treated like a gladiolus, the two following ornithogalums are frost-hardy and can be planted 5 cm (2 in) deep in autumn to flower the next spring. *O. nutans*, 25 to 30 cm (10 to 12 in) tall, bears starry, greenish-white flower racemes, and *O. umbellatum*, the star of Bethlehem, is pure white on 15 cm (6 in) stems. Like these, the dwarf *Puschkinia scilloides* belongs in the rock garden, at the front of borders or naturalized in grass; sometimes known as the striped squill, it resembles a scilla, but the flowers, on 10 to 15 cm (4 to 6 in) stems, are pale blue, striped darker blue. 'Alba' is a white cultivar.

Scillas themselves – the true squills – are unmistakable, ideal planted in broad drifts beneath shrubs or in woodland. They are so easy to grow and so gay with their nodding starry flowers in shades of blue that no garden should be without them. *Scilla bifolia*, 10 to 15 cm (4 to 6 in) high, is gentian-blue; *S. hispanica* (*S. campanulata* or *Endymion hispanicus*), the 30 to 45 cm (12 to 18 in) tall Spanish bluebell, is in various shades of blue, and there are also named forms in white and pink. The English bluebell, *S. non-scripta* (*S. nutans*, *Endymion nutans* or *E. non-scripta*) is a familiar sight in woodland glades with its violet-blue bells on 30 cm (12 in) stems. *S. peruviana* flowers in late spring and early summer, with massive blue flower-heads on stems up to 30 cm (12 in) high; it is sometimes called the Cuban lily. *S. sibirica* is up to 15 cm

(6 in) tall, each bulb producing several stems of brilliant blue flowers, white in 'Alba', while the dazzling blue *S. tubergeniana* (*S. mischtschenkoana*) is only 10 cm (4 in), with delicate soft blue flowers.

Sadly, the dainty harlequin flowers, *Sparaxis* (*Ixia*) *tricolor*, are not frost-hardy and must be planted in late autumn under a protective winter mulch in a warm and sheltered position and lifted again when the foliage dies down. Each 15 to 25 cm (6 to 10 in) stem produces a number of wide-open six-petalled flowers that are multicoloured in brilliant shades of white, yellow, red, orange and purple.

The smaller summer bulbs
The majority of short-stemmed bulbs flower in winter and spring, but there are still a surprising number to bridge the gap of summer and autumn. A number of ornamental garlics or onions (*Allium* spp) display themselves superbly in the summer garden and flower arrangements. Undemanding and/*continued*

The invaluable 'minor' bulbs (continued)

Brodiaea laxa

Begonia × *tuberhybrida* double variety

long-lived, they include the round-headed lilac-flowered *Allium albopilosum* on 45 cm (18 in) stems, the purple-blue *A. beesianum* of similar height, and the slightly taller *A. caeruleum* (*A. azureum*) with globes of sky-blue flowers. *A. neapolitanum*, which flowers earlier, sometimes even in spring, is similar but with scented white flowers, and is not always hardy in very cold climates. *A. ostrowskianum*, on the other hand, is native to Turkestan and therefore indifferent to frost and snow; reaching only 20 cm (8 in), it bears carmine-pink flowers. The Mediterranean *A. roseum* resembles the latter, with soft rose, mauve-tinged flowers, but is not so hardy.

Brodiaeas are among the earliest of the summer bulbs, with dainty tubular flowers, 5 to 10 cm (2 to 4 in) wide on 45 to 60 cm (1½ to 2 ft) stems, ideal for the wild garden, in large rockeries and for cutting. A number have been renamed in recent years, and you may find them catalogued under various names. *Brodiaea lactea* (*Triteleia hyacinthina*) is white flushed with lilac, and the dark blue *B. (T.) laxa* is almost violet in the variety 'Queen Fabiola'. *B. (T.)* × *tubergenii* has larger, pale blue flowers.

Another summer beauty is *Crocosmia masonorum* (see p 182), which for weeks on end, from late summer onwards, graces the border or wild garden with spikes of orange-yellow to red blooms. The hardy hybrids officially classed as *C.* × *crocosmiiflora* are commonly called montbretias, and may be catalogued as *Montbretia crocosmiiflora*. Many named forms are available in shades of yellow, orange, bronze and red; the narrow trumpet-shaped flowers appear alternately along wiry arching stems.

The deeply fragrant freesias (*Freesia* × *hybrida* or *F.* × *kewensis*) are recent introductions to the summer garden. The corms should be set 5 cm (2 in) deep in fertile and moist soil after all frost is over. They need a sunny sheltered spot and plenty of water to produce their delicate pastel blooms; although the corms must be discarded in the autumn and replaced with new stock the following spring, the exquisite flowers – on 25 to 40 cm (10 in 15 in) stems and available in mixtures – make freesias well worth experimenting with.

The South African corn lily, *Ixia viridiflora*, is a dainty little summer-bloomer, carrying a myriad of star-shaped pale flowers with contrasting centres on 30 cm (12 in) stems. It is not frost-hardy in cool climates, and should be protected in winter, but the taller hybrids, in shades of yellow, red and blue, are a little more robust. Confusingly, the plants commonly known as ixia lilies are species of *Ixiolirion* (belonging to a quite different family), notably *Ixiolirion tataricum* (*I. montanum*) with starry blooms of narrow backswept petals, violet-blue and borne in early summer on thin 40 to 45 cm (15 to 18 in) stems. They are good as cut flowers, but as they disappear completely after blooming they are best planted amongst ground-cover plants where they will leave no bare patch afterwards; like ixias they require a protective winter mulch.

The colourful ranunculus are not frost-hardy, and planting should be delayed until spring, with the claw-like tubers set – claws down – no more than 4 cm (1½ in) deep in rich soil and a sunny spot. Lift the tubers in autumn or, in areas where frost is only occasional, give them winter protection. Several strains are available, all developed from *Ranunculus asiaticus*, and usually in mixtures of semi-double or double forms spanning the colours of the rainbow.

Trilliums, or trinity flowers, are not true bulbs but grow from rhizomatous roots, ideally in lightly shaded woodland. The three-petalled flowers of *Trillium grandiflorum*, on 40 cm (15 in) stems, open pure white, later becoming suffused with pink. The slightly smaller *T. undulatum* is purple at the base of the white petals.

The fabulous begonias
The tuberous-rooted begonia hybrids, generally classed as *Begonia* × *tuberhybrida*, are extremely diverse. They are the biggest and showiest of shade-loving bulbous plants, blooming from midsummer into autumn. The large-flowered cultivars, with thick stems some 40 cm (15 in) tall and large leaves, are ideal for the partly shaded border; the smaller-flowered and more compact kinds, about the same height, can be used dramatically as foundation plantings, grouped in beds

and borders or grown in oudoor containers. The trailing Pendula begonias, with showers of smaller blooms in clusters on pendent stems, are superb for hanging baskets or raised containers.

Except in colder climates, the tubers can be planted outdoors in early summer, setting the surface-rooting tubers hollow side up about 2.5 cm (1 in) deep and giving them a mulch of peat. They require plenty of water throughout the growing period. In colder areas, start the tubers under glass in spring and move them outdoors in early summer; lift them after the foliage withers and store them in boxes of leafy soil in a frost-free place. For the largest blooms allow only the central bud to develop, removing all side buds as they appear.

Single-flowered begonias are sold by colour and come in white, yellow, copper, orange, salmon, pink, dark red and scarlet. Among the doubles are the camellia-flowered types, available in rich scarlet, orange, salmon, red, pink, white and yellow – or two-toned pink and white, as in 'Bouton Rose'. Fimbriated begonias, with fully double flowers and neat deckle-edged petals, are available in the same colours. Marmorata begonias are also double, with bicoloured ruffled petals, marbled violet-rose on carmine.

The Multiflora strain has smaller single or double flowers, several to each stem, compact and prolific. Named varieties are available in colours ranging from yellow through bronze to various shades of red. The Multiflora Maxima strain contains freer-flowering large double flowers, forming bushy plants ideal for bedding. Colours include light pink, rose, yellow, white, salmon and orange. The Pendula strain, available in crimson, scarlet, rose, salmon, orange, yellow and white, has a profusion of semi-double flowers on long trailing stems, and delicate foliage.

Tall summer-flowering bulbs
While shorter-stemmed bulbs admittedly have wider applications than the longer-

Ixia viridiflora

stemmed, the latter possess such exotic attributes, enchanting habits, glamorous features and striking styles that they can dramatically enhance any garden. They are restricted only in that they, with a few exceptions, are not suited to outdoor containers or naturalization, and that most dislike exposed sites.

Counterparts of the dwarf alliums mentioned above are found in several tall species, 0.6 to 1.25 cm (2 to 4 ft) high, with flower-heads in some as wide as 25 cm (10 in); for this reason, space the bulbs at least 15 cm (6 in) apart in mixed borders. *Allium aflatunense* bears starry flowers in round lilac-purple heads, while those of the 1.25 cm (4 ft) *A. giganteum* are ball-shaped and mauve. *A. rosenbachianum* has solid purple-rose heads, and the shorter (60 cm [2 ft]) *A. sphaero-cephalon* is crimson-purple.

Allium giganteum

For dramatic effect few plants surpass the North American camassias, which year after year produce their huge blue flower spikes. Plant the large bulbs in fairly heavy and moist soil, in sun or light shade, 10 cm (4 in) deep and 15 cm (6 in) apart in autumn. *Camassia cusickii* has pale blue flowers as early as late spring at the same time as the darker blue *C. esculenta*. *C. leichtlinii* comes later, with white or blue flowers, almost purple in 'Atro-violacea'. *C. quamash*, the quamash, has edible bulbs eaten for food by American Indians; its flowers range in colour from white to blue and purple.

Some crinums, such as *Crinum asiaticum*, are hardy in all but the coldest climates if planted 25 cm (10 in) deep in a sunny sheltered border of well-drained sandy loam and given a protective winter mulch. The beautiful funnel-shaped flowers, on stems up to 1.25 m (4 ft) tall, are fragrant, greenish-white and pink, and appear from midsummer onwards. *C. × powellii* is rose-pink, white in the form 'Album'; it is less hardy but ideal for contain-

Crinum × powellii

ers that can be moved under cover in winter.

The stately foxtail lilies (*Eremurus* spp) look like enormous hyacinths set on the upper half of stems that range from 0.6 to 2.7 m (2 to 9 ft). In spite of their height they should be planted shallowly, with the bud at soil level and about 60 to 90 cm (2 to 3 ft) apart. Plant in autumn and protect with a mulch, repeating this each winter. *Eremurus bungei* is bright golden-yellow, while the tallest of the species, *E. robustus*, is peachy-pink. There are also various hybrids.

Other beauties include the sweetly-scented white summer hyacinth, *Galtonia candicans* (see p 194), the lovely day lilies (*Hemerocallis* spp; see p 182), of which there are numerous varieties, and the various species and cultivars of *Alstroemeria* (see p 181), the Ligtu hybrids being popular. Probably the most outstanding of tall subjects, however, are the huge giant lily, *Cardiocrinum giganteum* (see p 198) and the lovely sky-blue agapanthus (see p 180).

Autumn-flowering kinds
Depending on the season, autumn snowflakes bloom in late summer or early autumn. *Leucojum autumnale* bears white, pink-flushed bells on erect 20 cm (8 in) stems; they resemble snowdrops but have a more rounded appearance, the six petals all being of the same length. (For other earlier-flowering species, see page 201.)

The misleadingly named autumn crocuses are not crocuses at all, but species of *Colchicum*. (To add to the confusion, they are sometimes called meadow saffrons, when saffron comes from a species of true crocus.) Plant the large corms 5 cm (2 in) deep and 15 cm (6 in) apart in late summer, in sun or light shade, or naturalized in grass. *Colchicum autumnale*, 15 cm (6 in) tall, has lilac-pink crocus-like flowers, deeper and more profuse in the form 'Major' and smaller and starry in 'Minor'; 'Album' is white. Also outstanding are the larger, more brilliantly coloured hybrids of *C. speciosum*, such as the lilac-pink 'Lilac Wonder', the mauve and white-blotched 'The Giant' and the double mauve 'Waterlily'. All these have much larger, wider leaves than true crocuses, but they die down before the flowers appear.

Colchicum autumnale

Eremurus bungei

The real autumn-flowering crocuses, 8 to 12 cm (3 to 5 in) high, resemble their spring-flowering cousins, the goblet-shaped flowers with striking styles appearing before the narrow leaves in some species. Plant as for colchicums. *Crocus longiflorus* is unusual in being strongly scented; it is rose-lilac with vivid orange stigmas. *C. pulchellus* is silvery-blue with white anthers, and the saffron crocus, *C. sativus*, has red-purple blooms that remain wide open displaying red stigmas and orange anthers. The easy lilac-blue *C. speciosus* has produced a large number of hybrids, such as 'Albus' (white), 'Artabir' (pale blue with darker markings) and 'Conqueror' (violet-blue with gold). The dainty little *C. zonatus* (*C. kotschyanus*) is soft lilac with a yellow throat.

The so-called autumn daffodil, *Sternbergia lutea*, is perhaps the least known of autumn bulbs. It bears open crocus-like golden-yellow flowers on 10 to 15 cm (4 to 6 in) stems. Plant 15 cm (6 in) deep in a sunny spot in midsummer.

Some unusual bulbs

Most of the bulbs described in this article are unusual only in so far as they are less commonly grown in cold areas because of the extra attention they need, firstly in hunting them down from specialist nurseries and secondly in their general cultivation. Still, the dedicated gardener is always on the look-out for rare and exotic plants to enhance his collection and seldom resents the care devoted to prized specimens. Unusual does not necessarily imply difficult, and while most of those mentioned here are tender – or rather unable to survive unaided sustained hard frosts – their cultivation programme differs from common bulbs only in the need for planting when spring frosts are past, lifting the bulbs in autumn, and cleaning and storing them under frost-free conditions during the winter.

Dwarf bulbs
The spikes of *Babiana stricta* resemble those of a gladiolus, numerous fragrant blooms being set on either side of the 15 to 30 cm (6 to 12 in) stems. The blooms are cup-shaped, however. They come in early summer and are white and blue. There are also hybrids in pink, rose, crimson, yellow or purple. Plant the corms about 10 cm (4 in) deep and the same distance apart, in well-drained soil and full sun. In warm areas, the bulbs can be left in the ground over winter, but elsewhere protect them with a heavy mulch of bracken or straw, and where hard frosts are common lift the bulbs in early autumn and store in dry peat.

Oxalis adenophylla hugs the ground with cushions of silvery-grey foliage above which rise in midsummer deep pink-lilac blooms on 10 to 15 cm (4 to 6 in) stems. *O. deppei* has red-spotted, clover-like leaves and copper-red blooms, white in the cultivar 'Alba'. Plant in autumn, 5 cm (2 in) deep and 10 cm (4 in) apart in warm, sunny spots; in cold climates planting should be delayed until spring and the bulbs lifted again in autumn.

The exquisite zephyr lilies (*Zephyranthes* spp) bloom in autumn. *Zephyranthes candida*

Oxalis deppei

Hymenocallis narcissiflora (Ismene calathina)

(sometimes called flower of the west wind) is the hardiest, with pure white open trumpet flowers on 20 cm (8 in) stems. Plant it – massed in borders, as edgings or in rock gardens – 10 cm (4 in) deep and the same distance apart in autumn or spring, and give a protective mulch in winter. *Z. robusta* (*Habranthus robustus*) is similar, but with blooms twice as large – 8 cm (3 in) wide. Being less hardy, do not plant in cold areas until spring, and lift again in late autumn.

Intermediate bulbs
One showy cultivated orchid is almost hardy even in cold climates; this is *Bletilla striata* (*Bletia hyacinthina*), which will usually survive most winters under a layer of bracken if planted 10 cm (4 in) deep and 15 cm (6 in) apart in a sheltered spot in sun or light shade. The bulbs can also be grown in pots, moved outdoors for the summer and stored over winter. It bears typical orchid flowers of pinkish-mauve petals and a purple lip, on 30 cm (12 in) arching stems in early summer.

The curious *Calochortus venustus* will not put up with winter conditions and must be

lifted in early autumn, dried and stored until the following spring. Then it can be planted 5 cm (2 in) deep and 10 cm (4 in) apart in a sunny rock garden. The flowers, on stems up to 60 cm (2 ft) high, consist of three broad petals, white, yellow, red or violet, with conspicuous markings. Several are borne to a stem in midsummer.

The blooms of *Chlidanthus fragrans* are lemon-scented, several appearing on slender stems, about 30 cm (12 in) tall, in summer. They are lemon-yellow, too, with broad back-swept petals, excellent for cutting or for sunny spots in the rock garden. They can be grown in outdoor containers or planted in borders 8 cm (3 in) deep and 15 cm (6 in) apart in spring, lifted in autumn and stored in dry peat. Clivias (see p 223) are also suitable for containers that can be moved outdoors in summer; the bulbs should be left undisturbed until they are really crowded.

Haemanthus, or blood lilies, are true curiosities, the flowers being crowded in dense umbels and having long stamens, so that they look like balls or shaving-brushes. They are tender and happiest when crowded in containers. Plant the bulbs in spring with the tips just above soil level and move outdoors in early summer, returning them to cover before autumn frosts. *Haemanthus coccineus* has red flower clusters in summer on 25 to 50 cm (10 to 20 in) leafless stems, while the pink *H. katharinae* blooms earlier, at the same time as the more vigorous hybrids in shades of pink and scarlet.

Also flowering in summer, *Hymenocallis narcissiflora* (*Ismene calathina*) resembles a daffodil, the pure white fragrant flowers being borne in umbels on 45 cm (18 in) stems. It is almost frost-hardy, and the hybrid 'Advance', with long reflexed segments, is even more robust. *H. × festalis*, also white but with gold-tipped anthers, is slightly taller. Plant the bulbs 15 cm (6 in) deep and twice as much apart in sandy soil in mixed borders; lift before the first frosts and store in dry peat.

Many species of *Pancratium* are now classified under *Hymenocallis*, which they resemble. The sea lily, however, *Pancratium maritimum*, has only a faint resemblance to the daffodil blooms of the former, the six pet-

Zephyranthes candida

Tigridia pavonia

kind is available, *Acidanthera bicolor murielae*, with 5 to 10 cm (2 to 4 in) wide star-shaped flowers, pure white with dark purple centres. Plant in late spring, 8 cm (3 in) deep and as much apart in sun.

Amaryllis belladonna (not to be confused with the indoor bulbs commonly called amaryllis but correctly species of *Hippeastrum*) also needs special attention. In most climates winter protection with bracken will be sufficient, but in very cold areas it is best to grow them in containers that can be moved indoors in winter. Plant the bulbs 15 to 20 cm (6 to 8 in) deep in late spring in a sheltered position at the foot of a sunny wall, or in a deep pot; allow them a year to become established. The fragrant pale rose to white trumpets are borne in loose clusters on 50 cm (20 in) stems in autumn, before the leaves.

ideally be started in a warm greenhouse in winter and moved or planted outdoors in early summer. They must be brought indoors again before frost, dried and stored in peat.

Nerines, although fairly hardy, are best grown against a sunny wall and only need lifting for the winter in very cold climates. They can be planted in autumn, 10 cm (4 in) deep and the same distance apart, and appreciate a top dressing of good compost and bonemeal in late summer. The hardiest is *Nerine bowdenii*, with loose clusters of scented, narrowly strap-shaped blooms on bare 60 cm (2 ft) stems (the leaves do not appear until spring). The flowers, which are excellent for cutting, are usually larger and more robust in the cultivars, such as 'Pink Triumph'. *N. sarniensis*, called the Guernsey lily though it is South African, is deeper pink

als being very narrow, often twisted, around a small inner cup. They are white and sweetly scented, and are carried in clusters on 30 cm (12 in) stems in summer and early autumn. Plant the bulbs about 10 cm (4 in) deep, either in a sheltered sunny border or rock garden or in containers; they must be lifted again before the autumn frosts.

Sprekelias, too, are best grown in pots, planted in either autumn or spring and moved outdoors after frosts finish. The leaves appear as flowering begins in early summer. *Sprekelia* (*Amaryllis*) *formosissima*, the Jacobean lily, is the only species. It bears a single blood-red flower on top of the 30 to 45 cm (12 to 18 in) stem, with one erect petal flanked by two recurving ones above three drooping petals.

One of the most curious summer-flowering bulbs is the tiger flower, *Tigridia pavonia*. Each 45 cm (18 in) stem carries several cup-shaped blooms, comprised of three large petals set round three smaller, heavily spotted petals that look somewhat like a tiger's face. Each flower only lasts a day, but the buds open in succession throughout the summer. There are several named cultivars, the predominant colours including white, yellow, red, purple and orange. Plant in sun and shelter in moist soil, in late spring in cold areas, and lift the corms before autumn frosts.

Two superb summer-flowering bulbs that in cool climates do best in containers are *Tritonia crocata* and *Vallota speciosa*. The former looks like a large crocosmia with orange flowers – or copper in 'Orange Delight' and white in 'White Glory'. It is sometimes called the blazing star. *V. speciosa*, the Scarborough lily, with clusters of bright scarlet lily-like flowers on 60 cm (2 ft) stems, is reminiscent of an amaryllis. In frost-free areas it may be grown permanently outdoors in a sunny position.

Tall bulbs

The corms of acidantheras must be lifted and stored every autumn in all regions where frost is experienced, but the dainty flowers, heavily scented, which open in succession over several weeks in late summer and early autumn, are ideal massed in the border, and are long-lasting in cut-flower arrangements. Only one

Sprekelia formosissima

× *Crindonna* is a bigeneric hybrid, and combines the characteristics of *Amaryllis belladonna* and crinums (see p 203). General cultivation is similar to that of amaryllis. The scented shell-pink trumpet blooms are borne in umbels on 90 cm (3 ft) stems, but appear a little earlier than those of amaryllis, in late summer.

The dragon arum, *Dracunculus vulgaris* (*Arum dracunculus*), has a highly exotic appearance, carrying on each 60 cm (2 ft) stem a huge crimson-maroon spathe offsetting the equally long brownish-black spadix. Unfortunately, it smells fouly after a few days, attracting pollinating flies. It needs sun and shelter and in cold areas it is advisable to lift and store the bulbs in winter.

Also highly exotic, the glory lily, *Gloriosa rothschildiana*, may reach a height of 1.8 m (6 ft) and will usually need support with canes. The conspicuous flowers of twisted, sharply recurved petals, crimson-scarlet fading to yellow at the base, appear in summer from among the upper leaves. The tubers should

Gloriosa rothschildiana

to red, but is tender and suited only to warm areas. Another autumn-bloomer is the Kaffir lily, *Schizostylis coccinea* and its cultivars (see p 185), flowering until late.

Possibly the most outstanding of unusual bulbs are the arum or calla lilies, *Zantedeschia* species. The waxy, elegantly curved spathes, which surround a prominent spadix, rise just above the handsome glossy leaves in early summer. *Zantedeschia* (*Calla*) *aethiopica* (*Richardia africana*) is pure white, the spadix yellow, and about 75 cm (2½ ft) high. *Z. (C. or R.) elliottiana*, of similar height, is golden-yellow, the leaves being marked with silvery spots. *Z. rehmannii* is a dwarf species, at 30 cm (12 in), with pink spathes, shading to green. Like other tender bulbs, zantedeschias are best grown in containers, setting the rhizomes just below the soil surface in early spring and moving them outdoors after the last spring frosts. Keep them moist. Return them to the greenhouse in autumn for drying and winter storage. *Z. aethiopica* 'Crowborough' can, however, withstand some frost.

The easy hardy annuals

Nature is rarely in a hurry, but when it is the reasons are good ones. The life-style of the true annual is an example. Some areas of the world – notably (so far as annuals are concerned) the near-desert parts of South Africa, California and Mexico – have short sharp rains with long spells between so arid that little will grow. Following the rain comes a spectacular explosion of colour as the dormant annual seeds germinate, mature and flower. The glorious colours are to attract insects and ensure fertilization. In a few short weeks all is complete, and with the coming of the ripened seed, the annuals die and leave the future of their kind to these seeds, which are by now freely scattered. Commonly used garden plants from such sources include clarkias and godetias.

Helianthus annuus 'Italian White'

Annuals are still a common feature where climates are less extreme, and, whilst less vividly brilliant than their desert kin, make up for this by a longer flowering period. As examples there are alyssums and calendulas (pot marigolds) from the Mediterranean region and annual poppies from colder areas. A direct result of the speed and sureness with which annuals germinate and grow in nature is the ease with which they can be cultivated in the garden – particularly the hardy kinds, which can be sown directly where they are to flower (see p 344). All the aftercare needed is to thin the seedlings, get rid of weeds and, in the case of only the tallest types, stake the stems. Other great virtues of the hardy annuals are the many ways they can be used (see p 114) and their relative cheapness.

Giant annuals

Because of their short season of growth, annuals more than 75 cm (2½ ft) tall are rare. But such as there are become doubly valuable to break the monotony of height in the border. The best-known are the sunflowers and hollyhocks. For the best results, both are sown under glass and planted out when a few inches high, but if you are prepared to wait until late summer they can be sown in early spring in the open ground 1 cm (½ in) deep, thinning to 60 cm (2 ft) apart.

With sunflowers (*Helianthus annuus*) you can have single flower heads of enormous size on stems up to 3 m (10 ft) tall, but better border value comes from the multi-branching medium-sized kinds such as 'Sunburst' and the pale yellow 'Italian White'. Colours range from pale yellow to maroon, and their wiry stems make them useful for flower decoration. The annual hollyhock, *Althaea* (*Alcea*) *rosea,* is related to the perennial hollyhock for long a familiar feature of cottage gardens. It is free of the deadly rust disease which often spoils the perennial kinds. You can expect 1.5 m (5 ft) spikes of yellow, pink or red shades when grown as an annual, but if treated as a biennial it can reach 2.5 m (8 ft).

Few plants are more lovely than the annual mallow, *Lavatera trimestris.* It does not transplant, so it must be sown in autumn or early spring where it is to flower. By midsummer it will be 75 cm (2½ ft) high and covered with rose-pink trumpet-shaped flowers in great profusion. You can even use it as a temporary hedge, especially the compact form 'Loveliness', which is remarkably wind-resistant, even beside the sea.

Annual lupins (or lupines) are not so well known as the perennial kinds (see p 180), but if you can obtain the seed of *Lupinus hartwegii,* they will give graceful spikes, up to 90 cm (3 ft) tall, in white, mauve and blue shades. There are also dwarf kinds. For early flowering, sow in the autumn.

The 90 cm (3 ft) shoo-fly plant, or apple of Peru, *Nicandra physaloides,* never fails to interest visitors as much for its (doubtful) reputation of repelling flies as for its midsummer abundance of pale blue, bell-shaped flowers followed by curious small, apple-shaped fruits. Branches carrying these can be dried for winter arrangements. Sow the seed in mid-spring.

The sweet scabious, or pincushion flower, *Scabiosa atropurpurea,* flowers from late summer in a wide range of colours from very dark maroon – which gave rise to yet another common name, mourning bride – to lavender, rose, red and white. It gives excellent results from an autumn sowing, and is a good cut flower. Normal varieties reach about 90 cm (3 ft) but dwarf types are half this height.

A number of annuals, although well worth growing, are not well known, and their seed may be difficult to find. Among them is a plant with really striking character, *Silybum marianum.* It has acquired a number of common names with a religious flavour: the blessed thistle, St Mary's thistle or Our Lady's milk thistle. It is about 1.25 m (4 ft) high, and bears spiny leaves that are bright glossy green, spotted and veined with white. The flowers are best removed, for they detract from the striking effect of the foliage. It is good for a wild garden. Sow in spring or autumn.

Agrostemma githago 'Milas' is a variety of the wild corn cockle collected near Milas in Turkey. It is an easy annual with showy rosy-lilac flowers borne on wiry stems which resist both wet and wind. The flowers are unusual in that they remain open day and night. They cut well for flower arrangements.

Althaea (*Alcea*) *rosea* double variety

Lavatera trimestris 'Loveliness'

It is something of an exaggeration to dub *Hibiscus trionum* the flower-of-an-hour, but certainly the individual flowers, usually primrose surrounding a maroon throat and up to 8 cm (3 in) across, are fleeting. It is a good back-of-the-border plant some 90 cm (3 ft) high with a loose habit, but because it flowers from late summer on is especially valuable. It often seeds itself.

Medium-tall kinds

The annuals described here range in height from 45 to 75 cm (1½ to 2½ ft), and are most useful in breaking the line of a bed or border. Love-lies-bleeding, *Amaranthus caudatus,* is an old-fashioned flower with most striking long drooping tassels of red (or greenish-white in the form 'Viridis'). They are much beloved by flower arrangers.

The prickly poppy, *Argemone mexicana,* is also called the devil's fig. About 60 cm (2 ft) tall, it has poppy-like flowers 5 cm (2 in) or more across in clear lemon-yellow. They are set against spiny, light green foliage often veined with white. It is happiest in the sun in a light soil, and will not transplant.

There are many good garden plants in the aster family. Among them is the biennial *Aster tanacetifolius,* the Tahoka daisy, which is perfectly satisfactory treated as an annual. It needs a warm dry spot where it will unfold

Hibiscus trionum

Centaurea cyanus 'Little Boy Blue'

and scarlet, white and rose. The flowers are double, delicately held by slender branches. Shorter and more delicate are forms of *C. pulchella,* with semi-double flowers in white, violet and rose-pink.

Coreopsis tinctoria, with the rather unpleasant common name of tickseed, is often listed as *Calliopsis.* It is one of the boldest of yellow annuals, and can be relied on for an abundance of yellow, maroon or crimson daisy-shaped flowers. Sow the seeds in succession from spring to early summer.

A useful plant to break up the border is the 75 cm (2½ ft) *Datura stramonium,* the thorn apple, also known as the stink-weed or jimson weed. Its flowers are funnel-shaped and white, the leaves toothed, ovate and green. The plant is an old medicinal herb, said to

Coreopsis (Calliopsis) tinctoria

have value in the treatment of asthma, but is deadly poisonous.

Whilst most foxgloves are biennial, *Digitalis purpurea* 'Foxy' reaches 75 cm (2½ ft) in about five months from sowing, with spires of carmine, pink, cream and purple flowers spotted with maroon. Foxgloves, too, are poisonous.

Euphorbia marginata is an annual spurge commonly known as snow on the mountain. A soft green, bushy plant, the leaves become veined with white and are valuable in flower arrangements. The cut stems exude an irritant milky sap, however; to stop this, plunge the cut ends briefly into hot water. Small white flowers appear in early autumn.

For the best results with larkspurs, or annual delphiniums, sow the seed outdoors in the autumn and enjoy the long attractive flower spikes the following summer. There are varieties in white, pink, red and blue shades, varying in height from 30 to 90 cm (1 to 3 ft). They are derived mainly from *Delphinium ajacis* and the generally taller *D. consolida* (both sometimes classified as species of *Consolida*). The foliage has a delicate grace about it which makes them welcome even before the flowers.

Everyone knows the field poppy, *Papaver rhoeas,* and once sown you probably have it in the garden for life, such is the prof-/continued

Clarkia elegans

its golden-centred lavender-blue flowers from early summer until the frosts. It is sometimes listed as *Machaeranthera*.

The cornflower, *Centaurea cyanus*, most brilliant of deep blues, is another prime favourite, vying for popular affection with love-in-a-mist, *Nigella damascena,* whose cornflower-like flowers peep out from a delicate tracery of light green foliage. These come in white, pink and purple as well as blue, and are followed by the curiously-shaped seed pods which delight the flower-arranger. A lesser-known relative of the cornflower, with very attractive fringed flowers in shades of white, pink, mauve and purple, is the sweet sultan, *Centaurea moschata* (often listed as *C. imperialis*). Like the cornflower, it is good for cutting. Both can be autumn-sown for early

flowering, as can love-in-a-mist if given cloche protection over winter.

Three species make up the gay and easy annual chrysanthemums: *Chrysanthemum carinatum* (*C. tricolor*), *C. coronarium* and *C. segetum*. They are similar in flower formation but have distinctive foliage. All have daisy-like flowers up to 5 cm (2 in) across, usually with a dark eye ringed with bands of three or four distinct colours. Some are pure gold, and a mixture of flame shades is a delight. Some other chrysanthemums can be treated as half-hardy annuals (see p 215).

If allowed only a limited choice, *Clarkia elegans* would be on most people's list of favourite annuals. A few individual colours are available, but usually it is sold in mixtures which make a riot of pink and salmon, purple

The easy hardy annuals (continued)

ligacy of its seed. The Shirley strain, in a brilliantly varied colour range, is about 60 cm (2 ft) tall; there are single and double forms. Under such names as 'Carnation-Flowered' and 'Paeony-Flowered', seedsmen list selections of the opium poppy, *P. somniferum*, so double as to resemble pink, red or purple powder-puffs. Unlike the perennial poppies (see p 180), the annual kinds do not normally need staking. Sow in autumn or spring.

Saponaria vaccaria 'Pink Beauty' is a 60 cm (2 ft) annual carrying graceful sprays of rose-pink flowers that are excellent for cutting. It associates well with white annual gypsophila (see below). One of the soapworts, its leaf sap will make a lather. There is also a white form, 'Alba'. They can be sown in autumn or spring.

The mainstream of annuals

The plants in this group range in height from about 20 to 45 cm (8 to 18 in). As height is reduced, it becomes easier for them to flower quickly from a spring sowing. For example, *Adonis aestivalis,* the pheasant's eye, flowers profusely from early summer. It is a graceful plant with anemone-like flowers forming deep crimson cups, and fern-like foliage.

Anchusa capensis comes from South Africa, and is a striking plant whose deep blue flowers remind one of forget-me-nots. It can be treated as a biennial. Other magnificent blues are the hound's-tongue, *Cynoglossum amabile,* sometimes called the Chinese forget-me-not, and also often given biennial treatment; *Convolvulus tricolor* (*C. minor*) 'Dark Blue'; and *Phacelia campanularia,* whose gentian-blue bell flowers are beloved of bees. Other varieties of the convolvulus, which is a bushy relative of the climbing morning glory (*Ipomoea purpurea*; see p 212), include 'Royal Ensign' (royal blue with a white and yellow centre), 'Crimson Monarch' and 'Cambridge Blue' (pale blue).

The blazing star, *Mentzelia lindleyi,* is better known as *Bartonia aurea.* Some 45 cm (18 in) tall, it has large golden-yellow flowers much like the rose of Sharon (*Hypericum*), in that both have a central boss of feathery stamens. It does not transplant, but associates well with blue flowers such as *Echium plantagineum,* whose ugly common name is viper's bugloss. This will thrive in poor dry soils; Australians are all too familiar with the *Echium* 'Pattisons Curse' which invades partially cultivated ground. It masses pink, blue, rose and intermediate shades on sturdy 30 cm (12 in) bushes.

The tassel flower, *Cacalia coccinea* (properly called *Emilia coccinea*), is one of the gayest of flowers, forming tassels of vivid orange-scarlet from early summer for months to come when sown out of doors in late spring. Or it can be treated as a half-hardy annual.

The common marigold, pot marigold or simply calendula, *Calendula officinalis,* has been loved ever since there have been gardens. It got its name from the Latin *calendae* – the first day of every month. The Romans had noticed that, whatever the month, its cheerful orange face could always be found in some sheltered corner. Most shades from cream to orange are available; the seed can be sown in autumn or spring. Dead-heading prolongs flowering and prevents self-set seedlings spreading like weeds.

Crepis rubra is a hawkweed from southern Europe, bearing masses of soft pink or white, dandelion-like flowers carried on single stems well above the pale green foliage. It appreciates an open sunny spot, and can be autumn- or spring-sown.

Dimorphothecas, commonly known as Cape marigolds or African daisies, are true natives of the African veldt, revelling in warm sunny spots. There are annual and perennial species, none of them truly hardy, but all can be treated as hardy annuals if sown after the danger of sharp frosts is past. In a good situation they will be in flower within six weeks and will keep on flowering until the autumn frosts. For even earlier flowering, treat as half-hardy annuals. The 5 cm (2 in) daisy flowers are best known in yellow, orange and brown shades, but there are also white and dark pink forms, often with blue or purple reverses to the outer petals and a blue central disc. The most commonly available seeds are of the perennials *Dimorphotheca aurantiaca* (*D. sinuata*), commonly called the star of the veldt, and *D. ecklonis* (*Osteospermum ecklonis*), both treated as annuals, and the true annual *D. annua* (*D. pluvialis*).

Equally brilliant is the Californian poppy, *Eschscholzia californica,* whose brilliant orange flowers, setting many a hillside aglow, gave rise to the term golden West. It needs a dry, sandy soil and a sunny position to bring

Dimorphotheca ecklonis

Echium plantagineum

Calendula officinalis

out the multitude of frilled and fluted poppy-like flowers, now available in many brilliant colours, set against delicately cut foliage. *E. caespitosa* is a dwarf species. Both can be sown in autumn or spring.

From the same part of the world come the godetias. Given a poorish soil and a few short twigs (through which the seedlings will grow) as a protection against wind damage, no annual is easier to grow from autumn or spring sowings. Forms mainly of *Godetia grandiflora* (*G. whitneyi*), their poppy-like flowers, many semi-double and prettily frilled, are a riot of red, pink, salmon and lavender. Many are delightfully dappled.

Gypsophila elegans needs no common name to introduce it. It bears innumerable tiny white or pink flowers in light and graceful clouds, making it a distinctive feature of any border. As a cut flower it has no peer as a foil for larger, brighter blooms, especially sweet peas. Again, sow in autumn or spring.

Another favourite, especially good in town gardens, candytuft has been developed from species of *Iberis,* notably the dwarf *Iberis umbellata.* However, the larger Hyacinth-flowered varieties derived from *I. amara* (*I. coronaria*) are better for borders, where they produce striking little columns of white, pink or carmine-red. For extended display, sow in autumn and then at intervals in spring.

From eastern North America comes *Layia elegans,* known as tidy tips, which is a reference to its yellow daisy flowers, each petal of which is tipped with white. It is very easy and bright, and has scented leaves.

Linaria maroccana is a splendid North African annual rejoicing in two delightful common names: toadflax and bunny rabbits. You can now buy only mixtures, such as 'Fairy Bouquet', of these gaily coloured flowers. They are like tiny snapdragons, in rose, crimson, pink, yellow, violet and white shades. Sow in autumn or spring; the plants will probably spread by self-set seedlings.

Mignonette, *Reseda odorata,* is also North African, and supplies a uniquely well-loved fragrance. Generally about 30 cm (12 in) tall, there are giant forms which are just as fragrant. Sow the seed (in autumn or spring) near the house where the breeze can waft the scent on a summer evening.

It is as well to give a similar position to the night-scented stock, *Matthiola longipetala*

Salvia horminum

(*M. bicornis*), whose richly scented mauve flowers open only in the evening. For appearance's sake, however, you should interplant it with the more showy Virginia stock (*Malcolmia;* see below).

Long-lasting flowers are unusual among annuals, so it is a wonder that clary, *Salvia horminum,* is not more widely planted. Its display is from long-lasting bracts – which in normal flowers protect the bud – rather than from petals. The colours – pink, purple and white – are recessive and blend well with others. It will dry for winter use.

Senecio (*Jacobaea*) *elegans* has carmine-rose flowers rather like those of cinerarias (*Cineraria cruenta* or *Senecio cruentus*). They are good for cutting, and look best in the garden if planted in bold groups.

The viscarias, which are of mixed hybrid origin derived mainly from *Viscaria oculata* (correctly called *Silene coeli-rosa*), are extremely free-flowering and colourful plants for near the front of the border. Most forms are about 30 cm (12 in) tall, but 'Nana Compacta' is a dwarf, as is the related *Silene pendula.* It is difficult to get viscarias in clear separate colours, but mixtures of pink, red, blue and white are brilliant indeed. /continued

Godetia grandiflora

Viscaria hybrids

Senecio (*Jacobaea*) *elegans*

The easy hardy annuals (continued) | Hardy biennials

Front-of-the-border annuals

Many of the most brilliant annuals are no more than a few centimetres high. Sweet alyssum, *Alyssum maritimum* (or, more correctly, *Lobularia maritima*), honey-scented and in purple, violet and rose-pink as well as the better-known white, is indispensable in the bed or border. Unless deprived of water, it will flower the whole summer through. On the rock garden or wall it will naturalize itself quite happily. There are varieties ranging from 5 to 15 cm (2 to 6 in) in height.

The scarlet pimpernel, *Anagallis arvensis,* is a familiar European weed, but its domesticated forms – especially the dark blue 'Caerulea' – make attractive prostrate plants. The annual woodruff, *Asperula orientalis* (*A. azurea* or *A. setosa*), covers itself in clusters of

Alyssum maritimum

lavender-blue, fragrant flowers from midsummer to autumn. It thrives in a damp, semi-shaded position.

The violet cress, *Ionopsidium acaule,* makes an excellent carpeting plant, as well as being good for rock gardens and for planting between paving stones. It has pretty pale mauve flowers. The *Kaulfussia amelloides* of catalogues is more properly *Charieis heterophylla.* It is a very pretty South African annual with tiny deep blue daisy-like flowers. It is very easy to grow and will flourish in any sunny spot.

Another commonly misnamed species is *Linanthus androsaceus luteus,* which may be listed as *Gilia lutea* or more often as *Leptosiphon luteus.* Its common name is stardust. Its small, bright flowers come in cream, yellow, orange, pink and red in such mixtures as 'French Hybrids'. It originates in California, as does *Limnanthes douglasii,* the meadow foam, known to children as the poached-egg flower. It is a low, spreading plant bearing a multitude of white flowers with yellow centres. Bees love it. It will grow in any odd corner, but to make it really happy give it a moist spot. Sow in spring or autumn.

As seedsmen, for economic reasons, tend to packet mixed seeds at the expense of individual colours, plants that appear only in pure colours – like the flax, which has only red,

white and blue forms – become even more valuable to the gardener planning colour effects in the border. *Linum grandiflorum* 'Rubrum' is brilliantly red on attractive slender growths, while 'Bright Eyes' is white with a carmine eye. Often listed at 30 cm (12 in) high, it rarely achieves this unless on rich ground. The common blue flax, *L. usitatissimum,* is slightly taller and produces a brilliant mass of pure blue. It is also a valuable crop plant, producing linseed and the fibre flax. Sow the seeds in autumn or spring.

Nemophila menziesii (*N. insignis*) has the improbable common name of baby blue-eyes. It is a Californian annual bearing clear sky-blue, cup-shaped flowers with white centres. It flowers quickly after sowing, and appreciates a cool, moist spot.

Tropaeolum majus Whirlybird strain

One of the easiest of all hardy annuals, and a favourite for children's gardens, is the Virginia stock, *Malcolmia maritima.* It is ideal for edging, or for growing in drifts through a bed or border. The showy flowers – cross-shaped and in clear shades of white, yellow, lilac, pink and red – appear only a month after sowing and continue for up to two months. For the longest show, from spring right through to the end of summer, sow seed in autumn and then successively from early spring to midsummer.

If you want to introduce a child to the mysteries of seed-sowing, however, the best choice is perhaps the nasturtium, *Tropaeolum majus.* It has few requirements and a large seed which will put up with neglect better than most. Even on a hot dry bank, a sheet of colour – red, pink and gold – is guaranteed. A rich soil is a disadvantage, as it encourages leafy growth which masks the flowers.

There are a multitude of cultivars. Many are dwarf and some strains, like Jewel and Whirlybird, both of which have semi-double flowers, tend to throw flowers well above the foliage. Some are scented, the Gleam strain are semi-climbers or trailers, and there is the old-fashioned single scrambler which will climb a hedge or hide a shed. And to add to the fun, you can eat the leaves in salads and pickle the seeds like capers.

Hardy biennials

The term biennial indicates any plant that is best grown by devoting one year to building up strength so that it may flower the following year. Such plants include true biennials that die after flowering and short-lived perennials that respond well to biennial treatment. The latter may be discarded after flowering or kept for a further year or two.

Since biennials lack flowers in their first year, they are best raised in an out-of-the-way corner in a reserve bed, or perhaps in the vegetable garden. They can then be planted out in their flowering positions in autumn. However, no biennials enjoy a damp cold climate; a temperature of 14°F (−10°C) is near their limit, though some will withstand colder conditions if dry. In more severe climates, they should be overwintered in a cold frame and transplanted in early spring.

Wallflowers

The common, or English, wallflower, *Cheiranthus cheiri,* is among the most useful of groundworks for spring-flowering bulbs since it has many cultivars in clear colours that will associate well with, say, tulips. There are four distinct strains – the 45 cm (18 in) tall Giant-flowered, the Normal or Regular (30 to 40 cm [12 to 15 in]) the Dwarf (about 25 cm [10 in]) and the Early, 60 cm (2 ft) tall and generally used for cut flowers. Colours include crimson, purple, orange, yellow, cerise, brown, ruby, salmon and white. The variety 'Blood Red' is very dark indeed, and may look black from a distance.

The 40 cm (15 in) Siberian wallflower, *Cheiranthus* (*Erysimum*) × *allionii,* is a hybrid relative that flowers right on the heels of the common wallflower and continues well into summer, especially if dead-headed regularly. It is a brilliant orange, best used as a contrast, and associates well with forget-me-nots. It is hardier than the ordinary wallflower, and can be grown as a perennial.

Forget-me-nots

The constant companion of the wallflower in spring beds and borders is the forget-me-not, *Myosotis alpestris.* Its misty-blue clouds perfectly enhance the clear greens of spring. It grows well except in hot dry spots, will tolerate shade and naturalizes readily. 'Royal Blue' is an outstanding cultivar of richest blue about 30 cm (12 in) tall. There also are dwarf (18 cm [7 in]) and miniature (12 cm [5 in]) forms in the same colour, and a number of colour breaks – white, lavender, pink and carmine – which have more limited uses.

Daisies

Gardeners in Europe spend so much time ridding their lawns of daisies that it may seem strange to grow *Bellis perennis,* the English daisy, as a garden plant. But seedsmen have developed this humble plant to an extraordinary degree. There are giant 15 cm (6 in) forms under such names as 'Enorma' and 'Monstrosa', with white, pink or red flowers up to 5 cm (2 in) across, so freely produced as to create a carpet of colour. The miniature 'Pomponette' range – about 10 cm (4 in) high

– bear a multitude of button-like small flowers in colours ranging from white through delicate shades of pink, often with deeper centres, to crimson. Dead-head regularly to prevent inferior self-set seedlings.

Other biennials

The Canterbury bell, *Campanula medium,* appears in the cup-and-saucer form beloved of the English cottage garden in blue, white and pink on a sturdy 75 cm (2½ ft) plant. There is also a compact single-flowered strain 40 cm (15 in) tall and known as 'Bells of Holland' or 'Musical Bells'. These are well suited to the small garden.

Dianthus barbatus, the sweet William, is generally 30 to 40 cm (12 to 15 in) high, and has been a favourite in English gardens since

the 16th century. It is loved for its brilliant colours in all shades from dark red to white, including bicoloured forms, its glorious scent and its good temper. With the Canterbury bell, it bridges the early summer gap.

The foxglove, *Digitalis purpurea* has been developed from the simple country hedgerow plant into a stately 1.5 m (5 ft) specimen worthy of its place in any border. The flowers may be in clear colours such as cream, pink and purple, whilst some are exotically spotted within the flower tube.

Find a plant with a simple, attractive common name like honesty – *Lunaria annua* or *L. biennis* – and you may be sure that it has a long history of affection in the cottage garden. Its spikes of spring flowers are a recessive purple, but for its best season you have to await the

Dianthus barbatus

Digitalis purpurea

Campanula medium

Papaver nudicaule

flat silver discs of the seed-pods, which dry well for winter decoration.

The evening primrose, *Oenothera biennis,* earned its common name for its habit of opening its pale yellow flowers at eventide. The kinds usually found in catalogues are day-flowering (diurnal), such as *O. lamarckiana* and *O. trichocalyx,* which has large sweetly-scented white flowers set on grey foliage.

The Iceland poppy, *Papaver nudicaule,* is a short-lived perennial that can be grown as a half-hardy annual but responds best to biennial treatment. In cold damp climates, however, it needs cloche protection in winter. The soft greyish-green foliage forms clumps from which the wiry flower stems rise to 60 to 75 cm (2 to 2½ ft). They need staking. The fragrant flowers, up to 8 cm (3 in) across, have the texture of tissue paper and come in pastel shades of white, pink, salmon, apricot, gold, orange and red. They are the only poppies good for cutting. Pick when the buds just begin to show colour, and immediately seal the stems by plunging the ends into boiling water. Good forms include 'Kelmscott Strain' and the F1 hybrid 'Champagne Bubbles'.

Another cottage-garden gem is the mullein, *Verbascum bombyciferum,* with sulphur-yellow flowers on 1.25 m (4 ft) silvery stems. Related hybrids range from white through pink to purple.

Other good garden biennials, or plants that do well treated this way, include hollyhocks (*Althaea,* or *Alcea, rosea*; see p 206), which grow even taller as biennials than as annuals; the sweet rocket, or damask violet, *Hesperis matronalis,* a short-lived hardy perennial (see p 180); Brompton stocks (*Matthiola incana*; see p 216); and many garden pansies and violets (forms of *Viola*; see p 184).

Climbers to grow from seed

Shrubby climbers play an important permanent role in the garden (see p 92), but quick-growing climbers that you can grow from seed – either true annuals or plants that can be treated thus – also have a multitude of uses. These range from the temporary covering of an ugly shed or other feature, through the production of blooms for cutting, to the creation of varied heights and focal points in the bed or border by training the plants up peasticks or tripods of larch poles.

In their natural surroundings, such climbers either haul themselves up another branch by twining or climbing by tendrils, or – if they lack anything to climb – they scramble down a bank. These are rather untidy methods for the gardener, so if you would see them in all their beauty, provide a suitable framework on which you can train them (see p 93). They include both hardy and half-hardy plants.

Sweet peas

Perhaps the best-loved of all annual climbers, the numerous garden varieties of sweet peas are derived from an Italian wild flower, *Lathyrus odoratus*. They all have the characteristic pea flowers, with large outer wing petals either side of the central keel petals. They are delicate, often with frilled or wavy edges, and coloured in a wide range of shades of white, pink, lavender, violet, red, orange and yellow. Some varieties are striped or mottled, and all of them are fragrant to a greater or lesser extent.

Remember, however, that some of the larger-flowered varieties, developed mainly for exhibition and having blooms up to 5 cm (2 in) across, have traded scent for size and number of blooms per stem. If you want the air to be perfumed as well as a showy display of cut blooms, grow both the large-flowered types and some of the smaller, heavily perfumed old-fashioned sweet peas. Combine the two in arrangements.

Although most sweet peas will climb to as much as 3 m (10 ft), there are also dwarf bushy kinds that need little or no support. Notable are the 45 cm (18 in) Bijou strain, the 0.6 to 1.25 m (2 to 4 ft) Knee-Hi and Jet Set types, and such varieties as 'Colour Carpet', which spreads to form a low mat 20 to 25 cm (8 to 10 in) high – excellent for rock gardens or for edging.

The normal climbing varieties should, however, be provided with support in the form of trellis, netting, strings, canes or twiggy sticks. Best known are the Spencer varieties, which are good for garden and cutting. They have four or five flowers on each stem and reach 1.8 to 3 m (6 to 10 ft). The Cuthbertson Floribunda strain are good for hot climates, or for growing under glass in cooler regions. The Galaxy strain grow well in both hot and cool climates, and have five, seven or even more flowers per stem. They are often fragrant.

Sweet peas are hardy annuals, and can be sown in their flowering positions in spring or (in mild climates) autumn, given cloche protection during winter if necessary. They are often treated as half-hardy annuals, however, and sown in pots or boxes under glass in autumn or late winter, pricked out into individual pots, and planted out (after hardening off) when about 10 cm (4 in) high. The seeds have hard coats, and to speed germination these may be nicked, or the seeds rubbed gently with sandpaper and soaked in tepid water for a day or two before sowing.

For best results, the soil should be cultivated deeply and plenty of bulky organic matter (such as leaf-mould) and well-rotted manure worked in. Regular application of dilute liquid fertilizer will help growth, and mulching will help to keep the roots cool (see p 334). Pinch out the growing tip when the young plants are about 15 cm (6 in) tall, to encourage branching growth. Most importantly, keep picking the flowers and do not allow any to go to seed; this will ensure the longest flowering season.

In regions with hot summers and warm winters, such as the South of the United States, sweet peas are best grown in winter. They are most difficult in areas with extreme climates, such as the American Midwest; there they need plenty of watering and mulching, and will probably not succeed at all unless night temperatures fall below about 20°C (68°F).

Convolvulus family

The morning glories and their relatives include some of the most beautiful, if ephemeral, flowers among the annual climbers. Most of them need a warm, sunny spot. Hardiest (but still unable to withstand any frost) is the morning glory itself, *Ipomoea purpurea* (sometimes called *Convolvulus major* or *Pharbitis purpurea*). It is a vigorous climber, and will quickly cover a fence or scramble through a hedge. Its 8 cm (3 in) flowers are funnel-shaped and purple, the colour fading as they age. There is also a red variety, 'Scarlett O'Hara', among others.

Few flowers deserve to be called breathtaking, but *Ipomoea rubro-coerulea* (*I. tricolor, P. rubro-coerulea* or *I. violacea*) 'Heavenly Blue' is one. Its trumpet flowers may be up to 10 cm (4 in) across, and are the purest, clearest sky-blue imaginable. Once seen it is never forgotten. The flowers open in early morning and are over by afternoon, but each succeeding morning brings more.

Also related to the morning glory, but having generally smaller flowers, mainly red, are species of *Quamoclit* (often, however, listed as *Ipomoea* or in some cases *Mina*). They need really warm spots, being popular in the South and West of the United States but also succeeding in sheltered places elsewhere. *Quamoclit lobata* (*Mina lobata*) has bright crimson flowers that fade to orange and finally cream. *Q. pennata* (*I. quamoclit*), the cypress vine, has red and yellow flowers; there is also a white variety. *Q. coccinea* (*I. coccinea* or *M. sanguinea*) is also red, as is the cardinal climber, *Q. sloteri* (*I. cardinalis*). These all have leaves of varied shapes, and give dappled shade in hot regions when grown on arbours, pergolas or porches.

Finally, there is *Calonyction aculeatum* (*I. bona-nox,* or *I. roxburghii*), the moonflower.

Lathyrus odoratus

Ipomoea purpurea (Convolvulus major)

This really needs warm conditions to survive – a minimum night temperature of 10°C (50°F) – so it is generally grown in greenhouses or conservatories in cool regions. Where it will grow, however, it rewards with huge convolvulus-like white flowers, 15 cm (6 in) across and heavily fragrant. The common name comes from the fact that they open in the evening and close next morning.

Other annual climbers

Cobaea scandens, commonly called the cup-and-saucer plant or cathedral bells, has flowers rather like large Canterbury bells

varieties of *Cucurbita pepo.* These close relatives of the edible marrow (see p 296) come in a variety of shapes and colours: apple, bottle, egg, orange, pear and others. When dried, such fruits can be polished or painted with wax or clear varnish for indoor decoration. The larger-fruited *Lagenaria* species may have provided ancient household utensils around the Mediterranean, for they dry iron-hard. Some varieties have such evocative common names as Hercules's club, bottle, calabash, powder-horn and syphon. You may also be able to obtain seeds of *Luffa aegyptiaca,* the source of the loofah or vegetable sponge, and some other species. Treat all as half-hardy annuals.

The Chilean glory flower, *Eccremocarpus scaber,* is an easy and attractive climber given a warm position in which to ramble. It bears clusters of orange tubular flowers. Treat as a half-hardy annual.

The Japanese hop, *Humulus scandens* (*H. japonicus*), is a perennial easily grown as a hardy or half-hardy annual to provide a quick screen of lime-green foliage. There is a form called 'Variegatus' in which the maple-like leaves are dappled with cream. Although not so decorative, the common hop used in beer-making, *H. lupulus,* is easy and fun to grow. The variety 'Aureus' has golden foliage.

Lathyrus latifolius, the perennial sweet pea, is a relative of the common sweet pea (see above), but can also have annual treatment. See also page 177.

Another plant for a warm, sheltered spot is

Cobaea scandens

come in clusters. Similar in appearance, but only distantly related, is the so-called hyacinth bean, *Dolichos lablab.* It needs warmer conditions than the runner bean, and will then give spikes of purple or white pea-shaped flowers.

Black-eyed Susan is a common name applied to a number of plants that have orange or yellow flowers with a black centre. Among them is the attractive South African climber *Thunbergia alata.* It comes in shades of cream, yellow and buff, as well as orange. Give it a sheltered spot and a light, rich soil if you can. *T. gibsonii* has similar but larger

Quamoclit (Mina) lobata

(*Campanula medium*). They have purple petals forming the 'cup' and a green calyx, the 'saucer'. They are unusual and certainly not flamboyant, but have an appealing charm. The plant is a rapid and effective climber on a sunny wall or trellis. It is perennial in frost-free regions, but elsewhere is treated as a half-hardy annual.

Gourds are grown for their quaintly shaped fruits. The most suited to growing outdoors – especially in a tub on a warm terrace – are

Maurandia (Asarina) barclaiana, a fast-growing Mexican climber also grown under glass. It has trumpet-shaped purple flowers 8 cm (3 in) long. It needs rich soil and half-hardy annual treatment.

Although confined to the vegetable garden in many countries, the runner bean (*Phaseolus coccineus* or *P. multiflorus*) also makes an attractive decorative plant. (It is often used in this way in the United States.) The brilliant scarlet, pink or white flowers

Thunbergia alata

flowers; it is an evergreen perennial that can be treated as an annual.

Climbing varieties of nasturtiums (*Tropaeolum majus*; see p 210) are perhaps the least demanding of all climbers. An entirely distinct climbing species is *T. peregrinum* (*T. canariense*), the canary creeper. The common name alludes to the attractively fringed yellow flowers, supposedly like canary birds. It needs richer soil than the nasturtium, and will happily climb in shade.

Half-hardy plants from seed

Half-hardy annuals include some of the garden's most colourful plants. Although in areas with warm climates they can be sown directly where they are to flower, gardeners in most temperate regions must raise them under glass. Sown from late winter to early spring, they should be germinated and grown on in gentle heat, and then hardened off in a cold frame. When big enough, and after the danger of frost is past, they can be set out in their flowering positions.

Although the majority of the plants described here are true annuals, a number are free-flowering hardy or half-hardy perennials that will flower in their first year if treated as described above. Apart from the plants covered on these pages, many everlastings (see p 245) are half-hardy annuals.

Tall-growing kinds

As with the hardy annuals, only a small proportion of half-hardy annuals grow taller than about 60 cm (2 ft). Among them are the 'Rocket Hybrid' snapdragons or antirrhinums, an F1 hybrid strain, and some forms of arctotis, African (or American) marigolds and schizanthus. These are all described, together with their medium-sized forms, below.

Cleome spinosa (*C. pungens*), the spider flower, is a 60 to 90 cm (2 to 3 ft) half-hardy from tropical America that is easily grown, given a warm corner and rich soil. Its common name comes from the six very long stamens that emerge from the centre of the flowers, looking rather like a daddy-long-legs (harvestman) spider. It is always a talking point. The four petals are pink, the upper pair rather like a startled rabbit's ears.

Cosmea, or the Mexican aster – forms of *Cosmos bipinnatus* – is a plant closely related to the dahlia, whose single-flowered cultivars it somewhat resembles. It makes a plant some

Penstemon × gloxinioides Monarch strain

Tithonia rotundifolia (T. speciosa) 'Torch'

90 cm (3 ft) high with delicate and fernlike foliage, and an excellent border backing. Its flowers are white, pink, orange or red, and there are bicoloured forms. There is also a double form, with small gem-like flowers in shades of orange-scarlet, that is only about 45 cm (18 in) tall.

The sweetly fragrant nicotianas, or tobacco plants, are decorative relations of smoking tobacco. Garden forms are mainly derived from *Nicotiana alata* (*N. affinis*), and are about 75 to 90 cm (2½ to 3 ft) tall. The tubular flowers range from white, through yellow and pink to crimson, and there is a greenish-yellow form called 'Lime Green'. They tolerate light shade, and their scent is strongest in the evening.

Like a number of tender perennials, the garden hybrid penstemons classed botanically as *Penstemon × gloxinioides* flower freely in the first year when sown early and treated as half-hardy annuals. The taller *P. barbatus* (often listed as *Chelone barbata*) can be

treated in the same way. The tubular white, pink or red flowers appear throughout the summer on 90 cm (3 ft) stems.

Although not very well known, *Tithonia rotundifolia* (*T. speciosa*), the Mexican sunflower, makes an impressive background plant. The 8 to 10 cm (3 to 4 in) orange-red flowers – resembling those of single dahlias – are held on 1 to 1.25 m (3 to 4 ft) stems.

Medium-sized half-hardies

Plants in a height range of about 25 to 60 cm (10 in to 2 ft) are, of course, the principal element in any bedding scheme, but remember that many of the plants described here have particularly tall or dwarf forms – or both. These can be extremely useful in introducing interesting variations of height to the border.

Alonsoa warscewiczii (*A. grandiflora*), the mask flower, comes from South America. It is bushy, 30 to 60 cm (1 to 2 ft) high, and has dark green foliage which admirably sets off the multitude of orange-scarlet flowers.

Nicotiana alata (N. affinis)

Perhaps its difficult specific name does this easy and excellent plant a disservice.

The snapdragon, *Antirrhinum majus,* in its many variations of height and form, was the most widely grown plant in this group until the dreaded rust disease (see p 367) struck in the 1930s. Its ability to give a good show even when attacked, together with the arrival of rust-resistant strains, has done much to preserve its popularity. The dwarf F1 varieties, often from Japan, are especially good, forming sturdy plants 30 cm (12 in) high and as much across, in a wide colour range. Even smaller are the 'Floral Carpet' snapdragons, only 15 cm (6 in) tall, while at the other extreme are the F1 'Rocket Hybrids', reaching 90 cm (3 ft) or more. The large-flowered types, including the Tetraploid (or Tetra Snaps) and Penstemon-flowered strains, are excellent for cutting, while the F1 hybrid Coronette type make 40 cm (15 in) bedders.

Arctotis, or African daisies, are great sun-lovers, and given a warm spot will grace the garden with their large daisy flowers from midsummer to the early frosts. Several species and hybrids are available, the latter classified as *Arctotis × hybrida*. A wide colour range includes ivory, cream, yellow, orange and red, many with contrasting zones, set on attractive grey foliage. Heights range from 30 to 90 cm (1 to 3 ft), but most are below 60 cm (2 ft).

Rather similar is the Namaqualand daisy, or *Venidium fastuosum* (also called the monarch of the veldt), another brilliant South African daisy. Its flowers come in white, orange, ivory, cream and yellow, with a black centre and a maroon ring superimposed upon the colour. It needs the sun to be seen at its best. A bigeneric hybrid between this plant and species of arctotis is called × *Venidio-arctotis*. It blends the characteristics of its parents, with a profusion of 8 cm (3 in) daisy

Arctotis × hybrida

flowers on sturdy, upright plants 45 cm (18 in) tall. Colours range from ivory to dark brown-reds. They make excellent summer bedding plants for sunny spots.

Callistephus chinensis, the China aster, has a multitude of different forms ranging from single daisy flowers with two or three rows of petals, through an infinite number of petal variations, to those resembling powder-puffs or incurve chrysanthemums (see p 187). Often listed in catalogues simply as asters, they vary in height from 60 cm (2 ft) down to 20 cm (8 in), and their uses include bedding, cutting, and growing in pots, tubs or boxes. They are indeed versatile, and come in a colour range which includes carmine, white, yellow, scarlet, red, blue and purple – and intermediate shades galore. The dwarf bedding varieties should be planted about 30 cm (12 in) apart, the larger Ostrich-Plume and Totem Pole types 45 to 60 cm (1½ to 2 ft) apart. For the hardy annual *Aster tenacetifolius,* see page 206.

Callistephus chinensis

Celosia argentea 'Plumosa' – the Prince of Wales feathers, often catalogued as *C. plumosa* – and *C. argentea* 'Cristata' (*C. cristata*) – the cockscomb – are usually associated with the cool greenhouse, but will stand bedding outdoors in a sunny place if grown to flowering size before planting out. The plumes, up to 60 cm (2 ft) high, are mainly scarlet or yellow.

Perennial chrysanthemums (*Chrysanthemum* cultivars) are generally grown from cuttings (see p 186), but you can also treat some kinds as half-hardy annuals to flower within the year, if sown in late winter in a heated greenhouse. Best types for this treatment are Koreans and early-flowering varieties of Charm chrysanthemums. The latter spread to form a carpet of autumn flowers. *Chrysanthemum parthenium,* the feverfew (often catalogued as *Matricaria eximia*), is a short-lived perennial that does best as a half-hardy annual. It grows 20 to 45 cm (10 to 18 in) tall, with single or button-like double

× *Venidio-arctotis* 'Flame'

Dahlia dwarf bedding hybrids

flowers, white or golden in colour. The foliage and flowers both smell pungently.

Most dahlias of the border type are half-hardy perennials grown from tubers overwintered in frost-free conditions (see p 188) Dwarf bedding strains have however been developed which will respond to half-hardy annual treatment. Of such confused parentage that they are simply classed/*continued*

Half-hardy plants from seed (continued)

Heliotropium arborescens (H. peruvianum)

Schizanthus pinnatus (S. grandiflorus)

as *Dahlia* hybrids, they can be single, semi-double or fully double, in a wide range of colours. Best known are perhaps the 45 cm (18 in) single 'Coltness Hybrids', but there are taller and shorter types. Unlike border dahlias, they are good for planting with other flowers, and do not need staking or disbudding, but they can be lifted and overwintered just as with the border types.

Apart from the hardy annual larkspurs (see p 207), certain species of *Delphinium* can be treated as annuals if sown early under glass. This is true of *Delphinium grandiflorum* and *D. tatsienense,* as well as such hybrids as the 75 cm (2½ ft) 'Connecticut Yankees'.

Didiscus caeruleus (*Trachymene caerulea*), the blue lace flower, comes from Australia. Its rounded umbels of lavender-blue scented flowers are 5 to 8 cm (2 to 3 in) across, on 60 cm (2 ft) stems.

Unlike *Euphorbia marginata* (see p 207), which is hardy, *E. heterophylla* (known as fire on the mountain, the Mexican fire plant or the annual poinsettia) is a half-hardy annual from Central America. As its common names suggest, it bears whorls of scarlet bracts around the small orange-red flowers, resembling the popular Christmas pot-plant.

The half-hardy annual gaillardias, or blanket flowers, have been developed from *Gaillardia pulchella.* (There are also perennial kinds; see p 182.) The commonest cultivars are double, in shades of yellow, orange, red and crimson, and 60 cm (2 ft) tall.

The heliotrope, or cherry pie, *Heliotropium arborescens* (*H. peruvianum*) is a tender perennial often used as a temporary bedding subject (see p 222). However, it is also treated as a half-hardy annual, giving large trusses of fragrant, mauve to purple flowers in summer from a sowing under glass in late winter.

The clove fragrance of the stock is one of the great scents of the garden. A universal favourite in many brilliant colours, derived mainly from *Matthiola incana* and *M. sinuata,* it is one of the few plants in which double-flowered forms rather than singles are generally considered essential for bedding purposes. To assist, seedsmen list '100% double' varieties whose seedlings are either pale or dark green; the pale will be double and the dark single, so selection can be made when pricking out. Another, the Trysomic strain, is even simpler; prick out only the strong seedlings to ensure double flowers. The single stock is, however, an attractive cut flower.

All stocks produce a column solid with flowers in pleasant shades of red, pink, yellow, white and mauve. Differences lie in flowering times. The summer-flowering Ten-Week stocks flower in about that period from a spring seed sowing. For late summer and autumn, the Intermediate or East Lothian strain is used, and for winter flowering under glass the Beauty of Nice strain. The latter can also be used, sown in late winter, for summer bedding; they make large plants with fine flowers. The spring-flowering outdoor stock is a biennial, the Brompton stock. Using normal biennial treatment (see p 210), it is best overwintered in a cold frame or under cloches and planted out in early spring.

Mirabilis jalapa, the marvel of Peru or four-o'clock plant, is a showy plant whose second common name comes from the fact that fresh blooms open in the afternoon and generally fade next day. (They last longer in dull weather.) The trumpet-shaped flowers, 2.5 cm (1 in) across, come in white, pink, red, yellow and violet. 'Jingles' has striped flowers on bushy 60 cm (2 ft) plants.

Molucella laevis, the bells of Ireland or shell-flower, is as attractive as its name, not for its flowers, which are not spectacular, but for the unusual calyces, or sepals, which support them. These are like shallow green shells, delicately veined and turning cream with age. They dry well for winter decoration.

Rudbeckia bicolor, the cone flower, best represents the annual forms of this family. There are many yellow daisy flowers, but this is one of the best. Its common name arises from the cone-shaped central disc, whose dark brown sets off and enhances the petals, which are mainly golden but can be bronze or lemon. About the same height – 60 cm (2 ft) – is *R. hirta,* black-eyed Susan, a perennial usually grown as a hardy or half-hardy annual. It has 5 cm (2 in) golden flowers and a dark brown central cone. *R. hirta* 'Gloriosa', the gloriosa daisy, is a bolder variety, good for borders and cutting, up to 90 cm (3 ft) tall. It has single or double flowers in shades of gold, bronze, chestnut and mahogany-red.

The painted tongue or velvet flower, *Salpiglossis sinuata,* has a claim to be among the finest of half-hardy annuals, yet it is little grown. Its trumpet-shaped flowers, up to 9 cm (3½ in) across, appear on 60 cm (2 ft) spires in crimson, blue and pink, with the most exquisite etchings of gold within the throat. 'Shalimar' and 'Splash' are among the sturdy F1 hybrid varieties. None of the varieties like wind, so they need a sheltered spot, and in areas with hot summers should be started early so that they are established before the hot weather.

Rudbeckia hybrids

Vying with these for intricacy of flower markings are the hybrid schizanthus derived from *Schizanthus pinnatus* (*S. grandiflorus*), commonly called the butterfly flower or the poor man's orchid. The orchid-like flowers come in shades of red, pink, white, mauve and purple, all beautifully blotched and marked in gold and other contrasting colours. The best varieties, such as 'Angel Wings' and 'Hit Parade', make bushy, 30 to 45 cm (12 to 18 in) plants.

The marigolds have innumerable inter-related strains basically divided into French, African (or American), and now Afro-French types – although the species from which they are derived both come from Mexico. Together they form the most widely grown annuals, providing cheerful colour all summer long in sunny positions. *Tagetes erecta,* the African marigold, once meant a solitary bloom on a 60 cm (2 ft) stem, looking as if it had been cut from a rubber sponge. Today the dwarfest are 20 cm (8 in) tall, and they graduate up to 90 cm (3 ft) tall, all fully double and with multiple blooms of immense size in orange, lemon, gold or near-white. The French marigolds, *T. patula,* are mainly 20 to 30 cm (8 to 12 in) tall, some single but mainly double. They come in the same colour range as the African, but with the addition of mahogany-red and many bicoloured forms. They are of superb colour and extremely easy if the dead blooms are regularly removed. Afro-French are between the two, having the habit and flower-type of the French, but larger, earlier and more double blooms.

Trachelium caeruleum is not unlike a lavender-blue gypsophila. It provides the lightest cloud of colour, with its multitude of flowers on stems some 60 cm (2 ft) high. Its common name of throatwort arises from the early belief it could cure diseases of the throat.

Ursinia anethoides is a showy South African daisy with dainty, finely cut foliage and brilliant 5 cm (2 in) flowers. It is available in various shades of gold and orange. It likes sun and well-drained, sandy soil.

Zinnias are excellent border plants from Mexico, but they rarely succeed in temporary bedding, so greatly do they resent being moved. They should therefore be sown, after all danger of frost has passed, where they are to flower, and then thinned to 30 cm (12 in) apart. Alternatively, sow under/*continued*

Tagetes erecta 'Gypsy Sunshine'

Zinnia angustifolia (*Z. mexicana*) 'Old Mexico'

Salpiglossis sinuata 'Shalimar'

Tagetes erecta 'Moonshot'

Half-hardy plants from seed (continued)

glass in early spring and carefully prick out the seedlings into peat pots; these can be set out in the garden with minimal root disturbance. Derived mainly from *Zinnia elegans*, they come in giant (up to 75 cm [2½ ft]), intermediate, and dwarf (25 cm [10 in]) forms in brilliant colours – plum, scarlet, pink, yellow, orange, white and all intermediate shades – with single or double flowers. 'Envy' is a chartreuse-green variety, while 'Persian Carpet' is a small variety of *Z. angustifolia* (*Z. haageana* or *Z. mexicana*) with bicoloured and tricoloured double blooms.

Dwarf kinds
The plants described here are generally below 30 cm (12 in) in stature, and are excellent for edging in annual borders and bedding schemes. Among the most beautiful is the floss flower, *Ageratum houstonianum* (*A. mexicanum*), whose numerous fluffy flower-heads are in recessive blues ranging from powder-blue to ultramarine. Some are so intense as to defy attempts to reproduce them accurately on colour film. This is a pity, as the attractive flowers could be even more popular. There are also whites and pinks.

Anagallis monelli linifolia (*A. linifolia*) is a 15 cm (6 in) pimpernel with deep gentian-blue flowers. A short-lived perennial, it is usually treated as a half-hardy annual. Anagallis means delightful, and so it is. A sunny spot is needed; it will then open its flowers at breakfast time and close for tea.

Begonias include two types that are commonly grown for outdoor use from seed. The *Begonia × tuberhybrida* Multiflora and Multiflora Maxima hybrids produce a tuber very quickly, and are of compact, bushy habit, about 25 cm (10 in) tall, bearing many brilliantly coloured double camellia-like flowers. They are especially good from late summer onwards. The other is *B. semperflorens*, the wax begonia, which is at present at the height of a surge of popularity – and rightly so, for, whether the year be wet or dry, this fibrous-rooted begonia can be relied upon. Its name means ever-flowering, and it does so from early summer to the frosts so freely that you can hardly see the waxy leaves. Many shades of red, rose and pink are available; also white. You can select for bronze or green foliage. The F1 hybrid varieties have much to commend them, the largest being about 30 cm (12 in) high, whilst the compact kinds are 15 cm (6 in). Open-pollinated cultivars are available; they are also good, and cheaper.

Brachycome iberidifolia is from Western Australia, as its common name of Swan River daisy suggests. Given a warm and sunny spot it will reward you with a multitude of daisy-like flowers in pale blue, pink and white from early summer till autumn. They are fragrant.

Calceolaria integrifolia (*C. rugosa*) and its relatives have suffered for years from too-close identification with Victorian bedding schemes. New strains, which do well as half-hardy annuals, seem likely to restore their popularity, for the yellows are clear (reds and bronze shades are also available), growth is even and flowering very free. Weather-

Ageratum houstonianum (A. mexicanum)

Begonia semperflorens

resistance too is good, and in a favourable winter it can survive to a second year.

Cotula (*Cenia*) *barbata,* the pincushion plant, has tiny yellow pincushion flowers rather like the central disc of wild daisies. They are held on wiry stems up to 20 cm (8 in) tall, above the narrow, silky, hairy leaves. It makes a pretty edger.

Far more showy – and often grown as indoor pot-plants – are two species of the so-called Mexican cigar-plant commonly available from seedsmen: *Cuphea ignea* (sometimes called *C. platycentra*) and *C. miniata* (more correctly *C. llavea miniata*). The flowers are narrow tubes, 2.5 cm (1 in) long, with black tips that are supposed to resemble the ash on a cigar. They make excellent bedding plants, flowering freely from when they are small seedlings. They need a well-drained sunny spot, and reach about 30 cm (12 in), or *C. miniata* slightly more.

Dianthus, or pinks, that are commonly raised from seed include the Japanese pinks

(listed as *Dianthus × heddewigii,* though they are strictly forms of *D. chinensis*), which are striking bedding and border plants submerged beneath fringed flowers from early summer onwards in crimson, white, pink, salmon and dappled bicolours; also the Indian pink (*D. chinensis,* or *D. sinensis,* itself), which is taller and looser than the Japanese pink, but equally attractive. In the same genus are the sweet Williams (*D. barbatus*), which are generally biennials, (see p 211). Such dwarf varieties as 'Wee Willie' can, however, be grown as half-hardy annuals, flowering in as little as two months from sowing.

Diascia barberae, the twinspur, is a free-flowering South African annual good for edging or as a pot-plant, but is listed by only a few seedsmen. Its soft pink flowers, somewhat like those of nemesias, have two spurs protruding behind. It reaches about 25 cm (10 in).

The kingfisher daisy, *Felicia bergeriana,* is a dwarf, almost creeping annual whose flashing steely-blue daisy flowers, with golden centres,

Begonia × tuberhybrida Multiflora Maxima variety

Gazania × hybrida

Mimulus 'Scarlet Gem'

Nemesia strumosa 'Funfair'

do no disgrace to the bird from which its common name comes. It is a true annual, whereas its relative *F. amelloides* (sometimes listed as *Agathaea coelestis* and commonly called the blue marguerite or blue daisy) is a perennial commonly treated as a half-hardy annual (though it will easily overwinter in mild areas or under glass). The sky-blue daisy flowers are held well above the foliage on 30 to 45 cm (12 to 18 in) stems.

Gazanias (derived largely from *Gazania splendens* but classified as *G. × hybrida*) are also tender perennials commonly used as temporary bedders and then overwintered under glass as young plants struck from cuttings. However, they respond equally well to treatment as half-hardy annuals if sown in warmth in late winter, pricked out into pots and planted out in early summer. The daisy flowers – generally bicoloured in shades of yellow, orange, brown, red and pink – are up to 8 cm (3 in) across. They grow about 25 cm (10 in) high.

Mesembryanthemum criniflorum

The outdoor forms of busy Lizzie (also known variously as patient Lucy, patience or sultan's balsam) have not achieved the popularity their beauty, ease of cultivation and tolerance of all kinds of weather justly merit. The most useful forms are dwarf cultivars of *Impatiens sultani* 'Nana'. They like reasonable moisture at the root, but given that will flower continuously for four or five months, and will not mind if it be a wet year or a dry one, or whether you plant them in sun or shade. Most strains are 15 to 20 cm (6 to 8 in) high and are available as orange, scarlet, pink, white, mixed or striped varieties. Somewhat taller are most varieties of *I. balsamina* (balsam), although 'Tom Thumb' and similar strains are only 25 cm (10 in) tall. They are slightly hardier than busy Lizzies, and many varieties have double flowers.

Lobelia erinus is one species in a vast family that is invaluable for beds and borders, as it supplies good shades of blue – colours not easily found among dwarf plants. It can be very dark, bright mid-blue or pale. The pink and white forms are less effective.

Though correctly *Dorotheanthus bellidiformis*, you will usually find the Livingstone daisy listed in catalogues as *Mesembryanthemum criniflorum*. It creeps along the ground with crystalline succulent leaves and an abundance of 2.5 cm (1 in) daisy-like flowers in an astonishing range of brilliant colours, almost shouting to be admired. They need the sunniest spot – as shown by their succulence and the fact that the flowers open only in sun. Some seedsmen also list certain other species of mesembryanthemums, such as *M. tricolor* (*M. gramineum* or *Dorotheanthus gramineus*) and *M. crystallinum* (*Cryophytum crystallinum,* the ice plant). Most of these sun-loving South African succulent plants – known as a group as fig marigolds – are low-growing and suitable for treatment as half-hardy annuals.

Mimulus hybrids (derived mainly from *Mimulus cupreus*, *M. luteus* and *M. variegatus*) are commonly known as monkey flowers because the blotched, trumpet-shaped flowers are supposed to resemble the faces of grinning monkeys. They are mainly in shades of red and yellow, and are generally under 30 cm (12 in) tall, though *M. luteus* (monkey musk; see p 185) can be taller. A common factor is the need for constant moisture, so they are ideal for pool-side spots.

There is probably no more brilliant half-hardy annual than *Nemesia strumosa* 'Suttonii'. This is a selection with larger flowers than most other varieties, on robust plants about 30 cm (12 in) high. Compact forms for bedding are 20 cm (8 in). The brilliant colours glow and echo the sunshine of its native South Africa in yellow, rose-pink, orange, cherry, scarlet and blue, and in bicolours and even tricolours. For long-flowering success it is imperative to have a moist root run, no check in growth from dryness or any other cause, and a climate that is not too hot.

Given a hot summer, petunias (a hybrid mixture classed as *Petunia × hybrida*) are among the best half-hardy annuals. (Their roots should not dry out, however.) Try to obtain weather-resistant strains, for there is wide variation in this characteristic. Their superb trumpet flowers have a/*continued*

Half-hardy plants from seed (continued)

Petunia × hybrida

Salvia splendens

very wide colour range. For very large flowers use the F1 Grandiflora varieties, which are also vigorous and a little taller than the F1 Multifloras. The latter in turn are freer-flowering and less prone to rain damage. The beautiful, exquisitely coloured doubles are best suited to pot culture under glass.

Phlox drummondii is the annual phlox from Texas (it is sometimes called Texas pride). It grows up to 40 cm (15 in) tall, but is best in the dwarf forms 15 to 20 cm (6 to 8 in) tall. The flowers, in dense heads up to 8 cm (3 in) across, come in an amazing colour range – from white, pink and red to yellow, lavender and purple, in self and bicoloured forms. They revel in sun and fertile soil. Space them 15 cm (6 in) apart, and remove dead flower-heads to prolong the season.

Polygonum orientale and *P. capitatum* are knotweeds well suited to treatment as half-hardy annuals. The former is from the Old World tropics and bears large leaves and drooping spikes of red flowers. The latter is strictly a perennial; it has bronzy foliage and pink flowers, and creeps along the ground.

More people should discover *Portulaca grandiflora*, commonly called the sun rose, sun plant, rose moss or sun moss. It is a dwarf spreading plant with slender fleshy spikes for leaves. The many-coloured cup-shaped flowers have an oriental splendour about them, the doubles looking like miniature roses. Both single and double forms may be yellow, white, pink, purple, red or orange. They are especially good for the hot dry spot, rivalling the nasturtium for a hot bank.

Salvias, flowering relatives of the herb sage, are easy and colourful half-hardies. *Salvia splendens* is the species commonly used for bedding. There are many cultivars which are very similar, varying slightly in height and earliness of flowering. All produce long spikes of brilliant scarlet flowers, which contrast well with the dark green foliage. One of the best blues in the garden, *S. patens* (a perennial in mild areas) can be used in the same way.

Most stonecrops (*Sedum* spp) are perennials and mainly suited to the rock garden, but *Sedum caeruleum* is a low-growing annual that often spreads by self-set seedlings. It is best treated as half-hardy, however. The pale green leaves and stems turn bright red as the

pale blue, star-shaped flowers with white centres emerge in midsummer. It likes well-drained, sandy soil, in full sun.

Tagetes tenuifolia (*T. signata*), commonly called simply tagetes, is a plant of much less formal appearance than the related French and African marigolds (see above). The finely cut foliage makes a neat, bushy plant, about 20 cm (8 in) tall in the dwarf varieties, which are the best. It bears a multitude of small golden, orange or lemon-yellow stars from early summer until the first frosts. The foliage is strongly fragrant.

The vervains (*Verbena × hybrida*) are superb bedding plants, especially for a hot dry place. The largest are the so-called Mammoth or Giant strain ('Grandiflora') about 30 cm

(12 in) high, whilst shorter ones are called 'Compacta'. The clear red, purple, violet, cream and mauve flowers are much enhanced by a clear white eye. *V. rigida* (*V. venosa*) is a deep mauve bedder bearing its flowers on little spikes which are very long lasting. Its colour is an attractive foil for many brighter colours in bedding schemes. Like the deep violet *V. canadensis,* it is a perennial easily grown as a half-hardy annual.

Violas and pansies (all forms of *Viola*) are best grown as biennials, but garden pansies or heartsease (classed as *Viola × wittrockiana*) can be treated as half-hardy annuals. If sown in the greenhouse in late winter and planted out in early summer, they will give a carpet of autumn colour.

Tagetes tenuifolia (*T. signata*)

Verbena rigida (*V. venosa*)

'Dot' and foliage bedding plants

Most plants used for colourful display in bedding schemes are less than 45 cm (18 in) in height. To avoid any tendency to flat monotony, plants of contrasting foliage colour, such as grey foliage among scarlet flowers, or plants of striking shape and greater height, can be spaced among the main display. These are referred to as dot plants. It is an easily understandable term, but should not be thought to indicate mathematical precision in distribution. An asymmetric arrangement is much more likely to be effective.

Dot plants include a number of annuals or other plants easily grown from seed, generally raised under glass. Others are tender perennials or shrubs that can be overwintered under glass for re-use or for cuttings next year.

Subtle foliage

The abutilons, or flowering maples, have remarkable colour variations in their maple-like, gracefully pendent leaves. *Abutilon striatum* 'Thompsonii' has a variegation akin to marbling in gold, green and cream. This is due to a transmittable virus, so stock grown from cuttings will closely resemble the originals. Well-grown plants may be 1 to 1.5 m (3 to 5 ft) tall and bear attractive bell-like orange flowers. *A.* × *hybridum* 'Savitzii' is equally useful, bearing cream and light green leaves on slender 45 cm (18 in) stems. Both are tender shrubs, except in the mildest areas.

Grevillea robusta, the silk oak, is a giant tree in its native Australia but as a young plant its fern-like leaves make it one of the most graceful of foliage plants for bedding. It needs to be overwintered in a frost-free greenhouse.

A plant which has little grace but much impact is *Kochia scoparia*, the summer cypress. It is a descriptive common name for this bright green plant shaped like a guardsman's busby. The cultivar 'Childsii' stays green all summer, whilst *K. scoparia* 'Trichophylla' turns beetroot-red as autumn approaches – hence the other common name, the burning bush. It is a half-hardy annual.

Grey and silver foliage is useful in this context. Plants like the brilliantly scarlet *Salvia splendens* associate well with silvery foliage such as *Senecio cineraria* (*Cineraria maritima*) or with the soft purple *Verbena venosa*, which will soften the one and enhance the other. Grey foliage is dealt with on page 240, and suitable plants for bedding purposes include species of *Senecio, Centaurea, Artemesia, Helichrysum* and *Eucalyptus*.

Miscanthus (*Eulalia*), *Festuca, Arundo* and other ornamental grasses are very useful dot plants (see p 244). In the case of the widely used *Zea mays* 'Quadricolor', resist the temptation to plant too many and too closely – certainly no closer than 2 m (7 ft) – or their multi-coloured impact is reduced.

Colourful kinds

Plants with brightly coloured foliage should be used sparingly, but effective bedding schemes are possible by reversing the kind of combination mentioned above – using, for example, colourful dot plants among principally white flowers and silver foliage.

Among such plants are the ornamental cabbages and kale (borecole) varieties – forms of *Brassica oleracea*. The former can have whitish or pink leaves, plain-edged or crinkled; the latter generally come in purple shades. Both are good for winter colour.

Two of the most brightly coloured foliage dot plants are the flame nettle, *Coleus blumei*, and *Amaranthus tricolor*. The latter is a half-hardy annual, the former a tender perennial easily raised from seed. Though quite different in shape, the foliage of both is brilliantly splashed in crimson, scarlet, bronze and other colours. Good forms of the coleus can be overwintered under glass and new specimens grown from cuttings taken in spring.

Dark and dramatic

Dark foliage is desirable where pale subjects form the groundwork. The half-hardy annual *Perilla frutescens* 'Atropurpurea Laciniata', for example, makes a 60 cm (2 ft) plant with bronzy-purple, deeply indented leaves. Perennials like *Lobelia cardinalis* 'Queen Victoria', with metallic crimson foliage, or the purple-leaved sea-kale, *Beta vulgaris* 'Rhubarb Beet', are well suited to this purpose.

If permanently potted and plunged speci-

mens are desired, then *Cordyline australis*, with a striking cluster of sharply pointed narrow leaves, or the New Zealand flax, *Phormium tenax*, are excellent 'architectural' plants. Both are hardy in mild districts. *Canna indica*, the Indian shot, and its hybrids also make dramatic plants. Their banana-like leaves – green, greyish, brown or purple – provide instant contrast. For bedding purposes, seek the shorter cultivars.

The red mountain spinach, *Atriplex hortensis* 'Atrosanguinea' ('Rubra'), is hardly the most graceful of plants, but its dark red foliage can form a useful contrast. It grows up to 1.25 m (4 ft) and, like the ornamental cabbages and kales mentioned above, its leaves can be cooked and eaten. Other strikingly dark red or purple foliage is found in a form of basil, *Ocimum basilicum* 'Dark Opal' and in *Hibiscus* 'Red Leaved'. Both are half-hardy annuals.

Finally, one of the most dramatic foliage bedding plants is the castor-oil plant, *Ricinus communis*, a tender shrub commonly grown as a half-hardy annual. Grown thus it seldom exceeds 1.5 m (5 ft), but in good conditions will treble this. The big palmate leaves can be green, bronze or reddish-purple.

Senecio cineraria (*Cineraria maritima*)

Ocimum basilicum 'Dark Opal'

Standards and half-standards
One old-established method of breaking border flatness is to grow plants on a tall base stem or leg. Up to 45 cm (18 in) they are termed half-standards; above this they are called standards.

They are easy to grow. Take cuttings a month or two earlier than usual, to allow more time for growth. Do not pinch out the top, but remove all side-shoots until the stem is the required height. Support it with a cane. Then remove the growing tip to cause it to bush out near the top. Suitable subjects include fuchsias, lantanas, streptosolen, heliotrope and, easiest of all, geraniums (*Pelargonium*).

Tender perennials for colourful bedding

Apart from the many annuals and biennials used for temporary bedding purposes (see p 210 and pp 214 to 219), a number of tender perennials are also popular for summer display. In cold climates these cannot go outside until all risk of frost is past, and in autumn they must either be discarded or lifted and overwintered under frost-free conditions. In favourable climates where frosts are rare or non-existent, however, tender perennials give longer displays and are often only renewed when they become straggly or flower badly. Apart from their use for bedding out, they are bright and attractive in window-boxes, jardinières, tubs and other containers, while the dwarfer kinds are sometimes used to make colourful patterns in carpet bedding. In warm places the climbers can be trained up lamp standards and over railings, or else allowed to wend their way across and over rocks.

Most tender perennials are renewed from cuttings, particularly the cultivars; these are

will flower for weeks in moist, partially shaded beds. The fairy primrose, *Primula malacoides*, with dainty whorls of pink, white or mauve flowers on slender 20 to 30 cm (8 to 12 in) stems, has an ethereal quality yet is strangely durable, the single kinds persisting longer than the doubles. There are also single and double forms of the 20 cm (8 in) Chinese primrose, *P. praenitens* (*P. sinensis*), in white, crimson, blush, salmon, scarlet, cerise and blue, as well as some taller starry-flowered Stellata forms. Double types are best propagated from root cuttings in a closed frame, but the single ones grow readily from seed. *P. obconica* bears its large and mostly blue or lilac flowers in umbels on 25 to 30 cm (10 to 12 in) stems. The leaves carry irritating hairs which cause a painful rash to some people.

Although usually regarded as an annual, the scarlet sage, *Salvia splendens*, is perennial in warm climates. Few plants match its vivid colouring. Lantanas (see p 175) are tiresome,

varieties with cream, pink, purple, mauve, red or yellow tubular flowers, and also a number of doubles raised by the Dutch. Specially treated bulbs which will bloom outside are available for cool climates, but must be discarded afterwards. These are planted in late spring for summer bloom. See also page 202.

But by far the most important tender perennials for massing – in warm and cold climates alike – are pelargoniums, commonly called geraniums. Most of the cultivars, which may be pink, mauve, orange, red or white, and may have single or double flowers, need sharp drainage and plenty of sun. Too much moisture encourages foliage rather than flowers. This is particularly apparent with zonal pelargoniums (*Pelargonium × hortorum* cultivars), which have horseshoe markings on the leaves. In humid climates these flower less freely than the ivy-leaved kinds (*P. peltatum*). The latter trail, and are ideal for hanging containers and to drape from rocks in warm climates.

Fuchsia 'Thalia'

Clatharanthus roseus (*Vinca rosea*) 'Bright Eyes'

Datura sanguinea

more dependable than seed as regards height, colour and general habit. No two seedlings are ever exactly alike, but cuttings, being pieces of the original plant, come true to type. Cuttings should generally be rooted under glass, in cold frames in late summer or in warm propagating units in spring.

Perennials for massing

Certain perennials require massing in order to create bold effects. Formal display beds in open positions particularly need this treatment when they are set in turf or paving. A few taller 'dot' plants are permissible to break the flatness, but the basic ground planting should be low. Plants suitable for massing in this way include dwarf bedding dahlias (see p 189) and cushion-type chrysanthemums (see p 215), both of which come in a wide range of colours. Tuberous begonias (see p 202) are highly successful in moist soil, but need shade from hot sun. The same conditions also suit the yellow and brown pouch-flowered shrubby calceolarias (*Calceolaria × herbeohybrida*), which range from 20 to 45 cm (8 to 18 in) in height.

In warm climates, several tender primulas that need greenhouse treatment elsewhere

rampant shrubs in such tropical countries as Kenya, yet have a place in summer bedding displays if kept dwarf – by pruning or frequent renewal – or trained as standards.

Florist penstemons (mostly derived from *Penstemon barbatus* and *P. hartwegii*, and usually listed as *P. × gloxinioides*) are normally reproduced from late summer cuttings. The foxglove-like flowers, carried on 60 cm (2 ft) leafy stems, persist until early autumn. Good garden sorts include 'Firebird' (scarlet), 'Southgate Gem' (blood-red), 'Garnet' (deep red), 'Pink Endurance' (clear pink), 'Catherine de la Mare' (lilac-pink) and 'White Bedder' (white).

Bedding fuchsias (mostly hybrids of *Fuchsia fulgens* and *F. magellanica*) can be grouped, and do well outdoors in mild climates provided the roots are kept moist and they are shaded from hot sun and protected from strong winds. Cultivars are legion, ranging from dwarfs around 30 cm (1 ft) tall to low shrubs and standards with single or double pink, white, red and purple flowers in a variety of shapes and colour patterns. (For hardy fuchsias, see page 157.)

Sweet-scented freesias, derived from *Freesia refracta*, also need shade. There are

There are also the more tender but very showy regal pelargoniums. Also called Martha Washingtons, these are classed as *P. × domesticum* varieties, and have large bunches of flowers in shades of pink, purple, red or white, usually patterned in several shades. They grow about 45 to 60 cm (1½ to 2 ft) high and have crinkly leaves that are thinner than in other pelargoniums. Other forms include the free-flowering Deacon and Irene cultivars, the former making bushes over 1 m (3 ft) tall if given plenty of head- and root-room. Named cultivars of all types should be regularly renewed from cuttings, otherwise they become straggly; they flower within a few months. Ordinary bedding geraniums of mixed colours can also be raised from seed.

Low-growing perennials

Low-growers make natural ground cover between the taller perennials, and some are suitable for edging purposes. Others are used in the making of floral clocks and other carpet-bedding schemes, although these may have to be kept dwarf by constant clipping. Suitable plants for carpet bedding include the fleshy-leaved echeverias; rosette-forming aeoniums; silvery-leaved acaenas, agaves,

Pelargonium × hortorum 'Carefree'

Agapanthus sp

helichrysums and raoulias; and *Thymus serpyllum* varieties. A useful edging plant is *Iresine lindenii*, which has deep crimson foliage, and *I. herbstii* (rich red with carmine stems) and its form 'Aureoreticulata', which is bright green with red veins and stems. They all grow about 30 cm (1 ft) high but can be kept more dwarf by pruning.

Nertera granadensis (*N. depressa*) depends for its effect on bright red berries, which look like scarlet beads on a green velvet bed of leaves. Hardy in frost-free climates, it also survives in places like southern Ireland if protected with a pane of glass in winter; but shade is essential.

Gazania splendens and *Dorotheanthus bellidiformis* (better known as *Mesembryanthemum criniflorum*, or the Livingstone daisy) are bedding subjects for sunny places and, being prostrate, may solve a problem in windy ones. The former has green or silver leaves and large orange, yellow or scarlet and green daisy flowers, which are often zoned with several colours. The latter is many-petalled, with carmine, white or yellow flowers.

Catharanthus roseus (better known as *Vinca rosea*) blooms continuously in warm climates, with large pink or white flowers (bicoloured in some forms) on 20 to 30 cm (8 to 12 in) stems. In cooler climates it makes a good long-flowering pot-plant.

Plants to give height
Taller perennials are useful at the back of one sided borders, before buildings or as 'dot' plants to break the flatness of conventional beds. Amongst those striking enough to use singly are the trumpet-flowered daturas, which have rough leaves and pendulous flowers 15 to 25 cm (6 to 8 in) long. *Datura suaveolens* and its semi-double variety 'Knightii' are both white and heavily fragrant; *D. sanguinea* is orange-red.

Strelitzia reginae, sometimes called the bird-of-paradise flower, is a noble plant 1.25 cm (4 ft) high. It has stiff glaucous leaves and orange and blue flowers arranged in an inflorescence shaped like the beak and crest of an exotic bird. Standard heliotropes (see p 221) are also useful, and *Hedychium gardnerianum*, a canna-like plant of the ginger family, has lanceolate leaves and 1.25 to 1.8 m (4 to 6 ft) stems carrying spikes of yellow flowers with long red stamens (see p 252).

Clivia miniata, with umbels of trumpet-shaped, red-orange flowers on 60 cm (2 ft) stems and broad strap-shaped leaves, does best in light shade. Known as the Kaffir lily, it is a favourite greenhouse pot-plant in cool regions, where it can also be grown in outdoor containers for the summer. It is propagated by dividing the fleshy roots, as are agapanthus. Some of the latter are hardy enough to grow permanently outdoors in cool regions (see p 180), but they and the more tender kinds really come into their own in a warm climate. Many species and hybrids are grown, particularly *Agapanthus africanus* and *A. praecox* and their forms. In some, the great globular heads of flowers – mostly bright blue – may reach a height of 1.25 m (4 ft).

Climbing perennials
These are useful to provide a living background for flower beds alongside walls, or to create lightweight shady arbours in summer. Among the plants suitable for these purposes are the blue *Plumbago capensis*; the evergreen, trumpet-flowered, orange-red *Streptosolon jamesonii*; and various solanums. These include the mauve *Solanum crispum* and its white counterpart 'Album'; *S. jasminoides*, which has blue-tinged white blossoms in bold clusters; and the deep blue, large-flowered *S. wendlandii*. They are all described elsewhere.

Primarily for foliage
Perennials with attractive foliage remain in character longer than flowers, and among the most useful for warmer climates are the cannas, with their red or green leaves as well as showy scarlet, yellow or orange inflorescences (see p 221). *Perilla frutescens* is purple-leaved, while *Cnicus casabonae*, the fishbone thistle, has dark green glossy leaves edged with golden spines and a tracery of white veins. Others include abutilons, eucalyptus, coleus and *Grevillea robusta* (all detailed on page 221), *Arundo donax* 'Variegata', a 3.5 m (12 ft) tall green and white striped grass (see p 244), and *Hebe* × *andersonii* 'Variegata', which has green and white patterned leaves and purple flowers.

Succulents
Succulent plants have fleshy leaves or stems or both, a characteristic that makes them vulnerable to frosts. In tropical and subtropical regions they thrive in hot, sun-baked areas, although they appreciate plenty of water in early summer. Plant them in well-drained soil. Many are increased from suckers, leaf-cuttings or seed; and although the mother plants often die after flowering there are usually plenty of side plantlets to take their place. Among the hardiest are species and cultivars of *Agave*, *Aloe*, *Cotyledon*, *Aeonium*, *Echeveria*, *Crassula*, *Euphorbia*, *Rochea*, *Sempervivum* and *Sedum*. Both aloes and agaves make good plants for containers.

Almost all cacti are also succulent, but most of them like cooler, drier winter conditions than the majority of other succulents (some in fact withstand slight frost; see p 252). Among the most attractive, many of them producing short-lived but colourful flowers in summer, are species of *Astrophytum*, *Cereus*, *Gasteria*, *Hamatocactus*, *Lobivia* and *Opuntia*.

Hebe × andersonii 'Variegata'

Agave × leopoldii

Rock plants for full sun

A very large proportion of alpine plants are sun-lovers, coming as they do from regions where the air is clear and the sunshine, if not hot, is fierce in its brilliance. There are also plenty of rock plants for shade (see p 226), and most rock gardens have shady spots where these will thrive. But the majority of the easily grown alpines like sun, and this is why the beginner is well advised to site his rock garden in an open, sun-drenched place.

Apart from light needs, it is necessary when choosing plants to differentiate between those that form great colour masses and the smaller treasures from the mountains. You will need a relatively large rock garden to accommodate many of the former, though such a rock garden will have odd corners where the smaller plants, too, can grow. A further factor is the

Aubrieta deltoidea

Primula 'Rufus'

desirability of having rock garden colour throughout the year, and not just in the spring and early summer, as explained on page 120. A number of dwarf bulbs (see p 200) are especially useful in extending the season.

Early colour masses
Specialists are inclined to look down on the old favourites like aubrieta, alyssum, saponaria and iberis, yet the very reason for these plants remaining favourites is that they are superb garden plants. There can be no finer spectacle – especially if one gardens on limy soil – than a blending of the old colour forms of *Aubrieta deltoidea*, such as the purple of 'Gurgedyke', the red of 'Mrs Rodewald' and the intense violet-blue of 'Dr Mules'. These have never been bettered.

Alyssum saxatile, in its various shades of yellow – and with a form called 'Compactum' that is particularly suitable for the small garden – supplies quite a different colour range, but one with which aubrieta associates well. So does the vast white-flowered mat of *Iberis sempervirens* – a good plant, incidentally, to cover up a garden manhole-cover. *I. saxatilis* is a diminutive beauty with the same lovely white flowers.

Aethionema pulchellum (*A. grandiflorum*) follows closely, with masses of pink, whilst the hybrid *A.* × 'Warley Rose' will satisfy the lover of smaller things. A superb colour combination with the aethionemas is *Lithosper-*

mum diffusum (now *Lithodora diffusa*) in its form 'Heavenly Blue'. It is strongly averse to lime, and benefits from a light cutting-back after flowering – as, indeed, do most of these plants, particularly aubrieta, which will then flower again later in the year.

Smaller treasures
If 'Heavenly Blue' is to be denied to those who garden on limy soil, they have a compensation in the similarly coloured *Polygala calcarea*, one of Britain's choicest native plants, seen at its best growing on tufa (see p 123).

Long before the great colour masses burst

Saxifraga collosa (*S. lingulata*) 'Albertii'

into flower, the tiny immaculate hummocks of the Kabschia saxifrages brighten the scree. Many of these are hybrids of *Saxifraga burseriana*, itself a plant boasting many fine forms like 'Gloria' (white), 'Major Lutea' (yellow) and the pink-flushed 'His Majesty'. The hybrids are legion, but one would do well to seek out 'Marie Louise' (white), which flowers in middle to late winter, 'Valerie Finnis', a good clear yellow, or the best of them all, 'Winifred' (rose-red).

Around such treasures may be planted *Gentiana verna*, the intense blue spring gentian, whose immense popularity is scarcely dimmed by it being short-lived, for it is easily raised from seed. Here, too, can be planted the smaller of the silver saxifrages, where the compact domes of *Saxifraga cochlearis* 'Minor' or *S. callosa* (*S. lingulata*), both white, will extend the flowering season.

The various colour forms of *Anemone blanda* flower in late winter, and their tubers are easily and cheaply obtainable, but for the finest of all the anemone clan you must look under *Pulsatilla*. *Pulsatilla vulgaris* (sometimes called *Anemone pulsatilla*), whose flowers of imperial purple sitting tight on their flat leaves once studded Britain's chalk downs, can be obtained in a variety of garden forms. They include rich reds, violets and pure whites, and these should be purchased in flower to ensure that you do not receive the washy lilac forms so often seen in gardens. All the pulsatillas, including that loveliest of flowers, the lady of the snows, *P. vernalis*, form tidy clumps suitable for the smallest rock garden. But they are tap-rooted, and should never be moved.

The primulas comprise one of the greatest of all the families for the rock garden, some easy, some difficult, and flowering almost throughout the year. But for early colour in the small rock garden it would be hard to better the Europeans like *Primula auricula* 'Dusty Miller' (in red or yellow forms) or the lovely farinose-leaved forms of *P. marginata* such as 'Linda Pope' (lavender-blue) or 'Shipton' (pale blue). Or there is the wonderful range of easy-going and colourful plants usually grouped under the name *P. × pubescens*; a gritty well-drained soil will provide a home

Helianthemum nummularium 'Ben Heckla'

for such classic beauties as 'Rufus' (brick-red), 'Faldonside' (crimson) and 'Carmen' (carmine).

Also among the pinks and reds at this time of year is a species of thrift, *Armeria caespitosa*, with showy pink flowers and grassy grey-green leaves in small hummocks. And for those with moist, lime-free soil there is the rosy-red *Rhodohypoxis baurii*, with its star-shaped flowers from spring right through to early autumn. It grows from a corm-like rhizome, and is not entirely hardy.

Later colour masses
As the season advances, the flaming carpets of *Phlox subulata* and its sister *P. douglasii* take over from the aubrietas and alyssums, in a range of colours from the white of the lovely *P. douglasii* 'Snow Queen', through soft pinks like *P. subulata* 'Betty' and the soft lilac of *P. douglasii* 'Boothman's Variety', to the shrieking magenta of *P. subulata* 'Temiscaming'.

Soon the magnificent brooms come into their own. Not all are yellow. For the hottest and driest place your garden has to offer, choose the slow-growing blue broom from Spain, *Erinacea anthyllis*; or, if space permits, the great billowing masses of cream flowers from *Cytisus × kewensis* or the deep yellow of *Genista lydia*. These are immensely long-lived shrubs that will maintain their perfection for fifteen or twenty years in moderate climates.

Geranium is a name so long attached to the

gaudy relatives of 'Paul Crampel' and other pelargoniums, that one forgets how valuable the real geraniums are in the rock garden. The cherry-red, black-eyed beauty *Geranium subcaulescens* will flower throughout the summer, and the raspberry-ice flowers of *G. endressii*, accompanied perhaps by the black-purple of the so-called mourning widow, *G. phaeum*, may well be planted amongst your hellebores to continue the season of flower.

Summer is also the season for two well-loved, vigorous and easily grown carpeting plants: *Saponaria ocymoides*, in various shades of pink, whose variety 'Compacta' is less rampant than the species; and *Gypsophila repens*, with white to deep pink flowers above a mat of wiry stems and grey-green leaves. Both do well where they can hang down over a rock-face or trail over a wall.

The same remarks apply to the colourful hordes of the sun roses or rock roses, the helianthemums, for those with the space to accommodate their exuberance. Four of the best cultivars of *Helianthemum nummularium* (*H. chamaecistus*) are 'Jubilee' (double yellow), 'The Bride' (creamy-white with yellow centre), 'Watergate Rose' (rose-pink with grey foliage) and 'Wisley Primrose' (yellow). There is also an excellent series of varieties with 'Ben' as part of the name, but all types will spread 60 cm (2 ft) or more. A dainty gem for the smaller rock garden is *H. lunulatum* (yellow).

Some of the less vigorous thymes can also find a place in rock gardens or among paving stones. Among the best are such forms of wild thyme (*Thymus serpyllum* or *T. drucei*) as 'Coccineus' (with crimson flowers in summer) and 'Annie Hall' (shell-pink), and the earlier *T. doerfleri* 'Bressingham Seedling' (clear pink). Another pink-flowered mat-forming plant of late spring and early summer is the moss campion, *Silene acaulis*.

One of the great rock garden families is that of the bellflowers. Since most gardens have some problem situation where almost nothing will grow, the first recommendation is for just such a situation: a combination of the rampant and free-seeding *Campanula poscharskyana* and the equally rampant *Alchemilla mollis*, whose flowers – in blue and greenish-

Campanula carpatica 'Pelviformis'

yellow respectively – blend together in perfect harmony. Much better behaved, though quickly spreading, is the deep blue of *C. portenschlagiana*, but the finest of the larger-growing campanulas is *C. garganica*, whose powder-blue flowers are seen at their best when the plant is grown in the chinks and crevices of a wall. An upright-growing, clump-forming species, with large flowers, is *C. carpatica*, selected forms of which in a wide variety of colours include 'White Star', 'Ditton Blue', and 'Blue Clips'.

Other small treasures
Bellflowers suitable for the small rock garden include the stocky little *Campanula nitida* 'Alba' (*C. persicifolia* 'Planiflora Alba' or *C. planiflora* 'Alba'), with 15 cm (6 in) spires of

Phyteuma comosum

pure white flowers, the small but spreading blue *C. arvatica*, and *C. pulla*, whose deep violet bells rise profusely above the mat of leaves on 8 cm (3 in) stems. A choice member of the campanula family for a well-drained limestone scree is a native of the high Dolomite crags, *Phyteuma comosum* (*Physoplexis comosa*), whose huge blue flowers are quite unlike those of any other plant in the family; it is a superlative species in a genus of weeds.

The dwarf *Dianthus* species, or rock pinks, have the advantage over the campanulas in that their tight hummocks are evergreen and a pleasure to look upon even when out of flower. There are some fine red hybrids to be had under martial-sounding names like 'Mars' and 'Brigadier', but it would be hard to exceed the beauty of two species from the Alps, *Dianthus alpinus* and *D. neglectus*, both pink in colour but the latter having an attractive biscuit-coloured backing to the petals.

An equally well-known alpine is the edelweiss, *Leontopodium alpinum*, with its curious off-white flowers with woolly petal-like bracts. Finally, and aptly, there are the evening primroses. *Oenothera riparia* has woody, floppy stems carrying masses of yellow flowers which remain open throughout the day, but the enormous yellow flowers, often 8 cm (3 in) across, of *O. missouriensis* are fleeting, and open only in the evening. But the constant succession of these glorious blooms continues for weeks to welcome the gardener home.

Rock plants for shady spots

Alpine pundits sometimes say that, if a choice had to be made between a rock garden in sun and a rock garden in shade, they would choose the shady site because of the outstanding beauty of some of the plants that love shade. But the shade must be light, ideally from deciduous trees that do not overhang, but which cast a shadow across the rock garden in the hottest months of the year.

Even the open, sun-drenched rock garden will also have the odd shady corner formed by an overhanging rock, or in the shadow of a shrub, where such treasures may be grown. A problem always to be borne in mind, however, is that plants in shade generally need moister soil than those in sun, and you may have to increase the water-retentive properties of soil pockets in shaded spots with peat or other humus-forming material.

Cassiopes and phyllodoces

Cassiopes are among the loveliest of carpeting plants, with their myriads of white bells suspended over deep green whipcord branches. Yet they are something of an enigma. They are basically sun-lovers, but need constant moisture at the root – two factors that are difficult to provide simultaneously in gardens. The more sun they get, the more freely they

Phyllodoce caerulea

flower, but if ever they dry out completely they will die. The easiest is probably *Cassiope lycopodioides*, with its hybrid relatives 'Edinburgh' and 'Muirhead'. *C. fastigiata* is more upright-growing and has larger bells, whilst *C. mertensiana* is more bushy.

Phyllodoces are some of the finest dwarf shrubs for the shady rock garden or peat bed, and grow throughout the northern hemisphere. *Phyllodoce caerulea* (*P. taxifolia*), one of the loveliest of them all, is a native of northern Europe and in spite of its misleading name (*caerulea* means blue) it carries heather-like bells of deep reddish-purple. From the American continent come the pink-flowered *P. breweri* and the popular *P. empetriformis*, with flowers of pink-purple. The yellow-flowered *P. aleutica* and the greenish-yellow *P. glanduliflora* come from the Arctic wastes of Alaska, Russia and the Aleutian Islands, whilst Japan contributes the dainty white-flowered and more upright shrublets *P. nipponica* and *P. tsugaefolia*.

An unusual bigeneric hybrid has occurred between *P. empetriformis* and a delectable but difficult gem from the Dolomite limestone, *Rhodothamnus chamaecistus*. It is called × *Phyllothamnus erectus*, and it has rather stiff upright branches and strangely crinkled pink flowers. A comparative newcomer to European gardens of a similar nature to the above plants, and one which should be sought far and wide, is the tiny pink-flowered *Kalmia microphylla* from the mountains of the western United States.

Trilliums and woodland phlox

The Trinity flower, so-called because the parts of the flower are grouped in threes, is a paragon of all garden virtues. The best known is the white, rarely pink, *Trillium gran-*

Shortia uniflora

diflorum, which has a splendid double-flowered form that might well be taken for a camellia. It is immensely long-lived, a clump prospering undisturbed for as much as thirty years. It is also of the easiest culture, though, like all trilliums, it is slow to settle down when first planted. Many species have mottled leaves of great beauty, and they cover a wide range of colour, from the mahogany-red upright-pointing flowers of *T. chloropetalum* to the ivory-white of *T. sessile*. There is even a yellow – albeit insipid – in *T. luteum*.

One tends to think of the phlox as a sun-lover, and forget how beautiful can be the spreading, self-rooting mats of such species as *Phlox adsurgens* and its new variety 'Wagon Wheel', raising their delicate pink flowers amongst dwarf rhododendrons and phyllodoces. Two other species are *P. divaricata* and *P. stolonifera* with, respectively, pink and blue flowers borne in clusters on 15 cm (6 in) stems. Their self-layering stolons are never so thick that they cannot be underplanted with

shade-loving bulbs like the erythroniums and snowdrops. Two fine new cultivars have recently been raised in the United States: 'Chattahoochee', with crimson-eyed flowers of pale violet, and an immaculate white beauty, 'Ariane'.

Some aristrocrats

There are so many wonderful plants for the shady rock garden or peat bed that it seems almost invidious to suggest that some of them be called aristocrats. Yet how else could one describe the double form of the North American bloodroot, *Sanguinaria canadensis* 'Plena'? Its ruff of leaves encircle the multi-petalled white chalices, which all too soon fall, to carpet the ground like fallen snow. Daphnes are real aristocrats of the rock garden, too,

and the creeping, sweetly-scented *Daphne blagayana* is tolerant of the deepest shade, but prefers limy soil.

The shortias from a genus that now encompasses the schizocodons, providing shade-loving plants that are as attractive in foliage as they are in flower. From Japan comes the aptly-named *Shortia* (*Schizocodon*) *soldanelloides*, whose flowers, if removed from the glossy autumn-hued beauty of the leaves, might well come from some heavenly pink soldanella of the Alps. The American species *S. galacifolia* has the largest leaves, but for the finest flowers one must turn again to Japan, to *S. uniflora* 'Grandiflora', whose single pink (or occasionally white) flowers can be as much as 4 cm (1½ in) across. To grow amongst such treasures one might well plant a few tubers of a wonderful form of the wood anemone, *Anemone nemorosa* 'Allenii', with flowers of diaphanous palest blue. A more rampant relative of the anemones, with red, mauve or white flowers, is *Hepatica nobilis* (*H. triloba*).

The dainty wild cyclamen from the mountains have a strong attraction for many alpine enthusiasts, and indeed the specialist can observe these dainty flowers for eight months of the year – though not all, alas, in the open garden. The species that do well in the open are of the easiest culture; of these, *Cyclamen hederifolium* (better known as *C. neapolitanum*) is probably the best because of the infinite variety of shapes and marbling patterns of its leaves, which carpet the ground in winter. Other reliable species for the open are *C. coum* (*C. orbiculatum*), whose variable flowers range from white to deepest carmine, *C. purpurascens* (formerly called *C. europaeum*) and a hybrid derived largely from *C. coum* that is usually listed as *C. × atkinsii*; its flowers range from white to crimson.

Arisarum proboscideum

shooting stars from North America. Most of these, like *Dodecatheon meadia*, are of purplish-pink colour, growing some 30 cm (12 in) high and always herbaceous in character. But the lovely little *D. dentata* is unusual in having white flowers that are rather cyclamen-like in appearance.

One should be cautious about planting species of oxalis, for they vary between free-seeding menaces to be avoided at all costs to fine plants like the pink-flowered *Oxalis adenophylla*. This loves the conditions of a damp scree, and its lovely grey foliage is second only to that of a new introduction from Patagonia, *O. laciniata*. The latter has 2.5 cm (1 in) wide flowers of imperial purple and will, if happy, soon spread its tiny white rhizomes across the surface of the scree.

Saxifraga oppositifolia

Primula auricula

Berries for late colour

The wise gardener knows the value of seed and the beauty of seed heads and berries, especially as the gardening year draws to a close and flowers are hard to come by. Then the berries on such dwarf shrubs as the gaultherias are the more appreciated. The great white clusters of fruit on *Gaultheria cuneata* and the pink-flushed berries of *G. miqueliana* are a real delight, but neither exceeds the fascination of *G. trichophylla*, with its great elongated berries of brightest blue. In the same category are two unusual though easily-grown similar plants from America, *Disporum oreganum* and *D. smithii*. Their tubular cream-coloured flowers are followed by berries of brightest orange.

The shady scree

Although the term scree generally implies exposure to sunshine, the well-designed scree bed should always allow for an area of sunless aspect, or even the shade cast by rocks or

shrubs. Here you can grow the purple-studded carpets of a superb British native, *Saxifraga oppositifolia*, in various forms ranging from plum-purple to white.

Shady vertical crevices in the rockwork can be planted with the crinkled evergreen rosettes of ramondas and haberleas; in such positions, where rain does not lodge in the rosettes, these plants – with their flower clusters commonly of bright mauve with golden anthers – are very long-lived. The easiest is probably *Ramonda myconi* from the Pyrenees, whose flowers may be found in various shades of mauve, pink or occasionally white. Its relatives *Haberlea ferdinandi-coburgii* and *H. rhodopensis* are both lilac-purple, the latter being smaller and more delicate. It also has a white form, 'Virginalis'.

Moist scree suits many of the primulas, such as the forms of *P. auricula* (commonly called auriculas and available in a wide range of colours) and the British native *P. farinosa*, and their relatives the dodecatheons, the

For the curious

Finally, because curious plants beget curiosity in a gardener, and curiosity begets knowledge and a deeper appreciation of the wonders of plant life, consider a couple of aroids. Where there are children there should always be the mouse-tail arum. *Arisarum proboscideum*, an easy-going carpeter for any shady place. Its strange browny-black pitcher flowers, each with a long curly proboscis, look for all the world like brown mice disappearing into the foliage.

Then, for the lover of flower arranging, an essential plant for a shady corner is *Arum italicum* 'Marmoratum'. Its beautifully marbled arrow-shaped leaves, so perfect for winter posy bowls, appear just as the leaves are falling from the trees, and last all winter long. As the days begin to lengthen, the strange ephemeral greeny-yellow spathes appear, to be followed a month later by the stiff stems of brilliant red berries, like the lords and ladies of a country lane.

Foliage plants for the rock garden

Compare a good rock garden and a good herbaceous border in the winter months. The first is full of interest, with evergreen shrubs, the varying habit of its dwarf conifers, its foliage plants and the occasional winter-flowering bulb beginning to peep above the ground. The other is dreary, dull and lifeless, and will remain so for many months to come, unless the gardener has compromised with his principles and introduced some shrubs among the herbaceous plants.

Some more 'architectural' shrubs and dwarf conifers for the rock garden are dealt with in the next article, while these pages consider the other plants whose foliage contrast forms so essential a part of the rock garden throughout the year. Many such plants are herbaceous in character, so evergreen winter foliage must be considered as a thing apart.

Gold in winter

There are those who feel that heathers have no place in any but the largest of rock gardens. But, although this may have been true of the older forms of the glorious winter-flowering *Erica carnea*, it is certainly not true of some of the remarkable new cultivars of dwarf and compact habit. There is, for example, *E. carnea* 'Ann Sparkes', whose golden, red-tipped foliage is a delight in the long cold months of winter. Other good forms include the golden 'Foxhollow', growing to some 60 cm (2 ft) in height, and the golden-yellow 'Aurea'. See also page 152.

The very real value of the heathers in the smaller rock garden is enhanced by the superb foliage contrasts provided by the various cultivars of *Calluna vulgaris* (ling). 'Golden Carpet', whose leaves are flecked with orange and red, is a good example, as is an old cultivar, 'Multicolor', sometimes offered under its far more appropriate name of 'Prairie Fire'.

Some of the dwarf 'whipcord' hebes can also give gold in the winter months. *Hebe hectoris* is dwarf and reasonably attractive, as are *H. lycopodioides* and *H. armstrongii*.

Silver in winter

Leucanthemum hosmariense represents one of the very finest plant introductions of post-war years. It comes from the Ben Hosmar Mountains of North Africa, but appears to be quite hardy. It is valuable both for its evergreen mat of sparkling silver leaves and for the fact that it carries its mass of yellow-eyed white daisy flowers all winter through.

The santolinas are immensely popular plants, and for the larger rock garden the stiff, upright-growing *Santolina neapolitana* makes a wonderful background plant. It does benefit from a fairly severe cutting back after flowering, however, lest its brittle branches be damaged by winter snow. Similar, though rather smaller, is the lavender cotton, *S. chamaecyparissus* (sometimes listed as *S. incana*), whose form 'Nana' makes an ideal silver plant for the smallest rock garden.

Ptilotrichum (Alyssum) spinosum is always a favourite. When it is planted in a hot dry position, its silvery hummocks are smothered in pink or white flowers in summer. It is nota-

Milium effusum 'Aureum'

ble how most of the silver-foliage plants revel in poor soil and hot dry places (see p 240). For just the reverse conditions, in cool damp woodland, the massive silvery rosettes of the statuesque celmisias of New Zealand may be tried. *Celmisia coriacea* and *C. spectabilis* are good examples.

The scree may be brightened in winter by some of the silver-leaved helichrysums, like the attractive, though not fully hardy, 'whipcord' *Helichrysum coralloides* or the soft whiteness of *H. plumeum*. There are a multitude of good hebes for the rock garden, too, most of them inclining to be rather large. One of the best is *Hebe* 'Pagei' (often listed as *H. pageana* or *H. pinguifolia* 'Pagei'), whose sprawling grey cushions are a delight at all times of the year.

Chrysanthemum (Tanacetum) haradjanii

Gold for later seasons

Having differentiated the golden-leaved plants that retain their colour in winter, now consider some that give gold effects for the rest of the year. Few of the maples are sufficiently small or slow-growing to be considered for the rock garden, but a glorious exception is *Acer japonicum* 'Aureum'. This will take many years to outgrow its position in the larger rock garden, and provides a touch of gold from spring until the leaves turn rich crimson before falling in autumn. Its gold is almost as bright as that of the new growth of the golden meadowsweet, *Filipendula (Spiraea) ulmaria* 'Aurea'. The leaves of this European native are so attractive that one is well advised to cut out the tall, lanky flower stems and so promote renewed leaf growth.

One of the dead nettles, *Lamium maculatum*, has a good form, 'Aureum', which will make an attractive carpet. There are also a number of golden sedges and grasses for the rock garden, one of the best being Bowles's golden grass, *Milium effusum* 'Aureum'. There is no finer sight than to see the sun shining through the swaying fronds of this bright and cheerful grass if it is allowed to seed along a rock garden path.

Silver for later seasons

The composites, the daisy family, give some of the best silver and grey-leaved plants. Among the artemisias, for instance, are *Artemisia armeniaca* and the rather similar *A. vallesiaca* both with billowing clouds of fine filigree foliage. For the smaller garden, *A. schmidtiana* 'Nana' makes a compact clump seldom exceeding 15 cm (6 in) in height and of a glistening silvery white. Its flowers are encased in woolly bracts to form tiny balls; they appear in autumn. The dwarf achilleas include *Achillea ageratifolia* and the neat *A. clavenae*, the latter being best in the variety 'Integrifolia'. Another composite of fairly recent introduction is *Chrysanthemum haradjanii* from Asia Minor, whose attractive spreading mats of grey leaves bear butter-yellow flowers in summer. It is sometimes listed as *Tanacetum haradjanii* or *T. densum* 'Amani'.

It would be a poor rock garden that did not

'Atropurpureum' and for the smaller garden the much more dwarf hybrid *S.* × 'Autumn Joy'. Another two outstanding hybrids are 'Ruby Glow' and 'Vera Jameson', making tidy hummocks of bronze-purple leaves some 30 cm (12 in) or so in height, with vivid pink flowers late in the summer. *S. spathulifolium* 'Purpureum' makes a prostrate mat of the same purplish colour, and the form 'Capa Blanca' has foliage which at certain times of the year almost approaches a white colour, making a lovely association with some of the golden dwarf conifers.

and bushy, seldom going over 30 cm (12 in), and has rich purplish-red deciduous leaves. They turn scarlet in autumn. There are small yellow flowers in spring, followed by small scarlet berries.

Two more for the scree – they are rather invasive in richer soil – are a couple of spurges. The cypress spurge, *Euphorbia cyparissias*, should also be starved for another reason: only then will it develop its brilliant red and orange colouration. *E. myrsinites* is blue-grey in colour and rather succulent. Both have greenish or yellow flowers in spring.

Sempervivum tectorum

Trifolium repens 'Purpurascens'

boast a few of the smaller willows to give height and background. Magnificent though the woolly *Salix lanata* may be, it soon grows too large, reaching a height and spread of 1.25 m (4 ft). Seek instead the form 'Stuartii', which has equally beautiful leaves of felted silver, but seldom exceeds 90 cm (3 ft) in height. *S. lapponum* is another and more delicate willow, upright-growing and all too seldom seen in rock gardens, while the prostrate *S. reticulata* shows silver only with the young leaves; these later become glossy green.

For the scree one can try the incomparable combination of two beautiful plants: *Veronica bombycina*, with flowers of palest blue above almost white foliage, and *Asperula suberosa*, with equally delicate flowers of pink above soft cushions of greyish-green. Here, too, you can grow *Raoulia hookeri*, whose leaves are white rather than silver, and the grey-leaved and easy *R. australis*, the ideal bulb cover for the delicate flowers of the early spring.

A miscellany of leaves

Podophyllum hexandrum (*P. emodi*) is always a much admired plant. Its large ornamental leaves, with their strange blotches of chocolate-coloured marbling, appear early, before the single pink-white flowers, which open in early summer. Then, to everyone's surprise, come the large orange-red fruits, like 'Victoria' plums on 30 cm (12 in) stems. The roots and rootstock are poisonous.

Some of the sedums, too, have interesting leaves, much beloved of flower arrangers. For the larger rock garden there are the mahogany leaves of *Sedum maximum*

The latter sedum has rosette leaves, and there are a wide range of houseleeks (*Sempervivum* spp) of similar form that make long-lived mats of fleshy foliage. They are ideal for the scree or for growing on dry walls. Among the most popular species is *Sempervivum arachnoideum*, whose common name of cobweb houseleek comes from the mat of white hairs that tangle among the green or pink-flushed leaves. In this the rosettes are a mere 2.5 to 4 cm (1 to 1½ in) across, but the common houseleek, *S. tectorum*, has rosettes up to 15 cm (6 in) across; in 'Commander Hay' they are maroon with green tips. There are many other species.

Most berberis are too big for the rock garden, but a colourful exception is *Berberis thunbergii* 'Atropurpurea Nana'. It is dense

Sedum 'Vera Jameson'

For those with plenty of room, the late-flowering, rose-red *Polygonum vacciniifolium* has leaves of good autumn colour, and it always seems a pity that the strange *P. capitatum*, whose large green leaves have a curious brown marbling, should be slightly tender. It will generally seed itself, however, and reappear the following summer.

Foliage for the curious

A weed, it is said, is merely a plant in the wrong place, so for those who find beauty in curious things, here finally are a clover, a thistle or two, and (almost) a dandelion. With children around, one should always grow the purple clover, *Trifolium repens* 'Purpurascens' – where three-, four- or even five-leaved lucky emblems can always be found. Its beauty is unquestionable, but it is best confined to a paved path where it cannot spread too far.

Hieracium maculatum is a hawkweed that should be grown strictly for its black-spotted leaves, which are ideal for posy bowls; its dandelion-like flowers are best removed lest an unnoticed seedhead spreads it far and wide. *H. villosum* is an equally desirable silver-leaved plant to which the same rules should be applied.

Finally the thistles: Garden visitors are always entranced by the white-flecked, pea-green leaves of the rosettes of the biennial thistles, *Cnicus diacanthus* and *C. benedictus*, which are such a delight in winter and spring. But enough is enough, and only a single seed-head should be allowed to seed around for future seasons.

Rock garden shrubs and trees

A rock garden, particularly one that is built on a flat site, needs shrubs and dwarf trees of architectural value to add height and form and to help give year-round interest. This is best provided by the dwarf conifers, which have both height and colour, but there are many shrubs which also give form and grace. There are, for instance the male form of *Salix apoda*, a prostrate willow whose great yellow catkins can crown a green mat tumbling down a rock face, and *Rhamnus pumilus*, the dwarf buckthorn, whose carpet of pale green follows every contour of the rockwork. Such plants are just as valuable in their way as the stately columns of *Juniperus communis* 'Compressa' or the evergreen statuesque beauty of some of the daphnes.

Background shrubs
Here the shrubby potentillas are valuable, being easy to grow and propagate, and easily pruned to size. They have long-lasting flowers ranging in colour from the deep yellow of *Potentilla arbuscula* (probably the best of the lot), whites such as *P. fruticosa* 'Farrer's White' and 'Mount Everest', through the faintly orange 'Tangerine' to red in the much-vaunted new 'Red Ace'. The dwarfer cistus (rock roses or sun roses), though sometimes inclined to be tender, are also good background shrubs. The well-known *Cistus* × 'Silver Pink' is a good example, though in somewhat short supply, and there are many other slow-growing cultivars with single rose-like flowers in various colours.

Statuesque shrubs
There must always be a place in the rock garden for the dwarf willows, and, where space permits, *Salix hastata* 'Wehrhahnii' (*S. wehrhahnii*) has catkins of the greatest beauty. It may be pruned to cultivate a horizontal habit, or allowed its more natural columnar shape. Even the smallest rock garden or trough should sport the gnarled and curious form of *S.* ×*boydii*. Some of the hollies are useful, too, ranging from the tiny slow-growing beauty of *Ilex crenata* 'Mariesii' to the spreading *I. crenata* 'Aureovariegata', whose new growth is gloriously tipped with gold in springtime.

The real aristocrats of the rock garden are the daphnes, and *Daphne collina*, *D. retusa* and its slightly larger-growing relative *D. tangutica* are all long-lived (unlike some daphnes), evergreen, sweetly-scented shrubs of great architectural worth. Lovers of the curious will want to grow also the slender-branched contortions of *Corokia cotoneaster*, the so-called wire-netting bush, which needs a sheltered place in fullest sun.

Evergreen shrubs
The dwarfer boxes are seldom seen in rock gardens, yet they can be quite admirable in a quiet way. *Buxus microphylla*, from Japan, forms a small rounded shrublet, and has some even smaller forms, such as 'Compacta' and the natural variety *B. microphylla koreana*, which are suitable even for trough gardens. *B. harlandii* is larger-growing and stately, with a

Salix hastata 'Wehrhahnii'

distinctive upright habit. Among the cotoneasters are two prostrate shrubs ideal for covering awkward places: *Cotoneaster microphyllus* for the small rock garden and, for the larger, *C. dammeri radicans*, which has the invaluable attribute of being able to tumble down a cold, sunless rock wall.

The barberries
The barberries, or berberis, are invaluable shrubs that include both deciduous and evergreen species. *Berberis* × *stenophylla* 'Corallina Compacta' is a lovely miniature evergreen, seldom exceeding 30 cm (12 in) in height, and has buds of flaming coral opening to yellow. *B. buxifolia* 'Nana' is somewhat similar, but much larger-growing, and no garden, let alone rock garden, should be without the beautiful spiny, purple-leaved *B. thunbergii* 'Atropurpurea Nana'. When obtaining

these shrubs, however, remember the vital importance of the word 'Compacta' or 'Nana' in the varietal name, for all three are micro-forms of much larger shrubs unsuitable for the rock garden.

Shrubs for the peat bed
It goes almost without saying that in acid conditions the dwarf rhododendrons reign supreme, but how is the gardener to choose from so many? The sheer delight of out-of-season flowers suggests that you should always take a gamble and plant some of the very early-flowering species, in the hope that a warm spell in early spring will suddenly produce a mass of flower. For the small rock garden, try *Rhododendron pemakoense* (purple) or *R. forrestii repens* (scarlet), or for the larger *R. leucaspis* (cream) or *R.* × Cilpinense (white, flushed pink).

Potentilla arbuscula

Rhododendron forrestii repens

Abies balsamea 'Hudsonia'

Cedrus libani 'Sargentii'

For later flowering in the small rock garden there is the pink-flowered *R. imperator*, the purple-crimson of *R. keleticum* and the rose-purple *R. radicans*. Where space permits, try the crimson-scarlet hybrid 'Little Bert' or the intense blue of 'Bluebird'. The choice is so wide that recommendations seem almost invidious. See also page 127.

Dwarf conifers

A rock garden without dwarf conifers would be incomplete. Indeed, anyone who has visited such famous collections as that of the Strybing Arboretum in San Francisco, or H. J. Welch's Pygmy Pinetum near Devizes, in the west of England, will know that conifers alone can make a garden beautiful throughout the year. Yet there is hardly any collection of such trees that does not eventually prove to be too closely planted. A tiny bun of *Chamaecyparis obtusa* 'Juniperoides', often recommended for troughs, will become 60 cm (2 ft) across in thirty years, whilst the popular and beautiful *C. pisifera* 'Boulevard' will need to be discarded from all but the largest rock garden in half that time.

A dwarf conifer is generally a sport of some sort, either an aberrant seedling propagated thereafter from cuttings, or a cutting from a so-called witch's broom (a kind of gall in which a tufted, dwarf outgrowth forms on a branch of an otherwise normal tree). In the latter case, different cuttings will have different characteristics. If vegetatively propagated from the same cutting, yet subsequently grafted onto different rootstocks, a fresh range of variations may occur. Hence the multiplicity of forms, shapes, sizes, colours and bewildering latinized and cultivar names. They have nothing to do with bonsai, which is a method of artificial dwarfing. They are true

dwarfs, even if they were once referred to by a distinguished tree expert as the 'miniature poodles of the rock garden'.

The dwarfer and more slow-growing the tree, the more costly it is to buy, because the nurseryman must grow his cuttings for many years before they even begin to look like dwarf trees. Yet, on the other hand, to plant the rock garden with comparatively quick-growing 'dwarf' trees like the popular *Chamaecyparis lawsoniana* 'Ellwoodii' is to court disappointment when they have to be discarded after comparatively few years. The best solution to this problem is to compromise by planting dwarf conifers of medium growth in the rock garden initially, but to keep a stock

of slow-growing replacements in a nursery bed or in pots in a frame. These can be transplanted when the originals have exceeded their allotted space.

The table represents a guide to some of the admirable dwarf conifers. Those described as of moderate growth and medium size will reach perfection in a decade, but may well prove too large for the rock garden of moderate size in thirty years. Those of slow growth and small size are the aristocrats which need patience – and perhaps the temporary home of a pot or nursery bed – to achieve perfection. But in no other form of gardening is patience so rewarding as in the growing of these fascinating dwarf conifers.

Recommended dwarf conifers

	Botanical name	Growth rate	Size	Habit	Colour
Firs	*Abies balsamea* 'Hudsonia'	Slow	Small	Spreading	Dark green
Cedars	*Cedrus libani* 'Nana'	Slow	Small	Spreading	Green
	C. libani 'Sargentii'	Moderate	Medium	Weeping (if trained)	Blue-green
False cypresses	*Chamaecyparis obtusa* 'Juniperoides'	Slow	Small	Bun-shaped	Green
	C. obtusa 'Nana	Moderate	Medium	Pyramidal	Dark green
	C. obtusa 'Nana Aurea'	Moderate	Medium	Pyramidal	Golden
	C. obtusa 'Tetragona Aurea'	Slow	Medium	Bushy	Bronze-gold
	C. pisifera 'Plumosa Aurea Nana'	Slow	Small	Round, bushy	Golden
Junipers	*Juniperus communis* 'Compressa'	Slow	Small	Columnar	Grey-green
	J. procumbens 'Nana'	Moderate	Medium	Prostrate	Green
Spruces	*Picea abies* 'Gregoryana'	Slow	Small	Bun-shaped	Green
	P. abies 'Nidiformis'	Slow	Medium	Spreading	Green
	P. glauca 'Albertiana Conica'	Moderate	Medium	Tall, conical	Green
Pines	*Pinus sylvestris* 'Beuvronensis'	Moderate	Medium	Spreading	Dark green
Thujas	*Thuja orientalis* 'Aurea Nana'	Moderate	Medium	Bushy	Yellow

Plants for ground cover

There is little point in retaining an area of bare soil around shrubs and other plants. For one thing it has no aesthetic appeal, but, even more important, it affords weed seeds too much opportunity for germination. It also creates aridity near plant roots, since there is nothing to shield the soil from hot sun or drying winds. Bare earth is rarely seen in nature where soil fertility and moisture are adequate; any land disturbance is quickly masked by a canopy of vegetation.

In gardens, grass is extensively employed as ground cover (see pp 84 to 87), and has two attributes which single it out from other plants. When properly grown it makes a uniform green carpet, and it is tough enough to withstand walking or ball games. However, there are many situations where grass will not thrive even if preferred. Extreme shade, dry ground underneath deciduous trees, and very damp areas are all poor places to grow grass, nor are some of these places easy to mow.

Fortunately there are other plants better able to survive under such unpromising conditions. Some of them make pleasing substitutes for grass (see p 234) and can be mown or walked on. Others, while often coarser-leaved and generally growing more unevenly, readily carpet the ground between larger plants, whether it is flat or sloping, and effectively smother weeds — providing practical as well as aesthetic gains.

Ground cover for shade

More ground-cover plants will grow in damp shade than in dry shade, so it may be necessary to work some moisture-retentive material like leaf-mould or damp peat into the soil before or during planting. In later years, if a little ground bark fibre or peat is packed under and around the plants as a mulch, they will root into this and spread.

The best types for dry shade are vincas,

Nepeta × *faassenii* (*N. mussinii*)

(periwinkles), hederas (ivies), and pachysandras, but even these do better where the soil is damp. *Vinca minor* (the lesser periwinkle) increases by means of runners, the type having flat blue, five-petalled flowers and small oval leaves. Cultivars exist with white and purple flowers, also a deep blue, compact, almost runnerless form called 'Bowles's Variety' ('La Graveana'). Several doubles occur, like the blue *V. minor* 'Coerulea Plena' and the wine-red *V. minor* 'Multiplex', and there are sorts with gold-variegated leaves and blue or white flowers.

Pachysandra terminalis is a weed-defying, scrambling Japanese evergreen about 30 cm (12 in) high, with spikes of small white flowers and diamond-shaped leaves. These are heavily variegated with white in the more garden-worthy form 'Variegata'. The taller

(30 to 45 cm [12 to 18 in]) but less spreading *P. procumbens* from North America is semi-evergreen, but if planted 30 to 45 cm (12 to 18 in) apart soon increases to a dense mass. Deprived of a suitable support, many ivies (see p 142) will trail across the soil to make dense ground cover.

In damp soil and shade, several members of the arum family thrive, including *Arisarum proboscideum*, which grows to about 10 cm (4 in), with glossy arrow-shaped leaves and brown and white long-tailed flowers that resemble the hindquarters of burrowing mice. The taller (45 cm [18 in]) *Arum pictum* (*A. corsicum*) has large green and cream leaves that are ideal for flower arrangements.

The round-leaved, aromatic wild gingers — *Asarum europaeum* and *A. caudatum* — form dense masses 10 cm (4 in) high and remain evergreen in temperate climates. If the leaves are parted in spring many curious three-petalled crimson flowers are disclosed.

The barrenworts (*Epimedium* spp) are other weed-defying and evergreen shade plants. They have wiry stems and heart-shaped leaves, mottled with chocolate brown in the yellow-flowered *Epimedium perralderianum* but plain green in the white-flowered *E.* × *youngianum* and crimson-flowered *E.* × *rubrum*. All grow 15 to 20 cm (6 to 8 in) tall.

Others for damp shade include the ajugas and *Hypericum calycinum*, described later; the white-flowered, 20 cm (8 in) foam flower, *Tiarella cordifolia*; blue-eyed Mary (*Omphalodes verna*), a stoloniferous trailer (reputed to have been Queen Marie Antoinette's favourite flower) with deep blue forget-me-not flowers and small oval leaves; also two trailing relatives of the raspberry, *Rubus calycinoides* (*R. fockeanus*) and *R. tricolor* (*R. polytrichus*), both with bristly stems, white flowers and red edible fruits.

Vinca minor

Pachysandra terminalis 'Variegata'

The yellow archangel, *Lamiastrum* (*Lamium*) *galeobdolon* 'Variegatum', although rampageous, is fortunately surface-rooting so can be kept in check without too much trouble. It has trailing stems, yellow nettle-like flowers and grey-green, white-splashed leaves. *Brunnera macrophylla* (*Anchusa myosotidiflora*) grows 30 cm (12 in) high, with deep blue forget-me-not flowers and rough heart-shaped leaves. It tends to seed itself about, however, a characteristic absent in the slower-growing variegated form.

Ground cover for dry spots
Dry banks and slopes are difficult to clothe with plants, but the steeper these are the more important it is to bind the soil with plant roots to prevent erosion. Those selected should be large enough and strong enough to stand up to such conditions. On very steep banks it may be necessary to plant at the foot of the slope and peg the stems upwards into the soil.

For gentle slopes suitable plants include aubrietas, *Cotoneaster dammeri*, helianthemums (rock or sun roses), catmint (*Nepeta* spp) and various creeping junipers like *Juniperus sabina* 'Tamariscifolia' and *J. horizontalis* and its varieties. For steep slopes some of the stronger roses may be pegged down (or upwards): kinds like *Rosa wichuraiana* and its varieties and *R.* × *paulii*. *Forsythia* 'Arnold Dwarf' makes a bold display in sunny situations. Several of the prostrate, white-flowered and red-berried cotoneasters like *Cotoneaster horizontalis*, *C. adpressus* and *C. microphyllus* are also suitable; similarly *Vinca major* (the greater periwinkle) and the golden-flowered *Hypericum calycinum*.

Dry ground on the flat should be mulched if possible in the early years of planting so as to establish quickly such plants as the double white *Arabis albida* 'Flore Pleno', with flowers like small stocks and silvery leaves; *Mentha requienii*, a peppermint-scented, moss-like mint with tiny mauve flowers; *Oxalis inops*, which has large shamrock leaves and rosy-pink flowers all through summer; and dwarf gypsophilas like the pink *Gypsophila repens* 'Rosea' or *G.* 'Rosy Veil'.

In sunny situations, aubrietas and the colourful moss phlox (*Phlox subulata*) form carpets of mauve, pink, red and white in early summer; pinks (*Dianthus plumarius* cultivars), being evergreen, are useful at all seasons; and in warm spots the Barbary ragwort, *Hertia* (*Othonnopsis*) *cheirifolia*, soon spreads to form 30 cm (12 in) silvery clumps topped by golden daisies.

Ground cover for wet soils
Not every plant thrives where the soil is constantly damp, although those that do are quick spreaders. Among the most reliable are the asarums and arisarums, *Cotoneaster dammeri* and *Rubus calycinoides* (all described earlier), also the ubiquitous creeping Jenny, *Lysimachia nummularia*, a trailer with small neat leaves and golden flowers. The golden-leaved form 'Aurea' is still more attractive. Callunas (ling or heather; see p 152) also

favour moist albeit lime-free ground; the spring-flowering creeping dogwood (*Cornus canadensis*), whose 5 cm (2 in) stems terminate in white, four-petalled blossoms, is another good choice for wet soil. In boggy areas, water forget-me-nots (*Myosotis palustris*), bog beans (*Menyanthes trifoliata*) and bog arums (*Calla palustris*; see p 256) are most reliable ground-covering plants.

Flowering ground cover
Ground-cover plants which flower have a double attraction for gardeners, and perhaps the most useful in this group so long as soil is not limy are the hardy heathers (see p 152). These not only provide a weed-defying, weatherproof mat of evergreen foliage but, by careful selection of varieties of *Erica carnea* and *E. cinerea*, you can have spikes of pink, red or white bell-shaped flowers throughout most of the year. Additionally, gold- and silver-leaved heathers give colour at all seasons. Set the plants, with a ball of soil

Cotoneaster microphyllus cochleatus

attached, 40 cm (15 in) apart in humus-rich soil and top-dress them annually with peat to keep them healthy.

Lilies of the valley, arabis, aubrieta, epimediums, tiarellas, nepeta and *Phlox subulata* all have attractive flowers in spring, and the dwarf *Iris cristata* is a gem for small areas, its 5 to 10 cm (2 to 4 in) sky-blue, white-crested flowers poised on 15 cm (6 in) stems between fans of small leaves in late spring.

Several low-growing campanulas, or bellflowers, are suitable for open places in rock gardens, for under-carpeting roses or for bordering flower beds. Among the most useful are *Campanula poscharskyana* and *C. portenschlagiana* – both blue-flowered. *Saponaria ocymoides* will trail over banks and rocks and also cover bare ground, but needs sun and sharp drainage to thrive. Its small pink flowers spangle the grey-green foliage in midsummer.

The evergreen *Hypericum calycinum* is ideal for sunless positions in damp soil, its golden, bowl-shaped flowers looking like pincushions with myriads of stamens. It grows about 30 cm (12 in) high. *Galium odoratum* (*Asperula odorata*) is the woodruff, a small plant 15 to 20 cm (6 to 8 in) tall with

masses of white flowers and whorls of needle-fine leaves which, when dried, smell like new-mown hay.

There are also a few sun-loving sweet-pea relatives like the prostrate brooms *Genista lydia*, *G. sagittalis* and the Spanish gorse, *G. hispanica*, all with bright yellow flowers. Equally useful are a few brooms of the genus *Cytisus*, particularly *Cytisus* × *kewensis*, creamy-flowered and spreading across the ground like a fan; *C. procumbens*, with whippy green shoots; and the taller (45 cm [18 in]) *C.* × *beanii*, both bright yellow.

Ground cover with coloured foliage
A number of these are evergreen, like *Pachysandra terminalis* 'Variegata' and the epimediums already mentioned, but there are also several conifers which are useful on rough ground and similar difficult situations. The best of these include *Juniperus sabina* 'Tamariscifolia', *J. procumbens* 'Nana', *Picea abies* 'Procumbens', *P. pungens* 'Procumbens'

Genista sagittalis

('Glauca Procumbens') and *Taxus baccata* 'Cavendishii' and 'Repandans'.

Deciduous kinds include *Ajuga reptans* 'Variegata', with cream-blotched foliage, a form of the blue-flowered bugle; also its forms 'Atropurpurea' (purple-leaved) and 'Multicolor' ('Rainbow'), with bronze, pink and yellow suffusions on its green foliage. There is a purple four-leaved clover called *Trifolium repens* 'Purpurascens'. The nettle-like 10 cm (4 in) *Lamium maculatum* has a silver stripe on the middle of every leaf and purple or pink flowers, and there are also several good silver-leaved plants for dry sunny positions. They include the evergreen *Artemisia stelleriana*, the dusty miller (45 cm [18 in]), *A. schmidtiana* 'Nana' (10 cm [4 in]), *A. brachyloba* (2.5 cm [1 in]) and the taller flowerless form of *Stachys lanata* (*S. olympica*), 'Silver Carpet', which is deciduous.

The silvery-grey *Cerastium tomentosum*, or snow-in-summer, is a rampageous plant, ideal for covering rough obstacles like broken rocks. It has white flowers. Although tender in hard frost districts, the variegated ground ivy *Nepeta* (*Glechoma*) *hederacea* 'Variegata' is useful in milder climates.

Substitutes for lawn grass

In Tudor times the fine lawns of today were unknown. Instead the 'flowery meads' of the period were, at their best, reclaimed meadow land, kept short with scythes and reserved for the ladies of the household. In the 16th century, lawns were as frequently made of chamomile as of grass, a plant which, as Falstaff noted, 'the more it is trodden on the faster it grows'. In the 17th century, low-growing plants which were fragrant became popular for 'spacious and fair walks', banks and seats; native thymes, burnet, mints and chamomile were the kinds most commonly used.

The advent of the mowing machine was the main cause of the disappearance of these alternatives to grass. Nowadays they are enjoying a revival, however, for most gardens have small areas which defy grass culture, such as beneath trees or overlaying brick rubble or gravel where there is little topsoil. Unless re-sown annually these always look unkempt. Turf substitutes are also useful for roof gardens – where weight is a problem – or in quadrangles; or a mixture of fragrant plants makes an attractive feature in city gardens.

Chamomile lawns

One of the most famous chamomile lawns in Britain is in the grounds of Buckingham Palace. This example is mixed with grass and cut with a mower. Even in the driest summer chamomile (*Anthemis nobilis*) stands up to hard wear, remaining green when grass has lost its verdure. The flowerless form known as 'Treneague' (propagated by division or cut-

Anthemis nobilis

tings) is the best as it remains compact – without the elongations of the stems other varieties undergo during flowering. Small plants should be set 10 cm (4 in) apart in spring, in ground previously dug and manured, allowed to settle for several weeks, then raked. The area must be carefully weeded the first season and watered if necessary. Make the first cut with shears. Other varieties of chamomile can be propagated from seed, sown in drills and later transplanted. The flowers are white and there is an attractive double form.

Thyme lawns

There are many varieties of thyme, all evergreen and all fragrant. In midsummer, when they come to flower, the small white, rose or red flowers are much visited by bees. Thyme lawns can be made of a single variety, or a mixture of kinds. *Thymus serpyllum*, (*T.*

Minuartia verna caespitosa 'Aurea'

drucei), a favourite for this purpose, is a flat carpeter with magenta, purple, pink or white flowers, the forms 'Pink Chintz' and 'Snowdrift' being particularly desirable.

T. × *citrodorus* 'Aureus', lemon-scented with gold-green leaves and pale lilac flowers, and the variegated 'Silver Queen' are others to note; also the lilac *T. herba-barona*, which smells of caraway, and *T. drucei pseudolanuginosus* (*T. lanuginosus*), with silvery, woolly foliage and pale mauve flowers.

Carpeters to walk on

A few low-growing plants will withstand occasional walking on, although this practice should not be abused. Those that are among the most tolerant of infrequent crushings are mentioned here. *Sagina glabra* (*S. pilifera*) 'Aurea', the pearlwort, is one of the most striking, with bright golden, finely cut foliage covered in summer with myriads of tiny white flowers. The closely related *Minuartia* (*Arenaria* or *Alsine*) *verna caespitosa* 'Aurea', a form of spring sandwort, is similiar; it is very hardy and likes moist but well-drained soil. Two acaenas are useful: *Acaena buchananii,* with grey-green leaves, a quick spreader with insignificant flowers, and *A. microphylla,* which has bronze-green foliage and small crimson, daisy-like flowers.

Sedum acre, the yellow stonecrop, spreads rapidly, as does *Phyla nodiflora* (*Lippea repens*), a trailer with tiny oval leaves arranged in pairs and small pink, scabious-like flowers. *Armeria caespitosa* is a 5 to 10 cm (2 to 4 in) thrift, with bright pink flowers and hummocks of needle-fine leaves. *Cotula squalida* has its foliage arranged in rosettes and tiny white, daisy flowers, and *Mentha pulegium*, the pennyroyal, is a much branched prostrate species for moist shade with whorls of lilac flowers and small leaves.

Carpeters to look at

Some low-growing plants will not tolerate pressure and develop fungal diseases if repeatedly trodden on. Ivies and pachysan-

dras are prime examples, but in point of fact most fleshy perennials resent this and rot if their stems are constantly broken. There are, however, a number of plants that make good carpeters away from the main path, including various heathers, ajugas, helianthemums and *Lysimachia nummularia.*

Others are *Chrysanthemum* (*Tanacetum*) *haradjanii,* a sun-lover with 10 to 15 cm (4 to 6 in) silver stems, silvery aromatic leaves and golden, buttonhole flowers; *Erigeron kar-*

Thymus serpyllum 'Argenteum'

vinskianus (*E. mucronatus*), 15 to 20 cm (6 to 8 in) tall, with white and pink daisy flowers on the same plant; *Frankenia laevis,* the pink sea heath, which forms dense mats from trailing stems, the heath-like leaves turning orange or red in autumn; and *Campanula cochleariifolia* (*C. pusilla*), a dainty bellflower with hanging blue blossoms on 10 cm (4 in) stems.

Parochetus communis, the shamrock pea, will succeed in moist, shaded spots in favoured locations, producing masses of brilliant blue pea-like flowers amidst clover-type foliage *Raoulia hookeri, R. australis* and *R. tenuicaulis* are silver and ground-hugging *Gypsophila repens* 'Fratensis', with grey-green leaves and pink flowers on 10 cm (4 in) stems and the lime-loving *Globularia meridionalis* (*G. bellidifolia*), the globe daisy, with rosettes of leaves and soft blue flowers on 5 to 10 cm (2 to 4 in) stems, are others to note.

Cushion plants for pavements

Flagstones, bricks and crazy paving stand up to continuous hard wear better than grass, which is one of the reasons they are so popular for small suburban and city gardens. In such situations the soil is usually poor or shallow – another reason for covering it with a hard surface, which also suppresses weeds and eliminates lawn maintenance.

To soften the hard effect, however, plants are often grown in the cracks between the paving, or planting pockets are left during construction. Where the soil is poor, excavate to a depth of 15 to 20 cm (6 to 8 in) and replace it with good potting mixture; you can then sow seeds in this or insert small plants. The cool moist conditions below and dry warmth above suits most plants, so that growth is rapid. There is generally no need to limit them to low spreading types, except in areas much used for walking, for the occasional taller plant or small shrub breaks the outline and relieves the monotony.

Easy crevice plants
For quick coverage and a riot of colour such plants as aubrietas, helianthemums and *Phlox subulata* are indispensable. Restrict the pockets to one variety of each in order to achieve bold splashes of pink, white, red, purple, orange or yellow – according to the kind of plant used. All of these should be cut back fairly hard to about 15 cm (6 in) after flowering, in order to induce blooming shoots later in the year or for the following season.

Others that are easy to establish and main-

Saxifraga paniculata (S. aizoon)

tain include several hummock-forming plants such as the thrifts (especially *Armeria caespitosa*), *Thymus serpyllum* and various dianthus – like *Dianthus gratianopolitanus* (*D. caesius*), the Cheddar pink, with bright pink flowers, *D. arenarius*, which has white, fringed flowers, and the single rose-pink *D. × arverensis* – all of them evergreen.

The prostrate-growing, evergreen *Veronica prostrata* (*V. rupestris*) has dark green leaves and tiny spikes of vivid blue – or rosy-pink in the variety 'Mrs Holt'. *Hypericum reptans,* a tiny St John's wort with yellow, red-budded flowers on 8 cm (3 in) stems, makes a 20 to 25 cm (8 to 10 in) spread; *Linaria alpina* is semi-prostrate with tiny violet, orange-tipped, snapdragon flowers above grey-green foliage; *Acantholimon glumaceum*, the prickly thrift, resembling an armeria except that its leaves are stiffer and more pointed,

Veronica prostrata

has rich pink flowers on 15 cm (6 in) sprays; and *Globularia meridionalis* (*G. bellidifolia*) is a shrubby, hummocky plant with masses of pompon, powder-blue florets on 5 to 10 cm (2 to 4 in) stems. It does well on chalky soils.

Some aristocrats
Plants of character that are a little more difficult to cultivate include the lime-hating *Lithodora diffusa* (*Lithospermum diffusum*) and its cultivars 'Heavenly Blue' and 'Grace

Limnanthes douglasii

Ward'. Of prostrate habit and slightly shrubby, these have small narrow leaves and myriads of vivid blue flowers in midsummer. They should be cut hard back after flowering.

Androsace sarmentosa, a primrose relative, increases by means of thread-like runners and blooms in spring, producing round heads of carmine-pink flowers on 10 cm (4 in) stems above rosettes of grey-green leaves. Well-drained soil is essential, with protection from winter wet – best afforded by propping a pane of glass on bricks over the crowns. This precaution is also necessary for species of *Raoulia*, a group of evergreen plants with stemless silver leaves and minute yellow flowers. These barely rise above the ground yet are of great decorative value. Pack them around with rock chippings or brick rubble at planting time, to ward off excessive moisture.

Gentiana acaulis (a name covering *G. clusii*

and *G. kochiana* [*G. excisa*]) is unpredictable in any situation, and much contrary advice is given as to the need for manure and lime, shade or sun. The fact is that it will flower profusely in one spot and not at all in another; but the large, vivid blue, trumpet flowers are so striking that it is worth trying plants in a variety of situations. Where happy they persist for years, flowering in spring and occasionally again in autumn. The less fastidious *G. septemfida* is suitable for most soils, given a well-drained open position. It flowers in late summer, bearing three or four deep blue flowers on each 30 cm (12 in) stem. *Campanula pulla* (single, purple) and *C. × haylodgensis* (double, mauve) are charming summer bloomers for sun and shelter.

Types for shade
The plants most likely to succeed in shady spots are the cushion-type saxifrages like *Saxifraga paniculata* (*S. aizoon*), whose mounded hummocks of silvery leaves are spangled in early summer with white, pink or yellow flowers, *S. burseriana*, white or yellow, or the clear pink *S. × 'Jenkinsae'*. These too benefit from collars of granite chippings and the protection of glass in winter. Another suitable plant is *Oxalis magellanica,* which has shamrock-like leaves of bronzy-red and delicate green-veined, pearly-white flowers. It increases rapidly from runners.

Fill-ups
Fill-up plants of short life for pavement crevices include several annuals like Virginian and night-scented stocks; white and purple forms of sweet alyssum; *Limnanthes douglasii*, which has white-edged golden flowers; *Anagallis monelli linifolia*, a scarlet pimpernel; the violet cress, *Ionopsidium acaule*; and *Nemophila menziesii*, blue with white eyes. Small bulbs are also useful, particularly crocuses, cyclamen, chionodoxas and snowdrops (see p 200), also prostrate-growing conifers (see p 233), dwarf lavenders and creeping willows like *Salix repens*.

Trailers for display and camouflage

Plants of trailing habit have a miscellany of uses in the garden. They look delightful spilling from the sides of window-boxes and hanging baskets, also tumbling down from their planting pockets in dry walls. In the rock garden some kinds can be used to drape large stones with mats of foliage and flowers, and others allowed to grow horizontally to provide carpets of colour.

To brighten flat areas and relieve the bareness of severe walls they can be inserted between stones or even allowed to spread over brick or concrete edgings. Trailing plants are also useful to mask eyesores and disguise irremovable tree stumps, foundations of buildings, broken verges and the like. They may drip down from crevices in well-heads, festoon balconies, ornament fountains and hang down from containers in a variety of other situations.

Ramonda myconi

ers for dry walls are aubrietas, helianthemums, *Phlox subulata, Iberis gibraltarica, Alyssum saxatile,* arabis and *Erigeron karvinskianus* (*E. mucronatus*), which are all described elsewhere in this work. All these are hardy, free-flowering, varied in colour and unlikely to attract snails and other pests because of their pendent mode of growth. Between them they provide the backbone of dry-wall drapes.

In sunless situations two good plants are *Haberlea ferdinandi-coburgii* and *H. rhodopensis.* Both form rosettes of leathery, toothed, spoon-shaped leaves and have umbels of tubular lilac flowers. *H. rhodopensis* 'Virginalis' is white. They require humus in the soil and should be planted at an angle so that water cannot collect in the rosettes and cause rotting. A similar situation suits the better-known *Ramonda myconi,* a plant

pink or rose flowers; the blue *Helichrysum bellidioides*; and, for light soils, *Frankenia laevis,* a heath-like plant with narrow leaves and clusters of flesh-coloured flowers.

Houseleeks (*Sempervivum* spp) of all kinds fit neatly into the pockets left between stones in dry walls, and although their foliage remains compact the flowers trail outwards in long spikes. *Sempervivum tectorum,* the common houseleek, with its countless cultivars, actually prefers an elevated position. In central Europe it has a reputation for healing, and is still planted on roofs to protect households against lightning.

Two campanulas – the rosette-forming *Campanula garganica,* with 15 cm (6 in) leafy sprays carrying a succession of starry blue flowers throughout the summer, and *C. portenschlagiana* (*C. muralis*; see p 225) – are others for dry walls. In warm areas, the

Arabis cyprius

Alyssum saxatile

Always give trailers a good start by planting them in rich loam, but if this is not naturally present improve the existing soil by the addition of moist peat, sand and a small quantity of well-rotted garden compost or a general fertilizer. Alternatively, use a proprietary potting mixture in the planting holes. Most of those described here are of lax habit, and in order to maintain their vigour the old stems should be shortened back immediately after flowering. This also keeps them neat and tidy. The shrubby kinds need careful pruning to preserve their shape, and should not be allowed to get out of hand.

Plants for dry walls
The best way of planting dry walls is to insert suitable trailers during construction (see p 124), when they can be set in place without the root disturbance likely to occur through forcing them into a restricted space. Before other stones or bricks hem them in, pack some good soil around the roots. Pot-grown specimens are likely to prove the most satisfactory, and after removal from their containers should be inserted sideways so that, as new shoots grow and elongate, they will droop gracefully down.

Among the easiest and most reliable trail-

something like the popular indoor African violet in general appearance. Between rosettes of crinkled, dark green leaves, which are hairy underneath, rise 10 to 15 cm (4 to 6 in) stems carrying a number of five-petalled mauve flowers in late spring. There are also pink and white forms.

Dryas octopetala is a splendidly good-natured evergreen for early summer flowering in pendent or horizontal positions. It forms broad carpets, rooting itself as it goes. The knotted branches are packed with small, dark green, crinkled leaves that are silvery-grey beneath and have masses of chalice-like, eight-petalled white flowers.

Others to try include *Gypsophila repens,* a low-growing, wiry-stemmed species which branches out in all directions to provide a grey-green drape of stems and leaves spangled in summer with myriads of small white,

Gypsophila repens

horizontalis 'Glauca', with blue-green foliage and whipcord branches that root where they rest on the ground – can be planted near the edge of the obstacle and will gradually inch their way forwards with overlapping fans of stiff, short, leafy branches.

In exceptionally dry places, such as beneath dense-canopied conifers, the creeping antirrhinum, *Asarina procumbens,* is particularly useful. It is a charming little snapdragon with rounded, hairy leaves and large yellow and white flowers.

For hanging baskets and boxes
With both hanging baskets and window-boxes, trailers are of paramount importance, for hiding the sides and edges as well as for improving the overall effect. Hanging basket plants will not survive winter outdoors in cold climates, so the baskets are usually made up

sheltered positions, while *Campanula isophylla*, with its starry blue or white flowers, is a beautiful but tender trailer.

Other useful plants include the pendent silver-leaved and silver-stemmed *Helichrysum petiolatum* and *Calocephalus brownii,* which looks like a jumble of silver-painted twigs, also the easy annual nasturtiums (*Tropaeolum majus*), especially the Tom Thumb strain. *Ballota pseudodictamnus,* another silver, may also be tried, as well as plants which develop trailing runners terminating in small plantlets. Examples of these are *Chlorophytum capense* (*C. comosum* or *C. elatum*), a favourite houseplant commonly known as the spider plant, the cream and green variegated *Nepeta* (*Glechoma*) *hederacea* 'Variegata', and the mother of thousands, *Saxifraga stolonifera* (*S. sarmentosa*), with rounded leaves, pink-edged in the

Helichrysum petiolatum

Zebrina pendula

form 'Tricolor'. Other houseplants, such as *Zebrina pendula* and various tradescantias, are also useful in warm spots.

For water features
Trailing plants can be useful in water features, particularly for masking the fabric of artificial pools and for making a natural transition between the water and the rest of the garden.

Some of the plants which succeed equally well in damp soil or shallow water are described on page 256, and include the bog arum, *Calla palustris,* the false loosestrife, *Ludwigia palustris*, and the bog bean, *Menyanthes trifoliata. Lysimachia nummularia* (see above) can also be used in this setting, as can the needle-leaved *Crassula* (*Tillaea*) *recurva*, a South African plant with tiny white flowers.

Some fountains have small pockets near the top capable of accommodating one or two small aquatics, and for such spots *Myriophyllum proserpinacoides* is ideal, dripping down in long trails of finely cut, pale green, water-repellent leaves. Each shoot turns up at the end like a monkey's tail. In autumn, as the weather becomes colder, this part of the stem turns crimson, accounting for the plant's common name, parrot's feather.

yellow-flowered, clover-leaved *Oxalis chrysantha* will thrive. The top of dry walls can be similarly planted, or small pinks (*Dianthus* spp), sedums and saxifrages can be used to give a neat finish.

Trailers for masking
Old tree stumps and the like may rapidly be hidden beneath robust trailers, especially if these are helped with a foundation of wire netting laid over the area and have their roots planted in pockets of rich soil. Most ivies can be trained to ramp over the wire, also *Lonicera japonica repens* 'Aureo-reticulata', a normally flowerless honeysuckle with green leaves veined and netted in gold, and many species and cultivars of clematis, notably *Clematis alpina*.

Creeping junipers – like the bright green *Juniperus sabina* 'Tamarascifolia' and *J.*

for summer enjoyment. Consequently, it is not essential to use hardy species, and tender plants – even some that are normally grown as houseplants – are often included.

Among the hardiest, however, for sunless or draughty positions are any of the small-leaved ivies (*Hedera helix* varieties), and creeping Jenny (*Lysimachia nummularia*) and its golden-leaved form 'Aurea'. These should be clipped back from time to time to keep the shoots thick and shapely.

For warm, sunny situations, trailing lobelias like *Lobelia erinus* 'Blue Cascade' (rich blue) or 'Sapphire' (blue with a white eye) are ideal. So are ivy-leaved geraniums (*Pelargonium peltatum* cultivars) like 'Galilee' (rose-pink), 'Blue Peter' (mauve), 'La France' (double, mauve), 'Sir Percy Blakeney' (crimson) and 'Madame Crousse' (double, pink). There are also trailing begonias and fuchsias for more

The shapely hardy ferns

In Victorian times ferns enjoyed a degree of popularity unparalleled in gardening history. Their varied shapes and different tones of green, their adaptability to cold rooms and poor interior lighting, plus an ability to grow outdoors in damp shady spots where few plants seemed (at that time) to flourish – all these factors endeared them to thousands. More books were written about ferns in the late 19th century than any other type of plant.

After a period in the 'wilderness', ferns are now enjoying a revival of popularity. Flower arrangers have been quick to appreciate the beauty of their leaves, but gardeners are also realizing what splendid foils they make for the bright flower colours of nearby plants. They are hardy, long-lived and easily grown, and never become rampaging nuisances.

Growing ferns

Most hardy ferns prefer a cool, rich soil that remains constantly moist without becoming waterlogged; such conditions can be obtained by working plenty of leaf-mould, peat and similar humus-forming materials into the existing soil. Very heavy ground may also need liberal applications of coarse sand to improve the drainage, but do not introduce animal manures unless these are so old that they crumble at the touch, nor lime or artificial fertilizers. A dressing of bonemeal at 135 g/m² (4 oz/sq yd), forked into the top 15 cm (6 in), gives new ferns a good start, but this is all the additive required.

Ferns should never be planted beneath the fringe of large trees, nor near a building from which constant drip may be expected in wet weather. Also, deep shade is not desirable; most thrive best in the dappled half-light cast by trees and shrubs. However, certain trees – such as limes – that can become infected by aphids, and consequently drip honeydew on plants underneath, should be avoided.

The best time to transplant ferns is during the dormant period between autumn and early spring. Try to move them with a ball of soil around the roots, particularly the evergreen kinds, and establish them at the old planting level – never deeper. Ferns can be propagated by division or from the spores found on the backs of the fronds (see p 345).

Deciduous ferns

Adiantum pedatum is the best of the hardy maidenhairs. It is a dainty species, with black, glistening, wiry 30 cm (12 in) stems carrying fan-shaped leaves divided into leaflets – like fingers on a hand. Each of these has countless opposite pinnules. *A. pedatum japonicum* is noteworthy for the pinkness of the younger fronds, whilst the smaller *A. venustum*, about 20 cm (8 in) tall, grows rapidly into carpets of green. All adiantums require a sheltered place and may merit a covering of dry leaves in severe winters.

Athyrium filix-femina is the lady fern, a common British species found in damp woods, hedgerows or nestling between rocks in hilly districts. It is an extremely variable species, and through the years numerous forms have been selected, some with such

Phyllitis scolopendrium undulatum

long names as to deter all but the most ardent enthusiasts. The species itself has a woody rootstock covered with dark brown scales and finely cut, vivid green fronds divided into pinnate pinnules (see illustration). Forms exist having the frond ends bunched into tassels or flat rounded crests. Sometimes the pinnules are reduced to round bunched domes, and one of the most remarkable forms, *A. filix-femina victoriae,* has narrow 60 to 90 cm (2 to 3 ft) fronds with all its parts – pinnules and frond edges – deeply cut into V-shapes. Discovered in Stirlingshire, Scotland, more than a century ago, divisions of the original plant are still in cultivation.

True waterside ferns include osmundas, the so-called flowering ferns, which bear their spores on separate stems, instead of their lining the backs of the fronds. *Osmunda regalis,* the royal fern, is the tallest and noblest, making a fine specimen plant by the waterside, where it will grow 2.5 to 3 m (8 to 10 ft) tall, given time and the right conditions. It will also thrive in an open border, given good, damp but lime-free soil. The barren fronds are divided into long, narrow pinnae, while the fertile fronds bear brown spores and look something like astilbe seedheads.

O. cinnamomea, the cinnamon fern from North America, grows to 1 to 1.5 m (3 to 5 ft)

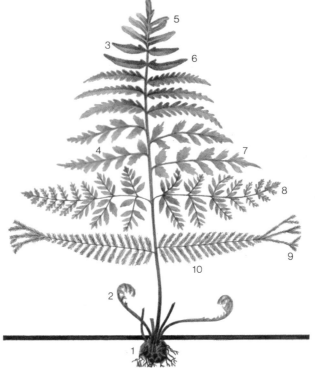

Anatomy of a fern

Because ferns are unrelated to other plants, their parts have distinctive names and descriptions. A 'leaf', for example, is a frond. The imaginary composite fern **left** illustrates some of the terms commonly encountered.

The stock **1** is the permanent underground part, from which 'fiddleheads', or croziers **2**, arise to form new fronds. The 'leaflets' branching from the stalk **3** are called pinnae. Where these are themselves divided, the small leaflets **4** are called pinnules.

Depending on the depth and degree of subdivision, the frond may be pinnatifid **5**, pinnate **6**, bipinnate **7** or tripinnate **8**. Fronds or pinnae may be crested at the end **9** or plumose (feathery) **10**.

tall, with rich green fronds 15 to 25 cm (6 to 10 in) wide; its young stems are densely covered with soft, cinnamon-brown scales. In the United States the young, uncurled fronds are a gastronomic delicacy, being cooked and eaten as 'fiddlehead' greens. (In general, fern fronds are poisonous.) *O. claytoniana* is another good American species. Many osmundas have striking autumn colours.

Another waterside fern is *Onoclea sensibilis,* variously known as the American oak fern (the true oak fern is *Gymnocarpium dryopteris*), bead fern and sensitive fern. The last name refers to its sensitivity to frost, and the term bead fern relates to the blue-green 'beads' or spores borne at the top of the 30 cm (12 in) fertile fronds. The barren fronds may be up to 60 cm (2 ft) in length, half of which is bare stem and the upper part pinnate with broad pinnae. The plant has a creeping rhizome which enables it to run in and out of shallow water and damp soil. It revels in humus-rich soil in full sun or light shade.

Matteuccia struthiopteris is the ostrich-feather fern, a fine graceful plant for damp woodland. The tall – 1 to 1.25 m (3 to 4 ft) – elegant, pale green barren fronds flare out from a central axis like the feathers of a shuttlecock; the fertile fronds, half their height, are crowded with dark brown sori (sporecases) in midsummer.

Woodwardias are called chain ferns because their sori are arranged on the frond pinnae like chains of sausages. They are normally woodland plants but, given damp, acid, near-swamp conditions, also do well in full sun. In early spring the sterile fronds are reddish-green, pinnatifid and spreading, but with age they develop to a glossy dark green. *Woodwardia radicans* has fronds up to 1.8 m (6 ft) long, with 30 cm (12 in) pinnae. These sometimes develop small plantlets at their tips; when pegged down into damp soil, these root and make new plants. *W. virginica* needs acid conditions and also makes a good pot plant. The 45 to 60 cm (1½ to 2 ft) fronds are reddish when young, then develop to glaucous-green.

For really tough conditions in wild or woodland gardens, or along a cool, sunless border, no ferns are more accommodating than the male or buckler ferns – species of *Dryopteris*. The majority are native to the British Isles, and are often incorrectly called *Lastrea*. Among the most garden-worthy is *Dryopteris*

Polypodium vulgare

aemula, the hay-scented buckler fern; it is so called because the dying fronds emit a pleasant scent like new-mown hay. It likes humus-rich soil and produces 30 to 60 cm (1 to 2 ft) fronds, 12 to 20 cm (5 to 8 in) across.

D. filix-mas, a robust 1.25 to 1.5 m (4 to 5 ft) species that is well known and widespread in Britain, is commonly called the male fern. (In medieval times, this and the lady fern were thought to be male and female of the

Adiantum pedatum

same plant; in fact, ferns do not have separate sexes.) It has given rise to many mutations, so that forms with crested, plumose or congested pinnae are common. They can only be kept true to type by division of the roots in spring.

Thelypteris phegopteris, the dainty little beech fern, has very pale green fronds 15 to 30 cm (6 to 12 in) in height and long, slender, underground rhizomes. It looks delightful growing near azaleas or in shady rock-garden pockets, but dislikes lime.

Evergreen ferns

The best-known evergreen ferns for the outdoor garden are the hart's-tongues, common plants of damp woodland in the west of England, Wales and Scotland. They are frequently but incorrectly known by their specific name, scolopendriums. *Phyllitis scolopendrium* (*Scolopendrium vulgare*), the common hart's-tongue, has shiny green, leathery, tongue-like fronds, but some 800

Onoclea sensibilis

varieties are known, many with crested, plumose or variously doubled or divided fronds. With few exceptions these are all suitable for moist or wet shady situations, such as damp woods, rock crevices and niches beside – or beneath – waterfalls or bridges, and in well mouths. They also make good pot plants.

Dryopteris borreri (*D. pseudomas*), the golden-scaled male fern, is a near or complete evergreen (according to conditions), and produces 0.6 to 1.5 m (2 to 5 ft) golden-green fronds which become darker with age and have orange-brown scales. There are many varietal forms – dwarf, crested, divided at the frond tips, narrow-leaved and the like. Most of them require damp, humus-rich soil and woodland conditions.

The polypody, *Polypodium vulgare,* has a wide distribution, being found under hedges, between bricks on old walls or on mossy rocks, or growing epiphytically on trees. Good drainage is essential for this species, so retain a little of the old soil when transplanting. The fronds are evergreen all winter, only fading when new ones appear in spring; they are long and narrow, with the pinnae in opposite pairs. Again there are many varietal forms with different frond modifications.

Ceterach officinarum, the scaly spleenwort or rusty-back fern, is a small-growing species found in nature on limy rocks or old mortared walls. The short-stalked fronds are deeply pinnatifid and 8 to 15 cm (3 to 6 in) long, with leathery sage-green pinnules that are rusty-brown beneath. Even when apparently dead through drought this fern will recover after a night's rain.

Dicksonias are the tree ferns of the southern hemisphere, only suitable for planting outdoors in very sheltered, maritime regions such as Ireland, the west of England and Scotland, and the west coast of the United States. *Dicksonia antarctica* is the hardiest and may ultimately grow a trunk 6 to 9 m (20 to 30 ft) high when well suited.

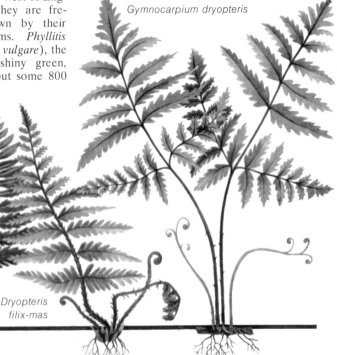

Gymnocarpium dryopteris

Dryopteris filix-mas

Plants of grey and silver

Although there are some who enjoy the challenge of growing 'difficult' plants in 'difficult' situations, the most successful gardeners are generally those who choose their plants to suit their climate and soil. Certainly this is true for those who have to deal with very dry plots, which can be turned into superb silver borders but fail miserably when planted in the conventional manner.

The reason why grey-foliaged plants can survive bad droughts is that their fundamentally green leaves are covered with fine hairs, wool or a dusting of bloom. This covering, which accounts for the silver or glaucous (greyish or bluish) effect, protects the foliage from the heat of the sun and thus prevents water loss by transpiration. Such plants are found in arid areas in all parts of the world. Obviously, those that come from tropical and subtropical parts cannot be considered hardy, but the majority will survive a −14°C (7°F) frost, or even −18°C (0°F) in ideal conditions.

In the past, species such as the silver-leaved cineraria, *Senecio cineraria* (also sold as *Cineraria maritima*) were considered delicate and were brought under cover at the first sign of frost. This may have been because it was not realized that the bark of silver-foliaged shrubs rots when it gets wet, and that the plants will collapse if the soil they are growing in becomes waterlogged. As with many plants, damp cold is fatal if the drainage is inadequate. Furthermore, different strains of the same species will react in different ways according to the habitat of the original parent, and gardeners in the past may well have been using weak stock.

Creating a grey border
Many gardeners have tried to copy the borders in the famous White Garden at Sissinghurst Castle, in Kent. This garden, created in the 1940s by Vita Sackville-West, relies entirely on contrasts in shape and texture, light and shade, for its effect. Nothing could be more lovely on a sunny day, but it does not look so good under cloudy skies, and many gardeners think that just a touch of colour brings a silver border to life. It is surprising how little is needed. A single rock rose such as *Helianthemum nummularium* 'Wisley Pink', a thin drift of blue flax (*Linum narbonense*) or even a few Californian poppies (*Eschscholzia*) will make a big difference, but the most suitable plants for this purpose are probably hybrid pinks like 'Doris', a clear salmon colour capable – if planted in fertile soil – of flowering from early summer until the very end of autumn (see p 183).

It is better not to depend too much on the flowers of the silvers themselves for colour. Many have uninteresting flowers, and the effort required to set seed tends to rob the leaves of their lustre and the plants of their vigour. Flowering growth must be cut out before the seed has a chance to set – preferably in some cases whilst in bud!

Planting and pruning
The best time to plant all the species mentioned in this article is in late spring. If the

The Sissinghurst White Garden has inspired many borders of grey and silver plants. Those visible here include *Artemisia purshiana* (foreground), *A. discolor* (to its left), *A. splendens* (low-growing, beyond path) and *Onopordum arabicum* (tall, in background).

ground is dry, sizeable holes must be filled and refilled with water 12 hours before planting. At the same time the plants to be set out must be well watered. With this start, no further water should be needed.

Mid-spring is the time for pruning the shrubs, when most of the previous year's growth should be removed. The young growth of those species that come from the warmer parts of the world, such as the Mediterranean, is not frost-resistant, and they should therefore not be dealt with quite so early. It is risky to prune any silver shrub in autumn, and all tidying must be completed by late summer.

Herbaceous subjects are best left untidy for the winter but need dividing every third year in spring. Dwarf alpines merely need deadheading, whilst biennials can be kept going for several seasons if not allowed to set seed.

Tall-growing types
Fierce annual pruning, though it makes for superb foliage, does prevent many of the silver shrubs growing to much more than 1 m (3 ft), and it is difficult to recommend any tall varieties. True, the heraldic thistle of Scotland, *Onopordum arabicum*, will grow to more than 2 m (7 ft), but it is a most difficult biennial to keep going. It has a multitude of big thistle heads, each set on a spine-covered stem, and these spines can give a very nasty prick. *O. acanthium* is similar. *Verbascum bombyciferum* on the other hand, though merely 1.5 m (5 ft) in height, is easy; if dead-

headed, it will produce a number of woolly spikes, heavily encrusted with little primrose-yellow flowers, over a long period.

Another suggestion is the Californian tree-poppy, *Romneya coulteri*, which has glaucous foliage and large white flowers with golden centres. Herbaceous in habit, it takes time to establish and the flowering stems become untidy when the heads wither. Once these are removed, the growth that has not flowered remains fresh for many months. Both *Senecio laxifolius* and *Artemisia arborescens* can be kept tidy by only light pruning if tall specimens are required. The

Onopordum arabicum

former is well known, but the latter is seldom seen; this is a pity, for it is a graceful, sparkling silver shrub somewhat reminiscent of the Japanese maple (*Acer palmatum*). Like *Senecio laxifolius* it is evergreen, though not reliably hardy in cold areas.

Left to itself, a young *Eucalyptus gunnii* will grow into a tall tree carrying narrow pointed leaves. Those of immature specimens are rounded, and this type of growth can be encouraged by regular 'tipping' in spring and summer. Some individuals can be kept as 2 m (7 ft) bushes for years, but they vary in habit, as all 'gums' have to be raised from seed.

If *Cynara scolymus* (globe thistle) and *C. cardunculus* (cardoon) did not require so

Artemisia splendens

much food and water they would be invaluable, for their huge silvery leaves are extremely decorative. *Teucrium fruticans*, on the other hand, is amazingly abstemious, but really needs an evergreen background to show off the beauty of its white stems, silver leaves and pale blue flowers.

Medium-sized kinds
All the shrubby helichrysums are reliable and good in winter. *Helichrysum fontanesii* grows to about 1 m (3 ft) and has heavily felted thin leaves about 5 cm (2 in) long. Those of *H. angustifolium* (*H. serotinum*), sometimes

Ballota pseudodictamnus

called the curry plant because of its smell, are smaller and silvery rather than white. Seedlings of *Senecio cineraria* are seldom hardy, and are often used as summer bedding plants, but two cultivars – 'White Diamond' and 'Ramparts' – seldom lose a leaf in moderate winters. The former looks like a snowball from a distance, and has nearly white leaves about 8 cm (3 in) long. 'Ramparts' is a bolder plant with larger leaves, but just as white.

Although the flowers of *Ballota pseudodictamnus* are almost invisible, the little round, dove-grey leaves that surround the whorls make this an attractive plant for the front of a border. Trimming back these flowering stems when they start to become untidy encourages a lovely crop of apple-green and dove-grey shoots which remain attractive throughout the winter.

There are a great number of artemisias with silver and grey leaves. The herbaceous types such as *Artemisia purshiana* are invasive, but the shrubby *A. maritima* 'Nutans' (*A. nutans*) and *A. splendens* should be in every dry border. The former grows to 45 cm (18 in) and throws out a wealth of delicate silver stems; the latter is shorter and has finely cut curly leaves. These are very dense, so that the effect from a distance is that of a cumulus cloud. Flowering ruins the shape of *Santolina chamaecyparissus* (cotton lavender) but it makes a neat little grey bush when disciplined. The dwarf form 'Weston' is much whiter and has a spreading habit.

The foliage of most lavenders is grey-green, though that of *Lavandula vera* 'The Dutch' (*L. angustifolia* or *L. spica* 'Vera') does go grey in winter, whilst that of *L. lanata* is not only heavily felted but also strongly scented. Sadly, the latter is often cut to the ground by frost. Much the same is true of *Centaurea gymnocarpa* (sometimes listed as *C. argentea*), but this spectacular shrub, which has long, white deeply cut leaves cascading from the stem, should most certainly be given a try.

The hybrid *Verbascum* 'Frosted Gold' is a perennial that grows to about 75 cm (2½ ft). It can, by judicious dead-heading, be persuaded to go on producing primrose-dotted spikes until late in autumn. *Convolvulus cneorum* is the most exciting of all the silver shrubs. Slow growing, it smothers itself with white flowers in early summer and again in autumn. Reputedly difficult, it seldom fails when planted on well-drained soil in a position where its roots can run down onto something hard, such as the footings of a wall. Best pruned after the summer flush, it can be grown to 60 cm (2 ft). Similar in size is *Senecio compactus*, an exquisite miniature version of *S. laxifolius* (see above).

Dwarf silver plants
Two low-growing species that warrant a position for the sake of their flowers are *Teucrium pulverulentum* and *Veronica incana*. The former has small silver leaves and panicles of rosy-mauve florets, while the latter produces pale grey spikes covered with dark blue florets out of a carpet of smooth grey leaves. The flowers of *Tanacetum* (*Chrysanthemum*)

densum 'Amani' and the related *T.* (*C.*) *haradjanii* are poor, but the individual leaves resemble tiny ostrich feathers, and the effect is that of a woolly rug. By contrast, *Artemesia lanata* (*A. nitida*) is silvery and silky.

The dwarf achilleas have a cushion-like habit. There are several varieties that all flower in early summer, but *Achillea×kolbiana* is probably the most desirable, as its foliage is aromatic. *Stachys candida* – a cousin of the well-known lamb's tongue, *S. lanata* (*S. olympica*) – is another treasure, for although the individual leaves and stems are very small, both give the feeling that they must have been cut out of the finest velvet.

Alyssum saxatile, with its bright yellow

Stachys lanata (S. olympica)

flowers in the spring, is often recommended for quick cover, but some feel that it is an uninspiring plant. *Cerastium tomentosum* is just as rampageous but much prettier, and warrants the name snow in summer for its tiny leaves are nearly as white as the flowers.

Finally, two biennials: *Salvia argentea* and *Glaucium flavum* both have beautiful basal leaves but dull flowers and ugly stems. If these are removed as they appear, more leaves develop. Those of the salvia are very furry, rounded and about the size of a hand, whilst those of the glaucium are deeply cut, long and narrow, and tend to curl at the tips.

Salvia argentea

Plants for foliage effect

Foliage is as important – perhaps more important – to the overall appearance of a garden as flowers. It provides a background and infilling to more flamboyant displays, and subtle foliage effects can make restful and extremely pleasing features in their own right.

Green is the basic colour of plant life, but the subtle variations in just this one colour are enormous. In addition, a wide range of plants have leaves that are speckled, mottled, splashed, striped or margined with contrasting variegations of white, silver, yellow, gold or red. Some are flushed or suffused with red or pink, while in many leaves the undersurface contrasts with the upper. A further range is provided by bluish, or glaucous, colourations, or from a covering of down or fine hairs that give a grey or silver appearance.

Apart from this silver effect, the colour of leaves depends on the various coloured pigments they contain. The amounts of these vary not only from variety to variety, but at different times of the year (the leaves often being rosy or lighter in spring, or tinged with purple or red in cold weather) and also according to the nature of the soil. Several plants that give fine displays of autumn colour on acid or neutral soil are disappointing when grown on chalk. Distance can also influence visual effect; variegated leaves commonly look very attractive close-to, but when small appear dull grey from a distance.

Details of many plants grown primarily for their foliage will be found elsewhere in this book. Foliage trees and shrubs form major structural elements in a garden design. Evergreen trees (see p 136) and shrubs (see p 150) are particularly important for their year-round value. The strongest foliage colour effects occur more commonly (if temporarily) in deciduous trees and shrubs; examples of these will be found on pages 140, 156 and 164. Some climbers (see pp 142 to 147) also have beautiful foliage, while spectacular displays are given by plants used as 'dot' subjects in bedding schemes (see p 221) or whose dramatic form gives a particularly 'architectural' and exotic effect (see p 252).

Pleasing small-scale foliage effects can be given by ferns (see p 238) and also by herbs with variegated or coloured leaves (see pp 272 to 275). Plants with grey and silver foliage (see p 240) can be used – particularly in dry situations – both for contrast with more colourful plants and also for creating whole borders punctuated here and there with a drift of colour. On the smallest scale of all are those plants that can be used to provide background foliage in a rock garden (see p 228), to provide ground cover between shrubs and other tall plants (see p 232), or to act as a substitute for grass (see p 234). In the herbaceous border, fine foliage sets off fine flowers, and some of the most striking of these are mentioned below. Many of them have further details elsewhere in this book.

Variegated, mottled or spotted

Cream or white leaf variegations are the chief attraction of *Iris foetidissima* 'Variegata', a useful shade evergreen with insignificant

Hosta spp

flowers but bright orange seeds. *I. pallida* 'Argenteo-variegata', with silver leaf suffusions, and the rarer *I. pallida* 'Aureovariegata' (gold) are both blue-flowered. *Lamium maculatum* has creamy bars on its foliage and there is a variegated lily of the valley, *Convallaria majalis* 'Variegata'. *Arum italicum* 'Pictum' is particularly handsome in spring, with its silver-marbled leaves, likewise the spotted-leaved lungwort, *Pulmonaria officinalis*.

The cream-splashed *Scrophularia aquatica* 'Variegata' thrives in damp soil, as do the variegated hostas, or plantain lilies. There are striped grasses like *Miscanthus sinensis* 'Variegatus' and 'Zebrinus', *Glyceria maxima* 'Variegata' and *Phalaris arundinacea* 'Variegata', all of which associate pleasantly with bright perennials. A number of bamboos (see opposite) also have variegated leaves.

If space permits, the milk thistle (*Silybum marianum*) is most striking, with spiny rosettes of large, white-veined, glossy green leaves and 1.25 m (4 ft) stems of violet thistle flowers in late summer. *Phormium tenax* 'Variegatum' should be treated as an accent plant in

---

Plants for autumn leaf tints

Autumn colouration of trees, shrubs and other plants varies from year to year according to weather, but the following are among the most reliable. Remember when planting that some kinds turn colour earlier than others.

Mainly yellow and gold	*Acer cappadocicum* (*A. laetum*; T); *A. lobelii* (T); some forms of *A. palmatum* (Japanese maple; S/T); *A. pensylvanicum* (*A. striatum*; T); *A. platanoides* (Norway maple; T); *Celastrus orbiculatus* (C); *Ginkgo biloba* (maidenhair tree; T); many *Hosta* spp (P); *Humulus lupulus* (hop; C); *Larix* spp (larches; T); *Liriodendron tulipifera* (tulip tree; T); many *Populus* spp (poplars; T)		
Variable yellow, orange and red	*Acer nikoense* (Nikko maple; T); *A. saccharum* (sugar maple; T); *Amelanchier laevis* (S/T); *Cercidiphyllum japonicum* (T); *Cornus florida* (flowering dogwood; S/T); *Enkianthus campanulatus* (S); *Fothergilla major* (S); *F. monticola* (S); *Hamamelis* spp (witch hazels; S/T); *Malus tschonoskii* (T); *Nyssa sylvatica* (tupelo; T); *Parrotia persica* (S/T); *Rhododendron luteum*		

(*Azalea pontica*; S); *R. schlippenbachii* (S); *Rhus trichocarpa* (S/T); *R. typhina* (stag's-horn sumach; S/T); many *Sorbus* spp (rowans and whitebeams; T)

Mainly russet, red and purple	*Acer capillipes* (T); *A. griseum* (paperbark maple; T); *A. japonicum* (S/T); many forms of *A. palmatum* (Japanese maple; S/T); *A. rubrum* (red or Canadian maple; T); *Cornus kousa* (S); many *Cotoneaster* spp (S); many forms of *Cryptomeria japonica* (Japanese cedar; T); *Euonymus alatus* (S); *Liquidambar styraciflua* (sweet gum; T); *Osmunda regalis* (royal fern; P); *Parthenocissus* spp (Boston ivy and Virginia creeper; C); *Polygonum vacciniifolium* (P); *Prunus sargentii* (Sargent's cherry; T); *Quercus rubra* (red oak; T); *Taxodium distichum* (swamp cypress; T); many *Vaccinium* spp (bilberries, blueberries etc; S); *Viburnum lantana* (wayfaring tree; S); many *Vitis* spp (vines; C)

Key: C = climber; P = herbaceous perennial; S = shrub; T = tree

a key position, where its sword-like, cream-striped leaves show to advantage. Under trees or in shady rock-garden pockets, the silver-patterned leaves of *Cyclamen neapolitanum* can never be duplicated, for no two are exactly alike.

Gold and yellow
Apart from a number of yellow-leaved heathers, such as *Calluna vulgaris* 'Gold Haze' and 'Golden Feather', *Erica ciliaris* 'Aurea' and *E. carnea* 'Aurea', there are a number of golden thymes, the best-known being *Thymus vulgaris* 'Aureus' and *T. × citrodorus* 'Aureus'. *Lysimachia nummularia* 'Aurea' is suitable for a damp spot, while *Origanum vulgare* 'Aureum' is a delightful foliage form of the common marjoram. *Milium effusum* 'Aureum' is a golden grass, and there are various yellow-variegated hostas, of which *Hosta fortunei* 'Albopicta' and 'Obscura Marginata' are among the most striking. *Solidago* 'Goldenmosa', a yellow-leaved form of golden rod, and the moisture-loving *Filipendula ulmaria* 'Aurea' are others to note.

Bronze, red and purple
Some of these are brightest at the beginning of the year, like *Salvia officinalis* 'Purpurascens', the purple sage; *Ajuga reptans* 'Atropurpurea' and 'Multicolor' ('Rainbow'), bugles with beetroot-red leaves and bronze, pink- and yellow-variegated leaves respectively; and the chocolate-blotched *Epimedium perralderianum*. There are also tulips with maroon- or purple-marked foliage, notably the *Tulipa greigii* hybrids. Others are best in late summer or autumn, particularly the bergenias and *Sedum maximum* 'Atropurpureum', which starts green, then develops to rich purple. *Lobelia fulgens* is uniformly crimson, and there is a purple-leaved *Phormium tenax* called 'Purpureum' and several houseleeks with red and green leaves, notably *Sempervivum tectorum* 'Commander Hay' and *S. tectorum calcareum*.

Seasonal plants for summer borders include the purplish-red castor oil plant, *Ricinus communis* 'Sanguineus'; *Amaranthus tricolor*, sometimes called Joseph's coat on account of its vivid leaf colouring; and several green and pink ornamental kales and cabbages. All of these can be raised from seed, although the red, bronze and purple foliage forms of *Coleus blumei*, the flame nettle, are best reproduced from cuttings.

Glaucous and blue-green
These include the 60 cm (2 ft) rue, *Ruta graveolens* 'Jackman's Blue', and the early-flowering, single yellow paeony *Paeonia mlokosewitschii*. *Hosta fortunei* and *H. ventricosa* also have greyish or blue foliage tints, as do various hebes, like the 90 cm (3 ft) *Hebe colensoi* 'Glauca' and the 20 cm (8 in) *H.* 'Pagei', and the dwarf lavenders. *Mertensia ciliata*, a 45 cm (18 in) plant with clusters of sky-blue pendulous bell flowers, has oval blue-green leaves, and *Lysimachia ephemerum* is white-flowered with smooth oblong glaucous foliage.

Other attractive leaf forms
Densely hairy leaves are found in several verbascums (mulleins), notably *Verbascum densiflorum* (*V. thapsiforme*) and the biennial *V. bombyciferum*, also in *Stachys olympica* (*S. lanata*, the lamb's tongue or lamb's ear). The yellow-flowered *Phlomis samia* is densely woolly, and so are most of the herbaceous anaphalis like *Anaphalis triplinervis* and *A. yedoensis*.

Particularly delicate effects are given by ferny or filigree foliage. Among the best for this are the pulsatilla anemones, pyrethrums, *Dicentra eximia*, *Santolina chamaecyparissus* (*S. incana*) and *Achillea millefolium* 'Cerise Queen', a red-flowered yarrow.

Origanum vulgare 'Aureum'

Amaranthus tricolor

The elegant bamboos
The graceful habit of these giant grasses belies their toughness. If protected against the worst of the elements they make fine windbreaks, particularly behind water gardens or in woodland situations. Being evergreen, they are also attractive as accent plants and can be grown in tubs or pots or used to mask ugly features.

Bamboos require deep, rich, loamy soil, kept fertile during their early years of development by annual mulches of rotted manure and leaves. It usually takes two to three years for a clump to become established, so regular feeding, watering and protection are essential at first.

Propagation is by root division in spring, retaining a ball of soil around each section. They can also be increased by stem or root cuttings. In some cases, they will grow from seed, although few bamboos flower, or if they do so may die afterwards.

There is often some confusion in identifying species of bamboo, since botanists have reclassified many species that were formerly known as *Arundinaria* and *Bambusa*. Among the most garden-worthy kinds are a number of sinarundinarias, notably *Sinarundinaria* (*Arundinaria*) *murielae* and *S. nitida*, both compact-growing with narrow leaves on 2 to 3 m (7 to 10 ft) stems. *Sasa* (*Arundinaria*) *palmata* has broad, bright green leaves with prominent veins and grows 1.5 to 2 m (5 to 7 ft) tall. *Pseudosasa* (*Arundinaria*) *japonica*, also known as *Bambusa metake*, is one of the best known, with smooth, glossy leaves, 20 to 25 cm (8 to

10 in) long by 5 cm (2 in) wide, on 3.5 to 6 m (12 to 20 ft) stems.

Particularly decorative species include *Arundinaria viridi-striata* (*A. auricoma*), which grows up to 1.8 m (6 ft) and has pea-green leaves striped with gold, while *Phyllostachys* (*Bambusa*) *aurea* has stiff 3.5 m (12 ft) gold or green canes, used in the Orient for umbrella handles. *P. viridi-glaucescens* is a cold-resistant bamboo with blue-green undersides to the leaves and arching 5.5 m (18 ft) canes, and the 1.8 m (6 ft) *Chimonobambusa* (*Arundinaria*) *marmorea* is noteworthy on account of its marbled beige, green and purple stems.

Among the smaller kinds are *Sasa variegata* (*Arundinaria fortunei*), to 1.4 m (4½ ft), *Sasa* (*Bambusa*) *veitchii* (*S. albo-marginata*), 1 to 1.25 m (3 to 4 ft), and *Shibataea kumasaca*, 60 to 75 cm (2 to 2½ ft) tall.

Sinarundinaria (*Arundinaria*) *murielae*

Ornamental grasses

Ornamental grasses include annual, perennial and shrubby garden plants. Their pale narrow leaves provide valuable contrast for more broad-leaved, dark green subjects. They are occasionally used for edging, but the airy grace of their leaves and flower panicles is more apparent in borders, and the larger types are impressive as specimen plants. Leaves and stems are ideal for fresh and dried flower arrangements.

Many grasses are ornamental forms of the common cereals – oats, barley and wheat – and even maize (*Zea mays*) has a variegated garden form. They all have very narrow leaves set on either side of hollow straight stems which carry the small flowers in terminal spikes, branched spikelets or silky plumes; in many cases the seeds are surrounded by long, bristly attachments known as awns.

Both annual and perennial species are best started in spring as soon as danger of frost is past. All do well in ordinary, even poor soil; the perennials are increased by division.

Annual grasses

As temporary fillers at the front of borders and beds, annual grasses make excellent foils for other plants. Seeds can be sown under glass in late winter for planting out, or sown outdoors when the soil has warmed up. Allow the seedlings a distance of about 25 cm (10 in) from other plants. None reach a height of more than 60 cm (2 ft).

The white, soft branchlets of *Agrostis nebulosa* justify its popular name of cloud grass; it does best in dry sunny spots, as does the animated oat (*Avena sterilis*) whose long awns agitate the seeds in the slightest breeze. *Briza maxima*, pearl or quaking grass, needs well-drained soil to develop its trembling, heart-shaped, brownish spikelets. The pearl-grey hard seeds of *Coix lacryma-jobi* (Job's tears) are used for stringing as bead curtains; its grass-green leaves are half-hardy and quickly ruined by frost. Native to cold northern regions, *Hordeum jubatum* (squirrel's-tail grass) fairly thrives in dry soil; long silky awns envelop the pale grey seed heads above sharply pointed leaves. The erect and fluffy spikes of *Lagurus ovatus* (hare's-tail grass) are favourites with florists, who dye them; it is not suitable for cold gardens.

Perennial and sub-shrubby grasses

The siting of these needs careful consideration, as many reach a height and spread that may encroach on other plants. Even where they are grown as specimen plants, some will be out of proportion on a small lawn. Most need full sun.

The evergreen *Cortaderia selloana* (pampas grass) is one of the most imposing specimen plants for a large lawn. It grows more than 2 m (7 ft) high, with blue-green rough leaves, above which rise the huge silvery plumes, most majestically on female plants. Pampas grass needs a sheltered position in exposed gardens. The fescues are striking edging grasses for poor soils and coastal gardens. *Festuca alpina*, no more than 15 cm (6 in) high, forms dense tufts of narrow green leaves beneath

Miscanthus sinensis 'Zebrinus'

graceful flower spikes; *F. glauca* has bristly, blue-grey leaves. Another good edger is *Holcus mollis* 'Albovariegatus', a dainty variegated variety only 12 cm (5 in) tall.

A good specimen plant for small gardens, *Molinia caerulea* (Indian grass) prefers moist soil and sun or shade; the violet, branched flower panicles are set on rigid 60 cm (2 ft) stems above the green and yellow leaves. More suitable for large gardens is the North American bamboo-like *Panicum virgatum* 'Strictum' which, at 1.5 m (5 ft), is equally happy in moist and dry soils; its shiny brown, branched panicles are outstanding. Apply a winter mulch to the roots in cold areas. Winter protection and shelter are also necessary for *Pennisetum alopecuroides*, with its dense hummocks of grey-green leaves and feathery, brush-like plumes. *P. orientale* is also attractive, with purplish flower spikes.

Somewhat invasive but superb as a large specimen plant, *Spartina pectinata* 'Aureomarginata' grows up to 1.5 m (5 ft); the gracefully pendent leaves are edged with gold-yellow, particularly in light shade. It flourishes on not too dry soil. Among the so-called

feather grasses, *Stipa pennata* is a good all-rounder on chalky soil, growing to about 60 cm (2 ft) and having green rolled leaves and long silvery plumes.

Moisture-loving grasses

A few grasses prefer moist, even wet soil. *Arundo donax* (giant reed), more than 3.5 m (12 ft) tall, has silky plumes that emerge red in late summer, fade to white, and last throughout winter. Another giant is *Miscanthus sinensis* (*Eulalia japonica*), which at up to 1.5 m (5 ft) makes an outstanding lawn specimen plant; the narrow blue-green leaves have white centres, while in 'Zebrinus' they are banded with yellow. Moist soil is preferable but not essential for *Phalaris arundinacea* 'Picta' (gardener's garters); although it grows to only 60 cm (2 ft), it spreads rapidly from creeping rhizomes. The narrow leaves are striped cream and bright green or rose.

The grass-like sedges and rushes are described among marginal water plants (see p 256), while the bamboos – which, although tough-stemmed, are classed as grasses – are covered on page 243.

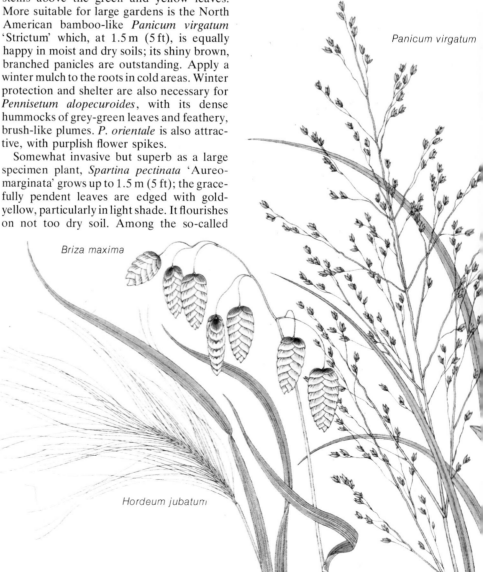

Panicum virgatum

Briza maxima

Hordeum jubatum

Everlasting flowers

Many gardeners have a deep-rooted aversion to having their precious blooms robbed for indoor flower decorations, which is perhaps why they are so grateful for the everlastings, or immortelles, that are grown expressly for indoor use. Truly immortal the immortelles are not; used continuously in dried arrangements the colours eventually fade and become encrusted with dust, or the brittle flower heads snap off unless attached to florists' wire. But for many dreary winter months, dried immortelles and ornamental grasses are invaluable to serious flower arrangers, and when not in use their lifespan can be extended by wrapping them carefully in tissue paper and storing them in cardboard boxes.

The true immortelles all belong to the daisy family and are characterized by the straw-like texture of the fully developed blooms. For drying purposes, they should be cut just as they reach perfection, often over several days from the same plant. Cut too immature they turn limp; harvested too late they quickly disintegrate. Tie the stems in small bundles with raffia or soft string and hang them upside down in a dark, cool but airy place until quite

Physalis franchetii 'Gigantea'

dry. Remove the shrivelled leaves before arranging or storing the flower heads.

Most immortelles are best grown as half-hardy annuals (see p 214) in full sun.

Pastel shades

Soft colours associate best with dried arrangements of silvery and grey foliage, branches and pale-coloured seeds set against a dark background. One of the finest pale immortelles is *Ammobium elatum* (sand flower), an annual with white, almost silvery bracts round the yellow centres, on 45 cm (18 in) stems. The daisy-like flowers of anaphalis (pearl everlasting) are carried in flat clusters in late summer; both *Anaphalis margaritacea* and *A. yedoensis* are hardy perennials with pearl-white blooms, *A. margaritacea* at 30 cm (12 in) achieving only half the height of *A. yedoensis*. Plant and increase both species by division in autumn.

Catananche caerulea (cupid's dart) is another hardy but short-lived perennial of up to 60 cm (2 ft); the form 'Major' has lavender-blue blooms like cornflowers, and there are also purple-blue and white varieties;

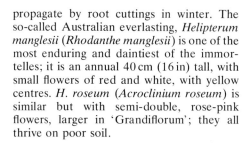

propagate by root cuttings in winter. The so-called Australian everlasting, *Helipterum manglesii* (*Rhodanthe manglesii*) is one of the most enduring and daintiest of the immortelles; it is an annual 40 cm (16 in) tall, with small flowers of red and white, with yellow centres. *H. roseum* (*Acroclinium roseum*) is similar but with semi-double, rose-pink flowers, larger in 'Grandiflorum'; they all thrive on poor soil.

Bold colours

For massed colour effects of yellow, red, orange, russet and purple, the following immortelles truly come into their own. The Spanish clover or globe amaranth, *Gomphrena globosa*, bears clover-like flowers on 30 cm (12 in) stems; this annual comes in white, pink, yellow, orange and purple, seeds being sold in mixtures or in single colours.

If one had to choose just one immortelle it would surely be the straw flower, *Helichrysum bracteatum*; this 90 cm (3 ft) half-hardy annual is outstanding in the wide colour range of the large daisy flowers with prominent yellow discs. It also comes in a dwarf form, 'Dwarf Spangle Mixed', ranging through white and yellow to rich pink, red and orange, or nearly brown. *Lonas inodora* (African daisy) is a hardy, yellow-flowered annual, 30 cm (12 in) tall, that deserves wider use.

Vying for popularity with helichrysum is the statice, now correctly classified as *Limonium*, though still listed as *Statice* in some catalogues. *Limonium sinuatum* is an annual, 45 cm (18 in) high, with blue- and cream-coloured flower-clusters on slightly arching stems. The strain 'Art Shades' includes mixtures of orange, red, blue and purple. Its relation *L. latifolium* (sea lavender) is a perennial, up to 60 cm (2 ft), with erect, wide-branching flower panicles of palest lavender-blue; it does best on poor soil, planted or increased in spring from root cuttings. The purple-blue daisy flowers of *Xeranthemum annuum* can also be had in double forms and in mixed colours.

Perpetuelles

This term embraces foliage, seeds and fruits of plants used in dried flower arrangements. Unlike the immortelles, which dry naturally when hung up, the perpetuelles need more care during the drying process, often involving chemicals, in order to preserve the colours, and they have a shorter life than the immortelles. Foliage such as beech and eucalyptus leaves can be preserved by standing the stems in a mixture of one part glycerine and two parts water. Many garden flowers can be dried by covering them with a mixture of borax and dry silver sand for a few days, while the seed heads of honesty (*Lunaria*), Chinese lantern (*Physalis*) and stinking iris (*Iris foetidissima*) need no special treatment. Bridging the border between the immortelles and perpetuelles is the sea holly, *Eryngium maritimum*, whose steel-blue, thistle-like flowers, surrounded by silvery bracts on 45 cm (18 in) perennial stems, can be dried like immortelles.

Helichrysum bracteatum

Eryngium maritimum   *Limonium sinuatum*

Plants for the flower arranger

A skilled flower arranger can use almost any plant, being limited only by those whose flowers or leaves drop prematurely, or refuse to take up water or to dry or preserve well. Nevertheless, it pays the flower arranger with a garden to plan plantings so that a wide range of varied material is at hand in every season of the year.

It is possible to use flowers that last only a day or two, or to grow the latest, most expensive varieties – or old-fashioned kinds no longer grown commercially. You can concentrate on winter flowers or on colours to suit home furnishings. Even flowers that are easy to buy are worth growing if you have the space, for they will be fresher and cheaper, and can be given proper treatment before arrangement. And foliage and branches that add individuality to an arrangement can be cut as needed.

Since the range is so wide, this article can mention only the more unusual or valuable plants that the flower arranger may wish to grow. Further details of a great many of them will be found on other pages.

Stems from shrubs and trees

Many of these have interest beyond that of their leaves, flowers or fruits. Among those that can be cut for (and pruned to exaggerate) their exotic shapes of stem and branch are the corkscrew hazel, *Corylus avellana* 'Contorta', and two Asian willows, *Salix matsudana* 'Tortuosa' and *S. sachalinensis* 'Sekka'. Several cornels, or dogwoods, are cut for their colourful bark, notably *Cornus alba* 'Sibirica' (red), *C. sanguinea* (purplish-red) and *C. stolonifera* (dark red) and its variety 'Flaviramea' (yellow). *Salix alba* 'Chermesina' (orange-red) and *S. daphnoides,* with a plum-coloured bloom, can be used similarly; they are known as the scarlet and violet willows respectively. As bark is brightest on young growth, prune most of the stems to within 5 cm (2 in) of the base of the plant in spring to ensure a supply with rich colour.

Stems of such flowering shrubs as lilac, Japanese quince (*Chaenomeles* spp), mock orange (*Philadelphus* spp), buddleias and roses (among the longest-flowering) need to take up water rapidly when cut. They do this best if the wood is young and sappy, so again relatively hard pruning is advantageous. Even so, the removal of foliage before arranging helps to prolong flower life; if you want leaves, cut separate shoots. Among shrubs worth cutting for their berries are many hawthorns (*Crataegus* spp), cotoneasters, pyracanthas (firethorns) and the sea buckthorn, *Hippophaë rhamnoides,* a tall deciduous shrub with silvery willow-like leaves. Plant it in a group containing both sexes to ensure a supply of the orange-yellow berries.

Alder, hazel and willow catkins open indoors, and so do the buds of horse chestnut, forsythia, flowering currants (*Ribes* spp) and witch hazels (*Hamamelis* spp). If you have a mild climate, you can grow *Eucalyptus gunnii* and *Pittosporum tenuifolium* for their juvenile foliage (and encourage this by hard pruning); the eucalypt is blue-grey, the pitto-

Euphorbia characias wulfenii

sporum pale green in the type but variegated, silvery, yellowish or purplish in its various forms.

Flat sprays of beech leaves can be pressed, while both beech and hornbeam can be preserved for winter use by standing sprays of the still green leaves in a mixture of one part glycerine to two parts water. Norway maple (*Acer platanoides*) and limes (lindens; *Tilia* spp) are useful for their greenish-yellow flowers; those of limes can be dried. Beech masts, and the fruits of elm and hornbeam are useful both green and dried.

The ivies, *Hedera helix, H. canariensis* and *H. colchica,* are all prized for the shapes and colouring of their leaves. The last two, particularly, have large leaves – up to 25 cm

Liriodendron tulipifera

(10 in) across – and good variegated forms; *H. colchica* 'Dentata Variegata', for example, is green, grey-green and cream, while 'Paddy's Pride' has a bold splash of yellow. The numerous forms of English ivy (*H. helix*), though not large-leaved, are very variable and most make excellent trails of foliage in arrangements.

Herbaceous foliage

Herbaceous plants with large leaves of striking shape or colour can be used in flower arrangements either fresh or preserved with glycerine as described above. Grey foliage is particularly useful. Variegated leaves look

Acanthus longifolius

best close to, and variegated, yellow and grey foliage all light up any arrangement where dark colours predominate or where the arrangement is poorly lit. See also pages 242 and 252.

For long, sword-shaped leaves, choose the phormiums – particularly *Phormium tenax* (New Zealand flax), which has varieties whose leaves are purplish-bronze or variegated with either cream or yellow stripes. On a smaller scale, use leaves of *Iris pallida* 'Variegata' (with either white or yellow stripes, sometimes listed separately as 'Argenteo-variegata' and 'Aureo-variegata'), or *Sisyrinchium striatum* 'Variegatum' (white-striped).

Arum italicum has green leaves with well-marked white veins; they die down in summer, but are available when foliage is scarce in winter. Somewhat similar is the milk thistle, *Silybum marianum,* an annual with large, prickly, white-veined leaves in summer. Other good variegations are found among the hostas, whose leaves preserve to pale yellow in glycerine. *Hosta albo-marginata* (*H. sieboldii*) and *H. crispula* are edged with white, *H. undulata univittata* has a broad cream stripe in the centre, and there are various variegated forms of *H. fortunei* such as 'Obsura Marginata' (gold-edged) and 'Albopicta' (yellowish, edged with pale green). The largest and most luxuriant of all hosta leaves are found in *H. sieboldiana* (not to be confused with *H. sieboldii*), whose greyish or bluish leaves are up to 30 cm (12 in) wide and even more in length.

With large leaves it is often the more mature ones that survive best in winter. This is especially true of the so-called bear's breeches (*Acanthus* spp); the flower spikes of these are also good for drying. Other leaves of exciting shape are those of *Melianthus major,* the rather tender South African honey bush, which – though shrubby – is cut down by frost but will usually sprout again from the base. However, its beautiful grey-green, deeply ser-

Bergenia sp

Allium albopilosum

Kniphofia 'Dawn Sunkiss'

rated leaves smell unpleasant when bruised. The grey leaves of cardoon (*Cynara cardunculus*) are very satisfactory when picked, as are the flower buds. You can similarly use the closely related globe artichoke (*C. scolymus*). The thick leaves of bergenias are usable throughout most of the year, and those of *Bergenia purpurascens* turn mahogany-coloured in winter. Thinner leaves, which tend to flag easily, sometimes respond to soaking in starch-water to stiffen them; this works with the red leaves of beetroot (*Beta vulgaris*).

Flowers and seed-heads

It is well worthwhile to grow a stock of flowers to give shades that are not commonly available at florists' shops. The most important of these for flower arranging are lime-green, greenish-white, cream and purplish-red shades. A variety of plants of various kinds that will provide such material are listed in the table. Since other flower colours, including white, pink, red, yellow and true blue, are more readily available, they are not listed.

Many seed-heads are worth saving, including those of the poppies *Papaver orientale* and *P. somniferum*, the lilies *Lilium martagon* and *Cardiocrinum giganteum*, onions such as *Allium albopilosum* and *A. porrum* (leek), and teasels (*Dipsacus* spp). Angelica, dill and carrots give good heads, as do many of the agapanthus, especially *Agapanthus praecox*. Rhubarb, both culinary and decorative (*Rheum* spp), gives large sprays. *Physalis alkekengi*, the winter cherry, provides its well-known 'lanterns'.

Iris foetidissima has bright orange seeds, as have such species of euonymus as *Euonymus europaeus*, *E. latifolius* and *E. yedoensis*, where they contrast with pink seed-cases. Fleshy fruits and seeds must be used fresh. Worth growing are the arums, crab apples, dwarf 'currant' tomatoes, 'wild'-type grapes such as *Vitis vinifera* 'Brandt', and the poison-

Unusual flower colours

Lime-green to greenish-white
Alchemilla mollis (HP); *Allium siculum* (HB); *Amaranthus caudatus* 'Viridis' (HHA); *Cobaea scandens* (cup-and-saucer plant) 'Alba' (HHPC or HHAC); *Daphne laureola* (spurge laurel; ES); *D. pontica* (ES); *Enkianthus campanulatus* (DS); *Euphorbia amygdaloides* (wood spurge; HP); *E. characias* (HP); *E. characias wulfenii* (*E. wulfenii* or *E. veneta*; HP); *E. myrsinites* (HP); *E. polychroma* (*E. epithymoides*; HP); *Galanthus* spp (snowdrops; HB); *Garrya elliptica* (ES); *Gladiolus* 'Green Woodpecker' (HHB); *Helleborus corsicus* (HP); *H. foetidus* (HP); *H. viridis* (HP); *Hydrangea quercifolia* (DS); *Liriodendron tulipifera* (tulip tree; DT); *Molucella laevis* (bells of Ireland or shell-flower; HHA); *Nicotiana alata* (*N. affinis*; tobacco plant) 'Lime Green' and 'Limelight' (HHA); *Ornithogalum nutans* (HB); *Polygonatum multiflorum* (*P. × hybridum*; Solomon's seal; HP); *Reseda odorata* (mignonette; HA); *Tiarella cordifolia* (foam flower; HP); *Tulipa* Viridiflora varieties (tulips; HB); *Veratrum album* (false helleborine; HP); *V. viride* (Indian poke; HP); *Zinnia elegans* 'Envy' (HHA)

(*Cheiranthus alpinus*) 'Moonlight' (HP); *Epimedium* spp (HP); *Hamamelis mollis* (Chinese witch hazel) 'Pallida' (DS); *Hydrangea arborescens* 'Grandiflora' (DS); *Kniphofia* (red-hot poker) 'Dawn Sunkiss' and 'Maid of Orleans' (HP); *Lilium* (lily) 'Limelight' (HB); *L. sulphureum* (HB); *Mahonia japonica* (ES); *Oenothera biennis* (evening primrose; HBl); *Pittosporum tobira* (HHES); × *Solidaster luteus* (× *S. hybridus*; HP); *Syringa vulgaris* (lilac) 'Primrose' (DS); *Yucca gloriosa* (ES); also cultivars of chrysanthemums, dahlias, gladioli, narcissi and daffodils, roses, sweet peas and tulips

Creamy yellow to sulphur yellow
Achillea × 'Moonshine' (HP); *Camassia leichtlinii* 'Plena' (HB); *Cephalaria gigantea* (*C. tatarica*; HP); *Cheiranthus cheiri* (wallflower) 'Ivory White' (HBl or HP); *Chimonanthus praecox* (winter sweet; DS); *Cimicifuga cordifolia* (HP); *C. racemosa* (HP); *Corylopsis* spp (DS); *Erysimum alpinum*

Plum and dark purple
Acanthus spp (bear's breeches; HP); *Cercis siliquastrum* (Judas tree) 'Bodnant' (DT); *Daphne bholua* (DS); *D. mezereum* (mezereon; DS); various forms of *Helleborus orientalis* (lenten rose; HP); *Leycesteria formosa* (DS); *Magnolia liliiflora* 'Nigra' (DS); *M. × soulangiana* 'Lennei' (DS); *Paeonia delavayi* (tree paeony; DS); forms of *Salvia horminum* (clary; HHA); *Veratrum nigrum* (HP); forms of *Vinca minor* (HP); also various cultivars of chrysanthemums, dahlias, gladioli, old roses (such as 'Cardinal Richelieu' and 'William Lobb'), sweet peas, tulips and wallflowers

Key: *A* = annual; *B* = bulbous; *Bl* = biennial; *C* = climber; *D* = deciduous; *E* = evergreen; *H* = hardy; *HH* = half-hardy; *P* = perennial or sub-shrub; *S* = shrub; *T* = tree

Echinops ritro

ous *Phytolacca americana*, a North American plant known as the poke weed.

Flowers worth drying (apart from the everlastings described on page 245 and many grasses on page 244) include those of acanthus, anaphalis, heathers (both *Calluna* and *Erica* spp), globe thistles (*Echinops* spp), eryngiums or sea hollies, hydrangeas, the plume poppy (*Macleaya cordata*), *Molucella laevis*, the knotweed *Polygonum vacciniifolium* and the reedmaces (*Typha* spp). These will all dry hanging upside-down in a cool, dry place, but there are very few garden flowers that cannot be dried by covering with dehydrated silica gel or borax powder.

The perfumed garden

Perfume is the most difficult plant attribute to discuss rationally because its production and effect are subject to so many vagaries. A flower that seems heavily scented on a warm, humid, still summer evening may seem far less so when conditions are different. People's personal appreciation also varies markedly, yet all would agree that perfume is the most evocative of qualities and one that can add greatly to the pleasures of the garden.

Good scents are to be found in every type of ornamental plant – trees, shrubs, climbers, herbaceous plants and annuals – and something can be found to cover every month of the year. Nor, as is sometimes said, are scented flowers always dull flowers; some do rely more on scent than on colour to attract pollinating insects, but a large number are bright and cheerful, as the following selections show. But of course there are many very popular flowers that are not scented and never have been. They have other qualities which make them desirable, and as most scented plants throw their perfume some distance they can, if well distributed, cover the unscented kinds and make the whole garden deliciously fragrant.

Spring
Some of the richest perfumes of the whole year come in the spring. Wallflowers (*Cheiranthus cheiri*) have lost none of their old charm, and bring a scent so heavy and yet so pleasing that it cannot be compared with any other. Much the same is true of the spring-flowering (biennial) Brompton stocks, except that their full fragrance is exactly repeated in summer by that of the annual Ten Week stocks: both types are derived from *Matthiola incana*.

Among the spring bulbs, hyacinths also have a heavy perfume, but it is much sweeter and less refreshing than that of wallflowers or stocks, so that some people find it sickly. Narcissi have a whole range of perfumes, from the light, slightly sharp fragrance of some of the trumpet and large-cupped daffodils to the richly sweet perfume of the Jonquils, *Narcissus tazetta* and its varieties, *N. poeticus* and its varieties, and the numerous hybrids between the last two. The crown imperial, *Fritillaria imperialis*, has a foxy smell which most people find unpleasant, but a few enjoy.

No one ever complains of the delicate fragrance of primroses and polyanthus, nor of the much sweeter, more penetrating perfume of lily of the valley (*Convallaria majalis*). The scent of the early-flowering broom, *Cytisus × praecox*, is however, another that most people dislike but a few find invigorating – especially outdoors and at a little distance.

The same could be said of the unmistakable scent of the leaves of box (*Buxus sempervirens*), which it is said Queen Anne had removed from Hampton Court Palace because it made her sneeze. Being evergreen this is not a distinctively spring perfume, but is one that can be in the garden all the year, as can the leaf aromas of various herbs and other evergreens such as rosemary, lavender, bay, eucalypts of various kinds, santolina (cotton

Cheiranthus cheiri

lavender), thymes, sage and rue, the last the least pleasant to some but not to all.

The scent of *Osmanthus delavayi* is universally approved, and it is one of those shrubs that seems more scented at a distance than close-to. The related hybrid × *Osmarea burkwoodii* has the same qualities and a sturdier habit. Of barberries, the sweetest is *Berberis × stenophylla*. In places where it thrives, the slightly tender *Cytisus × racemosus* contributes a lemon sharpness to the air. *Skimmia japonica* varies in its scent production, but is always pleasing and quite powerful in the male variety 'Fragrans'.

Numerous rhododendrons, including the opulent hybrid *Rhododendron* 'Loderi', are richly scented, but the spiciest perfumes come from rather tender kinds, such as *R. bullatum* and *R.* 'Fragrantissimum', and from the hardy yellow azalea (*R. luteum* or *Azalea pontica*). Some daphnes and spring-flowering viburnums also have this rich spicy quality, notably *Daphne mezereum*, *D. odora*, *D. collina* and the hybrid *D. × burkwoodii*, and *Viburnum carlesii*, *V. bitchiuense* and *V. × burkwoodii*. At the end of spring, lilacs (*Syringa* spp) bring their own sweet, pervasive, but never overpowering scent.

Ruta graveolens 'Jackman's Blue'

Rhododendron 'Loderi'

Summer

In summer, annuals make a considerable contribution to the perfumed garden. Sweet peas have their own fragrance so delicate that many aging people declare that sweet peas are no longer scented. It is a perfume that can be greatly affected by the atmosphere, so that it can come and go several times a day, and is best when the air is cool and moist. By contrast, sweet alyssum (*Lobularia maritima* or *Alyssum maritimum*) is most strongly honey-scented when the sun is hot. Nicotianas, or tobacco plants, release their scent at night, as does *Matthiola bicornis* (*M. longipetala*), the night-scented stock, but the annual varieties of *M. incana* make no distinction between day and night.

Magnolia sieboldii

Mignonette (*Reseda odorata*) is a flower so distinctive in perfume that it is used as a scent name. So is heliotrope, *Heliotropium arborescens* (*H. peruvianum*), really a half-hardy perennial but commonly grown as an annual. Its common name, cherry pie, inadequately describes its highly individual perfume.

Perhaps the most pervasive summer scent in temperate gardens is that of the various species and hybrids of *Philadelphus*, which is strong enough to earn them the common name of mock orange. These can fill a whole garden with sweetness, though in a climate warm enough to sustain them *Michelia figo* (*M. fuscata*) and *Osmanthus fragrans* can surpass them in this quality. The michelia is sometimes called the banana tree because of the supposed banana-like scent of its rather dull flowers. It is related to the magnolias, which make their own contribution, especially in early summer, with species such as *Magnolia sieboldii*, *M. wilsonii* and later with the evergreen lemon-scented *M. grandiflora*.

Among the brooms, *Cytisus battandieri* smells of pineapple and *Spartium junceum* is honey-scented. *Robinia pseudoacacia*, the false acacia, also has a pleasantly sweet scent. *Laburnum alpinum* emulates it and has contributed its sweetness to some of the summer-flowering garden hybrid laburnums.

But of all shrubs it is the roses that make the greatest contribution to the perfumes of the summer garden. Because of their very varied origins, rose scents cover an astonishingly wide range from the delicate so-called 'tea' scents, which some people are unable to detect and whose name in any case owes a certain amount to the imagination, to rich spicy perfumes that rival those of the 'clove' carnations and stocks. These, too, are perfumes that are highly sensitive to the atmosphere, best when it is damp and moderately warm and tending to disappear when it is dry, cold or hot. The recommended roses on page 148 and pages 158 to 163 include some of the most reliably scented kinds. The sweet briar, *Rosa rubiginosa*, also has scented foliage that is most pleasant after rain.

Some species of poplar, such as *Populus balsamifera*, *P.* × *candicans* and *P. trichocarpa*, give out a strong scent of balsam as they

Amaryllis belladonna

open their growth buds, and the common lime tree, *Tilia europaea*, fills the air with its sugary scent when it is in bloom. To the foliage scents of the evergreens already mentioned are added those of deciduous herbs such as the mints, fennel, clary (*Salvia sclarea*), aniseed (*Pimpinella anisum*), balm (*Melissa officinalis*) and lemon verbena (*Lippia citriodora*).

There are also richly scented summer-flowering climbers, including the summer jasmine, *Jasminum officinale*, and some, but by no means all, honeysuckles. Outstanding for rich spicy fragrance are *Lonicera japonica* and *L. periclymenum* in all their forms and hybrids (see p 145).

Scented herbaceous flowers for summer include the peppery lupins, the delicately scented varieties of *Paeonia lactiflora* – the Chinese paeony – and the pervasively sweet-scented border phloxes, forms or hybrids of *Phlox paniculata* and *P. maculata* that are often collectively called *P. decussata*. The pinks (derived from *Dianthus plumarius*) and border carnations (from *D. caryophyllus*) also make a varied contribution which includes the spicy perfume of the clove-scented varieties. Lilies are at their peak in summer, too, and many species and varieties are powerfully scented (see p 198).

Autumn

Of all the four seasons, this is the least well endowed with scents that are peculiarly its own. Many of the summer perfumes, including those of roses, will continue into autumn, though they may decline in intensity as the air gets colder. *Amaryllis belladonna* provides a perhaps too heavily sweet link between the two seasons, since it starts to bloom in late summer and continues into early autumn.

But of the true autumn flowers, some of the sweetest – *Elaeagnus pungens*, *E. macrophylla*, *E. glabra* and the hybrid *E.* × *ebbingei* – are so inconspicuous that many gardeners do not realize that they are there at all, and grow these evergreen shrubs solely as foliage plants. Another very sweet-smelling autumn flower is that of *Clerodendrum trichotomum*. It is fortunate that this throws its scent a considerable distance, for the leaves of this handsome shrub or small tree smell most unpleasant if one brushes against them.

Winter

Winter is far better endowed with scents of its own, and several of them are so well thrown that they can fill a garden on a still mild day. *Hamamelis mollis*, the Chinese witch hazel, and *Chimonanthus praecox*, the aptly named winter sweet, are two of the most popular, but two shrubby Chinese honeysuckles, *Lonicera fragrantissima* and *L. syringantha*, are equally generous with perfume.

Viburnum fragrans (botanists now want to call it *V. farreri*, but it seems a pity to lose a well-known name that signifies its superlative fragrance), *V. grandiflorum* and the hybrid between these, *V.* × *bodnantense*, are all sweetly scented. So is *V. foetens*, which comes later and continues into spring.

The flowers of the sarcococcas are almost as unassuming as those of elaeagnus and equally fragrant, so that it is the scent that makes one stop to look for them. The clusters of small yellow flowers of *Azara microphylla* would be easier to see if they were not half hidden by the leaves, but again it is their powerful vanilla scent that arrests attention. *Mahonia japonica* mimics the scent of lily of the valley. The diminutive but colourful *Iris reticulata* is violet-scented, and there are genuine violets also in flower in winter, though only varieties of *Viola odorata* and the double-flowered Parma violets are richly fragrant. They are ideal for winter posy bowls.

Hamamelis mollis 'Pallida'

The winter garden

In the winter months a garden can be a very drab and uninteresting place, but with a careful choice of plants, and some thought given to their siting, this need not be so. There will never be the riot of bright colour that one gets in summer, but many plants and shrubs do flower during the winter months, often bringing the bonus of perfume, and there are others that can make your garden attractive in a different kind of way with their foliage or coloured bark.

The positioning of winter-flowering plants and shrubs is of great importance, and this is not simply because some of them will do better with a little protection from cold winds and frost. It is, of course, exciting to stroll around the garden and discover the incredibly fragile-looking blooms of *Iris unguicularis* (*I. stylosa*) braving the worst of the weather in an out-of-the-way corner, and any garden should have such surprises. But during the winter you, and certainly your friends, will far more often look out at the garden from the house and see little of it from outside except the approach to the front or back doors. So site most of your winter-flowering plants where you can see them from the windows.

Their background – what you grow behind them – is a point to be watched carefully,

Hamamelis mollis

Prunus subhirtella 'Autumnalis Rosea'

particularly with a number of trees and shrubs. The winter-flowering cherry, *Prunus subhirtella* 'Autumnalis', in either its white or pink form, is a small tree which may reach about 5.5 m (18 ft) at most. It will flower on and off from late autumn to early spring whenever there is a mild spell. But it is a delicate, airy thing, and against a confused background – perhaps the bare, leafless twigs of another tree – half its beauty would be lost. Far better if you can site it – and shrubs like the 3 m (10 ft) Chinese witch hazel (*Hamamelis mollis*) or *Cornus mas*, the 4 m (13 ft) Cornelian cherry – against a background of evergreens if this is possible.

Both the latter shrubs have yellow flowers before the leaves come. The witch hazel blooms from early winter to early spring, its scented flowers coming unscathed through a

considerable degree of frost, and though it is slow-growing, it flowers when quite small. *Cornus mas*, a member of the dogwood family and native to Europe, blooms in late winter. It is a good shrub or small tree for poor soils.

Other shrubs for winter

Daphne mezereum, the mezereon, is a much smaller shrub than the above, reaching no more than 1.5 m (5 ft) high and 0.9 m (3 ft) through. Its stiff, erect branches closely studded from late winter onwards with small, fragrant, mauve flowers, it is something to put under a window so that the scent can drift into the room on mild days. There is also a white form, 'Alba'. Neither do well on acid soils.

Garrya elliptica is an evergreen and a useful shrub for sun or shade. It probably does best with some wall protection, however, for though it is quite hardy, its shiny, dark green leaves can become scorched by cold winds. It

will grow to 2 m (7 ft) and spread out to about 3 m (10 ft), and it bears pale green catkins fully 20 cm (8 in) long in the winter months.

A number of the honeysuckles (*Lonicera* spp) are winter-flowering, and *Lonicera × purpusii* is a good, scented, creamy-white one. Strong scent is, in fact, a characteristic of many of the winter-flowering shrubs.

The evergreen *Mahonia japonica* is probably the best member of its family that is hardy in a cool climate. On a plant 1.5 m (5 ft) tall by 2 m (7 ft) across, the small yellow, bell-shaped flowers, scented like lilies of the valley, are in long sprays. They last from early winter to spring, and are set off by the most striking, dark green, pinnate leaves. It will thrive in shade. The shorter-growing *M. aquifolium* has round clusters of yellow flowers in late winter and early spring. These are followed by berries which look like bunches of tiny black grapes, which have

Iris unguicularis

Magnolia stellata

given the plant the popular name Oregon grape. It will make good ground cover.

Several viburnums flower in winter. *Viburnum × bodnantense* 'Dawn', unlike some of the others, is better in sun than shade, though the flowers can be damaged where morning sun strikes after a night frost. It makes a big deciduous bush 2.75 m (9 ft) tall by 2 m (7 ft) across if the soil is well drained and preferably limy. It has small pink flowers in clusters from late autumn right through to spring. *V. × burkwoodii* blooms from early to mid-spring, the pink buds opening white against the evergreen foliage.

Other shrubs of the early part of the gardener's year include *Corylopsis pauciflora*, a 1.25 m (4 ft) spreading bush, with cowslip-scented, primrose-yellow flowers, and several rhododendrons. *Rhododendron* 'Christmas Cheer' is an old cultivar, but still one of the best. Low and rather sprawling, it carries in very early spring small, round trusses of warm pink flowers, paling to blush. *R. × praecox* is pale lavender-pink and more delicate-looking. About the same size, 1.25 m (4 ft) tall, it has small clusters of bloom rather than trusses, but the flowers of both rhododendrons can be damaged by hard frosts.

The same must be said for the earliest-

berschmelze' ('Molten Silver' or 'Silver Bells') have the advantage that they will grow on somewhat limy soil, which other heathers will not tolerate. See also page 152.

Foliage, berries and bark
For the winter garden, attractive leaves can be just as important as flowers. The variegated, yellow-splashed leaves of the evergreen *Elaeagnus pungens* 'Maculata' ('Aureo-variegata') will light up the garden when the sun shines. It makes a shrub 3 m (10 ft) tall and as much wide in time. It can be used for a hedge, though it should not be closely clipped. Any branches on which the leaves revert to all-green should be removed promptly.

Holly berries give cheery winter colour provided both male and female plants are grown, and *Ilex aquifolium* 'Fructoluteo' ('Bacciflava') has yellow ones in place of the usual red. There are hollies with variegated foliage, too. As well as those mentioned on page 151, there are *I. × altaclarensis* 'Silver Sentinel', with creamy-blotched and margined leaves, and such forms of *I. aquifolium* as 'Argenteomarginata' with silver edgings and 'Aureomarginata' with gold.

The berries of many varieties of pyracantha and cotoneaster make spectacular displays if

Border plants
Pride of place for winter flowering among herbaceous plants must go to the hellebores. With handsome leaves throughout the year and sculptured, incredibly long-lasting flowers, these all do best with some shade, but will make a good show even without. *Helleborus corsicus* is the largest and most showy, making a clump 60 cm (2 ft) high, with clusters of large, pendent green flowers early in the year. *H. niger*, the Christmas rose, may flower at any time during the winter, depending on how mild the season is. The flowers are pure white, with golden stamens, and the protection of a cloche may help it to come into bloom early in a bad winter. Manure in spring is beneficial, but most well-drained soils suit hellebores. There is also a variable group known as the Orientalis hybrids, or lenten roses, which are derived from *H. orientalis*. Growing to about 45 cm (18 in), they have flowers ranging from blush-white to plum, often attractively spotted inside with maroon. They will flower from early winter to spring.

Mention has already been made of *Iris unguicularis*, which will thrive on the poorest soil. It should have its long, spiked leaves cut hard back in early winter and as much of the tangle of old dead leaves pulled out of the

Erica carnea

Helleborus corsicus

flowering magnolias. The first on the scene, *Magnolia stellata* from Japan, will make a dense bush 1.8 m (6 ft) tall in time, and this will be smothered from early to mid-spring in star-shaped white flowers.

Of the winter-flowering heathers derived from *Erica carnea* (itself as good as any of its varieties), there is quite a selection, but none should be grown in the shade. Most will reach about 30 cm (12 in) in height, and 'Heathwood' is a good, rosy-purple, compact kind with coppery foliage. 'King George' is a rich pink and probably the first each year into flower. 'Springwood Pink' and 'Springwood White' are low, spreading growers, with long, horizontal sprays of flowers. They make good carpeters. The 45 cm (18 in) *E. × darleyensis* is rosy-lilac and flowers from early winter onwards. It and the fragrant white form 'Sil-

the birds do not get at them before winter sets in, and the ornamental value of rose hips should not be forgotten. Particularly striking and colourful are the long, bottle-shaped ones carried by shrub roses of the Moyesii group and the bright red round ones of the Rugosas that have single flowers (see p 158).

The bark of some shrubs and trees can give welcome winter colour, and even something as common as the silver birch (*Betula pendula*) gains an added attraction. Then there are two maples: *Acer grosseri*, with green and white striped bark, and the paper-bark maple, *A. griseum*, the mahogany bark of which peels off to reveal the new orange bark underneath. The shrubby *Cornus alba* has plum-red stems in winter, and if it is cut hard back in spring, these will be encouraged to make a dense thicket. It grows best in damp places.

clump as possible. *I. reticulata* is another miniature of the genus that sends up its deep purple flowers in late winter and early spring, when most plants are resting.

Among other winter bulbs, the tiny winter aconite, *Eranthis hyemalis*, does not mind shade and is best used for underplanting in a shrubbery where, once established, it can be left undisturbed to colonize. In midwinter, its star-like yellow flowers peep from whorls of green leaflets. Also colonizing well if left to itself is the common snowdrop, *Galanthus nivalis*. Snowdrops will seed themselves, but the seedlings will not flower for about three years. *G. byzantinus* has larger flowers and is one of the earliest into bloom. A number of crocuses also bloom in winter, and you will find some other bulbs that bloom extremely early on pages 191 and 200.

'Tropical' plants for temperate regions

Many people like to create the illusion that they live in a warmer climate than is in fact the case, and one way of doing this is to grow plants that have a tropical appearance. These may be either plants that are considerably hardier than they look, or plants that are readily produced and grow rapidly, so can be treated as disposable. The choice is widened still further if you have a greenhouse where plants that will not withstand frost can be overwintered.

Such pseudo-tropical plants can make a striking display if the situation is carefully chosen. They often look most at home in surroundings of uncompromisingly modern design, such as on the patio of a very modern house, in the company of elegant furniture – which can, however, well be of old-fashioned wicker and cane. It is for this reason that such plants are commonly termed architectural.

Palms and their like
Probably the first plant image created for most people by the word tropical is that of a palm tree. Most true palms are natives of the tropics or subtropics, and so are too tender to be grown in temperate regions, but there are exceptions. Most notable is *Trachycarpus fortunei* (*Chamaerops excelsa*), a Chinese species of fan-leaved palm that will survive a temperature of −12°C (10°F), or even lower if sheltered from wind. It grows slowly but will eventually make a very striking specimen.

Though not as hardy as this, the Mediterranean fan palm, *Chamaerops humilis*, will survive temperatures of −5°C (23°F). It is especially useful for patios and small gardens because of its modest height, often no more than 1 m (3 ft).

Then there are plants that create a palm-like impression, though they are not actually palms. One of the best of these is *Cordyline australis*, sometimes called the cabbage palm.

Hedychium gardnerianum

Stipa gigantea

It is a New Zealand member of the agave family with plumes of narrow, swordlike leaves, and thrives particularly well by the sea. It is undamaged by temperatures of −5°C (23°F) or even a little lower, but in cold, wet winters it is as well to tie the leaves in a bundle with raffia and wind burlap or sacking around them for protection. (Similar treatment can be given to *Chamaerops humilis* and some other woody plants.)

C. australis grows much faster than the true palms mentioned, easily reaching 5 m (16 ft) or more. It is readily increased by seed or cuttings, so that young plants are usually freely available. As a pot plant it is much used for interior decoration, having a very exotic appearance. Mature specimens flower freely; the flowers, individually small, creamy-white and scented, are crowded into large stiff sprays. *C. indivisa* has broader leaves but is less hardy.

Among the tender plants that can only spend the summer outdoors are two species of date palms, the dwarf *Phoenix roebelinii* and the taller Canary Islands species *P. canariensis*, which will eventually reach 2 m (7 ft) or more in a tub.

Stiff, fleshy foliage
The agaves are desert plants with thick fleshy leaves capable of withstanding long periods of drought, as are the somewhat similar aloes. None of these will withstand more than a degree or so of frost, and some are so barbarously armed that they are uncomfortable companions in the garden unless they can be kept well out of the way of unsuspecting passers-by. *Agave americana*, sometimes called the century plant, is the best known, most striking in its variegated form.

Much the same is true of some sword-leaved yuccas, such as *Yucca aloifolia* – not without reason called the Spanish bayonet – and *Y. gloriosa*, or Adam's needle. But *Y. filamentosa* is harmless and *Y. flaccida* is positively soft and yielding. Both these handsome plants are capable of standing temperatures as low as −20°C (−4°F), and both freely produce stiff spikes of ivory-white flowers. Equally striking though less hardy is the New Zealand flax, *Phormium tenax* (see p 177).

Cacti create the tropical image as effectively as palms, but few will survive much frost. Some of the hardiest will be found among the prickly-pears (*Opuntia* spp). They have thick bat-shaped stems which in most species are so sharply spined that they, like the agaves, must be placed with an eye to safety. One of the most suitable for small gardens is *Opuntia compressa*, which grows only 30 cm (12 in) high and will withstand temperatures as low as −15°C (5°F).

Large, striking leaves
Then there are plants with broad leaves like those of banana plants. These include the cannas, hedychiums and cautleyas. The cannas grown in gardens are mostly hybrids of *Canna indica*, with erect green or bronzy-purple leaves and stiff spikes of brightly coloured flowers. All have a West Indian parentage and are not very hardy, but these are plants with fleshy roots that can be lifted in autumn and stored out of harm's way all winter. Even more tropical in appearance, and actually a little hardier, is *C. iridiflora* from Peru. It has very big blue-green leaves and crimson flowers hanging from 1.8 to 2.5 m (6 to 8 ft) stems.

Hedychiums and cautleyas belong to the ginger family, and some species are decidedly tender. But *Hedychium gardnerianum*, with scented lemon-yellow flowers, and *H. densiflorum* (orange-red) will withstand several degrees of frost. So will *Cautleya lutea*, with yellow flowers followed by ice-blue seeds. If you can overwinter the roots in frost-free conditions, several bananas themselves (*Musa* spp) will grow in temperate regions, especially the Japanese *Musa basjoo*, the hardiest species.

First rate in tubs or large pots to stand on a terrace or patio are the various evergreen species of datura. Most spectacular are the double-flowered forms of *Datura cornigera*,

Cordyline australis

the horn of plenty, with large white night-scented flowers hanging from the branches in summer. *D. suaveolens*, known as angel's trumpet, is equally good, but both are injured by any frost. *D. sanguinea*, with almost tubular flowers that are orange-red towards the mouth, will survive a few degrees of frost and even when badly damaged will often grow again from the base in spring.

Although not very similar to the above, several other plants have large, decorative leaves. They include some plants that are completely hardy except in the coldest places, such as *Fatsia japonica* (*Aralia sieboldii*), sometimes wrongly called the castor-oil plant (see below). This has large, deeply divided shining leaves, rather like those of a fig but more sharply lobed. It is an evergreen shrub

Arundinaria viridi-striata

grass, makes elegant tufts of narrow leaves and has loose sprays of pinkish-brown oat-like flowers about 1.5 m (5 ft) high. There are also various species and varieties of *Miscanthus sacchariflorus* and *M. sinensis*, some variegated in different ways, that are quite hardy and yet capable of contributing a jungle-like air to the garden.

Exotic climbers and others
Among hardy deciduous climbers, two of the best to produce a tropical effect are *Actinidia chinensis*, the Chinese gooseberry, and *Vitis coignetiae*, the glory vine. Both have large rounded leaves, and both can grow so fast as to become an embarrassment, but their stems can be pinched in summer and cut back in winter to restrict their spread. They are

Fatsia japonica

Musa sp

related to the ivies (*Hedera* spp), and has globular heads of flowers in autumn, similar to those of ivy in shape but ivory-white. It has been hybridized with the large-leaved Irish ivy (*Hedera helix hibernica*) to produce a much laxer plant with almost equally handsome leaves. This is called × *Fatshedera lizei*, and it can be allowed to sprawl along the ground or be tied like a climber to a wall, fence or screen. Edible figs themselves, varieties of *Ficus carica*, are also worth growing either as shade trees or trained against a sunny wall (see p 323).

The true castor-oil plant, *Ricinus communis*, is actually a tropical tree, but it grows so rapidly from seed that it is frequently grown as a half-hardy annual. The leaves are similar in shape to those of the fatsia, but may be bronzy-green with white veins or purple all over, according to variety. Similarly there are coloured varieties of sweet corn (*Zea mays*) with multicoloured grains in their cobs, most notably 'Rainbow'.

Eucalypts are also trees which can be reduced to garden scale by hard pruning each spring. This preserves the juvenile form of leaf, usually very different from the adult form, and increases leaf size. Two of the best and hardiest species to grow in this way are *Eucalyptus gunnii* and *E. urnigera*, both capable of surviving temperatures of −6°C (21°F).

By the waterside no fairly hardy plant looks more tropical than *Gunnera manicata*, with its huge umbrella-like leaves (see p 257). But it needs a lot of space and protection against temperatures lower than −5°C (23°F).

There are several completely hardy species of acanthus, all herbaceous perennials with large, shining green, thistle-like leaves. The leaf divisions are narrow in *Acanthus spinosissimus* (*A. spinosus*), broad in *A. mollis*. But the most impressive of all is a variety of the latter, *A. mollis latifolius* with extra-large leaves and the typical stiff spikes of hooded maroon and white flowers. In this form, however, they are 2 m (7 ft) or more in height instead of the usual 1 to 1.25 m (3 to 4 ft).

Delicate form
Many bamboos (see p 243) are completely hardy and ideal for an oriental effect. The taller species, such as *Sinarundinaria* (*Arundinaria*) *murielae*, *S.* (*A.*) *nitida* and varieties of *Phyllostachys nigra*, can be used as backgrounds or screens. Short kinds, such as the gold- and green-leaved *Arundinaria viridistriata*, make good ground cover.

Other members of the grass family are worthy of consideration, too. Varieties of pampas grass (*Cortaderia selloana*) can be had in heights varying from 1.25 to 3 m (4 to 10 ft). *Stipa gigantea*, the Spanish feather

described on pages 145 and 147. Passion flowers (see p 146) also grow fast, but even the relatively hardy *Passiflora caerulea* is likely to be cut to near ground-level if the temperature drops below −8°C (18°F). If the base of the plant is protected, however, it will usually throw out new shoots in spring.

Other exotic-looking flowering climbers include *Cobaea scandens*, commonly called cathedral bells or the cup-and-saucer plant. It is hardy down to about −6°C (21°F), especially if protected at the base. The purple-flowered perennial morning glory, *Ipomoea learii*, is too tender to be grown outdoors where there is risk of any frost, but there are annual species with beautiful if ephemeral flowers that grow easily from seed. They include *I. purpurea* and *I. tricolor*, both often listed under other names (see p 212).

Finally, there are several bulbous and herbaceous flowering plants with flowers of exotic appearance. Among the best are the blue-flowered *Agapanthus africanus* and the hardier 'Headbourne Hybrids', the pink or white lily-like *Crinum* × *powellii*, the pink and white *Amaryllis belladonna* and the rose-pink *Nerine bowdenii*, both also lily-like, and the hardiest of the arum lilies, *Zantedeschia aethiopica* 'Crowborough'. These will all survive a few degrees of frost and are ideal for sunny patios.

Life in the garden pool

To bring the water garden to life requires the lively movements of fish plus a wide variety of plants. The latter include bog plants for damp soil outside the pool itself (see p257) and marginal aquatics which have their roots submerged but the rest of their growth emergent (see p 256). Within the water itself – or, at most, emerging a few centimetres from its surface – are ornamentals with floating flowers and foliage but anchored roots, like water-lilies and water hawthorns, for deep water; floating plants that are not anchored at all; and underwater oxygenators. These, with the fish, make the pool a small but complete world with a balanced environment.

For general information on planting and stocking water gardens, see page 130.

Deep-water aquatics

The most important of the aquatics with floating leaves are the water-lilies (*Nymphaea* spp), of which there are about fifty species and many cultivars. The hardy kinds have two types of rootstock: one an upright, squat tuber with leaves and flowers coming from the top, the other a rhizomatous tuber which grows horizontally after the fashion of a bearded iris (see p196). They must be planted correctly.

The first group includes most of the hybrids raised by Marliac (see p 33) and the European *Nymphaea alba*. The second group are mainly derived from two North American species, *N. tuberosa* and *N. odorata,* and usually have fragrant flowers.

It is important to select varieties that fit the size and depth of the pool, remembering not to exceed recommended quotas (see p 130). The hardy varieties listed in the table below are divided into four groups. The very strong growers need water 75 to 90 cm (2½ to 3 ft) deep, and each occupy a surface area of 0.75 to 1 m² (8 to 11 sq ft). The strong types are best for medium-sized pools, needing water 45 to 60 cm (1½ to 2 ft) deep and taking a surface area of 0.45 to 0.65 m² (5 to 7 sq ft). The moderate growers are suitable for small pools with water 30 to 40 cm (12 to 15 in) deep, and occupy 0.25 to 0.4 m² (3 to 4 sq ft). The dwarf kinds can be grown in tubs, bowls and rock pools with 10 to 25 cm (4 to 10 in) of water, and take a surface area only 30 to 50 cm (12 to 20 in) across.

Nymphaea 'Moorei'

Colours vary from white to cream, various shades of pinks and reds, and also yellow. There are no hardy blue water-lilies, only tropical ones suitable for indoor pools or for temporary residence outdoors in hot summers, for they need a water temperature of 21°C (70°F). None are frost-hardy, and they must be stored indoors in moist soil at about 13°C (55°F) in winter. They should be started into growth in tanks of water under glass in spring prior to moving outdoors.

Other aquatics for 30 to 45 cm (1 to 1½ ft) of water include the water hawthorn, *Aponogeton distachyos,* which has strap-shaped floating leaves and very fragrant white flowers with jet-black anthers borne on forked inflorescences. There is also the water fringe, *Nymphoides peltata* (*Limnanthemum nymphoides*), which spreads across the water surface and looks like a miniature water-lily with round, mottled, crinkly-edged leaves about 4 cm (1½ in) across. It has bright yellow, five-petalled flowers.

Floating plants

Floating aquatics are useful to shade the pool in summer, and also harbour many small insects which are greedily devoured by fish. The shade they cast deters algae, since light is essential for the multiplication of these primitive plants, and also benefits fish in the heat of the day. Some floaters, like the water hyacinth, *Eichhornia crassipes,* have long trailing roots which provide a nursery for fish eggs; the pearly eggs of goldfish, for example, are easily seen on their black roots. Although not frosty-hardy, water hyacinths are useful for summer display – their showy spikes of lavender-blue and gold flowers poised on rosettes of small heart-shaped leaves. The

Eichhornia crassipes

Recommended hardy water-lilies

Very strong growers	'Attraction' (garnet-red); 'Charles de Meurville' (red); 'Colonel Welch' (yellow); 'Gladstoniana' (white); 'Leviathan'* (pink); 'Picciola' (amaranth-crimson)
Strong growers	'Escarboucle' ('Aflame'; deep crimson); 'James Brydon' (carmine-red); 'Marliacea Albida'* (white); 'Marliacea Rosea'* (pink); 'Moorei' (yellow); 'Rose Nymph'* (pink); 'Sunrise'* (yellow); 'Virginalis' (white)
Moderate growers	'Eugenia de Land' (pink); 'Laydekeri Fulgens' (crimson); 'Laydekeri Purpurata'* (rosy-crimson); 'Marliacea Chromatella' ('Golden Cup'; yellow); *Nymphaea odorata* 'Alba'* (white)
Dwarf types	'Paul Hariot' (apricot, becoming pink and red); 'Pygmaea Alba' (white); 'Pygmaea Helvola' (yellow; chocolate-blotched leaves)

Recommended tropical water-lilies

Day bloomers	'Afterglow'* (orange); 'Baghdad'* (blue); 'Evelyn Randig'* (red; purple-mottled leaves); 'General Pershing'* (pink); 'King of the Blues'* (blue); 'Mrs G. H. Pring'* (white); 'St Louis'* (yellow); 'Trailblazer'* (yellow)
Night bloomers	'H. C. Haarstick' (dark pink); 'Missouri' (white); 'Mrs G. C. Hitchcock' (dark pink); 'Red Flare' (red)

*Scented varieties

Nymphaea 'Charles de Meurville'

Nymphaea 'Pygmaea Helvola'

Nymphaea 'Escarboucle' ('Aflame')

Ranunculus aquitilis

latter have large inflated stalks – rather like sausages – which make them buoyant, and the plants reproduce rapidly in summer from stolons. They need overwintering in moist soil at about 15°C (59°F).

Hardy floaters include the fairy floating mosses, *Azolla caroliniana* and *A. filiculoides*. These are almost identical plants with small lacy fronds of bright pale green leaves and tiny trailing roots. Towards the end of summer they become first pink, then red, then brown, before disappearing to the bottom of the pool for the winter.

Hydrocharis morsus-ranae is the frogbit, a European native with small, round, fleshy leaves and white three-petalled flowers in spring and early summer. It does best in small shallow pools, and forms winter buds or turions which lie at the bottom of the pond all winter and start growth again in spring.

The water soldier, *Stratiotes aloides*, only comes to the surface to flower, spending the rest of its time either as a dormant turon at the base of the pool in winter, or throughout spring, summer and autumn bobbing about in the water at various levels. It resembles the top of a pineapple in appearance, with translucent green, spiny-edged leaves in 10 to 20 cm (4 to 8 in) rosettes. The white male and female flowers are on separate plants.

Trapa natans, the water chestnut, is an annual from southern Europe that does best in warm, shallow water. It is raised from striking edible seeds about the size of a horse-chestnut seed (or 'conker') and with four protruding spines. These germinate in spring to grow long trailing stems clothed with triangular, toothed, floating leaves on spongy stems. The flowers are inconspicuous.

Submerged aquatics

Submerged aquatics play a key role in maintaining pool balance, which in turn is the secret of clear water. Their most important functions are oxygenating the water by the emission of oxygen through the leaf pores, using up carbon dioxide respired by fish and other pond occupants, and, by competition, taking food from more lowly plants such as algae, so preventing these from thriving. In addition, the submerged green masses make a suitable repository for fish eggs, and, after these hatch, hide the fry from their cannibalistic parents. Fish also nibble at some of the plants, partially for green diet, but also to seek out insects.

Submerged plants can be planted at any time during the growing season (see p 130), and are readily propagated from young pieces of new growth rooted in small pots of loam, submerged in tanks 30 cm (12 in) deep. Some

Hottonia palustris

are more efficient oxygenators than others, a few come to the surface to flower, but several may become weeds under very favourable conditions of warmth, shelter and shallow water. However, it is usually easy enough to pull out superfluous growth, either with the hands or using a garden rake.

Among the flowering oxygenators, one of the most attractive is *Hottonia palustris,* the water violet. In early summer, it has whorls of pale violet blooms on stems held about 15 cm (6 in) above the surface. *Ranunculus aquatilis,* the water crowfoot, is a plant tolerant of moving water as well as still. It has two kinds of leaves; the submerged ones are finely cut into hair-like segments, the floating leaves buttercup-shaped. The flowers are white.

The bladderwort, *Utricularia vulgaris,* needs still, rather acid water (as, for example, in pools in boggy land over peat or clay) for best results. It forms a mass of tangled stems furnished with tiny bladders which trap small insects. The flowers come in midsummer on spikes held 15 cm (6 in) above the water; they are bright yellow and like antirrhinums.

Most submerged aquatics have small, insignificant flowers, and amongst the most efficient oxygenators in this group are the milfoils (*Myriophyllum* spp); *Callitriche hermaphroditica* (*C. autumnalis*) and *C. palustris* (*C. verna*), the autumn and spring starworts, with pale green leaves forming starry masses; *Elodea* (*Anacharis*) *canadensis,* the Canadian pondweed, and an allied species *E. callitrichoides*; *Chara fragilis,* the stonewort, a rather brittle plant that is rough to handle; *Fontinalis antipyretica,* the willow moss, which usually grows on stones or from the side of a concrete pool; *Lagarosiphon major* (*Elodea crispa*), one of the most efficient, which resembles a curly-leaved anacharis; *Potamogeton crispus,* the curled pondweed, and *P. densus,* the frog's lettuce, both with oval translucent leaves; and *Crassula* (*Tillaea*) *recurva,* a succulent creeping plant with small leaves and white flowers.

Animal inhabitants

Fish for a small pool should be bright and colourful, should swim near the surface and should not grub around for food among plant roots, stirring up mud. The best-known kinds are the goldfish (*Carassius auratus*) and its allies. These originated in the Far East, where many varieties – some grotesque but others of great beauty – have been bred. They vary in colour from a rich golden-orange to almost silver and jet-black (as in the Moors). There are the multi-coloured Shubunkins and, most exotic of all, the Japanese Koi carp. Of the curiously-shaped goldfish forms, only the elongated Comets are hardy enough for outdoor pools. Other attractive species are the golden orfe (*Idus idus*) and the golden tench (a variety of *Tinca tinca*).

Snails are not essential members of the garden pool community. If you want to include them, the best kinds are freshwater winkles (*Paludina vivipara*) or ramshorns (*Planorbis corneus*). Never introduce freshwater whelks (*Limnaea stagnalis*), which eat plants.

Plants for the pool margin

Marginal aquatics are primarily ornamental. Besides displaying great variation in their flowers and foliage, they bloom at different times of year and so prolong the water garden's appeal. They are particularly useful in informal pools, where they break the flat surface of the water and also hide the edges. But with formal pools more restraint is necessary. The charm of the latter lies in their simplicity, so that water, fish and water-lilies are usually enough – although the odd clump of irises or rushes near a figure or fountain is permissible. Do not spoil the effect with too much vegetation, though. For details of planting marginal aquatics, see page 130.

Low-growing marginals
Some low-growing aquatics – that is, those under 30 cm (12 in) – are equally happy in shallow water or wet mud. They often scramble from one medium to the other, rooting into the soil as they go. Two with pencil-thick running rootstocks are *Calla palustris,* the bog arum, and *Menyanthes trifoliata,* the bog bean. The former has glossy heart-shaped leaves and white arum flowers, which, when pollinated by pond snails, go on to produce clusters of scarlet berries. The bog bean has trifoliate leaves and spikes of fringed white flowers that emerge from pink buds. Both flower in late spring and early summer.

Among the first marginals to greet the spring are the kingcups, *Caltha palustris,* their rich golden, buttercup-like flowers shining like fire at the water's edge. The double form is particularly effective, and there are whites.

The water mint, *Mentha aquatica,* blooms on and off all summer with spikes of pale lavender flowers, and its aromatic foliage is a joy to brush against at all seasons. *Ludwigia palustris,* the false loosestrife, has shiny, almost stalkless leaves with red reverses on creeping stems. The flowers are insignificant.

Later come the charming water forget-me-nots, *Myosotis palustris,* with pale blue florets – or rich blue in the cultivar 'Mermaid' – and various *Mimulus* hybrids such as 'Whitecroft Scarlet' and 'Bee's Dazzler', both scarlet and only about 15 cm (6 in) high. There is also the yellow, chocolate-spotted, 45 cm (18 in) *M. luteus* (see p 185).

Cotula coronopifolia, or brass buttons, is a small 15 cm (6 in) annual with lemon-scented leaves and flowers like the middle of a daisy with the outer florets removed. *Houttuynia cordata* 'Plena' ('Flore Pleno') flowers in late summer. Its pungent-smelling leaves are heart-shaped and purplish; the quaint double flowers are produced in spikes like miniature stocks (*Matthiola* spp; see p 216).

Medium-sized marginals
The earliest to bloom in this section, which grow to between 30 and 60 cm (1 and 2 ft), are the water plantains, *Alisma lanceolatum* and *A. plantago-aquatica,* and *Baldellia* (*Echinodorus*) *ranunculoides.* These plants are very similar in appearance, with acrid rootstocks, plantain-like leaves and loosely arranged spikes up to 45 cm (18 in) tall of small, three-petalled, rosy-pink flowers. All are inclined to

indiscriminate seeding, so remove the old flower heads.

The golden club, *Orontium aquaticum,* is an arum-relative without the normal wrap-round, petal-like flower spathe. Consequently the blooms look like yellow-topped pokers. The bluish-green leaves stand 30 to 45 cm (12 to 18 in) high in shallow water, but float if it is growing in deep water.

Few rushes are ornamental enough for a small garden pool, but exceptions are *Juncus effusus* 'Spiralis', commonly called the corkscrew rush because its fat green stems curl in spiral fashion, and *J. effusus* 'Vittatus', a gold and green striped rush.

Sagittarias are commonly called arrow-heads because of their leaf shape. All have spikes of three-petalled white flowers, which in *Sagittaria sagittifolia* 'Flore Pleno' are doubled so that they look something like stocks.

Cotton grasses (*Eriophorum* spp) are plants of the north, so do best in gardens with cool climates. They have narrow grassy leaves and 30 to 45 cm (12 to 18 in) slender stems terminating in silky, cotton-like inflorescences. Ludwigias belong to the evening primrose (*Oenothera*) family and have similar showy yellow flowers in the species *Ludwigia clavellina,* (frequently offered by growers as *Jussiaea repens*), a creeping plant, and its taller variety *L. clavellina grandiflora* (*Jussiaea grandiflora*). Neither are reliably hardy, so

Iris laevigata 'Variegata'

grow them outside permanently only in warm areas; elsewhere overwinter under glass.

Tall marginals
Among the best of the marginal aquatics that grow more than 60 cm (2 ft) tall is the non-rampant pickerel weed, *Pontederia cordata,* a striking 60 to 90 cm (2 to 3 ft) plant with smooth, heart-shaped leaves on long petioles and spikes of soft blue flowers.

Others with attractive flowers are the water irises – not only the golden *Iris pseudacorus,* which is most effective in the gold-variegated form 'Variegata', but also the rich blue *I. laevigata.* Among cultivars of the latter are the white form 'Alba', the pink 'Rose Queen' and several blue and white bicolours like 'Benekiron' and 'Colchesteri'. These all grow 60 to 75 cm (2 to 2½ ft) tall, require 8 to 10 cm (3

Glyceria maxima

to 4 in) of water and bloom in midsummer.

Ranunculus lingua is like a giant buttercup with rich yellow flowers on 90 cm (3 ft) stems, but *Cyperus longus,* the sweet galingale, has a grassy inflorescence, as has the green, pink and white variegated manna grass, *Glyceria maxima* (*G. spectabilis*). The flowering rush, *Butomus umbellatus,* has umbels of rosy-pink flowers on 60 to 90 cm (2 to 3 ft) stems, and smooth, stiff, grassy leaves.

Acorus calamus 'Variegatus' resembles a green and white variegated iris until it produces its strange brown poker-like inflores-

Zantedeschia aethiopica

cences. Two good bulrushes are *Scirpus albescens,* with fat 1.25 m (4 ft) stems longitudinally variegated in green and cream, and *S. tabernaemontani* 'Zebrinus', in which the stems are horizontally barred with alternate bands of green and white. Typhas or reed-maces (often misnamed bulrushes) should be banned from small pools unless the roots are confined. The least invasive are *Typha angustifolia* and *T. minima,* 1.25 m and 30 cm (4 ft and 1 ft) tall respectively.

Thalia dealbata, with canna-like foliage and slender spikes of nodding, reddish-purple flowers, makes a good summer-blooming aquatic, but is only hardy in warm climates, whilst in temperate regions *Zantedeschia aethiopica* 'Crowborough', the hardiest of the white arum lilies, is equally happy in damp borders or very shallow water.

Plants for the bog garden

Many familiar plants of the herbaceous border give even finer displays when grown under bog conditions. Being moisture-lovers, they need even growing conditions and in consequence produce more and finer blooms when freed from the risks of periodic drought. Included in their numbers are such well-known plants as day lilies (*Hemerocallis* spp), monkshoods (aconitums), *Filipendula rubra,* trollius, *Lobelia fulgens, Iris sibirica,* ajugas, aruncus, schizostylis and mimulus – all described elsewhere in this book.

In addition, there are certain truly water-loving plants which can be killed if the roots dry out, so must be given perennially damp or boggy conditions (see p 133). These are the plants described here. Group the smaller kinds for maximum effect, but only plant single specimens of such giants as gunnera and phormium. Most bog plants are best established in spring.

Smaller bog plants

Anagallis tenella 'Studland', a selected form of the British bog pimpernel, makes a mat of fine leaves studded on bright days with masses of deep pink fragrant flowers. In the related *A. monelli linifolia,* a half-hardy annual, they are deep blue. No pimpernels open their flowers when rain threatens, so they make good weather indicators.

The 25 cm (10 in) *Cardamine pratensis,* or

Astrantia major

cent plant for a wet situation. It develops huge, crenate, lobed leaves 1.5 to 2.5 m (5 to 8 ft) across on stems of similar height. Both stems and leaf-backs are covered with sharp bristles, and the greenish-brown flower spikes resemble giant bottle brushes. A single specimen makes an imposing accent plant in a key situation. *Phormium tenax,* the New Zealand flax, is almost as impressive (see p 177).

Rodgersias have spiraea-like plumes of pink, red or white flowers and variously shaped leaves. *Rodgersia podophylla* is known as bronze-leaf on account of its bronzy

flowered irises, *Iris kaempferi* and its forms. Their flowers are often doubled and with the petals held erect so that they resemble gay parasols at the pool's edge. The colours vary through shades of blue, red, violet, crimson, yellow and white, often striated and patterned with other shades. A rich lime-free soil is essential, with plenty of moisture during the growing season but dryer conditions in winter. Other bog irises include *I. bulleyana,* with grassy leaves and rich blue flowers and *I. sibirica* and the less hardy, copper-red *I. fulva,* together with their hybrids (see p 197).

Candelabra primulas need damp soil and shade from hot sun. They are dainty plants of ethereal appearance, particularly the *Primula pulverulenta* Bartley hybrids, with their pink and rose flowers in summer arranged in whorls on 60 cm (2 ft) mealy stems. Others to note are the sturdy *P. japonica* hybrids 'Millar's Crimson' and 'Postford White'; *P. helodoxa,* with 90 cm (3 ft) stems carrying whorls of golden-yellow blossoms; the rosy-carmine *P. beesiana,* rather smaller at 60 cm (2 ft) and with white-powdered stems; *P. burmanica,* of similar colouring but without the mealy stems; and the 90 cm (3 ft) *P. florindae* and the 60 cm (2 ft) *P. sikkimensis,* the Himalayan cowslip, both of which have terminal heads of yellow flowers.

The narrow leaves and tapering spikes of bright blue flowers of *Lobelia siphilitica* (or

Primula rosea 'Delight'

lady's smock, has an exquisite double form with spikes of soft lilac and delicate, deeply cut leaves. The best small bog primrose is *Primula rosea* 'Delight' (also known as 'Visser de Greer'), with 15 cm (6 in) stems carrying many bright rose-pink flowers in early spring. Some masterworts – astrantias – are also suitable for bog conditions, notably the 40 cm (15 in) *Astrantia carniolica* 'Rubra', with round heads of dark red flowers surrounded by silvery bracts – rather like a Victorian posy. Also good are the green and pink *A. major* and *A. minor* 'Moyra Reid', with green and grey flowers.

Taller bog plants

Some of these are noteworthy on account of their foliage, particularly the gunneras and phormiums. *Gunnera manicata* is a magnifi-

Gunnera manicata (young leaves and flower)

leaves with five to seven lobes, like those of the horse chestnut; its flowers are yellowish. *R. pinnata* has pinnate leaves and pink blossoms, which are white in the form 'Alba' or rosy-red in 'Superba' and *R. tabularis* (given by some authorities as *Astilboides tabularis*) has perfectly round leaves and 1.5 m (5 ft) spikes of creamy-white flowers.

Among the best flowering bog plants are the lovely 60 to 90 cm (2 to 3 ft) clematis-

Lysichiton americanus

white in 'Alba') associate pleasantly with astilbes. They are both summer-flowering. Growing 0.6 to 1.25 m (2 to 4 ft) tall (or 30 to 45 cm [12 to 18 in] in the dwarf cultivars), the latter have handsome, deeply cut leaves and feathery plumes of white, pink, red or crimson. There are many cultivars, generally listed under *Astilbe × arendsii,* of which 'Fanal' (deep crimson), 'Bridal Veil' (white), 'Cattleya' (pink) and 'Salland' (magenta) are a representative selection.

Rosy-pink lythrums, blue camassias and filipendulas (all described elsewhere) are others for the bog garden, also two splendid arums: *Lysichiton americanus* has deep yellow flowers 30 cm (12 in) tall in early spring, and *L. camtschatcensis* white flowers. They are succeeded by large glaucous leaves which need plenty of room to develop.

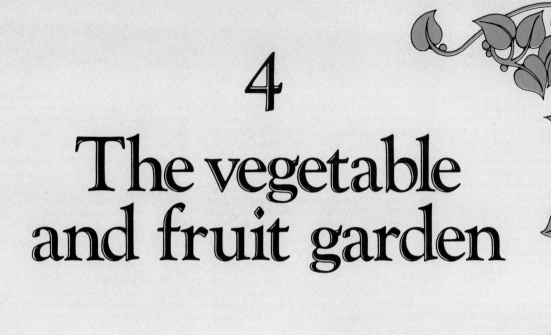

4
The vegetable and fruit garden

To many, an important – sometimes the most important –
aspect of gardening is growing their own food.
Whether you devote just a small plot to fruit and vegetables
or these occupy the major part of your garden,
this chapter shows you how to grow all the important types.
It ranges from the basic root and leaf vegetables
through the highly rewarding tomatoes, cucumbers and the like
to the more exotic kinds, such as asparagus and artichokes.
Recommendations are given of varieties for yield and flavour,
together with detailed information on sowing and growing,
protection, harvesting, storage and preservation.
A similarly wide range of fruits is covered,
including tree fruits and soft fruits, and also nuts
and such seldom-grown types as medlars, quinces and mulberries.
A series of articles deals with herbs and herb gardens,
but first of all comes a sequence of articles on
food-growing fundamentals: planning and basic cultivation.

Food from your garden

It is not only the opportunity of saving money that encourages large numbers of people to grow their own fruit and vegetables, but the lure of freshly harvested, tender, full-flavoured crops. The food you grow yourself can be picked when it is young, succulent and at the peak of its flavour. Freshness can transform many vegetables – sweet corn, for example, begins to lose sweetness within hours of harvesting – while the gardener can choose better-flavoured varieties of even common crops that are unobtainable in shops and markets because they will not stand the rigours of commercial cultivation and transportation, or do not give high enough yields. It is also possible to grow unusual vegetables, herbs and fruits that are otherwise difficult to obtain.

The corollary to the financial savings that can be made by growing your own food is the need to expend time and energy. However, the labour involved in a small vegetable garden is not much more than that required to give proper attention to a lawn. Moreover, the main growing season – when a small amount of regular attention is needed – coincides with the summer, when many people can get home from work before dark and spend an hour or two in the garden. (The long light evenings are more noticeable, of course, the farther from the equator you are.) Some crops that need training – tomatoes and melons, for example – require more attention than others, but they are often some of the most rewarding. In any case, to many people 'pottering' in the vegetable and fruit garden acts as an antidote to the pressures of modern life, and this, when combined with the satisfaction of harvesting their own crops, is reward enough.

Another major factor in the revival of interest in growing food is the increasing use of domestic freezers. While commercial food-freezing means that many vegetables and fruits are available in the shops out of season, freezers also enable gardeners to preserve surplus summer produce and to even out the gluts and shortages that are bound to occur. Nevertheless, it is still important to plan your food-growing programme sensibly, not only to ensure that you grow the right amounts of various crops, but to make sure that they mature at the best possible time and make maximum use of your land.

Basic requirements
Apart from the need to spend a certain amount of time, energy and money (to pay for seeds, fertilizers and pesticides), the one unalterable factor governing the feasibility of growing vegetables and fruit is the situation and aspect of the garden. Quite simply, if it is sunny then vegetables will generally grow; if shady, overhung by tall trees or shadowed for most of the day by tall buildings, then most vegetables will fail. It is also a heartbreaking task to grow most crops on stony or very light soils, though almost all soils can be improved and with many it is essential if you are to obtain the best results. For general information on soils and their cultivation, see pages 330 to 335; for particular aspects related to food-growing, see page 266.

If your own garden is not suitable for food-growing, it may be possible to find an allotment (see p 47) or part of a large garden that the owner cannot manage. If such a plot is available, it is as well to consider carefully the pros and cons before committing yourself. Are water and storage facilities available, is access easy and is the plot secure from vandalism? How far is it from your home, and does the state of the surrounding plots or garden suggest that weeds and soil-borne pests and diseases may be a problem?

How big is the plot available? With good management, intensive cropping and average soil conditions, a plot of 165 to 185 m² (1,800 to 2,000 sq ft) in an area with moderate winters and summers, such as the southern half of Britain, can supply all the vegetable needs of a family of two adults and two children, with the exception of maincrop potatoes and possibly winter greens. Somewhat more space will be needed if harsh winter conditions shorten the growing season, and with even greater space a fruit orchard is a possibility. Or you may be able to be completely self-sufficient in food – possibly with some to spare, which can be sold to friends – but of course this demands more time and labour. (This can, however, be saved by buying or hiring a mechanical cultivator; see p 377.)

Even with an allotment or similar plot, there are crops that it is best to grow close at hand, in your own garden – salad vegetables, for example – or where you can be sure that you have security of tenure for a considerable number of years, as with fruit trees and even soft fruit bushes. On the other hand, even the

smallest patio garden can provide some fruit and vegetables if it is sunny (see below).

Where the area cultivated is not too big, no elaborate equipment is needed to grow your own food. It is worth buying good quality tools of the right size and weight for easy use, however, as food-growing undoubtedly involves more cultivation than most other aspects of gardening. Apart from a spade and a digging fork, you will need a rake, long- and short-handled hoes, a trowel, a garden line and a wheelbarrow. You will eventually find it well worth while to invest in cloches, one or more frames and possibly a greenhouse (see p 380), as these greatly increase your scope and growing season where frosts occur.

Siting and layout
If you decide to grow vegetables in your own garden, you should consider a number of factors when siting the vegetable plot and planning its layout. Maximum light is essential for at least part of the day, and shelter will be necessary in cool climates or if the site is exposed to winds or draughts blowing around the side of buildings. The best site is one that the sun reaches and warms early in the day; shade is less important in the late afternoon. Avoid overhanging trees; they not only create shade, but their roots compete for food and water and drips from their branches damage the soil structure and cause capping.

Most people prefer to keep the vegetable garden out of sight of the main living rooms, and to be able to use the part of the garden nearest to the house for recreation, but a well-planned and well-maintained plot

Kitchen garden layout
The way you lay out your fruit and vegetable garden obviously depends on the size and shape of the land available, but it makes good sense to organize the space in a logical, orderly way. Here, three main vegetable plots are planted according to the three-year planting plan shown at the top of page 265. They are laid out with rows running north-south for even lighting. The central utility area has a potting shed, compost bins, greenhouse, cold frames and a hard-surfaced working area. To the left of this is the fruit garden, with one part devoted to tree and bush fruits and cordon apples. The other has raspberries and grape vines, permanently planted herbs, globe artichokes and rhubarb, and also a row of strawberries (which will have to be removed after about three years to avoid virus diseases). Blackberries and loganberries are trained along the side fence and fan-trained peaches on the sunny rear wall.

should not look unsightly. It can be both screened and sheltered by low ranch-style fencing, by fruit bushes or by shrub borders. Trained fruit trees – such as espaliers and cordons (see p374) – make a particularly attractive 'frame' without casting too much shade. Fast-growing hedges have invasive roots which rob vegetables of food and water, but sunken vertical barriers of galvanized steel or even thick plastic sheeting (or over-lapping plastic fertilizer sacks) inserted verti-cally to a depth of 60 cm (2 ft) will at least reduce the problem. Whatever type of screen-ing you use, take care to avoid creating shade or frost pockets (see p339).

Distance from the kitchen is no problem in a small or moderate-sized garden, but good paths (or stepping stones set in grass) are needed to provide clean, dry access in winter. A water supply is essential; if this is taken by hose from an outlet in or near the house, an uncluttered route will save time and temper. Site the compost heap or bins (see p334) near the vegetable plot, as much of the raw ma-terial for composting will come from there and much of the finished compost will be re-turned. It similarly makes good sense to posi-tion the shed and utility area, and frames and greenhouse if you have them, nearby.

Rectangular plots and an orderly, well-planned planting scheme look attractive and are efficient. Ideally, try to provide three or four equal-sized plots for crop-rotations of the main vegetables (see p262) and a fourth or fifth plot for long-term crops such as asparagus, rhubarb, mint and other perennial herbs (though many of these can be grown in the flower garden). If your garden is too small for separate sections, try to follow the same principles by changing the positions of the various crops in an orderly way year by year.

On sloping sites, the rows of vegetables should run up and down the slope, not across it, as this can result in frost pockets. Other-wise, the rows should run north and south as this gives even illumination to the crop. Some crops are better grown in blocks than in single rows. These include sweet corn, which is wind-pollinated; self-blanching celery, which can be surrounded by low boards to make a rough frame to assist blanching; and marrows, cucumbers and melons, which require beds of well-rotted organic matter and can also be grown on the remains of a compost heap.

Strawberries, which should be replanted every two to three years, can be included in the scheme of crop-rotation, but raspberries and other soft fruits need a separate plot (which should be in a part of the garden least likely to suffer late spring frosts, when the plants are flowering). Apart from the use of cordons or espaliers as attractive screens, it is better to site fruit trees elsewhere in the gar-den, where they can form decorative features. Make full use of fences to grow cane fruits such as blackberries and loganberries, and in cool regions use sheltered sunny walls to grow peaches, nectarines and figs. Where summers are warm and sunny, grape vines, Chinese gooseberries and passion fruit can be trained on walls and pergolas. Cob-nuts and filberts can be used to give privacy or to screen parts of the garden, but are not worth growing where squirrels are a pest.

Utilizing limited space

Even a paved patio or courtyard can be used to grow fruit and vegetables if it is sunny. Tubs, pots and growing bags of prepared growing mixture (see p117) enable a wide range of crops to be grown. The enthusiast can even use hydroponic methods of culture, in which the plants grow in containers of a com-pletely sterile 'soil' consisting of sand, ver-miculite or baked clay nodules, and nutrients are given in the form of balanced fertilizers dissolved in water.

Vegetables and herbs can be included in the flower garden. Parsley, chives, chervil, purple and green basil, globe artichokes, cardoons, golden and purple sage, lovage, angelica and borage all fit easily into the flower borders, and thymes and marjoram in paving, dry walls or rock gardens. Carrots, beetroot, Swiss chard (seakale beet) with broad white or (in 'Ruby Chard') scarlet stalks are both decora-tive and edible, and there are decorative vari-eties of cabbage and kale (borecole). 'Salad-bowl' lettuces – the pick-and-come-again type – can also be included in a well-prepared flower bed, and rhubarb could be grown among other 'foliage' plants.

A wigwam of canes will support runner beans at the back of a flower border to give attractive scarlet or white flowers and a useful crop. Purple-podded peas and purple-podded climbing French beans can be grown in the same way. However, an extremely important point to remember if you include vegetables with flowers, is that they need even better soil preparation and care in thinning and feeding than in more conventional settings.

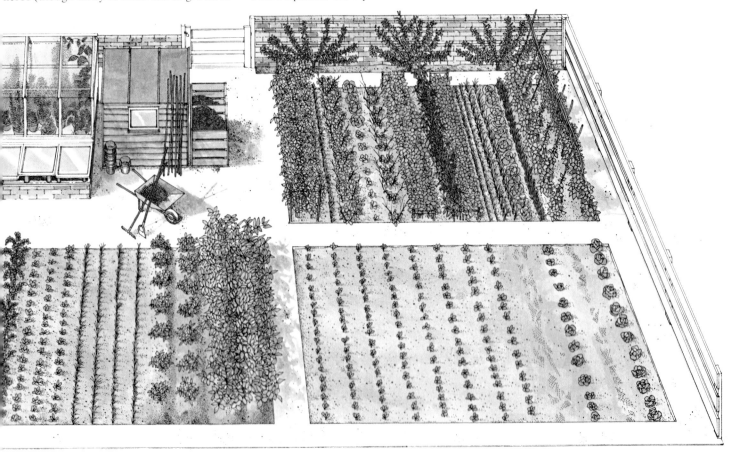

Planning your food-growing

What you grow in your vegetable and fruit garden obviously depends on what you want to grow, what the space and time available will enable you to produce, and what your soil and climatic conditions will permit. But very many gardeners fail to sit down and plan their growing programme logically. The result is that they have periods of glut and shortage, and they make poor use of their land's productive capacity.

The main climatic factors are the severity of winter cold, average summer temperatures and the period free from frost (see p 268). Where severe winters occur, full use must be made of summer and autumn crops to stock the freezer, and even in milder areas leaf crops may be so severely attacked in winter by pigeons and various mammals that winter crops are not worth growing. If possible, invest in a few cloches (see p 269) or a cold frame (see p 380) to extend both ends of the growing season.

Consider which vegetables are usually cheap and easily obtainable at particular seasons. Maincrop potatoes require a good deal of attention and on some heavy soils tunnelling of the tubers by black keeled slugs causes so much loss that the ground this crop occupies could be far better used. Winter broccoli and late cauliflowers occupy the land for a very long time; calabrese and autumn cauliflowers can be grown more rapidly, with more certainty of success, and both freeze well. Late cabbages, Brussels sprouts and swedes are of good quality grown commercially, and once again, where space is limited, other, more unusual crops can be substituted in the garden.

It is important to plan your crops to avoid over-production at one time and shortages at another, and to take into account holiday plans. Unless you do this on paper long before it is time to sow the first seeds you will be tempted irresistibly in the warm spring days to buy seeds on impulse and to sow them in any available space; as a result, the garden will be filled with a glut of lettuces and other unfreezable salad crops and no space will be left for later sowings to provide a succession.

Work out your approximate needs for various crops (taking into account storage or freezing capacity). Then, with the help of the information given in the chart on page 264, sow only as much of each as you need – or just a small surplus, to allow for losses. Pelleted seeds enable you to sow precise numbers of quick-growing salad crops every week or ten days for a succession of pickings. A useful alternative is to buy packets of mixed varieties of radishes, lettuces and some others; these not only mature at different times but also give varied eating.

Catch crops and intercropping

Most people are eager to start in the spring, but they do not take advantage of ground left empty when early crops are cleared and before later ones take their place; this can be used for 'catch crops'. Quick-maturing 'early' cultivars of peas, carrots, beet and salad crops, which are normally sown earlier in the season,

are suitable, as these will give a crop before it is time to sow or plant out longer-maturing types. Simply clear the old crop, hoe or lightly fork over the ground, firm, and rake in a base dressing of a balanced compound fertilizer before sowing. In areas with hot summers you must, however, take into account the maximum temperatures that certain crops will withstand (see p 268).

Endive, Chinese cabbage, spinach beet, seakale beet (Swiss chard) and 'Sugar Loaf' chicory (French or Belgian endive) are all sown soon after midsummer for use in autumn. The chicory will stand some frost but the endive should be protected from frost and wet weather by cloches in autumn. A few plants can be blanched as required by covering the cloches with black plastic sheeting. 'Witloof' chicory will provide salads in midwinter; sow in early summer, lift the roots in autumn, store in a cool place in sand or peat and force a few roots at a time in pots or tubs of sand or peat in a warm dark place.

Catch crops can also be taken after the ground has been prepared but before it is needed for late-planted maincrop vegetables

– for example, savoys and late broccoli – especially if an early start is made with cloches so that you can be sure that the catch crop will be mature by the time you need the ground.

Intercropping is another method of getting 'double mileage' out of the space you have available. It involves using the space that must be left between the rows of taller vegetables such as peas, runner beans and tomatoes by sowing rows of short, quick-growing salads or roots for pulling young – for example, lettuces, radishes, summer spinach, the shorter carrot cultivars and early turnips. In the same way, you can use the excavated earth between celery trenches to grow lettuces or courgettes (zucchini) (see p 287). It is particularly important to work out your cropping programme carefully when using intercrops, allowing the proper spacing between the rows and marking out the plan accurately on the ground.

Rotation of crops

However small your vegetable plot, never grow the same crop in the same place two years running, except in the case of the semi-permanent types like asparagus, rhubarb and

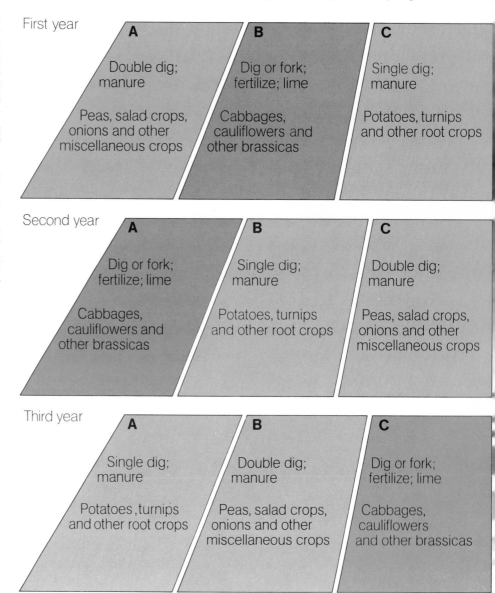

First year

A	B	C
Double dig; manure	Dig or fork; fertilize; lime	Single dig; manure
Peas, salad crops, onions and other miscellaneous crops	Cabbages, cauliflowers and other brassicas	Potatoes, turnips and other root crops

Second year

A	B	C
Dig or fork; fertilize; lime	Single dig; manure	Double dig; manure
Cabbages, cauliflowers and other brassicas	Potatoes, turnips and other root crops	Peas, salad crops, onions and other miscellaneous crops

Third year

A	B	C
Single dig; manure	Double dig; manure	Dig or fork; fertilize; lime
Potatoes, turnips and other root crops	Peas, salad crops, onions and other miscellaneous crops	Cabbages, cauliflowers and other brassicas

artichokes. Soil-borne pests and diseases will build up, and the amounts of plant foods in the soil will become unbalanced.

The system of ordered, pre-planned swapping-around of crop positions is called crop-rotation. At its very simplest, it can consist of alternating crops needing deep cultivation and manure with the leaf and root crops year by year. If you have enough space, the best system for the amateur gardener is a three-year rotation, because crops can be divided into three main groups according to their needs and each group can be given one-third of the total plot area.

Peas, beans, onions, leeks, celery, tomatoes, marrows, sweet corn and some others benefit from deep cultivation and plenty of organic manure or garden compost. Root crops for storage need single digging and fertilizer but not manure (which causes the roots to fork). Brassicas – cabbages, Brussels sprouts, cauliflowers, broccoli and their relatives – need firm soil with fertilizer and sufficient lime to reduce the risk of club root disease. By alternating these three groups of crops, not only do each get their ideal condi-

tions, but you also save yourself work, because it is only the 'miscellaneous' group that needs the ground to be double dug (see p 334); by moving these on a three-year rotation, the whole plot will be double dug once every three years and will be similarly limed (for the brassicas) if necessary. In the fourth year, the crops once again occupy their first-year positions.

If you want to grow quantities of potatoes, the system can be modified to spread over four years, the plot being divided into four parts, one of which is devoted to potatoes. Here, the whole plot is double dug once every four years. A four-year rotation may also be more appropriate if your family is much more fond of peas, beans, onions, sweet corn, salad crops and so on than of either root vegetables or brassicas. In this case, you can sub-divide the 'miscellaneous' group into peas and beans (the legumes, whose roots contain bacteria that put nitrogen into the soil) and the others. Each of these sub-groups can then be given a quarter of the site, the remainder being equally divided between roots and brassicas. In this scheme, you double dig half the total

area – the legume and miscellaneous beds – each year. Alternatively, a three-year cropping scheme is given on page 265 that omits main root crops and winter greens, and puts the emphasis on crops for freezing; this may be better where space is limited, since a four-year rotation clearly reduces the size of the individual plots.

Whatever system you use, try to arrange the order in which the crops occupy the ground year by year so that they gain the maximum advantage from what went before. For example, if you grow brassicas in ground previously occupied by legumes, they will benefit from the nitrogen-enrichment caused by the latter's root bacteria. Roots or potatoes can follow the brassicas.

The diagrams on these pages illustrate three systems of crop-rotation, based on three- and four-year cycles, in broad outline. On page 265 you will find more detailed suggested planting plans based on three-year rotation schemes, and including suggestions for catch crops, that will supply an average small family with a large proportion of its vegetable needs from a plot of moderate size.

Three-year crop-rotation
left Divide the plot into three equal parts, A, B and C. For the first year, A is double dug and manured for peas, beans, onions and other miscellaneous crops; B is single dug on heavy soils or forked over on light soils in the autumn, limed if necessary and left to settle through the winter to give the firm bed needed by brassicas; C is single dug for root crops; both B and C receive a base dressing of compound fertilizer before sowing or planting out seedlings.
In the second year, brassicas occupy bed A to take advantage of the nitrogenous foods 'fixed' by the previous year's peas and beans and also the residues of manure. The root crops move to bed B, which is single dug, and bed C is double dug for the miscellaneous crops. In the third year, the rotation is completed, brassicas moving to bed C, roots to A and the others to B, which is double dug and manured.
In areas with mild winters, the spring cabbages planted in autumn to follow the beans in the miscellaneous bed overwinter to reappear in what becomes the brassica bed the following spring. Other overwintering crops, such as leeks and purple sprouting broccoli, should be carefully sited at the end (or side) of the bed to avoid interrupting the continuity of digging. The time when these will be cleared is taken into account in planning the subsequent crops.
In each individual bed, root crops always follow brassicas, which follow miscellaneous crops.

Four-year crop-rotation
Here the plot is divided into four equal areas, A, B, C and D. If you want to devote one whole area to maincrop potatoes, follow the plan below. Only the first year is shown, when peas, beans, onions, salads and other miscellaneous crops are planted in A, brassicas in B, potatoes in C and other root crops in D. In the second year, put brassicas in A, potatoes in B, other roots in C and miscellaneous crops in D. In the third year, potatoes move to A, other roots to B, miscellaneous crops to C and brassicas to D. The fourth year completes the cycle with root crops in A, miscellaneous crops in B, brassicas in C and potatoes in D. The sequence of crops in each bed is: miscellaneous – brassicas – potatoes – other roots.
If you want fewer root crops but more of the miscellaneous group, you can divide the plot in four in the same way but follow the scheme shown bottom. In year one, plant legumes (peas and beans) in bed A.

brassicas in B, onions, salad crops and other miscellaneous crops in C and root vegetables in D. The second year, brassicas move to A, miscellaneous crops to B, roots to C and legumes to D. The rotation pattern continues in a similar way in the third and fourth years, so that the sequence of cropping in each bed is: legumes – brassicas – miscellaneous – roots. In any of these cropping schemes you can start in any 'year', but thereafter maintain the sequence suggested.

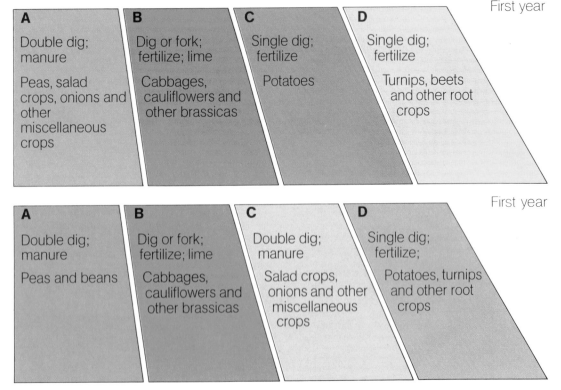

First year

A	B	C	D
Double dig; manure	Dig or fork; fertilize; lime	Single dig; fertilize	Single dig; fertilize
Peas, salad crops, onions and other miscellaneous crops	Cabbages, cauliflowers and other brassicas	Potatoes	Turnips, beets and other root crops

First year

A	B	C	D
Double dig; manure	Dig or fork; fertilize; lime	Double dig; manure	Single dig; fertilize;
Peas and beans	Cabbages, cauliflowers and other brassicas	Salad crops, onions and other miscellaneous crops	Potatoes, turnips and other root crops

Planning your food-growing (continued)

Vegetables for continuity of supply

	Crop*	Sowing or planting season	Harvesting season	Storage method if not consumed	Typical yield† per 3 m (10 ft) row
Spring and early summer crops to overwinter (in moderate) climates)	Broad beans	Late autumn	Early summer	Freeze	6 kg (12 lb; double row)
	Cabbage (spring)	Summer	Spring	Cut as needed	4 kg (8 lb)
	Lettuces	Early autumn	Early spring	Not storable	10 heads
	Onions	Late summer	Midsummer	Cool, dry place	2 kg (4 lb)
	Peas	Late autumn	Late spring	Freeze	5 kg (10 lb)
	Spinach beet (perpetual spinach)	Summer	Winter; spring	Pick as needed	4 kg (8 lb)
	Spring greens	Midsummer	Winter; early spring	Cut as needed	3 kg (6 lb)
	Spring (salad) onions	Early autumn	Early spring	Pull as needed	1 kg (2 lb)
	Turnip tops	Early autumn	Spring	Cut as needed	2 kg (4 lb)
Summer crops for consumption or storage	Artichokes (globe)	Perennial	Summer	Can be frozen	32 heads
	Asparagus	Perennial	Late spring; early summer	Freeze	4 kg (8 lb)
	Aubergines (eggplant)	Early spring‡	Summer	Freeze	3 kg (6 lb)
	Beetroot	From mid-spring	Summer; autumn	In sand; freeze; pickle	4 kg (8 lb)
	Broad beans	Early spring	Summer	Freeze	7 kg (15 lb)
	Broccoli (green; calabrese)	Spring	Late summer; autumn	Freeze	4 kg (8 lb)
	Cabbage (summer; autumn)	Spring	Summer; early autumn	Cut as needed	5 kg (10 lb)
	Carrots	From early spring	From early summer	In sand; freeze young	2 to 4 kg (4 to 8 lb)
	Cauliflowers (summer)	Late winter‡; spring	Summer	Freeze	5 heads
	Chinese cabbage	Early summer	Early autumn	Not storable	3 kg (6 lb)
	Chicory ('Witloof')	Late spring	From autumn	In sand; force as needed	10 chicons
	Courgettes (zucchini)	Late spring‡	Summer	Freeze	7 kg (15 lb)
	Cucumbers	Spring‡	Summer; early autumn	Not storable	14 kg (30 lb)
	Fennel (Florence)	Spring	Late summer	Cut as required	10 heads
	French beans	From late spring	Summer; early autumn	Freeze; dry	4 kg (8 lb)
	Kohlrabi	Spring; summer	From early summer	In peat	15 stems
	Lettuces	Spring; summer	Summer; autumn	Not storable	10 heads
	Lima beans	Early summer	Early autumn	Dry	2 kg (4 lb)
	Marrows; summer squashes	Late spring‡	Summer; early autumn	Cool, dry place	14 kg (30 lb)
	Melons	Late spring‡	Early autumn	Not usually storable	8 fruits
	Onions	Spring	Late summer	Cool, dry place	5 kg (10 lb)
	Peas	Spring	Summer	Freeze	5 kg (10 lb)
	Peppers (red; green)	Spring‡	Late summer	Freeze	3 kg (6 lb)
	Potatoes	Spring	Summer; autumn	Cool place	10 kg (22 lb; maincrop)
	Pumpkins; winter squashes	Late spring‡	Autumn	Cool, dry place	7 kg (15 lb)
	Radishes (summer)	From late winter	Late spring; summer; autumn	Eat immediately	2.5 kg (5 lb)
	Runner beans	Late spring; early summer	Late summer; autumn	Freeze; dry; salt	20 kg (45 lb; double row)
	Shallots	Late winter	Summer	Cool, dry place	3 kg (6 lb)
	Spinach (summer)	Spring to midsummer	Early summer to autumn	Freeze	1.5 kg (3 lb)
	Spinach beet (perpetual spinach)	Spring	Summer; autumn	Pick as needed	3 kg (6 lb)
	Spring (salad) onions	Spring; summer	From early summer	Eat immediately	10 bunches
	Sweet corn	Late spring‡	From late summer	Freeze	12 to 20 cobs
	Tomatoes	Spring‡	From midsummer	Not storable when ripe	10 kg (22 lb)
	Turnips (early)	From early spring	From late spring	In sand or straw	4 kg (8 lb)
Crops maturing in late autumn and winter (late types hardy to −10°C [14°F])	Artichokes (Jerusalem)	Spring	From late autumn	In sand; in ground	14 kg (30 lb)
	Broccoli (purple; white)	Late spring	Midwinter to spring	Cut as needed	5 kg (10 lb)
	Brussels sprouts	Spring	Autumn; winter	Freeze	5 kg (10 lb)
	Cabbage (winter; savoy)	Early summer	Late autumn; winter	Cut as needed	5 to 6 kg (10 to 12 lb)
	Cauliflowers (autumn; winter)	Spring	Autumn; winter; spring	Freeze	5 kg (10 lb)
	Celeriac	Spring‡	Autumn	In sand; in ground	4 kg (8 lb)
	Celery	Spring‡	Autumn; early winter	Cut as needed	5 kg (10 lb)
	Chicory ('Sugar Loaf')	Summer	Autumn; winter	Cut as needed	10 heads
	Endive (late)	Summer	Autumn; winter	Cut as needed	8 heads
	Kale	Late spring	Winter; early spring	Cut as needed	4 kg (8 lb)
	Leeks	Spring	Autumn; winter; early spring	Lift as needed	5 kg (10 lb)
	Parsnips	Spring	Winter	Lift as needed	5 kg (10 lb)
	Radishes (winter)	Summer	From mid-autumn	Lift as needed; in sand	3 kg (6 lb)
	Salsify	Spring	Autumn	In sand	2.5 kg (5 lb)
	Scorzonera	Spring	Autumn	In sand	2.5 kg (5 lb)
	Seakale beet (Swiss chard)	Summer	Autumn	Cut as needed	3 kg (6 lb)
	Spinach (winter)	Late summer	Autumn to early spring	Cut as needed	3 kg (6 lb)
	Swedes (rutabagas)	Early summer	From mid-autumn	In ground	5 kg (10 lb)
	Turnips (maincrop)	Midsummer	From mid-autumn	In sand	6 kg (12 lb)

For suitable varieties, see individual articles; †these figures will vary widely according to soil, climate, variety and other factors; ‡under glass in cool climates, transplanting as necessary; dates refer to moderate climates with some frost – different dates may apply in warm climates

Vegetable planting schemes
right Two alternative schemes for efficient land use, both based on a three-year crop-rotation. The one at the top of the page corresponds to that illustrated on page 263, with the site divided into three equal-sized plots devoted to root crops, brassicas and miscellaneous crops respectively. The lower scheme concentrates on crops for immediate eating and freezing, and omits maincrop root vegetables and winter greens.
In both cases, the diagrams represent a combination of space and time. The vertical arrangement, although not strictly to scale, shows the spacing of crops on the ground. (For details of planting distances, see the individual articles later in this chapter.) The horizontal scale is one of time, so that reading across the diagrams shows the sequence of crops in a particular piece of ground over a period of three years. (For example, the bars at the top of the first box in the upper diagram indicate that runner beans occupy this strip of ground from early spring to early autumn, followed by spring cabbages.) At the same time, since each box represents one year's planting for a bed, the diagrams show the overall planting pattern at any one time. (S/b = seed bed.)

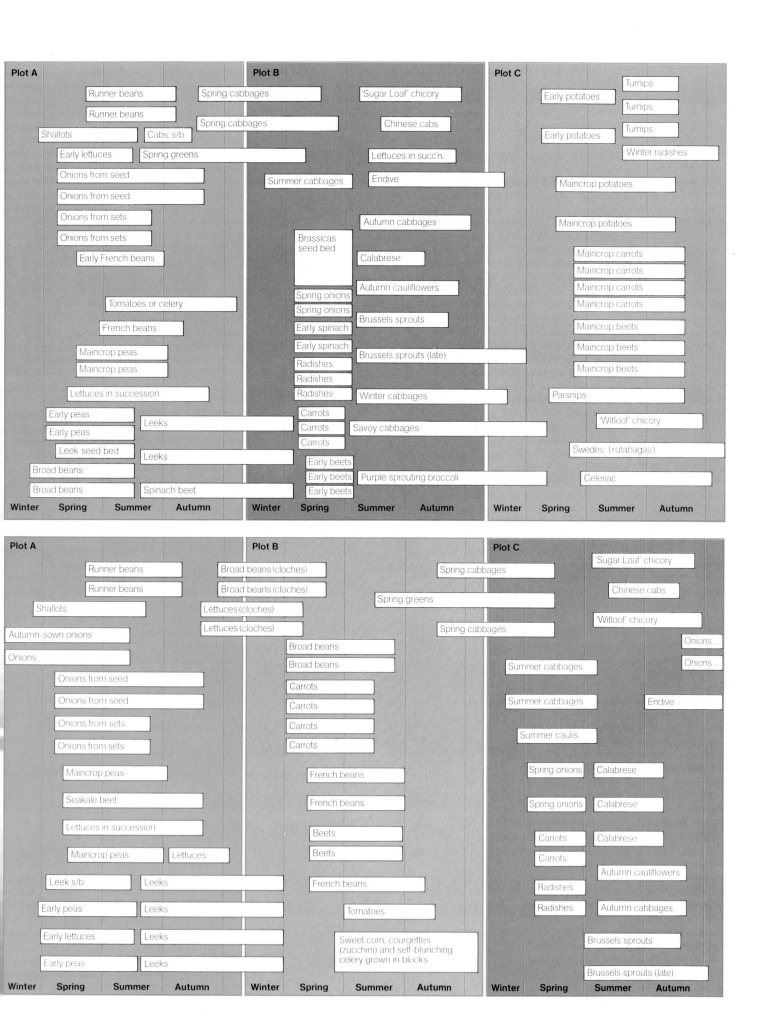

The fundamentals of food-growing

The growing of food crops – particularly vegetables – certainly demands closer day-to-day (or, at any rate, week-by-week) attention and more work than growing most kinds of decorative plants, but nothing especially difficult is involved. Much of the basic information and many of the techniques described in chapter 5 (beginning on page 328) are applicable to food-growing. The basic difference is, perhaps, that every stage of growth, right up to final harvesting of the crop, is critical to success with vegetables, whereas – barring serious accidents – permanent decorative plants can often recover from setbacks, even if they do give a poor show for a while.

Climatic and other factors are extremely important, and are examined on page 268, but the basis of successful vegetable-growing is your soil, its cultivation and the sowing or planting of your crops and their immediate after-care. The ideal soil for growing vegetables and fruits is a mixture of clay, sand and organic matter that forms a rich medium loam having a pH value of 6.5 – that is, just on the acid side of neutrality – and is well drained, easy to work, not too stony, quick to warm in the spring, yet retentive of plant foods and moisture in the summer.

Very, very few people are fortunate enough to begin with a soil like this, yet provided that drainage is adequate or can be improved (see p 333), there are few soils that cannot support at least some crops.

Light and heavy soils

The articles beginning on page 330 discuss in detail the characteristics of various types of soil and what can be done to improve them. To simplify and summarize the situation as far as growing food crops is concerned, soils can be divided into two basic types. Light soils drain quickly, are easy to work, warm easily in spring and are good for early crops. On the other hand, fertilizers and lime both wash out easily, so these soils tend to be both acid and 'hungry'. Basic treatment consists of digging in plenty of composted organic matter, mulching thickly, feeding little and often, and liming more frequently than average.

Heavy, clayey soils retain fertilizers and lime, and are potentially rich; they hold water longer than light soils and, in fact, may drain too slowly. They are difficult to work and warm up slowly in spring, so they are unsuitable for early crops. It is essential to time cultivations carefully, never working the soil when it is wet or compaction may occur. Dig early in autumn and leave rough for the weather to break down the lumps. Dig in well-rotted organic matter. If acid, they need heavier dressings of lime than sandy soils but they need it less frequently.

Acidity and liming

The acidity of your soil has an important bearing on crop-growing. (For information on testing for acidity, see page 332.) Most fruits will tolerate slightly more acid conditions than most vegetables. Among the most acid-tolerant crops, which will grow in soil with a pH value as low as 5, are apples, aubergines (eggplants), blackberries, cucumbers, currants, figs, gooseberries, grapes, marrows and squashes, potatoes, raspberries, rhubarb, strawberries, tomatoes and turnips. Most other crops will tolerate a pH value of 6 or even 5.5 in many cases.

Where acidity is too great for the crops you plan to grow, this can be corrected by liming, which has the effect of making many plant foods more easily available to crops. Free lime in the soil also reduces the risk of club root disease of brassicas, such as cabbages, cauliflowers and Brussels sprouts, but it increases scab disease of potatoes. For this reason, you should never lime ground before growing potatoes. A system of crop-rotation (see p 262) enables you to lime the vegetable plot in sections year by year, immediately before growing brassicas, so that the whole plot receives lime once every three or four years; this should be adequate unless acidity is a serious problem.

At the other end of the scale, most crops will grow well in soil with a pH as high as 7.5, but an excess of lime causes deficiencies of trace elements (see p 352) in some crops – for example, blackcurrants, raspberries, toma-

toes and turnips. Blueberries require exceptionally acid conditions, with a pH value of around 4.5 to 5, and on many soils you must grow them in containers of a special peaty growing mixture (see p 126); they will tolerate no lime and are even damaged if watered with hard water. Except in this extreme case, you can help to redress the balance where alkalinity is a problem – and a soil pH higher than 8 is rare – by using sulphate of ammonia whenever a nitrogenous fertilizer is needed (see p 352) and by using peat to supply bulky organic matter. It should never be necessary to use lime on chalky soils.

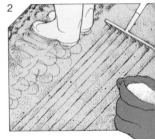

Soil preparation and planting

Free drainage is essential for crop plants, so the first need is to break up any soil pan (see p 332) whether conventional systems of cultivation or the 'no digging' method is followed. The latter relies on heavy mulches of organic material, such as garden compost, in which the crop is sown or planted. It is suitable for light soils, but is less successful on heavy ones; tests have shown that after some years there is a marked deterioration in crop yields in an undug plot compared with one that is dug conventionally.

As outlined on page 263 in connection with crop-rotation, double digging – in which the soil is cultivated to twice the depth of a spade's blade and organic material is dug into the lower spit – is only necessary for crops other than brassicas and root crops. For both of these, single digging is adequate or, in the case of cabbages on light soil, no more than light forking of the soil. Both digging techniques are described on page 334. In both cases, the soil should be allowed to settle before sowing – on heavy soils, preferably from autumn to spring. Then, when conditions are dry, the bed can be trodden firm, raked level to a fine tilth and drills taken out for sowing seed as described on page 344.

Broadcast sowing (scattering of the seeds) is inefficient, as weed control is so difficult. The individual articles on crops starting on page 276 suggests suitable spacing for the drills, which is governed by the height of the crop and the need for access. Wide spacing is wasteful and encourages weed growth, but too narrow spacing causes overcrowding and poor yields. Sweet corn is one of the few crops best grown in square blocks rather than rows, as this facilitates wind-pollination. Many gardeners favour growing a number of crops, such as squashes, cucumbers and melons, on shallow mounds over holes filled with soil enriched or layered with well-rotted manure or garden compost (see illustration).

Making a hill or mound

A good way of growing cucumbers, melons, marrows, squashes, pumpkins and some other crops is on low hills or mounds, spaced 1.25 to 3 m (4 to 10 ft) apart, depending on crop and variety. (Bush marrows and courgettes [zucchini] can be grown more closely.) Usually, about three plants are grown on each mound, each trailing in a different direction. Where seeds are sown directly, place eight to ten in a circle and later thin out the weakest of the seedlings.

To make a mound, 1 dig a hole 30 cm (12 in) deep and 60 cm (2 ft) across. Loosen the bottom with a fork, then 2 add a layer of well-rotted compost or manure 10 to 15 cm (4 to 6 in) deep. Finally, put back enough of the excavated soil to form a gentle

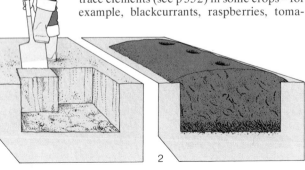

hill that is about 10 cm (4 in) higher at its highest point than the surrounding ground. For marrows and squashes, enrich the returned soil with one part well-rotted manure to three parts soil. The mound system ensures good drainage and plentiful food for the plants, but watering must be adequate.

Routine care

Successful vegetable-growing depends on regular care and attention to detail. Any checks to growth in the early stages, especially those caused by drought and starvation (which may result from overcrowding), will cause premature ripening and hardening of the tissues, and the plant may never recover. (This is especially true of seedling brassicas.) With few exceptions (such as pickling onions and peas sown the correct distance apart), all

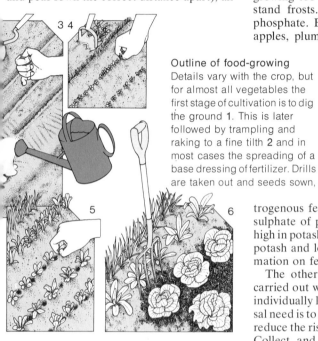

Outline of food-growing
Details vary with the crop, but for almost all vegetables the first stage of cultivation is to dig the ground 1. This is later followed by trampling and raking to a fine tilth 2 and in most cases the spreading of a base dressing of fertilizer. Drills are taken out and seeds sown, covered and watered in 3. Vital processes in the early stages of growth are watering, weeding and thinning the seedlings 4. A second thinning 5 is almost always needed, but these thinnings may be eatable. With many crops, mulching 6 is desirable, plus further feeding and watering as needed.

seedlings must be thinned as soon as possible to 2.5 cm (1 in) apart, or where seeds are sown in stations the weakest seedling at each must be removed. As soon as the seedlings touch again further thinning is necessary, but you can use these thinnings in salads or soups in the case of beets, carrots, onions and some other crops.

In dry weather, watering is essential and this should be a generous soaking, not a casual sprinkling which only brings the roots to the surface. A large can of water is needed for each 3 m (10 ft) row. If possible, water in the evening when the rate of evaporation is lower, but daytime watering will not hurt the crop if you apply the water generously. Mulching taller crops with a generous layer of garden compost, well-rotted manure or peat will help to retain soil moisture, and is essential to keep the roots of crops like tomatoes cool; but it should be done when the ground has been well moistened by rain. Similarly mulch fruit trees and bushes, as any soil disturbance will damage the roots. Black plastic sheeting can also be used as a mulch between rows of vegetables (see p 356); it will suppress weeds as well as retain moisture.

Take advantage of warm weather to feed the crops with a compound liquid fertilizer or manure; you can apply these with a dilutor attachment on the garden hose (see p 353). In very dry conditions, foliar feeding is safer than applying fertilizers to the ground, but soluble fertilizers can be used as top-dressings if a

sprinkler is available or you can water them in by hand. Set the sprinkler, if it is adjustable, to deliver small droplets of water to avoid causing capping of the soil.

In early spring, leaf crops benefit from nitrogenous fertilizers, but later in the summer potash is particularly necessary – especially in dull, overcast summers. Such crops as tomatoes need potash to ripen the fruits, but it also hardens off late leaf crops which are growing too vigorously, to help them withstand frosts. Root crops particularly need phosphate. Early in the year, feed cooking apples, plums and blackcurrants with a nitrogenous fertilizer; later feed all fruit with sulphate of potash or a compound fertilizer high in potash or a compound fertilizer high in potash and low in nitrogen. For more information on fertilizers, see page 352.

The other routine tasks that need to be carried out with particular crops are detailed individually later in this chapter. One universal need is to maintain cleanliness, for this will reduce the risk of attack by pests and diseases. Collect and compost all fallen and dying leaves, young annual weeds and so on, but burn any diseased material. A short-handled hand, or onion, hoe is convenient to use between the crops if you have no trouble bending; otherwise, use a long-handled 'push-pull' Dutch hoe or a draw hoe. Watch for any abnormal growth, discolouration of leaves or wilting of crops, as this frequently indicates attack by pests or disease. Lift suspect plants and examine the roots for grubs or root flies. Watch for attack by aphids and other leaf pests. Spray immediately, and on fruit trees use a tar oil wash when the trees are dormant in winter to destroy aphids' eggs. For more information on fruit and vegetable pests, diseases and disorders, see pages 358 to 368.

Protection from birds
1 Black cotton criss-crossed over the seed-bed is vital for the protection of many seedling vegetables; some gardeners combine this with bird-scarers ranging from the traditional scarecrow to spinning discs of propeller-shaped bright metal.
2 Fruit cages are excellent though somewhat expensive for protecting bush fruits; the mesh should be small enough to keep out birds but big enough to let pollinating insects pass.
3 Moderate-sized fruit trees can be draped with nylon nets.

Protection from wildlife

It is not only insects and similar small pests that may ruin your crop-raising efforts. In severe winters, hungry rabbits, hares and deer may damage fruit trees and bushes by stripping the bark. Perforated tree guards will protect the trees from these attacks, but in very cold areas it is also advisable to protect the bark of young trees from severe frost, which may cause splitting. Binding the trees with straw or dry bracken and dry hessian will give the necessary protection. Do not use plastic sheeting, as the bark must breathe.

Pigeons can devastate winter leaf crops such as cabbages and kale, while some birds may strip the buds of fruit trees and bushes in early spring. Unpalatable bird-deterrent sprays are available, while fine nylon netting draped over the tree or bush will prevent the birds settling. You must protect soft fruit crops with netting held well above the bushes. You can use permanent fruit cages, but a temporary structure can be made from strong bamboo canes joined by perforated rubber balls available from garden centres. Drape netting over the frame, pegging it down to the ground all round the edge, or some birds will get under. This is particularly useful for strawberries. Remove the netting in winter to allow birds to feed on harmful pests. Black cotton thread stretched cobweb-fashion across seedling vegetables will protect them from birds.

Moles, rabbits and other burrowing animals can cause havoc in the vegetable garden. Professionals can be called in to gas the animals underground, or they can be shot, but most amateurs would prefer to use deterrents. Chemical rabbit-deterrents are available, while mothballs (naphthalene balls) put down mole-runs distract the moles' sense of smell, by which they hunt for worms. Apart from shooting, the only way to deal with squirrels is to protect vulnerable crops – nuts and fruit, particularly – with netting.

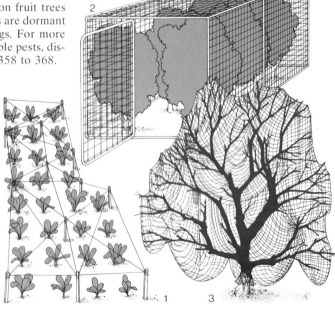

Climate and your crops

The range of food crops that you can grow in your garden depends very largely on climate. The unpredictability of the weather is almost a worldwide joke, but this can have serious consequences for the gardener. One late, unseasonal frost can ruin unprotected crops. Tender plants like tomatoes and cucumbers are most vulnerable, but even with hardy fruit trees flowers or immature fruits can be destroyed, and with them a whole year's crop. The abnormally early onset of cold winter weather or a particularly wet autumn can have an equally devastating effect at the end of the season, by cutting down unharvested crops or by preventing ripening.

In spite of the weather's vagaries, the sensible gardener gets to know the climatic conditions of his garden (which can, as explained in the article on page 338, differ quite markedly from those of gardens only a short distance away, and can even vary within its own confines). Such variations notwithstanding, the overall climatic features of the region in which you live are extremely important, and the information given on the endpapers of this book is designed to give you guidance. Supplement this with information from local weather stations and your own weather records. If you position a maximum and minimum thermometer in your garden – but out of direct sunlight – and record its readings, you will learn a great deal. Learn, too, how to recognize natural signs of weather changes, such as cloud conditions, and regularly listen to broadcast weather forecasts during the critical seasons.

As far as growing vegetables is concerned, the most important climatic factors are temperatures – both winter and summer – the number of frost-free days, day length and light intensity, and rainfall (especially in summer). While there is nothing the gardener can do to alter these (as he can soil conditions), quite a lot can be done to 'cheat' the weather and shield your crops from some of its effects, including the use of frames and similar protection described in this article and by growing in a greenhouse.

Winter conditions
Minimum winter temperatures – both absolute and average – will determine whether or not you can grow many crops outdoors over winter. In areas that experience very severe winters, crops must be grown intensively in the summer and stored in clamps, frost-free stores and freezers for winter use. In areas where winter temperatures do not usually fall below about −8°C (18°F), you can grow hardy vegetables such as cabbages, savoys, Brussels sprouts and purple sprouting broccoli over the winter season. Kale (borecole) and leeks will stand even lower temperatures. Spinach, seakale beet (Swiss chard) and spring hearting cabbages, all planted or sown in autumn, and 'Sugar Loaf' chicory sown in summer, will provide fresh green vegetables from late autumn to spring if the winter is not too cold. But all leaf crops need winter protection with nets where pigeons are a pest.

Day length and light intensity are particu-

larly important when growing winter crops under glass. The day length decreases in winter the farther you are from the equator, and the intensity of the sun's radiation is reduced as it drops lower in the sky. Light intensity is also affected by cloud cover, which is generally greater inland than on the coast, and light is further reduced in areas subject to industrial atmospheric pollution. Keen gardeners facing such problems may supplement daylight with artificial lighting in the greenhouse, particularly when starting seedlings in late winter. Special fluorescent tubes are available under such names as 'Gro-Lux', whose colour (a rosy-purple) has the best effect on plant growth. It is not difficult to arrange a battery of such lamps over one of the benches. Further information can be obtained from manufacturers.

Spring and autumn conditions
The number of frost-free days determines the length of the growing season for tender vegetables. This varies enormously, even in the same district, because of the effect of frost pockets. Low-lying areas act as pools where the heavier freezing air collects. In such areas, site soft fruits and strawberries in the highest part of the garden, and choose late-flowering varieties of apples and other tree fruits (see pp 316 to 322).

Vegetables sown or planted in spring can be destroyed when a severe radiation frost occurs in late spring – usually after very clear warm days, when air humidity is low and there is no cloud cover. When such conditions threaten, you must take precautions to protect young plants. Even a light covering of newspaper or netting will trap warm air around the plants, and watering the soil will allow better conduction of soil warmth to the air around them. Glass cloches (see below) give considerable protection, and this can be increased by covering with paper or straw. But plastic tunnels allow free heat loss by radiation, and by trapping cold air and reducing air movement may actually increase the damage, so give extra insulation. Many American gardeners use waxed-paper cups or plastic 'hot kaps', which are obtainable from garden centres and stores, instead of cloches; they are translucent and can cover individual plants or small clumps.

Sudden thawing is as damaging as freezing, and you should leave all covers on the plants to give some shade after a night frost. If a sprinkler system is available this will give considerable frost protection, especially to soft fruit bushes (see p 354). You can also use this to increase humidity around young plants which have suffered frost damage, and thus reduce the effect of strong sunshine.

Early autumn frosts occur in the same areas, and these will kill tender crops such as melons, marrows and squashes, cucumbers, tomatoes, aubergines, peppers and French and runner beans. It is important in such gardens to get as early a start as possible in spring by using cloches or other devices as described below, as these crops are more easily protected when young than when mature.

Summer conditions
An early start is also needed for a number of crops in areas where summer temperatures are high. This is because in the case of some root and leaf vegetables, the plants bolt into flower instead of forming good roots or heads, while some other crops are unable to set seed. The threshold temperature varies according to the crop, and details of such problems are given with the instructions for growing the individual kinds later in this chapter. In some cases, as with celery, planting is carried out later in the year in warm, frost-free regions, so that it can grow over the cool winter period to be harvested in spring. In the same way, a second sowing of a quick-maturing 'early' variety of such crops as peas may be made in regions experiencing extremes of summer heat and winter cold; if sown after the hottest period of the summer, the crop will have time to produce before winter comes.

Although a wet spring can cause problems with sowing and a wet autumn with ripening and harvesting, rainfall – or, rather, the lack of it – is mainly a summer problem. Very dry summers seriously affect the growth of crops if irrigation is not permitted, but those that succeed will be of good keeping quality. To make the most of winter rainfall, thickly mulch around crops while the soil is still moist in spring, using peat, garden compost or black plastic sheeting (see p 334). Set each plant in a shallow depression to collect moisture, and collect and give the plants as much rainwater as you can. Even bathwater will not harm most crops as long as it is allowed to cool. Do not use water containing chemicals (including bath salts or oils), however.

Aspect and shelter
The aspect of the vegetable garden has a considerable influence on the amount of light and warmth it receives from the sun. Sloping sites that receive maximum sunlight are much 'earlier' than those that receive sunshine for only part of the day. In winter, in northern Europe or northern North America, a site with a 15° (1:4) slope towards the morning sun receives twice as much warmth as a flat site. On exposed sites, wind both cools and causes the plants stress through increased water loss. Screens and shelter belts can increase warmth, but you must take care, especially on a sloping site, not to place them where they will trap pools of cold air. Nor should they shade the crops.

Hedges provide the best type of shelter by filtering the wind, but they take time to establish and compete for water and plant foods, so do not site them too close to the vegetable plot. In small gardens, slatted screens made from 10 cm (4 in) wide timber with 2.5 cm (1 in) gaps (either vertical or horizontal) are effective and attractive; if painted white, they reflect the maximum amount of light. They can also be used to support climbing plants. The effective range of such shelter is ten times the height of the screen, so that a screen 1.5 m (5 ft) high will reduce the force of the wind for 15 m (50 ft)

Light-textured, well-drained soil warms

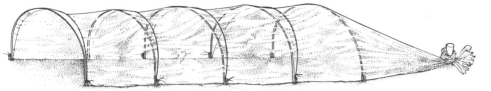

Types of cloches

Cloches consist of two or more sheets of glass or clear rigid plastic that can be placed together to protect crops. The simplest type is tent-shaped 1; it is made of two sheets of horticultural glass 3 mm (⅛ in) thick held together by a metal clip. A barn cloche 2 consists of four sheets of glass held together in a similar way, while others 3 have three pieces. Choose the shape that best suits the plants to be covered; tall cloches are available for covering crops like tomatoes. The ends of the rows and the gaps between the glass provide ventilation, and this can also be adjusted by moving the wires at the top. You should close the ends with panes of glass in cold weather. Rain and irrigation water run off the roof and reach the crop from the sides. The drier and warmer air conditions inside in winter enable plants to survive much lower temperatures than they could in the open. So that the plants receive the maximum light, regularly clean the glass.

more quickly in spring than wet clay, while dark-coloured soil that is rich in humus or has been darkened with weathered soot warms more rapidly than very light-coloured soil. With all these facts in mind, it is possible to construct raised, well-drained beds of light, organically-rich soil that slope in the direction of maximum light (to the south or the southeast in the northern hemisphere). The beds should be sheltered on the other sides from wind. In this way, you can start your growing season for vegetables significantly earlier – by several weeks – than you could otherwise, and the addition of temporary glass or plastic covers gives you an even earlier start.

Frames, cloches and tunnels

In cool climates, or ones with cold winters, the use of frames (see p 380), cloches and tunnels of plastic sheeting stretched over wire hoops can considerably increase the variety and quantity of fruit and vegetables you can grow in the garden. They enable seeds to be sown earlier and crops to be grown for a longer period. They ensure ripening of crops like melons in areas with cool summers. They not only give protection from cold, but also from heavy rain and wind (though the plastic types are not suitable for use on windy, exposed sites), and from birds. The water lost by transpiration from plants' leaves (see p 336) is reduced, and warm air is trapped inside as it rises from the soil warmed by the sun during the day, so that glass cloches, in particular, give good protection from spring radiation frosts. (The temperature under a closed glass cloche may be as much as 7°C [13°F] higher than outside.)

The choice of equipment will depend on various factors. If you have any young children who play in the garden, you may prefer unbreakable plastic to glass cloches and frames. The plastic substitutes, although cheaper, are less efficient than glass in giving frost protection, however, and have a shorter life. Unlike plastic, glass retains long infra-red heat rays. The result is that the air in plastic tunnels heats up very rapidly in sunshine but cools much more rapidly than that under glass cloches at night. For this reason, it is important to ventilate plastic tunnels by raising one side during the day, but close them again at night to retain as much soil warmth as possible. As mentioned above, extra protection is vital when frost threatens.

Glass cloches are relatively expensive – and frames even more so – so it is well worth planning a full cropping programme to make use of them throughout the year. Suggested crops for various seasons are given in the table. For winter and early spring crops, it is essential to warm the soil by covering with cloches for at least two weeks before sowing or planting. (This generally takes place in mid- to late winter.) This method of growing is only suitable where average winter temperatures exceed −2°C (28°F). After this, the cloches can be used to give an early start to spring-sown crops, which can be gradually hardened off by increasing ventilation as the weather improves, to finish in the open. Do not uncover tender crops until all risk of frost is past. You can then use the cloches in cool regions for tender, slow-maturing crops like cucumbers and melons, finally covering late outdoor crops to promote ripening or extend the season.

Plastic tunnels are relatively cheap to buy or make, and can be used to raise vegetables from seed earlier than would otherwise be possible. You should put them in position at least three weeks before seed is to be sown to help to warm and dry the soil so that a seed bed can be prepared. They are commonly used to produce early strawberries (see p 314). In summer, thin white plastic film is more suitable than the clear type; the tunnels can be used to raise plants from semi-ripe wood cuttings (see p 346) and for the production of melons. New plastic should be used each year, as it deteriorates in light.

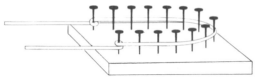

Making a plastic tunnel

You can make plastic tunnel cloches with clear or (for summer) white 150-gauge plastic film bought in rolls about 1.25 m (4 ft) wide. This will cover a 60 cm (2 ft) wide row. Form the supporting hoops with 8-gauge galvanized wire. Each hoop needs 1.65 m (5½ ft) of wire bent into a semicircle of diameter 60 cm (2 ft), leaving 25 cm (10 in) legs to be inserted into the ground. A simple former made of a board with nails inserted in a semicircle right can be used to shape the hoops. Make a small loop at the top of each leg around the first nail on each side. These will be used for securing lengths of polypropylene string to hold the plastic sheeting in place. Space the hoops 90 cm (3 ft) apart along the row, and cover with the plastic film. Bunch and secure this at one end to a strong stake 75 cm (2½ ft) from the end hoop. Stretch the film as tightly as possible over the hoops and secure it in the same way at the other end. Tie plastic twine between the small loops at the top of the legs, passing over the tunnel, so that the plastic is held between the hoops and the twine. This allows the film to be raised for ventilation or access.

Crops to grow under cloches in cool climates

Winter-sown crops (average at least −2°C [28°F])	Broad beans; carrots; lettuces; onions (maincrop; for transplanting); peas; radishes; spring (salad) onions
Early spring-sown crops (to finish in the open)	Beetroot; Brussels sprouts; cabbages; carrots; cauliflowers; celery; lettuces; marrows and squashes; sweet corn
Summer crops (where summers are cool)	Aubergines (eggplants); cucumbers; marrows and courgettes (zucchini); melons; peppers; strawberries (cover in winter for early crop); tomatoes
Late crops (covered in autumn)	Endive; French beans; haricot beans; lettuces; onions (to ripen); parsley; peas; potatoes (for late lifting); tomatoes (for late ripening)

The herb garden

Herbs have been cultivated almost as long as man has existed, and are inextricably bound up with a wealth of folklore based on ancient mythologies, religious ceremonies, witchcraft and superstitions. Some authorities argue that herbs were first grown for their medicinal qualities, others for their culinary purposes, but it seems logical to assume that the two developed simultaneously. The great majority of herbs are useful aids to the digestion, and many also have food-preserving and antiseptic qualities.

Monasteries had extensive herb gardens for medicinal purposes. To the medieval cook, a huge variety of aromatic herbs was equally important, employed as they were to disguise the taste and smell of rank meat and fish. Unscrupulous medicos brandished quack herbal mixtures, and witches brewed their concoctions at the dead of night from wild herbs gathered by moonlight.

The herb garden of later centuries was ornamental, finding its ultimate expression in the knot garden with its dozens of different herbs. Others were laid out in chequerboard patterns, each square of herbs alternating with a gravel square, or in sundial patterns. The advent of the Industrial Revolution in the 18th and 19th centuries spelt destruction for the herb garden, and by the 20th century only the faithful few herbs – parsley and mint, sage and thyme – were in general cultivation in most English-speaking countries.

Today there is an increased awareness of aromatic herbs, partly due to the subtle flavours they impart to mass-produced foodstuffs, and partly due to the free interchange of national cuisines brought about by expanding tourism. (In most parts of continental Europe and in various other parts of the world – notably the Middle and Far East – herbs have always played an important culinary role and never fell into disuse, unlike in Britain.) Apart from their uses in savoury (and a few sweet) dishes, herbs are used to flavour home-made vinegars. Herbal teas, tisanes or infusions are said to cleanse the system, relieve colds in the head and generally act as soothing tonics. Cosmetically, herbs are used for steam baths, face packs, bath essences and hair rinses. For details of individual herbs, see pages 272 to 275.

Herb garden designs

Few gardens have enough space to allow a replica of the Elizabethan knot garden, the geometrical design of which was based on individual, often irregular beds planted with a herb contrasting in colour and texture with that in the next bed. They were linked by paths of grass or gravel and edged with low hedges of box, lavender or santolina. A small paved herb garden can, however, be created on the same principle, dividing a square or rectangular plot into sections separated with paving stones or bricks and edged with violets, chives, parsley or thyme. A circular herb garden can be created around a central feature, such as a sundial or a bird bath. The individual beds are then laid out in wedge shapes and separated from each other with gravel or box

A knot garden
Medieval knot gardens were extensive, but most gardens can accommodate a smaller version, either of traditional design or with modern informal shapes. Choose dwarf hedging plants of contrasting textures and colours for the various strands – such as santolina, lavender, thymes, winter savory, sage and hyssop – planted so that the strands seem to interweave and pass over and under each other. In some knot gardens, other herbs are planted within the knots, while in others gravel or mulches of contrasting colours are used to fill the gaps.

A formal herb garden
A charming herb garden of formal design can be laid out with crossed paths of red brick or some other mellowed paving material. These form symmetrical corner beds for the herbs. A small statue, sundial or other ornament can make a centrepiece, while the whole feature can be surrounded by a close-clipped dwarf hedge of box edging (*Buxus sempervirens* 'Suffruticosa'). Many herbs are ornamental in themselves, but for additional colour you can introduce patches or a central planting of colourful annual flowers, bulbs or non-rampant perennials.

'spokes'. An interesting alternative is to use an old cart-wheel laid on the ground.

Where space is limited, many herbs can be grown in pots – expecially basil, chives, chervil, marjoram and parsley. Mint, rosemary and bay do well in tubs. Shrubby herbs like rosemary and sage can be integrated in the mixed border, where the creeping thyme also makes an attractive evergreen edging. The graceful dill and fennel alike can find a place among the annuals. Parsley seems to associate happily with roses, and can edge a rose bed.

In most cases, a small collection of herbs will be incorporated in the kitchen garden. Most of are Mediterranean origin and thrive in ordinary alkaline, well-drained soil. They generally prefer a sunny, sheltered spot, although angelica, balm, fennel, mint and parsley do better in light shade and moist soil. The ideal spot for a small herb garden is on a gentle slope where the sunloving and tall-growing herbs can be placed at the back, the lower herbs that need moisture at the front.

Planting and sowing

Early winter is the best time to prepare for a herb garden. The soil should be dug to a spade's depth; if it is heavy also incorporate well-rotted manure or garden compost at the

rate of two bucketfuls per square metre (sq yd). In spring, when the soil has warmed up, rake it to a fine tilth and at the same time add a general fertilizer (analysis about 7:7:7; see p 352) at two handfuls to every square metre (sq yd).

For most households one or two plants of the larger herbs will be sufficient. Perennial and shrubby herbs like bay, marjoram, mint, rosemary, sage, tarragon and thyme can be planted in early spring, but remember that young bay and rosemary can be damaged by late frosts and should preferably not be set out until late spring; better still, plant them in tubs which can be moved under cover when frost threatens. Take into account that perennials will be set in permanent quarters and allow them sufficient room to spread.

With the exception of parsley and chervil, annual herbs are seldom grown in large quantities, but luckily most seed merchants and certainly specialist herb farms market small quantities of seeds, sometimes in mixed selections which may include annual and perennial types. Sow seeds of hardy annuals in drills in the herb garden. Make the drills no more than 1 cm (½ in) deep and cover the seeds lightly with fine soil. As the seedlings grow, thin them to stand about 20 cm (8 in) apart. Half-hardy

A chequerboard herb garden
One of the simplest but most attractive of herb gardens is designed in a chequerboard pattern, alternating squares being paved and planted. For an old-fashioned effect, the paved parts can be of brick, as here, or well-worn square stone slabs. Alternatively, gravel can be laid between low retaining edges of brick or wood. Such a feature can form a self-contained element in the garden design, or an area of similar pattern can be incorporated in a patio or terrace. As with some other herb gardens, a few annual flowers can be introduced.

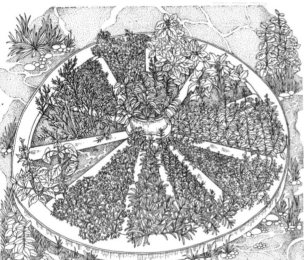

A wagon-wheel herb garden
If you have or can obtain an old wooden carriage or wagon wheel, this can be used to make an unusual frame for a bed of herbs. Simply paint or treat the wheel with wood preservative, then lay it down on a patch of well-cultivated ground. Plant a different herb between each pair of spokes. If you wish, the names of the individual herbs can be painted or burned with a red-hot poker on the segments of the rim. Other attractive situations for herbs include containers of all types – from simple pots, tubs and window boxes to strawberry pots and barrels and old sinks.

The use of herbs
Herbal teas (tisanes) can be made from both fresh and dried leaves, but fresh herbs give the better flavour. Steep one teaspoon of fresh leaves (slightly less if dried) in a cup of boiling water for five to ten minutes; the tea is then strained and drunk hot or cold. Chamomile tea, popular on the Continent of Europe, is made from the dried flowers and infused for fifteen minutes; the strained tea can be sweetened with honey or sugar.

Herb vinegars are particularly good in salad dressings. Fill a glass jar half-way up with fresh young leaves and top up with warm wine vinegar; cover the jar and let the herbs steep for about two weeks, shaking the jar daily.

For a herbal steam bath, place a large handful of mixed leaves – sage, mint and fennel – with some chamomile and lavender flowers in a bowl of boiling water and expose the face and neck to the steam for ten minutes. Face packs can be made from yoghourt or fuller's earth mixed with a herbal tea, and a relaxing bath tonic is obtained from a strong herb infusion strained and added to the warm bathwater.

annuals should be raised under glass in gentle heat and not planted out until frost is over. Seeds of perennial herbs are best sown in a separate seed-bed, thinned and left to grow on before transplanting the next spring.

Care and cultivation
Once the herbs are well established they need little attention, apart from weeding and, during long dry spells, watering those that need moisture. At the end of the season, pull up the annuals, cut the perennials to near ground level, and on acid soils give the herb garden a light lime dressing. Or wait until spring and rake in a general fertilizer. Shrubby plants like rosemary can be kept to a manageable shape by pruning long shoots back by half in spring; use the prunings as cuttings for new plants.

Few pests attack herbs, but sometimes maggots of carrot and celery fly burrow into stems and roots of parsley; treat affected plants with trichlorphon or malathion (see p 361). Rust (see p 367) can be a serious, non-controllable disease of mint, and once this occurs the plant must be destroyed. Purchase new mint roots certified as free of rust.

Harvesting and storage
During the summer, pick and use herbs while they are young and soft-leaved; as they mature many tend to lose their aroma and develop a bitter taste. Depending on sowing and planting, most leafy herbs are ready for harvesting from early summer onwards, before flowers develop, run to seed and flood the herb garden with self-sown seedlings. On herbs grown for their seeds as well as their leaves, such as dill and fennel, allow the flowers to mature and harvest the seeds before they drop from the plants.

While herbs release their best flavour when fresh, any surplus should be harvested and stored for winter use. For drying, cut the young stems in the morning after dew has vanished, tie them in small bunches enclosed in paper bags or muslin, and hang them upside down to dry in a dark, airy place for a week to ten days. Tender-leaved herbs with a high moisture content, such as basil, balm, mint and tarragon, must be dried quickly to prevent shrivelling. Spread them on muslin-covered trays and place in a warm room, over a radiator, in a ventilated airing cupboard or in a slow oven with the door left open. Turn the herbs daily until they are quite dry and brittle (a few days); then strip the leaves from the stems and crumble them into small, dark-coloured storage containers with airtight stoppers. Seeds are dried in the same way, being picked when they have turned brown, straight into a paper bag and hung up in an airy place until dry.

Some herbs, notably chives and parsley, do not dry well, but they can be had fresh throughout winter by keeping late-sown parsley and dug-up chive plant in pots in the kitchen. Both are also suitable for freezing, after blanching; place small quantities – enough for one use at a time – in small freezer bags, or freeze them in ice-cube trays and store the cubes in freezer cartons.

The classic herbs of cookery

The number of herbs grown for culinary purposes has dwindled to but a handful over the centuries; they have survived because they have remained in constant general use and because many are associated with national cuisines. Tarragon, for example, is essentially linked with French cooking, while basil, marjoram and rosemary are used frivolously in many Italian dishes. Sage and mint are associated with British cookery; mint is hardly used in any other parts of Europe, although it features strongly in Middle Eastern dishes. Fennel flavours fish irrespective of national frontiers, but chives and dill are chiefly traditional to Scandinavian and German cooking, the latter occurring frequently, together with caraway, in eastern European dishes.

Certain combinations of herbs are used internationally as the basic flavouring of stocks and soups. The French *bouquet garni*, known in Britain as a faggot of herbs and in Germany as *Krätersäckchen* or *Suppengrün*, is composed of the same classic ingredients: parsley, thyme and bay leaf. A classic flavouring for omelettes is *fines herbes*, which consists of fresh, finely-chopped chervil, chives, parsley and tarragon.

Annual herbs

All the annual culinary herbs need some shelter from prevailing winds and, with the exception of caraway and parsley, do best in full sun, especially in northern Europe. Basil (*Ocimum basilicum*), which is half-hardy except in Mediterranean regions and grows 60 to 90 cm (2 to 3 ft) high, should be sown under glass and not planted out until late spring. The highly aromatic, clove-like scent is most pronounced in young leaves, and for a steady summer supply make sowings every six weeks. The finely-shredded leaves are used in tomato and egg dishes and in fish marinades. Pack surplus leaves in jars and cover with oil.

Caraway (*Carum carvi*), which will grow up to 90 cm (3 ft) in fairly heavy but fertile soil, prefers a semi-shaded position. It is slow to germinate, but later in the year seeds itself abundantly unless gathered just as the seeds mature. The fern-like leaves may be used chopped in salads, but the plant is chiefly grown for the strongly flavoured seeds, which are traditional in breads, cakes, cheeses and cabbage dishes in Germany, Austria and eastern Europe.

Chervil (*Anthriscus cerefolium*), up to 45 cm (18 in) tall, is faintly reminiscent of parsley, but has a more delicate flavour which is quickly lost if cooked for long. The light green, dainty leaves are used in *fines herbes*, tartare sauce, as soup flavouring and for garnishes. It needs moist soil or the plants will run to seed.

Coriander (*Coriandrum sativum*) is one of the ancient herbs, and has been used in cooking and medicine throughout Europe, India and China for thousands of years. The faint orange flavour of this herb – height up to 45 cm (18 in) – is best preserved in the ripe seeds, although the young finely-cut leaves may also be used in salads. Ground coriander seeds are used for curries, beef stews and in northern Europe and America as a whole pickling spice.

Dill (*Anethum graveolens*), with bright green narrow leaves on 90 cm (3 ft) slender stems, is widely used in Scandinavian and German cookery, sprays of leaves complete with seeds being used in the pickling of cucumbers, with fish and in the preparation of vinegars. It is also used with new potatoes. It is a useful digestive aid and is best preserved frozen rather than dried.

Sweet, or knotted, marjoram (*Origanum majorana*) is really a perennial herb, but as it is hardy only in warm regions such as southern Europe (where it is known as oregano) it is usually treated as an annual. It grows up to 60 cm (2 ft) high; the small flower-heads are tightly bunched and surrounded by green bracts or 'knots'. The related species *O. onites*, pot marjoram, is fully hardy, but the leaves lack the sweet taste of knotted marjoram. Both are used to season and flavour meat and poultry stuffings, soups, tomatoes and mushrooms. Marjoram dries and freezes well. Sow the seeds under glass and delay planting out until frost is over.

Parsley (*Petroselinum crispum*) is so widely grown and so well known that it hardly needs a description. In fertile, moist soil it grows up to 30 cm (12 in) high and is available as either curly or plain-leaved varieties. The latter is the hardiest; curly or moss-leaved parsley often needs winter protection with cloches in very cold areas. Parsley seeds are slow to germinate, but it helps to soak them in lukewarm water for 24 hours or to moisten the seed drills with hot water prior to sowing. Thin the seedlings to stand 25 cm (10 in) apart. Sow several times a year to maintain supplies. Parsley is the ubiquitous garnish for all savoury dishes, and a must in *bouquets garnis*, *fines herbes* and *maître d'hôtel* butter.

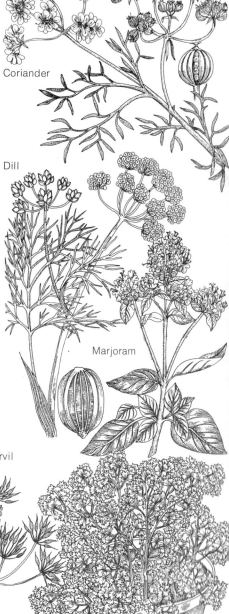

Coriander

Dill

Marjoram

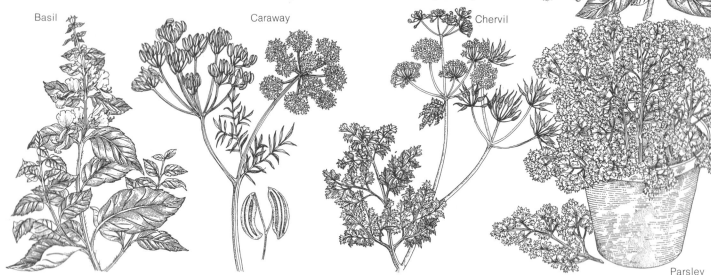

Basil

Caraway

Chervil

Parsley

Perennial herbs

These fall into seemingly natural, geographical areas, chives being not only a native of northern Europe, Canada and North America, but also a favourite herb in these areas while being practically unknown in southern Europe. Mint as a herb and a flavouring is almost indigenous to the British Isles, and while fennel will also grow there (and is naturalized in some parts) it is happier in warmer climates where it is more extensively used. Garlic and tarragon are essentially French.

Chives (*Allium schoenoprasum*) is a most attractive little herb, its grass-like tufts seldom growing more than 20 cm (8 in) high. The small, round pink flowers in early summer should be removed to ensure a steady supply of green leaves. These give a mild onion flavour to salads, sauces and dressings, herb butters, egg and vegetable dishes. Chives die down completely in autumn, but a clump can be lifted and grown on as a pot herb indoors for the winter. Dig up and divide every three or four years.

Fennel (*Foeniculum vulgare* or *F. officinale*) is a highly ornamental herb, up to 1.8 m (6 ft) high, with graceful, pale blue-green leaves. These have a sweet scent and the flavour of liquorice, which complement the richness of oily fish and at the same time act as a digestive. The leaves, which are suitable for drying, are also used for herbal teas, gripe water and in sweet liqueurs. The seeds have an even stronger flavour and may be used in pickling. New plants are best purchased young or raised from seeds in spring. (For Florence fennel, grown as a vegetable, see page 287.)

Garlic (*Allium sativum*) is related to the onion and like this is used for its bulbs, which are composed of a number of small segments known as cloves. From these comes the unmistakable smell and taste which permeate many Mediterranean dishes. It is less popular in America and Britain in spite of its antiseptic and digestive properties. Garlic combines with stews and casseroles, marinades and dressings, herb butters and vinegars. It cannot stand cold or damp soil, and needs both warmth and sun to mature; plant the small cloves about 2.5 cm (1 in) deep, 15 cm (6 in) apart in spring, and lift the bulbs for drying and storing in late summer. A recommended variety for cool climates is 'Continental'.

There are several kinds of mint (*Mentha* spp), the two most common being *Mentha spicata*, common or spearmint, with a height up to 90 cm (3 ft), and *M. rotundifolia*, apple mint, which in the best variety, 'Bowles' Variety', reaches 60 cm (2 ft). The rounded leaves of both are faintly hairy; they should be picked and used in the young stage, and as they lose much of their flavour in drying they are better frozen or preserved in vinegar. Apart from flavouring young vegetables and Middle Eastern meat dishes, mint is also used in sauces and chutneys, iced cups and drinks such as mint julep, and in tisanes. It needs a moisture-retentive soil and sun or light shade; mint can be increased by division or cuttings, but it spreads extensively unaided.

Tarragon (*Artemisia dracunculus*), one of the great classic herbs, deserves to be more widely grown. It reaches a height of 45 cm (18 in). In spite of its indefinable, strong aroma, the leaves of tarragon are chiefly used to flavour delicate dishes, especially egg and cream sauces, fish, chicken and salads. It is essential in *fines herbes* mixtures and is used commercially for vinegars, liqueurs and perfumery. The leaves are better frozen than dried. French tarragon is preferable to the coarser Russian form, but is becoming increasingly difficult to obtain. Cut the stems to ground level in autumn and protect with a winter mulch; in frost-prone regions, lift the roots and keep them in a cold frame. Tarragon deteriorates with age and should be divided every three or four years.

Shrubby herbs

These are all evergreen and native to southern Europe, and thus revel in light, well-drained soil and full sun. They are among the most ancient of herbs and have innumerable traditional uses and associations. Apart from the strong scent with which they perfume still summer days, they are attractive little shrubs, at home in borders and tubs as well as in the herb garden.

Bay (*Laurus nobilis*) is the laurel whose leaves adorned returning heroes and conquerors in ancient Rome; it was also the symbol of wisdom, perpetuated still in the English honorary title of Poet Laureate. In its native habitats, bay will grow as tall as 6 m (20 ft), but is usually kept to a lesser height as a cultivated shrub. It can be pruned into a round-headed standard or an attractive slender bush. It is not hardy in the northernmost parts of Europe or North America, but makes a good tub plants which can be moved under cover for winter. The leaves are used, /continued

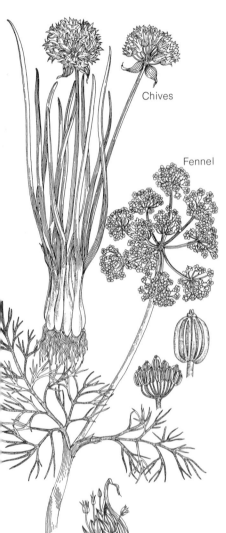

Chives

Fennel

Garlic

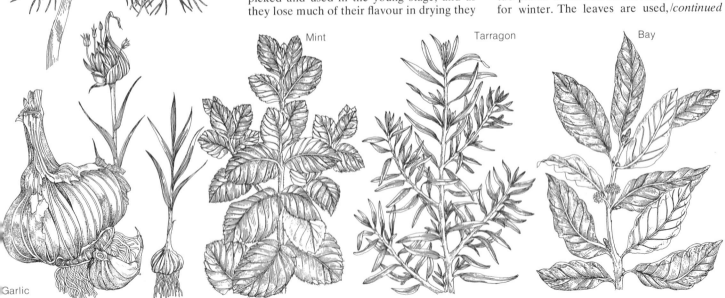

Mint

Tarragon

Bay

The classic herbs of cookery (continued)

Rosemary

Sage

Thyme

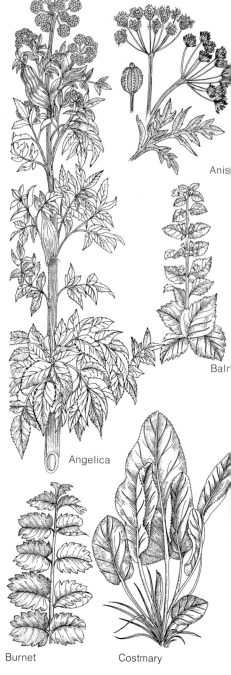

Anis

Balr

Angelica

Burnet

Costmary

fresh or dried, as flavouring for any type of savoury dish as well as for custards and other cream desserts, and it is always part of a *bouquet garni*. Bay needs shelter, and tub-grown plants should not be allowed to dry out in summer. It can be propagated by cuttings.

Rosemary (*Rosmarinus officinalis*) is for remembrance, once reputed to ease the brain and restore speech to the dumb. It may reach a height of 1.5 m (5 ft), but is usually pruned to less. Its narrow green leaves, almost white on the undersides, are highly aromatic and contain camphor. They were formerly burnt in sickrooms as a disinfectant. Today, sprigs of rosemary flavour first of all roast lamb, mutton and goose, but are also good with other types of meat, poultry and fish. The sprigs dry well but with a noticeable loss of flavour. Rosemary, which thrives on poor chalky soils, is not hardy in extreme cold areas. Propagation is by heel cuttings rooted in midsummer in sandy soil.

Sage (*Salvia officinalis*) was originally used medicinally, and a daily cup of sage tea was said to promote a long life. Growing up to 60 cm (2 ft), sage is hardy although it will not tolerate winter damp. The wrinkled, grey-green leaves have a pungent aroma which

becomes almost bitter when they are mature; they should be used before the blue or white flowers appear. Sage leaves both freeze and dry well and are mainly used in stuffings for fatty meats and fish. It responds fairly well to annual pruning, but as it is not a long-lived plant it should be replaced after a few years with young plants raised from seeds or late summer cuttings.

Thyme (*Thymus vulgaris*) grows wild over most of Europe and is one of the most important culinary herbs. It is a small, often creeping plant, very suitable for edging and window boxes. (There is a highly decorative golden variety, 'Aureus'.) Thyme contains a disinfectant oil known as thymol and was formerly used as incense, now more commonly together with rosemary in *pot-pourris*. Several varieties are available besides the common thyme: lemon, orange and caraway thyme, each with the additional flavours inherent in their names. Essential in a *bouquet garni*, fresh or dried thyme is also used in stuffings, vegetable soups, meat and fish dishes and in marinades. Although hardy and thriving on chalky soil, thyme does not succeed in damp areas; it can be increased by division, seeds or cuttings.

Home-grown tobacco

Growing your own tobacco is not difficult, even in cool climates, but processing the leaves for smoking poses more problems, and many amateur growers prefer to leave this to associations that exist in some countries (see the list of useful addresses at the end of this book).

The commercial tobacco plant, *Nicotiana tabacum*, is a relative of the tomato, and thrives in the same conditions: deep, well-dug and well-manured soil, plenty of sun and adequate moisture. Treat the plants as half-hardy annuals, sowing the seeds in spring under glass at 13 to 16°C (55 to 61°F), hardening off in a cold frame and planting out in early summer, when all danger of frost has passed. Alternatively, obtain seedling plants from amateur

associations. In warm regions, the seed may be sown outside in spring.

Set the plants 90 cm (3 ft) apart, in rows the same distance apart. give dilute nitrogenous liquid fertilizer (see p 352) at intervals through the summer. When the plants are 1.25 to 1.8 m (4 to 6 ft) tall, remove the flower-heads. Pinch out any side shoots immediately.

When the plants are about 1.8 m (6 ft) tall, begin harvesting the leaves, starting at the bottom and taking a few leaves once or twice a week. Yellow them by hanging them in a warm humid greenhouse, then dry them in a warm room. The final process of fermentation, or curing, sweetens the leaf. There are various methods, all needing heat and humidity; associations cure members' tobacco in kilns.

The almost-forgotten herbs

Many less-well-known herbs have passed into history. Betony (*Stachys officinalis*), wild bog myrtle (*Myrica gale*) and gillyflowers (clove pinks) were once used to flavour home-brewed ale. Ground ivy (*Glechoma hederacea*) was used as well for herbal teas, and lady's bedstraw (*Galium verum*) and dried lime or linden flowers – still sold in some European markets – were made into sleeping draughts. Samphire (*Crithmum maritimum*) has practically disappeared as a pickling herb, though it is still eaten as a regional delicacy in some parts of Britain. And the bitter-tasting tansy (*Chrysanthemum vulgare*), beloved in medieval milk sops, now exists only as a name for certain cream-based desserts.

Vervain (*Verbena officinalis*), believed by the ancient Persians to possess magical powers and therefore used in love potions, has lost its mystery, while wormwood (*Artemisia absinthium*), related to tarragon and originally used as a cure against worms, is still grown commercially and used in the preparation of vermouths and other related aperitifs. The latter is an example of a herb whose use in gardens is now almost solely decorative, but there are a number of other herbs that are slowly disappearing from garden cultivation in spite of their culinary qualities and continued (if in some cases declining) use.

purposes as the latter, have a rich lemon scent.

Burnet (*Sanguisorba minor*), or salad burnet, is now little used outside France and Italy. It is a hardy perennial, growing about 60 cm (2 ft) high, and the leaves, which have a faint cucumber taste, are used chopped in salads, vinegars and sauces.

Costmary (*Chrysanthemum balsamita* or *Balsamita vulgare*), also known as alecost, was once as popular as lavender for scenting linen cupboards and was also used for flavouring ale – hence the second common name. The leaves of this hardy perennial, up to 90 cm (3 ft) high, keep their aroma well when dried; they are used to flavour soups, stuffings, salads and wine cups.

The purple-black berries of juniper (*Juniperus communis*) have a pronounced pine flavour and are used throughout Europe, especially in mountain regions, to flavour meat marinades and stuffings, pâtés and cabbage dishes, and also gin.

Lovage (*Levisticum officinale*) is one of the most useful but neglected herbs. The leaves, stems and seeds of this hardy 60 cm (2 ft) perennial are used in cooking. The highly aromatic, slightly lemon-scented leaves are used fresh in soups and salads, dried for tisanes. The seeds are used like caraway seeds, and the stems like angelica. One plant would

by the ancient Egyptians and Romans. Today, this tufted hardy perennial, height 30 cm (12 in), is little used outside France, although sorrel soup was popular in medieval times. The bitter young leaves are added to salads or may be used to season vegetable soups. Moist soil and full sun are essential.

Decorative herbs

Some herbs, once used in both medicine and cooking, are now grown purely as ornamental plants, either in the herb garden or in herbaceous borders, their former uses virtually forgotten. The aromatic bergamot (*Monarda didyma*) is an example. It is a native of North America and was used to make tea by the Oswego Indians. It makes an attractive plant about 60 cm (2 ft) high with large, bright red flowers during summer. The dried leaves are suitable for *pot-pourris* and herbal teas.

One thing only detracts from the annual borage (*Borago officinalis*): its tendency to self-seed throughout the garden, even in the tiniest crevices. It is hardy only in warm and temperate climates, on chalky soil and in sun. The flowers, which are like blue forget-me-nots, can be candied. The leaves are covered in prickly hairs, and may be added to wine cups, but the plant is chiefly grown for its ornamental value.

The sweetly scented chamomile (*Anthemis nobilis*) was a popular lawn plant in Tudor days, the scent wafting gently as flowers and leaves were crushed underfoot (see p 234). It is not a hard-wearing plant, but makes a delightful addition to a large herb garden. The dried flowers can be used for herbal teas, bath tonics and hair rinses.

Hyssop (*Hyssopus officinalis*) is a perennial plant, up to 45 cm (18 in) high and hardy everywhere except in the extreme north. It has been used in medicine rather than cooking, and with its aromatic, mint-scented leaves and spikes of blue flowers is worthy of a place in the garden.

The highly pungent smell from the deeply cut blue-green leaves of the shrubby rue (*Ruta graveolens*) is unpleasant to many people. It grows up to 60 cm (2 ft) high, but can be cut back to ground level annually in spring. The small yellow flowers are of no importance, but the shape and colour makes rue a very decorative plant. It is a classic ingredient in the Italian *grappa* and was once regarded as an antidote to snake and scorpion bites.

Other plants which could be grown in the herb garden for their aromatic and decorative value might include the perennial sweet cicily (*Myrrhis odorata*), meadow-sweet (*Filipendula ulmaria*), cotton lavender (*Santolina chamaecyparissus*), southernwood (*Artemisia abrotanum*), the biennial clary (*Salvia sclarea*; see p 180) and the curry plant (*Helichrysum angustifolium*), which gets its name from the distinctive smell of its crushed leaves.

Finally there is lavender (*Lavandula* spp); although not a true herb, it is grown for the heady scent of its flower spikes – dried and sown into sachets to perfume cupboards and drawers – and is often used as a low-growing hedge around the herb garden.

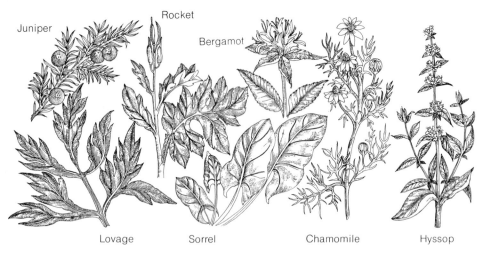

Juniper — Rocket — Bergamot — Lovage — Sorrel — Chamomile — Hyssop

Uncommon culinary herbs

Angelica (*Angelica archangelica*), a huge, short-lived perennial more than 1.8 m (6 ft) high, is hardy in the coldest areas. The young green stems are used candied for cake and dessert decoration. It needs good moist soil and light shade, and is best raised from seeds.

The dried seeds of anise (*Pimpinella anisum*), or aniseed, give the well-known liquorice flavour to alcoholic drinks; the seeds, however, seldom ripen in the short summers of the northern parts of Europe and North America. This annual – height 45 cm (18 in) – resembles a small celery and should be sown in a sunny spot in late spring.

Balm (*Melissa officinalis*), better known as lemon balm, is one of the ancient herbs, and when added to wine cups is said to relieve melancholy. It is a hardy perennial, up to 90 cm (3 ft) tall, that spreads quickly like mint; the leaves, which are used for the same

be enough in the average garden, but new plants can be raised from seeds and set in fairly moist soil and full sun.

Rocket (*Eruca sativa*) is an annual salad plant, up to 60 cm (2 ft) high, little used outside southern Europe although it grows wild in North America. It does best in moist, rich soil where the pungent leaves retain their crisp texture best.

There are two varieties of savory, *Satureja hortensis*, or summer savory, and *S. montana*, or winter savory. The first is a hardy annual, 25 cm (10 in) high, the latter a perennial of similar height. Both bear sweetly-scented leaves that add a minty, slightly bitter taste to soups, fish, egg and vegetable dishes. They dry successfully, but those of winter savory are inferior in taste and more bitter than those of summer savory.

Garden sorrel (*Rumex scutatus* and related species) was used as a digestive for rich foods

Potatoes

Potatoes are among the most important vegetable cash crops, but unless you have a large garden it is impracticable to grow them in large quantities. An early crop of delicious 'new' potatoes is another matter, however, and potatoes are also a useful ground-breaking crop in new kitchen gardens because the continual cultivation involved in earthing up the rows destroys weeds and exposes pests to birds and other predators. Potatoes are frost-tender, but extremely early crops can be raised in pots under glass. They are also grown successfully in growing bags (see p 117), tubs or window boxes, so long as they are deep enough for the roots to develop.

Originating in South America, the potato (*Solanum tuberosum*) is grown in many varieties throughout the temperate world. Potato varieties are divided into three groups: first early and second early (which follow each other, and are the best types for immediate eating in summer and autumn) and maincrop (which are stored for winter and spring eating). The parts that are eaten are the tubers that grow on underground stems, and they may be round, oval or kidney-shaped, with skin that is white, pink-flushed or tinged with red or purple. The flesh is white or yellowish, and the texture after cooking varies from waxy (when it stays firm) to floury (when it 'falls' easily).

Sprouting tubers
right Stand 'seed' potatoes in trays, eyes uppermost. Keep them cool but frost-free and well lit. When the shoots are 1 to 2.5 cm (½ to 1 in) long, thin them out to two or three sturdy sprouts per tuber. You can make the tubers go farther by cutting the larger ones into sections, each with two or three sprouts. Dust the cuts with lime.

Planting out
above far left Plant the sprouted tubers 10 to 15 cm (4 to 6 in) deep, 30 cm (12 in) apart in rows 60 cm (2 ft) apart for early types. Space maincrop potatoes (which need not be sprouted) more widely.
above left Cover the tubers, levelling the ground or leaving a slight ridge to protect them from frosts.

Soil and planting

A light, quick-warming soil with plenty of organic matter yields the best results. Improve 'hungry' sandy soils by working in peat, garden compost, well-rotted manure or leaf-mould; lighten heavy loam with gritty sand and manure that is not too wet. If the ground was organically manured with bulky waste for the previous crop, simply work a general fertilizer (analysis about 5:10:5; see p 352) into the top 15 cm (6 in) of soil. Do not lime; this encourages scab disease.

Potatoes are grown from 'seed' tubers, gen-

erally the size of a hen's egg. For best results, buy certified virus-free tubers. Most 'eating' potatoes are treated chemically to retard sprouting, and any you save from your own harvest may have developed disease.

Sprout early types in late winter and plant out as soon as severe frosts are over. In cold or exposed districts, it may help to plant potatoes between widely spaced rows of peas planted earlier and staked to support growth. The netting or brushwood used shelters the potatoes. In frost-free regions, plant from autumn to midwinter for winter or spring harvesting.

Growing under black plastic

This method is ideal on light soil, as the plastic retains moisture. There is no earthing up; the potatoes are picked off or unearthed with a trowel.
below First dig and fertilize a strip of ground 1 m (3 ft) wide. Plant sprouted tubers 30 cm (12 in) apart and 10 to 15 cm (4 to 6 in) deep, using a trowel. Water in slug-bait, as slugs enjoy the warmth and moisture under the plastic. Then unroll 1 m (3 ft) wide black plastic sheeting over the row. Tuck the edges into a slit in the soil made with a spade and pile earth on the edges to anchor them. When bumps in the plastic show that shoots have grown, make slits and ease the shoots through. Apart from spraying against disease, no attention is needed until harvesting. Lift the plastic to remove the biggest potatoes, allowing the smaller ones to grow on.

Sweet potatoes

Quite unrelated to the ordinary white (or Irish) potato, the sweet potato (*Ipomoea batatas*) needs a five-month growing season with night-time temperatures of 16°C (61°F) or preferably more. So it is a crop for places with hot summers, widely grown in the southern United States, tropical America, the Pacific and warm parts of Asia. It has long, trailing stems with pink or rose-violet funnel-shaped flowers. The tuberous roots, which are the crop, have white or yellow sweet, firm flesh.

Grow sweet potatoes from the sprouts (or slips) that grow from the roots when put in moist sand at 27°C (81°F), or by cuttings of the vine-like stems. Plant out about 40 cm (15 in) apart, preferably in light, sandy soil, as soon as minimum temperatures reach 16°C (61°F). Allow the stems to trail over the ground. Harvest in late autumn, or when the first frost blackens the leaves. Handle the tubers carefully (the skins are delicate), and 'cure' in a dry place at about 26°C (79°F) for 10 to 14 days before storing in cool, dry conditions.

Growing under glass

For the earliest crop, grow potatoes in 25 cm (10 in) pots in a cool greenhouse, starting in late winter.
right Set a sprouted tuber 2.5 cm (1 in) deep on 5 cm (2 in) of potting mixture over the drainage material. As the shoots grow, add more potting

Recommended potato varieties

First early	'Arran Pilot' (kidney-shaped; floury); 'Home Guard' (round); 'Pentland Javelin' (round-oval; eelworm-resistant); 'Pentland Lustre' (long-oval, waxy; eelworm-resistant); 'Sharpe's Express' (kidney-shaped; for heavier and fertile soils)
Second early	'Catriona' (kidney-shaped); 'Craig's Royal' (long-oval); 'Maris Peer' (resistant to common scab disease and some forms of blight); 'Maris Piper' (oval; disease-resistant)
Maincrop	'Desirée' (long-oval; prone to blight); 'King Edward' (kidney-shaped; blight-prone); 'Pentland Crown' (oval; resists common scab); 'Pentland Dell' (kidney-shaped; virus- and blight-resistant); 'Pentland Hawk' (oval; floury); 'Pentland Ivory' (long-oval; floury; virus-resistant)

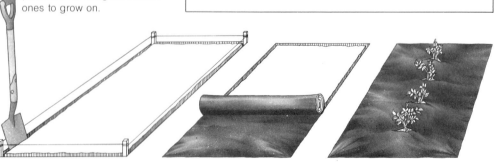

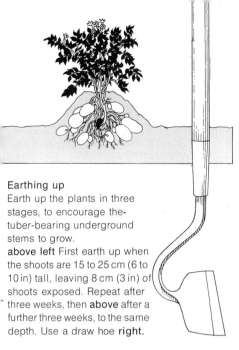

Radishes and carrots

Earthing up
Earth up the plants in three stages, to encourage the tuber-bearing underground stems to grow.
above left First earth up when the shoots are 15 to 25 cm (6 to 10 in) tall, leaving 8 cm (3 in) of shoots exposed. Repeat after three weeks, then **above** after a further three weeks, to the same depth. Use a draw hoe **right**.

Routine care and harvesting
Water potato plants freely in dry weather, and dose the ground with slug-bait if necessary. Earthing up the rows encourages more underground stems and thus more tubers to form. It also keeps down weeds, discourages blight and makes harvesting easier. At the second earthing-up, sprinkle on a high-nitrogen fertilizer to encourage a good crop of tubers. Remove any flowers that form. Apart from slugs, watch out for eelworms and wireworms (see p 362) and such diseases as blight, common scab, dry rot and wart disease

mixture until it is 2.5 cm (1 in) below the rim **left**. Water regularly and feed every two weeks with liquid manure. At 10 to 13°C (50 to 55°F) some potatoes will form in three months. Up-end the pot carefully and remove the largest; replace to allow the smaller ones to grow on.

(see p 365 and 366). In some regions, Colorado beetle is a destructive potato pest and, together with wart disease, is notifiable in some areas, including Britain.

Lift early potatoes when the haulms (tops) are still green, and the tubers are the size of hens' eggs and their skins are beginning to set. Lift only enough for a day or two's eating. Second earlies and maincrop varieties should be lifted later, when the leaves turn yellow – usually in late summer or early autumn. Be sure to harvest before frosts begin; in hot regions you should lift before average daytime temperatures reach 32°C (90°F). Make digging easier by cutting off the haulm – and burning it to prevent the spread of disease – a day before lifting. Dig from well to the side of the row to avoid damaging the tubers.

After harvesting maincrop potatoes, let them dry off for several hours before putting them in open net bags or boxes. Discard any that are diseased, speared or rotten. Store the rest in a cool, dark place; light turns them green and poisonous. Clamping potatoes – storing them in the open, protected by straw and earthed over – is only suitable for a very large crop, as a clamp should be 1 m (3 ft) high and 1.5 m (5 ft) across (see p 279).

Two easy root vegetables, neither radishes nor carrots take much space – though the former are much quicker growing. Neither like high temperatures: The limit for carrots is a daily average maximum of 30°C (86°F), for radishes 26°C (79°F).

Growing radishes
Ordinary summer radishes for salads can be round like a marble, taking about three weeks to mature; cylindrical like a thumb and slightly slower maturing; or narrow and tapered and up to 12 cm (5 in) long, taking just over four weeks. The larger winter radishes, 15 to 40 cm (6 to 15 in) long and up to 8 cm (3 in) thick, are dug for shredding in autumn and winter salads or for cooking like turnips. All are varieties of *Raphanus sativus*.

For tenderness, radishes must grow fast. But high temperatures cause bolting – with a fine crop of leaves and flowers but no root development – so it is best to grow in a moist place in the light shade of other crops (such as peas or beans). Best results come from spring and early summer sowings, but you can sow again in late summer and early autumn. An early crop can be raised in cold frames or under cloches by sowing in late winter. For constant supplies, sow every two weeks.

Most well-drained soils grow succulent radishes provided they are fortified with humus in the form of peat, garden compost or well-rotted manure. If the soil is poor, rake in general fertilizer (10:10:10; see p 352) at 135 g/m² (4 oz/sq yd) ten days before sowing. Water the ground well and then sow in drills 15 cm (6 in) apart and 1 cm (½ in) deep. Or broadcast among lettuces or other crops, in patches at ends of rows, or anywhere to fill vacant ground and prevent weeds. Thin the seedlings if necessary to allow good root growth, keep well watered, and pull as soon as they are big enough. Watch for flea beetle (see p 362) and dust with derris if necessary.

Sow winter radishes in mid- to late summer in drills 20 cm (8 in) apart. Thin the seedlings to 10 to 15 cm (4 to 6 in) apart. Lift the roots before the first frosts and store in boxes of damp sand. Alternatively, leave in the ground in areas where frosts are not too severe, giving protection with straw or other material on frosty nights. Peel winter radishes before use.

Growing carrots
There are three main groups of carrots: short varieties with finger-sized or large marble-sized roots, intermediate stump-rooted kinds up to 15 cm (6 in) long, and long kinds with tapered roots 30 to 60 cm (1 to 2 ft) long, usually grown for winter storage. All are derived from a poisonous wild plant, *Daucus carota sativus*.

You can enjoy a succession of pullings by sowing carrots every two weeks from the start of spring to the end of summer and, where winters are not too severe, by growing under cloches or in a cold frame through the rest of the year. The finest carrots grow on sandy soil that warms early in spring. They do not grow well on clay, but the shorter types grow on stony soils. Work in general fertilizer rich in

phosphate (5:10:10; see p 352) at 135 g/m² (4 oz/sq yd) about ten days before sowing.

Sow the seed thinly in drills 5 mm to 1 cm (¼ to ½ in) deep, 20 cm (8 in) apart for early varieties and 30 cm (12 in) for maincrop types. Pelleted seeds should be 2.5 cm (1 in) apart. Sprinkle a soil insecticide powder along the drill to deter carrot root fly, wireworms and other pests. Firm the soil down with the back of a rake.

Thin the seedlings to 2.5 cm (1 in) apart when manageable, and again to 8 to 10 cm (3 to 4 in) two or three weeks later. The second thinnings are big enough to eat, but always bury others deep in the compost heap to avoid attracting carrot root fly. Water freely in dry weather, spurring growth with a foliar feed (see p 353). Pack moist peat around the shoulders of the carrots to prevent splitting and greening. Pull when they are mature – about 14 weeks from sowing for early varieties, 16 weeks for maincrop kinds. Store maincrop carrots, after trimming off the tops, in sand in a frost-free place.

Recommended radish varieties

Summer	**Round**
	'Burpee's White'; 'Cherry Belle' (red); 'Crimson Giant' (large); 'Inca' (red); 'Saxa' (red); 'Sparkler' (red and white)
	Intermediate length
	'French Breakfast' (red and white); 'Half Long' (red and white); 'Yellow Gold' (yellow)
	Long
	'White Icicle'
Winter	'Black Spanish'; 'China Rose' (pink); 'Mino Early' (mild flavour)

Recommended carrot varieties

Short	'Amsterdam Forcing' (early); 'Early Nantes' (early); 'Frühbund' (very early); 'Oxheart' (maincrop); 'Parisian Rondo' (round; early); 'Short 'n' Sweet' (early); 'Tiny Sweet' (very early)
Intermediate length	'Danvers Improved' (maincrop); 'Goldinheart' (early); 'James's Scarlet Intermediate' (maincrop); 'Juwarot' (early/maincrop); 'Nantes' (early); 'Red Cored Chantenay' (early); 'Royal Chantenay' (early); 'Scarla' (maincrop); 'Spartan Bonus' (Fl hybrid; early/maincrop)
Long	'Gold Pak' (maincrop); 'New Red Intermediate' (maincrop); 'Saber' (Fl hybrid; early); 'Tendersweet' (maincrop)

Popular root vegetables

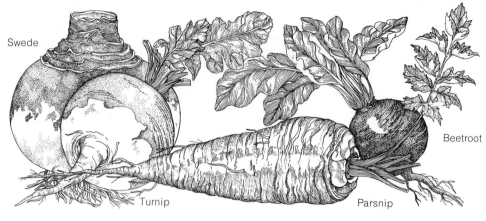

Swede

Turnip

Parsnip

Beetroot

Although they belong to three different families, beetroots or beets (*Beta vulgaris conditiva*); parsnips (*Pastinaca sativa*), and swedes (rutabagas) and turnips (*Brassica napus napobrassica* and *B. rapa rapa* respectively) have much in common. They are all botanically biennials that are grown as annuals for their thick, fleshy roots. They all thrive in cooler climates – hot, dry weather makes the roots tough and in warm regions they must be sown at least two months before average daytime temperatures reach 27°C (80°F). And they all thrive under the same conditions and methods of cultivation and harvesting.

All four grow best on a well-limed, well-drained soil that has been deeply manured for a previous year's crop. Fresh manure will make the roots fork. While excess water can cause rot, do not let them dry out, as any sudden fall of rain will then cause the roots to split. Broadly speaking, they are susceptible to the same pests and diseases – including mangold fly maggots, celery fly, swift moth caterpillars, flea beetles, crown gall, damping off, leaf spot, violet root rot, club root and soft rot – as well as certain mineral deficiency disorders and specific problems that are mentioned below.

Finally, all four store well for winter use, either in the ground where they grew, mulched with straw or hay against moderate frosts, or lifted and kept in clamps or in wooden boxes stored in a cool but frost-free place where winters are colder.

Beetroots

The juicy flesh of beetroots has long been popular in salads and for pickling, in both cases being boiled first. They can also be served as hot vegetables or made into a soup (as in the Russian *bortsch*), and the edible leaves are a crop in themselves, making a substitute for spinach. Most people are familiar with the dark red types, but varieties with golden or even white flesh are now available and make an interesting culinary diversion.

Beets are classified by their root shapes: globe-shaped, top-shaped (cylindrical or tankard-shaped) and long. Globes are the most popular, being quick to mature, highly resistant to bolting and possessing the tastiest leaves. The leaves of 'Burpee's Golden' are particularly recommended. Long-rooted types are best for winter storage and exhibition. Tankard-shaped varieties can be treated either way, but on the whole are better for storage than immediate eating.

Soil and sowing Beets flourish in organically rich soil that stays moist and cool in summer and warms early in spring. A good crop can be raised in most soils, provided they are not of heavy clay or very stony. Avoid frost pockets where icy air can check growth. Prepare the bed in early winter.

Globe and some tankard varieties can be sown successively every two weeks from spring to midsummer, providing a continuous crop of young roots for summer eating. For an extra-early crop, sow under cloches in early spring. Long-rooted kinds or globe types for later eating are sown in summer. In frost-free regions, autumn sowings will yield winter and spring harvests. Take out drills 2.5 cm (1 in) deep and 30 cm (12 in) apart. Beetroot 'seeds' are actually capsules of three or more seeds. Sow in groups of two or three, 10 cm (4 in) apart, thinning to one plant when the seedlings are manageable. If the ground is dry at thinning time, water a few hours beforehand. When they are about 15 cm (6 in) tall, pull alternate plants to eat young; do not forget the delicious leaves.

Routine care and harvesting Water regularly in dry spells, and pack moist peat around the shoulders of the roots to keep them tender and free from woodiness. Keep down weeds and give a foliar feed in summer if the rain does not come to wash in dry feeds given to the root area. Be particularly wary of boron deficiency (see p 368).

Young globe beets can be lifted as required (about nine weeks after sowing) when they are about the size of golf balls; young tankards can be taken when they are about 5 cm (2 in) across. Beets left to mature are ready four months after sowing. Scrape the soil away from them to see if the roots are ready, and lift them very carefully, as they bleed easily. Maincrop beets can be left in the ground for the winter, mulched with hay or straw, in moderate climates or lifted and stored in clamps or boxes of sandy soil.

Parsnips

Slow-growing parsnips are well worth cultivating for their sweet-tasting flesh for autumn and winter dishes. Three basic kinds are available – short, intermediate and long-rooted – though often no distinction is made. Short-rooted varieties are best for light, shallow or stony soils that would hinder the development of the long-rooted kinds. They are also the best choice if the soil is poor or where canker is prevalent. Long-rooted kinds need special care and are usually grown for exhibition only, although 'Tender and True' is a long-rooted type that resists canker and has a fine flavour. For most gardeners, intermediate parsnips are ideal, doing very well on normal, deep loamy soils and yielding a good return for minimum attention.

Soil and sowing Parsnips like a limy soil enriched with well-rotted organic manure during the previous season. Work in a base dressing of general fertilizer high in phosphate (see p 352) before sowing. Clear the soil of stones and other obstructions to a depth of at least 30 cm (12 in), more if you are growing

Recommended beetroot varieties

Globe-shaped	'Avonearly'; 'Boltardy'; 'Burpee's Golden'; 'Burpee's Red Ball'; 'Detroit Little Globe'; 'Divergina' (good for pickling); 'Early Bunch'; 'Early Wonder'; 'Golden Beet'; 'King Red'; 'Ruby Queen'; 'Snowhite'
Top-shaped	'Burpee's Redheart'; 'Burpee's White'; 'Cylindra'; 'Formanova'; 'Housewives' Choice'; 'Lutz Green Leaf'; 'Tendersweet'
Long	'Long Blood Red'; 'Cheltenham Green Top'

All varieties are red unless obvious from the name

Recommended parsnip varieties

Short	'Avonresister'; 'Evesham'
Mid-length	'Intermediate'; 'Offenham'; 'The Student'; 'White Gem'
Long	'Dobie's Exhibition'; 'Exhibition'; 'Hollow Crown Improved'; 'Leda'; 'Lisbonnais'; 'Tender and True'

Recommended turnip and swede varieties

Early turnips	'Early Purple Top Milan'; 'Early Red Top Milan'; 'Early Six Weeks'; 'Early Snowball Improved'; 'Early White Milan'; 'Early White Store'; 'Jersey Navet'; 'Sprinter'; 'Tokyo Cross' (F1 hybrid)
Maincrop turnips	'Golden Ball'; 'Greentop White' (good for leaves); 'Just Right' (F1 hybrid); 'Manchester Market'; 'Marbletop White' (good for leaves); 'Model White'; 'Purple Top White Globe'
Swedes	'American Purple Top'; 'Bronze Top Best of All'; 'Burpee's Purple Top Yellow'; 'Improved Long Island'; 'Macomber'; 'Purple Top Western Perfection'

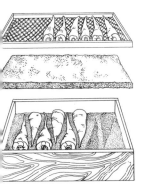

Storing root vegetables

Except in very cold or wet regions, maincrop and late varieties can be left in the ground **1** until needed. Spread dry hay, straw or grass clippings over the tops to protect from frost. If the vegetable garden is far from the house, heel in a few roots nearby to use in bad weather. For small to moderate crops, lift roots in late autumn or early winter and pack in large, deep boxes **2**, between layers of light soil, sand or barely damp peat. Keep cool but frost-free. With large crops, you can build a clamp **3** on well-drained soil in a sheltered spot. Stack the roots evenly, making a pyramid shape – or, for very large crops, a long ridge shape. Cover with a layer of dry straw 25 to 30 cm (10 to 12 in) thick all over, followed by 15 to 20 cm (6 to 8 in) of soil. Beat it down firmly with a spade. Leave a tuft of straw sticking through the soil at the top as a 'chimney' to allow the roots to breathe; otherwise they sweat and rot. If you build a long ridge-shaped clamp, provide several 'chimneys'.

Turnips under glass

An early crop of turnips can be raised by sowing Milan varieties in a heated frame in middle to late winter, in 1 cm (½ in) holes 12 cm (5 in) apart. Set two or three seeds to a hole, thinning to the strongest seedling. Keep the frame closed, but ventilate and water as weather and growth dictate. A temperature of 19°C (66°F) is necessary for rapid growth. The roots should be ready for pulling in about two months.

Alternatively, you can sow in the normal way in early-spring in soil warmed by cloches. Keep the plants covered for five to six weeks. You can make another sowing in midsummer and lift from early autumn onwards.

long-rooted varieties. Parsnip seeds are thin, papery and liable to rot in wet soil. Choose a sunny site, be generous with the seeds to ensure a reasonable crop and sow only in well-drained ground. If necessary, line the drills, which should be 30 cm (12 in) apart and 1 cm (½ in) deep, with sharp sand.

Parsnips take at least eight months to mature, and you should generally sow in late winter. However, you can sow quite safely up to mid-spring if the soil is slow to dry out. In frost-free regions, an autumn sowing will yield a harvest in early spring. Group clusters of seeds 20 cm (8 in) apart along the drill. As the seeds take a month or so to germinate, sow a marker crop of radishes to indicate the row. Water well, cover with fine soil or grass clippings and firm with the back of a rake.

Routine care and harvesting When they are about 2.5 cm (1 in) high, thin the seedlings to the one strongest in each cluster. Keep down weeds and mulch with organic material such as garden compost, peat or pulverized bark, to keep the shoulders of the roots soft and tender and to prevent them cracking in dry weather. Watch out for canker, which rots the shoulders of the roots.

When roots are fully developed, about 8 cm (3 in) across at the shoulders, they are ready for lifting. They have a sweeter flavour if lightly frosted and many people prefer to leave them in the ground for the winter, protecting them with a mulch of straw or hay. Although the roots are frost-hardy, they may be attacked by soil pests if it is very wet. Alternatively, you can lift the whole crop at once and store as for turnips. Whatever you do, make sure you lift the crop before the following spring, otherwise the plants will start into new growth, producing flowers at the expense of roots.

Turnips and swedes

Turnips and swedes have a long history of cultivation, the former being popular vegetables in the Middle Ages while the latter are still regarded in many countries as suitable only for cattle feed. They are often confused, both being commonly globular, but turnips are quicker-growing and smaller, with 5 cm (2 in) diameter roots which are usually white, and are topped with delicious edible leaves (a form of 'spring greens'). Swedes, also known as rutabagas, have larger, 10 to 12 cm (4 to 5 in) roots, which usually have yellow flesh, and inedible leaves. They take longer to mature but are hardier and excellent for

winter storage. They have a sweeter though coarser flavour than turnips.

There is only one group of swedes, but early-maturing and maincrop varieties of turnips are available. Early types have either globe-shaped, cylindrical or flattened roots, white to pale green. Their delicate flavour is much prized, but they will not store. Maincrop turnip varieties all have globular roots, usually dark green and white, but some with purple tops. They store well in winter and produce the best tops, which are cooked and eaten like cabbage.

Soil and sowing Choose a patch that has been well manured for a previous crop, well drained and limed if acid, as turnips and swedes are brassicas and liable to become infected with club root disease in wet, acid ground. Rake well and scatter general fertilizer before sowing. Phosphates are important for root growth, so if this plant food is lacking, work superphosphate into the soil at 135 g/m² (4 oz/sq yd) before taking out drills.

Treat turnips like beetroot, sowing early varieties successively every two weeks from early spring to midsummer, and maincrop varieties in one batch in mid- or late summer. Protect very early crops with cloches if necessary. They will be ready for harvesting from midsummer. Maincrops can be harvested in autumn or winter. In areas where winter temperatures never fall below −4°C (25°F), sowing in autumn will produce a winter crop. If you want to grow turnips primarily for their green leafy shoots, sow in late summer or early autumn for spring pickings. Swedes are sown all at once in late spring and early summer for pulling in mid-autumn.

Sow turnip seeds thinly in drills 40 cm (15 in) apart and 1 cm (½ in) deep, watering the drill beforehand if the soil is dry. Swedes need slightly deeper drills, 2.5 cm (1 in) deep, spaced 45 cm (18 in) apart. When they are about 2.5 cm (1 in) high, thin seedlings to 15 cm (6 in) apart for early turnips and 25 cm (10 in) for maincrop turnips and swedes. Further thinning may be needed as the plants develop, but varieties grown for their leaves need no thinning.

Routine care and harvesting Water freely and regularly, especially when young, mulching rows with peat to stop the roots splitting in dry weather. Keep down weeds, and make sure that the ground is well drained to discourage club root disease, which will kill any member of the brassica family, to which turnips and swedes belong.

Early turnips can be pulled as required, when they are about the size of golf balls. Maincrops are lifted in the autumn, for storing in boxes of dry peat or sand in a cool, frost-free shed or garage. They can be left in the soil, but if it turns wet they are liable to rot and become infested with pests such as millipedes, wireworms, and slugs. Turnip tops are cut when the foliage is about 20 cm (8 in) high. This is usually eight to ten weeks after sowing. Swedes, which take three months to mature, can be lifted for storage in autumn, or left in the ground for digging as required. Protect with a mulch of straw or grass clippings.

Some unusual root vegetables

There is a surprisingly large range of intriguing and tasty root vegetables which are reasonably easy to grow and make a refreshing change from the usual root crops. In truth, not all of them are botanically 'root' vegetables; the edible part of celeriac for example, is not the root but the swollen stem which grows underground. None of the plants described below are related, but they share certain similarities of cultivation both with each other and with the better-known crops described on page 278.

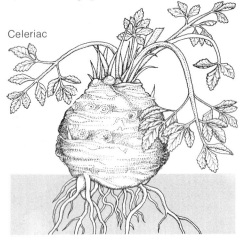
Celeriac

Celeriac
Although rather different in appearance, celeriac (*Apium graveolens rapaceum*) is very closely related to celery. It is also known as turnip-rooted celery on account of its swollen knob, or root, which grows to the size of a grapefruit, 10 cm (4 in) across. In North America it is called knob celery. It makes a good celery substitute if you have a thin, shallow or stony soil where celery cannot be grown. Although treated in the kitchen quite differently from celery – you grate or slice the roots and eat them raw, or boil them as a vegetable – the flavour is similar. The young top leaves may be used in a bouquet garni or to flavour soups in place of celery stems.

Celeriac does well in cool but relatively frost-free regions. Ordinary soil, enriched with well-rotted humus (not fresh manure or the roots will fork) and dressed with general fertilizer, is ideal for quick results. The plants take all the growing season to mature (about 200 days), so start in good time, in early spring. Prepare seed-trays of seedling mixture and sow thinly, germinating in gentle heat: 15°C (61°F). Prick out the seedlings when they are 1 cm (½ in) high. Space them 5 cm (2 in) apart in trays of loam- or soil-based potting mixture and harden off gradually, transplanting outdoors in late spring to early summer, as soon as frosts have finished. Position them 30 cm (12 in) apart in rows 45 cm (18 in) apart, setting the plants in shallow furrows if the weather is dry. Water in well.

Plump up the roots by feeding weekly with dilute liquid manure from midsummer to early autumn. Keep down weeds and pull off suckers and side-shoots to retain a clear, uncluttered root and a sturdy growing tip. Water liberally in dry spells, or the roots may

turn hard and woody. Lightly earth up the roots in mid-autumn to safeguard them from early sharp frosts. Watch out for the same diseases and pests that afflict celery – mosaic virus diseases, celery leaf spot and damping off. A suitable fungicide (see p 361) will protect plants from the two latter troubles.

Celeriac can be pulled when the roots are about 5 cm (2 in) across, but if the soil is light and drains well, leave the roots to harvest as required. In heavy soil that is liable to water-logging and areas prone to hard frosts, lift them in early winter, cut off any fibrous roots and store in boxes of moist sand or peat in a cool, frost-free place. Remove all the leaves but retain the central 'topknot' of foliage.

Chinese artichokes
These curious vegetables, known botanically as *Stachys sieboldii* (*S. affinis* or *S. tuberifera*), gained their common name because the spiral tubers taste like artichokes. They do best in temperate regions and, although easy to grow, are not often attempted.

A sunny position is desirable, as shade can cause an excess of top growth at the expense of tuber production. Any soil that is reasonably fertile and dressed with general fertilizer before the tubers are planted will ensure good results. Manure light soils well if they have not received a dressing of organic refuse for several years. The plants are grown from 'seed' tubers in the same way as potatoes. Set these 5 cm (4 in) deep and 25 cm (10 in) apart in rows 40 cm (15 in) apart in early spring. Water regularly in dry spells, top dress with fertilizer if growth is slow and keep down weeds to prevent them smothering the stems.

The tubers, from 2.5 to 8 cm (1 to 3 in) long and 2.5 cm (1 in) thick at the middle, are lifted as required, from late autumn onwards. They are a little frost-tender, so protect them with straw or sacking when severe frosts threaten. It is better not to lift and store the tubers as

Chinese artichokes

they will only throw out shoots and loose their flavour. If a few are needed for a week or two, pack them in boxes of barely moist peat or sand. Cook and eat as you would Jerusalem artichokes (see below).

Horseradish
This pungent, paddle-leaved perennial – so good as an accompaniment to roast beef and other dishes when it is grated and pickled or mixed with cream – is a native of Europe and is often found growing in rampant colonies. It is classified as *Armoracia rusticana* (*Cochlearia armoracia*).

Get the best results by planting the fleshy roots in well-drained, fertile soil enriched with old manure or waste from the compost heap. Soggy, wet ground, or soil that is excessively chalky or dries quickly, will produce poor results. A sunny spot is ideal, but horse-radish will thrive in a shady corner. It is such

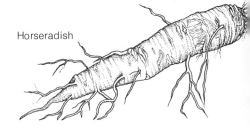
Horseradish

an invasive grower that it is a good idea to grow it in tubs, large pots or perforated buckets plunged to the rim in the soil.

The crop is raised from pieces of the thong-like roots planted in early spring. The thongs should be 20 to 30 cm (8 to 12 in) long and about the thickness of a finger. Limit the roots to one bud each. Set these 30 cm (12 in) apart with their tops 10 cm (4 in) below the soil. Firm the soil gently round them. As a clump forms quickly from a single root, very few roots provide ample pickings. Water freely in dry weather and scatter slug bait if it turns wet, as slugs and snails favour the succulent leaves. Keep down weeds and hoe to stir the soil and prevent it compacting after prolonged watering or heavy rain.

Lift the roots in autumn and store them in moist sand in a cool place to keep them plump and fresh. Use as required; do not bring from store more than you need, or the flavour will deteriorate. Peel and grate them immediately before use. Another way of storing the roots is to shred them, dry them in a slow oven, then pack them in a jar and keep the top tightly on.

Although it is a perennial, it is best to treat horseradish as an annual, clearing the crop from the ground each autumn and retaining some roots for replanting the following spring. Make sure they are planted the right way up by cutting them horizontally at the top and obliquely at the bottom.

Jerusalem artichokes
Handsome vegetables that are grown for their edible artichoke-flavoured tuberous roots and also as effective windbreaks or screens, these have nothing to do with the city of Jerusalem. Botanically, the plant is a kind of sunflower, *Helianthus tuberosus*, and was discovered in Nova Scotia by the French in the early 17th century; it grows up to 1.8 m (6 ft) and more but the flowers will only bloom in hot summers. The Italians gave them the name of *girasole del Canada* (Canadian sunflowers), which was gradually corrupted to Jerusalem. In North America, they are often called sunchokes. The tubers are irregularly shaped and very knobbly, about 10 cm (4 in) long and 5 to 8 cm (2 to 3 in) across. They usually have whitish-yellowish flesh, although there is a purple-skinned type, 'Fuseau'.

Ordinary soil is perfectly adequate for these plants and they do not need feeding with ni-

right Jerusalem artichokes make a splendid screen against cold winds, and are usefully planted where they will shelter a row of tomatoes, marrows or cucumbers. Their light shade also helps salad crops in a hot summer.

rogenous fertilizers as they make their own
rom the soil. Provided there is good drainage
nd lime is present, good roots are produced;
void waterlogged patches. If the soil is well
ndowed with humus, a particularly heavy
rop of tubers can be expected. Should the
lanting site be a little poor and the soil thin,
vork in plenty of humus-forming materials
uch as garden compost, old manure or spent
ops, plus a general fertilizer (analysis about
7:7:7; see p 352) at 135 g/m² (4 oz/sq yd)
before planting. If the soil is shallow and
tony, take out holes 30 to 60 cm (1 to 2 ft)
leep and replace the existing soil with well-
otted leaf-mould, garden compost or peat
nixed with soil.

Plant in late winter to early spring to give
he tubers a long time to develop and prolifer-
te. Treat them as potatoes, setting 'seed'
ubers 40 cm (15 in) apart and 10 to 15 cm (4
o 6 in) deep in rows 75 cm (2½ ft) apart.
Plant with a trowel. Large tubers may be
liced into sections, each with a healthy bud.

Keep free from weeds, water regularly in
lryish weather to encourage steady and
obust growth and top dress twice, in late

Jerusalem artichokes

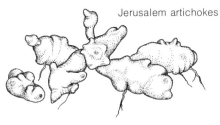

spring and in midsummer, with general fertilizer watered in to help tubers swell to a good
plump size. In late summer, especially if your
garden is windswept, secure the tall stems to
canes or poles. In a hot dry season, unless you
are growing the plants just for screening purposes, nip out the growing shoot tips to stop
flowers forming. These will only sap the
plant's strength and few top-quality tubers
will be produced. Watch out for sclerotinia
disease, causing fluffy white mould; destroy
affected plants. In winter, reduce the stems to
within 30 cm (1 ft) of ground level.

To harvest, carefully unearth a root of tubers, taking care to remove them all, otherwise they could be a nuisance sprouting the
following year. A good average yield would
be about 1.5 kg (3 lb) of tubers per root.
Leave the tubers in the ground until wanted.
If lifted, it is not advisable to store them for
more than two months as they have thin skins
and do not keep as well as potatoes. Pack the
tubers in boxes of barely damp peat or sand
and store in a cool, frost-free place. Pick out
some healthy tubers for replanting. Plant
them out straight away if you have the space.

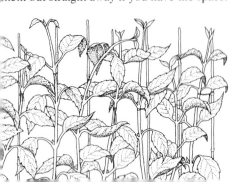

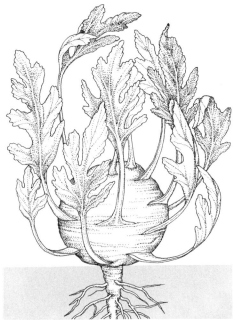
Kohlrabi

Kohlrabi
A superb, mild-flavoured, close relative of the
cabbage, kohlrabi (*Brassica oleracea gongylodes*) is often grown as an alternative to turnips on hot, shallow soil in which the latter
quickly run to seed. In fact, its nutty, turnip-
like flavour has given it the name of turnip-
rooted cabbage. Kohlrabi develops a large
greenish or purplish swollen stem base just
above ground level, and is best eaten when
this is little bigger than a tennis ball; allowed
to grow larger, it may be tough, fibrous and fit
only for cattlefeed. It is grown widely in
Europe, and 'Primavera White', which is
bolt-resistant, has fewer leaves and 'bulbs'
that are crisp, tender and remarkably free
from fibre, is particularly recommended.

Most soils that drain well and are fairly well
nourished with organic manure give good
yields, but, as already mentioned, it is highly
useful on stony or light soils. It thrives in soils
that warm up quickly, and is exceptionally
drought-resistant. Garden varieties mature
very quickly (between eight and nine weeks
from sowing), so successive sowings can be
made from early spring to midsummer to give
harvests from late summer to winter. Take out
drills 2 cm (¾ in) deep and 25 cm (10 in) apart
and sow thinly. Water the drill first if the
weather is dry. Thin the seedlings to 12 cm
(5 in), then to 25 cm (10 in), using the succulent thinnings to eat. Seedlings can be transplanted if great care is taken.

Water freely when young, top dress with
general fertilizer if the soil is poor, and keep
down weeds, especially chickweed and
groundsel. Very little watering is needed during the growing season. Look out for turnip
flea beetle and club root disease (see pp 362
and 365). Kohlrabi does not store well, so
leave the plants in the ground and lift as
required. Enjoy them peeled and sliced thinly
in salads, or boiled like turnips.

Salsify and scorzonera
Both these intriguing and tasty root vegetables are grown in a similar manner. They are
botanically distinct, though both are members
of the daisy family. Salsify, a biennial, is
Tragopogon porrifolius, a native of Algeria;
the perennial scorzonera is *Scorzonera his-*

panica, a native of Spain. The black-skinned
roots of scorzonera share the familiar sweet
flavour of parsnips; salsify, which has white-
skinned roots, is sometimes called the vegetable oyster because of its distinctive flavour.

For both crops, get the best results by growing in deep, rich soil preferably manured for a
previous crop like peas or celery. (The roots
will fork if the manure is too fresh.) Sow in
mid- or late spring. Make drills 2 cm (¾ in)
deep, 30 cm (12 in) apart, and sow thinly. If
the soil is shallow or stony, take out crowbar
holes and fill them with sifted loam and peat
plus a sprinkling of general fertilizer. The
holes should be 25 cm (10 in) apart in rows
40 cm (15 in) apart. Sow three seeds per hole,
thinning to the strongest seedling. Water and
liquid feed freely to encourage fat, fleshy
roots. Thin if necessary and remove any
flowering shoots. Keep down weeds and
mulch the rows with peat or compost if the soil
starts to become dry. There are no serious
pest or disease problems with either vegetable.

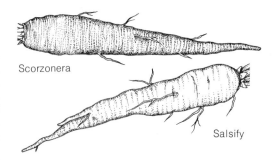
Scorzonera

Salsify

Lift the roots as required in autumn. In
sandy soil they can be left in throughout the
winter, protected by a mulch, but it is better to
lift and store them in boxes of peat or sand if
the soil is liable to become waterlogged. If
scorzonera fails to make usefully large roots in
its first year, leave them to grow on and
enlarge in the second year. Roots of salsify
will, however, have to be harvested after the
first year, even if they are small. The spring
following planting, if they are left in the
ground, both salsify and scorzonera roots will
push up vigorous flowering shoots. These are
a delicacy if covered with pots, blanched and
eaten with salads. Or they can be eaten green
like asparagus when about 15 cm (6 in) tall.

Recommended varieties

Celeriac	'Alabaster'; 'Claudia'; 'Giant Prague'; 'Globus'; 'Iram'; 'Marble Ball'
Horseradish	'Bohemian'; 'Marliner Kren'
Jerusalem artichokes	'Fuseau'; 'New White'
Kohlrabi	'Primavera White'; 'Purple Delicatesse'; 'Purple Vienna'; 'Suttons Earliest Purple'; 'Suttons Earliest White'; 'White Vienna'
Salsify	'Mammoth Sandwich Island'
Scorzonera	'Russian Giant'

Chinese artichokes are available only as the species

Green leaf vegetables

Between them, the leafy brassicas – members of the cabbage family – supply a year-round crop of pleasantly varied, nutritious green vegetables. Cabbage itself has been cultivated for centuries; Brussels sprouts, eponymous with the Belgian capital, have a similar long tradition, and kale, once thought of only as cattle fodder, now enjoys a respectable reputation as a table vegetable. Although not related to these, spinach enjoys almost equal popularity, while for those in hotter climates there are the unrelated New Zealand spinach and leaf beet (various forms of beetroot).

Brassicas are all biennials raised, with the exception of Brussels sprouts, as annuals. They are grown in the same way and appreciate the same conditions. They are easily raised from seed, in a nursery bed or under glass for an early crop, and transplanted to permanent quarters later. They are essentially mild-climate crops, and most will not survive severe frost or extreme heat; kale, however, withstands both heat and cold better than the other types. In hot regions, a crop of the less hardy varieties can be raised for winter use.

The most important thing with brassicas is the soil: they need firm, consolidated soil which is generously limed (unless already alkaline), well manured and drains well. This combats club root disease, the bane of all brassicas. Never grow them on a site used previously for another brassica (including turnips and some other root crops), as this encourages the disease. As a further precaution use calomel (mercurous chloride) liberally, either as a paste in which to dip seedling roots before transplanting, or applied as a powder direct to the soil. Root flies are also a serious problem (see p 362), and in many areas are resistant to BHC; the most effective measure is to treat the soil with trichlorphon once transplanted seedlings are established.

Cabbages

There are so many varieties of cabbage (*Brassica oleracea capitata*) that you need never be without them. Pointed (or cone-headed) and round-headed types predominate, although there are the flat-headed varieties that are especially popular in the United States. As a general rule, pointed varieties are harvested in spring in regions where winters are not too harsh, round-heads in winter, with the summer and autumn crops having a mixture of both. Red cabbages, which are picked for winter cooking and pickling, are round-heads.

Mid-season and winter cabbages are larger than spring crops, and Savoy cabbages (*B. oleracea bullata*) are a breed slightly apart. They are a winter crop, improved by a touch of frost, and are easily identified by their crinkly, dark green leaves and mild flavour. They are excellent shredded in salads or as coleslaw. Portuguese cabbage, or *couve tronchuda* (*B. oleracea costata*) is a loose-centred cabbage sown in spring and ready for harvesting in early autumn. 'Spring greens' are generally immature cabbages (though turnip-tops, broccoli leaves and Brussels sprout tops are used in the same way). They are usually taken from the spring crop, but an immature cabbage of any season can be eaten thus. Spring greens are also known as collards, although American gardeners reserve this term for plain-leaved kale (see below).

Sowing Cabbages are generally raised in a seed-bed, but sow under glass if you want to start really early or the weather is uncommonly frosty. Sow the seeds sparingly 1 cm (½ in) deep in short rows about 20 cm (8 in) apart. Thin out, and transplant – using calomel as mentioned above – when the plants are about 15 cm (6 in) tall and have a sturdy ball of roots. The smaller, compact varieties should be place 40 cm (15 in) apart in rows 45 cm (18 in) apart. Space all others 45 cm (18 in) apart in all directions. If you intend to take some for spring greens, set the plants only 20 cm (8 in) apart, and take every alternate plant for greens, leaving the remainder enough space to heart up.

Sow varieties for spring cutting in mid- or late summer, transplanting in early autumn; protect with cloches or plant them in the shelter of a wall if the weather is bad. Stagger your summer crops by planting some in late winter, under glass in frosty regions, to transplant in spring for cropping in early summer, and make a second sowing outside in early spring. Transplant these in early summer for a late summer crop. Autumn crops are sown in mid-spring and transplanted in early summer, and winter crops are sown in late spring and transplanted in midsummer.

Routine care and harvesting Protect seedlings from root flies as mentioned above, and from turnip flea beetles in hot dry weather (see p 362). Keep down weeds and earth up stems in autumn to protect winter and spring cabbages from blustery winds (the root system is very shallow). Spring cabbages appreciate a nitrogenous feed to encourage them after their lethargic winter growth. Protect them with cloches in cold windy spells. Unless you are picking spring greens, cut the hearts when they are firm and swollen. Winter cabbages from blustery winds (the root system is very shallow). Spring cabbages a cool place; if frost threatens to burst the hearts, quick action will save your crop.

Chinese cabbages

Not strictly a cabbage, *Brassica pekinensis* looks like a giant cos lettuce. A looser-leaved species is *B. chinensis*. Both can be eaten raw in salads or cooked like cabbage. They are raised in much the same way as cabbages, but are sown *in situ* rather than raised in a seed-bed and transplanted. Sow them in rows 30 cm (12 in) apart in late spring to midsummer. Beware of bolting. Water freely and feed with liquid fertilizer to promote rapid growth. Pick them when the hearts are full, and use straight away; they will not keep.

Brussels sprouts

Although very popular in Europe, Brussels sprouts (*B. oleracea gemmifera*) enjoy limited appeal in North America. The sprouts form compact buttons, like tiny cabbages, clustering thickly around stems that vary from 45 to 75 cm (1½ to 2½ ft) tall. They can be har-

Round-headed cabbage   Pointed cabbage

Savoy cabbage   Red cabbage

vested from early autumn to early spring in areas with moderate winters, and are excellent for freezing. The newly developed F1 hybrids (see table) produce very uniform buttons, but they tend to mature simultaneously. If you have no means to store them, or if you prefer to pick the buttons freshly, choose the ordinary varieties which crop in succession.

Soil and sowing Proceed as for cabbages, making sure that the crop is grown in a sunny but sheltered spot, so that cold winds or droughty spells will not delay growth. Early varieties are planted in early spring for a crop in autumn. For a really early crop, raise the plants the previous summer, protect them with cloches throughout winter and plant them out in spring. Mid-season and late varieties are sown in mid- to late spring for winter cropping. When transplanting, choose plants with good growing tips – some are 'blind', producing only a rosette of leaves and no tips.

Routine care and harvesting Keep down weeds and top dress the root area with high-potash fertilizer (see p 352) in early summer. If you have a windy garden, support tall stems with stakes. In early winter nip out a small piece of the growing tip, about the size of a sprout. This technique, known as cocking

Winter cabbages	'Burpee's Danish Roundhead'; 'Burpee's Surehead'; 'Christmas Drumhead'; 'Penn State Ballhead'; 'Premium Flat Dutch'; 'Seneca Danish Ballhead'; 'Winter Monarch'; 'Winter White' (good for storage)
Savoy cabbages	'Best of All'; 'Chieftain'; 'Dwarf Green Curled'; 'Ice Queen'; 'January King'; 'January Prince'; 'New Year'; 'Ormskirk Rearguard'; 'Perfection Drumhead'; 'Savoy King'; 'Wirosa' (F1 hybrid)
Chinese cabbages	'Burpee Hybrid'; 'Crispy Choy' (loose-leaved); 'Michihli'; 'Nagoaka'; 'Pe-Tsai'; 'Sampan'; 'Tip Top

Brussels sprouts

Early
'Achilles' (F1 hybrid); 'Early Dwarf'; 'Early Half Tall'; 'Fillbasket'; 'Focus' (F1 hybrid); 'Jade Cross' (F1 hybrid); 'Long Island Improved'; 'Rollo'; 'Peer Gynt' (F1 hybrid)
Mid-season
'King Arthur' (F1 hybrid); 'Irish Elegance'; 'Perfect Line' (F1 hybrid); 'Roodnerf Seven Hills'; 'Thor' (F1 hybrid); 'Vremo Inter'; 'Winter Harvest'
Late
'Citadel' (F1 hybrid); 'Fasolt' (F1 hybrid); 'Market Rearguard'; 'Prince Askold' (F1 hybrid); 'Sigmund' (F1 hybrid)

Kale

Curly
'Blue Curled Scotch'; 'Dwarf Blue Curled Vates'; 'Dwarf Green Curled'; 'Dwarf Siberian'; 'Extra Curled Scotch'; 'Fribor' (F1 hybrid); 'Frosty' (dwarf); 'Tall Scotch Curled'; 'Toga'; 'Verdura'
Plain-leaved
'Carolina Header' (collard); 'Cottager's'; 'Georgia' (collard); 'Hardy Sprouting'; 'Thousand Headed'
Rape kale
'Asparagus Kale'; 'Hungry Gap'; 'Ragged Jack'; 'Russian'

New Zealand spinach

Brussels sprouts

Curly kale

Plain-leaved kale

Chinese cabbage

Spinach

Spinach	**Summer** 'America'; 'Bloomsdale Long Standing'; 'Cleanleaf'; 'Dominant'; 'Forkhook'; 'King of Denmark'; 'Long Standing Round'; 'Monoppa' (low acid content); 'Noorman' **Winter** 'Broad-Leaved Prickly'; 'Greenmarket'; 'Long Standing Prickly'; 'Sigmaleaf' (round-seeded); 'Viking'; 'Winter Bloomsdale'
Leaf beet	'Burpee's Fordhook Giant'; 'Burpee's Rhubarb Chard' ('Rhubarb Beet'; red-stalked); 'Lucullus'

improves the quality of the crop and speeds up development. Pick the buttons when they are about the size of a walnut, taking a few from each plant, beginning at the bottom. Do not strip one plant. Remove 'blown' (loose-hearted) sprouts first and pull off yellowing leaves which obscure light and air. In spring cut the leafy tops to cook like cabbage.

Kale

Unlike other members of the brassica family, kale (*B. oleracea acephala*) can thrive in poor, thin, stony or sandy soil as long as it is well limed. It is much in demand in late winter when few green vegetables are available. There are several varieties: the extremely hardy curly kale, often listed as borecole, which is, incidentally, an attractive ornamental plant; plain-leaved kale (known in North America as collards), which is coarser in appearance, but more prolific and slightly more pest-resistant; rape kale, which looks like curly kale, but goes on cropping for longer; and 'Pentland Brig', a useful cross-breed of plain-leaved and curly kale, which not only produces copious leaves but yields the additional bonus of broccoli-like spears. All are improved by a touch of frost.

Sowing Raise all varieties except rape kale in a seed-bed. Sow the seeds in mid- to late spring in drills 2.5 cm (1 in) deep and 15 cm (6 in) apart. Transplant when the seedlings are 10 cm (4 in) tall. Sow rape kale *in situ*, as it does not take kindly to transplanting, in early to mid-spring. Make drills 60 cm (2 ft) apart, and thin the seedlings to 45 cm (18 in) apart when the plants are about 10 cm (4 in) tall. In warm regions, make a summer sowing of all varieties for a winter harvest.

Routine care and harvesting Water liberally, and in very dry weather stir the soil to make a dust mulch; this prevents water evaporating from lower levels. Spur on summer growth with a dressing of nitrogenous fertilizer. In the autumn, earth up stems to prevent them blowing over. Kale is ready for harvesting about six months after sowing. Pick side shoots as they form, taking a few from each plant in turn. Pinch out the growing tips of curly kale to encourage prolific side shoots. 'Pentland Brig' should be regularly picked over for non-flowering side shoots and leaves and later for budding spears, just as sprouting broccoli is gathered (see p 286). Collards are either picked as ordinary kale or allowed to fully mature and cooked whole, like cabbage.

Spinach and leaf beet

Once valued for medicinal purposes only, spinach (*Spinacia oleracea*) is now grown for its delicious taste. Year-round supplies can be obtained by sowing summer varieties, which have round seeds, and the prickly-seeded winter varieties (which are very hardy) in succession. Delicious alternatives are New Zealand Spinach (*Tetragonia tetragonioides*), a tender plant grown for picking in summer, and Malabar spinach (*Basella alba*). The latter is a vine-like plant which develops bright green glossy leaves; neither are true spinach.

One of the drawbacks with summer spinach is its tendency to bolt in hot dry weather. This can be prevented by careful soil maintenance, but in very hot or dry areas it is probably safer to grow New Zealand spinach, which does not bolt, or leaf beet (a form of *Beta vulgaris*), which yields profusely in dry seasons. This biennial, which produces swathes of paddle-shaped leaves, is known variously as silver beet, seakale beet or Swiss chard (but is quite different from seakale; see p 305). Spinach beet or perpetual spinach is also a form of leaf beet, but does not have the thick leaf stalks.

Soil and sowing The soil must be fertile and moisture-retaining yet well drained. Deep, loamy, well-manured soil is best. Leaf beet will survive if it is a little drier, as will New Zealand spinach. Sow true spinach in drills 2.5 cm (1 in) deep and 30 cm (12 in) apart, thinning the seedlings to 10 cm (4 in), then 20 cm (8 in) (the thinnings are delicious). Sow summer varieties from late winter to mid-summer for harvesting from early summer to autumn. In hot climates, sow only up to spring for an early summer crop. Winter varieties are sown from late summer to early autumn for harvesting from mid-autumn to mid-spring. Protect late sowings with cloches unless you live in a frost-free region.

New Zealand spinach can be raised in the greenhouse in late winter and planted out in late spring when the frosts are over. Alternatively sow outdoors directly in early spring, protecting with cloches to encourage robust growth. Space the plants 90 cm (3 ft) apart in all directions, as they spread rampantly. Leaf beet is sown in mid- to late spring in drills 2.5 cm (1 in) deep, 40 cm (15 in) apart. Thin the seedlings to 15 cm (6 in), then 30 cm (12 in). The thinnings can be eaten or transplanted. Make another sowing in late summer to overwinter, under cloches in cold regions.

Routine care and harvesting Water regularly and mulch with moist peat to keep roots cool. In early spring give winter spinach a nitrogenous feed to spur growth, and in early summer feed leaf beet in the same way. Keep down weeds and feed summer spinach in late summer to encourage a good second growth of leaves. Harvest by pulling or cutting a few of the outermost leaves from each plant in turn, starting at the bottom, so that more can grow. You will have to be patient with New Zealand spinach, which makes masses of tiny triangular leaves. The small tender leaves of leaf beet are delicious in salads. It is best to cook the larger leaves. The fat, fleshy leaf stalks can be cooked like asparagus.

Green salad vegetables

Leafy vegetables for salads are among the most popular of garden crops, and lettuces are undoubtedly the most popular of all. Unless you live in an area with harsh winters and do not have cloches or a greenhouse, there are lettuce varieties for every season. But there are many others that will bring salad-bowl variety, and some of these are particularly good for winter use.

Apart from those described here, there is watercress and land (or winter) cress, which are not commonly grown in gardens and are covered on page 307.

Lettuces
To the ancient Egyptians a pernicious weed, today's lettuce (*Lactuca sativa*) takes many forms. There are the oval-hearted Cos lettuces (named for the Greek island of Cos, where they are said to have originated); they are sometimes known as romaine lettuces in North America, and have the strongest flavour. The other main group are the round-headed or cabbage lettuces, which are subdivided into several groups. The butter-head types have moderately solid hearts of fairly soft leaves; the crisp-head varieties, such as 'Webb's Wonderful', produce a very solid heart of crisp, crunchy leaves; and the loose-head or 'cut-and-come-again' lettuces do not produce a head at all, but loose leaves that are harvested a few at a time.

The last two groups are particularly good in hot, dry conditions, but no lettuces do well if average temperatures exceed about 27°C (81°F); they are then liable to bolt prematurely into flower. At the other extreme, a number of varieties grow well over winter for early spring crops so long as temperatures average above −4°C (25°F); below this temperature, give cloche protection. Certain varieties, such as 'Kwiek', grow rapidly under cloches or in a cold frame or cool greenhouse, giving winter crops, while some others are good for forcing in a heated greenhouse.

Lettuces are excellent for catch-cropping and intercropping (see p 262). You can sow them with carrots in a cold frame or under cloches; there will be no overcrowding provided the carrots are sown thinly. You can flank a row of dwarf peas grown under cloches with two rows of dwarf lettuces. Or sow them on the ridge of soil between celery trenches (see p 287) or between rows of Brussels sprouts, beans or potatoes. Where space is limited, you can grow lettuces in plastic growing bags (see p 117).

Soil and sowing Lettuces need good, rich soil that has been well dug through with humus-forming organic matter – old mushroom compost is ideal – either prior to sowing or planting out, or for a previous crop. A cool, moist root run is essential for prolonged cropping and to prevent bolting of hearting varieties; in summer choose a lightly shaded spot between taller vegetables such as peas and beans. For winter crops, however, the soil should not be too heavy. The soil should be well limed if necessary; even if it is only moderately acid (below pH 6; see p 332), the plants will mature slimy and flaccid. Apply a

balanced fertilizer (analysis about 7:7:7; see p 352) as a base dressing at 135 g/m² (4 oz/sq yd) 10 days before sowing.

You can grow early lettuces by sowing seeds thinly from midwinter in trays or pots of loam- or peat-based seedling mixture in a cool greenhouse or cold frame. When the seedlings are just manageable, prick them out 5 cm (2 in) apart into further trays or pots of rich, gritty potting mixture. Set them outdoors about 20 cm (8 in) apart when they are 8 cm (3 in) high and the ground is suitable and the weather mild. Handle the seedlings carefully to avoid damaging the leaves and roots; they do not transplant very well.

For sowing directly outdoors in spring, summer and (with winter varieties) early autumn, take out drills 1 cm (½ in) deep and 25 to 40 cm (10 to 15 in) apart, depending on variety, and scatter a soil insecticide such as BHC or bromophos along them to keep down millipedes, wireworm and cutworms. Sow thinly, firm the soil with the back of a rake and water in if the soil is dry. Using pelleted seed makes subsequent thinning easier. The seedlings should be thinned to 5 to 8 cm (2 to 3 in) apart and then to 20 to 25 cm (8 to 10 in); the second thinnings are good to eat. For a continuous supply, sow short rows every two or three weeks.

Forcing chicory roots
To obtain tasty chicons – the tightly enfolded leafy hearts of witloof chicory – the needs are moisture, warmth and lack of light (so that the chicons are blanched). Plant sturdy roots lifted from the garden in pots or boxes of moist peat or sand. If you cut the roots back to 20 cm (8 in) and cover them to a similar depth **right** no further shading is needed, but if planted more shallowly put them in a dark cupboard or

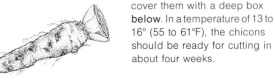

Crisp-head lettuce

Cos (romaine) lettuce

Butter-head lettuce

Loose-head lettuce

Routine care and harvesting Lettuces must have plenty of root moisture at all times so that there is no check to growth that might cause bolting. Mulch the rows to conserve moisture, remove all weeds and close the ends of cloches, if used, to prevent them becoming wind tunnels. If growth is slow, give a top-dressing of nitrogenous fertilizer or water weekly with dilute liquid manure. Control aphids with a non-toxic spray such as derris or pyrethrum (see p 361), and if growing under glass use a fungicide such as benomyl or

cover them with a deep box **below**. In a temperature of 13 to 16° (55 to 61°F), the chicons should be ready for cutting in about four weeks.

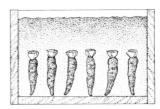
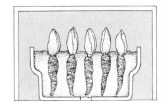

Recommended salad vegetable varieties

Lettuces	Butter-head		Loose-head	
	'All the Year Round'; 'Appia' (mildew-resistant); 'Arctic King'†; 'Aurelia'; 'Avondefiance' (mildew-resistant); 'Burpee Bibb'; 'Buttercrunch'; 'Cobham Green'; 'Constant Heart'; 'Continuity'; 'Dark Green Boston'; 'Emerald'‡; 'Fordhook'; 'Fortune'; 'Heartwell'; 'Helga'; 'Ilo'; 'Imperial Winter'†; 'Kloek'‡ (minimum 10°C [50°F]); 'Knap'‡; 'Kordaat'‡ (minimum 10°C [50°F]); 'Kwiek'‡; 'May Queen'‡; 'Premier'‡; 'Suzan'; 'Tom Thumb' (dwarf); 'Unrivalled'; 'Valdor'†		'Black-Seeded Simpson'; 'Burpee's Greenheart'; 'Ruby' (red-tinged); 'Salad Bowl'	
			Chicory	'Rossa de Verona' ('Red Verona'; red-tinted); 'Sugar Loaf' ('Pain de Sucre'; large-headed); 'Witloof' ('Brussels')
	Cos (romaine)		**Endive†**	**Batavian (escarole)**
	'Balloon' (large); 'Little Gem' (intermediate shape; dwarf); 'Lobjoit's Green Cos'; 'Paris Green'; 'Paris White'; 'Winter Density'† (intermediate shape)			'Batavian Green'; 'Broad-Leaved Batavian' ('Full Heart Batavian'); 'Golda'; 'Winter Lettuce-Leaved'
	Crisp-head			**Staghorn**
	'Burpee's Iceberg'; 'Great Lakes'; 'Imperial no. 44'; 'Minetto'; 'Oswego'; 'Webb's Wonderful'; 'Windermere'			'Exquisite Curled'; 'Green Curled' ('Giant Fringed Oyster'); 'Salad King'
			Corn salad†	'Broad-Leaved English'; 'Large-Leaved Italian'; 'Verte de Cambrai'

†Good for growing outdoors over winter (average minimum temperature −4°C [25°F] or more);
‡good for growing under glass in winter (unheated except as noted)

Dandelion

Staghorn endive

thiram to protect the plants from downy mildew and grey mould (see p 365).

Cut heart-forming lettuces when they feel firm and solid, but before the heart starts to elongate. (This is a sign that they are starting to bolt.) With loose-leaved varieties such as 'Salad Bowl', pick a few leafy sprigs from each plant in turn.

Chicory

Chicory and endive are often confused. Although quite different in appearance, they are related, and chicory is often known in North America as Belgian or French endive or as witloof chicory (from the Dutch for white leaf). Classified as *Cichorium intybus*, it is an easily grown hardy perennial usually grown as an annual and eaten raw in salads or cooked as a leaf vegetable. The variety 'Sugar Loaf' develops a leafy, tender-hearted head not unlike that of a large Cos lettuce. The other varieties are generally grown in two stages: First, a sturdy plant with a well-developed root is grown from seed; then roots are forced in warm, dark conditions to produce tender, slightly bitter-tasting succulent hearts known as chicons. The roots of some varieties are roasted and ground to produce a coffee-substitute.

As it is deep-rooted, chicory needs a well-cultivated, fertile soil; it likes a sunny position. Grow it in the same way as for lettuce, sowing in early summer; it needs the same routine care. In mid- to late autumn, lift the roots, which are rather like those of parsnips, and expose them to the weather for a few days to arrest growth. Cut off the top growth 2.5 cm (1 in) above the crown. Then heel them into the soil in a sheltered part of the garden to protect them from frost or – especially in areas with harsh winters – pack in boxes of sand in a cold but frost-free place.

Force a few roots at a time. Pack in boxes of moist sand or peat and put in a dark place at a temperature of 13 to 16°C (55 to 61°F). Or cut back the roots to 20 cm (8 in) and pack in moist peat, covering them to a depth of 15 to 20 cm (6 to 8 in); then only warmth is needed, not darkness. Cut the chicons when 15 to 20 cm (6 to 8 in) long (after about four weeks), cutting a slice of the crown with the tightly folded head of white leaves. Use them immediately.

Celtuce

A two-for-the-price-of-one vegetable, celtuce (*Lactuca sativa angustana*) is a versatile variety of ordinary lettuce combining the uses of lettuce and celery. It grows 30 to 60 cm (1 to 2 ft) tall, with a thick fleshy stem from which branch broad green leaves. The stem, when trimmed of its leaves, can be eaten cooked or raw like celery – though some people feel that it is slightly bitter. The leaves themselves can be eaten raw in salads when young, or cooked like spinach. Grow celtuce in the same way as lettuce, spacing the plants at a final distance of 20 cm (8 in).

Endive

A first-class lettuce-substitute for summer, autumn and winter salads, endive (*Cichorium endiva*) is a sun-lover from the Mediterranean region, and yet some varieties easily stand frost down to about −4°C (25°F). There are two main groups of varieties. Both resemble lettuces in shape, but the Staghorn, or curly endive, types have crinkled, fern-like leaves, while the Batavian varieties, often called escarole in North America, have plain, flat leaves. The latter are somewhat hardier than the curly varieties.

Grow endive exactly like lettuce, preferably on a light, sandy but humus-rich soil. Curly-leaved varieties can be sown from early or mid-spring, the plain-leaved as late as early autumn. Protect late-sown plants with cloches in hard weather. The leaves are rather bitter when green, so they should be blanched by shading them from light for 7 to 10 days in summer, or up to three weeks in winter; this whitens the leaves and makes them sweeter and more tender. Treat a few plants at a time. Either tie together the outer leaves with raffia so that they shade the inner leaves, or invert a box or large flower-pot over each plant (blocking the drainage hole). If they are

covered with cloches, you can use black plastic sheeting. Once the hearts are creamy-white, cut like lettuce.

Other kinds

Corn salad, or lamb's lettuce (*Valerianella locusta*), has been grown in north-western Europe as a winter salad crop for centuries, and was introduced to the British Isles by the Huguenots. It can, in fact, be harvested at any time of the year if sown in spring and again in late summer. Resembling a rosette of dandelions, with smooth-edged leaves, corn salad tastes somewhat earthy – stronger than a Cos lettuce but milder than dandelion itself (see below). The leaves can be blanched in the same way as for endive, and are picked a few at a time as with loose-leaved lettuces. Grow them in the same way as lettuces, except that they need spacing only 15 cm (6 in) apart.

Although universally despised as a weed in Britain and North America, the dandelion (*Taraxacum officinale*) has cultivated forms such as 'Thick-Leaved Improved' that are consumed with great relish in salads on the continent of Europe. The leaves are blanched as with endive (they are too bitter for most people when green), and – like chicory – the roots can be used to make a coffee-substitute. The roots can also be lifted and forced in the same way as chicory. Only a few plants will be needed, as the plant is a perennial, so do not sow many seeds. Like its wild relative, it is a profligate seeder, so remove any flower buds before they open to prevent your garden being invaded. It will grow in any normal soil.

The pleasantly pungent leaves of nasturtiums (*Tropaeolum majus*) – among the easiest and most popular of hardy annual flowers (see p 210) – make a spicy addition to salads. The flowers can be used in salads too, and the seeds can be pickled like capers. A variety called 'Red Eating Selected' is particularly good, and an especially good crop of lush leaves is given if you grow nasturtiums on moist, fertile soil. Chop them before use.

Mustard and cress

Invaluable as a salad garnish or sandwich filling, white mustard (*Sinapsis alba*) and cress (*Lepidium sativum*) are usually grown and eaten together. Rape (*Brassica napus*) is often substituted for mustard. All have a pleasantly pungent flavour. They are simplicity itself to grow, being cut 10 to 14 days after sowing, when they have one or two pairs of bright green leaves on 5 to 8 cm (2 to 3 in) stems.

You can grow mustard and cress outdoors in spring, summer and early autumn in a seed bed raked to a fine tilth, in trays or pots of seedling mixture in a greenhouse or cold frame, or indoors in small containers on pads of moist absorbent material – flannel, cotton wool, lint, thick absorbent paper and so on. The last method is ideal for showing children how seeds germinate. Simply sprinkle the seeds thickly and evenly over the surface, sowing cress

seeds three days before the faster-growing mustard or rape, so that both are ready together. Cover with brown paper, kitchen foil or black plastic sheeting and keep moderately warm. When the whitened stems are about 5 cm (2 in) long, uncover and place in the light so that the leaves green up. Cut a day or two later.

Cauliflowers and broccoli

Cauliflowers (*Brassica oleracea botrytis*) and broccoli (*B. oleracea italica*) are so closely related that it is often difficult to distinguish between them. Both produce clusters of crumbly-textured florets which grow in a tight clump called a head, curd or heart. Between them, they can provide a year-round supply, though neither vegetable flourishes in average daytime temperatures exceeding 24°C (75°F). Although not so easy or trouble-free as other members of the cabbage family, they are well worth trying.

Probably the most familiar is the summer cauliflower which grows a single large head, usually white but sometimes purple (this goes green in cooking). It is quicker-growing but less hardy than broccoli. Strains have now been developed which will mature in late spring or in autumn as well as the traditional midsummer type. Early varieties are small, tidy plants producing very white curds. Autumn-maturing varieties are usually taller and are surrounded by bluish, protective leaves, but the recently-developed Australian types are sturdy, compact and low-growing.

Winter cauliflowers, which are more correctly termed curding or heading broccoli, are virtually indistinguishable from summer cauliflowers, but are hardier, more suitable for cold-region gardening, and have duller-coloured curds that are enfolded by a protective envelope of leaves. They mature from early winter to late spring.

Sprouting broccoli, whose differences are more obvious, each produce many small heads, and go on producing them throughout their season. Conventional sprouting broccoli comes in white or purple varieties, the purple being hardier, and matures between mid-winter and late spring. Green sprouting broccoli, or calabrese, has the best of both worlds, producing one large cauliflower-type head in autumn and, after this has been cut, a succession of side shoots or spears until stopped by hard frost. Once a broccoli plant has stopped yielding spears, you can cut its leaves for use in the same way as cabbage. Perennial sprouting broccoli produces many small heads annually, in late spring, for several years.

Soil, raising and planting

For best results grow plants on a sunny but sheltered site in deep, rich soil, well supplied with organic matter. Hot, dry, gravelly or sandy soils yield poor results. If the soil needs improving, work in old manure or garden compost during winter. Top dress with lime, too, if the soil is acid, to guard against club root disease. Cauliflower and broccoli plants can be raised in a greenhouse, under cloches or in frames, or in an outdoor seed-bed in good friable soil. Early and mid-season summer cauliflowers are best raised in a greenhouse or cold frame. In a greenhouse, sow seeds in midwinter in trays of sterilized seedling mixture and germinate in gentle heat, about 10 to 16°C (50 to 61°F). When the seedlings develop a pair of leaves prick them out 5 to 8 cm (2 to 3 in) apart, and let them grow on in the same temperature. Harden off in a cold frame before shifting to their perma-

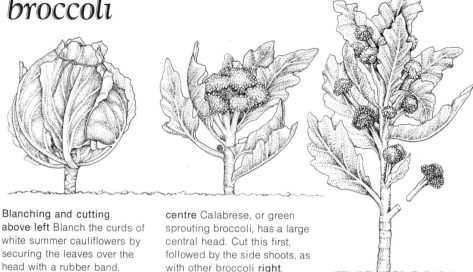

Blanching and cutting
above left Blanch the curds of white summer cauliflowers by securing the leaves over the head with a rubber band.

centre Calabrese, or green sprouting broccoli, has a large central head. Cut this first, followed by the side shoots, as with other broccoli **right**.

nent growing quarters in mid-spring, when they are 12 to 15 cm (5 to 6 in) tall. Where the soil carries a risk of club root, dip the seedlings' root ball in a calomel paste. Set them out 45 to 50 cm (18 to 20 in) apart in both directions, planting firmly, and water thoroughly.

For top yields in areas with moderate winters, sow seed in early autumn in cold frames or under cloches. Make drills 1 cm (½ in) deep and 12 to 15 cm (5 to 6 in) apart. Sprinkle with a soil insecticide (such as Bromophos or diazinon) to combat such pests as millipedes, wireworms and cabbage root fly, or use calomel, which will also effectively deter club root disease. Sow thinly and protect the seedlings from severe weather by covering the glass with sacking at night. Thin out the young plants as necessary and harden them off in early spring. When the weather warms

up, transplant them to permanent quarters as for greenhouse-raised varieties.

Late-maturing summer cauliflowers, winter cauliflowers and sprouting broccoli can also be raised under glass, but respond best if sown in an outdoor seed-bed in spring (late spring for winter cauliflowers). Sow in drills and, apart from giving glass protection, treat as described above. Transplant to the permanent site in early summer, or in midsummer for winter cauliflowers. As these types are larger, space them about 60 cm (2 ft) apart.

Routine care and harvesting

Hoe regularly to keep down weeds, water freely and earth up maturing plants in windy gardens to save them being blown over. It may also pay to stake tall plants. Top dress once or twice with a nitrogenous fertilizer in summer (and in early spring to push overwintering sprouting broccoli).

Protect the developing curds of summer cauliflowers, using the plants' own leaves as illustrated. This checks premature ripening and is essential for the successful blanching of white-headed varieties. Winter cauliflowers can be protected from hard frost by the same method. Apart from those already mentioned, troubles to beware include flea beetles, caterpillars, cutworms and various fungal diseases (see pp 362 and 365).

Cauliflowers are best harvested very early in the day. Cut when the heads are well-formed but compact. If too many ripen together, protect any surplus for a few days by breaking their inner leaves over them as for blanching. If necessary, lift out the whole plant (leaving earth on the roots), wrap the head in tissue paper, and hang it roots uppermost in a cool place; it should keep for up to three weeks.

White and purple sprouting broccoli should be cut when the side shoots have grown 10 to 12 cm (4 to 5 in) and the flower buds are just visible but not open. Cut about 5 cm (2 in) from the base. Regularly pick a few from each plant to ensure further growth. Leave the leaves on for protection. Harvest green sprouting broccoli by first cutting the large cauliflower-like head, then later dealing with the resultant side shoots as for conventional sprouting broccoli. The multiple curds of perennial broccoli are harvested all at once when they appear in spring.

Recommended cauliflowers and broccoli

Summer cauliflowers	**Early varieties** 'Classic'; 'Delta'; 'Dominant'; 'Erfurt'; 'Polaris'; 'Snowball'; 'Snow King'; 'Walcheren' **Mid-season varieties** 'Abuntia'; 'All Year Round'; 'Alpha Polaris'; 'Burpeeana'; 'Mechelse Arcturus'; 'Mechelse Classic'; 'Purple Head'; 'Snow Crown' **Late-maturing varieties** 'Autumn Giant'; 'Barrier Reef'; 'Bondi'; 'Brisbane'; 'Conquest'; 'Kangaroo'; 'Majestic'; 'Manly'; 'Veitch's Autumn Giant'
Winter cauliflowers	**For mild climates** 'Angers No 2'; 'Snow-White'; 'Summer Snow'; 'Superb Early White' **Extra-hardy varieties** 'English Winter – June Market'; 'English Winter – Late Queen'; 'English Winter – Reading Giant'; 'Newton Seale'; 'Roscoff St Agnes'; 'Veitch's Self Protecting'; 'Walcheren Manston'; 'Walcheren White Cliffs'; 'Walcheren Winter Thanet'
Sprouting broccoli	**Conventional varieties** 'Christmas Purple'; 'Early Purple'; 'Improved White Sprouting'; 'Late Purple'; 'Late White'; 'Purple Sprouting' **Green (calabrese) varieties** 'Autumn Spear'; 'Comet' (F1 hybrid); 'De Cicco'; 'Express Corona' (F1 hybrid); 'Italian Sprouting' **Perennial varieties** 'Bouquet'; 'Nine Star Perennial'

Celery and fennel

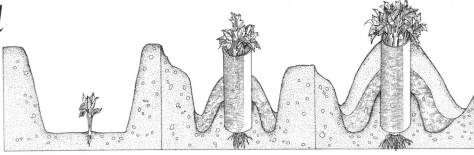

Crisp, crunchy celery (*Apium graveolens dulce*) is equally good raw in salads or braised as a vegetable, but it is not the easiest of crops to grow: it is prone to pests and diseases; it is liable to bolt; the seeds take a long time to germinate (although you can buy seedlings ready for transplanting); and the traditional method of cultivation in northern Europe, in trenches, is laborious and time-consuming.

Celery is grown in trenches to make it easier to blanch the stalks by earthing them up. Trench celery, also known as winter celery, comes in white, pink and red varieties, red being the hardiest. The development of self-blanching and green-stemmed varieties that need no earthing up has made growing easier. However, these varieties are not so hardy, mature earlier (in late summer in cool climates), and in some opinions are less crisp and have a less delicate flavour. The leaves of both types can be used for flavouring.

Soil and sowing

Celery needs a sunny position, rich, deep, moisture-retaining but well-draining soil, and plenty of feeding. It will not grow in heavy clay soils or thin sandy ones. It does best in a temperature range of 10 to 21°C (50 to 70°F), but trench varieties will withstand slight frosts when earthed up. In warm, frost-free climates, celery is grown as a cool-weather crop, planting out in autumn.

In cool climates, you can raise celery plants from seed in a greenhouse or propagator, in a frame, or under cloches. In all cases, sow the seed thinly – in early spring for trench varieties, a month later for self-blanching and green kinds – germinating at a temperature of 16 to 18°C (61 to 65°F) in the greenhouse, 21°C (70°F) in a propagator. Prewarm outside beds with cloches before sowing, and keep the cloches on until transplanting. The seedlings will appear as a fine green carpet; prick them out 5 cm (2 in) apart, making sure that you are not pricking out clumps rather than single plants. Allow the young plants to establish sturdy growth at 13 to 16°C (55 to 61°F). When they are about 8 to 10 cm (3 to 4 in) tall, harden them off in a cold frame for several weeks before transplanting in early summer. Alternatively, buy young plants.

Planting out

Plant out only when all danger of frost has passed and the plants are at least 15 cm (6 in) tall. Plant trench varieties either in a single central row or in multiple rows in a zig-zag formation. Space the plants 25 to 30 cm (10 to 12 in) apart and water them in. Self-blanching varieties can be planted out in a well-manured conventional bed, 25 cm (10 in) apart in all directions. Do not space them too widely, so that their leaves will shade each other's stalks and help in blanching.

Routine care and harvesting

Water freely, especially in dry spells, and feed with dilute liquid manure every two or three weeks, more frequently if growth is slow. Trench varieties may need more water and food. Weed regularly with a hoe, being careful

Trenching and earthing up Prepare celery trenches in winter (or at least a month before planting out) and before digging the garden, to ensure neat, firm sides. Make them 40 cm (15 in) deep and (for single rows) 45 cm (18 in) wide and 90 cm (3 ft) apart. Fork plenty of well-rotted manure or rich garden compost into the bottom, then add 8 to 10 cm (3 to 4 in) of good soil. **left** Plant the seedlings in this. **centre** Earth up first in mid- to late summer, when the plants are 30 to 40 cm (12 to 15 in) tall. Strip off any side shoots, tie the stalks loosely with raffia and fit protective paper collars. Pile earth up around each plant, leaving only the leaves exposed. Delay if the soil is wet, and slope the mounds to deflect rain. **right** Continue earthing up as the plants grow, until they are ready to lift.

not to break the stems, and remove any suckers that grow from the base of the plants. With non-trench types, mulching is useful. If self-blanching varieties need extra shading from the sun, you can enclose the bed with boards or stretch black plastic around it to form a sun screen. Trench celery should be first earthed up when the plants are 30 to 40 cm (12 to 15 in) tall, and progressively earthed up throughout the growing season. To prevent soil getting into the hearts, first wrap with heavy paper. Make sure that the soil is not wet, or the plants may rot.

Pests and diseases to look out for include carrot root flies, leaf-mining celery fly maggots, slugs and several fungal diseases. Deal with these as advised on pages 358 to 367, but also beware of boron deficiency (see p 368) and insufficient moisture, which causes split stalks and bolting. (Self-blanching varieties are particularly prone to the latter.)

Lift self-blanching celery as required in late summer and autumn (or from midwinter in warm regions). Fill up any gaps created by harvesting with soil, to prevent too much light reaching the rest of the crop. Trench varieties are ready about eight weeks after the first earthing up. Use a fork, and prise up the sticks carefully, taking care not to slice or spike the hearts. Cover any remaining plants with straw in earthed-up rows, to protect from frost. Trench celery tastes no better for a light frosting, as many people think, so there is no need to wait for frost before lifting.

Recommended celery varieties	
Trench types	'Clandon White'; 'Giant Pascal' (white); 'Giant Prize Pink'; 'Giant Red'; 'Giant White'; 'Ideal Pink'; 'New Dwarf White'; 'Prizetaker White'; 'Solid White'; 'Standard-Bearer Red'; 'Superb Pink'; 'Unrivalled Pink'; 'White Ice'
Green and self-blanching types	'American Green'; 'Burpee's Fordhook'; 'Golden Self-Blanching'; 'Greensleeves'; 'Lathom Self-Blanching'; 'Summer Pascal'; 'Utah'

Florence fennel

Florence fennel or finocchio (*Foeniculum vulgare dulce*) is grown for its swollen stem bases, which look somewhat like celery and are blanched and shredded for eating raw in salads, or braised as a vegetable; they have a mild aniseed flavour. The leaves are also used for flavouring in the same way as its close relative common fennel (see p 273), but are more pungent. It is grown as an annual in the vegetable garden, but needs a warm, sunny summer to thrive. It is sturdier than common fennel and grows only about 60 to 90 cm (2 to 3 ft) high.

Florence fennel needs a warm, sheltered spot where it can grow quickly and form its swollen stem bases at the end of summer. It likes well-drained soil, and if the soil is poor enrich it with generous dressings of old, well-rotted compost, old manure or peat fortified with bonemeal or some other slow-release fertilizer. Raise the plants in mid-spring, sowing the seed thinly in rows 50 cm (20 in) apart in their permanent positions. Thin the seedlings to 30 cm (12 in) apart. Water them liberally in dry weather and feed weekly with dilute liquid fertilizer if growth is slow. In late summer, when the bases of the stems begin to swell, draw soil around them to blanch them. Alternatively, you can cover the stems at the base with brown-paper collars. Cut as required when the stem bases are about the size of tennis balls.

Onions, shallots and leeks

Onions

Versatile, high-yielding and satisfying to grow, onions are one of the best kitchen-garden crops. They grow well in all climates that receive adequate sun to ripen the bulbs – which are, of course, the part used in cooking, along with the leaves of the virtually bulbless salad varieties. Onions are perennials (they are all varieties of *Allium cepa*) but are generally cultivated as annuals or biennials.

They can be raised from seeds or sets. Sets are specially developed immature bulbs that have been treated to stop the plants from 'bolting', or running to seed. They are invaluable for a quick return of high-quality bulbs, ripen earlier than bulbs grown from seed and are less liable to become infested with onion fly or infected with mildew.

Many varieties of onion are available, either as sets or seeds, and varying from brownish-red to straw-yellow and white in colour. Depending on the type, they can be sown or planted from early spring until autumn. With the introduction of the new Japanese varieties, which in areas that are not too cold in winter can be sown in late summer or early autumn for ripening the following midsummer, the onion 'chain' is now complete; these link up with the first of the spring-sown or planted varieties which are ready in late summer. A judicious combination will therefore yield a satisfyingly large and varied crop, providing a selection of globe-shaped or flattish onions for winter storage and consumption.

'Specialized' onions, such as the tiny silver-skins used for pickling or the small, mild-tasting spring onions eaten in salads, will also grow prolifically throughout the spring and summer. There are also such curiosities as the Egyptian onion, which produces edible aerial bulbils on tall stems, and the non-bulbous Welsh onion.

Recommended onion varieties

Sets	'Stuttgart Giant' (flattish); 'Sturon' (globular)
Spring-sown seeds	**Globular** 'Ailsa Craig'; 'Autumn Spice' (F1 hybrid); 'Bedfordshire Champion'; 'Buccaneer' (F1 hybrid); 'Hygro' (F1 hybrid); 'Polina'; 'Primodoro'; 'Red Globe'; 'Rijnsburger Robusta'; 'Rijnsburger Yellow Globe'; 'Showmaster'; 'Superba' (F1 hybrid) **Flattish** 'Giant Zittau'; 'Solidity'; 'White Spanish'
Autumn-sown seeds	**Japanese varieties** 'Express Yellow' (F1 hybrid); 'Imai Early Yellow'; 'Kaizuka Extra Early'; 'Senshyu' **Others** 'Ailsa Craig'; 'Autumn Queen'; 'Reliance'; 'Solidity'
Pickling types	'Barletta Barla'; 'Blood Red'; 'Cocktail'; 'Small Paris Silverskin'; 'The Queen'; 'White Portugal'
Salad types	'White Lisbon'; 'White Lisbon – Winter-Hardy'; 'White Portugal'

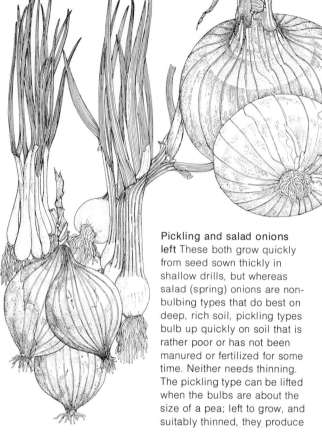

Pickling and salad onions
left These both grow quickly from seed sown thickly in shallow drills, but whereas salad (spring) onions are non-bulbing types that do best on deep, rich soil, pickling types bulb up quickly on soil that is rather poor or has not been manured or fertilized for some time. Neither needs thinning. The pickling type can be lifted when the bulbs are about the size of a pea; left to grow, and suitably thinned, they produce usually flattish white bulbs. Sow salad onions (also called scallions, a name shared with shallots) at three-weekly intervals throughout spring and summer for a continuous crop. In areas with moderate winters, a final autumn sowing will produce a fine spring harvest if given glass protection.

Culinary onions
top Large culinary onions vary from globular to flattish and from white to reddish-brown.

Soil and planting Well-manured soil that drains freely yet retains moisture in dry weather is ideal for growing onions. It should be firm, but there is no need to roll the bed as enthusiasts used to do many years ago to produce top-quality bulbs for exhibition. Keen gardeners prefer the same site from year to year, but if you do not rotate the crop around the vegetable garden you risk the build-up of disease, especially white rot. An open sunny site should be chosen. Dig the ground in winter, manuring if necessary, so that it has time to consolidate to a gentle firmness for spring plantings. Autumn sowings should be made on ground that is simply raked to a good tilth, and not dug deeply, or it will be too 'puffy'. It should be lightly limed unless it is already naturally alkaline.

Most seed varieties are sown in the early spring. Take out drills 30 cm (12 in) apart and 1 cm (½ in) deep, and sow thinly. When the seedlings are manageable and have grown about 8 cm (3 in) high, thin them to 5 cm (2 in) apart; later thin again to 10 to 15 cm (4 to 6 in) apart. Surplus plants from the second thinning can be used for salads. Fill in holes left by thinning to discourage onion flies from laying their eggs.

Early to mid-spring, when the soil is crumbly and warming gently under the sun's rays, is the ideal time to plant sets. Do not plant them in cold soil or growth may be checked. Position them 15 cm (6 in) apart in rows 30 cm (12 in) apart. Bury them just beneath the surface so that birds do not see them and scratch them up.

There are varieties of seeds that can be sown in summer or early autumn. Sow them at the same distance as for spring-raised plants,

Egyptian and Welsh onions

These are both grown as perennials, clumps being lifted, divided and replanted every three years or so, in spring. Egyptian onions, also called tree onions and classified as *Allium cepa aggregatum* (*A. cepa viviparum*), are curious plants that develop stems 1 to 1.5 m (3 to 5 ft) tall, carrying clusters of small bulbs in place of flowers. The stems need staking. These bulbs are the crop; to obtain new plants, plant them about 25 cm (10 in) apart in late summer in ordinary soil in sun. The first harvest will be ready the following summer.

Welsh onions originated in the Far East and have nothing to do with Wales. They are also called onion greens, ciboils or Japanese bunching onions, and are classed as *A. fistulosum*. They can be raised from seed sown under glass or obtained as young plants, which should be set out 25 cm (10 in) apart in spring. Harvest the leaves and stems for use in salads and for flavouring.

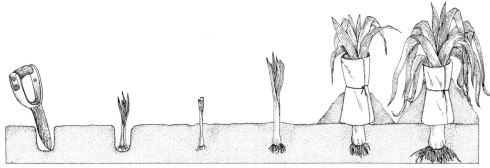

Growing leeks

right Rake a patch of soil to a fine tilth, working in 135 g/m² (4 oz/sq yd) of a balanced fertilizer of analysis about 7:7:7 (see p 352). Take out drills 15 cm (6 in) apart, and scatter the seed thinly in them; water them in if the soil is dry. No thinning is needed.

When the seedlings are 20 to 30 cm (8 to 12 in) tall, water them well, then lift with a trowel; the roots should disentangle easily. Cut off the top one-third of the foliage. Using a dibber or stick, set out the young plants 15 to 20 cm (6 to 8 in) apart. The dibber holes should be 15 to 20 cm (6 to 8 in) deep. Water in the transplants. Thereafter, water the plants regularly with dilute liquid fertilizer.

As the stems lengthen and thicken, blanch them by using a hoe to pile up dry earth around them a few centimetres (an inch or two) at a time, having first fitted paper collars around the plants to prevent soil getting in among the leaves.

Leeks

One of the most useful 'cold-weather' vegetables, leeks (*Allium porrum*) are incredibly hardy, suffer from very few pests and diseases, and give a valuable return of thick, fleshy, mildly onion-flavoured stems for very little outlay and effort. By choosing a succession of varieties, plants may be dug from early autumn to early spring in moderate climates. All they ask for is a good, rich, well-drained soil and some water during dry spells.

Raise leek plants in a seed-bed in spring. Early planting, if weather permits, produces robust plants. The ground should be prepared thoroughly and a general fertilizer worked in. Sow the seed thinly in drills. Transplant the seedlings during the summer, when they are 20 to 30 cm (8 to 12 in) tall and as thick as a pencil. When transplanting, cut off the top one-third of the foliage to reduce water loss while the roots are recovering and making fresh growth.

Water freely and keep down weeds. Encourage growth with a weekly feed of liquid fertilizer if the weather is dry and little natural progress is being made. For extra-long white stems, earth up the plants, a few centimetres (an inch or two) at a time, with dry soil. Do not use wet soil, which may cause the leaves to rot. Watch out for onion root fly maggots (see p 362), the only important pest.

Lift the crop as required, from early autumn onwards. The leeks can be safely left in the ground until needed, so storage presents no problem. However, if the ground is needed for another crop, dig up the leeks and heel them in in a convenient spot – close to the house, perhaps. Simply cover the stems, leaving the leaves free. Frost will not hurt them.

Recommended leek varieties

Early	'Early Market'; 'Malabar'; 'Regius'
Maincrop	'Musselburgh'; 'The Lyon'
Late	'Catalina'; 'Malines Winter'; 'North Pole'; 'Winter Crop'

in drills 30 cm (12 in) apart. Thin the seedlings to 15 cm (6 in) apart, again using the thinnings in salads. Do not transplant them as they may be checked and fail to grow satisfactorily.

Routine care and harvesting Do not water too much in an average season, or the bulbs may split and rot; the soil should, however, be watered well in dry conditions. Keep down weeds, especially among the grassy-leaved seedlings. In midsummer, top dress the rows with a general fertilizer (analysis about 7:7:7; see p 352) to spur growth and encourage the formation of good, solid bulbs. Watch for maggots of onion root fly, which may burrow into the stem bases and bulbs (see p 362), and eelworms, which cause swelling and distortion of leaves and bulbs. Mildew and other fungal diseases that cause rotting or smut may also attack onions (see p 365).

When the tops begin to bend at the necks, the bulbs will start to ripen and swell in size. Scrape the soil from around them to aid this. When the leaves are quite brown, accelerate the ripening process by forking under the bulbs to break the roots. Finally, when the foliage is quite dry, lift the bulbs and dry them off on suspended netting or lay them out with their roots and base plates towards the sun. Cover them at night and when it rains.

Eventually they will be ready for storing, but if not ripened thoroughly they may rot. The test is to squeeze the foliage at the neck of the bulb. If it shows no sign of moisture or squashiness it is dry enough for the bulbs to be stored, either roped together to make 'strings' or hung in open-net sacks. (Stockings are just as good.) A cool, airy, frost-free place will ensure that the bulbs stay in sound condition all winter long.

Shallots

Shallots are hardier but less sharp in taste than onions. They belong to a different species, *Allium ascalonicum*; like salad onions they are sometimes called scallions. Traditionally they are planted on the shortest day and lifted on the longest, but the soil is rarely fit for planting as early as this in cool climates. Although it is usual to grow them from bulbs, they can be raised from seed and grown like onions. 'Giant Yellow' is recommended for growth from bulbs and 'Giant Red' from seed. Both kinds root strongly in cold soil, and provided the ground can be worked there is much to be gained from planting early. Like onions, shallots can be dried and stored in an airy, frost-free place for use in winter and spring. They are used in cooking in much the same way as onions, or are sliced raw in salads or pickled.

Soil and planting A deep, fertile patch of ground in full sun yields the best results. It should drain freely. If it was not manured during the previous autumn, rake in a processed manure before planting. If you are raising from bulbs, plant them 15 to 20 cm (6 to 8 in) apart in rows 30 to 40 cm (12 to 15 in) apart. Set them with their 'noses' just below the surface so that they can grow on strongly, undisturbed by birds. The walnut-sized bulbs will not grow much larger, but proliferate into clusters of bulbs. You can raise plants from seed by sowing in drills 30 to 40 cm (12 to 15 in) apart in spring, in the same way as for onions. Thin the seedlings to 15 cm (6 in) apart when big enough to handle. The thinnings make good salad eating.

Routine care and harvesting Hoe carefully around the bulbs to keep down weeds. In early summer expose the bulbs to help them ripen. If growth is slow, top dress with a general fertilizer in late spring. Water freely in dry weather. The same range of pests and diseases may occur as for onions.

When the leaves turn yellow and flop, the bulbs have finished growing and begin to swell quickly. Scrape the soil from round the bulbs so the sun can reach them and aid ripening. Lift the clusters and dry them off completely on a framework of chicken-wire or plastic netting. Separate the bulbs and store them in netting bags for the winter. Make sure that the loose outer scales are removed as these trap moisture which can rot the bulbs. Keep smaller bulbs for planting the next year.

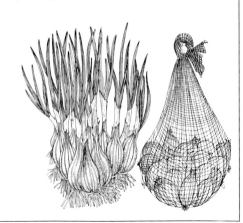

Beans and peas

French beans

Extremely nutritious and productive, beans are among the most popular of all garden vegetables, and without doubt the most popular bean worldwide for temperate regions is the French or kidney bean, *Phaseolus vulgaris*, in its many forms. These are known by many other names – snap bean, bush bean, green bean, wax bean and simply 'bean'. One old name, string bean, is now something of a misnomer; although there are still some stringy types, newer varieties are fleshy and stringless, and snap cleanly. These types, together with haricot and flageolet beans, have green, yellow or occasionally purple or mottled pods (which turn green on cooking), that are cooked and eaten fresh or frozen. Many types can also be dried; then the pods are discarded and the dried seeds – which may be white, green, brown, black, purple, reddish or mottled – are stored until required. One group specifically grown for drying are the shell, or horticultural, beans that are popular in North America. These include red kidney beans. The confusingly-named pea bean is also a variety of this one big species even though it resembles a pea.

French beans are available in both bush (dwarf) and climbing, or pole, varieties. The latter, which grow about 2 m (7 ft) tall, take the place of runner beans (see opposite) in most southern hemisphere, North American and continental European gardens. They yield heavily and, unlike runners, their flowers set very easily – very few blooms form without turning into plump, usable pods. Another advantage is their drought resistance – in a dry year, pole French beans will produce a record harvest while runners growing beside them may fail miserably. Bush varieties can be

sown successively throughout the season to provide a continuous harvest, and avid bean enthusiasts can get an early start by germinating seeds in the greenhouse before the frosts are over, or sowing under cloches a little later.

Soil and sowing All beans thrive on deep, fertile, well-fed and well-drained soil. You can create the right conditions in normal soil by taking out a trench 60 cm (2 ft) deep in winter and using it as a depository for organic waste from house and garden – soaked newspapers, peelings and so forth. In spring, you can top these with 8 cm (3 in) of good soil and a scattering of general fertilizer before sowing. The beans will germinate readily and make good, strong pod-bearing haulms. If the soil is light and sandy, dig in plenty of moist peat, garden compost or old manure. If it does not drain well, ridge it and sow on top of the ridges. Lime if the soil is very acid.

Make the earliest sowings in early spring in the greenhouse. Choose dwarf varieties. Set the seeds 5 cm (2 in) deep in 25 cm (10 in) pots of loam- or peat-based potting mixture. Germinate them in gentle heat close to the light. Stick twigs in among the plants to hold the leaves and stems high and help the pods form freely. In mid-spring, continue with early sowings outdoors under cloches, setting the cloches over the ground two weeks beforehand to warm the soil. Stagger the rows of cloches and set the seeds 15 cm (6 in) apart down the centre of the cloche run. Uncover once all danger of frost is past.

Begin direct outdoor sowings when frosts are over, in late spring or early summer. Germination is poor in cold soil, however, so wait until the ground is warm enough to encourage a rapid 'getaway'; nothing is gained by sowing too early in cold, wet ground, but conditions

can be improved by prewarming with cloches as mentioned above. Make successional sowings of bush types every two or three weeks until late summer. Climbing varieties are sown once only, in spring. In frost-free regions, you can make sowings of bush types from early autumn to early spring; the last should be made two or three months before average temperatures reach 27°C (80°F).

Take out drills for bush beans, or for climbing varieties grown along a fence or netting, 5 cm (2 in) deep and 40 to 45 cm (15 to 18 in) apart. Space the seeds 15 cm (6 in) apart in the drills, cover and firm the soil with the back of a rake. Water in if the ground is dry. If you are growing climbing beans up poles in rows or tripod formation, space the poles 45 cm (18 in) apart. Sow five or six seeds in a small circle around each pole, and thin out to the strongest three or four seedlings to each pole. They will twine anticlockwise around their supports as they grow.

Although seedlings grown in small pots sometimes transplant satisfactorily, avoid this if possible. There is usually a check to growth, and cropping is delayed.

Routine care and harvesting Beans do not normally need treatment with fertilizer if the ground is adequately prepared, since, like other legumes, their roots develop nodules containing bacteria that 'fix' atmospheric nitrogen into a form that can be used by the plant. In fact, ground that has grown beans is richer after harvesting than before. It may help, however, to scatter a commercial preparation of the bacteria such as 'Legume Aid' on the seeds before sowing; this is available from garden centres in some countries.

Water the plants freely (but not from overhead) in dry spells. Mulch the rows with

Beans for drying

Haricot and shell (horticultural) beans are grown specifically for their crop of seeds, which are dried out and stored for later use in soups, stews, cassoulets, baked beans and so forth. Grow them just like ordinary French bush or pole beans, sowing in early spring as soon as frosts have finished. As the pods are left on the plant to mature, successional sowings are unnecessary.

Most shell and haricot beans are late maturers. At harvest time, make sure that the pods are fully developed and the seeds have ripened to white or brown by opening one or two; then pull up the plants bodily. Hang them in a cool airy place until they are brittle dry, then remove the seeds from the pods and store in jars.

Although they are best dried, most of the shell and haricot bean varieties listed in the table can also be eaten as whole garden pods. Haricot beans are also delicious in their intermediate state, when the seeds are well developed but still green; they are shelled and used like peas and are known as flageolets. Conversely, an excess crop of any bean can be saved and stored by leaving the pods to mature and dry out on the plant.

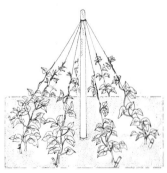

Supports for climbing beans
There are several methods of erecting stable supports for your climbing French or runner beans. If you have the space and want a large crop, plant double rows **above**, setting the poles, which should be about 2.5 m (8 ft) tall, in pairs with 40 cm (15 in) between the base of each pole in a pair and 30 to 40 cm (12 to 15 in) between each pair along the rows. Tie the pairs together about 15 cm (6 in) from the top, and stabilize the whole row with a horizontal pole at the top. For single rows, you can set one pole vertically at each end of the row and stretch two wires (top and bottom) between them. Tie strings vertically for the plants to climb or

stretch wire or plastic netting between the wires **top right**. In a restricted space, erect a 'maypole' with wires, string or poles fixed to a central pole **above**. In all cases, pinch out the growing tips when the plants reach the top.

d manure or compost to encourage rapid owth by keeping the roots cool in dry, hot eather, and give a liquid feed weekly if rowth is slow. Prop up pod-bearing shoots of ush varieties with twigs to keep the pods om the soil and from the mouths of hungry ugs. This also helps to support the plants uring heavy rain. In the autumn, you can xtend the season of dwarf beans by covering e plants with cloches.

Among the pests that may attack French eans are aphids, capsid bugs and greenhouse ed spider mite, while the principal diseases clude anthracnose, downy mildew, various orms of root rot and wilt, and virus diseases ee pp 362 to 366).

Pick snap beans – that is, all kinds to be aten whole – regularly when the pods are oung, about 10 cm (4 in) long, and succulent. hen more will quickly follow. Bush varieties egin cropping about two months after sow-g and go on for about two to three weeks. ole varieties take about two weeks longer to ome into bearing but go on cropping, so long s they are picked regularly, for about four eeks. Shell beans and others for drying are ft on the plant until fully mature (see the ox). When the crop of all types is finished, ut down the tops but leave the roots in the round to release their store of nitrogen.

Runner beans

he runner bean or scarlet runner, *Phaseolus occineus* (*P. multiflorus*), is less hardy than he French bean and enjoys less worldwide opularity – though it is more popular in the British Isles than climbing French beans. It annot be grown in very cold or very dry reg-ons, and its pods are coarser and larger, hough more tasty, than those of French beans. t would be a shame to neglect this hard-vorking member of the bean family, which rovides decoration (its principal use in North America), good eating and a protective screen or smaller, more vulnerable vegetables.

Runner beans are decorative self-clinging limbers with bright red, white or pink flowers n summer to brighten the garden. The looms are followed by a profusion of succu-ent pods which should be picked frequently, efore the seeds inside bulge and become oticeable, rendering the pod unpalatable nd stringy. The beans are usually grown up louble rows of criss-crossed poles or on wig-vams of poles or bamboos. They can also be rained over supports of netting fixed to stout osts or to warm garage, shed or house walls. f supports are unavailable, grow the naturally warf and bushy varieties, which produce ods the same length as the climbing kinds. Alternatively, pinch out the growing tips of limbing varieties and grow them as bushes.

Runner beans are ready from late summer o autumn. The roots are perennial, and can e lifted, boxed up and stored in a frost-free reenhouse for replanting the following year, ut in practice there is little to gain from this s it is just as easy, if not easier, to raise a fresh rop from seed each year. This is a frost-ender vegetable, so the first outdoor sowings re made in late spring when frosts no longer

Recommended French bean varieties

Bush types	Green-podded (flat)	Haricot types	'Brown Dutch'; 'Comtesse de Chambord'; 'Earligreen'; 'Granda'; 'Purley King' (baked or navy bean); 'Rembrandt' (brown); 'White Leviathan' (flageolet)
	'Bountiful'; 'Brezo'; 'Bush Romano'; 'Canadian Wonder' (long pods); 'Limelight'; 'Masterpiece'; 'The Prince'		
	Green-podded (pencil)		
	'Burpee's Richgreen'; 'Burpee's Tenderpod'; 'Canyon'; 'Chevrier Vert' (very hardy; good for drying); 'Cordon'; 'Cyrus'; 'Flair'; 'Glamis' (very hardy); 'Greensleeves'; 'Harvester'; 'Lika Lake'; 'Loch Ness'; 'Phoenix Claudia'; 'Processor'; 'Provider'; 'Remus'; 'Salem Blue Lake'; 'Sprite'; 'Stringless Green Pod'; 'Tendercrop'; 'Tendergreen'; 'Topcrop'	Shell beans	'Dwarf Horticultural'; 'French Horticultural'; 'King Horticultural' (pole variety); 'Pinto'; 'Red Kidney'; 'Seneca Horticultural'; 'Speckled Cranberry' (pole variety); 'White Marrowfat'
	Yellow-podded (wax beans)		
	'Burpee's Brittle Wax'; 'Cherokee Wax'; 'Goldcrop'; 'Golden Wax'; 'Kinghorn Wax'; 'Mont d'Or'; 'Pencil Pod Black Wax'; 'Surecrop Stringless Wax'		
	Other colours		
	'Blue Coco' (purple); 'Carmine King' (mottled red); 'Deuil Fin Précoce' (mottled violet); 'Royalty' (purple)		
Pole types	'Blue Lake'; 'Burpee Golden'; 'Coco Bicolor' ('Pea Bean'); 'Earliest of All'; 'Kentucky Wonder'; 'McCaslan'; 'Purple Podded'; 'Romano'; 'Violet-Podded Stringless'; 'Zebra'		

Recommended runner bean varieties

Standard types (climbers)	'Achievement'; 'As Long As Your Arm'; 'Best of All'; 'Challenge'; 'Cookham Dene'; 'Crusader'; 'Czar' (white flowers); 'Desirée' (white flowers); 'Emergo White' (white flowers); 'Enorma'; 'Fry' (white flowers); 'Goliath'; 'Kelvedon Marvel'; 'Mammoth White' (white flowers); 'Painted Lady' (red and white flowers); 'Princeps'; 'Scarlet Emperor'; 'Streamline'; 'Sunset' (pink flowers); 'White Achievement (white flowers); 'Yardstick'
Dwarf types	'Hammond's Dwarf Scarlet'; 'Hammond's Dwarf White'

bite. Earlier sowings can be made under glass – in frames, under cloches or in the greenhouse – for transplanting outdoors to their permanent sites when frosts are over.

Soil and sowing Like all beans, runners prefer deep, rich, well-manured ground that drains freely. In poor soil, it pays to take out a trench as for French beans, 60 cm (2 ft) deep and wide, during the winter and part fill it with old compost, or household waste, so that by sow-ing time all has decomposed well. Cover with an 8 cm (3 in) layer of soil and sow. Then in summer, the roots stay cool and growth flourishes. Choose a sheltered site to attract pollinating insects.

Before sowing or transplanting (or after removing cloches if these are used as de-scribed below), erect a supporting structure of poles or bamboo canes, or fix netting specially made for the purpose. Each double row should be 1.8 m (6 ft) apart, with 40 cm (15 in) between the individual rows. The poles should be 30 cm (12 in) apart.

You can raise the earliest crop by germinat-ing seeds in pots or boxes of loam-based pot-ting mixture. Fill containers with the soil mix-ture and push in the seeds 4 cm (1½ in) deep and 5 cm (2 in) apart in all directions. Water them in. Germinate in gentle warmth, at about 10°C (50°F). Harden off the seedlings

gradually and keep them close to the light to stop them growing leggy. Plant them out 30 cm (12 in) apart, either under cloches in mid-spring or directly in the open in late spring or early summer. Remove the cloches in late spring and erect supports for the plants.

If sowing directly in the growing position in late spring, either take out a hole 5 cm (2 in) deep adjacent to each pole (or at the same distance apart if using netting), or take out drills 5 cm (2 in) deep. Set two seeds in each hole or sow in pairs 30 cm (12 in) apart in the drills. Sow a few extra seeds at the end of each row in case germination fails. When the seed-lings emerge, single each pair to the strongest plant. Dwarf types should be planted about 25 cm (10 in) apart in rows 60 cm (2 ft) apart. Pinch out the tips to encourage strong, bushy growth. Whether sown directly or trans-planted, it is vital that the plants grow unchecked by frost or dry soil. If nights turn unexpectedly cold, with a hint of frost, drape sacking around the supporting framework or cover the seedlings with newspaper.

Routine care and harvesting Protect early sowings from cold winds that can brown their leaves. Water frequently in long spells of dry weather, and mulch rows with peat or garden compost to keep the soil moist and encourage a good set of pods. Do not worry/*continued*

Beans and peas (continued)

if the first blooms drop and pods fail to set; this is quite common, and subsequent flowers will usually set to ensure a good crop. White-flowered varieties such as 'Desirée' and 'White Achievement' usually set a heavier crop of pods than the red-flowered varieties. Hand-pollination is useful to make quite sure that the flowers set; spray the flowers with water and brush against them, either bodily or with a stick, to distribute the pollen. When the plants reach the top of their supports, pinch out the growing tips.

Look out for slugs, millipedes and especially the black bean aphid (blackfly), the bane of all beans. Deal with such pests as advised on pages 362 and 364. Runner beans are subject to the same diseases as those that afflict French beans (see p 291).

Pick the pods carefully, using one hand to hold the vine, the other to hold the pod – the last thing you want is to inadvertently pull off a flower truss. Pick frequently, before the seeds show through the pod walls. Then the pods are succulent and snap cleanly, without strings, and more pods are encouraged to form. If you do not need the whole crop at once, you can freeze them or layer them in salt. Alternatively, leave the pods on the plant to mature, and then pick them for drying.

Broad beans

Broad beans (sometimes dubbed English broad beans or fava beans, and classified as *Vicia faba*) are among the most venerable of all vegetables, their seeds having been found in Iron Age remains in many parts of Europe and the Mediterranean region. They are hardy, nutritious, tasty and easy to grow (though sometimes plagued by blackfly), and remain a favourite vegetable in many regions. Not least of their advantages is the fact that they are hardy enough to be sown outdoors in late autumn in places with moderate winters, such as the southern half of the British Isles, for harvesting in late spring and early summer. They are not much grown in North America, though they do well in the cooler areas where summers are short, making it difficult to grow other beans to maturity.

The name broad bean is an apt one, for the seeds are larger than those of any other garden beans except the limas (see opposite). They are either dark green or almost white (except for 'Red Epicure' which is reddish-brown); the flavour is the same but the dark green varieties are better for freezing. The varieties are divided (rather arbitrarily) into Longpods and Windsors. Windsor varieties have about four or five large round seeds in each rather short pod; the Longpods have twice the number of seeds per pod, but they are each smaller and oblong in shape. Windsor types are often preferred for their sweeter taste, but the hardier Longpods are useful for overwintering. Dwarf Longpod varieties are good for small or exposed gardens. They grow barely 40 cm (15 in) high, and need no staking; they can be grown right throughout the winter and up to cropping time under cloches.

Broad beans are normally harvested when mature but still succulent, the fresh seeds

Supporting broad beans
Both Longpod and Windsor varieties of broad beans can grow to a height of 1 m (3 ft) or more, and need to be supported. Erect poles at regular intervals down each side of a double row and stretch one or two lines of string at convenient spacing to hold up the plants. As soon as about four trusses of flowers and the first pods have set, pinch out the growing tips, together with about 15 cm (6 in) of stem. This will discourage both extensive growth and plagues of blackfly.

being removed from the fleshy pods before cooking or freezing. However, broad beans are also most delicious picked very young and cooked in the pods in the manner of fresh French or snap beans. Broad bean seeds also dry well for later use.

Soil and sowing Broad beans are a hungry crop, and repay sowing in ground that was well manured for a previous crop or in the winter before spring sowing. Make sure that the soil drains freely (especially if you plan an autumn sowing) and is not acid, and that the site is sunny. For autumn sowings it should be sheltered from cold winds. Dress the ground with a general fertilizer before sowing; no nitrogenous top-dressings are needed as the crop develops, because the roots – like those of other beans – have nodules containing bacteria that manufacture nitrogenous salts from the soil air.

When sowing directly outdoors, take out pairs of drills 5 cm (2 in) deep, allowing 25 cm (10 in) between the two drills and 60 cm (2 ft) between each pair. Space the seeds 15 to 25 cm (6 to 10 in) apart in the drills and sow a few extras at the end of the rows to transplant

---

Some unusual beans
For a different bean taste you can try some of the more out-of-the-ordinary members of the family, such as edible soya beans, tic beans, chick peas and lentils. Some of these do well only in warm climates but others are quite easy to grow wherever French beans will thrive.

Soya beans, classified as *Glycine max*, are extremely important oil and animal-feed crops, and have long been grown for human consumption in the Far East. They are extremely rich in protein, and are used to make a kind of flour and also 'textured vegetable protein' or meat-substitute. There are more than a thousand varieties altogether, but only a few edible types are available generally; recommended ones include 'Bansei', 'Kanrich' and 'Fiskeby V'. The last is a Swedish-bred variety that is especially good for cool climates where soya beans normally produce poor crops. The seeds can be eaten (removed from the pods) fresh, when they are green, or the pods can be left on the plant to ripen fully and the seeds dried to a yellow or brownish colour for storage. They are excellent baked.

Like bush lima beans, soya beans make compact plants, the pods growing up to about 8 cm (3 in) long. Raise them in late spring, sowing them after the last frosts 8 cm (3 in) apart in drills 4 cm (1½ in) deep. Space the rows 30 to 40 cm (12 to 15 in) apart and later thin the seedlings to 15 cm (6 in) apart. Alternatively, raise in gentle heat under glass in early spring, using peat pots, and plant out in late spring. Choose a sheltered position and treat in other respects as for bush lima beans. They may take up to four months to reach maturity.

The pods of tic beans (varieties of *Vicia faba*) may be eaten green, and are very tasty, but it is for their nourishing dried seeds that the crop is usually planted. The beans are like broad beans in appearance and cultivation. Sow them in spring or autumn, spacing them 15 cm (6 in) apart in rows 30 to 40 cm (12 to 15 in) apart. Make sure that the soil is well manured. 'Maris Bead' is a recommended variety.

Chick peas (*Cicer arietinum*) are extremely high in protein and are grown mainly for drying and cooking in traditional Asian and Mediterranean dishes. They have been grown for centuries in southern Europe and are gaining popularity in the southern half of North America – where they are known as garbanzo or chestnut beans because of their distinctive nutty flavour. Grow them in the same way as bush French beans (they form bushes 40 cm [18 in] high), sowing in late spring. The beans will be ready for picking after about four months.

Lentils (*Lens culinaris*) have been cultivated for thousands of years in the Mediterranean region and farther east, but will also grow in warm light soil in much cooler regions. The plants grow only 45 cm (18 in) tall, with small leaflets and very short, flattened pods. Each contains only one or two seeds, which are dried and sometimes split. They are very nutritious, and may be green, brown or reddish.

nto gaps if there are any failures. Water in if he soil is dry. Dwarf varieties can be close-spaced in the drills, but are then best sown in single rows.

If you live in an area where winters are not too cold or wet, you can sow early Longpod varieties such as 'Aquadulce Claudia' and 'Colossal' in late autumn. These will mature before the blackfly invasion that invariably contaminates spring-sown varieties. For the normal summer crop, sow Longpods and Windsors in mid- and late spring. A dwarf variety can also be sown in summer as a catch crop, perhaps after harvesting early potatoes, and will be ready to harvest in autumn.

For early crops where winter conditions are bad – and for less risk of winter losses even where autumn sowing is possible – you can gain a head start by sowing Longpods in early spring under glass. Germinate the seeds in individual small pots – clay, plastic or peat – in a loam- or peat-based seedling mixture. Maintain a minimum temperature of 7°C (45°F), and when the plants emerge keep them close to the light. Harden them off gradually in a cold frame before planting out in mid-spring (giving cloche protection if the weather is still bad). Use a trowel to make a hole large enough to take the root system without cramping, and water in.

Routine care and harvesting Autumn-sown plants should be covered with cloches or shielded with fine netting or hessian if the weather turns bitter. This will also protect them from birds. Tread the soil around the plants carefully after frost to re-firm the roots. Earthing up the stems to a depth of about 8 to 10 cm (3 to 4 in) will also give protection, while you can help to toughen the growth against adverse weather by working 40 g/m² (1 oz/sq yd) of sulphate of potash into the root area in autumn or winter. This can alternatively be given as a base dressing before sowing. Stake the plants against buffeting winds. In the spring, rows of autumn-sown broad beans can protect the seedlings of more delicate vegetables sown between them.

Spring and summer crops should be watered liberally in dry spells and mulched with garden compost or old manure to help conserve soil moisture. Hoe to keep down weeds as necessary, and stake the taller varieties. Blackfly is a serious pest (see p 362), and must be kept at bay, often by spraying. However, they feed mainly on the young growth, and you can reduce the problem by nipping out the growing tips when about four trusses of pods have formed on each plant. If clean, these shoot tops make an excellent vegetable which tastes delicious if lightly boiled. Sowing the herb summer savory between the rows of beans is also supposed to discourage blackfly, but most gardeners prefer to depend upon an insecticide such as malathion; this will also control weevils. Broad beans are susceptible to foot and root rot, especially if crops are not rotated; chocolate spot can also be troublesome in winter and is controlled by spraying with benomyl (see p 365).

As already mentioned, broad bean pods can be picked very young – when about 5 cm

(2 in) long – for cooking whole. Normally, pick them when the beans are well developed, about four months after sowing. When they are in their prime, the scar where the bean was attached to the pod is green or white; if it is black they are past their best. Make repeated pickings, beginning at the base of the plant; this encourages further growth. When the crop is finished, cut down the top growth and compost it; leave the roots to decay in the soil and release their valuable cargo of nitrogen to benefit the next crop.

Lima beans

Lima beans (*Phaseolus lunatus*) are extremely popular crops in the southern half of North America and other places with long, warm

---

Recommended broad bean varieties

Longpod types	**For autumn sowing** 'Aquadulce Claudia'; 'Bunyard's Exhibition'; 'Colossal' **For spring sowing** 'Cavalier'; 'Dreadnought'; 'Exhibition'; 'Imperial Green Longpod'; 'Longfellow'; 'Major'; 'Masterpiece Green Longpod'; 'Promotion'; 'Red Epicure'; 'Rentpayer' **Dwarf varieties** 'The Midget'; 'The Sutton'
Windsor types	'Broad Windsor'; 'Express'; 'Giant Four Seeded Green Windsor'; 'Giant Four Seeded White Windsor'; 'Giant Windsor'; 'Harlington'; 'Imperial White Windsor'; 'Unrivalled Green Windsor'

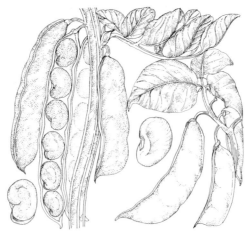

Broad beans   Lima beans

Recommended lima bean varieties

Bush types	'Baby Fordhook Bush Lima'†; 'Burpee's Improved Bush Lima'; 'Bush Fordhook'; 'Clark's Green Seeded'; 'Dixie Butterpea'; 'Fordhook no. 242'; 'Henderson's Bush'†; 'Jackson Wonder'; 'Kingston'†; 'Peerless'; 'Thaxter'; 'Thorogreen'†; 'Triumph'
Pole types	'Burpee's Best'; 'Burpee's Big 6'; 'Carolina'† ('Sieva'); 'Challenger'; 'Florida Butter'†; 'King of the Garden'; 'Large Speckled Christmas'; 'Prizetaker'

†*Small-seeded varieties*

summers, where they more or less take the place of the hardier, cool-climate broad bean. They do not usually do very well in cooler regions such as the British Isles, though they can be grown there in sunny situations if you choose the quicker-maturing bush varieties. Known variously as butter beans, butter peas or Madagascar beans, limas need a minimum night temperature of at least 10°C (50°F) for a minimum period of 2½ months for the bush varieties, and three months or more for the pole types. Where the climate is suitable, however, they reward with a bumper harvest; provided the weather stays warm, you can harvest the pole varieties over a period of a number of weeks.

Like many varieties of French beans, limas are often grown for drying and storage (the form in which they are most commonly seen in cool-climate regions). However, they taste their best when fresh; then they have a delicious nutty flavour and a dry, mealy quality. They are removed from the pods before cooking, like broad beans. Most varieties have seeds that are 2 to 2.5 cm (¾ to 1 in) long, but 'baby' types (which can be either bush or climbing in habit) have 1 to 1.5 cm (about ½ in) seeds. Both types are a rounded, rather flattened kidney shape, and are generally pale to medium green when fresh, drying to a white or creamy colour; beware of coloured seeds which may contain a poison.

Soil and sowing Like French beans, limas like a light, warm, but rich soil – one that is well drained and has had plenty of organic matter dug in deeply. In regions where frosts occur, sow the seeds in spring under glass or outdoors when all danger of frost has passed. In warmer areas, sow as soon as you can rely on minimum night temperatures remaining above 10°C (50°F). Bush varieties can be sown successively every two weeks until late summer, or up to about 2½ months before night temperatures can be expected to drop below 10°C (50°F) again. Pole varieties need only one sowing.

Also like French beans, they do not transplant easily, so it is best to sow *in situ* in warm, friable soil. For bush varieties, make drills 5 cm (2 in) deep and 60 cm (2 ft) apart; space the seeds about 8 to 10 cm (3 to 4 in) apart, water in and thin out the weaklings when they have germinated, to final spacings of 20 cm (8 in). For pole varieties, erect a framework of poles or wires as described for French and runner beans (see p 290), setting the poles about 45 to 60 cm (1½ to 2 ft) apart. Sow four to six seeds in a circle around each pole, later thinning to the three or four strongest plants. If using trellis against a wall or fence, space and thin the plants as for bush varieties.

An early crop of bush lima beans can be started under cloches, which should be removed once warm, reliably frost-free weather comes. This is useful for getting an early start in cool regions. Alternatively, you could try raising the plants under glass at a temperature of about 21°C (70°F); sow the seeds singly in peat pots of seedling mixture and transplant them carefully, pots and all, in early summer. /continued

Beans and peas (continued)

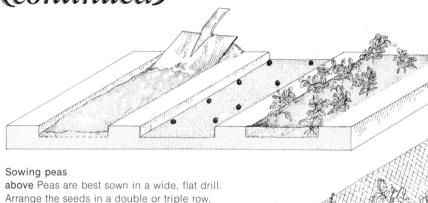

Routine care and harvesting Lima beans should be treated much like French beans, needing no nitrogenous fertilizer but benefiting from a mulch of rotted garden compost or manure. Water them well in dry weather, but keep water off the leaves, especially in strong sun. Give a feed of liquid manure if growth is slow. The bush varieties, which grow to about 60 cm (2 ft), need no support, but you can use twiggy sticks to help keep the lower pods off the ground. Pinch out the growing tips of pole types when they reach the top of their supports. Pests and diseases are the same as for French beans (see p 291).

Bush limas – both standard and small-seeded varieties – are generally ready for harvesting about ten weeks after sowing. Pole varieties take about three weeks longer but go on cropping for a longer period. Pick them when the seeds are well developed inside the pods but are still green and succulent. Alternatively, leave them to mature fully on the plants and harvest when the pods are dry and the seeds hard. Store the beans in jars. In cool regions, it may pay to cover bush varieties of lima beans with cloches in late summer in order to hasten ripening.

Peas

The green or garden pea (*Pisum sativum*) has been cultivated in Europe for several centuries and is today among the most popular of vegetables worldwide – consumed, unfortunately, mostly in canned, dried or frozen form. Eaten fresh from the garden and properly cooked, however, the pea is a particularly succulent vegetable.

Peas are climbing annuals ranging from 40 cm (15 in) to 1.5 m (5 ft) in height. They are divided into round- and wrinkle-seeded (marrowfat) types, depending on the appearance of the seeds when dried. The round-seeded types are the most hardy and where the climate is not too severe can be over-

Recommended pea varieties

First early	'Alaska'‡; 'Beagle'*†; 'Early Onward'*† 'Feltham First'†‡; 'Freezonian'*; 'Gradus'*; 'Kelvedon Wonder'*†; 'Little Marvel'*†; 'Meteor'†‡; 'Myzar'*; 'Pilot'‡; 'Pioneer'*†; 'Progress no 9'*†; 'Sparkle'*†; 'Sweetness'*;
Second early	'Chieftan'*; 'Dwarf Defiance'*; 'Hurst Green Shaft'*; 'Lincoln'*†; 'Lud'*; 'Miracle'*; 'Onward'*†; 'Wando'*; (suitable up to 27°C [81°F])
Maincrop	'Achievement'*; 'Alderman'* ('Tall Telephone'); 'Fordhook Wonder'*†; 'Giant Stride'*; 'Lord Chancellor'*; 'Recette'*†; 'Senator'*
Petit pois	'Cobri'; 'Gullivert'
Mangetouts	'Carouby de Maussane'; 'Dwarf de Grace'; 'Dwarf Gray Sugar'; 'Mammoth Melting Sugar'; 'Oregon Sugar Pod'; 'Sweet Green'†

Wrinkled seeds; †dwarf varieties, normally 60 cm (2 ft) or less tall; ‡very hardy – for very early sowing, in autumn or winter in moderate climates

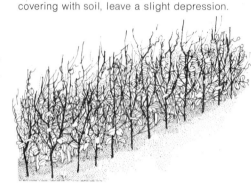

Sowing peas
above Peas are best sown in a wide, flat drill. Arrange the seeds in a double or triple row, spacing them about 8 cm (3 in) apart. When covering with soil, leave a slight depression.

Supporting pea plants
Peas are climbers, and all varieties – even the dwarfs – need support. As the seedlings emerge, insert twiggy sticks along the rows **above left**, avoiding damage to the roots. Spreading outwards in a V shape, the twigs should not impede growth and must allow light and air to reach the plants, while protecting them from wind damage and preventing them from falling over to become prey to pests. When suitable sticks are not available, and also for the medium- and tall-growing types that need extra support, use strong plastic or wire netting **above right** supported on stakes or strong canes. The self-clinging vines will pull themselves up the netting.

wintered in the open (or under cloches in some colder areas), reaching maturity in late spring or early summer. Elsewhere, they can be sown very early in spring. The wrinkle-seeded kind have a higher sugar content and a better flavour, but are less robust and must be sown in succession in spring to crop from early summer onwards. Maincrop types generally mature from midsummer, unless summer temperatures are too high; crops generally fail if average daytime temperatures exceed 24°C (75°F). In cool areas, a late sowing of quick-maturing 'early' varieties will give a crop well into autumn.

Becoming increasingly popular are the edible-podded *mangetout* varieties of peas (also known as sugar or snow peas) and the asparagus pea (a distinct species, *Tetragonolobus purpureus* or *Lotus tetragonolobus*). Both of these are cooked and eaten whole, pod and all, but the asparagus pea is inferior in taste to the *mangetout*. Also extremely succulent are the French-style *petit pois* varieties, with their tiny sweet seeds.

Soil and sowing Peas are not an easy crop to grow; best results are achieved in a well-manured, deeply dug and thoroughly tilled soil which should be loamy and well limed (peas grow best in soil with a pH of 6 to 7.5; see p 332). Avoid a heavy, wet soil, and be sure to change the site each season. Shortly before sowing, apply a general fertilizer with a low nitrogen content (see p 352) at the rate of 70 to 100g/m² (2 to 3 oz/sq yd). Nitrogen-rich fertilizer is unnecessary because peas, like other legumes, have bacteria in their root nodules that draw nitrogen from the air.

Dig a flat-bottomed drill about 15 cm (6 in) or a spade's-width across and 8 cm (3 in) deep. Sow the seeds in alternating rows of three, setting them about 8 cm (3 in) apart. Alternatively, plant the bottom of a single V-shaped drill with one row of seeds about 4 cm (1½ in) apart. The rows should be spaced according to the full height of the cultivar; for dwarf types, space the drills 45 to 60 cm (1½ to 2 ft) apart, increasing this to a much as 1.25 m (4 ft) for the tallest varieties. Where space is limited, repeated sowings of dwarf varieties at intervals of three weeks may be more convenient. Fill in the soil over the seeds, leaving a slight depression to protect the seedlings from cold winds and to collect rainwater, providing a moist, sheltered environment for germination. No thinning is needed; trials have shown that sowing the peas as closely as suggested above gives the best overall yield.

Sowing seed indoors You can gain a head start on spring by raising seedlings of wrinkle-seeded peas in trays of seedling mixture and transplanting them outside as soon as the soil is workable and the weather mild. You can raise them indoors, in a greenhouse or in a cold frame provided conditions are frost-free; no heat is needed. If you divide the tray lengthwise with plastic strips, the self-contained seedlings can be transplanted with

Sweet corn

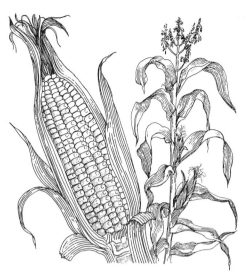

Sweet corn (*Zea mays saccharata*), also called Indian corn or maize, is a sturdy grass that grows to about 2.5 m (8 ft) tall and flourishes most successfully in regions blessed with long, warm summers. The sweet juicy corn cobs or ears grow in a sheath of protective leaves in the leaf axils of the main stem.

It is in North America, sweet corn's native home, that the potential of the plant has been truly exploited. There are varieties with golden-yellow, cream or white kernels, and even bicoloured types. And there are varieties that mature from midsummer to late autumn. Until recently, sweet corn has been a difficult and unreliable crop to grow in cool regions, but an influx of specially bred, quick-maturing F1 hybrids has made cultivation easier. The plants are shorter and sturdier, growing to about 1.5 m (5 ft), but crop very well as long as they are planted out or sown when there is no more danger of frost.

Soil and sowing

Raise a crop in soil that was well manured for a previous crop. Do not add too much bulky organic manure rich in nitrogen or the plants will make too many leaves and poor cobs. In cool climates, the site must be a sheltered sun-trap for warmth to speed growth to maturity and sunshine to swell the ears to succulent sweetness. Dress the area with superphosphate at 135 g/m² (4 oz/sq yd) ten days before sowing or planting out seedlings.

Plants can be raised under glass in mid-spring, sowing the seeds 1 cm (½ in) deep, two to a 8 cm (3 in) pot of seedling mixture. Thin down to the strongest on germination. Spur growth in gentle heat 16 to 18°C (61° to 64°F). Grow on strongly close to the light and harden off in a cold frame when 10 to 15 cm (4 to 6 in) high, before setting outdoors in late spring or early summer. Transplant them 45 cm (18 in) apart each way in a square block rather than a row, so that the cobs are well pollinated by the wind blowing pollen from the male spikes onto the female tassels.

Seeds can be sown directly outside once all frost danger has passed. Rake the soil to a tilth and group three seeds 1 cm (½ in) deep, 45 cm (18 in) apart. Again, sow in compact blocks rather than long rows. When the seedlings appear, thin out the weakest. A direct sowing can be made earlier in spring if the ground is covered with cloches to protect the emerging seedlings from frost and cold winds. If the spring weather is colder than expected, it is worth making a second sowing about two weeks after the first to ensure a crop. Later sowings should be sown a little deeper, as the soil surface will be drier.

In North America, mound planting is preferred, spacing the mounds 60 cm (2 ft) apart, 90 cm (3 ft) for taller varieties. Sow six seeds per mound, thinning down to the three strongest. In warm regions with long summers, a succession of crops can be raised, either by progressively sowing early-maturing varieties throughout the season, or by planting early, midseason and late varieties simultaneously in spring and harvesting them as they mature in succession.

Routine care and harvesting

Water freely in early summer to encourage rapid growth and dose weekly with liquid fertilizer rich in potash. Earth up the stem bases to cover the roots that sprout from them and help to anchor the plants. When the tassels appear, keep the soil moist. Keep down weeds. There are few diseases, but protect the corn from birds.

In midsummer the cobs begin to form in the axils between the leaves and stem. They develop as thin 'cigars', gradually fattening out. In time, the male spikes at the tops of the stems shed pollen which is caught by the sticky female tassels on top of the cobs. When a cob is fertilized the tassel turns brown and shrivels. The cob will be ready approximately a month later. To test for ripeness, peel back the outer sheath to reveal a few seeds. Press one with your finger-nail. If transparent watery fluid spurts out, it is not quite ripe; if the fluid is white, it is ready for eating; if the milky juice is thick and doughy, it is past its best. Carefully pick or cut the cobs from the stems. Careless pulling damages the plant, harming immature cobs. Use the crop immediately, otherwise it loses its sweetness.

Recommended sweet corn varieties

First early	'Earliking' (F1 hybrid); 'Early Golden Giant Hybrid'; 'Early Sunglow' (F1 hybrid); 'First of All' (F1 hybrid); 'Golden Beauty'; 'Golden Midget'; 'Honey Dew' (F1 hybrid); 'John Innes Hybrid' ('Canada Cross'; F1 hybrid); 'Kelvedon Glory' (F1 hybrid); 'Polar Vee' (F1 hybrid); 'Seneca Beauty Hybrid'; 'Silver Sweet'†; 'White Midget'†
Second early	'Barbecue'; 'Early Extra Sweet' (F1 hybrid); 'Spancross'; 'Sugar and Gold'‡
Mid-season	'Burbank Hybrid'; 'Burpee's Snowcross'† (F1 hybrid); 'Carmelcross' (F1 hybrid); 'Golden Bantam'; 'Honey and Cream'‡ (F1 hybrid); 'Marcross'; 'Tastyvee Hybrid'
Late	'Burpee's Honeycross' (F1 hybrid); 'Burpee's White Evergreen'†; 'Country Gentleman'†; 'Golden Cross Bantam'; 'Ilini Xtra Sweet'; 'Ioana'; 'Iochief'; 'North Star' (F1 hybrid); 'Silver Queen'† (F1 hybrid); 'Stowell's Evergreen'† (F1 hybrid)

Popcorn 'Japanese Hulless'; 'White Cloud'

† White-seeded variety; ‡ bicoloured

Mangetouts and asparagus peas

Edible-podded sugar peas, or *mangetouts*, are simply special varieties of ordinary garden peas. They range from about 60 cm (2 ft) to 1.5 m (5 ft) in height, and are grown in exactly the same way as normal peas. The pods are picked when still flat, the peas inside being almost indiscernible, and are cooked whole like green beans.

The asparagus pea is not a pea at all, but belongs to a related genus. It is a half-hardy annual from southern Europe grown for its edible seed-pods, which have four wavy-edged flanges or 'wings'. The plants are best raised under glass in mid-spring, sowing the seeds shallowly. Plant them out in an open, sunny position in rich but light soil in late spring, when no more hard frosts are expected. They form bushes 30 cm (12 in) high. Harvest the pods when about 5 cm (2 in) long and cook them whole.

out root disturbance. Sow the seeds 2.5 cm (1 in) deep, and plant out the seedlings when they are 10 to 15 cm (4 to 6 in) high.

Routine care and harvesting Aerate the soil and keep down weeds by hoeing regularly; water freely in hot weather and in cold spray leaves with foliar feed (see p 353) to encourage growth. Protect the roots from extreme heat by mulching with lawn mowings, old garden compost or peat – they must remain moist if growth is not to become stunted. Stake even dwarf varieties with twiggy sticks to keep the pods from the ground and being consumed by slugs; alternatively, use pea netting, which also gives some protection against birds. The foliage of second early and maincrop varieties is heavy and will collapse after rain unless staked firmly. The main pests to watch for are aphids, pea moth caterpillars, pea thrips and millipedes, but a number of fungal diseases may also strike, including downy mildew, fusarium wilt, grey mould and root rot (see pp 362 to 367).

The pods of the green pea should be picked when firm but still succulent; they should not be allowed to become yellowish or shrivelled. Edible-podded varieties are harvested when the pods are still flat and the seeds within barely formed. When picking either type, hold the stem with one hand and pull the pods with the other. When all the pods have been picked, cut the stems to soil level, leaving the nitrogen-rich roots in the earth. Put the stems on the compost heap.

Marrows, squashes and pumpkins

Marrows, squashes and pumpkins have a special fascination, generated in part by the gratifying speed with which they grow, in part by their versatility in cooking, jams, pickles and chutneys and in part by the surprising variety of shapes and colours they achieve. They are all closely related, but can resemble anything from a lemon to a starship; there are varieties that look like scallop-edged cakes, large acorns or even oriental turbans. Some types can be cultivated to practically any size, sometimes with dramatic results. Huge ones – weighing anything up to 35 kg (75 lb) – have hardly any taste, however, consisting of as much as 99 per cent water.

The term marrow is used only in Britain, and was originally applied as it was thought that the flesh of the vegetable resembled bone-marrow. The prefix vegetable was added to avoid confusion. Any such semantic difficulty is firmly ruled out in North America, where the vegetable is known as a squash. This name comes from an American Indian word, *askutasquash*; unfortunately even this is a misnomer, as it means *eaten raw, not cooked* – which squashes are not.

There are two main types of American squashes. Summer squashes include the green, smooth-skinned long kinds that the British call marrows. They also include such varieties as 'Patty Pan', with its attractive scallop-edged white fruits, and many more. All are eaten young, straight from the plant, and all are forms of *Cucurbita pepo*; they are closely related to the ornamental gourds. Winter squashes, on the other hand, are derived from *C. maxima* and *C. moschata*; these take longer to ripen, have more solid flesh, and are grown for winter storage.

To add to the confusion, what the British call a pumpkin is a form of *C. maxima*, a winter squash, whereas the American pumpkin is a form of *C. pepo*, a summer squash. Both are orange, but only the round, traditional 'jack-o'-lantern' is known in Britain, whereas American pumpkins are more variable. Finally, courgettes (known in North America by the Italian name, zucchini) are simply dwarf or immature versions of the English marrow picked when only 10 to 15 cm (4 to 6 in) long. Left to grow, even the special dwarf varieties become normal marrows, but the more they are harvested the more young fruits replace them.

Fortunately, however, the confusion over names does not extend to cultivation, where marrows, squashes and pumpkins all have similar needs. These are, primarily, a very rich soil, plenty of water and ample sunshine.

Given these – and, in the case of winter squashes, a lengthy period of ripening that makes them more difficult in cool climates – they are adaptable and reasonably easily grown vegetables. There are bush varieties, dwarf types and trailers (which can be induced to climb) to fit most gardens. They can be started outdoors or under glass, and they will provide both a continuous crop throughout the summer and autumn season and a stock of fruits for winter storage.

When growing any kind of marrow, squash or pumpkin, an important point to remember is that only the female flowers – which have a swelling behind the petals – can set fruit, and you may need to aid pollination to ensure this.

Soil and sowing

Choose a site rich in moisture-holding humus so that growth is uninterrupted in summer when hot spells tend to dry out the soil. A sheltered position in full sun is preferable to one in light shade, as more leaves and fewer fruits appear if plants do not receive good light. If the ground is poor, take out square holes 30 to 45 cm (12 to 18 in) deep and the same across, making sure that they will not turn into sumps if the area is not well drained. Fill in with a mixture of topsoil and good, well-rotted garden compost, bagged processed manure bought from a garden centre or fortified hop-manure. This is a job that can be done in early spring in preparation for sowing or planting out in early summer.

Cavities in a compost heap make good planting positions, provided the heap itself does not dry out in summer. Wherever you plant, do not make the common mistake of setting plants on pyramids of soil; these dry out quickly and consequently growth suffers. If you are planting on the flat, it is preferable to make a depression 8 to 10 cm (3 to 4 in) deep and to plant in the centre, then what rain falls will collect in the hollow and invigorate the plant. The spacing of the planting positions depends on the type and vigour of the plants you grow, but for bush marrows and squashes the typical distance would be 1 m (3 ft) and for trailing kinds 1.8 m (6 ft). Dwarf courgette varieties can be planted as close as 50 cm (20 in).

Plants can be raised in gentle heat indoors in late spring for setting outdoors when frosts are over. Or you can sow them *in situ* outdoors

---

Recommended marrows, squashes and pumpkins

Marrows		Squashes	
Trailing varieties		**Summer squashes**	
'Long Green'; 'Long Green Striped'; 'Long White'; 'Table Dainty'; 'Vegetable Spaghetti'		'Baby Crookneck' (F1 hybrid); 'Custard Pie'; 'Early Golden Summer Crookneck'; 'Early Prolific Straightneck'; 'Seneca Butterbar'; 'Patty Pan'	
Bush varieties		**Winter squashes**	
'All Green Bush'; 'Custard White'; 'Custard Yellow'; 'Early Gem' (F1 hybrid); 'Green Bush Improved'; 'Green Bush – Smallpak'; 'Little Gem'; 'Prokor' (F1 hybrid); 'Tender and True'; 'White Bush'; 'Zephyr' (F1 hybrid)		'Butternut'; 'Blue Hubbard'; 'Gold Nugget'; 'True Hubbard'	
		For summer and winter	
		'Burpee's Bush Table Queen'; 'Royal Acorn'; 'Sweet Dumpling'	
Dwarf bush varieties			
'Burpee Golden Zucchini'; 'Goldneck' (F1 hybrid); 'Green Bush' (F1 hybrid); 'Zucchini'		**Pumpkins** 'Big Max'; 'Big Tom'; 'Cinderella'; 'Golden Delicious'; 'Hundredweight'; 'Mammoth'; 'Small Sugar'	

Raising plants under glass above Prepare 8 cm (3 in) pots of a free-draining loam- or peat-based seedling mixture, and sow two seeds on end to a pot, 2.5 cm (1 in) deep. Cover with a pane of glass and place in a temperature of 16 to 18°C (61 to 64°F) to germinate. When the seedlings have grown two strong cotyledons (seed-leaves), pull out the weaker of each pair, allowing the stronger to develop. Harden off gradually, in a cold frame or under cloches, and transplant

into good, rich soil when all frosts have finished.

Raising plants *in situ* Set the seeds 2.5 cm (1 in) deep – two or three to each station – in their final growing positions, and cover with cloches **above** or jam jars to keep the soil warm and to encourage germination. Ideally, prewarm the soil by covering with cloches for about two weeks before sowing. When the seedlings appear, thin them out to leave the strongest at each station.

Hand-pollination above Remove the male flower and, after stripping back the petals, dab its pollen-laden anthers over the stigmas of three or four females. Or use a small fine brush, preferably of camelhair, to transfer pollen from males to females.

under cloches in late spring, or unprotected in early summer. This is especially advisable if you are growing winter squashes or pumpkins, which do not appreciate transplanting. Fruiting will suffer if growth is checked.

Routine care and harvesting
Marrows and squashes thrive in warm, moist conditions. Water the plants freely and keep the roots cool and moist with a mulch at least 5 cm (2 in) thick of old manure, garden compost, moist peat or damp lawn clippings (but do not use these if the lawn has been treated with weedkiller unless they have rotted for at least six months). If the plants fail to make good growth it is either because they are growing in poor soil lacking in sufficient plant foods, or they have been raised too early and it is too cold for them to prosper. If there is an unexpected cold spell after plants have been set out, protect them and encourage their growth by covering them with cloches or erecting sacking along the windward side of the row. If prolonged dry weather threatens, water copiously, using a sprinkler if necessary, and increase the layer of mulch to about 10 to 12 cm (4 to 5 in).

Unlike the bush varieties, which form compact, free-fruiting plants without trouble, trailers need a certain amount of training. They tend to wander all over the place and can become a nuisance. Avoid this by pinching out the leading shoots when they are 45 cm (18 in) long. This promotes the growth of lateral shoots, which means more female flowers and consequently more fruits. You can encourage the growth of larger fruits by heaping soil over the leaf axils of the side shoots, which will then root. Over-exuberant tendrils can be directed up free-standing tripods of canes or poles, or over netting fixed to a fence or wall, where they make very attractive and effective screens.

Normally, fruits set unaided by the gar-

dener, but should the female flowers wither without their embryo fruits (situated just behind the blooms) swelling, it could be through lack of pollinating insects. You can easily overcome this and get a crop on the way by hand-pollinating. Do this on a warm sunny day when both male and female flowers are fully open. Repeat the operation periodically until the weather is conducive for pollinating insects to visit the flowers.

When fruits are setting well, encourage plentiful and robust growth by feeding with liquid fertilizer twice weekly from summer to autumn. If you use any artificial fertilizer, choose one that is rich in phosphate, having an analysis of about 5:10:5 (see p 352). Watch out for signs of powdery mildew, grey mould and cucumber mosaic virus (see pp 365 to 367). Pests are few, but aphids (which carry the mosaic virus) and slugs may attack (see pp 362 to 364).

Bush varieties mature three weeks earlier than trailers, and squashes and pumpkins ripen later than marrows. Pick the fruits of marrows, summer squashes and small-fruited pumpkins throughout the season, as you need them. The optimum size for marrows is 20 to 30 cm (8 to 12 in) long; after that the flesh becomes woody and the flavour deteriorates. Regular harvesting ensures a continuous crop of delicious young vegetables and clears the way for further fruiting. Courgette (zucchini) varieties are best picked when they are 10 to 15 cm (4 to 6 in) long. Left to grow they will become mere marrows. At the end of the season, leave three or four marrows on the plant to mature. These can be picked in autumn and stored in a frost-free shed for use in the winter.

Large-fruited pumpkins and winter squashes, which develop hard shells, are ideal for winter storage. These are best left to ripen on the plant before cutting. Hang them in a cool, frost-free place in netting bags.

Mushrooms

Mushrooms are the ideal vegetable to grow if you have little space. They are easy to raise in containers of special compost bought ready prepared or (if you have room) freshly made from horse manure or straw. The containers can be positioned in any moderately warm place – a temperature of 10 to 13°C (50 to 55°F) is best – that is well ventilated and dark or only dimly lit. Ideal places include sheds, garages, cellars, under the greenhouse staging or even in buckets indoors. Or mushrooms can be colonized outdoors in a lawn or rough grass so long as it is not treated with fungicides, weedkillers or moss-killers. Although many fungi are edible, the species generally cultivated is the field mushroom, *Agaricus (Psalliota) campestris*.

Cultivation indoors
Mushrooms are very primitive plants that must obtain their food from rotten organic matter. Sterile mushroom compost is sold by garden centres. Alternatively, make a heap outdoors of wheat straw that has been saturated with water and dusted in layers with special conditioning chemicals sold for the purpose. Add a little animal manure if possible or, best of all, make the whole heap from fresh horse manure; this needs no chemicals.

As the manure or straw rots, it generates heat, and the inside may reach 38°C (100°F) or more. Turn it after a week – sides to middle, top to bottom – and keep it moist; repeat every few days for two or three weeks. A straw heap is prevented from getting sticky by mixing in 1 kg of gypsum (sulphate of lime) to each 100 kg of straw (1 lb to each hundredweight). During one of the turning operations, dust the heap with BHC (see p 361) to prevent infestation by the almost invisible mushroom mite. When the compost is crumbly, brown and odour-free, it is ready for use. Pack it firmly into boxes or other containers to a depth of 25 cm (10 in), or make a heap a similar or greater depth on a clean shed or garage floor. When its temperature falls to 24°C (75°F) it is ready for spawning.

Mushroom spawn is available in lumps which are broken into 2 cm (¾ in) pieces and set 25 to 30 cm (10 to 12 in) apart and 4 cm (1½ in) deep. Alternatively, sprinkle 'grain' spawn on the compost surface. After a week, thread-like hyphae spread through the compost, and in another week it should be 'cased'. This consists of covering it with a layer of soil – which must be sterile, to prevent disease – 2.5 to 5 cm (1 to 2 in) thick to retain moisture and warmth. In a further two months the first mushrooms can be cut; they continue for two or three months. Fill holes left after picking with more sterile soil. Once exhausted, use the mushroom compost in the garden for mulching and soil-improvement.

Cultivation in grass
Lift small squares of turf 5 cm (2 in) thick and 30 cm (12 in) apart. Set lumps of spawn underneath and replace the turf firmly. Water in if the soil is dry. So long as weedkillers, pesticides and moss-killer are not used, you can look forward to a crop each year.

Melons

Melons belong to the same family as squashes and cucumbers. They produce round or egg-shaped fruits, with smooth, netted or ribbed skins, and sweet, succulent flesh varying in colour from green and almost white to yellow, orange and pink. Although eaten as fruit, they are grown in much the same way as their vegetable relatives; however, they need a much longer period of warmth to grow and reach full maturity.

The main categories of ordinary melons are the Cantaloupes (sometimes called musk-melons in the United States and classified as *Cucumis cantalupensis* or *C. melo reticulatus*), which are generally round, with white netting and/or broad ribs in the skin; and the Casaba group (*C. melo inodorus*), which are generally oval, with smooth but often finely-ridged skins. The latter include the honeydew varieties and the somewhat slower-maturing 'winter' melons, such as the Crenshaw and Persian types, that will store for up to a month. Watermelons are quite distinct from other melons and are classed as *Citrullus vulgaris* (*C. lanatus*).

Melons will not grow outdoors without protection in cold or cool temperate climates. In northern Europe, some varieties can be grown in a greenhouse or, in the case of particularly hardy types, under frames or cloches. Melons thrive outdoors in regions with hot summers, such as southern Europe, Australia and most of the United States, but early varieties must be chosen where summers are short. Outdoors, they trail over the ground, but in a greenhouse they are best trained up canes and wires in the same way as cucumbers. Like their relatives, they thrive in well-manured soil that is moist and cool in summer but drains well.

Methods of growing

All melons grown in cool climates must be started in a greenhouse, and most are best left

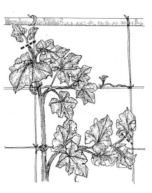

Melons in a greenhouse
Sow two seeds 1 cm (½ in) deep in each 8 cm (3 in) pot of seedling mixture. Keep moist at 18°C (64°F) – higher for watermelons – and close to the glass. Remove the weaker of the two seedlings and pot on to 12 cm (5 in) pots of potting mixture before they are

pot-bound. When the seedlings have five leaves, plant out in the greenhouse border 90 cm (3 ft) apart, or in deep boxes or 25 cm (10 in) pots. In all cases use rich but well-drained soil or potting mixture. Maintain at least 16°C (61°F), more for watermelons
above left Train up strong canes or wires and stop the

main shoot at the top. Pinch out laterals at five leaves to encourage flowering sublaterals. **left** Provide nets to support the fruits.

Melons in a frame
right Harden off well-branched seedlings and plant two to an average frame, in well-manured free-draining soil. Plant at the opposite ends and allow them to grow together, or plant centrally and train in opposite directions. Ventilate in the day.

Melons on mounds
Make a mound as described on page 266. Sow the seeds 1 cm (½ in) deep and about 8 cm (3 in) apart in a ring some 30 cm (12 in) across. Thin to the two strongest seedlings **right** and train in opposite directions.

there until they reach maturity. Seeds can be sown monthly from midwinter to late spring. Pot on the strongest seedlings as they grow, discarding the weaker, and transplant them to their permanent quarters when they have about five leaves.

In cool regions, only certain Cantaloupe varieties can be grown in frames. Raise seedlings as for greenhouse growing, but do not pot on. Lower the temperature to 16°C (61°F) when the seed-leaves are fully formed. Pinch out the growing tip to leave only five leaves on the main stem, and similarly stop the side shoots at three leaves. Harden off gradually and in late spring set out the plants in frames. A frame set on top of a hotbed (a stack of rotting manure that generates heat; see p 380) is an excellent place to grow melons, while in warmer areas they can be grown in a sunny,

sheltered border, protecting them with cloches when necessary.

You can grow melons in the open only if the average temperature remains about 13°C (55°F) at night and above 27°C (80°F) by day throughout the growing season of three months or so. Plants can be raised in a hotbed or greenhouse for a month before these temperatures are reached, and temporary cloche protection can be given when needed. (Or use the translucent waxed paper cups sold for this purpose in some countries.) The American method is to plant the melons on low mounds about 1.25 to 1.8 m (4 to 6 ft) apart – or up to 3 m (10 ft) for the larger watermelons. Grow two robust plants on each mound.

Routine care and harvesting

All melons need hand pollination in exactly the same way as for marrows and squashes (see p 297). The male flowers generally occur in small groups, while the females are solitary; they also have a swelling (the immature fruit) behind the petals. Pollinate several female flowers at the same time; then they will all set fruits well and will develop at the same pace. A single pollinated female tends to suppress the production of further female flowers. Pollinate on warm sunny days, allowing four to six fruits to form on each plant, or up to ten on a vigorous variety such as 'Ha-Ogen'.

All melons, wherever they are grown, need plenty of water and a humid environment in the early stages of growth. Water and spray greenhouse-grown varieties, but never let water collect around the stems as they are prone to rotting. When the fruits are fist-sized, feed weekly with liquid manure, until they reach full size. After that, give less water, but keep the soil moist; warm, fairly dry conditions hasten ripening (a problem if you are raising cucumbers in the same greenhouse; see p 300). Support the fruits with netting.

With varieties raised outside, under frames or not, water well until the flowers open. Give less water after pollination until the fruits set.

Growing watermelons

With delicious red flesh and glossy green rind, watermelons range in weight from a convenient 'family size' of 2 to 3 kg (4 to 6 lb) up to gigantic 20 kg (45 lb) specimens. Seedless varieties (which often contain a few seeds) rarely exceed 9 kg (20 lb).

Although raised in much the same way as Casaba and Cantaloupe melons, they need even more heat, and outdoor cultivation is possible only in areas with long, hot summers. Elsewhere, a heated greenhouse – reaching 30°C (86°F) for germinating the seedless types – is essential. Seeded varieties can be sown in their outdoor growing positions as soon as minimum night temperatures exceed 13°C (55°F). Grow on mounds, as for other melons, setting the mounds 1.8 to 3 m (6 to 10 ft) apart, according to the size of the variety grown.

Hand pollination may be needed, and with seedless varieties it is essential to plant a normal seeded type nearby to provide pollen. 'Sugar Baby' is a good variety for

this. Water well and feed every two weeks with liquid manure. Mulch with dry straw or grass clippings. In late summer, remove young fruits that are unlikely to reach maturity; then all the plants' energies will be devoted to swelling the remainder.

Rhubarb

Like melons, rhubarb (*Rheum rhaponticum*) is grown like a vegetable but eaten as a fruit. It is gratifyingly easy and convenient to grow, and is hardy almost everywhere, but will not grow in regions where the daytime temperature regularly exceeds 32°C (90°F) and requires a cool winter to satisfy its dormancy needs. The delicious red stalks are much prized, but beware of the inedible leaves, which contain poisonous oxalic acid. Rhubarb is a perennial, and can be left to crop annually on the same site for many years.

Soil and planting
Rhubarb will obligingly grow on any site, provided that the soil is dug deeply and well manured a few weeks before planting. Naturally rich, heavy soil is an advantage, as is an open position sheltered from cold winds.

It is best to start your crop from purchased roots, or crowns, although propagation from seed is possible. Make sure that the crowns each have one or two stout buds and strong root thongs. Plant them out in early autumn or early spring, spacing them 75 to 90 cm (2½ to 3 ft) apart, or up to 1.25 m (4 ft) for larger varieties. Spread the roots out in a hole deep enough to leave the buds no more than 2.5 cm (1 in) below the soil level. Plant firmly and water freely if the soil is dry.

Several varieties have been specially bred for growing from seed, but on the whole it is not a good plan; the crop is usually inferior and it is often several years before it is harvestable. The seeds are sown thinly, 2.5 cm (1 in) deep, in a frame in early spring or in an outside seed-bed in mid-spring. Thin the seedlings out to 20 cm (8 in). The young plants will not be ready for removal to the permanent site until the following spring.

Routine care and harvesting
Rhubarb is a greedy feeder, revelling in applications of farmyard manure or generous helpings of artificial fertilizer at up to 200 g/m² (6 oz/sq yd) of analysis about 5:5:10 (see p 352). Water freely in dry weather and conserve moisture with a deep mulch of semi-decayed straw. Keep down weeds and be sure to remove any flower-buds and seed-stalks as soon as they appear, as these only weaken the plant's growth. When picking has finished, mulch the roots with a layer of manure or give a pick-me-up feed of 25 g/m² (¾ oz/sq yd) of sulphate of ammonia. Stem and bulb eelworm and certain caterpillars may attack rhubarb, so look out for these; crown rot and leaf spot are the most likely diseases to afflict your plants (see pp 362 to 367).

Growth is fairly rapid, and you will be able to pull your first rhubarb stalks six weeks after the crowns start into growth each spring. Resist pulling any sticks in the first year. Pull sparingly in the second year, too, and from then on take only three or four sticks at a time from each plant. Make sure that they are fully grown, about 2.5 cm (1 in) thick, and leave a few sticks on the plant. These will die down in the winter and ensure good, sturdy growth in later years.

After five to eight years, the stalks will become generally thinner. Then is the time to lift the crowns and divide them, providing yourself with new crowns to start a new rhubarb bed elsewhere.

Recommended rhubarb varieties

Roots **Early**
'Hawke's Champagne'; 'Merton Foremost'; 'Timperley Early' (all good for forcing)
Maincrop
'Chipman's Canada Red'; 'Cawood Castle'; 'Cherry' (good for mild climates); 'Honeyred'; 'MacDonald'; 'The Sutton' (good for forcing; never sets seed); 'Valentine'; 'Victoria'

Seed 'Glaskin's Perpetual'; 'Victoria'

When they are the size of walnuts, start watering freely again. Encourage ripening by feeding weekly with a high-potash fertilizer (see p 352). Rest the swelling fruits on a tile or piece of wood, to keep away slugs and other pests. Beware of cucumber mosaic virus and verticillium wilt, which causes collapse. When weeding, remember that the roots are shallow and the stems fragile.

Unlike marrows and squashes, melons should be left to mature on the plant. You can tell when Cantaloupes are ripe by their honeyed aroma and the fact that the fruit slips from the stem at the slightest touch. Casaba melons indicate ripeness by a yellowing of the skin, while the Crenshaw and Persian varieties smell sweetly. Watermelons are ripe when the fruit gives a dull, slightly echoing sound when it is tapped.

Recommended melon varieties

Cantaloupe melons
'Burpee Hybrid Cantaloupe'; 'Burpee's Fordhook Gem'; 'Cantaloupe No Name'; 'Charantais'; 'Golden Crispy' (F1 hybrid); 'Ha-Ogen' ('Mini Cantaloupe'); 'Honey Rock'; 'Mainerock Hybrid' (early); 'Pride of Wisconsin'; 'Resistant Joy' (early); 'Samson Hybrid'; 'Sweetheart' (F1 hybrid; early); 'Tiger' (early)

Casaba melons
'Blenheim Orange'; 'Burpee Early Hybrid Crenshaw' (early); 'Emerald Gem'; 'Golden Beauty Casaba'; 'Hero of Lockinge'; 'Honeydew'; 'Honey Drip' (F1 hybrid); 'Honey Mist' (early); 'King George'; 'Persian'; 'Ringleader'; 'Sungold Casaba' (early); 'Superlative'

Water-melons
Normal varieties
'Burpee's Fordhook Hybrid'; 'Charleston Gray'; 'Crimson Sweet'; 'Dixie Queen'; 'New Hampshire Midget' (early); 'Northern Sweet' (early); 'Sugar Baby' (early)
Seedless varieties
'Burpee Hybrid Seedless'; 'Triple Sweet Seedless Hybrid'

Forcing rhubarb
An early, though small, crop of sweet and tender rhubarb can be obtained by forcing, either outdoors *in situ* or under cover. The essentials for forcing are warmth, moisture and darkness, so that the stems draw upwards. Start in midwinter. Outdoors, cover roots with a large inverted lightproof container such as a deep box, barrel, bucket or metal drum *right*. Pack insulating material such as hay, straw or bracken around and over the cover.
Alternatively, lift a few strong roots in late autumn or winter for forcing in a greenhouse or shed; they must be three or more years old. Let them stand above ground, exposed to frost, for a few days before taking them indoors. Trim excessively long roots and pack them close

together in moist peat, either in boxes or directly on the floor. Cover with boxes or black plastic sheeting to keep out the light. Maintain a temperature of 10 to 13°C (50 to 55°F) and keep moist. The rhubarb should be ready to pick in four to five weeks. Roots forced indoors must be discarded afterwards;

those forced *in situ* will yield few sticks the following year.

Picking rhubarb
above Unforced rhubarb stalks are ready to pick when 2.5 cm (1 in) thick. Grasp near the root, pull outwards and twist at the same time, separating cleanly from the root.

Cucumbers

Cucumbers (*Cucumis sativus*), extremely popular in salads or pickles, are versatile vegetable fruits which can be grown as trailers or climbers and cultivated indoors or out, according to the dictates of climate. In mild regions, they are generally grown in the open, on mounds or ridges of banked-up soil. In fact, outdoor cucumbers are often called ridge cucumbers. In colder regions, until recently, a reasonable crop could be raised only in a heated greenhouse; varieties bred for a hardier life in a cold frame were limited.

Greenhouse cultivation presents problems, as the degree of heat and humidity demanded by cucumbers is incompatible with nearly all other greenhouse crops, which means devoting the whole house to one crop or screening off a section of the house with plastic sheeting. However, the recent development of a range of F1 hybrids and Japanese varieties of ridge cucumbers has extended the cucumber repertoire. These new types are not as long as greenhouse varieties, but crop heavily. They are not frost-hardy so usually have to be raised indoors or under glass before transplanting in early summer. Grown under frames they crop early and even more copiously than outside, and so provide a more satisfactory and less expensive way for the amateur to raise a successful crop where summer sunshine is not so plentiful.

Outdoor cultivation

For successful outdoor cropping, the soil must be deeply fertile, well drained but moisture-retaining, and easily warmed. A sunny, sheltered spot is best, near a wall or a fence if the cucumbers are to be trained as climbers. Provide poles or tripods if a boundary site is impossible. Raise the plants either on ridges or in the preferred American fashion on gentle mounds, as used for melons, marrows and squashes (see p 298).

In mild and frost-free regions, sow outside directly in a prepared bed, planting groups of two or three seeds 2.5 cm (1 in) deep, spacing the groups about 60 cm (2 ft) apart. Cover with inverted glass jars to encourage growth. When two or three leaves have formed, thin to the strongest seedling in each group. If using mounds, sow five or six seeds in a circle on top of each mound, thinning down to the strongest two or three seedlings in late spring or early summer, when all danger of frost is past. (In very warm areas, you can also sow in autumn to obtain a crop the following winter or spring.)

In cooler climates, germinate the seedlings indoors or under glass about three weeks before transplanting. Proceed as for frame cultivation (see below). Do not set out the young plants before the night temperature can be guaranteed to remain above 13°C (55°F). Space the seedlings about 45 to 60 cm (1½ to 2 ft) apart on ridge beds, or two or three per mound.

Frame or cloche cultivation

In mid- to late spring, prepare 8 cm (3 in) pots of potting mixture and sow two seeds on edge to a pot, 1 cm (½ in) deep. Grow them close to the light, at a temperature of 18°C (64°F). Thin out the weaker seedling in each pot and harden off gradually. When the plants are 8 to 10 cm (3 to 4 in) high and equipped with two or three well-developed 'rough' leaves, transplant them to prepared beds in frames or covered by cloches. Allow one plant per standard-sized frame, 1.8 by 1.25 m (6 by 4 ft). As they grow, train as described below and stake out the trailing stems to use all the available space. If you are using cloches, set the plants 1 m (3 ft) apart. Staking out may not be necessary with these.

Training and pollination

Encourage the fruit-bearing side shoots by pinching out the growing tip when seven or eight leaves have formed. Continue to pinch out the tips of side shoots if any fail to bear fruits when they are six or seven leaves long. Frame-grown cucumbers will need more extensive training; pinch out the main growing tip after three leaves have formed and the side shoots after four or five. You may need to pinch out the tips of the sub-laterals, too, to encourage further branching to make best use of the available space.

Unlike greenhouse and some frame varieties, whose male flowers must be removed to prevent pollination of the females, which causes the fruits to be bitter and swollen with

Cucumbers in the greenhouse

Sow the seeds singly in 8 cm (3 in) pots. Place them in a good light, where they will germinate quickly. When the seedlings have three true leaves, pot on to 12 cm (5 in) pots of sterilized potting mixture, being sure to cover the lower part of the stem. The seedlings will be ready for planting out three to four weeks after sowing.

Prepare the growing bed at least two weeks before you need it. Make a raised bed about 75 cm (2½ ft) across and 50 cm (20 in) high, sandwiching layers of bulky, strawy manure with good rich soil. Sprinkle with lime, water well and increase the greenhouse temperature to 21°C (70°F). Set out the plants 1 m (3 ft) apart and water them in. Alternatively, use growing bags (see p 117) or 30 cm (12 in) pots of good growing mixture. In all cases, provide wires or netting for the plants to climb up.

The flowers of greenhouse varieties must not be fertilized, otherwise the resultant fruits will be bitter and swollen. Remove all male flowers (which have no embryo fruits behind) as soon as they appear. Pinch out the main growing tip at about 75 cm (30 in) so that the side shoots develop. Pinch these out after the second leaf, and allow only two fruits to set on each lateral shoot.

Water the plants freely, feed them every two weeks with a nitrogenous fertilizer, and protect the shallow fibrous roots with a thin mulch. Maintain the temperature at 21°C (70°F) and spray to maintain humidity, but ventilate the house on very hot days. Shade the glass from strong sunshine in the summer, as the plants scorch easily. Harvest as for outdoor varieties.

Greenhouse cucumbers are particularly troubled by red spider mite, a fungal infection of the fruits known as gummosis and verticillium wilt, as well as the usual cucumber pests and diseases.

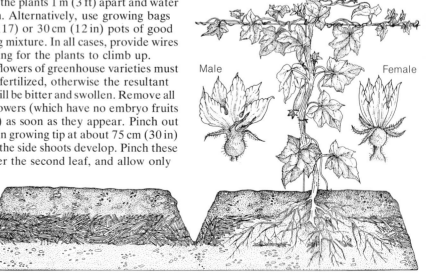

Male   Female

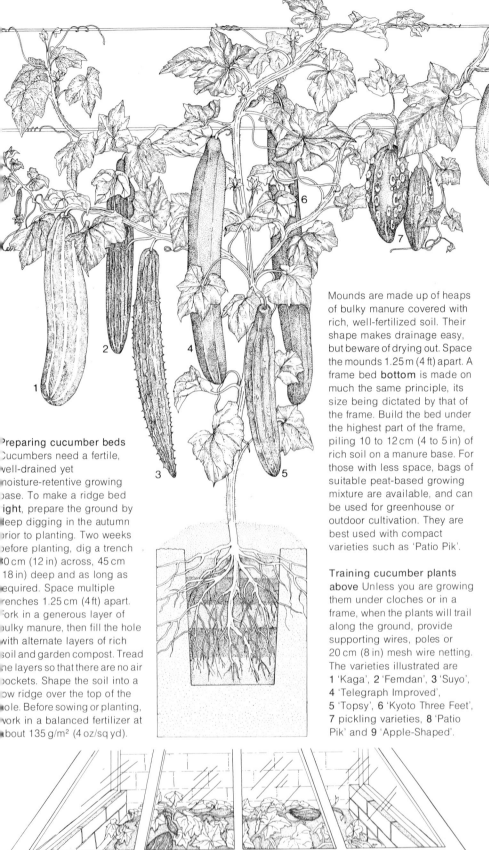

seeds, outdoor cucumbers must be pollinated for fruits to develop. So do not remove the males. If the weather is dull or there is a dearth of pollinating insects, you may have to hand-pollinate, as for marrows and squashes (see p 297). Repeat as necessary if fruits fail to set. Some outdoor varieties (notably 'Victory Hybrid', 'Prolific', 'Burpless Tasty Green', 'Marion' and 'Spartan Valor Hybrid') produce only female flowers; be sure to plant at least one male-bearing plant nearby to provide pollen, and mark it to avoid accidental thinning out.

Routine care and harvesting

Water cucumber plants freely, using a fine spray to avoid washing away soil from the shallow roots. Take care that water does not collect around the stems, thus causing rotting. Mulch with old manure or compost to conserve moisture and stimulate rapid growth and fruiting. Keep the prostrate stems covered with soil so that they root well and supplement the main root system. Feed weekly with a dilute liquid fertilizer rich in nitrogen when the fruits are swelling. Cucumbers under glass may be attacked by red spider mite, while in the open or under cloches woodlice may eat the leaves. In North America, cucumber beetles may be bothersome; they overwinter in garden debris, so an autumn clean-up will aid control of this pest. Other pests are few, but a wide variety of fungal diseases may strike the plants or their fruits, while cucumber mosaic virus causes mottling and distortion of leaves and fruits and stunted, non-climbing growth. Treat these as described on pages 362 to 367.

Outdoor cucumbers can be protected from hard rain and unseasonal frosts by wax-paper cups or glass cloches. If using frames, shade the glass to prevent scorching when the sun is strong; ventilate on hot days, closing the frames at night. Cucumbers trained to climb are automatically protected from soil contamination, but you can protect the fruits of trailers by placing tiles or pieces of wood underneath.

Cut the fruits regularly to encourage more to form. Fruits left on the plant too long go to seed, preventing the development of more fruits, so it is essential that they are picked young, and at their sweetest. You can generally start harvesting ten weeks after sowing. Cut pickling cucumbers when they are immature, about 5 to 8 cm (2 to 3 in) long.

Preparing cucumber beds
Cucumbers need a fertile, well-drained yet moisture-retentive growing base. To make a ridge bed **right**, prepare the ground by deep digging in the autumn prior to planting. Two weeks before planting, dig a trench 30 cm (12 in) across, 45 cm (18 in) deep and as long as required. Space multiple trenches 1.25 cm (4 ft) apart. Fork in a generous layer of bulky manure, then fill the hole with alternate layers of rich soil and garden compost. Tread the layers so that there are no air pockets. Shape the soil into a low ridge over the top of the hole. Before sowing or planting, work in a balanced fertilizer at about 135 g/m² (4 oz/sq yd).

Mounds are made up of heaps of bulky manure covered with rich, well-fertilized soil. Their shape makes drainage easy, but beware of drying out. Space the mounds 1.25 m (4 ft) apart. A frame bed **bottom** is made on much the same principle, its size being dictated by that of the frame. Build the bed under the highest part of the frame, piling 10 to 12 cm (4 to 5 in) of rich soil on a manure base. For those with less space, bags of suitable peat-based growing mixture are available, and can be used for greenhouse or outdoor cultivation. They are best used with compact varieties such as 'Patio Pik'.

Training cucumber plants above Unless you are growing them under cloches or in a frame, when the plants will trail along the ground, provide supporting wires, poles or 20 cm (8 in) mesh wire netting. The varieties illustrated are 1 'Kaga', 2 'Femdan', 3 'Suyo', 4 'Telegraph Improved', 5 'Topsy', 6 'Kyoto Three Feet', 7 pickling varieties, 8 'Patio Pik' and 9 'Apple-Shaped'.

Tomatoes

Once grown only for its ornamental beauty, the tomato (*Lycopersicon lycopersicum*, or *L. esculentum*) has become one of the most popular crops of the amateur vegetable gardener. This is at least partly due to the amateur's ability to go for quality and flavour, unlike the commercial grower, who must concentrate on quantity production. Yet for a long period after it was introduced from South America in the 16th century, the tomato's fruit was considered downright poisonous. Cautious gardeners did have a point; tomato leaves and stems do contain toxins, but the fruits are completely harmless. Later it acquired a reputation – unjustified – as an aphrodisiac, and became known as the love apple. Today it is simply one of the most useful salad and culinary crops.

Tomatoes range from tiny, deliciously-flavoured fruits no bigger than a cherry up to monsters of 750 g (1½ lb) each. Most varieties are red, but there are also orange, yellow, pink and even striped types, some with pear- or plum-shaped fruits. They are real sun-lovers, coupling this with a need for ample water to swell the fruits. They dislike cold and are killed by frost, so they are marginal outdoor crops in areas with cool climates. In the British Isles and the north-west of North America, for example, some varieties will do well outdoors in the sunnier southern parts, but in the colder north a greenhouse or at least a cold frame or cloches are necessary for a worthwhile crop. Even in more favoured areas, greenhouse cultivation prolongs the season and greatly increases the yields.

Varieties differ in their habit of growth, too, and you should choose the type best suited to your method of cultivation. Best known are the cordon, or standard, varieties, which are allowed to develop a single stem, supported by string or a stout cane. This involves regularly pinching out any side-shoots that form in the axils of the leaf-stalks and only pinching out the main growing tip when enough trusses of fruit have set – anything from four to six or even more, depending on climate, variety and conditions. Cordons are the best for greenhouse growing and for outdoors in a restricted space. The bush varieties are allowed to branch out and do not grow so tall – as little as 25 cm (10 in) in some cases – and some are virtually trailers. They need no staking but tend to sprawl. They are good for growing outdoors if you have the space and do not want the trouble of staking, and are particularly useful for growing under cloches.

Raising tomato plants

Garden shops and centres sell young tomato plants, but for some of the best varieties you must raise them from seed. Begin in early spring if you plan to grow the mature plants outdoors or in an unheated greenhouse, in midwinter if you can maintain a minimum greenhouse temperature of 10°C (50°F).

Sow in trays or pots of seedling mixture, spacing the seeds 4 cm (1½ in) apart and 5 mm (¼ in) deep. Water carefully and cover with glass and brown paper until they germinate, maintaining a temperature of about 16°C (61°F). Prick out the seedlings into 8 cm (3 in) pots of potting mixture as soon as the seed-leaves are fully expanded. Handle the seedlings by the leaf tips. Grow on close to the light in a minimum temperature of 13°C (55°F), watering them evenly. They should develop into sturdy, dark green, 15 cm (6 in) plants within about six weeks. Discard any diseased or distorted seedlings, or ones with 'ferny' foliage, caused by a virus (see p 366).

Planting outdoors

In cool regions, choose a warm, sunny spot, preferably sheltered by a wall. The soil should be deep, fertile, well dug and enriched with organic matter. On thin, poor soils you would be well advised to use growing bags, large pots or the ring culture method (see illustrations). Two weeks before planting out, rake in 135 g/m² (4 oz/sq yd) of general fertilizer (analysis about 7:7:7; see p 352). If you use cloches to prewarm the soil and protect the young plants, you can plant out two weeks earlier than the normal time, which is in early summer, after all danger of frost is past. Make sure the plants are hardened off thoroughly before planting out. Water them well the day before transplanting.

When removing the plants from their pots, be careful not to disturb the roots. Set them in rows 40 cm (15 in) apart for cordon types, 60 cm (2 ft) for bush varieties; the rows should be 45 cm (18 in) apart. Insert stout 1.25 m (4 ft) canes or stakes before planting cordons. Then use a trowel to position the plants in holes adjacent to the canes, setting them just below soil level. Firm in and water well. Scatter slug bait around the stems.

Training cordon tomatoes

1 Cleanly pinch out side shoots developing in axils and 2 any shoots at the end of fruit trusses 3 Pull out any suckers. 4 When enough fruit trusses have set (depending on climate and situation), pinch out the growing tip to prevent further growth. 5 Regularly tie in the stem to its supporting stake with soft string or special ties every 25 to 30 cm (10 to 12 in).

Tomatoes in pots

Tomato plants can be grown in 25 cm (10 in) pots of good potting mixture, while such varieties as 'Tiny Tim' and 'Small Fry' can be grown in smaller pots or in window boxes. If you are growing cordon varieties, insert a cane in each pot, and tie another cane along the top of the row to hold them steady. Pot-grown tomatoes need very frequent watering – perhaps twice a day in hot weather; add a little liquid tomato fertilizer each time once the fruits have set.

Tomatoes in growing bags

Plastic bags filled with a special peat-based growing mixture containing a balanced fertilizer suited to tomatoes are an excellent way of growing these plants in a greenhouse or on a patio. You can usually grow three plants to a bag indoors, four outdoors. Follow the maker's instructions, cutting holes in the plastic that are not too big to avoid too-rapid drying out – and, conversely, swamping of the bag in heavy rain. There are no drainage holes, though you can make some in the sides. Make sure that the growing mixture remains moist. Start feeding when the first truss of fruit has set.

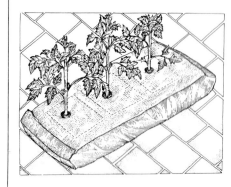

Ring culture of tomatoes

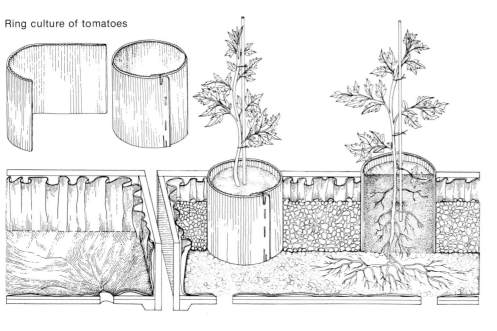

In ring culture, the plant is grown in an open-ended ring of whalehide (tarred paper), roofing felt or plastic 25 cm (10 in) long and the same across. These stand on a bed of gravel or peat, and the plants develop coarse roots that absorb water from the gravel and fine roots that absorb nutrients from the growing mixture in the ring. It is an excellent method both outdoors and under glass, though the latter is more common. Prepare a bed 60 cm (2 ft) wide, with 15 cm (6 in) high sides of boards, and line with plastic sheeting **above left**. Make a drainage hole every 90 cm (3 ft) and fill with 5 mm (¼ in) washed gravel, coarse peat or weathered boiler ashes. **above** Set the rings 45 cm (18 in) apart on the bed and half-fill with a good peat- or loam-based potting mixture. Position the tomato plants in the rings and top up with potting mixture to within 2.5 cm (1 in) of the rim. Water the plants in well. For the next ten days, water sparingly through the rings, to encourage roots to grow down. After that, water the bed of gravel or peat regularly to keep it moist; do this directly, not through the rings. Once the first truss of fruits has formed, begin feeding with a liquid tomato (high-potash) fertilizer through the rings once or twice a week.

Planting in a greenhouse

Growing bags, ring culture or large pots are ideal for greenhouse tomatoes, as these methods avoid the inevitable contamination of the greenhouse border's soil with pests and diseases if tomato plants are grown there. This entails soil sterilization or renewal after every three years (see p 384). If you do grow in the border, prepare it as for an outdoor bed, digging in well-rotted manure or garden compost, followed by a general fertilizer two weeks before planting. Set the plants out 40 to 45 cm (15 to 18 in) apart.

Support the plants – which should normally be cordon varieties – with 1.8 m (6 ft) canes or by winding the stems up strong, soft strings attached to the roof. Maintain a minimum night temperature of 10 to 13°C (50 to 55°F) and preferably 16°C (61°F). Ventilate when the temperature exceeds 21°C (61°F), and shade the glass in summer. Spray the plants occasionally with water to aid pollination.

Routine care and harvesting

Tomatoes need regular watering but not overwatering; once or twice a week is usually enough. Irregular watering causes uneven fruit growth and splitting. When the first truss shows its tiny fruits, start giving a high-potash tomato fertilizer (see p 352), applied weekly in water. In hot weather mulch the root area of both outdoor and greenhouse tomatoes with moist peat.

Tie in the stems of cordon varieties to their stakes every 25 to 30 cm (10 to 12 in) and remove any side-shoots cleanly when 2.5 cm (1 in) long. Do neither of these with bush varieties, but use straw or plastic sheeting to prevent fruits touching the soil. In cool climates outdoors, pinch out the growing tip of cordons two leaves above the topmost truss once four or five trusses have formed. In hot climates or in a greenhouse, you can allow as many as eight or ten trusses to form – or stop the plant when it reaches the roof.

Tomatoes are prone to a rather wide range of pests and diseases (see pp 362 to 367). Pests include caterpillars, thrips, aphids and potato cyst eelworms, while whiteflies and red spider mites may be a problem in a greenhouse. Aphids spread mosaic viruses, while a variety of fungal diseases may strike. These include leaf mould, grey mould and blight, which all first appear on leaves and stems. Plants can be grafted onto a disease-resistant rootstock (see p 351). Physiological disorders include blossom end rot and greenback, both of which affect the fruits, and magnesium deficiency (see p 368).

Pick fruits – sharply snapping the stalk from the stem – when they have turned colour but are not quite ripe; they will quickly ripen indoors and frequent picking speeds development of subsequent fruits. Any green tomatoes remaining on outdoor plants at the end of the season should be picked before the first frost and ripened indoors on a windowsill or in a drawer. Alternatively, cover the plants with cloches (laying cordon types down on straw), or lift the whole plants – roots and all – and hang in a cool, dark place until ripe.

Tomatoes under cloches

You can grow tomatoes – preferably bush types – outdooors in cool climates under tall barn cloches. If you set the plants in shallow trenches about 15 cm (6 in) deep, lined with straw, you can use cloches of more modest size.

Recommended tomato varieties

Cordon (standard) varieties	'Ailsa Craig'*‡; 'Alicante'‡; 'Beefsteak'† (large); 'Big Boy'† (F1 hybrid; large); 'Burpee Globemaster'† (F1 hybrid; large); 'Burpee's Delicious'‡; 'Carters' Fruit'‡; 'Cura'† (F1 hybrid); 'Davington Epicure'*† (F1 hybrid); 'Eurocross A'† (F1 hybrid); 'Eurocross BB' (F1 hybrid); 'Gardener's Delight'*‡ ('Sugar Lump'; 'Sugarplum'; small); 'Gemini'‡ (good for cold regions); 'Golden Boy'*† (golden-yellow; F1 hybrid); 'Golden Queen'*‡ (yellow); 'Herald'*† (F1 hybrid); 'Marmande'*‡ (large); 'Moneymaker'‡; 'Outdoor Girl'*‡; 'Oxheart'† (pink); 'Pagham Cross'*† (F1 hybrid); 'Ponderosa'† (pink; large); 'Red Ensign'*† (F1 hybrid); 'Red Whoppa'† (large); 'Ronaclave'‡ (F1 hybrid; good for cold regions); 'Saint Pierre'*‡; 'Spring Giant'*† (F1 hybrid; large); 'Supercross'† (F1 hybrid); 'Tangella'*‡ (orange); 'Tigerella'*‡ (red and gold striped)
Bush types	'French Cross'* (F1 hybrid); 'Pixie'*‡ (F1 hybrid; early); 'Roma' (plum-shaped); 'Sigmabush'* (F1 hybrid); 'Sleaford Abundance' (F1 hybrid); 'Small Fry'*‡ (miniature); 'Sub Arctic Plenty' (good for cold regions); 'The Amateur'; 'Tiny Tim'*‡ (miniature)

*Sizes refer to fruits. * Best flavour; †best grown under glass in cool climates; ‡suitable for growing under glass or in the open*

Aubergines and peppers

Both members of the potato and tomato family, aubergines (or eggplants) and peppers (sometimes called capsicums) are somewhat exotic but increasingly popular vegetables. They are both natives of tropical regions and do best where summers are long and hot, but they are not too difficult to grow in cooler climates. They naturally do best in a sunny spot or under glass – either tall cloches or in a greenhouse. Peppers are in general easier to grow and slightly hardier than aubergines. Both form bushy plants about 60 cm (2 ft) tall, and cultivation is generally similar to that of tomatoes (see p 302).

The aubergine or eggplant (*Solanum melongena*) originated in Asia. Known in India as the brinjal, it has long been eaten as a meat-substitute. Aubergine is the French name; it is widely used in Mediterranean, Balkan and Middle Eastern cookery. The fruits, which are the part eaten, vary from egg-shaped to oblong and sausage-shaped. A single plant will produce four or more fruits 10 to 20 cm (4 to 8 in) long and weighing up to 500 g (1 lb), or sometimes more, each. The skins are generally purplish-black, with a slight bloom, but some varieties are white. The firm whitish flesh contains many fine seeds, but these are not removed before cooking. Aubergines are a versatile vegetable that can be used in much the same way as marrows.

Peppers – not to be confused with the pepper of peppercorns, which come from a tropical vine – originated in the Americas. There are two main species, and their classification is somewhat confused. Sweet red, yellow and green peppers, and also the mild-flavoured paprikas and pimentos, are forms of the annual *Capsicum annuum*. The hot chillis and cayenne peppers are fruits of *C. frutescens*, a perennial usually grown as an annual. Sweet peppers are always green when under-ripe, and are often picked and eaten in this condition. When fully ripe, they are usually red, but some varieties are golden-yellow.

The fruits are hollow, containing white seeds that are generally removed (together with the inner ribs) before eating, and vary from the size of a tomato up to about 15 cm (6 in) long by 10 cm (4 in) wide. They may be heart-shaped or chunky and lobed. Sliced thinly, they are excellent in salads, while they are equally good cooked in stews or stuffed with minced meat and/or rice.

Raising young plants

Raise young plants of both aubergines and peppers under glass at a temperature of 16 to 19°C (61 to 66°F). If you intend to keep the plants in the greenhouse, begin in late winter or very early spring, but wait a month for plants destined to grow outside. You can sow the seeds (which are quite large) in trays of sterilized seedling mixture, and transplant to individual 8 cm (3 in) pots when they are big enough to handle. Alternatively, sow two seeds to a small peat pot and thin out the weaker of the two seedlings that emerge. In all cases, grow on the seedlings after they have germinated in good light to ensure sturdy, short-jointed growth.

Growing outdoors

Both aubergines and peppers like a deep, rich but well-drained soil, plenty of sun and shelter from winds. Enrich the soil with old manure or garden compost, and rake in 135 g/m² (4 oz/sq yd) of superphosphate before planting. In late spring, harden off the young plants carefully in a cold frame, and in early summer (or whenever the danger of frost is over), set them out 60 cm (2 ft) apart. If possible, pre-warm the planting site with cloches for 10 days before planting out. Pinch out the growing tips when they are about 15 cm (6 in) tall, to encourage bushy growth.

Aubergines are more tender than peppers, and should be covered with cloches after planting unless the weather is very warm. If you have them, keep tall barn cloches permanently over aubergine plants – and peppers, too – in cool regions, for more reliable cropping. Aubergines are particularly prone to rotting of the roots in cold, wet soil, so water in the transplanted plants only if the soil is warm and dry. It is a good idea to help them recover while their roots are growing afresh by spraying the young plants with a foliar feed (see p 353).

With both types, aim to keep the roots moist but not wet. Once growth is well under way, give a weekly feed of liquid manure; once the fruits start swelling you can use a high-potash tomato feed. Peppers can be encouraged to flower (and thus fruit) more freely if the first flowers are nipped off. With aubergines, however, you should allow only four fruits to set on each plant – or one or two more in warm regions – to ensure that they reach a good size. With both kinds, be prepared to control aphids and fruit tree red spider mites (see pp 362 and 363). In some areas, cutworms are a problem; you can protect the young plants' stems by slipping bottomless paper cups over them.

As an alternative to growing directly in the ground, both aubergines and peppers can be grown outdoors on a sunny patio in 20 to 25 cm (8 to 10 in) pots, preferably plunged to the rim in damp peat. In this case, pot on the seedlings as described below for growing under glass.

Growing in a greenhouse

If the plants are to remain in pots under glass or outdoors, pot on the seedlings from 8 cm (3 in) pots or peat pots to 15 cm (6 in) pots of good potting mixture, and then, in early summer, to 20 to 25 cm (8 to 10 in) pots. Alternatively, use growing bags (see p 117). When the plants are about 15 cm (6 in) tall, nip out the growing tips as for outdoor plants.

You can encourage the flowers to set fruits by spraying with tepid water on hot days when they are fully open. Spraying of the leaves also helps to control greenhouse red spider mite (see p 364), which can be a nuisance under glass. But, like tomatoes, these plants do not like too humid an atmosphere, which may encourage grey mould (see p 365). Feed and water regularly, but do not let the pots become waterlogged. Maintain a minimum night temperature of 18°C (60°F). Stake the plants if necessary, and shelter from draughts.

Harvesting

Sweet peppers may be eaten green, yellow or red, and there is no culinary advantage in leaving them to ripen on the plant. Pick aubergines when the skin is glossy and a good colour; as the shine fades the fruits become bitter. With both, use secateurs (hand pruners) or sharp scissors to cut the stalks.

Recommended aubergine and pepper varieties

Aubergines (eggplants)	'Black Magic' (F1 hybrid); 'Burpee Hybrid' (F1 hybrid); 'Early Beauty Hybrid' (F1 hybrid); 'Long Purple'; 'Long Tom' (F1 hybrid); 'Money-maker' (F1 hybrid); 'Short Tom' (F1 hybrid); 'Slice-Rite no. 23' (F1 hybrid)
Peppers (capsicums)	**Sweet varieties** 'Bell Boy Hybrid' (F1 hybrid); 'California Wonder'; 'Canape' (F1 hybrid); 'Golden Calwonder' (ripens yellow); 'Merrimack Wonder'; 'New Ace' (F1 hybrid); 'Pimento' (spicy); 'Slim Pim' (F1 hybrid); 'Worldbeater'; 'Yolo Wonder' **Hot varieties** 'Cayenne Chilli'; 'Hungarian Yellow Wax'; 'Large Cherry'; 'Long Red Cayenne'

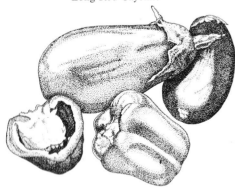

Hot peppers

Hot peppers, often generally termed chillis, are essential ingredients of many cuisines from India to Mexico. Over three centuries of cultivation have given rise to a range of varieties differing in shape, size, flavour and pungency – from the merely hot to ones that even irritate the hands of those who harvest them. They are generally smaller than sweet peppers, and are usually elongated and pointed. Like sweet peppers, they start green, but may ripen red or yellow.

They are even more tender than sweet peppers, and are best grown in a greenhouse except where summers are long and hot. Otherwise, cultivation is as for sweet peppers. The fruits will be ready for harvesting in late summer – they can be used fresh, or dried in the sun and stored in jars. They can be ground to make chilli powder, or pulped and pickled in brine or

Globe artichokes, cardoons and seakale

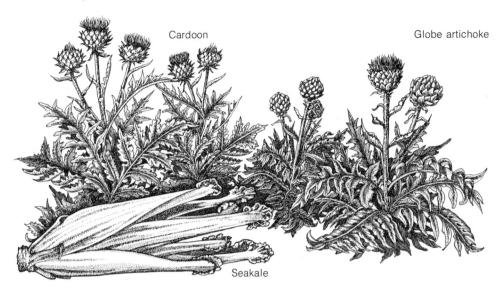

Cardoon

Globe artichoke

Seakale

The globe artichoke (*Cynara scolymus*), an attractive and imposing silver-leaved perennial, is as much at home backing a herbaceous border as it is in the vegetable garden. The large leaves are particularly popular with flower arrangers. The delicious 'globes' are the immature flower buds, cut before the middle portion unfolds. The young leaf shoots, called chards, can also be eaten. Left to flower, the buds form large cushions of rich purple, beloved by bees and other insects.

The plants can reach 1.8 m (6 ft) in height and each need around 1.5 m² (16 sq ft) of growing space, so they are not for small gardens. There are few varieties, but the following are recommended: 'Grande Beurre'; 'Green Ball'; 'Green Globe'; 'Gros Camus de Bretagne'; and 'Gros Vert de Laon'.

The cardoon (*C. cardunculus*) is closely related, and is grown as a vegetable for its blanched leaf stalks. It, too, is also a decorative plant, and resembles the globe artichoke in habit and cultivation. Seakale (*Crambe maritima*), though unrelated, is also a perennial savoured for its delicious blanched leaf shoots, eaten in winter and spring.

Globe artichokes

Happily, globe artichokes are very drought-resistant, as are most silver-leaved plants. They therefore grow successfully on thin, light, sandy soils, though they do best in medium to rich deep loam, well manured in winter to supply nourishment throughout the growing season. Top dress with a general fertilizer before planting.

Raise the plants on a nursery bed in early spring, sowing in 2.5 cm (1 in) deep drills, spaced 30 cm (6 in) apart. Thin the seedlings to 15 cm (6 in) apart to grow on strongly, and shift sturdy plants to their permanent quarters the following spring. Plant them firmly, watering in if the soil is dry. Feed with a balanced fertilizer after plants have recovered from transplanting, water liberally to establish growth, and keep down weeds. Support the stems with canes. In late autumn, protect

established plants from severe weather by cutting them back and tucking straw around them to safeguard the crowns and roots.

Cut the flower buds when their outer bracts (scale leaves) are just unfolding; do not leave them too long. Plants raised from seed will not produce edible buds until the autumn after sowing, but plants in their second and third year of growth will yield good globes in midsummer. It is best to discard plants after three years, first taking rooted suckers to propagate. The young edible leaf shoots, or chards, can be taken from plants two or three years old after the globes have been cut. Reduce the leaf shoots to 15 cm (6 in) and water well. Side shoots will sprout freely; when 60 cm (2 ft) long, tie them together loosely. Wrap in strong paper or black plastic and earth up. Blanching takes about six weeks.

Cardoons

The finest, juiciest stems are raised on soil well supplied with organic material. Raise plants from seed sown under glass in early spring at a temperature of about 15°C (59°F). Harden off before planting out 45 cm (18 in) apart in mid- to late spring. Alternatively, sow outdoors in late spring, sowing groups of three to five seeds, 45 cm (18 in) apart. Single to the strongest plant in each group when about 5 cm (2 in) high.

Cultivate as for celery, growing the plants in trenches 30 cm (12 in) deep. The stems need blanching by earthing up in autumn. When the plants are dry, tie the leaves together at the top, wearing gloves (they are extremely prickly). Then wrap the stems with thick brown paper and earth up with straw and soil in two stages to exclude light for about six

weeks. They are then ready for eating, raw in salads or cooked as a vegetable.

Seakale

Seakale can be grown from seed, but takes two years to crop this way. You can enjoy a quicker return by planting crowns taken from an established plant. Each crown has a terminal bud. Cut this off to prevent flowering and set the crowns 60 cm (2 ft) apart in well-manured soil in early spring. Apart from liberal feeding and watering through the summer, and applying a small dose of salt, no more needs to be done until autumn.

When their leaves wither in autumn, tidy the ground and cover the plants with large flower-pots or boxes and a layer of leaves. After about a month, replace the leaves with fresh manure about 30 cm (12 in) thick; rotting provides gentle heat for forcing new white shoots. This takes about two months in a moderate winter, but if left until early spring (essential where winters are harsh) takes only about three weeks. Cut the shoots when 15 to 20 cm (6 to 8 in) long; they must be completely blanched or they taste bitter. In spring, also cut away the crowns of any plants that have not been forced, to prevent flowering, and on all plants reduce the eyes that have formed around the stem bases to the three strongest per plant; these will form crowns the next year.

You can also force seakale indoors, in the same way as chicory (see p 284). Lift the roots as you need them, cut off side roots to provide root cuttings to grow new plants (see p 348) and pack the main roots in soil or peat in pots. Keep them completely dark at a temperature of about 10°C (50°F) for five to six weeks.

vinegar to make tabasco sauce. If you put some hot chillis in a small jar and fill it with olive oil, after a few months the oil can be used like tabasco sauce for flavouring stews. But be careful how much you use initially with any chillis – some varieties are *extremely* hot!

Propagating globe artichokes
In spring, suckers sprout from the base of the plant. When about 20 cm (8 in) long, scrape back the earth and cut them off with a portion of root. Plant out 1 m (3 ft) apart. More suckers may appear and can be taken in autumn. In cool areas, overwinter these in a cold frame in 12 cm (5 in) pots of soil.

Asparagus

The beloved 'sparrow grass' of diarist Samuel Pepys and a delicacy loved by gourmets everywhere, asparagus has been grown and eaten in Europe for at least 2,000 years. Classified as *Asparagus officinalis*, it is a perennial of the lily family that, left to its devices, grows pretty ferny foliage rather like a giant version of the florist's asparagus fern. For eating, however, the shoots – or 'spears' – are cut very young, when they are only about 10 to 15 cm (4 to 6 in) high. They are then stood upright in bundles in a tall saucepan or asparagus pan of boiling water to cook, so that the tougher bases are boiled but the tender tips merely steamed.

Asparagus is an expensive vegetable to buy for several reasons. Plants take several years to begin cropping (though they may then go on for 20 years or more before they need to be split up or replaced). It is space-consuming, needing at least 60 cm (2 ft) between the roots, or crowns, in the rows. And it occupies a patch of ground permanently for a cropping season of only six to eight weeks in late spring and early summer. If you have ample room, however, it is not a difficult crop to grow provided your soil is fertile and at the same time very well drained, and you have a site that is protected from cold winds and receives ample sunshine. It will not grow where winters are warm, however, for it needs a cool dormant period. Good varieties include 'Argenteuil', 'Brock's Imperial', 'Connover's Colossal', 'Martha Washington', 'Mary Washington', 'Viking' ('Mary Washington Improved'), 'Waltham Washington' and '500W'.

Raising and transplanting

You can raise asparagus plants from seed, but they will take three or four years to produce a crop. Sow the seeds in spring in a nursery bed that was well manured the previous autumn. Apply a pre-seeding dressing of superphosphate at 135 g/m² (4 oz/sq yd) 10 days before sowing. Space the seeds 2.5 cm (1 in) apart in drills 4 cm (1½ in) deep and 30 cm (12 in) apart; first soak them in tepid water for 24 hours to hasten germination. Thin the seedlings to 8 cm (3 in) apart, grow on over the summer, and cut them down close to the ground when the foliage yellows in autumn. Transplant to the permanent site early the following spring.

Prepare a bed for the transplanted seedlings or one- or two-year-old crowns bought from a nurseryman (which will give crops in one or two years) very thoroughly. A bed 1.25 m (4 ft) wide will accommodate two rows. Dig in autumn, working in plenty of organic matter, such as old mushroom compost, rotted cow manure, or fresh seaweed. If your soil is rather heavy, also add coarse sand or grit, but for better results use a raised bed. Lime if necessary; asparagus dislikes acid soil, and you should aim for a pH in the range 6 to 8 (see p 332). Get rid of all perennial weeds.

In early spring, take out trenches as illustrated, and set the crowns on a gently sloping mound with the roots well spread out. Do not expose them to the air more than absolutely necessary; cover with soil only shallowly. During the summer gradually fill in the trench as the plants grow.

Routine care and harvesting

In early spring, scatter the bed with 70 g/m² (2 oz/sq yd) of a general fertilizer (analysis about 7:7:7; see p 352). To increase the length of the blanched spears, draw a ridge or slight mound of soil about 10 cm (4 in) high over the rows. Throughout the year, keep down weeds and water freely in dry weather. Watch for the grubs or adults of the asparagus beetle, and for rust; treat as recommended on pages 362 and 367 respectively.

Do not cut any spears for eating until the plants are well established, and then only a few from each in the first year of harvesting. Cut when the spears are 10 to 15 cm (4 to 6 in) tall – or less if you mound up the earth – starting in late spring. The buds at the tip of the shoots should be still tightly closed. Cut with a sharp, serrated knife about 10 cm (4 in) below the normal soil level or as much as 20 cm (8 in) below the top of the ridge. Be careful not to damage neighbouring shoots; scrape back the soil so that you can see what you are doing. Once the plants are established, you can cut every shoot for a period of six weeks, but you should then stop to allow top growth to develop and feed the crown for next year's crop.

In autumn, this top growth – or 'fern' – will turn yellow. Cut it down to ground level before any berries on female plants drop, and burn it, or you will find the ground carpeted with asparagus seedlings – a menace when weeding. Then mulch the bed with 8 cm (3 in) of rotted manure. If the soil was ridged in spring, level this first.

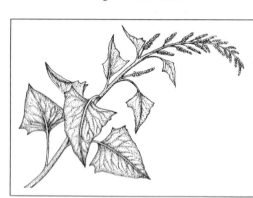

Mercury, or Good King Henry

A British native, mercury (*Chenopodium bonus-henricus*) is also known as Lincolnshire asparagus because it has long been grown in cottage gardens of that county. It is a herbaceous perennial growing 30 to 60 cm (1 to 2 ft) tall that is easily raised from spring-sown seed. The young shoots can be cut and eaten in spring exactly as with true asparagus. The leaves also make good eating if treated like spinach, while the sprouts can be used like sprouting broccoli.

Growing and cutting asparagus

1 Take out straight-sided trenches 25 cm (10 in) wide, spaced 60 cm (2 ft) apart. Fork the soil in the bottom and rake it into a slight mound. 2 Set the crowns on top of the mound, with the fleshy roots spread well out. Space them 60 cm (2 ft) apart and cover immediately with 8 to 10 cm (3 to 4 in) of soil. 3 As they grow, increase the soil depth gradually until it is level with the surrounding ground. 4 In subsequent years, mound soil over the rows in spring to increase the spears' length.

5 Use a sharp, serrated knife to cut the shoots below ground level, taking care not to accidently harm nearby stems or the crown. 6 At the end of the season, when the leaves and stems turn yellow, cut down the whole top growth or 'fern' before seeds fall.

1   2   3   4   5   6

Some unusual garden vegetables

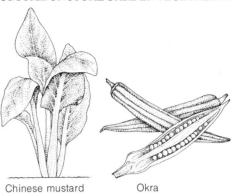

Chinese mustard   Okra

Do not be put off by unusual-sounding vegetables – they are often easier and less troublesome to grow than familiar crops. If chosen carefully, they can help you fill parts of the garden that are otherwise unusable, or take advantage of particular climatic conditions. In hot, dry regions, large crops of okra (gumbo) can be raised; Chinese mustard is another fast-growing, drought-resistant vegetable. If the opposite conditions prevail, try chop-suey greens in a moist, cool area. Watercress, although it could not be called unfamiliar, is ideal for a very damp patch or a slow-flowing, clear, clean stream, but land cress is a useful alternative. See also the unusual root vegetables on page 280.

Watercress and land cress

A favourite salad ingredient rich in vitamins and protein, watercress is the ideal crop for cool, damp regions. There are two varieties – the hardy, bronze-green type (*Nasturtium microphyllum* or *Rorippa microphylla*) and the dark green 'summer' type (*N. officinale*, or *R. nasturtium-aquaticum*), which is usually easier to obtain from seedsmen. The key to successful watercress cultivation is shallow, clear, pollution-free water. Watercress will not grow in stagnant water, though it will succeed in constantly damp soil. If your garden conditions are not suitable, you could try the similar-flavoured American land cress or winter cress (*Barbarea verna* or *B. praecox*).
Growing watercress Sow seeds of the summer variety in spring in drills 8 cm (3 in) apart in a prepared bed as illustrated. Just cover the seeds, and thin to 10 cm (4 in). The bronze type is raised from cuttings of fresh shoots bought from the greengrocer. The latter must be inserted 5 cm (2 in) deep in the soil before they wilt. The cuttings should be 8 cm (3 in) long, cut across at a joint and with the lower leaves removed. Do this in midsummer.

Shade from hot sunshine until the cuttings have rooted. Flood the beds with a hose pipe daily, or fit some system of trickle irrigation, to keep plants moist at all times. There are very few pests or diseases to look out for. In late summer prune away straggling growth and flowering stems. Harvest from late autumn onwards. When cutting, leave a few

centimetres (an inch or two) of basal shoot to branch afresh and produce new growth.

Watercress is a perennial, but you should renew the bed after nine to twelve months, digging in fresh compost and building it up as described. Heel in the plants while doing this, then replant the sturdiest outermost portions, complete with vigorous roots.
American land cress This crop is easily grown in ordinary garden soil, but choose a patch that keeps moist in dry spells and is shaded from hot sunshine. Take out drills 2.5 cm (1 in) deep and 15 to 20 cm (6 to 8 in) apart in prepared soil, and sow thinly in midsummer or early autumn. Thin the seedlings to 15 cm (6 in) apart and cut the leafy shoots when about 15 cm (6 in) high. Alternatively, lift clumps and transplant to a cold frame and grow on for later pickings when the weather turns cold. Or cover rows with cloches if severe weather threatens. This also is a perennial, and can be grown on for several seasons if protected from severe cold.

Okra

Also known as ladies' fingers or gumbo, okra (*Abelmoschus*, or *Hibiscus*, *esculentus*) is a native of North Africa and is grown for its cone-shaped, ribbed seed-pods, which are eaten fresh, cooked or preserved. It is cultivated extensively in the southern states of America and other warm, frost-free regions, where long warm days spur growth and encourage a prolific crop. In cooler regions, it is best raised under glass and protected for the eight to nine weeks it takes for the pods to reach harvestable size. Ideally, grow it in a cool greenhouse where the 0.6 to 1.25 m (2 to 4 ft) tall plants can grow unhindered. Recommended varieties are 'Long Green', 'Clemson Spineless', 'Emerald', 'Louisiana Green Velvet' and 'Dwarf Green Long Pod'.

If plants are being grown outdoors, the soil should be enriched with old manure and garden compost and dressed with 135 g/m² (4 oz/sq yd) of superphosphate. In frost-free regions, sow the seeds outside directly, grouping three or four seeds 1 cm (½ in) deep, 45 cm (18 in) apart, in rows 90 cm (3 ft) apart. Thin to the strongest seedling in each group and feed when they begin to blossom.

If raising plants under glass, sow two or three seeds to an 8 cm (3 in) pot. Thin to the strongest and pot on to a 12 cm (5 in), then a 20 cm (8 in) pot, if plants are being grown to maturity in pots. Use a loam- or peat-based seedling mixture for raising the plants and loam- or peat-based potting mixture for growing them on. Sow in early spring, in a temperature of 16°C (61°F). Alternatively, use a hotbed (see p 380). If the plants are to be shifted to a cold frame or cloches, harden them off well before transplanting in late spring or early summer, when frosts are over and the soil is warm.

Pick the pods when they are still immature, about 8 cm (3 in) long, before the seeds begin to bulge. The pods will ripen to 20 cm (8 in), but this prevents the plant producing more, and the mature 'fingers' are unpalatable.

Chop-suey greens

Also called shungiku or Chinese shungiku, chop-suey greens are an edible, fleshy-leaved variety of a common flowering annual, *Chrysanthemum coronarium*. They make bushy plants about 15 to 25 cm (6 to 10 in) high. Raise a patch by sowing seeds in spring and summer, in drills 2.5 cm (1 in) deep and 30 cm (12 in) apart. Thin the seedlings to 15 cm (6 in) and mulch the rows with damp peat to keep the roots cool and moist, as the plants are liable to bolt in hot, dry soil. Beware of aphids (see p 362). Harvest by cutting whole plants when they have grown sufficiently large and bushy. Use them immediately, as the flavour deteriorates quickly, treating them like spinach.

Chinese mustard

A large, leafy plant some 30 cm (12 in) high, Chinese mustard (*Brassica juncea*) is also called pac-choy, tender green, mustard green or mustard spinach. It is similar to Chinese cabbage (see p 282), except that it has a looser, more open heart and is a great deal more resistant to long bouts of drought and the resultant hot soil. Recommended varieties are 'Burpee Fordhook Fancy', 'Florida Broad Leaf', 'Green Wave', 'Southern Giant Curled' and 'Tendergreen' ('Spanish Mustard').

Give it an open, sunny site on deep, rich soil that drains freely in wet weather. If the ground was not manured for a previous crop, work in plenty of well-rotted garden compost, old manure or processed organic manure. Sow the seeds thinly, at any time from early spring to summer, in 1 to 2.5 cm (½ to 1 in) drills spaced 40 cm (15 in) apart. Thin out the seedlings to 20 cm (8 in) apart and harvest the hearts after six weeks or so. It also resembles spinach, but both these last two vegetables are also used extensively in Chinese cuisine.

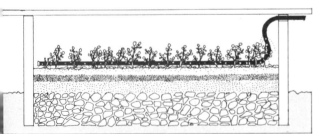

Land cress

Watercress

Making a watercress bed
above Take out soil to a depth of 45 cm (18 in) over an area of about 2 m² (20 sq ft) and box in with planks. Fill in the base with firmed rubble and cover with 15 cm (6 in) of well-rotted garden compost and 10 cm (4 in) of peaty soil. Finish with 5 cm (2 in) of equal parts of topsoil and coarse vermiculite. Add superphosphate at 70 g/m² (2 oz/sq yd) and soak with water. Fit a cross-piece to support glass and if possible a 'leaky hose' for irrigation.

Currants and gooseberries

These closely related bush fruits are some of the most useful, suitable and productive fruits for the garden. Black currants are derived from *Ribes nigrum*, a widespread European and Asian species, while red and white currants have three main parents: *R. petraeum*, *R. spicatum* and *R. sylvestre* (*R. sativum*). Gooseberries, although their fruits are quite different from currants, are equally closely related; the European sorts are derived from the bushy *R. uva-crispa* (*R. grossularia*), while North American varieties come mainly from *R. hirtellum*, which has long arching canes. Another American species is *R. divaricatum*; this is sometimes called the Worcester berry, and although its growth habit is like that of other American gooseberries, its fruit is like a large black currant. It is available from a few specialist nurserymen and is well worth growing as a tasty novelty.

Gooseberries and currants are hardy and easy to grow. They are, however, liable to spread a fungal disease called white pine blister rust, which can devastate pine forests. For this reason, their cultivation is banned in many parts of North America, though there are no restrictions in Europe. If in doubt, consult your local official horticultural or agricultural advisory service. Where they are permitted, they begin producing within two or three years of planting and, although black currants have a useful life of only 12 to 15 years, the others go on cropping for 25 to 30 years. Black currants are fairly space-consuming but are commensurately prolific. Red and white currants and gooseberries are more compact, and in the smallest gardens can be grown as single or double cordons or as fans. The difference in habit of black currants from the others is related to fruiting, and they need different methods of pruning.

Gooseberries are among the earliest fruits in the garden, being harvestable for culinary use from late spring or very early summer; dessert kinds go on until late summer. Red and white currants follow the early gooseberries, ripening over a period of four to six weeks in high summer. Black currants are later still, ripening from midsummer to the end of summer. All these fruits can be bottled or frozen, and all make excellent jams, jellies and pie fillings. The currants are extremely good in fruit salads, black currants particularly adding a rich flavour. The sharp-flavoured red currants make an especially good jelly and the strained juice is used to help other jams set because it contains a lot of pectin. The sweeter white currants are delicious for dessert if sprinkled with sugar and allowed to stand overnight. All currants are rich in vitamin C, but black currants are especially so and are commonly made into a syrup for later diluting with water.

Soil and planting

Currants and gooseberries tolerate a wide range of soils but prefer well-drained but moisture-retentive loam. Black currants are gluttons for nitrogen and revel in rich soils; the others need a more balanced supply of nitrogen and potash. All of them are likely to be short-lived and poor producers on thin,

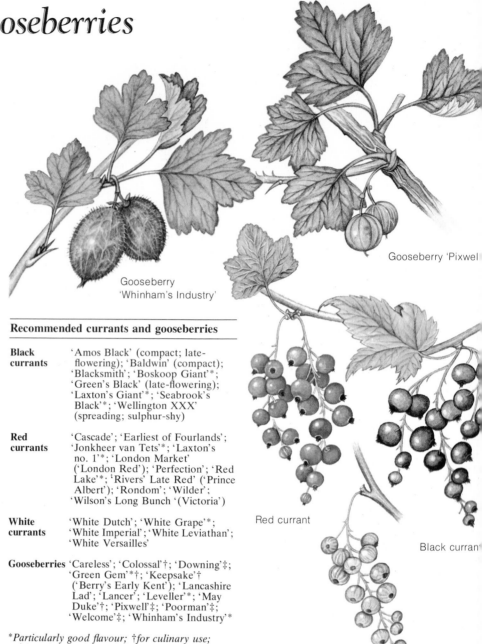

Gooseberry 'Whinham's Industry'

Gooseberry 'Pixwell'

Red currant

Black currant

White currant

Recommended currants and gooseberries

Black currants	'Amos Black' (compact; late-flowering); 'Baldwin' (compact); 'Blacksmith'; 'Boskoop Giant'*; 'Green's Black' (late-flowering); 'Laxton's Giant'*; 'Seabrook's Black'*; 'Wellington XXX' (spreading; sulphur-shy)
Red currants	'Cascade'; 'Earliest of Fourlands'; 'Jonkheer van Tets'*; 'Laxton's no. 1'*; 'London Market' ('London Red'); 'Perfection'; 'Red Lake'*; 'Rivers' Late Red' ('Prince Albert'); 'Rondom'; 'Wilder'; 'Wilson's Long Bunch '(Victoria')
White currants	'White Dutch'; 'White Grape'*; 'White Imperial'; 'White Leviathan'; 'White Versailles'
Gooseberries	'Careless'; 'Colossal'†; 'Downing'‡; 'Green Gem'*†; 'Keepsake'† ('Berry's Early Kent'); 'Lancashire Lad'; 'Lancer'; 'Leveller'*; 'May Duke'†; 'Pixwell'‡; 'Poorman'‡; 'Welcome'‡; 'Whinham's Industry'*

Particularly good flavour; †for culinary use; ‡American variety with long arching canes

dry, sandy soils, but if your soil is rather light, digging in plenty of well-rotted manure or other humus-forming material will make it more to their liking. Such soils will need heavy mulches and ample watering in dry spells – particularly for black currants. Currants dislike acid soils, a pH of about 6 being ideal (see p 332); gooseberries, on the other hand, dislike lime and tolerate slightly more acid conditions. They all prefer an open, sunny site sheltered from strong winds, but partial shade will only have the effect of delaying ripening. Red and white currants, gooseberries and certain black currants are rather early flowering, so should not be planted in frost pockets where spring frosts may damage the blossom.

Clear the ground of all perennial weeds before planting, and work deeply, digging in ample humus-forming material. A dressing of 100 g/m² (3 oz/sq yd) of bonemeal, the same amount of hoof and horn and 35 g/m² (1 oz/sq yd) of sulphate of potash worked into the soil prior to planting will help the bushes to establish more quickly. If possible, plant in autumn, otherwise in early spring. The best age of bush

to plant is two years; black currants should be certified virus-free. Set the bushes 1.5 m (4 ft) apart in rows 1.8 m (6 ft) apart. When planting single cordons of red or white currants or gooseberries, set them about 45 cm (18 in) apart, allowing appropriate extra space for double cordons and fans. All these latter forms need the support of wires on walls or fences or between posts (see p 374).

Black currants should be planted 2.5 to 5 cm (1 to 2 in) deeper than the existing soil mark on the stem to encourage the growth of shoots from below soil level. In Europe, red and white currants and gooseberries are normally grown with a short 'leg' or trunk, and so should be planted at the same depth as grown in the nursery. However, the practice in North America is to plant those fruits also slightly deeper. Firm the soil for all types.

Prune after planting, cutting back black currants hard to 5 cm (2 in) from the ground. For the other fruits, European practice is to cut back the branches by half to a healthy bud. But American gardeners cut them all back to about 15 or 20 cm (6 or 8 in) from the ground

anting and initial pruning
Plant black currants 2.5 to
cm (1 to 2 in) deeper than in
e nursery and **2** cut back
ard to 5 cm (2 in). The British
ethod with other currants
nd gooseberries is to **3** plant
t normal height and **4** cut
ack the main branches by
bout half. North American
ractice is to cut back these
15 to 20 cm (6 to 8 in) after
lanting, and then to cut the
d growth of gooseberries
ack hard the next winter.

runing established bushes
ethod **A** is used for black
urrants, and for
ooseberries to produce a
rge crop of berries for
ulinary use; it is used in
lorth America for all currants
nd gooseberries. In the
utumn or winter after
lanting **1** cut back weak new
rowth, leaving about six
turdy shoots. The following
nd subsequent years **2** cut
ack weak young growth plus
few of the oldest shoots.
lethod **B** is used in Britain for
ed and white currants and for
op-quality gooseberries. In
ummer **1** prune side shoots
o five leaves, but do not
rune the leaders. Next
inter **2** shorten the leaders
y one-third of their new
rowth to a healthy
utward-facing bud (or to an
pward-facing one with
ooseberries of drooping
abit) and reduce the side
hoots to two or three buds.

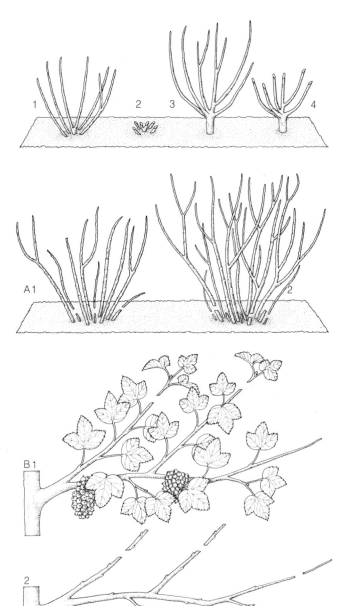

nd then, in the case of gooseberries, cut these
hoots and all but the six strongest new canes
ack to ground level in winter.

Routine care and harvesting

Apart from pruning, the principal attention
hese fruits need is to keep the soil around
hem free of weeds, to water and feed them
dequately and to protect the blossoms and
ruits from frosts and birds. The plants are all
hallow-rooting, so do not hoe weeds; if they
annot be pulled up, use simazine and/or
araquat weedkiller, making sure that the
ushes are not splashed (see p 356). A thick
mulch of well-rotted garden compost or man-
re will help to suppress weeds, as well as
etaining moisture and improving the soil. A
mulch of straw or plastic sheeting can also be
sed for both purposes.

Black currants particularly respond to
pplications of poultry manure, but for all
urrants and gooseberries you can give dres-
ings of sulphate of ammonia in the spring – at
0 g/m² (2 oz/sq yd) for black currants and
5 g/m² (1 oz/sq yd) for the others – plus sul-

phate of potash at 35 g/m² (1 oz/sq yd) for all
types in autumn. A good alternative for
gooseberries is John Innes base fertilizer (see
p 353) applied in spring at 135 g/m² (4 oz/sq
yd). Red currants are particularly susceptible
to potash deficiency, which shows up as brown
edges to the leaves. But never give them
muriate of potash (commercial potassium
chloride); it contains impurities that can kill
the bushes. A deficiency of nitrogen with
black currants results in short, weak shoots
and reddish bark.

For protection against frosts in the spring,
old curtains or sheets of sacking can be draped
over the bushes, but for gardens that are
prone to spring frosts, choose late-flowering
varieties. Birds may attack the buds during
winter and spring, and later the fruits themselves. The best protection is to grow the
bushes in a fruit cage (see p 267), uncovering
during blossoming time so as not to discourage pollinating insects. Alternatively, use netting over the bushes. Blackcurrant bushes that
are insufficiently pollinated – often because
bad weather or strong winds deter bees and

other insects – suffer from 'running off' – the
currants shrivelling and dropping off before
they are ripe. Where the bushes are growing
well but not fruiting to capacity it can pay to
plant a different variety nearby to increase the
chances of cross-pollination. Although these
fruits are self-fertile, the flower formation of
some varieties tends to defeat self-pollination
because the stigma of each flower is above the
pollen-bearing anthers.

Other troubles that may afflict the bushes
include aphids, mites that cause a condition
called big bud, and, in the case of gooseberries, sawfly and magpie moth caterpillars;
diseases include a number of fungal infections
including leaf spot, mildew and grey mould.
For further information, see pages 362 to 367.
With black currants, a virus disease called
reversion may cause reduced cropping and
leaves that are crumpled and have fewer veins
than healthy leaves, giving a nettle-head
effect; affected bushes should be burned.

Pruning of currants and gooseberries, as
with all fruits, has the aim of both promoting
strong, healthy growth and maximizing crops.
Two methods of pruning are used on these
fruits, depending on fruiting habits, and
common practice differs on the two sides of
the Atlantic. The first method is used in
Britain only for black currants and for gooseberries when a large crop of under-ripe fruits
is wanted for bottling or jam-making, but in
North America it is commonly used for all
types of currants and gooseberries. Black currants fruit best on one-year-old wood – both
main shoots and laterals – so about a quarter
to a third of old, fruited wood is cut back hard
to ground level each winter, together with any
weak young growth. This stimulates plenty of
new fruit-bearing shoots. Although gooseberries fruit on both one- and two-year-old
wood, they can be treated similarly. North
American gardeners also prune red and white
currants in the same way after allowing an
initial period of two or three years for sturdy
growth to become established, when only
weak stems are removed.

The second method, used in Britain for red
and white currants and for gooseberries
where top-quality dessert fruit is wanted, is
somewhat similar to the pruning of apples.
The fruit is produced on established spurs
(short side shoots), so the aim of early pruning
is to establish a framework of evenly spaced
branches on which fruit spurs are encouraged
to form. Laterals are cut back to about five
leaves in summer, and then to two or three
buds in winter. Leaders are shortened only in
winter. Only when the main branches are
ageing or becoming congested are a few
removed and new young shoots allowed to
replace them. The training of cordons is similar to that of cordon apples (see page 374).

Pick the currants and gooseberries as they
ripen for dessert use; gooseberries can be
picked under-ripe for cooking. Red currants
make the best jam when they have turned
colour but are still somewhat sour. If you
intend to use the fruits immediately, strip
them from the stalks as you pick them; otherwise, snip the stalks with scissors.

Grapes

'Black Hamburgh'

'Perle de Czaba'

Contrary to popular opinion, grapes are not tender and difficult plants to grow if the right variety is chosen for the particular climate. They undoubtedly give greater yields in cool climates if grown under tall cloches or in a greenhouse, but it is quite feasible to grow them in the open in most areas – though the shelter of a sunny wall may be needed. Ideally, they need long, dry, warm summers during which to develop fruit, and cool, rainy winters when they can lie dormant; only the very tender varieties should be given any artificial heat in winter. Although the majority can survive considerable winter frost (down to less than −18°C [0°F] in some cases) spring frosts after the vines have started growing can easily kill them. Humid rainy summers encourage disease, and rain during ripening and harvesting can rot the fruit.

Of the three species from which modern fruiting grapes are derived, the American bunch or fox grape, *Vitis labrusca*, tolerates humid summers and cold winters better than the European wine grape, *V. vinifera*; and the other North American species, the muscadine grape, *V. rotundifolia* (used commercially to make muscat wines), thrives best in very warm regions. Because the European species is prone to grape phylloxera, a disease of the roots caused by a gall-forming soil aphid, it has been crossed with the disease-resistant labruscan species and the resulting hybrids are now used all over Europe as rootstocks in commercial vineyards.

Grape plants are tendril-climbing shrubs, which, if left to their own devices, grow to enormous heights. They fruit best on one-year-old wood, however, and for this and reasons of convenience methods of pruning have been developed that keep them within bounds. Dense bunches of small green flowers, which are usually hermaphrodite and self-pollinating but in some varieties self-sterile, are followed by similarly bunched fruits which swell and ripen from late summer to late autumn, according to variety. Under tall cloches, they will even bear fruit until midwinter. Ripe colour ranges from green and yellow to red and almost black. If grapes are planted as year-old cuttings or rooted 'eyes' (see p 347) they require four to five years to establish a good enough root system to reach full fruit production, but they often bear some fruit in their second and third years. They can also be purchased as pot-grown vines which will fruit more quickly.

Grapes can be used to make wine, they can be eaten as a dessert, or they can be made into jelly, jam or juice, or dried to make raisins, sultanas and currants. Wine grapes, which are small but have a high sugar content, also make good eating grapes. The larger, thicker-skinned and more pulpy dessert grapes, on the other hand, usually do not make good wine.

Soil, site and planting

Grapes will grow outdoors in a wide variety of soils, but extreme types should be avoided – heavy clays, for example, produce inferior grapes. The soil should not be too rich, bu above all good drainage is essential; water logging is anathema to the vines. Choose warm site in full sun, sheltered from hig winds, and plant the young vines against a wa or fence or on a post-and-wire support.

Pot-grown vines can be planted at any time others in late autumn or (if winters are harsh very early spring. Water the roots well befor planting, dig a hole about 30 cm (12 in) wid and deep, gently spread out the roots, an after mixing rotted compost with the topsoi firmly pack this around the roots. For th Guyot training system using a single rod (o stem), allow 1.25 m (4 ft) between the vine and the same distance between the rows Muscadine varieties and some vigorous var ieties of other species need almost twice a much room between individual vines. Afte planting prune all vines back to two or thre buds and train the new growth according t the system chosen (see illustrations).

Routine care and harvesting

After a mulch of compost when the soil ha warmed up in spring the vines will start t grow. Water them well in the dry spells, bu reduce watering when the grapes begin t swell to avoid them splitting. If the grapes ar grown against a sunny wall they can b allowed to spread out more vigorously than i planted completely in the open, and should b summer pruned as for indoor vines. Thi involves pinching out side shoots at two leave

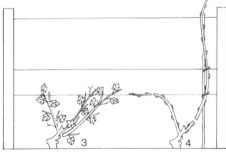

Guyot training system
This method, where either one or two fruiting canes (rods or stems) are tied along a single wire, best suits European and wine grape varieties. It needs horizontal wires about 0.5, 0.75 and 1.25 m (20, 30 and 50 in) above the ground. Tie bamboo stakes to the wires for extra support for the canes.
In the spring after planting, **1** remove all but the strongest young cane growing from the cut-back plant. Pinch out side shoots and for the first year allow only the one cane to grow. **2** The next winter, cut this back to two or three buds.
For the Single Guyot system, **3** remove all but the two strongest resultant canes in the spring. Pinch out all laterals and tie the two canes in. One will bear fruit the following year, while the other will produce replacement canes. **4** In the third winter, tie the fruiting cane along the lower wire and cut back to six buds.

Prune the other cane to two or three buds and **5** in the spring allow the two strongest new canes to grow up against the upper wires as before.
6 In the Double Guyot system, two fruiting canes are tied in opposite directions along the bottom wire, so three replacement canes are needed – two for fruiting and one to produce further replacements. Each winter cut away the fruited canes. Tie in and prune the

replacements, cutting the third cane back to three or four buds; then in spring allow three new replacement canes to grow as before.
In both systems, prune all but the strongest lateral shoots when flowers appear; in later years more and more laterals can be retained. If you wish, the fruiting canes can be covered with cloches while the replacements are trained up the gap in between.

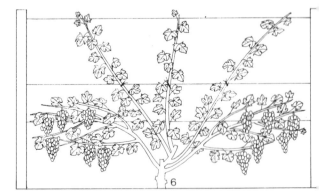

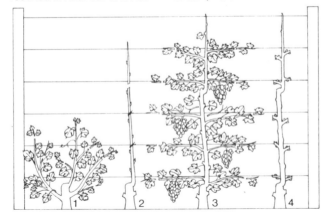

Kniffin training system
This method, where the vine is pruned to four canes that are each tied to a wire, suits American grapes and some European varieties. Two wires, .5 and 1.25 m (20 and 50 in) above the ground, are needed. In principle, it is not unlike a 'quadruple' Guyot system. Allow one main stem to grow, and in the spring after it reaches the first wire **1** cut off, close to the stem, all side shoots except for the two next to the wire; cut both of these shoots back to two buds. One of the buds will produce a fruiting cane, the

other a cane that will once again be cut back to two buds to produce two further replacement canes.
2 Follow the same procedure at the top wire, but stop the upward growth as well. **3** In later years, allow the four fruiting

canes to each produce six to ten laterals – or up to 15 on mature vines. After fruiting, **4** remove the fruited canes, tie in the replacements and cut back the second replacement canes to two buds. Each year, remove all other side shoots.

beyond the point at which they produce a lower truss.

Soon after the grapes have set, the bunches should be thinned to avoid undersized grapes. Using special pointed vine scissors and a forked stick to hold and turn the bunches, cut out one berry in every three, leaving the intact fruits room to swell. Cover exposed fruit with bird-proof netting and trap wasps in jam jars baited with beer and honey. An alternative is to protect each bunch with a perforated plastic bag. In cool climates, covering the vines with tall cloches from late summer aids ripening. When harvesting the grapes, handle them as little as possible. Shake Muscadine varieties onto a cloth and with others use hand shears or secateurs to remove whole bunches.

The yearly winter pruning must be done while the vine is dormant, otherwise sap may bleed from the cuts. Should this occur, a wound sealant can be applied. Whatever the shape of the vine the reason for pruning is to establish a permanent framework of old wood and to ensure that the previous year's growth provides the current year's fruiting shoots as well as replacement shoots for fruiting the following year. Vines grown in the open are subject to few pests, but you should spray to prevent mildew and dust with sulphur to get rid of grey mould (see pp 366 and 367).

Training greenhouse grapes
The simplest method is to allow a single main stem to grow laterals that fruit the same year and are then cut back. The first spring **1** pinch out the tips of all shoots except the leader at six leaves and all further laterals at one leaf.
2 After leaf-fall, shorten the leader to 0.9 to 1.25 m (3 to 4 ft) and cut off all side shoots close to the main stem. Each year allow the leader to grow an extra 60 cm (2 ft) until it reaches the roof ridge.
In spring, select side shoots next to the wires and train these horizontally, cutting out all others. As soon as the first flowers appear, stop the shoots

at two leaves beyond the first truss **3**; stop non-flowering shoots at five to seven leaves. Remove all tendrils, as they are redundant. After the vine has

fruited **4** cut the canes back to two buds and in the following year allow the strongest of each pair of new shoots that grow to carry fruit.

Growing grapes indoors

To achieve maximum quality and colour with indoor grapes, the greenhouse or sun-lounge should preferably face south in the northern hemisphere, or north in the southern hemisphere, so that it receives all available sunlight in summer and early autumn. Vines are commonly planted outside and trained through the side wall, but planting in an inside border or even a large tub is preferable. Although an outside border requires less attention, it allows no control over water and warmth. A clay subsoil should be conditioned by incorporating coarse gravel and peat, and a poor soil should be completely replaced with a bed of good loam, such as that from a well-decayed stack of turves. Otherwise incorporate farmyard manure. Unless already alkaline, apply 270 g/m² (8 oz/sq yd) of lime.

Pot-grown vines can be planted at any time, but others should be planted in late autumn. For the simple, single-stem training system allow 1.5 m (5 ft) between the vines and support their growth with horizontal wires at 30 cm (12 in) intervals. After cutting back the plants to just above the ground, train and prune them as illustrated.

An annual mulch in late winter and a feed of 100 to 200 g (4 to 8 oz) of bonemeal per plant promotes healthy growth, and a farm-

yard manure mulch will release nutrients at each watering. Feed with a proprietary vine fertilizer in spring; later, when the grapes have set, dilute liquid manure can be given once a week. If your greenhouse is heated, aim for a night temperature of 7°C (45°F) in late winter, rising to 16°C (60°F) in early spring, with a daytime temperature then of 18 to 21°C (64 to 70°F). Syringe the growth and soil at least once a day in warm weather to promote a moist atmosphere, and to deter red spider mite (see p 364). Keep the roots moist. Ventilate freely in summer to ward off mildew attack, but avoid creating draughts. Pollinate the flowers by tapping the stems at midday to release the pollen.

After the berries have set, feed with liquid manure, and start to thin out the bunches two weeks after the fruitlets have formed. Black grapes may need a proprietary liquid shading material applied to the glass in the hottest weather; some varieties, such as 'Muscat of Alexandria', are best without shade.

Recommended varieties of grapes

Hardiest varieties (outdoors even in cooler climates)	**Wine or dessert** 'Brandt'† (blue-black); 'Brighton'‡ (red); 'Buffalo' (blue-black); 'Catawaba' (red); 'Chambourcin 26–205' (black); 'Chasselas d'Or' ('Golden Chasselas'); 'Gamay Hâtif des Voges' (black); 'Madeleine Royale'; 'Müller-Thurgau' ('Riesling Sylvaner'); 'Noir Hâtif de Marseilles' (black); 'Pirovano 14' (purple); 'Seyve Villard 12–375'; 'Seyve Villard 18–315' (black); 'Siebel 5279' ('Aurora'); 'Siegerrebe' **Dessert** 'Baco no.1'† ('Baco Noir'; black); 'Chasselas Rose Royale' (red); 'Concord' (blue-black); 'Golden Muscat'; 'Interlaken Seedless'; 'Perle de Czaba'; 'Van Buren' (black)
Less hardy varieties (cloches or cold greenhouse in cooler climates)	'Black Hamburgh' (blue-black); 'Chasselas d'Or' ('Golden Chasselas'); 'Datier de Beyrouth'; 'Foster's Seedling'†; 'Higgins'‡; 'Himrod Seedless'; 'Hunt'‡ (black); 'Madeleine Noir' (black); 'Madresfield Court' (black); 'Muscat Hamburgh' (black); 'Red Malaga' ('Molinera'; purplish-red); 'Reine Olga' (pink); 'Ribier' (black); 'Thompson Seedless' ('Sultanina'); 'Tokay' ('Flame Tokay'; red)
Tender varieties (heated greenhouse)	'Alicante'† (black); 'Black Hamburgh' (blue-black); 'Gros Colmar'† (black); 'Muscat of Alexandria'‡

Unless otherwise stated, varieties are 'white' (that is, green to golden); †vigorous type needing wide spacing; ‡self-sterile variety needing a self-fertile type for pollination.

The cane fruits

Blackberries and related cane fruits, which include raspberries (see opposite), make an invaluable addition to the garden as they can provide a convenient screen for unsightly objects, a division between plots, clothing for a pergola, or even ornamental subjects tied to single posts in the flower garden – as well as being prolific fruit-bearers from a young age. They are particularly well worth growing because the taste of the freshly-picked fruit is incomparable. They also freeze well.

Blackberries and their hybrids

There are a number of species of blackberries that grow wild in the northern hemisphere in both the New and Old Worlds, and the origin of the cultivated forms is somewhat obscure; one of the main British species is *Rubus ulmifolius*, while a major American type is *R. alleghéniensis*. As far as the gardener is concerned, they are divided into two main groups: the clump-forming vine type, in which canes arch or trail outwards, and the bush type, which is more stiff and upright, with branching canes. Clump-forming varieties are the only ones cultivated in the British Isles for their fruit and also do well in the milder parts of North America. In the central and north-eastern parts of North America, however, the bush type are grown as they withstand colder winters.

The loganberry, classified as *R. loganobaccus*, is probably a hybrid between a blackberry and raspberry. It first appeared in 1881 in the garden of a Judge Logan in California, and has been grown in Europe since 1897. It is less sprawling and better suited to small gardens than many blackberries. Like blackberries, loganberries can be stewed, bottled and made into jam, jelly or wine, but they have a flavour all of their own. Only those with a taste for tartness, however, delight in eating them raw – unlike blackberries. A number of other hybrid 'wonder berries' have been developed, generally with a similar dull red colouring to that of the loganberry; the boysenberry and youngberry are the best known, the latter being derived in part from the dewberry, *R. flagellaris*. The boysenberry has particularly delicious large, almost black, sweet berries with very little core, and is very ornamental; moreover, it survives dry conditions better than its relatives. It should otherwise be treated like the loganberry.

Soil and planting Blackberries and loganberries need similar growing conditions, and because they are late flowering they are particularly suitable for low-lying areas prone to spring frosts. The loganberry generally needs more shelter than most blackberries. They both tolerate a shaded position, but if possible choose an open, sunny site shielded from cold winds.

They will grow in a wide range of soil types but prefer a deep, fertile loam that is moist but well drained. Chalk, however, induces iron and manganese deficiencies in loganberries and insufficient moisture precludes the berries swelling adequately. Absence of perennial weeds, especially bindweed, is important, and generous manuring promotes heavy cropping. Thornless varieties need more feeding and are slightly less productive. Prior to planting blackberries in the autumn (or spring in very cold climates), dig deeply and enrich the soil with farmyard manure, garden compost or well-rotted straw.

Allow 2.5 to 3.5 m (8 to 12 ft) between clump-forming plants, according to vigour and training, and 2 m (7 ft) between rows. Provide horizontal wires 0.9, 1.25 and 1.5 m

Blackberry

Loganberry

(3, 4, and 5 ft) above the ground, stretched between strong posts 1.8 m (6 ft) high where there is no fence or wall against which to train the canes. Shorten the canes to 25 cm (10 in) after planting, and give a dressing of fish meal or blood, meat and bone meal and a sprinkling of sulphate of potash to help rapid establishment. Plant loganberries in spring on a post and wire support, on pergolas or arches, or against fences or walls, allowing 1.8 to 3 m (6 to 10 ft) between the plants. Shorten the canes as for blackberries and give a deep mulch. When planting bush-type blackberries, space the plants 1.25 to 1.5 m (4 to 5 ft) apart and cut back to 15 cm (6 in) from the ground. No supporting wires are needed.

Routine care and harvesting Keep the soil weed-free but avoid deep cultivation that might sever roots near the surface. You can use paraquat and simazine weedkillers (see p 357) between established plants, taking care not to wet their leaves or stems. Their chief food is nitrogen, and can be applied either as a thick mulch of farmyard manure or as fish meal or sulphate of ammonia. Also give a dressing of sulphate of potash every two or three years. Correct chlorosis in plants growing on chalky soils by dressing with sequestered iron (see p 353).

Both loganberries and blackberries fruit on year-old canes, and pruning and training is designed to facilitate and promote this. With bush types, pinch out the tips of young canes when they are about 75 cm (2½ ft) tall, in summer; then, next spring, thin out the side shoots to 25 cm (10 in) apart and shorten these to 45 cm (18 in). They will bear this year's fruit, and as soon as this is harvested these canes should be cut out and burned. Meanwhile, new canes will have developed.

With clump-forming kinds, individual canes must be tied in to the wires about 15 cm (6 in) apart. There are various methods of training designed to separate fruiting canes (which will be cut out after harvest) from new canes that will bear the next year's crop; two are illustrated. Loganberries are trained in the same way, allowing 10 to 12 bearing canes per plant. In parts of North America where winters are cold, the canes are usually allowed to trail along the ground for the first season, where they can be covered with a protective mulch in winter.

A number of fungus diseases may attack, including cane spot, which shows as small dark spots on the canes that develop into white blotches, grey mould, spur blight and rust; affected canes should be burned. Virus

Training blackberry canes
The aim is to keep fruiting canes separate from the current year's growth, which will fruit next year. One method is to train all growth of one year to one side **below left**. In autumn, cut out all the fruited canes, leaving the other side of the wires free for the subsequent year's growth to be tied in.
Alternatively, the fruiting canes can be trained left and right along the wires **below right**, leaving the centre free for tying in new growth. After removing the fruited canes, the new supply of canes can be fanned out from the middle. It is best to leave this until early spring in cold areas, so that the young canes, tied in a bundle, can be protected from hard frosts with sacking or burlap.

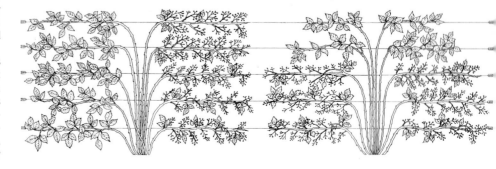

diseases may cause stunting. Raspberry beetle maggots may attack the fruits, and it is advisable to use nets to protect them from birds. For further information, see pages 362 to 367.

Harvest the fruits when they are fully ripe, in late summer; blackberries come away from the core when they are ripe but loganberries do not. Cut back the fruited canes immediately afterwards. New plants can easily be raised by tip layering (see p 350).

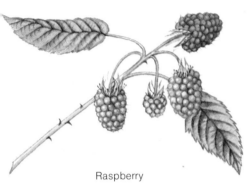

Raspberry

Recommended blackberry varieties

Blackberries	'Bedford Giant'; 'Brainerd'; 'Darrow' (bush); 'Eldorado'; 'Himalaya Giant' ('Theodor Reimers'); 'John Innes'; 'Lawton' (bush); 'Lucretia'; 'Marion'; 'Oregon Thornless' (thornless); 'Smoothstem' (thornless); 'Snyder' (bush)
Related hybrids	'Boysenberry' (reddish-black); 'Cascade' (red); 'Kings Acre Berry' (dark red); 'Loganberry LY59' (red); 'Malling Hybrid 5316' (purplish-black); 'Thornless Loganberry L654' (red; thornless); 'Youngberry'

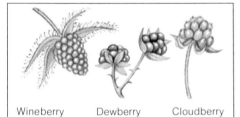

Wineberry   Dewberry   Cloudberry

Unusual cane fruits

The Japanese wineberry, *Rubus phoenicolasius*, is a highly decorative plant with long canes clothed in red bristles. It can easily be grown on a trellis or fence. The initially golden-yellow berries turn wine-red in late summer and make a refreshing dessert served with cream. The dewberry (*R. flagellaris*) is a slender plant that scrambles over the ground. Its small blackberry-like fruits have a white bloom and ripen early. The cloudberry (*R. chamaemorus*) is different from its relatives in being herbaceous. It is low growing, and its small golden berries have long been used in northern parts of Europe and North America in puddings and for jam-making.

Raspberries

Raspberries (derived from *Rubus idaeus*) are an even better dessert fruit than blackberries. They also freeze probably better than any other fruit, and are ideal for pies and jam-making. They are easy to grow and produce heavy yields less than two years after planting. As well as the familiar red kinds, there are yellow varieties and distinctively flavoured purple and black raspberries (the latter known as blackcaps). They all grow on erect canes, the summer-fruiting kinds producing fruit on the previous year's growth, the autumn-fruiting on wood produced in the current season. The latter are also known as perpetual or ever-bearing, because it is possible to get an early summer crop on one-year-old wood as well as an autumn crop; however, this weakens the plants and it is best to make do with one heavy autumn crop, growing a separate variety for earlier eating.

Soil and planting Raspberries prefer a moist heavy soil with plenty of humus, but good crops can be obtained on sandy soils if watering and mulching are adequate. They will not tolerate poor drainage, however, and will soon die. Slightly acid soils are best; chalk can cause chlorosis (see p 352). A sunny site is ideal, but partial shade only has the effect of delaying ripening. Shelter from strong winds is most important to prevent the fruiting lateral shoots being broken.

Select a site not previously occupied by cane fruits, or by potatoes, tomatoes, aubergines (eggplants) or peppers, to avoid infection by soil-borne virus diseases. The ground must first be treated with herbicides to kill perennial weeds, particularly couchgrass, bindweed and creeping thistle. In view of the raspberry's shallow rooting habit, it is imperative to prepare the soil well before planting, by working in large amounts of organic matter. Provide post and wire supports as for blackberries. Alternatively, the canes can be grown without tying between double wires attached to either side of the two supporting posts, so that they are 10 to 15 cm (4 to 6 in) apart, the wires themselves being held together with hooks every 60 cm (2 ft) or so.

Buy certified virus-free canes and preferably plant them in autumn, or in spring in areas where winters are harsh. Set them 45 cm (18 in) apart, giving black and purple varieties 15 cm (6 in) more room, in rows 1.8 m (6 ft) apart. The roots should not be more than 8 cm (3 in) deep and the soil around them must be well firmed down. After planting, or in early spring, shorten the canes to 25 cm (10 in)

Pruning raspberry canes

With summer-fruiting varieties **1** cut old canes down to ground level after fruiting, together with weak young canes. Tie in the strongest new canes, using soft fillis string. In late winter **2** tip-prune these canes. At this time, too, prune autumn-fruiting varieties, **3** cutting back all of the canes to about 15 cm (6 in) above ground level.

above the ground and after they have made sufficient growth tie them to the wires.

Routine care and harvesting Mulch deeply with rotted straw in the spring to conserve moisture, to keep the roots cool, and to suppress weeds, and feed with a fertilizer rich in nitrogen and potash (see p 352). Water in dry weather. Preferably use herbicides to kill weeds, as with blackberries, for although it is safe to use a hoe between the rows, the shal-

Recommended raspberry varieties

Summer-fruiting	'Allen' (black); 'Amber' (yellow); 'Black Hawk' (black); 'Bristol' (black); 'Clyde' (purple); 'Delight'; 'Dundee' (black); 'Glen Clova'; 'Hilton'; 'Lloyd George'; 'Malling Admiral'; 'Malling Jewel'; 'Malling Orion'; 'Norfolk Giant'; 'Sodus' (purple); 'Taylor'
Autumn-fruiting	'Durham'; 'Fallgold' (yellow); 'Fallred'; 'Heritage'; 'Indian Summer'; 'Lloyd George' (if pruned in late winter); 'September; 'Zeva'

low roots of raspberries are easily damaged.

Allow the plants to grow unpruned for their first year, merely removing weak canes. In late winter, prune the tips of the canes to promote fruit-bearing side growths. After fruiting, cut the fruited canes of summer-fruiting varieties down to ground level. Reduce the young unfruited canes to the six to eight strongest per plant, and tie these in 8 to 10 cm (3 to 4 in) apart. Shorten their tips in late winter as before or, alternatively, bend the tips over and tie them down to the top wire. Prune autumn-fruiting types in late winter by cutting all the canes back to about 15 cm (6 in) above the ground. They will make new fruiting growth which must be tied in as before. They do not need tip-pruning. With all types, pull up suckers that grow between the rows; do this when they are young and easy to pull out.

Pests and diseases are much as for blackberries, but aphids can be troublesome and spread virus diseases, which are a serious problem with raspberries, and raspberry beetles are common. Winter spraying with tar-oil as well as the use of insecticides in summer will aid control. Birds eat the opening fruits, and should be deterred with nets. Pick the fruits when ripe, going over the plants every few days; they come away easily from the core. After eight to ten years, it is best to plant new virus-free canes in a new site to prevent virus infection setting in. Burn the old canes.

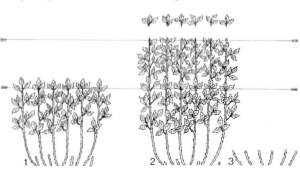

Strawberries

Strawberries are among everyone's favourite fruit, whether eaten fresh or made into jam. They will grow in most climates providing they have enough sun and moisture. They are relatively easy to manage, they take up little space in the garden and they will bear fruit in less than a year after planting. Their main vice is that they are very prone to virus diseases. Commercial strawberries are descendants of two American species, *Fragaria chiloensis* and *F. × ananassa,* and are classified as *F. × ananassa.* They are perennial plants that grow to about 20 cm (8 in) high and increase by runners that form plantlets at the ends.

The two- to three-week season of the summer-fruiting varieties, or 'June bearers', is all too short, but it can be extended by planting both early and late types or by planting the so-called perpetual, everbearing or remontant types, which fruit in early summer and again in autumn, with a few berries on and off in between. The tiny-fruited, but delicious, alpine or wood strawberries, a distinct European species, also have an extended season, while growing plants in a greenhouse or under cloches or plastic tunnels can force early crops and extend the autumn season. With good management, it is possible to have strawberries for six months of the year or more.

Be sure to buy certified, virus-free plants, or runners, from a reliable nursery, and varieties that are suited to the local climate. Summer varieties are best planted from midsummer to autumn, except where winters are harsh, when spring planting is best. Small plants planted in summer will give a better yield the following summer than larger ones planted in autumn. Perpetuals planted in spring will give a crop in the autumn; those planted in autumn will bear fruit from the next spring. It is best to remove the first flush of flowers from spring-planted strawberries to ensure establishment of sturdy plants.

Soil and planting
Choose a sunny site that is not shaded by trees or invaded by their roots, is freely drained, devoid of perennial weeds and, preferably, was previously well manured for vegetables. Avoid planting where chrysanthemums,

potatoes, tomatoes, melons or raspberries previously grew, as these might have carried eelworm or other soil pests or diseases. Dig the site two or three weeks before planting, adding 35 g/m² (1 oz/sq yd) each of sulphate of potash and superphosphate, but no nitrogenous fertilizer (see p 352) – virus-free runners do not need it and would grow leaves at the expense of fruit. Mix in a generous amount of decayed garden compost or peat on dry soils.

Just before planting, spray paraquat (see p 357) to kill annual weeds that have germinated, thereby leaving a weed-free plot for the autumn and winter. Using a garden line, plant the runners of summer varieties about 45 cm (18 in) apart in straight rows about 60 cm (24 in) apart. Soak pot-grown runners in water; do not break up peat pots but remove plastic ones. Dig holes deep enough to take the roots of the plants and plant with the crowns exactly at soil level. If they are too high the roots dry out; if they are too low the crowns rot. Thoroughly firm the soil. Water well every day until the plants are established.

Perpetuals should be planted in the same way as summer varieties, but the plants should be 45 to 60 cm (1½ to 2 ft) apart and the rows 90 cm (3 ft) apart, and the two types should not be grown together.

Routine care and harvesting
The spring after late summer planting, hoe to prevent weeds, and conserve soil moisture by laying a 1 cm (½ in) mulch of moist peat or black plastic sheeting. With the latter, it will be unnecessary to lay straw to keep the fruit clean but if frost is expected cover the plants at night with newspaper or a thin layer of straw. Where plastic is not used, lay straw (from wheat or barley – oat straw may carry eelworm) or saltmarsh hay under the plants after the fruits have set to prevent them being dirtied by soil. Do not lay straw before fruiting as this insulates the plants from soil warmth and increases frost risk.

Water the plants well when the berries are swelling. The berries must now be protected from birds by draping netting on posts over the whole crop. Of other pests and diseases that may threaten the crop, slug pellets will

combat slugs, derris will kill virus-carrying aphids, and various sprays prevent mildew (see pp 362 to 367).

Pick the fruits gently; for jam, pick them without the calyx (ring of 'leaves') and stalk. After harvesting, cut back the dying leaves and remove old straw and rotting fruit – especially in warm, humid climates where grey mould is a serious problem. Or set fire to the straw and burn off this and all top growth. Leave only healthy strong plants to reform a new bed, replacing weaklings with new plants grown from runners. After three years buy new certified plants to ensure that virus disease does not build up; plant them in a new plot. Where winters are severe, protect plants with 10 cm (4 in) of dry straw or hay.

Feed second- and third-year plants in early spring with 135 g/m² (4 oz/sq yd) of John Innes base fertilizer or a similar low-nitrogen, high-potash feed (see p 353). Perpetuals should be treated in just the same way as summer varieties but there is as yet no certification scheme for them and it may be best to treat them as annuals in case they are carrying disease; root a good supply of runners – up to four from each plant – in pots in early summer (see p 349), and plant out in a new plot.

Recommended strawberry varieties

Summer-fruiting	'Cambridge Favourite'; 'Cambridge Late Pine'*; 'Cambridge Prizewinner'†; 'Catskill'; 'Cyclone'; 'Domanil'; 'Dunlap'; 'Fairfax'; 'Grandee'†; 'Marshall'; 'Merton Herald'*†; 'Midland'; 'Northwest'; 'Red Gauntlet'; 'Royal Sovereign'*; (good pollinator; vulnerable to disease); 'Siletz'; 'Sparkle'; 'Spring Giant'*† (good pollinator); 'Surecrop'; 'Tamella'†; 'Temptation'*; 'Tennessee Beauty'; 'Trumpeter'; 'Vesper'
Perpetual	'Gento'*; 'La Sans Rivale'; 'Ogalala'; 'Ozark Beauty'; 'Red Rich'; 'St Claude'; 'Superfection'
Alpine	'Alexandria'; 'Baron Solemacher'; 'Dobie's Delicious'*; 'Harsland'; 'Yellow Alpine'

*Especially good flavour and quality; †early

Forcing and plastic mulching
For an early strawberry crop, grow under plastic or glass cloches. In late summer plant pot-grown runners in a row in well-prepared ground. Thoroughly water if necessary before scattering slug pellets and laying black plastic sheeting. Unroll a strip 75 cm (2½ ft) wide over the row, making crossed slits at each plant and gently teasing the leaves through them. Secure the edges in the soil.

In late winter, cover the row with cloches or erect a plastic tunnel (see p 269) and lay more slug pellets. Ventilate the cloches on warm days (by raising the sides in the case of the plastic tunnel) to help ensure pollination, but protect plastic tunnels at night in frosty weather with newspaper or sacking. Under plastic, the plants fruit about two weeks earlier than normal, under glass cloches about three weeks.

For an even longer season, grow in pots in a greenhouse with a minimum night temperature of 7°C (45°F). Then it will be necessary to hand-pollinate the conical female flowers with a brush.

Alpine strawberries
Alpine strawberries, *Fragaria vesca semperflorens*, do not produce runner and must therefore be grown from seed. The plants give aromatic, miniature berries from summer onwards and they are ideal for garnishing fresh fruit salads and are excellent for making jam. In autumn or early spring, sow the seeds in pots or trays in a greenhouse or cold frame; do not cover the seeds with soil mixture. Plant out in late spring (or earlier from an autumn sowing) in order to gather fruit in the late summer of the same year. Plant 30 cm (12 in) apart as an edging to a border, in pockets in a rock garden or in a strawberry pot (see p 117). If growing on the ground, mulch these woodland plants with leaf-mould.

Blueberries, barberries and golden berries

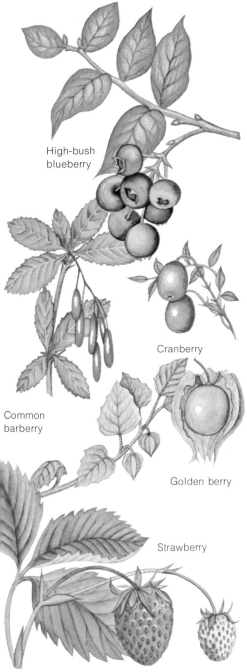

High-bush blueberry

Cranberry

Common barberry

Golden berry

Strawberry

Although commonly grown in some parts of the world, and in some cases traditional pie-fillers of many years' – even centuries' – standing, these delicious fruits and their close relatives could be grown by many more gardeners. The main problem with blueberries, and the related cranberries and bilberries, is that they demand very acid, moist growing conditions, but this can be overcome in all but areas with really chalky soil by growing them in peat beds or containers of very peaty growing mixture. Barberries are much easier to grow, though they are more common today for ornament than eating, as is the related Oregon grape. The golden berry, or Cape gooseberry, is easily grown from seed in the same way as tomatoes.

Blueberries and their relatives
North America is the home of blueberry pie, and of the blueberry species that give the best fruits. However, *Vaccinium myrtillus*, the bilberry, whortleberry, whinberry or blaeberry, is a native of northern Asia and Europe. It grows wild on acid heaths and moors, and its small blue-black fruits, though acid, make good tarts, pies, sauces and jams. There is also a European cranberry, *V. oxycoccus*, a low-growing shrublet with red berries that make good tart and pie fillings, sauces and jams. However, the best types for the fruit garden are two American species of blueberry, *V. corymbosum* (the high-bush blueberry) and, for warm climates *V. ashei* (the rabbiteye blueberry), together with the American cranberry, *V. macrocarpum*. The low-bush blueberry (*V. angustifolium*) is extremely hardy, but the high-bush type has the best flavour; particularly good varieties include 'Berkeley', 'Bluecrop', 'Blueray', 'Collins', 'Coville', 'Darrow', 'Dixi', 'Earliblue', 'Goldtraube', 'Herbert', 'Ivanhoe', 'Jersey' and 'Pemberton'. Good rabbiteye varieties include 'Angola', 'Callaway', 'Croatan', 'Homebell', 'Murphy', 'Scammell', 'Tifblue', 'Walker', and 'Wolcott'.

All blueberries need a moist, acid, peaty or sandy loam with a pH value of between 5.5 and 4.3 (see p 332). Most garden soils need plenty of peat and sand digging in, while it is possible to increase acidity by raking in 135 g/m² (4 oz/sq yd) of sulphur powder (flowers of sulphur) per pH unit requiring adjustment; do this several months ahead of planting. It is often easier, however, to grow the plants in peat beds or in containers of acid, peaty growing mixture (see p 126). Large tubs are suitable, but to make it easier to ensure constant root moisture, sink them almost to the rim in the ground; provide drainage holes.

Plant between autumn and early spring, allowing a spacing of 1.8 m (6 ft) for high-bush blueberries, which reach a height of 1.5 to 2 m (5 to 7 ft). Interplant at least two varieties to ensure cross-pollination. Pruning is unnecessary in the first two years; subsequently shorten one or two branches and remove dead wood each winter to encourage basal growth – blueberries fruit on one-year-old wood. Mulch with garden compost plus 35 g/m² (1 oz/sq yd) of sulphate of ammonia in spring, or use sawdust plus a double dose of fertilizer. Give 15 g/m² (½ oz/sq yd) of sulphate of potash in winter. Blueberries ripen from midsummer to early autumn, when the foliage turns a glorious red. As soon as the berries begin to colour, net the bushes to keep off birds. The berries can be eaten fresh with sugar and cream, can be stewed or made into jelly, jams, pies or tarts, or can be frozen.

Cranberries are grown in the same way, but make somewhat smaller bushes. The berries are used to make the traditional sauce to accompany turkey and game.

Barberries and mahonias
Several barberries (*Berberis* spp) produce edible berries as well as being decorative shrubs. *Berberis asiatica* berries are used for making raisins in India, the evergreen *B. buxifolia* produces large black berries of good flavour and those of the ornamental *B. darwinii* are also edible. But the common barberry, *B. vulgaris*, is most used for tarts and pies and for making sauces and refreshing drinks. It grows to a maximum height of 3.5 to 4.5 m (12 to 15 ft), and has spined, upright to arching growth sporting drooping racemes of yellow flowers. They are followed by scarlet to purple oblong berries. They are acid but of good flavour, and are sometimes seedless.

The related Oregon grape, *Mahonia aquifolium*, also has golden-yellow flowers that are followed by clusters of grape-like black berries. These are excellent for jellies, jams and flavouring pies, for their juice and for making wine.

Golden berries
Otherwise known as the Cape gooseberry (because it has been long cultivated in the Cape of Good Hope) or Peruvian cherry (for its original home), the golden berry (*Physalis peruviana edulis*) can be grown from seed for cultivation either outdoors in a sunny spot or in a greenhouse. Sow in early spring at 18°C (64°F), and pot the seedlings into 8 cm (3 in) pots and then 20 cm (8 in) pots. Stake the sprawling growth – it may reach 1.25 m (4 ft) outdoors in temperature climates or 2.5 m (8 ft) under glass – and treat as for tomatoes (see p 302). Water freely and regularly, and feed with liquid fertilizer.

Pick the berries in late summer, when the parchment-like husk (which betrays the plant's relationship to the Chinese lantern, *P. alkekengi*) changes from green to golden-brown and has become papery. Store them for two to three weeks to enable the intriguing, rich flavour to develop. They are delicious in fresh fruit or vegetable salads, or stewed, preserved in syrup or used in pies. They can be frozen or stored by hanging in a cool, dry place for several months. You can expect 1 to 2 kg (2 to 4 lb) of fruit per plant. The plant is perennial if protected from frost, and can be multiplied by cuttings in spring.

Related species with rather similar fruits are the North American ground cherry, *P. pruinosa*, and the tomatillo or jamberry, *P. ixocarpa*. Both are annuals whose berries are usually used in sauces and preserves.

Apples

Apples, derived mainly from the wild *Malus sylvestris* of Europe and Asia, are the most widely grown of all fruit trees in gardens in temperate climates. They are hardy and thrive on a wide range of soils so long as the aspect is reasonably sunny and the soil drains well. They are the last of the tree fruits to blossom, the flowers of the various varieties appearing over a period of about a month in late spring. They are therefore less prone to frost damage than, say, the stone fruits, but the buds and flowers can still be caught by late frosts where these occur, as can the fruitlets of some varieties. So it is best to site them in slightly elevated positions where freezing air can drain away downhill. In cool climates, such as that of the British Isles, however, they do best below an altitude of about 120 m (400 ft) above sea level. They also prefer moderately dry conditions, with an annual rainfall of between 50 and 75 cm (20 and 30 in).

The flavour of apples extends from sweetness in dessert fruit (preferably combined with slight acidity, or the taste is rather bland) to extreme acidity for cooking and cidermaking. Dual-purpose varieties have moderately high acidity as well as sweetness. Some varieties should be eaten within a few weeks of picking, while others can be easily stored for six months or more – and, in fact, are woody and flavourless if eaten too quickly. So by choosing a range of varieties it is possible to have home-grown apples for nine months of the year – from midsummer to late the following spring.

It is always wise, in fact, to plant two or more varieties, to ensure adequate pollination. Many apples will give reasonable crops if planted alone, but all do better if there is another variety nearby that blooms at the same time; then each will pollinate the other. With some varieties, this is essential, as pollen from a tree of the same variety will not start the development of fruits. These self-sterile varieties (see the table) are also poor pollinators of others; their pollen may even be completely sterile, and with these you should plant at least three simultaneously flowering varieties – the self-sterile one plus two normal kinds. It is possible to buy 'family' trees that have two or three cross-compatible varieties grafted onto one trunk – generally three main branches of each; these are useful where space is restricted.

Tree sizes and shapes

Young apple trees are propagated by budding or grafting (see p 351) on rootstocks that have themselves been propagated by layering (see p 349), so that they are identical; they should be certified to be free of virus diseases. Apple trees grown from seed are extremely variable in size of tree – and their fruit, too, is frequently worthless. By using numbered rootstocks, the vigour of a tree in a given soil can be forecast and planting distances gauged accordingly. The most popular rootstocks in Britain are Malling 9 (or simply M9; very dwarfing), Malling 26 (M26; dwarfing), Merton-Malling 106 (MM106; semi-dwarfing), Merton-Malling 111 (MM111;

'Blenheim Orange'
'James Grieve'
'Worcester Pearmain'
'Bramley's Seedling'
'Charles Ross'
'Lord Derby'

Apples for cider

Cider is made commercially by blending the juices of special cider apple varieties – generally sharp and sweet ones with bitter varieties having a high tannin content. Most cider varieties are unsuitable to use on their own, but either the bitter-sweet 'Dabinett' or 'Kingston Black', which is a medium-acid, high-tannin variety, will make acceptable cider if used alone.

Alternatively – and more practically for most gardeners – the dessert varieties 'Cox's Orange Pippin' and 'Laxton's Superb' can be used in equal parts with the culinary 'Bramley's Seedling'. As a further alternative, you could use 'Cox's Orange Pippin' and 'Worcester Pearmain' plus any russet apple.

vigorous) and Malling 25 (M25; vigorous). When buying a tree that has already been partly trained to a particular shape, it should be on a suitable rootstock; if buying a one-year-old 'maiden', make sure that the nurseryman knows what size and form you want to achieve. Soil conditions also influence size, so tell him if your soil is particularly fertile or particularly poor.

Tree shapes and sizes range from large standard trees that may reach 7.5 m (25 ft) through half-standards and bushes to dwarf bushes, dwarf pyramids, espaliers and other artificially-shaped geometric forms, and upright and oblique cordons (see p 374). The last are ideal for very small gardens, as they can be planted very close, but they give the smallest individual yields (see the small table). Dwarf forms have the general advantage of being more easily sprayed, pruned and

harvested without using a ladder; it is also easy to cover them with nylon nets to prevent bird damage and to protect from frost.

In general, cooking apples are inherently more vigorous than dessert sorts, so for planting in gardens it is particularly important to buy only trees grafted on dwarfing rootstocks.

Soil and planting

Deep loamy soils are ideal for apples, but they tolerate sandy soils provided that water is given during drought and heavy clays provided that you improve drainage as described on page 333. They also tolerate a wide range of soil acidity (see p 332). They do not like exposed conditions or salt-laden winds, however, and you may need to erect a semipermeable screen or plant a windbreak as protection. Culinary apple trees are less sensitive to soil conditions than the dessert varieties, and will tolerate heavy soils even where drainage is poor. They do not rely on sunshine so much and accept higher rainfall.

Trees may be planted at any time when they are dormant and the soil is workable and not waterlogged. In areas where winters are harsh it is best to leave planting until early spring; elsewhere late autumn planting gives a better start. If your soil is poor, mix well-rotted farmyard manure or garden compost with the soil, but elsewhere save this for a surface mulch. Make a hole large enough to take the roots without cramping, and insert a supporting stake. Plant really firmly by ramming each spadeful of soil down around the roots with a baulk of timber (being careful not to damage the roots themselves); use the best topsoil. Make sure that the point of grafting (shown by a swelling in the trunk) is above soil level to prevent the top growth rooting. Tie the tree securely to its stake.

Routine care and pruning

In areas prone to spring frosts, be ready to take protective measures from when the flower buds begin to swell. These methods include draping the trees with nets and sprinkling water as described on page 354.

At the beginning of the growing season, cover the root area with a thick mulch of garden compost, peat, straw or farmyard manure to conserve soil moisture and (in the first year) to induce rapid re-establishment. If conditions are dry, make sure that the trees receive adequate water in spring and early summer. Depending on vigour, as judged by the amount of growth being made and fruit set, apply a general fertilizer around the tree; nitrogen tends to promote growth, while potash boosts fruit production (see p 352). With cooking apples, nitrogenous fertilizers can be applied more liberally, particularly on poorer soils; they improve fruit size and promote a texture especially good for cooking.

Prune new apple trees hard in the early spring after planting, cutting back leaders by one-half and side shoots to 2.5 cm (1 in) or less. Subsequently, for all except the larger trees, most varieties of apples benefit from pruning in mid- to late summer. Leave the leaders unpruned, but shorten side/continued

Apples in containers

You can grow miniature apple trees trained as dwarf pyramids or vertical cordons on a paved garden or terrace in large pots or wooden tubs filled with a good potting mixture, preferably a loam-based type such as John Innes no. 3 (see p 345). Renew some of this annually during the dormant season by carefully teasing away the old potting mixture from the root ball, repositioning the tree in its container and repacking with fresh. It is advisable to protect the roots of such containerized trees from frost with sacking or by plunging the whole pot in ashes for the winter.

Forms of apple tree

	Mature height	Planting distance	Row distance	Typical yield
Standard	6 m (20 ft)	10 m (33 ft)	12 m (40 ft)	125 kg (275 lb)
Half-standard	4.5 m (15 ft)	6 m (20 ft)	6 m (20 ft)	50 kg (110 lb)
Bush	3.5 m (12 ft)	3.5 m (12 ft)	3.5 m (12 ft)	40 kg (90 lb)
Dwarf bush	3 m (10 ft)	1.8 m (6 ft)	4 m (13 ft)	12 kg (25 lb)
Dwarf pyramid	2.5 m (8 ft)	1 m (3½ ft)	2 m (7 ft)	3 kg (7 lb)
Espalier	2.5 m (8 ft)	5 m (16 ft)	(on walls)	6 kg (14 lb)
Oblique cordon	2 m (7 ft)	75 cm (2½ ft)	1.8 cm (6 ft)	2 kg (4½ lb)

Figures for yields are very approximate, and will vary widely with variety, soil and climate

Recommended apple varieties

	Variety	Season of use	Flavour	Texture	Cropping	Flowering season	Pruning
Dessert varieties	'American Mother'	Mid-season	Good; aromatic	Crisp; juicy	Irregular	Late	Normal†
	'Ashmead's Kernel'	Late	Excellent	Firm	Light	Mid-season	Normal†
	'Beauty of Bath'	Early	Good from tree	Soft	Sometimes irregular	Early	Light*†
	'Cox's Orange Pippin'	Late	Superb	Tender	Fair to good	Mid-season	Hard†
	'Discovery'	Early	Pleasant aroma	Firm	Regular once started	Mid-season	Light*†
	'Egremont Russet'	Mid-season	Choice; nutty	Firm	Very good	Early	Normal†
	'Ellison's Orange'	Second early	Good	Crisp	Good; sometimes biennial	Mid-season	Light
	'Fortune'	Second early	Aromatic; sweet	Tender; crisp	Prolific; sometimes biennial	Mid-season	Minimal*†
	'George Cave'	Early	Pleasant	Firm	Heavy; regular	Early	Minimal*
	'Golden Delicious'	Late	Excellent; sweet	Crisp; juicy	Regular; best in hot summers	Mid-season	Normal
	'Ingrid Marie'	Very late	Moderate	Firm	Good	Mid-season	Normal
	'Irish Peach'	Early	Good from tree	Soft	Irregular	Early	Light*
	'James Grieve'	Second early	Good; refreshing	Soft	Regular; very good	Mid-season	Normal†
	'Laxton's Superb'	Late	Good; aromatic	Soft	Good; sometimes biennial	Mid-season	Light†
	'Lord Lambourne'	Mid-season	Excellent	Fairly soft	Very good	Early	Light*†
	'Merton Charm'	Second early	Excellent	Soft; juicy	Good; regular	Mid-season	Light†
	'Merton Russet'	Very late	Acid	Crisp	Good	Mid-season	Normal†
	'Miller's Seedling'	Early	Good; fresh	Crisp	Heavy	Mid-season	Light
	'Orleans Reinette'	Late	Aromatic; excellent	Crisp	Fair	Mid-season	Normal†
	'Ribston Pippin'	Late	Aromatic; excellent	Firm	Moderate	Early‡	Hard†
	'Spartan'	Late	Acceptable	Firm	Precocious; heavy	Mid-season	Normal
	'Sunset'	Mid to late	Very good	Fairly firm	Heavy	Mid-season	Normal†
	'Worcester Pearmain'	Second early	Very good	Firm	Regular; very good	Mid-season	Light*
Dual-purpose varieties	'Allington Pippin'	Late	Good; acid	Firm	Very good	Mid-season	Normal
	'Belle de Boskoop'	Very late	Good; aromatic; acid	Firm	Moderate to heavy	Mid-season‡	Normal
	'Blenheim Orange'	Late	Nutty; acid	Crisp	Good; regular	Mid-season‡	Light
	'Charles Ross'	Mid-season	Sweet	Tender	Good; regular	Mid-season	Normal†
	'Peasgood's Nonsuch'	Second early	Good	Soft	Irregular	Mid-season	Light†
	'Rival'	Mid-season	Moderate	Firm	Fair	Mid-season	Light†
	'Wagener'	Very late	Fair	Firm	Fair	Mid-season	Normal
Cooking varieties	'Arthur Turner'	Early	Good; acid	—	Very good	Mid-season	Light†
	'Bismarck'	Mid-season	Good; semi-acid	—	Good	Mid-season	Light
	'Bramley's Seedling'	Late	Excellent; acid	—	Heavy	Mid-season‡	Minimal*
	'Crawley Beauty'	Very late	Good	—	Very good	Very late	Hard†
	'Crimson Bramley'	Late	Excellent; acid	—	Very good	Mid-season‡	Minimal*
	'Edward VII'	Very late	Good	—	Very good	Late	Normal
	'Grenadier'	Early	Good; acid	—	Very good	Mid-season	Normal†
	'Lane's Prince Albert'	Late	Very good; acid	—	Very good	Mid-season	Hard†
	'Lord Derby'	Mid-season	Excellent	—	Good	Late	Light
	'Newton Wonder'	Very late	Very good	—	Rather irregular	Late‡	Minimal

Tip bearer – do not shorten laterals, but thin out; †suitable for growing as a cordon or in other special shapes; ‡self-sterile and will not pollinate other varieties (all apples benefit from cross-pollination by another variety flowering at the same time)

Apples (continued)

Pruning spur bearing apples
Most apple trees bear fruit on spurs (short side shoots) from the main branches. To encourage these, prune back all laterals in winter to between two and six buds of their base, depending on the variety (see the table). The terminal shoot on each branch may be shortened by about one-third except on vigorously growing varieties.

Pruning tip bearing apples
Some varieties (see table) bear fruit at or near the ends of lateral shoots. These should be shortened only if they are growing vigorously; otherwise simply thin out overcrowded or crossing laterals in winter.

shoots to leave five leaves. Then, in winter, shorten the leaders by one-third and the side shoots to between two and six buds, depending on variety. Trees not summer pruned are winter pruned by first removing dead, diseased and crossing branches and then cutting out sufficient to maintain an open crown. The leaders may be shortened by one-third during the first four winters but, afterwards, are best left unpruned on bushes and standards to induce a drooping, more fruitful habit.

There are certain exceptions to the above, however. If a tree is making poor growth, hard pruning will stimulate new development provided the tree is healthy. On the other hand, excessively vigorous trees and most cooking apples should receive minimal pruning. (Other curbing measures include withholding nitrogenous fertilizers, growing regularly-mown grass around the trees, removing a ring of bark no more than 5 mm (¼ in) wide from around the trunk in late spring, and root pruning in late autumn.) One other group of apples should receive little pruning of the side shoots. These are the so-called tip bearers, a high proportion of whose fruit is borne at the very end of one-year-old lateral shoots; these clearly must not all be removed or yields will suffer. In this case, simply thin out overcrowded side shoots and cut back only enough of the longest ones to maintain vigour. These are indicated in the table, together with general pruning needs. Since training into special shapes such as espaliers inevitably involves a lot of pruning, these kinds should generally be avoided for training.

Apples are prey to a depressingly wide range of pests and diseases, so it is wise to take preventive measures with regular spraying and by applying grease bands to the trunks of the trees in winter (see p 359). The principal insect pests are aphids, red spider mites,

sawflies, codling moths, woolly aphids and various caterpillars. Diseases include mildew, scab, canker, brown rot and various viruses. In addition, russeting and bitter pit of the fruits – both physiological disorders – may be troublesome. And birds attack the unopened flower buds, the blossom and the fruit. For further information, see pages 362 to 368.

Harvesting and storage
Where too many fruitlets are set, many drop naturally. Nevertheless, hand thinning in stages in summer may be necessary to achieve acceptable fruit size. Also, if a tree crops excessively in one year, it may have few fruits the next, falling into a biennial habit. First thin the fruit clusters to at least 8 cm (3 in) apart, remove the largest 'king' fruit from each cluster and then reduce to two fruitlets per cluster. With cooking apples, leave single fruitlets spaced 15 to 20 cm (6 to 8 in) apart.

Gather apples when well coloured and when they part readily from the parent spur when lifted and twisted slightly. All the fruits on one tree may not be ready for picking at the same time; go over each tree every few days. Early-ripening varieties need to be eaten within a few weeks, in late summer. Store keeping sorts in a frost-proof, cool dark place with a moist atmosphere, in trays or boxes lined with newspaper. If possible, wrap each apple in waxed paper after allowing to stand for a week to 'sweat'. Or put them in plastic bags pierced with holes; this decreases 'breathing' and prolongs storage life. Inspect the apples regularly for rotting, however, and remove any with blemishes. Do not try to store bruised fruits in the first place. Mid-season varieties are good to eat throughout autumn, while late sorts will keep, if properly stored, through winter and well into spring in some cases.

Pears

Pears (varieties of *Pyrus communis*) are more fickle than apples and require a more sheltered, warmer position to fruit well and achieve quality. They revel in sunshine and low summer rainfall; they sulk in cold and damp. However, they tolerate heavier soils than apples but, equally, demand good drainage, while enjoying a cool root run. On alkaline soils they may suffer from chlorosis, necessitating spraying of the young leaves with sequestered iron (see p 353).

Flowering commences before apples, making pear blossom more vulnerable to damage by frost, so that air drainage to a lower level is vital in frosty climates and protection from cold winds a necessity. Pear blossom – and even the fruitlets – can be killed if the temperature remains only 2°C (4°F) below freezing for an hour or more. Unfortunately, there are no very late-flowering, frost-avoiding pear varieties.

Many pear varieties are only partially self-fertile, not being able to pollinate themselves adequately, but planting two more more varieties flowering at the same time ensures cross-pollination and more reliable cropping. Quinces (see p 325) also pollinate pears. A few varieties (marked in the table) have very poor pollen and need a third variety. On the other hand, 'Conference' often fruits unaided even when the embryo seeds have been killed by frost. In general, pears do not keep as well as apples, but varieties are available for eating from high summer to midwinter, and the cooking varieties keep even longer.

Pears are available in the same range of forms – from standards down to dwarf bushes and cordons – as apples, but the larger types are slow to bear and not recommended for gardens. As with apples, 'family' trees bearing two or three different varieties are available. The quince is used as a dwarfing rootstock for pears. Apart from cordons and bush trees, pears fruit particularly well as espaliers against walls or fences. Allow for a spread of 2.5 to 3.5 m (8 to 12 ft). Occasionally the side branches on opposing sides of an espalier get out of step in vigour, the strongly growing branch carrying less fruit than its partner opposite. To correct this, either release the weaker branch from its support and secure it temporarily at an angle above the horizontal, or tie the more vigorous branch down below the horizontal. As soon as a balance in vigour is restored, reposition the branches horizontally on their permanent supports.

Planting and routine care
Plant pear trees in the same way as for apples (see p 316), but take even more care not to bury the grafting union; set it 8 cm (3 in) above soil level to preclude roots forming from the pear top growth – if they do, they will nullify the dwarfing effect of the quince rootstock. Pear trees rarely thrive in grass; keep an area around the trunk at least 1 m (3 ft) across free from weeds and grass. Mulch this area annually with garden compost, straw or rotted farmyard manure to help conserve soil moisture. Give more nitrogenous fertilizer, but less potash, than to apples (see p 352).

Just as with apple trees, pears should be pruned fairly hard in the early spring after planting. Thereafter, pruning need only be light until fruiting commences. Then most varieties respond to being spur pruned – that is, having the new lateral shoots cut back to about five leaves in summer, followed by pruning to two buds in winter. As with apples, a few varieties (indicated in the table) are tip-bearers, fruiting at the ends of lateral shoots, and should have a proportion of their laterals left unpruned each year.

Pears should be regularly sprayed against pests, as with apples, the main ones being aphids, pear leaf-blister mite, caterpillars, pear midge and birds. The last can cause much trouble by pecking immature fruits just below the stalk; wasps then frequently take over and enlarge the holes; brown rot fungus finally ruins the fruit. To prevent bird damage on bush trees, a home-made cardboard or plastic disc having a slit to the centre can be slid over the stalk of each fruit. Alternatively, enclose each pear in a small clear plastic bag secured by a wire tie at the stalk. With cordon or espalier trees, a bird-proof net, or a sheet of muslin, can be draped over the whole tree. The most troublesome diseases are pear scab, pear canker (which can be severe when drainage is poor), fireblight and brown rot. For more information, see pages 362 to 367.

Harvesting and storage

Fruit-thinning may be necessary where the set is prolific; otherwise, a heavy crop of small pears is likely. Thin the fruitlets to leave two or three pears per fruit spur, snapping the stalks of rejected fruitlets rather than attempting to sever them from the spurs, as the latter break easily. Thinning to one fruit per spur is advisable in dry seasons on light soils if fruit size is not to suffer.

Timing when to pick the fruit is less easy than with apples. Pears picked too early do not mature properly, shrivel and lack flavour and juice; pears picked too late go mealy, begin to rot from the centre and are equally inedible. The earliest-ripening varieties can be picked and eaten straight from the tree as soon as the skin begins to turn yellow – as early as midsummer. They will then come away from the tree with a gentle pull. Do not expect them to remain delicious for more than a few days. Mid-season pears, too, should be picked as soon as the colour changes, despite feeling firm and unripe, but late varieties should remain on the tree as long as possible to preclude shrivelling in store. With all types, hold the pear by the stalk, lift and twist sideways; this avoids bruising and damage to the fruiting spurs.

Mid-season pears need to be stored for at least a week to mature off the tree; they can be eaten in early to mid-autumn. Keep them and late types unwrapped, preferably in a moist atmosphere and as cool as possible; 5 to 7°C (41 to 45°F) is ideal. Finally, keep them at room temperature for a few days to achieve full flavour. Individual pears off the same tree may ripen at widely different times; test by gently pressing near the stalk.

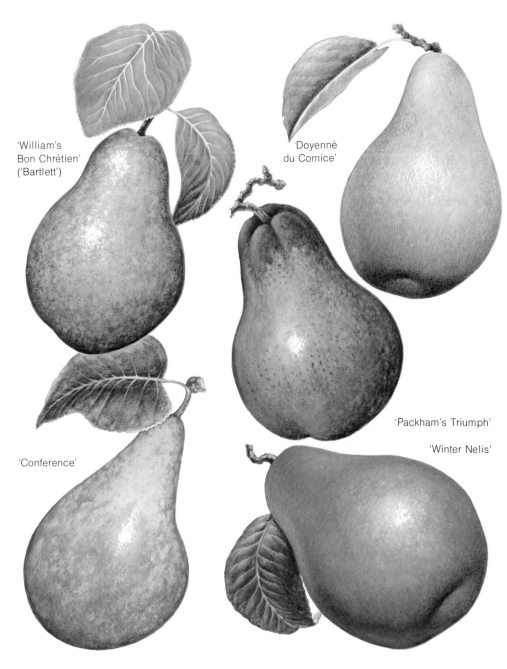

'William's
Bon Chrétien'
('Bartlett')

'Doyenné
du Comice'

'Conference'

'Packham's Triumph'

'Winter Nelis'

Recommended pear varieties

	Variety	Season of use	Flavour	Cropping	Flowering season	Pruning
Dessert varieties	'Beurré Hardy	Mid-season	Excellent	Excellent	Late	Light
	'Beurré Superfin'	Mid-season	Excellent	Good	Mid-season	Fairly hard†
	'Conference'	Mid-season	Good	Excellent	Mid-season	Normal†
	'Dr Jules Guyot'	Early	Good	Good	Mid-season	Fairly hard
	'Doyenné du Comice'	Mid-season	Superb	Light	Late	Fairly hard†
	'Fondante d'Automne'	Second early	Good	Excellent	Mid-season	Hard†
	'Gorham'	Late	Excellent	Good	Late	Fairly hard†
	'Jargonelle'	Early	Good	Excellent	Mid-season‡	Light*
	'Joséphine de Malines'	Late	Excellent	Good	Mid-season	Light*
	'Louise Bonne of Jersey'	Mid-season	Excellent	Excellent	Early	Normal†
	'Merton Pride'	Mid-season	Superb	Light	Mid-season‡	Fairly hard
	'Packham's Triumph'	Mid-season	Good	Good	Mid-season	Moderate*
	'William's Bon Chrétien' ('Bartlett')	Early	Very good	Excellent	Mid-season	Normal‡
	'Winter Nelis'	Late	Excellent	Good	Late	Hard†
Dual purpose	'Pitmaston Duchess'	Mid-season	Fair	Light	Late‡	Normal
	'Fertility'	Mid-season	Poor	Excellent	Late	Fairly hard
Cooking varieties	'Bellisime d'Hiver'	Late	Good	Reliable	Mid-season	Normal
	'Catillac'	Late	Good	Variable	Late‡	Light
	'Vicar of Winkfield'	Late	Excellent	Good	Early	Light

*Tip bearers – do not shorten laterals, but thin out; †suitable for training as cordons, etc; ‡self-sterile and will not pollinate other varieties (all pears benefit from cross pollination)

Stone fruits

The stone fruits – plums, cherries, peaches, nectarines and apricots – are all closely related, being classified by botanists in the genus *Prunus*, which also contains the almond. The pedigree of some of them is uncertain, however, for they have been grown and interbred by man for hundreds – even thousands – of years. These are some of the most popular and delicious tree fruits, varieties of most kinds being available for both dessert and culinary purposes. Apart from those cultivated specifically for their fruits, some ornamental prunus species also have useful fruits. The cherry plum, *Prunus cerasifera*, for example, is exceptionally ornamental, with an abundance of pure white flowers in early spring, and these are followed by soft, juicy, sweet round fruits. The blackthorn, *P. spinosa*, gives small, damson-like sloes, used in jams and for flavouring gin.

Stone fruits are all hardy, but they bloom very early – in late winter in some cases – so that frosts may ruin the blossom, and with it the year's crop of fruit. Furthermore, some types – apricots, nectarines and peaches in particular – need long, sunny summers to produce good yields. In cool areas, such as the British Isles, they generally need to be grown against a warm wall, where plants trained as espaliers or fans (see p 375) can be protected from late frost with nets or sacking, and where they can catch the maximum summer sunshine. They do even better under glass, and this is essential for reliable cropping in such areas as northern England and Scotland; an unheated greenhouse is adequate. Cherries and plums are more suited to growing outdoors in cool climates, but you must avoid frost pockets (see p 339) with all these fruits. In North America, apricots are commonly grown on north-facing slopes, where blooming is delayed to a period when frost damage is less likely, and slightly elevated sites (where frosty air can flow away downhill) are preferable for all stone fruits.

Most of these are available on dwarfing or semi-dwarfing rootstocks (see p 350). An excellent type for the various types of plums and for peaches, nectarines and apricots is 'St Julien A', which gives a medium-sized tree with early cropping. Until recently, however, only a very vigorous rootstock has been available for sweet cherries, so that these form large trees unsuitable for the average garden. However, the development of a dwarfing rootstock called 'Colt' in the 1970s promised the availability of more manageable trees.

The soil and fertilizer needs of stone fruits vary slightly, but they all need an adequate and steady supply of moisture during the period when the fruits are swelling; uneven watering may cause splitting in some kinds. Mulch thickly around the trunks with peat, garden compost or well-rotted manure to help conserve soil moisture. Many of their pests and diseases are also similar. Silver leaf, bacterial canker and brown rot diseases may afflict them all, as may aphids; other problems are mentioned individually below. Birds are a pest with all these fruits, but especially cherries and plums, attacking both flower buds and fruits. These should be protected with netting; deal with other troubles as advised on pages 362 to 367.

Apricots

The delicious orange fruits of the apricot are perhaps the most adaptable stone fruits, all the varieties being equally good in desserts (raw or stewed), for bottling or for jam-making. A native of China, the apricot is classified as *P. armeniaca*. It is the earliest-flowering of all the stone fruits, so it is only safe to grow apricots as free-standing bushes or standard trees where spring frosts are unlikely. Fan-trained trees tend to be excessively vigorous, however, unless you restrict growth by regularly pinching back the laterals (side shoots from the main branches) in summer, or check root growth. Most apricots are

Recommended cherry varieties

	Variety	Season of use	Flavour	Colour	Cropping	Flowering season	Varieties not pollinated†
Dessert varieties	'Amber Heart' ('Kentish Bigarreau')	Mid-season	Rich	Yellow and red	Good	Late	—
	'Bigarreau de Schrecken'	Early	Good	Black	Good	Early	A
	'Bigarreau Gaucher'	Mid-season	Rich	Black	Good	Late	0
	'Bigarreau Napoleon' ('Royal Ann')	Mid-season	Very good	Yellow and red	Good; regular	Mid-season	B
	'Bing'	Late	Excellent	Dark red	Heavy	Mid-season	C
	'Black Tartarian'	Mid-season	Excellent	Black	Good	Early	D
	'Bradbourne Black'	Mid-season	Rich; meaty	Black	Heavy	Late	E
	'Early Rivers'	Early	Excellent	Black	Good	Early	D
	'Emperor Francis'	Mid-season	Rich; aromatic	Dark red	Good	Mid-season	B
	'Frogmore Early'	Early	Good	Yellow and red	Good	Mid-season	A
	'Géante de Hedelfingen'	Mid-season	Rich	Black	Good	Late	E
	'Governor Wood'	Mid-season	Good	Yellow and red	Good	Mid-season	F
	'Lambert'	Mid-season	Good	Black	Heavy	Mid-season	C
	'Merton Bigarreau'	Mid-season	Excellent	Black	Heavy	Mid-season	A
	'Merton Glory'	Early	Good; juicy	Yellow and red	Good	Mid-season	0
	'Merton Heart'	Early	Rich	Black	Heavy	Early	F
	'Noir de Guben'	Mid-season	Very good	Black	Fair	Early	0
	'Roundel Heart'	Mid-season	Very good	Dark red	Heavy	Mid-season	D
	'Waterloo'	Early	Rich	Black	Sometimes biennial	Early	A
	'Windsor'	Late	Good	Dark red	Heavy	Early	A
	'Yellow Glass' ('Stark Gold')	Late	Good	Yellow	Heavy	Late	†
Dual-purpose	'Late Duke'	Late	Fair	Dark red	Good	Late	0
	'May Duke'	Early	Fair	Black	Good	Mid-season	0
Sour varieties	'Kentish Red'	Mid-season	Acid	Red	Good	Mid-season	0†
	'Meteor'	Late	Acid	Red	Heavy	Late	0
	'Montmorency'	Mid-season	Acid	Red	Indifferent	Late	0
	'Morello'	Late	Acid	Dark red	Prolific	Late	0
	'North Star'	Late	Acid	Red	Good	Late	0

Cherry

Apricot

Peach

†*Pollination: Almost all sweet (dessert) varieties are self-sterile, and need pollinating by a compatible variety flowering at the same time. Incompatible varieties are indicated by a code letter (A, B, etc); varieties with the same code letter will not pollinate each other even if they flower simultaneously. A zero means that the variety will pollinate any other that flowers at the same time; a dash means that no incompatible varieties are included in this list. 'Bing' and 'Lambert' are recommended for pollinating 'Yellow Glass' ('Stark Gold'). Sour cherries are mostly self-fertile as well as pollinating sweet varieties flowering simultaneously; 'Kentish Red', however, has two forms, one self-fertile, the other not. Dual-purpose varieties are partially self-fertile and give better crops if cross-pollinated. If in doubt, consult a specialist nurseryman.*

self-fertile and can be planted singly; 'Moongold' and 'Sungold' are self-sterile but will pollinate each other if planted in a pair.

The best soil for apricots is a slightly alkaline, moisture-retaining but well-drained loam; they dislike heavy soils. Plant early, in late autumn if possible, especially if you are growing them under glass. They respond to annual feeding with fertilizer rich in potash and phosphate, but you should use nitrogenous manures very sparingly or growth will become too leafy (see p 352). Prune regularly, shortening the leading shoots of newly-planted young trees by a half to two-thirds in autumn, and cutting back laterals to about 10 cm (4 in). With established trees, shorten leaders by one-third and pinch back side shoots to four leaves repeatedly from early summer onwards. Apart from the problems mentioned above, wasps and flies can be troublesome pests.

Thinning the fruitlets to 8 to 12 cm (3 to 5 in) apart ensures good fruit size and an adequate crop the following year. The mature fruits are ready to pick in late summer, when they are a good colour and part from the fruit spurs without tearing.

Cherries

There are two principal types of cherries – the sweet dessert varieties derived from *P. avium* and the sour culinary kinds such as 'Morello' derived from *P. cerasus*. Both come from Asia Minor. Intermediate between these, however, are the dual-purpose 'Duke' varieties. As already mentioned, sweet cherry trees normally grow very large – up to 12 m (40 ft) tall – and the situation is made worse by the need to plant at least two trees that flower simultaneously and are compatible, to ensure pollination. Sour cherries are much less vigorous and are self-fertile, as well as acting as good pollinators to any sweet kind flowering at the same time. It is possible to train sweet cherries

as fans, with permanent branches clothed in fruiting spurs, so long as you regularly prune both roots (in autumn) and shoots (in summer) to restrict vigour. The new dwarfing rootstock will, however, make cherries a more attractive proposition for many more gardeners. Sour cherries do well in bush form, or as fan trees with a few main branches supporting annually-replaced young fruiting shoots.

Cherries prefer a deep, light to medium loam. The sour varieties, however, tolerate poor soils provided drainage is good. A spring application of nitrogenous fertilizer, followed in the autumn by a potash-rich type, will keep the plants happy. Shorten the leading shoots of young sweet cherry trees in spring, but merely remove unwanted, crossing or diseased branches of mature ones. With sour

cherry bushes, prune in spring, cutting back wood two or more years old to stimulate the growth of new shoots that will bear the following year's crop. With sour cherries trained as fans, allow a lateral shoot to grow from the base of each fruiting branch, pinching back other laterals except for a 'sap-drawer' at the top. At the end of the season, remove the branches that have fruited and tie in the replacements. Apart from those mentioned above, cherry pests include winter moth caterpillars and diseases include blossom wilt.

Pick the fruits, with their stalks, when fully ripe – from early to midsummer, depending on variety – and consume quickly. Use scissors when harvesting sour cherries.

Peaches and nectarines

These are closely related, the nectarine being simply a smooth-skinned natural sport (or mutation) of the peach, *P. persica*, a native of China. Nectarines bear smaller fruits with a more delicate flavour; both fruits may have white or yellow flesh, though the skins are yellow or orange, flushed red. The nectarine generally needs a warmer situation than the peach, and must be trained on a warm wall even in areas (such as southern England) where peaches can be grown as free-standing bushes. Both do well under glass. In most parts of the United States except the north-central areas where winters are very harsh, the peach is considered the easiest garden stone fruit, but everywhere frost pockets must be avoided. Both peaches and nectarines are self-fertile, so only one tree need be planted, but it is advisable to hand-pollinate the fully-opened blossom, using an artist's brush.

The ideal soil is a deep, well-drained medium loam; chalky soils are unsuitable. Give a little nitrogenous fertilizer in spring, but no further feeding is needed on fertile soils. The pruning of peaches and nectarines is similar to that of sour cherries./*continued*

Apricots under glass
Apricots can be forced in a heated greenhouse by maintaining a temperature of 13°C (55°F) from late winter, rising to a minimum of 18°C (65°F) in summer. However, a cool period with full ventilation is needed later to ensure leaf fall and full dormancy. Spray with water daily in the growing period and hand-pollinate with an artist's brush.

Pruning fan apricots, sweet cherries and plums **above** Prune the lateral shoots regularly from early summer by pinching back to within three or four leaves of the main branches. A few well-placed laterals can, however, be left and tied in to the supporting trellis or wires, either to form new branches or to replace old ones. Remove any dead or diseased branches and tie in their replacements in early summer to avoid the risk of silver leaf disease. At the same time, thin out overcrowded fruit spurs.

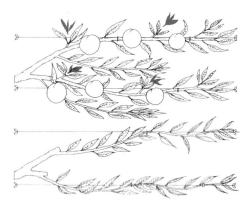

Pruning fan sour cherries and peaches With these, refurbish the main branches with new fruiting laterals annually. **top** On each fruiting branch, allow a strong lateral shoot to grow from near the base and another near the end to draw sap, but pinch back the others to three or four leaves; with long branches, a third central lateral may be retained. **above** Cut back the fruited branches to just above the basal laterals immediately the fruit has been picked, and tie in the new shoots as replacements for next year.

Stone fruits (continued)

They fruit on year-old wood, so prune in late spring, cutting back two-year-old or older wood hard enough to induce new shoots about 30 cm (12 in) long annually. Always cut above new shoots, after removing all dead wood and crossing branches. Treat fans as for fan sour cherries, tying in new young shoots at the end of the season to replace those that have borne fruit. Apart from those mentioned above, peaches and nectarines may be affected by peach leaf curl disease, die-back, red spider mite and caterpillars.

Peaches commonly set too many fruitlets, resulting in small fruits and a poor crop the following year. Avoid this by thinning out gradually to a final distance apart of about 20 cm (8 in) for nectarines and 25 cm (10 in) for peaches. In mid- to late summer, test fruits for ripeness by lifting gently, avoiding finger-tip pressure which easily bruises them; when ripe they come away easily from the spurs. Alternatively, pick when just beginning to get soft around the stalk, and ripen in a cool place.

Plums

Garden plums are divided loosely into three main groups, all now regarded as forms of *P. domestica* (which may well, however, be a hybrid). These groups are the sweeter gages (mainly green or yellow), the less sweet dessert plums and the highly acid culinary plums that are so good for cooking and jam-making. The small, generally round bullaces, which may be green, yellow or black, can be eaten raw but are used mainly in the kitchen. The oval damsons, though unsuitable for use as fresh dessert fruit, have a rich flavour compounded of spiciness and bitterness, and are delicious for stewing and making jams and jellies. A number of plums set fruit when planted alone; the others do best when cross-pollinated. With these, plant any two varieties that flower at the same time.

In many areas, choice gages are commonly planted against a sunny wall for protection. These are usually fans, but free-standing trees may be bushes, standards or pyramids, the last being ideal for minimal branch breakage. Trees overloaded with plums often break branches unless the fruitlets are thinned; this also increases the fruit size. Even so, you should support heavily-laden branches with individual wooden props or by ropes, maypole-fashion, from a central pole lashed to the trunk of the tree.

Plums thrive on deep, moisture-retentive but free-draining medium to heavy loams containing a little lime. They dislike dry sandy soils, heavy clay or very chalky soils. Give ample nitrogenous fertilizer, together with a moderate amount of potash, in late winter. A little lime is beneficial on acid soils, but too much causes chlorosis, necessitating treatment with sequestered iron; manganese deficiency may also occur (see p 368). When pruning young plum trees, shorten leading shoots by one-half to one-quarter in spring to encourage branching. Thereafter, merely remove dead, diseased or crossing branches to maintain an open crown. Do this in mid-summer, to reduce the risk of cuts becoming infected with fungal diseases, especially silver leaf. Apart from the common troubles of stone fruits, red spider mites may be a pest.

The season for plums extends from mid-summer to mid-autumn. Pick culinary plums, including damsons and bullaces, when under-ripe, dessert plums when firm and fully coloured prior to ripening off in a warm room for a few days. Leave gages to ripen fully, almost to the point of splitting, to ensure maximum sweetness, but then use them immediately; if you want them for jam-making, they should be picked earlier.

Gage

Dessert/culinary plum

Damson

Recommended plum varieties

	Variety	Season of use	Flavour	Size; shape; colour	Cropping	Flowering season
Gages	'Bryanston Gage'	Mid-season	Very good	Medium; round; greenish-yellow	Good	Mid-season†
	'Cambridge Gage'	Mid-season	Excellent	Medium; round; green to yellow	Good	Late‡
	'Coe's Golden Drop'	Mid/late	Rich; sweet	Large; oval; yellow	Adequate	Early†
	'Count Althann's Gage'	Mid-season	Sweet; juicy	Large; oval; crimson	Good	Late†
	'Denniston's Superb'	Early	Fair	Medium; round; greenish-yellow	Good	Early
	'Early Transparent'	Early	Very sweet	Small; round; orange-yellow	Fair	Late
	'Golden Transparent'	Late	Sweet; rich	Large; round; yellow	Fair	Early
	'Green Gage' ('Reine Claude')	Early	Excellent	Medium; round; green	Adequate	Early
	'Jefferson'	Mid-season	Excellent	Large; oval; yellow	Adequate	Early†
	'Late Transparent'	Mid-season	Rich; juicy	Large; round; greenish-yellow	Adequate	Late†
	'Laxton's Gage'	Early	Rich	Medium; round; golden-yellow	Good	Mid-season
Dessert plums	'Delicious'	Early	Sweet; juicy	Large; oval; bright red	Good	Late†
	'Kirke's Blue'	Mid-season	Excellent	Medium; round; reddish-purple	Fair	Mid-season†
	'Oullin's Golden Gage'	Early	Fair	Large; round; green to yellow	Heavy	Late
Dual-purpose plums	'Early Laxton'	Very early	Sweet; juicy	Medium; oval; yellow and red	Adequate	Mid-season‡
	'Marjorie's Seedling'	Late	Sweet	Large; long; blue-black	Good	Late
	'President'	Late	Sweet	Large; oval; deep purple	Moderate	Early†
	'Severn Cross'	Mid-season	Sweet; juicy	Large; oval; greenish-yellow	Heavy	Mid-season
	'Victoria'	Early	Good	Large; oval; bright red	Good	Mid-season
Culinary plums	'Belle de Louvain'	Early	Fair	Large; oval; red	Good	Late
	'Black Prince'	Early	Damson-like	Medium; round; blue-black	Good	Early†
	'Blaisdon Red'	Mid-season	Tart	Medium; oval dark red	Heavy	Late
	'Czar'	Early	Moderate	Medium; round; dull red	Heavy	Mid-season
	'Giant Prune'	Mid-season	Fair	Large; oval; deep red	Good	Late
	'Pershore'	Early	Good for jam	Medium; oval; yellow	Heavy	Mid-season
	'Pond's Seedling'	Mid-season	Fair	Large; oval; dark red	Good	Late†
	'Rivers' Early Prolific'	Very early	Damson-like	Small; round; blue-purple	Good	Mid-season‡
Bullaces	'Black Bullace'	Very late	Sour; juicy	Small; oval; black	Good	Late
	'Langley Bullace'	Very late	Damson-like	The largest; oval; blue-black	Prolific	Early
	'Shepherd's Bullace'	Late	Good	Medium; round; greenish-yellow	Good	Late
	'White Bullace'	Very late	Some sweetness	Small; round; pale creamy-green	Good	Late
Damsons	'Farleigh'	Mid-season	Good	Small; oval; black; green flesh	Heavy	Early†
	'Merryweather'	Mid-season	Good	Medium; round; blue-black	Excellent	Mid-season
	'Shropshire'	Late	Excellent	Small; oval; purple; green flesh	Good	Late

†Self-sterile and must be planted with another variety flowering at about the same time; ‡partially self-sterile – cropping improved if planted with another variety flowering at the same time

Some unusual garden fruits

Kumquat

Tangerine   Lemon   Blood orange   Sweet orange

Citrus fruits

Although they grow outdoors only in regions where frosts are virtually unknown, oranges, lemons and a number of their relatives are easy to grow in a greenhouse or conservatory. The drier the atmosphere can be kept, the lower the winter temperature the trees or bushes will tolerate. The hardiest types generally are the kumquat (*Fortunella* spp, and not a true citrus but a close relative) and various types of tangerine (*Citrus reticulata*), including the mandarin and satsuma. These and others need only be kept under glass in winter; if grown in large pots or tubs, they can be moved to a sunny, sheltered spot outdoors for the summer. The calamondin orange, *C. mitis*, sometimes grown as a house-plant, does much better in the greenhouse than the home, and seldom exceeds 1 m (3 ft). It gives very small, acid oranges that can be used in drinks or made into preserves.

Orange, lemon and other citrus plants can be bought from nurserymen, but can also (with less predictable results) be grown from seeds germinated in a warm, dark place. Lemons take a year or more – and oranges two or three years – to produce their fragrant white flowers. Bushes of fruiting size can be housed in 20 to 25 cm (8 to 10 in) pots of good, well-drained potting mixture, and eventually in even larger pots or tubs, when they will reach a height of 2.5 m (8 ft) or more.

Give copious amounts of water in summer and, since the plants are evergreen, a little also in winter. If kept under glass, syringe the leaves with water daily during the summer, and shade the greenhouse in the hottest period. The young shoots carry the blossom; lemons bloom almost continuously under glass and are exceedingly fragrant, while oranges bloom in spring and early summer. Fruits are generally set whether the flowers are pollinated or not; they take at least nine months to mature, depending on whether they ripen before winter or not. Trees carrying fruit should be fed once a week with dilute liquid manure from late summer until the end of the season. Cut back straggling shoots in late autumn; otherwise, minimal pruning is needed. Allow the fruits to ripen fully on the tree before picking. Beware of aphids, scale insects and mealy bugs; all can be controlled with malathion (see p 361).

Crab apples

Numerous species and hybrids related to the dessert and culinary apples (see p 316) bear small 'crab apples' that are not generally edible raw but can be made into excellent jelly. Most of these are grown primarily as decorative trees (see p 138), but a number of varieties give particularly good fruits. These are doubly decorative, for not only do they bear attractive spring blossom but the fruits are generally extremely colourful in autumn. *Malus* 'John Downie', for example, has scarlet conical fruits with a yellow flush; unfortunately, it is prone to scab disease. Other good fruiting varieties and hybrids include 'Chilko' (with crimson fruits), 'Crittenden' (scarlet), 'Dartmouth' (reddish-purple), 'Dolgo' (deep red), 'Gibb's Golden Gage' (waxy, yellow), 'Hyslop' (red), 'Kerr' (red), 'Veitch's Scarlet' (bright red) and 'Wickson' (red; edible raw).

They should be grown as for dessert apple trees except that no thinning of the fruitlets is needed. Some nurserymen supply bush trees as well as standards and half-standards.

Crab apple 'John Downie'

Fig

Although figs (*Ficus carica*) are generally regarded as warm-climate fruits, they are not difficult to grow in areas where winter temperatures do not normally fall below about −10°C (14°F), particularly if they are given some winter protection. They do need plenty of warmth to ripen the fruits, however, so in areas with cool summers are best grown as fans against a warm, sunny wall. Then the deliciously sweet and syrupy brown, purplish or whitish-green fruits ripen in late summer or early autumn. Where the weather is warmer, they do well as bushes, and two crops may be obtained – one in early summer, the second in late summer on new growth. In a heated greenhouse, it is even possible to achieve three crops per year if forcing is started in early winter at 18°C (64°F), rising to 27°C (81°F) by late winter; this is expensive in terms of fuel, however, and figs also do well fan-trained against the wall of an unheated lean-to greenhouse.

Among the best-known hardier varieties of figs are 'Brown Turkey' (also known in North America as 'Black Spanish' and 'San Piero') and 'Brunswick' ('Magnolia'); another North American variety is 'Celeste' ('Blue Celeste'). Less hardy types for growing under glass in cool climates or outdoors in warm regions include 'Negro Largo' and 'White Marseilles'. All are self-fertile, so only one plant is needed.

In cool climates, it is important to restrain figs' potential vigour in order to promote short-jointed, fruitful growth; do this by restricting their root run. They can be grown in large tubs, or in a sunken brick or concrete trough about 1 m (3 ft) wide and 1.25 m (4 ft) deep. Both should have drainage holes in the bottom, plus a layer of stones, broken bricks or gravel – 30 cm (12 in) deep in the trough – topped by inverted turves and good potting mixture or fibrous loam fortified/*continued*

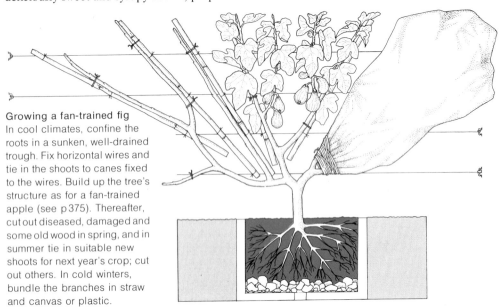

Growing a fan-trained fig
In cool climates, confine the roots in a sunken, well-drained trough. Fix horizontal wires and tie in the shoots to canes fixed to the wires. Build up the tree's structure as for a fan-trained apple (see p 375). Thereafter, cut out diseased, damaged and some old wood in spring, and in summer tie in suitable new shoots for next year's crop; cut out others. In cold winters, bundle the branches in straw and canvas or plastic.

Some unusual garden fruits (continued)

with a few handfuls of bonemeal. If positioned at the base of a sunny wall, reckon on the fig tree occupying a 5 m (16 ft) run of wall space. If planted in the open in warmer climates, figs thrive on many soils but prefer a light to medium loam.

The best time to plant pot-raised figs is early spring. After planting, water well and give a mulch of peat to conserve moisture. Tie the shoots in to horizontal wires on the wall during summer. Feed annually in autumn, giving 175 g (6 oz) of basic slag and 40 g (1½ oz) of sulphate of potash per plant; alternatively use a proprietary fertilizer rich in phosphate and potash but low in nitrogen (see p 352). In alternate years, sprinkle about 225 g (8 oz) of ground chalk around the tree unless the soil is already alkaline.

Figs are tip bearers, forming embryo figs on the present season's young growth. These remain on the tree during winter and then develop throughout the following spring and summer. Embryo figs larger than garden peas will not overwinter and should be removed. Even so, the pea-sized figlets and the young growth are liable to be frosted. Except in mild areas, it is a good idea to bundle the young growths carefully together, tie straw around them and keep the whole top growth dry by wrapping in plastic sheeting, canvas or tarred paper. Such protection – together with mounding of soil to a depth of 60 cm (2 ft) over the crown of the plant – is essential where winter temperatures are liable to dip to −12°C (10°F) or lower. Remove all protection directly conditions improve, however.

Prune in early spring, when frost-damaged shoots can be clearly seen and cut back, together with any that are weak or diseased. Preserve as many unpruned shoot tips as possible for fruiting. Each year cut out a small proportion of the old wood to maintain young shoot production. When pruning a bush tree, aim to promote many horizontal laterals. Figs may be attacked by various insect pests in the greenhouse, but outdoors the principal problem is grey mould, which may attack young shoots and fruits (see p 366).

Loquat

Sometimes called the Japanese medlar, the loquat (*Eriobotrya japonica*) is widely grown in Japan, China, northern India and the Mediterranean area for its yellow, pear-shaped fruits. They are about 4 cm (1½ in) long and have a delightfully refreshing flavour. The small evergreen tree or large shrub is fairly hardy but needs a good summer to flower in cool temperate regions and a long one for the fruits to ripen. You stand the best chance of success where summers are not long and hot if it is planted against a sunny wall. Any average garden soil is suitable.

Even where the loquat's fruits cannot be relied upon, it makes an extremely handsome specimen shrub or tree. Its beautiful dark grey-green, ribbed and toothed leathery leaves are up to 30 cm (12 in) long, and the flowers, when they do appear, are delightfully fragrant; they are yellowish-white, are tightly packed in woolly panicles 8 to 15 cm (3 to

6 in) long and appear over a long period. Young loquats make good indoor plants in cool, well-lit situations.

Medlar

Like the loquat, the medlar is related to the apple, pear, quince and rose. Classified as *Mespilus germanica*, it is a native of Asia Minor and south-eastern Europe, but is naturalized over many other parts of Europe. It lives to a great age, specimens at least 300 years old being known. Three main varieties are in cultivation. 'Dutch' ('Monstrous') makes a very ornamental and vigorous tree,

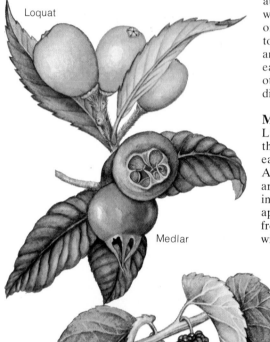

Loquat

Medlar

Mulberry

Persimmon

good for providing shade; it has good flavour but is not such a heavy cropper as the other two. 'Nottingham' has an upright habit but is less vigorous and not so ornamental as 'Dutch'; it is, however, a regular, heavy cropper with the best flavour. 'The Royal' has medium growth and is also upright and less ornamental than 'Dutch', but it is a heavy cropper from an early age, with fruit of a good, acid flavour.

Whichever variety you choose, however, its rough, ash-grey bark, its crooked and drooping branches, its thick, oval, dark green and downy leaves and its spreading habit make the medlar useful for planting alone in a lawn. Large, five-petalled, single, white or pinkish-white flowers, each with a centre of deep red anthers, are displayed from late spring to midsummer. The foliage turns through a rich yellow to golden-brown in autumn. The unusual brown, flattened and indented fruits are not picked until late

autumn before frosts start to become keen. In warm, Mediterranean-type climates, they ripen on the tree and can be eaten immediately they are picked. In cooler regions, allow them to dry indoors before storing in a cool, airy place, stalks upwards, for up to four weeks for the flesh to soften and turn brown. Medlars in this condition retain their very distinctive, slightly acid flavour for dessert use for several weeks; alternatively, jelly, sauce or wine can be made from them.

Medlars prefer a rich, well-drained soil, but the trees succeed almost anywhere where the soil is not cold and wet. Plant between early autumn and early spring when the ground is workable. Medlars fruit both on old spurs and on young growth, so restrict winter pruning to removing dead, diseased, inward-growing and rubbing growth. Caterpillars and leaf-eating weevils may need controlling, but otherwise the tree is refreshingly pest- and disease-free.

Mulberry

Like the fig, and belonging to the same family, the black mulberry (*Morus nigra*) has been eaten since ancient times. A native of western Asia, it is quite hardy and grows over a wide area, though wall protection gives best results in cold areas. It forms a smallish tree of quaint appearance, with gnarled branches growing from a short, rugged trunk. It is deciduous, with large, toothed, dark green leaves. The

fruits resemble those of the loganberry, and are a dark purplish-red with a delicious, piquant flavour. They are extremely good eaten straight from the tree when fully ripe (in late summer), or can be used for pie fillings, delicious jam and wine. They are very juicy and easily squashed, however, and the juice is very staining – to hands, lips, clothes and paving. So do not plant the tree where it will overhang paths, patios or other places where people pass. The easiest way to harvest the berries is to lay sheets of cloth or plastic below the tree and shake the branches.

The mulberry needs deep, fertile soil and a sunny site. Buy a pot-grown young tree, for the roots dislike even slight damage, and plant out in late spring. The mulberry resists drought well. Pruning consists merely of keeping the tree in good shape. Trees can be grown successfully for fruiting in dwarf pyramid shape in large pots or tubs. Protect the fruits from birds with netting if possible.

Persimmon

Persimmon fruits look rather like large tomatoes, with a yellow to red skin and jelly-like flesh that is highly astringent until fully ripe, when it becomes sweet. They only ripen outdoors in hot summers, but can be picked in autumn even if under-ripe and ripened indoors for eating or making into preserves.

The best fruiting species is the Oriental persimmon, *Diospyros kaki*, which forms a highly ornamental deciduous tree with glossy oval leaves up to 20 cm (8 in) long, attaining an eventual height of 6 to 12 m (20 to 40 ft). Good varieties include 'Chocolate', 'Eureka', 'Fuyu' ('Gaki'), 'Hachiya', 'Tamopan' and Tane Nashi'; most have glorious autumn colouring. It is fairly hardy, withstanding frosts down to about −12°C (10°F) or even slightly lower if the wood is well ripened, but in cool areas the protection of a sunny wall or cold greenhouse is advisable and will give a better chance of good fruiting. The American persimmon, *D. virginiana*, is hardier, occurring wild as far north as the Great Lakes; its fruits are smaller and less tasty than those of the Oriental species, but it also has good autumn colouring. Good varieties include 'Early Golden', 'Garrettson' and 'Killen'. A third species, *D. lotus* or the date plum, is less commonly grown, but is also quite hardy and produces small yellow or purple fruits.

Persimmons need a good, loamy, well-drained soil. Plant in late autumn or early

branches. Attractive white flowers in early summer make it a good ornamental tree.

A number of varieties are available from specialist nurserymen. 'Bereczki' ('Vranja') has large fruits with the best flavour, and crops young. Other good croppers with large fruits are 'Champion' and 'Meech's Prolific'. 'Portugal' produces a light crop of early-ripening, very large tender fruits that turn an attractive purplish-crimson on being cooked. Others include the exceptionally heavy-cropping 'Apple-Shaped' and the small 'Pear-Shaped', both of which store very well, and 'Smyrna', which is less astringent than the others and a heavy cropper.

A highly moisture-retentive soil, or even one subject to flooding, is ideal for growing quinces, provided the site is in full sun and does not form a frost pocket. However, they tolerate a wide range of soil types and sites, but in colder areas benefit from some shelter. Cropping is improved if you interplant different varieties, spacing the trees 3 to 5 m (10 to 16 ft) apart. Preferably plant in autumn, but delay until spring if the soil is too wet. Mulch thickly with straw or garden compost; feed as for pears (see p 318). Lightly tip-prune the leading branches of young bushes in winter to encourage extension growth, and shorten side shoots to 20 cm (8 in). Once fruiting starts, merely remove dead wood and mildewed shoots, together with any growth congesting the centre of the bush. Apart from mildew,

duct of another vigorous climber, the passion flower (see p 146). There are various species, the most popular fruit being that of the purple *Passiflora edulis* and the greenish *P. quadrangularis*. Although tropical in origin, the former fruits even in Mediterranean climates and can be grown elsewhere in a greenhouse where a minimum winter temperature of 7 to 10°C (45 to 50°F) can be maintained. The fruits ripen in early autumn. Other species, such as *P. caerulea*, which grow outdoors in areas where winters are not too harsh, produce edible fruits only after hot summers.

The pomegranate, *Punica granatum*, can similarly be grown outdoors in areas with mild winters, but even with the protection of a sunny wall rarely produces ripened fruits in cool climates. It will do so in a cool greenhouse, however, so long as an autumn temperature of at least 13°C (55°F) is maintained. In areas where summers are hot but winters cold, such as much of the United States, it can be grown outdoors in a tub in the summer months and moved under cover for winter. It is an attractive evergreen shrub with scarlet flowers from early summer.

Various species of elder (*Sambucus* spp) are planted as decorative plants, and most of them produce black or red berries that are good for wine-making. In Europe the species most used is the black elder, *Sambucus nigra*, while the berries of the American elder, *S. canadensis*, are also used in combination with

Passion fruit

Quince

Chinese gooseberry

Pomegranate

Elderberry

spring, being sure to plant two different varieties of the American persimmon to ensure fruiting; the Oriental kind is normally self-fertile. The best plants are those grafted onto seedling rootstocks (see p 351). Prune as for apples. Pot-grown plants grown under glass fruit freely; they need copious amounts of water after the fruit has set, but keep them on the dry side in winter.

Quince

The quince (*Cydonia oblonga*) is another relative of the rose, medlar and apple, and has also been cultivated since ancient times. It produces knobbly apple-like or pear-like fruits that are golden-yellow when ripe and have an extremely distinctive, acid and astringent flavour but make excellent jams, jellies and preserves. They ripen outdoors in autumn in reasonably mild climates. The trees are small, seldom exceeding 6 m (20 ft), and often have crooked and seemingly deformed

pests and diseases to look out for include caterpillars, codling moth, leaf blight, leaf blotch and brown rot (see pp 362 to 367).

Defer picking the fruits until mid- to late autumn. Store in a frost-free place away from all other fruits; quinces exude a powerful aroma which is liable to be absorbed.

Other kinds

A number of plants more usually grown for decoration can yield interesting and often delicious fruits, and specialist nurserymen can often supply selected forms for especially good fruiting. Among them is the Chinese gooseberry, fruit of the vigorous climber *Actinidia chinensis* (see p 145). Its fruit is brown, hairy, egg-shaped and up to 5 cm (2 in) long; the flesh is semi-transparent, and looks and tastes rather like that of a normal gooseberry. Plant in pairs to ensure pollination, and grow against a sunny wall.

The granadilla, or passion fruit, is the pro-

apples for jam and pies. Much less commonly collected are the red berries of the mountain ash, or rowan, *Sorbus aucuparia*, but in parts of Scotland and northern Europe they are made into jelly, alone or with apples, that is a traditional accompaniment to game. Its close relative the service tree, *S. domestica*, has small brownish fruits that must be allowed to get over-ripe before eating, as with the more distantly related medlar. These trees are related to the rose, and the large hips of many shrub roses – particularly the Rugosas (see p 159) – make vitamin-rich syrups, preserves or sauces. Another related genus are the thorns (*Crataegus* spp), most of whose fruits – or haws – are inedible; but those of the azarole, *Crataegus azarolus*, have an apple-like flavour and have long been used to make preserves in southern Europe; it is quite hardy though not common in cultivation.

Some other unusual fruits will be found among the bush fruits on page 315.

Nuts

Nuts in general are a highly nutritious food in a very concentrated form. They are an invaluable source of protein, many contain considerable quantities of fats or oils, and they are rich in iron, calcium and other elements. Most are fairly expensive to buy – a reflection of the costs of gathering a commercial crop – so it makes good sense to grow some of your own. Most grow on trees – very substantial and decorative ones in some cases – but cob-nuts and filberts (both forms of hazel) form no more than large bushes. In regions with hot summers, peanuts can be grown as an annual crop. There are some exceptions, but many nut tree varieties are self-sterile; to be sure of a good crop, plant trees of at least two varieties of the same species.

Almonds

The common almond, *Prunus dulcis* (*P. communis* or *P. amygdalus*), is one of the first and prettiest trees to bloom, its pink blossom appearing in late winter or very early spring, but this makes it prone to frost damage. The

Almond

most susceptible stage is in late spring, when the young fruitlets are the size of a pea; as a result, nut production is uncertain in areas where late frosts occur, such as most of the British Isles. When nuts are produced, those of the species and the culinary varieties are sweet and nutritious. Almond oil is extracted from the nuts of the bitter variety, *P. dulcis amara*. These nuts are inedible, the strong unpleasant bitterness resulting from the presence of poisonous hydrocyanic acid. Some of the ornamental varieties of almonds produce nuts containing small amounts, but there is no danger if they are not eaten raw, as the heat of cooking dissipates the poison.

Almonds are deep-rooting, and prefer a light, warm, fairly rich soil with an abundance of humus, but they will thrive where conditions are too dry for related species such as peaches and plums. They dislike heavy, poorly drained or very alkaline soils. Most almonds are self-sterile, requiring cross-pollination from a nearby tree. The trees are budded or grafted on plum rootstock (see p 351), and may bear from the third or fourth year onwards. After pruning to a good, natural shape, light thinning of the branches is all that is needed from the third year. They will typically achieve a height and spread of 6 m (20 ft) in about 15 to 20 years.

The nuts are enclosed in a dry and leathery outer case, and are ripe when the husk begins to split in early autumn. The kernels are generally removed immediately for drying in the sun; they are dry enough for storing in jars when they break without bending.

Chestnuts

Variously known as the common European, Spanish or sweet chestnut, *Castanea sativa* is a handsome tree sporting smooth, glossy, large-toothed leaves and a profuse show of catkins in midsummer. These are followed by a crop of nuts enclosed in prickly burs. The Chinese chestnut, *C. mollissima,* also produces excellent nuts, and is favoured in parts of North America for its blight resistance. They are self-fertile.

A fairly light, non-calcareous soil is preferred, but the sweet chestnut will grow on the heavier and clayey soils provided that drainage is not impeded. The trees rarely suffer from drought. With light pruning in the early years and minimal pruning subsequently, nuts can be expected at six years old, with increasing quantities to full crops at thirty years. A distance of 12 to 15 m (40 to 50 ft) between trees gives room for mature development.

The nuts are rich in sugar and starch and, unlike most other nuts, have a minimal fat and

Chestnut

oil content. They can be boiled, but give the finest flavour when roasted. They can be stored in an earthenware jar, mixed with dry sand, for many months.

Cob-nuts, filberts and hazels

Where the soil is unsuitable for growing fruit trees, you should try cob-nuts and filberts – varieties of *Corylus avellana* (the common hazel) and *C. maxima* respectively. They perform excellently on poor, stony soils, whether acid or alkaline, forming robust bushes, whereas on rich soils vigour may be excessive. Most varieties need cross-pollinating, so plant more than one bush. Several other species of hazel also produce excellent nuts, including the very hardy American hazel, *C. americana,*

Filbert

Cob-nut

and the Turkish hazel, *C. colurna*; the former is a medium-sized shrub, the latter a striking pyramidal tree.

Plant two- to three-year-old bushes of cob-nuts or filberts between late autumn and early spring, spacing them at least 3 m (10 ft) apart. Thoroughly firm the soil around the roots and stake and tie securely. Give a mulch of garden compost in the spring, and water thoroughly if the soil becomes dry. New stock can easily be propagated from mature bushes by layering in spring, and the young bushes are severed from the parent in the autumn. Their single stems are shortened to 45 cm (18 in) to induce branching at the top of a clean leg. The best six resulting shoots are retained and, in turn, shortened by half the next winter. All pruning is to outward-pointing buds to obtain an open centre. This is the stage for planting out.

Continue shortening the stems by half annually until a bush 2.5 m (8 ft) tall is achieved. Subsequent pruning consists of cutting out crowded, dead and rubbing branches, plus shortening of growth carrying the yellow male catkins sufficient to maintain production of young shoots; retain as many growths carrying the tiny crimson female flowers as possible. To promote fruitfulness, any long, vigorous shoots can be snapped midway in mid- to late summer, but left hanging. Check overall excessive vigour by growing regularly-mown grass around the bushes. Feed them only if growth is poor, using a fertilizer moderately rich in potash, such as John Innes base fertilizer (see p 353) at 135 g/m^2 (4 oz/sq yd). The bushes may be attacked by caterpillars, nut weevil and brown rot fungus (see pp 362 to 367), also by squirrels and some birds.

Defer gathering the nuts until the husks are hard and quite brown. Spread them out in a single layer to dry prior to removing the husks and storing them (in their shells) in tins or jars, preferably layering them with salt.

Peanuts

The peanut or monkey nut, *Arachis hypogaea,* is also known as the ground nut or earth nut because of its peculiar, ostrich-like habit of burying its head in the ground to ripen its pods. It is an annual, a member of the pea family, and the 'nuts' are in fact seeds akin to peas or beans. After producing yellow, pea-like flowers, the stems bend down to the soil and lengthen, pushing the pods beneath the ground. For this reason, a friable soil with a loose surface is necessary; lime is desirable and plenty of humus.

Peanuts also need a long, hot summer to thrive; for this reason, they can be grown outdoors only in regions such as the southern half

Peanut

of the United States. They are planted in early summer about 5 cm (2 in) deep and 20 to 25 cm (8 to 10 in) apart in rows 90 cm (3 ft) apart. You can either sow in the husk, thinning to the strongest seedling, or carefully shell them and sow individual seeds, taking care not to damage their thin skins. They form low, sprawling bushes. The crop takes about four months to mature. Elsewhere, peanuts can be grown in a warm greenhouse. Sow in heat in early spring and pot on singly when large enough. You can, in fact, grow plants from shop-bought peanuts – provided, of course, they are not roasted!

Pecans and hickories
The pecan, *Carya illinoinensis* (*C. pecan*) yields the best nuts of all the hickories; they are rather like those of its near relative the walnut, but are smooth-shelled. They are much used in cooking and confectionery, and are the most widely grown nuts in the United States. Unfortunately, it is the least amenable of the hickories to cool, damp climates, such as that of the British Isles. It is adequately frost-hardy, but yields the best crops where summers are long and warm, as in its native

Pecan

regions of the midwestern and southern United States. Some varieties mature more quickly than others, however, and are better suited to cooler climates. The pecan is a very large, long-lived deciduous tree, reaching up to 45 m (150 ft), but demands a deep, well-drained soil. The nuts are enclosed in round to oval husks, and develop from the insignificant female flowers after being self-pollinated by the male catkins.

Both the nutmeg hickory, *C. myristicae-formis,* and the shag-bark hickory, *C. ovata,* are more hardy than the pecan, and are first-class ornamental and nut-producing trees. They are ideal for siting as specimen trees. They like a deep loam and should be planted when quite small – or sown direct where they are to be grown – as they resent being transplanted. The leaves turn a beautiful yellow colour in autumn.

Walnuts
There are few trees that can vie with the walnut for beauty of bark, ornamental foliage and sheer majesty. Varieties of three main species are grown for their nuts – the most delicious of all temperate nuts: the common walnut of Europe and Asia, *Juglans regia;* the black walnut of North America, *J. nigra;* and the extremely hardy butternut, or white walnut, *J. cinerea.* The black walnut is the fastest-growing, reaching up to 45 m (150 ft) and living 100 years or more. The butternut is the shortest and shortest-lived, lasting 50 to 75 years. They are all generally self-fertile, but crops may be improved by planting two different varieties with similar flowering periods.

Walnuts thrive in light soil over gravel; they object to soils that are waterlogged. Basically hardy when established (though frost can split the bark in severe winters), the dormant shoots of young European walnut trees may be frosted and the young growth scorched by cold winds on exposed sites; if the flowers are damaged, fruiting may suffer. Varieties that come into leaf and flower late (see table) are least prone to damage. Do not plant walnuts in a low-lying frost pocket or near old tree stumps liable to be harbouring the lethal honey fungus (see p 366). Pot-grown walnut trees transplant readily, lifted trees less so, particularly if their roots are allowed to dry out to any extent. Firm planting and staking plus mulching promote rapid establishment.

Keep winter pruning to a minimum to preclude bleeding, merely cutting out shoots which spoil the shape. Summer pruning induces an earlier start to nut bearing – a

Walnut

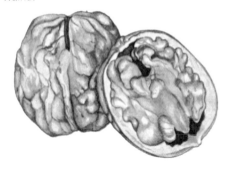

Butternut

worthwhile operation unless you are prepared to wait for 15 to 20 years! Repeatedly pinch out the tips of the stronger shoots (not the thin ones) whenever five or six leaves have grown. Squirrels should be prevented from stealing walnuts by fitting an aluminium projecting collar around the trunk. Bacterial blight may attack the leaves, shoots and green husks.

Gather immature nuts for pickling in early to midsummer, while still soft enough for a needle to pierce them. Ripe walnuts are ready for gathering when the green husks have turned black and the nuts have loosened. Wear rubber gloves as a precaution against stains when removing the husks. Scrub the nuts with a wire brush to remove all fibres liable to go mouldy. You can bleach the shells by immersing for one minute in dilute household bleach. Dry with a fan heater. Store in a net bag hung in a dry, airy place or in a wooden box filled with dry sawdust.

Recommended varieties of nuts

Almonds	The type species, *Prunus dulcis*, is commonly grown, but the cultivar 'Macrocarpa' has excellent large nuts. American culinary varieties include 'Davey'; 'Hall' ('Pioneer'; 'Ridenhower'); 'Ne Plus Ultra'; 'Nonpareil'; 'Texas' ('Mission')
Chestnuts	**European chestnut varieties** 'Darlington'; 'Devonshire Prolific'; 'Gros Merle'; 'Marron de Lyon'; 'Paragon' **Chinese chestnut varieties** 'Abundance'; 'Crane'; 'Kuling'; 'Nanking'
Cob-nuts, filberts and hazels	'Barcelona'; 'Bixby'; 'Buchanan'; 'Cosford' (good pollinator); 'Italian Red'; 'Lambert's Filbert' ('Kentish Cob'); 'Red Filbert'; 'Reed'; 'Royal'; 'Rush'; 'White Filbert'; ('Kentish Filbert'); 'Winkler'
Peanuts	'Early Spanish'; 'Jumbo Virginia'; 'Red Tennessee'
Pecans	**For very long summers** 'Desirable'; 'Moneymaker'; 'Stuart' **Earlier-maturing varieties** 'Greenriver'; 'Hodge'; 'Major'; 'Starking Hardy Giant'
Walnuts	**European walnut varieties** 'Broadview'; 'Franquette' (late); 'Lady Irene'; 'Leeds Castle' (good for pickling); 'Mayette' (late); 'Northdown Clawnut'; 'Parisienne' (late; frost-resistant); 'Patching' (good for pickling); 'Secrett'; 'Sutton Seedling' **Black walnut varieties** 'Adams'; 'Elmer Myers'; 'Grundy'; 'Snyder'; 'Stambaugh'; 'Thomas' **Butternut varieties** 'Lingle'; 'Sherwood'; 'Van de Poppen

See text for information on self-fertility

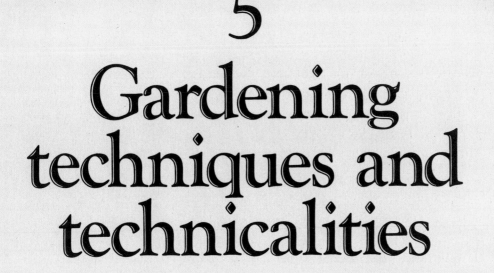

5
Gardening techniques and technicalities

Gardeners, it has sometimes been said, fall into two categories:
the green-fingered, who can do no horticultural wrong,
and the black-thumbed, to whom gardening is a mystery.
This chapter aims to clear away the mystery
and explain the fundamentals of gardening success.
It covers the basic nature of soil and plants,
and how these and other environmental factors interact.
It then goes on to more practical aspects:
choosing plants and raising them from seed, cuttings and so on,
providing food, water, shelter, support and other needs,
dealing with weeds and plant pests, diseases and disorders,
and how to prune and train your plants for best effect.
There are articles on tools, machines, frames and greenhouses.
Following this technical section, you will find
a series of charts to help you select plants for your needs,
a glossary, lists of useful addresses and books for further reference
and extensive indexes of general topics and plant names.

Understanding your soil

The most important part of your garden is the soil, and the most important factor governing your success or failure as a gardener is the soil's condition. These may seem obvious truisms, but vast numbers of gardeners fail to get the best results from their plants – both decorative types and food crops – because they do not understand the characteristics of their soil, and neglect to treat it accordingly. They tend to regard it as an inanimate mass that can be taken for granted except for the occasional digging, watering and application of fertilizer 'to help the plants grow'.

It is true that plants obtain food chemicals (see p 352) and water from the soil, and are anchored in position by the roots that grow into it. But the relationship is far from one-sided. Soil is a living, changing structure, and its health depends just as much on plant life as vice-versa. The disintegrated, pulverized rocks that provide the mineral bulk of soil cannot be converted into fertile soil itself unless life is present. All life needs air, water, food and warmth, so these also are essential.

Life in the soil

It may be difficult to believe that a handful of soil is teeming with millions of living creatures. The larger soil animals that you can see – the worms, insects, millipedes and so on – play their part, but it is the invisible creatures, the soil micro-organisms, that are of the greatest importance. Without the bacteria in soil, life would not be possible, for they are responsible in large part for disintegrating the remains of dead plants and animals and the

latter's excreta. This enables the organic material to be used as food and thus recycled by a new generation of plants – the ultimate food source of all living things.

Apart from the bacteria, there are single-celled soil animals; also fungi, which are plants devoid of the green colouring matter chlorophyll. The latter range from mushrooms and toadstools (with their extensive underground thread-like hyphae) to moulds and mildews. Unlike green plants, which build up simple chemicals from soil and air into more complex food materials, fungi have to obtain their nourishment from organic material. Those which do this parasitically from living tissues cause many plant diseases (see p 358). The vital soil fungi live on dead material, which they digest chemically. Fungi play an important part in the breakdown of woody plant material, and they tolerate more acid conditions than bacteria. Decomposition produces acids, making the soil 'sour', so lime is needed on some soils to neutralize this effect.

Earthworms are the most useful of the soil animals. They play an important part in maintaining good soil structure, and by drawing dead leaves into their burrows increase the amount of organic matter in the soil. This occurs particularly on grassland, where far more worms live than in cultivated soil. They feed on dead vegetation, which passes through their bodies mixed with soil. Those that make casts bring this enriched soil to the surface, amounting to the equivalent of a layer 5 mm (¼ in) thick each year – 50 tonnes per hectare (20 tons per acre). The earth-

worms' digestive processes make the casts alkaline, helping to counteract soil acidity. Consequently, the soil is continuously being moved, mixed, aerated, drained and fertilized without any mechanical interference.

Soil fertility

The part of the soil that is most fertile and best able to support plant life is that nearest the surface. This is the part exposed to the air and warmed by the sun, and it has much the greatest concentration of soil organisms. Most important of all, it is the part most enriched by plant remains and animal manure, so that it contains the nutrients plants need. It is called the topsoil; it varies in thickness from 5 to 60 cm (2 in to 2 ft), depending on the underlying strata. Below it lies the subsoil.

If you dig a trench or hole in your garden, the topsoil is usually obvious by its darker colour. This is due to the presence of humus, a dark, sticky material that is the result of the disintegration of organic matter. Humus coats soil particles, and is able to bind them together to form crumbs. This assists the aeration, drainage and cultivation of the soil. Working the soil in very dry or very wet conditions can result in a breakdown of its crumb structure, with a resultant loss of fertility.

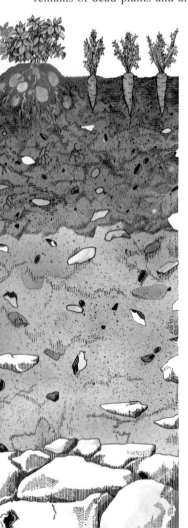

A portrait of fertile soil

A typical soil profile shows three main layers: the uppermost layer of dark, fertile topsoil, which varies in thickness according to soil type, vegetation, cultivation and other factors; the infertile and usually lighter-coloured subsoil; and the bedrock, which may be anything from a few to many hundreds of metres (yards) deep.

Soil is in intimate mixture of many components. Minerals include clay, silt and sand particles and stones of various sizes; the latter help to maintain an open, freely draining structure and are a nuisance only on the surface of seed-beds or where excessively numerous. Many soils contain lime or chalk; where, as here, the bedrock is chalk, an excess occurs and the soil is alkaline, or 'sweet'. A soil lacking lime may be acid, or 'sour'; a neutral soil, which is neither acid nor alkaline, suits the majority of plants.

Living organisms and their dead remains are a vital part of soil. Topsoil's dark colour comes from humus, a sticky material that results from decay of plant and animal remains by fungi (both visible and microscopic) and bacteria. Humus retains plant foods so that roots can absorb them, and also holds soil particles in crumbs that improve drainage and aeration, so that roots and soil organisms can 'breathe'.

Earthworms increase soil fertility by aerating the soil and drawing plant remains down into their burrows. Proper cultivation, with the incorporation of rotted manure or garden compost, also increases the depth of fertile soil left.

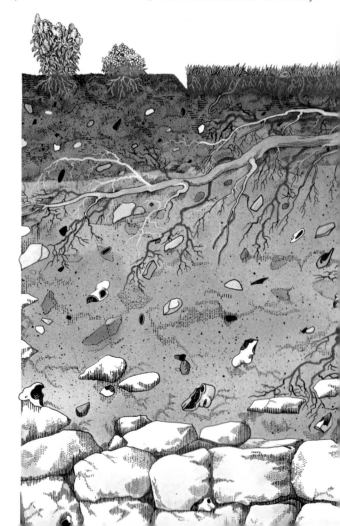

Soil types

Although the factors mentioned above influence the fertility of all soils, their nature also depends on the size and origin of the mineral particles. These can have a profound effect on drainage, the rate at which plant food materials are leached out and the soil's chemical nature – its acidity or alkalinity, and the availability of mineral salts that plants need. These in turn affect the types of plants that can be successfully grown.

The characteristics of the principal types of soils are described below. It is a mistake, however, to think that there are precisely six different sorts of soil. In fact, the variations are infinite, so that, for example, there is a more or less continuous gradation from pure clay through various grades of sandy loam to pure sand. The articles on pages 332 and 334 show you how to identify your soil type and how to maximize its fertility.

Clays Clay soils are easily identifiable. In the extreme, they stick to your boots when wet, drain slowly, and are heavy and difficult to work. When dry, they set brick-hard, shrink and crack.

The reason for these characteristics lies in the extremely small size of the individual mineral particles – less than 0.002 mm in diameter. They pack closely together, leaving very little space between the particles, so that the movement of air and water is very slow. Water is held tightly in a film around the particles, so that it is difficult for the plant to obtain, and growth is slow. The shrinking and cracking when clay dries may damage plant roots. Because so much water is held in clay, these soils warm up slowly in spring, but plant foods are also held, so that if the texture is improved they are potentially fertile soils.

The naturally occurring plants are coarse-rooted, including such trees as oaks, ash and elder, and such perennials as dock, thistles and creeping buttercup. These give a guide to the kinds of garden plants that will succeed. Roses and the fleshier-rooted kinds of herbaceous plants do well. Maincrop vegetables can be rewarding, but the soil is unsuited to early crops. However, plants with delicate roots systems and those requiring good drainage will not succeed.

Silts The particles in silty soils are slightly larger than those of clay – up to 0.02 mm – and, although they pack together so that drainage is slow, they lack the chemical qualities of clay. Fertilizers and lime are more easily lost, so that silty soils are less rich and also tend to be acid. The surface 'caps' after rain, affecting permeability, so that erosion can occur and aeration is impeded.

Loams These are the ideal soils for the gardener, as they contain a mixture of different-sized particles and good reserves of organic matter. Plant foods are held by the latter and by the clay particles, and drainage and aeration are helped by the coarser sand particles that are also present.

Sandy soils These vary from pure sand in gardens near the sea to sandy loams and the very acid sands of heathland. They are composed of grains of silica from 0.02 up to about 2 mm in diameter; these are chemically inactive and contain no plant foods. The character of the soil depends on the proportion of other substances it contains – organic matter, clay and iron or aluminium compounds.

Because drainage is so rapid, soluble plant foods – especially nitrates and potash – are lost and the soil is said to be 'hungry'; plants make poor growth. In areas of high rainfall, calcium is lost, too, so acidity is another problem. This may result in iron and manganese being washed out of the soil, which bleaches; the salts then accumulate in a rusty band which forms an impervious 'pan' at a lower level, impeding drainage.

The native plants include heaths (*Erica* spp) and heathers (*Calluna* spp), conifers and birch. Cultivated forms of these plants do well, as will other plants needing light acid soils, such as the rhododendrons and azaleas and some alpines. These soils warm early in spring if drainage is free, and provided you add lime, fertilizers and organic matter, are ideal for early vegetable production if irrigation is available.

Chalk and limestone soils The soft chalk and harder limestone rocks originally formed under the sea from deposits of dead marine animals. Later upheavals brought them to the surface, where they form distinct geological areas. The resulting soils are well-drained and strongly alkaline. This prevents iron and manganese from being absorbed by certain plants, such as azaleas and camellias. Potash deficiency also occurs; organic matter is rapidly decomposed.

Native plants include beech, clematis, viburnums, scabious, rock roses (*Helianthemum* spp) and thyme. A wide range of plants tolerant of calcium can be grown, and such soils are especially good for species that require good drainage. The topsoil is commonly very shallow, and solid chalk may lie near the surface; if this is broken, roots can penetrate to find reserves of water. It is worth considering importing topsoil to increase its thickness.

Peat and fen soils These are composed of partially decomposed organic matter with little mineral content. Peat is formed in areas of high rainfall and bog conditions where few plants can grow because of the extreme acidity. Fen soils developed in areas with lower rainfall, in low-lying bogs over alkaline soils. Drainage enables bacterial activity to resume and the resulting soils are among the most fertile, but they lack phosphates.

Soil tests and treatment

The ideal soil for growing the widest range of garden plants is a medium loam combining the advantages of sandy and clayey soils and containing plenty of organic matter – the type of soil sometimes referred to as 'vegetable' soil because it gives the greatest crop yields. Few gardeners are lucky enough to have such soil, however. They must adjust their ambitions to the soil conditions in their garden, or they must begin a programme of soil improvement – or both.

However, soils can vary in their characteristics even between different parts of the same garden. So to find out the kind or kinds of soil you have, the treatments needed and the types of plants that will do best, you should first carry out a series of soil tests, combining these with general observations of your own and neighbours' gardens and the kind of plants that flourish there. Some soil tests are best done with a test kit bought from a garden centre or shop, but you can learn a lot about your soil without any special equipment or materials. Test soil from various parts of your garden that have not been cultivated or fertilized recently. Scrape back the top 5 cm (2 in) or so, and take your samples from the 10 cm (4 in) below this.

Identifying soil type
Take a handful of moist but not waterlogged soil; squeeze it tightly, then release it. If it keeps its shape then some clay is present. If you could model with it and it feels smooth, it contains a lot of clay. If it crumbles, feels gritty

Identifying your soil
Squeeze a sample of moist but not wet soil in your hand. Pure clay **1** feels smooth, sticks to your hand and can be shaped like putty. Silt **2** is also smooth but does not keep its shape like clay. Sand **3** just crumbles and runs through your fingers, leaving nothing sticking to them. Loams and other soils containing a mixture of sand and clay **4** feel gritty and crumble to some extent, but also stain the skin.

the extent of root penetration and the nature of the subsoil. You will also discover whether there is a hard 'pan' that will impede drainage. Blue-grey patches streaked with rusty marks indicates very poor drainage at some time, with lack of oxygen. Any water rising in the bottom of the trench shows you the depth of the water table – the level of the underground 'lake' of water which collects over an impervious layer. If this is near the surface, it will restrict the growth of roots, and artificial drainage or raised beds may be advisable.

General site observations
If your garden is attached to a new house, or if there have been earth-moving operations in connection with building work, are there areas of light-coloured soil lying on the surface? If so – and particularly if there is no

below). On very small sites it is better to make raised beds and to use gravel instead of grass on areas used as paths or for sitting; in wet conditions turf is useless and paving can be dangerously slippery.

Is the soil 'thin' and dusty in summer, and is plant growth stunted? This indicates a severely impoverished soil due to lack of organic material; treatment is similar to that for sandy soil (see below). It may also indicate a very shallow topsoil.

Checking soil acidity
It is extremely useful to find out how acid or its opposite, how alkaline, your soil is before selecting plants for a new or existing garden, and it is vital if you want to grow certain plants that are intolerant of extreme conditions. Most heathers, for example, will not grow on alkaline soils, whereas gypsophila is a well-known lover of alkaline conditions. For some food crops, too, the degree of acidity is important for good yields and freedom from certain diseases (see p 266).

Soil acidity is measured on a scale of pH numbers. The neutral point, where acidity and alkalinity are equal, is represented by a pH of 7. The higher the pH, the more alkaline the soil is. A pH of 6 is ten times more acid and a pH of 5 is a hundred times more acid than the point of neutrality. The most acid conditions are found in some peat soils, which may have a pH value of 3. In climates with moderate rainfall it is rare to find an alkaline soil with a pH higher than 8.

To test soil acidity you need a special test kit. With some types, you simply moisten a soil sample and dip a strip of test paper in the soil; then compare the colour of the test strip with the numbered chart provided. Other kits use an indicator liquid. A small amount of soil is placed in a glass tube and mixed with one or more liquids supplied, according to the instructions. The tube is shaken, allowed to stand, and the solution is then matched for colour against the chart. Some test kits of this type enable you also to test for the amounts of plant nutrients in your soil (see p 352).

It is possible to influence soil acidity. To raise the pH, add lime or use alkaline fertilizers such as bonemeal, basic slag or nitrochalk. The amount of lime needed depends on soil type as well as acidity. In order to increase the pH by 0.5, add hydrated lime (calcium hydroxide) at about 180 g/m² (5 oz/sq yd) to

Measuring soil components
1 Place a soil sample in a jar and three-quarters fill with cold water. **2** Shake well and leave to stand, watching as the soil settles. **3** When completely settled you should be able to see several more-or-less distinct layers: the coarsest sandy particles at the bottom, gradating to the finest clay. Organic material will float.

and stains your hand, it is a mixture of sand and clay. A silty soil feels smooth but cannot be modelled, whereas a very sandy soil will simply slip through your fingers.

Next take a large screw-top glass jar and fill it about one-quarter full of soil (first removing large stones). Fill the jar three-quarters full with cold water, replace the lid and shake vigorously. Observe what happens as the soil settles. Stones and coarse sandy particles which assist drainage settle first. Silt settles more slowly, while clay remains in suspension for a long time and settles only very slowly. Organic matter floats. This test will show the proportion of these different materials, and will help you to judge whether you have a sandy soil, a loam or a clay.

Examining the soil profile
Excavate a trench 75 cm (2½ ft) deep with clean-cut sides. This will show you the depth of topsoil (which is darker than the subsoil),

natural vegetation growing on them – then infertile subsoil may have been dumped and must be removed to expose the fertile topsoil. Or the builders may even have removed and sold the topsoil, leaving only the subsoil.

Does water lie on the surface after heavy rain? This may indicate poor absorption due to capping, which can be remedied by cultivation and the addition of organic material such as peat as a thick mulch (see p 334). It may be caused by heavy compaction, especially in ground around newly-built houses, where heavy machines have operated. Deep cultivation is needed to aerate the soil, and large quantities of organic material such as rotted straw, pulverized bark, and so on will be needed if the soil structure has been damaged.

Does the ground flood in winter? Unless it is low-lying beside a river, this indicates that drainage is faulty, due to a pan, compaction, or heavy subsoil below a shallow topsoil. On clay, artificial drainage may be needed (see

light, sandy soils; 250 to 350 g/m² (7 to 11 oz/sq yd) to loams; and about 450 g/m² (13 oz/sq yd) to clayey soils. Double these quantities if using ground chalk. The best time to add lime is in autumn or winter, but do not do so less than two months after manuring or one month after applying fertilizer, and do not apply manures or fertilizers until at least one month after liming. You can reduce pH (increase acidity) by adding flowers of sulphur, by choosing sulphate of ammonia when a nitrogenous fertilizer is required – a rate of about 50 g/m² (1½ oz/sq yd) gives a reduction of 0.5 in pH – or by digging in liberal quantities of peat. (The above figures are very approximate; re-test the soil about six weeks after treating, and remember that heavy rain can wash lime out of the soil.)

Treating problem soils
The first thing you must put right in any garden where it is a problem is drainage. Water that cannot run away becomes stagnant underground just as it does in surface pools. The soil becomes sour and airless, so that plant roots may 'drown'. Where the problem is not too severe, double digging (see p 334), which breaks up any hard pan and aerates and introduces organic matter into the subsoil, may be sufficient. On heavy clay, you may need to aid drainage by digging a deep stone-filled sump at the lowest part of the garden and possibly elsewhere. For best results, lay one or more lines of unglazed land-drainage pipes on a gently sloping bed cut into the subsoil – at least 60 cm (2 ft) deep – leading to a pond, ditch or artificial soakaway. The pipes should be laid just touching and covered with a 15 cm (6 in) layer of coarse gravel or stones – increased to 30 cm (12 in) under a lawn – before the topsoil is returned. On very badly drained soils it may be necessary to lay side drains in a herringbone pattern.

With clayey soils, thorough cultivation is essential. Do this in autumn, ridging the soil to expose the maximum area to weathering and breaking up by winter frost. Liming in winter makes clay more workable, by encouraging the formation of soil crumbs. But this will not help if there is free lime in the soil, so test for this first. Mix a handful of soil with distilled water and stir to remove air bubbles. Add ordinary vinegar; bubbling indicates that free lime is present. If distilled water is not available, vinegar can be used alone; listen for a distinct fizzing sound. Other treatments for heavy clay are to improve natural drainage by digging coarse boiler ash, mortar rubble, coarse sand and so on into the topsoil. And work in plenty of bulky organic manure, well-rotted compost or coarse peat in order to increase the humus content and open up the soil structure.

At the other extreme, sandy soils are 'hungry' and 'thirsty' and are commonly also acid. Large quantities of organic manure (which must be well rotted), regular liming and feeding are required. Generally, the greatest need is for nitrates and potash applied little and often. If you can obtain clay – even subsoil from excavations – mix this with coarse peat and lime and spread it on the surface in winter. Green manuring (see p 335) is beneficial, and the soil should never be left uncovered – especially on sloping sites – otherwise erosion will occur. You can use ground-cover plants (see p 232) or a mulch of organic matter such as pulverized bark, mushroom compost or spent hops.

Some stony soils are also free-draining, but this depends mainly on the soil between the stones. However, you should only remove the larger surface stones, as the stones do help to maintain an open soil structure. Otherwise, treat according to the type of soil in between. Most chalk soils are also free-draining, and therefore hungry, and ample bulky humus-forming material (either composted or from green manuring) will be needed. In addition, they are very alkaline – so much so that you would be well advised not to attempt growing lime-hating plants except in raised peat beds or containers of lime-free growing mixture (see p 126). Some degree of pH adjustment may be attempted, however, as described above; in addition, some plants may need treatment with sequestered iron (see p 352).

At the opposite extreme from chalky soils, peaty ones are very acid and generally poorly draining. Certain plants, such as heathers and rhododendrons, will do well, but these soils, even if drained and limed, lack many nutrients and are seldom suitable for the cultivation of fruit and vegetables. The somewhat similar fen soils are, however, very fertile if drained.

Aiding drainage
A drainage sump **1** should be dug at the garden's lowest point, or wherever drainage is the greatest problem. It should be at least 1 m (3 ft) deep and as much across; 1.25 m (4 ft) is preferable. Fill to half its depth with large stones or broken bricks, covered with a layer of smaller stones and inverted turves. Then replace topsoil to a depth of at least 30 cm (12 in). Lay land drainage pipes **2** at least 60 cm (2 ft) deep in trenches with a 1:100 slope. The pipes should just touch end to end. Cover with stones or gravel 15 to 30 cm (6 to 12 in) deep, followed by at least 30 cm (12 in) of topsoil. Lead to a very deep soakaway **3**, ditch or other drain. Where two lines of pipes join, cut one end at an angle and place together at a joint between two pipes. Extensive systems should be laid herringbone-fashion **4**.

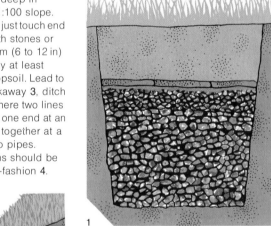

1

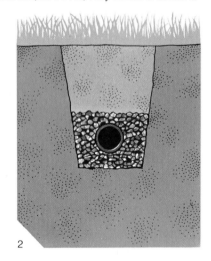

2

3

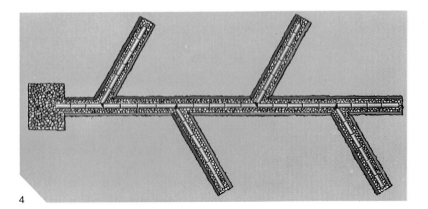

4

Soil cultivation and enrichment

Digging is a basic gardening operation that aerates the soil, improves drainage and makes root penetration easier. It also exposes the soil to the action of frost and winds, helping the formation of a good crumbly soil structure. Aeration helps the soil to warm up more quickly in the spring, accelerating plant growth, and speeds the decay of organic matter to nutrients that plants can absorb and use. Digging also enables you to find and remove the roots of perennial weeds and to incorporate quantities of manure or compost.

Digging is particularly important in the initial preparation for any long-term planting, particularly of plants such as shrubs that are destined to occupy the same ground for many years. Then it is advisable to double dig (see below) in the autumn. However, the development of selective weedkillers and the use of mulches has eliminated the need for regular deep cultivation except on areas from which crops are removed. (This includes areas planted with annuals, biennials and bedding plants as well as the vegetable garden.) Only a few vegetables need deep cultivation, and if their position is moved over a three- or four-year period (see p 262), the whole area will be double dug once in that time. Where a large area is cultivated, a powered rotary cultivator (see p 377) saves much labour, but over-enthusiastic use may damage soil structure. In any case, many gardeners feel that occasional double digging is still worthwhile.

How to dig
Double digging is so called because two layers of the soil are disturbed, each layer being the depth of a spade's blade – a 'spit'. This is about 25 cm (10 in). In single digging, only the top spit is turned over. In both cases, however, the topsoil remains on top. As shown in the illustrations, in double digging the top spit is removed and the lower spit broken up; it is then re-covered with topsoil. By working in trenches, the plot is covered systematically.

If turf is growing on the land being dug, skim this off as you work, invert it in the trench and chop it up. It will decompose to form humus. You can treat annual weeds in the same way, but be careful to remove the roots of perennial weeds. In the same way, place manure or compost in the trench, and fork it in, before the turf and topsoil from the next trench. If well rotted, these materials can also be mixed with the topsoil.

Use of mulches
It has been shown that far better growth is made if the roots of trees, shrubs and bush fruits are not disturbed by cultivation, but are protected by mulches of organic matter. These keep the soil open, preserve and improve soil structure, add humus, increase the availability of phosphates and potash, help in the absorption and retention of water, keep a more equable soil temperature and reduce weed growth. Mulches should be removed temporarily in spring where early warming of the soil is important.

Suitable material for mulching around woody plants includes peat, shredded bark, spent hops, leaf-mould, partially decomposed garden compost or farmyard manure, mushroom compost, chopped fern fronds, rotted

Building a compost heap
If you have a large garden that produces a lot of waste, build a free-standing heap **above**; otherwise, use ventilated bins so that air can reach the compost but it does not dry out. If you have three bins **above right**, one can be filled with refuse while the second is

sawdust or wood shavings (fresh woody material will reduce the soil's nitrogen content), straw (which should be sprinkled with a nitrogenous fertilizer to reduce nitrogen depletion of the soil) and pecan shells. They should all be applied when the soil is warm and moist. The thickness depends on the material used; the looser, coarser kinds such as garden compost and straw, which will compact, should be 15 cm (6 in) thick initially, while with peat (which should be thoroughly moistened before application) and shredded bark 5 to 8 cm (2 to 3 in) is sufficient. (For mulching for weed control, see page 356.)

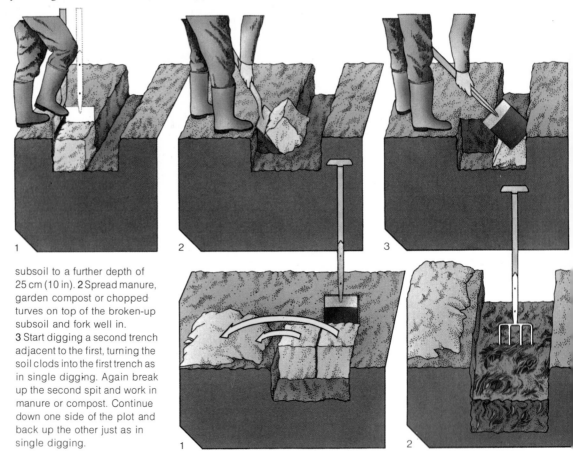

Using the spade
When digging, insert the spade vertically **1** to ensure the deepest possible cultivation. Thrust it with your foot to the full depth of the blade. Then drive it in again at right-angles to cleanly cut off a clod of soil. **2** Lever the spade back to lift the clod and, with a flick of the wrist, **3** turn it over completely into the adjacent trench so that any weeds are completely buried. Do not try to work too fast, and cut off only small clods of earth at a time – 15 to 20 cm (6 to 8 in) is quite enough. See also page 378.

Double digging
This needs wider trenches than single digging so that you can stand and work in them; 60 cm (2 ft) wide is suitable. All the trenches must be the same width and depth, so mark out the plot first, dividing it into two parts as for single digging. **1** Dig a straight-sided trench to the full depth of the spade's blade, removing the soil and piling it up as before. Then use a strong fork to break up the subsoil to a further depth of 25 cm (10 in). **2** Spread manure, garden compost or chopped turves on top of the broken-up subsoil and fork well in. **3** Start digging a second trench adjacent to the first, turning the soil clods into the first trench as in single digging. Again break up the second spit and work in manure or compost. Continue down one side of the plot and back up the other just as in single digging.

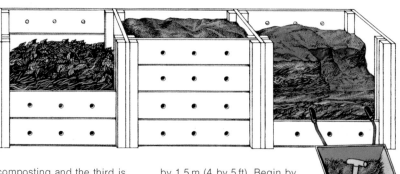

composting and the third is being used. Plastic or wire bins (the latter best with a perforated plastic lining) **left** are ideal for small gardens.
The principles of construction are the same in every case. Choose a well-drained, sheltered site and for a heap peg out a rectangle at least 1.2 by 1.5 m (4 by 5 ft). Begin by spreading a layer of coarse material – straw, stalks, etc – 30 cm (1 ft) deep, and tread firm. Next add a layer of nitrogenous matter (lawn mowings, young weeds, non-greasy kitchen scraps, or animal or poultry manure), then 5 cm (2 in) of soil, or water and a sprinkling of nitro-chalk, ammonium sulphate or a proprietary compost activator. Continue to build up the heap like a sandwich, keeping the sides sloping gently inwards and a little higher than the centre. Sprinkle occasionally with powdered chalk or bonfire ash to counteract acidity, but keep this away from the fertilizer or manure to avoid loss of ammonia. Tread firmly as each layer is added, to retain moisture, as a dry heap will not rot. Water if necessary.
When the heap is 1.2 m (4 ft) high, cover with 2.5 to 5 cm (1 to 2 in) of soil and a plastic sheet to prevent it becoming too wet. As decomposition takes place it will heat up and shrink. It should then be turned, sides to middle, onto an adjoining area of ground (or to another bin). In normal conditions, the compost will be ready to use in four to six months; decomposition is most rapid in warm weather.
Apart from those already mentioned, good materials to compost include soft leaves and hedge clippings, vegetable waste, fruit and vegetable peelings, tea and coffee grounds, shredded cotton or woollen waste, and vacuum cleaner emptyings. Avoid plastics, anything contaminated with salt, paint or creosote, tough plant material such as pine needles, diseased plants, and the roots of perennial weeds.

Compost-making
A healthy soil depends on adequate supplies of organic matter, and while rotted farmyard manure has long been used for this, well-made garden compost is an excellent alternative. Apart from diseased material and the roots of perennial weeds, which should be burned, most garden plant residues – and much kitchen waste, too – can be composted and returned to the soil, except where they have been treated with weedkillers. Allow ample time for these to break down – at least six months in the case of selective lawn weed-killers – before adding to the compost heap.

Various methods can be used to make garden compost, but all require good aeration, free drainage, adequate moisture and a balance between dry, strawy material and soft, green plant tissues such as lawn mowings. Dry material cannot rot unless soft plant material, or animal manure, or nitrogenous fertilizers and water are added. If too much soft plant tissue is used without the drier, coarser material, the compost will lack aeration and become a slimy, smelly mess. When a lot of grass mowings are available buy a few bales of straw, or some sawdust or wood shavings to mix in layers and keep the heap open.

Green manuring
Another good way of increasing the amount of organic material in the soil is by green manuring. A quick-growing, cheap crop such as mustard, rape, clover or lupins – the kind used by farmers for this purpose, not the decorative sort – is sown, preferably in early autumn, and dug into the ground a few weeks later, while still green. Lupins and clover are able to enrich the soil with nitrogen, which is fixed by bacteria in their roots, but they will not do this if fed with nitrogenous fertilizer. This is however needed by the other crops to encourage lush growth.

Single digging
This thoroughly turns over the topsoil, but does little to increase the depth of fertile soil.
right Begin by dividing the plot to be dug lengthwise in two with a strong garden line. Digging begins on one side and continues in the reverse direction on the other side of the line. Remove a trench 30 cm (12 in) wide and the full depth of the spade – 25 cm (10 in). Make the sides straight and vertical, and pile the soil to one side, adjacent to the opposite side of the plot. Spread manure or garden compost in the bottom

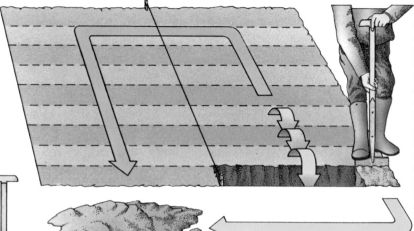

of the trench. Then start digging a second trench adjacent and parallel to the first, turning the clods of soil over into the first trench. Dig a third trench, turning the soil over into the second, and continue in this way until you reach the end of the plot. Spread manure, garden compost or chopped turves in each trench. Then dig a trench on the opposite side of the line, turning the soil over into the adjacent trench. Work back up to the top of the plot, filling the very last trench with the soil taken from the very first.

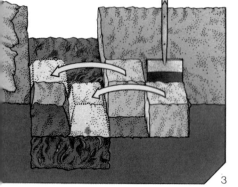

Ridging
This is done in autumn to maximize the exposure of heavy soils to the weathering action of frost and rain. There are several methods, each resulting in the clods of soil being piled in threes to form ridges and furrows. In the method shown **right** you work backwards down a wide trench, throwing clods forwards, to the right and to the left so that they rest on each other.

Understanding your plants

The plants in your garden may be as diverse as a pine tree and a clump of grass, a cabbage and a carpet of aubrieta, a crocus and a wisteria. And yet they resemble each other more than they differ. At the most fundamental level they share most characteristics with each other and with all other living things.

Like all other plants – and like animals – they are made of minute cells, which can range in size from one-tenth to one-hundredth of a millimetre. Under a microscope, these cells show almost as much diversity as individual plants, ranging from the hollow tubes that form part of the plant's internal transport system to the closely fitting jigsaw-like cells of the leaf surface and the rapidly multiplying cells of its growth zones. It is in these growth zones that all plant cells are formed, at first identical and with the thin wall of tough cellulose that distinguishes them from animal cells. These young cells quickly differentiate to form the varied tissues of the plant. Most mature living plant cells have a large central cavity filled with watery sap, but the stems and trunks of many plants consist largely of dead woody and corky cells that transport water and give strength and protection.

There are many other similarities between plants and other living organisms. They all use oxygen from the air to respire, or 'breathe', and to break down food materials such as sugar and starch to produce the energy needed to carry on such activities as growth, flowering and seed production. The major difference between green plants and animals is that the former make their own food – and the materials needed to build their own bodies – from simple substances from the air and soil.

The basis of this is a process called photosynthesis, by which plants convert water and carbon dioxide (from the air) into sugar. The sugar is then converted into starch or cellulose, or combined with other substances to make a whole range of materials from waxes and aromatic oils to proteins. It is a process we and all other animal inhabitants of the Earth depend upon, because it is the ultimate source of all our food – and of the oxygen we (and plants) breathe, for oxygen is an important by-product of photosynthesis. This process itself needs energy to drive it; this comes from sunlight, so photosynthesis takes place only in the day, and at that time more oxygen is produced as its by-product than is consumed by respiration. At night, photosynthesis stops, and plants become net consumers of oxygen. That is why it is sometimes said that plants breathe out oxygen during the day and carbon dioxide at night.

Photosynthesis is just one of the activities constantly going on in plants' tissues. Apart from growth and reproduction, other, subtler processes are taking place, including the uptake of water by the roots and its evaporation into the air (a process called transpiration); the movement of food supplies from one part of the plant to another; the storing away of such food in stems, roots and special storage organs to tide over lean periods of dormancy when photosynthesis cannot take place and to provide the energy for a renewed

The leaf is the plant's food factory and lung. It contains green chlorophyll which absorbs the energy of sunlight to drive the process of photosynthesis. This combines water (absorbed by the roots and carried up the stem) with the gas carbon dioxide (which enters from the air via minute pores called stomata) to make sugar, starting point of all food materials and plant structures. Oxygen, a by-product of photosynthesis, passes out by the same route. At the same time, the reverse flow takes in oxygen to be consumed in the respiration or 'burning' of food material to provide energy; this releases carbon dioxide.

The stem, stiffened in various ways, is a major structural part and contains two distinct sets of tube-like transport vessels (visible as leaf veins) – the xylem, which carries water and dissolved minerals from roots to leaves, and the phloem, which carries food made in the leaves to other parts of the plant.

The roots anchor the plant in the soil, so have to be strong yet flexible. They absorb water and mineral salts from the soil – the raw materials to build up sugars into more complex substances. The fine root hairs just behind the growing tips are the main water-absorbing parts. Roots, like other parts, need oxygen to 'breathe'; except in bog plants, they cannot do this in waterlogged soil, so drown and die.

Buds are potential or actual growth points. Containing stored food, they may remain dormant for long periods. Terminal buds at the ends of shoots tend to repress growth of lower buds; hence removing these by pruning or pinching out promotes bushy growth. Some buds form flowers.

Most plant cells **1** are box-like, with a tough cellulose coating, a thin layer of living tissue – the cytoplasm – which contains the nucleus (the control centre) and the green chloroplasts (site of photosynthesis), and a large central fluid-filled vacuole. In drought, this may lose water, so the cells become flaccid, or limp, and the plant wilts. On the lower leaf surface **2**, openings between cells form the stomata. Water evaporating from these creates a 'pull' that draws water up from the roots via the xylem vessels **3**; this process is transpiration. In dry conditions, the stomata close, reducing water loss.

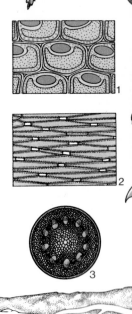

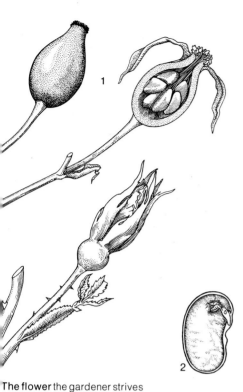

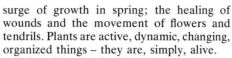

surge of growth in spring; the healing of wounds and the movement of flowers and tendrils. Plants are active, dynamic, changing, organized things – they are, simply, alive.

Being alive, much of their activity is concerned with producing the next generation, to ensure survival of the species. The life cycle of all flowering plants is basically the same: a seed germinates to produce a plant, which grows and develops flowers that, after pollination and fertilization, produce new seeds. In annuals, this whole cycle is over in a season; the seeds containing embryo plants are the only parts to survive over winter to begin anew the next year, or whenever favourable conditions return. Such plants are called

monocarpic; they die after flowering and setting seed. Biennials are similar, but they take two years to reach the flowering stage from germination. Perennials last many years, generally flowering and producing seed repeatedly. They vary in their methods of overwintering. Shrubs and trees are woody and have dormant overwintering buds above ground level; they may or may not shed their leaves in autumn. Most herbaceous plants have soft tissues that die back in winter, their dormant buds being at or below ground level. Some of them have special food storage organs such as bulbs or tubers to help them survive. And survival is the most fundamental characteristic of all life.

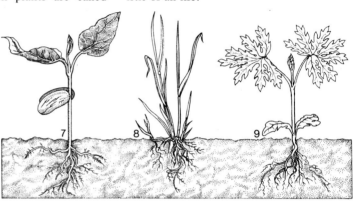

The flower the gardener strives to perfect is the plant's organ of reproduction. Its colour and scent attract insects seeking pollen and nectar as food; they transfer pollen grains (containing male reproductive cells) from the outer male stamens to the inner stigmas – the upper parts of the female carpels. Most flowers have male and female parts, but their structure may make self-pollination impossible. Some plants have separate male and female flowers on one plant; some have separate male and female plants. Some flowers, such as grasses, are wind-pollinated; they are not colourful or scented, but produce vast amounts of pollen and have feathery stigmas to which it easily adheres. Conifers are pollinated similarly but the female flowers (strobili) resemble tiny cones. After pollination, the pollen grain grows a pollen tube down to the female ovule, where male and female cells join, the process of fertilization. The resultant embryo becomes a seed, the surrounding tissues a fruit – any structure that aids seed dispersal. The remaining parts of the flower, their job completed, wither.

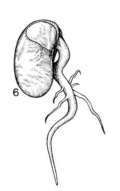

The seed **2** contains an embryo plant, with root (or radicle), shoot (plumule) and one or two seed-leaves (cotyledons). In seeds with two cotyledons, these may be swollen with food, as in beans. Others, including all with one cotyledon, have a separate store of food. The ripening seed loses water, and in this dormant state can survive harsh conditions. The fruit surounding the seed **1** gives protection and aids dispersal. Fleshy fruits such as tomatoes and rose hips may be eaten by animals; the seeds survive passage through the creature's digestive system and are thus dispersed. Other seeds have such dispersal aids as the 'wings' of maples **3**, the 'parachutes' of dandelions **4** and the 'shaker' of poppies **5**.

Germination **6** needs water, air and warmth. The seed swells, its cells become active and the root starts to grow. It bursts through the seed coat and begins to absorb soil water. The shoot then starts to grow. It may carry the cotyledons above the ground, as in the tomato and French bean **7**, or these may stay underground, as in broad and runner beans. Flowering plants with one seed-leaf are called monocotyledons, or monocots. Characteristically their leaves are strap-shaped, with parallel veins; examples are grasses **8** and irises. Many monocots have bulbs or corms but there are few trees or woody plants except for the palms, cordylines and bamboos. Dicotyledons, or dicots, have

two seed-leaves, and include all the other plants with true flowers. They have diverse leaf shapes but, as in pelargoniums **9**, all have branching leaf veins. There are many trees and shrubs but no true bulbs. Gymnosperms or conifers **10** are a separate group. Their 'flowers' are quite different and the seeds naked; they generally develop within the scales of a cone. The seedlings have many cotyledons, and the woody stems are different in structure from that of flowering trees. Ferns **11** belong to an even more primitive group, producing spores on the back of fronds. These produce heart-shaped prothalli (see p345) in which occurs a second, sexual stage of reproduction.

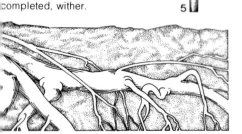

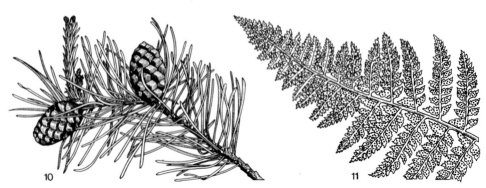

Climate and the gardener

It is the weather and the soil together that control the growth of plants. Although it is convenient to refer to the weather factors, such as temperature and rainfall, individually, it must be remembered that it is their combined effect that determines whether a plant will thrive, survive or die. Therefore, given certain soil conditions (as modified by cultivation), it is the climate of your garden that determines the types of vegetables, fruits and decorative plants that you can grow.

Climate is the summary of all the weather likely to be experienced at a particular place, but it is important to remember that the likely extremes are often more important than the average throughout the year. For example, two places with an average annual temperature of 12°C (54°F) might have widely differing climates, one fluctuating a mere 10°C (18°F) either side of the average from summer to winter, while the other has sweltering summers and bitterly cold winters. In the former, frost-tender shrubs might thrive that would perish in their first winter in the latter, while in the hot summers it might be possible to grow a crop that would not ripen in the more equable climate.

No weather is constant. It varies from day to day, and even from hour to hour. The only plant influence with any degree of consistency is the day-length, or ratio of day to night (see p 341). All other weather factors are far less dependable, and their relative importance varies from one geographical region to another. In most temperate regions, temperatures (in the air and in the soil) are determining factors, since they control the start and end of the growing season, and also the time taken for a plant to develop through its various stages of growth. The rate of food production, however, is more dependent on the amount of energy provided by sunshine.

Another major limiting factor on plant growth – the principal factor in many areas with warm climates – is the amount of soil moisture available to the plant through its roots. This is controlled by the frequency and amounts of rainfall and artificial irrigation, and by the rate of water loss by evaporation from the soil and by transpiration from plants' leaves (see p 336), both of which losses are largely determined by temperature, though wind strength and humidity of the air also have a considerable influence.

Major climatic zones

It is the combination of all these aspects of weather over a period of years that determines the garden climate. Climate cannot be satisfactorily split up into rigid divisions, because in most places the climate of one area merges almost imperceptibly into that of its neighbour. On the other hand, differences can occur over short distances – even between two adjacent gardens or two parts of the same garden. Nevertheless, some form of generalization of climatic type does help to bring out the meteorological possibilities, and for this reason a set of maps indicating important climatic factors are printed on the endpapers of this book.

The main variations in climate are associated with latitude (proximity to the poles or equator), with continentality (closeness to major seas or oceans), and with altitude (height of ground above sea level). The coldest climates are found in high latitudes near the poles, with long winters of low temperatures and short day-lengths (and perpetual night within the Arctic and Antarctic circles). The summers are short, with very long day-lengths and generally cool temperatures, although high summer temperatures can occur in high latitudes in the middle of continents. The growing season is very short, but aridity is rarely a problem. Hot climates, on the other hand, occur in lands near the equator, chiefly between the tropics of Cancer and Capricorn. They may be very dry (as in desert areas), very wet (as in the rain forests) or have alternate wet and dry seasons (as in the monsoon belts). There is little change in day-length throughout the year, and temperatures too show relatively little variation, though low night temperatures can occur in arid regions. Rainfall is the main factor controlling plant growth.

In between these two extremes lie the temperate zones, cooler towards the poles and warmer towards the equator. The word temperate implies the absence of extremes, but this type of climate only truly occurs on islands or in coastal areas to the lee side of large oceans. (These are on the western coasts of continents in the northern hemisphere, but the situation is more complex in the southern.) In the middle of large continents there is a far greater range of temperatures, from hot summers to cold winters, which overrides the effect of latitude. It is for this reason that islands in the Hebrides, near 60°N off the west coast of Scotland, can experience a frost-free winter while areas in southern Europe can suffer devastating cold.

Western coastal districts in the higher latitudes of the northern hemisphere have an additional advantage, as in the British Isles and the north-west of North America, in that they can have a rainfall pattern more or less equally distributed throughout the year. Continental areas tend to be drier in the summer than in the winter, a feature that is also very marked in a so-called Mediterranean climate. This occurs around much of the Mediterranean basin, on the American West Coast, in the Western Cape area of South Africa, and in south-western and part of southern Australia. Other temperate regions with fairly even rainfall include New Zealand, the south-eastern coastal belt of Australia and a small coastal area of South Africa around Port Elizabeth and East London.

On the other hand, there are some very significant arid or semi-arid areas within the temperate zones. The only ones in western Europe are in northern Spain, but a large part of the central-western United States, much of western South Africa and a vast area of central Australia, extending to the coast in the west, receives very little rain. What does fall is generally very erratic. In many cases, the world's arid areas lie in the 'rain shadow' of a mountain range; moist winds deposit a lot of rain on one side, so that by the time they descend on the other they contain little moisture. This occurs in North America to the east of the Rocky Mountains.

Local climatic differences

Even within a climatic zone there are significant differences in the weather over quite short distances. The most rapid changes occur when moving up or down a hill, when a difference of 30 m (100 ft) in altitude can cause a change as great as over 100 km (60 miles) along level ground. As altitude increases, the amount of sunshine, average temperatures and the length of the growing season all decrease (spring comes earlier in the valleys than the hills), while wind strength and rainfall increase. There are also significant changes over short distances near a coast. Next to the sea, the weather is more equable, so that temperature extremes are avoided; it is generally sunnier than inland, but winds are stronger and in times of gales the salt spray can cause vegetation damage. The day temperatures are therefore likely to be the highest in non-coastal low-lying areas, but on calm clear nights these will probably have the lowest night minimum temperatures. However, temperatures are generally some degrees higher in urban areas than in nearby rural areas; this due partly to the heat-absorbing properties of concrete and partly to the warmth generated artificially in buildings.

Apart from the above, the aspect to the sun and the exposure to wind can make significant differences. In the northern hemisphere, land on a south-facing slope will receive more solar energy and have an earlier spring and warmer soil than on one facing north. The reverse is true in the southern hemisphere. There is little to choose between east and west slopes in this respect, but prevailing winds make a significant difference whatever the slope. The sides of hills facing prevailing winds will have a much windier climate than the more sheltered slopes in their lee; if the prevailing winds are moist oceanic ones, the climate will also be wetter. This is a small-scale version of the effect mentioned above in connection with arid regions, and distinct dry 'rain shadows' can occur in the lee of quite low hills. In winter, the lee slopes facing a continent are liable to be bitterly cold, while the more 'exposed' slopes facing an ocean may be comparatively mild.

Wind always tends to increase with height, but when slope has to be taken into consideration it is the relative height that is important and the extent to which neighbouring hills provide some form of shelter. When visiting an area for the first time, you can judge the extent to which it is subject to strong winds from any distortion in the shape of hedges or trees (see p 340). If an isolated, exposed tree is symmetrical in form, with good, equal growth on all sides, there is not likely to be a wind exposure problem. Very sheltered areas can be good sites for gardens, but you must also remember that they are also much more liable to night frosts.

Frost liability

In most parts of the temperate zone frosts are liable to occur, and one of the most important ways in which the climate of two gardens can differ – even if they are separated by only a short distance – is in their liability to frost, especially the first and last ones of the winter. (These can be the most damaging, because your plants may be in an 'accident-prone' state.) Generalized maps showing average dates of first and last frosts give only very inadequate guidance to most individual gardeners. This is because such averages refer to open sites such as airfields, and cannot take into account the all-important local details. Moreover, since they show average dates, there is a 50-50 chance that in any particular year the last spring frost may be as much as a month earlier or later than the predicted date. When using such maps to judge when it is safe to plant out frost-tender plants it is therefore wise to err on the side of caution, and certainly to be ready to give protection in the form of glass cloches, netting, or one of the other methods mentioned in the article on page 354 should late frosts threaten.

In general, spring frosts are likely to occur later on sites farthest from the coast, and in localities lower in altitude than the neighbouring ground. The reason for the latter is that cold air at night flows downhill like water, filling a dell or valley like a pool. Little can be done to alter the frost risk of a garden on a level site, but one on a slope should always be planned to allow good 'air drainage'. In particular, it should not have a wall or dense hedge as a boundary on its lower side, as this will obstruct the flow of cold air and create a 'frost pocket'. A solid boundary along the upper side, especially one that diverts the downhill flow of cold night air sideways away from the garden and does not merely block it, can be a distinct advantage.

Late frosts are more likely in a dry spring than a wet one. Frost is also more severe over sandy or peaty soils, and is least likely over heavy clay. In the northern hemisphere, the nights when late frosts are most likely are those which follow a day when the wind has come from a northerly quarter and has died away at nightfall to nearly calm conditions. If at the same time the sky has cleared of clouds, then a low night temperature is likely before dawn unless the wind picks up again or the cloud returns. A quick inspection of the sky at dusk can give a gardener, after a little experience, a good idea of the risk of frost. With an ear to the broadcast weather forecast and an eye on his own thermometer he may be able to save his more valuable plants.

Climatic extremes

Catastrophic weather conditions can ruin a garden in a matter of minutes. Gardeners in the more equable climate of the British Isles are fortunate in being spared the most violent extremes of drought, flood, storm and blizzard – though all of these can on occasion do damage enough.

There is little the gardener can do to protect his garden from floods or from the kind of tropical storm – hurricane in the Atlantic, typhoon in the Pacific – that are liable to lash the Gulf and East coasts of North America and to a lesser extent eastern Australia and the North Island of New Zealand. This is less true of heavy hailstorms, however, which are liable to occur in many areas, including parts of North America and the High Veld region of South Africa. Gardeners in such areas should fit hail screens made from fine-mesh wire stretched on a wooden frame over all glass structures, such as greenhouses and frames. It is worth having a few portable screens available to protect small plants.

The British Isles

The climate of the British Isles reflects their midway position between the cold north and warm south and between the temperate Atlantic Ocean and the more variable European continent. There are almost subtropical conditions in the extreme south-west and almost subarctic on the Scottish hills. Rainfall is overabundant on the higher ground to the west but virtually in the semi-arid class in East Anglia. The day-lengths also vary considerably, from 6 hours in winter to over 21 in the summer in the far north, and from 8 to 16 hours in the south.

Thanks to the warming influence of the Gulf Stream, spring comes earliest in the south-west, and the growing season (which can be defined in terms of soil temperatures, approximately 6°C (43°F) being necessary for many plants) lingers on longest in the same regions. Indeed, in south-western Cornwall, the Scilly Isles and the south-western coasts of Ireland these conditions often prevail throughout the year. At the other extreme, in the northern hills the main growing season may be less than six months. Generally speaking, altitude retards the start of spring by about a week for every 50 m (160 ft) increase in height above sea level, but in all parts there may be a variation of about a month either side of the average dates.

In practice, the effective end of the growing season for many plants is caused by the first autumn frost, which tends to occur in late October over much of England, but earlier in Scotland and northern England and much later in coastal gardens. Increasing rains also hamper autumn gardening, and it is wise to be ahead of the calendar in your gardening work, but the opposite is true in spring. The last frost may occur as early as February or March on western coasts, around late April or early May over much of lowland Britain, and in June in northern areas. However, these dates can be very variable, as explained above; for inland gardens, even in southern England, mid-May is the very earliest that all danger of frost may be said to be past, and early June is safer, especially in midland and northern areas. On the coast far greater risks can be taken.

Summer temperatures are rarely high enough to cause the gardener problems in the British Isles, so long as plants are given adequate water in dry spells, which can frequently occur. On the other hand, winters can vary from the surprisingly mild (as in the mid-1970s) to the severe (as in 1962–63). Generally, the north and the hills are colder than the south and the valleys. However, in a very cold winter, with icy south-easterly winds from continental Europe, it is the east and south-east of England that experience the lowest temperatures and only sheltered spots in the west that escape the brutal cold. For further information, see the maps printed on the front endpapers of this book.

The southern hemisphere

Of the English-speaking temperate countries in the southern hemisphere, New Zealand has the most equable climate. Northland is the mildest part, having a subtropical climate with year-round growing season and very few frosts, though North Island is prone to tropical storms. The most severe conditions occur in the Southern Alps, but frost is liable to occur during a period of more than three months (and mostly five months or more) over the whole of South Island. New Zealand has a generally moist climate, and droughts are rare. Some parts are extremely wet, with 5,000 mm (200 in) or more of rain per year. The dryest parts are the east-central area of South Island. In the north, rain falls predominantly in the winter, summer rains becoming more and more predominant towards the south. See the climatic maps on the front endpapers.

Both Australia and South Africa show great climatic variations. In Australia, climatic zones range from the cool temperate climate of Tasmania (similar to that of north-western Europe) to the wet-and-dry tropical monsoon climate of the north and the wet tropical north-east. A vast central area is arid or semi-arid, but the most highly populated regions show two main climatic types: the south-east, including the whole coastal belt of New South Wales, has a warm temperate climate with mild winters and hot summers, and rain at all seasons. The extreme south-west, in the vicinity of Perth, and also the south-eastern part of South Australia, including Adelaide and the Spencer Gulf, have a Mediterranean climate with mild, wet winters and hot, dry summers. Most of Victoria lies between these two extremes, with some rain at all seasons but summer rainfall being rather erratic. To a greater or lesser extent, almost all of Australia is prone to droughts. See the climatic maps on the back endpapers.

South Africa similarly has extremes of desert and humid tropical climates, with an area around Cape Town having Mediterranean conditions. The large central plateau has a rather continental climate with fairly wide extremes of conditions. Frosts are common at night here between April and mid-October (though accompanied by warm days), while summer temperatures reach an average daily maximum of 30°C (86°F) or more over a wide area. Only the Port Elizabeth–East London coastal strip has appreciable rainfall throughout the year. The Cape Town area has very dry summers, but the rest of the country has most rain in summer. See the maps on the back endpapers.

Your plants and their environment

As can be seen from the details of the various processes constantly taking place in plants that are given in article on page 336, plants are in what scientists call dynamic equilibrium with their environment. They are continuously exchanging materials with their surroundings – the soil and air – and are affected by changes in them. Unlike animals, they cannot run away or shelter themselves from adverse conditions, but they do react in ways that help to ensure their own survival. For example, a plant reacts to drought by cutting down its water losses.

Such reactions may not be adequate, however, and the plant may still die. The gardener can clearly help here, and by understanding how the environment affects his plants can put his husbandry on a sound basis. He can also take steps to ensure that some of his plants' protective measures – such as premature ripening that causes leaf crops to bolt into seed – do not act to his own detriment.

Water balance

One of the most important things that must be kept in balance is the plant's intake of water by the roots and its loss by transpiration through the leaves (see p 336). This balance is affected by the amount of water in both soil and air, by air and soil temperature, by exposure to sunlight and wind, and by the efficiency of the root system. This last factor may be affected if the plant has recently been transplanted, if the roots have been attacked by pests or disease, or if insufficient food from the leaves is passed down to the roots to enable new growth to be made. Similarly, if a plant is not planted firmly, its root ball can remain isolated and the roots unable to benefit from moisture in the surrounding soil.

Wilting occurs when transpiration exceeds water intake. This may be only temporary, and can occur when the soil is quite moist. Large-leaved plants such as cabbages may flag at midday when the roots cannot absorb water quickly enough to replace that lost in hot dry atmospheric conditions. Watering the soil will have no immediate effect, and wilting can only be reduced by shading or spraying with a fine mist to reduce the temperature and increase the humidity. For the same reason, newly planted conifers (which are never completely dormant) should have their foliage sprayed regularly to counteract the effect of root disturbance.

Nevertheless, the availability of soil water is an important factor. Water is held more tightly by clay soils than sandy ones; this not only affects drainage (see p 331), but also the ease with which plants can absorb the water available. Where large amounts of inorganic fertilizers are used, especially in drier regions, excess salinity can be a problem as the fertilizer levels build up. The result is that, even if the soil does contain some moisture, the concentration of salts is higher in the soil than in the cell sap of the plants' roots. As a result, the roots cannot absorb even what soil water there is. So you must be sure to irrigate as necessary if you add inorganic fertilizer to the soil – though too much water can have the opposite effect, of washing valuable plant foods away.

Inadequate water results in the stomata (see p 336) closing to reduce transpiration even before wilting occurs, and this also reduces the intake of carbon dioxide so that the production of sugars by photosynthesis is cut down and all growth is checked. This is why it is important to irrigate the ground whenever water loss is greater than rainfall. The young growing plant, in particular, needs a lot of water, and any deficiency will stunt growth, harden the plant by producing tough fibrous tissues and precipitate premature flowering – for example, in lettuces, spinach and beetroot. Copious watering, if nitrates are available (see p 352), produces soft lush growth. So long as the plant manufactures enough sugars by photosynthesis, however, ripening and flowering will eventually occur. Bulbs, and also plants grown for their seeds, need less water as they ripen, and geraniums (pelargoniums) given too much water produce leafy growth at the expense of flowers. Excessive watering will also reduce the flavour of fruit and vegetables.

The effect of wind

As any housewife who hangs out her washing knows, wind greatly increases the evaporation of moisture, and in plants transpiration is much more rapid in windy conditions than when the air is still. Plants on exposed sites appear to grow away from the wind because they make no growth on the windward side. This is due to dehydration of the buds, and it may be essential to establish shelter before a garden can be made. However, the effect of solid barriers is to increase air turbulence and this may cause more damage. A permeable screen – whether an openwork fence or a hedge – reduces the wind speed and consequently reduces the rate of evaporation.

A combination of frost and wind increases transpiration in evergreens; they cannot obtain water from the soil due to the low temperatures, and they may die as a result. Pollination of fruit trees is also affected by wind, which dries up the flowers and prevents the flight of pollinating insects. And apart from the drastic damage caused by gales and hurricanes, continuous exposure to wind places a severe strain on plants and inhibits their growth.

Light, air and ripening

Plants need space not only for their roots to grow without excessive competition with neighbouring plants, but also to admit light and air. If they are crowded together they shade each other and the air between them becomes moist and stagnant. This provides an ideal environment for the spread of fungal diseases, which have no difficulty in penetrating the soft tissues that result from the reduced rate of transpiration caused by the humid conditions.

When a plant is exposed to full light it is able to manufacture the substances derived from sugars that are needed for ripening the tissues. This gives a greater resistance to disease and increased frost-hardiness, partly because of a greater concentration of sugars and other substances within the cell sap and also because of a reduction in the amount of water in the tissues. As a woody stem ripens the proportion of thick-walled and dead cells increases; these show much greater frost-hardiness than young sappy stems.

Plants grown in a greenhouse must be hardened off before being planted outside. This is a ripening process as the temperature and humidity are gradually reduced (see p 345), increasing the concentration of the cell sap. The plant also develops a thicker cuticle – the tough outer coating – on the leaves, reducing water loss by transpiration.

Light and growth

Plants grow because their cells multiply. This takes place mainly at the tips of roots and shoots, in buds (resulting in lengthening), and in certain layers of the stems and roots (resulting in thickening). Plant shoots grow away from the force of gravity, but the reverse is true of roots. Shoots grow faster in the dark because light produces a chemical in the plant's tissues that slows down cell multiplication. One result of this, however, is that plants appear to grow towards a source of light. This is because cells on the shaded side of the stem grow more quickly and 'push' the plant towards the light. As a result, seedlings grown near a window lean towards it and herbaceous plants close to a dark fence are 'drawn'.

In poor light, plants become leggy, and because sufficient food materials cannot be made flowering is also poor. A sunless summer will reduce the number of flower buds made by fruit trees, which provide the crop in the following year. On the other hand, a heavy crop will follow after a very warm sunny summer which enables both the current year's fruit to develop and many new buds to form. Certain plants are, however, adapted to grow in moist shade, where they benefit from the more humid atmosphere. Their leaves are usually thinner than those of plants which grow in open situations, and if grown in full sun they will quickly wilt.

Alpine plants in their natural environment are exposed to high light intensities, wind and, in many cases, quick-draining soil. They adapt by producing hairy or waxy coverings to their leaves, which may also be a silver colour to reflect sunlight and reduce transpiration. These plants quickly die in wet conditions although they can tolerate extremely low temperatures. Silvery foliage usually indicates that a plant requires a well-drained, sunny situation. You should also avoid hairy-leaved plants where the air is polluted with soot and chemicals that will clog the hairs.

Excess light is harmful to plants, especially those with thin leaves and those with variegated foliage. Variegation is due to the absence of chlorophyll in certain parts of the leaf. Scorching commonly occurs if these plants are grown in exposed positions. Copper-coloured and purple pigmentation are adaptations developed in conditions of strong light. The leaves of a copper beech or

Watering the garden

The most important way you can modify your plants' environment is by irrigation. Water falling on dry soil saturates each layer before moving down. A small amount wets only the top layer and in hot weather evaporates before being of any use to the plants. So it is better to water thoroughly once or twice a week than inadequately every day. To gauge how much water you have given from a sprinkler, stand a jam jar in the area being watered. The water level in the jar will tell you the amount in millimetres or inches. In dry conditions, the minimum worthwhile application is about 10 mm (½ in).

The size of the water drops and the rate of application are important. Large drops or too fast a rate of application will break down the soil crumbs into a wet slurry which eventually covers the surface. This becomes more and more liquid and on a slope erosion may occur. The breakdown of the crumb structure also results in 'capping' of the soil, interfering with the passage of water and air. All these problems are reduced by mulching (see p 334), which also reduces evaporation. Nevertheless, ensure that your watering equipment delivers a fine spray and is preferably adjustable.

Watering equipment

1 A watering can with a fine rose is essential for planting and watering small seedlings. Hand-held sprays 2 are useful for watering awkward places and spraying foliage in hot weather, but they need to be used for a considerable time to usefully moisten dry soil. The cheapest and simplest sprinklers 3 work in a similar way and cover only a small area at a time – up to about 6 m (20 ft) in diameter, or 30 m² (325 sq ft); they generally have a spike to stick in the ground. A rotating sprinkler 4 will cover an area up to 15 m (50 ft) across, or 175 m² (1,900 sq ft); it may or may not have adjustable nozzles. The oscillating type of sprinkler 5 may cover an even bigger area – up to 225 m² (2,400 sq ft) or even more – in an oval shape; some models have adjustable coverage. For the longest range, and especially to reach over tall plants, choose a pulsating sprinkler on a 1 m (3 ft) leg 6. A 'leaky hose' 7 is useful to install permanently in beds and borders where sprinklers cannot easily reach. For ease of use and storage, it is worth storing your hose on a wall-mounted reel 8 permanently connected to a water supply.

In hot, dry climates, make a shallow depression 9 around your plants – especially those that need most water – to direct water to their roots.

purple berberis that grow in shade are much greener than those in sun. To obtain the richest colour, such plants should always be grown in full sun. Golden-foliaged plants are similar in their requirements, as most will go green if grown in a shady spot.

The effect of day length

Plants not only respond to different light intensities but also to day length. Those that are natives of countries near to the equator experience days and nights of equal length, and many of them will not flower if the nights are short. Chrysanthemums flower as the nights increase in length in the autumn, but by subjecting them to artificial 'day' and 'night' conditions in a greenhouse they can be brought into flower at any time of year. On the other hand, many summer flowers of the temperate regions require long days and short nights, and annuals of this kind will not flower if sown late.

A combination of longer nights and lower temperatures prepares deciduous plants to shed their foliage in order to reduce transpiration. These are plants native to areas which experience cold winters, when the plant may be unable to obtain water from the soil. Many bulbous plants complete their growth before midsummer, when days are longest. Some of these are natives of countries with hot dry summers; others are plants of deciduous woodland which must complete their growth before the full leaf canopy develops and cuts down light intensity.

The effect of temperature

The most obvious effect of low temperatures is to slow down or stop almost all processes in plants, and in particular growth. This ceases in most plants when the temperature falls below about 5°C (41°F). Some alpine plants are exceptional, however, and the heat generated by their breakdown of food in respiration can be enough to melt thin snow in spring. Many plants must experience winter conditions before their resting period can be broken, although the temperature need only fall to 5°C (41°F). This is because inhibitory chemicals produced in the autumn to prevent premature bud burst are broken down, and as soon as conditions are suitable again the buds are able to grow. A similar thing happens with some seeds (see p 345).

Both excessive heat and excessive cold can harm plants. During transpiration, the plant is naturally cooled as water evaporates from the leaves. But if both soil and air conditions are very dry the plant may be unable to reduce its temperature, the cell sap will overheat and the cells die. This is quite apart from excessive water loss causing wilting, but the remedy is the same: cooling the plant by shading and by spraying with a fine mist of water.

Shading and spraying can also be used to reduce the effect of radiation frosts, which occur when there is no cloud cover to reflect heat back to the earth. These are most damaging when they occur after warm spring and autumn days. For further information, see page 354.

Choosing your plants

If you want the best results from your horticultural efforts, take as much care over the choice of your plants, seeds, bulbs and other stock as over their subsequent planting and care. In that way, you will have a head-start in the quest for healthy, sturdy plants – which will, in turn, give you the best display and best crop yields.

The first consideration in choosing plants is their suitability for the climate of your garden and for your soil conditions. For example, it really is important to know the acidity of your soil (see p 332) as there are many shrubs and other plants that will not tolerate alkaline conditions. It is possible to overcome these problems with raised beds and containers, but you would do far better to select plants that will grow happily in the naturally occurring conditions; these will demand much less attention and, more important, will fit in with other plants in the neighbourhood. The charts beginning on page 386 give details of the needs and special features of a wide range of decorative plants.

A second general principle is to buy from growers and suppliers who have a reputation to maintain – and do not be afraid to complain if you receive poor-quality stock. Healthy, well-grown plants may cost more initially than 'special offers', but the time and effort you expend on growing the plants can be wasted on shoddy material. Also, stock from disreputable sources may introduce serious pests and diseases to your garden. One safeguard when choosing a particular kind or variety of plant is the mention in catalogues of any awards it may have received from expert judges (see p 343). But such an award is no guarantee that a particular example of that variety will have been grown well. Be your own judge when it comes to the final selection.

Deciding what to buy

With some plants, choosing which precise form to buy is easy: only the natural wild type, or species, is available. With others, you may be faced with a bewildering range of varieties and cultivars – all with apparent advantages. Quite apart from differences in colour and flower form, they may be taller, dwarfer, larger-flowered, earlier, later, more strongly scented, hardier or better suited to certain other climatic conditions – or, in the case of fruit and vegetables, may mature at a certain part of the season, have a particularly high yield or good flavour, or any number of other characteristics. The only way out of this dilemma is to find out about the available varieties and decide which best suit your own garden conditions and needs. Where necessary, seek the advice of reputable suppliers.

In any case, you should not be content to select plants from illustrations in books and catalogues. Try to see them growing. Visit gardens – both public and private, when these are open to visitors – and ask about plants that are not labelled. Visit nurseries and garden centres. Many seedsmen have trial grounds where you can see new and established varieties growing. A visit to the fields of a specialist rose nursery after a few days of wind and rain will soon show you those varieties that drop their dead petals cleanly and do not 'ball' and rot in bud in wet weather. In the same way, visits to gardens out of season will give you ideas for plants to extend the period of interest in your own garden.

National and regional horticultural and agricultural shows generally provide shop-windows for the bigger nurserymen, and their staff will be present to give information and advice. Remember, however, that plants will have been specially prepared for the early summer shows and some will be in flower earlier (or later) than usual. The more specialist flowers – dahlias, chrysanthemums, sweet peas and so on – and also the annuals will have received exhibition treatment, while the flowers of bush roses will have been as carefully groomed and prepared for show as any entrant in the 'Miss World' contest. However, the trees, shrubs, herbaceous plants and alpines should present a realistic picture.

Where to buy

Garden centres that specialize in container-grown plants usually offer a reasonable selection, and you have the advantage of being able to see and select your plants, even when they are in flower. The rarer species will probably not be available, however, and you may even be restricted to a few of the most popular varieties of better-known plants. These are not necessarily the best, and if you want a particular variety that is not among the commonest you will have to go to a specialist nursery. (One British tree and shrub nursery – admittedly one of the biggest in the world – has 14,000 species and varieties in cultivation, a figure many times greater than that of a big garden centre.) A further advantage of the specialist is that staff are on hand who have a far deeper knowledge of their plants than is usual in garden centres.

However, the advantage of choosing your own plants, and of not having to wait until the dormant season for delivery, is considerable. Plants may be cheaper in a garden centre, and

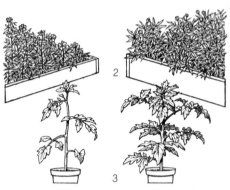

Choosing the best stock
With most types of plants, there are clear signs that distinguish poorly grown plants (shown here on the left of each pair) from good specimens. With a tree lifted from open ground 1, look for an undamaged and well-branched fibrous root system and a shapely, evenly branched crown. A box of bedding plants 2 should be deep enough to hold good roots, and the plants should not be stunted or in flower. With tomato plants 3, choose

there are no delivery charges to pay. But do make sure that container-grown plants really have been grown in the container and have not just been potted up for sale. Lift the plant very gently by its stem (near soil-level); the container should come too. If there is any movement, you will not be able to transplant it with an intact soil ball – an essential when moving plants during the growing season.

Buying trees and shrubs

Standard trees grown in open ground will be on sale in the dormant season. Choose those with a well-shaped crown, a strong leading shoot, no damaged branches, and a good

---

Hybrid plants

Many plants are described in catalogues as hybrids. Any plant whose parents are distinctly different is a hybrid, and may show some of the characteristics of each, possibly with some features of its own. Commonly – but not inevitably – it may have what is called hybrid vigour; that is, it grows more vigorously, often with bigger flowers, fruit and so on.

This is most pronounced in F1 hybrids (often written F_1), which are the offspring of a cross between two pure-bred strains. (F1 is simply shorthand for first filial generation). The F1 hybrid cannot be reproduced from its own seed, but only by repeating the original cross. Since this often has to be carried out by hand-pollination, F1 hybrid seed is generally more expensive than seed from open-pollinated plants. The plants it produces may be 'bigger and better', but some gardeners prefer 'old-fashioned' types which may have more scent or flavour, or be more delicate or less uniform in colour and so on.

Some plants are described as tetraploid. This means that they have twice as many chromosomes – the tiny bodies in the plants' cells that govern heredity and growth – as normal. The result is usually exceptionally large plants. In the case of triploid fruit trees, the number of chromosomes is 1½ times the normal. This again gives bigger yields, but one side-effect is that the pollen is generally completely sterile – the tree cannot pollinate itself or other trees. Since even many normal (diploid) varieties are self-sterile – they can pollinate other varieties but not themselves – two different diploid trees plus the triploid should be planted to ensure pollination and fruiting of all three.

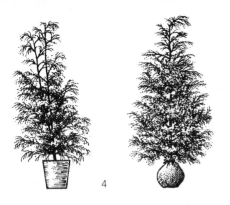

the sturdy, leafy, dark green specimen in preference to one that is tall, thin and spindly, with long internodes and limp foliage. Conifers **4** should not have forked leading shoots, unevenly spaced branches or dead foliage; avoid any that are loose in their containers; balled and burlapped plants should be firmly tied in sacking. With a container-grown flowering shrub **5**, choose a well-branched bushy plant with plenty of good foliage that is not spindly, stunted or pot-bound.

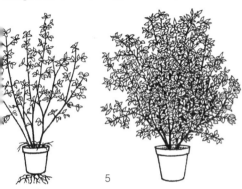

Trials and awards

Garden plants of all kinds are regularly tested and compared in trials organized in many countries. The best receive awards, and this fact is often mentioned in nurserymen's and seedmen's catalogues, together with the date.

Trials of flower and vegetable seeds are held at a number of centres spread over a country or even a continent. The All Britain Trials, for example, are conducted at more than a dozen places in Britain, while many of these centres also take part in the European Fleuroselect Trials, which are also held at centres in Denmark, France, the Netherlands, Sweden, Switzerland and West Germany. In the same way, trials are held at centres in various parts of the United States for the All-America Selections.

Judges gauge the performance of each cultivar or variety at each centre, the points gained at each centre being added together. Awards or selections are given – in some cases with gold, silver and bronze medals – on the basis of the total score. Winning plants can be considered to be of exceptional quality and have proved themselves over the range of growing conditions spanned by the trials.

All types of plants – flowers, fruit, vegetables, shrubs, trees and others – are also eligible for awards given by the Royal Horticultural Society (RHS) of Britain. The awards are given on the recommendation of specialist committees, who examine specimens submitted. The highest award, only given to plants of 'great excellence', is the First Class Certificate (often abbreviated in catalogues to FCC). Plants judged 'meritorious' to the society's very stringent standards are given the Award of Merit (AM).

The RHS also runs field trials of flowers, fruit and vegetables, and the best plants may receive a Highly Commended (HC) or Commended (C) award. Finally, and best of all, established decorative plants that are judged to be 'of good constitution and have been proved excellent for ordinary garden decoration' may receive the Award of Garden Merit (AGM); this implies that the plant has shown its value as a garden plant over a number of years.

Other societies may also give awards to plants, including various specialist societies. In some cases, however, these plants may be more suited to exhibition than garden decoration.

---

fibrous root system. The trees should have been lifted regularly in the nursery to encourage the development of fibrous roots, and any with badly torn or damaged roots should be rejected. There is no long-term advantage in buying 'heavy standard' trees, which, because of possible vandalism, have to be planted in streets and parks; they are expensive and difficult to establish. Young healthy specimens grow away more quickly and eventually overtake the heavy standards, and losses are much less likely. Conifers should be sold in containers or with the roots balled in sacking. Make sure that the foliage clothes the plants to soil level. Badly-grown plants lose their lower branches and develop an unsightly 'leg'.

Broadly the same rules apply to container-grown shrubs. With both these and young trees, check that there are no obvious blemishes on foliage or stems which may indicate disease. The growth should be well spaced, firm and ripe, and there should be plenty of leaves and new shoots. Thin, hard, stunted plants with sparse foliage have been starved. The largest plant is not necessarily the best: look for a good overall shape.

The roots of all lifted plants should be protected by damp straw or wet sacking. Do not accept plants without such protection.

Buying herbaceous and bedding plants

Herbaceous plants may be bought in containers at any time, or in spring and autumn with their roots packed in moss and plastic film. These suffer from neglect in many stores and garden centres. Reject those with blanched leaves and stems (caused by lack of light and too high temperatures) or with decaying leaves and shoots.

Summer bedding plants are sold in vast quantities, often long before the risk of night frosts is over. The plants should have been hardened off before sale by gradually acclimatizing them to conditions in the open. 'Soft' plants which will be damaged if planted outside are generally a bright green colour and have soft, fleshy shoots and leaves. 'Hardened' plants are a darker green and look sturdy. Avoid plants sold on draughty street-corners or from stands exposed to cold winds.

Boxes of plants in flower look attractive and sell well, but avoid these as flowering indicates a precocious maturity brought about by some check to growth. Well-grown plants, not in flower, will transplant better and grow into much stronger specimens which will give a far longer season of flower. Some biennials for spring bedding, such as wallflowers, are field-grown and lifted for sale in autumn; make sure that the ones you buy have an adequate root system and are not too limp or they will never recover.

Buying seeds, bulbs and tubers

The seeds of many plants keep for a number of years, but for best results obtain fresh seed. (In many countries, seed packets must be dated by law.) All except large seeds with tough coats deteriorate rapidly in damp conditions, so it is an advantage to buy them in hermetically sealed packets. Do not open the packets until you want to use them, and keep any unused seed in a dry, cool place. Pelleted seed (see p115) of plants whose seeds are very small is easier to handle, and you will be able to sow more thinly, thus wasting fewer plants; also, fungicide in the coating may help ensure healthy germination. However, pel-

leted seed is more expensive and you get fewer seeds per packet, and it is essential that the soil remains moist to break down the clay coating and ensure germination.

When buying bulbs, corms and tubers, ensure that they are plump, firm and free from any sign of mould, rotting or mildew. Look for any sign of attack by boring insects. For further information, see page 110.

Buying fruit and vegetables

It is especially necessary to buy certified disease-free 'seed' potatoes, strawberry plants and fruit trees and bushes from reliable sources, as all these plants can be infected with virus diseases. These may not be visible at the time of purchase but they seriously affect cropping potential and will be a source of infection to other plants. In Britain, the Ministry of Agriculture issues lists of nurserymen that supply certified stock. When buying seedling plants of such vegetables as tomatoes, the same rules apply as for buying bedding plants: choose sturdy, dark green specimens that do not look 'drawn' and have been properly hardened off.

The eventual size and vigour of fruit trees is an important consideration; this depends on the rootstock onto which they are grafted, and a good nurseryman will be able to advise on the best rootstock for each purpose. He will also suggest suitable cultivars to ensure pollination. Tell him if you have a low-lying garden that forms a frost pocket, or are subject to late frosts for other reasons, so that he can suggest late-flowering cultivars that will escape damage. Then you can be sure that your choice will have the best possible chance of giving you good yields.

Growing plants from seed

The cheapest way of introducing new plants to your garden is to grow them from seed. In the case of many types of plants, notably hardy annuals and most vegetables, it is the only way. In other cases, such as half-hardy annuals and bedding plants, it offers a far wider range than can be bought ready-grown at a garden centre. At the other extreme, it may also be the only way to acquire extreme rarities among plants such as alpines that even specialist nurserymen do not stock.

The majority of plants can be raised from seed, but the resulting progeny may not always be replicas of their parents. You may have discovered this if you have sown seed collected from a particularly fine lupin or a named delphinium cultivar. The disappointing results have sometimes been blamed on the bees! Many of the best garden plants have been produced by the deliberate or accidental crossing of different strains of the same species, or by a cross between species. If the seeds produced by these hybrids are grown, they seldom 'come true'. Only by propagating from cuttings or similar vegetative methods (see pp 346 to 350), or by repeating the original cross, can results be duplicated. The latter is true in particular of F1 hybrids (see p 342).

Some plants can, however, be grown satisfactorily from home-saved seed. These include many alpines, some annuals and biennials, and herbaceous plants and shrubs that are true species. Gather the ripe seed-heads into paper bags on a dry warm day and hang them up in a dry airy place; later packet and label the seeds which are shed. Use paper bags and packets rather than plastic, because the seeds lose water as they dry and would go mouldy in plastic bags. Deal with berries and fruits as described below.

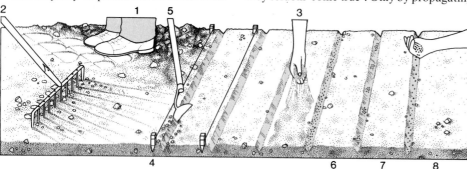
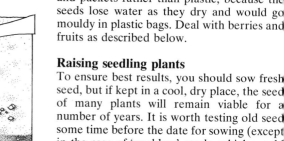

Sowing seed in open ground

Ground is ready for sowing as soon as earth no longer sticks to your shoes. 1 Break down clods and level and firm the ground by treading. 2 Rake the soil to a fine tilth. If the seeds are to be sown in drills (furrows) 15 cm (6 in) or less apart, broadcast a base dressing of fertilizer and rake in; with wider spacing, apply fertilizer beside the drills 3. 4 Mark out the row with a tight garden line. 5 Make a shallow drill of even depth and width alongside this with a draw hoe or sharp stick. Most normal-sized seeds need drills about 1 cm (½ in) deep, but larger seeds may need to be sown 2.5 cm (1 in) deep. In dry weather and for pelleted seeds water the drill well before sowing.

With plants susceptible to damping off or root pests, dress the drill with a soil fungicide or insecticide respectively. 6 Sow seeds thinly along the drill or 7 place larger and pelleted seeds in groups (stations) of two or three corresponding to the final spacing of the plants; later thin out all but the strongest seedling at each station. It helps to mix very fine seed with silver sand or peat to aid thin sowing; sprinkle the mixture along the drill. Seed-dispensing devices are available, but you can sow most seeds from the packet or by hand 8. Sow large seeds in individual holes made with a dibber or stick. Finally cover all seeds lightly with fine soil and firm with the back of a rake. For how to sow seed tapes, see page 115.

Raising seedling plants

To ensure best results, you should sow fresh seed, but if kept in a cool, dry place, the seed of many plants will remain viable for a number of years. It is worth testing old seed some time before the date for sowing (except in the case of 'problem' seeds, which would take too long; see below). Then you can avoid wasting valuable growing time. Place a few seeds – 10 to 15 of normal types – on damp cotton wool in a closed clear plastic box. Keep it warm. If no germination occurs within two weeks the seed is probably dead. If only half germinate, they are 50 per cent viable and should be sown more thickly than usual.

All seeds require moisture, air and a certain amount of warmth for germination. A few, such as petunias and nicotianas, germinate best in the light, but others prefer shading. The temperature needed varies with the type of plant. Hardy annuals need only low temperatures, so they are normally sown in the open ground in spring when the ground is workable and not waterlogged. The site

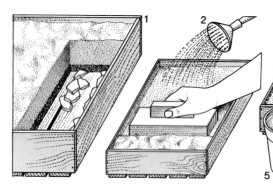
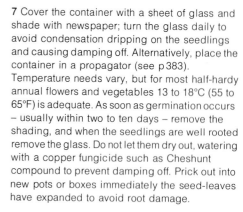

Raising seedlings in containers

1 Wooden seed trays (flats) and clay pots need a layer of broken crocks over the drainage holes, followed by a thin layer of fibrous peat; these are unnecessary in plastic containers with many small drainage holes. Fill the container with seedling mixture (see opposite) and tap firmly to settle it. Scrape off any surplus with a board to leave it full but level. 2 Use your fingers or a board with a handle to firm down the mixture without compacting it; it should be level and about 1 cm (½ in) below the rim. Water well with a fine rose and allow to drain thoroughly for several hours; the mixture should be just moist.
Sow the seeds very thinly. 3 Larger seeds and

pellets should be spaced about 5 cm (2 in) apart in each direction. When sowing minute dark seeds, such as those of begonias, sifting a thin layer of silver sand over the surface shows up the seeds; these then need no other covering since they settle between the grains of sand. 4 With normal-sized seeds, cover very lightly with more seedling mixture shaken from a 2 mm (⅛ in) sieve; it is worth practising this on a sheet of paper, as the seeds should be covered to a depth equal to only about twice their own diameter. 5 You can sow large seeds in pairs in individual clay, plastic or peat pots, or in peat blocks (which are sold compressed, and expand when wet). 6 When the seedlings emerge thin out the weaker of each pair.

7 Cover the container with a sheet of glass and shade with newspaper; turn the glass daily to avoid condensation dripping on the seedlings and causing damping off. Alternatively, place the container in a propagator (see p 383). Temperature needs vary, but for most half-hardy annual flowers and vegetables 13 to 18°C (55 to 65°F) is adequate. As soon as germination occurs – usually within two to ten days – remove the shading, and when the seedlings are well rooted remove the glass. Do not let them dry out, watering with a copper fungicide such as Cheshunt compound to prevent damping off. Prick out into new pots or boxes immediately the seed-leaves have expanded to avoid root damage.

should be open, sunny and well drained. The ground should have been prepared by digging the previous autumn and trampled and raked to a crumbly tilth before sowing. Once the seedlings are big enough to handle easily, thin out the weaker ones to leave the sturdiest to grow on at the distance apart advised on the seed packet or in literature. Allowing the plants to grow too closely only results in weak, spindly specimens and poor crop yields, and increases the risk of disease.

Half-hardy annuals can be sown outdoors once there is no more danger of frost, but for an earlier display in areas with cool climates they are generally sown in pots or trays in a greenhouse, propagator or heated frame (see p 380) at a temperature of 16 to 18°C (61 to 65°F). Such vegetables as tomatoes are treated in the same way. Do not sow too early, as half-hardy annuals should not be planted out before all risk of frost is over (although temporary cloche protection can be given if necessary) and they suffer if held in the boxes. It is better to grow plants quickly for eight weeks before planting out than to sow too early and have rootbound hardening plants which never grow away so well.

Once big enough to handle, the seedlings of plants raised under glass are pricked out about 5 cm (2 in) apart in containers, to give them room to grow. When they are growing well and about three weeks before planting out, the seedlings must be hardened off – gradually accustomed to cooler temperatures. First place the boxes in a cold frame which is given slight ventilation by day but closed at night. Gradually increase ventilation until the frame is open day and night.

The seeds of hardy perennials, alpines and shrubs vary greatly in their needs. Some germinate best at a temperature of up to 20°C

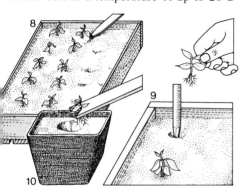

Pricking out seedlings
Prepare pots or boxes as before, but use potting mixture. **8** Lift the seedlings carefully with a pointed flat stick or a kitchen fork; handle only by the seed-leaves. Very tiny seedlings can be held in a notched plant label. **9** Make holes about 2.5 cm (1 in) deep with a small dibber or thick pencil. Leave 5 to 8 cm (2 to 3 in) between each seedling to allow sturdy plants to develop. Carefully place the seedling's roots in the hole and gently firm down with the dibber. Water with a fine rose and shade lightly until new growth is apparent. **10** Seedlings can be planted singly in peat pots; the roots grow through the peat and can eventually be planted out pot and all.

(68°F), while others are best kept in a cold frame or sown in open ground. You should follow the seedsman's advice.

Dealing with 'problem' seeds
The seed of many hardy shrubs and trees needs special treatment if it is to germinate. This may involve exposure to winter cold – either outdoors or in a refrigerator – possibly combined with abrasion of the seed coat so that it can absorb moisture. If the seeds are thus prepared as soon as the fruits ripen (commonly in autumn) and stored outdoors until spring they will then be ready for sowing.

You can separate seeds from soft, fleshy fruits by rubbing them through a fine nylon sieve. Wash the seed, dry it and store it in well-drained containers mixed with sharp sand. Berries, such as those of holly, hawthorn and cotoneasters, and also rose hips contain seeds with very tough coats that must be softened by stratification. The simplest way to deal with them is to mix the fruit with very coarse sharp sand (three parts sand to one part seed) on a hard surface and then 'mill' the

Seedling and potting mixtures
When raising plants from seed under glass, it is best to use a special soil mixture, or compost, that is sterile and has a predetermined fertilizer level. When growing on the seedlings in pots, potting mixtures with higher fertilizer levels are used, the 'strongest' being suitable for permanently potted plants. You can buy such mixtures in bags at garden centres and shops; they are based either on loam or on peat (with or without the addition of sand or vermiculite). The latter type are sometimes called soil-less mixtures.

Excellent loam-based mixtures are prepared by various manufacturers to formulae devised by the John Innes Horticultural Institute, in Britain. There is a John Innes seed mixture and a series of potting mixtures. John Innes no. 1 potting mixture is suitable for young seedlings, but for growing more vigorous plants, such as chrysanthemums, in pots, use no. 2; no. 3 (which has treble the fertilizer level of no. 1) is suitable for large plants in tubs. Lime-free versions are available for lime-hating plants.

Similar ranges of peat-based mixtures are available, many based on formulae devised in the United States at the University of California (incorporating sand), and at Cornell University (using vermiculite). One reason for their increasing popularity is the shortage of good loam. It is possible to make up your own mixtures of either type, but it is not worth the time and trouble for most amateurs. A reasonable compromise is to buy packs of specially formulated base fertilizer and blend it with medium- to fine-grade peat, adding one-third of its bulk of sand if you wish.

fruit with a smooth brick or a plasterer's float. This rubs away the flesh and begins the abrasion of the seed coat. The whole messy mixture of seed, sand and the remains of the fruit should then be put into perforated tins and overwintered in a cold place outside, protected from mice and birds with wire netting. Untreated, such seeds may take two to three years to germinate.

A few seeds of ordinary annuals also need to experience 'winter' before they will germinate. This process of vernalization involves exposing the seed after it has been sown to a period of cold. *Molucella laevis* (bells of Ireland) sometimes responds to this treatment. The very hard coats of seeds such as those of sweet peas need chipping or abrasion to allow the penetration of water. A quick way is to rub the seed between two pieces of coarse sandpaper, taking care of course not to damage the seed itself. The seed of beet and spinach contains an inhibitor which must be washed away before germination can occur. Soaking the seed for a few minutes in lukewarm water before sowing will speed germination.

Ferns from spores
Ferns do not produce seeds, but make spores in spore capsules on the back of the fronds. You can obtain the spores by picking a suitable frond in late summer and laying it between two sheets of white paper in a dry, warm place. The dust-like spores should fall onto the paper. Prepare pans or trays of loam-based seedling mixture and sterilize with boiling water. When cold, sprinkle the spores very thinly on the surface from the tip of a penknife blade. Cover with glass immediately and put in a shady place in a greenhouse, cold frame or indoors. If at any point it is necessary to water, stand the container in a bowl of a very weak (palest pink) potassium permanganate solution. (This is a disinfectant.)

After two to three months, a green film should form on the surface of the potting mixture, and after a further three to four months this will have developed into small heart-shaped prothalli. From these, in a further three months or so, tiny ferns develop; prick these out 2.5 cm (1 in) apart in sterilized pans or trays of potting mixture and grow on in shade. Keep covered with glass right up to this stage, and water from below. Once new fronds appear, gradually harden off. Transfer to individual pots and pot on progressively until, a year or more after sowing, they are ready to be planted out.

Multiplying your plants

If you want to quickly and easily increase your stock of plants – particularly if you want to duplicate exactly perennial plants that are already in your garden – the answer is to use plants' natural ability to propagate themselves vegetatively. This means growing a whole new plant from a portion of the parent. Anyone who has tried to rid a border of a perennial weed such as a dock or dandelion has seen this in action: even a small piece of root is enough to regenerate a whole new specimen. Other plants, such as ivy, develop roots on their stems and these, if severed from the parent plant and planted, can continue a separate existence. Strawberry runners form whole plantlets on the end, and these too grow roots and can carry on independently.

Softwood cuttings
1 Take a section of tip growth and trim immediately below a node (leaf joint or bud, often with a swelling of the stem), using a sharp knife or razor blade. Its length may range from 2.5 to 8 cm (1 to 3 in).
2 Remove the lower one or two pairs of leaves, then dip the cut end in hormone rooting powder, shake off the excess and insert in a hole made with a small dibber or sharp stick in the sand and peat mixture in a propagator or mist unit. Alternatively, 3 insert in a pot or seed tray of rooting medium, standing this directly over a source of heat (not on top of the peat and sand in a propagator).
4 Cover with a clear plastic cover to increase humidity. Allow geranium (pelargonium) cuttings to dry before insertion to avoid fungal infection; they need no mist treatment.

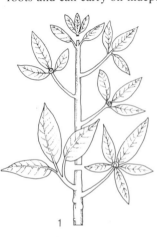  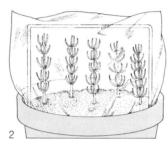

Semi-hardwood cuttings
1 Take terminal growth, cutting well into ripening wood. Trim below a node as with softwood cuttings and remove any soft tip growth above a bud, leaving a finished length of 8 cm (3 in).
2 Alternatively, take similar-sized lateral shoots with a heel of old wood attached, by pulling gently from the plant; trim off ragged tissue from the heel. With both types, remove the lower pair of leaves. 3 Insert four or five cuttings around the sides of an 8 cm (3 in) pot of a mixture of peat and sand. Water well and cover with a clear plastic bag supported internally with a bent wire or two canes; or use a clear plastic pot-cover. Alternatively, insert the cuttings in seed trays of rooting medium, in rows 4 cm (1½ in) apart. Place the trays in a light, closed garden frame; keep them moist.

Gardeners can make use of this ability by taking portions of plants' stems, roots or even leaves as cuttings, and treating them – generally by inserting the ends in a suitable medium, such as a mixture of sand and peat – so that they form roots. The plants can then be potted up individually or planted out and grown on to make substantial specimens. The plant produced is identical with the parent, so this is a way of duplicating hybrid plants that are sterile or do not come true from seed (see p 342). Another advantage is that a larger plant is obtained more quickly than would be possible from seed. But plants chosen for propagation must be healthy; virus diseases are transmitted with other characteristics.

Although taking cuttings is one of the most familiar forms of vegetative propagation, it is not the only method. When you divide a clump of Michaelmas daisies, this is a form of vegetative propagation. So is the multiplication of bulbous plants from the small bulbils that grow around the parent, and the chopping of a 'seed' potato or an iris rhizome into a number of pieces, each of which forms a new plant. In some cases, suckers and other types of side growth can be detached from a parent plant together with already-formed roots. These methods are very useful for plants that are difficult to propagate from cut-

tings. Finally, in the technique of layering, a shoot is induced to form roots while still attached to its parent and is only then detached and grown on; the parent plant supports the part being propagated until it has its own root system. Grafting is also a form of propagation (see p 350).

Softwood and semi-ripe cuttings

Techniques of taking and rooting stem cuttings differ according to whether the stems used are soft and fleshy, have begun to ripen

Internodal cuttings
Take cuttings of clematis in early summer, choosing young growth that is about to ripen.
1 Trim at the bottom 5 cm (2 in) below a node and at the top just above the same node, leaving a pair of leaves attached, together with their buds. 2 Slit the cutting vertically downwards between the pair of buds to produce two cuttings from each section. 3 Insert up to the bud in peat and sand in an 8 cm (3 in) pot. Water and place in a light closed propagating case over bottom heat.

and become woody, or have completed this process of ripening. The different methods suit different kinds of plants and different rooting methods. Whatever type is used, the cuttings must be taken from vigorous, healthy plants growing in good, well-lit conditions and collected from the younger parts of the plant. Collect soft and semi-ripe cuttings in the early part of the day in plastic bags to prevent excessive loss of water.

The first general need is a suitable rooting medium. This must be open and well drained, and many gardeners use a mixture of equal parts (by bulk) of moss peat and sharp sand, while the John Innes formula for rooting cuttings consists of one part loam, two parts peat and three parts coarse sand; no fertilizer is needed. With many plants you can speed rooting by dipping the lower end in hormone rooting powder (available in various proprietary forms) before inserting it in the rooting medium. Finally, with softwood and semi-hardwood cuttings, water loss by transpiration through the leaves (see p 336) is great, so a moist atmosphere is generally needed to prevent wilting. The best method is with a mist unit, but this is expensive, and a propagating case is a good alternative; both are described on page 383. With many plants you can achieve success with simple clear plastic covers to fit over pots or seed-trays, while covering the whole pot in a clear plastic bag serves the same purpose. Unlike the germination of seeds, the rootings of cuttings needs light (but not direct sunlight) so that the

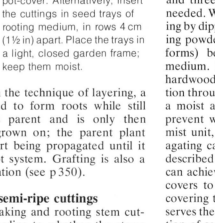 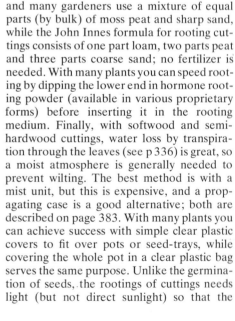

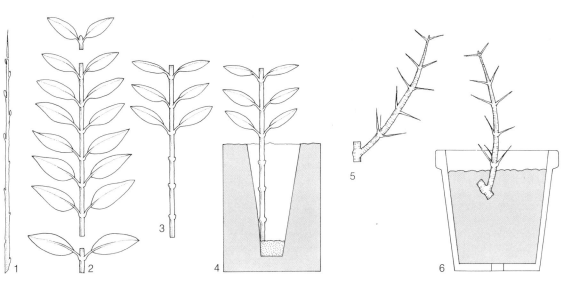

leaves can go on producing food by photosynthesis (see p 336); this is particularly true of softwood cuttings which contain very little of the food necessary to make new growth.

You can take softwood cuttings from early spring until late summer, when conifers root most satisfactorily. Many perennials and sub-shrubs can also be increased this way. Cuttings vary in size from 8 cm (3 in) down to 2.5 cm (1 in) for some alpines. Trim the bottom immediately below a bud or leaf joint, using a sharp knife or razor blade. Geraniums (pelargoniums) root very easily from softwood cuttings, and do not need mist treatment. Most others need both moisture and heat. Basal cuttings are softwood cuttings taken from shoots arising around the base of a plant in spring. Delphiniums and lupins are propagated in this way before their stems become hollow, and similar cuttings are taken from chrysanthemum stools and dahlia tubers brought into growth in spring after overwintering indoors (see pp 186 and 188).

Semi-ripe cuttings are taken from deciduous and evergreen shrubs, heathers, many conifers and climbers when the young growth has partially ripened and is beginning to become woody. The time for this is from midsummer to early autumn, depending on climate and the particular plant concerned. The trimmed length of the cutting should be about 8 cm (3 in), except for heathers, which should be 2.5 to 5 cm (1 to 2 in) long. The cutting can be of terminal growth or of a lateral shoot, both non-flowering, taken with a heel of old wood from the main stem attached. Generally, cuttings should be trimmed at the bottom just below a node (leaf joint or bud). Clematis are among the few plants where cuttings should be trimmed between two nodes. All these partially ripened cuttings contain some reserves of food, and can be rooted without heat or mist treatment. If your soil is well drained, you can root them outdoors under a white plastic tunnel; otherwise use a propagator, pot-cover or plastic bag.

As soon as softwood or semi-hardwood cuttings have rooted well, you should transfer them to individual 8 cm (3 in) pots of peat- or loam-based potting mixture and water them. Place them in a greenhouse or closed frame for a few days to recover, then grow on in a cold frame before planting out in spring.

Hardwood cuttings
Take these in late autumn, after leaf-fall in the case of deciduous subjects, choosing well-ripened wood of the current year's growth.
1 Remove soft tip growth above a bud and make the bottom cut immediately below a node; average length is 20 to 30 cm (8

Hardwood cuttings
These can be taken from a wide range of trees, shrubs (including many shrub, old-fashioned, miniature and Floribunda roses) and bush fruits in late autumn or (in mild climates) winter. Choose plump, well-ripened wood of the current season's growth, remove soft tip growth and trim at the bottom immediately below a bud. The length varies according to the plant. Apple rootstock cuttings are generally 75 cm (2½ ft) long, for example, while poplar, willow and privet are about 30 cm (12 in), currants, gooseberries and forsythia 20 cm (8 in), and berberis and weigela only 10 cm (4 in).

In regions with moderate climates where very hard frosts are rare, you can insert the larger cuttings in a slit made with a spade in well-drained ground and part-filled with coarse sand. If the soil is poorly drained, however, pack the prepared cuttings in bundles in peat and sand and store them over winter in a well-drained but cold situation in the shade of a building. In countries with severe winters, the cuttings can be prepared in autumn, dipped into hormone rooting powder and the bottoms wrapped in plastic sheeting with damp peat. Store them between 0 and 4°C (32 and 39°F) until ground conditions improve in

to 12 in). If the plant is to be grown on a short stem, or leg – as with red currants and gooseberries – remove the lower buds, leaving just the top four. 2 With such evergreens as privet, trim in the same way and 3 remove the leaves from the lower half to two-thirds of the cutting. 4 With a spade, make a slit of suitable depth in well-drained open ground. Pour about 2.5 cm (1 in) of coarse sand into the bottom and insert the cuttings to half to two-thirds their length. Tread in firmly and water if necessary. 5 With thin shoots, such as those of deciduous berberis, take 'mallet' cuttings with a short section of main stem. 6 Insert these and other small cuttings in pots of peat and sand.

the spring. Even if planted in the autumn, roots will probably not develop until spring. The cuttings should then be watered if the weather is dry. During the following autumn (a year after taking the cuttings), they can be transplanted to a nursery bed to grow on.

The smaller hardwood cuttings are best rooted in peat and sand in an open frame and potted on as for semi-hardwood cuttings. Where stems are very thin (as with some berberis), you are more likely to succeed if you take 'mallet' cuttings – short side shoots similar to heel cuttings with a small 'hammerhead' piece of the main stem attached – and insert these in peat and sand.

Eye and leaf-bud cuttings
These methods are very similar, and involve using only a very short piece of stem with a bud attached. With leaf-bud cuttings, a portion of semi-ripe stem with a leaf and its bud is taken and inserted in rooting medium. This is useful for camellias. With eye cuttings – used mainly for grape vines – sections of ripe wood of the previous season with a good bud are taken in late winter (when the plants have no leaves). The sections are laid horizontally on the surface of sand and peat, bud on top, in a warm greenhouse or propagator./continued

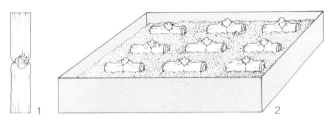
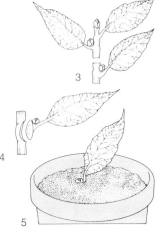

Eye and leaf-bud cuttings
1 Take cuttings from the previous season's wood of grape vines in late winter, trimming 2 cm (¾ in) either side of a plump bud. 2 Lay them on sand and peat, the buds uppermost, and keep warm and moist. 3 Take similar cuttings from camellias in spring, but with a leaf as well as a bud attached; 4 alternatively, leave only a small heal of wood attached to the leaf and bud. 5 Insert in peat and sand in a propagator over heat.

Multiplying your plants (continued)

Root cuttings

Fleshy-rooted herbaceous plants and trees and shrubs that tend to produce suckers can be propagated by root cuttings, so long as they are not grafted onto a different rootstock. With the smaller types, this generally involves lifting the whole plant during the dormant season – usually between autumn and early spring, but in late summer in the case of the oriental poppy (*Papaver orientale*) – and cutting sections of root. You can expose the roots of trees and cut them in the same way. Pot the root sections in peat and sand or potting mixture, burying the large cuttings vertically but the smaller ones taken from such plants as phlox and *Primula denticulata* horizontally and shallowly. Water them and place them in a cold frame to grow. Further suitable plants include anchusa, *Anemone hupehensis japonica,* sea holly (*Eryngium* spp), *Catananche caerulea,* lupins, verbascum, *Romneya coulteri* and, among trees, *Paulownia tomentosa* and the sumach, *Rhus typhina*.

Bulbs, corms and tubers

Bulbs and corms multiply naturally. The young bulbs of daffodils, for example, which develop as offsets beside the parent bulb, may be removed and planted separately. The very

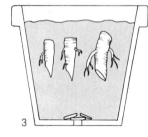
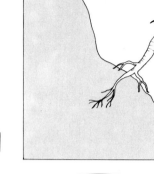
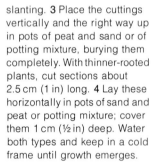

Root cuttings
1 Lift the crowns of fleshy-rooted perennials when they are dormant or 2 expose their roots; the latter method is suitable for some trees. Cut sections of healthy roots about 1 cm (½ in) thick and 8 cm (3 in) long; make the top cut directly across the root, the lower one slanting. 3 Place the cuttings vertically and the right way up in pots of peat and sand or of potting mixture, burying them completely. With thinner-rooted plants, cut sections about 2.5 cm (1 in) long. 4 Lay these horizontally in pots of sand and peat or potting mixture; cover them 1 cm (½ in) deep. Water both types and keep in a cold frame until growth emerges.

Bulbs, corms and tubers
Offsets – small bulbils or cormlets – grow from the sides of many bulbs and corms 1. If left, these will eventually grow to flowering size and naturalize to form a clump. 2 If removed and potted up or planted out they will also flower in time. 3 Lilies can be propagated similarly from fleshy scales removed from the sides of the bulbs. 4 Cut or break iris rhizomes into sections in late summer, each section having at least one, and preferably two or three, sprays of leaves; discard the old, woody central parts of the rhizomes. 5 Cut back the leaves to about 15 cm (6 in) and plant out shallowly and horizontally.

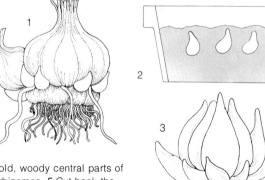
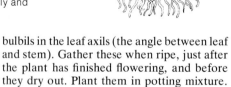
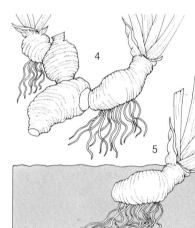

small bulbs will not flower but may be grown on to produce a new flowering-size bulb after one or two years. Gladiolus and crocus corms multiply by the new corm formed on top of the old exhausted one, as well as by the little cormlets that develop around it. If these are detached and grown on they will also eventually achieve flowering size. Hyacinths increase slowly but can be induced to produce large numbers of young bulbs by wounding – making three deep cuts up through the basal plate into the bulb scales to destroy the main shoot. This technique is used commercially, but it is hardly worthwhile for the amateur as it involves keeping the wounded bulbs at high temperature and humidity for several months and then takes four or five years to produce flowering-size bulbs.

It is not difficult to propagate lilies by removing the fleshy outer scales of the bulbs, potting them in peat and sand to root and then growing on the young plants until big enough to plant outside. Some lilies produce aerial bulbils in the leaf axils (the angle between leaf and stem). Gather these when ripe, just after the plant has finished flowering, and before they dry out. Plant them in potting mixture.

Tubers are food stores formed on underground stems or roots, and often have buds or 'eyes' that are each capable of development into a separate plant if the tuber is cut up, each piece having at least one eye. The best-known examples of these are potatoes (see p 276) and Jerusalem artichokes (see p 280). Paeonies and dahlias have root tubers that have no buds, so it is essential to retain a piece of the original stem with a bud if they are divided (see p 188). Rhizomes are specialized stems which grow horizontally at or just below the soil surface. The 'flag' iris (*Iris germanica*), lily of the valley, bergenias and many grasses can be propagated by division of the rhizomes. Divide flag irises immediately after flowering, selecting young rhizomes. Reduce the foliage by half its length and do not plant the new plant too deeply (see p 196).

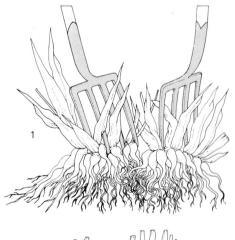
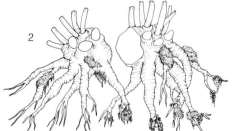

Division and offsets

Many herbaceous plants form crowns. These consist of new shoots that arise at the base of the old flowering shoots and produce side roots that enable the plant to spread. With some vigorous types, such as Michaelmas daisies, if the crown is not divided and replanted every few years the soil soon becomes impoverished and flowering suffers. The crowns may be divided in spring or autumn. Spring-flowering plants which make new growth after flowering are generally divided in early autumn; summer- and autumn-flowering plants which make no new growth until the spring are divided when growth is beginning in spring. You may be able to divide the lifted crowns by hand, but tougher types need to be split by using two garden forks inserted back to back in the clump and levered apart. Discard the older, inner part of the plant in favour of the younger outer portions. Plants to be replaced in a herbaceous border should have about six shoots. You can use smaller pieces to build up stocks in a nursery bed.

Offsets are short shoots that end in a cluster of growth. These form at the base of the plant, and should be removed in the spring. On heavy soil it is best to box them up in potting mixture until well established on their own roots. On lighter soil they may be set out in a nursery bed to grow on. Sempervivums, chrysanthemums, achilleas, anthemis and *Aster × frikartii* are among the plants that may be propagated from offsets. In much the same way, suckering shoots developing from the roots of many trees and shrubs can be dug up with a section of root attached, but do not do this with any plant grafted onto a different rootstock; the sucker will be of the rootstock, not the shrub.

Runners are stems which arise from the axil of a leaf in the crown of a plant and grow along the ground, rooting and producing new plants at the nodes. When well rooted these can be lifted and transplanted. Strawberries are one of the best-known examples.

Layering

1 Peg down lateral shoots of plants like border carnations and many shrubs about 15 cm (6 in) from the end, stripping off some leaves if necessary; separate when well rooted. Cutting or notching the lowest part of the stem helps to induce rooting. 2 Serpentine layering is a way of producing several plants from a single stem of such climbers as clematis and wisteria.

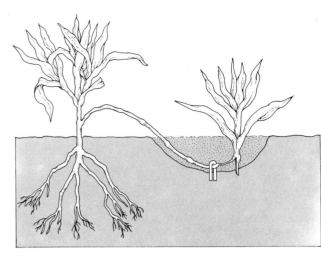

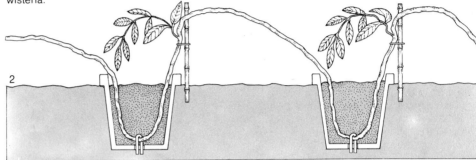

Layering

Many plants root along their stems if these lie on the surface of the soil. This horizontal position assists rooting, as the chemical substances needed to promote it collect on the lower side of the stem. To obtain new plants, peg down one-year-old branches of shrubs and stems of climbing plants onto well-prepared soil; this should contain peat or well-rotted garden compost and sharp sand if it is at all heavy. Hold the branch firmly in place about 15 cm (6 in) from its tip using bent wire, a wooden peg or a stone. Keep the end of the shoot upright by tying it to a stake. Cover the pegged-down portion with 5 cm (2 in) of soil. This treatment is adequate for *Cornus alba, Cotinus coggygria,* forsythia, winter jasmine, heathers and many other shrubs. Border carnations and the longer-stemmed pinks can be increased in the same way (see p 183). In the case of some shrubs rooting is assisted if you first twist the stem and then hold it sharply upright with a firm stake. The underside of the stem should be cut or notched as this also stimulates rooting.

Layering is best done in autumn or before growth starts in the spring, except in the case of carnations, which are layered in summer. By the following autumn the stems will have taken root and can be severed from the parent plant. You can then lift the young plants carefully and overwinter them in pots in a cold frame. Alternatively, lift the young plants in the spring. The top growth should be reduced as this has been supported by the parent plant and the new root system may not be adequate.

You can produce numbers of such climbing plants as clematis and wisteria by serpentine layering in early spring. This involves pegging the stem down at intervals into a/*continued*

Division and offsets

Crown-forming herbaceous plants should be lifted and divided when dormant. Small clumps of fibrous-rooted plants can be gently pulled apart by hand. With old, tough crowns 1 use two forks back to back to prise the clump apart. 2 Such plants as lupins have tough crowns that must be cut with a sharp knife, ensuring that each part has roots and shoots; dust the cut with flowers of sulphur to discourage rotting. 3 Separate offsets of such plants as sempervivums with some roots attached, and pot up. 4 Treat strawberry runners similarly. 5 Suckers from shrubs growing on their own root system can be separated from the parent plant together with roots.

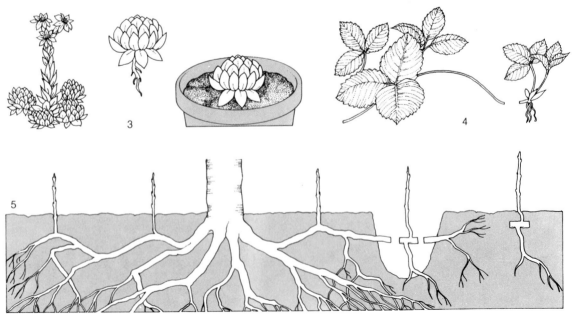

Multiplying your plants (cont)

Further methods of layering
1 In tip layering, bury the end of a blackberry cane in a pot of potting mixture to facilitate transplanting when rooted. In aetiolation layering of such plants as holly, 2 peg down a branch in a trench over winter, but do not bury. When new side shoots develop in spring, 3 begin earthing up, leaving the tips uncovered. Separate and pot up in autumn.

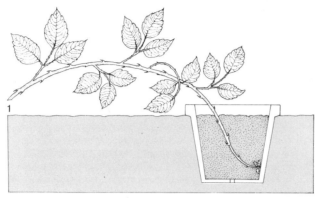

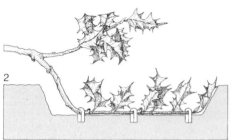

series of 12 cm (5 in) pots of peat and sand sunk into the ground. The stem dips in and out of the pots like a snake – hence the name. You should tie the emergent parts of the stem to supporting canes. It helps to promote rooting if you remove a thin band of bark from the lowest portion of each stem, where it is pegged down. Fill the pots with rooting medium, firm well and keep moist. By autumn, roots should have formed and the stem can be cut in sections, separating each new plant. Overwinter them in their pots in a cold frame, sunk to their rims in peat.

Loganberries and blackberries can be tip layered in late summer. Bury the ends of the current year's growth in the ground or, more satisfactorily, in pots prepared as above and sunk into the ground. The end of the shoot should be buried touching the side of the pot. Roots develop quickly and will fill the pot by the spring. The new plants can then be severed and transplanted with the minimum of root disturbance.

Some plants, such as magnolias, will not root unless the stems are blanched. In French or multiple layering, for example, a branch is pegged down in autumn or late winter in a shallow trench, but it is not earthed up. In the spring new shoots rise vertically from each node. When these are 8 cm (3 in) high they should be gradually earthed up – the way you would earth up celery – always leaving the tips uncovered. By the autumn these buried shoots will have rooted and in the following spring you can sever the whole branch from the shrub and pot up or plant out each shoot.

Air layering

This technique is used in propagating some indoor and greenhouse plants, such as the rubber plant, but can also be used outside – for example with magnolias, camellias, holly, azaleas and lilac. It is a slow process, however, taking up to two years. You can carry it out in spring on the previous year's wood or in late summer using ripened shoots of the current

year. As in normal layering, it involves inducing a shoot to develop roots while still attached to the parent plant. However, the part being layered is not pegged down into the soil but instead is surrounded with moist sphagnum moss enclosed in a sleeve of plastic sheeting tied firmly top and bottom.

The shoot should either have a shallow cut made in it, just below a bud, or have a narrow ring of bark removed. In either case, dust this portion with hormone rooting powder and keep the cut open with a wisp of sphagnum moss before wrapping in moss and a plastic sleeve (which can be made from a bag with the bottom cut off).

The layered branch will need supporting with a cane; or tie it to another branch. When eventually roots are formed, take great care of the new plant when it is severed from its parent. It should be potted and kept under mist, or in a propagator or closed frame with frequent spraying, until the plant is well established. Then harden it off slowly by reducing atmospheric humidity.

Air layering
Strip leaves from a section of a suitable branch 15 to 30 cm (6 to 12 in) from the end, and make a shallow cut up into the centre just below a bud. Alternatively, remove a ring of bark 1 to 2.5 cm (½ to 1 in) wide. Sprinkle on hormone rooting powder and pack moist sphagnum moss into and around the cut. Enclose the whole in a sleeve of clear plastic sheeting, tied securely top and bottom. Support with a cane or by tying the branch to another. The layer is ready for removal and potting when roots are visible.

Grafting

There is nothing new about grafting sections of one plant onto another so that they grow as one; it has been performed for nearly 3,000 years. Yet it is a technique many amateur gardeners are hesitant of using. Certainly, it is primarily carried out by professionals, but certain methods of grafting are quite simple and straightforward. The term grafting is generally used when sections of stem of one plant (called the scion) some centimetres (several inches) or more long are joined onto another (the stock or rootstock). Budding is no different in principle, but uses mere slivers of the scion with buds attached.

Growing one plant on the roots of another has a number of advantages. In some cases, it is the only reliable way of propagating 'difficult' plants, and it is almost always the quickest way to produce a mature specimen of a particular cultivar. In the case of bush roses and some other plants it is the most economical method of increasing numbers, for one bud can quickly form a new bush on the roots of a suitable rose stock.

Fruit trees are normally budded or grafted onto specially selected or bred rootstocks. Choice of stock – there are a range of named and numbered types available – affects the size, vigour and fruiting time of hardy fruit trees. Some rootstocks are resistant to pests and diseases (for example, to root-borne woolly aphids, which are a particularly serious pest in New Zealand), while some are certified virus-free. Some – such as those used for citrus fruits – influence frost-hardiness or the texture, flavour and skin thickness of the fruit, while others give tolerance of certain soil conditions. These variations show the importance of selecting the correct rootstock for your garden conditions and of discussing your choice with a specialist nurseryman if you are unsure.

Although grafting is performed mainly with woody plants, cacti and tomatoes are sometimes grafted. In the latter case, F1 hybrid rootstocks derived from wild tomato species have been developed that are resistant to certain soil-borne diseases such as wilt and some eelworms. They confer immunity to fruiting varieties grafted onto them, quite an easy process for the amateur. At the other extreme, in top-grafting and frame-working, the branches of an established fruit tree are replaced or augmented with scions of quite another variety – or more than one variety. These methods are sometimes used in orchards to change the trees to more commercially desirable varieties; they reach full production more quickly than newly planted trees.

How grafting works

Grafting sometimes occurs naturally, and is in fact a form of wound-healing in which the tissues of two separate but closely related plants become merged. When a woody plant is damaged, live cells close to the injury divide rapidly to produce a mass of thin-walled cells called callus tissue. In budding or grafting, callus tissue is produced by both the stock and the scion. The merging of this callus tissue is the first stage in the union of stock and scion.

Grafting tomato plants

Sow seed of the rootstock a few days in advance of that of the fruiting variety, as germination tends to be slower. When pricking out, place one stock and one scion seedling 2.5 cm (1 in) apart in the same pot.
1 When the stems are about 2 mm (⅛ in) thick and the plants are 8 to 12 cm (3 to 5 in) tall, remove the top from the stock plant, leaving two leaves. Make a slanting cut about 1.5 cm (¾ in) long down into the stem of the stock between the two leaves, and a matching cut upwards into the stem of the scion. Insert the tongue of the stock into the cut in the scion to unite the cut surfaces and
2 bind the join with adhesive tape. Because both plants are still on their own roots, no

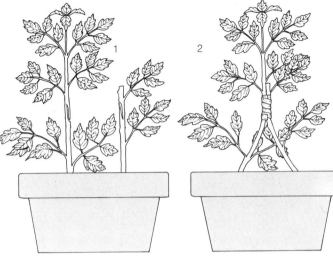

special facilities such as a propagator are needed. After 10 to 14 days the graft should have taken. Later the scion can

be severed just below the graft, leaving it to grow on the rootstock, but you can leave this until just after setting them out.

Grafting in practice

There are many methods of grafting, differing mainly in how the scion and stock are shaped and joined. The easiest and most useful for the amateur include whip and tongue grafting, used for a wide range of fruit and ornamental trees, crown grafting, used for rejuvenating old fruit trees, and budding, used for various ornamental trees and shrubs but notably roses, ornamental cherries and crab-apples.

Timing is important. Graft deciduous woody plants when the stock plant is about to begin growth in the very early spring. The scion wood must be still dormant, however, so collect this in winter and store it in plastic bags at 0°C (32°F), or at 5 to 10°C (41 to 50°F) if it is to be used within one month. Do not store it in a freezer as damage will occur. Choose healthy, well-ripened shoots made during the previous growing season; they should be about 6 to 12 mm (¼ to ½ in) in diameter. Discard the terminal part of the shoots as this has insufficient food reserves, cutting above a bud. Shape the bottom end according to the type of graft; the scion should have about four buds for whip and tongue or crown grafting.

Budding takes place in the growing season when the bark of the stock can be lifted easily; this indicates active cell division in the cambium. The usual time is in late summer, although it can be performed earlier. Obtain scion material by selecting bud sticks from vigorous shoots of the current season's growth. Remove the leaves immediately to reduce water loss, but leave on the leaf stalks to help handling the individual buds. The material must be used fresh. The buds at the top of the stick are too succulent and should be discarded.

If the process is to be successful, the first essential is that the stock and scion must be compatible. In general, the closer the botanical relationship the more chance there is of success. Any apple can be 'worked' on any other apple, but an attempt to graft an apple to a pear, although apparently successful for a short time, will eventually fail. Pears, however, are always grafted onto quince rootstocks, which are also used to produce a dwarf form of the loquat (see p 324). Incompatibility occurs between certain pears, such as 'William's Bon Chrétien' ('Bartlett'), and the quince rootstock, and a pear 'interstock'

which is compatible with both has to be used in between; this is double grafting.

The second essential in budding or grafting is to expose and unite the part of the stems where cell division is active. This is the cambium layer just below the bark, where growth occurs, increasing the girth of woody stems. The cut surfaces must be held tightly together. The third essential is to prevent the cut surfaces from drying. This may be done by placing the newly grafted material in a humid atmosphere such as a closed frame, or by covering the graft with a waterproof strip, binding or grafting wax.

to a bud. Then make a short vertical incision about one-third of the way down from the top of this cut, to form the tongue.
2 Make a sloping cut of the same size in the stock, ending just above a bud, and make a vertical incision downwards about one-third of the way from the upper end of this cut to take the tongue from the scion.
3 Unite the two stems, matching the cambial tissues and slotting the tongues into the matching incisions. **4** Bind with raffia or adhesive tape, and cover with grafting wax.
In crown grafting, scions are inserted in the newly cut stubs of branches – two or more in each stub if desired. **5** Prepare the bottom of the scion by making a slanting cut about 2.5 cm (1 in) long opposite a bud. **6** Make a vertical cut in the bark of the stock, down from the cut end of the branch, and lift the bark. Push the scion down under the bark so that the cut surfaces touch. Bind with tape and seal the whole area.

Methods of grafting trees

For whip and tongue grafting, the stock and scion should be more or less the same thickness. **1** Make a slanting cut 4 to 5 cm (1½ to 2 in) long downwards at the lower end of the scion, on the opposite side

Budding

1 Hold the bud stick by the top end and, using a sharp knife, make a shallow cut, starting 1.5 cm (¾ in) below the bud and emerging about 2.5 cm (1 in) above it. Cut off the leaf, leaving a stub of stalk. Make a 2.5 cm (1 in) T-shaped incision in the bark of the stock, as near the ground as possible unless you are forming a standard tree. Lift the bark with the flat handle of a budding knife and **2** slide the bud into position as far down as possible. Cut off any protruding part of the bud 'shield' and **3** bind firmly, leaving the bud uncovered.
After two to three weeks, examine the buds. The leaf stalk will have fallen from those that have taken, and there will be some swelling of the bud; loosen the tie, and the next spring cut back the stock plant to just above the scion bud. Failed buds shrivel.

Feeding your plants

Plants need at least 16 chemical elements in order to grow and remain healthy; all are equally vital, but the amounts used vary widely. Major plant nutrients, needed in large quantities, are carbon (obtained from carbon dioxide in the air; see p 336); hydrogen and oxygen (the constituents of water); and nitrogen, phosphorus and potash. These last three, like water, come from the soil, as do calcium, magnesium and sulphur (which are needed in moderate quantities), and the so-called trace elements, which are necessary only in tiny amounts (and are often harmful in excess). The trace elements are iron, manganese, boron, zinc, copper, chlorine and molybdenum.

The amounts of these individual nutrients needed by plants vary according to conditions of light, temperature and water supply, and according to the plant type, situation and soil. Where crops are harvested and all debris removed from the soil, nutrient levels will fall unless the gardener replenishes them in the form of fertilizer or manure. This applies to beds of annuals, biennials or herbaceous plants, which are pulled up or trimmed back at the season's end, as well as to fruit and vegetable patches. Even pruning removes food, as does removing dead leaves. If fallen leaves are not removed, trees and shrubs are more or less self-supporting, although extra food is needed for vigorous growth.

You should also remember that such factors as soil temperature, moisture, acidity and aeration affect the availability to a plant of whatever food is present in the soil (see p 330). So maintaining good soil conditions is just as important as adding plant nutrients. Bulky manures and garden compost – applied as mulches or worked into the soil – supply some plant foods, but only at low concentration, and this function is less important than that of soil improvement. Organic and inorganic fertilizers supply much higher concentrations, and are also needed on many soils if cropping is to be satisfactory. Generally speaking, soils need both fertilizers and bulky organic material.

The need for fertilizers

Except in cases of specific deficiency (such as the well-known inability of lime-hating plants to obtain iron and other trace elements from alkaline soils), the three plant nutrients that most concern the gardener are nitrogen, phosphorus and potassium. Nitrogen (chemical symbol N) makes up 80 per cent of the atmosphere, but plants can use it only in the form of nitrates, which dissolve easily in water – and are just as easily washed out of light soils. Certain soil bacteria turn chemicals found in animal and plant wastes into nitrates, and an important group that live in the root nodules of beans, peas, clover and other leguminous plants are able to 'fix' nitrogen from the air and make it available to the plant. Some nitrates also come from the air as a result of lightning flashes in thunderstorms.

Nitrogen is particularly important for rapid growth, good green foliage, and plentiful leaves, fruit and seeds; it is also essential for soil bacteria to break down plant wastes. Deficiency is shown by thin, upright, spindly growth with few laterals; small, pale green leaves that later turn orange, red or purple; and early loss of leaves on fruit trees, with less blossom and (on apples) small, hard fruits. Excess nitrogen produces soft, lush growth prone to frost damage, and large, dark green leaves; flower and seed production suffers because potassium deficiency results.

Phosphorus (symbol P) occurs as phosphates, some of which will not dissolve and are thus unavailable to plants, but mulches (see p 334) increase the natural availability of phosphates. These are involved in all plant processes, but are particularly important for root growth, and also assist germination, ripening and seed formation. Deficiency results in spindly, stunted growth, with thin shoots and poor roots (and few tubers with such crops as potatoes). Leaves are a dull bluish-green, purple or bronzed. Apples have soft, acid fruits, often green with a red flush.

Potassium (symbol K) occurs in clay minerals, and various natural materials boost its level, including composted young weeds, dry wood ash, grass clippings and straw. Potassium availability is measured in terms of the equivalent amount of a chemical called potash, which does not itself occur free in soil. Potassium seems to be particularly important in leaves and at the growing points, and especially in the formation of flowers and fruit, improving their quality. It also helps to ripen and harden plant tissues and promote resistance to disease and frost. Deficiency leads to scorching of leaf edges; poor, thin growth, possibly with the death of whole branches in fruit trees; poor flowers; and tasteless, woody and sometimes blotchy fruits. Excess can cause calcium or magnesium deficiency.

Trace elements are needed for various plant processes, and signs of deficiency vary. The commonest is chlorosis – yellowing between the leaf veins – which occurs in iron and magnesium deficiency, for example.

The performance of your plants will thus often give clues as the plant nutrients needed. If, however, you want to know more precisely, soil test kits are available for simple measurement of nitrogen, phosphate and potash levels (see p 332).

Types of fertilizers

Fertilizers are commonly classed as organic and inorganic – though many proprietary brands contain mixtures of both types. Organic fertilizers come mainly from animal wastes (some come from plants), and include materials like bonemeal (see the table). They are generally slow-acting but long-lasting, and there is little danger of applying too much. They tend to be expensive, however.

Inorganic fertilizers come either from natural mineral sources or are manufactured. They generally dissolve easily and are quick-acting, so they are useful when a quick boost is needed. But they are often very concentrated and need to be applied carefully or excess salinity may occur. They tend to be cheaper, but some may inhibit the activity of natural

Methods of application
1 Dig in well-rotted organic manures, or use as mulches.
2 Broadcast base dressings of pre-seeding or pre-planting fertilizers evenly over the bed and rake in; or 3 apply in

soil organisms. When using inorganic fertilizers, it is particularly important to increase the humus levels with bulky organic manures or compost, or soil structure will suffer.

'Straight' fertilizers contain only one of the major nutrients, so they are useful in correcting a particular deficiency or if a specific type of growth is required. For example, nitro-chalk (which is rich in nitrogen) can be used to boost the leaf growth of cabbages in the spring. Where more than one nutrient is required – and for general purposes, or where you do not know the soil's deficiences – you can buy a 'compound' fertilizer containing a range of plant foods. Alternatively, you can apply a mixture of straight fertilizers, with the exceptions noted in the table.

The content (and thus the value) of a fertilizer is frequently stated in percentage terms on the package or in literature. For example, hoof and horn contains 13 per cent nitrogen, so 100 g of fertilizer provides 13 g of nitrogen (and 100 oz contains 13 oz). With compound fertilizers, the percentages are always given in the same order: first nitrogen, then phosphate and finally potash. These may be abbreviated to their chemical formulae – N, P_2O_5 and K_2O (or simply N, P and K) respectively. For example, a fertilizer might contain 15 per cent N, 10 per cent P_2O_5 and 10 per cent K_2O, so that 100 g of fertilizer provides 15 g of nitrogen, 10 g of phosphate and 10 g of potash. This may be further abbreviated to 15:10:10, still always in the order N:P:K. Note that a 7.5:5:5 fertilizer has exactly the same proportions of nutrients, but in half the quantities, and you would need to use twice as much for the same results. In more general terms, a 'high-phosphate' fertilizer might have an analysis of about 5:10:5, and so on. Where growing instructions specify simply the use of a 'balanced' fertilizer, one with approximately equal N, P and K figures is appropriate; a good example is Growmore, devised in Britain to boost food production during World War II and having an analysis of 7:7:7.

A final type of plant 'food' is not really a fertilizer as such, but is a source of the intermediate and trace nutrients, such as magnesium and iron. A simple example is Epsom salts, which supplies magnesium, either via the soil or when sprayed on the leaves. Also extremely useful are sequestrols or chelates – most commonly sequestered iron, but sometimes containing other elements as well. These are in a chemical form that plants can absorb even from limy soils, thus overcoming trace element deficiencies.

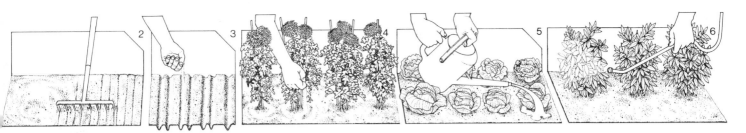

shallow drills 5 cm (2 in) to each side of seed drills, or mix with topsoil to make a planting mixture for trees, shrubs and herbaceous plants. **4** Sprinkle top dressings around plants to stimulate growth, flowering and fruiting; water in if it does not rain within a few days.
5 Liquid feeds act quickly and are better than top dressings in dry weather; do not exceed the recommended concentrations. Foliar feeds are special liquid fertilizers that are sprayed onto leaves with a pressure sprayer **6** or hose dilutor **7**. They are excellent as quick-acting boosts to growth if roots are damaged, and for applying trace elements. Do not use in hot sun, and water first if the soil is very dry. Apply sequestered iron and other trace elements similarly, or water into the soil. Correct magnesium deficiency by spraying Epsom salts mixed with weak liquid soap.

Manures and fertilizers

	Name	Nitrogen (N) %	Phosphate (P$_2$O$_5$) %	Potash (K$_2$O) %	Normal rate of application*	Comments†
Organic manures	Chicken manure (dry)	4	3	1.5	270–400 g/m^2	Can be used to make liquid manure (diluted)
	Cow manure (rotted)	1–1.5	0.4	0·5–1	2.5–5 kg/m^2	Bulky; improves soil structure
	Farmyard manure (rotted)	0.5–1	0.25–0.5	0·5–1	2.5–5 kg/m^2	Variable; urine increases N and K$_2$O content
	Guano (dry)	2–12	10–20	2–4	70–100 g/m^2	For liquid manure, use 6 g/litre; difficult to obtain
	Horse manure (rotted)	1–1.5	0.25–0.5	0·5–1	2.5–5 kg/m^2	Improves soil structure; best quality from racing stables
	Pig manure (rotted)	1.75	0.75	1	2.5–5 kg/m^2	Analysis variable; best for light, sandy soils
	Seaweed (fresh)	0.5	0.1	1.2	5 kg/m^2	Contains 1.2% salt; good for asparagus
	Shoddy (wool waste)	5–15	—	—	1 kg/m^2	Improves soil structure; nitrogen released slowly
	Spent hops	0.5	1–2	Trace	2.5–5 kg/m^2	'Hop manure' has chemical fertilizers added – follow maker's instructions
Organic fertilizers	Blood, fish and bone meal	6.5	6	5	Up to 70 g/m^2	High quality complete organic fertilizer
	Bonemeal	2–5	20–25		Up to 135 g/m^2	Speed of action depends on how finely ground (up to three years); contains lime; handle with gloves
	Dried blood	10–13	—	—	Up to 70 g/m^2	Fast-acting; for liquid fertilizer, use 6 g/litre
	Fish meal (fish guano)	7–10	4–10	Trace	70–100 g/m^2	Fish manure may have chemical fertilizers added – follow maker's instructions
	Hoof and horn meal	12–14	1–3	—	Up to 70 g/m^2	Lime-free; speed of action depends on fineness of grinding
	Meat and bone meal	7	16	—	70–100 g/m^2	Meat wastes increase nitrogen content; handle with gloves
	Oil cake (rape meal)	5–6	—	—	Up to 135 g/m^2	Good for mixing with concentrated inorganic fertilizers
	Wood ashes	—	—	4–15	Up to 270 g/m^2	Must be stored dry; ash from young wood richest
Inorganic fertilizers	Ammonium nitrate‡	35	—	—	Liquid feed	Also called nitrate of ammonia; use 0.75 g/litre in water
	Ammonium sulphate‡	21	—	—	15–35 g/m^2	Sulphate of ammonia; makes soil acid; can affect soil bacteria
	Basic slag‡	—	8–20	—	135–270 g/m^2	Slow-acting; solubility (thus availability to plants) varies; alkaline
	Calcium cyanamide	21	—	—	35–70 g/m^2	Contains 20% free lime; damages plants on direct contact
	Calcium nitrate	16	—	—	35 g/m^2	Nitrate of lime; can be used to aid rotting of compost
	'Gold N' ('Harvest Gold')	32	—	—	35–70 g/m^2	Slow-release nitrogenous fertilizer for lawns, vegetables
	Nitro-chalk‡	16	—	—	35 g/m^2	Contains 48% lime; can be used to aid rotting of compost
	Potash nitrate (Chilean)	About 15		About 10	15–35 g/m^2	Impure potassium nitrate
	Potassium chloride	—	—	Up to 60	15–35 g/m^2	Muriate of potash; avoid direct contact with roots; not for potatoes
	Potassium sulphate	—		50	15–35 g/m^2	Sulphate of potash; best general source of potash
	Sodium nitrate‡	16	—	—	15–35 g/m^2	Nitrate of soda; burns foliage; quickly washed out of soil
	Soot	Up to 6			Up to 200 g/m^2	Store dry for several months before using
	Superphosphate (of lime)‡		18–20		35–100 g/m^2	Contains no free lime; burns delicate foliage; base dressing
	Urea‡	45	—	—	5–8 g/m^2	Richest source of nitrogen; use 0.75 g/litre in water; can be used as foliar feed
Compound fertilizers	Chrysanthemum base fertilizer	4.5	11.5	7.25	15–35 g/m^2	For top dressing chrysanthemums; other strengths available
	'En-mag'	5	23.5	10	35–70 g/m^2	Contains 10% magnesium; pre-seeding and pre-planting base dressings; top dressing, especially for trees and shrubs
	Growmore	7	7	7	35–70 g/m^2	General-purpose; for pre-seeding, pre-planting; top dressing for brassicas and root vegetables
	John Innes base fertilizer	5.1	7.2	9.7	35 g/m^2	Contains hoof and horn meal, therefore slow release of N; used in potting mixtures; pre-seeding; pre-planting; top dressing
	'Maxicrop "Plus N"'	17.7	2	3	Liquid feed	Liquid organic fertilizer with iron; for foliar and liquid feeds
	'Phostrogen'	9.7	10.6	26.5	Liquid feed	For use dissolved in water; contains iron and magnesium
	Rose fertilizer (Tonk's)	4	6.75	13	70–140 g/m^2	For top dressing roses in summer; contains iron and magnesium
	Sequestered elements				As advised	Formulation of trace elements; see text
	Tomato fertilizer	6	5	9	Liquid feed	Liquid feed at 1 teaspoon per 4.5 litres (1 gallon)

*Conversion to Anglo-American measures: 5 g/m^2 = ⅛ oz/sq yd; 8 g/m^2 = ¼ oz/sq yd; 15 g/m^2 = ½ oz/sq yd; 35 g/m^2 = 1 oz/sq yd; 70 g/m^2 = 2 oz/sq yd; 100 g/m^2 = 3 oz/sq yd; 135 g/m^2 = 4 oz/sq yd; 200 g/m^2 = 6 oz/sq yd; 270 g/m^2 = 8 oz/sq yd; 400 g/m^2 = 12 oz/sq yd; 550 g/m^2 = 16 oz/sq yd; 1 kg/m^2 = 2 lb/sq yd; 2.5 kg/m^2 = 5 lb/sq yd; 5 kg/m^2 = 10 lb/sq yd

†Conversion of liquid measures: 6 g/litre = 1 oz/gallon; 0.75 g/litre = ⅛ oz/gallon.

‡Do not mix any of the following with lime or basic slag: ammonium nitrate, ammonium sulphate, nitro-chalk, superphosphate or urea. Do not mix superphosphate with sodium nitrate

Protecting tender plants

In any one garden you may find tulips from the mountains of Turkestan, heathers from the Alps of central Europe, rhododendrons from China, schizanthus from Chile, Californian poppies from (of course) California and geraniums (pelargoniums) from South Africa. It is a credit to the adaptability of these and thousands of other garden plants that they will thrive far from their natural environment and often in climatic conditions quite different from those in which they originated. Many of them, however, need the gardener's help to survive the worst excesses of the weather in their new home, and this usually means protection from winter conditions.

The plants from warmer countries that can be grown outside in summer but need protection from winter cold are termed tender or half-hardy. (The term half-hardy generally implies an ability to withstand somewhat colder conditions than the term tender, but the demarcation line is blurred.) There are, indeed, varying degrees of hardiness among those plants that can survive frost. Some can stand intense cold but are killed by wet soil or damp atmospheric conditions – so that they might survive in the American Midwest but succumb in Scotland. Others will survive in light sandy soil which is very sharply drained, but will die in cold heavy clay. Still others are not very concerned by cold or even damp soil and air conditions so long as their crowns are protected from direct wetting by rain.

So it is not simply a matter of preventing your plants getting too cold – though that is an important factor with many kinds. Shelter from wet and wind are equally important for others. This article is concerned primarily with the protection of decorative plants; the article on page 268 deals with related aspects when growing food and also contains information (such as on the protection of tree-trunks) that is applicable to the decorative garden. It also describes various kinds of cloches, which are useful for protecting some plants. Other related articles include those on the relationship between a plant and its environment (p 340), climate and the gardener (p 338) and greenhouses and frames (p 380).

Protection from wind

Strong winds – especially cold winter ones – can be extremely damaging to plants, particularly if speeded up by being funnelled between buildings or clumps of trees like a river in a narrow ravine. Tall buildings and walls also cause severe turbulence on both the leeward and windward sides. Wind striking a building is forced both up and down; the down-draught batters plants on the windward side while that forced upwards descends again on the other side to create more turbulence. These are important factors to take into account when positioning plants that are not completely hardy.

Shelter belts of trees or tall shrubs, or hedges, can be planted on the windward side of the garden, and will give better protection (by filtering the wind) than a solid fence. You should make sure, however, that these barriers neither cut off sunlight nor cause frost

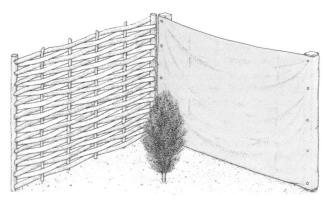

pockets. You can erect windbreaks of woven wattle hurdles, hessian or sacks fixed to stakes, or even plastic sheeting similarly supported. These are particularly useful to shelter newly-planted shrubs and young trees – especially evergreens, which are often difficult to establish in exposed places. Any such screening should shelter but not coddle the plant; it must not touch the foliage.

Shelter with walls

Although they cause turbulence, walls if sheltered and sunny – that is, generally south-facing in the northern hemisphere – can give considerable protection to plants growing close to them. This is because the wall absorbs the sun's heat and gives it out again slowly. (The effect is increased considerably if the wall is that of a centrally-heated house.) As a result, many plants will survive in such places that would be killed by frost in open situations; many examples are given in the article beginning on page 170.

You should take care, however, about the siting of winter-flowering shrubs; these should be shaded from the early morning sun, as rapid thawing of frozen flowers will destroy them. Early-flowering wall-trained fruit trees such as apricots, peaches and nectarines should be protected from frost by light curtains of fine netting. This traps warm air around the plants and shields the flowers from morning sun. In severe weather, wall-trained shrubs can be protected by hessian draped in front of the plants and tied to the supporting wires. If necessary, dry straw, bracken or similar material can be packed behind the hessian to give added insulation. All such protection should, however be removed as soon as particularly cold weather is over.

Protection from radiation frosts

Radiation frosts occur when there is no cloud cover and are most damaging when they occur in late spring after warm days. On clear, still evenings frost can be expected and tender plants must be protected. Newly planted vegetables can be protected with tents of newspaper held down with stones; even a light covering will reflect back warmth. Seedlings can be protected with jam jars, plastic bottles or waxed-paper cups sold specially for the purpose in some countries. Strawberry flowers can be covered with straw pulled from between the rows. Cloches can be used, but as explained on page 269, the plastic kind gives little protection and must be covered with sacking, newspapers or other insulation.

The best wind screens for newly planted trees and shrubs filter the wind and reduce its force without cosseting them too much. Good materials include wattle hurdles **far left** and burlap (hessian or sacking) supported on strong stakes **left**. Unless the position is extremely exposed, arrange the screen on two or three sides, leaving the sunniest aspect open.

You can protect soft fruit bushes by covering them with fruit netting, old curtains, dust sheets or anything else that will trap warm air rising from the soil around the plants. Mulches should if possible be drawn to one side and the soil watered as this will increase the conduction of ground warmth to the air around the plants. Fruit blossom can be saved by being covered with spray from sprinklers. Water freezes around the flowers but gives out heat as it does so and they will be unharmed as long as the sprinkler runs and they do not fall more than a degree or two below freezing point.

Radiation frost is most severe in winter where there is little air movement. Trees provide an overhead canopy that retains warmth, and many evergreen shrubs will survive in woodland gardens when they would be severely damaged in open situations. In summer these shrubs benefit from the cooler, moister environment. Tender deciduous shrubs and trees in more exposed situations can be protected from severe frost with dry material such as straw, which should be packed loosely around the plants and held in place with hessian or wire netting – but not plastic sheeting, which prevents 'breathing'.

One of the most adaptable methods of frost protection is to use glass cloches 1, which can be augmented with newspaper or sacking. Waxed paper cups 2 are useful for seedlings, while rain is kept off alpines by a single pane of glass 3.

Supporting your plants

In areas which experience very severe winters, such as the north-central United States and Canada, roses need protection as described on page 101, but it is essential that the plants be kept cold enough to remain dormant until the spring. To prepare it for the winter, rose wood must be well ripened by witholding nitrogenous fertilizers (see p 352) and water from late summer onwards. Many tender Mediterranean and New Zealand plants will stand some frost if grown in well-drained soil in a sunny position which similarly ensures that the wood has ripened. And in fact it is true generally that plants both outside and under glass can be conditioned to tolerate lower temperatures by reducing the amount of nitrogenous fertilizers, increasing the amount of potash and gradually reducing the amount of water that they receive. Thinning and pruning also help ripening by admitting light and air to the plant.

Protecting herbaceous and alpine plants
The crowns of herbaceous plants are protected by the dead flowering stems, and these should not be cut down until spring in cold areas. This can be supplemented with dry straw or bracken. Slightly tender herbaceous plants such as *Lobelia fulgens* can be protected by covering the crowns with dry ashes, or the plants can be lifted and packed into boxes of peat or dry potting mixture, and stored in a cold frame or greenhouse. *Salvia patens*, *Centaurea candidissima* and Korean chrysanthemums can be stored in boxes in the same way. Zonal pelargoniums (geraniums) can be dried off and hung up in a frost-free shed or cool room. In spring new shoots will appear and the plants can be started into growth to provide cuttings. Bedding chrysanthemums and dahlias are treated similarly (see pp 186 and 188).

Many alpine plants – especially those with hairy leaves – loathe winter wet but may stand intense cold if kept dry. You can protect them by fixing a large pane of glass above the plant; it can rest on wooden pegs and be held down by pieces of brick. Alternatively, use an open-ended cloche. Rosette-forming plants, such as sempervivums are best grown in a vertical situation, such as a dry wall, so that water does not collect among their leaves.

Protection from heat
The need to protect plants from summer sun is not restricted to those areas with very hot summers. Large-leaved plants and newly-planted trees and shrubs are particularly vulnerable and should be shaded with heavy plastic netting of the type used for shading greenhouses, or with slatted structures supported above the plants, and should have their foliage sprayed frequently with water. And, of course, you should choose the planting situation of shade-lovers just as carefully as that of frost-tender types. Most of the species rhododendrons, for example – and certainly the taller ones – need to be planted under a canopy of tall trees. Woodland plants will not survive in hot, sunny situations any more than tender plants will survive harsh winters.

Many plants need support of some kind either to stop them falling or being blown over, or to encourage their growth in the direction you want. In the case of most decorative trees and shrubs, staking is only necessary – if at all – in the early years, before the roots establish themselves properly and in some cases the top growth achieves enough strength. Others, such as standard (tree) roses, need permanent support, as do the taller herbaceous plants and some annuals throughout their season of growth. This applies both to decorative types such as delphiniums and to such crop plants as tomatoes and beans.

Among annuals and herbaceous perennials, many modern hybrids have extra-large flowers and long stems; these obviously are more in need of support than dwarf forms or, in many cases, the original species. Plants grown in full or partial shade are more likely to grow 'leggy' and need staking than those in full sun, while many herbaceous plants can be encouraged to form compact, bushy growth by pinching out the growing tips in early summer. Climbing plants need some kind of support to climb on, though they vary in how much assistance they need in the way of tying-in; for methods of supporting climbers, see page 93. The plant-selection charts beginning on page 386 give an indication of plants that generally need staking.

Methods of support
It is important to choose a support to suit the plant. It must be strong enough and tall enough without being unsightly. With plants that have one or a few stems, canes or stakes are the most appropriate; they should end just below the flowering head or bushy top – not only for appearances' sake but so that the top of the stake does not damage the flowers in

wind. Thick canes are usually adequate for delphiniums, but giant varieties of dahlias need stakes of 2.5 cm (1 in) square cross-section. With tall plants of more branching habit, you can position three canes around the plant, linked with string or wire, and tie the stems to the canes. For standard trees and large shrubs you will need stakes 5 cm (2 in) thick, or similar-sized larch poles.

Treat the bottom of a stake or pole with preservative before driving it firmly into the ground and if possible insert it before planting, not afterwards, to avoid damaging the roots. When tying plants to such stakes, make sure that the tie does not damage the plant's stem. With soft-stemmed plants, use soft fillis string or wired-paper twist ties, and tie firmly but not tightly. When using thicker cord for trees and shrubs, protect the trunk with a piece of sacking or rubber inner-tube. Patent adjustable plastic or rubber ties are excellent and are available in various sizes. Never use nylon or wire, which will cut into the stems.

With weak-stemmed branching or clump-forming plants, twiggy branches of birch, elm or hazel make ideal supports. Sharpen the bottom ends and insert them between the plants before these have made their full growth; they can surround and be bent over clumps of herbaceous plants. The plants will then grow up through the twigs, concealing them. Patent supports in the form of horizontal wire grilles on legs work on the same principle, while home-made versions can be made from chicken-wire fixed to short wooden stakes. In large herbaceous borders, wide-mesh string or nylon netting stretched horizontally between stakes can be used similarly. Finally there are patent wire ring supports that are good for such plants as border carnations; their height can be adjusted.

You can support slender-stemmed tall perennials with a single cane **1**, but with a clump of plants arrange three or four canes around the plants and join with string or wire **2**. Patent plastic ties to attach young trees to sturdy stakes **3** can be adjusted for growth, and avoid stem damage. Twiggy sticks **4** are ideal for bushy perennials, and wire grille supports **5** are good for carnations and similar plants. In a large herbaceous border, use string netting **6**.

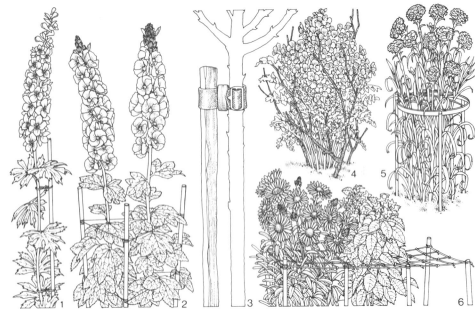

Dealing with weeds

Weeds are successful plants growing in the wrong place. Some are native wild plants, others introduced aliens which have taken too well to their new environment. All possess an ability to survive adverse conditions and an aggression which enables them to compete effectively with cultivated plants. They not only compete for food, water and light but also act as sources of infection for diseases and pests which can nullify the cleaning effects of crop rotation. Weeds such as shepherd's purse (*Capsella bursa-pastoris*), which is related to brassicas such as cabbages and cauliflowers, can be infected by club root, and potato cyst eelworm can live on the roots of black nightshade (*Solanum nigrum*). There is no place for weeds in cultivated land, but in wild areas they provide food for insects and birds and so are important in the ecological food chain.

Weeds produce prodigious quantities of seed. One annual nettle can produce 40,000 seeds and the great plantain (*Plantago major*) can produce 30,000. On the other hand, in very adverse conditions a minute plant with only two leaves could still produce eight seeds. Not only are these enormous numbers of seeds produced, but their germination is spread over a long period, so that having cleared one batch of seedlings, another batch appears still from the same parent, and this can continue for months. Buried seeds may germinate at any time for 60 years or more.

Most weeds are tolerant of extremely low temperatures as plants, but especially as seeds, and most are quite insensitive to day length, so they can flower and seed in most months of the year. They have solved the problem of pollination when no insects are about either by self-pollination, or by being able to produce seed without pollination (the dandelion can do this). Perennial weeds spread mainly by vegetative means. The roots and underground stems contain food stores so that even small pieces can regenerate if broken up or incompletely removed. Some perennial weeds have very deep roots which survive when the rest of the plant is destroyed.

Methods of control

Until relatively recently, cultivation was the only method of controlling weeds. It is still important to remove entirely the roots of perennial weeds when digging a patch of ground, and the hoe is a convenient tool for regular removal of shallow-rooted annual weeds among crops or decorative plants. (Even many perennial weeds will succumb to continual beheading.) But the modern gardener has other weapons, notably the use of mulches, ground-cover planting and herbicides (chemical weedkillers).

Ground-cover planting (see p 232) is designed to give complete cover that will smother weeds in two or three years, but all perennial weeds must be removed before planting. Mulches similarly smother annual weeds, and can be used to cover the soil between shrubs, roses, fruit bushes, herbaceous plants and vegetables. The best known are organic materials such as peat (see p 334), but black plastic sheeting is an excellent weed-

suppressant. It is particularly suitable for laying in strips between rows of vegetables, being removed in winter. If plastic sheeting is used to cover the ground between permanent shrubby plants and is completely covered with gravel or stones to give a more attractive appearance and hold down the plastic, annual weeds cannot grow and no maintenance is needed. Make a shallow depression around each plant to allow water to reach the soil, but the plastic reduces evaporation, resulting in better growth. The only problems are slugs and woodlice, which enjoy the dark, moist conditions under the plastic.

Precautions with weedkillers

Take the very greatest of care in storing and using weedkillers. Some are deadly poisonous to man and animals – in some cases, even prompt medical attention may not be enough to save life. If, however, any person or pet is poisoned (or suspected of being poisoned), give milk and raw egg or simply water to drink, and get the victim to a hospital, doctor or vet immediately. Take the container and any unconsumed herbicide with you for identification. Induce vomiting only if medical help is distant.

Precautions in storage Keep all weedkillers under lock and key. If possible, store them in a locked shed on a shelf too high for children to reach. If this is not possible, they must be kept in a locked cupboard. Do not store near peat, seedling or potting mixtures, seeds, plants or bulbs.

Always keep them in the maker's containers, clearly labelled. NEVER keep them in lemonade bottles, wine bottles or similar containers; deaths of children and adults have resulted from drinking weedkiller by mistake. Most taste nasty, but one sip can be fatal.

Precautions in use Never use a stick to stir a solution and leave this where a child or pet may get hold of it. Keep a special watering can for use only with weedkillers, and keep it and its sprinkler bars as securely as the weedkillers themselves. Use weedkillers only in calm weather to avoid spray drift, and do not use in hot weather in enclosed areas where vaporization can occur. Do not use a fine spray.

Measure accurately; never exceed stated quantities. Avoid contaminating puddles from which animals may drink, children's paddling-pools or pools stocked with plants or fish. Wear rubber gloves and avoid herbicide contact with the skin; immediately wash off any splashes. Wash out all spray equipment immediately after use, using washing soda. Do not pour the solution down drains or ditches where it may contaminate water-courses. Wash your hands afterwards, and especially before eating, drinking or smoking.

Weedkillers are basically chemicals that are poisonous to plants. Some only affect certain kinds of plants, while others are indiscriminate; they differ also in the way they are absorbed by the plant and therefore the method of application. In a private garden the great variety of plants limits the use of selective weedkillers. (Commercial growers can match the herbicide to the crop.) Consequently some cultivation is still required in the vegetable garden, flower borders and rock garden, although even here spot treatment with selective weedkillers can be the most effective method of dealing with some deep-rooted perennial weeds. However, there are obvious areas in any garden where a careful choice of weedkillers can reduce labour, and it is possible to design a garden of shrubs, fruit, lawns and trees which can be kept entirely free of weeds by the use of weedkillers and mulches. But this does require an understanding of the herbicides available and strict accuracy in their application.

Choosing and using weedkillers

The basic rules when using herbicides are to choose the chemical to suit the job you want done and to follow the manufacturer's instructions exactly. Herbicides are sold as granules to be used dry, as wettable powders, as soluble powders or as concentrated liquids that must be mixed with water. You can apply the types that are mixed with water either with a watering can fitted with a sprinkler bar or with a low-pressure sprayer that has a spray boom and coarse fan nozzle (which reduces the risk of spray drift). Keep such spray equipment only for use with weedkillers. It is important to find out how much weedkiller your equipment delivers over a given area when moving at a specific speed, and to use this information when calculating the amount of weedkiller to be used. Mark out the area to be sprayed so that no overlapping occurs.

Herbicides may be applied to the plants' leaves or to the soil, depending on how they act. Leaf-acting contact herbicides kill all green plant material they touch and are non-selective, but have no residual effect on the soil. Examples are diquat and paraquat. Paraquat kills only the parts it touches, and does not move within the plant, so it acts like a chemical hoe, killing off top growth but not affecting the roots of perennial weeds. It will damage decorative plants if it touches green stems or foliage, so use it with a dribble bar under shrubs to kill annual weeds. It acts most quickly in bright sunshine. It is inactivated on touching soil. It is most effective used on seedling weeds, and can be used as a pre-seeding weedkiller (alone or with diquat) before sowing lawn grass or vegetables. Prepare the seed-bed and leave for a week or two before sowing seeds. Water in dry weather to encourage the germination of weed seeds. Spray these with paraquat, then take out seed drills with minimum disturbance, or broadcast lawn seed. Experienced gardeners may use paraquat as a pre-emergence weedkiller; the seed-bed is prepared and the seed is sown, and spraying with weedkiller is timed to take place a few days before the crop germinates.

A second group of leaf-acting herbicides are termed translocated herbicides because they are absorbed by the plant and are carried to its various parts. As a result, complete spray cover is not needed. Examples include 2,4-D, 2,4,5-T, mecoprop and MCPA. Their effect varies on different plants, and some can be used to control weeds in lawns, where they act as selective weedkillers. They are most useful in killing deep-rooted perennial weeds, and spot treatment can be used on these. Grass itself is not affected, but mowings from treated grass must be composted efficiently for at least six months and should never be used as a mulch. These weedkillers should be used when plants are actively growing in warm weather and when no rain is expected for several hours. Most broad-leaved cultivated plants are highly susceptible to even tiny amounts, so you must be extremely careful when using them. They have some residual effect on the soil.

The third and in many ways most useful group of herbicides are those that are soil-acting; they persist in the soil and are absorbed by the plant's roots. Examples include sodium chlorate, dichlobenil, simazine and propachlor. These may be selective or non-selective, depending on their type and the way they are used. Sodium chlorate, for

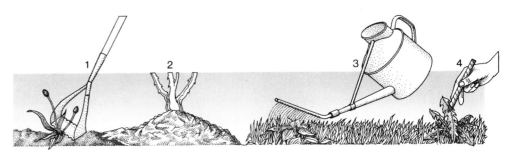

Ways of killing weeds
1 Hoe shallow-rooted annual weeds; collect and burn them if in flower. Dig up perennials, being sure to remove all parts of the roots or they will re-grow. 2 Mulch thickly with organic material to prevent annual weeds germinating. A mulch of black plastic sheeting is efficient between rows of vegetables. 3 Sprinkle weedkiller solution from a watering can fitted with a sprinkler bar; choose the weedkiller carefully and apply at a measured rate. Lawn weedkillers can be applied dry with a fertilizer spreader; it is more effective to apply a weedkiller alone two weeks after fertilizer than to use a combined formulation. 4 Spot treat single weeds with a weedkiller-impregnated stick or brush a suitable solution on their leaves.

example, is a total weedkiller that kills all plant life and can spread sideways and downwards in the soil. It can be used on paths and waste ground. Simazine used at the right strength, on the other hand, can be used on established rose beds and shrub borders (except on light soils or certain susceptible shrubs noted on the packet) to kill germinating weeds. It is held in the top 5 cm (2 in) of soil and does not spread downwards or sideways. It persists for several months, and provided there are no herbaceous plants with the shrubs, one spraying each spring is usually enough to control all annual and most peren-

nial weeds; hoe the ground in autumn. Propachlor is the first selective weedkiller safe to use among some root vegetables and certain herbaceous and bulbous plants if applied before the bulbs emerge.

Always study manufacturers' literature carefully when choosing and using weedkillers. They are sold under various proprietary names but the active ingredient, which has an internationally-recognized name, should also appear. Note advice concerning susceptible plants; it does not matter whether you consider them weeds, ornamentals or crops as far as the herbicide is concerned.

Garden weedkillers and their uses

	International name(s)	Some proprietary names	Weeds controlled and comments
Foliar contact herbicides	Diquat + paraquat	'Weedol'	Total kill of foliage and annuals; repeated treatment needed for perennials; lethal poison to humans and animals
Translocated leaf-acting herbicides for lawns and spot treatment	2,4-D	'Lornox'; 'Vigon DC'; 'Dicotox'	Daisy, dandelion, docks, buttercup, creeping thistles, plantains, bellbine, convolvulus, annual nettle; harmful to fish
	2,4-D + mecoprop	'Lornox Plus'; 'Mecodox'; 'Verdone'; 'Supertox'	As above, plus clevers, clover, pearlwort, yarrow, mouse-ear chickweed; harmful to fish
	Dicamba + MCPA	'Cambadex'	Knotweeds, spurrey, chickweed, pearlwort, yarrow and weeds controlled by 2,4-D; harmful to fish
	Ioxynil	'Acrilawn'	Speedwells, knotweeds; may be used on young grass to control many seedling weeds; harmful to fish
Other translocated leaf-acting herbicides	2,4-D + 2,4,5-T	'Brushwood Killer'; 'Silvitox'; 'Spontox'	Stinging nettles, brushwood, brambles, ivy, regrowth from felled trees; poisonous to fish, animals and humans
	Dalapon	'Dalapon'; 'Dowpon'	Couch grass and other perennial grasses; can be used among dormant fruit bushes (blackcurrant, gooseberry) and 'Cox's Orange Pippin' apple
Soil-acting total weedkillers	Ammonium sulphamate	'Amcide'	Persists 12 weeks
	Sodium chlorate		Persists six months or more; moves in soil water; used on derelict land; inflammable when dry (but some brands have fire depressant)
	Dichlobenil	'Casoron G'	Total at high strength; persists several months; does not move in soil; harmful to fish
	Simazine + aminotriazole	'Super Weedex'	Persists 12 months; does not move in soil
	Simazine + aminotriazole + MCPA	'Kilweed'; 'Combat Path Weedkiller'	Persists 12 months; does not move in soil; can be used around established apple and pear trees
Soil-acting selective weedkillers	Dichlobenil	'Casoron G'	Selective at lower strength; controls ground elder, docks, couch grass, coltsfoot, horsetail; does not move in soil; harmful to fish; avoid on susceptible shrubs
	Lenacil	'Venzar Lenacil'	Annual weeds among shrubs and some herbaceous plants on light soils; harmful to fish
	Propachlor	'Ramrod'	Germinating weeds among some established vegetables, some bedding and herbaceous plants and shrubs; persists six weeks
	Simazine	'Weedex'	Selective at lower strength to kill germinating annual weeds in rose beds and shrub borders (but some shrubs susceptible); not suitable for light or newly cultivated soils; otherwise does not move in soil.
Lawn moss killers	Ammonium sulphate + ferrous sulphate	Various, including many lawn sands	Moss, pearlwort; ammonium sulphate is a fertilizer that raises soil acidity; see p 393
	Mercurous chloride (calomel)	'Mos-tox'; 'MC Moss Killer'; mercurized lawn sands	Moss; poisonous; harmful to fish; also a lawn fungicide
	Mercurous chloride + ferrous sulphate	'Berk Mosskiller'; 'Mosstoll'	Moss; poisonous; harmful to fish; also a lawn fungicide

Problems with your plants

Every gardener comes up against the problem of plant pests, diseases and disorders at some time; there is no way of keeping them out of even the most carefully tended plot. But your general standard of plant care and the cleanliness of your garden can have an important influence. Plants grown from good stock, suitably placed and spaced so that sun and air can ripen their stems, and well fed and watered, will not succumb as quickly to disease and will not be as badly damaged by pests as plants that are struggling. They will also recover faster when control measures are applied. Thus everything that you do to make your garden beautiful and productive will also help to keep it healthy.

Nevertheless, it will be necessary to counter-attack on occasions. Then you will need to know, firstly, what the problem is, secondly, what to treat it with and, finally, how to apply the treatment. This article gives you general guidance on recognizing and treating plant pests and diseases, while those on pages 362 to 367 deal more specifically with the troubles that are most likely to afflict your plants. The article on page 368 deals with disorders – constitutional troubles of plants that are not caused by specific insect pests or disease organisms.

Recognizing pest damage
Most plant pests fall into one of three groups: the sap-feeders, the leaf-eaters and the soil-dwelling root pests. Sap-feeders do not usually make holes in plants but they can weaken them and stunt their growth. Aphids such as greenfly and blackfly are the most common type of sap-feeding insect and they often cause leaves to become curled up. Together with scale insects and whiteflies, aphids excrete honeydew which makes the host plant sticky. Sooty moulds often grow on the honeydew and this is a good indication that one of these pests is present somewhere on the plant, usually on the underside of the foliage.

Two other sap-feeding pests are red spider mites and thrips. These both attack the leaves and cause the upper leaf surface to become mottled with tiny white, yellow or pale green spots, but they do not produce honeydew. Thrips generally live on top of the leaves and cause a silvery discolouration, whereas red spider mites are usually found under the leaves where they spin a fine silken webbing. Capsid bugs are a type of sap-feeder that do cause holes to be made in the leaves. They have a toxic saliva that kills plants cells, and this makes the foliage distorted, with many small holes. This damage mainly occurs at the tips of the shoots.

Leaf-eating pests such as caterpillars, slugs and snails are capable of eating large pieces out of leaves, stems and flowers. Caterpillars are the larvae of either moths, butterflies or sawflies. They can usually be found on the plant near the damaged tissues, and this makes their identification easy. Slugs and snails tend to feed at night and hide during the day. They often leave behind a silvery slime trail on the foliage, and this is a useful indication that this type of pest has been at work.

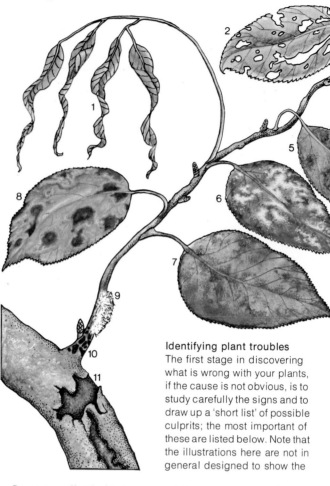

Identifying plant troubles
The first stage in discovering what is wrong with your plants, if the cause is not obvious, is to study carefully the signs and to draw up a 'short list' of possible culprits; the most important of these are listed below. Note that the illustrations here are not in general designed to show the results of attack by specific pests and diseases.
Leaves and shoots: 1 Leaves curled or rolled: aphids; peach leaf curl disease; sawflies.
2 Holes or notches in leaves: caterpillars; capsid bugs; earwigs; flea beetles; sawflies; slugs; snails; weevils. **3** Leaf blisters or white 'trails': leaf

Some pests live inside leaves, and these are called leaf miners. They are usually the larvae (maggots) of flies, and they cause 'mines' or tunnels of various shapes and patterns. The mined area often appears as a white or discoloured zone. If you pick a mined leaf and hold it up to the light, it is possible to see the maggot at the end of its tunnel.

Soil pests such as chafer grubs, cutworms, leatherjackets and root flies eat roots and chew the tissues at the base of plant stems. This causes the plants to grow slowly and in severe attacks they may wilt and die. Plants which are making poor growth should be dug up and the roots carefully examined. If the root system has been damaged, the culprits can usually be found in the root ball or in the soil from which the plant was lifted.

Recognizing plant diseases
Plant diseases are not so easy to diagnose as pests, since you cannot directly identify the culprit, nor are the signs of attack so clear-cut. So recognition is to some extent a question of elimination. If a plant is obviously not well, and there are no signs of pests on leaves, stems or roots, then it is probably suffering from either a disease or a disorder! Diseases of plants are caused, just like diseases of people, by micro-organisms – principally, in the case of plants, by fungi, bacteria and viruses. The commonest everyday diseases are caused by fungi – not, generally, the familiar toadstool type, but mildews, moulds and the like.

The most easily recognized diseases are the powdery mildews. These coat plants with a superficial white mould. They disfigure, but

they also stunt growth because they interfere with the functioning of the leaves. Other common diseases cause spots on leaves. The colour and shape of the spots identify the disease. Often, but not always, mould can be seen on the upper or lower surface of the spot. The spots are usually soft, sunken or of different texture from the rest of the leaf. If left unchecked they spread or multiply and cause leaf fall. Some diseases, such as downy mildew and grey mould, produce areas of discoloured tissue rather than definite spots, but they can be identified by a mould on the surface.

Leaf curl can be caused by a disease, but it is more likely to be the result of insect attack. Always look carefully on the inner surface of a rolled and discoloured leaf; you will very often find a pest. As already mentioned, wilting or sudden death usually indicates trouble at the roots. This could be due to a pest or disease. Usually the only way to find out is to dig the plant up and have a look.

Diseases caused by bacteria and viruses are mainly of concern to the really keen gardener and the commercial grower. However, it is important to be able to recognize them because they are difficult or impossible to control and the best advice is often to dig up and burn the affected plant to remove the source of infection – which, if left unchecked, may often spread to other plants in the garden. The most common bacterial disease is bacterial canker of stone fruits such as plums; it is described on page 366. Another is fireblight, which may attack apples, pears and other members of the rose family (see p 366). Virus diseases cause a variety of symptoms, ranging

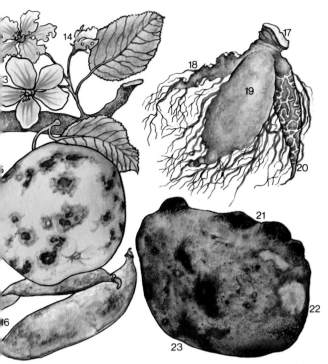

on leaves or stems:
anthracnose; apple scab; black
spot; cane spot; chocolate spot.
11 Soft wound on branch or
trunk: canker.
Flowers and fruits: 12 Flowers
eaten: caterpillars; earwigs;
slugs; snails. **13** Flowers
unnaturally mottled or streaked:
thrips; virus disease. **14** Flower
buds eaten or distorted: aphids;
birds; capsid bugs;
caterpillars; earwigs; weevils.
15 Brown marks on fruits: bitter
pit; bitter rot; brown rot; codling
moth; sawflies; scab. **16** Bean
or pea pods distorted: thrips.
Roots and stems: 17 Stem
eaten through at base: chafer
grubs; cutworms;
leatherjackets; root fly larvae;
slugs. **18** Roots, bulbs, etc,
eaten: chafer grubs; slugs.
19 Swollen roots: turnip gall
weevil; club root disease;
eelworms. **20** Roots, bulbs, etc,
tunnelled: leatherjackets;
millipedes; root flies;
wireworm. **21** Outgrowth on
potato tubers: wart disease.
22 Soft patches on potato
tubers: potato blight. **23** Scabs
on potato tubers: scab disease.

miners. **4** Leaves and/or stems
deformed: aphids; capsid
bugs; virus diseases
(reversion; fern leaf of
tomatoes); weedkiller damage.
5 Sticky honeydew with sooty
moulds on leaves: aphids;
scale insects; suckers; whitefly.
6 White, grey or yellowish
deposit on leaves: downy or
powdery mildew; grey mould.
7 Mottled or discoloured
leaves: red spider mite; silver
leaf disease; thrips; virus
diseases. **8** Brown or yellowish
leaf patches: blight; frost
damage; leaf mould (tomatoes,
on upper leaf surface); scorch.
9 White 'wool' on stems: mealy
bugs; woolly aphids. **10** Spots

from mottling and streaking of leaves or
flowers to stunted and abnormally shaped leaf
growth (see pp 366 and 367).

Recognizing disorders

Disorders appear when there is something
wrong with the conditions in which plants are
growing. This could be an unsatisfactory balance of plant foods, too much sun, irregular
water supply or an accidental dose of weedkiller. Obviously it is difficult to generalize
about symptoms resulting from such a diversity of causes. Sometimes tissue damaged
by a disorder will then be invaded by a disease, which complicates diagnosis.

Nutritional disorders result in a change of
colour, size or even shape of leaves and a
consequent reduction in growth or fruitfulness of the plant as a whole. Colour changes
may affect the edges of leaves or diffuse areas
between veins (spots or more clearly-defined
patches of colour generally indicate a disease). Irregular watering can cause fruit to
split. Sun scorch usually blanches and kills the
tissues of leaves, fruits or even flowers.

Choosing and using pesticides

It is sometimes possible to stop a pest or disease attack in its early stages by removing the
diseased leaves or by squashing the offending
insects. Unfortunately, attacks have often got
beyond this stage by the time you see them or
can do anything about them. This is where
pesticides – principally insecticides to kill
insects and certain other related animals, and
fungicides to treat fungal diseases – are
needed. Sensibly used, pesticides are a very

valuable aid to gardening and particularly to
week-end gardeners. They are not intended
to be used to eradicate every insect and fungus
in the garden; they should be used to stop the
pests getting more benefit from your garden
than you do.

Modern pesticides are fairly expensive
chemicals, so the wise gardener gets the best
value he can out of them. With most insect
pests, it is sufficient to keep a sharp eye out for
trouble and then counter-attack with the
appropriate pesticide. The same is true of
many diseases. However, some plants are so
prone to attack from certain pests and diseases that it makes good sense to take preventive measures in anticipation of attack.
Examples include the winter and spring spraying of fruit trees against aphids and other
troubles (see the box on this page) and the
spraying of roses with fungicides to prevent
mildew, black spot and rust. Some other preventive measures applicable to particular
plants, especially vegetables, are mentioned
in the relevant articles elsewhere in this book.
With plant diseases in particular, improved
growing conditions are just as important as
the application of pesticide.

Choosing pesticides Choosing the most suitable pesticide calls for a little knowledge and a
little thought. It should control the particular
pest or disease, be suitable for the plants
which are attacked and, in the case of food
crops, have an acceptable harvest interval –
that is, the period that must elapse between
treatment and harvesting. It is obviously
important to identify the trouble, and the following articles describe the troubles and

recommend suitable pesticides and other control measures.

The table on page 361 gives details of the
most important generally available pesticides
and their effects, and should help you to select
a small range to keep at hand. Pesticides are
usually sold under trade names, but the name
of their active ingredients are printed somewhere on the label, and you should always
check this to make sure that you are in fact
using what you intended.

Pesticides are available as liquids or wettable powders for dilution with water to make
a spray, as dusts in puffer packs, as aerosols, as
powders and granules for combating soil pests
and as baits. The last are used principally
against slugs and snails. Formulations for
spraying are usually the cheapest to use and
the most effective against most pests and diseases. Dusts and aerosols are expensive but
are a useful standby for small-scale spot and
emergency treatments; they are always ready
to use without any measuring or mixing. Dusts
leave a slight deposit even when very carefully
applied; aerosols must be held at the correct
distance or they may scorch plants. A pesticide may control a slightly different range of
troubles if it is formulated in a different way –
another reason to study the manufacturer's
instructions.

Some plants are sensitive to certain pesticides and may be damaged by them. Some
pesticides, while not damaging the plants,
may taint the flavour of fruit or vegetables.
Pesticide labels list the plants which should
not be treated. Some pesticides break down
quite quickly after being applied,/*continued*

Protecting fruit trees

Fruit trees and bushes are prey to a wide
range of pests and diseases that seriously
affect crop yields and quality, and it is
wise to carry out a systematic programme
of preventive spraying. If, in spite of these
precautions, certain pests are
troublesome, specific control measures
must be used in addition.

Dormant period Winter spraying of tar
oil controls the overwintering eggs of
aphids, scale insects, suckers and winter
moths. Alternatively, use a
dinitro-ortho-cresol (DNOC) winter
wash, which controls the above plus the
eggs of the fruit tree red spider mite. Note
that these winter sprays are not suitable
for use on the myrobalan plum (*Prunus
cerasifera*) or on strawberries.

Spring At bud burst, use a systemic
insecticide such as dimethoate or
formothion to control aphids and suckers.
Do not spray during the flowering period
to avoid harming pollinating insects. At
petal fall use a systemic insecticide again
to control aphids, suckers, leaf-hopper
and capsid bugs.

Autumn Apply a band of special grease
around the trunks of trees to trap the
wingless females of winter moths and
prevent them laying their eggs in the tree.

Problems with your plants (continued)

Ways of applying pesticides
For spot treatments, you can use an aerosol 1 or a puffer pack of pesticide powder 2. Small lever-action plastic sprayers 3 have largely superseded old metal types, just as the larger plastic pump-up pressure sprayer 4 has replaced the old-fashioned syringe. Pressure sprayers are available in various sizes, some with a trigger or other on-off control; preferably choose one with a long spray lance and an adjustable nozzle. Back-pack sprayers 5 are needed only for the spraying of large numbers of fruit trees and bushes. Powders and granules to combat soil pests and diseases are simply sprinkled on the soil surface and raked in, or are applied direct to seed drills.

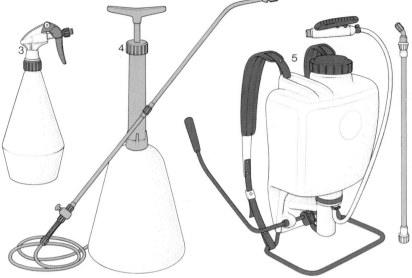

and treated fruit and vegetables can be picked and eaten within a day or two. Others are more persistent; they give longer protection but are not suitable for crops that are almost ready for eating. The harvest interval can vary from nothing to four weeks, and again this is stated on the label.

Using pesticides Pesticides must be used at the recommended rate. Underdosing is a waste of time and money; overdosing is also a waste of money and may damage the plants. When mixing sprays, measure carefully both the amount of chemical used and the amount of water it is mixed with. As a general rule, do not mix two or more pesticides unless you know that they are compatible; if you really need a 'broad-spectrum' insecticide that will kill a wide range of pests, combined formulations are available from manufacturers. It is, however, normally permissible to mix any one fungicide and one insecticide in the same spray without harm, though to be safe it is advisable to consult the charts issued by manufacturers. Each should be at full strength, so first mix one component with the correct amount of water, then stir in the correct amount of the second.

Most pesticides act by direct contact with the pest or disease organism, so it is important when applying sprays to wet the whole plant — stems, buds and both upper and lower surfaces of leaves. However, some insecticides and one or two fungicides have so-called systemic action – that is, they are absorbed into the plant, where (so long as the plant is not a type that is sensitive) they do no harm but are carried by the plant's internal transport system to all its tissues; then, any susceptible pest attacking the plant is poisoned as it does so. Some systemic insecticides can even be watered into the ground, to be absorbed by the plant's roots. However, it is foolish to rely on such systemic action where infestation is heavy – be sure then to thoroughly spray the plant as described above – but systemic pesticides do give more prolonged protection than contact types.

The best time to spray is in early morning or late afternoon, when beneficial insects such as bees are least active. (Never spray fruit trees and bushes when they are in blossom, for the same reason.) Do not spray in bright sun-shine, when even plain water may scorch foliage. Do not spray when it is windy, or much of your spray may miss its target and drift onto other plants. Dull, still weather is best. Use common sense when utilizing pesticides, and observe the precautions mentioned in the panel on this page.

Beneficial insects
Some of the creatures that appear on plants are not harmful, but are useful friends which either parasitize or prey on pests. The best known predator is probably the ladybird. Both adult ladybirds and their larvae feed on greenfly and other aphids. Towards the end of summer, ladybirds and other insects that feed on aphids, such as hoverfly larvae and small parasitic wasps, can become sufficiently numerous to control this pest. Insecticides should be used wisely and in moderation, spraying only affected plants and their near neighbours, in order to preserve as many beneficial insects as possible.

Biological control is the deliberate use of predators and parasites to control pests. Most beneficial insects, although useful, do not exert enough control on their own to prevent damage occuring. With two specific examples, however, biological control is feasible as an alternative to the use of pesticides. These are greenhouse red spider mite (a distinct species from the red spider mite that infests fruit trees) and greenhouse whitefly. They can be controlled respectively by introducing onto the infested plants a predatory mite called *Phytoseiulus persimilis* and a parasitic wasp called *Encarsia formosa*. These beneficial creatures are available in some countries from commercial suppliers whose advertisements can be seen in the gardening press.

Precautions with pesticides
Take the very greatest of care in storing and using pesticides. Do not use products marketed for use by farmers or growers; some are deadly poisons. Pesticides sold for garden use are safe when used as directed, but remember that they may poison if misused. Most are poisonous to fish and bees. If any person or pet is poisoned (or suspected of being poisoned), get them to a hospital, doctor or vet as soon as possible, taking the pesticide container and any unconsumed pesticide with you for identification. Give the patient milk and raw egg or simply water to drink. Induce vomiting only if medical help is distant.
Precautions in storage Keep all pesticides under lock and key. If possible, store them in a locked shed on a shelf too high for children to reach. If this is not possible, they must be kept in a locked cupboard. Always keep them in the maker's containers, clearly labelled. NEVER keep them in lemonade bottles, wine bottles or similar containers; they usually taste nasty, but by the time someone has noticed the taste the damage may be done. Keep aerosols out of direct sunlight and away from any source of heat.
Precautions in use Never use a stick to stir a solution and leave this where a child or pet may get hold of it. Keep special spray equipment for use only with pesticides, and keep it as securely as the pesticides themselves. Use pesticides only in calm weather to avoid spray drift; do not use in hot weather in enclosed areas where vaporization can occur, or in strong sunshine when foliage may be scorched. Adjust the spray equipment to give a spray suitable for the conditions – not so fine as to drift away from the plants but fine enough to wet them properly.

Measure accurately; never exceed stated quantities. Avoid contaminating puddles from which pets may drink, children's paddling pools or fish ponds. Do not lay slug pellets where children or pets may find and eat them. When mixing and spraying, keep arms covered. If spraying extensively overhead, as when treating fruit trees, wear a face mask if possible and work with your back to the breeze. Avoid all pesticide contact with skin and eyes; immediately wash off any splashes with large amounts of water. Do not leave any unused solution in the sprayer; wash it out immediately after use. Wash all exposed skin, especially before eating, drinking or smoking.

Garden insecticides and other pest-killers

Name; alternative names	Pests controlled	Comments
Benzene hexachloride (BHC; gamma-BHC; HCH; 'Gammexane'; 'Lindane')	Most insect pests	May taint fruit and root vegetables; rather persistent; 'Lindane' is a purified form less liable to cause tainting
Bioresmethrin	Aphids; caterpillars; whitefly	Non-persistent
Bromophos	Most root pests	Available as a powder for soil application
Carbaryl ('Sevin')	Caterpillars; earwigs; flea beetles; leaf rollers; leatherjackets; sawflies; wasp nests; weevils; etc	A broad-spectrum insecticide often used as a substitute for DDT; also available in some countries as an earthworm killer
Chlordane	Ants; earthworms; leatherjackets	Persistent; use alternatives if possible
Chlorpyrifos ('Dursban')	Most soil pests	Persistent granular soil pesticide applied at planting time
Derris	Wide range of insects; red spider mite	Safe; non-persistent; poisonous to fish
Diazinon	Aphids; capsid bugs; cockroaches; leaf-hoppers; leaf miners; mealy bugs; millipedes; red spider mite; scale insects; thrips; whitefly; soil pests	Rather persistent; poisonous to animals and humans
Dichlorvos	Aphids; caterpillars; thrips; red spider mite; whitefly	Impregnated plastic strip used as greenhouse fumigant
Dimethoate ('Cygon'; 'Rogor')	Aphids; leaf-hoppers; leaf miners; red spider mite; scale insects; thrips	Systemic; relatively non-persistent; poisonous to fish
Dinitro-ortho-cresol (DNOC)	Eggs of aphids, capsid bugs, caterpillars, red spider mites	Used as winter wash in place of tar oil; stains skin
Fenitrothion	Aphids; caterpillars; codling moth; pear midge; sawflies; thrips	Rather persistent
Formothion ('Anthio')	Similar to dimethoate	Systemic; poisonous to fish
Lime sulphur	Big bud mite; gall mites; pear leaf-blister mite	Primarily a fungicide (see below); mainly used as winter spray
Malathion ('Cythion')	Aphids; capsid bugs; red spider mite; scale insects; thrips; whitefly	Safe; non-persistent; poisonous to fish
Menazon ('Saphos')	Aphids	Available mixed with BHC; systemic
Mercurous chloride (calomel)	Root flies	Poisonous; primarily a fungicide (see below); 4% dust relatively safe for garden use
Metaldehyde	Slugs; snails	Available as pellets and liquids; poisonous to fish, birds, animals and humans
Methiocarb	Slugs; snails	Available as pellets only; harmful to fish
Nicotine	Aphids; capsid bugs; caterpillars; leaf-hoppers; leaf miners	Poisonous but non-persistent
Oxydemeton-methyl ('Metasystox')	Aphids; leaf-hoppers; red spider mite	Systemic; poisonous to animals and humans; available as aerosol
Petroleum oil (white oil)	Capsid bugs; red spider mite; scale insects; thrips	Different formulations available for winter and summer use
Pirimicarb	Aphids	Non-persistent; very selective; most beneficial insects unharmed
Pirimiphos-methyl	Aphids; beetles; caterpillars; leaf miners; red spider mite; whitefly	Non-persistent; useful for vegetables and fruit
Pyrethrum	Aphids; caterpillars; leaf-hoppers; thrips; whitefly	Safe; non-persistent; poisonous to fish
Tar oil	Aphid's eggs; winter moths; other overwintering insects	Used as winter wash on dormant fruit trees, etc; harms swelling buds and leaves
Trichlorphon	Ants; caterpillars; cutworms; earwigs; root flies; leaf miners	Non-persistent; poisonous to fish

Garden fungicides

Name; alternative name	Diseases controlled	Comments
Benomyl ('Benlate')	Anthracnose; black spot; grey mould; lawn diseases; leaf spots; powdery mildews; scab	Systemic, but regular applications needed
Bordeaux mixture	Bacterial canker; black spot; blight; leaf spots; scab; most mildews; some rusts	May scorch foliage; for formula, see p 392; harmful to fish
Burgundy mixture	As for Bordeaux mixture, but especially rusts	Use immediately on mixing; for formula, see p 392; harmful to fish
Captan ('Orthocide')	Black spot; grey mould; peach leaf curl; scab	Do not use on fruit to be bottled; poisonous to fish; also used as a seed dressing to protect from damping off
Carbendazim ('Bavistin')	Anthracnose; grey mould; powdery mildew; scab	Systemic action
Cheshunt compound	Damping off of seedlings	For formula, see p 392; harmful to fish
Copper, colloidal	Similar to Bordeaux mixture	Harmful to fish and animals
Copper sulphate	Rose black spot and rust	Use only when plants dormant in winter at 5 g/litre (1 oz/gallon) of water; kills spores; harmful to fish
Dichlofluanid ('Elvaron')	Black spot; grey mould; paeony wilt; tulip fire	Harmful to fish; do not use on strawberries under cloches
Dinocap ('Karathane')	Powdery mildews	Poisonous to fish; also helps to control red spider mite
Folpet ('Phaltan')	Black spot; powdery mildews; rust	For roses; similar to captan; wettable powder
Formaldehyde (formalin)	Soil-borne fungi	Soil sterilizer; do not use near plants; poisonous
Iron sulphate (ferrous sulphate)	Some lawn diseases	Component of lawn sands (see p 393)
Lime sulphur	Peach leaf curl; powdery mildews; scab	Sulphur-shy fruit varieties harmed; do not use on fruit to be preserved
Mancozeb	Black spot; blight; downy mildew; rust	Also provides trace elements zinc and manganese
Maneb	Similar to mancozeb	Sometimes combined with carbendazim
Mercurous chloride (calomel)	Club root; some lawn diseases	Poisonous; component of mercurized lawn sands; harmful to fish, may cause skin irritation
Oxycarboxin	Rust	Systemic action
Quintozene	Soil-borne fungal diseases	Including diseases of lawns and bulbs
Sulphur	Powdery mildews; scab; rotting of stored roots, etc	Precautions as for lime sulphur; powder used on roots and plants; proprietary liquid formulations available
Thiophanate-methyl	Similar to benomyl	Systemic
Thiram	Black spot; downy mildew; grey mould; paeony wilt; peach leaf curl; rust; scab; tulip fire	Do not use on fruit to be preserved; also used as seed dressing to protect from damping off
Triforine	Black spot; powdery mildews	Systemic; especially for roses
Zineb ('Dithane')	Black spot; blight; downy mildew; peach leaf curl; rust	Similar to maneb

NB: Some of the above may be unavailable in certain countries; trade names may be different.

Plant pests

The pests that afflict garden plants are principally insects, though members of some other groups of creatures also cause problems. Details are given below of the most common pests that the gardener is likely to encounter, together with recommended preventive measures or treatment. If you have problems with identification, consult the article on page 358 to try to narrow the field down. The chart of pesticides on page 361 also gives details of alternative treatments. Bear in mind that this book is designed for readers in many countries, and not all the pests detailed here may occur in your region. Where a pest is not covered specifically here, follow the general advice in the article on page 358.

Vegetable pests

Aphids Also known as plant lice, these are small, plump, sometimes winged insects of various colours. Greenfly can attack most vegetables, but the most troublesome are blackfly on beans and grey aphids on brassicas (cabbages and their relatives). They suck sap from the leaves and stunt the plant's growth. Aphids excrete honeydew which makes the plants sticky and encourages the development of sooty moulds. Control the pest by spraying with dimethoate or malathion before the plants become heavily infested.

Asparagus beetle This beetle and its grubs attack asparagus plants and can strip the foliage. Spray or dust as necessary with derris.

Caterpillars Caterpillars – the larvae of various butterflies, moths and sawflies – are mainly a problem on brassicas. The plants should be regularly inspected during the summer and sprayed with fenitrothion as soon as caterpillar damage is seen.

Colorado beetle This pest has been kept out of Britain by vigilance and prompt action against any outbreak, but it is common in much of Europe and North America. The yellow and black striped beetles and their orange-coloured grubs feed on potatoes, and they can defoliate the plants. Control by spraying or dusting with BHC, but if they are seen in Britain, report their presence to the Ministry of Agriculture immediately.

Cutworms These are soil-dwelling caterpillars that sever lettuce roots and chew pieces out of root crops. The caterpillars are a dirty brown colour and they grow up to 4 cm (1½ in) in length. Control methods are the same as for root flies (see below).

Eelworms The potato cyst eelworm is a very persistent pest which can damage potatoes and tomatoes to the extent that the entire crop is lost. The pest attacks the roots, and the adults are just visible to the naked eye as white, yellow or brown spherical cysts on the roots. There are no effective chemicals available to home gardeners but some eelworm-resistant potato cultivars such as 'Maris Piper' have been developed (see p 276). Onion eelworm causes affected plants to become soft, swollen and distorted. Affected plants should be dug up and burned. Crop rotation is important as a way of avoiding eelworm problems (see p 262).

Flea beetles These are small beetles which

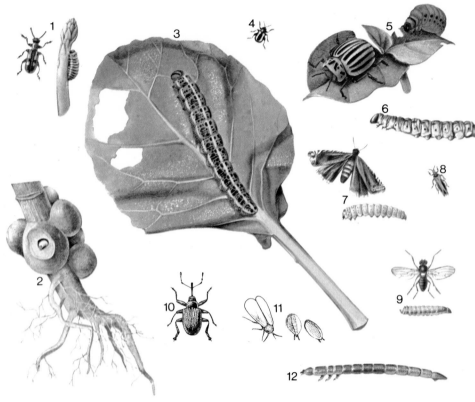

eat holes from the seedling leaves of brassicas, turnips and swedes. Heavy attacks can slow the young plant's growth and may destroy the seedlings. Prevent damage by dusting the seed rows with BHC, and water the seed bed to encourage rapid growth.

Pea moth This moth is active during the summer months and lays its eggs on the flowers. When they hatch, the caterpillars enter the pods and feed on the peas. Damage can be prevented by spraying with fenitrothion when most of the flowers have set pods.

Pea thrip This pest is similar to the thrips that may infest decorative plants (see below). The resultant mottling affects pods as well as leaves, and plants can become stunted, with poor cropping. Control by spraying with dimethoate, malathion or nicotine as soon as you see any sign of damage.

Root flies These are flies that overwinter as pupae in the soil; it is their larvae, or grubs, that do the damage. They attack the roots of brassicas, onions, beans and carrots. The carrot root fly larvae are thin yellow maggots which make rusty brown tunnels in the carrot surface. The other types of root fly are white maggots which eat the roots of their host plants; they can kill young plants. They can be controlled by treating the seed rows and planting holes with diazinon granules.

Weevils Adult pea and bean weevils are greyish-brown beetles about 5 mm (¼ in) long that make U-shaped notches in the leaf edges. They mostly feed at night, and drop off the plant when disturbed. Mature plants can withstand damage, but attacks on seedlings delay growth. If damage is seen, dust the seedlings with BHC or derris.

Grubs of the turnip gall weevil attack the roots of most brassicas, not only turnips and swedes, and may cause small rounded swellings on the roots. These may be confused with the swellings caused by club root (see

Vegetable and fruit pests
Illustrations are from life-size up to 1½ times life-size, except where stated. 1 Asparagus beetle and larva; 2 turnip gall weevil grub (half-size); 3 cabbage white caterpillar; 4 flea beetle; 5 Colorado beetle and grub; 6 cutworm; 7 pea moth and larva; 8 pea thrip (×3); 9 carrot root fly and larva; 10 pea or bean weevil (×3); 11 whitefly and larvae (×3); 12 wireworm; 13 greenfly (×3); 14 blackfly (×3); 15 woolly aphid; 16 big bud mite (affected bud at bottom); 17 mussel scale; 18 brown scale; 19 apple suckers (×3); 20 winter moth (winged male, wingless female and caterpillar); 21 raspberry beetle and larva (×3); 22 codling moth and caterpillar; 23 gooseberry sawfly and caterpillar

p 365). With the former, if you cut the swelling in half you will see either a small white grub or the hollow centre where it has been feeding. The pest is prevented by a BHC seed dressing, and further control measures are not usually necessary.

Whiteflies The adults of these pests resemble tiny white moths; they fly up readily from infested plants. The greenhouse whitefly can be found on outdoor tomatoes and members of the cucumber family as well as on greenhouse crops, and the cabbage whitefly on brassicas. Both the adults and the scale-like larvae are sap-feeders and they cause similar damage to aphids. They are best controlled by spraying with pyrethrum or BHC. Cucurbits (marrows, cucumbers, pumpkins and so on) should be sprayed with pyrethrum only. Frequent applications will be necessary if a heavy infestation has developed.

As an alternative to chemicals, the greenhouse whitefly can be controlled biologically with a parasitic wasp called *Encarsia formosa* (see p 360).

Wireworms These are the larvae of click beetles. They make many small holes in

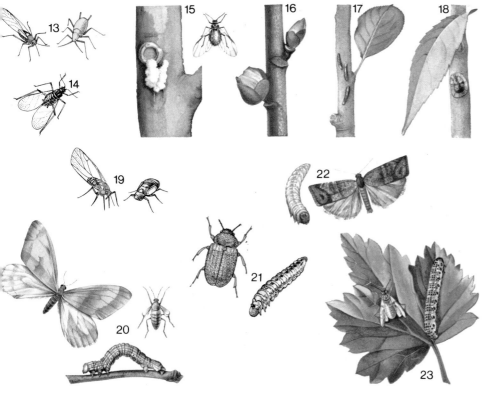

potato tubers. Wireworms are a rusty brown colour and grow up to 3 cm (1¼ in) long. They are most common in new gardens that were formerly grassland. Treat the soil with diazinon granules at planting time.

Others Leaf vegetables are prone to attack by slugs and snails, while greenhouse crops – particularly tomatoes and cucumbers – may suffer from greenhouse red spider mite. Both of these are described later among the pests of ornamental plants, as are leaf miners, which can attack celery, and millipedes, leatherjackets, chafer grubs and other root pests, which attack a wide range of plants.

Fruit pests

Aphids All types of fruit are attacked by these sap-feeding insects. They often cause leaf-curling and soiling of the foliage with sooty moulds, and they are important carriers of virus diseases of soft fruits. Woolly aphid is a pest of apples which lives in crevices in the bark and covers itself with a white fluffy wax material. Most aphids overwinter as eggs on their host plant and these eggs can be destroyed by spraying with a tar oil wash during the winter when the trees are dormant (see p 359). Systemic insecticides such as dimethoate should be applied to the young foliage in the spring before aphids begin to cause damage.

Big bud mite This is a serious pest which spreads the virus causing black currant reversion disease (see p 367). The microscopic mites live and feed within the buds, which become swollen and rounded in shape. Affected buds are most readily seen in the winter, when they can be removed and burned. Spraying with lime sulphur as the first flowers open, and subsequently at two 14-day intervals, will help to control the mites.

Birds and mammals Many birds will damage ripening fruits, and bullfinches will eat flower buds during the winter. Bird-repellent sprays may have some success, but netting is the most effective remedy in situations where this is possible. For further information on these and other animal pests, see page 267.

Codling moth The caterpillars of this moth feed inside apples and sometimes pears, and they are the cause of maggoty fruit in the late summer period. Control by spraying with fenitrothion four weeks after petal-fall and again three weeks later.

Fruit sawflies The caterpillars of these insects tunnel into the fruitlets of apples, plums and pears in the early summer period, and damaged fruits usually fall from the tree without developing further. This type of pest is controlled by spraying with BHC at petal-fall (but not before, to avoid harming pollinating insects).

Gooseberry sawfly The black-spotted green caterpillars can rapidly defoliate gooseberry bushes during the summer. Check regularly for this pest during the late spring and summer, and spray with fenitrothion or pyrethrum if it is seen.

Pear leaf-blister mite This pest is too small to be seen without a microscope, but it causes a row of pale green or pink blotches along either side of the midribs of young leaves. Later, the blotches become brown or black and the whole leaf area may be affected. Control by thoroughly spraying the tree with lime sulphur as the buds begin to open in spring.

Pear midge This is a tiny gnat-like fly that lays its eggs in the unopened blossoms. The larvae feed inside the fruitlets, which initially grow more quickly than normal, then begin to turn black and after a few weeks fall off the tree. The grubs, which are white or pale orange and about 2 mm (¹⁄₁₀ in) long, leave the fallen fruitlets and pupate in the soil. Attacks can be prevented by spraying with fenitrothion when the blossom is at the white bud stage. Regularly collect any fallen fruitlets and burn them.

Raspberry beetle This small beetle lays its eggs on the flowers of raspberries, blackberries and hybrids such as loganberries. These hatch into small brown and white grubs that feed on the ripening fruits. The pest is controlled by spraying with malathion when the first fruits are ripening. Spray late at night in order to avoid harming pollinating insects.

Red spider mite This is a quite distinct species – *Panonychus ulmi* – from the pest of the same common name that infests greenhouse plants and certain outdoor ornamentals. The effect is similar, however. It attacks the foliage of apples, plums and other fruit trees, sucking sap and causing the leaves to turn a mottled yellow and fall prematurely. Hot summers favour this pest. It can be controlled by spraying with dimethoate.

Scale insects These are small sap-feeding insects which have a shell-like covering over their bodies. They usually feed on the bark, and two common types are mussel scale on apples and brown scale on peaches, vines and currants. Winter treatment with tar oil will deal with these pests, or they can be sprayed with malathion in the summer.

Suckers Apple and pear suckers are sap-feeding insects that become active in the spring, attacking the blossom trusses and young leaves. Heavy infestation can kill the blossom, turning it brown as though frosted. The adults are pale green and the size of greenfly, but are flattened rather than rounded and have conspicuous wing pads.

Apple sucker has only one generation a year and damage is confined to the spring period. Pear sucker, however, has two or three generations during the summer, and heavy infestations can lead to the foliage and fruit being coated with sooty mould, which grows on the honeydew excreted by the pest. Both insects can be controlled by spraying the trees with a systemic insecticide shortly before the blossom opens.

Wasps These are beneficial early in the summer, because they catch caterpillars and other insects. At the end of summer, however, they can be a real nuisance when they develop a taste for sweet things, including ripening fruits. The best solution is to trace them back to their nest and place carbaryl dust in the entrance hole at dusk.

Winter moth The looper caterpillars of this pest feed on the young foliage and blossom of most tree fruits. They finish feeding by early summer and pupate in the soil. The moths emerge during the winter and the female adults, which are wingless, can be prevented from climbing into the branches to lay their eggs by placing a sticky grease band around the trunk. This should be used between autumn and spring. The caterpillars can be controlled by spraying the young leaves with fenitrothion.

Others Slugs and snails commonly attack strawberry plants, eating leaves and fruit, while capsid bugs may attack fruit trees, discolouring fruit and leaves. Both are described over with pests of ornamentals. /continued

Plant pests (continued)

Pests of ornamentals

Ants Ants can be a nuisance by building their nests directly beneath choice plants and by crawling over plants in search of aphids and their sweet honeydew. They cause little direct damage to plants, however. If necessary, ants can be controlled by dusting or drenching the nests with BHC.

Aphids and caterpillars Most ornamentals can suffer from various types of aphid and caterpillar, and these can be controlled as described above for vegetable and fruit pests.

Capsid bugs Hydrangeas, roses, fuchsias and dahlias, as well as fruit trees, are among the plants that are damaged by these sap-feeding insects. The green or brown bugs, which are up to 1 cm (⅜ in) in length, inject a toxic saliva into the buds on which they feed. This causes the leaves which subsequently develop to be distorted and tattered. Malathion or diazinon should be applied at the first sign of damage.

Chafer beetles The adult beetles sometimes damage plants by eating foliage and flowers, but it is the root-feeding larvae that are the more serious pest. One of the largest species, the cock-chafer, has grubs which grow up to 6 cm (2½ in) in length. They are white grubs with three pairs of legs and brown heads. Their bodies are characteristically curved like a letter C. Cock-chafer grubs will attack most plants – ornamental and food crops – while a smaller species, the garden chafer, is usually found eating the roots of grass. Chafer grubs can be controlled by watering the soil with BHC when damage is seen, but with root crops use diazinon.

Chrysanthemum eelworm This microscopic pest can be very destructive to chrysanthemums and some other plants, including asters and paeonies. Infested parts of leaves become brown and are often sharply divided from healthy parts by leaf veins – a distinctive feature. The eelworms rapidly spread up the plant in wet or humid weather, disfiguring the plant. There are no effective chemicals available to home gardeners. Burn affected plants, and obtain new stock from reputable growers; plant them in a different part of the garden.

Earwigs These feed by night on young foliage and the petals of flowers such as dahlias and chrysanthemums. When damage is noticed, the plants and soil beneath them should be dusted with BHC. Earwigs can also be trapped by placing straw-filled flower pots among the plants. The earwigs will hide in the straw during the day and can be picked out.

Leaf-hoppers These small insects jump off plants when disturbed. They are sap-feeders related to aphids, and like these transmit virus diseases. Attacked leaves show white or pale green spots. They attack roses and geraniums (pelargoniums) and also soft fruits such as strawberries and raspberries. Control with dimethoate, formothion or malathion when damage is seen.

Leaf miners These are usually the grubs of small flies and they tunnel in the foliage of a number of plants. The shape of the tunnels varies acording to the species of leaf miner, but they generally take the form of blotches,

as on holly, or sinuous 'mines' or tunnels, as on chrysanthemums. The grubs can be controlled by spraying with BHC or diazinon when damage is noticed.

Leatherjackets These fat grubs of craneflies or harvestmen (daddy-longlegs) live in the soil, particularly in lawns and newly cultivated land. They feed on roots and can be very damaging to lawns, causing brown patches in summer. Control by watering the turf with BHC during warm damp weather in spring or autumn. On cultivated ground, deep cultivation exposes them to birds, or you can use BHC or bromophos powder.

Millipedes These live in the soil and can damage seedlings by feeding on the roots and

Pests of ornamentals
1¼ to 1½ times life-size, except where stated.
24 Capsid bug; 25 chafer beetle; 26 cock-chafer grub; 27 leaf miner (effect); 28 millipede; 29 leaf-hopper; 30 leatherjacket (×3)

young shoots. They also cause harm to larger plants when they enlarge on damage started by other pests and diseases. Millipedes grow up to 5 cm (2 in) long, are often black in colour and they have many pairs of legs all along the length of their bodies. When disturbed, they curl up like a watch spring, unlike their close relatives the beneficial centipedes, which tend to run for cover. If millipedes are causing trouble they can be controlled by dusting the soil with BHC.

Red spider mite This is a different species to that which occurs on fruit trees, being classified as *Tetranychus urticae*, and is a great nuisance in the greenhouse. The tiny mites are a yellowy-green colour and they suck sap from the underside of the leaves of many plants outdoors as well. The foliage develops a mottled yellow colour and plants may be killed or defoliated. Control by spraying with malathion or derris, or by using biological control with a predatory mite called *Phytoseiulus persimilis* which can be introduced onto the infested plants (see p 360).

Sawflies A number of sawflies attack roses. One of the most common, the leaf-rolling sawfly, causes the leaves to become tightly rolled at the beginning of summer, each leaf containing a green caterpillar. The caterpillars of another species feed on the lower surface of leaves. Spray with trichlorphon or fenitrothion; pick off and burn rolled leaves.

Slugs and snails These feed mainly at night on the leaves and flowers of most herbaceous plants and leaf vegetables and also attack stems, roots, bulbs and tubers. They can be controlled by scattering slug pellets among the plants, especially on warm humid nights when these pests are most active.

Thrips These are tiny thin yellow or black insects, about 2 mm (⅒ in) in length, which suck sap from the leaves and flowers of many plants such as roses, lilac, gladioli and dahlias. They cause a white mottling on the leaves, and heavy infestations in the flowers can destroy the blooms. Hot summers favour this pest. Control by spraying with dimethoate or BHC.

Woodlice Woodlice are common soil animals which feed mainly on dead plant material, but they sometimes damage seedlings. If necessary, dust with BHC; tidy up dead leaves and other debris, which attracts and shelters woodlice. Established plants are unlikely to be harmed by these animals.

Others Ornamental plants may be attacked also by cutworms and wireworms, as described above for vegetables, and by scale insects, as described for fruit.

Plant diseases

The main diseases that afflict garden plants are caused by fungi whose microscopic spores are constantly in the air. Details are given below of those most likely to be encountered. Where treatment by unspecified spraying is advised, choose a suitable fungicide from among those in the table on page 361. Where you are advised to burn the plant, make sure that you do so promptly and completely, or you risk allowing the disease to spread to other plants in the garden. Bear in mind that the incidence of plant diseases varies greatly with climate; as this book is designed for readers in many countries, not all of them may occur in your region. Where a disease is not covered specifically, follow the general advice given in the article on page 358.

Vegetable diseases

Anthracnose This disease attacks a number of vegetables in wet weather, but is usually only serious on French beans. Dark spots with a lighter edge appear on leaves, seeds and pods. They become paler with age and may coalesce to form a slimy mass. Plants should be sprayed thoroughly with benomyl at the first sign of trouble, and the spray repeated regularly during wet weather. Burn infected plants at the end of the season. Do not save seed from them. Buy good-quality seed.

Bacterial blight This disease of beans can affect all parts of the plant, including seeds. Large irregular brownish patches occur, especially in wet weather, on the leaves, while similar but smaller spots with a reddish margin occur on seed pods. Destroy infected plants. Ensure that disease-free quality seed is sown and never work around the crop in wet weather. Also clean up after harvesting.

Black rot Cabbages, Brussels sprouts and other members of that family growing in warm moist conditions are attacked by black rot. It is not very common in Britain. Infected plants virtually stop growing and their leaves turn yellow, particularly at the edges. If the stalk of an infected plant is cut through, a characteristic black ring will show in the tissue. Infected plants should be burned. The bed in which they were growing should not be replanted with any members of the cabbage family for at least two years, preferably longer. Again, buy good-quality seed.

Blight This is a serious disease of potatoes which will also attack tomatoes. It only becomes troublesome during periods of warm wet weather, and some varieties of potato are resistant to blight (see p 276). Large dark brown spots appear on the leaves of infected potatoes. They spread and can kill the top of the plant if left unchecked. The infection will spread to the tubers if these are not properly earthed up, causing dark-coloured sunken patches and rotting. Tomato leaves also develop dark spots, but the main damage is on the fruits, which develop irregular, dark brown marbled spots and are unusable.

Potatoes should be sprayed with zineb as a precaution when the plants start to meet between the rows, or at the first sign of infection. Sprays should be repeated at 10- to 14-day intervals during warm humid weather.

Tomatoes should be given a protective spray if infected potato plants are growing nearby.

Chocolate spot This is a disease peculiar to broad beans, autumn-sown plants in poorly-drained soil being the most likely to be damaged. Brown spots up to 5 mm (¼ in) across appear on the leaves and sometimes on the flowers. Brown streaks can be seen on the stems. The whole plant may collapse and die. Plants should be sprayed thoroughly with benomyl at the first sign of trouble. It is often worthwhile to give overwintered plants a spray in the spring, even though they may look healthy. Old plants should be burned at the end of the season.

Club root This serious soil-borne disease attacks all members of the cabbage family. Cabbages, sprouts, cauliflowers, broccoli, turnips, swedes and kale are all attacked and so are wallflowers, stocks, candytuft and weeds like charlock and shepherd's purse. It is worst in poorly-drained, acid soils. Attacked plants make little growth and their leaves become discoloured. Large swellings appear on the roots, which eventually decay to an evil-smelling rot. These swellings gave rise to the common name 'finger-and-toe disease'. The flesh inside the swellings is mottled. (The round swellings caused by turnip gall weevil have a grub inside; see p 362).

This disease persists in the soil, and ideally members of the cabbage family should not be planted in the same bed more often than every seven years. A three- or four-year crop rotation (see p 262) will, however, help to reduce the build-up of this disease, as will liming of the soil immediately before sowing. Seedlings should be raised in soil which is free from the disease, and their roots should be dipped in a paste of calomel dust (mercurous chloride) before planting out.

Damping off This is a disease of very young seedlings. The stems turn black and shrivel at soil level. The seedlings topple over and die. Do not sow seed too thickly and do not overwater. Use sterilized or peat-based soil mixtures for seed-sowing in containers. If the disease does appear, water all the seedlings with a solution of Cheshunt compound (see p 392) to prevent it spreading. It is a good idea to water newly sown seeds with this fungicide as a routine preventive measure.

Downy mildew This disease attacks many plants, including leafy vegetables, peas,

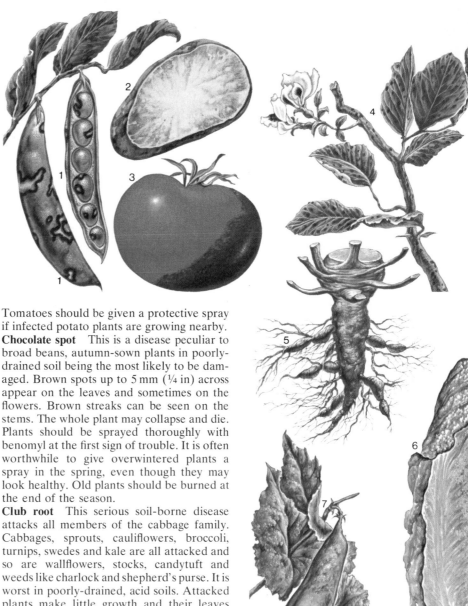

Diseases of vegetables
1 Anthracnose; 2 potato blight; 3 tomato blight; 4 chocolate spot; 5 club root; 6 downy mildew; 7 grey mould (botrytis)

onions and leeks. Yellow spots appear on the upper surface of the leaves, with corresponding greyish, downy areas on the underside. Leaves and pods rot, and sometimes the whole plant may be killed. It is worst in cool, moist conditions. Remove and burn any damaged leaves. Greenhouses and frames should be ventilated whenever possible. Spray with a suitable fungicide early in the day so that the plants are dry before the temperature falls in the evening.

Grey mould (botrytis) A common disease in cool damp conditions, and in poorly drained soils, this often enters through wounds and leaf scars. A grey furry mould grows on areas of rotting tissue on leaves, stems and pods. Remove all dead and rotting tissue from affected plants. In the greenhouse or frame, give as much ventilation as pos-/*continued*

Plant diseases (continued)

sible. Spray thoroughly and repeat sprays at recommended intervals while conditions remain cold and wet.

Potato scab There are two different forms of scab, but both of them give potatoes a rough unattractive skin. Scabby potatoes should not be used as 'seed'; they can be eaten so long as the scabby parts are cut off. This disease persists in the soil, so to prevent it building up potatoes should not be planted in the same place more often than once every three years. It is more likely in alkaline soil.

Potato wart disease This is a serious disease that cannot be controlled; fortunately it is not very common. Large warty masses grow on the tubers, and the stems become gnarled. In Britain it is a notifiable disease and must be reported to the Ministry of Agriculture.

Smut This disease disfigures and may kill. Onions and sweet corn are the vegetables most commonly attacked. Plants are deformed and produce masses of black spores. Destroy affected plants and rotate crops (see p 262).

Tomato leaf mould A very common disease of greenhouse tomatoes and sometimes seen on plants grown in the open, this starts as yellow spots on the leaves. The underside of these spots develops a pale, greyish mould. It is encouraged to spread by warm moist conditions, so greenhouses should be well ventilated. They should also be shaded in hot weather. Diseased leaves should be removed and the plants sprayed thoroughly. Some tomato varieties are resistant to this disease.

Virus diseases Many vegetables may be attacked by virus diseases, but only potatoes, tomatoes and cucumbers are likely to show noticeable symptoms. Potato leaves may be rolled, crinkled or spotted. Nothing can be done to cure affected plants and they will produce few tubers. Spray all plants at the first sign of aphid attack, as these pests can spread viruses. Avoid these diseases by buying new seed potatoes each year, rotating crops and keeping the plants free of insects.

Tomatoes sometimes develop strange narrow leaves which look almost like ferns. This is caused by cucumber mosaic virus, and other symptoms include dark mottling of the leaves. The same virus also attacks cucumbers, causing mottling and distortion of the leaves and stunted, non-climbing growth. Destroy any affected plants and wash your hands before touching any other tomatoes or cucumbers; sterilize or replace soil before replanting. Weedkillers may cause similar distortion of leaves. The commonest tomato virus is tobacco mosaic virus, which causes yellow or brown mottling or spots on the leaves. Plants only slightly affected may still bear fruits, but again destruction is desirable.

Further plant diseases

8 Potato virus disease; 9 tobacco mosaic virus of tomatoes; 10 cucumber mosaic virus (fern leaf) of tomatoes; 11 fireblight; 12 armillaria root rot (honey fungus); 13 brown rot; 14 canker; 15 leaf curl; 16 powdery mildew; 17 reversion virus disease of black currants; 18 tulip fire (tulip blight); 19 rose black spot; 20 rust

Fruit diseases

American gooseberry mildew This disease attacks the leaves, shoots and fruit of gooseberries. It starts as a white mould, which turns brown. Growth of the bushes is checked and the fruit is disfigured. Infected shoots should be cut out during pruning and burned. The bushes should be sprayed, preferably with a systemic fungicide such as benomyl, to prevent the disease getting a hold. The most important sprays are in early spring and when the very small fruits have just set. Two more sprays, at intervals of two weeks, should be given if the bushes have been badly attacked during previous seasons.

Anthracnose Grapes and raspberries are attacked by anthracnose. Dark greyish angular spots appear on their leaves and on the canes. Spray the plants thoroughly in early spring, just as the new shoots start to grow. If the disease has been bad in other years, re-spray every 10 to 14 days, particularly during periods of wet weather.

Armillaria root rot (honey fungus) This is a killer disease which will attack fruit and ornamental plants – both woody and herbaceous. Honey-coloured toadstools may be seen, but these do not normally spread the disease directly. Roots are attacked either by 'boot-laces' of black fungus which grow through the soil, or by direct contact with infected roots. Plants may survive the attack for many years or collapse quite suddenly. A white, fan-shaped growth may be found just under the bark near soil level. Dead plants should be removed, together with their

neighbours, and burned. As much root as possible should be removed. Sterilize the soil with formaldehyde before replanting.

Brown rot Mainly a problem on apples, this can attack stone fruit. Soft brown patches appear on the fruits as they ripen on the tree or in store. Pale concentric rings of spores grow on the affected areas. If the fruit is not picked, it dries out and may hang on the tree through the winter. There is no satisfactory control in the garden, but spraying for scab (see below) and control of fruit-eating insects such as wasps (which allow the disease to attack) will reduce it. Burn diseased fruits and cut out the spurs on which they grew.

Canker This may be caused by a fungal infection or by bacteria. It appears as sunken patches of dead bark on the trunk and branches of trees. These gradually enlarge and if they girdle a limb all the growth above will die. Cut out all the dead bark and wood to leave a smooth, white wound. Cover this with a tree paint to protect it while it heals. Always collect rotting fruit and burn or bury it.

Fireblight A bacterial disease, this may affect many trees and shrubs of the rose family, including apples and pears; it is a notifiable disease in Britain that must be reported to the Ministry of Agriculture. Infection starts in the flower spurs and spreads rapidly. Affected parts turn brown before shrinking and dying. Leaves turn blackish and after death remain on the branches. Local infections can be pruned well below the level of infection and diseased parts burned. In some countries, antibiotic sprays are available, while Bor-

deaux mixture or canker solution can be used. Do not over-fertilize susceptible plants.

Grey mould (botrytis) This disease is worst in wet weather and in humid conditions. Attacked fruit rots and a grey fur of fungus grows on the surface. Hygiene, and good ventilation of greenhouses and frames, is essential to the control of this disease. Spray well with benomyl at the first sign of rotting.

Leaf curl This is best known as a disease of peaches, but it also attacks almonds, apricots and nectarines. It appears in the early spring. Young leaves curl and thicken, and then turn red. (This damage should not be confused with the leaf curl caused by the feeding of aphids on the underside of the leaves.) Collect fallen leaves and compost them thoroughly or burn them. Spray trees thoroughly with zineb in early spring as the leaves unfold, and repeat two weeks later. Spray the trees again when the leaves start to fall.

Powdery mildew Apples, peaches and grapes are attacked by powdery mildew, but the disease does not spread from one to another. A thin white 'fur' of fungus grows on the surface of leaves, stems and occasionally fruit. The disease is worst in hot, dry weather. Cut out and burn infected shoots in winter. Spray thoroughly with benomyl at the first sign of trouble and repeat at 14-day intervals while the weather remains dry. If the disease was bad in the previous year, spray as the buds start to open in the spring, even if the growth appears to be healthy.

Scab This is an important disease of apples in wet seasons. Matt, greenish-black spots grow on both leaves and fruit. If attacked early, the fruit may split. If possible fallen leaves should be collected and burned at the end of the season. Spray trees with benomyl or captan every 10 to 14 days during wet weather in spring and early summer.

Silver leaf This is a disease of stone fruit trees such as cherries and plums. Leaves develop a silvery, metallic look, and branches or the whole tree will gradually die. To avoid infection, stone fruit trees should be pruned in summer to give them a chance to heal before the winter, when the spores of this disease are around. The wood in the centre of a diseased branch is stained brown. The diseased branches must be cut back until the wood is white and healthy. Burn the diseased wood and protect the wounds with a tree paint.

Virus diseases So-called reversion of black currants is the virus that causes most damage to fruit grown in gardens. Leaves appear with fewer lobes and fewer veins than normal. The affected bushes produce poor crops and act as a source of infection for other plants; dig them out and burn them. The disease is spread by the big bud mite (see p 363).

Diseases of ornamental plants

Black leg Geranium (pelargonium) cuttings usually root very easily, but occasionally they rot instead. The stem goes soft and black at soil level. This condition can be greatly reduced by using a sterile rooting medium and taking great care not to overwater. The soil should be kept barely moist until they root.

Black spot This is a common disease of roses which is worst during wet weather. Some varieties are more susceptible than others. Large black spots with a fuzzy edge appear on the leaves. The spotted leaves become yellow and fall. In a severe attack a rose can be completely defoliated. Roses should be sprayed thoroughly at the first sign of attack and the spray should be repeated at the recommended interval during wet weather. If the bushes were badly attacked during the previous year, they should be sprayed thoroughly in early spring just as the leaves unfold, even though they may appear to be perfectly healthy.

Dutch elm disease Affected elm trees take on autumn colours in the summer, when leaves quickly turn yellow and wilt. Diseased branches die back from the tip and the wood immediately below the bark is darkly stained. These trees should be felled and the bark and twigs burned on site. The disease is spread by elm bark beetles. Healthy trees can be injected with a fungicide to protect them, but this is expensive and not always effective. Some species and varieties are more resistant than others.

Rust This disease attacks roses and a number of herbaceous plants; it can be very damaging. There are varieties of antirrhinum and hollyhock which are resistant, however. Yellow spots appear on the upper surfaces of leaves. On the underside there are corresponding little cushions of 'rust'. Badly attacked leaves will fall and if the disease is left unchecked the plant may be killed. Diseased leaves should be picked off and burned. The plants should be sprayed very thoroughly with a suitable fungicide. If rust attacks just one variety of rose in a mixed bed it is advisable to remove that variety rather than leave it to act as a source of infection for the others.

Tulip fire (tulip blight) This is the most common disease of tulips, grey or scorched-looking patches appearing on the leaves, which rot in wet weather. Flowers are deformed or fail to open. Spray plants with zineb at the first sign of infection. Bulbs should be dipped in benomyl after lifting and before planting as a control measure.

Wilt This causes plants to wilt suddenly and die. Clematis, asters, paeonies, carnations and pansies are among the plants affected. It is a soil-borne disease probably due to several different fungi. If possible, grow susceptible plants in a different part of the garden each year. If one type of plant, say asters, have been badly attacked, do not plant them in the same bed again for at least four years. Affected clematis will sometimes send out new healthy shoots if the dead top growth is cut back and the soil around the roots is drenched with a fungicide.

Other troubles Among the diseases of fruit and vegetables that may also afflict certain ornamental plants are powdery mildew (especially on roses and chrysanthemums), club root (in wallflowers and stocks), downy mildew (anemones), smut (dahlias), armillaria root rot (privet and other shrubs and trees), fireblight (cotoneasters and ornamental thorns [*Crataegus* spp]) and damping off of seedlings of all kinds.

Plant disorders

Disorders can stunt and disfigure plants, or kill them. Some can be avoided, but others are beyond a gardener's control. They are caused by unsatisfactory growing conditions.

Balling

In wet weather the flowers of some plants, notably roses, fail to open properly. The petals colour and grow, but they do not separate. The flower remains a soft ball of petals which eventually rots. There is nothing you can do about this. If a variety does this year after year in a particular garden it should be discarded. If possible, see your chosen rose varieties growing in the open after a spell of bad weather before committing yourself to buy.

Deficiency disorders

Plants need a balanced diet of a large number of minerals if they are to develop and grow properly. Some are needed in comparatively large amounts, others as the merest trace (see p 352). They are all essential, however, and lack of one can upset the whole plant.

The diagnosis of deficiencies in garden plants is usually difficult. The symptoms may be different in different plants. Often two deficiencies occur together and the symptoms of one mask or modify the symptoms of the other. Poor growth and discolouration are common signs. Leaves may be small or mis-shapen, or may show chlorosis (yellowing between the veins), and roots may be reduced or discoloured.

It is not unreasonable to assume that plants which are looking poorly and not growing well, but are not suffering from any identifiable pest or disease, are suffering from some sort of deficiency, but the trouble is often due to poor roots or soil conditions rather than a real lack of plant food. Some plants have difficulty in absorbing vital minerals from alkaline soils, but in other cases a lime deficiency may be the cause.

The short-term treatment is to spray the plants with a foliar feed containing trace elements. These will be taken straight into the plant's system. Sequestered iron can be used where you have good reason to believe this is the element lacking – as with camellias or rhododendrons on soil that is not acid enough for them. The long-term treatment is to increase the organic content of the soil, apply lime if it is needed, and rake in a suitable fertilizer before planting or sowing.

Die-back

This is a condition which affects many plants, including roses and stone fruit trees. The ends of shoots die and the length of dead stem gradually increases. There are various causes, but the presence of die-back indicates that the plants are not growing in ideal conditions. Drought, waterlogging, starvation, root damage or pest attack can all induce die-back.

The dead ends should be cut off and the wounds sealed with a tree paint. This is to prevent infection getting in. The plants should be fed and cossetted to encourage new healthy growth, and soil conditions should be improved where necessary.

Disorders of fruits
1 Bitter pit of apples; 2 greenback of tomatoes;
3 blossom end rot of tomatoes

Frost damage

The young leaves and flowers of many plants are damaged by frost. The damaged parts show brown and crisp a few days later. Usually these plants recover and no treatment is needed. Other, tender, plants are very sensitive to frost; they go black and soft when they thaw after a frost. They may regrow if they have a good undamaged root system. Tender plants should be covered (with cloches, leaves, straw, newspaper, and so on; see p 354) when frost is likely to occur. Do not plant out tender young plants too early.

Fruit troubles

Bitter pit This is a disorder of apples. Small dry brown patches occur in the flesh and on the skin of the fruit. They may not develop until the fruit is stored. It is worst in hot dry summers. Young trees which are growing vigorously and cropping lightly are more likely to be affected than mature trees. It is caused by calcium shortage in the fruit. Regular sprays of calcium nitrate while the fruit is developing are required in hot dry areas to control this disorder. In other parts of the world an occasional foliar feed containing calcium will be beneficial, particularly for young trees.

Blossom end rot This is one of several disorders of fruit caused by an irregular water supply. It is most commonly seen in cucumbers and tomatoes. Fruits develop this disorder if they are fairly small when the plant suffers a shortage of water. The symptoms appear later when the part farthest from the stem fails to develop with the rest of the fruit. Ripening tomatoes show a flat black bottom; cucumbers have a small, brown and usually rotting end. Plants grown in containers are obviously most prone to this condition. It should be prevented by adequate, regular watering, particularly during hot weather.

Fruit drop Most trees set many more small fruitlets than they can carry to full maturity. As these little fruits start to swell the tree simply sheds many of them, to reduce the crop to a manageable size. In apples this is known as 'June drop' (it occurs in November or December south of the equator). It is a natural and normal process. Young trees which are still growing vigorously may drop all their fruit. Bush and cane fruits, and vegetables such as tomatoes and peppers, will drop fruit if the air and the soil are too dry. Improved watering, and increased humidity under glass, will rectify this.

Greenback This is fairly common on tomatoes grown in hot conditions. The stalk end of the fruit remains green and hard while the rest ripens normally. Some varieties are resistant to greenback. It can be reduced in greenhouse tomatoes by applying external shading to reduce the temperature.

Splitting Tomatoes are most commonly affected by this disorder, but apricots, plums and other fruits may also split. It is caused by sudden heavy rain or watering after a comparatively dry period. If the fruit skin has started to harden it may split when the flesh inside swells as a result of increased water uptake by the roots. There is little you can do to control the weather, but you can try to ensure that your plants do not get dry while they are carrying fruit.

Sun scorch

This is usually seen on greenhouse plants, but can also occur out of doors during very hot weather. Plant tissue is simply scorched by heat from the sun; it becomes bleached and thin. Tomatoes and peppers are scorched if the leaves which normally protect them are removed. (De-leafing does not make them ripen any faster!) Heat can be reduced by shading the glass either with a spray or with blinds or netting (see p 383).

Water scorch

Drops of water on leaves can act as magnifying glasses, concentrating the sun's rays and burning the tissues. The following day the burnt tissue shows pale, thin and crisp. Plain water, pesticide sprays and particularly oil sprays will all cause this damage if applied in hot sunshine. The best time to use them is in early morning or, better still, late afternoon.

Weedkiller damage

Hormone weedkillers may drift in the wind from treated lawns. Traces may also remain in sprayers and watering cans, and may be spread when they are subsequently used for pesticides. The answer is obvious: equipment used for weedkillers should never be used for anything else.

Tomatoes are particularly sensitive to weedkiller damage, but all flowering plants can be harmed. The youngest growth is the mostly severely affected. Leaves and stems twist, curl and may swell. Fruits may grow mis-shapenly. Leave damaged plants alone. If the damage is not too great, fresh shoots of normal growth will appear and the damaged shoots can then be cut away or ignored.

Pruning your plants

Most plants with woody stems – whether trees, shrubs or climbing plants – will need pruning, or cutting back of some or all of the stems, at some time or another during their lives, though with many – perhaps the majority – it is not a regular annual need. Pruning has various purposes, and the importance of these may differ from one kind of plant to another. In all types, it is necessary to remove dead or diseased branches. In many, lopping may be necessary to prevent wind damage to the roots caused by excessive top growth. Thinning the branches helps to build resistance to disease by admitting light and air to the centre of the plant to help ripen the wood. Where plants differ most markedly is in the pruning needed to maintain vigour and to keep a balance between leafy and flowering or fruiting growth. Finally, of course, some plants may need pruning simply to maintain a balanced shape or to train them into one of the special shapes described on page 374.

The special ways of dealing with individual kinds of plants are covered below, except for the techniques of pruning rose bushes, which will be found on page 161, climbing and rambling roses (p 149) and clematis (p 145). There are, however, a few basic rules that apply in every case.

Pruning techniques

The tools you use for pruning must be sharp, because all cuts must be made cleanly in order to heal; crushed wood dies and allows fungal diseases to enter. When the stems are cut correctly, the plant produces a waxy substance that protects and waterproofs the wound. Later, a special protective growth called callus tissue will form over the surface of all but very large wounds. However, you should paint any cuts more than 1.5 cm (½ in) across with special bituminous compound obtainable from garden centres and shops; creosote and tar are not suitable.

Branches up to about 10 mm (³⁄₈ in) in diameter can be cut with sharp, well-adjusted secateurs. There are two main types: one where the blade cuts against a flat surface, the other having a 'scissors' action. Most people prefer the latter, but they must be used carefully or the blades will not meet properly, damaging the branch they are supposed to cut cleanly. Branches thicker than this should be cut with long-handled lopping shears, with a sharp, finely-set pruning saw or, in the case of very large branches, with a bow saw or power saw. When pruning a large branch, saw upwards from below first, then down from above to join the cut; this severs the bark and inner tissues cleanly and prevents tearing.

Never prune in very cold weather, as the cut surface will freeze, damaging the tissues; in severe frost the bark may split. If you need to remove large branches from a tree, do this in autumn or in a frost-free period in winter with deciduous trees, and not when the sap begins to rise in the spring. Spring is, however, the best time for such surgery of evergreens.

Removing unwanted wood

Before you start pruning any tree or shrub, stand back and look at it carefully from all sides. Note any obvious imbalance in growth, and whether the plant is damaging its neighbours. The first priority is to remove any dead, diseased or damaged branches; burn them. Diseased branches usually show some staining on the cut surface; cut these back until the wood is free from stains. Look for branches that cross and chafe, and any that grow across the centre of the plant, and remove these, too, at their base. Finally cut weak branches back to a well-developed bud which points in the direction in which you want the branch to grow; the shaping of the tree or shrub is achieved in this way.

Pruning shrubs and climbers

Apart from the removal of branches that are in bad health, or are distorting the shrub's shape, as described above, the main purpose of pruning decorative shrubs is to maintain their vigour and to accentuate and promote their decorative features. Little pruning is needed after planting except to remove any damaged branches back to sound wood and to reduce any very long or weak shoots by about one-third. Thereafter, the method and timing of pruning depends on the vigour, growth habit and other characteristics of the shrub. Many need no attention at all, or need pruning only every few years.

For the purposes of pruning,/*continued*

How to prune
Cut just above a side branch **1** or a bud pointing the way you want growth to develop **2**. Do not cut too close to the bud **3** or too far away **4**. A long snag will die, allowing fungal disease to enter, as will a ragged, torn cut **5**; eventually, the die-back will extend down the whole branch. Do not slope the cut towards the bud **6**; if you slope it slightly away (as in **2**), sap is drawn to the cut surface, promoting rapid healing.

Tools for pruning
A pruning knife **7** needs skilled handling. Secateurs may have two blades **8** or a single blade that cuts on an 'anvil' **9**. The latter may bruise thick stems, but the former may also not cut properly if ever used with a wrenching action. Lever-action loppers **10** will cut branches up to 4 cm (1½ in) thick, but for thicker branches use a fine-toothed saw **11**. A bow saw **12** or even a power saw is needed for really heavy work. For trimming hedges, choose lightweight hand shears **13** – preferably stainless steel – or a mains or battery electric hedge-trimmer **14**.

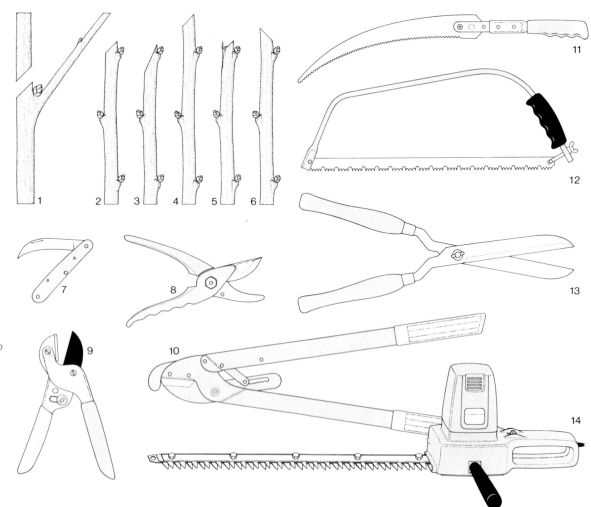

Pruning your plants (continued)

Removing a large branch
Do this in several stages **1**, reducing the branch's weight progressively to avoid it splitting under its own weight and damaging the trunk. The final section to be removed should be about 45 to 60 cm (1½ to 2 ft) long. Cut this off almost flush with the trunk. First cut upwards from below **2** about one-third of the way through.
3 Then cut downwards to meet the first cut so that the stump comes away cleanly. **4** Pare the edges of the wound with a very sharp knife to facilitate the formation of protective tissue.
5 Treat the whole wound with a sealant immediately it is dry.

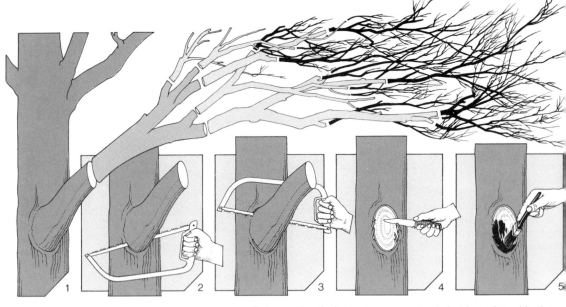

Rejuvenating fruit trees
A fruit tree that has not been regularly and correctly pruned may have developed a mass of weak, leggy branches **left**, and will need more or less severe pruning over one or two years – in winter with apple and pear trees, but in spring with plums and cherries. First remove any dead or diseased branches and any that cross the centre, congesting the crown. Then cut back weak branches hard, so that a framework of strong new growth is formed **below**.

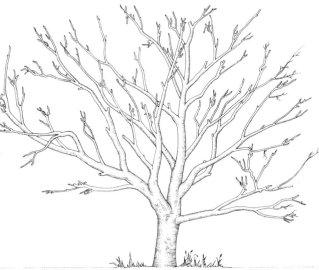

shrubs can be divided into six groups. Details of how and when to prune them are given on pages 372 and 373. The table on the same pages gives details of which shrubs come into which category. The first two groups include the vigorously-growing types that need regular pruning; when you prune depends on whether they flower early in the year on the previous year's wood (when you should prune immediately after flowering), or after mid-summer on the current year's wood (when you should cut back hard in early spring to stimulate new growth).

Then there are two groups of shrubs that need minimal pruning beyond the removal of very old, spindly or diseased wood. These are some of the winter-flowering deciduous shrubs and certain others that do very well if left alone, and most evergreen shrubs; the latter can be cut back very hard if they are

overgrown and neglected, but will then take some time to return to flowering. The fifth group consists of shrubs grown primarily for the coloured bark of their young stems; these need to be cut down very hard in late winter or early spring to encourage new shoots to grow. A few flowering shrubs are treated in the same way. Finally there are the small-leaved and generally low-growing shrubs that can be tidied with shears at varying times of the year.

Many shrubby climbers fall into similar categories, but others, including the very vigorous types, such as the Russian vine, *Polygonum baldschuanicum,* and *Vitis coignetiae,* need no pruning at all except to keep them within bounds. These form a seventh group in the illustrations and table. One exception to the normal is wisteria; as with other plants that flower on new wood, this is pruned hard in late winter or early spring, to

within two or three buds of the main stems, but the growing tips of young lateral shoots should also be regularly pinched out in summer when they are about 30 cm (12 in) long.

Pruning hedges
Formal hedges need regular grooming to keep them neat and compact, whereas informal hedges can be treated in the same way as flowering shrubs. However, both kinds need fairly severe pruning after planting, to establish bushy growth.

Quick-growing hedges, such as hawthorn, privet and prunus species, should be cut down to 10 cm (4 in) after planting, and the new growth halved in height the following winter. Holly, yew and the conifers should be left unpruned after planting, and the following year the sides only should be shaped; the tip growth should not be touched until the final

Pollarding and stooling

This is the hard cutting back of a tree or shrub, with the result that vigorous young growth is stimulated. The results are often extremely ugly when a tree is beheaded because it is too big. However, cutting back hard to ground level can have highly decorative results. For example, a young tree of heaven (*Ailanthus altissima*) **right** responds with luxuriant sucker-like growth and beautiful leaves up to 90 cm (3 ft) long, each with up to 30 leaflets. Others to treat this way include forms of the Norway maple (*Acer platanoides*) and *Paulownia tomentosa*.

A different problem is that of the apple or pear tree **right** that, as a result of regular spur pruning over many years, has developed excessive, congested fruiting spurs **below 1**. These produce a large number of inferior fruits, and for best results should be thinned out. Over one or two years, cut out up to half the spurs **below 2** and shorten the remainder to stimulate strong new lateral shoots **far right**.

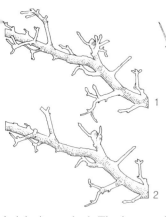

Root-pruning of trees

This may be necessary to bring over-vigorous fruit trees into bearing. **1** In late autumn, dig a trench to expose the roots on the leeward side of the tree, about 1.25 m (4 ft) from the trunk. **2** Cut the roots with a saw or long-handled lopping shears. Do not touch the roots on the windward side of the tree or you may affect its stability.

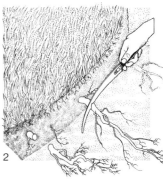

height is reached. The intermediate group – for example, beech, hornbeam, viburnum and cotoneaster – should have the tips cut back by a third after planting and in the following year, but the sides should be pruned hard.

Established hedges of the quick-growing plants need clipping about four times between early summer and autumn, the intermediate group twice, once in late summer and again in autumn. Hollies and the Lawson and Leyland cypresses can be included in this group, as they grow more rapidly once established. Yew and the laurels need pruning only once, in the autumn, and the large-leaved shrubs should always be pruned with secateurs, not shears, to avoid slicing the leaves in two. Always trim a formal hedge so that it is slightly narrower at the top than the bottom; this will help to keep it clothed with leaves all the way down. See also the article on page 90.

Pruning fruit trees and bushes

Just as with flowering shrubs, fruit trees and bushes vary in the age of wood on which they bear flowers and fruit. For example, peaches and sour cherries fruit mainly on one-year-old wood, while sweet cherries and apples fruit on wood two or more years old. Pruning thus has an important influence on fruitfulness. Information on how to prune the various types is given in the articles on the individual fruits in chapter four.

With most tree fruits and also such bushes as red currants and gooseberries, fruit is borne mainly on short side shoots, or spurs, from the branches. These either occur naturally or are encouraged to form by pruning the lateral shoots. The severity of this spurring back can influence fruiting. With some varieties of apples and pears, for example, the fruiting buds grow at or near the tips of the laterals, so these must not be cut back but merely thinned out. Others respond best to having the laterals pruned to two or three buds from the base. On the other hand, the crowded spurs of an old tree should be thinned out to prevent large numbers of inferior fruits being set.

Normally, spur pruning is carried out in winter. In the case of sweet cherries and plums, however, winter pruning results in too vigorous growth and may allow silver leaf disease to strike. When grown in the open, these need minimal pruning once established; if grown as fans or espaliers against a wall, perform any necessary shortening of laterals by pinching out the growing tips in the summer. In general, summer pruning retards growth while winter pruning encourages it, and the former is usually carried out on apples and pears only if they are trained in a restricted form, including dwarf pyramids. *continued*

Pruning your plants (continued)

Pruning ornamental shrubs
Group 1 These are vigorous shrubs that flower before midsummer on young wood – for example, *Deutzia* species and hybrids, and flowering currants (*Ribes* spp). Prune as soon as flowering is over. Cut out worn-out stems completely to the base. Remove weak shoots and cut back flowering shoots to strong young growth.

Group 2 These are vigorous shrubs that flower after midsummer on the same year's stems – for example, *Buddleia davidii*, the butterfly bush. Prune these shrubs back hard when severe weather is over. Remove weak shoots and in some years thin out the oldest stems to the base. Cut back the previous year's shoots to two or three buds from their origin.

Group 3 This includes winter-flowering and various other shrubs that generally need little pruning except dead-heading, but may benefit from thinning out of old, worn-out wood – for example, the common hydrangea. This is generally done in spring, but may be performed after flowering in some cases.

Group 4 This includes most evergreen shrubs – for example, the spotted laurel (*Aucuba* spp). Here, little or no pruning is needed except for the removal of weak or old wood in spring and the removal of dead flower-heads from rhododendrons, camellias and similar types. Where the shrub becomes very large and unkempt, it can be cut back very hard – almost to the ground – in spring, and will make new growth, but flowering types may take several years to flower again. Paint the wounds with a suitable sealant.

How to prune shrubs and climbers

Botanical name	Common name	Is regular pruning needed?	Pruning group	Botanical name	Common name	Is regular pruning needed?	Pruning group
Abelia spp	—	No	3	*Cotoneaster* spp	—	No	3; 4
Abeliophyllum distichum	—	No	3	*Crataegus* spp	Ornamental thorn	No	3
Abutilon spp	Flowering maple	No	3	*Cytisus* spp	Broom	Yes	1; 2
Acer spp	Maple	No	—	*Daphne* spp	—	No	3; 4
Actinidia spp	Chinese gooseberry, etc	No	7	*Desfontainea spinosa*	—	No	4
Akebia spp	—	No	4	*Deutzia* spp	—	Yes	1
Amelanchier spp	Shadbush, etc	No	3	*Disanthus cercidifolius*	—	No	(2)
Ampelopsis spp	—	No	7	*Eccremocarpus scaber*	Chilean glory vine	No	4
Arbutus spp	Strawberry tree	No	4	*Elaeagnus* spp	—	No	4
Aristolochia spp	Dutchman's pipe, etc	No	(2)	*Embothrium coccineum*	Chilean fire bush	No	4
Aucuba spp	Spotted laurel	No	4	*Enkianthus campanulatus*	—	No	3
Azara spp	—	No	4	*Erica* spp	Heath; heather	Yes	6 (see text)
Berberidopsis corallina	Coral plant	No	4 or 7	*Escallonia* spp	—	No	3; 4
Berberis spp	Barberry	No	3; 4	*Eucryphia* spp	—	No	—
Bignonia capreolata	—	No	7	*Euonymus* spp	Spindle	No	3
Buddleia alternifolia	—	Yes	1	× *Fatshedra lizei*	—	No	4
Buddleia davidii	Butterfly bush	Yes	2	*Fatsia japonica*	False castor oil plant	No	4
Buddleia spp (others)	—	No	4	*Feijoa sellowiana*	—	No	4
Buxus sempervirens	Box	No	4	*Forsythia* spp	—	Yes	1
Callistemon spp	Bottlebrush	No	4	*Fothergilla major*	—	No	—
Calluna spp	Heather; ling	No	6 (see text)	*Fremontodendron californicum*	—	No	4
Camellia spp	—	No	4	*Fuchsia magellanica*	—	No	2; 5†
Campsis spp	Trumpet vine	No	7	*Garrya elliptica*	Tassel bush	No	4
Caragana arborescens	—	No	3	*Gaultheria procumbens*	—	No	—
Carpenteria californica	—	No	4	*Genista* spp	Broom	No	3
Caryopteris × *clandonensis*	—	Yes	2	*Griselinia littoralis*	—	No	4
Ceanothus spp (deciduous)	—	Yes	2	*Halimium* spp	—	No	—
Ceanothus spp (evergreen)	—	No	4	*Hamamelis* spp	Witch hazel	No	3
Celastrus orbiculatus	Staff vine	No	7	*Hebe* spp	Shrubby veronica	No	4
Ceratostigma spp	Hardy plumbago	No	5	*Hedera* spp	Ivy	No	7
Chaenomeles spp	Japanese quince; japonica	No	(1)	*Helianthemum* spp	Rock rose; sun rose	No	6
Chamaecyparis spp	False cypress	No	—	*Helichrysum* spp	Curry plant, etc	Yes	6
Chimonanthus praecox	Winter sweet	No	3	*Hibiscus syriacus*	—	No	3
Choisya ternata	Mexican orange-blossom	No	4	*Hippophaë rhamnoides*	Sea buckthorn	No	3
Cistus spp	Sun rose; rock rose	No	6	*Hydrangea macrophylla*	—	No	3
Clematis spp	—	Yes	(see p 144)	*Hydrangea paniculata*	—	Yes	2
Clethra spp	Sweet pepper bush	No	3	*Hydrangea* spp (climbing)	—	No	7
Clianthus spp	Parrot's-bill; glory pea	No	7	*Hypericum calycinum*; H. elatum	Rose of Sharon	Yes	5
Colutea arborescens	Bladder senna	Yes	2	*Hypericum patulum*; H. 'Rowallane'	—	Yes	2
Cornus spp (coloured-stemmed types)	Cornel; dogwood	Yes	5	*Ilex* spp	Holly	No	4
Cornus spp (others)	Flowering dogwood	No	3	*Itea ilicifolia*	—	No	4
Corokia cotoneaster	Wire-netting bush	No	4	*Jasminum nudiflorum*	Winter jasmine	Yes	1
Corylopsis spp	—	No	3	*Jasminum officinale*	Common white jasmine	Yes	3
Corylus spp	Hazel	No	3*				
Cotinus spp	Smoke bush						

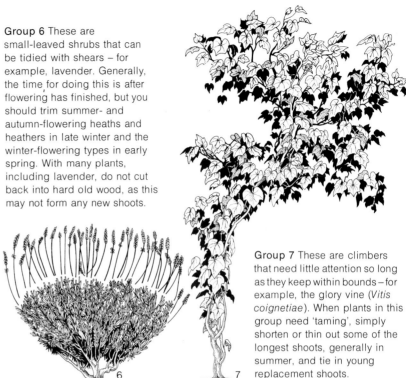

Group 6 These are small-leaved shrubs that can be tidied with shears – for example, lavender. Generally, the time for doing this is after flowering has finished, but you should trim summer- and autumn-flowering heaths and heathers in late winter and the winter-flowering types in early spring. With many plants, including lavender, do not cut back into hard old wood, as this may not form any new shoots.

Group 5 These shrubs are grown mainly for their colourful young stems – for example, some dogwoods (*Cornus* spp). Promote plenty of this young growth by cutting them down to about 5 cm (2 in) above the ground in early spring, before bud-burst. You can treat some flowering shrubs similarly.

Group 7 These are climbers that need little attention so long as they keep within bounds – for example, the glory vine (*Vitis coignetiae*). When plants in this group need 'taming', simply shorten or thin out some of the longest shoots, generally in summer, and tie in young replacement shoots.

Botanical name	Common name	Is regular pruning needed?	Pruning group	Botanical name	Common name	Is regular pruning needed?	Pruning group
Juniperus spp	Juniper	No	—	*Rubus* spp	Flowering bramble	Yes	1*
Kalmia latifolia	Calico bush	No	—	*Ruscus aculeatus*	Butcher's broom	No	4
Kerria japonica	Jew's mallow	Yes	1	*Salix* spp (coloured-stemmed)	Willow	Yes	5
Kolkwitzia amabilis	Beauty bush	Yes	3				
Laurus nobilis	Sweet bay; bay laurel	No	4	*Salix* spp (others)	Willow	No	3
Lavandula spp	Lavender	Yes	6	*Salvia officinalis*	Sage	No	6
Leucothoë fontanesiana	—	No	4	*Sambucus* spp	Elder	No	2; (5)
Leycesteria formosa	Flowering nutmeg	Yes	2; 5	*Santolina* spp	Cotton lavender	Yes	4
Ligustrum spp	Privet	(Trim hedges)	4	*Schizophragma* spp	—	No	7
				Senecio spp	Shrubby silver cineraria	No	1
Lippia citriodora	Lemon-scented verbena	Yes	2	*Skimmia* spp	—	No	—
Lonicera nitida	Shrubby honeysuckle	No	6	*Solanum* spp	Potato vine; jasmine nightshade	Yes	4 or 7
Lonicera spp (climbing)	Honeysuckle	No	7				
Magnolia spp	—	No	3; 4	*Sophora* spp	Kowhai, etc	No	—
Mahonia spp	Oregon grape, etc	No	4	*Sorbaria* spp	—	Yes	(5)
Mutisia spp	Climbing gazania	No	4	*Spartium junceum*	Spanish broom	Yes	2; 6
Nandina domestica	Heavenly bamboo	No	4	*Spiraea* × *arguta*	Bridal wreath; foam of May	Yes	1
Olearia spp	Daisy bush	No	4	*Spiraea* spp (others)	—	Yes	(5)
Osmanthus spp	—	No	—	*Stachyurus praecox*	—	No	3
× *Osmarea burkwoodii*	—	No	—	*Stephanandra* spp	—	Yes	1; 3
Pachysandra terminalis	—	No	—	*Stranvaesia davidiana*	—	No	3
Paeonia spp	Tree paeony	No	3	*Sycopsis sinensis*	—	No	4
Parrotia spp	—	No	—	*Symphoricarpos* spp	Snowberry, etc	No	3
Parthenocissus spp	Boston ivy; Virginia creeper	No	7	*Syringa* spp	Lilac	Yes	3
Passiflora spp	Passion flower	Yes	2	*Tamarix* spp (spring-flowering)	Tamarisk	Yes	1
Pernettya mucronata	—	No	4	*Tamarix* spp (summer-flowering)	Tamarisk	Yes	2
Philadelphus spp	Mock orange; 'syringa'	Yes	1				
Phillyrea spp	—	No	4	*Taxus baccata*	Yew	No	4
Phlomis fruticosa	Jerusalem sage	No	4	*Thuja* spp	Arbor-vitae	No	—
Photinia × *fraseri*	—	No	4	*Trachelospermum* spp	—	No	4 or 7
Pieris spp	—	No	4	*Ulex europaeus*	Gorse; furze	No	4
Piptanthus laburnifolius	—	No	4	*Vaccinium* spp	Blueberry	No	3*
Polygonum baldschuanicum	Russian vine; mile-a-minute vine	No	7	*Viburnum* spp (deciduous)	—	No	3
				Viburnum spp (evergreen)	—	No	4
Potentilla fruticosa	Shrubby cinquefoil	No	3	*Vinca* spp	Periwinkle	No	6
Prunus laurocerasus	Cherry laurel; common laurel	No	4	*Vitis* spp	Glory vine, etc	No	7
				Weigela florida	—	Yes	1
Prunus spp (other shrubby)	Ornamental almonds	No	1*	*Wisteria* spp	—	Yes	(see text)
Punica granatum	Pomegranate	No	—	*Yucca* spp	—	No	—
Pyracantha spp	Firethorn	No	4	*Zenobia pulverulenta*	—	No	4
Rhododendron spp	(Including azaleas)	No	4				
Rhus spp	Sumach	No	(2)				
Ribes spp	Flowering currant	Yes	1*				
Rosa spp	Roses	Yes	(see text)				
Rosmarinus officinalis	Rosemary	No	6				

*When no group number is given, pruning is generally unnecessary; a number in brackets indicates that this method should be used if pruning is ever necessary, or that it is optional. *For pruning of fruiting species, see chapter four. †To be carried out only if shoots are damaged by frost.*

Training your plants

The training of plants into special shapes depends on the treatment of terminal buds (the buds at the ends of the stems and shoots). As mentioned on page 336, these buds produce a chemical substance within the stem that inhibits the development of buds lower down the stem into side shoots. The effect gets less the farther the buds are down the stem, so that the lower buds break to form side shoots. If you remove the terminal bud, the inhibiting chemical is no longer produced, and all the lateral (side) buds can develop. Pruning to form a tree into a desired shape is based on this fact. It may be used simply to form a well-balanced, sturdy tree with a strong leading shoot, or – particularly in the case of fruit trees such as apples and peaches – it may be used to form a special shape such as a cordon, espalier, fan or dwarf pyramid.

However, it is not only with woody plants that removal of the terminal bud produces branching; herbaceous plants, too, are made to bush out by pinching out the growing tip. The same principle is used when forming 'mop-headed' standards of such plants as geraniums (pelargoniums). On the other hand, the removal of side shoots channels food to the main stem, and this is used to produce extension growth when standards are to be grown, and to produce smaller quantities of high-quality flowers or fruit – as, for example, in the training of sweet peas and tomatoes. In the same way, the removal of all but a selected few flower buds by disbudding results in the production of specimen blooms

Single oblique cordons
1 Plant the maiden at an angle of 45°, pointing away from the midday sun and with the scion part of the graft union on top. Place a 1.8 m (6 ft) cane at the same angle and tie it to the supporting wires. Tie the young plant to the cane.

No pruning is needed until the end of the following summer, when the new lateral growths are ripe. 2 Cut these back to three or four buds. 3 The following year, treat newly produced laterals in the same way, and cut back extension growth from the older laterals to

two buds. Alternatively, prune more lightly in summer to six or seven buds, and then in winter reduce these to three or four for new laterals and one or two in the case of extension growth. Stop the terminal growth of the main stem only when it reaches the desired height.

– as, for example, in the case of roses, chrysanthemums and dahlias.

The suppressive effect of the terminal bud depends on gravity – the inhibiting chemical moves downwards rather than simply back along the shoot. As a result, if a shoot is bent so that its terminal bud is lower than the others, these are able to grow. This is used in French layering (see p 350), and also has an effect on flowering and fruiting; this can be used to bring over-vigorous plants into flower and to stimulate fruiting in some methods of training fruit trees.

Decorative trees
Decorative trees may be raised from seed or by budding or grafting onto a suitable rootstock (see p 350). The shoot which develops

may be allowed to grow naturally, or it may be 'headed back' at the desired height (by removing the terminal bud and a short section of stem) to encourage the production of side branches. The new terminal shoot is then taken up as the leader and should be supported by a cane to make sure that it grows straight upwards.

If all the lower buds were allowed to develop when the tree was headed back, this would result in overcrowded upright branches lacking in strength. So you should select those buds that will produce a balanced head with wide-angled branches. It is most important to remove any shoots that compete with the leader. Shoots which break below the head or around the base of the tree should be rubbed out with your thumb as soon as you see them.

Topiary specimens
Small-leaved evergreen shrubs such as yew, box and *Lonicera nitida* (shrubby honeysuckle) are suitable. Training begins with young plants; the aim is to achieve steady, compact growth by clipping the young shoots to produce solid, bushy plants. To form pyramids, balls and cones needs only a good 'eye' and regular attention. The more fanciful shapes need to be trained on a framework of strong

wire **above**. A loop of wire will be needed to form a circle; for a bird you will need two pieces of wire, one to shape the head and neck, the other in a loop to shape a fanned tail. A bunch of shoots is allowed to develop; these are then divided and tied to each side of the frame. They need to be regularly tied in and clipped as they grow. The key to success is frequent light clipping to stimulate plenty of dense new growth.

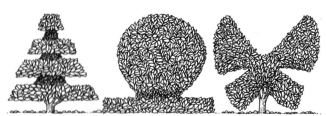

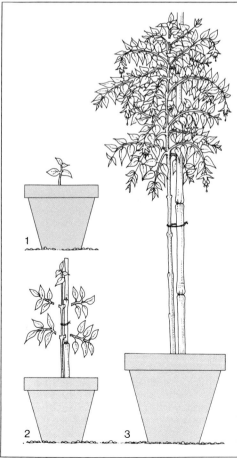

Mop-headed standards
Fuchsias, coleus, geraniums (pelargoniums), bay, *Centaurea gymnocarpa*, citrus species and some other shrubby and sub-shrubby plants make elegant specimens if trained as mop-headed standards. Many of them need protection from frost in winter, so it is a good idea to grow them in pots.
In the first season, pot rooted cuttings singly 1 and grow them on in the greenhouse, taking care that they receive no check to growth. 2 Remove all lateral shoots as they appear and support the single stem with a cane, tying it in as it grows. After two or three years – or less in the case of coleus and geraniums – the stem may be long enough, and should be stopped by pinching out the terminal bud 3. Allow laterals to grow at the top of the stem and pinch these back to encourage further branching. Potting on and repotting (see p 384) will be necessary from time to time, and you should take care to support the plant's stem well.

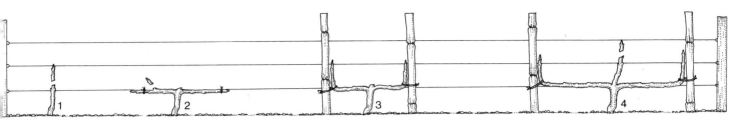

Horizontal and double cordons

1 After planting with two opposing buds in line with the training wires, cut the stem of the maiden back to these two buds. 2 Train the two shoots that break horizontally along the wires, removing any other shoots. Then treat horizontal cordons like oblique cordons;

Espaliers and fans

To form an espalier, 1 cut the maiden to a bud above the chosen pair, as for double-U cordons. 2 Train the centre shoot vertically and the side shoots diagonally on canes.

they come into bearing quickly. Begin double cordons in the same way but when the shoots are about 45 cm (18 in) long, train the tips upright along vertical canes 3.
To form a double-U cordon, cut the maiden back to a bud above the chosen pair, so that three shoots develop. 4 Train the centre shoot vertically but treat

3 Then, in winter, tie these horizontally to the lowest wire. Cut back the centre shoot when 45 cm (18 in) long, as before, and train the two new lower shoots diagonally. 4 Next winter, tie these horizontally to

the others as before, except that the horizontal length should be increased to 90 cm (3 ft) on each side. When the central shoot is about 40 cm (15 in) long, cut it back in winter to a further pair of buds to form another pair of shoots. 5 Train these horizontally as before, but only to 30 cm (12 in) before taking them up vertically.

form the second tier. Repeat until there are enough tiers. You can form a fan 5 similarly, by tying the first pair of branches horizontally and each succeeding pair at steeper and steeper angles.

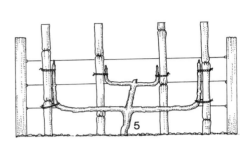

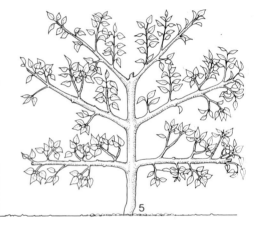

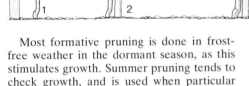

Most formative pruning is done in frost-free weather in the dormant season, as this stimulates growth. Summer pruning tends to check growth, and is used when particular forms of fruit trees are to be trained.

Fruit trees

Fruit trees may be supplied from the nursery as two- or three-year-olds that are already trained, or as one-year-old 'maidens' or 'whips' with a single main shoot. In either case, correct treatment is necessary to maintain and form the desired shape, but in the latter case the gardener has both more to do and a wider range of possibilities. It is essential, however, to ensure that the young plants are budded or grafted onto a suitable rootstock – in particular, onto a dwarfing type if you want to grow cordons, espaliers, fans or dwarf pyramids, and a suitably vigorous kind for half-standards and standards.

The formation of standard and half-standard fruit trees is very much like that of decorative trees described above, the difference between the two depending on whether the leader is stopped at a height of about 1.8 m (6 ft) or only 1.25 m (4 ft). In the case of a bush, the main shoot is cut back at the end of its first year to a height of about 75 cm (2½ ft). Once side shoots have broken and begun to form the tree's or bush's head, after a further year, you can remove side shoots lower down the trunk to leave a clear trunk of about 1.8 m (6 ft) for a standard, 1.25 m (4 ft) for a half-standard or 60 cm (2 ft) for a bush.

If necessary to form evenly spaced branches, encourage dormant buds in suitable positions on the main trunk to break by cutting a shallow notch in the bark just above the bud in early spring. By cutting back the side shoots the following winter, sub-laterals are induced to form, filling in the head of the tree or bush. However, remember that with apples the branches should be about 30 cm (12 in) apart to allow plenty of light and air to reach the centre of the tree.

In order to form a cordon, espalier or fan, the maiden tree needs to be planted in autumn on well-prepared ground and provided with strong posts and horizontal wires 30 to 60 cm (1 to 2 ft) apart for support. If an espalier or fan is planted against a wall, stretch the wires between vine eyes, but remember that the footings of walls are very dry; plant the tree a little way in front and prepare the ground especially well. Oblique single cordons should be planted at an angle of 45°, sloping to the north in the northern hemisphere, to the south in the southern; this gives the plant maximum sunshine. Plant with the sloping graft union between the rootstock and scion (fruiting wood) about 10 cm (4 in) above soil level and with the latter on top, to prevent the scion rooting.

Double cordons, espaliers and fans are formed from maidens planted vertically, and should be trained at right-angles to oblique cordons, with the plane of the tree lying approximately east-west. This ensures even illumination. Whenever planting whips to be

Dwarf pyramids

Dwarf pyramid trees are formed in much the same way as fans and espaliers, cutting back the maiden 1 to stimulate side growth. However, make no attempt to restrict this to two laterals at each level; indeed, you may have to encourage further buds to break by cutting notches in the bark above them so that balanced, all-round growth is made 2. Also, allow the side shoots to grow naturally rather than tying them in. Do, however, train one central leading shoot upwards each year, stopping it in autumn or winter to produce a further tier of side growths. Shorten the side shoots themselves to encourage further branching.

trained in any of these more complex ways, look for a pair of buds on opposite sides of the stem about 40 cm (15 in) above the planting level. Arrange the tree so that these buds are in line with the training wires, for they will form the basic framework of side shoots for the tree. Throughout the period of training, cut back any shoots that develop out of the plane of the tree.

For the general principles of pruning various kinds of fruit trees once established, see page 371. See also pages 308 to 327.

Garden tools and machines

Gardening tools, like those used in any other activity, exist to help the gardener perform his various tasks in the most efficient manner, and like any other tools their usefulness is judged by how well and how easily they do their job. There is a wide range of choice, including both traditional and modern designs, and it pays to study them carefully before buying.

The first principle to follow is to choose a tool that is within your capability to use with comfort. If you are a big, strong, active person you should be able to handle a full-sized spade or fork without difficulty. But if you are a sedentary worker, are getting on in years, or are of slight build, a smaller type may be a better buy, even if it takes longer to do the job. It is, in any case, a good principle to buy a lightweight tool; it is not the weight of a spade, for example, that forces it into the soil, but the pressure applied by the gardener. At the same time, ensure that your choice is strong enough for its expected use. Many tools are available in stainless steel, and in most cases these are well worth the extra expense; not only do they keep in good condition with the minimum of attention, but in the case of digging implements they are lighter to use since the polished surface is easier to push into the soil.

Garden machinery includes such near-necessities as lawn-mowers as well as motorized equipment that many gardeners consider luxuries; but this is mainly a question of the area that has to be maintained and the time, money and energy available. Any lawn larger than a tennis court and its surrounds – about 400 m² (4,500 sq ft) – really needs a 45 cm (18 in) motor mower if grass-cutting is to be a relatively pleasant activity rather than a tiresome chore. With a cultivated area of about 75 m² (800 sq ft), a powered cultivator (or rotovator) is a real boon to someone who does not have much spare time or is not very physically strong. Since it is costly, powered equipment needs even more careful choice than hand tools, and it is well worthwhile trying to arrange with a main distributor of horticultural machinery to have a demonstration of some machines in your own garden. For occasional use, many machines can be hired.

Garden tools, machinery and other equipment fall into two broad classes: those of general everyday use in many aspects of gardening, which are the ones principally covered in this article, and those with more specific functions, details of which you will find elsewhere. Lawn-mowers and other equipment used in lawn care, for example, are covered in the article on page 86; equipment for watering on page 341; plant supports on page 355; spraying equipment for pesticides and fungicides on page 360; and secateurs, shears and other pruning and trimming equipment on page 369. The article on page 378 describes aids and techniques for gardeners who are handicapped or unable through age to use more conventional methods, and many of these are equally useful for more active people.

Basic cultivating tools

Apart from a trowel (mentioned below among planting aids), there are five basic hand tools that every gardener needs – a spade, a fork, a rake, and long-handled and short-handled hoes. Of course, there are plenty of others that can be added as needs arise, but the above are essential for the proper cultivation of beds and borders.

Forks and spades generally have T-shaped or D-shaped handles; the latter are more popular in Britain, but the reverse is true in many other countries. In the same way, most British spades have a square-ended blade with a tread at the top on which the foot can push. Other spades may be rounded or pointed at the end, and may or may not have a tread. There are especially narrow spades that are easier to use in heavy soils, and in most countries there are regional variations. One excellent non-traditional spade is the 'Terrex', which works by lever action and is an ideal labour-saver for able-bodied as well as handicapped gardeners (see p 378). Forks, too, vary, the square-pronged type being easier to push into heavy soils than the flat.

For lighter, shallower cultivations there are many types of tined cultivators which are drawn through the soil towards the operator to loosen the top few centimetres (2 or 3 in). The tilth made is generally fine enough for making a seed-bed, though for this a rigid-tined rake is more commonly used. Tined cultivators can also be used for keeping down weeds and to prevent capping and drying of the soil in hot, dry weather. Rakes for gathering up weeds or leaves, or for teasing out moss, dead grass and other debris from a lawn are best with flexible wire tines (see p 87). One useful type of rake has two parts that can be brought together by manipulating a grip on the handle, and thus grab a load of weeds or leaves; they are just as easily released.

Hoes fall into two main types: the draw hoe, or swan-necked hoe (see p 277), which you draw towards you through the soil or operate with a downwards chopping motion, and the Dutch hoe, which has a flat blade used with a push-pull action through the soil, chopping off weeds and loosening the surface. The advantage of the Dutch type is that by using it while walking backwards you leave the hoed ground clear of footprints. There are stainless steel models, and a particularly good design has a wavy-edged cutting blade that increases efficiency. There are long-handled hoes and short-handled types (sometimes called onion hoes) for close work; the latter are particularly useful to weed between individual vegetables in a row and for work in the rock garden and similar confined places.

With long-handled hoes and rakes it is important to choose the right length of handle, so that you can use it standing upright with the minimum strain on the back muscles. As a rough test, the tallest person likely to use the implement should stand it with its head on the floor. If the top of the handle comes up to at least ear level, it is long enough.

Powered cultivators

There are many types of powered cultivators, or rotovators, but they fall into three basic categories. The simplest, suitable for relatively small gardens, has a rotating cultivator on an extended arm in front of the power unit. For heavy soil and a rather larger area – up to, say, 1,000 m² (¼ acre) of cultivated ground – there is the type with the power unit mounted over the digging tines or rotary blades. The third type has the blades mounted farther back, and is capable of heavier work; it is also a more stable machine that is easier to control. Some cultivators have power-driven wheels.

Among the points to watch when buying a cultivator are the ease (or difficulty) of getting at the belt or chain drive and the carburettor, and the ease of fixing and removing the various attachments. Ask to see (and if possible have demonstrated) all available attachments, such as hoes, ridgers, furrowers, long-grass cutters and lawn scarifiers and aerators.

Planting aids

A dibber and a garden line on a reel are necessary aids when planting and sowing, together of course with a garden trowel. It is desirable

Tools for cultivation
1 Square-bladed garden spade with D-shaped handle;
2 pointed spade with T-shaped handle; 3 full-sized fork;
4 border or 'lady's' fork;
5 Dutch hoe (long-handled);
6 rigid-tined rake; 7 tined cultivator; 8 push-pull hoe with zig-zag blade; 9 onion hoe

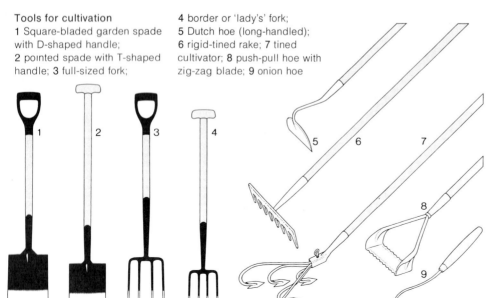

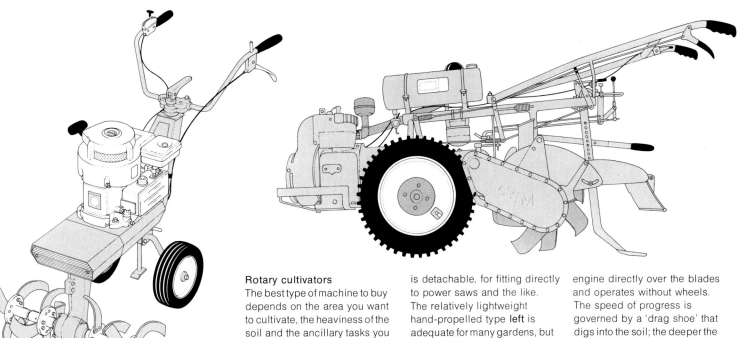

Rotary cultivators

The best type of machine to buy depends on the area you want to cultivate, the heaviness of the soil and the ancillary tasks you want it to perform. Many have a power take-off point to operate other equipment, while with some small models the engine is detachable, for fitting directly to power saws and the like. The relatively lightweight hand-propelled type **left** is adequate for many gardens, but a more powerful self-propelled model **above** will deal better with large areas. An intermediate type has the engine directly over the blades and operates without wheels. The speed of progress is governed by a 'drag shoe' that digs into the soil; the deeper the operator pushes this, the slower and deeper the machine digs. Wheels are fitted for hoeing and other operations.

to have two trowels: a wide one for taking out a hole large enough to accommodate a plant from a 10 to 12 cm (4 to 5 in) pot, and a narrow trowel only about 5 cm (2 in) wide and sometimes called a bulb-planting trowel. The latter is splendid for planting bulbs, obviously, and for small seedlings; it is more versatile than a special bulb-planting tool. Here again, it is worth paying the extra for stainless steel. A small hand fork, preferably also of stainless steel, is useful for loosening soil among small plants, and many people like to use a long-handled type – known as a weed fork – when tending a large herbaceous or shrub border, a rock garden, areas between vegetables or similar inaccessible places.

Barrows

Much time and effort are spent, mostly grudgingly, in barrowing garden compost, grass cuttings, leaves and other materials about the garden. Obviously, the more you have to carry, the bigger the barrow (within reason) it pays to have, while ensuring that it will pass through any narrow spaces between buildings, gateways and so on. The traditional single-wheeled barrow is still very popular, and the larger models can be fitted with a temporary extension top that greatly increases the capacity for lightweight bulky material such as mowings or leaves. Solid wheels are most common, but pneumatic ones are much easier to manoeuvre over rough or muddy ground; one design has a wheel in the shape of a ball.

Two-wheeled barrows, which are available in various sizes, are a boon because all the weight is taken on the wheels. (With a single wheel you are still carrying half the load.) The two-wheeled type is therefore ideal for the elderly or handicapped gardener, but with all barrows you should test for balance by loading them up with anything available, lifting them a few times and (in the case of single-wheeled types) tilting them from side to side. For the larger garden there are truck attachments for towing behind certain types of cultivator, and even motorized ride-on trucks.

Other aids

Other, more specialized powered equipment is available to perform virtually every gardening task, from lopping trees to 'chewing' weeds. There are motorized lawn scarifiers, edge cutters and leaf sweepers. Electric hedge trimmers are a boon where there is perhaps 50 to 100 m (yds) of hedge to cut. Among the most versatile are those that have a rechargeable power-pack into which can be slotted instantly a variety of working heads: hedge and shrub trimmer, grass shears, powerful torch, drill head capable of driving drill bits up to 3 mm (¼ in) diameter, and sprayer. Some may feel that these devices are gimmicks, but it is surprising how 'essential' some of them become once you own them!

Planting and other aids

1 Garden line for marking seed rows; 2 dibber to make holes for planting seedlings, etc; 3 trug, or garden basket; 4 plastic-bodied wheelbarrow with wheel in the form of an inflated ball; 5 short-handled trowel and 6 hand fork for planting, weeding, etc; 7 long-handled weed fork for use in herbaceous and shrub borders

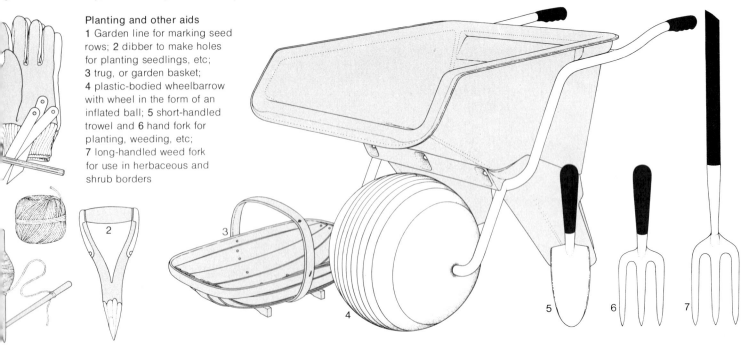

Aids for the elderly and handicapped

A garden can be made much easier for an elderly or handicapped person to maintain and enjoy by thoughtful design and the elimination of features that are difficult to tend, as explained on page 56. However, the choice of the right tools and techniques can turn a tedious – sometimes impossible – chore into a valuable and enjoyable form of occupational therapy. Of course, people's disabilities – and therefore the solutions to their gardening problems – differ widely. One person may be unable to bend, another may have the use of only one hand, while a third may be confined to a wheelchair or may have to work while seated on a stool.

Most of the tools and other pieces of equipment mentioned here are not produced specifically for handicapped gardeners, though a few items that must be specially made are described. Where brand names are mentioned, it is because no exact equivalents made by other manufacturers are known. It is likely that readers in some countries may have difficulty in obtaining certain specific items, though the addresses of manufacturers given at the end of this book should help, while the illustrations may help you to find equivalent aids by other makers. Always consult major horticultural equipment distributors.

Soil cultivation

Cultivating the soil by digging or other means normally demands a great deal of muscle power and bending. The Wolf 'Terrex' spade, with its unique lever action, eliminates lifting spadefuls of soil while your back is bent. All you need to do is to push the blade into the ground with your foot on the pedal, and then pull back the handle sharply; the pedal acts as a fulcrum, propelling the dug soil forwards from the trench. In light soil it may be possible to use the hands only, but pushing on the

The Wolf 'Terrex' spade
This works by a unique lever action, the gardener pushing it down into the soil with the pedal **1**, then levering back **2** to throw the soil forwards **3**. No bending down is needed.

handle-bar, which is more like that of a bicycle than a normal spade handle. A fork head can be fitted in place of the spade blade.

With forks and spades of traditional design you can have a D-shaped handle fitted halfway along the shaft. This cuts out some of the bending, as you need only pull on this handle instead of reaching down to the lower position normally used. It can be a very helpful aid when digging from a wheelchair or stool.

You can easily cultivate lighter soils with a soil miller, which has a row of star-shaped wheels with a hoe blade behind. The latter digs down into the soil when pushed forward, and when pulled back changes its position and cuts into the ground again. The combined action of starred wheels and cutting blade reduces the soil to a fine tilth. Unlike raking, it can be done one-handed, and combines the action of a hoe, chopping down annual weeds. The depth to which it works the soil can be controlled by raising or lowering the shaft. If the width of the bed is restricted you can cultivate the whole area without treading on the soil. With heavier soils, it is best to tackle the job in two stages, leaving a day or two between the millings.

Sowing, thinning and planting

To help sowing seed with the minimum of bending, it is worthwhile making a special garden line attached to 1 m (3 ft) handles as illustrated, instead of the normal short ones. The line can be kept wound on a fishing reel near the top of one handle and fed to a position near the bottom end through two screw eyes; the other handle needs only one screw eye, to which the line is tied, near the point. This is easily positioned and wound in again without bending.

You can take out drills for sowing small seeds with the back of a rake or with a lightweight draw hoe. For sowing the seeds a plastic wheel-type seed distributor on a 1 m (3 ft) or longer shaft is extremely useful; this is generally adjustable for spacing of the seeds. A small spring-tine rake can be used to cover the seeds and the back of the same rake used to firm the soil afterwards. To make deeper drills for large seeds such as beans and peas, a wooden 'sledge-runner' device like that illustrated can be quite easily made. Pushed backwards and forwards through well-cultivated ground, it will leave a narrow trench 8 cm (3 in) deep ready to receive the seeds. You can direct these to their positions in the trench by using a length of lightweight

but rigid plastic pipe of the type used in plumbing systems; 2.5 cm (1 in) diameter is suitable. The same aid can be used for pelleted versions of smaller seeds. Seeds in the trench can be covered by treading the soil either side to fill it in. You can thin out unwanted seedlings with an 'onion' hoe (a small draw hoe; see p 376), preferably only about 5 cm (2 in) wide, on a 1 m (3 ft) shaft. You can also use the so-called scuffle hoe, which has a diamond-shaped blade.

To plant out from an erect position, you can use a trowel head mounted on a 1.25 m (4 ft) shaft. When you have made the hole by cutting out a bowl of soil with the trowel, you can place the plant in the trowel head and guide it into the hole. For firming, the Wolf double hoe is useful; this has a normal draw hoe blade on one side and two sharp-pointed tines (normally used as a soil cultivator) on the other. With the stem of the plant between the two prongs, you can firm it by pressing down. Another useful device is the 'Dibba'; this makes a hole suitable for planting bulbs or pot-grown plants without having to kneel.

Some gardeners do, however, prefer to kneel down to plant out using a short-handled trowel, but then find difficulty in getting into

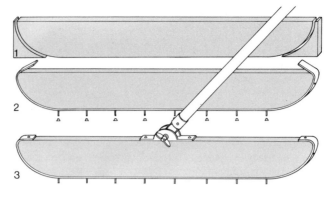

Making a seed-trencher
Take a piece of wood about 1 m (3 ft) long, 10 cm (4 in) wide and 2 cm (¾ in) thick, and shape it like a sledge runner **1**. Cover the working surface with a thin metal strip **2** and drive eight nails 5 cm (2 in) into the base, leaving them about 1 cm (½ in) proud. Cut off the heads of the nails. To the other side fit a pivoted 1.25 cm (4 ft) handle **3**. For the method of use, see text.

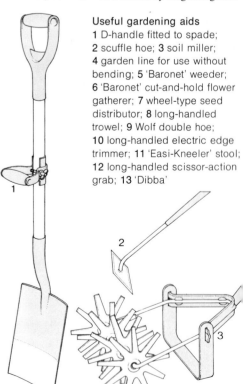

Useful gardening aids
1 D-handle fitted to spade; **2** scuffle hoe; **3** soil miller; **4** garden line for use without bending; **5** 'Baronet' weeder; **6** 'Baronet' cut-and-hold flower gatherer; **7** wheel-type seed distributor; **8** long-handled trowel; **9** Wolf double hoe; **10** long-handled electric edge trimmer; **11** 'Easi-Kneeler' stool; **12** long-handled scissor-action grab; **13** 'Dibba'

an upright position again. The 'Easi-Kneeler' stool has a platform on which you can kneel and arm supports to help you stand up again; used the other way up it makes a seat, and is recommended for any gardener who finds difficulty in standing for long periods.

Routine care and maintenance

A large number of gardening tasks can be done while sitting by using remote-controlled tools. Two sold under the name 'Baronet' are now well-established favourites with disabled gardeners. One is a cut-and-hold secateur for gathering flowers, pruning light wood, dead-heading and so on. The other is a weed puller; you push the blade into the ground beside the weed, close the jaw by squeezing the trigger and can then extract the weed complete with unbroken root system. The same tool can be used as a 'long arm' to reach for flower-pots and deposit plants in holes without bending.

Of course, the disabled gardener can make use of chemical weedkillers (see p 356) to rid the garden of weeds, and a plastic bottle (such as a liquid detergent bottle) with a needle hole pierced in the cap can be used to direct a contact weedkiller such as paraquat from a wheelchair. Soil weedkillers such as simazine are also very useful, especially on paths and under shrubs, but there are those who say that chemical weed control should be used only as a last resort – not on ecological grounds, but because the exercise gained from hoeing is excellent therapy!

Gathering up garden rubbish such as leaves and hoed weeds can be a tiresome chore, however. To make it easier, several versions of long-handled grabs have been introduced. All are based on the time-honoured design of two boards which gardeners have used for generations, but with the addition of 1 m (3 ft) scissor-action handles. Wheelbarrows to be managed with only one hand need two wheels; they come in a variety of sizes, some low-loaders, others mobile scoops that can be tipped easily for loading and unloading. Operating a wheelbarrow from a wheelchair is no easy task; the best solution is to use a lightweight two-wheeled barrow with a single 'walking-stick' handle that can be temporarily clipped over the back of the chair and used as a trailer.

As shown on page 56, a hose is most easily managed if coiled on a rotating wall-mounted hose reel near the centre of the garden. As an alternative, a semi-permanent water-distribution system can be laid around the garden using standard hose and snap-on fittings, with take-off points positioned conveniently. There are sprinklers which can be adjusted or switched on and off without turning the supply off at the tap; for those who cannot move quickly or cannot bend down, the pulsating type on a 1 m (3 ft) leg are a good choice, since they sweep around the garden only slowly, allowing time to reach and adjust the sprinkler without getting wet.

Another tiresome chore is the staking of herbaceous plants, and the not-so-agile gardener would be wise to avoid those that need staking. However, a number of devices make the job simpler, as shown on page 355.

Lawn care

The lawn is a hard task-master for any gardener, let alone the elderly or handicapped, and the lawn-mower needs to be chosen especially carefully. There are many factors to be considered, but for many a lightweight 30 cm (12 in) electric machine is the ideal choice, especially one where the power drives the cutters only, leaving you free to choose your own speed of working. Mains electric machines are light to push and easy to control, but you must take great care to ensure safe handling of the cable. Battery models are safer but heavier to handle, while petrol-engined types suit few elderly and disabled gardeners because of difficulties in starting and controlling.

An electric-powered rotary mower that floats on a cushion of air is particularly suitable for the wheelchair gardener. You can push it sideways as well as backwards and forwards, and from a wheelchair you can swing it in an arc, thus cutting a large area without the need to move the chair. For any handicapped or elderly gardener, the extra weight of a grass box added to the machine makes handling difficult, especially when it is full. In dry summer weather it does no harm to leave the grass cuttings on the lawn, but for lawn health they should not be allowed to form a sodden mat. Perhaps the best answer is to use a separate sweeping machine (which can also be used to collect autumn leaves).

Cutting grass edges can be a problem – and worse for gardeners with the use of only one hand. The answer may be a battery-powered trimmer mounted on a long handle. One model can be adjusted to also cut the grass around trees, close to walls or in other places inaccessible to mowers, while one of the best and safest types uses a whirling length of nylon fishing line as its cutter; this efficiently trims grass and weeds but does no harm to more solid objects – including the gardener's shoes. Hand-operated long-handled lawn shears and edging shears are suitable for gardeners who can use both hands but are unable to kneel or bend down to work. Finally, there are a wide range of other machines powered from rechargeable batteries, ranging from small grass-trimmers and hedge-cutters to the versatile type that has interchangeable heads and is described on page 377.

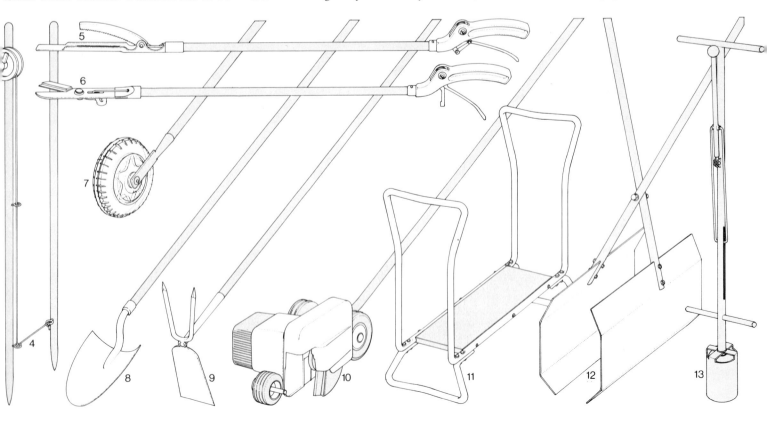

Frames and greenhouses

If you want to make the most of your garden, and especially if you live in an area where frosts occur, some method of growing plants under glass is essential. As explained on page 269, cloches – either glass or plastic – are extremely useful for protecting and promoting early growth of plants in open ground. But you will have much greater versatility – especially for raising half-hardy plants from seed, for raising early vegetable seedlings and for overwintering half-hardy and tender perennials such as fuchsias, geraniums (pelargoniums), dahlias and chrysanthemums – with a garden frame, preferably one fitted with air- and/or soil-warming cables. In summer the frame can be used for rooting cuttings or for growing tender crops such as melons and cucumbers. Even if you germinate half-hardy seeds indoors or in an unheated greenhouse perhaps in a small propagating case (see p 383), the seedlings will need to be transferred to a cold frame to grow on sturdily and become properly hardened off before being planted out.

Although a heated frame provides adequate protection for many plants, a greenhouse offers far more scope and provides a better environment for the gardener, allowing scope for 'pottering' when outside conditions are unpleasant. The two fixtures are not interchangeable, and one or more garden frames are desirable in addition to a greenhouse, but a greenhouse of adequate size can be used for seed-sowing and potting (though not for storing garden chemicals), and will even give you space to sit and enjoy the early spring sunshine. Many gardeners use a greenhouse as a kind of conservatory for growing exotic and flowering pot-plants, ranging from orchids and chrysanthemums to cacti and to the kind of foliage plants commonly used as houseplants. With the exception of using a cold greenhouse for growing alpines, which is discussed briefly on page 122, this kind of greenhouse gardening is beyond the scope of this book. However, as explained in chapter four, the greenhouse is extremely useful for raising a variety of food crops – especially melons, cucumbers, tomatoes, aubergines (eggplants) and peppers.

The garden frame

It is possible to buy complete frames in kit form or to build them yourself. Some ready-made cold frames have glass to the ground; these admit the maximum light, and light-weight aluminium-framed versions are portable, but they are not suitable for giving winter protection. More commonly, the sides, particularly of home-built types, are of brick or wood. (Brickwork 20 to 25 cm [8 to 10 in] thick has the same heat insulation as 2.5 cm [1 in] wood.) A convenient size is 1.5 m (5 ft) square; this will take two Dutch lights (wooden or aluminium frames each glazed with one large pane of horticultural glass to admit the maximum amount of light). Such a frame will accommodate 24 standard seed trays plus 72 small pots 8 cm (3 in) in diameter, or alternatively 400 pots alone. The normal height is about 20 cm (8 in) at the front and 25 or 30 cm (10 or 12 in) at the back, so that the lights slope gently to allow rain to run off. Frames should be sited in full light in a well-drained, sheltered position.

If you have room for two such frames, one can be equipped with a soil-warming cable laid on 5 cm (2 in) of sand and covered to the same depth with more sand. This can be used for seed raising and for rooting cuttings, boxes and pots being simply stood on the sand. Alternatively, you can lay 20 cm (8 in) of a mixture of peat and sand over the wires and insert cuttings directly in this (see p 346). The second frame can have air-warming cables attached to the side walls and allows the maximum headroom for pot-plants, tender fruit and vegetables and so on. To ensure the minimum use of electricity, a thermostat should be fitted. In all cases, make sure that

you use the special waterproof armoured cable made for the purpose, and that it is fitted according to the manufacturer's instructions; if in doubt, have it installed professionally. Always switch off the electricity before you cultivate the soil.

An old-fashioned alternative to electrical soil warming that is useful if you have a handy source of fresh stable manure is to build a hotbed (see illustration) on which a portable frame is stood. Alternatively, straw can be used if it is treated with the chemicals used to prepare mushroom compost (see p 297). In either case, the heat of rotting warms the soil laid over the manure or straw. This is particularly useful for raising melons and similar crops that relish a rich growing medium.

Generally, all frames should be ventilated during the day when there is no frost. With Dutch lights, you can raise the lower end on small wooden blocks, but some proprietary frames have adjustable stays. In severe weather, you should cover the lights at night with mats of hessian or other insulating material, but remove this during the day to admit light to plants that are in leaf. (Dormant plants, tubers and so on can remain covered.) As the outside temperature rises you can switch the heating off and gradually increase ventilation, at first during the day only, until by late spring or early summer, when all danger of night frost is past, the lights are left off day and night. This allows half-hardy plants to be hardened off before being planted out. If you are using a frame for rooting cuttings, however, the lights should be left on. Some shading will then be necessary to prevent overheating and scorching of foliage; fine plastic netting or straw roller blinds are best.

Choosing and siting a greenhouse

The first principle when choosing a greenhouse is to buy one of adequate size; small greenhouses do not have enough room to work in properly, and temperature fluctua-

Types of garden frame
A metal-framed model **above** is ideal for growing cucumbers and melons because it admits the maximum light. It is shown on a hotbed – a flat-topped heap of fresh stable manure 60 to 90 cm (2 to 3 ft) high, topped with 15 cm (6 in) of good soil. Brick and timber frames **right**

provide better winter insulation. In cold areas, the walls should be particularly thick – two courses of bricks or at least 2.5 cm (1 in) timber. In all cases, make the glazing bars as thin as possible to admit the most light. The wooden frame has soil- and air-warming cables and a thermostat.

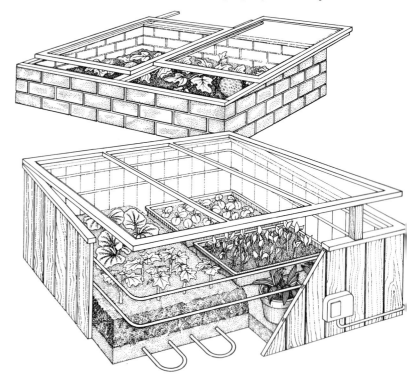

tions are much greater than in large ones. If you are a keen gardener it is worth waiting until you can afford a greenhouse that is at least 2.5 m (8 ft) square, or preferably 2.5 by 3.5 m (8 by 12 ft), rather than start off with one half this size.

The type of construction you choose should depend on the range of plants you want to grow. The glass-to-ground type is good if you wish to grow plants such as tomatoes in the borders or in containers on the floor, but the heat loss is greater than in the type with half-walls of brick or wood. (Metal or plastic walls lose as much heat as glass.) This is of less importance if the greenhouse is to be used for seed-raising, food-growing and so on in early spring, summer and autumn, but if you want to grow pot-plants needing a minimum winter temperature of 7°C (45°F) or more, the potential heat loss is important. In the latter case, a lean-to or three-quarter span greenhouse built against a sunny wall would be a good choice.

Wooden lean-to greenhouses generally have a thicker framework than modern free-standing ones of metal or lightweight wood. This reduces the amount of light admitted, but this is less important in the production of pot-plants; maximum light is essential for fruit and vegetable production. Very light-weight wooden greenhouses may not be as strong as metal-framed ones, but neither need much maintenance. Both need a brick foundation to prevent uneven settlement. Wooden greenhouses tend to be slightly warmer than metal ones, but the latter are extremely durable. If possible, avoid the type that needs regular painting. Much the same applies to the staging (benches) inside; aluminium is more expensive but more durable than timber; with either, many gardeners like to use metal gravel trays even if they do not have an automatic capillary watering bench, as described below.

The appearance of the greenhouse is, of course, important, as it will be a dominant feature in most small gardens. There are some attractive hexagonal and octagonal designs, but consider carefully whether one of these will be as practical in use as it is attractive. For the area covered, the cheapest but least attractive type of greenhouse is that resembling a giant plastic tunnel cloche (see p 269). As with the smaller type, the plastic sheeting does not give good frost protection, but such a tunnel is useful in the larger garden for growing large amounts of tomatoes and similar crops. One advantage, if you have the space, is that it can be dismantled at the end of the season and re-erected on a fresh patch of gound, making frequent soil sterilization unnecessary. (This is, however, quite a heavy job.) A snag, however, is that the plastic sheeting needs to be replaced every two to five years, depending on its thickness.

The siting and orientation, as well as the structure of the greenhouse, affect the amount of light that is received. Even clean horticultural glass in a well-designed greenhouse will transmit only 75 per cent of the available light, so you should avoid any site shaded by trees or buildings. Because the sun shines from a lower angle, the maximum winter light is obtained if the greenhouse is orientated east and west. Frost hollows or draughty, exposed positions will increase heat losses. The distance from mains supplies of electricity and water are important cost factors, since both can be expensive to install; the former is essential in a modern automated greenhouse and the latter highly desirable.

Heating and ventilation

The object of a greenhouse is to provide a controlled environment in which plants can be grown, but outside conditions of light and temperature affect the conditions inside. This means that, in the absence of automatic controls, the gardener must always be on hand to increase or reduce ventilation and shading, to turn heating up or down, to damp down the greenhouse (sprinkle water on the floor and staging) in order to increase humidity, and to attend to the watering of plants. The alternative is to install automatic equipment, the first essentials being heating and ventilation.

There are several ways of heating a greenhouse. The traditional one of hot water from a boiler circulating through pipes is only suitable for a large greenhouse unless it is built on to the walls of your home, so that it is a practicable proposition to extend the house's central heating system to the greenhouse. Better suited to a small greenhouse is direct air heating by natural gas (not coal gas, which produces poisonous fumes), bottled propane gas or kerosene (paraffin). These all increase humidity and carbon dioxide in the atmosphere, so that some ventilation is always needed. With small kerosene heaters, the wick needs regular trimming and the fuel tank refilling; larger types have automatic fuel feed from an external tank, thermostatic control and an external flue to take away fumes.

Although more expensive to run than any of the above, electrical heating is generally the easiest to install and certainly the easiest to control, since a sensitive rod-type thermostat can be easily fitted. (It should be placed about one-third of the way from the door, out of direct sunlight, above the plants and away from the draught of ventilators.) The most reliable, because they have no moving parts, are the waterproof tubular aluminium heaters. These are mounted around the walls of the greenhouse, the bottom tube being about 25 cm (10 in) above the floor. With this type of heater, there must be a 15 cm (6 in) gap between the glass and the back of the staging, so that air can circulate. This is improved if fans are fitted. Electric fan heaters are cheaper and produce good air movement (combating fungus diseases) and even warmth, but are less reliable. The heater should be placed on the floor at the end of the house opposite the door and away from the staging. In summer, the fan can be used without the heat switched on to help air circulation. Always use a heater designed for greenhouse use; domestic fan heaters are unsafe in moist greenhouse conditions.

Whatever form of heating you choose, it is wise to consult the manufacturer (or that of the greenhouse) to ensure that your installation is powerful enough to maintain the desired winter temperature. This depends entirely on the size and construction of the greenhouse and the outside temperature that can be expected. In Britain, calculations are commonly based on a normal outside minimum of −7°C (19°F), so that in order to maintain an inside temperature of 7°C (45°F), the heaters need to be able to maintain a temperature difference of 14°C (25°F). This in turn means that outside temperatures need to drop to −14°C (7°F) before the inside of the greenhouse reaches freezing point.

As the temperature differential that must be maintained increases, so does the cost of heating – at an ever-increasing rate. The result is that in areas where winters are harsh it may be uneconomic to try to keep the greenhouse warm throughout the winter, though double 'glazing' with a layer of clear plastic sheeting held a few centimetres (an inch or two) inside the glass will reduce heat losses considerably. Even better insulation is given by double-layer sheeting that has air bubbles trapped between the layers. It is also a good idea to fit draught excluders to doors and ventilators, while a large greenhouse can be divided into sections with sliding doors and only the central part heated. If heating is uneconomic, tender plants may have to be taken indoors or kept frost-free in a small heated frame or propagating case (see below).

Ventilation is as important as heating for plant health, and automatic ventilation of a small greenhouse is provided very simply by thermostats which work on an expansion system, without electricity, to open ventilators in the roof of the greenhouse, near the ridge. An extractor allows the most efficient temperature control, but a well-sealed house may need to have hand-operated louvres near the door to allow fresh air to enter during warm conditions. Again, it is advisable to consult an equipment manufacturer when deciding the size of fan needed; this should be capable of changing the greenhouse air completely once a minute, to cope with hot summer conditions. Normally controlled by thermostats, extractor fans should be set to come on when the internal air temperature rises above the optimum level for the plants being grown – commonly 18°C (64°F) in summer and 13°C (55°F) in winter. When the fan is used, however, the roof ventilators should be closed, or air will simply be drawn in through the ventilators and expelled by the fan, with little effect on the overall atmosphere. The fan should close completely when not in use.

Other greenhouse equipment

A capillary bench provides a simple automatic method of watering pot-plants, and also helps to keep the atmosphere moist. The staging must be strong enough to support a solid waterproof bench with raised sides. A perforated plastic pipe supplies water to the bench from a header tank equipped with a ball valve. The perforations in the pipe are protected by glass wool and it is covered with a/*continued*

Frames and greenhouses (continued)

Types of greenhouses

right The full-span timber-framed house is a traditional design built on a brick base. The lightweight aluminium-framed Dutch light has sloping walls, making it ideal for border crops. The hexagonal cedar-wood design is attractive but relatively small. Three-quarter span and lean-to types are good if you have a convenient sunny wall. The plastic tunnel is not attractive, but is cheap in relation to the area covered, and will grow large amounts of tomatoes, early flowers and so on.

Greenhouse equipment

The cutaway drawing shows some of the more important items of greenhouse equipment. (In some cases, items are unnecessarily duplicated for the purposes of illustration.) **1** Staging; **2** wall ventilator; **3** tubular heaters; **4** kerosene (paraffin) heater; **5** electric fan heater; **6** mist unit with thermostatically controlled heated bed; **7** capillary bench; **8** fluorescent plant lights (normally a battery of three or more tubes is needed); **9** pesticide vaporizer; **10** rod thermostat for controlling electric heaters; **11** maximum and minimum thermometer; **12** plant shelf; **13** external slatted blind; **14** extractor fan; **15** thermostatically controlled roof ventilators

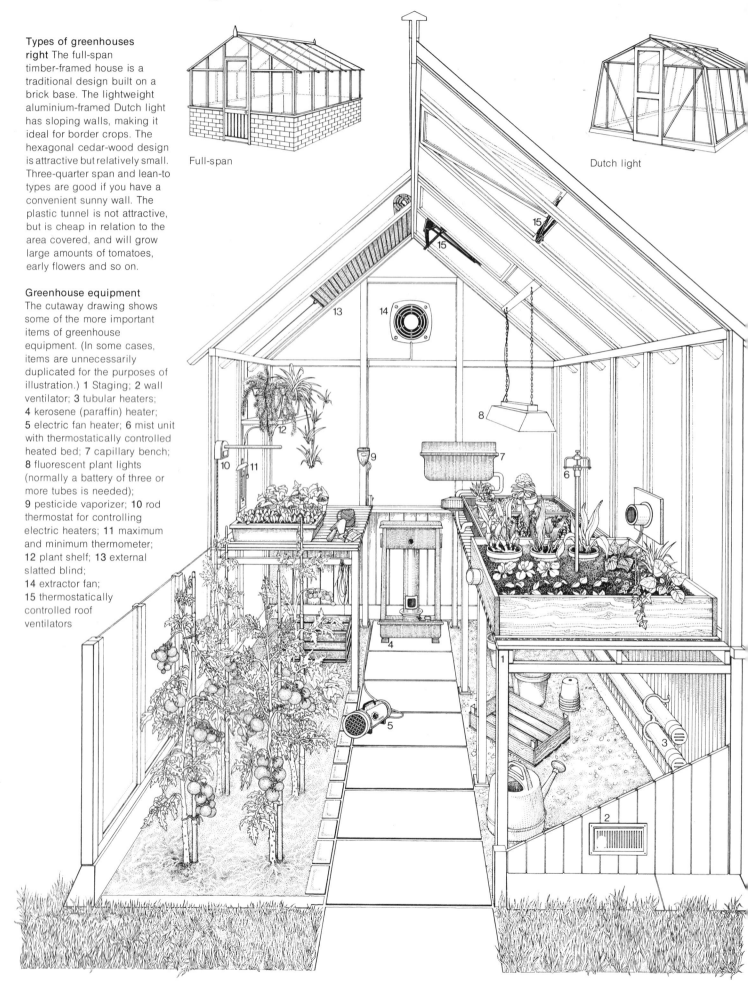

Full-span

Dutch light

Hexagonal

Three-quarter span

Lean-to

Plastic tunnel

layer of fine washed sand. The tank and its valve are positioned so that the water level is maintained just below the surface of the sand. Pots placed on the sand should have no drainage material. Instead, provide clay pots with a glass-fibre 'wick' buried in the potting mixture and passing out through the drainage hole; press this into the sand. Plastic pots with multiple drainage holes need no wick but are simply pressed into the sand. You must water the pots in the normal manner when first placing them in position, as dry pots will not take up water, but thereafter water is taken up as needed by capillary action. Proprietary systems are available using a synthetic fibre mat in place of sand.

External shading is necessary in summer to help keep the temperature down and to prevent the plants being scorched. (Internal shading stops direct sunlight but does little to stop overheating.) The most expensive type is provided by slatted cedar-wood blinds operated by a thermostat or photoelectric cell, but manually operated wooden or bamboo blinds are just as effective if you are on hand to raise and lower them according to weather conditions. The cheapest method is to spray or brush on shading material in early summer and remove it in early autumn. Apart from the traditional 'whitewash' type, which is washed off with water, there are proprietary products that are not affected by rain but wipe off easily when dry. Avoid green plastic blinds, which absorb the colours of light that are essential for plant growth.

A minimum winter temperature of 7°C (45°F), which is the lowest (and therefore most economical) useful temperature for growing a wide range of plants, is too low for germinating seeds of half-hardy plants. But heating costs would soar enormously if you tried to raise the level to the optimum of 18°C (64°F) most seeds need. This problem is solved by using a heated propagating case on the greenhouse bench. Various proprietary models are available, including a simple thermostatically-controlled heater plate on which one or two seed trays can be placed, covered with domed plastic lids or simply sheets of glass to increase humidity. The more complex (and rather expensive) type have a clear plastic or (preferably) glass structure not unlike a miniature greenhouse with a sliding door for access.

However, it is quite simple to construct a propagator yourself from timber lined with plastic sheeting, as illustrated. It should be fitted with a soil-heating cable, embedded in sand and controlled by a thermostat, just as described for a garden frame on page 380.

The case in fact resembles a small frame. An air-warming cable is a useful extra when raising seedlings of plants like begonias, petunias and tomatoes. A glass lid maintains humidity, and the case can be used later in the season for rooting cuttings; for this, a 15 to 20 cm (6 to 8 in) layer of moist peat and sand can be provided in the bottom so that you can insert the cuttings directly.

A more sophisticated way of providing the humid conditions needed for rooting softwood cuttings (see p 346) – though really only worthwhile if you want to do so in large numbers – is to install a mist unit on a bench with soil-warming cables. The mist unit sprays a very fine mist of water over the cuttings at intervals. Some units are controlled by a sensor that increases the frequency of misting in bright, sunny weather, while others have an artificial 'leaf' that switches on the mist whenever conditions become too dry.

Apart from such essentials as a maximum and minimum thermometer and possibly a hygrometer (humidity meter), other useful greenhouse equipment includes an automatic pesticide vaporizer, a small electrical device with a heater that evaporates doses of insecticide or fungicide placed inside. However, vapour distribution may be uneven unless you have some kind of fan that circulates the air, and a small hand-held fan device may be more efficient. In any case, these are no substitute

for maintaining clean, healthy conditions, but they do keep many pests and diseases at bay. For the keen gardener living at high latitudes, where winter days are particularly short, artificial lighting as well as heating greatly increases greenhouse productivity. Flowering pot-plants can be grown for the home at every season (though some, such as chrysanthemums, will not flower if given long 'days', as explained on page 341), and good yields of salad crops such as lettuces can be grown. It is not usually economic or necessary for the amateur to light the whole greenhouse; fittings suspended over one section of staging will be adequate. The best are fluorescent fittings with 'Gro-Lux' or equivalent tubes, whose mauvish light is the best for promoting plant growth. Once installed, these are not expensive to run, but it is advisable to consult manufacturers' literature for guidance on the number of tubes, their distance from the plants, and other details.

Greenhouse management

Although automation can do much to reduce the day-to-day attention that plants in an enclosed environment require, the skill of the gardener is still needed. The artificial environment created by a greenhouse provides ideal conditions for pests and diseases, as well as plants, to thrive, and you need to be constantly on the lookout for signs/*continued*

Propagating cases
The essentials of a propagator are a source of bottom heat, preferably thermostatically controlled, and a cover that admits light but maintains a humid atmosphere inside. You can buy proprietary types ranging from a simple heated plate on which a seed tray with a rigid transparent cover can be placed, through the type shown **above right**, which has a clear polyethylene cover on a metal supporting frame, to glass or plastic structures resembling miniature greenhouses. For most gardeners, a better investment is a self-built propagator of wood lined with plastic sheeting **right**, with a simple glass lid. This is fitted with soil- and air-warming cables, the former embedded in sand, and soil and air thermostats (only one of the latter is needed).

Frames and greenhouses (continued)

of attack. Good greenhouse management can reduce these troubles, not only by the correct use of pesticides but also by avoiding the conditions that favour them.

A stagnant, over-humid atmosphere increases the risk of fungus diseases, which attack stems and foliage. This can result from inadequate or inefficient ventilation and also from placing the plants too close together on the bench or in the borders. If dead or diseased parts are left on plants, the risk of infection is greatly increased. The dull moist days of late autumn create the most difficult conditions, and you may need to turn on the heating simply to allow ventilators to be opened and to encourage a more buoyant atmosphere. In these circumstances, keep the atmosphere as dry as possible by disconnecting capillary beds and by not damping down.

On the other hand, an atmosphere that is too dry in the growing season allows infestations of greenhouse red spider mite (see p 364) to build up. This is one of the most difficult pests to control, as it can easily become resistant to sprays. As explained on page 360, biological control by a predatory mite is possible, but you must take care not to use sprays against other pests that will also kill the predator. Good hygiene, in removing all weeds inside and outside the greenhouse, which can be a reservoir of infection, together with careful damping down in hot weather to maintain air humidity, will help to reduce the chance of attacks.

Hygiene is important in the control of all pests and diseases, and if possible the greenhouse should be emptied and cleaned once a year, before the new season, by washing down and fumigation. All cracks in the glass must be sealed, and of course the ventilators and door kept closed, for fumigation to be effective. Various proprietary fumigant 'candles' or 'bombs' are available, or alternatively place 175 g (6 oz) of potassium per-

---

Growing on straw bales

Good results can be obtained with tomatoes, cucumbers, aubergines (eggplants), sweet peppers and chrysanthemums in the greenhouse by growing on a bale or a wad 25 cm (10 in) thick of partially decomposed straw impregnated with nutrients. The straw must be free from persistent herbicides. Damp it down over a period of two or three days until it is thoroughly wet, and then to each 50 kg (1 cwt) of straw apply 500 to 700 g (1 to 1½ lb) of nitro-chalk, 350 g (12 oz) of superphosphate, 700 g (1½ lb) of potassium nitrate and 350 g (12 oz) of

---

manganate in a can and pour on 250 ml (½ pt) of formalin (formaldehyde) solution; this is enough for a greenhouse 3 by 4.5 m (10 by 15 ft). Close the house for 24 hours, keeping the temperature at 10°C (50°F). Then ventilate freely for two or three days before replacing the plants.

If your greenhouse has an open border, the soil in this should also be sterilized annually to control soil-borne fungus diseases and pests, unless it is completely renewed to a depth of 60 cm (2 ft). Chemical methods are easiest, and of the chemicals available, formalin is the oldest established but still effective. If using a 40 per cent solution, dilute it with fifty times its volume of water (1 litre in 50 litres, or 1 pt in 6¼ gallons) and apply at the rate of 25 litres/m² (4 pt/sq ft). Cover the soil with plastic sheeting for 48 hours, and then ventilate the greenhouse well for 10 to 14 days. Before sowing or planting crops, test the soil by making a trial sowing of mustard seed; it should germinate within two or three days if the fumigant has all dispersed. Granular soil sterilants based on dazomet may be more convenient than formalin, but should only be

---

magnesium sulphate. Water these carefully into the straw.

Close the greenhouse ventilators to conserve warmth; in a few days the bales will heat up to 45° to 55°C (110° to 130°F). When their temperature falls below 38°C (100°F), place a layer of potting mixture on top of the straw deep enough to take the plants. Rather more nitrogenous fertilizers may be needed in the early stages of growth than with more conventional methods of cultivation, but otherwise methods are the same as when using growing bags (see p 117) or raised greenhouse beds (see p 300).

---

used in well-cultivated light or medium soil where the temperature does not fall below 7°C (45°F) at a depth of 15 cm (6 in). They are not suitable for heavy or peaty soils. Follow the maker's instructions carefully.

After any method of sterilization, the bed must be washed free of deposits of fertilizer, which can accumulate in greenhouse conditions and cause root damage. This is done by spraying water for a period of two to three days at a rate that can be absorbed without flooding. (The latter will damage the soil structure.) The total amount of water needed is some 250 to 300 litres/m² (45 to 55 gals/sq yd) – the equivalent of 25 to 30 cm (10 to 12 in) of 'rainfall'. Many gardeners prefer to avoid the need to sterilize or renew border soil by growing all their plants in containers – ranging from clay and plastic pots and the ring culture system (see p 303) to growing bags (see p 117) – or in bales or wads of straw impregnated with fertilizers. Such methods enable the gardener to control the growing medium, feeding and watering of his plants as closely as the greenhouse enables him to control other aspects of his plants' environment.

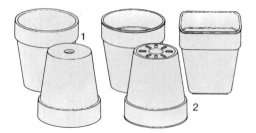

Growing pot-plants
Flower pots are made of 'clay' (earthenware) or plastic. The former 1 have a single drainage hole, and unless you are using a capillary watering bench (when a wick is inserted 3) need a good layer of drainage material, or crocks, covered with a layer of 'roughage' such as fibrous peat. Plastic pots 2 have several small holes and need no crocking, but it is easier to overwater them. You can judge the need for water by

lifting the pot, but for the inexperienced a moisture meter 4 is a useful aid.
Pots are measured by the diameter across the top, a convenient range of sizes being 6 cm (2½ in), 9 cm (3½ in), 12 cm (5 in), 18 cm (7 in), 25 cm (10 in) and 30 cm (12 in). Square pots are useful for small plants as they save space. Always grow pot-plants in a sterile potting mixture (see p 345). Use the smallest pot that will comfortably accommodate

the root ball; stagnant conditions are more likely in too big a pot. If a plant becomes pot-bound 5, with roots matted thickly and twining around the pot, growth will be slow, even in good conditions. It needs potting on to the next size of pot 6; do not fill the pot completely, but leave a space for watering. Plants in pots need regular feeding during the growing season, but do not over-feed. Liquid and foliar feeds are convenient (see p 353).

The year in the garden

The jobs to be done in your garden and their timing depend on many variables, particularly position and aspect, climate and its year-by-year variation, and of course the design and planting scheme. However, these notes give reminders of the most important tasks. Gardeners in areas with harsh winters should note that many jobs indicated for autumn in milder parts should be left until early spring.

Winter programme

Specific jobs are fewer and their timing less urgent than at other seasons, but take advantage of good weather. Overhaul equipment.

Maintenance Continue with routine care as long as weather permits, leaving the soil alone if it is very wet or frozen. Apply manure in late winter, especially to permanent plantings; do not put it on too early, or nutrients will wash away before the plants can reactivate and take advantage of it. In areas with harsh winters, protect vulnerable vegetables, roses and other plants from frost with cloches, hay, straw or other appropriate methods; remove protection as weather improves.

Planting and propagation Order seeds. In good weather, plant any trees and shrubs (including fruit trees) left over from autumn. If earth is too wet or frozen, leave everything until early spring. Sow slow-growing plants under glass in midwinter and the bulk of half-hardy annuals in late winter. Bring chrysanthemum stools into growth to provide basal cuttings. Take scions for grafting in early spring; store in plastic bags in a refrigerator.

Pruning Prune deciduous trees, including most fruits except *Prunus* species, in frost-free weather. Prune vines before sap rises (late winter in moderate climates). Prune roses at any time in mild regions, but leave until early spring in cold areas. Cut back some summer-flowering clematis in late winter.

Vegetables and fruit Prune autumn-fruiting raspberries. In cold regions lift and store mature root crops in early winter. Give fruit trees a routine winter spray to destroy the overwintering eggs of aphids and other pests (see p 359); do this in calm, dry weather.

Spring programme

This is the busiest time of the gardener's year, with a great deal of sowing to get through as well as a heavier maintenance routine.

Maintenance Apply quick-acting fertilizer to awakening plants, watering it in if rain is scarce. Be ready to protect tender plants and early fruit blossom from sudden late frosts. Watch for emerging pests and diseases and spray as necessary. Mulch between shrubs and perennials when soil is moist but warm.

Lawns Sow new lawns and patch up old ones. Alternatively, lay turf. Aerate, fertilize, weed and resume mowing, lightly at first.

Sowing and planting As early as possible, finish sowing under glass any slow-growing plants, including half-hardy annuals. Prick out seedlings, grow on and, in late spring, harden off prior to planting out. Sow hardy annuals directly outside in mid-spring and faster-growing half-hardies in late spring where frosts are unlikely. Sow biennials in late spring so that they have time to make good growth but not to flower before autumn. You can sow tree, shrub and herbaceous perennial seeds now if you wish. Lift and divide overcrowded perennials; plant herbaceous perennials. Plant evergreen shrubs and trees, making sure that the root ball is intact, and other container-grown trees and shrubs as early as possible (especially in areas with hard winters). Plant summer-flowering bulbs in mid-to late spring, and restart begonia tubers into growth prior to planting out. Plant aquatics in late spring.

Propagation Take softwood cuttings, particularly from herbaceous perennials and sub-shrubs. Restart dahlia tubers in very early spring in warmth under glass to provide cuttings to root in time for outdoor planting in early summer. Graft scions of trees and shrubs, especially fruits, that were taken earlier and kept in a refrigerator.

Pruning Prune certain trees, shrubs and climbers, including roses and some clematis if they were not pruned in winter.

Vegetables and fruit Begin a planned programme of sowing vegetable seeds, the majority where they are to crop, others in an outdoor seed bed and tender types under glass in areas experiencing spring frosts. Plant 'seed' potatoes when danger of hard frost is over. Continue with the routine spraying of fruit trees and bushes. Hand pollinate bush fruits if bad weather inhibits pollinating insects.

Summer programme

The plants do most of the work in this season; the gardener's main task is to encourage and regulate them, and to control pests and weeds.

Maintenance Feed, water and stake active plants. Make sure climbers are well supported. Thin out over-enthusiastic plants. Keep down weeds by hand, hoe or (where safe) herbicide. Dead head decorative plants. Combat pests and diseases, but do not overdo it. Feed, water and apply weedkiller to lawns, and continue mowing at frequent intervals.

Planting and propagation Plant out half-hardy annuals and perennials as soon as danger of frost is past. This is not a good time to plant trees, shrubs and herbaceous perennials; only do so if you have to and only if they are well established in containers and you can give them close after-care. However, you can lift, divide and replant iris rhizomes immediately after flowering. Plant autumn-flowering bulbs. If early-flowering bulbs are to be lifted, do so immediately the foliage withers. Take half-ripe cuttings from woody plants, making sure they do not wilt. Propagate carnations by layering, roses and fruit trees by budding.

Pruning Prune certain early-flowering shrubs and climbers as soon as they cease flowering. Prune fruit trees that are trained in restricted forms such as cordons as soon as the first flush of summer growth begins to harden. Prune cherries, plums and other *Prunus* fruits whether or not trained in a restricted form. (They are prone to disease entering through pruning wounds if pruned in autumn or winter.) Trim formal hedges two or three times.

Vegetables and fruit Sow or plant out tender vegetables in early summer. Continue with successional sowings of quick-maturing types. Plant out maincrop brassica and leek seedlings. Harvest green vegetables and soft fruits when in peak condition for immediate use. Harvest early root vegetables and lift shallots and onions. Take advantage of empty spaces to sow late 'catch' crops such as lettuces and spinach. Peg down strawberry runners and plant out these, or bought runners, in late summer. Cut back summer-fruiting strawberries after harvesting to get rid of pests and diseases, or burn off top growth with straw. Cut down the fruited canes of summer-fruiting raspberries and prune black currants after the harvest is over. Pick early apples and pears in late summer. Throughout the season, protect developing crops from birds.

Autumn programme

The summer routine is continued and many crops are harvested, but the bulk of autumn work is clearing up and preparing the garden to face the winter.

Maintenance Continue as for summer. Dig vacant ground as early as possible to allow maximum weathering. Apply lime and slow-acting fertilizers. Clear away dead leaves to the compost heap and cut back the dead tops of most herbaceous perennials. Carefully fork the ground between perennials and shrubs, avoiding damaging roots. Scarify and aerate lawns; apply phosphate-rich fertilizer to encourage strong root growth in winter.

Sowing and planting Plant spring-flowering bulbs, lilies and (in mild areas) tender types such as early-flowering gladioli. Sow seeds of hardy trees, shrubs and perennials outdoors so that they can experience winter cold and break dormancy. Except where winters are harsh, plant evergreens in early autumn, deciduous trees (including hardy fruits), shrubs, roses and cane fruits in late autumn. Transplant such plants after leaf fall. In moderate winter areas, divide and/or plant most herbaceous perennials, plant out spring- and early summer-flowering biennials and sow seeds of some hardy annuals to overwinter outside as seedlings.

Propagation Take and plant out hardwood cuttings of trees, shrubs and climbers. Propagate shrubs and climbers by layering; dig up and plant out rooted suckers.

Storage and overwintering Lift tender perennials (including chrysanthemums), bulbs and tubers before the first frosts. Prepare to protect vulnerable plants that are to remain outside before severe frosts begin.

Pruning Prune once-flowering roses and lightly prune repeat-flowering roses once flowering is finished; leave full pruning until later. Prune cane and tree fruits (except autumn-fruiting raspberries and *Prunus* species) and currants after leaf fall.

Vegetables and fruit In mild areas, sow such hardy vegetables as broad beans, giving cloche protection if necessary. Complete harvesting of fruits and most vegetables; store those suitable. Clear away remains. Apply grease bands to trunks of fruit trees.

Plant selection guide: woody plants

This chart summarizes the basic cultural needs and decorative features of some 150 trees, shrubs and climbers to help you choose plants to suit your requirements and garden conditions. To find further details, refer to the index. Abbreviations and symbols are as follows:–

Type C = climber or rambler; H = hardy; HH = half-hardy; P = perennial; S = shrub; T = tender; Tr = tree

Light needs ○ = full sun; ◉ = partial or open shade; ● = full shade; + = sun or shade

Soil needs + = most soils suitable; △ = tolerates or likes light, sandy soil; ▲ = needs light or well-drained soil; ▽ = tolerates or likes heavy soil; ▼ = will not tolerate light, sandy soil; ★ = needs moist (but not necessarily wet) conditions; ◇ = tolerates or likes acid soil; ◆ = needs acid or neutral soil and will not

tolerate lime; □ = tolerates or likes limy (alkaline) soil; ■ = needs alkaline or neutral soil and will not tolerate acid conditions

Other needs D = drought-tolerant; P = pollution-tolerant and good for gardens in cities or industrial areas; S = salt-tolerant and good for coastal gardens; ‖ = needs staking or support

Size − − = less than 60 cm (2 ft); − = 0.6 to 1.8 m (2 to 6 ft); + = 1.8 to 3 m (6 to 10 ft); ++ = 3 to 9 m (10 to 30 ft); +++ = 9 to 15 m (30 to 50 ft); ++++ = more than 15 m (50 ft) when mature

Seasons of interest 1 = winter; 2 = spring; 3 = summer; 4 = autumn

Flowers W = white or cream; Y = yellow or gold; G = green; O = orange; R = red; P = pink; M = mauve or purple; B = blue; Br = brown;

+ = multi-coloured or a wide range of colours; * = scented

Foliage A = autumn colouring; C = coloured (other than green, grey or silver); E = evergreen; G = grey, silver or glaucous; V = variegated, mottled, etc; † = attractive in some other way (especially leaf shape, shine or texture); * = scented or otherwise smelling (in some cases unpleasantly)

Other features ☆ = striking, graceful or otherwise attractive overall plant form; ¶ = attractive stems or bark; ∞ = attractive fruits, seed heads, cones, etc

Brackets around a symbol or abbreviation mean that it applies only in certain circumstances or situations, or to only certain species or varieties among those covered, or that it is of subsidiary importance; an oblique stroke means 'or'.

Name; common name(s)	Type	Cultural needs Light	Soil	Others	Size	Season(s) of interest	Decorative features Flowers	Foliage	Others
Abelia spp	H/HHS	○	+		+	3 4	W P (*)	(E)	
Abies spp (fir)	HTr	◉	▲ ★ ◆		− to ++++	1 2 3 4	(P R)	E (G)	☆ ¶ ∞
Abutilon spp (flowering maple)	HHS	○ ◉	+ ▲		+	2 3 4	W Y O R	E †	
Acer spp (maple)	HTr	○ ◉	+ ▲ ★ (□)	P (S)	− to +++	(1) 2 3 4	(Y)	A (C) †	(¶)
Actinidia spp (Chinese gooseberry, etc)	HC	○ ◉	+ ▲ ◆	‖	++	(2) 3 (4)	W Y *	(C) †	∞
Ailanthus altissima (tree of heaven)	HTr	○ ◉	+ △	P	++	2 3 4		†	(☆)
Akebia spp	HC	+	+	‖	++	2 (3 4)	M *	E †	∞
Alnus spp (alder)	HTr	+	+ ★ (◆)	(P) S	+++	2 (3 4)	Y	†	(∞)
Amelanchier spp (snowy mespilus; shadbush)	HS/Tr	○ ◉	+ ★ ▲		+	2 (3) 4	W	A	∞
Ampelopsis spp	HC	○ ◉	+	‖	+++	2 3 4		(V) †	∞
Araucaria araucana (monkey puzzle)	HTr	○	+ ★	S	+++	1 2 3 4		E	☆ ∞
Arbutus spp (strawberry tree)	H/HHTr	○ ◉	(◆)(□)		++	(1) 2 (3) 4	W (P)	E †	(¶) ∞
Aristolochia macrophylla (Dutchman's pipe)	HC	○ ◉	+	‖	++	(2) 3 (4)	Y G Br	†	
Atriplex halimus (tree purslane)	HS	○ ◉	+ △	S	+	1 2 3 4		E G	
Aucuba japonica (spotted laurel)	HS	+	+ ▽	P S	+	1 2 3 4	G	E (V)	∞
Bamboos	HS	○ ◉	+ ★		− − to ++	1 2 3 4		E (V) †	(☆)(¶)
Berberis spp (barberry)	HS	○ ◉	+ △	S	−/+	1 2 3 4	Y O	(A)(C)(E)(†)	∞
Betula spp (birch)	HTr	+	+ △ ◇		++	1 2 3 4	Y G	(A)	☆ ¶
Buddleia spp (butterfly bush, etc)	HS/Tr	○	+ □	D P (S)	+/++	3	W (O) P M *	(E)	
Buxus spp (box)	HS	○ ◉	+	P	−/+	(1) 2 (3 4)	G *	E (V)	
Calluna vulgaris (heather; ling)	HS	○ ◉	△ ◆		− −/−	1 (2) 3 4	W P M	(C) E (G)	
Camellia spp	H/HHS	◉	+ ◆		+/++	1 2 (3 4)	W R P	E	
Campsis spp (trumpet vine)	H/HHC	○	+ ▲	(‖)	++	3	O R		
Carpenteria californica	HHS	○	+ □		+	(1) 2 3 (4)	W *	E	
Carpinus betulus (hornbeam)	HTr	○ ◉	+ ▽ □		+++	2 3	G		☆ ¶ ∞
Caryopteris × *clandonensis*	H/HHS	○	+ ▲ □		−	3 4	M B	G *	
Catalpa spp (Indian bean tree)	HTr	○	+ ▲	P	++/+++	3	W Y M	(C) † *	∞
Ceanothus spp	H/HHS	○	+ ▲ (◆)		−/+	2 3 4	B (*)	(E) †	
Cedrus spp (cedar)	HTr	○ ◉	+	S	−/++++	1 2 3 4		E (G)	☆ ∞
Cercis spp (Judas tree, etc)	HTr/S	○	+	D	++	2 3	P M		∞
Chaenomeles spp (Japanese quince, japonica)	HS	○ ◉	+		−/+	2 4	W O R P		∞
Chamaecyparis spp (false cypress)	HTr/S	○ ◉	+ △		− to ++++	1 2 3 4		(C) E (G)	☆
Chimonanthus praecox (winter sweet)	HS	○	+ □		+/++	1	Y M *		
Choisya ternata (Mexican orange blossom)	H/HHS	○ ◉	+	D	+	(1) 2 3 (4)	W *	E † *	
Cistus spp (sun rose; rock rose)	H/HHS	○	+ △ □	D S	− − to +	2 3	W Y P M	E (G)	
Clematis spp	HC	○ ◉	+ ▲ ★ □	‖	− to +++	1 2 3 4	+	(E)	
Cordyline australis (cabbage palm)	H/HHS/Tr	○	+	S	++	(1 2) 3 (4)	W *	E †	☆
Cornus spp (cornel; dogwood)	HS/Tr	○ (◉)	+ (★)		+/++	(1) 2 3 4	W Y G P	(A)(C)(V)	(¶)(∞)
Corokia cotoneaster (wire-netting bush)	H/HHS	○	+ △		−/+	(1) 2 3 (4)	Y	E	☆ ∞
Corylus spp (hazel)	HS/Tr	○ ◉	+ ▲		++	2	Y	(C)	(☆)(¶)
Cotinus coggygria (smoke tree)	HS	○ ◉	+ ▲		+	3 4	P M	A (C)	
Cotoneaster spp	HS	○ ◉	+		− to ++	1 2 3 4	W P	(A)(E)	(☆) ∞
Crataegus spp (hawthorn; thorn)	HS/Tr	○ ◉	+	D P S	++	2 3 4	W R P	A	∞
Cryptomeria japonica (Japanese red cedar)	HTr/S	○ ◉	+ ▲ ★ ◇		+ to ++++	1 2 3 4	(R)	E	☆ ¶
× *Cupressocyparis leylandii* (Leyland cypress)	HTr	○ ◉	+ ▲ □	S	++++	1 2 3 4		(C) E (G)	☆
Cupressus spp (true cypress)	H/HHTr	○ ◉	+ ▲ (□)	(S)	++ to ++++	1 2 3 4		(C) E (G)	
Cytisus spp (broom)	HS	○	+ (◇)	D S	− − to +	2 3	W Y O R P (*)		¶
Daphne spp (mezereon, etc)	HS	○ ◉	+ ▲ ★ □		− −/−	1 2 3	W P M *	(E)	
Deutzia spp	HS	○ ◉	+		−/+	2 3	W P M (*)		
Elaeagnus spp	HS	+	+	S	+/++	1 2 3 4	W	(E)(V) †	
Erica spp (heath; heather)	H/HHS	○ ◉	△ ◆ (□)		− −/−	1 2 3 4	W R P M	(C) E	
Escallonia spp	H/HHS	○	+	D S	+	3 4	W R P	E	
Eucalyptus spp (gum tree)	H/HHS/Tr	○	+ (◇)	(‖)	++ to ++++	1 2 3 4	W *	E (G) † (*)	¶
Eucryphia spp	H/HHS/Tr	○ ◉	+ ★ ◇		++	3	W *	(A)(E) †	
Euodia hupehensis	HTr	+	+	P	+++	3 4	W	†	¶ ∞
Euonymus spp (spindle)	H/HHS/Tr/C	○ ◉ (●)	+ □	D P S	+/++	1 2 3 4	(W)	(A)(E)(G)(V) (∞)	
× *Fatshedera lizei*	HS/C	+	+ ‖	P ‖	−/+	1 2 3 4		E (V) †	☆
Fatsia japonica (false castor oil plant)	H/HHS	+	+	P	+	(1 2 3) 4	W	E †	☆
Forsythia spp	HS/C	○ ◉	+	P (‖)	+	2	Y		
Fothergilla spp	HS	○ ◉	▲ ★ ◆		−	2 4	W *	A	
Fremontodendron californicum	HHS	○	+ ▲ □		+/++	2 3 4	Y	E †	
Fuchsia spp	H/HHS	○ ◉	+ □		−/+	3 4	R P M W		
Garrya elliptica (tassel bush)	H/HHS	+	+	P S	+/++	1 2 3 4	G	E G †	∞
Genista spp (broom; gorse)	HS	○	+ ▲	D	− to ++	3	Y		☆
Ginkgo biloba (maidenhair tree)	HTr	○	+	P	+++	2 3 4		A †	☆
Gleditsia triacanthos (honey locust)	HTr	○	+ ▲	P	++/+++	1 3 4		A †	☆ ∞

Name; common name(s)	Type	Cultural needs			Size	Season(s)	Decorative features		
		Light	Soil	Others		of interest	Flowers	Foliage	Others
Griselinia littoralis	HHS	+	+	S	+ +	1 2 3 4		E †	
Halesia monticola (snowdrop tree)	HTr	○ ◉	◆		+ +	2 (3)	W P	†	∞
Hamamelis spp (witch hazel)	HS/Tr	○ ◉ (●)	★ ◆	P	+	1 2 (4)	Y O R (*)	(A)	
Hebe spp (shrubby veronica)	H/HHS	○ ◉	+ □	P S	− − / −	(1) 2 3 4	W P M B	(C) E (V) †	
Hedera spp (ivy)	HC/S	+	+	P	+ + to + + + +	1 2 3 4		E (V) †	
Helianthemum spp (rock rose; sun rose)	HS	○	+ △	D	− −	3	Y O R P	E (G)	
Hibiscus syriacus	HS	○	+ ▲	S	+	3 4	W R P M B	†	
Hippophaë rhamnoides (sea buckthorn)	HS/Tr	○ ◉	+ ▲	S	+ / + +	1 2 4	(Y)	G	¶ ∞
Hydrangea spp	H/HHS/C	(○) ◉ (●)	+ ★ (◇)	P S	− / + / + + +	3 4	W R P B	(E)	
Hypericum spp (St John's wort; rose of Sharon)	HS	○ ◉	+ ▲		− − / −	3 4	Y	(E)	(∞)
Ilex spp (holly)	HS/Tr	+	+ (◆)	P S	+ / + +	1 2 3 4	(W G)	E (V) †	☆ (∞)
Jasminum spp (jasmine)	HᵀC/S	○ ◉	+	P ‖	+ / + +	1 / 3 4	Y W (*)		(¶)
Juniperus spp (juniper)	HS/Tr	○ ◉	+ △ □		− − to + +	1 2 3 4		(C) E (G)	☆ ∞
Kalmia latifolia (calico bush)	HS	○ ◉	+ ★ ◆		+	(1 2) 3 (4)	P	E †	
Kerria japonica (Jew's mallow)	HS	○ ◉	+		−	(1) 2 (3 4)	Y		¶
Kolkwitzia amabilis (beauty bush)	HS	○	+ ▲		+₊+	(1) 2 3 (4)	Y P		☆ ¶
Laburnum spp (golden rain)	HS/Tr	○ ◉	+	D P	+ +	2 3	Y *		
Lagerstroemia indica (crape myrtle)	HHS/Tr	○	◆		+ +	4	P		¶
Larix spp (larch)	HTr	○	+ ★		+ + + +	1 2 3 4		A †	☆ ∞
Laurus nobilis (bay)	H/HHS	○	+ △	S	+ +	1 2 3 4		† *	☆
Lavandula spp (lavender)	HS	○	+ ▲	D S	−	(1) 2 3 (4)	M B W *	E G *	
Leycesteria formosa (Himalayan honeysuckle)	HS	○ ◉	+		− / +	3 4	W R	G	∞
Ligustrum spp (privet)	HS/Tr	+	+	P	+ / + +	1 2 3 4	W (*)	(C) E (V)	
Lippia citriodora (lemon-scented verbena)	HHS	○	+ ▲		−	2 3 4	M	*	
Liquidambar styraciflua (sweet gum)	HTr	○ ◉	▲ ★ ◆		+ + +	(1 2 3) 4	(Y G)	A (C)(V)	☆ ¶
Lonicera spp (honeysuckle)	HC/S	(○) ◉ (●)	+ ▲	(P)	− to + +	2 3 4	W Y M (*)	(C)(E)(V)	
Magnolia spp ('tulip tree')	HS/Tr	(○) ◉	▲ ▽ ★ ◆ (□)	P	+ / + +	2 3 (4)	W R P M (*)	(E)	
Mahonia spp (Oregon grape, etc)	HS	○ ◉	+ ★	P	−	1 2 (3 4)	Y (*)	E †	∞
Malus spp (crab apple)	HTr	○ ◉	+ ▲	P	+ +	2 4	W R P	(A)	∞
Nandina domestica (heavenly bamboo)	H/HHS	○	+ ▲ ★		− / +	3 4	W	A E	∞
Nyssa sylvatica (tupelo)	HTr	○ ◉	★ ◆		+ + +	3 4	(Y G)	A †	☆
Olearia spp (daisy bush)	H/HHS	○ ◉	+ ▲ □	P S	+	(1) 2 3 (4)	W Y (*)	E †	
Osmanthus spp	HS	○ ◉	+ ▲		+	2 / 4 (1 3)	W *	E	☆
× *Osmarea burkwoodii*	HS	○ ◉	+		+	(1) 2 (3 4)	W *	E	
Parthenocissus spp (Virginia creeper, etc)	HC	+	+	P	+ + / + + +	4	(Y G)	A	(∞)
Passiflora spp (passion flower)	HHC	○ ◉	+ ◆	‖	+ +	3 4	W M B Br	E †	∞
Paulownia tomentosa	HTr	○	+ ▲		+ + +	2 3	B *	†	
Pernettya mucronata	HS	○ ◉	★ ◆		−	1 (2 3) 4	W	E †	∞
Philadelphus spp (mock orange)	HS	○ ◉	+ ▲		− / +	3	W (M) *	(C)	
Phlomis fruticosa (Jerusalem sage)	H/HHS	○	▲		−	(1 2) 3 (4)	Y	E G	
Picea spp (spruce)	HTr	○ ◉	★ ◆		− to + + + +	1 2 3 4	(R)	E (G)	☆ ∞
Pieris spp	HS	◉	★ ◆		− / +	(1 2) 3 (4)	W	(C) E	
Pinus spp (pine)	HTr	○ ◉	▲ ◆ (□)	(D)(S)	− − to + + + +	1 2 3 4		(C) E (G)	☆ (¶) ∞
Pittosporum spp	H/HHS/Tr	○ ◉	+ ▲	S	+	(1) 2 3 (4)	Y Br *	E †	(∞)
Polygonum baldschuanicum (Russian vine)	HC	+	+ □	P ‖	+ + +	3	W P	(G)	
Potentilla spp (cinquefoil)	HS	○ ◉	+ ▲		− − / −	3 4	W Y O R		∞
Prunus spp (cherry, common laurel, etc)	HTr/S	○ (◉)	+ □	(P) (‖)	+ +	1 2 (3 4)	W P (*)	(A)(C)(E)(V)	(☆)(¶)(∞)
Pseudolarix amabilis (golden larch)	HTr	○	◆		+ + +	(1 2 3) 4		A	☆ ∞
Pyracantha spp (firethorn)	HS	○ ◉	+ ▲	P (‖)	+ / + +	1 2 3 4	W	E	∞
Rhododendron spp (including azalea)	H/HHS/Tr	(○) ◉	▲ ★ ◆	P	− − to + + +	(1) 2 3 (4)	+ (*)	(A)(E) †	
Rhus spp (sumach)	HS/Tr	○	+	(P)	+ +	3 4	(R)	A	☆ ∞
Ribes spp (flowering currant)	HS	○ ◉	+	P	+	2	W R P	*	∞
Robinia pseudoacacia (false acacia)	HS/Tr	○	+ ▲	D P	+ + +	3	W *	†	☆
Rosa spp (rose)	HS/C	○ (◉)	+ ▽	P (‖)	− − to + +	3 4	+ (*)	(E)(†)	∞
Rosmarinus officinalis (rosemary)	H/HHS	○	+ ▲	D S	−	1 2 3 4	W B M	E *	☆
Rubus spp (ornamental bramble)	HS	○ ◉	+ ▲	(‖)	+	2 3	W P M		(∞)
Salix spp (willow)	HS/Tr	○	+ ▽ (★)		− − to + + +	(1) 2 3 (4)	(W Y)	(G)(†)	(☆)(¶)
Salvia officinalis (sage)	HS	○	▲		− −	1 2 3 4	(M)	(C) E G (V) *	
Sambucus nigra (elder)	HS/Tr	○ ◉	+ □		+ +	3 4	W *	(C)(V)	∞
Santolina spp (cotton lavender)	HS	○	+ ▲		− − / −	(1 2) 3 (4)	Y	E G *	∞
Schizophragma spp	HC	○ ◉	+ ★		+ +	3	W	†	
Senecio greyi; S. laxifolius	H/HHS	○ ◉	▲	S	−	(1 2) 3 (4)	Y	E G †	
Skimmia spp	HS	(○) ◉	+ ▲ (◇)	P	+ + + +	1 2 3 4	W P *	E †	∞
Solanum spp (Jasmine nightshade, etc)	H/HHC	○	+	‖	+ +	(1 2) 3 4	W B M	E †	
Sophora spp (Japanese pagoda tree, etc)	HS/Tr	○	+	(‖)	+ / + +	2 3 4	W Y	†	(☆) ∞
Sorbus spp (rowan, etc)	HTr	○ ◉	+	P	+ + +	2 3 4	W	(A) †	∞
Spartium junceum (Spanish broom)	HS	○	+ ▲ □	D S	+	3	Y *		¶
Spiraea spp	HS	○	+		− / +	2 3	W R P		
Stachyurus praecox	HS	○ ◉	+ ▲		+	1 2	Y R		¶
Stranvaesia davidiana	HS/Tr	○ ◉	+ ▲	P	+ +	(1 2) 3 4	W	A E †	∞
Styrax spp (storax)	HTr	○ ◉	★ ◆		+ +	2 3	W		☆
Syringa spp (lilac)	HS/Tr	○ ◉	+	P	+ / + +	2 3 (4)	W P M B (*)	†	
Tamarix spp (tamarisk)	HS	○	+ ◆	D S	+ +	2 3	P	†	☆
Taxodium distichum (swamp cypress)	HTr	○ ◉	+ ★ ◆		+ + +	(1 2 3) 4		A †	☆ ¶ ∞
Thuja spp (arbor-vitae)	HS/Tr	○	+		− − to + + + +	1 2 3 4		(C) E *	☆ ∞
Tilia spp (lime; linden)	HTr	○ ◉	+	P	+ + +	(1 2) 3 (4)	Y *	†	☆
Trachycarpus fortunei (Chinese fan palm)	HTr	○ ◉	+ ▲		+ +	1 2 3 4	(Y)	E †	☆ ¶ ∞
Tsuga spp (hemlock)	HTr	◉	+ ▲ ★ (◆)		− to + + + +	1 2 3 4		E	☆ ¶ ∞
Ulex europaeus (gorse)	HS	○	+ ▲	S	+	2 (3 4)	Y *		¶
Vaccinium spp (bilberry, blueberry, etc)	HS	○ ◉	▲ ★ ◆		−	2 3 4	W P	(A)(E)	∞
Viburnum spp (wayfaring tree, etc)	HS	○	+ ▼	D S	+	(1)(2 3)(4)	W P (*)	(A)(E)	(∞)
Vitis spp (vine)	HC	○ ◉	★ ■	‖	+ + to + + + +	(2 3) 4	W G (*)	(A) †	∞
Weigela florida	HS	○ ◉	+	P	− / +	2 3	W R P (*)	(C)(V)	
Wisteria spp	HC	○ ◉	+	‖	+ + +	2 3	W M B *		☆
Yucca spp	H/HHS/Tr	○	+ ▲	D P S	− / +	(1 2) 3 (4)	W	E (G) †	☆

Plant selection guide: border perennials

This chart summarizes the basic cultural needs and decorative features of some 150 herbaceous and evergreen perennial border plants (including hardy bulbs) to help you choose plants to suit your requirements and garden conditions. To find further details, refer to the index.
Abbreviations and symbols are as follows:–
Type B = bulbous (including tuberous, etc); C = climber or rambler; H = hardy; HH = half-hardy; P = perennial; S = shrub
Light needs ○ = full sun; ◉ = partial or open shade; ● = full shade; + = sun or shade
Soil needs + = most soils suitable; △ = tolerates or likes light, sandy soil; ▲ = needs light or well-drained soil; ▽ = tolerates or likes heavy soil; ▼ = will not tolerate light, sandy soil; ★ = needs moist (but not necessarily wet) conditions; ◇ = tolerates or likes acid soil;

◆ = needs acid or neutral soil and will not tolerate lime; □ = tolerates or likes limy (alkaline) soil; ■ = needs alkaline or neutral soil and will not tolerate acid conditions
Other needs D = drought-tolerant; P = pollution-tolerant and good for gardens in cities or industrial areas; S = salt-tolerant and good for coastal gardens; ‖ = needs staking or support
Size – – = less than 30 cm (12 in); – = less than 60 cm (2 ft); + = 0.6 to 1.25 m (2 to 4 ft); + + = 1.25 to 3 m (4 to 10 ft); + + + = more than 3 m (10 ft) when mature
Seasons of interest 1 = winter; 2 = spring; 3 = summer; 4 = autumn
Flowers W = white or cream; Y = yellow or gold; G = green; O = orange; R = red; P = pink; M = mauve or purple; B = blue; Br = brown;

+ = multi-coloured or a wide range of colours; * = scented
Foliage A = autumn colouring; C = coloured (other than green, grey or silver); E = evergreen; G = grey, silver or glaucous; V = variegated, mottled, etc; † = attractive in some other way (especially leaf shape, shine or texture); * = scented or otherwise smelling (in some cases unpleasantly)
Other features ☆ = striking, graceful or otherwise attractive overall plant form; ¶ = attractive stems or bark; ∞ = attractive fruits, seed heads, cones, etc
Brackets around a symbol or abbreviation mean that it applies only in certain circumstances or situations, or to only certain species or varieties among those covered, or that it is of subsidiary importance; an oblique stroke means 'or'.

Name; common name(s)	Type	Cultural needs Light	Soil	Others	Size	Season(s) of interest	Decorative features Flowers	Foliage	Others
Acanthus spp (bear's breeches)	HP	○ ◉	+	P	+	3	W M	†	☆
Achillea spp (sneezewort, yarrow, etc)	HP	○	+	D	+	3	W Y	†	
Aconitum spp (monkshood)	HP	◉	+ ★		+/++	3	W M B	†	☆
Adonis amurensis; *A. vernalis*	HP	○ ◉	+ △		– –	2	Y	†	
Agapanthus spp (African lily)	H/HHP	○	+ △		+	3	B W	(E)	∞
Ajuga reptans (bugle)	HP	○ ◉	+ ★		– –	3	B	(C)(V)	
Alchemilla mollis (lady's mantle)	HP	○ ◉	+ ★		–	3	Y	†	
Allium spp (ornamental onion)	HBP	○	+	(‖)	– –/–/+	2 3	+	*	
Alstroemeria spp (Peruvian lily)	H/HHBP	○ ◉	+ △	(‖)	+	3	+	†	
Alyssum saxatile (gold dust)	HP	○	+		– –	2 3	Y	E G	
Amaryllis belladonna	HHBP	○	▲		+	4	P W *		
Anaphalis spp (pearl everlasting, etc)	HP	○ ◉	▲		–	3	W	G	
Anchusa azurea	HP	○	+	D ‖	+	3	B		
Anemone spp (fibrous-rooted)	HP	◉	+ ★		+	3 4	W P M		
Anemone spp (bulbous)	HBP	○ ◉	+		– –	2	+		
Aquilegia spp (columbine)	HP	○ ◉	+ ★		–	3	+	G	
Arabis albida	HP	◉	+ △		– –	2 3	W R	G	
Armeria spp (thrift)	HP	○	+ △		– –	2 3	P W	E	
Artemisia spp	HP/S	○ (◉)	▲ (★)		– –/–/+	(1 2) 3 (4)	(W)(Y)	(E)(G) *	
Arum italicum	HP	◉ ●	+ ★		–	1 2 3	(W G)	V	∞
Asclepias tuberosa	HP	○	▲ ★ ◆		–	3	O	†	
Aster spp (Michaelmas daisy)	HP	○	+	(P)(‖)	–/+	3 4	R P M B W	(G)	
Astilbe spp	HP	+	+ ★		–/+	3	W R P	†	
Aubrieta deltoidea	HP	○	△ ■		– –	2 3	R M	E	
Ballota pseudodictamnus	HP	○	▲		–	2 3	(W)	G	
Bergenia spp	HP	○ ◉	+ □	P	–	2	W R P M	(A) E †	
Brodiaea spp	H/HHBP	○	+ ▲		–	3	W B		
Brunnera macrophylla	HP	◉	+ ★		–	2 3	B	(V)	
Camassia spp (quamash, etc)	HBP	○ ◉	▼ ★		–/+	3	B		
Campanula spp (bellflower)	H/HHP	○ ◉	+ △ (◇)		–/+/++	3	W M B		
Catananche caerulea (Cupid's dart)	HP	○	▲	(‖)	–/+	3	W M B	G	
Centaurea spp (knapweed)	H/HHP	○	+	(‖)	–/+	2/3	W Y P M B	(G)	
Centranthus ruber (red valerian)	HP	○	△ ◇	D	+	3	R P W		
Cerastium tomentosum (snow-in-summer)	HP	○	▲		– –	2 3	W	E G	
Chionodoxa spp (glory of the snow)	HBP	○	+		– –	1 2	B P W		
Chrysanthemum coccineum (pyrethrum)	HP	○	▲	‖	+	3 4	W R P		
C. haradjanii	HP	○	+ ▲		– –	3	(Y)	G	
C. maximum (Shasta daisy)	HP	○	+ ◇	‖	+	3	W Y		
Cimicifuga spp (bugbane)	HP	◉	+ ★	(‖)	++	3 4	W Y	†	
Clematis spp (herbaceous clematis)	HP	○	+ ◇	‖	+	3	B (*)		
Colchicum spp (meadow saffron)	HBP	○ ◉	+		1/4		W P M		
Convallaria majalis (lily of the valley)	HBP	◉ ●	+ ★		–	2	W P *		
Coreopsis spp	HP	○	+ △	‖	–	3	Y O	(†)	
Cortaderia selloana (pampas grass)	HP	○ ◉	+		++	3 4	W	E G	☆
Crambe cordifolia (giant seakale)	HP	○	+ ▲		++	3	W *	†	☆
Crocosmia spp; *Montbretia crocosmiiflora*	H/HHBP	○ ◉	▲ ★		–/+	3	Y O R		
Crocus spp	HBP	○ ◉	+ ▲		– –	1/2/4	+		
Cyclamen spp	HBP	◉ ●	▲ ★		– –	1/2/3/4	W P M (*)	E V	
Cynara spp (cardoon; globe artichoke)	H/HHP	○	+ ▲	‖	++	3	M	G	☆
Delphinium spp (larkspur)	HP	○	+ □	‖	+/++	3	W P M B		
Dianthus spp (carnation; pink)	HP	○	▲ ■	P S (‖)	–/+	3 (4)	W Y O R P (*)	E (G)	
Dicentra spp (bleeding heart)	HP	○ ◉	+		–/+	2 3 (4)	R P M	(G)	
Doronicum spp (leopard's-bane)	HP	○ ◉	+ ★	(‖)	–/+	2 3	Y		
Echinops spp (globe thistle)	HP	○	+	D	+	3	B	G	
Epimedium spp (barrenwort)	HP	○	▲ ★		– –	1 2 3 4	Y R P	A C E V	
Eranthis spp (winter aconite)	HBP	◉ ●	★		– –	1 2	Y (*)		
Eremurus spp (foxtail lily)	HBP	○	+ ▲		+/++	2 3	W Y O P		
Erigeron spp (fleabane)	HP	○	▲ ★	(‖)	–	2	P M B		
Erodium spp (heron's-bill)	HP	○	+ ▲ □		–	3	P M	†	
Eryngium spp (sea holly)	HP	○	+ ▲	D S	–/+	3	B	†	
Erythronium spp (dog's-tooth violet, etc)	HBP	◉	▲ ★		– –	2	W Y P M	(V)	
Euphorbia spp (spurge)	HP	○ ◉	+ △	D	–/+	2 3	Y G		☆
Ferns	HP	◉ ●	★		– – to ++	2 3 4		(A)(E) †	(☆)
Ferula communis (giant fennel)	HP	○	▲		++	3	Y	†	☆
Filipendula spp (meadowsweet)	HP	○ ◉	+ ★ (□)	‖	+/++	3	W R P		
Frankenia laevis (sea heath)	HP	○	▲	D S	– –	3	P	†	

Name; common name(s)	Type	Cultural needs Light	Soil	Others	Size	Season(s) of interest	Decorative features Flowers	Foliage	Others
Fritillaria spp (fritillary)	HBP	○◉	▲(★)		-/+	2	W Y O R M		
Gaillardia aristata (blanket flower)	HP	○◉	+△	(‖)	+	34	Y O R	G	
Galanthus spp (snowdrop)	HBP	○◉	+▽★		--	12	W G		
Galtonia candicans (summer hyacinth)	HBP	○	+		+	3	W *		
Gentiana spp (gentian)	HP	○◉	★(◆)(■)		--	234	B		
Geranium spp (cranesbill)	HP	○◉	+▲	(‖)	-	3	R P M B		
Geum spp (avens)	HP	○◉	+	(‖)	-	3	Y O R		
Gunnera manicata	H/HHP	○◉	★		++	34	(R Br)	†	☆
Gypsophila spp (baby's breath)	HP	○	+▲■	(‖)	-/+	3	W P	G	
Helenium autumnale	HP	○	+		+/++	34	Y O R Br		
Helichrysum spp (curry plant, etc)	H/HHP	○	+▲		-	3	(W Y)	G(*)	
Helleborus spp (hellebore)	HP	◉●	▲★		-	12	W G M P	(E)	
Hemerocallis spp (day lily)	HP	○◉	+		+	3	Y O R P(*)		
Hermodactylus tuberosus (snake's-head iris)	HBP	○	▲		-	2	G		
Hesperis matronalis (damask violet)	HP	○◉	▲★		-/+	3	W M *		
Hosta spp (funkia; plantain lily)	HP	+	+▲★		-/+	2	W M(*)	(C)(G)(V)†	☆
Hyacinthus orientalis (hyacinth)	HBP	○◉	+		--	2	W Y R P B *		
Incarvillea spp	HP	○	▲		-	23	P	†	
Ipheion uniflorum	HBP	○◉	▲		--	2	W B *	*	
Iris spp	H/HHBP	○(◉)	(varied)		--/-/+	1234	+(*)	(E)(V)	
Kniphofia spp (red-hot poker)	HP	○	+▲	S	-/+/++	34	W Y O R	E	
Lamium maculatum (dead nettle)	HP	+	+		-	2	W P M	(V)	
Lathyrus spp (everlasting pea)	HP/C	○	+▲	‖	++	3	W R P M		
Leucojum spp (snowflake)	HBP	+	+▲★		--/-	234	W G		
Liatris spp (gayfeather)	HBP	○◉	+▲★		+	34	R P M		
Ligularia spp	HP	○◉	+★	(‖)	+	3	Y O		
Lilium spp (lily)	H/HHBP	○◉	+▲(◆)(□)	(‖)	+/++	3	+(*)	†	
Limonium latifolium (sea lavender)	HP	○	+▲	DS	-	3	M B		
Linum narbonense (perennial flax)	HP	○	+▲		-	3	B	G	
Lobelia fulgens	HHP	◉	+★		-/+	34	R P	C	
Lupinus spp (lupin)	HP	○◉	+◆	(‖)	+	3	+		
Macleaya spp (plume poppy)	HP	○	+	(‖)	++	3	W P		
Meconopsis spp (Himalayan blue poppy)	HP	◉	▲★◆	(‖)	+/++	3	B(+)		
Mertensia virginica (Virginian cowslip)	HP	◉	+★		-	2	M B		
Milium effusum 'Aureum' (golden grass)	HP	◉	+		-	23	(W)	C	
Mimulus spp (musk)	HP	○◉	+★		-	23	Y O R		
Miscanthus spp	HP	+	+		+/++	34		V	☆
Molinia caerulea (Indian grass)	HP	+	+		-/+	34	G M	C V	
Monarda didyma (bergamot)	HP	○◉	+★	‖	+	3	R W P M	*	
Muscari spp (grape hyacinth)	HBP	○	+		--/-	2	W B M		
Narcissus spp (daffodil, etc)	HBP	○◉	+		--/-	12	W Y O(*)		
Nepeta spp (catmint)	HP	○◉	+		-	34	M	G *	
Oenothera spp (evening primrose)	HP	○	+▲	(‖)	--/-	3	Y *		
Ornithogalum spp (star of Bethlehem, etc)	H/HHBP	○◉	+▲		--/-	23	W *		
Paeonia spp (paeony)	HP	○◉	+▲★□	(‖)	-/+	23	W Y R P M(*)		
Papaver orientale (oriental poppy)	HP	○	+▲	‖	+	23	R W O P		∞
Pennisetum alopecuroides	HHP	○	+▲		+	34	Y	G	
Phlox paniculata	HP	○◉	+▲★	‖	+	3	W R P M		
Phormium tenax (New Zealand flax)	H/HHP	○	+▲★		++	1234	(R)	(C)E(V)	☆
Physalis alkekengi (Chinese lantern)	HP	○◉	+		-	34	W		∞
Physostegia virginiana (obedient plant)	HP	○◉	+★	(‖)	+	3	W P M		
Platycodon grandiflorum (balloon flower)	HP	○	+▲	‖	-	3	W P B		
Polygonatum multiflorum (Solomon's seal)	HP	○◉	+		+	3	W	†	☆
Polygonum spp (knotweed)	HP	○◉	▽★		-/+	34	R P	A	
Potentilla spp (cinquefoil)	HP	○	+▲		--/-	23	Y O R P	G	
Primula spp (polyanthus; primrose)	H/HHP	○◉	+★		--/-/+	23	+(*)		
Pulmonaria spp (lungwort)	HP	◉●	+★		--	2	P M B	(V)	
Pulsatilla vulgaris (pasque flower)	HP	○◉	+▲		--	2	R P M	†	
Puschkinia scilloides (striped squill)	HBP	○◉	+		--	2	B		
Ranunculus aconitifolius (fair maids of France)	HP	○◉	+★		-	23	W		
Rheum palmatum (ornamental rhubarb)	HP	○◉	+★		++	23	R P	C †	☆
Romneya spp (tree poppy)	H/HHP	○	+▲		+/++	3	W(*)		
Rudbeckia spp (coneflower, etc)	HP	○	+▲	‖	+/++	34	Y O		
Salvia spp	H/HHP	○◉	+▲		-/+	3	B	(G)†	
Saxifraga umbrosa (London pride)	HP	◉●	+▲		-	2	P	(V)	
Scabiosa caucasica (pincushion flower)	HP	○	+▲	(‖)	-/+	3	W M B		
Schizostylis coccinea (Kaffir lily)	H/HHBP	○	+★		+	4	R P		
Scilla spp (bluebell; squill)	HBP	○◉	+▲★		--	23	B W P		
Sedum spectabile; S. telephium	HP	○	+	(D)	-	34	R P	†(V)	
Sidalcea spp	HP	○◉	+	(‖)	+	3	R P		
Sisyrinchium striatum	HP	○	+		-	3	Y		
Solidago cutleri (golden rod)	HP	○◉	+	(‖)	-/+/++	3	Y		
Sternbergia lutea (autumn daffodil)	HBP	○	+▲		--	4	Y		
Stipa spp (feather grass)	HP	○	+▲		+/++	3	W Y	†	☆
Stokesia laevis (Stokes' aster)	HP	○◉	+▲	‖	-	34	W M B		
Thalictrum delavayi (meadow rue)	HP	○◉	+★		+	3	W M	†	
Tradescantia × andersoniana	HP	○◉	+▲★	(‖)	-	3	W P M B		
Trillium spp (trinity flower)	HBP	◉	+▲★		--/-	23	P W	(V)	
Trollius europaeus (globe flower)	HP	○◉	+★		+	23	Y O		
Tulipa spp (tulip)	HBP	○◉	+□	(‖)	-/+	2	+	(V)	
Veratrum spp (helleborine)	HBP	◉●	+▲★		+/++	3	W Y G M	†	☆
Veronica incana	HP	○◉	+▲★	(‖)	-	3	B	G	
Vinca spp (periwinkle)	HP	○◉	+		--	234	B W M	E(V)	
Viola spp (pansy; violet; etc)	HP	○◉	+▲★		--	1234	+(*)		
Zauschneria californica (Californian fuchsia)	HHP	○	+▲		-	34	R	G	

Plant selection guide: temporary plants

This chart summarizes the basic cultural needs and decorative features of some 150 temporary bedding plants (mainly annuals and biennials, but also some tender and bulbous perennials) to help you choose plants to suit your requirements and garden conditions. To find further details, refer to the index of plant names.
Abbreviations and symbols are as follows:–
Type   A = annual; B = bulbous (including tuberous, etc); Bl = biennial; C = climber or rambler; H = hardy; HH = half-hardy; P = perennial; S = shrub; T = tender
Light needs   ○ = full sun; ◉ = partial or open shade; ● = full shade; + = sun or shade
Soil needs   + = most soils suitable; △ = tolerates or likes light, sandy soil; ▲ = needs light or well-drained soil; ▽ = tolerates or likes heavy soil; ▼ = will not tolerate light, sandy soil;

★ = needs moist (but not necessarily wet) conditions; ◇ = tolerates or likes acid soil; ◆ = needs acid or neutral soil and will not tolerate lime; □ = tolerates or likes limy (alkaline) soil; ■ = needs alkaline or neutral soil and will not tolerate acid conditions
Other needs D = drought-tolerant; P = pollution-tolerant and good for gardens in cities or industrial areas; S = salt-tolerant and good for coastal gardens; ‖ = needs staking or support
Size   −− = less than 30 cm (12 in); − = less than 60 cm (2 ft); + = 0.6 to 1.25 m (2 to 4 ft); ++ = 1.25 to 3 m (4 to 10 ft); +++ = more than 3 m (10 ft) when mature
Seasons of interest   1 = winter; 2 = spring; 3 = summer; 4 = autumn
Flowers   W = white or cream; Y = yellow or gold; G = green; O = orange; R = red; P = pink;

M = mauve or purple; B = blue; Br = brown; + = multi-coloured or a wide range of colours; * = scented
Foliage   A = autumn colouring; C = coloured (other than green, grey or silver); E = evergreen; G = grey, silver or glaucous; V = variegated, mottled, etc; † = attractive in some other way (especially leaf shape, shine or texture); * = scented or otherwise smelling
Other features   ☆ = striking, graceful or otherwise attractive overall plant form; ¶ = attractive stems or bark; ∞ = attractive fruits, seed heads, cones, etc
Brackets around a symbol or abbreviation mean that it applies only in certain circumstances or situations, or to only certain species or varieties among those covered, or that it is of subsidiary importance; an oblique stroke means 'or'.

Name; common name(s)	Type	Cultural needs Light	Soil	Others	Size	Season(s) of interest	Decorative features Flowers	Foliage	Others
Acidanthera bicolor	HHBP	○	+ ▲		+	3	W M *		
Adonis aestivalis (pheasant's eye)	HA	○	+ ▲		−	3	R		
Ageratum houstonianum (floss flower)	HHA	○	+ ★			3 4	B W P M		
Alcea rosea (hollyhock)	HA/Bl	○ ◉	▼ ★	‖	++	3	W Y R P		
Alonsoa warscewiczii (mask flower)	HHP/A	○	+ △		−	3 4	R		
Alyssum maritimum (sweet alyssum)	HA	○	+ ▲		− −	3 4	W P M *		
Amaranthus caudatus (love-lies-bleeding)	HA	○	+ ▽		+	3 4	R G		☆
A. tricolor (Joseph's coat)	HA	○	+ ▽		+	3 4	(R)	C	
Anagallis arvensis (scarlet pimpernel)	H/HHA	○	+ ▲		− −	3	R B		
Anchusa capensis	HA/Bl	○	+		−	3	B		
Antirrhinum majus (snapdragon)	HHA/P	○ ◉	+ △	(‖)	−/+	3 4	+		
Arctotis × hybrida (African daisy)	HHA	○	+		−	3	+		
Asperula orientalis (woodruff)	HA	◉	+ ★		−	3	B *		
Aster tenacetifolius (Tahoka daisy)	HA	○	+ △		−	3 4	Y B		
Atriplex hortensis (mountain spinach)	HA	○ ◉	+	(‖)	+	3 4		C	¶
Begonia semperflorens (wax begonia)	HHA/P	◉	+ ▲ ★		− −	3 4	W R P	E †	
B. × tuberhybrida (tuberous begonia)	HHBP	○ ◉	+ ▲ ★	(‖)	−	3	W Y O R P		
Bellis perennis (English daisy)	HP/Bl	○ ◉	+ ▲		− −	2 3 4	W R P		
Beta vulgaris (ornamental beet)	HA/Bl	○	+ ▲		−	(1) 2 3 4		C	
Brachycome iberidifolia (Swan River daisy)	HHA	○	+		−	3	W P M B *		
Brassica oleracea (ornamental cabbage)	HA/Bl	○	+ ▲ □		−	(1) 3 4		C	
Calceolaria spp	HHA/P	○ ◉	+ ▲ ◆	(‖)	−	3	Y O R		
Calendula officinalis (pot marigold)	HA	+	+		−	2 3 4	Y O		
Callistephus chinensis (China aster)	HHA	○	+ ▲	(‖)	−	3 4	P W R M		
Campanula medium (Canterbury bell)	HBl	○ ◉	+ ▲		−/+	2 3	W P M B		
Canna spp (Indian shot)	HHBP	○	+		+/++	3	Y O R	(C)	☆
Celosia argentea (Prince of Wales feathers, etc)	HHA	○	+ ▲		−	3	Y O R		
Centaurea cyanus (cornflower)	HA	○	+ ▲	(‖)	−/+	3	W R P M B		
C. moschata (sweet sultan)	HA	○	+ ▲ ■	(‖)	−	3	W Y P M *		
Cheiranthus spp (wallflower)	HBl	○	+ ▲ ■		−	2 3	+ * (O)		
Chlorophytum capense (spider plant)	TP	○ ◉	+		−	3	(W)	E V	
Chrysanthemum spp	H/HHA/HHP	○	+ ▲ (★)	(‖)	−/+	3/4	+ (*)		
Clarkia spp	HA	○	▲ ◆		−	3	W O R P M		
Cleome spinosa (spider flower)	HHA	○	+ ▲		+	3 4	Y W P *		
Clivia miniata (Kaffir lily)	HHP	○ ◉	+ ★		−	2 3	O R	E	
Cobaea scandens (cup-and-saucer plant)	HHA/PC	○	+ ▲	‖	+++	3 4	M W G		
Coleus blumei (flame nettle)	TP	○ ◉	+ ▲		−	3	(W B)	E C V	
Convolvulus tricolor	HA	○	+ ▲		−	3	B W Y R		
Coreopsis tinctoria (tickseed)	HA	○	+ ▲		−/+	3	Y O		
Cosmos bipinnatus (cosmea; Mexican aster)	HHA	○	▲	‖	+	3 4	W O R P	†	
Crinum spp	HHBP	○	+ ▲		−	3 4	W P *		
Crocus spp	HBP	○ ◉	+ ▲		− −	1/2/4	+		
Cucurbita pepo (gourd)	HHAC	○	+ ▲	‖	++	3 4			∞
Cuphea spp (Mexican cigar plant)	HHA/P	○	+ ▲		−	3	R		
Cynoglossum amabile (hound's-tongue)	HA/Bl	○ ◉	+ ▲		−	3	B	†	
Dahlia × variabilis	HHA/BP	○	+ ▽	(‖)	−/+/++	3 4	+		
Datura spp (angel's trumpet; thorn apple)	HA/HHP/S	○	+	(‖)	+/++	3	W R (*)	(E)	
Delphinium spp (larkspur)	H/HHA	○	+	‖	−/+	3	B W R P M	†	
Dianthus barbatus (sweet William)	HBl/P	○	+ ▲ ■	(‖)	−	3	+ *		
D. chinensis (Indian and Japanese pinks)	HHA/P	○	+ ▲ ■		− −	3 4	W R P		
Diascia barberae (twinspur)	HHA	○	+ ▲		− −	3	P		
Didiscus caeruleus (blue lace flower)	HHA	○	+	(‖)	−	3	B *		
Digitalis purpurea (foxglove)	HBl/P	◉	+ ★		+/++	3	W R P M		
Dimorphotheca spp (Cape marigold)	HA/HHP	○	▲		−	3	W Y O Br		
Eccremocarpus scaber (Chilean glory vine)	HHPC	○	+ ▲ ★	‖	++	3 4	O		
Eschscholzia spp (Californian poppy)	HA	○	+ ▲		−	3 4	W Y O R	G	
Felicia spp (kingfisher daisy, etc)	HHA/P	○	+ ▲		− −/−	3	B	(G)	
Freesia spp	HHBP	○	▲		−	3	+ *		
Fuchsia spp	HHS	○ ◉	+ ▲ ★		−/+	3 4	R P M W		
Gaillardia pulchella (blanket flower)	HHA	○ ◉	+ △		−	3 4	Y O R		
Gazania splendens	HHA/P	○	▲	S	− −	3 4	Y O R P Br		
Gladiolus spp	HHBP	○	+ ▲	(‖)	−/+	3	+		
Gloriosa rothschildiana	HHBPC	○	+ ★	‖	++	3	Y R		
Godetia grandiflora	HA	○	▲ ★		−	3	W R P M		
Grevillea robusta (silk oak)	HHS	○	◆		+/++	3		†	☆
Gypsophila elegans	HA	○	+ ▲ ■	‖	−	2 3	W P	G	

Name; common name(s)	Type	Cultural needs			Size	Season(s) of interest	Decorative features		
		Light	*Soil*	*Others*			*Flowers*	*Foliage*	*Others*
Hedychium gardnerianum (ginger-wort)	HHP	○	+ ▲		+	3	Y *	†	☆
Helianthus annuus (sunflower)	HA	○	+ ▲	‖	+/++	3	W Y Br		
Helichrysum bracteatum (straw flower)	HHA	○	▲		+	3	+		
Heliotropium spp (cherry pie; heliotrope)	TS	○	+ ▲	‖	–	3	B W M *		
Helipterum spp (Australian everlasting)	HHA	○	+ ▲		–	3	W Y R P *	G	
Hibiscus 'Red Leaved'	HA	○ ◉	+ ▲		–	3 4		C	
H. trionum (flower-of-an-hour)	HA	○	+ ▲		+	3	W Y Br		
Hyacinthus orientalis (hyacinth)	HBP	○ ◉	+		– –	2	W Y R P B *		
Iberis spp (candytuft)	HA	○	+ ▲	P	–	3	W R P M (*)		
Impatiens spp (balsam; busy Lizzy)	HHA/P	○ ◉	+ ▲		–	3	W O R P M		
Ionopsidium acaule (violet cress)	HA	◉	+ ★		– –	3	W M		
Ipomoea spp (morning glory)	HHAC	○	+ ▲	‖	++/+++	3	R M B		
Iris spp (bulbous – Dutch, English & Spanish)	H/HHBP	○	+ ▲ (★)		–	3	+		
Ixia viridiflora	HHBP	○	+ ▲		–	2 3	+		
Ixiolirion tataricum	HHBP	○	▲		–	3	B		
Kochia scoparia (burning bush)	HHA	+	+ ▲		–	3 4		C A	
Lantana camara	TS	○	+ ▲ ★	‖	+	3	W Y R P		
Lathyrus odoratus (sweet pea)	HAC	○	+ △ □	‖	–/+/++	3	+ *		
Lavatera trimestris (annual mallow)	HA	○	+ △	S	+	3	P W		
Layia elegans (tidy tips)	HA	○	+ △	D	–	3 4	Y W *		
Limnanthes douglasii (meadow foam, etc)	HA	○	+		– –	3	W Y *		
Limonium sinuatum (statice)	HHA	○	+ ▲	D S	–	3	+		
Linaria maroccana (bunny rabbits; toadflax)	HA	○	+ ▲		– –/–	3	+		
Linum spp (flax)	HA	○	+ ▲		–	3	R W B		
Lobelia erinus	HHA	◉	▽ ★		– –	3 4	B W R		
Lunaria spp (honesty)	HBl	◉	+ ▲		+	2 3 (4)	M W P *	(V)	∞
Lupinus hartwegii (annual lupin)	HA	○ ◉	+ △ ◆		–/+	3 4	B W R M		
Malcolmia maritima (Virginia stock)	HA	○ ◉	+		– –	2 3 4	+ *		
Matthiola spp (stock)	H/HHA/Bl	○ ◉	+ □	(‖)	– –	2 3 4	+ *		
Mentzelia lindleyi (blazing star)	HA	○	+ △	D	–	3	Y *		
Mesembryanthemum criniflorum	H/HHA	○	+ ▲		– –	3	+		
M. crystallinum (ice plant)	HHA	○	+ ▲		–	3	W P		
Mimulus spp (monkey flower)	HHA/P	○ ◉	+ ★		– –/–	3	Y R Br		
Mirabilis jalapa (four-o'clock plant, etc)	TBP/HHA	○	+ ▲		–	3	+ *		
Molucella laevis (bells of Ireland)	HHA	○	+ △		–	3 4	W G *		
Myosotis alpestris (forget-me-not)	HP/Bl	+	+		– –	2 3	W P B *		
Narcissus spp (daffodil, etc)	HBP	○ ◉	+		– –/–	1 2	W Y O (*)		
Nemesia strumosa	HHA	○ ◉	+ △ ◇		–	3	+		
Nemophila menziesii (baby blue-eyes)	HA	○ ◉	+ ★		– –	3	W B		
Nicandra physaloides (apple of Peru; shoo-fly) ..	HA	○	+ ★		+	3 4	B		∞
Nicotiana alata (tobacco plant)	HHA	○	+ ▲	(‖)	+	3	+ *		
Nigella damascena (love-in-a-mist)	HA	○	+		–	3	B W P M	†	∞
Oenothera biennis (evening primrose)	HBl	○	+ ▲ ★	S	+	3 4	Y W		
Papaver nudicaule (Iceland poppy)	HHA/HBl	○	+ ▲	(‖)	–/+	3	W Y O R P		
P. rhoeas (field poppy)	HA	○	+ ▲		–	3	R (+)		
P. somniferum (opium poppy)	HA	○	+ ▲		+	3	W R P M	G	∞
Pelargonium spp (geranium)	TP	○	+ ▲	D	– –/–/+	3 4	+	(C) (V) (*)	
Penstemon spp	HHA/P	○	+ ▲		–/+	3	R W P		
Petunia × hybrida	HHA	○	+ ▲		– –/–	3 4	+		
Phaseolus coccineus (runner bean)	HHA	○	+ ▲ ★	‖	++	3	W R P		
Phlox drummondii (annual phlox)	HHA	○	+ ▲		–	3	+		
Plumbago capensis	TPC	○	+ ▲	‖	++	3	B	E	
Portulaca grandiflora (sun rose)	HHA	○	+ ▲		– –	3	+		
Quamoclit spp	HHAC	○	+ ▲	‖	++	3 4	R Y O	†	
Ranunculus asiaticus	HHBP	○	+		–	2 3	+		
Reseda odorata (mignonette)	HA	○	+ △ ■		–	3 4	G Y R *		
Ricinus communis (castor-oil plant)	HHA/P	○	+	‖	++	3 4		(C) †	(¶)
Rudbeckia spp (black-eyed Susan; cone flower) .	HHA/P	○	+ ▲	(‖)	–/+	3 4	Y O Br		
Salpiglossis sinuata (velvet flower)	HHA	○	+	‖	–	3	+		
Salvia spp (clary, etc)	H/HHA/P	○	+ ▲		–	3 4	W R P M B		
Scabiosa atropurpurea (sweet scabious)	HA	○	+ ▲	(‖)	+	3	R W P M B		
Schizanthus pinnatus (butterfly flower)	HHA	○	+ ▲	‖	–/+	3 4	+	†	
Senecio cineraria (silver-leaved cineraria)	HHA/P	○	+ ▲		–	(1 2) 3 4		E G	
S. elegans	HA	○	+	(‖)	–	3	M		
Silene spp (viscaria)	HA	○ ◉	+ ▲		–	3	W R P B		
Silybum marianum (blessed thistle, etc)	HA	○ ◉	+		+	3 4	M	V	
Sparaxis tricolor (harlequin flower)	HHBP	○	+ ▲		–	2 3	+		
Tagetes spp (African and French marigolds, etc)	HHA	○	+		–/+	3 4	Y O R	(*)	
Thunbergia spp (black-eyed Susan, etc)	HHAC	○	+ ▲	‖	++	3 4	O Br		
Tigridia pavonia (tiger flower)	HHBP	○	+ ▲ ★		–	3	+		
Tithonia rotundifolia (Mexican sunflower)	HHA	○	+ ▲		+	3	O R		
Trachelium caeruleum	HHA	○	+ ▲		–	3	B		
Tropaeolum majus (nasturtium)	HA(C)	○	▲	(‖)	–/++	3 4	Y R P	*	
T. peregrinum (Canary creeper)	HAC	○	+	‖	+++	3 4	Y		
Tulipa spp (tulip)	HBP	○ ◉	+	(‖)	–/+	2	+	(V)	
× Venidio-arctotis	HHA	○	+ ▲		–	3 4	+		
Venidium fastuosum (Namaqualand daisy)	HHA	○	+ ▲	‖	–	3 4	O W Y	G	
Verbascum spp (mullein)	HBl	○	+ ▲		++	3	Y	†	
Verbena spp (vervain)	HHA	○	+		–	3 4	+ *		
Vinca rosea	TP	○	+ ▲		–	3	W R P	E	
Viola × wittrockiana (pansy)	HHA/HBl	○ ◉	+ ▲ ★		– –	1 2 3 4	+		
Zantedeschia spp (arum lily)	H/HHBP	○ ◉	+ ▲ ★		+	2 3	W Y G P	† (V)	
Zea mays (ornamental corn or maize)	HHA	○	+		+/++	3 4		C V	∞
Zephyranthes candida (flower of the west wind) .	HHBP	○	+ ▲		– –	3 4	W		
Zinnia spp	HHA	○	+ △		–/+	3	+		

Glossary

Acid The chemical opposite of alkaline (see p 332).

Aerial Above ground level.

Alkaline The chemical opposite of acid (see p 332). Alkalinity in soils is generally caused by chalk or lime.

Alpine In the strict sense, a plant that grows naturally on mountains above the tree line, but used generally for any plant suitable for a rock garden.

Alternate Having parts (such as leaves) arranged at different points on opposite sides of a stem, in contrast to opposed.

Annual A plant that completes its life cycle, from germination of the seed, through growth and flowering, to the production of more seeds, within one growing season, then dying. The term is also used generally for any plant that can be grown in this way.

Anther The pollen-bearing part of a stamen.

Aquatic A plant whose natural home is wholly or partly in water – floating, submerged or with its roots covered with water.

Awn A bristle-like attachment, as on some seeds, fruits and the seed-heads of some grasses.

Axil The angle between a leaf or its stalk (petiole) and the stem, or between a side shoot and a main stem.

Axillary bud A growth bud in an axil.

Bearded Having stiff hairs, as on the lower petals of some irises (see p 196).

Bedding plant A plant used for temporary display that is planted out, generally for the warmer seasons.

Bicoloured Having two contrasting colours on the same petals.

Biennial A plant whose natural life cycle spans two growing seasons, or which can be treated thus. Seed is sown in one year, and the plant makes vegetative (leafy) growth; it overwinters in this state and flowers the next year, then dying.

Bigeneric Deriving from two genera; a bigeneric hybrid's parents belong to two different genera.

Bipinnate See page 238.

Blade The flat part of a leaf or petal.

Blanching Whitening of stalks and/or leaves of certain vegetables (such as celery) by excluding light. Without it, many vegetables are bitter.

Blind Lacking a central growing tip.

Bog plant A plant whose natural home is in soil that is constantly wet but not submerged, or one that can be grown in such conditions.

Bole Trunk of a tree.

Bolting Premature formation of flowers and seeds by a vegetable.

Bordeaux mixture A useful general-purpose fungicide for spraying plants attacked by various fungal diseases (see p 361). It may be bought ready to mix with water or may be made as follows: Dissolve 40 g copper sulphate in 4 litres water (1½ oz in 1 gallon). Slake 40 g quicklime (beware – caustic to skin) slowly with water, then make up to 1 litre (1½ oz made up to 2 pints). Add the latter solution to the former, stirring, and use immediately. See also Burgundy mixture.

Bracts Modified leaves surrounding a flower; in such plants as euphorbias they are the major decorative features.

Brassica Member of the cabbage family.

Break Formation of side shoots after stopping.

Broadcast Sprinkle (generally seeds) evenly over the surface of the soil rather than in straight rows.

Broken Describes a flower with an elaborate pattern of colour on a contrasting background, often caused by an otherwise harmless virus, as in Rembrandt tulips

Bud A condensed shoot containing immature leaves and/or flowers and a store of food so that growth can quickly start in suitable conditions.

Bulb A swollen underground bud formed from fleshy scales or leaf bases that enables various plants to rest in a dormant state. The word is also used loosely for any similar underground organ, such as a corm or tuber.

Bulbil A small, immature bulb, generally forming at the base of a parent bulb but sometimes above ground in leaf axils (known as aerial bulbils), as in some lilies.

Burgundy mixture A similar fungicide to Bordeaux mixture, and easier to make since it uses washing soda instead of quicklime. However, it is stronger, and may scorch tender foliage. Make in the same way as Bordeaux mixture, using 50 g copper sulphate in 4 litres water (2 oz in 1 gallon) and 60 g washing soda in 1 litre water (2½ oz in 2 pints).

Calcifuge Lime-hating; describes a plant that will not grow on alkaline (chalky or limy) soil.

Callus Protective tissue formed by woody plants over wounds such as saw cuts.

Calomel Common name for mercurous chloride, a poisonous substance used in the garden generally as 4% powder, in which form it is relatively safe. A useful soil fungicide and insecticide.

Calyx The outer ring of flower parts, consisting of sepals, often inconspicuous but in many flowers highly decorative. Plural calyces. See also Corolla.

Carpel One of the complete units (stigma, style and ovary) of a pistil, the female part of a flower.

Cell See page 336.

Chelated compounds See Sequestrols.

Cheshunt compound A fungicide used (by watering on) to protect seedlings from fungal diseases such as damping off. It may be made by mixing (dry) 2 parts powdered copper sulphate and 11 parts ammonium carbonate (by weight). Store the mixture in a jar for at least 24 hours, then dissolve 15 g in a little hot water and make up to 5 litres with cold water (1 oz to 2 gallons). Use immediately.

Chlorosis Yellowing of leaves, often caused by mineral deficiency.

Clone A group of plants identical in character that are produced by vegetative propagation (eg, cuttings). The majority of named cultivars of trees, shrubs and perennials are clones, tracing their ancestry back to a single parent plant.

Chromosomes The minute rod-shaped bodies in the nucleus of a cell that control the cell's – and the whole plant's – inherited characteristics.

Collar The part of a plant where the roots meet the stem(s); also called the neck.

Composite A member of the daisy family, having compound flowers.

Compost Either decomposed plant remains, the product of a compost heap (garden compost) or a mixture of soil, peat and other materials used for growing pot-plants (potting mixture).

Compound Describes leaves, flowers or fruits made up of a number of distinct, similar parts. See Floret, Inflorescence, Leaflet, Simple.

Cordon Any plant, such as a fruit tree or tomato plant, restricted to one (or sometimes two or three) straight stem(s). See pages 302 and 374.

Leaves and stems
1 Alternate; 2 opposed; 3 axil;
4 node; 5 internode; 6 axiliary bud;
7 petiole; 8 leaf blade

Corm An underground storage organ similar to a bulb but consisting of a swollen stem base.

Cormlet A small, immature corm forming at the side of a parent corm.

Corolla The inner ring of flower parts, consisting of petals. See also Calyx.

Corymb A more or less flat-topped inflorescence (see illustration).

Cotyledon A seed-leaf (see p 337).

Crocks Drainage material such as broken pots placed in the bottom of a flower-pot.

Cross The offspring of two different parents. See also Hybrid.

Cross-pollination Pollination of a flower by pollen from a different plant, as opposed to self-pollination (see p 337).

Crown The upper part of the roots of a herbaceous perennial, from which the shoots grow. The term is also used loosely for a root of such plants as rhubarb lifted for forcing.

Cultivar A *culti*vated *var*iety; a distinct form of a plant bred and/or maintained in cultivation. Cultivars may be hybrids or sports.

Cutting A piece of a plant cut from its parent and inserted in a soil mixture to induce root formation, resulting in a whole new plant. See page 346.

Cyme A rounded or flat-topped inflorescence in which the inner or topmost flower opens first.

Damping off The wilting of seedlings due to fungal attack at soil level.

Dead-heading Removal of faded flowers.

Deciduous Describes a plant that sheds all its leaves at once, generally in autumn.

Decumbent Having stems that lie horizontally but rise at the tip.

Dibber A tool used for making holes in soil for planting seedlings, bulbs, etc.

Dicotyledon, dicot See page 337.

Die-back Progressive death of a shoot or stem backwards from the tip.

Dioecious Having distinct male and female flowers on different plants, as in holly.

Diploid Having the normal number of chromosomes.

Disbudding Removal of flower buds around a central bud to form an extra-big bloom.

Division Propagating plants by cutting their crowns into two or more parts.

Dormancy State of temporary cessation of growth and other activity in a seed or whole plant, usually but not always in winter.

Dot plant Tall, striking plant used in bedding schemes for accent and contrast.

Double Describes a flower having more than the usual number of petals, or a form having such flowers.

Drawn Describes a plant that, due to lack of light, becomes lanky and weak.

Drift An informal planting of a single species or variety stretching through a border or patch of grass.

Drill A shallow furrow scraped in the soil in which seeds are sown.

Dwarf A form of a plant that, due to an inherited characteristic, is shorter and/or slower-growing than normal forms.

Earthing up Drawing earth up around the stems of plants, for support, blanching or other purposes, such as frost protection.

Epiphytic Describes a plant that lives on another plant or other support without being a parasite, but obtaining food and moisture from rainfall, etc.

Ericaceous Belonging to the heather family; most such plants are calcifuges (lime-hating).

Espalier Correctly, a system of posts and horizontal wires used for training fruit trees, but loosely used for such a tree trained with tiers of horizontal branches (see p 375).

Evergreen Describes a plant that retains leaves at all seasons, shedding a few more or less continually.

Exhibition Describes forms of plants having a few large, perfectly formed flowers, fruits, etc., that are more suitable for horticultural shows than garden decoration.

Exotic Strictly, describes any plant that is not a native of the region where it is grown.

Eye The coloured centre of a flower (eg, a garden pink); a growth bud on a tuber (eg, potato); a bud on a stem used for propagation (see p 347).

F1 hybrid See page 342.

Family A major grouping in plant classification, consisting of one or more genera that share broadly similar characteristics.

Fancy Describes a flower with variegated markings.

Fastigiate Having branches that grow almost vertically and close together, forming a column shape (as in the Lombardy poplar). Such a variety is often named 'Fastigiata'.

Feathered Having branches all the way down the trunk to ground level.

Fertile Describes plants or flowers able to produce seeds and/or fruits, and soils containing abundant plant nutrients.

Fillis Soft string used for tying plant stems.

'Flore Pleno' The name commonly given to a variety of plant having extremely double flowers.

Floret An individual flower forming part of a compound flower; each 'petal' of a daisy or chrysanthemum flower is such a floret.

Floriferous Free-flowering; producing flowers freely.

Forcing The use of warmth and usually darkness to induce abnormally early or tall growth.

Foundation plantings Either the basic structural and shelter plantings of a garden, or plantings of bulbs or other plants along the footings of a wall.

Friable Describes soil that is light and crumbly without being dry.

Fruit Botanically, the whole seed-bearing organ, whatever its form; tomatoes, poppy seed-capsules and pea pods are all fruits.

Fungi A major division of the plant kingdom that includes mushrooms, toadstools, moulds and many plant disease organisms. They cannot make their own food materials, unlike green plants, and either feed on rotting matter or are parasites of other living things – hence the diseases caused.

Fungicide A chemical that kills fungi, particularly those responsible for various plant diseases.

Genus One of the most important groupings in the classification of plants. It consists of one or more (and sometimes thousands) of species, all of which are distinct but closely related. Plural genera.

Germination The first stage in the development of a seed into a plant.

Glaucous Bluish-green to bluish-grey.

g/m² Abbreviation for grammes per square metre. 100 g/m² equals approximately 3 ounces per square yard.

Habit The overall shape or form of a plant, such as upright, rounded, spreading, etc.

Half-hardy Unable to withstand frost. There is no clear distinction, but the term generally implies an ability to withstand somewhat lower temperatures than the term tender.

Half-standard A plant grown on a clear trunk or leg, but one that is not as tall as that of a standard.

Hand pollination The use of a soft brush, piece of fur, cotton wool or other material to transfer pollen from the stamens to the stigmas, thus ensuring fruit formation.

Hardy Able to withstand frost, though of an unspecified severity.

Haulm The top growth of a plant such as a potato.

Heeling-in Temporary planting until a plant can be put in its permanent position.

Herbaceous Describes a plant with non-woody stems that dies down to ground level during its dormant period.

Herbicide A chemical that kills plants; a weedkiller.

Hormone A chemical, natural or artificial, that controls or influences some aspect of plant growth or development. The best-known types are those that induce root-formation and hormone weedkillers.

Hose-in-hose Describes a flower that has one perfect set of petals within another. It is generally an abnormality, but varieties of plants such as azaleas with attractive hose-in-hose flowers have been bred.

Humus The dark, sticky material that results when organic matter decays. It is important for good soil structure (see p 330).

Hybrid A plant resulting from crossing two distinctly different parents – different varieties, species or genera. See also Bigeneric, F1 hybrid.

Hybridization The deliberate production of hybrids by cross-pollination, often with the aim of producing new varieties.

Incurving Having the petals curving inwards to form a ball-like flower; the opposite of reflexed.

Inflorescence Flower; the term is generally used for a compound inflorescence made up of a number of flowers arranged on a single stem.

Insecticide A chemical that kills insects.

Internode The portion of stem between two nodes (joints).

Joint See node.

Keel A boat-shaped petal commonly found in flowers of the pea family.

Lanceolate Lance-shaped.

Lateral Describes a shoot, bud, etc, at the side of a stem or main shoot.

Lawn sand A mixture of 20 parts fine silver sand to 3 parts ammonium sulphate and 1 part iron sulphate. It is applied dry at 135 g/m² (4 oz/sq yd) to lawns in spring and summer to combat weeds, including moss, and provide fertilizer. Some commercial preparations – described as mercurized – contain calomel, which increases their effectiveness against moss.

Lax Loose or floppy in habit.

Leaching The washing away of plant nutrients from the soil by water.

Leader, leading shoot The terminal (end) shoot of a branch, which, left to grow, will extend in the same direction as the branch itself.

Leaflet An individual 'leaf' that is part of a compound leaf.

Leaf-mould Partially decayed leaves, also called leaf-soil.

Legume A member of the pea family.

Life cycle The series of forms and processes a plant passes through from one particular stage to the same stage in the next generation. In the case of flowering plants it includes germination of the seed, development of the seedling plant into an adult, the production of flowers containing male and female sex cells, pollination and fertilization of the female cells by the male, and the development of more seeds. Ferns have a different life cycle (see p 337).

Lights Windows or glazed panels, as in a garden frame.

Lime Strictly, quicklime (calcium oxide) or slaked lime (calcium hydroxide). Gardeners commonly use the term also for ground chalk or limestone. All these may be used for 'liming' the soil to combat acidity (see pp 266 and 332), but quicklime and slaked lime are needed in half the quantities of chalk or limestone.

Lime-hating See Calcifuge.

Loam See page 331.

Monocarpic Describes a plant that dies after flowering and fruiting once, although this may take several years, as in the giant lily, *Cardiocrinum giganteum*.

Monocotyledon, monocot See page 337.

Monoecious Having separate male and female flowers, but on the same plant. See also Dioecious.

Mulch A covering of peat, leaf-mould, garden compost or plastic sheeting applied to the soil around and between plants. See page 334.

Mutation Any spontaneous change in a plant's inherited characteristics. One type is a sport. Another is a true-breeding species that produces a variation that is not due to cross-pollination.

Naturalize Permanently plant; particularly applied to bulbs allowed to grow undisturbed.

Flowers and inflorescences
1 Corymb; 2 cyme; 3 panicle
4 raceme; 5 spike; 6 umbel;
7 whorl; 8 single; 9 double

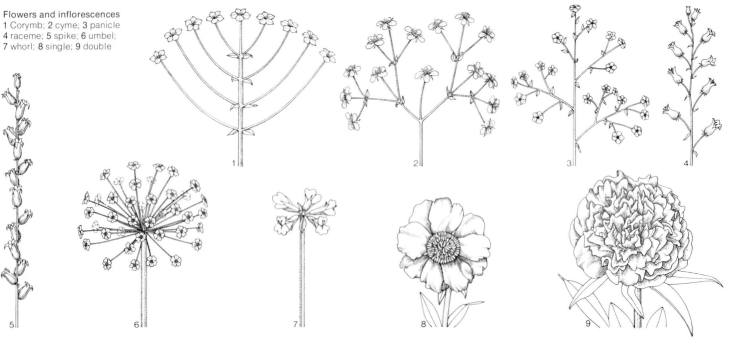

Glossary (continued)

Neck See Collar.

Neutral Neither acid nor alkaline.

Node A joint in a stem, from which a leaf, a bud or another stem branches. The stem is often slightly thickened here.

Offset A young plant that grows from the side of its parent and can be detached and grown on.

Opposite Having parts (such as leaves) arranged in pairs on either side of a stem, in contrast to alternate.

Ovary The part of the pistil that contains one or more ovules, which are the parts that develop into seeds. The ovary develops into a fruit.

Panicle Similar to a raceme, but with a branched cluster of flowers in place of each single flower of a raceme.

Peat Partially decomposed remains of mosses and sedges whose decay has been stopped. It is dug from boggy areas and used for mulching, soil improvement, making potting mixtures and so on. It is known in the United States as peat moss.

Pedicel, peduncle Both names for flower stalks.

Pendent Hanging or drooping.

Perennial A plant that lives for a number of years, generally being able to flower each year. May be woody, as in trees and shrubs, or soft-stemmed, as in herbaceous perennials.

Perianth The whole calyx and corolla of a flower.

Pesticide A chemical that kills garden pests, principally insects (insecticide) and mites (acaricide). The term is also used loosely to include fungicides.

Petal Any of the leaf-like, usually coloured, segments of the corolla.

Petiole A leaf-stalk.

pH A measurement of acidity or alkalinity (see p 332).

Pinching out Removal of the tip of a growing shoot, or the terminal bud, with the aim of causing branching, bushy growth.

Pinnate See page 238.

Pistil The female part of a flower. It consists of the ovary at the base and stigma at the top, joined by the style.

Plume A feathery inflorescence.

Pollarding Severe pruning of a tree back almost to its trunk, resulting in the growth of new young branches. See page 371.

Pollen The dust-like particles produced by male flower parts, and carrying the male sex cells.

Pollination The transfer of pollen from male anthers to female stigma of a flower, the first stage in the sexual reproduction of plants.

Pompon A small, globe-shaped flower.

Procumbent Creeping.

Propagation Increasing one's stock of plants by any means.

Raceme An unbranched inflorescence having flowers on stalks arranged up a long stem.

Reflexed Having the petals bending backwards; the opposite of incurving.

Rhizome An underground, often horizontal, stem serving the same purpose as a bulb or tuber.

Ripening Commonly applied to maturing fruits, but also to stems that harden and become woody.

Runner A shoot that grows along the ground, rooting to form new plants. Properly called a stolon.

Running to seed The same as bolting.

Sap Firstly, the fluid that fills the cavity in plant cells (see p 336). Secondly, the watery fluid that moves through a plant's phloem and xylem vessels (see p 336).

Scandent Climbing, but not self-clinging or twining.

Scion See page 350.

Secateurs Known in the United States as hand pruners.

Seed A fully developed ovule containing a dormant embryo plant that is capable of germinating and growing into an adult plant.

Seed-leaf A leaf of an embryo plant, which may emerge on germination and is generally different in shape from the true, or 'rough', leaves that follow. Also called cotyledon (see p 337).

Seedling Any plant, especially a young one, grown from seed.

Seed-tray A flat box used for growing seedlings. Known in the United States as a flat.

Self Term applied to a flower of one pure colour, with no markings.

Self-fertile Describes a plant – generally a fruit bush or tree – that can be pollinated by its own pollen or that of another plant of the same variety.

Self-sterile Incapable of being pollinated by the same variety, and needing pollen from a different, compatible variety.

Semi-double Describes a flower with rather more petals than normal but not so many as in a fully double type.

Semi-evergreen Describes a plant that sheds most, but not all, of its leaves in winter, or sheds them only in harsh climates.

Sepal Any of the leaf-like segments of the calyx, usually green and inconspicuous but sometimes colourful.

Sequestrols Chemical preparations of trace elements used to combat mineral deficiencies, especially of iron and magnesium. Their chemical form is such that they can be absorbed by plants from soils – mainly alkaline ones – that normally 'trap' these elements. They are also called sequestered compounds, sequestrated compounds or chelated compounds.

Sessile Not having stalks, as with some flowers that are attached directly to the stem.

Set, setting Terms applied to fruits and certain vegetables such as tomatoes when they are pollinated and the fruits start to develop.

Shrub A plant with woody branches but no distinct trunk (as in a tree).

Simple The opposite of compound; describes a leaf not divided into separate leaflets or a flower not forming part of a compound inflorescence.

Single Describes a flower having only the normal number of petals for the species, in contrast to double.

Slip An alternative name for a cutting, especially a heel cutting (see p 346).

Sour Of soils, acid.

Spadix A thick, fleshy flower spike with small flowers; it is generally surrounded by a spathe, as in members of the arum family.

Spathe The showy bract that generally surrounds a spadix.

Species The fundamental division of the living world, consisting of distinct, similar individuals that can breed together to produce offspring like themselves. One or more species make up a genus.

Specimen A plant placed on its own in a position where it can be admired from all sides.

Spike A raceme in which the individual flowers have no or almost no stalks.

Spit The depth of a spade's blade. See page 334.

Spores The dust-like 'seeds' of ferns and some other lower plants (not botanically seeds).

Sport A sudden change in a plant's characteristics. For example, a plant may produce different-coloured flowers on a particular branch, or a branch of climbing habit. Plants propagated from the sported branch will carry on the new characteristic, thus estabishing a new cultivar.

Spray A term applied to a plant with many flower-heads on branching stems, as in some chrysanthemums.

Spur A short, stiff, thin branch, particularly of the kind that bears fruit on many apple and other fruit trees.

Spur back Thin out unwanted clusters of buds.

Stamen The male flower part, consisting of a thin filament with a pollen-bearing anther at the end.

Standard A plant grown on a single tall stem, as with many fruit trees and roses (known in the United States as tree roses). Also, the uppermost, usually erect, petal or petals of certain flowers.

Sterile Of plants, unable to produce seeds. Of soil or potting mixture, having had all pests and disease organisms destroyed.

Stigma The female part of a flower on which pollen is deposited. Part of the pistil.

Stock See page 350.

Stolon Correct name for a runner.

Stool A plant used purely for propagation, such as overwintered chrysanthemum roots.

Stooling Cutting down to ground level to induce new lush young growth. See page 371.

Stopping Pinching out flower buds to induce the production of many more buds.

Strain A specially selected group of seed-raised plants, consisting either of a special selection (eg, for size or hardiness) from within a named cultivar or of a group of closely related varieties differing perhaps only in flower colour.

Strike To root a cutting.

Strobilus The flower of a conifer. The males are commonly catkin-like, the females like dwarf cones.

Style The part of a pistil linking ovary and stigma, often narrow and elongated.

Sub-shrub A plant that is partly woody and partly herbaceous in character, or which becomes woody in certain climatic conditions – generally high temperaures – as in the case of pelargoniums.

Subspecies A distinct sub-division of a species occurring in the wild.

Succulent Having fleshy stems and/or leaves that store water, as in cacti and (to a lesser extent) such plants as mesembryanthemums. Also describes soft, unripened stems.

Sucker A shoot growing from an underground stem or root.

Suffruticose Describes a plant that is partially woody, but with new growth coming from the soft terminal parts, not the woody base. Thus such plants must not be cut hard back or new shoots will not form. Examples are pinks and lavender.

Sweet Of soils, alkaline.

Systemic Describes a pesticide that acts through a plant's tissues, poisoning a pest that attacks the plant.

Tap root A strong vertical root.

Tender In general terms, describes a plant that is sensitive to cold, normally used for one that needs higher temperatures than one that is half-hardy.

Tendril A thin twining appendage that helps some plants to climb up supports.

Terminal Describes a bud, shoot or other structure at the end of a shoot, as opposed to lateral.

Tetraploid Having twice the normal number of chromosomes. Such plants are commonly larger and more vigorous than normal diploid types.

Tilth Crumbly soil produced by good cultivation and ideal for sowing seeds.

Trace elements Chemical elements needed by plants in only small (though vital) amounts.

Transpiration See page 336.

Tree A woody plant with a distinct trunk, as distinct from a shrub.

Triploid Having 1½ times the normal number of chromosomes. Such plants are commonly self-sterile and cannot pollinate other varieties.

Truss A term applied loosely to some fruit or flower clusters.

Tuber A swollen underground food storage organ serving much the same purpose as a bulb. It may derive from a stem, as in the potato, or from a root, as in the dahlia.

Type The basic original form of a plant in the wild, as opposed to forms raised in cultivation, or later introduced.

Umbel An inflorescence – round or flat-topped – in which all the flower stalks branch from one point.

Variegated Patterned with two distinct colours or shades. Mostly applied to yellow and green or white and green leaves, but can also refer to flowers.

Variety Botanically, a sub-division of a species similar to a subspecies. In horticulture (and in this book), the term is used more loosely for any variation of species or a hybrid; the correct term in such circumstances is usually cultivar.

Vegetative propagation The use of cuttings, division and other methods with the exception of seeds or spores for increasing plants.

Whorl An arrangement of leaves, flowers, etc, in a circle like the spokes of a wheel.

Useful addresses

The addresses below are given as an aid to readers, and are not meant to endorse individual firms, products or nurseries. Notes in brackets after the address indicate one or more specialities; many of the nurserymen also supply a range of other plants. Most of the firms listed issue catalogues, but a charge is usually made for these – a substantial charge in the case of some catalogues, which are virtually books.

General
Disabled Living Foundation, 346 Kensington High Street, London W14 (information for disabled gardeners)
Royal Horticultural Society, Vincent Square, London SW1. Fellowship is open to anyone interested in gardening, and gains free admission to shows (including Chelsea Flower Show) and monthly magazine. Details of the many affiliated specialist horticultural societies are available from the secretary
Scottish Amateur Tobacco and Curing Association, 39 Milton Road, Kirkcaldy
Tobacco Curing Cooperative, Tilty, Dunmow, Essex (tobacco seeds, plants, curing)

Seedsmen
D. T. Brown & Co, Poulton-le-Fylde, Blackpool, Lancs
Thomas Butcher, Shirley, Croydon, Surrey
Chiltern Seeds, Sunnymede Avenue, Chesham, Bucks
Samuel Dobie & Son, PO Box 2, Liverpool 4
M. Holtzhausen, 14 High Cross Street, St Austell, Cornwall (many exotic seeds)
Suttons Seeds, Torquay, Devon
Thompson & Morgan, London Road, Ipswich, Suffolk (general and botanical)
W. J. Unwin Ltd, Histon, Cambridge (general; speciality sweet peas)

Nurserymen
Allwood Bros, Clayton Nurseries, Hassocks, Sussex (carnations, pinks)
Anthony Estate Nurseries, Torpoint, Cornwall (camellias, day lilies)
Steven Bailey, Eden Nurseries, Silver Street, Sway, Lymington, Hants (carnations, pinks)
Barnhaven, Brigsteer, Kendal, Cumbria (primulas)
Bees, Sealand, Chester (roses; general)
Blackmore & Langdon, Twerton Hill Nursery, Bath (begonias, delphiniums, phlox)
Bressingham Gardens, Diss, Norfolk (perennials, dwarf conifers, etc)
Butterfields Nurseries, Harvest Hill, Upper Bourne End, Bucks (dahlias)
Thomas Carlile, Twyford, Berks (perennials, alpines)
Beth Chatto, White Barn House, Elmstead Market, Colchester, Essex (moisture-loving and drought-resistant plants)
Clifton Geranium Nurseries, Cherry Orchard Road, Chichester, Sussex (pelargoniums)
Cranmore Vineyard, Yarmouth, IOW (grapes)
Elm House Nurseries, Walpole St Peter, Wisbech, Cambs (chrysanthemums)
Fisk's Clematis Nursery, Westleton, nr Saxmundham, Suffolk
Great Dixter Nurseries, Northiam, Sussex (perennials)
C. Gregory & Son, The Rose Garden, Toton Lane, Stapleford, Nottingham (roses)
Grovemount Alpine Nursery, Montrose Road, Auchterarder, Perthshire (alpines, heathers)
R. Harkness & Co, The Rose Gardens, Hitchin, Herts (roses)
Don Hatch, Chantry Nursery, Combe Raleigh, Honiton, Devon (conifers)
Hayward's Carnations, The Chase Gardens, Stakes Road, Purbrook, Portsmouth (pinks and carnations)
Hillier & Sons, Winchester, Hants (very wide range of trees and shrubs)
C. G. Hollett, Greenbank Nursery, Sedburgh, Cumbria (alpines, primulas, etc)
Home Meadows Nurseries, Martlesham, Woodbridge, Suffolk (Iceland poppies, etc)

Hydon Nurseries, Hydon Heath, nr Godalming, Surrey (dwarf rhododendrons)
W. E. Th. Ingwersen, Birch Farm Nursery, Gravetye, East Grinstead, Sussex (alpines)
M. Jefferson-Brown, Whitbourne, Worcester (grape vines)
Kahn's Herb Farm, Broad Oak Road, Canterbury, Kent
Reginald Kaye, Waithman Nurseries, Silverdale, Carnforth, Lancs (alpines, hardy ferns)
Kelways Nurseries, Langport, Somerset (irises, paeonies)
Knap Hill Nursery, Barrs Lane, Knap Hill, Woking, Surrey (rhododendrons and azaleas)
The Knoll Gardens, Stapehill, Wimborne, Dorset (unusual and half-hardy shrubs and trees)
S. E. Lytle, Park Road Nurseries, Formby, Lancs (grape vines)
John Mattock, Nuneham Courtnay, Oxford (roses)
Millais Nurseries, Crosswater Farm, Churt, Farnham, Surrey (rhododendrons & azaleas)
Morehavens, Sway, Hants (chamomile)
Ken Muir, Weeley Heath, Clacton-on-Sea, Essex (strawberries and other soft fruit)
Notcutts Nurseries, Woodbridge, Suffolk (trees and shrubs)
Oldfield Nurseries, Trowbridge Road, Norton St Philip, Somerset (lime-tolerant plants)
Orpington Nurseries, Rocky Lane, Gatton Park, Reigate, Surrey (irises, etc)
Oscroft's, Sprotborough Road, Doncaster, Yorks (dahlias, pelargoniums)
The Palm Farm, Thornton Hall Gardens, Ulceby, Lincs (hardy exotica)
A. R. Paske & Co, Regal Lodge, Kentford, Newmarket, Suffolk (asparagus, seakale)
Pennell & Sons Ltd, Princess Street, Lincoln (clematis)
Pennyacre Nurseries, Crawley House, Springfield, Fife (heaths, heathers)
Perry's Hardy Plant Farm, Enfield, Middx (aquatics, perennials)
G. Reuthe Ltd, Jackass Lane, Keston, Kent (rhododendrons, azaleas, camellias, etc)
Thomas Rivers & Son, Sawbridgeworth, Herts (fruit)
Robinsons Hardy Plants, Greencourt Nurseries, Crockenhill, Swanley, Kent (alpines, small border plants)
L. R. Russell, Richmond Nurseries, Windlesham, Surrey (trees and shrubs, etc)
W. Seabrook & Sons, Boreham, Chelmsford, Essex (fruit trees)
Stapeley Water Gardens, London Road, Stapeley, Nantwich, Cheshire (aquatics, fish)
South Down Nurseries, Redruth, Cornwall (trees, shrubs, etc; plants for flower arrangers)
F. Toynbee, Yapton Road, Barnham, Bognor Regis, Sussex (trees and shrubs)
James Trehane, Stapehill Road, Hampreston, Wimborne, Dorset (camellias, azaleas, magnolias)
Treseder's Nurseries, Truro, Cornwall (trees and shrubs)
Tumblers Bottom Herb Farm, Kilmersdon, Radstock, Somerset
Mrs Desmond Underwood, Colchester, Essex (pinks, silver-leaved plants)
Wansdyke Nursery (and Pygmy Pinetum), Hilworth, Devizes, Wilts (dwarf conifers)
The Weald Herbery, Park Cottage, Frittenden, Cranbrook, Kent (herbs)
Wells of Mertsham, The Nurseries, Mertsham, nr Redhill, Surrey (chrysanthemums)
Wildwoods Water Gardens, Theobalds Park Rd, Crews Hill, Enfield, Middx (aquatics, fish)
Wills Fuchsias, The Fuchsia Nursery, West Wittering, Chichester, Sussex
H. Woolman, Grange Road, Dorridge, Solihull (chrysanthemums)
Zelah Nurseries, Zelah, Truro, Devon (coastal plants)

Bulb growers and merchants
Walter Blom, Leavesden, Watford, Herts
Broadleigh Gardens, Barr House, Bishops Hull, Taunton, Somerset (dwarf bulbs)

P. de Jaeger & Sons, Marsden, Kent
Groom Bros, Spalding, Lincs
J. A. Mars, Haslemere, Surrey (hardy cyclamen and other miniature bulbs)
Spalding Bulb Co, Horseshoe Road, Spalding, Lincs
Van Tubergen, Willowbank Wharf, Ranelagh Gardens, London SW6
Most seedsmen also supply bulbs

Equipment, furniture and sundries
Agriframes, Charlwood Road, East Grinstead, Sussex (fruit cages)
Alexpeat, Burnham-on-Sea, Somerset (potting mixtures, peat blocks, etc)
Allen Power Equipment, The Broadway, Didcot, Oxon (power tools)
Alton Glasshouses, PO Box 3, Bewdley, Worcs (greenhouses)
Andrews Lawn Edgers, Sunningdale, Berks (power tools)
Autogrow, Quay Road, Blyth, Northumberland (greenhouse equipment)
Joseph Bentley, Barrow-on-Humber, South Humberside (horticultural chemicals, sundries)
Chempak Products, Brewhouse Lane, Hertford (fertilizers)
Chilstone, Sprivers Estate, Horsmonden, Kent (reconstituted stone ornaments)
Danarm, London Road, Stroud, Gloucestershire (power equipment)
Diplex, PO Box 172, Watford, Herts (greenhouse instruments, etc)
Fisons Ltd, Harston, Cambs (potting mixtures, chemicals, etc)
Fox Pool International, PO Box 7, The Floral Mile, Twyford, Berks (swimming pools)
Haddonstone, The Manor, East Haddon, Northants (reconstituted stone ornaments)
Hayters, Spellbrook, Bishop's Stortford, Herts (mowers)
Howard Rotavator Co, Saxham, Bury St Edmunds, Suffolk (rotary cultivators)
Humex, 4 High Road, Byfleet, Surrey (greenhouse equipment)
ICI Plant Protection Ltd, Woolmead Walk, Farnham, Surrey (pesticides, etc)
Kirk-Dyson Designs, Leafield Trading Estate, Corsham, Wilts ('Ballbarrow', etc)
Lindsey & Kesteven Fertilizers, Wigford House, Brayford Pool, Lincoln (potting mixtures, chemicals)
A. W. Maskell & Sons, Stephenson Street, London E16 (fertilizers, etc)
Minsterstone, Ilminster, Somerset (reconstituted stone ornaments)
G. D. Mountfield, Reform Road, Maidenhead, Berks (power mowers, cultivators, etc)
Murphy Chemical, Wheathampstead, Herts (pesticides)
Pan Brittanica Industries, Waltham Cross, Herts (potting mixtures, pesticides, fertilizers)
Phostrogen, Corwen, Clwyd (fertilizers)
F. Pratten & Co, Charlton Road, Midsomer Norton, Bath (greenhouses, frames)
Charles H. Pugh, Coleridge Street, Sunnyhill, Derby (mowers)
Rolcut, Horsham, Sussex (secateurs)
Sheen, Greasley St, Bulwell, Nottingham (flame guns)
Spear & Jackson, St Pauls Rd, Wednesbury, West Midlands (tools)
Stanley Garden Tools, Woodhouse Mill, Sheffield
Stapeley Water Gardens – see above (pool equipment)
C. Sutton (Sidcup), North Mills, Bridport, Dorset (fruit cages, nets)
Wilkinson Sword, Totteridge Rd, High Wycombe, Bucks (tools)
C. H. Whitehouse, Buckhurst Works, Frant, Sussex (greenhouses)
Wildwoods Water Gardens – see above (pool equipment)
Wolf Tools, Ross-on-Wye, Herefordshire
Wolseley Webb, Electric Avenue, Witton, Birmingham (mowers, trimmers)
A. Wright & Son, 16–18 Sidney St, Sheffield 1 ('Baronet' tools)

Bibliography

This selective bibliography is designed mainly to guide readers wishing to find out more about particular specialist topics.

General reference books
L. H. and Ethel Zoe Bailey, *Hortus Second* (The Macmillan Co, New York, 1972)
Michael Chinnery, *The Natural History of the Garden* (Collins, 1977)
Royal Horticultural Society, *Dictionary of Gardening* (four volumes, Oxford University Press, 1965) and *Supplement* (1969)
The Royal Horticultural Society also publishes a useful series of booklets on various topics (30 titles to date) under the general title of Wisley Handbooks

Garden design
P. L. Carpenter, T. D. Walker and F. O. Lanphear, *Plants in the Landscape* (W. H. Freeman, 1975)
Sima Eliovson, *Gardening the Japanese Way* (Harrap, 1970); for Western readers
Peter Hunt (editor), *The Book of Garden Ornament* (Dent, 1974)
Edward Hyams, *A History of Gardens and Gardening* (Dent, 1971)
The Easy Path to Gardening (Reader's Digest, London, with The Disabled Living Foundation, 1972); garden design and techniques for the disabled
Denis Wood, *Practical Garden Design* (Dent, 1976)

Decorative plants and gardening
L. H. Bailey, *Manual of Cultivated Plants* (Collier Macmillan, 1949)
Peter Barber and C. E. Lucas Phillips, *The Trees Around Us* (Weidenfeld & Nicolson, 1975)
W. J. Bean, *Trees and Shrubs Hardy in the British Isles* (eighth edition edited by Sir George Taylor, four volumes, John Murray 1973–); the standard reference work, with a section on rhododendrons the equal of almost any specialist book on the subject
Judith Berrisford, *Gardening on Chalk, Lime and Clay* (Faber, 1977)
Alan Bloom, *Hardy Perennials* (Faber, 1968); *Moisture Gardening* (Faber, 1966)
C. O. Booth, *An Encyclopaedia of Annual and Biennial Garden Plants* (Faber, 1957)
Stephen Dealler, *Wild Flowers in the Garden* (Batsford, 1977)
Sima Eliovson, *Shrubs, Trees and Climbers* (Macmillan, 1975); written for South African gardeners but useful elsewhere
Alfred Evans, *The Peat Garden and its Plants* (Dent, 1974)
Muriel E. Fisher, E. Satchwell and Janet M. Watkins, *Gardening with New Zealand Plants, Shrubs and Trees* (Collins, 1970)
Jim Fisk, *The Queen of Climbers* (Fisk's Clematis Nursery, 1975); clematis
S. Millar Gault, *The Dictionary of Shrubs in Colour* (Ebury Press and Michael Joseph, 1976)
S. Millar Gault and Patrick M. Synge, *The Dictionary of Roses in Colour* (Ebury Press and Michael Joseph, 1971)
Roy Genders, *Bulbs: a Complete Handbook* (Robert Hale, 1973); *The Rose: a Complete Handbook* (Robert Hale, 1965)
Michael Gibson, *Shrub Roses for Every Garden* (Collins, 1973); covers old and modern types
Anna N. Griffith, *Collins Guide to Alpine and Rock Garden Plants* (third edition, Collins, 1973)

Roger Grounds, *Ferns* (Pelham Books, 1975)
Hardy Plant Directory (Hardy Plant Society, c/o Colt House, High Cross, Thurgarton, Nottingham); information on sources of 2,000 hardy plants, including rarities
Roy Hay and Patrick M. Synge, *The Dictionary of Garden Plants in Colour* (Ebury Press and Michael Joseph, 1969; paperback edition 1975)
Hillier's Manual of Trees and Shrubs (third edition, paperback, Hillier and Sons, Winchester, England, 1973; hardback, David and Charles, 1972)
Will Ingwersen, *Classic Garden Plants* (Hamlyn, 1975); *The Ingwersen Manual of Alpine Plants* (W. E. Th. Ingwersen Ltd, 1978)
Reginald Kaye, *Hardy Ferns* (Faber, 1968)
A. H. Lawson, *Bamboos* (Faber, 1968)
Christopher Lloyd, *Foliage Plants* (Collins, 1973)
Frances Perry, *Flowers of the World* (Hamlyn, 1972); a beautifully illustrated large-format book; *Water Gardening* (3rd edition, Country Life, 1961)
Noël J. Prockter, *Climbing and Screening Plants* (Faber, 1973)
Reader's Digest Encyclopedia of Garden Plants and Flowers (Reader's Digest Association, 1971)
Sanders' Encyclopedia of Gardening (22nd edition revised by A. G. L. Hellyer, Colligridge, 1966); an alphabetical guide to garden plants first published in the 1890s; not illustrated
Graham Stuart Thomas, *Colour in the Winter Garden* (revised edition, Dent, 1967); *Climbing Roses Old and New* (Dent, 1966); *Perennial Garden Plants* (Dent, 1976); *Plants for Ground-Cover* (Dent, 1970); *Shrub Roses of Today* (new edition, Dent, 1974); *The Old Shrub Roses* (Dent, 1963)
T. L. Underhill, *Heaths and Heathers* (David and Charles, 1971)
Mrs Desmond Underwood, *Grey and Silver Plants* (Collins, 1971)

Vegetables, herbs and fruit
Handbook on Tobacco Production (Tobacco Curing Cooperative)
Fred Potter and Frank Shacke, *Suttons Encyclopaedia of Vegetables* (Pelham Books, 1976)
Kay N. Sanecki, *The Complete Book of Herbs* (Macdonald, 1974)
The Fruit Finder and *The Vegetable Finder* (Henry Doubleday Research Association, Convent Lane, Bocking, Braintree, Essex); information on sources of varieties new and old, including rarities
The Fruit Garden Displayed (Royal Horticultural Society, 1974); *The Vegetable Garden Displayed* (Royal Horticultural Society, 1961)

Techniques and technicalities
George E. Brown, *The Pruning of Trees, Shrubs and Conifers* (Faber Paperbacks, 1977)
Gwen Conacher, *Food Freezing at Home* (The Electricity Council, London, 1976)
M. H. Dahl and T. B. Thygesen, *Garden Pests and Diseases of Flowers and Shrubs* (Blandford, 1974)
Ronald Menage, *Woolman's Greenhouse Gardening* (Hamish Hamilton, 1975)
Noël J. Prockter, *Simple Propagation* (new edition, Faber, 1976); includes details of how to propagate 550 types of plants
A. M. Toms and M. H. Dahl, *Pests and Diseases of Fruit and Vegetables* (Blandford, 1976)
Ian G. Walls, *The Complete Book of Greenhouse Gardening* (Ward Lock, 1970)

General index

General index (continued)

Index of plant names

A

Index of plant names (continued)

Belladonna lily: see *Amaryllis belladonna*
Bellevalia (Hyacinthus) dalmatica: 194; *B. romana (Hyacinthus romanus, Hyancinthus orientalis albulus,* Roman hyacinth): 194
Bellflower: see *Campanula* spp; bellflower, chimney: see *Campanula pyramidalis;* bellflower, Chinese: see *Platycodon* spp; bellflower, giant: see *Campanula latifolia;* bellflower, great: see *Campanula latifolia;* bellflower, Japanese: see *Platycodon* spp; bells of Ireland: see *Molucella laevis*
Bellis perennis (common daisy, English daisy): 107, 210–211, 390; *B. p.* 'Enorma': 210; *B. p.* 'Monstrosa' varieties: 113, 210; *B. p.* 'Pomponette' varieties: 210–211
Bent grass: see *Agrostis* spp
Berberidopsis corallina (coral plant): 146, 372
Berberis spp (barberry): 17, 34, 48, 54, 91, 99, 150, **156**, 229, 230, 248, 315, *315*, 340, 347, 372, 386; *B. asiatica:* 315; *B. buxifolia:* 315; *B. b.* 'Nana': 230; *B. chillanensis:* see *B. montana; B. darwinii:* 90, *90*, 150, 315; *B. gagnepainii:* 164; *B. montana (B. chillanensis):* 156; *B. sargentiana:* 165; *B.* × *stenophylla:* 150, 169, 248; *B.* × *s.* 'Autumnalis': 169; *B.* × *s.* 'Coralina Compacta': 230; *B.* × *s.* 'Pink Pearl': 169; *B.* × *s.* 'Semperflorens': 169; *B. thunbergii* 'Atropurpurea': 165; *B. t.* 'Atropurpurea Nana': 229, 230; *B. t.* 'Erecta': 165; *B. verruculosa:* 167; *B. vulgaris:* 315
Bergamot (*Monarda didyma*): 275, *275*; see also *Monarda* spp
Bergenia spp: 25, 41, **184**, 247, *247*, 348, 388; *B.* 'Abendglut' ('Evening Glow'): 184; *B. cordifolia:* 48; *B. c.* 'Purpurea': 184; *B.* 'Evening Glow': see *B.* 'Abendglut'; *B. purpurascens:* 247; *B.* 'Silberlicht' ('Silver Light'): 184; *B.* × *schmidtii:* 184
Beta vulgaris (ornamental beet): 247, 390; see also Beetroot, Seakale beet, Spinach beet; *B. v. conditiva:* see Beetroot; *B. v.* 'Rhubarb Beet': 221, 283; see also Seakale beet, red; *B. v.* 'Ruby Chard': see Seakale beet, red
Betonica spp: see *Stachys* spp
Betony (*Stachys officinalis*): 275
Betula spp (birch): 15, 31, 41, 88, **141**, 155, 331, 386; *B. jacquemontii:* 141; *B. medwediewii:* 141; *B. pendula* (silver birch): 23, 29, 30, 40, 42, 55, *89*, 91, **141**, 251; *B. p.* 'Dalecarlica' (cut-leaf birch, Swedish birch): 141; *B. p.* 'Youngii' (weeping birch): 46, 47, 141; *B. utilis* (Himalayan birch): 141
Bignonia capreolata: 146, 372
Bilberries (*Vaccinium myrtillus*): 315; see also Blueberries, European
Birch: see *Betula* spp; birch, cut-leaf: see *Betula pendula* 'Dalecarlica'; birch, Himalayan: see *Betula utilis;* birch, silver: see *Betula pendula;* birch, Swedish: see *Betula pendula* 'Dalecarlica'; birch, weeping: see *Betula pendula* 'Youngii'
Bird-of-paradise flower: see *Strelitzia reginae;* bird-of-paradise plant: see *Caesalpinia gilliesii*
Bishop's hat: see *Epimedium* spp
Bittersweet, climbing: see *Celastrus orbiculatus*
Blackberries *(Rubus allegheniensis; Rubus ulmifolius):* 168, 261, *261*, 266, **312–313**, *312*, 350, 363; black-eyed Susan: see *Rudbeckia fulgida speciosa, Rudbeckia hirta, Thunbergia alata;* blackthorn: see *Prunus spinosa*
Bladder senna: see *Colutea arborescens;* bladderwort: see *Utricularia vulgaris*
Blaeberries: see Blueberries, European
Blanket flower: see *Gaillardia* spp
Blazing star: see *Mentzelia lindleyi, Vallota speciosa*
Blechnum spicant (hard fern): 40
Bleeding heart: see *Dicentra* spp, *D. spectabilis;* bleeding heart, fringed: see *D. eximia*
Bletia hyacinthina (B. striata): 204
Blood flower: see *Haemanthus katherinae;* blood lily: see *Haemanthus* spp; bloodroot: see *Sanguinaria* spp
Bluebell, English: see *Scilla non-scripta;* bluebell, Spanish: see *Scilla hispanica*
Blueberries, European (bilberries, blaeberries, whinberries, whortleberries, *Vaccinium myrtillus*): 266, 315, *315*; blueberries, high-bush *(Vaccinium corymbosum):* 315; blueberries, low-bush *(Vaccinium angustifolium):* 315; blueberries, rabbiteye *(Vaccinium ashei):* 315; see also *Vaccinium* spp; blue-eyed Mary: see *Omphalodes verna;* blue grama grass: see *Bouteloua gracilis;* bluegrass, Canadian: see *Poa compressa;* bluegrass, Kentucky: see *Poa pratensis;* blue gum, Tasmanian: see *Eucalyptus globulus;* blue lace flower: see *Didiscus caeruleus*
Bocconia microcarpa: see *Macleaya microcarpa*
Bog arum: see *Calla palustris;* bog bean: see *Menyanthes trifoliata;* bog iris: see *Iris bulleyana, Iris fulva, Iris kaempferi, Iris sibirica;* bog myrtle: see *Myrica gale;* bog pimpernel: see *Anagallis tenella*
Boltonia asteroides: 176
Borage *(Borago officinalis):* 261, 275; see also *Borago* spp
Borago spp (borage): 184; *B. laxiflora:* 184; *B. officinalis:* see Borage
Borecole: see Kale
Boston ivy: see *Parthenocissus* spp, *Parthenocissus tricuspidata* 'Veitchii'
Bottlebrush: see *Callistemon* spp
Bougainvillea spp: 51, 113, 173; *B. glabra:* 173, *173*
Bouncing Bet: see *Saponaria officinalis*
Bouteloua gracilis (blue grama, mosquito grass): 85
Box: see *Buxus* spp, *Buxus sempervirens;* box, ground: see *Polygala chamaebuxus;* box edging: see *Buxus sempervirens* 'Suffruticosa'; box elder: see *Acer negundo*
Boysenberry: 312
Brachychiton acerifolium (flame tree): 174
Brachycome iberidifolia (Swan River daisy): 218, 390
Bramble, flowering (ornamental): see *Rubus* spp
Brass buttons: see *Cotula coronifolia*
Brassica chinensis: see Cabbages, Chinese; *B. juncea:* see Mustard, Chinese; *B. napus:* see Rape; *B. n. napobrassica:* see Swedes; *B. oleracea* (ornamental cabbage, ornamental kale): 221, 243, 261, 390; see also Cabbages; *B. o. acephala:* see Kale; *B. o. botrytis:* see Cauliflowers; *B. o. bullata:* see Cabbages, Savoy; *B. o. capitata:* see Cabbages; *B. o. costata:* see Cabbages, Portuguese; *B. o. gemmifera:* see Brussels sprouts; *B. o. gongylodes:* see Kohlrabi; *B. o. italica:* see Broccoli; *B. pekinensis:* see Cabbages, Chinese; *B. rapa rapa:* see Turnips
Brassicas (cabbage family): 262, 263, 264, 266, 267, **278–279**, **281**, **282–283**, **286**, 362, 365
Bridal wreath: see *Spiraea* × *arguta*
Briza maxima (pearl grass, quaking grass): 114, *114*, 244, *244*
Broccoli (calabrese, *Brassica oleracea italica*): 262, 263, 264, 265, 268, **286**, *286*, 365; broccoli leaves: 282
Brodiaea spp: 200, 202, 388; *B. lactea (Triteleia hyacinthina):* 202; *B. (Triteleia) laxa:* 202, *202*; *B. l.* 'Queen Fabiola': 202; *B. (Triteleia)* × *tubergenii:* 202; *B. uniflora (Ipheion uniflorum):* 200
Broom: see *Cytisus* spp, *Genista* spp, *Spartium junceum;* broom, butcher's: see *Ruscus aculeatus;* broom, Madeira: see *Genista tenera (Genista virgata);* broom, Mount Etna: see *Genista aetnensis;* broom, Spanish: see *Spartium junceum;* broom, Warminster: see *Cytisus* × *praecox*
Brunnera macrophylla (Anchusa myosotidiflora): 184, 233, 388
Brussels sprouts *(Brassica oleracea gemmifera):* 262, 263, 264, 265, 266, 268, 269, **282–283**, *283*, 284, 365
Buchloë dactyloides (buffalo grass): 85
Buckeye: see *Aesculus* spp
Buckthorn: see *Rhamnus* spp; buckthorn, dwarf: see *Rhamnus pumilus;* buckthorn, sea: see *Hippophaë rhamnoides*
Buddleia spp: 34, **157**, 175, 246, 372, 386; *B. alternifolia:* 97, *97*, 157, 372; *B. asiatica:* 175; *B. davidii* (butterfly bush): 157, 372; *B. d.* 'Royal Red': 157; *B. d.* 'White Profusion': 157; *B. globosa* (orange ball tree): 94, *94*, 157; *B. madagascariensis:* 175
Bugbane: see *Cimicifuga* spp
Bugle: see *Ajuga* spp, *Ajuga reptans*
Buglossoides (Lithospermum) purpureo-caeruleum: 184
Bulbocodium (Colchicum) vernum: 200–201
Bullaces *(Prunus domestica):* 322
Bulrush: see *Scirpus* spp, *Typha* spp
Bunny rabbits: see *Linaria maroccana*
Burnet: see *Sanguisorba obtusa;* burnet, salad *(Sanguisorba minor): 274*, 275
Burning bush: see *Dictamnus* spp, *Kochia scoparia;* burning bush, white: see *Dictamnus albus*
Busy Lizzie: see *Impatiens sultani*
Butcher's broom: see *Ruscus aculeatus*
Butomus umbellatus (flowering rush): 256
Buttercup: see *Ranunculus* spp; buttercup, creeping: see *Ranunculus repens*
Butterfly bush: see *Buddleia davidii;* butterfly flower: see *Schizanthus pinnatus;* butterfly weed: see *Asclepias tuberosa*
Butternuts (white walnut, *Juglans cinerea*): 327, *327*
Buxus spp (box): 43, 52, **90–91**, **230**, 374, 386; *B. harlandii:* 230; *B. microphylla:* 230; *B. m.* 'Compacta': 230; *B. m. koreana:* 230; *B. sempervirens* (common box): 91, 248, 372; *B. s.* 'Suffruticosa' (box edging): 90, *90*, 91, 270

C

Cabbage, skunk: see *Lysichiton americanus;* cabbage palm: see *Cordyline australis;* cabbage rose: see *Rosa* Centifolia varieties; cabbages *(Brassica oleracea capitata):* 261, 262, 263, 264, 265, 266, 267, 268, 269, **282**, *282*, 283, 340, 362, 365; cabbages, Chinese *(Brassica chinensis, Brassica pekinensis):* 262, 264, 282, *283*; cabbages, ornamental, see *Brassica oleracea;* cabbages, Portuguese (couve tronchuda, *Brassica oleracea costata*): 282; cabbages, Savoy *(Brassica oleracea bullata):* 265, 268, 282, *282*; cabbages, tree: see Kale, plain-leaved; cabbages, turnip-rooted: see Kohlrabi
Cacalia (Emilia) coccinea (tassel flower): 208
Cacti: *15*, 37, 51, **223**, 252, 350, 380; see also *Astrophytum* spp, *Cereus* spp, *Gasteria* spp, *Hamatocactus* spp, *Lobivia* spp, *Opuntia* spp
Caesalpinia (Poinciana) spp: 52; *C. gilliesii (Poinciana gilliesii,* bird-of-paradise plant): 173; *C. japonica:* 173
Calabrese: see Broccoli
Calceolaria spp: 29, 112, 116, 390; *C.* × *herbeohybrida:* 222; *C. integrifolia (C. rugosa):* 218
Calendula spp, *C. officinalis* (common marigold, pot marigold): 43, 53, 113, 114, 115, 206, **208**, *208*, 390
Calico bush: see *Kalmia latifolia*
Californian fuchsia: see *Zauschneria californica;* Californian poppy: see *Eschscholzia* spp, *Escholzia californica;* Californian tree poppy: see *Romneya coulteri*
Calla aethiopica: see *Zantedeschia aethiopica; C. elliottiana:* see *Zantedeschia aethiopica; C. palustris* (bog arum): 233, 237, 256
Calla lily: see *Zantedeschia* spp
Callicarpa bodinieri giraldii: 95
Calliopsis tinctoria: see *Coreopsis tinctoria*
Callistemon spp (bottlebrush): 175, 372
Callistephus chinensis (annual aster, China aster): 113, 115, 184, **215**, *215*, 364, 367, 390; *C. c.* Ostrich-Plume varieties: 215; *C. c.* Totem Pole varieties: 215
Callitriche hermaphroditica (C. autumnalis, autumn starwort); 255; *C. palustris (C. verna,* spring starwort): 255
Calluna spp, *C. vulgaris* (heather, ling): **152–153**, 228, 233, 247, 331, 372, 386; *C. v.* 'Alba Plena': 152; *C. v.* 'Alportii': 152; *C. v.* 'Barnett Anley': 152; *C. v.* 'County Wicklow': 152; *C. v.* 'Golden Carpet': 228; *C. v.* 'Golden Feather': 152, 243; *C. v.* 'Gold Haze': 152, 243; *C. v.* 'Hammondii': 152; *C. v.* 'Hirsuta Typica': 152; *C. v.* 'J. H. Hamilton': 152; *C. v.* 'Multicolor' ('Prairie Fire'): 228; *C. v.* 'Peter Sparkes': 152; *C. v.* 'Prairie Fire': see *C. v.* 'Multicolor'; *C. v.* 'Robert Chapman': 152
Calocephalus brownii: 237
Calochortus venustus: 204
Calonyction aculeatum (Ipomoea bona-nox, Ipomoea roxburghii, moonflower): 212–213
Caltha palustris (kingcup, marsh marigold): 33, 52, 256
Camassia spp: 179–180, 203, 257, 388; *C. cusickii:* 203; *C. esculenta:* 203; *C. leichtlinii:* 180, 203; *C. l.* 'Atroviolacea': 203; *C. l.* 'Plena': 247; *C. quamash* (quamash): 203
Camellia spp: 29, 42, 94, 151, **153**, 172, 331, 347, 350, 372, 386; *C.* × 'Cornish Snow': 153; *C. japonica:* 153, 172; *C. j.* 'Adolphe Audusson': 153; *C. j.* 'Alba Plena': 153; *C. j.* 'Alba Simplex': 153; *C. j.* 'Apollo': 153; *C. j.* 'Contessa Lavinia Maggi': 153; *C. j.* 'Donckelarii': 153, *153*; *C. j.* 'Duchesse de Rohan': see *C. j.* 'Preston Rose'; *C. j.* 'Elegans': 153; *C. j.* 'Gloire de Nantes': 153; *C. j.* 'Lady Buller': see *C. j.* 'Nagasaki'; *C. j.* 'Lady Clare': 153; *C. j.* 'Nagasaki' ('Lady Buller'): 153; *C. j.* 'Preston Rose' ('Duchesse de Rohan'): 153; *C. j.* 'Rubescens Major': 153; *C.* × 'Leonard Messel': 153; *C. reticulata:* 153; *C. r.* 'Captain Rawes': 153; *C. r.* 'Robert Fortune': 153; *C. saluensis:* 153; *C. sasanqua:* 153, 172; *C.* × *williamsi:* 153; *C.* × *w.* 'Donation': 153, *153*; *C.* × *w.* 'Golden Spangles': 153; *C.* × *w.* 'J. C. Williams': 153; *C.* × *w.* 'Mary Christian': 153; *C.* × *w.* 'November Pink': 153; *C.* × *w.* 'St Ewe': 153
Camomile: see Chamomile
Campanula spp (bellflower): 109, 121, **179**, **225**, 233, 388; *C. arvatica:* 225; *C. carpatica:* 225; *C. c.* 'Blue Clips': 225; *C. c.* 'Ditton Blue': 225; *C. c.* 'Pelviformis': *225*; *C. c.* 'White Star': 225; *C. cochleariifolia (C. pusilla):* 234; *C. garganica:* 125, 225, 236; *C. glomerata:* 105, 179; *C.* × *haylodgensis:* 120, 235; *C. isophylla:* 125, 237; *C. lactiflora: 105*, 176, 179; *C. latifolia* (giant bellflower, great bellflower): 176; *C. medium* (Canterbury bell): 29, 107, 115, **211**, *211*, 390; *C. m.* 'Bells of Holland' ('Musical Bells'): 211; *C. muralis:* see *C. portenschlagiana; C. nitida* 'Alba' *(C. persicifolia* 'Planiflora Alba', *C. planiflora* 'Alba'): 225; *C. portenschlagiana (C. muralis):* 225, 233, 236; *C. poscharskyana:* 225, 233; *C. pulla:* 225, 235; *C. pusilla:* see *C. cochleariifolia; C. pyramidalis* (chimney bellflower, steeple bells): 176; *C. rotundifolia* (harebell): 40
Campernelle: see *Narcissus* × *odorus* 'Campernelli', *Narcissus* × *odorus* 'Campernelli Plenus'
Campion: see *Lychnis* spp, *Silene* spp
Campsis spp (trumpet creeper, trumpet vine): 143, 372, 386; *C. grandiflora (C. chinensis):* 146; *C. (Tecoma) radicans* (trumpet vine): 143, 146; *C.* × *tagliabuana* 'Madame Galen': 146
Canary creeper: see *Tropaeolum peregrinum*
Candytuft: see *Iberis* spp; candytuft, perennial: see *Iberis sempervirens;* candytuft, Persian: see *Aethionema pulchellum*
Canna spp: 112–113, 252, 390; *C. indica* (Indian shot): 221, 252; *C. iridiflora:* 252
Canterbury bell: see *Campanula medium*
Cape figwort: see *Phygelius capensis;* cape gooseberry: see Golden berry; cape marigold: see *Dimorphotheca* spp
Capsicum annuum: see Peppers; *C. frutescens:* see Peppers, hot
Capsicums: see Peppers
Caragana arborescens: 372; *C. a.* 'Lorbergii': 169
Caraway *(Carum carvi):* 272, *272*

Index of plant names (continued)

Index of plant names (continued)

Index of plant names (continued)

Index of plant names (continued)

Index of plant names (continued)

Index of plant names (continued)

Index of plant names (continued)

Acknowledgements

The artists and photographers who contributed the illustrations in this book are listed below. Where more than one artist or photographer contributed the illustrations to a two-page spread, these are listed from A to Z, starting with the picture farthest to the left and nearest the top of the page, and working down each column in turn.

2–3: Donald Myall
10–11: Michael Wright/New Leaf
12–13: A: Jeremy Whitaker; B: John Chandler/New Leaf; C: Tania Midgley; D: Harry Smith Horticultural Photographic Collection (Harry Smith Collection)
14–15: A, C: Venner Artists; B: A–Z Botanical Collection; D: Jeremy Whitaker; E: Elly Beintema; F: A. du Gard Pasley
16–17: A, C, D: Harry Smith Collection; B, E: Tania Midgley
18–19: Venner Artists; B: Elly Beintema; C: Michael Wright/New Leaf; E: Arthur Hellyer; F: Harry Smith Collection
20–21: A, E: Harry Smith Collection; B, D: Tania Midgley; C: Fisons Ltd
22–23: A, E: Michael Warren; B, D, F: Harry Smith Collection; C: A–Z Botanical Collection
24–25: A, B, F: Harry Smith Collection; C: Michael Warren; D, E: Florapic
26–27: A, E: Michael Warren; B, C: Harry Smith Collection; D: Florapic; F: A–Z Botanical Collection
28–29: A, B: Harry Smith Collection; C: Florapic; D, E: Michael Warren
30–31: A, B, C, D: Harry Smith Collection; E, F: Noël J. Prockter
32–33: A, E: Michael Wright/New Leaf; B, C: Harry Smith Collection; D: A–Z Botanical Collection
34–35: A, E: Stephen Dalton/NHPA; B: Moira Savonius/NHPA; C: E.A. Janes/NHPA; D: Carole Vaucher
36–37: A, E: Harry Smith Collection; B: Florapic; C: Iris Hardwick Library; D: Michael Warren
38–39: A: Michael Warren; B: Harry Smith Collection; C: Iris Hardwick Library; D, E: Tania Midgley
40–41: A: Rosemary Roberts; B, D: Michael Warren; C: Alfred Evans; E: Harry Smith Collection
42–43: A, E: Iris Hardwick Library; B, C: Michael Warren; D: Nelson Hargreaves; F: Tania Midgley
44–45: A, B, D: Harry Smith Collection; C: A. du Gard Pasley; E: Michael Wright/New Leaf
46–47: A: Arthur Hellyer; B: A. du Gard Pasley; C: Tania Midgley; D: Stadt Frankfurt/Main; E, F: Robert Fels
48–49: A: Tania Midgley; B, C: Harry Smith Collection; E: Elly Beintema; F: Michael Wright/New Leaf
50–51: A: Michael Wright/New Leaf; B: Jeremy Whitaker; C, D: A–Z Botanical Collection; E: Michael Warren
52–53: A: Wolfram Stehling; B: Michael Warren; C: Tania Midgley
54–55: A, B: Michael Warren; C, D: Harry Smith Collection; E: Tania Midgley
56–57: Gary Hincks
58–59: Elsa Megson/A–Z Botanical Collection
60–61: A, B: Peter Russell; C: E.W. Tattersall
62–63: Jack Elliott
64–65: A, C: Gillian Platt; B: Michael Warren; D: A–Z Botanical Collection
66–67: Venner Artists
68–69: A, C: Venner Artists; B: Peter Russell
70–71: Gary Hincks
72–73: A, C: Gary Hincks; B, D: Michael Warren
74–75: A, D: Gary Hincks; B: Harry Smith Collection; C: Malcolm Smythe/New Leaf
76–77: A: Tania Midgley; B, E: Venner Artists; C: Florapic; D: Jeremy Whitaker; F: A. du Gard Pasley
78–79: Gary Hincks
80–81: A: John Chandler/New Leaf; B, F: Harry Smith Collection; C: Florapic; D: A. du Gard Pasley; E: A–Z Botanical Collection
82–83: A: Fox Pool International; B: Harry Smith Collection; C: Gary Hincks; D: Donald Myall
84–85: A: Harry Smith Collection; B, C: Donald Myall
86–87: A, B: Rodney Paull; C: Donald Myall
88–89: A: Malcolm Smythe/New Leaf; B: Michael Wright/New Leaf; C: Bees Ltd; D: Harry Smith Collection
90–91: A: John Chandler/New Leaf; B: Harry Smith Collection; C: A–Z Botanical Collection; D: Donald Myall
92–93: A, B: Harry Smith Collection; C: Michael Warren; D: Noël J. Prockter; E: Donald Myall; F: John Chandler/New Leaf
94–95: A, B: Harry Smith Collection; C: Noël J. Prockter; D, E: Michael Warren
96–97: A: Julie Stiles; B: Harry Smith Collection; C: A–Z Botanical Collection
98–99: A, C, D: Michael Warren; B: Michael Gibson; E, F: Michael McGuinness
100–101: A: Harry Smith Collection; B, C, E: Michael McGuinness; D: Carole Vaucher
102–103: A: Florapic; B: A–Z Botanical Collection; C: Vana Haggerty; D: Harry Smith Collection
104–105: A, C: Gary Hincks; B: Michael Warren
106–107: A: Florapic; B, C, D: Harry Smith Collection; E: Vana Haggerty

108–109: A: John Chandler/New Leaf; B: Michael Warren; C: Gary Hincks; D: Florapic; E: Alfred Evans; F: Michael Wright/New Leaf
110–111: A, B, C, D, F: Bulb Information Desk; E: Gary Hincks
112–113: A: Harry Smith Collection; B: Vana Haggerty; C: Michael Wright/New Leaf
114–115: A, C: Norman Barber; B: Elsa Megson/A–Z Botanical Collection; D, E: Gary Hincks
116–117: A, F: Fisons Ltd; B: Michael Wright/New Leaf; C, E: John Chandler/New Leaf; D, G: Carole Vaucher
118–119: A: Gary Hincks; B: Michael Warren; C, E: Michael Wright/New Leaf; D: Julie Stiles
120–121: Norman Barber
122–123: A: Sue Rawkins/New Leaf; B: Florapic; C, F, G: Roy Elliott; D: Donald Myall; E: Colin Gray
124–125: A: Michael Wright/New Leaf; B: Venner Artists; C, F: Roy Elliott: D, E: Harry Smith Collection
126–127: A, E: Alfred Evans; B: Roy Elliott; C: Tania Midgley; D: Donald Myall
128–129: A: Harry Smith Collection; B, C: Gary Hincks
130–131: A: Harry Smith Collection; B, D: Donald Myall; C: A–Z Botanical Collection
132–133: A, F: Jim Robins; B: Florapic; C: Michael Wright/New Leaf; D: Fisons Ltd; E: A–Z Botanical Collection
134–135: Bulb Information Desk
136–137: A, B, F: Alan Mitchell; C: Malcolm Smythe/New Leaf; D: Fisons Ltd; E: Carole Vaucher
138–141: Alan Mitchell
142–143: A, C, F: Malcolm Smythe/New Leaf; B: Michael Wright/New Leaf; D: Florapic
144–145: A, B, D, E: Fisk's Clematis Nursery; C: John Chandler/New Leaf; F, H: Noël J. Prockter; G: Michael Wright/New Leaf
146–147: A, B, C: Florapic; D: Michael Warren
148–149: Michael Gibson
150–151: A: Michael Smythe/New Leaf; B, E: Malcolm Smythe/New Leaf; C, D: Michael Wright/New Leaf; F: John Chandler/New Leaf
152–153: A, B, D: F.P. Knight; C, E: Michael Wright/New Leaf
154–155: A: Michael Wright/New Leaf; B, C: F.P. Knight
156–157: A: Sue Rawkins/New Leaf; B: Fisons Ltd; C, D, H: Michael Wright/New Leaf; E: Malcolm Smythe/New Leaf; F: Noël J. Prockter; G: Florapic
158–159: A, C, D: Michael Gibson; B: Fisons Ltd
160–161: A, D: Bees Ltd; B: Michael Gibson; C: Donald Myall
162–163: A, B: Bees Ltd; C: Carole Vaucher; D: Michael Wright/New Leaf; E: Harry Smith Collection
164–165: A, B, C, D: John Chandler/New Leaf; E: Malcolm Smythe/New Leaf; F: Florapic
166–167: A: Noël J. Prockter; B, C: Florapic; D, E: Michael Wright/New Leaf; F, G: John Chandler/New Leaf
168–169: Florapic
170–171: A, B: Noël J. Prockter; C, F: Florapic; D, E: Michael Wright/New Leaf
172–173: A: John Chandler/New Leaf; B: Noël J. Prockter; C, E: Florapic; D: Michael Wright/New Leaf
174–175: A, B, C, D, F: Michael Wright/New Leaf; E: Florapic; G: Malcolm Smythe/New Leaf
176–177: A, D: Florapic; B: Blackmore and Langdon Ltd; C, E: Michael Wright/New Leaf
178–179: A: Rod Shone/New Leaf; B: Malcolm Smythe/New Leaf; C: Fisons Ltd; D: Michael Wright/New Leaf; E: Florapic
180–181: A, D, E: Michael Wright/New Leaf; B, C: Florapic
182–183: A, B, H: Michael Wright/New Leaf; C: Florapic; D, E, F, G: Allwood Bros
184–185: A, E: Malcolm Smythe/New Leaf; B, F: Florapic; C, D: Michael Wright/New Leaf
186–187: A, C, E: Elm House Nurseries Ltd; B, D: Carole Vaucher
188–189: A, F: Philip Damp; B, C, D: Vana Haggerty; E, G, H: John Chandler/New Leaf
190–191: A, B, D, E, F, G: Bulb Information Desk; C: Carole Vaucher
192–195: Bulb Information Desk
196–197: A, B, E, G: Bulb Information Desk; C: Florapic; D: Carole Vaucher; F: Michael Wright/New Leaf
198–199: A, B, C, D: Bulb Information Desk; E: John Chandler/New Leaf
200–203: Bulb Information Desk
204–205: A: Michael Wright/New Leaf; B, C, D, E, F: Bulb Information Desk
206–207: A: Thompson & Morgan; B, D, E, G: W.J. Unwin Ltd; C: A–Z Botanical Collection; F: Fisons Ltd
208–209: A, G: John Chandler/New Leaf; B, C, D, E, F: W.J. Unwin Ltd
210–211: A: W.J. Unwin Ltd; B, C, D, F: Thompson & Morgan; E: Michael Wright/New Leaf
212–213: A: Harry Smith Collection; B, C, D: Florapic; E: John Chandler/New Leaf
214–215: A: Michael Wright/New Leaf; B, C, E, G: W.J. Unwin Ltd; D: John Chandler/New Leaf; F: Thompson & Morgan

216–217: A, C, G: W.J. Unwin Ltd; B, D: Thompson & Morgan; E: Suttons Seeds Ltd; F: Michael Wright/New Leaf
218–219: A: John Chandler/New Leaf; B, C, F: Michael Wright/New Leaf; D: W.J. Unwin Ltd; E, G: Thompson & Morgan
220–221: A, C, D: Michael Wright/New Leaf; B: John Chandler/New Leaf; E, G: W.J. Unwin Ltd; F: Harry Smith Collection
222–223: A, B, E, G: Michael Wright/New Leaf; C: Florapic; D: Thompson & Morgan; F: John Chandler/New Leaf
224–225: A: Thompson & Morgan; B: Roy Elliott; C, D: Michael Wright/New Leaf; E: John Chandler/New Leaf; F: Florapic
226–227: Roy Elliott
228–229: A: Roy Elliott; B: Rod Shone/New Leaf; C, D, E: Michael Wright/New Leaf
230–231: A, C: Roy Elliott; B: Florapic; D, E: Michael Wright/New Leaf
232–233: A, C, D, E: Michael Wright/New Leaf; B: John Chandler/New Leaf
234–235: A: Harry Smith Collection; B, C, E: Michael Wright/New Leaf; D, F: Florapic
236–237: A, C: Florapic; B: Roy Elliott; D, F: Michael Wright/New Leaf; E: John Chandler/New Leaf
238–239: A, D: Michael Wright/New Leaf; B, C: Carole Vaucher
240–241: A, B, C, E, F: John Chandler/New Leaf; D: Michael Wright/New Leaf
242–243: A: Thompson & Morgan; B: Michael Wright/New Leaf; C: W.J. Unwin Ltd; D: Sue Rawkins/New Leaf
244–245: A: Michael Wright/New Leaf; B: Harry Titcombe; C: Thompson & Morgan
246–247: A, C, D, F, G: Michael Wright/New Leaf; B: Malcolm Smythe/New Leaf; E: John Chandler/New Leaf
248–249: A: Thompson & Morgan; B, E: Michael Wright/New Leaf; C: Fisons Ltd; D, F: Florapic
250–251: A: Noël J. Prockter; B, F: Michael Gibson; C, D, E: Florapic
252–253: A: Florapic; B, C, D, E, F: Michael Wright/New Leaf
254–255: A, B, D, E, F, G: Florapic; C: Michael Wright/New Leaf
256–257: A, B, C: Michael Wright/New Leaf; D, F: Florapic; E: Malcolm Smythe/New Leaf; G: Fisons Ltd
258–259: John Chandler/New Leaf
260–261: Jim Robins
262–265: Anthony/Reid Partnership
266–267: Jim Robins
268–269: Rodney Paull
270–275: Vana Haggerty
276–277: Gary Hincks
278–279: Vana Haggerty
280–281: Julie Stiles
282–285: Lee Robinson
286–287: A: Julie Stiles; B, C: Vana Haggerty
288–303: Vana Haggerty
304–307: Lee Robinson
306–307: Julie Stiles
308–309: A: Julie Stiles; B: Andrew Popkiewicz
310–311: A, C, D: Julie Stiles; B: Julie Stiles
312–313: A, C, D: Julie Stiles; B, E: Andrew Popkiewicz
314–315: A: Donald Myall; B: Julie Stiles; C: Suttons Seeds Ltd
316–317: A: Julie Stiles; B: Andrew Popkiewicz
318–319: A: Donald Myall; B: George Thompson
320–321: A: Julie Stiles; B, C: Carole Vaucher; D, E, F: Andrew Popkiewicz
322–323: A, B: Carole Vaucher; C, D, E: Julie Stiles; F: Andrew Popkiewicz
324–325: Julie Stiles
326–327: A, G: Carole Vaucher; B, C, D, E, F, H, I: Ingrid Jacob
328–329: John Chandler/New Leaf
330–331: Gary Hincks
332–333: A, C: Venner Artists; B: Andrew Popkiewicz
334–337: Gary Hincks
340–341: Andrew Farmer
342–343: Norman Barber
344–345: Venner Artists
346–349: Andrew Popkiewicz
350–351: A, C: Andrew Popkiewicz; B: Lee Robinson; D, E: Michael McGuinness
352–353: Jim Robins
354–355: A: Lee Robinson; B, C, D: Andrew Popkiewicz; E, F: Michael McGuinness
356–357: Gary Hincks
358–359: George Thompson
360–361: Andrew Popkiewicz
362–364: Donald Myall
365–367: George Thompson
368–369: A: George Thompson; B: Andrew Popkiewicz
370–373: Gary Hincks
374–377: Andrew Popkiewicz
378–379: Jim Robins
380–383: Gary Hincks
384: Andrew Popkiewicz
392–393: Gary Hincks
Endpapers: Venner Artists